Masterpieces of Latino Literature

Masterpieces
of
Latino Literature

Edited by
Frank N. Magill

HarperCollins*Publishers*

FIRST EDITION

Library of Congress Cataloging-in-Publication Data

Masterpieces of latino literature / edited by Frank N. Magill. —
    1st ed.
        p.   cm.
    Includes indexes.
    ISBN 0-06-270106-1
    1. Latin American literature—History and criticism.   2. American literature—Hispanic authors—History and criticism. I. Magill, Frank Northen, 1907–   .
    PQ7081.A1M29   1994
    860.9'98—dc20   94-8803

---

94 95 96 97 RRD 10 9 8 7 6 5 4 3 2 1

PREFACE

Masterpieces of Latino Literature is a companion volume to *Masterpieces of World Literature* (1989), *Masterpieces of African-American Literature* (1992), and *Masterpieces of American Literature* (1993). Designed to highlight the literary achievements of Latino authors from the seventeenth century to the present, the essays in *Masterpieces of Latino Literature* were developed in response to the growing need for reference works capable of presenting information on ethnic literature in an accessible format. A rich tapestry of Latino literary culture is surveyed—from the early poetry of Sor Juana Inés de la Cruz to the contemporary poetry of Jimmy Santiago Baca; from classic fiction by such authors as Alejo Carpentier and Eduardo Mallea to contemporary novels by Laura Esquivel and Sandra Cisneros; and from early agitprop drama of Luis Miguel Valdez to plays by Dolores Prida and Luis Rafael Sánchez. Analysis of works by authors of the Latin American literary boom appear alongside articles about works that are garnering awards and critical attention for contemporary authors such as Abraham Rodriguez, Jr., Cristina Garcia, and Oscar Hijuelos. By presenting aspects of the vitality and diversity of Latino culture, these works, when taken together, assume a universal appeal.

This latest volume in the *Masterpieces* series presents 173 standardized articles—140 on classic and newly popular works of fiction and nonfiction and 33 general essays about the poetry, plays, short stories, and essays of notable Latino writers and thinkers—all arranged alphabetically, by title for individual works or by genre in the case of essay reviews covering all the works of an author in a particular genre. Designed primarily for reference, the format allows the reader to find the most appropriate information as quickly as possible. A plot summary format is employed for works that tell a single story. Each plot digest is preceded by carefully checked reference data that furnish at a glance the author, type of work, type of plot, time of plot, locale, and first publication date. The first major section of each essay introduces the reader to the story's principal characters, providing an extended description of each major character and his or her relationships to the other characters. The text itself is divided into three sections. The first section, consisting of approximately 700 words, provides a well-rounded introduction to the work, giving the reader an overview of its contents. Immediately following the plot summary, the "Analysis" section discusses, in about 600 words, the author's approach to characterization and the important themes and stylistic devices employed by the author. The "Critical Context" section, constituting approximately 500 words, places the work in its literary and historical context, evaluates its contribution to the understanding of Latino life, and assesses its significance within the author's literary career. Articles concerning works of nonfiction or collections of stories follow a similar format but omit the section dealing with literary characters.

The remaining essays, those that evaluate authors and their work in the genres of poetry, short stories, drama, and essays, are presented in an essay-review format. Following the ready-reference data (author, type of work, and a listing of major publications in the genre, arranged chronologically by date of original publication), an essay of approximately 2,500 words identifies the primary themes and images and integrates them with a discussion of the literary merits of the author's individual works in a clear, expository style.

Each of the essays in this edition has been written with an eye to the currency of the ideas presented, requiring an enormous amount of assistance from a carefully selected staff that included scores of faculty members from universities and colleges throughout the United States. All these contributors deserve recognition; in particular, we would like to acknowledge: Diane M. Almeida, Debra D. Andrist, Jane H. Babson, Margot Gayle Backus, JoAnn Balingit, Barbara G. Bartholomew, Margaret Kent Bass, Emilio Bejel, Stephen Benz, Ksenija Bilbija, Nicholas Birns, Kevin Boyle, Ludger Brinker, Silvester J. Brito,

Keith H. Brower, David Buehrer, Roberto Cantú, Jean S. Chittenden, David Conde, Virginia Crane, Peter Crawford, Martha J. Cutter, Susan Jaye Dauer, Jo Culbertson Davis, Linda Prewett Davis, Michael Dickel, Sandra L. Dixon, Margaret V. Ekstrom, Eduardo F. Elías, James Feast, Joseph A. Feustle, Jr., Gustavo Pérez Firmat, Kelly Fuller, Jean C. Fulton, Marc Goldstein, Joyce Ann Hancock, Stephen M. Hart, Tace Hedrick, Rebecca Stingley Hinton, Dennis Hoilman, Janice Jaffe, Jonathan Johnson, Jane Anderson Jones, Ludmila Kapschutschenko-Schmitt, Steven G. Kellman, Vera M. Kutzinski, David C. Laubach, Marketta A. Laurila, Linda Ledford-Miller, Marcus "C" López, Michael Loudon, James McCorkle, Andrew F. Macdonald, Gina Macdonald, Ron McFarland, Paul D. Mageli, Edward A. Malone, Barry Mann, Andres Mares, Sr., George Mariscal, Antonio C. Marquez, Joan F. Marx, William Matta, Warren L. Meinhardt, D. Jan Mennell, Margarita Nieto, Rafael Ocasio, Walter Oliver, Phillip Parotti, Rosemary M. Canfield Reisman, David Rigsbee, Elsa Saeta, Kenneth Seib, Wilma Shires, R. Baird Shuman, Francisco Soto, Teresia Langford Taylor, Evelyn Toft, Daniel Torres, Luis A. Torres, Rebeca Torres-Rivera, Rafael Venegas, and James M. Welsh.

The volume concludes with two indexes to aid the user in locating all works by author (author index) or title (title index).

Frank N. Magill

ACKNOWLEDGMENTS

The following plot summaries are used by permission of the publishers and copyright holders.

Broad and Alien Is the World by Ciro Alegría (Rinehart & Co., Inc., and Farrar & Rinehart, Inc., 1941)
Don Segundo Sombra by Ricardo Güiraldes (Rinehart & Co., Inc., and Farrar & Rinehart, Inc., 1935)
Epitaph of a Small Winner by Joaquim Maria Machado de Assis (The Noonday Press and William Leonard Grossman, 1952)
Fiesta in November by Eduardo Mallea (Houghton Mifflin Company, 1942, and Angel Flores)
The Foreign Girl by Florencio Sánchez (Alfred A. Knopf, Inc., 1927) *The Gaucho Martín Fierro* by José Hernández (Rinehart & Co., Inc., 1936)
The Itching Parrot by José Joaquím Fernández de Lizardi (Doubleday & Co., Inc., 1942)
The Underdogs by Mariano Azuela (Coward-McCann, Inc., 1929)
The Villagers by Jorge Icaza (Editorial Sol and Imprenta Nacional, 1936, and Jorge Icaza)
El Zarco, the Bandit by Ignacio Manuel Altamirano (W. W. Norton & Co., Inc., and Raymond L. Grismer, translator)

CONTENTS

CONTENTS

CONTENTS

Masterpieces of Latino Literature

ALBURQUERQUE

Author: Rudolfo A. Anaya (1937-   )
Type of plot: Magical Realism
Time of plot: 1992
Locale: Albuquerque, New Mexico
First published: 1992

Principal Characters

Abrán González, a twenty-one-year-old boxer from the barrio who has given up fighting because he feels responsible for the death of a sparring partner. Abrán learns that he is adopted and that his mother was Cynthia Johnson, a talented painter. She dies from cancer just as Abrán discovers the truth about his birth. He sets out to discover the identity of his father. He agrees to return to the ring in exchange for information about his father and is thus drawn into the world of Albuquerque wealth and politics. Two women are attracted to him: the mayor, who represents the power and glamour that can be his as a successful fighter, and a poor nurse from a small village in the mountains, who represents a simple life of service to others and the traditional Mexican values of family and land. In the end, Abrán discovers that it is not through biology that one gains one's identity; rather, he learns, one defines oneself through the choices one makes.

Ben Chávez, Abrán's biological father, a writer and teacher at the University of New Mexico. A poor boy from the barrio, Ben fell in love with Cynthia Johnson, an Anglo girl and the mother of Abrán, but her father insisted that the baby be put up for adoption, and she never revealed the identity of her lover to anyone. Even though he learns that Abrán is his son, he respects Cynthia's silence. Ben is an observer with a compulsion to write, rather than a man of action. He represents the artist in society, and through his stories he tells people who they are; his art enables them to understand themselves and their values.

Frank Dominic, a wealthy attorney running for mayor of Albuquerque. Although he was a high-school classmate of Ben and Cynthia, Dominic is unaware that Ben was Cynthia's lover. He promises to find out who Abrán's father was—if Abrán will return to the ring for a fight that will be the centerpiece in the celebration kicking off Dominic's campaign. Running on a platform of urban development that envisions the Albuquerque of the future as a gambling and entertainment center of canals and casinos, Dominic conceals his ruthlessness and hunger for power behind a good-old-boy façade. He is interested in using Abrán to further his political plans, but those plans are doomed to failure because they have not grown out of the character of the city but out of Dominic's insatiable ego.

Lucinda Córdova, a nurse from a small village in northern New Mexico who befriends Abrán after the death of his mother. She represents the traditional ideal of womanhood: She is selfless and devoted to family, and she wants to devote her life to healing. When she learns that Abrán has been unfaithful to her, she breaks off their relationship. On the night of the fight, however, she realizes that she has no future without him, and she rushes to ringside to be near him. Her presence inspires him, enabling him to make a comeback and win the match.

Marisa Martínez, the beautiful, competent, honest mayor of Albuquerque. She represents the new woman: She is divorced and lives alone, devoting herself to her work. When she meets Abrán, she is attracted to him and invites him to her home, and they make love. A detective hired by Dominic takes photographs, which Dominic then uses to try to make Marisa withdraw from the mayoral race. She is determined to see it through, however, and her courage and devotion to the city will probably be rewarded by reelection.

Jose Calabasa, a Santa Domingo Indian and loyal friend of Abrán. A Vietnam veteran who has not been able to escape the evils of the war, Jose is a student at the university and has lost touch with his pueblo and family. When Dominic attempts to buy the pueblo's water rights, Jose returns home to try to prevent the sale. He is unsuccessful, but he discovers that his future lies in helping his people.

He discovers that Ben is Abrán's father when he recognizes a picture of Ben in one of Cynthia's paintings.

Walter Johnson, a wealthy businessman and also a candidate for mayor. Johnson represents Anglo business interests and bigotry. He never learns that his wife had an affair with her gynecologist and that Cynthia was not his daughter. He enters the race for mayor to oppose Dominic, whom he hates, and he wants nothing to do with Abrán after Abrán learns that Cynthia was his mother.

The Novel

Alburquerque is Anaya's exploration of the ethnically and culturally diverse world of New Mexico in the 1990's. The book focuses on the conflict between the heritage of the past and the challenges to it posed by economic growth unscrupulously promoted by developers and politicians. In its structure, the novel parallels a young man's search for the identity of his father to the city's search for a sense of community amid divisive political and ethnic tensions. Anaya's spelling of the city's name in the title reflects the city's history; according to legend, a gringo stationmaster dropped the first "r" from the town's name "in a move," Anaya says, "that symbolized the emasculation of the Mexican way of life."

Near death from cancer, Cynthia Johnson, a highly respected New Mexico painter, sends for Abrán González, a former Golden Gloves boxing champion who is now a college student. She tells him that he is the son she gave up for adoption twenty-one years ago. Intensely proud of his Mexicanness and of the culture of the Barelas barrio where he was reared by his adoptive parents, Abrán is shocked to learn that he has an Anglo mother and naturally wants to know who his father is. By the time he arrives at the hospital, however, Cynthia is too weak to speak, and she dies without revealing the identity of her lover, a secret she confided to no one, not even her parents. Abrán turns for help and

companionship to Lucinda Córdova, a nurse who had been close to Cynthia during her final days and to whom he is deeply attracted. Together, they begin a search for the identity of Abrán's father.

This quest takes Abrán first to one of Cynthia's high-school classmates, Frank Dominic, who is now a wealthy lawyer running for mayor on a platform of legalized gambling and commercial development. Dominic promises to use his resources to find Abrán's father, but only if Abrán agrees to return to the ring for a fight to be held as a part of an elaborate celebration Dominic has scheduled to kick off his campaign.

Drawn into the orbit of power, Abrán succumbs—but only once—to the charms of the present mayor, Marisa Martínez, a beautiful and highly capable woman whose election was in large part the result of Cynthia's support. Unaware of Abrán's intimacy with Marisa, Lucinda takes him to northern New Mexico to meet her parents in the small village where they live. Dominic, furious when he learns that Abrán has broken training, arranges for Lucinda to be told about Abrán's infidelity, causing Lucinda to break off their relationship.

Additional complications result from Dominic's attempts to convince the Indian pueblos to sell their water rights to supply enough water for the canals envisioned in his urban development plan. Abrán's friend Jose Calabasa has returned to his pueblo to try to dissuade its council from selling out, but he is unsuccessful. Discouraged and depressed, he awakens after a two-day binge to learn that it is the day of Abrán's fight. Having promised to be there, Jose rushes back to Albuquerque. After a series of wildly comic adventures, he learns that a lawyer from Santa Fe has been trying to get in touch with Abrán about one of Cynthia's paintings, which may depict Abrán's father. Jose remembers having seen the painting at the house of Ben Chávez, a writer and teacher at the university who was another of Cynthia's high-school classmates. Rushing there, Jose confronts Ben, who admits to being Abrán's father. Hoping to reveal Ben's secret to Abrán and make it unnecessary for him to go through with the fight, Jose rushes to the convention center where the fight is being held. Lucinda, having talked with Marisa and forgiven Abrán, is also rushing to the convention center. She arrives to find that Jose has been badly beaten trying to get to Abrán. As he is being taken to a waiting ambulance, Jose manages to tell Lucinda that Ben Chávez is Abrán's father.

The match has already started, and Abrán is taking a bad beating. It is not until the end of the ninth round that Lucinda is able to make her way to ringside, where she is joined by Ben. Together they tell Abrán the truth. Still, he decides to continue the fight although he no longer needs Dominic's help. Inspired by the discovery of his father's identity and the return of Lucinda, Abrán makes an incredible comeback, knocking out his opponent in the tenth round and giving the people of Albuquerque the hero they need. Dominic's plans to change the city collapse, and both Abrán and the city have found their true identities.

Analysis

The novel is a complex weaving together of themes and meanings and even of literary styles. On one level, it is the love story of Abrán and Lucinda. Related closely to this theme is the conflict between urbanization, with its ethnic diversity and impetus toward continual expansion and flux, and pastoralism, which leads Abrán and Lucinda to see their future in terms of a return to the mountains, to the simplicity and cultural purity of village life, and to the spirituality that is engendered through a closer contact with nature than the city allows.

The novel also presents a critique of New Mexico politics and politicians. Many of its characters are drawn from real life. It presents an especially harsh indictment of Anglo bigotry and of unscrupulous and materialistic politicians. Contrasted to the politicians are the artists, primarily Ben and Cynthia, whose function is to interpret the people to themselves, to show them who they are and thus to give them the sense of identity and cultural heritage of which the politicians constantly threaten to rob them. It is in this light that Anaya's use of Magical Realism can best be understood. He introduces la Llorona, the wailing woman of Mexican folklore, the trickster figure of Coyote from Indian mythology, two "fictional" characters—Juan and Al—from Ben's poetry, and a figment of Ben's imagination, doña Loneliness, who suddenly becomes a flesh-and-blood whore dressed in red. These fantastic characters function side-by-side with the "real" characters to emphasize Anaya's view that the artist's creation is as much a reality as is the so-called reality it imitates. In the struggle to create the future, the artist is more important and much more to be trusted than the politician.

The man of the future that the artist has created—Cynthia as mother, Ben as father, and Anaya as author—is Abrán. He is to be the father of the people; as Anaya says, "Abrán, born of the Mexican father and the gringa mother, was the new Chicano, and he could create his own image, drawing the two worlds together, not letting them tear him apart." The future belongs not to the urban developers but to the people of mixed blood who can find a common ground for community within the diversity of ethnic heritages that threatens to tear it apart. Albuquerque, Anaya implies, is not merely a city in New Mexico; it is a microcosm of the United States and even of the planet.

Critical Context

Alburquerque brings Anaya's history of his people and of New Mexico up to the present. The history begins with his first and most famous novel, *Bless Me, Ultima* (1972), and continues in *Heart of Aztlán* (1976) and *Tortuga* (1979), between which and *Alburquerque* there is a lapse of some twenty years. It contains the elements for which Anaya has become best known—the celebration of the Mexican heritage of the Southwest, including its folklore and its deep commitment to family, to the land, and to the sense of mystery beyond the reach of science to explain. As does *Heart of Aztlán*, *Alburquerque* makes use of Old Testament typology. Clemente Chávez, the protagonist of *Heart of Aztlán*, leads the workers in a strike against the railroad, much as Moses led his people out of bondage, and Abrán, his grandson, is the Abraham who will be the founder of a new nation of chosen people, people of mixed blood.

The literary influence most apparent in this novel is that of the school of Magical Realism, an influence that places Anaya in the company of many distinguished Latin American writers. Perhaps equally important is the influence of a number of New Mexico writers who have anticipated vari-

ous themes developed in *Alburquerque*. Leslie Silko, in her well-known novel *Ceremony* (1977), developed the theme of the person of mixed blood as the progenitor of a race better suited to the needs of the future than people of "pure" blood. Silko's sense that it is the storytellers who will find the answers to the problems of mankind, who will create out of the materials of the past stories to defeat the powers of the destroyers who threaten the future, represents a somewhat mystical faith in the power of art similar to that developed by Anaya in *Alburquerque*. The influence of Frank Waters can be seen in Anaya's depiction of life in the Mexican villages of the North and in his sensitivity to the spiritual as well as the physical beauties of the land. The influence of N. Scott Momaday is apparent in Anaya's treatment of the rituals and ceremonies of Indian and Mexican life as well as in the theme of the creative power of the word, a theme that is thematically as well as structurally central to *Alburquerque*.

In this novel, Anaya takes his place in the forefront not only of Latino writers but also of all those writers who celebrate the beauty of the people and the land of the American Southwest.

ALL GREEN SHALL PERISH

Author: Eduardo Mallea (1903-1983)
Type of work: Novel
Type of plot: Existential
Time of plot: The 1930's and early 1940's
Locale: Ingeniero White, Bahía Blanca, and Nicanor Cruz's *estancia* (ranch) on the southern pampa near Bahía Blanca, Argentina
First published: *Todo verdor perecerá*, 1941 (English translation, 1966)

Principal Characters

Ágata Cruz, the protagonist, a once strikingly beautiful woman grown pallid and harder-featured from the frustration of her barren fifteen years of married life. She accepted the marriage proposal of Nicanor, whom she did not love, as a means of escaping life with her father. Life with Nicanor stifles her inner passion. When she is thirty-five years old, Ágata's anguish reaches a point of crisis. She leaves doors and windows open in winter when Nicanor is inside delirious with fever. After his death from freezing, she falls into a brief affair with the lawyer Sotero. She finds fleeting happiness, but Sotero callously discards her. She returns to the town in which she was reared and ends up as a street person. Her suicidal tendencies are restrained by the fear that the emptiness of her earthly existence will persist after death.

Nicanor Cruz, a dry, unimaginative landowner. A failure as a farmer, Nicanor has to abandon his estate for a smaller, even less productive farm. He is passionless and uncommunicative as a husband. His stoic attitude brings on his final illness, pneumonia, as he obsessively walks over his dead land for an entire day in a chilling rain.

Dr. Reba, Ágata's father, an inept medical practitioner. A Swiss immigrant, Dr. Reba married an Argentine woman who died at the birth of Ágata, their only child. He communicated better with his tavern companions than with his daughter, who loved him despite the gulf that separated them. In later life, Dr. Reba drank heavily. He died some years before the present time of the novel.

Dr. Sotero, a worldly, opportunistic lawyer who seduces Ágata when she is a widow. Handsome, deep-voiced, good-humored, and self-assured, Sotero claims to like diffident women such as Ágata, who completely subordinates herself to him. Sotero's mysterious business dealings for a Buenos Aires entity called the Organization take him out of Bahía Blanca and give him an excuse to leave Ágata.

Ema de Volpe, a frivolous but strong-willed woman who attaches herself to Ágata in Bahía Blanca. She is open about her own promiscuous life and does her best to wheedle intimate information out of the reticent Ágata. Conceited, perpetually overdressed, and having an exotic air about her, Ema calls herself a courtesan.

Dr. Romo, a short, heavy, sarcastic lawyer and associate of Sotero. Romo addresses everyone in an insinuating tone, and he habitually and cryptically calls Sotero "Sycophant." Romo visibly disdains Ágata for her docility. He is vulgar and has a taste for off-color jokes.

The Novel

All Green Shall Perish is divided into two parts. Each depicts a crucial period in the life of Ágata Cruz, and virtually all the action of the novel takes place within Ágata's anguished consciousness.

The theme and tone are established in the somber description of the desolate landscape of Nicanor Cruz's *estancia* (ranch) at the beginning of part 1. The drought suffered by the barren land is mirrored in the barren relationship of Nicanor and Ágata Cruz, who remain childless after fifteen years of marriage and estranged from each other by their inability to communicate and by a growing sense of isolation and resentment. Nicanor has lost his battle with the sterile land, although he stubbornly refuses to admit the defeat that has transformed him into a withdrawn and bitter man. Ágata, more sensitive and intelligent than her husband, asks more from life than he does and would have liked to help him during the early years, but Nicanor's pride would not allow him to accept her help. Ágata suffers from depression and resents being condemned to live out a life that she would never have chosen.

From this vantage point in time, Ágata reexperiences her past life in a series of flashbacks: first, the lonely childhood with her alienated father in the small port of Ingeniero White; then, her precipitous decision to marry Nicanor Cruz, a limited and taciturn man whom she did not love but who provided her with an escape from the stifling atmosphere of her childhood and the dreary prospect of life with her widower father, whom she loved but with whom she had never been able to communicate; and finally, a series of grim and worsening incidents from her fifteen years with Nicanor. The cumulative effect of this introspection is to deepen Ágata's depression.

In his unrelenting struggle with the land, Nicanor contracts pneumonia. While nursing him, Ágata reaches a crisis of desperation. Hoping to destroy herself and end her unhappiness, Ágata

opens all the windows to let in the cold. Nicanor dies, but Ágata is found unconscious on the porch at the end of part 1.

The second part of the novel begins in the southern metropolis of Bahía Blanca, where Ágata has moved following the sale of the *estancia*. Through the intervention of Ema de Volpe, a predatory and superficial woman who insists on taking Ágata under her wing, Ágata meets the lawyer Sotero. Ágata passively allows Sotero to seduce her, and, to her own surprise, she enjoys a brief period of happiness with this charming but shallow opportunist. Sotero, however, is incapable of committing himself to anyone for long, and he coldly abandons Ágata, leaving her with a note as he departs for Buenos Aires on business. His desertion confirms Ágata's worst fears, as she is again forced to provide for and nurture herself. After her happiness with Sotero, Ágata finds solitude even more difficult to bear, and she gradually withdraws still further into her own consciousness, caring nothing for those around her or for her surroundings. In her desperate obsession with understanding what is happening to her, she is drawn irresistibly back to the Ingeniero White of her childhood. Having lost all sense of time, wandering the streets of Ingeniero White like a madwoman, she is attacked by a gang of vicious children, who taunt and chase her. At the end of the novel, Ágata has lost all contact with reality except for the increasing intensity of her suffering. Her plight is poignantly captured in the last sentence of the novel: "It was very late when she got up suddenly, as if called by a scream, and, without direction or discernment, started running against the darkness."

Analysis

Theme, language, tone, and mood are the controlling elements of *All Green Shall Perish*. Mallea is essentially a lyric writer, a poet, who conceives the human, novelistic material of all of his works in musical terms that he controls thematically, like

an essayist. In structure, the novel's division into two parts allows for greater intensity and control in each. Indeed, the two halves can be read as interrelated novellas; the only link is the tortured self-awareness of Ágata, which informs the whole.

She is the sole survivor of part 1. In part 2, Ágata is given what amounts to a chance for a new life in Bahía Blanca, with a new cast of characters. Unfortunately, Ágata remains the same. She cannot forget her past, which colors her present and foreshadows her future.

In *All Green Shall Perish*, character cannot be separated from theme. This is ritual narration in which the central character is offered as a sacrifice to the universe. The near consummation of part 1 is fulfilled in part 2. The rite is complete.

In *La vida blanca* (1960; the sterile life), Mallea describes what he calls the "inner war": "A sweet immanent charity illumines the lives of men; all the rest is uncertainty, pettiness and betrayal." This sentence beautifully synthesizes the theme, tone, and message of *All Green Shall Perish*. The somber conclusion is never in doubt. What draws and holds

the reader's attention is the lyric affirmation of the human condition that is sensed throughout Mallea's requiem for Ágata Cruz.

Another theme, secondary in *All Green Shall Perish* but central to Mallea, is the search for authenticity in a specifically Argentine context. In *Historia de una pasión Argentina* (1937; history of an Argentine passion) and other essays that probe the Argentine national character, Mallea advocates a spiritually authentic Argentina as opposed to a shadowy and successful materialism. In this context, it is clear that Ágata and, to a lesser extent, Nicanor represent aspects of the "invisible Argentina" as opposed to the inauthentic "visible Argentina" of Sotero, Romo, and Ema de Volpe.

It is in universal terms that *All Green Shall Perish* is equated with authenticity and emerges as the supreme human value of Mallea's fiction.

Critical Context

All Green Shall Perish has been Mallea's most popular single work of fiction, as well as the novel that received the greatest critical acclaim. It was written at the peak of Mallea's creative powers, along with the autobiographical essay *Historia de una pasión Argentina* and the novels *Fiesta en noviembre* (1938; *Fiesta in November*, 1942) and *La bahía de silencio* (1940; *The Bay of Silence*, 1944).

Mallea was an extremely prolific writer who continued to publish novels, short stories, essays, and plays up to his death. He enjoyed his greatest popularity during the 1930's, 1940's, and 1950's, anticipating the "boom" of the Latin American

novel in the 1960's and 1970's. Mallea did not share the preoccupation with technical innovation of such novelists as Julio Cortázar, Carlos Fuentes, and Mario Vargas Llosa, although several of his works are innovative and experimental, most notably *La ciudad junto al río inmóvil* (1936; the city on the motionless river), *Fiesta in November*, and *All Green Shall Perish*. The themes of Mallea's fiction did not change significantly in the course of his career, and, in general, his work has fallen from fashion since the 1950's. Nevertheless, the titles cited in this article continue to enjoy a wide readership and are the subject of many critical studies.

ALWAYS RUNNING: La Vida Loca, Gang Days in L.A.

Author: Luis J. Rodriguez (1954-   )
Type of work: Autobiography
Time of work: The 1950's through 1992
Locale: Los Angeles, California
First published: 1993

Principal Personages

Luis Rodriguez, the author and protagonist. He tells his story of growing up in the barrios of Los Angeles as a Mexican immigrant. His use of the Spanish language was punished in school, and his knowledge of English was at first minimal, resulting in his virtual abandonment by his teachers.

As a child, Luis begins stealing, and by the age of ten he has formed his own gang. He sees one of his friends killed before he reaches the age of ten. Later, he takes an interest in reading, in art, and in music, but by then his life has lost much of its hope. Much of his time is spent in jail rather than in school. He becomes involved in community activism and attempts to stop the gang warfare. A note of despair remains at the end of the book, for even though Luis has made it out of the barrio, he must work to keep his young son from falling into the same kind of life.

Chente Ramirez, a man hired to run the local community center and a positive role model for the author. Although from the White Fence Barrio, considered to be among the most violent of the barrios, ruled by the oldest street gang in the Los Angeles area, Ramirez has never been involved in a gang himself, but has instead concentrated on education, including martial arts training and revolutionary theory. He appears about midway through the book and represents the turning point in the author's life. He offers Luis his first socially useful job, running a work crew of other teens to clean up the area. Ramirez is always there to help, bailing the author out of jail after he shoots another youth, explaining the situation in the barrios as he sees it, and stressing that the system must be changed. He arranges Luis' escape from the barrio and is instrumental in helping the boy to lead a successful and productive life.

Miguel Robles, one of the author's first and closest friends in the barrio. Miguel is the leader of the first gang Luis is involved in, a relatively innocent club formed when the boys are eleven years old. Throughout the story, Miguel is portrayed as a leader. He is always in that position as the gangs escalate into major military forces. Miguel is shot to death by a deputy sheriff near the end of the book. This becomes the impetus for the first real attempt at unity among the various street gangs in the area and the identification of society, especially the police, as the enemy.

Chava, a leader of the Sangra gang, the major rival to the Las Lomas gang of which the author is a member. Chava is portrayed as a ruthless warlord. Luis' first serious act of violence is aimed at Chava. As the chief of the enemy forces, he becomes the target of revenge after a member of the Las Lomas gang is killed in a fight. Luis takes part in the burning down of Chava's house. Chava is slaughtered in a gang war, stabbed repeatedly and bludgeoned to death.

Mr. Madison, the principal of the author's high school. Madison approves the addition of a course in Chicano history and culture to the school curriculum. He resists change when it seems to be coming too fast and opposes a number of projects the students attempt to initiate. Although portrayed as sympathetic to the students, Madison is found to be of little help because he wants to work within the system rather than changing it.

Rano, the author's older brother. Rano is portrayed as an angry young man. He takes out his frustrations by torturing Luis. At the same time, he is Luis' protector when other children attack him. Rano becomes successful at sports and runs with an older crowd than does his brother. The two become estranged.

Viviana, the author's first girlfriend. Viviana is a member of Sangra, the rival street gang. Although they love each other, the two are doomed to break up because of the gang rivalry. She moves away from Luis, choosing her loyalty to Sangra over her loyalty to her boyfriend.

Form and Content

Always Running is essentially an autobiography, although the author admits in the preface that names have been changed because he does not wish to hurt people. Most of the major characters in the book are gang members and criminals; many were also the author's friends. Some of the characters are identified only by first names, or even nicknames. In addition, some of the incidents in the story have been "synthesized"; they are based on real events in the author's life, but details such as particular street names and exact sequences of events have been altered. This is a common method of writing, often (though not in this case) indicated by a disclaimer to the effect that "names have been changed to protect the innocent." In this book, names have been changed to protect the guilty as well.

The book is mostly sequential, as an autobiography should be, but there are many asides referring to earlier events and foreshadowing later ones. There is a prologue and an epilogue, both referring to the time, 1991 through 1992, in which the book was written. Most of the book, however, takes place in the 1960's and early 1970's, during the author's youth.

The content of *Always Running* is far from cheerful. This is the story of a boy growing up in the barrios of Los Angeles and the horrid events he experiences and participates in. The story begins in Watts, where the author spent his first years in the United States.

Luis was a Mexican immigrant who spoke little English. He finds himself in a society in which Spanish is considered not only alien but also inferior. Luis' teachers are unfamiliar with his native language, and its use in school is punished. For a boy who cannot get along in English, this is devastating.

Luis' older brother, Rano, is placed in a class for retarded children because he is incapable of learning in an atmosphere in which he cannot understand the teacher. Luis himself is relegated to a corner of his own classroom, where he accomplishes nothing and learns nothing.

Most of the story takes place in and around a barrio called Las Lomas (the hills), an area of Los Angeles inhabited almost entirely by Chicanos. This is where Luis spends his childhood and teens, and where he learns that he is unwelcome in American society. By the age of seven, he is stealing candy and toys. By the age of ten, he has formed his first gang.

The gangs originally were no more sinister than the clubs that children in better circumstances form. They began with secret codes, clubhouses, and the like, but before long the gangs became criminal. Stealing candy accelerated to car theft, holdups, and burglary. Education was virtually nonexistent among gang members and other barrio children. Dropout rates in that part of Los Angeles were about 50 percent before students even reached high school.

Deprived of a proper education and not allowed to be a real part of American society, Chicanos formed their own society. It was not a pretty one. The Chicanos of Los Angeles were not primarily migrant agricultural laborers. They lived in shacks in the outskirts of the city. Their major sources of income were odd jobs at low wages, for those who could find them, welfare, and crime.

Sex is a major theme of this work, but it is nothing like the romantic sex and love of many mainstream novels. Sex is often violent, and rape is more common than romantic relationships. In male relationships, true friendship is rare, often replaced by what amounts to military alliances. When true, positive emotions surface, they generally end in betrayal, violence, or even death.

In one particularly telling scene, the author falls in love, for the first time, with a young lady named Viviana. Theirs is the classic *Romeo and Juliet* situation. Viviana is part of the Sangra gang, a rival to the Las Lomas gang of which Luis is a member. At a high school dance, the two hug and kiss on a rooftop while a gang war rages below on the dance floor.

Drugs were also a major factor in the barrio culture. The young people in the barrios, driven by despair, sought a way out. Drugs provided a means of escape. As in most levels of culture, alcohol was the first drug with which adolescents, and even children, experimented. There are few scenes in the central chapters of *Always Running* in which the author is completely sober. Alcohol is often not the endpoint. Rodriguez tells the story of his first trials with marijuana, with the variety of synthetic drugs usually called "angel dust," and finally with heroin.

The major theme of this book is violence. A variety of Latino gangs forms as the book progresses. They fight for territory, for drugs, for girls, for anything they can get. Luis witnesses his first death of a friend when he is ten. He sees people shot, stabbed, and raped before entering high school. Finally, he becomes a participant in the violence that surrounds him.

Even within a particular gang, violence was the order of the day. Entry into the Las Lomas gang involved running a gauntlet of kicks and punches by fellow gang members. The authorities who were supposed to be keeping the peace often did the opposite. Rodriguez cites several instances in which the Los Angeles police and the sheriff's department deliberately instigated fights among Chicano gangs.

In later chapters, some hope is offered, but it is usually short-lived. The author, in the midst of taking part in fights and seeing people die, takes an interest in reading, in art, and in music. A few adults are helpful and encourage his studies, but even then there is little hope. The people in charge of the boy's life constantly bring him down. He spends little time in school and much time in jail. Along the way, he becomes interested in trying to help end the gang wars and becomes a leader of the peacekeeping forces trying to address the real problems of the community. Rodriguez joins in political protests, strikes, and other community actions.

Throughout the book, the author's best efforts are met with defeat. Every attempt at peace seems to end in violence, often instigated by the very authorities that are supposed to prevent people from hurting one another. The usual response by the author is to return violence with violence. His arrests for drug use and petty theft become arrests for grand larceny, assault, and finally attempted murder.

Ultimately, Rodriguez makes it out of the barrio. He becomes a successful poet and publisher, working hard to aid those who are trying to end the violence in Los Angeles and other areas. The book ends on a note of hope, as the author tries to keep his young son from following the same sort of life that he himself led. At the same time, however, a note of despair remains. The epilogue is set in 1992, in the wake of the Los Angeles riots following the beating of black motorist Rodney King and the acquittal of the police officers who beat him.

Analysis

Always Running sends a mixed message of hope and despair. Most of the time, the reader is shown the lives of people living at the lowest levels of society, with little hope of change. On the other hand, the author himself is a living example of someone who did find his way out of the barrio and is now a successful member of society.

The book seethes with anger, but there is also a sign of hope. Although attempts at reform are often met with failure, things do seem to be getting better, at least for some people. It is interesting to note that the book was completed in the aftermath of one of the bloodiest riots in American history, by an author who probably would have been personally involved in those riots if they had occurred during his teen years.

The style of *Always Running* mirrors this mixed signal. There are graphic scenes of rape and murder. Children die bloody deaths. The police are shown clearly as the enemy, but most of the violence takes place among the Chicanos themselves. There are also characters in the book, some of them Hispanic, some English-speaking, some black, who try to make peace and try to address the real problems.

Ultimately, this book is a cry for help, but it is not by any means a call for charity. Rather, it is a call for understanding. The phrase in the book's subtitle, "La Vida Loca" (the crazy life), summarizes the author's point of view. Driven by despair, hopelessness, and anger, the inhabitants of the barrios turn against one another rather than against the real villains. They actually are crazy, because there is no sane way of dealing with a society that will not accept them.

At one level, this book is an autobiography of someone born into a hell on Earth who has managed to escape. At another level, it is the story of a subculture of American society. At the most important level, *Always Running* is an indictment against a society that will not accept change, that will not tolerate differences, and that will meet attempts at assimilation with violence and discrimination. It is especially an indictment against a legal system that assumes that people from minority groups are criminals by nature.

Always Running is also a book about escape, escape from a society that will not tolerate differences, escape into drugs and a fantasy world that is better than reality, and escape from society through creation of a subculture, one that is even more violent. Gang members react to their persecution by persecuting one another. Ultimately, they react to police brutality and to intolerance of Americans who happen to be of Spanish-speaking origin by killing and raping members of their own ethnic group.

The story here is not pretty, but it is real, and it applies to much more of American society than the Chicano subculture of Los Angeles. It applies to any group of people who are not allowed to live their lives. It is a comment on the American Dream, which in some cases is the American Nightmare. It is written in rage, but also in love. The message is that there is hope. Few can escape the barrios by themselves as the author has, but with help from the successful members of society, life can be better.

The message of this book is encapsulated in the title. Chicanos and other minorities are always running, because it is impossible to stay in the same place and succeed in life. The book ends with a two-word paragraph, addressed by the author to his teenage son, in the wake of the latest series of riots: Stop running. As long as you continue running, you will get nowhere. Only by addressing the real problems can solutions be found.

Critical Context

The barrios of Los Angeles are not the only ones in the United States. On the East Coast, there are similar cultures of Puerto Rican immigrants and their descendants, particularly in New York City. African Americans, the nation's largest minority group, have their own slums and a history of oppression that is just as severe. Although the author concentrates on his own group, *Always Running* is a commentary on all minorities in American cities.

It is important to consider that the author's teen

years were during the 1960's, a time of turmoil different from later decades. Times have changed in some ways. Spanish is now accepted as a second language for many Americans, or even as a language of primary use. Black and Hispanic subcultures are now considered to be parts of the American heritage, and there are courses taught relating to them in our schools. Schoolchildren are often taught in multilingual and multicultural classrooms. Problems, however, remain.

The barrios still exist, and riots still occur. Police officers still persecute members of minority groups.

Rodriguez is part of a movement urging that social problems be addressed, and *Always Running* is a statement of his commitment. In a broader context, the author mentions his involvement in protests against the Vietnam War and his involvement in other social issues. American society is perhaps the most democratic in the world, yet it still has subcultures that are violent and condemned or ignored by leaders. Rodriguez urges that all Americans be accepted as Americans. Then, and only then, will there be peace. In the meantime, minority groups will always be running.

THE APPLE IN THE DARK

Author: Clarice Lispector (1925-1977)
Type of work: Novel
Type of plot: Mythic
Time of plot: The late 1950's
Locale: A remote, desolate farming region of Brazil
First published: *A Maçã no Escuro*, 1961 (English translation, 1967)

Principal Characters

Martim, a middle-aged statistician from São Paulo. A heavyset blue-eyed man, he is in hiding because he believes that he has killed his wife in a jealous rage. He hides out for two weeks in a nearly empty hotel in central Brazil that is otherwise occupied only by a German and a servant. When he thinks they have gone to report his presence to the police, he flees and finds a job doing manual labor on a small farm in exchange for board and room. He spends a long time on the farm, which is owned and run by Vitória. He is involved for a while with Ermelinda, Vitória's younger cousin. Most of the action takes place in Martim's mind, as he tries to understand who he is and how he relates to his circumstances.

Vitória, a tough woman in her fifties who inherited a farm from an aunt and uncle whom she had visited in childhood. She spent her youth caring for her father, and only after his death has she been free to choose to move out to the country and run the farm herself. The farm is an isolated one,

and until Martim appears, Vitória has lived with only the company of her cousin Ermelinda, Francisco the hired man, and a mulatto cook with a small daughter. Attracted to Martim, Vitória is impelled to explain her life to him and, in the process, comes to a better understanding of herself.

Ermelinda, a young woman from Rio de Janeiro who has come to live on her cousin Vitória's farm after being widowed three years before Martim appears. Her sensuous indolence and vague spiritualism are attributed to her bedridden childhood and consequent overindulgence. Ermelinda falls in love with Martim, is sexually involved with him for a time, then falls out of love and distances herself from him. Opposite in personality from her cousin Vitória, who works very hard on the farm and continually barks out orders to Martim and Francisco, Ermelinda drifts about eating candied almonds, sentimental and idle, believing in her vague presentiments about the future.

The Novel

On the surface, the story in *The Apple in the Dark* could not be simpler. A man commits a crime, flees into the desolate interior of Brazil, arrives at a remote farm, is taken on as a farmhand, is reported to the authorities, and is arrested and returned to face the law. It is not the minimal action of the plot that intrigues the reader but rather the process of searching for some meaning in life, for

some definition of the world and of one's place in it, that provides the interest of the novel.

Primarily, it is Martim's quest for self-awareness that forms the core of the story. The mythic nature of his quest is straightforwardly indicated by the titles of the three sections into which the book is divided: "How a Man Is Made," "The Birth of the Hero," and "The Apple in the Dark." The author, in a stroke of brilliance, has managed to combine parallels to at least two major complementary views of man's existence in the unfolding of Martim's symbolic journey: the biblical story of the garden of Eden and the Darwinian theory of evolution.

From the beginning of the book, the reader is alerted to these two viewpoints. Martim awakes from sleep "on a night as dark as night can get," immediately after fleeing from a crime that he will come to see as an act that frees him to start all over again in life. The nature of the crime is revealed to the reader only toward the end of the novel. Martim's flight takes him first through total darkness over unknown terrain, permitting him to focus exclusively on his sensual feelings and to ignore the burden of civilization behind him. As the sun comes up, he begins to appreciate an even closer identity with nature in its most primitive forms: stones, dirt, searing heat, silence. Bereft of language, he discovers a great joy in repeating meaningless statements to the flora and fauna around him. By the time, early in the novel, that he comes upon the farmhouse where most of the story takes place, he has duplicated a sort of climb up the evolutionary ladder. Having shed the trappings of a man, he has begun to learn what it is to be like "a creature [who] does not think and does not get involved, and is still completely there."

The farm is owned and run by Vitória, an unmarried woman in her fifties who appears to be a tower of strength and self-reliance. Staying with her is her cousin Ermelinda, a dreamy, ethereal woman recently widowed, whose rather poetic manner of approaching life is a constant source of uneasiness for Vitória. The bulk of the novel consists in observing, through the eyes of the three principal characters, the slow process of change in Martim and the effect that he has on Vitória and Ermelinda. By the novel's end, however, the reader cannot be sure that the two women have experienced any genuine enlightenment, although it is probable that the protagonist now at least realizes that he has missed gaining a firm grip on the meaning of existence. In the last paragraph of the book, Martim finally understands that "we are not so guilty after all; we are more stupid than guilty." The quest for knowledge, he learns too late, is like "reaching for an apple in the dark—and trying not to drop it."

Analysis

Vitória has spent much of her life caring for her dying father, and as a result, she has never had, or at least has never reached for, a love of her own. She now fears love and has hardened herself against all possibility of it. The confrontation with Martim finally forces her to face her empty and near-tragic existence. At the climax of the novel, which occurs rather melodramatically during a rare and violent rainstorm, Vitória, unable to bear her dearth of love, races to the woodshed where Martim sleeps. Martim, however, has fled into the woods during the storm, like King Lear, distraught and seeking cleansing and purification in nature. It is not long after this episode that Vitória calls for the authorities to pick up Martim.

Ermelinda has an elliptical way of talking to people. Unlike her cousin, she embraces love; in fact, she falls in love with Martim almost at first sight, and before long they have become lovers. Her way of expressing her feelings for him is strangely indirect. She explains that if she comes up and says to him, "Look at that fern!" she is really saying, "I love you." Ermelinda is so frightened of death that she has retreated into a world of private symbolism.

Lispector read her existentialists closely. One can pick up veiled allusions to novels by Jean-Paul Sartre and Albert Camus in *The Apple in the Dark*. The character of Martim contains elements of both Meursault in Camus' *The Stranger* (1942) and Roquentin in Sartre's *Nausea* (1938). The protagonist has set out in search of his own essence. What Martim fails to realize, and what will ultimately bring him up short in his quest for a new Eden, is that he has deluded himself from the beginning. It is almost as if he is telling the reader that his crime was necessary as a means of escaping from a banal and deadening existence into a chance for true, human essence. His error lies in thinking that the initial act will not color subsequent events; indeed, it will determine them.

Critical Context

Lispector achieved her first general acclaim for the collection of stories *Laços de Familia* (1960; *Family Ties*, 1972), in which many of the protagonists, like Martim, struggle—often unsuccessfully—for a sense of self and harmony with the outside world. This concern with the subjective world, which receives its most complex articulation in *The Apple in the Dark*, is also examined in *A Paixão Segundo G. H.* (1964; *The Passion According to G. H.*, 1988) and *Água Viva* (1973; *The Stream of Life*, 1989). Lispector is among the Brazilian revisionists, postwar writers whose move away from the regionalism of the 1920's and 1930's and whose focus on more universal themes have been major forces in mainstreaming Brazilian literature. Indeed, Gregory Rabassa, in the introduction to his translation of *The Apple in the Dark*, includes Lispector among contemporary Brazilian novelists who are "in tune with . . . international currents."

AUNT JULIA AND THE SCRIPTWRITER

Author: Mario Vargas Llosa (1936-   )
Type of work: Novel
Type of plot: Comic realism
Time of plot: The 1950's
Locale: Lima, Peru
First published: *La tía Julia y el escribidor*, 1977 (English translation, 1982)

Principal Characters

Mario, the narrator-protagonist, a confident college student who is underemployed as a radio newswriter. He is waiting for the chance to devote himself completely to a literary life, preferably in Paris. Hardly anything distinguishes Mario— indiscriminately and purposely called by the author's nicknames as a young man—from the real Mario Vargas Llosa. Mario/Varguitas/Marito serializes comically and romantically his courtship of Julia, an aunt by his uncle's marriage, and his apprenticeship as a writer under the guidance of Pedro Camacho, a scriptwriter for radio soap operas. Mario's "autobiography" is an exercise in indiscretion, even though his depiction of himself as an intelligent, tall, dark, and handsome extrovert is rendered truthful by the other characters. Mario sees marriage alternately as a challenge or as an adventure, the material of which can be turned into literature, specifically short stories. As the narrator of the final chapter, he summarizes in one page how he reunites with Julia to share a life that would last eight years.

Aunt Julia, a divorced Bolivian who cannot bear children. She is fourteen years older than Mario. Physically attractive, she dazzles the young Mario with what he perceives to be healthy cun-

ning and spontaneity. Despite the close family ties that would prevent their ever getting together, it is Julia who is decisive and ultimately responsible for their union. She is warm and brave, and she has a wonderful sense of humor, which is what allows her to continue, despite her awareness that their relationship will not last. Her divorce from a marriage to Mario that lasted three more years than she expected is described strictly from Mario's point of view.

Pedro Camacho, a Bolivian working in Peru, brought in by the radio station in which Varguitas works single-handedly to organize and produce the soap operas they broadcast. Introverted and rather mechanical, he thinks only in catastrophic terms. His stories rely on extensive melodramas that are so repetitive and lacking in imagination that at times he loses characters or switches them from one program to another without knowing he is doing it. In the final analysis, he is his own excessive creation. The readers know little about the true Pedro but can intuit a certain madness. Marito, echoing the real Vargas Llosa, attributes his own ability to organize a narrative's totality to Camacho's type of truly professional, even if perverse, influence.

The Novel

Aunt Julia and the Scriptwriter is a comedic novel about the education of young Mario (called variously Marito and Varguitas) that combines nu-

merous elements of Vargas Llosa's own life with the fictional relationships with Aunt Julia and Pedro Camacho in Lima in the 1950's to form an autobiographical fable of identity that is neither autobiography nor history but rather an artistically rendered portrait of the artist as a young man. The primary narrator of the work, Mario, recounts, from a distance of at least twelve years, his youthful love for his aunt by marriage, their improbable courtship and hilarious attempts to circumvent the law to get married, and his own life as a law student, radio newswriter, and would-be short-story writer. Each of the novel's twenty chapters, except the last two, which conclude Mario's narrative, are arranged so that the odd-numbered ones are Mario's attempts to describe his life and fortunes and the even-numbered ones are scripts of soap operas by Pedro Camacho, an indefatigable and prolific Bolivian scriptwriter.

The work begins with a semiserious Mario introducing himself as a student and news director of Radio Panamerica, the lesser of Lima's two radio stations owned by the Genaro family. Pedro Camacho has just been brought from Bolivia to write original radio serials to replace those the Genaros brought from Cuba. Mario's initial encounters with Camacho and his aunt Julia, who has just been divorced and has moved to Lima from Brazil, are equally unpromising but turn out, in true melodramatic fashion, to be important first steps in forming a professional bond between Mario and the scriptwriter and a very personal one with Aunt Julia.

The story of the furtive courtship between Mario and Julia forms the central portion of Mario's narrative, as the two fall quite hopelessly, passionately, and madly in love with each other. Their love, when it is finally discovered after their ill-starred elopement, brings down upon them a family catastrophe that competes, in all of its ab-

surdity and odd manifestations, with elements of Camacho's soap operas, the stories that are recounted throughout the novel. The comedy of errors of their elopement—they dash about the countryside to find a mayor who will, for a bribe, marry the underage Mario without parental consent—has exactly enough improbability about it to make it resemble the vicissitudes of real life. So does life often resemble bad literature and B-pictures.

Meanwhile, Pedro Camacho's soap operas make him the toast of Lima. The stories and the fortunes of their characters are on everyone's lips when Camacho begins to show signs of fatigue and then madness. His villains all turn out to be Argentines or Peruvians with Argentine proclivities. Despite official protests to Radio Panamerica by the Argentine ambassador, Camacho persists in vilifying Argentina and its people. Far more serious is the growing bewilderment among his listeners. Characters who died in one serial are resurrected in another, sometimes with different professions; other characters move in and out of several serials; still others change their names in mid-script. Public confusion and dismay grow as, one by one, the principal continuing characters are killed off in one catastrophe after another until, after a series of disasters, each worse than the one before, all of fictional Lima is destroyed cataclysmically, and Camacho is finally committed to an insane asylum.

The work's final chapter serves as a neat conclusion to all the cliff-hanger questions about Mario's narrative and explains what has happened, over a twelve-year period, to Mario, Julia, Pedro Camacho, and lesser characters. In so doing, it serves both to provide a neat summary of much of the novel's action and to mark a decidedly new phase in Mario's fortunes.

Analysis

The central theme of the work, clearly a *Bildungsroman* in nature, is the act of writing, of telling one's story and a succession of stories. The novel's epigraph, from Salvador Elizondo's *El grafógrafo* (1972), is a perfect introduction to the work, as a classical statement of the metaphysical

and epistemological state of contemporary literature in which writers write about writing about writing and invite readers to imagine them imagining themselves writing about writing. Surely an invitation to formalist and deconstructive critical interpretation, the epigraph reinforces the perfect

Viconian circularity of the novel, in which Mario the narrator is a character of Mario the novelist and in which both are writing about being writers and about one notorious writer, the tireless but insane scriptwriter, whose creations are also those of Mario the novelist.

All other elements of the novel—the themes of romance, uproariously amusing misadventures, accidental meetings, amorous assignations, love unrequited and gloriously requited, ambition and entertainment—are subservient to the overmastering passions of Mario, Pedro, and the novelist to memorialize experience, fictionalize life, and artfully reinvent identity. The final chapter is supremely important in setting several records as straight as they can be in Mario's narrative, in the supposed events and motives of Pedro Camacho's life and works, and in the ultimately enigmatic life and adventures of the ineluctable Aunt Julia.

Critical Context

Aunt Julia and the Scriptwriter has been variously hailed as a "ribald classic," a pure example of the "literature of exhaustion" that reflects upon itself, and a postmodern novel that ratifies Vargas Llosa's early preeminence in *el boom latino americano* of the 1960's and 1970's. It is likely to become an international classic and one of the basic works upon which Vargas Llosa's literary reputation will ultimately rest. Unlike most of his previous and subsequent novels (especially *La guerra del fin del mundo*, 1981; *The War of the End of the World*, 1984), it is a distinctly comic work, handled with a light touch, testimony to his versatile imagination.

Vargas Llosa has produced a consistently first-rate series of works in the fields of criticism, journalism, fiction, and drama, explicating and elucidating the varied facets of Latin American life and culture both to fellow Latin Americans and to an increasing number of European and North American readers. Although he shares, surely and clearly, the Magical Realism of such pioneering figures as Gabriel García Márquez and Julio Cortázar, he has transmuted this technique into a more immediately accessible form of fiction that has been widely accepted in the last half of the twentieth century.

AURA

Author: Carlos Fuentes (1928-   )
Type of work: Novel
Type of plot: Fantasy
Time of plot: The early 1960's
Locale: Mexico City
First published: 1962 (English translation, 1965)

Principal Characters

Felipe Montero, a young historian and part-time schoolteacher. Bored with his present job of teaching "useless facts" to "sleepy pupils," he desires a change from his daily routine, and he is drawn to an advertisement that seems addressed personally to him. He accepts the job of translating the memoirs of Señora Consuelo Llorente's dead husband. In the mysterious, gothic setting of Consuelo's dark, moldy home, he meets Aura, the ancient woman's niece. Gradually, he is drawn into a series of bewildering, grotesque occurrences that suggest the fantastic bond between the two women. His growing desire for Aura is consummated when he makes love to her and swears, "Nothing can separate us." Eventually, Felipe realizes that this "sterile conception" engenders another self, his own double, the embodiment of Consuelo's late husband General Llorente. Through his sexual union with young Aura and his promise of undying love, Felipe completes his role in Consuelo's morbid scheme to perpetuate her youth and passionate marriage to the general.

Señora Consuelo Llorente, Aura's strange, eccentric aunt, who Felipe figures is about 109 years old. Obsessed with prolonging her youth and unwilling to relinquish the past, Consuelo dabbles in the occult. She married General Llorente at the age of fifteen and was widowed thirty-four years later in 1901, but she has remained ageless through her illusory double, Aura, waiting for the fated reappearance of her beloved groom.

Aura, Consuelo's young niece, pale and beautiful, with loose black hair and astonishing green eyes. Aura seduces Felipe, luring him into the old widow's plot to re-create her dead husband and preserve their love. Felipe sees her only in shadows; he senses her more than he actually feels her. In loving her, Felipe loses himself, for Aura is merely Consuelo's imagined self, a materialization of the old woman's past.

The Novel

The fantastic nature of this short novel is indicated at its very beginning, when Felipe Montero, an indigent young man, reads a newspaper advertisement requesting the services of a historian. The advertisement is so suited to his own experience, needs, and skills that it seems to be addressed to him and to no one else; all that is missing is his name. The sense of Montero's being especially summoned by the advertisement is further emphasized when he arrives at an ancient mansion in the old section of town where no one lives. As he enters, he takes one last look to try to "retain some single image of that indifferent outside world" before entering a realm of magic and imagination.

Although the incredibly old Consuelo Llorente ostensibly wishes Montero to edit the memoirs of her dead husband for publication, one suspects that she has other, more profound plans for the young historian. With the appearance of her beautiful young niece, Aura, who immediately exerts a hypnotic hold on Montero, the reader's suspicion that this is a sort of modern fairy tale or parable is confirmed. The mysterious, old, witchlike crone, the quietly beautiful young girl, and the summoned young man establish an archetypal fairy-tale situation.

The house itself is typically gothic and always in darkness. The old woman's room is filled with religious relics and lighted only with votive candles; in private she engages in occult rituals and makes entreaties to Gabriel to sound his trumpet. She continually caresses a pet rabbit, whose name is Saga, and the trunk that contains her dead husband's papers seems always to be covered with rats. Montero feels a pleasure in the house that he has never felt before. He decides that the old woman has some secret power over her niece, and he is obsessed with the desire not only to set her free but also to possess her himself. Consuelo's witchlike nature is further emphasized when, as Montero studies her husband's papers, he discovers that she must be at least 109 years old.

The mystery of the relationship between Consuelo and her niece deepens when Montero sees Aura skinning a young goat in the kitchen. He goes to the old woman's room only to find her performing the same skinning action in mime. When he dreams of Aura, he sees the old lady's image superimposed on the image of Aura. Although Montero believes that Aura is kept in the house to preserve the illusion of youth for the old woman, the truth of the matter is even more occult and mysterious. Aura seems to age each day. One day, she appears to be a girl of twenty, the next, a woman of forty. When Montero makes love to her, the act is prefaced by Aura's rubbing a wafer against her thighs and offering him half of it to eat. He falls upon her naked arms, which are stretched out on the side of the bed like the crucifix on the wall: "Aura opens up like an altar." To complete this carnal communion, she makes him promise to love her forever, even if she grows old and dies.

As the actions of Consuelo and Aura become more and more blended, as if one is an echo of the other, Montero realizes that the "sterile conception" of their lovemaking has created another double, his own other half which he now seeks. He finally discovers the secret of the old woman's relationship to Aura on the last page of General Llorente's papers, where he reads of Consuelo's growing herbs that will perform the magic of creating Aura as an image of her own youth. Moreover, he discovers portraits of the young couple. He realizes that the old woman is Aura and that the old general is himself. Montero fears that the hand of the past will wipe away his own features, "the cardboard features that hid your true face, your real appearance, the appearance you once had but then forgot." He rejects the human vanity of clock time and accepts what seems fated to happen to him.

In the final scene of the novel, Montero goes to Consuelo's room and calls for Aura. The voice he hears from the darkness tells him that she is gone and will not come back: "I'm exhausted. She's already exhausted. I've never been able to keep her with me for more than three days." Montero tears off Aura's robe and embraces and kisses her. As the moonlight falls on her face, he discovers it to be as brittle and yellowed as the memoirs—to be the body and face of Consuelo. He accepts this, however, for he has promised to love Aura even when she is old. He embraces her and waits until the cloud covers the moon, when the "memory of youth, of youth reembodied, rules the darkness." In the last line of the story, Consuelo promises that Aura will come back again: "We'll bring her back together."

Analysis

There are several levels of meaning in the novel. On one level, it is a love story in which the desires of youth and beauty triumph over the reality of old age and death. In a basic sense, this is a story of the power of pure desire to overcome the limitations of external reality. On the unconscious level, it is an archetypal parable about a man seduced into the loss of the ego, enabling him to enter completely into the world of the woman, for it is the imaginative reality of the woman that constitutes both erotic and supernatural transcendence over the external world. Culturally, the story suggests a theme that Fuentes has explored in other works, the simultaneous existence of the old Mexico superimposed upon the new.

The novel is narrated in the second person, in the present tense, as if Montero were recounting the events as they occur. For example, as he looks into the eyes of Aura for the first time, he sees them surge and change: "You look into them and tell yourself it isn't true. . . . But you can't deceive yourself: those eyes do surge, do change, as if offering you a landscape that only you can see and desire." This unusual narrative strategy not only creates a sense of gradually engulfing mystery, much like that in a detective novel, but also effectively eradicates Montero's own personal past and creates a sense of the presentness of the past. Moreover, the second-person narrative stance emphasizes both the concrete detail of Montero's experience and his growing sense of being lost in a dream reality. As he becomes engulfed in the eerie atmosphere of the old house, the reader becomes absorbed in the eerie tone of the novel itself.

As a historian, accustomed to studying the past as it is preserved in documents—a past, that is, kept at a certain distance—Montero finds himself drawn into a past that is maintained in the present by the imaginative creation of the old Consuelo, a past that is not preserved in historical texts but that lives in the mind and the reality of the other. Although he desires to take Aura outside the occult and hermetically sealed world of the old woman, the imagination and the realm of the sacred prove more powerful than external, profane reality.

The action of the novel hovers uneasily between reality and fantasy, as both Montero and the reader search futilely for realistic explanations for the mystery of Aura and Consuelo. Just as Montero is caught up in an increasingly occult reality, so also is the reader, who finally must accept the magical nature of the events and the ultimate reality of the imagination. The sense that the novel has of existing somewhere between the real world and the world of the imagination is emphasized not only by the gothic house, the occult Aura, and the old Consuelo, but also by Montero's being caught up in obsessive dreams that become so blended with the fantastic nature of his actual experience that the two realms cannot be distinguished.

Critical Context

Although many of Fuentes' novels have been concerned with political and social reality, his short stories and novellas have more often been mythic and symbolic. *Aura* is perhaps his best-known work in which magic, the occult, and particularly the witch archetype are of central importance. In an earlier collection of short stories, *Los días enmascarados* (1954; the masked days), the same witch figure appears, as does the prevailing theme developed in *Aura* of the dominance of the past over the present.

Various sources for the story have been noted by critics. Perhaps the most commonly mentioned are Henry James's *The Aspern Papers* (1888), Alexander Pushkin's *Pikovaya dama* (1834; *The Queen of Spades*, 1858), and H. Rider Haggard's *She* (1887). The single most important source, however, as Fuentes himself has noted, is Jules Michelet's *La Sorcière* (1862; *The Witch of the Middle Ages*, 1863), in which a woman is depicted as a witch who has the ability to give birth to a being identical to herself.

Aura was practically ignored by reviewers when first published because it appeared almost at the same time as Fuentes' best-known and most controversial novel, *La muerte de Artemio Cruz* (1962; *The Death of Artemio Cruz*, 1964). *Aura* became recognized as a central text in Fuentes' continuing exploration of history, myth, and the anima archetype, as well as a particularly fine example of the genre of the fantastic.

THE AUTOBIOGRAPHY OF A BROWN BUFFALO

Author: Oscar Zeta Acosta (1935?-   )
Type of work: Autobiography
Time of work: The 1940's to the 1960's
Locale: California, Idaho, and Texas
First published: 1972

Principal Personages

Oscar Zeta Acosta, the narrator, whose life from the ages of five to thirty-three has resulted in an angst and myriad dilemmas. As a Chicano growing up first in Texas and then in California, he endured racism from whites. He even experienced discrimination from other Chicanos for not fitting their Anglicized version of an acceptable Chicano. Such experiences lead him to define himself as a "Brown Buffalo," an outsider removed even from his ostensible group. Following service in the Air Force, he attends college and becomes a lawyer, practicing as a legal aid attorney in Oakland, California, for one year. He increasingly suffers from angst until he nears physical and psychological collapse. His physical problems are exacerbated by an ambivalence about his cultural status: He is proud of being Chicano yet suffers for such affiliation. He desperately wants to effect systemic change to improve the lives of Chicanos and others victimized by what he has endured. By journeying into his memory concurrently with his trip of escape from San Francisco to Idaho to El Paso (his birthplace), he comes to understand his past and its importance for his future.

Pauline, Acosta's secretary in his Oakland, California, legal aid office. Her limited involvement in the narrative belies her significance to Acosta. Other than his grandmother, Pauline is the gentlest and most understanding woman he has ever known. She is fifty-seven years old and suffers from what Acosta at first thinks are "female problems" but actually is cancer, from which she dies early in the autobiography. Without her assistance, he can no longer put up what he calls the

pretense of being a lawyer, suffering as he does from conflicts he must resolve.

Dr. Serbin, Acosta's longtime psychiatrist. At the beginning of the book, Serbin has begun haunting Acosta's psyche. Acosta is increasingly angry and sarcastic about Serbin's inability to alleviate Acosta's angst. He fires Serbin as his psychiatrist on the day of his escape, but Serbin reappears in Acosta's fantasies during significant flashbacks of memory. Such recurrences decrease as Acosta's journey develops.

June MacAdoo, Acosta's lover in the period before he passed his bar exam and became a lawyer. He describes her as his only serious love affair of the 1960's. She broke up with him the year prior to his escape. He assumes that the breakup resulted because he had not yet set a date for their wedding. On the day of his escape he calls her, and she tells him that she is going to be married.

Jane Addison, the girl with whom Acosta is hopelessly in love in grade school. She is the archetype of other white girls and, later, women with whom Acosta will be obsessed until late in the book. She is blonde, beautiful, and intelligent. After Acosta fights with and beats a white racist boy in the school sandlot, Jane humiliates him by telling the teacher in front of the class that Acosta "stinks," forcing him to confront his social place as an outsider.

Alice Joy, Acosta's high-school sweetheart. His experience with her is a turning point in his life that haunts him until the conclusion of the book. He is so entranced by her that he asks her to marry him within days of their meeting. Upon learning

Acosta's name, Alice's mother rejects the possibility of the two youngsters dating. With self-deprecating humor, Acosta decides that he will change his name, but the change will be from Oscar to another first name. It is his last name, identifying him as a Brown Buffalo, that is the crux. Although Alice returns his affection, her stepfather hates Mexicans, so Acosta is rejected by her family. Acosta traces his angst and other ensuing problems to experiences attendant upon that rejection.

Form and Content

The Autobiography of a Brown Buffalo is the narrative of a dynamic and vibrant but tormented thirty-three-year-old Chicano who journeys both geographically (from California to Idaho to El Paso) and through his memory, in a search to understand his past and its influence upon his future. Of the book's sixteen chapters, the first five, interspersed with flashbacks, describe the events of July 1, 1967, the day of his "escape" from his present. Beginning with chapter six, the chapters alternate from his childhood to his current journey, with the chapters about his past merging chronologically with those about his present at the end of chapter fourteen. The remainder of the autobiography reaches its conclusion in January, 1968.

In content, *The Autobiography of a Brown Buffalo* is the author's search to end his angst. First, he must find its cause. His problems are varied: racism; his ungainly physique; ulcers; intermittent sexual impotence; alcohol and other drug abuse; and a crisis with his profession. He begins his search with the first stark sentence, as he stands naked before his mirror contemplating the deterioration of his physical self.

As the autobiography unfolds, Acosta, having passed the bar exam a year previously, is working as a legal aid lawyer. He has become progressively dependent on his psychiatrist, but the therapy is at an impasse. Therapy sessions often involve silence, as if he has lost whatever interpersonal voice he previously had in contending with his dilemma.

In the first section, Acosta's attitude toward his legal career helps shape the narrative. Although on the surface he is deprecatingly sarcastic toward his law practice and his clients in Oakland, California, he very much wants to assist his poverty-stricken, socially victimized clients. He suffers from psychological and professional paralysis caused by his inability to provide systemic social change to improve his clients' lives. His practice has been one of keeping creditors from repossessing the automobiles and furniture of the poor and securing temporary restraining orders for women against abusive husbands. The year spent at his profession coincides with his physical affliction, the agony in his stomach.

At this crisis point for him, Acosta's secretary Pauline, whom he deeply appreciates, dies from cancer. With her death as a catalyst, he realizes that he can no longer endure his law practice and must break from his present situation. He "escapes" on July 1, 1967, which he declares as a day of rebellion. He quits his job, fires his psychiatrist, and leaves his life and friends in San Francisco.

At the beginning of this journey, the effects of discrimination, lingering since childhood, become an even greater theme. Despite the fact that he has been a proud "Brown Buffalo" since childhood, he must reevaluate his attitude toward his Chicano culture. Remembering when his family first moved from El Paso, Texas, to Riverbank, California, when he was a child, he recalls feeling like an outsider because of his ethnicity. He held "outsider" status even among the Chicanos in California because he was from Texas and did not speak English. As a result, he identified himself not just as a Chicano but as a "Brown Buffalo," the definition of which he has elaborated now to mean an outcast even from his or her own group. The buffalo is used symbolically: It was a member of a large herd, indigenous rather than foreign, but now, virtually extinct, it is an isolated member of an anachronistic minor group. Acosta identifies with that group and with the outcast buffalo.

The central part of the book describes his travels. He picks up Karin Wilmington, who is hitchhiking despite being wealthy. Her destination, more than his design, takes him to Idaho. Reverting again to memory, he recalls a turning point in his life. When he was in high school, he fell in love with Alice Joy, but he soon realized that her stepfather hated Chicanos. He now blames his problems on how he was treated by Alice's parents and the police, whom her stepfather called because Alice was dating Acosta, a Chicano. A policeman warned Acosta to stay away from Alice. Before parting, the policeman asked, "Savvy?" Acosta recalls that the convulsions and agony in his stomach began that night, upon that remark. The fact that the policeman used the word "savvy" in place of the Spanish "¿Sabes?," translatable as "Do you understand?" or "Got it?," makes this rejection culturally visceral for Acosta. This treatment was representative of his past and, he sensed, of his future. The treatment and denigration of his Chicano background was realized in even the most personal realm, love, and by the symbol of white authority, the police officer.

Acosta had decided earlier that his trip of escape would be a mapless journey, in counterpoint to his past, which was charted by the directional lines of ethnicity, his parents' and his first language, his skin color, and his hometown. To begin reversing this direction, he experiments with others' presuppositions of his ethnicity: He calls himself "Henry Hawk" and asserts that he is Samoan (as people assume) or a Blackfoot Indian from Oklahoma. Although it appears that this is a flippant attempt to disguise his Chicano identity from strangers, it is instead a mapping out of his future. Acosta suspends the determination of his identity until he has finished the search of his past.

Structurally, the chapters alternating between his past and his present merge following his experience in the Air Force, which he joins after his rejection by Alice's parents. He becomes a Baptist missionary, converting natives in Panama until his religious disillusionment. His experiences in un-

dergraduate and law school bring him to the year of legal aid work from which he is now fleeing. Following binges with alcohol and illicit drug use in Idaho and Colorado, Acosta realizes that such experiences are not the answer to his dilemma and decides to seek the answer in his birthplace of El Paso, Texas.

After arriving in El Paso, he visits his childhood home. He remembers suffering, even at the age of five, a "sickness" known to brown buffalos and sons of kings, manifested when he had thrown away anniversary rings his father had purchased for his mother. He was beginning to understand the social pressures weighing on his family and himself. This "sickness" at the age of five spanned his life, becoming the angst he feels at the age of thirty-three.

His restoration begins immediately after his reminiscences. On a streetcar in Juarez, the Mexican city separated from El Paso by the Rio Grande, he finally feels as if he belongs among the Mexicans. A young boy seeking tips boards the streetcar and sings "Adelita," a traditional song of the Mexican Revolution. Acosta remembers his mother singing such songs. As a child and commencing his memorial journey, he had thought such songs were "corny," but now, in a lyrical passage, he asks himself how much such a memory is worth. This is an emblematic memory poising him for cultural reaffirmation.

Enraptured by the Mexican women, whom he describes as the most beautiful women he had ever seen, he asserts that whatever his grade-school and high-school sweethearts, Jane Addison and Alice Joy, had meant to him, now they were merely memories, as distant as the possibility that the society they represented would ever fully accept him. His affirmation of the Mexican women toward whom he had been ambivalent since childhood signals a reintegration with his culture, and therefore with himself.

After this cultural re-encounter and subsequent experiences, he describes his feelings in the language of a conversion, cultural rather than religious, but with a rapidity reminiscent of St. Paul's in the Acts of the Apostles. The depth of his changes is revealed in a repetition of the book's beginning scene, as he stands naked before a mirror. This time, he weeps because of the changes he has failed to make in the world. He determines to go to East Los Angeles, involve himself with and write about Chicanos, and attack the causes of the systemic problems affecting himself and the millions of Chicanos for whom he is representative.

He concludes by inverting the usual process of the individual adopting a group identity: He proposes that the group adopt the "Brown Buffalo" identity he has claimed for himself. He ends up in Los Angeles, intending to run with the Brown Buffalo herd not toward extinction but toward creation, in a world he and they will make.

Analysis

The Autobiography of a Brown Buffalo is a vivid rendering of a Chicano's dramatic experiences. The overarching theme of the book is a deep, even obsessive, concern with the effects of social discrimination. With unsparing honesty, Acosta shows how such a legacy affects the group and from there filters into every aspect of the individual's most personal life. Especially poignant is his alienation from members of his own Chicano cultural group, who ostracize him because they have internalized stereotypes of Chicano "outsiders." Although Acosta reveals the immense pain, suffering, and confusion with which discrimination afflicts the individual, he also shows that positive cultural roots, engendered despite great social pressure, can overcome such afflictions. Although the work is ostensibly addressed to Chicanos, this thematic development enlarges the work's audience not only to victims suffering from discrimination but also to their victimizers.

Acosta is especially effective in showing the narrator's development as he progresses from confusion to understanding. For example, the narrator's physical journey ends geographically in El Paso and Juarez, where his understanding begins. Acosta's belligerence, part of a superiority complex adopted against Mexicans because he is from

the United States, lands him in a dungeon below the streets of Juarez. This symbolic vertical descent, a counterpoint to his horizontal ramblings throughout the book, forges an additional perspective from which to view his transformation. This scene is representative of Acosta's artistic ability to amplify the varieties of thematic development in his work.

The tone of the book is another of its major strengths, varying for example from ribaldry to compassion to sarcasm and seriousness, even frequently engendering humor. Passages in the book, if taken from their context, could be described as sexist, racist, and homophobic, but such an interpretation fails to realize that such passages reflect a world that neither Acosta nor its other victims made. Although the narrator is apparently self-indulgent and obsessed with sensuality, as a counterpoint readers see that at the beginning his inability to prevent his female clients from being victimized is at the heart of his current deeply troubled state. His acute reaction to omnipresent discrimination is to act as a mirror to society's prejudices: He adopts the society's persona. By creating the autobiography, he realizes that he must and can re-create himself in another image.

Critical Context

The Autobiography of a Brown Buffalo recounts one individual's life from the mid-1940's to the late 1960's, but it also represents the experiences of a

group, that of Chicanos. It also can stand as a paradigmatic recounting by any individual, from any group, who is subjected to outsider status. The work is aligned in many respects with established autobiographical writings, more so than is at first apparent, especially considering such subject matter as illicit drug abuse. The work falls strongly into the mode of ethnic autobiographers who concentrate on the communal "we" rather than the autonomous "I." In this respect, while Acosta's work is vastly different in tone and persona from that of Frederick Douglass, the escaped African American slave and later statesman, his work shares affinity with *Life and Times of Frederick Douglass* (1881) in the narrators' insistence on reintegrating themselves into and speaking for their communities.

The Autobiography of a Brown Buffalo was followed by *The Revolt of the Cockroach People* (1973), Acosta's only other major work to be published before his disappearance in 1974. *The Revolt of the Cockroach People* is essentially the second volume of Acosta's autobiographical account, covering the period from January, 1968, when the earlier book leaves off, to the spring of 1972. *The Revolt of the Cockroach People* depicts his involvement as a leader in the Chicano civil rights movement in Los Angeles and his tumultuous attempt to create systemic change, especially in the legal system's treatment of Chicanos. He thereby brings to fruition what had been a haunting failure for him at the beginning of *The Autobiography of a Brown Buffalo*.

Although eminently significant to the field of Chicano autobiography particularly and the Chicano literary movement generally, *The Autobiography of a Brown Buffalo* deserves a wide audience because it depicts various themes arising from one of the most significant social concerns in the nation's history, ethnic discrimination and its legacy.

THE AUTUMN OF THE PATRIARCH

Author: Gabriel García Márquez (1928-   )
Type of work: Novel
Type of plot: Satire
Time of plot: The late nineteenth and early twentieth centuries
Locale: An unnamed Caribbean country
First published: *El otoño del patriarca*, 1975 (English translation, 1975)

Principal Characters

The patriarch, also called **the general**, the **"All Pure,"** and **the "Magnificent,"** an unnamed Latin American dictator who is somewhere between the ages of 107 and 232. He rules from a palace that has been converted into a marketplace. It is overrun with soldiers, prostitutes, cows, and lepers seeking miraculous cures from the patriarch. The novel fluctuates between third-person reports of his actions, first-person statements made to the patriarch, and first-person interior monologues of the general's responses to characters and events. He is the history of his nation, and, as he becomes increasingly senile, he even remembers the arrival of Europeans in the New World. The novel begins with and repeatedly returns to the discovery of his body, mutilated beyond recognition by vultures.

Manuela Sánchez, a beauty queen of the poor whose supernatural beauty astounds the nation. The patriarch dances with her out of ceremonial obligation, then becomes obsessed with her.

Bendición Alvarado, the patriarch's mother by an unknown father, a former prostitute who paints common birds in order to sell them as exotic songbirds. During most of her son's reign, she lives frugally in a suburban house in the capital city, coming to the palace to clean up after and criticize her son. After her death, her son has her embalmed and sends her corpse on a tour of the provinces. Rumors of her miraculous preservation lead to his insistence on her sainthood.

Leticia Mercedes María Nazareno, the patriarch's wife, a former nun. She becomes the power behind his throne. As a result of her influence, the cult of his mother is overthrown in favor of a reinstitution of the Catholic church, yet flowers wilt, vegetables rot, and meat festers at her touch. Her extravagance in shopping threatens to bankrupt the government. In a plot laid by a cabal of the ruling junta, she is torn to pieces in the marketplace, along with the patriarch's son, by dogs trained to attack her outfit and the heir's uniform.

Patricio Aragonés, the general's perfect double, who is arrested in the provinces for impersonating the leader. When Aragonés is fatally poisoned (relatively early in the patriarch's reign), he castigates the general in a deathbed speech. The general uses the confusion following the fake state funeral to launch another of his political purges. Aragonés' death presages and becomes confused with that of the patriarch.

General Rodrigo de Aguilar, an artilleryman and academy graduate, the general's right-hand man. During a period of political unrest, he is late for a palace dinner held in honor of the high command. After the officers fret for a while, he is brought in on a silver tray, cooked and stuffed.

José Ignacio Saenz de la Barra, a sadistic torturer.

Emanuel, the patriarch's infant son. At birth, he is appointed a major general.

The Novel

The Autumn of the Patriarch, published eight years after Gabriel García Márquez's highly praised

Cien años de soledad (1967; *One Hundred Years of Solitude*, 1970), was a novel for which both general readers and critics had waited. It was, however, a project that García Márquez had put aside earlier to write *One Hundred Years of Solitude* because, as he has commented, he was writing it at first without any clear idea of what he was doing. García Márquez has said that he got the idea for writing the work two or three days after the fall of Venezuelan dictator Marcos Pérez Jiménez, when the ruling junta met. He was in the anteroom of the presidential office with other journalists when an officer in battle fatigues came out walking backward with a machine gun in his hand and mud on his boots. It was at that moment, García Márquez reveals, that he had a sudden insight into the mystery of power.

Consequently, he wanted to write a "poem on the solitude of power," in which a mythical Latin American dictator would be used as an embodiment of many such dictators, from "Papa Doc" Duvalier of Haiti to Juan Vicente Gómez of Venezuela. His first attempt at the structure of the book—a long monologue by the aged dictator as he is waiting to be executed—he abandoned for the existing structure of blending voices in six sections that make the book begin and end in a spiral fashion with the discovery of the patriarch's body. The result is a difficult book to read, for each of the six episodes of which it is composed is a single paragraph. There are no other breaks in the novel, and many of the sentences go on for several pages in a run-on, seemingly rambling and disconnected fashion, much like some of the novels of William Faulkner or the stream-of-consciousness works of James Joyce. The stylistic experiment of the book goes even further than Faulkner or Joyce, however, for the point of view of the work shifts constantly, sometimes even within a single line, from first-person participant to third-person author to first-person-plural choral response. García Márquez has called *The Autumn of the Patriarch* the most experimental of his novels and the one that interests him most as a poetic adventure; it is, he says, a book that he wrote like a poem, word by word, sometimes spending weeks on a few lines.

The novel begins with the discovery of the body of the aged patriarch, pecked at by vultures. Be-

cause he has not been seen by anyone in many years, and because this is the second time he has been found dead (the first time was with the death of Patricio Aragonés, his exact double), those who find him are not sure if he indeed is the dictator. Although the patriarch's entire life is recounted in the six chapters of the work, the primary plot line (if that is possible in such a multifaceted novel as this) focuses on the twenty-four-hour period from the discovery of the body to the final celebration and jubilation at the end of the book.

There is no real sense of chronological time in the novel, for the various voices that recount the events that characterize the patriarch's life blend into a kind of grotesque tone-poem in which time becomes a mythical cycle, ranging throughout the supposed two centuries of the patriarch's mythic life and even beyond to one scene when the patriarch looks out the window and sees the ships of Columbus beside a modern battleship. This world of mythic reality, like the worlds of many of García Márquez's other works, is one of violence and grotesquely brutal events. A few examples indicate the nature of the details of the novel and show the mythically mad world that the patriarch creates around himself.

There is, for example, the execution of General Rodrigo de Aguilar after he is suspected of instigating an attempt on the patriarch's life. On the night when he is to be the honored guest at a banquet for the palace guards, he makes his entrance on a silver platter decorated with cauliflower and laurel branches, marinated in spices, browned in the oven, then carved and served up with the order to eat heartily. There is the death of Bendición Alvarado, the patriarch's mother, who rots away of some mysterious disease but whose body is preserved and displayed throughout the country, revived and, according to some, still alive as the patriarch attempts to have her canonized as a saint. There is the death of Leticia Nazareno, the patriarch's wife, and his small son, Emanuel, devoured by a pack of trained dogs.

After this murder, José Ignacio Saenz de la Barra, who is hired to find the killers, sends the patriarch numerous bags of what appear to be coconuts but are really the heads of some of his enemies. There are the two thousand children who have been used by the patriarch as a way to cheat on the national lottery and who, because of their innocent complicity, must all be killed—an atrocity achieved by placing them in a ship filled with concrete that is then exploded. The horrors become so numerous that the reader can no longer take them completely seriously but must allow them to blend together in a kind of lyrically maintained mythical world of madness and extremity.

Analysis

Certainly *The Autumn of the Patriarch* is a political novel concerning the nature of the paradigmatic Latin American dictator. It is less a novel that focuses on particular political realities than it is about the most universal truth that underlies political reality, the truth of absolute power. Moreover, it is about the need of the people to create a supernatural leader who, although his decisions are often arbitrary, represents a sense of destiny and a source of control or responsibility for all the seemingly unpredictable absurdities that dominate life. It is a book about power and the ultimate solitude of power.

There are social themes in this novel. Petty corruption is magnified to the gigantic, there are dark hints at the threat of American imperialism, and the fundamental unjustness of the rigid economic and class distinctions in Latin America is revealed. *The Autumn of the Patriarch* is a grotesque lyric poem, a richly metaphoric and mythical experience that overpowers the reader who has the fortitude and the dedication required to read it and become lost in its comic absurdity and its horrific reality. The reader who allows the rhythm of the poetic prose to engulf him or her becomes carried away by the continuous and unrelenting assault on the sense of reality. *The Autumn of the Patriarch* is a book so richly and completely imaginative that it seems to be a palpable embodiment of the mind of García Márquez; indeed, the author has called it an autobiography in code, "the only book I always wanted to write and never could."

Critical Context

García Márquez has admitted that his primary literary debts are to the lyric, stream-of-consciousness style of William Faulkner, the restrained and stylized realism of Ernest Hemingway, and the nightmarishly concrete world of Franz Kafka. After the publication of *One Hundred Years of Solitude*, a work that astonished critics and the reading public with its fantastically realized world of myth and magic, many wondered how García Márquez could go beyond the experimental narrative style of that work. *The Autumn of the Patriarch* did not disappoint them, although many found it much less readable than his earlier works. Professional critics have had a field day with the book, for it is ripe for explication. They have itemized the obsessively repeated symbolic motifs of the novel, have suggested historical sources for the patriarch himself, and have delighted in demonstrating their ability to "read" and then to clarify what seems to be an extremely demanding book. Although the book has been generally praised, it has also been criticized for being too long, often too self-indulgent, and too stylistically idiosyncratic to be widely read. Although it is a book more often referred to than actually read, it reaffirms García Márquez's place as the most famous and respected figure of the Latin American literary renaissance.

AVALOVARA

Author: Osman Lins (1924-1978)
Type of work: Novel
Type of plot: Existentialism
Time of plot: 200 B.C., 1908-1940, and 1938-1970
Locale: Pompeii, France, Holland, Italy, Germany, English, São Paulo, Recife, and Rio Grande do Sul, Brazil
First published: 1973 (English translation, 1979)

Principal Characters

Abel, a writer from northeastern Brazil, where he was born in 1935. He makes love with three women at different times in his life. He is married to but separated from a woman who kills herself. He is murdered by Hayano.

Anneliese Roos (Rose), his German lover in Paris. She leaves Abel for her husband, who is in a Lausanne sanatorium.

Cecília, Abel's androgynous Brazilian lover. Her brothers, one a policeman, beat her and Abel. Pregnant by Abel, she dies in an accident.

Ⓞ, his twenty-three or thirty-two-year-old lover in São Paulo. She married Hayano when she was still in school and attempted suicide on her wedding night. Her lovemaking with Abel is rendered in strong physical detail, during which she recalls her previous life of first love, husband, grandparents, and feeling for the bird Avalovara. She is killed with Abel by her husband, who finds them in sexual embrace.

The Fat Woman, Abel's mother, who had been a prostitute. She got married but refused to give up sleeping with other men. She had many children by different men.

Raul Nogueira de Albuquerque e Castro, The Treasurer, married to The Fat Woman. He helped care for her children while working for a bank. He is killed by a truck, and it is unknown whether it was suicide or an accident.

Publius Ubonius, a Pompeiian merchant in 200 B.C. He offers Loreius freedom if he invents a phrase that can be read left to right and right to left.

Loreius, a slave who discovers the mysterious phrase that unites the novel. He kills himself after his phrase is stolen.

Tyche, a Pompeiian courtesan who steals the mystical phrase from Loreius and sells it to Ubonius.

Julius Heckethorn, a German clockmaker. He makes the clock, which he began constructing in 1933, found in the room where Ⓞ and Abel make love.

Olavo Hayano, the husband of Ⓞ, whom he met when they were both children. According to Ⓞ, he is a "yolyp," or sterile freak of nature.

Natividade, a black maid in the Hayano household, a virgin when she dies at the age of seventy-five. It is her funeral procession that winds through the streets of São Paulo during the novel.

Hermelinda and **Hermenilda,** old women of Recife. Though not twins, they look alike. They introduce Cecília to Abel.

The Novel

The structure of Osman Lins's *Avalovara* is at once astonishingly complex and altogether transparent. The sequence of events is predetermined by a geometric design that appears before the first page of text, consisting of a Latin palindrome of five five-letter words with a spiral superimposed on it. To visualize this palindrome, draw a large square subdivided into twenty-five smaller squares—five across and five down. In the first row of squares place the letters S-A-T-O-R; in the second, A-R-E-P-O; in the third, T-E-N-E-T; in the fourth, O-P-E-R-A; and in the fifth, R-O-T-A-S. The entire square is centered over a fourteen-ring spiral.

Each letter of the palindrome represents one plot line. When the spiral touches a letter, a passage of that plot line appears. Since some letters are more frequent than others, plot segments vary in number of episodes from twenty-four (letter "O") to two (letter "N," which is in the center of the design). In addition, episodes increase in length each time a plot line reappears. Most are ten lines long in the first episode, twenty lines long in the second, and so on.

Such a contrived structure would make *Avalo-vara*'s plot seem to be an extremely easy one to recount, but in fact the reading experience is nearly impossible to describe, because the reader is simultaneously witnessing a dazzling display of literary legerdemain and being led in and out of eight very different but interrelated plot lines. Plots of such visible artifice often turn out to be admirable failures, but Lins never sacrifices his fiction to the contrivances that order its unfolding. The novel betrays none of the self-centeredness of many cleverly concocted novels.

Six of the eight plot lines involve the protagonist Abel directly, two dealing with his love affairs with Roos (largely set in Europe) and Cecília (largely set in Recife). The other four are all in some way concerned with the enigmatic $\mho$, with whom Abel lives a consuming passion and in whose arms he dies, at the hands of Olavo Hayano. One of the other remaining plot lines deals with the Pompeiian Publius Ubonius, who offers to free his slave Loreius if the slave can construct a magic sentence that reflects the mobility of the universe and the immutability of the divine. The sentence Loreius invents is "Sator arepo tenet opera rotas" ("The farmer carefully maintains his plow in the furrows"). The square in which it lies is space; the spiral superimposed on it is time. The final subplot is the story of the obsessed clockmaker Julius Heckethorn, who early in the twentieth century attempts to devise a clock unencumbered by the bothersome ticks of ordinary clocks. He abandons the scheme but does design a clock with a complex triple sound system that will, someday, play Domenico Scarlatti's Sonata in F Minor.

As the reader approaches the end of the book, the spiral approaches the center of the square, and the various narratives, separated in time and space, draw together as Abel approaches something like an erotic transcendence in the arms of his mysterious and oddly polymorphous lover. The moment of this epiphany coincides with the beginning of a solar eclipse and is precisely the second that the intricate clock, now in the same room with Abel, begins the sonata.

Analysis

Avalovara is clearly a very ambitious work. Two themes—time and space—are suggested by the geometric design at the front of the text, and the entire structure of the novel is determined by the relationship of the physical space of the squares and the progression of the spiral of time over that space. Julius Heckethorn's clock is a variation on the theme, since he decides to set the device in motion at the exact second that will cause its musical culmination to coincide with Abel's moment of fruition. That moment of fruition is a contrary one, since in the process of attaining paradise, he must die. The title itself suggests that the philosophical framework for Abel's quest is rooted in a mysticism more encompassing than can be found in Roman Catholicism, though there are allusions to Western notions of transcendence, which might indicate that the substructure of the inquiry is not exclusively Buddhist but eclectic.

The interrelationship of time and space is, then, the overriding conceit in *Avalovara*, but numerous other kinds of questions are included. Each major theme is elaborated contrapuntally by secondary ones: The cities embodied in Roos are part of the search for Absolute City; the names and non-names of the characters (many do not have sur-names; one is known only as a symbol) suggest a search for *the* name, the Word; the spiral reappears in the shape of a unicorn's horn and in the spiraling descent of a vulture; time is viewed both as the linear progression marked by the ticks of a clock and as a (spiral) flow toward fruition. The geomet-ric design itself suggests two different views of the cosmos, one rooted in symmetry and cosmic order,

the other based on the unforeseen and unforesee-able chance meeting of the spiral and one of the squares.

Time and space are really only the setting for the central theme, which is contained in the meta-phor of a fish that leaps from the water and is devoured—at the moment of its plenitude. Abel's route to plenitude is through the sexual act, and his fruition is a cosmic orgasm and the moment of death and knowing, counterpointed by the eclipse and the chiming of the clock.

Critical Context

Osman Lins published his first novel, *O Visi-tante* (the visitor), in 1955, and his second, *O Fiel e a Pedra* (the faithful and the stone), in 1961. His first novel won for him several literary prizes, and two of his books of short stories, *Os Gestos* (ges-tures, 1957) and *Nove, Novena* (nine novena, 1966), contributed substantially to his reputation as a serious and talented writer. His works also enjoyed notable success abroad, especially the French translation of *Nove, Novena. Avalovara* itself was ready for publication in Italian, French, and German before the Brazilian edition appeared.

Lins has not been a "popular" writer in Brazil because his works are all, like *Avalovara*, intellec-tually and philosophically challenging. He does, however, have a solid reputation as one of Brazil's most accomplished, as well as one of its most difficult, authors. *Avalovara* is legitimately re-garded as the culmination of a brilliant writer's career. Although he published one more novel before his death in 1978, *Avalovara* had obviously been germinating in its author's mind for some time, since some tentative suggestions of it ap-peared in earlier works, notably short stories. Bra-zilian critics have consistently admired his works, though there have been reservations expressed about some of his technical innovations, occasion-

ally so complex as to produce not much more than perplexity in his readers.

Avalovara can be seen as belonging to two important but apparently contradictory literary tra-ditions: apocalyptic fiction and utopian fiction. It is in some ways comparable to such apocalyptic works as Thomas Pynchon's *Gravity's Rainbow* (1973)—there is even a symbolically suggestive Nike rocket launch in *Avalovara*, reminiscent of Pynchon's symbolic V-2's. It also fits into the more established utopian tradition. What is unusual about *Avalovara* is that it presents the apocalypse as the means of achieving the utopian state.

Avalovara is also a distinguished example of yet another literary fashion, one with particular impor-tance in the twentieth century: the self-referential novel. It is so intensely self-referential that some are reluctant to call it a novel at all, preferring to see it more as a tour de force of fiction about writing fiction than as a story about characters. There is some validity to this point, since few novels obey such a rigid and elaborate predeter-mined structure. The stories are so densely evoca-tive and so symbolically suggestive that readers become so involved as to overlook the artifice. Even those who do not are likely to remember *Avalovara* as an incomparable reading experience.

THE BAY OF SILENCE

Author: Eduardo Mallea (1903-1983)
Type of work: Novel
Type of plot: Picaresque
Time of plot: 1926-1940
Locale: Buenos Aires, Argentina; London, England; Paris, France; Brussels, Belgium; and Italy
First published: *La bahía de silencio*, 1940 (English translation, 1944)

Principal Characters

Martín Tregua, the narrator, a young former law student. Disgusted with the unscientific and spiritless faculty and their unproductive teaching methods, he leaves the law school and takes up writing. In his first venture, *The Forty Nights of Juan Argentino*, he attempts to give meaning to the life and suffering of the average Argentine. *The Bay of Silence* then grows out of the inspiration of a young woman to whom he writes, telling the story of his life. In three parts, he takes his correspondent from the uncertainties of his younger days ("Youth"), through his travels about Europe ("The Islands"), and into the disillusioned wisdom of his middle years ("The Defeated").

Gloria Bambil, a librarian in whom Martín Tregua vainly seeks to instill self-confidence. His failure in this effort makes him one of the defeated in the final section of *The Bay of Silence*.

Anselmi, a fellow law student.

Jiménez, an office employee.

César Acevedo, a wealthy Argentine.

Blagoda, an associate on the student magazine *Enough*.

Mercedes Miró, an unsettling companion of Martín Tregua.

The Novel

In *The Bay of Silence*, a roomer in a student boarding house, the aging Dr. Dervil, expresses his sentiments when he declares that Argentina is a lost nation, still colonial in spirit. He wonders when the healthy but submerged country, which exists because men believe in it, will rise from depths of ignorance and sloth. Mallea's own hope, like that of the young former law student supposedly writing *The Bay of Silence*, is that the re-creation of Argentina will come from the unspoiled rural areas.

Martín Tregua, who had stopped attending law school because of his disgust with methods of teaching and the unscientific, spiritless faculty, turned to writing. His first project was to give meaning to the life and suffering of the average Argentine in a volume called *The Forty Nights of Juan Argentino*. The sight of a lovely woman of his own age, never once mentioned by name, but called only "You," then inspired Martín to write to her, telling her the story of his life and letting her see her effect upon him. So *The Bay of Silence* comes into being.

The book is divided into three parts. The first, "Youth," covers Martín's life from his birth in Río Negro, through his student days, to his first success as a writer in 1932. Part 2, "The Islands," tells of his trip to Europe. The last section, "The Defeated," brings his life up to 1939. The novel ends as it began, with the narrator's glimpse into a flower shop in Buenos Aires and of the woman he had adored in silence for twelve years.

The story is developed with a wealth of detail. When Martín takes a walk, the streets he traverses and the buildings along the route are named, and the casual actions of unimportant people along the way are fully described. There is very little action in the first part. It is mostly an exchange of ideas about the fundamental problems of the world that the students discuss endlessly in their boarding house or pass around the editorial table of the magazine *Enough*, which they have founded with the financial assistance of a wealthy man of the city.

In the course of Martín's European trip, the author contrives to get him into conversations with a Czech munitions millionaire, several fascist un-

derlings, and a disillusioned surgeon in Brussels. Martín returns, in the final section, to his own country, the destiny of which he feels as keenly as his own fate, to write a sequel to his *Juan Argentino*. This task becomes complicated when he is attracted to a lending librarian named Gloria Bambil, one of many women in his life. Earlier, the unsettled and unsettling Mercedes Miró had been his companion at art exhibits, French theatrical performances, and musicales, circumstances related with many details and references that reveal Mallea's wide acquaintance with contemporary culture.

Analysis

Because Gloria is unconsciously an existentialist, Martín must occupy his time by reassuring her, in taking her from the mountains to the seashore in an attempt to give her confidence in herself and her future. Failure in this effort makes him one of the many "defeated" in the final section of the novel. Meanwhile, Martín Tregua has been finding his way from the uncertainties of youth to the disillusioned wisdom of middle age.

The title is twice explained. Once, in discussing

The Forty Nights of Juan Argentino, Martín declares that his book is to be a sea, rich and abundant, in which there are storms and stresses along with delightful bays of silence, filled with the dreams and sufferings of his people. Again, at the end, he tells the unnamed woman to whom he is writing that she has reached that place at which the angry sea of persecution beats in vain; the place, a bay of silence, where those who have turned their failure into triumph may wait.

Critical Context

Mallea was an outstanding Argentine writer, one of the most important figures in the literature of Latin America. He was a skilled technician in fiction and the literary editor of the Buenos Aires *Nación*. Among his experiments, he has written short stories such as those in the collection *La ciudad junto al río inmóvil* (the city on the motionless river, 1936) and essays such as *History of an Argentine Passion* (1937), both seeking, behind the faults and the grandeur of a new country, the basic principles of Argentine life. This theme pervades most of Mallea's writing.

Of the group of young writers of his era who considered individual freedom and responsibility, Mallea revealed the greatest power and possessed the greatest technical skill, though his work is

sometimes marred by a turgid style. He demonstrated these qualities as early as 1938, with the publication of *Fiesta in November*, an impressionistic portrait of the decadent upper class of the Argentine capital. Into the small talk and the evidences of corruption that reveal the "buyers and the bought" is woven an incident of fascist violence, presented with complicated technique.

The Bay of Silence is far more optimistic, and has more plot, than *Fiesta in November*. Mallea had seen a decline in the moral quality of Argentine national life. Even those only casually acquainted with the nation can recognize how Argentina had deteriorated economically, culturally, and spiritually even before the era of Juan Perón. This decline is noticeable particularly in the country's theater.

BETRAYED BY RITA HAYWORTH

Author: Manuel Puig (1932-1990)
Type of work: Novel
Type of plot: *Bildungsroman*
Time of plot: 1933-1948
Locale: Vallejos, a provincial town in Argentina
First published: *La traición de Rita Hayworth*, 1968 (English translation, 1971)

Principal Characters

José Casals (Toto), the main character. The novel follows him from infancy in the small provincial town of Vallejos, Argentina, to the age of fifteen at George Washington High School, a boarding school. Bright and inquisitive but self-centered and spoiled, he grows up being first in school and having his own way. He matures into adolescence and is exposed to an ever-widening world in which he is not always the center of attention. Confused about his own sexuality and the more intimate details of sex, his own sexual predilections are still to be determined. As a child, he fantasizes about romantic images of the world that come to him through Hollywood films, novels, and the influence of his doting mother.

Mita, Toto's mother, a college graduate. She marries Berto, a man with less education who reminds her of an Argentine film star with whom she had danced. When the family is finally financially secure, Berto forces her to quit her job and devote herself to family. She rears her husband's nephew Héctor, dresses down, uses little makeup, gains weight, and accepts the matronly role assigned by her husband. She fantasizes and escapes her small-town existence through novels, films, and her son Toto.

Berto, Toto's father, a proud Spaniard. When he is pulled out of school to work in his brother's factory, he is deprived of an education. When his brother sells the factory, he is forced to emigrate to Argentina. He marries above himself but refuses to accept help from his wife's family. He keeps his family in Vallejos and, through great effort and sacrifice, gradually becomes a successful businessman.

Héctor, Toto's cousin. He lives with Toto's family until the age of twelve, when his is sent away to a boarding school. Héctor returns to Vallejos during school breaks and summer vacation. He is moved by the thrill of girls and soccer.

Paquita, a lower-class schoolmate of Toto who is three years older.

Esther, a student from a humble Buenos Aires suburb who wins a scholarship to George Washington High School. There she is a classmate of Toto. She is enamored of Héctor and eagerly awaits an encounter arranged by Toto. Toto has designs on her, however, and has only used Héctor as bait.

Cobito, a schoolmate of Toto. He is vulgar, crude, and mean. Jealous of the intelligence, wealth, and success of Toto, he twice tries to sodomize him.

The Novel

Although *Betrayed by Rita Hayworth* does not resemble a traditional novel in form, its subject matter is highly conventional: the maturation and education of a sensitive young man. Because this is Puig's first novel, and because he shares the birthdate of his protagonist, most readers suspect that *Betrayed by Rita Hayworth* is autobiographical to some degree. The novel reveals the world of young José Casals, nicknamed Toto, by exploring not only his fantasies and daydreams but also those of his parents, aunts, cousins, schoolmates, and teachers. Through this sometimes indirect method, the reader absorbs the multitude of influences that shape Toto's life. At the same time, Puig delineates the spectrum of provincial life in Argentina, providing insight into such facets of that culture as the meaning of machismo, the importance attached to education, and the pervasive influence of romantic fiction and Hollywood films.

Most of the novel's sixteen chapters are internal monologues of the major and minor characters. A few chapters are made up of dialogues (consisting mostly of revealing gossip) between female characters. The novel also includes excerpts from diaries, two letters, and a school essay by Toto on the topic "The Movie I Liked Best."

A minimal plot emerges from this collage of material, although it may be difficult to discern on a first reading. Toto's mother, Mita, marries Berto even though he has less education than she, because he resembles a film star. As a consequence of the marriage, she leaves her large family in a busy town and moves to sleepy Vallejos. During the early years of her marriage, she works (to Berto's discomfort), but she increasingly becomes absorbed in her children and in going to films. Instead of bedtime stories, she recites to Toto the plots of films. As soon as he is old enough, Toto also becomes a cinema buff, especially enjoying films with beautiful female stars such as Rita Hayworth. The first half of the novel revolves around the female characters who make up Mita and Toto's world.

As Toto gets older, he naturally grows curious about sex and is given many opportunities to hear about its mysteries from his older playmates and cousins. A neighborhood girl, Paquita, teases him with salacious stories. One of his teachers, helping him to draw a model of the digestive and reproductive systems, explains the biological processes to the confused nine-year-old. Even at this early stage of his life, Toto is perceived by others as small for his age and as effeminate. He prefers to play with girls, does not like sports, and spends much time with his mother. Eventually, Toto is sent away to school where, as revealed by the sexually knowledgeable Héctor and the rough Cobito, he becomes the target of sadistic older boys. The savage voices of Héctor and Cobito provide a marked contrast to the predominantly female voices of the earlier chapters.

When the novel ends, Toto is still only fifteen years old, and thus no final word can be said about his sexual or social development. He remains immersed in the world of books, film, and music, and like a typical sensitive adolescent has begun to be scornful of the lowbrow tastes of others and of the pieties of religion. Almost the last word, however, is given to Toto's music teacher, who writes in her commonplace book that "Toto reminds me more and more of that unfriendly homosexual."

The final chapter of the novel consists of a letter written by Berto to his brother shortly after Toto's birth. This is the only chapter that is not placed in chronological sequence, and it poignantly reveals an unexpectedly tender side of Berto. Particularly emphasized are his love for his son and his hope to educate him to a proud place in society. Berto, like many of the other characters, has been in some fashion betrayed, not by Rita Hayworth, as the novel's title suggests, but by the gap between his dreams and reality. He had hoped to get a good education; instead, he left school at the age of fifteen to work for his brother.

Analysis

Berto's disillusionment, as revealed in his letter, is typical of the loss of innocence exhibited in many of the chapters in the second half of the book. In this generally depressing litany, the one note of romantic hope is suggested by Toto's essay on "The Movie I Liked Best." Toto's favorite film appears to be a version of *The Great Waltz*, the life of Johann Strauss. Toto's retelling emphasizes not only Strauss's musical genius but also his passionate love affair with a brilliant soprano. Although the love affair ends sadly, the film goes on to detail Strauss's ultimate triumph as an artist, ending in a scene in which the emperor leads him onto a balcony before the cheering crowds of Vienna. Near death now, Strauss has a vision of his lost beloved, and he is torn between the agony of dying without real knowledge of love's meaning and the ecstasy of remembering his beloved's beauty. Thus ends Toto's version of the film. In its extreme romanticism and emphasis on exquisite variations of feeling, Toto's favorite film provides a strong counterpoint to the brutality and discouragement glimpsed elsewhere in the novel.

In *Betrayed by Rita Hayworth*, the method is part of the meaning. By presenting each of his characters from a variety of perspectives, Puig underscores the complexity of human personality. Part of this complexity, he asserts, is the struggle between the raw impulses and factors that bring people down and those that uplift. Puig shows suffering in the form of illness, death of loved ones, economic hardship, and spiritual poverty. He suggests redemption through art, intellectual sensitivity, and meaningful work. The triumph of good over evil is by no means clear as the novel ends, however, even for Toto, who still has many years to develop before his fate will be certain.

Critical Context

Puig's first novel, *Betrayed by Rita Hayworth*, established themes that would be evident in later works including *Boquitas pintadas* (1969; *Heartbreak Tango,* 1973) and *El beso de la mujer araña* (1976; *Kiss of the Spider Woman*, 1979): the rough-and-tumble world of political and economic survival versus the sensuous dream of art, often symbolized in lushly filmed Hollywood motion pictures. In his exploration of these themes, as well as in his experimentation with the form of the novel, Puig is working in concert with other important Latin American writers such as Gabriel García Márquez, Julio Cortázar, and Mario Vargas Llosa. Puig also repeatedly explores the traditional social understanding of sexuality, with a particular interest in the development of the homosexual personality. In *Betrayed by Rita Hayworth*, he indirectly explores this theme through the composite portrait of the somewhat effeminate Toto. In *Kiss of the Spider Woman*, the subject of homosexuality is directly addressed through a series of scholarly footnotes.

Betrayed by Rita Hayworth also shows the beginnings of Puig's characteristic experimentation with the use of dialogue as a replacement for conventional narration. The opening chapter consists of a conversation between a group of women at Mita's parents' house; another chapter consists entirely of the conversation of two maids; still another shows the reader one side of a telephone call. The speaker must always be determined from context: no explicit attributions are given. Puig's use of this stylistic device increases in his later fiction and indicates his desire to reduce authorial intrusion.

BLESS ME, ULTIMA

Author: Rudolfo A. Anaya (1937-)
Type of work: Novel
Type of plot: *Bildungsroman*
Time of plot: 1943
Locale: Guadalupe, New Mexico
First published: 1972

Principal Characters

Antonio Márez y Luna, a child at the threshold of a larger world. Although he is only seven, Antonio's brothers are already fighting in World War II. Before his first day of school, Antonio sees a traumatized veteran killed by an enraged mob. In school, Antonio must master a new language, since classes are taught in English. At the end of the year, he is promoted an extra grade. The larger world proves more difficult to master, however. Antonio witnesses the deaths of several people he loves, endures the nauseating fears that beset local children in response to nearby atomic testing, and shares his father's anguish when his brothers return from the war only to wander away again, their cultural roots severed. Finally, he watches as Ultima, his spiritual mentor, dies, defeated by an opponent who hates her healing powers.

Ultima, an aged *curandera* (healer), trained by el Volaré, the flying man from las Pasturas. Ultima is a friend of Antonio's mother, Maria Luna. In her old age, she is left behind in a village that has lost many members through the war and economic migration. The Márez y Luna family invites Ultima to stay with them. Ultima is loved by a faithful few whom she helped in the past, especially Maria and Narcisco. She is also the object of community mistrust. Even many of those she once healed, including Maria's brothers, the Lunas, refuse to oppose those who seek to harm her.

Through Ultima, Antonio finds a path through the morass of injustice, chaos, and dogma that surrounds him. Ultima accepts her death because she has devoted her life's energies to life itself.

Ultima shows Antonio that even amid the catastrophic social and economic upheavals that have rent their region since the onset of Spanish colonization, one can contribute to healing within one's community.

Tenorio Trementina, an evil *brujo* (witch) who seeks to destroy Ultima. Tenorio first comes into conflict with Ultima when his daughters place a curse on Lucas, Maria's brother. Although Ultima tells Tenorio that she plans to lift the curse and warns that his daughters will be endangered if he does not order them to lift it, Tenorio remains intransigent, denying that his daughters have caused Lucas' ailment. Tenorio's pride blinds him to his daughters' peril. In refusing to acknowledge his daughters' involvement, Tenorio, in effect, signs their death warrant. When Ultima lifts the curse, the malevolent energies of the Trementina sisters are released, and the sisters are, one by one, consumed by the forces with which they trafficked.

As his three daughters sicken and die, Tenorio's chief concern is for his honor. He organizes three initiatives against Ultima, claiming that she has cursed his daughters. In his first attack, Tenorio's eye is gouged out by Ultima's owl. In the second, he kills Narcisco but nearly stands trial for murder. In his third attack, he kills Ultima's owl, and hence Ultima. In attempting to finish his work against the life force Ultima represents, however, he seeks to kill Antonio, and he is shot dead.

Narcisco, the town drunk. He is also one of a circle of visionary characters who are conscious of a spiritual realm in which the forces of life struggle against the forces of death. Like the other major characters, Narcisco undergoes a sequence of three transformative events. In a series of confrontations, Narcisco argues for calm in the face of riotous passions. In the first of these, Narcisco is ignored, and the demented veteran Lupito is killed. In the second, a confrontation with drunken witch hunters, Narcisco reasons with an angry mob

and exorcises the ugly passions that Tenorio has aroused. In the third confrontation, in which Narcisco is caught between two irrational obsessions—Tenorio's passion for vengeance and domination and the addiction of Antonio's brother Andrew to prostitutes—Narcisco gives his life in Ultima's defense.

The Novel

In *Bless Me, Ultima,* Rudolfo A. Anaya draws upon memories of his childhood in Pastura, New Mexico, during World War II to present one year in the life of seven-year-old Antonio Márez y Luna. Events in the novel are interspersed with allegorical dreams and are recounted from the perspective of an older Antonio. During this pivotal year, Antonio experiences the abrupt return of his three brothers from the battlefields of World War II and their subsequent departures, three senseless, violent deaths, his first year of school, and his first communion.

Antonio's maturation begins with the arrival of Ultima, a *curandera,* or healer, with whom he shares a mystical bond. Shortly before her arrival, Antonio dreams of his own birth. In the dream, his mother's brothers, the Lunas, bless him with offerings of fruit and claim him as a "man of the people," perhaps even a priest. Into this dream scene, however, enter his father's brothers, the Márezes. They arrive on horseback, shouting and shooting, laughing and drinking; they smash the fruit, wipe away the earth with which the Lunas have blessed Antonio, and claim Antonio for the Márezes. When he awakes, he intuits that Ultima, present at his birth, is also connected to his future.

Following Ultima's arrival, Antonio encounters an increasingly complex social universe. His father is summoned to join a vigilante group that is searching for a traumatized World War II veteran, Lupito, who shot and killed the local sheriff during a psychotic episode. Antonio secretly follows the vigilantes and watches as Lupito, still deranged, is killed by the angry

crowd despite the pleas of the town drunk, Narcisco.

Antonio starts school and weathers a difficult transition from Spanish to English in an environment in which divisions between town and country and between Chicano and Anglo-American culture fix students within a complex hierarchy of prestige. Outside school, Antonio becomes embroiled in a growing conflict between Tenorio and Ultima. Their feud begins when Ultima travels to the village of the Lunas to cure Antonio's Uncle Lucas, who has been cursed by Tenorio's daughters. Before healing Lucas, Ultima visits Tenorio's saloon to inform him of her plans. In a classic Western-style showdown, Ultima walks down the main street of El Puerto to confront Tenorio and advise him to order his daughters to remove their curse. Tenorio denies their involvement. After Lucas is healed, Tenorio's three daughters sicken and die.

Tenorio seeks revenge against Ultima, reviling her as a witch. Since Ultima rectifies situations that even priests cannot, even those she has healed fear to protect her. Initially, Tenorio arrives at the Márez y Luna home with a drunken lynch mob. Ultima is defended by Narcisco and by Antonio's father, who prove that Ultima is not a witch by applying an accepted folk standard: Ultima can pass through a door that is protected by the sign of the cross.

When Tenorio plans a second attack, Narcisco braves a snowstorm in search of Antonio's brother, Andrew. Andrew, the last of Antonio's older brothers to remain in Guadalupe, frequents Rosie's, a local brothel. Narcisco, silently followed by Antonio, begs Andrew to warn Ultima. Antonio is shocked and horrified to witness his brother at Rosie's door. Like the rest of the family, Antonio has denied Andrew's daily visits to Rosie's. Now, as Antonio watches, Andrew refuses to leave Rosie's to spare the aged Narciso a journey through a raging blizzard. As Narciso struggles on, Tenorio appears in his path. Antonio witnesses as the men struggle, and shots echo in the air. Moments later, Antonio holds the dying Narciso and, at his request, hears his last confession. Narciso dies at peace; Antonio returns home delirious with fever. In the dreams that follow, he repeatedly shouts out the story of how Tenorio killed Narcisco. Antonio reflects that he had to tell the story to purge the fever, foreshadowing that he will be a writer rather than a priest.

Tenorio finally destroys Ultima, but at the cost of his own life. He kills Ultima's owl, a magical creature to which she is sympathetically connected. As Tenorio takes aim at Antonio, however, Antonio's Uncle Pedro shoots Tenorio, an act that redeems the Lunas' earlier failure to protect Ultima. Antonio is with her as she dies. He buries her owl in a juniper, following her instructions; he reflects that "Ultima was really buried here. Tonight."

Analysis

Bless Me, Ultima thematically juxtaposes two moral systems. In the novel, the transcendent, binary ethics characteristic of Christianity and European high culture are juxtaposed against an immanent, nondualist ethos characteristic of the European folk tradition and of most pre-conquest religions in the Americas. Antonio struggles to resolve contradictions between the two traditions, especially in his allegorical dreams. A movement back and forth between figures from the Chicano oral tradition (such as the Virgin of Guadalupe, la Llorona, and the *curandera* tradition) and romantic figures such as Tenorio, the evil wizard whose horse is trained to kill, heightens a central asymmetry between Ultima's earth magic and Tenorio's transcendent wizardry. Tenorio and his daughters are classically evil; the daughters' performance of a conventional Black Mass in which they physically copulate with the devil clearly aligns them with romantic notions of absolute, ahistorical evil. The church and its rituals, on the other hand, are securely identified with a transcendent, if sometimes distant and inscrutable, good that is, alas, often distorted beyond all recognition by its adherents. A set of characters who seem to draw their energies from pre-Christian, folkloric traditions, however, fall outside the romantic good/evil dichotomy altogether. Narciso, Cico, and Samuel worship an earth deity called the Golden Carp. Antonio experiences the mystical "presence" of a river when he gathers herbs with Ultima. These characters, especially Ultima herself, all derive from a distinctly different narrative tradition and therefore operate according to different rules.

The novel's romantic perspective evaluates characters according to their ultimate allegiance to the forces of good or evil. Even Antonio's brother, Andrew, is relegated to the realm of evil in a dream in which Antonio sees him ensnared in the seething hair of a prostitute. Whenever this romantic good/evil dichotomy comes into contact with Ultima, however, the system breaks down. Particularly notable for its ambiguity is the episode in which, in order to prove that she is not a witch, Ultima passes through a doorframe in which needles blessed with holy water have formed the shape of a cross. Following the test, Antonio notices that the needles have fallen to the floor. In this episode, Ultima appears as a spiritual force outside the jurisdiction of Christianity. The hybridized folk religion that Ultima embodies emphasizes and celebrates the bicultural oral roots of Chicano culture.

Critical Context

Bless Me, Ultima is the best-selling and arguably the most popular Chicano literary work ever. The novel received the second annual Quinto Sol national Chicano literary award in 1971. The novel has been critically celebrated, probably in part owing to Anaya's "universalization" of Chicano experience through the use of mythical archetypes. Two novels that followed it, *Heart of Aztlán* and *Tortuga,* depict the struggles of the Chicano working class and have received less critical attention.

Although Anaya is one of the generation of writers whose work is associated with the Chicano movement of the mid-1960's, *Bless Me, Ultima* is frequently treated by movement writers and critics as a deviation, a distraction, or even as a betrayal. The novel's treatment of "universal" themes appealed to a number of critics who cared little about Chicano civil rights; some critics within the movement observed that the novel's fantastic, romantic depictions of a pastoral Chicano boyhood permitted such critics to ignore uncomfortable political questions. Chicano writers, critics, and activists who wanted to get racism and exploitation onto the national agenda were, perhaps inevitably, offended by Anaya's romanticization of rural poverty, his glossing over of the Spanish-speaking Antonio's disorientation and humiliation in an English-only and overtly racist classroom, and his representation of some migrant farmworkers as enthusiastically embracing this life as well-suited to the wanderlust they inherited from their vaquero progenitors.

Bless Me, Ultima does, however, incorporate the colonial and contemporary historical and social relations that it was accused of omitting. The fault of the novel's idealized, apolitical reception surely lies at least partly with a liberal white readership that focused on elements in the novel that were comfortable and familiar while ignoring or dismissing other aspects of the book. Antonio is, after all, only seven, and his ignorance concerning the origins of injustice is excusable. Rudolfo Anaya may have trusted his adult readers to think more carefully and reason more critically.

THE BOW AND THE LYRE: The Poem, the Poetic Revelation, Poetry, and History

Author: Octavio Paz (1914-   )
Type of work: Literary criticism
First published: *El arco y la lira*, 1956; revised, 1967 (English translation, 1973)

The Work

The Bow and the Lyre is a densely written, three-part scholarly study with an epilogue and appendices. It concerns Paz's own conception of poetry, the poetic, and history. The first five chapters constitute a series of bold and often compelling generalizations on the nature of poetry and the poetic, as well as commonly accepted attributes of poetry: poetic language, rhythm, verse, and imagery. This already broad field broadens further with three aspects of what is generally called "inspiration" and culminates in four chapters on poetry's relationship to history. Paz obviously considers these the most crucial parts of his work, for he concludes with three specific discussions, written as appendices: on poetry, society, and state; on ease and euphony in poetry; and on Walt Whitman, who for Paz combines all the constituents of an ideal poet.

In content, *The Bow and the Lyre* is a far-ranging work that deals with fundamental questions such as the differences between poetry and prose, the nature of inspiration, the relationship of poetry and history, and, by extension, the relationship of the epic and the modern novel. Although the book addresses the same concerns that André Breton considers in *Manifeste du surréalisme* (1924; *Manifesto of Surrealism*, 1969), the first of his three pronouncements on the nature and aims of the Surrealist movement, Paz's work is by no means tied to this ideology of his youth. He has, instead, written his own highly personal and ultimately incontrovertible study of the development of poetry and its nature in the contemporary world.

In the early chapters of *The Bow and the Lyre*, Paz seeks as much common ground with his readers as possible by enumerating the attributes poetry is commonly thought to have. He accepts Aristotle's broad and generic view of poetry and is careful to distinguish between poetry and poetic forms; the latter, for example, include the sonnet, but a sonnet is a poem only to the extent that it has been touched by "poetry." According to Paz, poetry is a use of language poised between tension (which he likens to the taut string of a bow) and resolution (the strings of the lyre, the ancient symbol of Apollo as guardian of the Muses). This is not to imply that for Paz the best poetry is that which is most agreeable to the reader; on the contrary, the poet's job of using language in unusual ways, particularly through metaphor, often causes hostility or, worse, indifference in readers. Every human being can, and often does, express ideas through metaphor. The poet, however, makes an art of subverting language, of using it in a highly original way that nevertheless evokes certain similar, though never identical, responses in readers. This causes the majority of readers to view the poet as a revolutionary and the poem itself as something suspect.

Poets, then, are constantly in the position of declaring the relationship of this, that, and the other. Violence is implicit in such verbal gymnastics because such declarations are not of the conventional variety. The poet usually does not say that this girl is like the other, but he might well compare a virgin to an unplowed field. All language has certain rhythms in the very patterns of speech, but the poet as magician knows when to create rhythmic irregularity or even interruption in the dance of words.

Rhythm prefigures language just as poetry prefigures prose; by Paz's definition, even nonliterate societies have a poetry, even if they do not have a prose. Paradoxical though it seems, the most primitive (or, more accurately, the least technological) societies have the richest poetry, rich because it is oral and therefore mythic and based on imaginative analogy. This leads Paz to accept much broader definitions of what constitutes verse, even in modern literature. Lewis Carroll's *Alice's Adventures in Wonderland* (1865), because of its rhythm and as much for its mythic content, becomes for him a poem. D. H. Lawrence's and William Faulkner's prose works have, as Paz reads them, the rhythmic unity of free verse.

Paz, as might be expected from the foregoing, views poetic imagery as the product of a participation between poet and reader—union potentially akin to religious experience. A poet might choose to place the word "chair" before readers, but this bare image compels readers to summon up the object as each individually perceives it at a given time. Obviously, each perception differs, though all will be within the limits the word "chair" imposes. No readers will perceive "table" if the poet directs that they perceive "chair"; thus, the poet's task is to guide rather than to describe in order to force the active participation of readers in creating the image. Paz's understanding of poetic imagery clearly springs from his reading of Plato's theory of imitation.

The second half of Paz's book deals primarily with the poet's role in creating, just as the first examined the reader's reception of what the poet created. Just as he sees the reader's encounter potentially akin to religious experience, so he views the poet as producing a work of timeless history. Homer's poems, for example, describe a Mycenaean Greece that had passed out of existence half a millennium before Homer was born; yet they reflect a poetic vision of that world even as they timelessly describe the behavior of their heroes. Paz, like many writers, notes the odd feeling a writer has when a text suddenly assumes a life of its own, when a given phrase is correct and the only one permissible, while another, though it

satisfies formal requirements such as meter, is unquestionably wrong. One could call this inspiration or "alien collaboration," but it is a regular phenomenon for creative writers. It serves to create a historical view that is true in the artistic sense. No reader could doubt that Dante made his journey through Hell, Purgatory, and Heaven, because, despite whatever lapses critics may discover, every element of his poem is inspirationally and (by a poet's understanding of the word) historically correct.

Further unifying his association of poetry, religion, and history, Paz argues that the poet's task is to render the instant sacred. Poems mediate between a given original experience and a cluster of subsequent experiences to privilege a moment based on all of these. The loves of Sappho have their primary identification in history and are unrecoverable, but her poetry continues to create these as sacred moments that live in new form each time her poems are read. Poetry thus incarnates history to yield a changing present with each reading and reader. The poems become archetypal history because they transcend the epoch in which they are composed, and poetry reproduces this tension of having been, and being again, "like the bowstring or the strings of the lyre."

Uncanny prophecy appears in Paz's final chapters. He views the period in which he writes as the end of the modern age and concludes that Karl Marx's apocalyptic vision of the end of the labyrinth of history, humanity's ability to create and modify its own existence, has come to pass. He believes, however, that the technology which has allowed this, and which Marx had viewed as essentially liberating, has had a devastating effect on the creation of poetry. Because technology imposes empiricism (proof by demonstration) on all that it touches, it privileges the "I" at the expense of the imaginable "Other." Carried to its furthest refinement, technology allows the "I" not only to exist by itself but also to control every aspect of its being without external referents. This reduces not only the imaginative capacity of the individual but also, more dangerously, the mythos (place of story or legend) within the group of individuals once considered a society. Heroes cannot exist because their flaws are all too clear; rites and rituals lose their meaning because technology respects no symbols but its own jargon. These frightening prospects show how far Paz has come from his association with the Surrealists, who had heralded technology as a form of art. They reveal Paz at his philosophical best.

Analysis

It is nearly impossible to argue against the positions Paz takes, even if one differs with his conclusions, because each is clearly grounded in a premise, admittedly his own, based on a lifetime of reading psychology, history, and aesthetics as well as literature. Although his foreword to the first edition traces the origins of his study to a series of lectures in 1942 and Spanish poet José Bergamín—with some of these thoughts finding their way into Paz's *El laberinto de la soledad: Vida y pensamiento de México* (1950, 1959; *The Labyrinth of Solitude: Life and Thought in Mexico*, 1961)—it is clear that by the time of the revised edition, Paz was more concerned with the poor state of poetry in his native Mexico, where its poets were generally despised or ignored. Thus, true to his Surrealist background, Paz turns inevitably to the course of politics and the appearance of modern technology in his account of this phenomenon.

With consummate irony, his work on poetics indirectly mounts an attack (though it is never called that) on Mexican intellectuals and presents a view of poetry in their chosen medium: prose. Never naming his opponents, Paz formulates broad theses backed by his own readings of a welter of sources cited in rapid succession but almost never argued in close detail. He clearly wishes to avoid the tone of academic argument or traditional literary criticism, just as he tries to skirt narrow, limited invective of the sort he had, in 1954, aimed at Antonio Castro Leal's academic view of Mexican poetry.

More than anything, *The Bow and the Lyre* is a prose synthesis of Paz's poetics, but one that extends far beyond the traditional limits of poetry. Both explicit and implicit in his arguments is the notion that the poet is essentially subversive, most often disdained or ignored by the powerful elite rather than actively persecuted. The contradiction, which Paz notes and argues, is that the nature of poetry is to avoid cliché through metaphor, an instinctive desire of all who use language, even those not considering themselves to be poets. If one accepts the premise, it follows either that there are no poets or that everyone has some claim to being one. Paz is willing to accept either conclusion with a delight exceeded only by the consternation of his adversaries.

Paz saw *The Bow and the Lyre* as a summation of his own *poesis*; this is clearly the reason it draws its examples and sources more heavily from continental literature than from less widely known poets writing in Spanish. Although the book was originally a response to the cultural values of his country, Paz authorized the distinguished translation by Ruth L. C. Simms because he saw similar dangers in academic criticism in the English-speaking world.

Critical Context

One can easily read *The Bow and the Lyre* as the kind of impersonal autobiography many poets could have written at the dawn of the technological age. Although poets have always been outcasts, the denial of the imaginative power of language creates a labyrinth of solipsism (the belief that the self can know only its own experiences). Joseph Campbell, the eminent writer on myth and ritual, reached exactly the same conclusions as Paz in noting the disappearance of mythos in the contemporary

Western world. In *The Labyrinth of Solitude*, Paz had called this modern phenomenon *soledad* (solitude, which implies alienation) and opposed it to *comunión* as the fruit the contemporary world will reap. Although Paz marshals a staggering variety of philosophers and poets to support his argument, conspicuous by his absence is the French existentialist Jean-Paul Sartre. This omission is strangely pleasing, as though Paz is still willing to entertain some hope of *comunión*.

Paz's diffuse theory of poetry sprang indirectly from his involvement with French and Spanish Surrealists during the years 1937-1942. With the writing of *The Bow and the Lyre*, Paz showed that he had passed not only beyond the Surrealist involvements of his youth but also beyond the circle of *poètes maudits* (cursed poets), the revolutionary poets damned for their antiestablishment values. Although he continues to hold that all poets are revolutionaries, this book marked Paz's return to Mexico and established him as its reigning philosopher-poet. The surprisingly favorable criticism it received from academic critics such as Helen Vendler, not to mention its broad circulation in English and French translations, transformed a revolutionary into a respected literary figure.

THE BOY WITHOUT A FLAG: Tales of the South Bronx

Author: Abraham Rodriguez, Jr. (1961-　　)
Type of work: Short stories
Type of plot: Social realism
Time of plot: The late twentieth century
Locale: The South Bronx, New York City
First published: 1992

Principal Characters

The Rodriguez boy, a gifted student and would-be rebel in "The Boy Without a Flag." The Rodriguez boy and his friend Edwin have a crush on their young teacher, Miss Colon, and they help her decorate her classroom at Halloween, earning her gratitude. They also defame her by producing and distributing a comic book called "Slut at the Head of the Class." To earn his father's respect, the Rodriguez boy reads voraciously and writes novels and plays. His father, a poet, tries to discourage him, knowing that he will not be able to earn a good living as a writer. Influenced by one of his father's tirades against American imperialism, he decides not to salute the American flag at school.

Nilsa, a fiery tomboy in "No More War Games." She loves to play war games and cringes at the thought of giving them up, but her friend Cha-Cha, formerly a tomboy, insists that she must act sexy and feminine if she wants to get a boyfriend. As she stalks her prey in one last battle inside a dilapidated building, she feels powerful and sexy. She imagines herself as a new type of woman, one who can play soldier and dress in tattered clothes and still look beautiful and date boys. When she commands Patchi, her prisoner, to tell her she is pretty, he says, "Yuh all right." His response devastates her. She realizes that boys are not attracted to powerful women.

The unnamed narrator, a sixteen-year-old heroin addict in "Babies." Abused as a child, she uses heroin to escape her painful memories. She is torn between a desire to become a mother and the realization that her world is "no place for babies."

Her maternal instinct is manifested in her compassion for others. Her abortion signals her surrender to the powerful environmental forces working against her. Like the flame on her birthday candle, she shimmers precariously, about to expire.

Angel, the adolescent narrator of "Birthday Boy." He is physically and mentally precocious and has a sense of humor, which he displays in the police station. For more than eleven years, he enjoyed a happy relationship with his father, but then his father became mean and abusive, blaming him for his mother's infidelity and eventually driving him onto the streets. Although he steals, he is not a bad person. His refusal to stab his father during a violent beating indicates his morality. He struggles to remain independent of Spider's crack operation. His burglary of an apartment is probably to get money for his pregnant girlfriend, Gloria, and to support himself.

Marty, a railway motorman in "Short Stop." He stops his train to help a suicidal teenager. Unlike the female conductor, who refuses to announce the stops correctly, or the two transit cops, who release the obviously distressed and suicidal teenager, Marty cares about people and his job. His capacity for affection and his desire to nurture are evident in the camaraderie he shares with his fellow motorman, Clint, his fondness for his wife, Melissa, and his yearning to be a father.

Dalia, a junior-high-school student in "The Lotto." She is shy, nervous, and superstitious. When boys talk to her, she averts her eyes. She is especially vulnerable to peer pressure. At her friend's prodding, she has sex with a street boy and later feels guilty about it. Her guilt manifests itself as morning sickness, which she interprets as a sign of pregnancy. Infected by her mother's distorted religious beliefs, she worries that God will reveal her pregnancy to her parents.

Elba, a teenage wife and mother, the title character of the last story. Although she once loved her husband, Danny, she now despises him, so much so that she scrubs her body clean of his unpleasant touch and dries herself off with a "virgin" towel, one not used by him. She views their cramped, roach-infested apartment as a prison cell. Although she tries to be a mature and responsible mother, Danny refuses to cooperate. He frequently comes home drunk and treats her like a whore. Her revulsion for Danny undercuts her affection for their baby, who looks like his father. Elba's act of rebellion takes the form of a symbolic prison break.

The Stories

The Boy Without a Flag is a collection of seven short stories, all set in the South Bronx, about Americans of Puerto Rican descent. In the title story, an adolescent boy refuses to salute the American flag at school because his father has convinced him that the United States is an enemy of Puerto Rico. Although his friend, Edwin, admires his defiance, his teachers, Miss Colon and especially Mr. Rios, are horrified. They send him to the principal, Mr. Sepulvia, who summons the boy's father to school. Rather than defend his son, Mr. Rodriguez apologizes to the principal; the boy feels betrayed.

"No More War Games" is about an eleven-year-old girl, Nilsa, who enjoys being a tomboy and playing war games but also desires a boyfriend. Walking past an abandoned building one day, she and a friend, Maria, are ambushed by two boys, Eddie and Patchi, who fling bottles at them from a third-story window. Nilsa storms the building and surprises the boys, capturing Patchi. She orders her prisoner to kiss her or tell her she is pretty, but he refuses. Embarrassed, she resolves to dress and act sexy, like her friend Cha-Cha, to "catch" boys.

In "Babies," an unnamed narrator lives with her boyfriend, Smiley, who supplies her with "H" (heroin). Her upstairs neighbor, Sara, an unwed mother, neglects her baby. Another neighbor, Diana, is being pressured by her mother to get an abortion against her will. The narrator tries to counsel both friends. Diana, after a violent struggle with her mother in the street, goes into premature labor and is rushed to the hospital, where her baby dies. In the weeks that follow, Sara gets rid of her baby mysteriously, Diana goes in search of "H," and the narrator, pregnant herself, decides to have an abortion because she does not want to bring another "zero" into the world.

"Birthday Boy" takes place on the narrator's thirteenth birthday. Sitting on a stoop at dawn, waiting to burglarize a man's apartment, Angel thinks about his sixteen-year-old girlfriend, Gloria, who informed him the night before that she is pregnant. His thoughts are interrupted by Spider, the local crack dealer, who comes by to offer him a job, but Angel wants to remain independent of Spider's organization. Inside the man's apartment, Angel finds a large stash of money, which he quickly pockets, but he is arrested almost as soon as he exits the building. He calls Spider, who bails him out, but not until Angel agrees to work for him.

In "Short Stop," Marty, a motorman for the New York City elevated railway, spots a girl sitting on a maintenance catwalk just inside a tunnel that his train is approaching. Certain that she intends to throw herself in front of his train, he stops, gets out, and manages to coax her into one of the passenger cars. He then radios for the transit police as he continues on his way. At the Brooklyn Bridge station, his last stop, he turns the girl over to the authorities, who question her routinely and release her. The girl immediately heads for another tunnel, and Marty runs after her. "Short Stop" is the only story in the collection that has an adult as its main character.

The sixth story, "The Lotto," is a tour de force.

Young Dalia thinks that she is pregnant and wants desperately to find her boyfriend, Ricky, who has disappeared. After a restless night in which she dreams about doctors pulling babies out of top hats, she searches unsuccessfully for her boyfriend and then meets her friend Elba at the local pizzeria. Also fearing herself pregnant, Elba has an appointment at Planned Parenthood. She buys Dalia a home pregnancy test, and they agree to meet later that night to share their findings. As her parents, Rosa and Camilo, watch the lotto drawing on television, Dalia conducts her own "lottery" in the bathroom, discovering to her good fortune that she is not pregnant. Moments later, Elba arrives with bad news.

In "Elba," a sixteen-year-old wife and mother is awakened by her son's sirenlike wailing, which foreshadows the trouble to come. Tired and angry, she goes to the baby's crib and picks him up. Immediately, her anger subsides, but then she notices how much he looks like his father, Danny, and she becomes angry again. She recalls a recent fight with her husband and his verbal and physical abuse. Then she thinks about their relationship, beginning with their first sexual encounter in the eighth grade and ending with the present unpleasantness. Infuriated by her husband's irresponsibility and cruelty, she decides to rebel by dressing provocatively and going out on the town. She shuts the windows, turns up the radio, and leaves the crying baby alone in the apartment.

Analysis

The Boy Without a Flag is social commentary and art at their finest. The title reflects the alienation of Puerto Ricans in a country that too often rejects and oppresses them. Their subordinate position in society is symbolized by the large American flag carried beside the small Puerto Rican one in the first story. The movies they watch and the literature they read are products of the dominant culture, which controls them and often determines their success or failure. When they try to rebel, they are beaten back by powerful economic and social forces.

The conflict between rebellion and submission organizes many of the stories and unifies the collection. The Rodriguez boy rebels unsuccessfully against the establishment and is forced to accept compromise. Searching for compromise, Nilsa tries to resist a sexual stereotype, but male expectations crush her rebellion. Angel struggles to stay out of Spider's web, but he is pushed in by external forces. To protest her submissive position in her family, which is a microcosm of the larger society, Elba abandons her baby for a night of freedom. Her act of rebellion is perhaps the most costly one of all because it creates another victim.

Several of the stories have initiation as their theme. The main characters pass from one stage in life to another, often losing something precious in the transition. In "The Boy Without a Flag," the Rodriguez boy matures as he learns the necessity of compromise, but he also loses some of his respect for his father. "No More War Games" is basically a coming-of-age story in which a pubescent girl discovers her sexuality and the constraints of womanhood, but she also sacrifices part of her identity as she resolves to imitate Cha-Cha. In "Birthday Boy," Angel undergoes a rite of passage as he receives a police record and joins Spider's organization on his unlucky thirteenth birthday.

The stories collectively identify teenage pregnancy as the greatest threat to the New York Puerto Rican community. The South Bronx, as Rodriguez depicts it, is a breeding ground for adolescents, who multiply at an alarming rate; Rodriguez includes many references to rabbits and cockroaches as reminders. Dalia's mother keeps a lucky rabbit's foot in her magic box, and Elba curses an entire generation of cockroaches. There is supreme irony in the fact that Marty, a suitable parent, cannot impregnate his wife. The characters in these stories live in a world in which birth control is scorned and in which babies beget babies. Dalia and Ricky have sex in a crack dealer's "tiny crib," and Ricky "cradle[s]" her like a baby. Diana's mother affectionately calls her daughter "my baby."

Pregnancy means a loss for these characters, who too often dismiss abortion as a solution. Young mothers and fathers are forced to quit school, take low-paying jobs or resort to crime, and live in abject poverty. Nor do they learn from their mistakes. Elba and Danny already have one un-wanted child, but Danny still refuses to wear condoms when he has sex with Elba, and Elba deliberately "forgets" to take birth control pills because she resents always having to be the responsible partner. Only by using birth control, accepting the necessity of abortion, and staying in school and off drugs can these characters break the pattern of poverty and despair.

Critical Context

Rodriguez is the son of a Puerto Rican poet who gave him his first typewriter at the age of ten and inspired him to become a writer. He grew up in the South Bronx, dropped out of high school when he was sixteen years old, worked at various jobs, later earned his high-school equivalency diploma, and attended City College of New York, where he wrote several prize-winning short stories. His writing reflects an intimate knowledge of the people and landscape of the South Bronx. He writes from experience but also from research, observing his surroundings and talking with young people in his old neighborhood. To give his writing the unmistakable flavor of truth, he often invites his young friends to read and critique his stories.

The Boy Without a Flag is Rodriguez's first book. It is not unusual for a writer to inaugurate his career with a volume of stories and then follow with a novel. Rodriguez's second book, *Spidertown: A Novel*, was published in 1993. It greatly expands the role of crack-dealing Spider, a minor character in "Birthday Boy." Unlike *Spidertown*, which was vigorously promoted by its publisher, *The Boy Without a Flag* did not receive the attention it deserved, but reviews, while few in number, were generally favorable, even laudatory. Although Rodriguez was not able to erase all evidence of his apprenticeship, particularly in the first half of "No More War Games," his stories succeed as art and poignant social commentary. In "The Boy Without a Flag" in particular, he distinguishes himself as a talented author.

Rodriguez's collection of stories can be grouped with the works of other New York Puerto Rican authors, such as Piri Thomas' *Down These Mean Streets* (1967), Nicholasa Mohr's *Going Home* (1986), and Victor Hernandez Cruz's *Red Beans* (1991). It has a special kinship with Piri Thomas' *Stories from El Barrio* (1978) and Mohr's *El Bronx Remembered: A Novella and Stories* (1975). *The Boy Without a Flag* also fits into the larger context of contemporary works by Latino writers.

THE BRICK PEOPLE

Author: Alejandro Morales (1944-   )
Type of work: Novel
Type of plot: Historical
Time of plot: The 1890's to the 1940's
Locale: Southern California
First published: 1988

Principal Characters

Octavio Revueltas, a Mexican immigrant who comes to Simons brickyard during the Mexican Revolution. He becomes an expert brickmaker and learns to gamble in order to supplement his income. When he weds Nana de León in 1926, they begin a family whose children will be first-generation Chicanos and Chicanas, people of Mexican descent born and reared in the United States. Octavio becomes increasingly interested in the union movement because he believes that the Simons family exercises too much control over the workers' lives in what is essentially a company town. During the Great Depression, Octavio makes contact with several unions. The Simons workers strike in 1937, but the strike is broken by scabs, and union solidarity disintegrates. Octavio retreats to his family convinced that working conditions will never improve. His direct experience of exploitation and racism makes him wary of the Anglo-American world outside the brickyard. Unlike his wife, Octavio struggles to resist assimilation into the dominant culture.

Nana de León Revueltas, a strong and intelligent woman who is determined to establish her family's independence and better its economic situation. As a young woman, she elopes with Octavio Revueltas, marries him, and moves to his parents' home. For the next few years, much of her energy is spent trying to set up an autonomous existence for her husband and children, away from the extended family and the authority of her mother-in-law; at one point, she actually moves the family without advising Octavio. Nana believes that the stubborn dominance of the Chicano-Mexicano male is a product of his oppression and low self-esteem.

Walter Robey Simons, one of the heirs of the family business, who competes with his brother Joseph until the latter's death. Unlike his brother, Walter is interested in Mexican culture, because he believes that an understanding of his employees' mentality will allow him to maintain control of them. After the death of his first wife, Sara, he marries a classical pianist who compares the adaptability and persistence of the Mexican worker to that of the cockroach. Both the Great Depression and the strike at Simons drive Walter into the role of absentee owner; his business affairs are managed by others as he travels through Europe with his wife. In Paris, he chokes to death on a swarm of brown insects.

Malaquias de León, one of the first workers who challenges the authority of the Simons company and its surrogates. His confrontation with the foreman, Gonzalo Pedroza, sets the stage for his eventual firing and departure from the brickyard. Because he attains a relative economic independence through the sale of horses, he is able to move his family to a nearby barrio; however, he fails to raise the money for the land he had always wanted to own.

Rosendo Guerrero, the first foreman, who helps Joseph Simons learn the brickmaking business and who designs the first brickyard. Rosendo's parents were killed in Mexico during the Napoleonic occupation, and Rosendo escaped to Los Angeles, where he met a Simons cousin who taught him the basic procedures for making bricks. He later becomes friends with Walter Simons, to whom he is close in age, and urges him to travel to Mexico in order to learn more about the culture. His death is mysterious and seems to have been part of a sacrificial ritual linked to ancient American Indian religious practices.

Arturo Revueltas, the firstborn son of Nana and Octavio. Arturo experiences racism in the school system and drops out at the age of fourteen. As a young child, he is labeled "retarded" by Anglo-American schoolteachers who are unaware of or uninterested in the problems of bilingual students. During World War II, he is drawn to the young Chicanos known as zoot-suiters, but his mother forbids him to wear the zoot-suiter's distinctive wardrobe. The final scene of the novel finds Arturo listening to his father's memories of the journey north as the two men prepare to build the family's new home.

The Novel

Based in part on the actual experiences of the author's parents (to whom the book is dedicated), *The Brick People* is the story of several generations of Anglo-American and Chicano/Mexicano families and their interactions in Southern California in the first half of the twentieth century. Representing the capitalist and working classes respectively are the Simons and the Revueltas families, the principal clans.

The novel begins in 1892, with Rosendo Guerrero laying out the ground plan for the original Simons brickyard in Pasadena, California. The coordinates of the plan are based on an Aztec mandala, suggesting that the legacy of the indigenous cultures of the region lies buried under the ground. This idea is reinforced by the figure of Doña Eulalia, who identifies with an ancient oak tree and who turns into millions of brown insects upon her death.

Joseph Simons, the eldest son of the brickmaking dynasty's founder, makes every attempt to keep his workers complacent. One of his greatest concerns is the worldwide increase in radical unionism. When a mass grave of Chinese workers is found on the brickyard grounds, Joseph notifies the authorities and orders that the bodies be burned so as to preclude any labor unrest. Joseph's relationship with his younger brother Walter is strained at best; he finds Walter to be arrogant and at odds with his own political views. A third brother, Orin Elmer, is a physical and intellectual weakling who is unable to participate in the family business.

Walter Simons is an "enlightened capitalist" who seeks to understand Mexican culture in order to make better use of his workers. On the suggestion of Rosendo Guerrero, Walter undertakes a fact-finding trip to Mexico, where he experiences at first hand the daily workings of U.S. imperialism under the dictator Porfirio Díaz. In the state of Chihuahua, he confers with William Randolph Hearst and other California businesspeople and witnesses the abuses of the hacienda system, including a massacre of peasants by government forces.

Upon Walter's return, the Simons company begins construction on a new brickyard in the Los Angeles suburb of Montebello. In the wake of the San Francisco earthquake of 1906, demands for building materials increase dramatically, and the Simons business expands at an incredible rate. Rosendo decides to promote one of his workers, Gonzalo Pedroza, to the status of foreman. Gonzalo will become one of the most powerful and hated figures at the brickyard. The arrival of Malaquias de León and his family marks a significant moment in the history of the brickyard, for it coincides with the Mexican Revolution of 1910, the tremendous rise in immigration to the United States, and the dissemination of socialist and communist ideology throughout the Southwest. Orin Elmer's death (and the consumption of his body by brown insects) marks an end to the initial stage of the narrative.

The tension between the Simons brothers, Joseph and Walter, is aggravated when the two compete for economic control of the family assets. Walter's decision to build a home in Los Angeles essentially makes him an absentee owner at the Montebello brickyard, where recently arrived workers from Mexico are becoming more politicized. The departure of Malaquias de León coincides with the increased importance of Octavio Revueltas, who marries Malaquias' daughter, Nana, in 1926. The stock market crash of 1929 and the resulting depression worsen economic conditions for the entire country. Some of the Simons workers (with Octavio as their leader) establish contact with various union organizers, despite harassment from the Simonses and the foreman Gonzalo Pedroza. The Long Beach earthquake of 1933 marks the symbolic end of the boom in the brick industry, since newer and more reliable building materials have been invented.

The Simons workers finally walk out, but the strike is broken with the use of poor African American workers. The Simons workers break ranks, some of them return to work, others are reduced to desperation and cynicism. The events of World War II overshadow problems that had existed previously: Mexican Americans serve proudly in the U.S. military, Japanese Americans are interned, the Zoot Suit riots (in which Anglo-American sailors attacked Chicanos) break out in Los Angeles, and Simons workers leave the brickyard to take jobs in wartime industries. Once outside the walls of the yard, Mexican families experience racial discrimination with regard to housing and bank loans. The Revueltas family is forced to move back to the home of Octavio's parents. News arrives of Walter Simons' death by choking on brown insects.

The final chapter consists of Octavio's memories of his family's original journey north from Mexico. The novel ends on an optimistic note: The Revueltas family is building a new home and moving tentatively into the middle class.

Analysis

The novel is a fictional treatment of Chicano/Mexicano history, specifically the period immediately surrounding the Mexican Revolution. *The Brick People* represents for the reader Chicano involvement in a series of key historical events, ranging from the Díaz dictatorship in Mexico, to the Mexican Revolution, to the Great Depression, to successful and unsuccessful strikes organized by Mexican, Japanese, and Filipino farmworkers in the 1930's, to World War II. The novel's historical sweep is grounded in the everyday lives of engaging and lifelike characters.

The text is structured upon the relationship between the Simons and Revueltas families. If the Simons family represents (on a small scale) the powerful U.S. industrialist class and, by extension, capital itself, the Revueltas family (the name means "uprisings" in Spanish) is the Chicano/Mexicano working class whose interests are necessarily opposed to those of their bosses. In addition to this political subtext, the novel incorporates images of nature (insects, earthquakes, serpents) and American Indian societies (Aztec deities, the mandala) that suggest that there are more powerful forces at work than the dominant Anglo-American culture may be equipped to recognize. The recurring image of the brown insects may be linked to the Chicano people in general (as it has in other works of Chicano literature)—the despised yet persistent "cockroach people" who survive against all odds.

In the character of Nana, the novel constructs a model for Chicanas that incorporates specific values of traditional Mexican society even as it breaks with certain limitations placed on women. The entire question of gender is an important undercurrent throughout the text.

By linking the important issues of class, gender, and ethnicity within the frame of a historical novel, *The Brick People* provides readers with a fascinating account of a particularly rich episode of Chicano history.

Critical Context

The Brick People, Alejandro Morales' fourth novel, is undoubtedly his most personal in that it is a fictionalized account of his parents' life. Unlike his earlier texts, which often have a fragmented structure, *The Brick People* is organized as a relatively straightforward historical novel; it follows the chronology of the early twentieth century with references to key events such as the Great Depression and World War II. The combination of historical fact and elements of fantasy places the novel in the Magical Realist tradition of contemporary Latin American literature associated with Alejo Carpentier, Gabriel García Márquez, and others.

Morales was one of the first Chicano novelists at a time (the late 1970's) when Chicano literature was not yet accepted as an important area of American studies. Chicano texts were not included in the curriculum of major universities, and Chicano writers and scholars in many English and Spanish departments were greeted with outright hostility. In a real sense, Morales' role in the U.S. academy was to be one of the founders of an emergent discipline. By the time *The Brick People* appeared (written entirely in English), Chicano literature enjoyed an international readership and academic respectability, and Morales was counted among the most influential Chicano critics and writers of fiction.

A BRIEF LIFE

Author: Juan Carlos Onetti (1909-   )
Type of work: Novel
Type of plot: Fantasy
Time of plot: The twentieth century
Locale: Buenos Aires, Argentina, and the fictional town of Santa María
First published: *La vida breve*, 1950 (English translation, 1976)

Principal Characters

Juan María Brausen, the protagonist, who is suffering an existential crisis at the time that both his vacuous advertising job and his marriage are dissolving. To save himself from the outer void, he takes on two new identities: an impersonation that he assumes so as to enter the life of the prostitute who lives in the apartment adjacent to his own, and his fictional surrogate, the protagonist of a film scenario that he is alternately writing and imagining over the course of the novel. All three levels of his identity merge ambiguously at the end of his story. Brausen ends up in the imaginary town of Santa María, the setting of the scenario.

Juan María Arce, the name under which Brausen moves in with Queca, the prostitute, who is unaware that he lives next door as Brausen. He virtually becomes a kept man. He develops a sadistic relationship with Queca and plans to kill her, essentially as a gratuitous act but also because she taunts him as a perpetual cuckold. Ernesto, one of Queca's lovers, kills Queca on the night Arce had planned to murder her.

Dr. Díaz Grey, Brausen's fictional alter ego, a slim provincial physician with thinning blond hair. Díaz Grey, like Brausen, is middle-aged and repressed. He is a bachelor but is awakened to love by the appearance of Elena Sala in his life. Quite corruptible, Díaz Grey supplies Elena with regular injections of morphine and after her death accompanies her husband to Buenos Aires to procure drugs for illicit trade. Díaz Grey is last seen in Buenos Aires, having left behind his fictional habitat, Santa María, and effectively changed places with his creator, Brausen.

Gertrudis, Brausen's wife. She has had a mastectomy just previous to the action of the novel. Brausen is put off by her new physical state and by the routine of marriage that Gertrudis represents.

Raquel, Gertrudis' younger sister. Brausen seduces her on a trip he takes to her city, although she has recently married.

Enriqueta "Queca" Marti, the diminutive prostitute who lives and works in the apartment next door to Brausen's. As time goes on, Arce routinely beats Queca, and she verbally abuses him and seems to intuit his desire to kill her.

Ernesto, a tall, bony, dark-haired, impulsive young man, one of Queca's lovers. He finds Brausen-Arce with her in her apartment one night, beats him up, and throws him out. Eventually Ernesto kills Queca, and after the murder, Brausen-Arce takes charge of the disoriented young man and attempts to help him escape via Santa María.

Elena Sala, the tall, blonde, married woman with a lewd smile who one day shows up in Díaz Grey's office to get morphine, and who continues to receive it from the doctor, along with his discreet attentions and his devotion.

The Novel

A Brief Life presents the inner conflict of a man who, after suffering a traumatizing experience, feels lost and seeks an identity. He splits into two selves, and, at the same time, he finds refuge in his own fantasy.

Juan María Brausen is about to be fired from his job. His wife, Gertrudis, has undergone surgery on her left breast, and her scarred body is so repulsive to him that it has become an obsession. He begins to realize that he is not the same person he thought he was and suffers a crisis of identity.

Through the wall of his apartment, Brausen can listen to the incidents that take place in the world of Queca, a prostitute. He decides to enter this adjacent world as an alternative to his tortured existence. In his imagination, Brausen becomes Juan María Arce, a new man who will exist simultaneously but apart from Brausen. Arce will live "a brief life in which time could not be enough to engage him, to make him repent, or grow older."

The agency for which Brausen works has ordered him to write a screenplay. For that purpose, he has invented the imaginary world of Santa María at the shores of the Río de la Plata. There, an imaginary alter ego, the mediocre forty-year-old Dr. Díaz Grey, spends his life selling morphine to Elena Sala, the woman with whom he is in love. Brausen repeatedly escapes to this world and projects himself into the doctor.

These "brief lives" exist primarily in Brausen's consciousness, rather than in the real world. The conclusion of the novel completes the image of failure presented at the beginning: Brausen has been fired from his job and has been abandoned by his wife. Queca has been killed, and Elena Sala also has died. The novel ends with Brausen walking along the streets of Santa María, integrated into his own fantasy.

Analysis

Onetti concentrates on Brausen's psychological problems, fears, and fantasies, rather than on a narrative description of his life. For this reason, Brausen's internal life, depicted through his reflections and through passages of stream of consciousness, predominates over action in the book.

Juan María Brausen, like many of Onetti's protagonists, is an imaginative man who refuses to develop the practical qualities that his world demands of him. Brausen is an alienated, existentially tortured man, an outsider. He knows that the world in which he lives is full of falsehoods, but he does not fight it. Brausen creates other selves through which he evades his anxiety, taking refuge in his fantasy as a self-defense mechanism, but he does not undergo change in the course of the novel.

The noises and voices to which Brausen listens through the wall of his room invite him to enter the world of sex, a world from which his wife's scars have separated him. Brausen—transformed into Arce—will visit Queca, the prostitute, to overcome the impotence that he feels with his wife.

A Brief Life, with its complex narrative structure, suggests that a person is one and many, a multiple being made of a series of distinct and alienated selves. As the title of the book indicates, a person can live many short lives.

Fatalism and failure govern Brausen's world. It is a world in which people are surrounded by deception that makes futile any fight against the natural obstacles of life. (The book begins and ends symbolically during carnival; life is a masquerade.) There is no way to succeed. The only possibility of salvation is in fantasy: "I had in my hands the paper, the blotter, and the fountain pen necessary for my salvation. . . . I would be saved if I began to write the plot. . . . If I wrote only one phrase." Salvation through the act of imagination is a recurring theme in Onetti's work.

Critical Context

Onetti belongs to a group of writers, born in Uruguay and Argentina, who reached maturity during the politically tumultuous 1930's and who became known as "the lost generation." They share a nihilist vision of the world, expressed through the solitary, alienated characters they create. These writers practice a kind of existentialism; their conflict with society is reflected in the deliberately fragmentary quality of their fiction. A good example of such fragmentation is Onetti's *A Brief Life*.

A Brief Life is considered to be a pivotal work in Onetti's career. His previous works—including *El pozo* (the well, 1939) and *Tierra de nadie* (no man's land, 1941)—sketch the psychological conflicts that are fully developed in *A Brief Life*. Many of the works that follow—including *Los Adioses* (1954; *Farewells*, 1992), *Para una tumba sin nombre* (1959; *A Grave with No Name*, 1992), and *Juntacadáveres* (1964; *Body Snatchers*, 1991)—base their plots on the inventions created in Juan María Brausen's mind. The world of Santa María, first introduced in *A Brief Life*, appears as a constant in Onetti's following works. Santa María, like Macondo in Gabriel García Márquez's books, becomes a mythical place. Onetti succeeds in transporting the reader to his character's fantasy world, because, although nonexistent, it seems perfectly real.

A Brief Life explores a man's search for an answer to his existence. "People believe they are condemned to one life until death. But they are only condemned to one soul, to one identity. One can live many times, many lives, shorter or longer." By creating an imaginary world, and imaginary selves, Brausen can enjoy several lives, although he remains the same person, the same soul.

BROAD AND ALIEN IS THE WORLD

Author: Ciro Alegría (1909-1967)
Type of work: Novel
Type of plot: Social criticism
Time of plot: 1912-1926
Locale: Peru
First published: *El mundo es ancho y ajeno*, 1941 (English translation, 1941)

Principal Characters

Rosendo Maquis, mayor of the Peruvian Indian village of Rumi. He fights a losing battle to keep his people from losing their ancestral lands. He is a peaceful man who seeks only justice from the white men. Seeking to recover the village's prize bull, he is imprisoned as a thief. He dies in prison, victim of a brutal beating administered when he is erroneously thought to be responsible for helping another prisoner, Fiero Vásquez, escape.

Bismarck Ruiz, an unethical lawyer. He is retained by the Indians to help them in court to keep their lands from falling into the hands of Don Amenabar, a white rancher. Ruiz is halfhearted in his efforts, as he is also in the employ of Don Amenabar.

Don Amenabar, a greedy, ruthless rancher. He treats the Indians as an inferior people and robs them of their cattle and lands. He tries also to make slaves of them for his mines.

Correa Zavala, a zealous young lawyer. He, filled with indignation, undertakes to help the Indians, but his well-meant efforts are unsuccessful.

Fiero Vásquez, a notorious Peruvian bandit. Implored by an Indian woman from Rosendo's village who loves him, he offers to help the Indians fight eviction by force. The peaceful villagers, knowing that violence will not bring them any lasting peace, reject his offer.

Benito Castro, the successor to Rosendo as the leader of the Indians of the village of Rumi. He is killed by soldiers who evict the poor people from their lands.

La Castelaña, a notorious woman, mistress of the lawyer Bismarck Ruiz.

The Novel

In *Broad and Alien Is the World*, Rosendo Maquis is the mayor of Rumi, a small Indian town in the Peruvian uplands. The village is a communal organization, as it has been for centuries. Its life is peaceful. Rosendo's only troubles are personal. Because his wife is dying, he has been sent into the mountains to find herbs to be used in making medicine. On his way back to the village, he sees an evil omen in the passage of a snake across his path.

That same night, Rosendo's wife dies. Her death marks the beginning of many misfortunes for the mayor and his people. A few days later, it

becomes known that Don Amenabar, whose ranch borders the Indian village, is filing suit to take away the best of the land belonging to Rumi. Rosendo and his selectmen saddle their horses and ride to the nearby town to get a lawyer to defend them. They hire Bismarck Ruiz, a man who has a poor reputation in the town because of his love affair with La Castelaña, a notorious woman of very expensive tastes. In return for a large fee, Bismarck Ruiz promises to win the suit for the Indians.

Life goes on as usual in the village during the days before the trial. There is a cattle roundup, to which Don Amenabar sends men to collect cattle belonging to him. Although he has not paid the grazing fee, and the Indians know it would be futile to ask it of him, he charges them a high fee to redeem any cattle that accidentally wander onto his lands. The Indians are also busy building a school, for the commissioner of education of the province has promised them a schoolmaster as soon as they have a hygienic place for the school to convene.

In an effort to learn what Don Amenabar is plotting against them, the Indians send one of their number to the ranch to sell baskets and woven mats. When Don Amenabar sees the Indian on his ranch, he orders his overseers to give the unlucky fellow a hundred lashes, a punishment that would have killed many men.

Finally the case comes to court. The Indians believe at first that they will win. Don Amenabar's men had removed the stones marking the community boundaries, but the Indians had returned them. The return, they thought, was indicative of their success. The case ends quickly, thanks to a large number of perjuring witnesses who testify against the Indians, claiming that the people of Rumi had encroached on Don Amenabar's land.

The Indians' lawyer immediately makes up a brief for an appeal to a higher court, but Don Amenabar's men, disguised as the followers of Fiero Vásquez, an outlaw, steal the mailbag containing the documents. Don Amenabar does not want the authorities in Lima to hear of the affair because he wants to send his son to the legislature and eventually to become a senator himself.

Correa Zavala, a young lawyer fired with zeal for the cause of the Peruvian Indians, takes up the villagers' case. It had become clear to the Indians that Bismarck Ruiz was not helping them, and they had evidence that he was in the pay of Don Amenabar. Zavala drafts a long brief including many documents from the history of the village. This is sent to the capital with a guard of troops and Indians, for its loss would have made it difficult to prove the village's legal existence as a community.

These efforts fail, and a court order, enforced by troops, is delivered to the Indians. They are to leave the most fertile of their lands and move to what is left to them in the higher areas. After one of the village women goes to her lover, Fiero Vásquez, the notorious highwayman and bandit, he arrives with his band of cutthroats to help the Indians drive off the people who are forcing them to leave. Rosendo refuses aid from the outlaws because he knows that resistance is useless. His point is made when a villager is machine-gunned to death for daring to kill one of Don Amenabar's men with a rock.

Even in the highlands, the Indians are not safe from Don Amenabar, who wants to make them slaves to work a mine that he owns on another piece of property. His men raid the Indians' cattle herds, even creeping up to the corrals in the village at night. The prize bull of the village disappears, and the Indians find the animal on Don Amenabar's ranch. In spite of branding on the animal, Don Amenabar refuses to return the bull and orders Rosendo off the ranch. That same night, the mayor returns, determined to regain the animal for his people. He finds the bull, but as he leads the animal away, he is captured. Taken into town, Rosendo is jailed on a charge of thievery. At his trial, he is found guilty and sentenced to a long term in prison.

While Rosendo is in jail, Fiero Vásquez is captured and placed in the cell with Rosendo. Having plenty of resources to make bribes, the highwayman makes arrangements to break out of prison. When he escapes, Rosendo is blamed. The prison guards beat the old man so severely that he dies within a few hours.

Not long after the death of Rosendo, a young Indian he had reared comes back to the village after an absence of many years. Benito Castro, a soldier and a gaucho, is quickly accepted as a leader by the Indians, who need the wisdom and aid of someone who has been outside the mountain village. Under Castro's leadership, the people drain swampy meadows and rebuild their village in a better location in the highlands. Their relative prosperity is short-lived, for Don Amenabar still plans to enslave them or drive them into hiding. A large detachment of troops, augmented by men convinced that the Indians were mutinous against the government, attacks the village. In a long battle with the forces sent against them, the Indians are utterly defeated, their leaders are killed, and the village is destroyed. The few survivors, told by the dying Benito Castro to save themselves, have no idea where they can go to seek a refuge in the harsh, lawless land.

Analysis

Ciro Alegría's panoramic novel mirrors life in the Peruvian Andes early in the twentieth century. Its many themes include defense of the downtrodden, justice against injustice, the tragedy of human life, dishonest lawyers and courts, litigation over land boundaries, suffering, villainy and heroism, and racism.

The novel's power lies in its defense of the abused Indian populace of Rumi. The reader lives with Rumi's people throughout the story and identifies with them. Unforgettable is the noble old leader of Rumi, Rosendo Maquis. Grave and good like the community of Rumi itself, Rosendo incarnates his people, who are idealized by Alegría. In addition to its many regionalist qualities, *Broad and Alien Is the World* has a well-developed plot and generally convincing characterization that make it one of the better contributions to the literature of *Indianismo*, which defends the Indian peoples of Latin America. The plot reaches a final crescendo with the destruction of Rumi and all that the recently murdered Rosendo stood for, but the noble Rosendo, his pathetic wife Pascuala, black-clad Fiero Vásquez, and Benito Castro still live and stand out in the reader's memory.

Alegría's style has its virtues. His language is poetic, lively, and colorful. He uses standard Spanish laced with occasional regionalisms, including Quechua words, to good effect. Dialogue is authentic. The reader's interest is captured from the opening sentence, which is "Danger!" The novel is nevertheless unwieldy and structurally chaotic. It betrays a lack of careful planning resulting from its hasty composition, which took only months.

Geography is always a silent presence in the novel. At times it is almost a dominant character, reflecting the importance of geography in Peru's culture. One thus sees the lofty Andean sierra with its crisp, thin air, gaunt landscapes, sparse vegetation, and rocky soil. One also sees Rumi, with its cobbled, windswept streets and huddled houses. Rumi's people grow potatoes and tend their llamas, but they chew coca to cope with hunger and the cold, and their chests are like those of pouter pigeons since the air has so little oxygen.

Alegría was born and reared in the same region in which he set this novel. Although his parents were his first teachers, he later credited the whole Peruvian people with having molded him and causing him to understand their grief. In *Broad and Alien Is the World*, Alegría penetrates the Indian mind, revealing the native's feeling for the soil, poverty, stoicism, dignity, superstition, and occasional lapses into alcoholism or sexual license. Unfortunately, Alegría ladles out some crude propaganda by lambasting safely unpopular types such as white men, priests, and landowners. These stock, one-dimensional figures are reminiscent of Diego Rivera's murals with their pasty-faced, evil whites, bloated priests, cruel-faced landowners, and clean-cut Indians. Alegría reveals unconscious prejudice in this respect, even though his own family owned land and was Nordic-Caucasian in appearance. Thus, as is so often the case in Spanish-American literature, a talented writer has produced an inspired and sincerely motivated work but simultaneously betrays the fact that he himself belongs to a privileged social class.

One of Alegría's great contributions is his depiction of rural Peruvian society. One sees many social types and their folkways, traditions, mentality, society, and sorrows. In Rumi, readers see the kaleidoscopic results of four centuries of blending between Inca and Spaniard. One of the finest examples is the colorful sketch of Rumi's village meeting, with its touches of imagery wherein bronzed Indian faces mingle with those of mestizos and an occasional white, against a background of Inca and Spanish dress, manners, postures, and gestures. The novel is thus a storehouse of all that has happened to Peru from the days of the mysterious Inca Empire, through the dramatic conquest by the Renaissance men of Spain and the four ensuing centuries of racial and cultural blending. It is said that all of Alegría's works demonstrate a determination to create an original literature that not only interprets the Peruvian reality but also expresses contemporary Peru's peculiarities. A mestizo is the central personality in all of Alegría's novels, with the possible exception of *Broad and Alien Is the World*. Even in this work, the mestizo Benito Castro inherits Rosendo Maquis' role and develops into the most significant personality late in the novel.

Broad and Alien Is the World is essentially a novel of the high sierra. It nevertheless broadens the social and human conflict beyond the bounda-ries of the community of Rumi to Peru's coast and jungle—nowhere under the Peruvian flag is there a place that is not hostile to the Indian. Benito Castro is regarded as an extremist agitator in Lima; one of Rosendo's sons is blinded by the explosion of a rubber ball in the eastern jungles; Calixto Páucar dies in a mine shaft; and other emigrants from Rumi meet misfortune in many parts of the Peruvian Republic, for "broad and alien is the world." Alegría's great achievement is that his masterpiece has undoubtedly helped to implement reform in favor of the mountain-dwelling Indians and mestizos of Central Peru. Their lot has slowly but surely improved since the day when, while writing a scene for another novel concerning the expulsion of some Indians from their community, Alegría was struck with such force "by an intense gust of ideas and memories" that the inspiration for his masterpiece was born.

Critical Context

This novel won for its author a $2,000 award offered in 1941 by the Division of Intellectual Co-operation of the Pan-American Union. Although the book and author are Peruvian, the novel was submitted by the Chilean committee. Stephen Vincent Bénet later dramatized part of the novel. Underlying the story is Alegría's plea for justice for the Peruvian Indians, a group exploited and injured by racial, social, and political self-seekers.

When the novel appeared, it was frequently referred to as a South American version of John Steinbeck's *The Grapes of Wrath* (1939). In addition to the sociological elements, the novel is a veritable storehouse of Peruvian lore, giving a detailed picture of the social structure of the Indian community, its innate dignity, its traditions, and its overwhelming tragedy. Alegría was exiled from Peru in 1934 because of his political views.

BUFFALO NICKEL: A Memoir

Author: Floyd Salas (1931-   )
Type of work: Memoir
Time of work: 1933 to the early 1980's
First published: 1992

Principal Personages

Floyd Salas, the author and protagonist, a novelist, poet, essayist, and creative writing professor. He teaches in various colleges in the San Francisco Bay Area. In this memoir, he recounts his life from the age of two through the early 1980's. The memoir focuses on his relationships with members of his family, especially with his two brothers, Albert in particular. Another theme of the memoir is a chronicle of his development as his own person with an identity separate from those of his brothers.

Floyd was born in 1931, during the Depression. When he was eight years old, his family moved from Colorado to California, finally settling in Oakland. The first part of the book tells of his turbulent early life. His mother dies when he is eleven years old. The death devastates the family. His father's remarriage changes Floyd's relationship with him because the new wife does not allow the closeness they once had to continue. Floyd is the youngest of the boys, and he loves his brothers.

Floyd finally takes Eddy's early advice and attends college, but not before becoming an accomplished boxer. Floyd is awarded two boxing scholarships. His boxing skills prove to be an asset later, when he becomes a boxing coach for the University of California. He becomes a writer and writing instructor.

Eddy, Floyd's brother, older than Floyd by eleven years. Floyd fondly and proudly calls Eddy a prodigy. Eddy becomes a naval officer, puts himself through Harvard, and is a successful pharmacist with his own pharmacy. The prodigy who accomplished so much in the troubled family commits suicide, tormented by his homosexuality that is not tolerated by American society.

Albert, Floyd's brother, older than Floyd by nine years. Al is a boxer, con man, and heroin addict who fathers nine children and all but abandons them. Four of his children commit suicide. Floyd calls Al a social psychopath for his failure to take responsibility for his actions. Nevertheless, it is Al whom Floyd idolizes. Floyd spends much of his time helping Al out of predicaments and trying to get him to change his life for the better.

Form and Content

Floyd Salas was born in 1931 in Walsenburg, Colorado, where he spent his early childhood. When he was eight years old, the family moved to California. Although Floyd Salas is the main person in this memoir, his interactions with members of his family are of prime importance, particularly those with his two brothers, Eddy and Albert. The book is dedicated to his two brothers and to his father.

Salas calls *Buffalo Nickel* an autobiographical memoir. The work has eight "Parts" (the author does not call them chapters), with several sections in each part. Parts 1 through 4 chronicle Salas' developing relationship with his brothers. Parts 5 through 8 relate primarily Salas' story of coming of age.

In the first section of the book, Salas relates the incident from which the book takes its title. The incident took place when Floyd was six years old, and it foreshadows the relationship between Floyd and his brother Albert, who is a boxer. Floyd goes with Al to the gym and has to wait for him for two hours. When Al finally emerges from the gym, he is heard to say, "My brother can whip yours!" Floyd is talked into fighting a bigger boy and is immediately smashed on the nose. As blood spurts from his nose, he is knocked down. Al stops the fight. As he quiets Floyd down, he gives him a buffalo head nickel to compensate him. On the way home, Al asks for the nickel back. As Floyd says, "He'd do that a lot to me, also, before it was over."

In the memoir, Salas addresses the importance of family. Even when a family is dysfunctional, the relationships among family members are important. Family members react to each other. Floyd has two sisters. Annabelle is younger than Floyd, and Dorothy is seven years older. Curiously, the influence of his sisters is not evident in this memoir. The sisters and other women are not as well developed as are the male characters; they are merely stick figures.

Floyd makes role models of his brothers. Eddy, eleven years older than Floyd, is an intellectual prodigy. He was a naval officer, has a degree from Harvard, and now runs his own successful pharmacy. Al, nine years older than Floyd, does not set the same example as Eddy. Al was in the Army, but he faked insanity and was discharged. Al is a promising boxer, a Golden Gloves champion, but his boxing career is interrupted by his drug selling and drug addiction. He ends up in prison. As a result, he does not make the "big time" in boxing. In fact, Floyd is constantly rescuing him from predicaments, or Al is getting Floyd into trouble. Clearly he is not one to emulate. Floyd is caught between the "good" brother whom he loves and his "bad" brother whom he also loves, and it is Al to whom he becomes attached. It is Al who teaches Floyd how to exist in the world, a world in which survival comes through fighting, hustling, and running confidence games. Floyd sees that it is not a good world and that he and Eddy should not be part

of it. Nevertheless, Floyd is drawn to Al.

The second section of the book chronicles Floyd's struggle to keep Al out of trouble and to get him to take care of his wife and nine children. Much of the time, Floyd struggles to steer Al in the right direction, away from crime and drugs. Salas' working title for the book, in fact, was "Brothers' Keepers." With Floyd's urging, Al almost makes a successful comeback in his boxing career.

Although he loves Al, Floyd must develop his own identity and must make some decisions. Is he to follow his brother Al and become a boxer, or should he follow the earlier advice of his college-educated brother Eddy and go to college? The book ends very hurriedly. It relates the suicide of four of Al's children and the deaths of five other family members and friends, including Eddy. Floyd becomes closer to Al after Eddy commits suicide, unable to deal with his homosexuality in a society that did not tolerate his way of life. Floyd finally takes Eddy's advice and goes to college, earning two boxing scholarships and eventually attending the University of California. He becomes a successful novelist, a boxing coach for the University of California, and a creative writing professor teaching for various colleges in the San Francisco Bay Area. Floyd still, however, must come to terms with Al.

The final scenes in the book show Floyd's raw feelings toward Al. In a moving narrative, Floyd and Al are in a boxing ring. With each punch, Floyd reminds Al of what he has done to him. As Floyd punches Al, he says, "That's for getting my nose broken for me at six!," and "That's for punching on me at Aunt Dolly's house!" Floyd thus reconciles his feeling toward his brother: After their fight, Floyd grabs Al and hugs him. He tells his brother, "You don't shoot dope anymore! And you don't steal! And you don't go to jail! That's a lot! That's really a lot!"

Analysis

Buffalo Nickel is an important work for Salas. It covers his personal life from the age of two until the early 1980's as well as his writing life. He

published his first book, *Tattoo the Wicked Cross*, in 1967. That book is partly autobiographical and discusses a boy's life in prison. Twenty-five years later, he published *Buffalo Nickel*. The quarter-century mark is an important literary point in Salas' life, one at which he has come to terms with himself. Salas believes that he is finally recognized as a writer. He begins the next quarter century with another autobiographical novel scheduled to be published in 1994, again by Arte Público.

As one reads *Buffalo Nickel*, it becomes apparent that some of the descriptions of characters and names of places are similar to those in *Tattoo the Wicked Cross*. Aaron, the protagonist of *Tattoo the Wicked Cross*, and Floyd have some of the same characteristics: Both are fighters and both are short for their age. Aaron was sent to "Golden Gate Institute of Industry and Reform" for his crimes, and Al escapes from "Golden Reform School," a prison farm.

The anguish that is depicted in the 347 pages of the memoir is alluded to in the following lines from the poem found on the page before the dedication, talking about his tears on the page.

> But I'll spread them for you
> Give the why
> Why?
> Because I ache in my guts

The autobiographical memoir is primarily a *Bildungsroman* literary piece. It details how Floyd Salas grew up, how he had to choose between Al, representing chaos, destruction, drugs, and the fist, and Eddy, symbolic of intelligence and fulfillment, tenderness and sensitivity. Al lives, and Eddy commits suicide. While they are both alive, he must choose one brother over another. Even after Eddy's death, he must struggle with the choice of a life path. The story is the pathos of a lost brotherly love, Al's love. Can a lost love ever be regained? Can it ever be reconciled? Can it be forgotten? Floyd says later in the poem at the beginning of the book, "And that memory is greased with brain and blood. . . ."

Salas' memoir shows the many facets of Latino literature. He has selected the parts of his life that he wishes to emphasize, but not without some glaring omissions. There are some issues that need elaboration. He says little of the importance of his sisters, the women in his life, his brother Eddy, and his literary career. Salas may have omitted discussion of these topics with an eye toward elaborating on them in later memoirs. A memoir records one's life and experiences and does not limit the writer to follow a strict, all-inclusive chronological format, as does the autobiography. The literary format of the memoir that Salas uses is common among Latino writers, many of whom have used memoir to tell selected portions of their stories.

Critical Context

Latino writers have had a difficult time gaining recognition for their writing. One area in which they have been recognized is autobiography. Some excellent examples of Latino writing with autobiographical overtones are Richard Rodriguez's *Hunger of Memory* (1981) and *Days of Obligation: An Argument with My Mexican Father* (1992), Victor Villaseñor's *Rain of Gold* (1991), and Piri Thomas' *Down These Mean Streets* (1967). These writers all wanted to tell their stories and to control their futures. Salas has done exactly that.

Latino writers enjoyed a literary renaissance beginning in the late 1970's. The Latino renaissance includes the fiction writers Sandra Cisneros, Ana Castillo, Luis Rodriguez, Oscar Hijuelos, and Alejandro Morales, to name only a few. In 1992, Salas' *Buffalo Nickel* became part of this Latino literary movement. Its importance is paramount. Even though *Buffalo Nickel* is not fiction, the memoir reads like a well-crafted novel.

Latino writers need to express themselves in as broad a context as possible. Salas has done this in his memoir. Fiction can also be a means of self-expression, but personal true accounts have more of an impact on the reader. Honest, personal, and sensitive writing, such as Salas', is important in Latino literature, as it is in all literature.

CHRONICLE OF A DEATH FORETOLD

Author: Gabriel García Márquez (1928-　　)
Type of work: Novel
Type of plot: Mystery
Time of plot: The early twentieth century
Locale: An unnamed Colombian village on the coast of the Caribbean
First published: *Crónica de una muerte anunciada*, 1981 (English translation, 1982)

Principal Characters

The narrator, a friend of Santiago. Returning to his hometown, he investigates Santiago's murder twenty-seven years after its occurrence. The narrative summarizes the results of his efforts.

Santiago Nasar, a member of the Arab community, slim and pale, with dark curly hair. He is killed in front of his own house at the age of twenty-one. Although he is killed as the deflowerer of Angela Vicario, his innocent behavior up to the moment of his death suggests that he was wrongly accused of the act.

Angela Vicario, the youngest and prettiest daughter of a poor family. She resists the prospect of marriage to Bayardo San Román and unsuccessfully attempts to pass as a virgin on their wedding night. After Bayardo brings her back home, she is beaten by her mother, Purísima (Pura) del Carmen Vicario. Questioned by her brothers, she names Santiago as the man responsible for deflowering her. In the aftermath of the murder, she grows from a hapless spirit to a mature and witty woman. Previously disinterested in Bayardo, she becomes obsessed with him and remains unmarried, writing hundreds of letters to him in the years after their separation.

Bayardo San Román, Angela's husband. About thirty years old, he has a slim waist, golden eyes, and tanned skin. A drinker, he seems to lack a steady occupation but exhibits familiarity with railway engineering, telegraphy, frontier illnesses, card games, and swimming. Soon after seeing Angela, he courts her and proposes to her. When he discovers on their wedding night that she is not a virgin, he carries her to her mother. Although he never opens any of Angela's letters, he saves them and eventually returns to her.

Pedro Vicario and **Pablo Vicario,** brothers of Angela, identical twins who support their family by slaughtering pigs. Told that Santiago has dishonored their sister, the brothers undertake to stab him to death. Although they are unrepentant after the deed is done, the narrator notes that they seemed reluctant to carry it off: By informing more than a dozen villagers of their intent, they seem to have been hoping to be stopped. In jail, they are haunted by an odor of Santiago that lingers after his death.

Clotilde Armenta, a milk vendor who appeals to the Vicario twins to refrain from killing Santiago. In an effort to prevent the crime from taking place, she asks all the people she sees to warn Santiago of the danger he is in, attempts to intoxicate the brothers, unsuccessfully tries to restrain Pedro, and shouts a warning to Santiago.

Don Rogelio de la Flor, Clotilde Armenta's husband. He disappoints Clotilde because he does not take strong measures to prevent the murder from occurring. He dies from shock after seeing Santiago's bloody corpse.

Purísima (Pura) del Carmen Vicario, Angela's mother, who beats her daughter harshly after Bayardo returns her.

Luisa Santiaga, the narrator's mother, Santiago's godmother and a blood relative of Pura. She is initially impressed with Bayardo, but her regard for him gradually ebbs. On the day of the murder, she tries to warn Santiago of the threat to his life but is told that she is too late.

The Novel

The "chronicle" of the title is the attempt by the narrator to piece together events leading up to the murder of Santiago Nasar by Pedro and Pablo Vicario. He does so by drawing on his own memories as well as on the accounts of those who witnessed the murder and whom he sought out twenty-seven years after the event. Thus, the novel bears many of the trappings of a murder mystery, but it is hardly a conventional representative of that genre: The murderers had announced their intentions to everyone they met hours before the event. What the narrator needs to learn is how a murder so publicly announced could have occurred, with so many well-meaning people doing nothing to stop the Vicario brothers, who had little heart for carrying out the deed and who, by their open announcements, were in effect asking to be stopped.

As the novel begins, the narrator recounts Nasar's waking about an hour before his death and telling his mother his dream of walking in a drizzle through a timber forest. Although she is a renowned interpreter of dreams, she fails to recognize the ominous foreboding of death. Her failure is the first of many to come, culminating in her barring the door through which Nasar is about to escape from his attackers. She thinks her son is already safe inside the house when she hears the crowd approaching at the end of the novel.

The narrator's reconstruction of the events of that morning is complicated by the varying accounts of people's whereabouts, their awareness of the brothers' intentions, and their feelings toward Nasar. They cannot even agree on the weather that morning, whether it was radiantly pleasant or oppressively funereal. The narrator objectively records all details, scarcely weighing them for consistency or import, possibly because he is attempting a purely journalistic account and possibly because he resembles his mother in the way, as he notes, "she is accustomed to noting . . . superfluous detail when she wants to get to the heart of the matter."

Nasar is murdered by the Vicario brothers to avenge their sister Angela's dishonor. She had married Bayardo San Román the previous day, but after a day and a night of extravagant feasting by the village, the groom discovers that his bride is not a virgin and returns her to her home. Her mother beats her, and upon questioning by her brothers, Angela Vicario identifies Santiago Nasar as her "perpetrator." Their duty is clear. They take two of the knives they use in their trade of slaughtering pigs, sharpen them at another butcher's shop, then wait in Clothilda Armenta's milk shop, from which they can watch Nasar's bedroom window. When Nasar goes out to see the bishop who has come to bless the village, they carry out their simple plan, butchering Nasar at his front door and profoundly changing the lives of everyone who has gathered to watch.

Analysis

Where García Márquez's highly regarded novel *Cien años de soledad* (1967; *One Hundred Years of Solitude,* 1970) has the large, episodic scope of a Greek epic, *Chronicle of a Death Foretold* has the concise brevity of a Greek tragedy. It shares with tragedy the theme of guilt and its purging through recognition of the truth. At the political level, the book is an allegory for tyranny made possible through uncritical obedience to established codes: No one is able to step out of the accustomed modes of behavior to stop the murderers.

Most of the characters reason that affairs of honor exclude all but those involved, a circular logic that admits no intervention. The fictional narrative, however, points to a very active involvement by supposed bystanders. For example, Nasar's maid, Victoria Guzmán, wakens him as ordered at 5:30 in the morning but fails to warn him because she pays no heed to what she considers drunken boasts. In fact, Nasar had asked her to send her daughter Divina Flor, a nubile girl whom Nasar has repeatedly manhandled, to wake him, but Guzmán herself had suffered the advances of Nasar's father, and so goes in her daughter's place. While Nasar eats breakfast, she disembowels rabbits before him and throws the entrails to the dogs; at the end of the novel, Nasar's mother orders the dogs to be killed as they howl for his intestines. Although the narrator does not draw a conclusion, evidence is strewn through the book that Guzmán would sooner see Nasar dead than have him repeat his father's conquest and that she maliciously withholds the warning that would easily save his life. Her righteous disregard of drunken boasts plays into her maternal instinct and her secret loathing of her helplessness. Although she cannot act on feelings she scarcely acknowledges, her inaction in not warning Nasar is fatally effective.

García Márquez challenges the reader to look more deeply than does the narrator at the pattern of chance that produces fate. The reader is prompted to reconsider the excuses, denials, and self-justifications that blind the narrator, who seeks through his chronicle of superfluous information to understand how a death so foretold could be allowed to take place.

Critical Context

Because many characters reappear in his works, because many of the works are set in Macondo (unnamed here, but recognizable as the fictional counterpart of his birthplace, Aracataca), and because of the persistently fabulous nature of his Magical Realism, García Márquez's novels and short stories can be said to constitute one grand fiction, of which *Chronicle of a Death Foretold* is a significant part. García Márquez's treatment of isolation and solitude in previous work extends to this novel. Macondo's search for a way inland to other villages in *One Hundred Years of Solitude* is ended here with the coming of the railroad, on which many of the characters will leave following the murder. The novel also is linked by contrast with the short story "El ahogado más hermoso del mundo" (1972; "The Handsomest Drowned Man in the World," 1972), in which a drowned man is taken in by the inhabitants of a stagnant town after he washes up on shore, becoming a source of community pride. Care for the drowned man removes the villagers from their individual and collective solitude, as contrarily the community's witnessing the death of Nasar jolts its members out of their "linear habits" and into an obsession with their guilt. Where in *El otoño del patriarca* (1975; *The Autumn of the Patriarch*, 1975) the aging dictator is isolated by his tyrannical power, here the villagers are cut off from one another by their failure to use their power to prevent Nasar's death.

In interviews, García Márquez has often equated his fiction with journalism (he began his career as a journalist in 1948) and has said that the fantastic elements in his work are merely the reality of Latin America, faithfully transcribed. In *Chronicle of a Death Foretold*, he has written an investigative report of the circumstances of a murder. He turns the genre of the mystery novel inside out in order to create his own convoluted, cyclical form of storytelling. It begins when the victim rises and ends one hour later with his death, but in between the narrator retraces the impossible labyrinth of circumstances and chance and the unwinding of its terrible consequences.

CITY OF NIGHT

Author: John Rechy (1934-   )
Type of work: Novel
Type of plot: *Bildungsroman*
Time of plot: The 1950's
Locale: El Paso, New York, Los Angeles, San Francisco, and New Orleans
First published: 1963

Principal Characters

The narrator, the nameless protagonist, of Mexican American background. His ethnicity does not play a significant role during his years as a male prostitute, but subconsciously it manifests itself in a sense of guilt, fostered by his mother's fervent Catholicism and by his father's death. Much of the narrator's career is a rebellion against his family background and religious promises of eternal life and redemption. The death of his dog and his mother's claim that dogs do not go to heaven push the narrator into a crisis of faith that he acts out through open rebellion—and emotional withdrawal. This pattern repeats itself throughout the narrator's wanderings through the homosexual underground. On one hand, the narrator thrives on the life of the streets and the desire that other men express for his body; on the other hand, he rents rooms away from this environment so that he can always have an emotional refuge. The need to have his body adored by as many people as possible stems from his loss of religious faith. If there is no afterlife, no possibility of redemption and resurrection, as he often tells himself, then his youthful body is his only weapon against the forces of time; thus, as long as he is young and desirable, he engages in an orgy of desirability. Despite his intent to kill compassion in himself and wear a mask of insensitivity, the narrator cannot do so. He thus becomes a confessor figure to his clients, because there is an aura about him that other male prostitutes do not possess.

Pete, a typical young male prostitute who initiates the narrator into the life of the streets. Despite his tough exterior, he is vulnerable and lost. His one display of affection toward the narrator serves to separate the two, because they feel that they have violated the code of toughness their trade demands.

The Professor, a client. Despite his ability to deceive himself through a torrent of words, he is as lonely and craves love as much as all the narrator's customers.

Jeremy Adams, a man who empathizes with the narrator's psychological dilemma. He makes the narrator realize that there is no real difference between prostitute and client; both are symbiotically linked through shared loneliness.

The Novel

Based in part on John Rechy's own experiences as an itinerant male prostitute in the late 1950's, *City of Night* is a powerful evocation of a nameless narrator's journey through the underside of America's urban wastelands and a haunting description of the different people he encounters there.

City of Night is divided into four parts, roughly equivalent to the narrator's stays in New York, Los Angeles, Hollywood, and New Orleans. It is further divided into short character sketches—named after the individuals who are described—that alternate with sections entitled "City of Night," which propel the action forward. The entire novel is a first-person narrative told by the nameless narrator-protagonist, and all actions are filtered through his consciousness.

The novel begins in El Paso, Texas, the narrator's hometown, with the death of his dog, an event that shapes his consciousness and to which he returns repeatedly throughout the novel. When the child is told that dogs cannot go to heaven, he experiences a loss of faith that is exacerbated by the fact that the dog's decaying carcass has to be reburied because of its smell.

Both parents are impoverished Mexican immigrants, and the home offers the child no escape from the mother's suffocating Catholicism and fierce, protective love and the father's increasingly erratic and threatening behavior, which often manifests itself in terrifying rituals of affection. The narrator's hatred of his father leads to both acts of rebellion and withdrawal from life. This emotional withdrawal increases his isolation so that his mirror becomes the most important object in his life; for him, it narcissistically confirms the reality of his undecayed, youthful body.

Restless after a tour of duty in the Army, the narrator hurls himself into the large cities of America, where he quickly learns to earn his livelihood as a male hustler. It is in New York that the characteristic pattern of the adult narrator's life begins. He is obsessed by a need to be with and wanted by as many people as possible. Hustling seems to be the easiest way to fulfill these desires; as a hustler, the narrator maintains a heterosexual front, although in moments of intense introspection he sees through his own self-deception. His customers, called "scores," neither expect reciprocal sexual acts nor wish him to appear gay. Doing so would destroy their own sexual fantasies.

Most of the narrative provides a guided tour through different sections of the 1950's gay subculture. In the hundreds of people the narrator encounters, he detects an overpowering loneliness camouflaged by various poses of defiance. Mr. King, one of the narrator's first clients, pretends not to care about any human interaction; at the same time, though, he desperately tries to impress the narrator by dressing up for him, and during their second meeting even asks the narrator to move in with him. The Professor both disguises and articulates his feelings of hurt; he talks of love and keeps a scrapbook with pictures of his "angels," but considers himself ugly and thus forced to buy sex. Even a fellow hustler, Pete, who has spent most of his life on the streets and is supposed to be tough and uncaring, drops his mask of heterosexual masculinity with the narrator; as a result, they never speak to each other again, because they both feel that they have violated the code of their trade.

Relentlessly, the narrative continues to explore the narrator's hustling in Los Angeles, San Francisco, Chicago, and New Orleans. In between, he returns to El Paso. This city becomes a refuge for him, a retreat offering sanctuary from the life of the streets and a place to contemplate life behind the protective security of his window.

From Los Angeles to New Orleans, the narrator observes some of the more bizarre aspects of gay life, from the world of transvestites (Miss Destiny) to the sadomasochistic underground (Neil). The men who offer more than money for sex, that is, the possibility of bonding and affection, are immediately rejected. It is in New Orleans, during Mardi Gras, that the narrator encounters Jeremy Adams, a man who finally—although only briefly—breaks through most of the emotional barriers the narrator has erected. Yet even Jeremy does not succeed. Nevertheless, Mardi Gras brings about an emotional crisis of such proportions that the narrator calls a number of Catholic churches, only to be rejected by all but one, in a desperate attempt to find spiritual solace. At the end of the novel, he returns to El Paso and his window to give meaning to his life and experiences, aware that his quest is not yet over.

Analysis

At the most basic level, the novel is a psychological study of the narrator and his quest for meaning in life. The makeup of his family—the mother's fierce love and the father's inexplicable hatred—seem designed to push the narrator into homosexuality, thus giving expression to a view commonly held at the time of the writing of the novel. Seen in its entirety, the novel is an elaborate investigation of the narrator's fragmented identity. Since he refuses to reveal his name throughout the narrative, he deliberately frustrates a reader's normal expectations to get to know him fully. In fact, all the more elaborately described characters the narrator encounters during his wanderings are carefully chosen to create a contrast to his murky identity. At the same time, this narrative technique allows the reader to imagine the life of a hustler. Like the narrator, the reader meets a character, is drawn into his life for a short period of time, and then as abruptly withdraws. This is underscored by the fact that the narrator attempts to create complicity between the reader and himself by addressing the reader several times directly as "you"; he seems to crave the reader's approval (or, perhaps, absolution). In the same way that the narrator assumes the role of confessor for his clients, the reader becomes the narrator's confessor (or psychologist). Thus the novel can be read as a sustained cry for help, and the comfort that is wished for comes through the telling of the tale; that is, the narrative itself can be read as part of the therapy to heal the narrator's wounded self.

The novel explores the narrator's refusal to accept death and decay. His inability to face this most basic of human conditions leads him, by his own explanation, into hustling; he has lost faith in religion, so other people's desire for his youthful body becomes a substitute for salvation. This crisis of faith is not brought to a complete and satisfying resolution, but the loneliness that the novel so eloquently investigates provides a thematic and structural unity.

Apart from toying with questions of identity, the novel critiques a social system that by law discriminates against those with a different sexual orientation. Although the novel tends to fixate on the pathological nature of the people the narrator encounters, the cry against social injustice, not yet fully articulated in political and social terms, cannot be ignored.

All these ideas are tightly interwoven in a circular structure. The novel begins and ends with the narrator's memory of his dog's death and the unresolved crisis of faith that this event precipitated. After all, the anarchy the narrator senses in himself throughout the novel is nothing but the fear of sharing the dog's fate: to grow old and to die. His inability to form meaningful relationships with other people must be seen in light of this. Relationships seem futile to him, because they offer what he considers false hope: the idea of permanence. Yet since the novel ends where it began, it also offers an element of hope. The narrator has come back to where his psychological crisis started, and the reader is left with the impression that when the narrator ventures forth again from his window, he will do so with a fuller understanding of himself and even greater compassion for the people he will encounter.

Critical Context

City of Night was John Rechy's first novel, and it almost overnight became a best-seller and an underground classic. Its description of parts of the gay subculture was more honest and detailed than had been attempted by writers before. In addition, the novel's narrative framework and technical experimentation show Rechy's indebtedness to other twentieth century writers such as James Joyce and John Dos Passos.

The novel demonstrates the growth of a gay

awareness, although this awareness is not yet fully evolved in the book. Through the form of the *Bildungsroman,* the novel of the development of a protagonist's character, Rechy captures the tortured life of his narrator and imbues it with dignity and meaning. The novel's protagonist and structure are also indebted to the picaresque novel. Like the picaro, a hustler lives on the fringes of the law and survives by his wit and resourcefulness.

In several subsequent works, including *Numbers* (1967), *This Day's Death* (1969), and *Rushes* (1979), Rechy continued his attempt to define gay male sexuality and identity. In all these works, questions of Latino identity were almost completely pushed aside. Although Rechy has claimed that all of his main characters are Latino, the emphasis on their ethnic, rather than sexual, identities came much later. There are few indications in *City of Night,* for example, apart from the narrator's lapsed Catholicism and his recurrent feelings of guilt, that ethnic identification is central to his self-understanding. More recently, though, Rechy has investigated questions of Latino identity in his novels *Bodies and Souls* (1983) and *The Miraculous Day of Amalia Gómez* (1991). He has also written a best-selling nonfiction work, *The Sexual Outlaw* (1977), and several plays.

CONVERSATION IN THE CATHEDRAL

Author: Mario Vargas Llosa (1936-   )
Type of work: Novel
Type of plot: Social criticism
Time of plot: The late 1940's and early 1950's
Locale: Peru
First published: *Conversación en la catedral*, 1969 (English translation, 1975)

Principal Characters

Santiago Zavala, also known as **"Skinny"** and **"Superbrain,"** the protagonist. Much of the narrative is rendered in his voice and from his perspective. He is a disillusioned intellectual and self-disinherited son of the bourgeoisie, determined to forge an authentic existence. When he is unable to break with his past, however, he slowly sinks into despair and cynicism. His preoccupation throughout the novel is with how both the nation and the individual have been betrayed by the same degrading and corrupt political forces.

Ambrosio Pardo, a *zambo* (part black and part Indian), first a chauffeur for Santiago's father, then a worker at a dog pound. He is both a victim of Peru's social order and a victimizer who adapts to a corrupt system in order to survive. Ambrosio's inability to break the social, political, and economic bonds that shackle him illustrates one of the novel's major themes: how a politically corrupt society can succeed in shaping and determining its members in perverse and inhuman ways.

Trinidad Lopez, a textile worker and political fanatic. He appears to be aware of the political reality of his time, but the narrative raises serious doubts concerning the validity of his assertions. Never really understanding the deeper implications of the *aprista* movement for which he fights, he is nevertheless beaten, tortured, and finally killed for his revolutionary activities. His death, therefore, is completely meaningless.

Amalia Cerda, a servant, later the wife of Trinidad Lopez, then of Ambrosia. Neither she nor Trinidad understands the functions of the institutions that determine their lives.

Don Fermín Zavala, Santiago's father, a rich Peruvian industrialist. He is deeply involved in deals with the government strongman, Cayo Bermúdez. His are the middle-class values against which his son revolts. He is involved in a homosexual relationship with Ambrosio.

Don Cayo Bermúdez, the minister of security and right-hand man of Peru's dictator, General Manuel Odría. He represents evil in its most sordid aspects, since he takes charge of the regime's dirty work. His character is without guilt or conscience. He functions both as the chief instrument of corruption and as one of its victims.

Hortensia, a wealthy prostitute and the mistress of Cayo Bermúdez. She and Queta, another prostitute, engage in homosexual relations for the voyeuristic purposes of Cayo Bermúdez. She is murdered by Ambrosio in order to protect Don Fermín from the possibility of blackmail. This act of murder forever dooms Ambrosio to his marginal social status and forces a confrontation between Santiago and his father.

The Novel

Conversation in the Cathedral is an ambitious novel. Vargas Llosa presents a "private history" of Peru. The book is long, the social canvas broad. The major interest is the Zavala family—Don Fermín the father, Doña Zoila the mother, and the three children: Santiago, his sister Tete, and his brother Sparky. A vertical picture of Peruvian society is drawn by including the servants of the Zavala household, Ambrosio and Amalia, who end up leaving the family to work for other employers, with the narration continuing to follow their lives and adventures. The structure of the novel somewhat resembles the English television series *Upstairs, Downstairs*, alternating the story line between the "masters" or wealthy bourgeoisie and the disadvantaged servants; it is not, however, quite so schematic.

Near the beginning of the novel, Santiago accidentally meets Ambrosio, and they go to The Cathedral, a café for poor people, to talk, drink beer, and catch up on each other's activities. This conversation is the most forward moment in the chronology of the novel. What follows is a narrative reenactment in detail of the events they were only able to touch upon in the conversation. In the first scene of the book the reader learns that Santiago, the protagonist, is dissatisfied with his life, believing that somewhere he has taken a wrong turn. He has a good job, a relatively happy marriage, and what appears to be a comfortable middle-class life. Six hundred pages later, the novel returns to the same point in time. The reader knows much more about Santiago, Ambrosio, and a host of other characters—the "conversation" has been fleshed out, and Santiago's problem has been vividly dramatized. Time will continue to pass without change or hope for anything different as long as Peruvian society remains enmeshed in corruption and gross inequities.

Although the bulk of the novel is set in the past, it has a remarkable forward drive. No answers or plot endings are revealed in the opening "conversation" (Santiago becomes partly drunk, Ambrosio is reticent), and thus each convolution of the narrative comes as a surprise.

Santiago's wealthy parents want their bright son to succeed in life; they hope he will go to the Catholic University, favoring it over the state university, San Marcos. Santiago, however, who has lost his faith and dislikes priests, goes to San Marcos and soon joins a Marxist discussion group. He becomes ashamed of his own family, although his father in particular still treats him with great consideration. The group is arrested, and his father obtains Santiago's release through his political contacts. Santiago then leaves the university and goes to work for a newspaper, *La Crónica*, having broken completely with his family.

The rest of the novel is a detailed probing of South American history and politics. This is not done through Santiago's reportorial activities—when Santiago breaks with his family, he also breaks with politics. Instead, as noted above, there is an expansion of the plot and cast of characters, with a counterpoint developing between those who are wealthy and those who are trapped in poverty. Ambrosio, Don Fermín's chauffeur, becomes the chauffeur of Don Cayo Bermúdez, the minister of security. Don Fermín is acquainted with Don Cayo, who turns against him, depriving him of government contracts. A plot is organized against Don Cayo, not by the poor or leftists but by a coalition of wealthy landowners including Don Fermín, who plays a significant role in the group. The plot is discovered, yet it partly succeeds—Don Cayo leaves the country. His mistress, the prostitute Hortensia, is murdered by an unknown culprit (he turns out to be Ambrosio).

The question arises, then, of why Santiago has broken with his family if his father is a basically tolerant man who even plays an important role in a plot against the military dictatorship. A full and satisfying answer is never given. Partial answers are suggested—Don Fermín is opposed to Don Cayo for business, not ethical, reasons; Don Fermín tolerates the prostitutes, thugs, and corrupt politicians who saturate Peruvian politics; Don Fermín turns out to be a homosexual. None of these, however, justifies Santiago's break, which comes to dominate the father's life, torturing him until he finally dies.

It may be significant that Santiago's break with his family coincides with his break from all politics; perhaps these two actions have the same motivation, resembling that which fueled his original attraction to Marxism and subsequent repudiation of it. He was seeking a kind of purity, an immunity from corruption. The son tries to avoid the political system entirely while the father tries to work within it, preserving what honor he can. Is the Zavala family so permeated by corrupt values of Peruvian bourgeois society that Santiago is compelled to make a total break with the family? Vargas Llosa succeeds in dramatizing the poignancy of Santiago's dilemma, but the question receives no satisfactory answer.

Analysis

The political and social meaning of *Conversation in the Cathedral* is unambiguous: A large part of the population of the country is trapped in a system of continuous exploitation, and most individuals, no matter what their origin, must adapt to the system and themselves become exploiters if they are to survive. Vargas Llosa clearly condemns this condition, yet in the novel he holds out little hope for change—it appears that Peru is destined to continue in its underdevelopment, in the crudity of the exploitation of the poor by the rich. Vargas Llosa has spoken of Peru's "cultural apartheid," and the monied caste considers itself apart from the world of half-breeds, Indians, and blacks, resembling the Southern whites in the United States before the Civil War.

Like Santiago, Vargas Llosa revolts against the moneyed caste, but he sees no way out of the spiral of exploitation. As a college student, Santiago goes through a Marxist phase, but he soon sees that Marxism requires a leap of faith just as large as that required by religion. He feels no spontaneous faith either for religion or for Communism. He is united with the other student revolutionaries by his sense of revolt and by his rejection of the injustices of the military dictatorship. Santiago must reject Communism for the same reason that he rejects priests: Both exploit blind faith and irrational obedience. The students' Marxist discussion group has a striking similarity to that described by the Polish Nobel Prize-winner Czesław Miłosz in his book *Rodzinna Europa* (1959; *Native Realm: A Search for Self-Definition*, 1968). In both books, existing social injustices cried out for a remedy, almost any remedy it seemed, that would obliterate the garish abuses. After joining the Communist government, Miłosz broke with it; similarly, in 1971, at a crucial stage in his career, Vargas Llosa repudiated the Cuban revolution and founded the magazine *Libre* with other Latin American and European writers. Vargas Llosa's political credentials are impeccable—a critic of both Right and Left, he has consistently spoken out in favor of social justice. His nonfictional writings in particular are models of fairness and clarity.

Vargas Llosa has recognized the dangers to fiction of political commitment: Art can easily be sacrificed on the altar of politics. To a certain extent, this happens in *Conversation in the Cathedral*. The revolt of Santiago becomes a matter of principle and is shrill. His search for a family secret or skeleton in its closet does not end in any new discoveries or knowledge. The brothel scenes, Don Fermín's "secret," and the mindless and rather unattractive way in which the children of the wealthy are reared are far less shocking than the details of real exploitation as they are presented in the lives of Ambrosio, Amalia, and others. The novel has a nineteenth century, sensationalist aura that seems commercial. If the worst criticism of Peruvian society is that wealthy landowners, cabinet ministers, and army officers frequent brothels, then the country might be a very happy one. The ills, however, are much deeper. Other works by Vargas Llosa, in particular his nonfiction, have addressed these ills with greater clarity.

In addition, the characters are rarely seen from the inside. The density of consciousness, thoughts, feelings, or reactions is indicated rarely; instead, unflagging varied action is the main feature of the narration, probably its strongpoint. It is somewhat mysterious that a talented novelist who wrote a baccalaureate thesis on Rubén Darío of the *Modernismo* movement and a doctoral thesis on

Gabriel García Márquez should write a novel that is technically so old-fashioned. The book's conspicuous devices—the lack of strict chronology, the crisscrossing fragments, and the constant references to the original conversation in The Cathedral—are only the superficial paraphernalia of *Modernism*. If, in part at least, the novel has been successful for the wrong reasons—for its sensationalism, fast-moving subplots, and mockery of easy targets—it is nevertheless impressive, with fine characterization and an evenhanded, profound, human vision of an entire society.

Critical Context

After writing *Conversation in the Cathedral*, Vargas Llosa's career skyrocketed. *Conversation in the Cathedral* was a pivotal book that made him known to a broad Spanish-speaking readership. Since that time, Vargas Llosa's concept of social and political justice has deepened and become, if anything, more acute. This is most evident in his novel *Historia de Mayta* (1984; *The Real Life of Alejandro Mayta*, 1985) and in essays such as "Inquest in the Andes," "A Passion for Peru," and "In Nicaragua." The novel *La guerra del fin del mundo* (1981; *The War of the End of the World*, 1984) is a major effort, a polyphonic novel almost as long as *Conversation in the Cathedral*. Like the earlier book, it is peculiarly old-fashioned, owing much to Honoré de Balzac and nineteenth century realism. It is conceivable that this important, famous writer, who possesses a moral vision more profound than that of almost any other American writer, still has not found the style or genre that best suits him.

CORONATION

Author: José Donoso (1924-   )
Type of work: Novel
Type of plot: Social realism
Time of plot: The 1950's
Locale: Santiago de Chile and Valparaiso, Chile
First published: *Coronación*, 1957 (English translation, 1965)

Principal Characters

Andrés Abalos, the middle-aged neurotic heir of a proud Chilean family now in decline. Rich and free of any strong familial ties or occupational obligations, he devotes himself to the reading of French history, his collection of walking sticks, and the avoidance of any type of emotional entanglement or commitment. His complacency changes to panic, however, when he realizes that, after his grandmother's death, he will be left entirely alone, without any links to the past and no promise for the future. This psychological crisis is further triggered by his growing obsession with the servant girl Estela, whom he sees as a symbol of youth and hope. His final humiliation at her hands leads him to accept madness as the only escape from a sordid, meaningless world.

Misiá Elisa Grey de Abalos, Andrés' regal nonagenarian grandmother. Once known for her beauty and modesty, she now poisons the atmosphere of their household with the delusions of her madness.

Estela, a nursemaid to Misiá Elisa. Estela seems overwhelmed by the big city of Santiago until she meets and falls in love with Mario. She lies and steals for him to prove her love and, finally, must choose between blind devotion and self-respect. She is desired by both Andrés and Mario; their passion for her forces both men to reevaluate the direction of their lives.

Mario, Estela's lover. Young, handsome, and carefree, Mario is known for his dalliance with many women, but the innocence and adoration of Estela quickly break down his defenses. The fear that he will be unable to overcome the cycle of poverty and will be drawn into the criminality and despair of his brother René's world becomes reality. He agrees to a plot to rob the Abalos mansion even though it means Estela's betrayal and humiliation.

René, Mario's manipulative half brother. His life is a series of scams and petty frauds. He yearns to escape from a wife and family he despises in order to enjoy himself, free from all responsibility. Jealous of his brother, he deliberately tries to ruin Mario's future prospects and sets out to turn him against Estela.

Dora, René's pitiful wife, beaten down by the harshness of her life and her ridicule by René. The pathetic love she still retains for her husband is her only hope.

Carlos Gross, Andrés' friend and confidant, a doctor. His self-satisfied comparison between his full life and the vacuum of his friend's precipitates Andrés' psychological trauma.

Adriana, Carlos' wife. Disillusioned by her husband's infidelity, she has converted herself into the perfect wife and mother. This façade is her protection against any emotional participation.

Lourdes, Estela's aunt and longtime servant to the Abalos family. Without any life outside the mansion, she, along with Rosario, lives in the past and devotes herself to the care of her mistress, whom she considers to be a saint.

Rosario, the longtime cook to the Abalos family. Her life also revolves around the gratification of any whim of Misiá Elisa and Misiá Elisa's grandson, Andrés, whom the servants still treat as a child.

The Novel

Most of the action of the novel takes place in the Abalos mansion, occupied by Misiá Elisa Grey de Abalos and her three servants, and in the working-class neighborhoods where Mario, who loves the young servant Estela, struggles to maintain his human dignity. The Abalos house represents the enclosed space of repressed characters; the outside constitutes that space where they would find liberation. *Coronation* consists of three parts. The first, "The Gift," introduces the characters who gather in the upper-class house to celebrate a birthday. The guest of honor is Misiá Elisa, a demented lady in her nineties. Despite her old age and her confinement in bed, Misiá Elisa dominates all those who frequent the house, including Andrés, the orphaned grandson whom she and her husband reared. Still a bachelor in his fifties, Andrés lives comfortably on his inheritance and occupies his idle life by collecting fancy walking sticks and carrying on philosophical conversations with his lifelong friend Carlos Gross. Misiá Elisa also controls three servants who live in the mansion: Estela, a young girl whose sole duty is to care for the aging lady; Rosario, who has cooked for the Abalos family for nearly half a century; and Lourdes, an aging housekeeper.

The second section, "Absences," follows the fates of Andrés and Mario, Estela's boyfriend, as they undergo major crises in their lives. Andrés is aroused from his complacency by the presence of Estela, the young, sensual servant recently arrived from the country. Mario, the young delivery boy who aspires to lead an honest happy life with Estela, finds himself increasingly entangled in the world of his brother René's illicit yet unprofitable dealings. While Andrés becomes obsessed with his

newly found sensuality and a preoccupation with death, Mario seeks to escape the fate of poverty and crime that now encircles him. Both men feel persecuted and trapped, Andrés by his grandmother, and Mario by Estela. The women seem to have joined forces under the banner of morality and religion to find shelter from abandonment and solitude. This section develops the characters and signals the eventual disintegration of the men. At the end of *Coronation*, the men find a questionable deliverance from their fate as Andrés loses his mind and Mario steals Estela and disappears in the streets of the dark city.

Having opened with the preparations for Misiá Elisa's birthday, the novel concludes with "The Coronation," a celebration of her saint's day. The guests never arrive, and the house becomes a stage for the final phase of the already evident decay. In the final scene, the two old servants, now drunk and unmindful of the power that their mistress exerts upon them, crown Misiá Elisa in a grotesque pageantry that erases the boundaries between reality and fiction, decay seamlessly blending life into death. Donoso describes the downward moral path of the upper class by its decadence and that of the lower class by its degradation. Masters and servants coexist in the dilapidated old house, and both Andrés and Mario seek salvation through Estela, only to have their expectations crushed. By drawing a parallel between the two men, the novel goes beyond the issue of class conflict to evoke the universal quest for happiness. In Donoso's world, the moment when dreams fail marks the passage into another, less clearly defined form of existence. In *Coronation*, flight leads the characters into madness and the unknown.

Analysis

Images of madness and crowning reappear throughout the novel to signify a transcending of or escape from the lot of the characters' lives. In her madness, Misiá Elisa insists that her family

descends from the crowns of Europe and that she deserves to be treated as royalty. The aging lady fills the silence of the house with violent accusations against Andrés and Estela for being lustful and of dubious morality, while she, on the other hand, stands as a model of purity, a saint. It is no surprise that her maids, attentive to her every whim, crown her on her saint's day. The ancient lady contaminates her grandson with the same kind of madness. They become obsessed with perverse sexuality because neither has enjoyed sex in a meaningful way. Ironically, they constitute each other's only source of affection and love; since they are both incapable of feeling or giving love, their deprived existence expresses itself in a condemnation of precisely that which they desire most. For this same reason, Andrés—an emotional cripple—collects walking sticks. Misiá Elisa's obsession with being crowned indicates a need to flee her impoverished reality of isolation and immobility. This immobility propels her into a world where she reigns over and controls her subjects.

When Andrés first feels the incongruity of his surroundings, he creates the world of Omsk, where harmony rules all circumstance: Through madness, he escapes. Later, he assumes this madness in a very conscious fashion—he is conscious of the creative process and, hence, of his madness. When he feels rejected by his grandmother and Estela, he abandons his ties with reason and enters a domain where his own fictions blur with the reality of the house. Soon after the coronation scene, Andrés stages his own masquerade and convinces his doctor friend that he is mad, thus becoming a character in a world of his own invention. Once Andrés attains the coherence that he desires through a conscious assumption of madness, he then slips completely into his own world. The novelist portrays a social milieu of fragmented families and a decaying upper class. The characters who inhabit the novel escape that world by assuming madness. Likewise, Donoso transcends his Chilean reality by creating characters that repeat the liberating act of invention.

Critical Context

Coronation, Donoso's first novel, was awarded the 1963 Faulkner Foundation Prize as best postwar Chilean novel. Two years later, it was published in English. This first work repeats some of the themes developed earlier in short stories, but most important, it foreshadows some of the author's most marked obsessions. The metaphor of the boarded-up house signifying a world closing in on the character becomes a dominant force in *El obsceno pájaro de la noche* (1970; *The Obscene Bird of Night*, 1973). It appears in *Coronation* as Andrés locks himself in the old mansion when he finds that Estela loves Mario. There is in this first novel great emphasis on the contrast between the outside and the inside of the house, representing internal, repressed forces and external possibilities for liberation. This play on internal/external spaces reappears in 1980 with *La misteriosa desparición de la marquesita de Loria* (1980). Similarly, a dramatically staged scene, such as that of the coronation at the end of the novel, becomes the basic structuring model for *Casa de campo* (1978; *A House in the Country*, 1984).

The novel has been praised for its portrayal of the stratification of Chilean society and for its vivid incursion into a surrealistic world of dreams and the repressed unconscious. At a first reading, *Coronation* falls within the context of other novels written in Chile during the 1950's and following the trend of social realism. Donoso departs from this trend, however, by creating a self-referential work in which the characters invent their own worlds. In *Coronation*, Donoso writes about himself when he writes about Andrés. This complex vision finds its fullest expression in Donoso's masterpiece, *The Obscene Bird of Night*.

THE CUTTER

Author: Virgil Suarez (1962-   )
Type of work: Novel
Type of plot: *Bildungsroman*
Time of plot: 1969
Locale: Cuba and the United States
First published: 1991

Principal Characters

Julian Campos, the major character, a twenty-year-old university student. He longs for freedom and attempts to attain it legally, but he eventually realizes that he will never be allowed to leave Cuba. Although Julian's parents were deeply distressed about having to leave their son behind when they left the country, they made the choice to leave. Despite Julian's own desperation to leave Cuba, he never forgives his parents for leaving for the United States without him. Julian is a good, responsible young man. He cares deeply for his ailing grandmother Bernarda and for Carmina, Bernarda's housekeeper and nursemaid. Julian tries to do what is right and obtain his freedom legally, but he suffers for his efforts.

Bernarda Del Rio, Julian's grandmother. She represents that group of people who believed in the system but became disillusioned after the repressive government began to retaliate against those who opposed the revolution. After Julian's father, Ernesto, was imprisoned for organizing "antirevolutionary activities," Bernarda renounced Cuba and the revolution. She longed for a reunion with her son in the United States.

Carmina, Bernarda's faithful housekeeper and friend. She nurses Julian's grandmother until she dies, then cares for Julian after his return from a work camp. Although Carmina sympathizes with Julian's desire to leave Cuba and assists him in his efforts, she refuses to leave. Cuba is her home, and Carmina suggests that she has a kind of freedom there.

Blancarosa Calderon, a former classmate of Julian. She inspires no sympathy, for she betrays her friends. Although government officials and party sympathizers call Julian a *gusano*, a traitor, it is clear that Blancarosa is the only traitor in the novel: She deliberately deceives those who entrust their lives to her.

Ofelia, Julian's neighbor. She tells Julian about a planned escape from Cuba. Ofelia believes herself to be in love with Julian and is jealous of Blancarosa, toward whom Julian seems to have romantic inclinations.

Fermin, Ofelia's father. Fermin goes to the cane fields with Julian to serve as a "voluntary" worker as a means of earning the right to emigrate. He and Julian spend time together in the camp jail cell. At the camp, Fermin is caught buying *aguardiente*, an illegal alcoholic drink. Fermin, who drinks to ease his frustration, tells Julian, while they are in detention, that he wants to die drunk. Fermin dies mysteriously, apparently getting his wish.

Nicanor, a Communist Party cadre. Nicanor is in charge of *El Comite*, "the community watchdog." He is the only major black character. He is a widower who lost his pregnant wife in a fire ten years before the action of the novel. Before the revolution, Nicanor was unemployed. He refuses a chance to flee Cuba after the revolution, vowing to attain a position in which he is powerful enough to "get even" for his wife's death. Nicanor watches Julian carefully and suspects, near the end of the novel, that Julian plans to leave Cuba illegally. Nicanor represents the repressive, ruthless government. He is clearly responsible for thwarting Julian's attempts to leave Cuba legally.

The Novel

The Cutter is the story of a young man's desperate attempt to leave what he believes to be a repressive Communist regime in Cuba. The novel is divided into five sections that mark the stages of Julian's journey away from Cuba. An omniscient third-person narrator relates the story.

The book begins when protagonist Julian Campos is twenty years old. Julian is a university student who has recently returned to Havana after having completed his years of mandatory military service in the Young Pioneers. Julian drifts off into the "freedom of sleep" only to be abruptly awakened by his ailing grandmother, Bernarda Del Rio, who informs Julian that someone is at the door. The visitor is a government official who hands Julian a telegram from the Ministry of the Interior. Julian has been waiting to leave Cuba ever since his parents received an "exit notice" five years earlier. Julian resents the fact that his parents left him behind. Although Elena and Ernesto, Julian's parents, wanted to take their son with them to the United States, the authorities at the airport demanded that they leave Julian in Cuba or forfeit the privilege of leaving the country themselves.

Although Julian is disenchanted with the government in Cuba, he still believes that the legal system works. He is therefore convinced that if he goes through the proper bureaucratic channels, he will be rewarded with an exit notice from the Ministry of the Interior. Heartened by the receipt of the telegram, Julian plans a new life in the United States for himself and his grandmother, but he is told that he must do additional "voluntary work" if he wants to leave Cuba.

In the second section, "The Fields," Julian spends months cutting cane for Cuba's "Ten-Million-Ton Sugarcane Program." The work is slave labor, and Julian and his coworkers are mis-treated. The men arise early and work all day, regardless of weather conditions. The workers receive substandard food, live in overcrowded housing, and are monitored by characters reminiscent of cruel overseers on Southern plantations before the Civil War. This section of the novel depicts Cuba at its worst, leading the reader to understand why Julian is compelled to leave the country. He grows increasingly despondent about his prospects for leaving Cuba, particularly when he receives the belated news of his grandmother's death.

When Julian is finally released from the fields and permitted to go home, he realizes that he will never receive an exit notice. He learns from Ofelia, his neighbor, that she and her mother, Silvia, are planning to escape. In the third section, "The Operation," Julian joins them in this quest. Blancarosa Calderon, Julian's former classmate, is a key figure in the escape plan and offers her assistance to Silvia, Ofelia, and Julian. Julian and his friends discover too late that Blancarosa works for the government. She betrays the group of escapees, resulting in the deaths of Silvia and Ofelia. Julian, however, survives. "The Shore," the novel's fourth section, describes his continued move toward the United States and freedom.

In the novel's final section, "The Refuge," Julian reaches the United States. In contrast to most of the Cuban characters, those in the United States are kind to him and are eager to help him adjust to his new country. Padre Marcelo, the priest at the Catholic Refugee Center, finds Julian a temporary job at a small cafe in Miami. Julian clearly enjoys his newfound freedom. The section implies that the story will have a happy ending. Although Julian appears reluctant to search for his parents, the novel ends with a suggestion that ultimately he will find refuge with them.

Analysis

The Cutter is a scathing critique of the Communist government in Cuba. The events in the novel take place after Fidel Castro's revolution that made him the head of state. The novel takes a vehemently anti-Communist position, with the repressiveness and evil of Communism as a recurrent theme. Other themes surround the dominant political one. The novel concerns the desire for personal freedom and independence, but it is also about the loss of innocence and of the belief that if one does the right thing, good will necessarily be the end result.

Julian moves from an attitude of hopeful skepticism to despair and rebellion, and he comes to understand, by the end of the novel, the value of freedom. Despite his ambivalence about his parents' abandonment of him, it seems clear that Julian and his parents will not only meet again, but they will also reunite as family.

The struggle between the forces of good and evil is clear throughout the novel. Julian, along with his grandmother and friends, are repre-sentations of good, as are the opponents of Castro's regime. The democratic society of the United States, which Julian strives to join, stands in stark contrast to the repressive regime of Cuba, which he seeks to escape. Blancarosa and members of the Communist Party are the forces of evil. They are unredeemable, uniformly corrupt and cruel.

The themes of escape and exile take curious twists. Escape becomes a necessity, and exile becomes a relief. Julian feels no ambivalence about leaving his native soil. Once in the United States, he has no fond memories of Cuba and no longing to return. He associates that "home" with pain and misery. The plot of the novel is rather simple, and its messages are clear: Communism is bad, escape from it is essential, and freedom is worth any price.

Critical Context

The Cutter, Virgil Suarez's second novel, is his attempt to come to grips with his native Cuba and reflects his bitterness toward the country from which he and his parents were exiles. Suarez's own family left Cuba in 1970, about the time at which this novel is set. Suarez is unrelenting in his criticism of the Cuban government and of Castro's Cuba as a harsh, repressive, and cruel place where a semblance of freedom exists only for those ruthless characters who follow the Party line to save their own skins. He has no favorable character to speak for or represent the government.

What seems conspicuously absent from the novel, as it is often found in works by writers from the Caribbean, is a detailed description of the island itself. Cuba is a beautiful island, but Suarez chooses not to depict that natural beauty, indicative of his treatment of the entire life and culture of the island. Suarez's portrayal of Cuba is perhaps too harsh and the novel itself too preachy and melodramatic. It is, however, obviously heartfelt.

Suarez's first novel, *Latin Jazz* (1989), was not favorably received and was relatively unsuccessful. *The Cutter* has had a similar fate.

DAYS OF OBLIGATION: An Argument with My Mexican Father

Author: Richard Rodriguez (1944-   )
Type of work: Essays
First published: 1992

Form and Content

Days of Obligation is a compilation of previously published essays that appeared in magazines and academic journals. They are collected in the format of an introduction and ten chapters. Ranging from eight pages to thirty pages in length, these loosely connected essays vary in tone, purpose, and audience. Some are intimate, confessional narratives, others are journalistic pieces, and several are intellectual essays with literary, political, or philosophical overtones. The overriding subjects are Mexican and Mexican American cultural history, the relations between Mexicans and Mexican Americans, the relations between Mexico and the United States, and Rodriguez's personal quest for ethnic identity.

The introductory chapter recounts Rodriguez's visit to Mexico and his visit to his parents' native village. It introduces the central concern with the historical differences and cultural clashes between Mexican and American societies. Using terms in the sense of Greek classical drama, he introduces his major thematic metaphor: Mexico is a country of tragedy because it is fatalistic, and the United States is a country of comedy because it is optimistic. The author's strategy is to explore these opposites and to find, if possible, a resolution.

"India" deals with racial issues and racist attitudes historically present in both cultures. Taking off from a description of his dark skin, Indian features, and mestizo heritage (a mix of Indian and European), Rodriguez explores the question of "Indianness." He notes the different attitudes historically present in what he calls Protestant America and Catholic Mexico, underscoring the racial and cultural interbreeding that occurred in Spanish America and its absence in Anglo America. He

concludes that the Indian in the United States disappeared into a Hollywood stereotype born of the American imagination and that the Indian in Mexico disappeared into a romanticized Aztec past. Neither Indian exists in the present; modernity has relegated them to the distant past.

"Late Victorians" is an introspective account of the tragedy that has befallen the gay community of San Francisco. Rodriguez is explicit about his homosexuality, and it marks an important juncture in his autobiographical writings. This is the most personal essay in the collection. Rodriguez's remembrances of friends who died from the ravages of acquired immune deficiency syndrome (AIDS) provoke empathy in the reader. The essay also expresses Rodriguez's conflicting feelings about his life as a homosexual and his life as a Catholic. Intellectually, he questions the medieval and moralistic prescriptions of Catholic doctrine, but he feels a sense of guilt that cannot be discarded easily.

"Mexico's Children" and "In Athens Once" can be paired thematically and stylistically. These essays explore Mexican and Mexican American themes dealing with social and cultural history. In "Mexico's Children," the longest essay and the cornerstone of the book, Rodriguez identifies the Mexican Revolution of 1910 as a watershed in modern history. He presents the historical panorama of four generations of Mexicans who left villages in Mexico to venture north in search of the American Dream. These immigrants crossed a border river into a different world that offered both opportunity and disturbing uncertainties. As the forces of assimilation and acculturation took hold, the question of ethnic identity became crucial.

Foremost, family and personal identity were changed as the immigrants became part of the "melting pot" and dreamers of the American Dream. The closing vignette has Rodriguez visiting a small village in Michoácan, now practically empty because most of the villagers have left Mexico for the United States. They return for the festival of the patron saint of the village, the men dressed in dark suits and the women in evening gowns and high heels. The scene sums up Rodriguez's point: Much of Mexico has disappeared, and Mexico is now mostly memory. It has disappeared into the modernity exemplified, for better or for worse, by the United States.

If the old Mexico has disappeared by force of history and necessity, the new Mexico is being made in the image of the United States. This is the thrust of "In Athens Once," the title being an allusion to Tijuana as a Trojan horse that has silently arrived with unexpected possibilities. The essay's historical sweep spans from prehistory to the proposed North American Free Trade Agreement and discusses Mexico-United States relations, with a focus on Tijuana and San Diego. The essay suggests that border towns such as those represent confluences of nations and cultures. Giving emphasis to Tijuana, he outlines the transformation of a seedy little town on the edge of the "land of mañana" to a teeming metropolis with American-style shopping centers, traffic jams, industrial parks, pollution, industrial waste, and every form of urban sprawl. The past has met the present. In Rodriguez's metaphor, tragedy and comedy are fused at the border. It is here that the term Mexican American is the most relevant and the bridging of two cultures and two nations is most dynamic and confusing, and also most promising.

"The Missions" and "The Head of Joaquín Murrieta" are also companion pieces; they are journalistic essays on early California history. The first part of "The Missions" focuses on the accomplishments of Father Junípero Serra, the founder of twenty-one missions stretching across the state. The second part takes a satirical turn as Rodriguez purviews the Anglo-American creation of a ro-

mantic Spanish California. Quaint missions, dashing *caballeros*, and beautiful *señoritas* became the staples of historical romances. His acerbic point is that Anglo-Americans created and commercialized what historian Carey McWilliams has called "California's fantasy heritage," and they denied or obliterated the true histories and legacies of the people who originally settled California. "The Head of Joaquín Murrieta" uses the legend of the nineteenth century Mexican miner who took up arms to fight the Anglo invasion during the gold rush. To the Mexicans, Murrieta became a Robin Hood type of hero. Murrieta was captured and decapitated, but his head has never been located. Legend has it that it is still unburied. Murrieta's story is part of the lasting legacy of cultural resistance.

"Sand," the shortest and slightest piece in the collection, is a comparison and contrast of Los Angeles and San Francisco. It focuses on Los Angeles as a paradoxical city that has become, for better or for worse, a cultural metaphor for America itself.

"Asians" stems from Rodriguez's memories of Chinese families in his childhood neighborhood in Sacramento and expands to a consideration of the Chinese immigrant experience and the ethnicity of Chinese Americans. Not satisfied with the cliché that the United States is a nation of immigrants, Rodriguez seeks an understanding of the unique character of the Chinese American experience and the impact of assimilation and acculturation on their traditional culture and beliefs.

"The Latin American Novel" is about the extraordinary growth of Protestant evangelical churches and church members in Latin America and among Hispanic communities in the United States. The rise of evangelical faiths and the diminution of the Catholic church presage important social, cultural, and political changes in Hispanic America, according to Rodriguez.

"Nothing Lasts a Hundred Years" creates a narrative frame by returning to the subject matter of the introduction: Rodriguez's family and cultural identity, and his argument with his father. When Rodriguez was fourteen years old and his father was fifty, they had an argument based on their different attitudes. His Mexican father was fatalistic, often telling Richard that life is very hard; Richard was an American optimist and thought that his father was wrong. Now in middle age, Rodriguez looks back and admits that his father was right. He has become his father's son. He now respects and reveres his father, and he has met an obligation.

Analysis

Days of Obligation is a sequel to Rodriguez's most famous work, *Hunger of Memory: The Education of Richard Rodriguez* (1981). Like its predecessor, it is a collection of essays marked by an autobiographical persona and distinguished by Rodriguez's mastery of the English language. Rodriguez's language and style are modulated by his audience, as exemplified in the essays in *Days of Obligation*. Some are journalistic pieces that appeared, for example, in *Reader's Digest* and *California Magazine*; in contrast, the full-fledged essays appeared in *Harper's, The American Scholar*, and *The New Republic* or were anthologized in *Political Passages: Journeys of Change Through Two Decades, 1968-1988* (1988). The different audiences account for the range of topics and authorial voices, and for the extreme unevenness between "Sand" and "Mexico's Children." Clearly, the crux of *Days of Obligation* rests with "India," "Mexico's Children," "In Athens Once," "The Latin American Novel," and "Nothing Lasts a Hundred Years." These essays are threaded on a unifying theme and reflect Rodriguez's most earnest concerns as a writer and intellectual. Both *Hunger of Memory* and *Days of Obligation* project Rodriguez's interests in and knowledge of history, sociology, literature, and ethnopoetics. His prose style is not dense or academic, but his signal essays are laced with literary allusions, theological references, and philosophical speculation. These multiple devices and layers of metaphor and imagery are used to present or dramatize his major concerns: the contradictions and paradoxes that attend the definition of America; the deep divisions and equally deep commonalities of the multicultural United States; the disparity between minority and majority cultures; the racism, ethnocentrism, and nativism at large in the country; and the dilemmas that confront the individual in the face of social fragmentation. Thus, his writings are often didactic and argumentative: Rodriguez holds strong opinions and expresses them with conviction. Avoiding ideology or political doctrines, his writings are responses to socioeconomic realities and are cast in introspective personal criticism.

The scope of Rodriguez's social commentary and criticism has steadily widened, and the expansion is evident in *Days of Obligation*. Whereas *Hunger of Memory* was strictly autobiographical and exclusively about Rodriguez's Mexican American heritage, the sequel branches to investigations of the AIDS crisis, relations between the United States and Mexico, hemispheric socioeconomic conditions, and complex social and political issues that affect diverse ethnic and cultural groups. Collectively, the essays in *Days of Obligation* indicate Rodriguez's intellectual maturity and increasing sophistication as a writer. His maturity can also be discerned in the modulated subjectivity of his later essays. The self-centeredness of *Hunger of Memory* has given way to sympathetic understanding of others. At crucial moments, Rodriguez takes a secondary role and gives primacy to the struggles of nameless multitudes. *Days of Obligation* is a sequel, but it is not a replica.

Critical Context

Days of Obligation solidifies Rodriguez's reputation as a major figure in Mexican American (Chicano) literature, an important voice in contemporary American letters, and a master stylist.

Highly praised when published and later widely anthologized in college readers and other academic texts, *Hunger of Memory* made Rodriguez one of the most famous and controversial writers in the history of Chicano literature. Less controversial or polemical, the essays in *Days of Obligation* that focus on the Mexican American experience are keenly sensitive and judicious; specifically, "Mexico's Children" is a significant contribution to Chicano literature and scholarship. Equally notable is Rodriguez's ability to transcend ethnic boundaries and extend his vision to the larger terrain of American literature and culture. *Days of Obligation* sustains the critics who have placed Rodriguez with James Baldwin, Saul Bellow, Alice Walker, and other American writers who have used their ethnic or racial heritages as springboards for literary art. That literary art comes in Rodriguez's mastery of the essay form. *Days of Obligation* lacks the emotional charge and lyrical force of its predecessor, but it still presents the best qualities of Rodriguez's prose style. Rodriguez offers a terse, vivid, lucid, and intelligent prose style that commends *Days of Obligation*.

DEAR DIEGO

Author: Elena Poniatowska (1933-   )
Type of work: Novel
Type of plot: Epistolary
Time of plot: The 1920's and 1935
Locale: Paris, France, and Mexico City, Mexico
First published: *Querido Diego, te abraza Quiela*, 1978 (English translation, 1986)

Principal Characters

Angelina Beloff (Quiela), a Russian painter of landscapes, still lifes, and portraits who also works as an engraver, lithographer, and book illustrator. She is Diego Rivera's lover in Paris from 1910 to 1920. After he leaves her, she writes to him for a period of nine months until she realizes that he is neither coming back nor sending for her. More than ten years later, she travels to Mexico, where he has gone, but she does not look for him.

Diego Rivera, a Mexican painter who lives with Beloff in Paris. He returns to Mexico in the wake of the Mexican Revolution. His ten-year relationship with Beloff (Quiela for him) is portrayed in *Dear Diego*, but as a character he appears only through her letters. He is judged in the novel because he leaves her and never writes back to her; he merely sends money once in a while. He represents the freedom of expression in contemporary Latin American art that Beloff lacks as a result of her European background.

The Novel

Dear Diego is based on one chapter of Bertram Wolfe's *The Fabulous Life of Diego Rivera* (1963). The novel is a fictionalized portrayal of Quiela (the Russian painter Angelina Beloff) as a broken-hearted lover waiting for the well-known painter Diego Rivera to send for her from Mexico City.

Dear Diego is divided into twelve love letters dated from October 19, 1921, through July 22, 1922—nine months in which Quiela, in spite of her desperation and longing for her lover, creates her own work as an illustrator for the Parisian magazine *Floreal*. By painting in nine months exactly, she affirms her identity through the art that Diego Rivera represents for her. The letters are followed by a brief narrative at the end of the book.

The book begins as Quiela is waiting for her lover. She expects him to send for her, but toward the end of the novel she realizes that he does not need her anymore. On one level, the narrative is about one woman in love with someone who does not want her; at the same time, it is about the aesthetic process of painting without the influence of her lover, a process that makes Quiela a newborn woman at the end.

The plot of the novel is fairly straightforward: Angelina Beloff (Quiela), a Russian painter in Paris, falls in love with the Mexican painter Diego Rivera. They live together for ten years. Diego Rivera goes back to Mexico in order to participate in the new beginning of his country after the Mexican Revolution, and he forgets about her. Although he sends some money for Quiela, he answers none of her letters. Quiela (the nickname Rivera gave her) writes him several times about how much she loves him and how important his ideas about painting have been for her. In a sense, he becomes a mentor for her. These episodes are brought out in Quiela's letters. The short concluding narrative describes Quiela's trip to Mexico in 1935, thirteen years after she has stopped writing. She does not look for Rivera, but she runs into him at a theater in Mexico City. He does not recognize her. The incident can be interpreted in two ways: Either Rivera has forgotten her to the point that he does not even recognize her, or, alternately, the woman he sees is no longer the heartbroken lover of Paris but a new Angelina Beloff, an artist who has her own life and art and who does not need him anymore.

Analysis

The novel is a feminist outline of the oppression in which women live when they love too much. Quiela waits endlessly for someone she knows is not coming back. The fact that the novel deals with two artists gives the work implications about art and love that extend beyond the melodramatic discourse of the letters and Quiela's process of forgetting about Diego.

During the nine months covered by the letters, Beloff tells her whole story. She has been an independent woman who has developed her technique as a painter as the only real center of her life. She grew up in Russia; her father was an important influence in her life because he always insisted that she have a profession. As an independent woman at the beginning of the twentieth century, she is something of a pioneer and role model, even though her longing for Diego makes her appear weak.

In her letters, she expresses the anger and the mixed emotions she feels toward Diego, but she eventually realizes that she has to find her center again; significantly, it takes nine months for her to be reborn. Life will not stop for this woman simply because Diego Rivera does not want her.

In Quiela's last letter, the tone changes completely. She writes to Rivera for the last time and tells him about her already finished illustrations for the Parisian magazine *Floreal*. Her artistic work is done; she has recuperated with dignity. It is not until 1935, when she goes to Mexico, that she again comes into contact with Rivera; even then, she does not seek him out. By going to Mexico City, Angelina Beloff becomes a woman in control of her own life and strong enough to face her past. (According to Bertram Wolfe's biography of Rivera, Beloff did in fact contact Diego Rivera in Mexico City because she needed his signature in order to sell some of his paintings that belonged to her. In the novel, this scene is not even mentioned; Poniatowska's version of the story is more dramatic, since Rivera does not recognize Beloff when they finally run into each other.)

The novel is also about the fascination of Angelina Beloff with anything Mexican. Colors are important also, especially gray and blue. Gray is her color before Diego's eyes, and blue is the bright color in which Diego describes her. Gray is Europe for Diego, and blue is Mexico.

Critical Context

Dear Diego is a testimonial work of fiction in the Latin American tradition of the *novela testimonio* (testimonial novel) developed by the Cuban author Miguel Barnet with his famous *Biografía de un cimarrón* (1966; *The Autobiography of a Runaway Slave*, 1966). The most important element in this kind of literature is the use of a "witness" to provide the writer with the basic monologue in which the character tells his or her story. In *Dear Diego*, the "witness" is the chapter dedicated to Quiela by Bertram Wolfe in his biography of Rivera. Poniatowska read Wolfe's biography and from this material developed the story line of her novel; she thus created a work in which it is the written word itself that acts as the "witness" of the story; The basic monologue is derived not from an interview with Angelina Beloff herself but from research on Beloff done by Poniatowska. The final monologue presented by the narrator is the collection of letters. In this respect, the novel does not follow the testimonial fiction structure of the first voice telling the story. In *Dear Diego*, the letters to Diego Rivera from Angelina Beloff constitute the narrative discourse.

DEAR RAFE

Author: Rolando Hinojosa (1929-   )
Type of work: Novel
Type of plot: Social realism
Time of plot: The mid-1950's to the early 1960's
Locale: The Rio Grande Valley of southern Texas
First published: *Mi querido Rafa*, 1981 (English translation and revision, 1985)

Principal Characters

Jehu Malacara, the head loan officer at Klail City First National Bank, the center of Belken County politics. A Mexican American with a military background, he has chosen to work his way up into the Texas Anglo-American world of politics and money, but he finds himself unable to live with the underhanded games played by the Anglo-American power brokers. Despite his efforts in support of the Texas Mexican struggle to gain higher economic and political status, he proves a disappointment to the Mexican American community. He quits his job at the bank; at the book's end, it is not known why he leaves the valley.

Noddy Perkins, a self-made man and bank owner who thrives on controlling the politics of Belken County. He is behind the Anglo-American power plays to keep the area's real estate out of the hands of Texas Mexicans. The reader is led to believe that he wants to exploit Jehu, his chief loan officer, by using him in the same manner as he does Ira Escobar. Although his sinister intentions do not bear fruit, Noddy is able to manipulate and control other important characters in his political schemes, even breaking off a love affair between his daughter, Sammie Jo, and Jehu.

Ira Escobar, a Texas Mexican employed at the Klail City First National Bank who falls prey to the political exploitation of Noddy Perkins. His desire to be a county commissioner makes him vulnerable to exploitation, and he becomes a pawn in Noddy's political schemes. Ira never understands why Jehu ever got a job at the bank or why he leaves this post.

Becky Caldwell-Escobar, the daughter of a prominent Mexican American family. She marries Ira Escobar, who is also from a prominent Mexican American family in Belken County. Their union creates a strong political bond between the two influential families. She is allowed to become part of the social circles of Anglo-Texan women. This achievement does not impress her people, but her affair with Jehu does. In the end, she breaks off her relationship with Jehu and is devoted to her husband. The members of the Mexican American community, however, never accept her affair with Jehu, which they see as a negative reflection on their social values.

Sammie Jo Perkins-Cooke, Noddy's spoiled daughter. Her social activities are essential to the Anglo-Texan power brokers. Although she has good reason to have an affair with Jehu (her husband is having a homosexual affair), her actions are unacceptable to the Anglo-Texan society of the valley. After she breaks off her relationship with Jehu, she goes back to her husband. She will not jeopardize the security and the economic welfare of her father for the fulfillment of their own personal needs; hence, she is a reflection of Anglo-Texan values.

Rafe Buenrostro, the silent sounding board for messages sent to him in letters by Jehu Malacara. The author's life reflects that of Rafe: Both lived in and left the Rio Grande Valley at about the same time, both went to the University of Texas, and both fought in the Korean War.

The Novel

Dear Rafe is based on Rolando Hinojosa's vivid experiences in the Rio Grande Valley of southern Texas from 1929 to 1946 as well as on his knowledge of the Korean War. *Dear Rafe* is a fictionalized portrayal of the area's white power brokers and what they are doing to control the economy in the lower Rio Grande Valley.

Dear Rafe is divided into two parts, forming a total of forty-seven chapters and a conclusion. The first part consists of twenty-three chapters made up of Jehu Malacara's letters to Rafe Buenrostro. The second part is made up of twenty-four chapters that deal mainly with speculation on Jehu Malacara's mysterious departure from Klail City First National Bank in Belken County.

The book begins with Jehu's letters to his cousin Rafe, who is recovering in Belken County War Memorial Veteran's Hospital from wounds incurred during the Korean War. Both are now employed; Rafe, although convalescing, is an attorney and a lieutenant of detectives in the district attorney's office in Belken County, while Jehu is the chief loan officer of the Klail City First National Bank. Jehu tells Rafe of the political activities going on in the valley. He focuses on the subtle games played by the area's power brokers, mainly Noddy Perkins and Ira Escobar. Jehu is indirectly involved in various political power plays, for he not only knows who is manipulating whom but is also in charge of money being lent to selected businesses that are subsequently taken over by Klail City First National Bank. During these socioeconomic and political fracases, Jehu becomes involved with two women, the beautiful Becky, the Mexican American wife of Ira Escobar, and the younger Sammie Jo, the white, spoiled daughter of Noddy Perkins. Ira is so caught up in his quest to be county commissioner—giving his undivided attention and services to Noddy, who can and does make his ambitions reality—that he is not aware of his wife's love affair with Jehu. Sammie Jo, who has been married before and who is known to be promiscuous, is also having an affair with Jehu, perhaps because she is being neglected by her husband, Sidney. Sidney is having a homosexual relationship with a high-ranking state official, Hap Bayliss, who is also controlled by Sammie Jo's father, Noddy. During this time, Jehu is also dating, off and on, Olivia (Ollie) San Esteban, an aspiring pharmacist in Klail City.

There are also two important minor characters in the novel. Morse Terry eventually takes Hap's position as a Texas state representative. Terry, once a successful real-estate broker, let a big land deal fall into the hands of a group of Mexican Americans, an economic and political faux pas that caused him to fall from grace with the white power brokers, especially Noddy Perkins. The price he had to pay was to become a politician who would be controlled by Noddy. Viola Barragan is a powerful white figure in the real-estate business in Belken County and also a key figure in Jehu's rise to a prestigious role in the Klail City First National Bank's money-lending sector, an upward move unusual for a Mexican American. She is also Jehu's firm supporter, regardless of his political and personal activities.

In the latter portion of the series of letters to Rafe, the reader is led to believe that Jehu gets so tired of the underhanded ploys of the white power brokers, especially Noddy, that he resigns his position as head loan officer at the Klail City First National Bank and also breaks off his relationships with Becky and Sammy Jo—especially since he has good reason to believe that Noddy has found out that he has been having an illicit affair with Noddy's daughter. Jehu goes back to his ever-faithful Ollie, who, it is believed, sells her part in a drugstore business to her brother so as to pursue a medical degree at the University of Texas at Austin. Jehu goes with her to give her his full support.

Part 2 is based on interviews with various characters in Belken County. The unnamed interviewer is trying to determine why Jehu Malacara left his post at Klail City First National Bank; hence, what follows is speculation on the part of several characters who are either only briefly mentioned in part 1 or who have not been heard of before. Each of the chapters in part 2 begins with a brief descriptive background on each character. Most of the time, these characters speak to Galindo, who serves as the author's listener. The characters give their views as to why Jehu Malacara left the Klail City First National Bank, with a few opinions about Jehu's relationships with Becky and Sammie Jo included.

"A Penultimate Note" brings the novel to its basic closure, a few following paragraphs, included under the heading "Brass Tacks Are Best; They Last Longer," include speculation by most of the Klail City Mexican Americans as to the guilt of Jehu. As in part 2, there are voices that speculate as to Jehu's whereabouts—and so the novel ends.

Analysis

The novel is an astute critique of the questionable tactics used by power brokers to control the socioeconomic and political lives of Mexican Americans in the Rio Grande Valley, of which Belken County is a microcosm. The events of the book reflect the real source of conflict between Anglo-Texans and Texas Mexicans, the latter of whom have been politically controlled since Texas became a state. The novel symbolizes the plight of Texas Mexicans who are subjected to the political dictates of Anglo-Texan power brokers and who are socially segregated from Anglo-Americans.

The novel is also about growing up Mexican American, about honor, loyalty, bravery, and love. The chronicles of the Texas Mexicans who work and live in the valley represent a lifestyle that is a cross between Anglo and Mexican society, from a sociological and political perspective. The young people will grow up, go to war for their country,

and come back to the valley with little change in their socioeconomic and political status, which means that they will fulfill the roles that Anglo-Texan society has designed for them. There will be few surprises, for only a few Mexican Americans will ever be accepted as equals in the ranks of Anglo-Texan society. This sense of inequity pervades the novel; growing up Mexican American means coming to terms with this reality, trying to conform to the dictates of Anglo-American society while still maintaining a cultural identity. The educated Mexican Americans accept leadership roles to challenge their people's subjugation; the moment they need help, however, their elders turn on them, breaking whatever cohesion existed between the older generation and the changing new breed of upward-bound valley Mexican Americans.

Critical Context

Dear Rafe, Hinojosa's first attempt to use the epistolary form, earned him wide recognition. The epistolary novel has not been much used in the twentieth century, but Hinojosa's work champions this literary form. Furthermore, Hinojosa avoids using formal English. When making reference to local things, he uses elliptical expressions; for

example, he shortens words (writer is shortened to "wri," for example). These usages can be confusing to the reader at first; however, Hinojosa employs these stylistic devices so cleverly that the reader is soon able to figure out their meaning. This approach has helped to earn Hinojosa a reputation as the writer of the understatement.

THE DEATH OF ARTEMIO CRUZ

Author: Carlos Fuentes (1928-   )
Type of work: Novel
Type of plot: Philosophical realism
Time of plot: 1889-1959
Locale: Mexico
First published: *La muerte de Artemio Cruz*, 1962 (English translation, 1964)

Principal Characters

Artemio Cruz, a wealthy, corrupt landowner in postrevolutionary Mexico. He remembers significant episodes of his seventy years while on his deathbed. He searches for his own identity, which is, like the Mexican national identity, based on the rape of the mother. Cruz joins the Mexican Revolution determined to fight against the landowners and for the rights of the peasants who work on the land. He associates himself with the winning faction of General Álvaro Obregón and during the first years of the revolution meets Regina. After she is brutally killed, he becomes a selfish opportunist who never opens his heart to anyone. Two years later, he is captured. While awaiting execution, he discusses the meaning of life and revolution with Gonzalo Bernal. Cruz saves himself by offering to turn traitor. Later, he introduces himself to Gonzalo's wealthy family and marries his sister Catalina. That marriage gives him a ticket to the upper class. He comes to epitomize the class that he fought in the revolution. He dies as an extremely prosperous man, surrounded by the people who despise him, lovers and business partners who want to use him, without any real friends and without any ideals.

Gonzalo Bernal, a young idealist who joins the revolution in order to fight against the establishment represented by his rich father. He dies disillusioned, in solidarity with other prisoners, realizing that the revolution will not bring desired changes. He exemplifies honesty and spiritual strength.

Lorenzo, the son of Artemio Cruz. He is faced with situations similar to those of his father, but he always chooses an honorable solution. In that sense, he can be seen as a redeemer of his father's spiritually and morally wasted life. Lorenzo dies in the Spanish Civil War.

Regina, Cruz's first love. She is hanged by Cruz's opponents at the beginning of the revolution. With her dies a romantic, open, and honest side of Artemio Cruz.

Catalina, Cruz's wife and Bernal's sister. She and Cruz never open up to each other, because she sees herself as property given to him by her father. Neither will she forgive the betrayal of her brother. Although Cruz claims that his love for her is genuine and honest, he has several mistresses during their marriage and stays with her only because of social status and the political implications of a breakup.

The Novel

Artemio Cruz is on his deathbed when the novel opens. Stricken by a gastric attack after his return from a business trip to Hermosillo on April 9, 1959, he lies in his mansion in a fashionable section of Mexico City, the moral corruption of his life causing as much stench in his nostrils as the processes of decay already at work in his body. An officious priest tries to administer the last sacrament in spite of his protests; Cruz had abandoned the church years before. Doctors subject him to the indignity of their instruments as they examine his body. In the background are his estranged wife and the daughter who despises him. Although they pretend concern for the dying man, their greatest concern is the whereabouts of his will, and he refuses to tell them. His only hold on reality is a tape recording, an account of business deals and proposed transactions, played by his secretary, Padilla. While these people jostle about his bed, Cruz drifts between past and present, not in any coherent order but in a series of flashbacks tracing the course that has brought him to his present state.

Thus readers see him in 1919, an ambitious young veteran of the revolution arriving at the home of the Bernal family in Perales, ostensibly to bring to a bereaved father and sister an account of Gonzalo Bernal's death before a Villista firing squad, in reality to insinuate himself into the confidence of the old *haciendado*, marry his daughter, and get possession of the Bernal estates. His wife, Catalina, never fully realizes that Artemio had really fallen in love with her; influenced by Father Páez, the family priest, she believes that her marriage bought her father's security and her own at the cost of her soul, and she hates herself for the passion to which Artemio moves her at night. In the end the two despise each other, and she blames him when their son, whom he has removed from her control, is killed while fighting in the Spanish Civil War. Before Catalina there was Regina, the camp follower he also loved, taken hostage by Villa's troops and hanged. After her death there were other women: Lilia, the young mistress he took on a holiday in Acapulco and who betrayed him there, and Laura, who later married someone else.

Artemio's adventures are not all with women. Readers see him ruining his neighbors at Perales and getting possession of their lands, using bribery and blackmail to buy his first election as a deputy, giving lavish parties where the guests who mocked him behind his back were not supposed to bore him with their conversation, negotiating big deals, ruining competitors, and all the while preparing himself for the loneliness and desolation he feels when his time comes to die. Close to the end of the novel, Fuentes presents two episodes that throw light on the later years of Artemio's career. One is the story of his capture by a Villista troop. Sentenced to death, he decides to give information to the enemy. Although he later kills the officer to whom he had promised betrayal, he had at least been guilty by intent. Some justification for his deed is given in the words of Gonzalo Bernal, the disillusioned idealist who nevertheless goes bravely to his death. Bernal declares that once a revolution has been corrupted by those who act only to live well, to rise in the world, the battles may still be fought and won, but the revolution without compromise has been lost to the ambitious and the mediocre. The last episode tells how it all began. Artemio Cruz was born on the *petate*, the mat symbolic of the peon's condition, the son of a decayed landowner and a half-caste girl. His only friend during his early years is Lunero, a mulatto who serves the needs of Artemio's half-crazed old grandmother and his lazy, drunken uncle. After the boy accidentally shoots his uncle, he runs away to Veracruz. There, a schoolmaster tutors Artemio and prepares him for the part he is to play in the revolution before he loses his ideals and makes the choice of betrayal and rejection that leads him to the corrupting use of power in other men's lives and his own.

Fuentes' meaning in this final episode seems clear. The revolution, in the end, was betrayed by the common people who had made it.

Analysis

The character of Artemio Cruz is handled with a considerable degree of subtlety and skill. Fuentes does not gloss over his cynicism, opportunism, or brutal ruthlessness. Artemio is saved from becoming a monster of pure abstraction and calculation by his relationships with the three people who mean most in his life: Lunero, the devoted mulatto for whose sake he committed a murder; Regina, the girl killed by Villistas; and his son Lorenzo. Through the novel, like a refrain, runs a reference to the time just before Lorenzo went off to fight in the Spanish Civil War, when father and son took a morning ride toward the sea. By the end of the novel, Artemio's story has been told as one man's journey with no real beginning or end in time, containing love, solitude, violence, power, friendship, disillusionment, corruption, forgetfulness, innocence, and delight. There is also the realization of how at the end a man's death is joined to his beginning.

To get his story told, Fuentes employs three voices. The first is the obvious third person, used to present in dramatic form the events of Artemio's life as they are pieced together in past time. The second is the "I" of the present as the old man lies dying, shrinks from the decay of his body, and takes fitful account of what is going on around him. The third is a vatic presence that is never identified—conscience? consciousness?—addressing Artemio as "you." This presence is the unrealized Artemio, the man he might have been. He is a lover of the land that the real Artemio Cruz robbed and raped, the product of history, perhaps the re-created moral conscience of the revolution. He speaks in metaphors, poetry, and prophecy about history and time, places and people, because they belong to the beautiful but sad and tragic land of his birth.

The Death of Artemio Cruz is a divided book, terse yet chaotic, passionate, ironic. Too much has been made, undoubtedly, of Fuentes as one of Mexico's angry young men. In spite of his Marxist beliefs, he is essentially a romantic. He is also the possessor of an exuberant, powerful talent.

Critical Context

Mexican intellectuals of the mid-twentieth century were often self-conscious in much the same way William Faulkner and writers of his generation were self-conscious: obsessed by feeling for place, burdened by the past, uneasy in the new society, seeking to reclaim in their stories and poems old values lost in the processes of change. Believing that history had isolated them in a particular moment in time, the parochialism of the revolution, Mexican writers often turned inward to create a literature veering between moods of fury and outrage and the poetry of nocturnal silence, living, to borrow a phrase from poet Octavio Paz, in a "labyrinth of solitude." It was José Luis Cuevas, the avant-garde painter, who first used the term "Cactus Curtain" in protest against the isolation of the Mexican artist. In an earlier novel, *Where the Air Is Clear* (1958), Fuentes said that it is impossible to explain Mexico. Instead, the artist believes in it with anger and a feeling of outrage, with passion, and with a sense of alienation.

This statement carries the reader a long way toward an understanding of Fuentes' fiction. It is clear that he rejected Mexican life as constituted in the 1960's, but at the same time he uses it in his novels to test his sensuous powers and dramatic vigor. The country he writes about is not the land that tourists see or a land of tradition; it is a country of art, a place and people transformed by compelling imagination into something rich and strange and meaningful. This is one reason for his restless experiments with technique, the broken narrative structures, the shifting points of view, his lovely, solemn hymns to landscapes and time, the interior monologues by which he tries to probe the national conscience as well as the consciousness of the people. If he has not yet assimilated in his own writing the influences he has absorbed from such varied figures as Marcel Proust, James Joyce, William Faulkner, and John Dos Passos, he has nevertheless put his borrowings to brilliant use in catching the tempo of Mexican life in a stage of uncertainty and indirection.

DELIA'S SONG

Author: Lucha Corpi (1945-   )
Type of work: Novel
Type of plot: *Bildungsroman*
Time of plot: The late 1960's to the mid-1970's
Locale: Berkeley and the San Francisco Bay area in California
First published: 1989

Principal Characters

Delia Trevino, a Mexican American student at the University of California, Berkeley. A freshman from a Mexican background, Delia becomes an activist for Third World liberation, participates in campus revolution, and falls in love with one of the idealistic heroes of the revolution.

Jeff Morones, also a young activist at the University of California, Berkeley. He is the object—and ultimate winner—of Delia's affections.

Roger N. Hart, alias "James Joyce." Hart is a marine biologist around whom Delia's fantasies turn after an erotic encounter at a Day of the Dead costume party at a friend's home.

Professor Mattie N. Johnson, Delia's mentor. Mattie is a sociologist and activist and is influential in Delia's intellectual, political, and personal growth.

Marta Trevino de Ciotti, Delia's beloved aunt. Delia lives with Aunt Marta in Monterey after leaving Berkeley; Aunt Marta serves as Delia's connection with her Mexican heritage and provides family background.

Samuel Corona, a graduate student in sociology. The intellectual leader of the student revolution, Samuel wins Delia's trust, but he crumbles into alcoholism after the political riots.

Julio Singer, a conga-playing poet. A member of the student activist group with which Delia becomes associated, Julio later becomes a published poet.

Sara Gonzalez, Delia's roommate and member of the liberation movement in Berkeley.

The Novel

Delia's Song recounts a young woman's maturation during the turbulence of student riots and civil rights movements in academic institutions during the late 1960's. The novel is divided into three sections and consists of twelve chapters.

The story begins with a flashback in an italicized passage that suggests the intensity of Delia's emotional state. The book then switches immediately into the central event of the main plot, which took place earlier in the novel's chronology. The disjointed nature of the plot requires the reader to remain attentive to cues within the narrative in order to make chronological sense of the sequence

of events, but the unconventional structure is one of the novel's best features.

Delia, dressed as the Carmelite Santa Teresa and overwhelmed by suddenly erupting memories of fire, terror, and threatening predators, has an emotional blackout as she contemplates a tenacious single yellow rose hanging to its branch in November. (The rose is a unifying symbol throughout the narrative.) She swoons and is rescued by none other than James Joyce himself, or so it seems to the distracted Delia, who is herself not who she seems in this scene. Gathering her wits, she continues to her destination, a "Day of the Dead" costume party given by Mattie Johnson, her mentor.

The narrative then shifts to the story's chronological beginning, as Delia is introduced to the
highly charged political campus life of Berkeley.
She meets Samuel, Jeff, and Sara and begins her
involvement with the social movement to establish
a department for Third World studies at the university. The students and idealistic activists of MASC
(the Mexican American Student Confederation)
are taken with Delia's mysterious but intelligent
personality.

The political and sexual tensions build. The
confrontation between the students and the administration culminates in a conflict with the police, the sting of tear gas, and sudden mayhem. In
the midst of the upheaval, Jeff and Delia kiss,
ostensibly to divert attention from themselves as
activists, but obviously with much passion. Their
kiss creates a romantic connection that forms the
love theme of the novel, but the could-be lovers are
soon star-crossed, separated by youthful misunderstandings when Jeff, heroically carrying a wounded
Delia away from the rioting, takes amiss a comment she makes. The two become increasingly
sensitive, estranged, and huffy, and the chapter ends
with Delia's pride smarting when she learns that
Jeff has requested a transfer to another campus.

The group disintegrates after the revolution, as
internal and external pressures create personality
conflicts and inevitable disillusionment. Samuel
begins to drink heavily, and Delia, involved with
an abusive lover (the most disturbing of several
disappointing lovers), becomes more and more
depressed, agonizing over her failures with Jeff.
Delia's decline parallels the decline of the student
activist group, and Delia's despair echoes the difficulty of the group's idealistic dreams.

The narrative returns to the Day of the Dead
costume party, where Delia has gathered her wits
enough to proceed on her journey after her fall in
the first chapter. She arrives late at the party and
again encounters the mysterious "James Joyce,"
who, like herself, is in costume. She and "Joyce"
consummate their desires by making love in the
back yard under the barbecue pit (a spicy reference
to Delia's country of origin, its folklore, and her

sexuality), after which "Joyce" gives Delia his
card, encouraging her to call him; she does not.

The second major movement of the novel takes
Delia away from Berkeley, away from the two men
of whom she is enamored—Jeff Morones of the
kiss and now "James Joyce" of the barbecue pit—
to her Aunt Marta's home in Monterey, California.

The history of Delia's family occupies the center of the novel and is related through conversations with Aunt Marta. Delia's growing commitment to her writing parallels her healing focus on
herself and her heritage. When the lost lover Jeff
appears, invited to the house by an unsuspecting
Aunt Marta, the interrupted romance resumes on a
stronger beat, but Delia remains unsettled because
of her obsession with "James Joyce," who, it turns
out, is a distant relative of Mattie and a widower.

Delia and Jeff, however, begin a courtship and
engage in a number of lovers' quarrels, which serve
in part to develop the novel's social criticism of
sexism. Delia decides, upon receiving an invitation
from Mattie, to return to Berkeley for a visit and to
look up her "Joyce," the tormenting object of her
fantasies since their erotic encounter.

The third section of the novel narrates Delia's
return to Berkeley to say farewell to Mattie (who
has decided to move to Honduras) and to meet
Roger N. Hart, alias "Joyce," in order to settle the
question of her attraction to him. After much indecision, she does call him. She discovers that although he is a decent and worthy man who has held
her in his own mind all this while, she is not, in
fact, in love with him. Thus she returns to a rather
nervous Jeff, but not without first coming to terms
with a lifetime of conflict through her writing.

She returns to Monterey, completes her book
(one very like *Delia's Song*), shares the story and
manuscript with a concerned Aunt Marta, and
eventually hands the typed manuscript over to a
mystified and upset Jeff, who has not understood
his lover's odd behavior. The book is Delia's statement of personal liberation, saying to Jeff, in effect, "this is who I am, take me as I am or not at
all." Aunt Marta questions the wisdom of such a
brash and honest move, but Delia is for once certain of her actions.

Analysis

Delia's Song describes the political, sexual, and emotional tensions characterizing America in the late 1960's and early 1970's. Divided into three major sections, *Delia's Song* outlines the pain and excitement of this turbulent period through the experiences of its eponymous principal character, Delia, as she emerges from naïveté into a new social and sexual maturity.

The events of Corpi's first novel are strongly autobiographical, echoing a young Mexican woman's quest for literary respect, sexual identity and equality, an academic degree, and a fulfilling love during the political transformations of late-1960's California. One of the most effective social themes of *Delia's Song* is the disturbing reality of sexism as it is experienced in Chicano culture. Delia must struggle against her own family's limiting attitudes as well as those of her colleagues. Her two brothers, both dead (one shot as a soldier in Vietnam, the other from a drug overdose), receive the affections from her mother that Delia desires and deserves. The deepest expression of her struggle for sexual and intellectual identity takes place in herself, as she moves from being an idealistic girl carrying many resentments and low self-esteem into a fully developed artist, academic, and partner in love.

The narrative structure suggests a field of awareness rather than a linear, historical sequence of events. Dreams, flashbacks, sprinkles of family history, and memories all interrupt the plot. Stream-of-consciousness flashbacks, vignettes of dream imagery, bits of journal entries, family oral histories, and even newspaper clippings are used as narrative elements. The entire story is presented in a limited-omniscient point of view, filtered principally through the emotions and mind of Delia, but taking liberties by revealing the inner thoughts of other characters as well.

The structure of the novel presents one of the main themes: that life happens all at once, at the level of consciousness, and has meaning to the degree that people have awareness of it. Delia's life makes sense only when looked at as an entire fabric, not as a series of logically related events.

The three sections create a circular narrative structure, suggesting the heroic "monomyth" typical of James Joyce's work. This structure takes the heroine from her fall into illusion and experience, into an incubation period leading to severe soul-searching, finally returning her to the initial locale, Berkeley, so that she can be released from the past and rejoin her first love as a fully individualized woman.

With the presence of Joyce felt from the first pages, both in the stream-of-consciousness narrative technique and the actual appearance of "James Joyce," a costumed man who lifts Delia from a dizzying fall, *Delia's Song* traces the cyclical heroic path in its three main sections. After the first "fall" when Delia meets "Joyce" in the first pages of the novel, Delia continues her heroine's journey through an initiation into academia, life, and sexuality to her three-part return: her return to her true love, Jeff; her "return" to campus, to Mattie's, and to her fantasy; and finally her "return" to a sense of wholeness, a sense of selfhood, which is what the journey is all about. Her journey back to Berkeley completes the heroine's quest cycle, allowing her to complete the novel she has been writing, to understand the difference between the illusory lover and the real one, and to resolve the inner tensions that have kept her distant and tormented. As the novel ends, readers are promised that the truth has set Delia free, that Jeff will understand her evasive and erratic behavior, and that Delia's heroic quest has ended at last with a Joycean "yes," uniting her not only with her lover but also, more important, with an enduring sense of her own worth as a woman and as a writer.

Critical Context

Delia's Song is the first published novel of a well-established poet, but it is not a strong work. Lucha Corpi has gained critical acclaim for her *Palabras de mediodia/Noon Words* (1980) and is well respected as a poet and fiction writer, with works appearing in numerous journals. Yet *Delia's Song*, while fascinating in its efforts, fails to live up to Corpi's artistic reputation.

Delia's Song has much to recommend it, but as a fully grown, full-blown novel, it fails. One senses that it may have been hastily written, if gathered over three decades; one senses that the author may have been purging a past as much as creating a work of art. These speculations come to mind because the characters stay, for the most part, flat and undeveloped, even though the characterization of Delia does compel attention and respect.

The psychological complexity of Delia—even though she never quite becomes a flawed, endearing, complete human being—holds the key to the novel's contribution to modern literature. The importance of the novel is its celebration of the intellect and sexuality of a Mexican (and, by extension, any) woman. In the description of Delia's self-doubt, her tormenting concern about her talents, and her erratic (sometimes saintly, sometimes sexy) personal development, the novel indicates the jagged inner life of any young woman with a mind trying to maintain integrity in a world that is given to devaluing her.

THE DEVIL IN TEXAS

Author: Aristeo Brito (1942-   )
Type of work: Novel
Type of plot: Historical realism
Time of plot: The 1850's to the 1970's
Locale: The Texas-Mexico border towns of Presidio and Ojinaga and the surrounding area
First published: *El diablo en Texas*, 1976 (English translation, 1990)

Principal Characters

Ben Lynch (Don Benito), an Anglo-American landowner who represents everything undesirable. He acquires his land in a legal but unethical agreement with Tía Paz, who was in no shape mentally to resist his overtures. In order to secure his position among the Mexican American population, he marries Francisco's sister. The story of his vengeance against anyone who opposes him reveals the extent to which he will go in his exploitation and manipulation of the minority population. By virtue of his Anglo-American heritage, he is able to find support from law enforcement agencies. His character personifies everything evil.

Francisco Uranga (Don Pancho), a pathetic figure whose life as a journalist and a lawyer is spent trying to correct the injustices he sees perpetrated upon the Chicano population. Francisco speaks for himself, his family, and the Mexican American population in general. It is through his acts of resistance, which are reinforced by his sons and their sons, that the reader sees a panorama of abuse that extends over several generations and clearly is suggestive of similar abuses in other communities with the same racial mix. What Francisco's character lacks in depth, it makes up for in intensity. His persistent dedication to exposing abuse and cruelty along the Texas border, despite the alienation he experiences on both sides of the river, helps to establish him as a sympathetic character whose determination to right wrongs merits respect.

Jesús and **Reyes,** Francisco's sons, who continue the resistance effort in their own manner.

Jesús is killed by Lynch's men because he refuses to stop transporting Mexican workers across the border. Reyes becomes a part of a renegade band of Mexican Americans who sabotage Lynch at every opportunity by organizing resistance to the Texas Rangers.

José Uranga, the unborn fetus who "speaks" from Marcela's womb and returns to Presidio when his father José is dying in 1970. His character represents the typical Chicano youth (perhaps inspired by the author's own experiences) who escapes from an oppressive environment and experiences some success in the dominant Anglo-American culture, only to realize as a mature adult the strong ties he still feels for Chicano culture.

Marcela Uranga, who is married to José Uranga. Like many Mexican American wives, she is trapped in a society that often deprives her of physical and emotional support. When her husband escapes to Mexico, she is left to deal with deprivation and physical discomfort. Upon attending a mass, she sees an apparition of the Devil winking at her with a mocking grin. The emotional trauma she experiences pushes her to the edge of insanity.

Chente, Marcela's uncle, dies an untimely death that is brought about by extreme working conditions, reinforcing the prevalence of exploitation across all aspects of Mexican American life. His conversations with Vicke, Marcela's mother, are poignant reminders of the hopelessness and helplessness of the Mexican laborer.

The Devil, the most powerful character in the

story. He takes many forms, both real and symbolic. He is the snake coiled around the cross that stands high on the mountain overlooking the river; the river and later the bridge that control the destiny of the Mexican Americans; Ben Lynch, who has more power than God himself in Texas; the goat-footed stranger who appears at a party; the tall cowboy who winks at Marcela in church; the train conductor; and the Green Devil who operates the capitalistic agrarian system. In fact, the Devil is anything and everything evil and oppressive and symbolizes the blatant insensitivity and evil intention of the Anglo-American population along the border with Mexico.

The Novel

No plot, as such, exists in this short novel, but the activities of the two main families named in the work can be traced through almost 120 years (1853-1970). The book begins with a prologue, told in the stream-of-consciousness technique, that sets the stage for the following narrative, told from multiple points of view. The next three parts, "Presidio 1883," "Presidio 1942," and "Presidio 1970," illustrate the conflict between Anglo-Americans, represented by the Lynch lineage, and Mexicans (who eventually become Mexican Americans, or Chicanos), represented by the Uranga family. The action throughout the book takes place in the border towns of Presidio, Texas, and Ojinaga, Mexico, on opposite sides of the Rio Grande. No main character, except perhaps the Devil, is introduced in the prologue, but the barrenness and desolation of western Texas, which will be the locus for years of conflict between the neighboring communities, is emphasized. Since Aristeo Brito was reared in this same environment of antagonism and conflict and, as an adult, returned "home" to research the book, many similarities between the author's life and the narrative appear.

"Presidio 1883" details the Anglo-American domination of the area, introducing Ben Lynch (Don Benito), whose wealth and influence enable him to threaten, cajole, or cheat the Mexicans. He is powerful and has the strong arm of the Texas Rangers on his side whenever there is a conflict between him and the Mexicans he employs. At one point, he discovers a ring of horse thieves and proceeds to host a party to which they are given a special invitation. Much to their surprise, the thieves are summarily slaughtered. The only person willing to stand up to Don Benito is Francisco Uranga, a lawyer and journalist who encourages the Mexican Americans to resist oppression; at one point, Francisco becomes a representative for the Mexican government. His efforts are in vain: One of his sons, Jesús, is ambushed and drowned in the Rio Grande one night; another becomes a part of a subversive band of roaming outlaws. His own sister Rosario marries Ben Lynch, the devil incarnate. Throughout this part of the book, incidents detail the misfortune and abuse experienced by the Chicanos. One such incident is the death of a twelve-year-old who dies as a result of a lung disorder contracted while working long hours in the mines. Descriptions of several key locations, symbolic as well as real, are provided in "Presidio 1883": a cave situated deep in the Santa Cruz Mountains, a train station, and a fort where devils and spirits roam at night telling their sad life stories and where tourists are taken (for a fee). In addition to the human characters from the two main families, the Devil in many disguises appears in this section of the book.

In "Presidio 1942," life continues much the same, although the Texas Rangers are replaced by the Border Patrol and some farm laborers, such as Teléforo and his son Chale, acquire a degree of professional status. Because these Hispanics have the responsibility of controlling the undocumented workers, their position in the social hierarchy is somewhat enhanced. Life in the little agrarian community continues to be boring and depraved. The young people who do not flee to a better existence somewhere else in Texas spend their time as shiftless bums in bars or brothels. Francisco Uranga's grandson José, a sharecropper on the land his family used to own, abandons his home and pregnant wife in order to dodge the draft by escaping across the border. His wife Marcela dies in childbirth, but the fetus speaks fervently from the womb about social injustices perpetrated on generations of Urangas. The surreal presence of a powerful and malignant devil continues to stalk the land.

Years later, in "Presidio 1970," José Uranga (the fetus in section 2) returns to the deathbed of his father. In a fantastic dialogue with the dead man, José learns of his father's reasons for fleeing and of his experiences in prison. Obviously, the plight of the Chicano has never improved, despite the passage of time and changing generations. Although he is initially bitter and resentful, the younger José decides to remain in Presidio to combat the wrongs perpetuated on his genetic and cultural fellow sufferers.

Analysis

The Devil in Texas might be described as a collage of images, dates, events, and characters who people the towns of Presidio and Ojinaga. The three dates used to divide the book do more to suggest timelessness than fixed time, and the historical and spiritual journey of Mexican Americans effected by the Treaty of Guadalupe Hidalgo in 1848 is a fractured one.

The theme of exploitation (past, present, and future) is illustrated by the life stories of the Uranga family, whose accident of birth causes them to lose lives, prestige, land, power—even human dignity. The fetus in "Presidio 1942" who returns in "Presidio 1970" may represent a sign of hope for the Chicano, because he seems to have in his blood the same resistant spirit of his ancestors, despite his earlier abandonment of the cause.

Many images appear and reappear: a haunted fort that is used as a tourist attraction for the few visitors who find their way to the remote land; a river that symbolizes life but also division and death; a bridge that is built more for control of the traffic between the two countries than for convenience; a cave where the Devil surely lives. By far the most dominant image is that of the Devil, who takes on various guises but who, for the purposes of this social commentary, is represented by Anglo-Americans in general and Ben Lynch in particular. In fact, everything evil, painful, or in any way restrictive is credited to the power of the "Devil in Texas." Initiated in the prologue, these symbols carry more narrative momentum than do the named characters. One of the most impressive features of the text lies in its "holographic" effect: One can begin reading almost any section and experience the impact, if not the details, of the other sections.

Critical Context

The Devil in Texas, first published in Spanish in 1976, is an experiment in narrative technique in the tradition of Juan Rulfo's *Pedro Páramo* (1955) and works by such other writers as Agustín Yáñez and Carlos Fuentes, who cast their stories in a semifantastic ambience. Brito's work differs, however, in that it defines the Chicano experience. Its Texas border setting does not restrict it to a regional audience; its powerful emotional message of alienation and powerlessness should be familiar to the "hyphenated" citizen of any race or location. Brito was one of the first to use (in the original Spanish version) Mexican Spanish, Chicano Spanish, English, and a mixture of English and Spanish in a written linguistic pattern typical of oral linguistic expressions, hence capturing the spirit of the issues together with the prosaic reality. The myriad narrative voices that tell the story also contribute to the mosaic experience of the novel.

Aristeo Brito's unique blend of fact and fiction laced with mythical and symbolic overtones transforms an apparently simple story line into a collage of images that project a powerful social message. With its rich intricacy of plot, theme, and symbolism, *The Devil in Texas* qualifies as an integral part of the canon of Chicano literature.

THE DEVIL TO PAY IN THE BACKLANDS

Author: João Guimarães Rosa (1908-1967)
Type of work: Novel
Type of plot: Psychological realism
Time of plot: The late nineteenth and early twentieth centuries
Locale: The Brazilian backlands
First published: *Grande Sertão: Veredas*, 1956 (English translation, 1963)

Principal Characters

Riobaldo, the narrator and protagonist. His life takes a major turn when, at the age of fourteen, he meets Diadorim, a girl who passes for a boy and who belongs to a family heavily involved in politically oriented armed movements in the backlands. After the death of his mother, he goes to live with his godfather, who teaches him the ways of the *jagunço*, or gunman. He then enters the *jagunço* life. In his travels, Riobaldo again meets Diadorim and joins her band. With her support and the strength he gains from a supposed encounter with the devil, he wins the leadership of the band and achieves victory over Heremógenes, the murderer of Diadorim's father, Joca Ramiro. As a wealthy old farmer, Riobaldo tells the story that is the novel as a way of discovering if he, in fact, sold his soul to the devil.

Diadorim, the daughter of Joca Ramiro. She lives her life as a man. She befriends Riobaldo and later becomes his faithful companion. After the murder of her father at the hands of Heremógenes, she becomes obsessed with taking revenge. Riobaldo's rise to leadership is the vehicle by which she is given the opportunity to realize her goal. During the last battle, she meets Heremógenes in hand-to-hand combat. Both die in a bloody scene. After her death, Riobaldo discovers that she is a woman.

Zé Bebelo, an outsider who seeks to bring law and order to the backlands. He also wants to become an elected official after his days as a *jagunço* leader. He fails in both of his attempts to achieve dominance. In the first, he is defeated by Joca Ramiro, and in the second, he is deposed by Riobaldo. He makes a third appearance at the end of the novel as a cattle buyer and entrepreneur.

Heremógenes, the leader of a band under Joca Ramiro. He is there when Zé Bebelo is defeated and speaks against him at the trial. He becomes disgruntled when Joca Ramiro allows Zé Bebelo to go free. Heremógenes later murders Joca Ramiro. Many of the characters believe that his success as a leader comes from having made a pact with the devil. His physical appearance lends credence to that notion. His death leaves the lingering question of whether the devil really exists and whether he can have dominion over a person.

Madeiro Vaz, a strong and committed leader with an impeccable reputation. The followers of Joca Ramiro rally to him after the death of Joca Ramiro. His commitment is so absolute that he burned his possessions before he departed to become a leader.

Joca Ramiro, the leader of the *jagunço* bands in the backlands. He is revered even during his life. His death sets the stage for the climax of the story.

The Novel

The Devil to Pay in the Backlands is narrated by the protagonist, Riobaldo, who tells his story in an attempt to resolve the psychological torment caused by the possibility that he sold his soul to the devil. João Guimarães Rosa's novel merges the psychological journey of the protagonist with his epic adventures in the lawless backlands of northeastern Brazil around the beginning of the twentieth century.

The action of the novel is narrated to a fictional interlocutor during a three-day period. The reader is aware that there is an interactive listener to the narration because the narrator appears to react to the listener's comments, even though the comments themselves are not communicated to the reader. The goal of the narration appears to be to discover whether the devil exists and whether a person can sell the authority over his or her soul to this entity. These challenging questions, intimately involved with the notion of good and evil, are unresolved at the end of the novel.

Chronologically, the story begins with Riobaldo as a fourteen-year-old who frequents a landing on the Janeiro River, begging for money to pay for a vow his mother made for his recovery from an illness. There he meets Diadorim, a girl who masquerades as a boy named Reinaldo. She invites him for a boat ride on the Janeiro and the São Francisco rivers. With Diadorim's encouragement, Riobaldo is able to overcome his fear of the churning and treacherous waters of the São Francisco and reach the other side. On the other side, Riobaldo forges a special relationship with Diadorim that lasts until her death in a battle with Heremógenes.

After the death of his mother, Riobaldo goes to live with his godfather, Selorico Mendes. Selorico Mendes teaches Riobaldo how to shoot and how to handle a knife and a club. He tells Riobaldo stories about *jagunço* life in the backlands. He also introduces Riobaldo to Joca Ramiro and Heremógenes, who lodge at their place for a time.

Eventually, Riobaldo decides to leave his godfather's side to join Zé Bebelo, the leader of an armed band. Zé Bebelo hires Riobaldo as his teacher and introduces Riobaldo to the violence of the backlands. Zé Bebelo has come to the backlands not to accept its way of life but to impose a new order. This appears to contradict Riobaldo's own reasons for being there. Riobaldo leaves Zé Bebelo's band and goes his own way.

Riobaldo again meets Diadorim and joins her band. Their band and other groups come together under the overall leadership of Joca Ramiro to defeat Zé Bebelo. Zé Bebelo asks for a trial, a request granted by Joca Ramiro. At the trial, Zé Bebelo manages to convince the majority of the leaders to set him free. Joca Ramiro sets him free with the condition that he is not to come back during Joca Ramiro's lifetime. Some of the leaders do not agree to freeing Zé Bebelo. Among them is Heremógenes, who later murders Joca Ramiro and plunges the backlands into a new state of violence.

The followers of Joca Ramiro, including Riobaldo and Diadorim, hurry to join Madeiro Vaz for a march of vengeance against Heremógenes. They serve first under Madeiro Vaz and then under Zé Bebelo, with equally negative results. Madeiro Vaz dies after an aborted attempt to cross the Sussuarão desert. On the other side is Heremógenes' home, which they sought to destroy. Zé Bebelo, on his second attempt to lead, manages to get everyone lost in the depths of the backlands.

Frustrated by the lack of progress against Heremógenes, Riobaldo goes to the middle of a crossroads one night and calls for the devil. Riobaldo does not see the devil but does feel a new sense of power. He soon deposes Zé Bebelo and assumes command of the band. His newfound strength is seen in his attempt to cross the Sussuarão desert. Even with extensive preparations, the previous attempt to cross, under the leadership of Madeiro Vaz, had failed. Now Riobaldo, without any preparations, easily crosses the desert. His band burns Heremógenes' house and takes his wife prisoner.

The last great battle occurs on the plains of Tamanduá-Tão, in the town of Paredão. The clash ends in hand-to-hand combat that sees Diadorim fight Heremógenes to their mutual deaths. It is after her death, when she is being prepared for burial, that the truth of Diadorim's sex is discovered. This deepens Riobaldo's sense of loss and causes him to retrace the steps of their travels together in order to find solace.

Analysis

Theme and structure come together in the novel to depict a journey on the part of the narrator-protagonist in search of spiritual and psychological wholeness. The narrator, a wealthy farmer, relates the story of his life as a young *jagunço* in the Brazilian backlands in order to discover whether he, in fact, made a pact with the devil and whether the devil really exists. The psychological journey of the narrator is mirrored by the journey to manhood and leadership of the young protagonist, Riobaldo. The end of the novel sees the questions relating to the pact and the existence of the devil go unanswered, as good and evil are demonstrated to be integral parts of the human condition.

The story is narrated in three days, consistent with the structure of Riobaldo's adventure, which includes three threshold experiences. In his first experience, Riobaldo meets Diadorim and goes for a boat ride with his new friend on the Janeiro and São Francisco rivers. The event transforms Riobaldo and symbolically initiates him into the world of the backlands. In the second experience, Riobaldo goes to a crossroads at midnight and calls for the devil. Although the devil does not appear, Riobaldo comes back invigorated with a power that allows him to take the leadership of the outlaw band. The last threshold experience is also a three-day affair. Riobaldo's band defeats part of Heremógenes' group and prepares for the final battle. After the initial victory, Riobaldo hears that there is a young girl traveling along a river nearby. Believing her to be Otacilia, his betrothed, Riobaldo leaves the group to look for her. In leaving the group, he also leaves behind the power that made him invincible. He later returns to the group but is only a minor participant in the last battle, in which Diadorim and Heremógenes die at each other's hands.

The aftermath of the battle sees the protagonist resolve a situation that had been of major concern throughout his relationship with Diadorim. Since their first meeting on the Janeiro and São Francisco rivers, Riobaldo and Diadorim shared special feelings for each other. Those feelings eventually grew to a love and passion with erotic overtones. Their attempts to hide their feelings are, to the reader, at best clumsy and transparent. The discovery that Diadorim is a woman resolves the confusion caused by Riobaldo's feelings for her. It also leaves Riobaldo with a deep sense of unfulfillment as a man and a new question of how it would have been between them had he known her true sex.

The narrator also experiences a lack of fulfillment because he finds no answers to the question of whether he lost his soul to the devil. The question is unanswered because the result of the symbolic struggle between good and evil was a draw and because the protagonist was reduced to the role of spectator at that climactic moment of the novel. The narrator will have to either accept the notion that good and evil are part of the reality of the human condition or tell the story again, hoping for a different ending.

João Guimarães Rosa displays novelistic genius in making the regional and historical both magical and universal. The backlands that he calls the *sertão* becomes a dominating and transpersonal world in which the physical and metaphysical join to create a human experience with archetypal implications. Language is enriched with established and invented regionalisms as well as classical and symbolic references. Language also becomes a vehicle structured in a dialogue-monologue framework to successfully portray the theme and structure of the quest.

Critical Context

The Devil to Pay in the Backlands, Guimarães Rosa's only novel, excited and continues to excite the literary public. The novel was published ten years after the publication of *Sagarana* (1946), a volume of short stories selected from another collection organized in 1938 but not published. In the same year that the novel was published, Guimarães Rosa also published *Corpo do Baile*, a collection of seven long stories that together with *The Devil to Pay in the Backlands* established the author as the standard of excellence in modern Brazilian prose fiction. His works represent a break with the opposing trends of rural versus urban and regionalism versus universalism traditionally part of the literary narrative in Latin America. For example, the novel, although set in the Brazilian backlands, transforms its immediate reality into spiritual and metaphysical symbols with universal implications. It uses literary techniques such as manipulation of both language and plot chronology and a monologue-dialogue that features a first-person narrator and an interlocutor.

Guimarães Rosa's contribution puts him into the company of such Magical Realism innovators as Miguel Ángel Asturias and Alejo Carpentier and the important contributors to the literary movement known as the boom of the 1960's and 1970's.

Before his death in 1967, Guimarães Rosa published *Primeiras Estórias* (1962; *The Third Bank of the River and Other Stories*, 1968) and *Tutaméia* (1967; trifle), both collections of short stories. *Estas Estorias* (1969; these stories) and *Ave, Palavra* (1970; hail word) are collections of short stories published after his death. The latter works served to embellish his well-established place in the history of Brazilian letters.

DIARY OF THE WAR OF THE PIG

Author: Adolfo Bioy Casares (1914-   )
Type of work: Novel
Type of plot: Satire
Time of plot: The near future
Locale: Buenos Aires, Argentina
First Published: *Diario de la guerra del cerdo*, 1969 (English translation, 1972)

Principal Characters

Don Isidro Vidal, an elderly widower, the novel's protagonist. Don Isidro is the leader of a social group of elderly men, the "pigs" referred to in the novel's title, who are under attack and are being murdered by a group of young men.

Isidorito Vidal, Don Isidro's son. His meager earnings support both his father and himself. When a gang of youths begins to terrorize the town, Isidorito tries to placate both sides. He participates in the group's activities but sometimes warns the old men targeted as victims. He is murdered by the group when he tries to save his father's life; they consider Isidorito a traitor.

Nélida, the young woman who falls in love with Don Isidro. She is engaged to a young man but breaks the engagement in order to be with Don Isidro, to whom she is increasingly drawn, as he is to her. When he attempts to hide from the youth group, she shelters him in her apartment.

Arturo Farrall, the leader of the gang of youths, the "Young Turks," whose death squads terrorize and murder the town's elderly citizens. The reasons he gives for the "war on the pigs" is that the population is growing too large and that the elderly are becoming a burden on society.

Néstor Labarthe, an elderly friend of Don Isidro. He is the first of Vidal's group to be murdered. His brutal murder, in the presence and pos-

sibly with the consent of his own son, causes a serious split in the Young Turks between those who attempt to avoid danger by conforming and those who try to rebel against the terrorism of this youth-oriented society.

Leandro Rey, a Spanish-born elderly friend of Don Isidro. He is nicknamed "The Thinker" by the group of aging men. Unlike the others in the group, he is not retired: He works as a baker.

James Newman (Jimmy), a member of the group of elderly men. He is kidnapped by the youth gang for a time and allegedly turns informer in order to obtain his release.

Dante Révora, a member of Don Isidro's group who tries desperately to look young by dyeing his hair. He has a reputation for being an educated man. He is terrified for his life and thinks that he can escape death by attempting to look younger.

Lucio Arévalo, another member of Don Isidro's group, formerly a newspaperman. He is described as being extremely ugly. Usually ill-shaved, he has cigarette-stained hands and flecks of dandruff on his poncho. He is the picture of an asthmatic, ailing old man. Don Isidro considers it strange that no member of their group has ever set foot into Arévalo's house. Because of his longtime affair with a teenage girl, he ends up in the hospital, kicked and beaten by a gang of youths.

The Novel

A nightly card game in a Buenos Aires café opens the action of the novel. Here, members of an elderly group discuss the topic that dominates the ensuing narrative: Members of a youth movement are exterminating old people. On their way home from the game, Don Isidro and his friends witness an encounter with one of the repressive squads of youths. In an alleyway, amid the turmoil of yelling and brutal sounds of sadistic aggression, they discover the body of an old newspaper vendor, Don Manuel. This nightmarish experience is repeated throughout the story as Don Isidro slowly discovers his precarious position in this absurd war of the pigs; that is, of the elderly.

Soon, Don Isidro feels the threat of his own extinction as the warring bands of youths raid the squalid tenements. After the death of Señor Huberman, the neighborhood upholsterer, the youth organization attacks members of Isidro's own group of cronies. First, Néstor Labarthe is killed while attending a soccer game with his son. His brutal murder, in the presence and by consent of his own son, bitterly divides the group into those who try to avoid the danger by conforming and those who try to rebel against the harassment of the youth-oriented society. The second tragedy caused by the juvenile squads sends Dante Révora, another elderly gentleman in the group, to the hospital.

In the midst of all these devastating events, Don Isidro finds refuge from his frustration in the arms of Nélida, a beautiful and young neighbor who falls in love with the protagonist. This erotic adventure becomes a turning point in the novel, for it provides the background for the examination of the polarization of the old people and their delinquent enemies: "It was as if with her beside him he would be safe, not from the young people—this threat had almost ceased to alarm him—but from the contagion to which he was clearly susceptible (given the sensitivity he felt for his environment), the insidious and terrible contagion of old age."

Love, then, becomes the catalyst that neutralizes the protagonist's pessimistic response to the biological, if not spiritual, process of decay, of aging and ultimate death: "Young people cannot understand how having no future to look forward to eliminates everything that is important in life to an old person. *The sickness is not the sick person*, he thought, *but an old man is old age, and there is no other way out but death*." More than simply providing a happy conclusion to an otherwise fantastic tale of tragic dimension, the love motif between Isidro and the young Nélida treats the stock literary convention of the power of love with such subtlety that it becomes a modern parable of frustrated desire.

Analysis

Adolfo Bioy Casares' unique interpretation of the problem of aging serves as the basic motif for a much more important and universal theme of the novel: death. The author exploits the polarization of the young and the old in an attempt to decipher the meaning of life as it draws near its end.

In the abstract and fanciful game played by the characters of the novel, the reader quickly notes the morbid symptoms of a youth-oriented society. In this fantastic world of persecution, everyone is a victim. Even the young, as Dr. Cadelago explains to the protagonist, "come to understand that every old man is what one young man or another will someday become." This fatalistic notion, in turn, provides the motive for the persecution, for in the intricate campaign to annihilate the old people, the juvenile members of this inhuman society become self-destructive. Dr. Cadelago explains the hostile obsession of the young when he clarifies the problem: "killing an old man is a kind of suicide."

Furthermore, in this oppression of the old by the young, the author delineates a universal pattern for persecution. Author D. P. Gallagher notes that the reader of this novel observes "the volatility of crowds, the persuasive power of demagogy, the problem of the divided family, the dilemma of those who believe they are not one of the victims (the old man who believes he is not yet old, like the Jew who believes he isn't a Jew), or of those who try to alter their appearance in order not to look conspicuous (the old man who dyes his hair, like the Jew who alters his nose)."

Critical Context

Bioy Casares' *Diary of the War of the Pig* brought almost immediate national and international acclaim to its author. Often dismissed as merely a disciple of and collaborator with Jorge Luis Borges, he has suffered greatly from a lack of critical attention. It was shortly after the publication of *Diary of the War of the Pig*, however, that Bioy Casares began to be recognized for his highly original contribution to the Latin American "boom" in literature. Evidence of the author's growing international popularity can be seen in the many translations of this novel into English, French, Italian, German, Portuguese, and Dutch.

Although Bioy Casares' contribution to the type of literature known as Magical Realism is weighty, especially after the 1940 appearance of *La invención de Morel* (*The Invention of Morel*, 1964), in *Diary of the War of the Pig*, he deemphasizes the magical elements of his previous writing. In its indirect satirization of social corruption and its effect on humanity *Diary of the War of the Pig* finds its most poignant message of societal reform.

DISTANT RELATIONS

Author: Carlos Fuentes (1928-   )
Type of work: Novel
Type of plot: Magical Realism
Time of plot: The early 1980's
Locale: Paris, France; Mexico; and the Caribbean
First published: *Una familia lejana*, 1980 (English translation, 1982)

Principal Characters

The Comte de Branly, a wealthy French aristocrat whose main interest is foreign travel. Most of this complex novel of parallel lives and reincarnations concerns the Comte's surrealistic adventure in a strange mansion outside Paris where he is confined as a result of an auto accident. It is probable that much of what he believes to have occurred is actually hallucinations. Although he is the viewpoint character, he is the passive victim of circumstances throughout the novel.

The narrator, a Latin American author who has taken France as his adopted country. Only at the end is it revealed that this character is a version of Carlos Fuentes. The narrator is supposedly writing out an account of incidents described to him by his friend Branly, and parts of what Branly tells him were narrated to the Comte by others. By this device, the author is able to maintain a distance from the events described and is therefore not committed to vouching for them. The reader is forced to make his or her own interpretations and thus become involved as an active participant.

The Mexican Victor Heredia, a twelve-year-old upper-class Mexican student. He is the catalyst of most of what happens in the novel. This handsome and aristocratic youth has been badly spoiled by a doting father. Victor displays violent outbursts, in one crucial instance deliberately slamming the door of Branly's Citroën on the chauffeur's hand. When Branly tries to drive the car himself, he runs into a tree and is confined to bed as an involuntary guest of the French Victor Heredia.

The French Victor Heredia, a wealthy businessman with social pretensions who proves to be vulgar and sadistic. He is old but has a youngish face, suggesting an immortal nature like that of a vampire.

André Heredia, the son of the French Victor Heredia, a boy about the same age as young Victor. Like his father, André is cruel and overbearing. At one point, Branly catches the French boy sodomizing the Mexican boy in the backseat of the wrecked Citroën. After this unnatural copulation, the two boys somehow merge into a single new supernatural individual, evidently symbolizing a merging of French and Latin American cultures. The Mexican Victor Heredia disappears for the rest of the story.

Hugo Heredia, a Mexican archaeologist, father of the Mexican Victor Heredia. Hugo is absent throughout most of the story, leaving his son in the care of the Comte de Branly. When his son vanishes, however, having merged identities with André Heredia, the father reacts in a strange manner that makes the reader believe he was in enforced collusion with the French Victor Heredia and anticipated what was going to happen.

The Novel

Most of *Distant Relations* takes place during one long afternoon in Paris, but the events that it recounts take place in Mexico and the Caribbean as well as in France and extend two centuries into the past. The title refers not only to the familial connections between the characters in the novel but also to the historical relationship between the French and Spanish American traditions. Fuentes puts particular emphasis on a series of French writers born in Spanish America—writers who, to a greater or lesser degree, bridge the distance between the two cultures. A poem by Jules Supervielle (1884-1960), a French poet born in Uruguay, is recited by one of the characters and serves as a leitmotif for the entire novel. The poem, "The Adjacent Room," refers to the notion, central to the plot of the novel, that there is an infinite series of contiguous possibilities for each historical event and for every personal destiny. This premise allows *Distant Relations* to be read as an entertaining and compelling ghost story. At the same time, by replacing a stable vision of the past with a precarious one in which alternate possibilities struggle to exist, it permits Fuentes to carry out a critical and imaginative interrogation of history.

Although the structure of *Distant Relations* is complex, it consists primarily of one long conversation between the Comte de Branly and the narrator, who then reports the exchange to the reader. Branly, a cultured and cosmopolitan French aristocrat, has been deeply shaken by his recent involvement with the Heredia family and by an experience that culminated in the mysterious disappearance of twelve-year-old Victor Heredia. Branly explains that he met the Mexican archaeologist Hugo Heredia and his young son Victor while visiting the Toltec ruins of Xochicalco in Mexico. Branly was impressed by the father's universal grasp of culture and love for the Indian past and was intrigued by the son's "imperious innocence" and childish games. Branly explained the closeness of the two by the recent deaths of Hugo Heredia's French wife and older son in a plane crash. He excused their arrogance when they appropriated a valuable, if broken, artifact that Victor found among the ruins.

Several months later, when the Heredias accept his invitation to come to Paris, a series of events make Branly an unwilling guest in the suburban home of another Victor Heredia, a rude and resentful Frenchman who appears in Branly's room only at night. For several days, while the Mexican boy plays with the French Heredia's son André, Branly is forced to recall forgotten details of his own life and listen to the chaotic and incoherent family stories of a man whom he finally realized never existed. The inconsistencies in Heredia's stories of the changing fortunes of his family in the nineteenth century Caribbean are never resolved, but they do show that in some way, Branly's destiny is intertwined with that of the Heredias.

This explanation of the French Heredia's raging insistence on the forgotten injustices of the past also accounts for his desire to bring about the birth of a new being, one previously denied existence, by joining his son and the Mexican boy. Before leaving Heredia's house, Branly tells the narrator, he witnessed the union of the two boys, each of whom brought half of the artifact from Xochicalco to form a whole. Branly was shocked to learn that Hugo had agreed to surrender his son to the French Heredia.

Despite this disturbing experience, Branly is somehow satisfied personally by the interrogation of his own past that he has carried out twice: once at the home of Victor Heredia, and once in the presence of the narrator. Branly, who is childless, leaves the story of the Heredias as a legacy to the narrator, who accepts it reluctantly. The narrator is someone who has refused the legacy of the past by turning his back on his Latin American roots. The reader learns in the last two chapters that he is an alternate destiny of Carlos Fuentes, but that the other Fuentes is constantly at his side, refusing to allow him to forget the legacy of the past. In the striking last scene of the novel, Fuentes is escorted by his phantom presence to the pool of the Club, where he sees a vision of the American jungle and also of the two boys, floating in the pool, oblivious of time. Their mystery is not explained, but Fuentes realizes that the destiny of the Heredias has included him as well.

Analysis

Distant Relations can be read on several levels—as a mystery, as a fantasy or metaphysical speculation, and as an essay about the literary and historical relationship between the Old World and the New. The archaeologist Hugo Heredia says at one point: "If you want me to summarize the most profound lesson of Mexican antiquity, it is this: all things are related, nothing is isolated; all things are accompanied by the totality of their spatial, temporal, physical oneiric, visible and invisible attributes." In looking at French culture and history in relationship to Spanish America, Fuentes shows a desire to find equilibrium and balance—in the perfect spherical object from Xochicalco, in the phantom presence that lives beside people, and in the order and reason that Branly tries to bring to the telling of his story. This sense of balance seems to elude him; the story remains incomplete.

This preoccupation with memory and inheritance animates all of Fuentes' works. In elaborating a genealogy of the New World, Fuentes struggles to discover how the past determines the identity of a nation. The uneasy and often violent legacy of the New World is a difficult one with which to come to terms.

Critical Context

Fuentes is without a doubt the most widely read Mexican writer on the international scene. As Branly says in *Distant Relations* when he suggests that the narrator might have chosen to stay in Mexico instead of going to France, "You write about Mexico, about Mexicans, the wounds of a body, the persistence of a few dreams, the masks of progress. You remain forever identified with that country and its people." Fuentes is a prolific writer who is both cosmopolitan diplomat and erudite professor. He is well known for his essays on contemporary Mexico as well as for his literary criticism.

In many of Fuentes' earlier novels, he discusses present-day Mexico by looking at its relationship to its violent and often brutal past. In later novels, he has looked at Mexico in relation to other nations and cultures, without ever abandoning the historical question. In *Terra Nostra* (1975; English translation, 1976), a massive and encyclopedic novel, he examines Mexico's relationship with Spain. In *El gringo viejo* (1985; *The Old Gringo*, 1985), he looks at Mexico's relationship with the United States. In *Distant Relations*, Fuentes pays homage to French culture and literature, to what he calls "that strange love for France which supposedly saves us Latin Americans from our ancient subordination to Spain and our more recent subordination to the Anglo-Saxon world."

DON GOYO

Author: Demetrio Aguilera Malta (1909-1981)
Type of work: Novel
Type of plot: Fantasy
Time of plot: An undefined time, probably between the mid-eighteenth and mid-nineteenth century
Locale: A group of islands on the coast of Ecuador, near Guayaquil
First published: 1933 (English translation, 1942)

Principal Characters

Don Goyo Quimi, the first inhabitant of the islands and founder of the town of Cerrito de Morreños. He is a 150-year-old patriarch who commands the respect and obedience of all the *cholos*. Although he hears unfavorable reports about the conduct of white men, he recruits *cholos* to help Don Carlos. When he sees that the *cholos* are being exploited, he convinces them to abandon Don Carlos to work for themselves again. He tells them to stop harvesting mangrove trees. By cutting down mangrove trees, the *cholo* cuts himself down because he is made of mangrove. After the *cholos* indicate that they will resume cutting down mangrove trees, Don Goyo disappears and dies with the oldest mangrove tree. The *cholos* find him entangled in its fallen branches.

Cusumbo, a young highlander who comes to the islands to escape prosecution for murdering his boss and his wife when he had caught them making love. As a highlander, he had worked for the landowner by cultivating rice, fishing, and caring for dairy cattle. After he comes to the islands, he fishes for a livelihood until he falls in love with Gertru,

who insists she will only marry a mangrove cutter. He becomes a mangrove cutter to please her and to make enough money to marry her. He asks Gertru to marry him after they both witness an apparition of a triumphant Don Goyo after his death.

Gertrudis (Gertru) Quimi, the sensible daughter of Don Goyo and his second wife, Doña Andrea. She resists Cusumbo's amorous advances at first because she wants a commitment from him. She accepts Cusumbo's marriage proposal after her father's death.

Don Carlos, a tall, blond, blue-eyed white man who settles on the islands with his family. He claims to want to improve life on the islands for everyone and solicits Don Goyo's help in securing the cooperation of the *cholos*. After some initial prosperity, Don Carlos begins to cheat the workers. Before Don Goyo's death, he plots the seizure of Don Goyo's island, trying to find out if Don Goyo has papers to substantiate his claim on the land.

Don Leitón, a mangrove cutter who leads the opposition to Don Goyo's sanction against mangrove cutting.

The Novel

This work combines the realism of the life of the *cholos* in the coastal areas of Ecuador with the fantastic elements of the legends that prevail in those tropical regions. The action evolves around two central characters, Don Goyo and Cusumbo. The former is the patriarch of the island region and

of the town of Cerrito de Morreños, which he founded after leaving his native town and which he helped develop into a peaceful and harmonious community. During the action of the novel, Don Goyo, nearly 150 years old, is still the virile man and the authority figure who makes the inhabitants listen and obey. He is admired for his manly qualities, which have yielded for him many children. He has stood up to white people and has prevented abuse of his people. Misfortunes come to the region, however, when, after having a vision in which a mangrove tree tells him that white people will ultimately ruin and own the land, Don Goyo orders the mangrove cutters to turn their livelihood to fishing. This proves to be disastrous since they do not have the skills or the interest to succeed. When they disobey and go back to cutting, the largest and oldest mangrove tree falls to the ground. Don Goyo is found tangled in its branches.

Cusumbo, the other main character, is Don Goyo's counterpart, in that he represents the average man of the region. When the novel begins, Cusumbo reminisces about his life in the highlands before he emigrated to the islands. There, after inheriting his drunken father's never-ending debt to a white landowner, he had become a drunk himself. Rehabilitated by Nica, his wife, he had gone back to work, only to realize that he would never pay his debt in full, because the white bosses cheat the workers mercilessly, taking advantage of their illiteracy. The final blow came when he found his wife in bed with a white man; killing them both with his machete, he fled to the islands, where he settled as a fisherman. In the course of the novel, he falls in love with Gertru, Don Goyo's daughter, and decides to become a mangrove cutter, only to go back to fishing on Don Goyo's orders. At the end of the novel, Cusumbo sees the specter of Don Goyo at the exact time the dead man's coffin, which the men transport in a canoe, falls in the river. Although it is clear that Cusumbo will never achieve the old man's legendary status, he will carry on his traditions as well as his line, since the reader is led to believe that he and Gertru will marry.

Analysis

Don Goyo treats social-protest themes with a unique approach. *Cholo* life in all of its facets is portrayed realistically as well as poetically. The true-to-life descriptions of the action and local customs, as well as the authentic dialogue, convey an accurate picture of the Ecuadoran coastal region. The style of the novel, however, gives the narrative a lyric quality. Technique brings about the creation of an emotive reality, one that transcends its limitations. The characters are not so poetic, however, that they are mere abstractions. Aguilera Malta's world is imbued with magical qualities while it maintains its firm footing in reality.

At the same time, *Don Goyo* is a socially conscious and committed novel that denounces the disappearance of *cholo* life, with its reliance on nature and simple things, and the emergence of white society. White people, Aguilera Malta says, are interested only in exploiting those whom they consider to be their inferiors. Even though he respects Don Goyo, Don Carlos, a white man who comes to Don Goyo's island, has no sense of community or sympathy for his neighbors. In Cusumbo's early life, another white landowner transfers his father's unpayable debt to Cusumbo, thus keeping him in chains. When Cusumbo murders the landowner and his own adulterous wife, there is neither retribution nor any indication that Cusumbo is a fugitive from justice. He apparently feels no remorse. The white man's abuses seem to justify both the murders.

The love theme is represented by Cusumbo's relationship to two women, Nica and Gertru. The former is mentioned as the embodiment of the betrayer and the reason for Cusumbo's exile. She is the unfaithful wife who deserves no pity. Gertru, on the other hand, is the humble, naïve girl who gives herself to Cusumbo in spite of her fear of losing him. Ña Andrea, Don Goyo's wife, is the faithful spouse who obeys her man and makes coffee for the men. Overall, love is a simple thing to the people in those regions, says Aguilera Malta. It is based on sexual attraction and loyalty to one's mate. Unfaithful spouses deserve to be killed. In the world of the *cholo*, there are no gray areas, love being no exception.

Finally, nature plays a very important role in *Don Goyo*. Not only are all the characters intimately bound to their environment, but they also believe in its magic qualities. From the beginning of the novel, the fishermen are described as water creatures: "Now they were naked again. Deep in the water, swimming—more fish than men—they raised the nets above the level of the water." Don Goyo is the embodiment of this symbiosis between people and nature. As he obeys the commands of the mangrove, the charcoal-giving tree, to stop the exploitation and the destruction, he demonstrates the relationship that all the inhabitants of the islands have with their surroundings. The fact that they do as he says reinforces their beliefs in nature's powers. Moreover, as islanders escape to Guayaquil in their frustration, they see the ugliness of the city, which they say should be called "Guayastink." At the end of the novel, the men defy Don Goyo and go back to cutting trees, but they learn a lesson as the old man dies. With this novel, Aguilera Malta reminds both those of his country and those outside Ecuador that the exploitation of natural resources ultimately destroys people and that as the countryside falls to the city, the soul of the nation dies.

Critical Context

Don Goyo was one of Aguilera Malta's early novels in a career that spanned four decades. Representative of the works of a group of writers of the 1930's, the Guayaquil Group, to which Aguilera Malta belonged before leaving Ecuador for Mexico, *Don Goyo* also bears many typical characteristics of the writer's style. It is a short, impressionistic work that seeks to convey a powerful message through understatement. The absence of anecdotal detail, the precise descriptions of the region, and the social message place Aguilera Malta with his group, stylistically and politically.

While drawing attention to their country's social problems, the writers of the Guayaquil Group also wanted to preserve the characteristics of their native region in detailed and precise descriptions of flora, fauna, and native customs. In this sense, *Don Goyo* fulfilled its mission but ultimately stood out among the rest, as it is the best-known work of the entire group's production.

DON SEGUNDO SOMBRA

Author: Ricardo Güiraldes (1886-1927)
Type of work: Novel
Type of plot: Adventure
Time of plot: The late nineteenth century
Locale: Argentina
First published: 1926 (English translation, 1935)

Principal Characters

Don Segundo Sombra, an elderly Argentine gaucho who for five years allows Fabio to accompany him in his wanderings, instructing Fabio in the life and the culture of the pampas. He then persuades Fabio to accept the responsibility of the ranch Fabio has inherited, staying with him until he gets established.

Fabio, a waif who turns to Sombra for understanding. Through many adventures, he learns courage and self-reliance.

Don Fabio Cáceres, Fabio's father, who ignores him as a child but later wills him a ranch and a fortune.

Pedro Barrales, a onetime gaucho companion who brings Fabio news of his inheritance.

Don Leandro Galván, a rancher and later Fabio's guardian.

Paula, a fickle country girl over whom Fabio duels with a rancher's son.

The Novel

Don Segundo Sombra concerns Fabio, who at the novel's opening is a young boy living with his two maiden aunts in a small Argentine village. He dislikes his aunts, who believe, in their turn, that he is simply a bother. He is not sure that the two women truly are his relatives, for they pay him little heed as long as he does not give them trouble. Don Fabio Cáceres, a rancher, occasionally comes to see the boy and takes him into the country for a day, but the man ceases coming when Fabio is about eleven years old.

Fabio grows up to be a cheeky youngster who shows off for the worst element of the town. He knows all the gossip and spends his time hanging around saloons. No one seems to care that he never goes to school. The village loafers hint that he was an illegitimate, unwanted child. At best, he seems destined to be a ne'er-do-well who carries a chip on his shoulder in defiance of the rest of the world.

One night, a gaucho rides into the town as Fabio is going home from fishing. The man impresses the boy at first sight. A little later Fabio earns the gaucho's interest by warning him of an ambush laid by a knife-wielding bully. The kind words spoken by the gaucho, Don Segundo, go to the boy's heart. Fabio immediately decides to follow the man when he leaves town. Gathering together his meager possessions, which fortunately include a saddle and two ponies, Fabio quietly leaves without telling anyone where he is going, in order to escape his hated aunts. He rides to the ranch belonging to Don Leandro Galván, where he knows that Don Segundo is going to spend a few days breaking wild horses.

When he arrives, the boy applies for work and is hired. By the time Don Segundo is ready to leave the ranch on a cattle drive, Fabio has convinced Don Leandro and Don Segundo that he is a willing worker. They let Fabio go with the other gauchos on half pay. At the end of the drive, Fabio is well along in his apprenticeship as a gaucho.

For five years, Fabio continues under the tutelage of Don Segundo. Traveling from ranch to ranch, they work for a number of landowners. From the older man, Fabio learns to care for himself and his horses, to work cattle under various conditions, to live courageously, to get along with all kinds of people, and to have a good time singing songs, dancing , and telling stories. It is more than a way of making a living that the man passes on to the boy; it is an entire culture, a culture as old as the cattle industry and in some respects even older, going back to the culture of Spain.

There are many incidents in their wanderings, including the time that Fabio wins a large bet by picking the winning bird in a cockfight when everyone else bets against the bird. He remembers also a long drive with cattle to a ranch on the seashore. There Fabio finds a country he detests and a young woman he loves, as well as a great store of bad luck. He had picked up quite a respectable string of horses, the tools of the gaucho's trade, and he was very proud of them. In working the cattle at the seashore ranch, two of the horses are injured, much to the young gaucho's dismay. One of them is badly gored by a bull. When Fabio comes across the bull one evening while exploring with another young man, he vows to break its neck. He lassos the beast and breaks its neck with the shock, but in doing so he injures himself severely.

Fabio remains at the ranch convalescing from his injuries. He falls in love, or so he thinks, with Paula, a pretty young girl who lives there. Unfortunately, she leads him on, as she does the rather stupid son of the rancher. The other boy takes advantage of Fabio's crippled arm and attacks him with a knife. Fabio, not wanting to injure the owner's son, to fight over a woman, or to violate the father's hospitality, avoids the other boy's thrusts until they become deadly. Then, with a quick thrust Fabio slashes the boy's forehead slightly, taking the will to fight out of him very quickly. Paula, over whom the fight began, rebukes the crippled Fabio. Disgusted at her and at himself,

Fabio, crippled as he is, mounts his horse and rides away to rejoin Don Segundo, who is working at a nearby ranch until Fabio is ready to travel.

Don Segundo and Fabio arrive in a small village on a day when people have gathered from miles around to race horses. Fabio bets and loses a hundred pesos, then another hundred, and finally the third and last hundred he possesses. Still not satisfied that he is a hopeless loser, he gambles five of his horses and loses them as well. He comes out of the afternoon's activity a sad young man.

He and Don Segundo are hired to trail a herd of cattle from a ranch near the village to the city to be butchered. It is a long, hard drive, even for experienced gauchos. It is made even more difficult for Fabio by the fact that he has only three horses, for the animals soon become fatigued from the work of carrying him and working the cattle on the road. When the herd stops to rest one afternoon, Fabio decides to see if he can get another horse or two.

While looking around, he finds Pedro Barrales, a gaucho who had traveled with him and Don Segundo several times before. Pedro Barrales has a letter addressed to Señor Fabio Cáceres, a letter that he gives to Fabio. The boy looks blankly at the letter, not believing it is addressed to him, for he does not know his true surname. Don Segundo opens the letter to find that the maiden aunts truly had been Fabio's relatives and that Don Fabio Cáceres, who had visited him at his aunts' home, was really his father, from whom he had inherited a fortune and a large, well-stocked ranch. The news saddens Fabio because he sees that it will take him away from the life he loves. He is angered, too, because he had been left so long under the impression that his parentage was a source of shame.

Acting upon the good advice of Don Segundo, Fabio returns to his native town, and from there to the ranch where he had begun work under Don Leandro Galván, who has become his guardian. When Don Segundo agrees to remain with him for three years on his own ranch, Fabio becomes willing to settle down. The three years pass all too swiftly, and at the end of that time Fabio is exceedingly sad when Don Segundo, answering the gaucho's call to wander, rides away.

Analysis

This novel is considered to be the classic novel of the gaucho. It has the clean lines of Ernest Hemingway's *The Old Man and the Sea* (1952), for Don Segundo Sombra, the patriarchal old gaucho, and Fabio, the boy, are thrown into relief as they ride across the billowing pampa. Don Segundo is introduced into the novel dramatically. When first seen by the boy, he looms enormously, a giant and almost overwhelming horseman. When Don Segundo rides off at the novel's end, readers see only him, the pampa, and the sky as he disappears, shadowlike, into the distance.

One theme is the passing of a breed, as represented by Don Segundo himself, the last of the true gauchos. Freedom is still another theme—the wild wandering of the duo across the pampa; the freedom, now disappearing, once enjoyed by the dying gaucho; the gradual smothering of such freedom by civilization. *Don Segundo Sombra* is simultaneously set late in the day of the gaucho's traditional frontier enemy, the wild Indian tribes, who have already been pushed up against the setting sun into the Andean foothills. Thus, while entertaining, the novel has various social and historical messages.

Güiraldes made unusual use of water imagery. The pampa itself is presented as an ocean of land, the reflecting sky overhead being an overhead ocean. Ponds and streams add other touches of water imagery. Don Segundo and Fabio even reach the Atlantic Ocean itself once and stare raptly at it. Life itself is symbolized by water: Life flows like water, as does the novel's action.

Adventure and travel give another element, in this case Quixotesque. The two riders wander at will, much like Don Quixote and Sancho Panza, satiating the human yen to travel and see what lies over the horizon. The appeal to wanderlust is so intense that it has a strong mystic touch. The novel is realistic and true to life, but it can almost be classified as a romance of chivalry since it exalts the virtues of Don Segundo and his adventures with Fabio in the field of struggle of a gaucho's daily labor, and in battle against the inclemencies of weather and nature.

The vocabulary has many Argentinisms, some of colonial vintage, but is never difficult. The plot develops serenely to a logical climax. The novel's style is good but not distinctive: The few characters are well done, or are deliberately shaded out so as not to distract from the protagonist, Don Segundo, and his young companion, Fabio. The reader thus identifies easily with both.

Güiraldes' use of nature is not equal in some respects to that of, say, Louis L'Amour, but it is blended so well into the narration that one can almost hear the rustle of leaves in the trees, the murmuring of the streams, and even the sound of the wind. There is some use of colors and tints, as for the green ombú trees and the colors of the steers and horses. Gaucho lore is presented extensively and authentically without any touch of "drugstore gauchoism." In general, relatively little of the milk of human kindness or warmth is presented, for Fabio is very much alone in a cold world until he meets Don Segundo.

As genres, the gaucho novel and poetry are extensive. They are important not only because of their intrinsic worth as genuine, regional products of the American hemisphere but also because they have tinged other aspects of Argentine literature, even the theater and essay. Gaucho literature and culture flourished throughout the area. In southern Brazil, an entire gaucho literature exists in Portuguese, forming a natural component to the unique gaucho genre. To this day, one even finds a certain impregnation of gaucho culture in southernmost Paraguay.

Although moving even further from the classic gaucho age in time, and despite paved roads and mechanization, Argentina, Uruguay, southern Brazil, and Paraguay's southernmost tip retained gaucho flavor in dress and speech. Novels in the tradition of *Don Segundo Sombra* were being published in southern Brazil late in the twentieth century, while a faint gaucho tinge spread northward into Brazil's immense "wild west" of Minas Gerais, Goiás, and Mato Grosso. Gaucho novels remained favorites of urban Argentine readers. The modern gaucho uses barbed wire and rides a jeep, but the average ranch still has gauchos in whose hearts beat the spirit of Don Segundo.

Critical Context

Don Segundo Sombra has been called the South American counterpart of *The Adventures of Huckleberry Finn* (1884). Like the hero of Mark Twain's novel, Fabio wanders on his own through youth in a new country, giving the author a chance not only to tell a story but also to present a vivid and varied documentation of details about the people, the customs, and the countryside. In Argentina itself, the book was immediately popular. It is one of the best narratives dealing with the gaucho, the South American cowboy. The hero of Güiraldes' novel was drawn from a real-life gaucho whom the author had known and loved in his own childhood on his father's ranch, La Portena, in the province of Buenos Aires. The novel reflects a pastoral form of life that has all but disappeared in Argentina, and the story will probably fascinate later generations much as Owen Wister's picturesque narrative of the North American cowboy, *The Virginian: A Horseman of the Plains* (1902), caught the fancy of postfrontier readers.

DONA FLOR AND HER TWO HUSBANDS: A Moral and Amorous Tale

Author: Jorge Amado (1912-   )
Type of work: Novel
Type of plot: Social morality
Time of plot: The 1960's
Locale: Salvador, in the state of Bahia, Brazil
First published: *Dona Flor e Seus Dois Maridos*, 1966 (English translation, 1969)

Principal Characters

Dona Flor dos Guimarães, a cook of genius. Flor's Cooking School of Savor and Art attracts pupils from all over the state of Bahia, Brazil, and ensures her a measure of dignity and independence. Flor is very feminine and at the peak of her charms when her husband of seven years, Vadinho, dies, leaving her chilled and lonely in her grief, with no outlet for her sensuality. Her instinct for order and propriety is satisfied by her second husband, and her life is complete when Vadinho is called back from death by the power of her desire to fulfill the other, hidden side of her double nature.

Waldomiro Guimarães (Vadinho), Dona Flor's first husband, a gambler and profligate. The bastard scion of an important family, Vadinho lives a life that is a series of picaresque adventures. Good for nothing except making love and friends, he initially courts Flor in a cynical attempt at defloration but ends with as much tenderness as nature has granted him to give. He is a bad husband, unfaithful and spendthrift, but a wonderful lover.

Dr. Teodoro Madureira, Flor's second husband, part owner and druggist-in-charge of the Scientific Pharmacy, and an enthusiastic member of the Amateur Orchestra of the Sons of Orpheus. Gentlemanly and upright, an outstanding member of the community, the doctor's watchword is order.

Dona Norma de Ze Sampaio, the neighborhood guardian angel. She helps Flor marry, establish her school, and survive her widowhood.

Dona Gisa, a teacher, ingenuous, stuffed with book learning, and incapable even of comfortable lies. Born a *gringa* in America but now a Brazilian citizen, Dona Gisa keeps up a commentary on the events of Flor's life.

Dona Rozilda, Flor's mother, a malicious harridan. Her daughter's widowhood offers her an opportunity to get Flor back under her thumb, and Flor's second marriage offers the means of basking in the social success she has bitterly craved.

Dionisia, a mulatto model and whore, a votary of the god Oxossi. Beautiful and a powerful worker of magic, she helps Flor conjure Vadinho back.

The Novel

As the novel begins, it is the first Sunday of Carnival in Bahia, and Waldomiro Guimarães, known by everyone as Vadinho, husband of Dona Flor, has just died while dancing the samba, dressed as a woman, with a large cassava tuber tied under his skirt. With this beginning, Amado introduces the reader to a rollicking, bawdy world.

The novel is divided into five parts, each chronicling a segment of Dona Flor's life. The first deals with Vadinho's death, wake, and burial, and with the stirring of Dona Flor's fears of life without her husband. The wake is a great success, with people streaming in and out to pay their respects. Everyone, it seems—from politicians to members of the exalted professions and the inhabitants of gambling parlors and houses of ill repute—has a story to tell of Vadinho and his deeds. The wake pales in comparison to the burial procession, which appears to draw half the population of Bahia.

For Dona Flor this is small solace. With Vadinho's burial, the reality of his absence becomes more pronounced. Dona Flor struggles through a period of deep mourning. Through flashbacks (and certain pertinent digressions by the author), her life as a young girl, her whirlwind courtship, and her subsequent marriage to Vadinho is recounted. The memories of her life with Vadinho haunt her at every turn. To be sure, not all of her memories are happy ones. Now, with Vadinho gone, it seems as if she lies buried with him, and only the shell of Dona Flor remains, going through the motions of living. Not until she has pushed these memories aside, plunged them deep into the bottom of her consciousness, is she able to resume her life. In a symbolic gesture at Vadinho's grave, she lays a bouquet of flowers and at the same time buries desire, love, and things of the bed and the heart, in order to take up life again.

Dona Flor settles into a routine that is slowly broken up by the insistent talk of matchmaking, marriage, men, and sex that her friends and neighbors continuously conduct in her presence. Although outwardly a respectable, upright woman, inwardly and at night, alone with her dreams, she is consumed by desire, by matters of the flesh. Even the most innocent of novels provokes in her all the desires she thought she had buried with Vadinho. Into her life at this time—when Dona Flor knows that to remain in this state may lead to insanity, while to do anything else would mean a loss of respectability or, worse, total ruination—comes Dr. Teodoro Madureira, the local pharmacist.

To Dona Flor, and indeed all the women in the neighborhood, this comes as a shock, since in all the talk of matchmaking not one of them has mentioned Dr. Teodoro as a possibility. Once the possibility is entertained, everyone agrees that he is perfect for Dona Flor.

She finds him acceptable, and a courtship, very different from her first one, ensues: a formal, proper, and respectable courtship. At the wedding, everyone agrees that this time Dona Flor has achieved her deserved status and that finally she will have the happiness she deserves.

Dr. Teodoro and Dona Flor settle down to a life of respectability after their honeymoon, a honeymoon that Dona Flor finds a little disconcerting. She expects blazing lights and a night of complete abandonment, something of what she has known before; instead, it is a night of restraint, modesty, and discreetness. To everyone who knows them, Dr. Teodoro and Dona Flor are a happy couple, he busy with his pharmacy, she with her cooking school. On occasion, Dona Flor attends conventions of pharmacists, where Dr. Teodoro reads learned speeches railing against the giant pharmaceutical companies, and where Dona Flor struggles to stay awake. At other times, she is host to the amateur orchestra, in which Dr. Teodoro is a featured bassoonist. So Dona Flor's life goes, with the unexpected never happening, with no tears or sorrows, until, on the night of the first anniversary of her marriage to Dr. Teodoro, she walks into her bedroom and sees Vadinho lying in her bed, nude. From this point, the struggle that Dona Flor has been conducting within herself since Vadinho's death becomes a full-scale battle between order and disorder, between love as represented by Dr. Teodoro and love as represented by Vadinho, a struggle that, before it is over, turns the entire society of Bahia upside down, involving everyone from the poorest ragamuffins to the richest social and political circles, even the entire pantheon of Bahian gods.

Analysis

Although its style is comedic, the novel deals with serious themes. It is a story of two worlds; of a clash between good and evil, where good and evil are not so sharply defined that a person can easily distinguish them; of love in all of its forms; of the meaning of happiness and respectability; of a battle between spirit and matter. Above all, however, it is a celebration of life.

By embodying the struggle between good and evil, between spirit and matter, in the character of Dona Flor, Amado is able to point out and attack the hypocrisy of a society that makes such a struggle necessary. Dona Flor finds it necessary to bury desire, love, and the things of the bed and of the heart when Vadinho dies, in order not to be tempted by the part of her that Vadinho so generously satisfied. She does so because if tempted, she might succumb, and if she succumbs, outside the institution of marriage, she loses (in the eyes of her neighbors, that is) the other side of herself—the decent, honorable, respectable side. In the society that she inhabits, it is the outward appearance of these qualities that counts more than the actual possession of them.

For Vadinho and Dr. Teodoro, no such problem exists. For Vadinho, a child of the street, illegitimate, there are no restraints whatsoever. He knows at first hand the hypocrisy that exists in the world, and he will have no part of it. Generous to a fault, with his physical love and prodigious in his excesses, he suffers no disgrace, not only because he is a man but also because, unlike Dona Flor, he has nothing to protect.

Dr. Teodoro, Vadinho's opposite, is a very respectable gentleman. In everyone's mind (including Dona Flor's) he confers his respectability on her when they marry, yet before he marries, he tarries with prostitutes without inflicting damage on his reputation. There is no doubt that he is decent, honorable, and respectable, but he embraces these traits so tightly that spontaneity and unbridled joy have no room to penetrate. It is to Dona Flor's sorrow that he brings his respectability to bed with him.

Dona Flor's nature encompasses both these extremes—indeed, she has need of them in order to survive—but she must have them in balanced measures, not in extremes. To choose the unbridled passions of Vadinho means death to the decent, honorable side of her; to choose the monotonous happiness of the respectability and security of Dr. Teodoro means death to her spirit.

Amado expresses these themes not simply with his characters but with his skillful use of narrative structure and clean, graceful, poetic language. In the recounting of Vadinho's escapades and his life with Dona Flor, the story moves with the rhythms and sounds of Bahian popular music, Vadinho's music. The story slows before and during Dona Flor's marriage to Dr. Teodoro, in tune with his amateur orchestra. During the climactic struggle of the novel, the mood is discordant and chaotic. When Dona Flor emerges victorious, at peace with herself, in balance, walking down the street to the seashore, arm in arm with her two husbands, the sense of sound is harmonious, in balance.

Critical Context

In the beginning of his career, Jorge Amado concerned himself with the themes of social justice and class struggle. It was not until the appearance of *Gabriela, Cravo e Canela* (1958; *Gabriela, Clove and Cinnamon*, 1962) that this emphasis shifted and Amado began to explore and expand the rich, comic literary territory that he pursues in *Dona Flor and Her Two Husbands*. The themes of social justice and class struggle are still present in *Dona Flor and Her Two Husbands*.

As Amado's themes have become universal, he has moved from being a regional or Brazilian writer to being one of international stature. *Gabriela, Clove and Cinnamon* and Dona Flor and Her Two Husbands are among the most widely read contemporary novels from Latin America. *Dona Flor and Her Two Husbands* has served as the basis for a successful Broadway play, *Sarava* (1978), and two films, a 1977 Brazilian production and *Kiss Me Goodbye* (1982), an American film in which the story is shifted from Bahia to New York City.

DÔRA, DORALINA

Author: Rachel de Queiroz (1910-   )
Type of work: Novel
Type of plot: Psychological realism
Time of plot: The 1930's and 1940's
Locale: Brazil
First published: 1975 (English translation, 1984)

Principal Characters

Maria das Dores (Dôra or Doralina), the narrator and central character, who recounts her life. She shelters and protects a wounded bandit, Raimundo Delmiro, when she is fourteen and at twenty-two marries a young surveyor, Laurindo Quirino, who courts both Dôra and her mother. After Laurindo dies, she leaves the ranch and joins an itinerant company of actors. They tour Brazil, and Dôra meets a handsome ship captain and falls in love. She and the Captain settle in Rio. When he dies of typhoid, she seeks refuge at Soledade and busies herself putting the long-neglected ranch back into good running order.

Senhora, Dôra's mother, widowed when Dôra was young. Dôra thinks that her mother is cold and uncommunicative and that she considers her daughter to be a competitor.

Laurindo Quirino, a distant relative of Senhora, an agricultural engineer and surveyor who covets the Soledade ranch and becomes Dôra's husband and Senhora's lover. He dies in a mysterious shooting accident for which Delmiro may be responsible.

Asmodeu Lucas (the Captain), the great love of Dôra's life. Lucas is captain of a ship when Dôra meets him. When he loses that job because he is caught smuggling diamonds, Lucas moves in with Dôra in Rio and becomes involved in a new smuggling enterprise. He and Dôra live together in Rio for many years, until he dies of typhoid.

Raimundo Delmiro, a bandit pursued by the police when he first appears at Soledade. He lives out his life on an isolated corner of the ranch. Delmiro is with Dôra when she discovers Laurindo's liaison with her mother. He continues to live a hermitlike existence on the ranch and dies shortly before Dôra's return to Soledade.

Carleto Brandini, a man of great charm and generosity, impresario of the theatrical company Dôra joins.

Estrela Vésper Brandini, the leading actress of the theatrical company and wife of its impresario.

Francisca Xavier Miranda (Xavinha), a distant relative of Senhora, the faithful housekeeper and seamstress at Soledade. Xavinha writes to Dôra during her years away from Soledade.

The Novel

The action of *Dôra, Doralina* is located in the consciousness of the protagonist, Maria das Dores (nicknamed Dôra or Doralina), who broodingly remembers the pleasures and pains that she has experienced as a daughter, a wife, and an actress.

The novel's first section revolves around Dôra's bitter struggle with her mother, whom she always formally calls Senhora. A beautiful widow, Senhora tyrannically manages the family ranch, Soledade, while showing no love toward her daughter.

Dôra's desire for love seems to be realized when Laurindo Quirino, a handsome surveyor, enters Dôra's life. Investing him with the aura of a film star, she sees Laurindo as a release from her emotionally stunted life on the ranch. Moreover, he becomes a way for Dôra to defeat her mother, especially since Senhora is also attracted to him. Thus, Dôra gloats: "I was twenty-two years old, she was forty-five—Laurindo married me." This joy, though, soon sours as she realizes that he is a violent, morally hollow opportunist. The climax of this section occurs when Dôra discovers that he is having an affair with her mother. Dôra is shattered by this revelation, and her sense of imprisonment deepens, only lessening when her husband is killed in a mysterious hunting accident. Although Queiroz never explains this mystery, she implies that Laurindo is murdered by Raimundo Delmiro, a former bandit now living on the ranch and devoted to Dôra because she once saved his life.

No longer able to tolerate her mother, Dôra leaves the ranch. The second section of the novel describes how she increasingly escapes her haunted past. Whereas the claustrophobic first section is filled with images of death, imprisonment, and alienation, this part is a picaresque affirmation of the human spirit, especially after Dôra joins a ragtag theater group as a fledgling actress. For the first time, as the company travels across Brazil, Dôra begins experiencing the larger world. Just as important, the company gives her the sense of family that she has always desired. Dôra becomes more independent and tests her society's mores by coming to the realization that "my body was mine, to keep or to give, as I wished. . . . This change made a tremendous difference to me. . . ." Eventually, three years after Laurindo's death, this section reaches its fullest expression when Dôra meets the man who fulfills her dreams, Asmodeu Lucas, a handsome, volatile, even demonic river captain. The two grow increasingly intimate as they travel down the São Francisco River, and finally they "marry"—neither worrying about obtaining any legal sanction for their union.

Their relationship is the heart of the novel's final section. When the pressures of World War II force the theater group to disperse, Dôra and the Captain begin to live together in teeming Rio de Janeiro. Queiroz initially depicts the idyllic nature of their everyday life, which, as Dôra stresses, "centered around just the two of us. But it wasn't a prison; it was more like a hedge protecting a garden, which made it fun." In contrast to her marriage with Laurindo, she gives herself to the Captain not out of duty, but out of love. She feels free, even though the demands of their relationship cause her to abandon her theater career, to accept his occasionally violent behavior, to acquiesce to his jealousy, and to close her eyes to the dangers of his new profession of smuggling. In short, she makes him a god whom she wants to possess totally, and as she says, "That could have been a mistake, I don't know. In the end love is like that: We get a man or a woman just like all others, and endow that creature with everything our heart wishes."

Their Edenic existence, however, is precarious. This becomes increasingly apparent as one shadow after another begins haunting Dôra. Besides the Captain's violence, which always threatens to destroy him, memories of Dôra's past begin to stalk her again. Her mother dies, leaving the responsibilities of the ranch to her, and Delmiro is gruesomely killed, thus bringing the death of Laurindo to the forefront of her consciousness. The novel climaxes with the Captain's death from typhoid, a disaster that makes Dôra , for the rest of her life, see the world as "one vast nothing." Unable to cope with her grief in Rio, she returns to the more familiar solitude of the ranch and becomes the new Senhora. The novel has come full circle as Dôra, again in prison, tries to endure by rebuilding the deteriorating homestead.

Analysis

In the striking first paragraph of the novel, Queiroz introduces the tragic vision that will color much of Dôra's story: "And so, as the Captain used to say, it's natural to be in pain. I was always in pain. Pain always hurts, and the only time it doesn't is when you are dead." This statement points to Dôra's realization that she, like all human beings, has been doomed to suffer and to die in a harsh, mutable world. She sees this truth through the deaths of the Captain, Senhora, Laurindo, her still-born daughter, and Delmiro; through the perpetual changes of nature; through the slow deterioration of her ranch; through the deterioration of human beings from old age; and through the dissipation of human emotion. Her obsession with time is rooted in the everyday reality that Queiroz successfully creates through her episodic, extremely concrete narrative.

Queiroz's artistic vision resists morbidity be-cause it also depicts, with the same vivid detail, the characters' deep-seated need to struggle against time. This struggle enlivens the novel, especially since Queiroz plays the comic second section off the tragic first and third parts. Dôra's love for the Captain and his bristling masculinity are attempts to challenge the horrors that inevitably come. Even more important, throughout the novel there is a kind of tragic exultation in Dôra's persistent, un-sparing, and honest attempt to remember and to confront her fading past. By trying to rescue her memories—an act that brings more pain to her already desolate existence on the ranch—she rejects the temptation to give in to time. Thus, she keeps the rosebud that the Captain once gave her: "I still have it pressed between the leaves of the dictionary; and even if it turns to dust and disappears, the impression that it made on the pages of the book will never leave."

Critical Context

Critics have associated Queiroz with a group of writers, including José Lins do Rego, Jorge Amado, and Graciliano Ramos, who were bred in the remote northeastern areas of Brazil and who burst onto the Brazilian literary scene in the 1930's to create what has been called "the novel of the Northeast." As Fred P. Ellison explains, this genre of the Brazilian novel is "characterized by its interest in man in his regional environment, by its implicit (and sometimes explicit) note of social protest, and by its endeavor to discover psychological truths in man, no matter what his walk of life. . . ." *Dôra, Doralina* can be seen as a late and interesting addition to this genre. The novel begins and ends with graphic descriptions of Dôra's life in the Northeast as she is both repulsed by and drawn to her family's ranch. Moreover, through Dôra's struggle to find individual freedom, Queiroz once again explores a social issue that is in all of her novels: the degrading secondary status of most women in this region.

Dôra, Doralina, which has rightly been called Queiroz's most ambitious and accomplished novel, goes far beyond being merely a regional work. It contains her broadest vision of Brazilian society, as Dôra travels to many cities as an actress before settling in Rio de Janeiro with the Captain. In addition, it continues Queiroz's movement from the sociological emphases of her earliest works toward the psychological realism of *As Três Marias* (1939; *The Three Marias*, 1963). With unflinching honesty, Queiroz reveals the subtleties of Dôra's character and in the process develops some of the prevailing themes within her fiction: the ambivalent nature of memories, the human need for nurturing maternal love, the difficulties and beauties of male-female relationships, and the individual's painful existence in a universe where the "good things in life occur less often, the evil ten times more."

DOWN THESE MEAN STREETS

Author: Piri Thomas (1928-   )
Type of work: Autobiography
Time of work: The late 1930's to the mid-1950's
Locale: New York, New York
First published: 1967

Principal Personages

John Peter "Piri" Thomas, a young New Yorker of Puerto Rican parentage. He is tormented by the issue of racial identity because of his partly black origins and negroid appearance. He becomes increasingly alienated from his father and his siblings as a result of his search for his racial identity. He quits high school after experiencing social rejection from white teenagers in Babylon, Long Island, where his parents had moved to get away from the Spanish Harlem barrio after World War II. Involved in street gang activity from an early age, he gradually descends, during his teenage and young adult years, into a life of drug pushing, drug abuse, and violent crime. Piri's aimlessly drifting life culminates, in his early twenties, in his arrest during a bungled gang robbery of a nightclub. In prison, he becomes more thoughtful and appreciative of learning, finally deciding to turn his life around. Prison is portrayed as changing Piri from a totally present-oriented individual to a future-oriented one; this change in personality gives him a chance to stay out of trouble once he is, after seven years, paroled.

James Thomas, Piri's father. During Piri's childhood years, his father, although a diligent unskilled laborer, has great difficulty finding and keeping a job. This is partly because of the Great Depression and partly because of discrimination against him as a black Puerto Rican. Because of self-hatred caused by being black, and because Piri is more negroid-looking than his other children, James tends to punish Piri more than the other children; at least, Piri believes that these are the reasons. In a climactic confrontation with Piri, he

finally admits to himself that he is black; at the same time, he is disgusted with Piri's aping of Southern black speech patterns. The bad relations between Piri and his father are worsened by the father's affair with a white woman.

Delores Montañez Thomas, Piri's mother. A plump, kindhearted woman, she tries to console Piri, but cannot truly empathize with his plight because she is white. Her death hastens Piri's downward spiral into a young adulthood of criminality.

Brewster "Brew" Johnson, a young black man from the South who becomes Piri's close friend. Brewster convinces Piri that Piri is black and persuades him to join him in entering the merchant marine.

José Thomas, Piri's white-looking brother. José's refusal to admit to being black sparks a fistfight with Piri. José is portrayed as eager to become part of white America and as somewhat embarrassed by the negroid-looking Piri.

Trinidad, Piri's first girlfriend, a white-looking girl who was born in Puerto Rico. After Piri goes to prison, Trina marries someone else, much to Piri's disappointment.

Louie, a white Puerto Rican friend of Piri. He is able to get a salesman's job when Piri, because of his color, cannot. Later on, he becomes part of a multiracial gang of robbers that Piri joins while in his twenties.

Miriam Thomas, Piri's white-looking sister.

Gerald Andrew West, a light-complexioned northern black man whom Brew and Piri meet in a bar. From his own experience, West argues that racial distinctions are artificial. He does not convince Brew and only partially convinces Piri.

Kent, a college-educated prisoner whom Piri meets. From Kent, Piri learns to appreciate the value of formal learning.

Waneko, an old friend of Piri and a former drug addict. He helps Piri kick the heroin habit.

Carlito, an old friend of Piri who tries unsuccessfully to tempt him back into heroin use shortly after Piri is paroled.

Dulcien, a Puerto Rican girl whom Piri gets pregnant.

The Work

Down These Mean Streets is a deeply moving and sometimes shocking account of a Puerto Rican boy growing up in New York City from the late 1930's to the mid-1950's. It presents not only an outsider's view of white American society but also a pioneering first-person account of youthful criminality and drug addition. Although written in English, it is liberally spiced with Puerto Rican Spanish words; there is a glossary of such words at the end of the book. A two-page prologue, almost poetic in quality, expresses Piri's lifelong quest for dignity and his love-hate relationship with Spanish Harlem, Manhattan's Puerto Rican neighborhood.

The narrative begins with Piri at about twelve years of age, during the end of the Great Depression. For a while, the family goes on relief after Piri's father loses a job digging ditches for the Works Progress Administration. The father gets a good job after America enters World War II. The narrative ends just after Piri is paroled from prison at the age of twenty-eight, in 1956. Although the chapters are arranged roughly chronologically, they do not follow the order of time rigidly. Thus chapter 7, illustrating Piri's disillusion with the educational system as a small boy, follows a chapter discussing his early involvement in gangs, although the former occurrence probably preceded the latter.

One can see a certain unity to the book as the story of one person's ever-growing alienation from mainstream society, from childhood to criminal youth, and back again to mainstream society after a spell in prison. Some of the chapters contribute much less to the main flow of the narrative than do others. Chapter 4, "Alien Turf" (on Piri's childhood encounter with Italian neighborhood bullies);

chapter 5, "Home Relief" (on Piri's childhood encounter with the Depression-era welfare system), and chapter 7, "Little Red Schoolhouse" (on Piri's maladjusted behavior in elementary school, which leads to a beating from the teacher) can each be read alone and have been anthologized separately.

One of the principal themes of *Down These Mean Streets* is the search for racial identity. Thomas suffers a terrible inner conflict resulting from his position as both the American-born son of Spanish-speaking immigrants and as the negroid-looking son of a black Puerto Rican father and a white Puerto Rican mother. He lives in a society that, unlike his parents' Puerto Rico, is sharply divided by race. This conflict is the root of Piri's growing alienation from both his own family and white American society.

As chapters 9 and 10 show, a sharp awareness of racism hits Piri when, during World War II, the family moves to the previously all-white suburb of Babylon, Long Island. Here, many of Piri's fellow high-school students see Piri, with his flat nose and woolly hair, as black rather than as Puerto Rican and snub him socially. Disillusioned, Piri drops out of school. While working at a briefly held job in a hospital, he meets and befriends a young white woman, but after overhearing hostile remarks from strangers, he ends the relationship. In another incident, recounted in chapter 11, Piri fails to get a job as a door-to-door salesman while a white-looking Puerto Rican friend of his is hired.

Embittered by racism, Piri flees Long Island and hangs around Spanish Harlem, bouncing from one temporary residence to another. A developing friendship with Brewster "Brew" Johnson, an African-

American born in the South, leads Piri to dig deeper into the question of his racial, as distinguished from cultural, identity. Their conversations about the issue are recounted in chapters 13 and 14. Piri's growing realization that he will face prejudice all his life, a sobering experience for anyone, is rendered all the more painful by the fact that neither his white mother nor his lighter-complexioned siblings can truly share in this experience: The color line cleaves Piri's own family. When, in chapters 15 and 16, Piri confronts his family over the issue of racial identity, he gets into a punching match with his white-appearing brother José and gets his father to admit to being black. In chapter 20, ironically titled "Home, Sweet Harlem," Piri recounts how he was expelled from the family home for ripping up a picture of his father's extramarital white girlfriend and for defiantly speaking to his father in black American dialect. From chapter 12 onward, he is infatuated with a white Puerto Rican girl, the island-born Trina.

Piri's desire to explore his black identity spurs him to go to the South to join the merchant marine with his black friend Brew. During this adventure, recounted in chapters 17 through 19, Piri encounters Gerald Andrew West, a light-skinned northern black man who insists on the artificiality of racial distinctions; patronizes a white prostitute in Galveston after telling her that he is a Puerto Rican, and then, upon leaving, triumphantly announces that he is black; is denied permission to eat at a whites-only restaurant; and gets into fights with a white crew member on board a ship. He returns to New York City filled with anger and hatred.

The other main theme is the tug-of-war for Piri's allegiance between street life, with its gang fights, crime, drug use, and casual sex, and the conventional lifestyle of school, work, and marriage. Throughout most of the book, the streets win out. At various points in the narrative, Piri ably re-creates for the reader the pleasure he felt in belonging to a gang and in gaining a reputation for courage by fighting back physically and committing petty crimes. Gang life is described in far more detail than is any legitimate job he held. On a dare, the teenage Piri engages in homosexual intercourse for money. After his return from the merchant marine, he sires a child out of wedlock by one Puerto Rican girl (Dulcien), even though he really loves another (Trina). While still a teenager, Piri begins to support himself by selling illegal drugs. After returning from the merchant marine, he becomes addicted to heroin. There are no episodes given from his childhood or adolescent years that indicate any positive attitude toward either school or book learning.

A low point is reached when Piri, back from the merchant marine, joins a multiracial gang of armed robbers. During the gang's bungled attempt to rob a nightclub in February, 1950, Piri is captured by the police. The experience of being in prison for seven years (1950 to 1956) leads Piri to sober reflection. In prison, Piri acquires from a college-educated prisoner, Kent, a love of words and of books; learns a trade; keeps his temper in order to qualify more easily for parole; and resists homosexual exploitation by fellow prisoners at all costs. As the book ends, the reader is confident that the recently paroled Piri will stay out of crime and free of drugs.

Analysis

Written between 1962 and 1967 with the aid of a foundation grant, *Down These Mean Streets* was the first book of an autobiographical trilogy that would include *Savior, Savior, Hold My Hand* (1972) and *Seven Long Times* (1974). The narrative presents Piri's particular view of the world: The reader is limited to what the author was able to see and experience while growing up. The reader learns nothing about how Piri's parents met and married and learns about Puerto Rico only through overhearing Piri's mother impart her nostalgic memories to him. This Piri-centered view, which forces the reader to experience Spanish Harlem vicariously rather than observe it from afar, may be responsible for the complaint raised by some reviewers that many of the characters are mere names, with no real personalities of their own. The aunt who was kind enough to shelter Piri after he was paroled is not even identified by name.

In style, *Down These Mean Streets* is neither learned nor genteel. Enriched by Puerto Rican Spanish vocabulary and black American street slang, it is also peppered with obscenities. The language is so coarse that self-appointed censors attempted, in the 1970's, to get the book banned from high school libraries. With its vivid descriptions of drug abuse and violence, *Down These Mean Streets* has an exciting quality missing from many autobiographies: Parts of it read like a crime thriller. The description of heroin withdrawal symptoms in chapter 21 ("Hung Down") is gut-wrenching, and the verbal portrait of conditions in prison are searing in their intensity. Addressed to sheltered, white, middle-class readers who want to understand how America's big-city ghettos produce juvenile delinquents, the book shows the psychological reasons for such delinquency more effectively than any dry sociological treatise ever could.

Although admitting that he did terrible things in his youth, Piri implies that society as a whole bears some responsibility for his going astray. At least one critic (John Clark) has attacked *Down These Mean Streets* for suggesting that racial discrimina-

tion and the alienation from family brought about by a divided racial identity led inexorably to Piri's deviant career. Disadvantage, such critics argue, neither predetermines nor excuses criminality. Thomas is aware of the existence of free will. The final chapter concludes with the recently paroled Piri's rejection of heroin offered by an old street buddy, Carlito.

As the story of how a youth from a foreign culture adapts to American life, *Down These Mean Streets* has something in common with autobiographical narratives by white immigrants and members of ethnic minorities that also treat the issues of poverty and of father-son conflict, yet the differences outweigh the similarities. In many ethnic and immigrant autobiographies, and in such Hispanic autobiographies as *Hunger of Memory: The Education of Richard Rodriguez* (1981), by the Mexican American author Richard Rodriguez, assimilation to Anglo-American ways is seen as the way out of poverty. By contrast, *Down These Mean Streets*, like *The Autobiography of Malcolm X* (1965), testifies to the tragic failure of the assimilationist ideal in the America of the 1940's. In Piri's racially mixed family, the promise of assimilation is profoundly divisive: Piri, unlike his siblings, can assimilate into American life only by joining the oppressed black caste, not by entering the white mainstream.

Critical Context

Down These Mean Streets is an early example of the so-called "Nuyorican" literature, that written in English by individuals of Puerto Rican parentage born or reared in New York City. Its development is roughly contemporaneous with the emergence of English-language Mexican American literature. The earliest autobiographical works in English by Puerto Ricans were *The Son of Two Nations: The Private Life of a Columbia Student*, by Pedro Juan Labarthe (1931), and *A Puerto Rican in New York, and Other Sketches* (1961), by Jesus Colon. Both authors went to New York in late

adolescence, and neither work had anything like the impact of Thomas' book. After Thomas' landmark book, other Nuyorican works appeared, including *Run, Baby, Run* (1968) by Nicky Cruz; the short stories and novels of Nicholasa Mohr, such as the collection *El Bronx Remembered* (1975); and *Family Installments* (1982), a work of autobiographical fiction by Edward Rivera. Nuyorican literary heirs of Thomas include the playwright Miguel Piñero and the short-story writer Abraham Rodriguez. Nor is Thomas' influence confined to Nuyoricans: In *Always Running: La Vida Loca,*

Gang Days in L.A. (1993), Luis Rodriguez, an American-born son of Mexican immigrants and a former gang member, points to a youthful encounter with *Down These Mean Streets* in the library as an early inspiration for his writing.

Much English-language Latino literature is printed by obscure ethnic presses and is not commercially successful. *Down These Mean Streets* was published by Alfred A. Knopf, a mainstream New York City publishing house. It was widely reviewed in the mainstream media and sold well. Unlike most Hispanic autobiographies, *Down These Mean Streets* touched on the crisis of black-white relations that erupted into urban riots in the late 1960's. Some contemporary reviewers saw it as an example of black ghetto protest autobiogra-phy. Thomas' treatment of his identity crisis as the child of a biracial family spoke to widespread white worries about miscegenation. His vivid depiction of violent crime and drug abuse drew sensation-hungry middle-class readers. *Savior, Savior, Hold My Hand*, which discussed marriage, fatherhood, and his working as a youth counselor, and *Seven Long Times*, about prison, did not sell nearly as well.

Down These Mean Streets came to be required reading in many college courses on Latino literature or the Puerto Rican experience in New York. The book is more widely read as a sociological document than as literature, and its author has not received much critical literary attention.

DREAMING IN CUBAN

Author: Cristina Garcia (1958-   )
Type of work: Novel
Type of plot: Historical realism
Time of plot: 1972-1980
Locale: Santa Teresa Del Mar and Havana, Cuba; New York, New York
First published: 1992

Principal Characters

Celia Del Pino, an old Cuban woman, a staunch supporter of Fidel Castro and the Cuban revolution. She is first seen sitting on her front porch peering through a pair of binoculars, guarding the coast against an invasion by the United States. Throughout the novel, Celia remains steadfast in her support of her country's government, even working in the sugarcane fields to aid the revolution despite her advanced age. Celia is a widow, having lost her husband to cancer just before the opening of the story. Her early life is revealed through her letters written to Gustavo Sierra de Armas, her first lover. The letters begin in 1935, immediately after Gustavo's return to Spain and Celia's marriage to Jorge Del Pino.

Lourdes Puente, Celia's oldest daughter. Lourdes lives in New York and is a firm opponent of the Communist regime in Cuba. Until the end of the book, Lourdes neither sets foot in Cuba nor expresses any desire to do so. Lourdes is a capitalist to the extreme. She owns a bakery in New York and opens a second midway through the book. She dreams of running a nationwide franchise of bakeries, named Yankee Doodle Bakeries. When she finally travels to Cuba, for her sister's funeral, Lourdes falls in love with her nephew, Ivanito, and gives him money to get out of Cuba.

Pilar Puente, Lourdes' daughter. Pilar lives in New York with her mother but is far from agreeing with her mother's point of view. Pilar is the most Americanized character in the novel, painting in abstract style and playing bass guitar. She is a devotee of punk rock. As part of a rebellion against her mother, Pilar considers Communism as a viable way of life and decides eventually that she is an atheist. Pilar wants to return to Cuba, and she even tries to do so by taking a bus to Miami, where she finds members of her family; however, she is brought back to New York. Pilar's most graphic rebellion against her mother occurs when she is told to paint a sign for the opening of the second Yankee Doodle Bakery; instead, she paints a punk version of the Statue of Liberty.

Felicia Villaverde, Celia's second daughter. Felicia spends the entire novel in Cuba. She is not, however, in favor of the revolution or of Fidel Castro; she refers to the government of her country as "tyranny." Felicia married Hugo Villaverde in 1962 and had three children with him. In 1966, she dropped a burning rag on Hugo's face, then locked herself and her children in the house. Felicia has strange visions and hears mysterious voices, and she spends some time in an insane asylum. Although she is critical of her mother's devotion to the Santeria religion, Felicia, at her own request, is buried in a Santeria ceremony.

Jorge Del Pino, Celia's husband. Although deceased before the opening of the story, Jorge still plays a major part in events. He regularly appears as an apparition, and he gives advice to his wife and daughters. Jorge's advice seems to confirm whatever the living characters feel; ironically, though, the only supernatural character in the novel often comes across as the most rational one.

Ivanito Villaverde, Felicia's son. Ivanito is five years old when the story opens and thirteen as it closes. Ivanito is the only character in *Dreaming in Cuban* for whom the reader feels unquestioned sympathy. When Felicia sets her husband on fire and locks the children in the house, Ivanito is the only one of her children to stand by her. As the youngest character in the novel, Ivanito is the only one who has not yet formed political opinions. He loves and is loved by all the adult members of the family. In this sense, Ivanito is a major focus of attention, symbolizing the human aspects of a complex society torn apart by social, political, and religious differences.

The Novel

Dreaming in Cuban is the story of three generations of a Cuban family, told from a variety of points of view. The story begins with Celia Del Pino, an aged woman, watching the waters off the north coast of Cuba with binoculars. She is on guard, devoted to The Revolution and El Lider (Fidel Castro, who is never mentioned by name in the book).

The novel is not told in straightforward, narrative terms, although there is a clear narrative thread running through the story. The book shifts between scenes, and the narrative is told from a variety of points of view. Some of it is told in the first person by Celia, Lourdes, and Pilar, including a number of extracts from Pilar's diary. There are also numerous flashbacks to the past, mostly Celia's past.

One device that is used to re-create the past is a series of letters that Celia wrote over a period of more than two decades. All these letters were written to Gustavo Sierra de Armas, her first lover, a Spanish lawyer. After Gustavo returned to Europe in 1935, Celia wrote to him monthly up until 1959, when the revolution succeeded and Celia became a dedicated Communist. Throughout the book, Celia speaks of The Revolution (always capitalized when Celia's point of view is espoused) in the present tense.

Felicia, Celia's second daughter, still lives in Cuba and never leaves that country; unlike her mother, however, she continuously refers to the present political state of her country as one of tyranny. Felicia is married three times, but never happily. Her first husband, Hugo Villaverde, the father of Felicia's three children, is never seen during the time covered by the story, although he is alluded to a number of times. In 1966, Felicia threw a burning rag into Hugo's face, then locked herself and her children in the house.

Felicia marries her second husband, Ernesto Brito, in 1978. Ernesto dies in a grease fire shortly after the marriage. Felicia then blacks out a period of months of her life and finds herself living at an amusement park, married to Otto Cruz. He works at the amusement park and apparently found Felicia wandering aimlessly there. She has no memory of the marriage.

Both Celia and Felicia have spent significant periods of time in insane asylums. They also both have regular visions of Jorge Del Pino, Celia's husband, who died in a New York hospital of cancer just before the story's beginning. Lourdes and Pilar, in New York, also have recurring visions of this man. He gives all of them advice, although the advice varies according to who is having the vision. All of them are reassured that they are thinking the right thoughts and taking the right actions, even though these actions are at cross purposes.

Lourdes, Celia's oldest daughter, is a marked contrast to her mother. Lourdes lives in New York with her daughter, Pilar, and runs a bakery. About midway through the book, she opens a second bakery and names her enterprise Yankee Doodle Bakeries. She is an emerging capitalist, and she dreams of a franchise of bakeries throughout the country.

A large part of the book is told by way of Pilar's diary. Pilar brings the story full circle, in a sense. She is the most obviously American character in the book; she wears jeans and sneakers and plays bass guitar. Nevertheless, she feels much more strongly tied to her grandmother than to her mother. At one point, she gets as far as taking a bus to Miami in the hope of finding a way to return to Cuba.

In this sense, *Dreaming in Cuban* is also a political story. Pilar's rebellion against her mother ironically brings her to consider atheism and to decide that Communism may not be such a bad idea. The third generation of characters is rather confused. Ivanito, the youngest child, is only thir-teen at the closing of the story, and thus of all the characters is least interested in politics.

The novel ends with the last of Celia's letters, written in 1959, a few weeks after the success of the revolution. Celia celebrates this success, de-cides to devote the rest of her life to the cause, and thus has no further need to write letters to her former lover.

Analysis

Dreaming in Cuban works on three levels. At the surface, it is a melodrama, the story of various members of a large family scattered among New York, Florida, and Cuba. This, however, is the least intense part of the story. The fact that this is a Cuban family, wherever its members may live, is central to the work.

The political level of the novel is close to the surface. The characters include Communists work-ing hard for El Lider and capitalists who despise the Cuban government. The author's own political stance is never made clear. Communism is both praised and criticized. The major point is that the characters themselves, both those who remain in Cuba and those who emigrate to the United States, are somewhat confused. The members of the third generation, especially Pilar, are torn between a way of life in Cuba that is uncomfortable and a longing for a return "home."

The most intense part of the story, and the reason for the title, is spiritual. Cuba, as a Commu-nist country, is supposed to be atheistic; however, spiritual values are not changed instantly by an altering of the political climate. Most Cubans in the story are Roman Catholics; only Pilar, the most American of the family and the youngest character portrayed in detail, considers atheism as a possible way of life.

Underneath Catholicism, however, lies an even older religion. The story begins and ends with rites of Santeria, an ancient religion with roots in Africa.

In its Latin American form, Santeria has taken on some of the trappings of Christianity. Most nota-bly, ancient gods are represented by Christian saints, the legacy of attempts to cover up the prac-tice of the ancient rituals.

Despite appearances, the ancient rites are still practiced. Animals are sacrificed, and magical herbs are used as remedies for a variety of illnesses. Even the family members in New York consult Santeria priests and priestesses when they have spiritual or physical problems. Felicia, who re-fused to take the rites seriously while she was alive, is buried in a Santeria funeral.

Many of the characters have supernatural vi-sions. Jorge Del Pino, Celia's dead husband, ap-pears regularly to a number of the characters, both in Cuba and in New York. The characters so visited invariably take these appearances as real. Although there is a certain amount of insanity in the family (two of the women have been institutionalized), the supernatural seems to play a real, seemingly rational, part in everyone's lives. In some ways, Jorge appears as the most rational character in the novel, despite his supernatural form.

Dreaming in Cuban, at its deepest level, is a consideration of reality and the way humans per-ceive that reality. Dreams, waking life, supernatu-ral visitations, and insanity are so intertwined in the narrative that it is often difficult for the reader to decide which events are actually taking place and which are imagined.

Critical Context

Cristina Garcia, the author of *Dreaming in Cuban*, was born in Cuba in 1958, shortly before the revolution. Her parents were among the many Cubans who emigrated to the United States following that revolution, and the author spent her childhood in New York. She has worked as a journalist for *Time* magazine; *Dreaming in Cuban* is her first work of fiction.

Dreaming in Cuban is not about Cuba but rather about Cubans and the strange social and spiritual attitudes that pervade Cuban society. The Communist government of Cuba retained power even after the breakup of the Soviet Union and the elimination of support from that country. At the same time, Roman Catholicism has remained the dominant religion, with an underpinning of ancient African rites. The seeming conflict between rational Marxism as espoused by the government and the private practice of secret rituals involving ancient magic makes Cuban society unique.

Dreaming in Cuban is a study in contradictions. The book opens with Celia Del Pino guarding the coast against an attack from the north; the failed Bay of Pigs invasion is still a recent memory. Yet some of her family lives in the United States. Her husband, in fact, had gone to New York for medical treatment when he discovered he had cancer; he dies there just before the opening of the story. When the family members all return to Cuba for Felicia's funeral, there is no real sign of reconciliation. The members of the New York branch of the family are still culturally tied to the land of their birth, but they have no intention of remaining in Cuba. Lourdes, the most extremely anti-Communist member of the family, ends the story by giving Ivanito, her young nephew, money to get out of Cuba.

THE EAGLE AND THE SERPENT

Author: Martín Luis Guzmán (1887-1976)
Type of work: Historical
Time of work: 1913-1915
Locale: Mexico and the United States
First published: *El águila y la serpiente*, 1928 (English translation, 1930)

Principal Personages

The narrator ("Luisito" Guzmán), a Mexican intellectual with no official position at first. The narrator records his impressions of the principal figures in the Mexican Revolution of 1910. He also logs the movement's history from its early successes against Victoriano Huerta (under Venustiano Carranza and Alvaro Obregón), through the stormy sessions of the Aguascalientes Convention, which finally established a compromise government, up to the collapse of that government following its break with Francisco "Pancho" Villa. The narrator pictures himself as the representative of the pure idealism of the revolution, sometimes sullied by forced associations with self-seeking rebels. Guzmán's final escape from the clutches of Pancho Villa is a hair-raising tale of reckless daring.

Victoriano Huerta, an old-guard general kept on by Francisco Madero after the victory of 1910. His thirst for power and his subservience to U.S. interests lead him to assassinate Madero and usurp the presidency for himself.

Venustiano Carranza, the first chief of the Constitutionalist Revolution. Tall, with a bovine expression and a patriarchal air, he is opinionated, domineering, and totally devoid of greatness. He brooks no opposition to his wishes. When the narrator declines an appointment to his staff, he earns Carranza's lasting disfavor.

Rafael Buelna, one of Carranza's officers. Beardless and boyish, he reflects the sadness of the Mexican Revolution and introduces the narrator to the tragedy of the movement during a trip by rail on his "flying machine," a motorized handcar that kills two military officers as it speeds through the night without lights.

Alvaro Obregón, the general of the Army of the Northwest. Obregón proves himself to be Carranza's ablest commander. He is convinced of his own importance, yet he feigns not to take himself seriously. Undoubtedly a brilliant military strategist, Obregón nevertheless is insincere and plays the role of a comedian.

Francisco "Pancho" Villa, the general of the Division of the North. The narrator recognizes that Villa's world and his own are irreconcilable. Villa is a savage animal dominated by his instincts.

Rodolfo Fierro, a *villista* who is a mirror of his commander's violent personality and one of Villa's bloodthirstiest officers. Smiling and self-assured, Fierro speaks in quiet tones even when issuing murderous orders.

Eulalio Gutiérrez, an able military officer named president by the Aguascalientes Convention. He appoints Villa as commander in chief of the army, then has to find a way to "escape from Villa without falling into Carranza." This leads to the absurd situation in which his government must support its enemies (*carrancistas*) to control its supporters (*villistas*). When Villa realizes what is going on, he issues orders to arrest Gutiérrez and his cabinet.

José Vasconcelos, an ardent supporter of Villa. Vasconcelos is named minister of education in the government of Eulalio Gutiérrez. The narrator calls him the "only great minister the Revolution produced."

Roque Gonzáles Garza, Villa's personal representative at the Aguascalientes Convention. To solve the impasse between Villa and Carranza, he suggests that the two generals commit suicide together. He is named provisional president by Villa after the fall of the presidency of Eulalio Gutiérrez.

The Work

The Eagle and the Serpent, a work that brings together literature and history, truth and fiction, is divided into two parts: "Revolutionary Hopes" and "At the Hour of the Triumph." In the first part, consisting of seven books, Guzmán tells of his adventures during the period preceding the peak of fighting in the Mexican Revolution. In the second section, also of seven books, he tells of deeds that occurred during the most turbulent years of the conflict.

The book opens when Guzmán, apparently the narrator of most of the work because of its strong autobiographical structure, escapes from Victoriano Huerta's usurping government and flees incognito from Veracruz to the United States, with the intention of reaching the northern Mexican states of Sonora or Coahuila and helping Venustiano Carranza in his fight against Huerta. Aboard ship, he meets four Mexicans, one of them a physician who shares his political views. They establish relations with a beautiful American woman who turns out to be a spy of the Huerta government. When this fact becomes known to Guzmán and his associates, the physician, in order to get rid of her, pretends ardent love for the lady and proposes that they marry in Havana, the next stop on the voyage. The trick fails because the ship delays her departure in that port. Again aboard ship, the revolutionaries are afraid of being imprisoned upon their arrival in New York. The physician feigns intent to kill the spy, but the woman does not appear when they go ashore. The fate of the woman is perplexing, but the author does not add to what already has been told.

Guzmán, unable to carry out his plan to contact Carranza, returns to Mexico City. His enthusiasm for the revolution causes him to embark again for Havana and later for New Orleans. After traveling to San Antonio, Texas, he meets José Vasconcelos, a writer and the only great minister produced by the revolution, according to Guzmán. Finally, in Ciudad Juárez, the author meets Pancho Villa, who is for him the chief hero of the revolution. The encounter is not as dramatic as could be expected, but an intimate, deep impression about Villa remains with the writer. Later he is introduced to Venustiano Carranza, first chief of the Constitutionalist Army. The author meets another revolutionary leader, Alvaro Obregón, whom he considers to be an impostor. Gradually, Guzmán realizes that sooner or later deep disagreement will arise among the fighters. He thinks that everything can be reduced to the fact of Mexicans looking for power and the accomplishment of personal ambitions instead of being disinterested leaders with communal goals.

A large number of episodes are intermingled in this part of the work. Perhaps they are the most interesting and representative material in the novel. Among them, "A Night in Culiacán," "The Murdering Spider," "A Race in the Darkness," and "The Feast of the Bullets" emerge as masterpieces of suspense and narrative vigor. This part of the work ends when the author is again in Ciudad Juárez, under the influence of Villa, after a journey to New York.

The second part of the novel deals with the triumph of the revolution. The schism between the leaders of the movement is inevitable, chiefly between Villa and Carranza. Guzmán joins Villa because he thinks that, in spite of the revolutionist's instinctiveness and moral blindness, he is the only possible leader who can give a democratic and impersonal character to the revolution, in contrast with Carranza, who is too prone to oligarchy. The author arrives again in Veracruz, taken by American soldiers, and finally makes his way to Mexico City. Guzmán exultantly writes the most lyric pages he has ever composed. The sight of the city and the volcanoes, the inhalation of the thin air of the plateau, and the bath of clarity are some of the unforgettable impressions of the "rebel who returned," as Guzmán calls himself. He goes again to Chihuahua and meets Villa anew. He gets the impression that the legendary warrior could never exist if there were not a gun in the world. Villa and his pistol are a single thing; from his gun all his friendships and enmities were born. To fight now against Carranza, the writer goes to Mexico City again. For him, Carranzaism is synonymous with ambition, lack of ideals, systematic corruption, and theft. Imprisoned by Carranza's orders, he is sent to Matamoros, but the Convention of Aguascalientes, a meeting of revolutionists to decide the future action of the movement, sets him free. Having been appointed minister of war by President Roque González Garza, Guzmán rejects the post and is threatened with the penitentiary. He escapes and goes to see Villa, who has been estranged by the Convention of Aguascalientes. The writer, caught between loyalty to the convention and friendship toward Villa, expatriates himself to the United States.

Analysis

The symbolism of the book's title can be found in the origins of Mexican nationality. The Aztecs, the main indigenous ancestors of Mexico, had as a legendary core of their nomadic period the belief that they should found their capital city in a spot where they would find an eagle, devouring a serpent, perched upon a nopal. Guzmán took these images and turned them into symbols for his book to show the bipolarity of Mexican history, in constant conflict between aggressive passions and an ascension of the spirit.

Guzmán explained the genesis and spirit of this book in a speech at the time of his reception as a member of the Mexican Academy of the Language. He declared that from early childhood he was accustomed to beauty from having lived in Tacubaya, one of the most charming suburbs of Mexico City, near the Chapultepec Castle, scene of many decisive moments in Mexican history.

This environment imposed on him a feeling for history in all of its grandeur. Some years later, when he embraced the cause of the revolution, he had at his disposal raw historical material of the first quality, out of which he took the subject for his most representative books.

For a long time, Guzmán hesitated to write about the revolution. He had witnessed ruthless crimes, usurpations, and disloyalties, but he also had seen in many participants of that movement a great spirit of service, purity of intention, and patriotic goals. This knowledge finally moved him to write about the revolution, to transform into literary values those violent deeds against the Porfirio Díaz dictatorship. He finally decided to embody what he had seen or done. He thought that if the chief leaders of the revolution had not been as faulty as they were, the revolution would not have become what it did.

Critical Context

The Mexican Revolution affected in different ways the Mexican writers of those days. Some remained indifferent, others defended its motives and facts, and a few engaged themselves actively in its vicissitudes. No one can be attributed with greater and more direct participation than Martín Luis Guzmán. Executor, witness, chronicler, interpreter, critic, and novelist, he embraced all the possible angles of relationship with the Mexican Revolution. For this reason, his work about the movement is the closest, most objective, and most penetrating of all the literary productions written on the subject.

Guzmán wrote three books—at the same time

biography, history, and novel—about the revolution: *The Eagle and the Serpent, La sombra del caudillo* (1929; the shadow of the commander), and *Memorias de Pancho Villa* (1938-1940; *Memoirs of Pancho Villa*, 1965). Of these, the nearest to a work of the creative imagination is the first.

THE EDGE OF THE STORM

Author: Agustín Yáñez (1904-1980)
Type of work: Novel
Type of plot: Social realism
Time of plot: Spring, 1909 to Spring, 1910
Locale: Near Guadalajara, Mexico
First published: *Al filo del agua*, 1947 (English translation, 1963)

Principal Characters

Don Dionisio, a parish priest who gives unity to the separate chapters describing the people and festivals of a small Mexican town. He is stern and upright, yet understanding and compassionate. He can combine the best of the contrasting philosophies of his two priestly associates.

Padre Reyes, his liberal and progressive assistant. He enjoys seeing the parishioners marry and shocks Padre Islas with his earthy talk. He has advanced ideas about such things as the value of life insurance, though he cannot convince any of the town of its value.

Padre Islas, Don Dionisio's narrow-minded and conservative associate. Unable to meet the townspeople on a personal basis, he scurries along the sun-baked streets with eyes averted. As the sponsor of the church organization for unmarried girls, he exerts tremendous influence on the community by urging the girls to stay pure by remaining single, and he threatens them with damnation for even wholesome thoughts about the men of the town. After achieving a reputation for saintliness, he ends up in an epileptic fit on the church floor, after which he is separated from the priesthood.

María, an orphan niece of Don Dionisio who rebels against the drab life of the community and secretly reads newspapers from Mexico and the forbidden *The Three Musketeers*. Her final rebellion takes the form of running away with the widow of Lucas González, a woman of doubtful reputation, to follow the revolutionary army fighting against dictator Porfirio Díaz.

Marta, the other niece of Don Dionisio, twenty years old and unmarried, who follows the monotonous village pattern, working in the hospital, looking after children, and accepting the social and religious restrictions.

Damián Limón, who has returned from the United States "where Mexicans are treated like dogs." He retorts that at least they get paid in money instead of promises, as in Mexico. Through the machinations of a political boss, he gets a light sentence after killing Micaela Rodríguez following a scandalous love affair. He manages to escape while on his way to jail at the capital and brazenly returns to María. She helps him escape again in order to join the revolutionary army.

Timoteo Limón, a prosperous landowner and father of Damián. He dies of a heart attack following a violent quarrel with Damián over his will.

Micaela Rodríguez, a spoiled only child who learned about freedom while on a visit to Mexico City and tries to reproduce the gay life of the capital in her little town. She shocks it with her indecent dress and shameless flirtations. In the end, stabbed to death by jealous Damián, she dies forgiving him and putting the blame for her death on her own actions.

Gabriel, young man reared by Don Dionisio. His religious life is upset by four talks with Victoria, a young widow from Guadalajara visiting the town.

Luis Gonzaga Pérez, at one time a talented seminary student. Convinced by Padre Islas of the evil of his natural desires toward the opposite sex, he ends up drawing obscene pictures on the walls of his cell in an insane asylum.

Lucas Macías, a fortune-teller whose prophecies concerning Halley's Comet upset his fellow villagers. Just before his death, receiving news of a revolt, he declares in the words of the title: "The rains are coming. We'll have a fine clearing shower."

Mercedes Toledo, a young girl of the town.

Victoria, a young widow who is visiting from Guadalajara.

The Novel

The action in the story begins in 1909, as people prepare for their Lenten and Easter activities. The panorama of people and events proceeds through the year, displaying the special religious days of June, the expected deaths, illnesses, and bad luck of August, the celebration of patriotic holidays in September, the scandalous pranks of the students home for vacation in November, and the Christmas season with its festivities. The story continues on into the New Year, at which time the people await the appearance of Halley's Comet. This event is anticipated so intently by Lucas Macías, a fortune-teller, that the rest of the people prepare for trouble, for Lucas has from the start associated the appearance of this comet with the stepping onto the scene of Francisco Madero, the man who is to lead the revolution against the tyranny of Porfirio Díaz.

The person who can most nearly be described as the main character is Don Dionisio, the stern and upright, but just and compassionate, parish priest. He touches in some way the lives of all the other characters in the book. His main ecclesiastical help comes from two assistant priests who present a vivid contrast. Padre Reyes is liberal and forward-looking; Padre Islas is narrow and conservative beyond belief. Although Padre Reyes is much more likable, it is Padre Islas, scurrying along the street from church to home so as to avoid meeting his parishioners on a personal basis, who wields more influence on the lives of the townspeople, for it is he who directs the organization to which all the unmarried girls belong. Into their minds he instills the urgent need to stay pure by remaining single. He imbues them with a sense of guilt for even thinking wholesome thoughts connected with the opposite sex. This narrow man will never use the chapel of the Holy Family, preferring the chapel of the Virgin Mary. Padre Reyes, the other assistant, is not above teasing him by asking if he thinks that María and Juan will make a nice couple, of if he is aware that Mercedes is just about ready to make someone a good wife. These questions are calculated to enrage Padre Islas.

Padre Reyes, with his modern ideas about such things as life insurance—too far removed from the imaginations of the people to be noticed—is largely ignored, while Padre Islas is revered as a saint beyond the temptations and afflictions of ordinary people. Great is the disillusionment when the good Father Islas is found collapsed on the floor of the church in a fit of epilepsy, which results in his having to be removed permanently from the priesthood. The archbishop had chosen wisely in making Don Dionisio the head priest, with the authority for making final decisions, for he approaches the problems of his parishioners with the best elements of the philosophies of his two assistants—an urgent sense of responsibility for their souls accompanied by a forgiving and understanding heart.

Two other personalities who present a study in contrast are María and Marta, the orphaned nieces of Don Dionisio, who has reared them since they were very small. At the time the story begins, they are in their twenties, unmarried, and on the verge of taking opposite paths in life. Marta, the contented, with her love for children and her work in the hospital and other gentle occupations, is the ideal end product of the social and religious forces at work in her environment. María, the rebellious, who has always read forbidden literature (*The Three Musketeers* and newspapers from the capital) behind her uncle's back, finally runs away with a woman of questionable reputation to follow the revolutionary army. She is a creature of reaction against this unnatural environment.

What happened to María happens, with variations, to nearly all the young people who have had contact with the outside world. Luis Gonzaga Pérez, a young and talented seminary student, is unable to reconcile his inhibitions concerning the opposite sex with his natural desires. At the end of the novel, he is drawing lewd pictures on the walls of his room in the insane asylum.

Damián Limón, the young son of a fairly prosperous landowner, leaves home and goes to the United States to work. Upon his return home, when criticized for going to such a sinful place where Mexicans are treated like dogs, he counters by stating that at least they are paid in money instead of in promises, as in Mexico. Damián becomes scandalously involved in a flagrant love affair with Micaela Rodríguez and kills the girl, after having just caused his father to have a fatal heart attack over an argument about his father's will. A corrupt political boss has a disgracefully light sentence placed upon him and, at the end of the story, he rides away to join the ranks of the revolutionaries.

The parents of Micaela Rodríguez, a spoiled only child, make the mistake of taking her to Mexico City for a few months. There she sees the parties, pretty clothes, and merriment of the capital's young people. Never again is she satisfied to stay in her dreary hometown. Failing to force her parents to move away to a gayer place, she threatens vengeance on the environment that binds her and shocks the town to its roots with her shameless flirting and indecent dress. She ends up being stabbed by a jealous lover. She dies forgiving him and putting the blame for her death on her own actions.

Doubt seems to be the villain that causes the downfall of these unfortunate young people. They have tasted of the world, compared it with their narrow surroundings, and found them wanting. Being few in number, these unlucky ones have fallen under the weight of a relentless social system that brooks no questioning. The time is near at hand, however, when many doubters will join together with enough force to make a crack in this teetering wall of hypocrisy, a crack that will become ever wider as education and enlightenment seep through. In this thought is captured the essence of the title, *Al filo del agua*.

Analysis

Al filo del agua is a Spanish phrase with two meanings, one literal, the other figurative. Literally, it signifies the moment that the rain begins. It is in its figurative sense that it takes on meaning as the title of this book: the imminence of something about to happen. The event about to take place was brought on by a growing dissatisfaction with the political situation and the unnaturalness of the environment imposed by the church as reflected by life in a small town in Mexico.

In 1910, Porfirio Díaz had been dictator of Mexico for more than thirty years. He had ruled with an iron hand; only now had the dream of political freedom and social improvement begun to filter through to the many semi-isolated towns of Mexico. The same few families had always been the social leaders and political bosses in the communities, and Díaz's thirty-odd years of rule had done nothing to lessen this stranglehold or to improve the lot of the common people. Education was only for the privileged few, and superstition was rampant.

Another force that held the people in its grip was the church, a circumstance especially true in rural areas where the long arm of Benito Juárez's 1859 Reform Laws seldom reached. These laws had greatly reduced the political power of the church and forbade such things as processions and public religious festivities. In the small towns, however, with the ever-present threat of arrest hanging over their heads, the priests often continued their regular clerical activities in spite of the law.

Each morning, the church bells in this town call

the people out of their beds as early as four o'clock to begin another dreary, quiet, prayerful day. Life is very serious. The women wear dark somber colors and do not leave their houses except to go to church or to do necessary errands. There is no visiting except in the case of extreme illness or a death in the house of a neighbor. There is little laughter, dancing, or singing. Strangers and strangeness are suspect. Nonconformity, even in small things, starts tongues wagging. At the end of each unvarying day, the church bells send the people to bed, an act which for many means the onset of sleepless hours or wrestling with guilty consciences, wondering when and in what form God's wrath will be brought down upon their heads.

Critical Context

Agustín Yáñez has given an unprejudiced and intricately detailed view of life in a Mexican town just after the beginning of the twentieth century. The book is not a call to arms to reform. It presents an understanding, not necessarily sympathetic, but always touching story. Yáñez has painted a series of character studies portraying the effects of a narrow and rigid as well as dull and conventional life on people of different ages, with varying degrees of education and exposure to outside influences. These influences, being outside ones and therefore bad, make up a long and varied list, including such things as Free Masonry, bright clothing, strangers, uncensored written material, fun, spiritualists, and people who had been to the United States. Yáñez creates a sense of monotonous gloom with the sure hand of an artist who has experienced this kind of life himself. The fictitious, but very typical, town in which the action takes place is set in the state of Jalisco, of which the author was a native.

EPITAPH OF A SMALL WINNER

Author: Joaquim Maria Machado de Assis (1839-1908)
Type of work: Novel
Type of plot: Philosophical realism
Time of plot: 1805-1869
Locale: Rio de Janeiro, Brazil
First published: *Memórias Póstumas de Braz Cubas*, 1881 (first translated as *The Posthumous Memoirs of Brás Cubas*, 1951; better known as *Epitaph of a Small Winner*, 1952)

Principal Characters

Braz Cubas, a wealthy Brazilian who writes his autobiography after his death, in order to while away a part of eternity. He has had several mistresses but no wife, since his fiancée died in an epidemic. He decides that in the game of life he has been a small winner, for he has brought no one into this world of misery.

Marcella, a courtesan and Braz's first mistress. She will not accompany him to Spain for study. Before his return, she is disfigured by smallpox.

Virgilia, a lame heiress chosen by Papa Cubas as Braz's wife. She prefers Neves but later becomes Braz's mistress. Their child dies at birth.

Lobo Neves, Virgilia's ambitious husband, who is blind to the infidelity of his wife.

Doña Placida, Virgilia's servant, at whose house Virgilia and Braz have their meetings.

Quincas Borba, Braz's down-at-the-heels former schoolmate, who is reduced to begging and thievery. With improved economic status, he becomes a philosopher.

The Novel

Braz Cubas, the chronicler of *Epitaph of a Small Winner*, is a wealthy Brazilian who dies of pneumonia in his sixty-fifth year. After his death, he decides to write his autobiography, to while away a part of eternity and to give mankind some record of his life.

Braz was born in 1805. His childhood was an easy one, for his father was extremely wealthy and indulgent, only pretending to be severe with his child for the sake of appearances. One of the earliest experiences the boy remembers is the elation of the Brazilians over the defeat of Napoleon, an occasion marked in his memory by the gift of a small sword. Braz remarks that each person has a "sword" that makes an occasion important.

As a child, Braz Cubas does not like school. In his seventeenth year, he has his first love affair, with a courtesan named Marcella. Trying to please his mistress, Braz spends all the money he can borrow from his mother, and then gives promissory notes that come due on the day he will inherit his father's estate. His father, learning of the affair, pays off his son's debts and ships him off to a university in Spain. At first, Braz hopes to take Marcella with him, but she refuses to go.

Braz admits that he knows very little after he is graduated from the university and awarded a degree. He takes advantage of his father's liberality and wealth and spends several years traveling around Europe. Called back to Rio de Janeiro by news that his mother is dying of cancer, he arrives homes in time to see her before she dies. After her death, he goes into retirement, remaining in seclusion until his father comes to him with plans for a marriage and a seat in the Brazilian legislative body. After some vacillation, Braz decides to obey his father's wishes. The reason for his hesitation is a love affair with a beautiful girl. His discovery that she is lame, however, turns him away from her. On his return to social life, he learns that the young woman his father had picked out for him, a girl named Virgilia, has position, wealth, and beauty. It was through her father's influence that the elder Cubas expected his son to get ahead politically. Unfortunately for the schemes of both father and son, Virgilia meets Lobo Neves, a young man with more ambition and greater prospects. She decides to marry him, a decision that ends, at least temporarily, prospects of a political career for Braz.

Disappointed and disgruntled with life, he accidentally meets Marcella, his former mistress. He finds her greatly changed, for smallpox has destroyed her beauty. After losing her looks, she had left her earlier profession to become the keeper of a small jewelry shop.

Disappointment over his son's failure to win Virgilia is too much for his father, who dies shortly afterward. The death caused commotion in the family, because Braz's brother-in-law turned out to be an avaricious man who wanted his wife, Braz's sister, to have as much of the estate as possible. Braz accepts calmly the selfish and unfortunate aspect of human nature thus revealed and agrees, for his sister's sake, to be reconciled with his greedy brother-in-law.

Not very long after his father's death, Braz learns from Virgilia's brother that Virgilia and her husband are returning to Rio de Janeiro. Braz is pleased, as he is still in love with her. A few days after the return of Virgilia and her husband, he meets them at a ball. Virgilia and Braz dance several waltzes together and fall more deeply in love than they had ever been while Braz was courting her. They continue to meet, and before long Virgilia becomes his mistress.

One day Braz finds a package in which are several bundles of banknotes. He keeps the money and later uses it to establish a trust fund for Doña Placida, a former servant of Virgilia's family who maintains the house in which Virgilia and Braz kept their assignations. They manage for several years to keep their affair a secret. In fact, he and Lobo Neves are good friends.

Braz meets Quincas Borba, an old schoolmate who has been reduced to begging. The man takes some money from Braz and, as Braz discovers later, also steals his watch. That night, Braz suggests to Virgilia that they run away. She refuses to do so. They have a lovers' quarrel, followed by a tender scene of repentance.

A short time later, Lobo Neves is offered the governorship of a province, and he suggests that Braz accompany him as his secretary. The situation is inviting to the two lovers, but they know that in the smaller provincial capital their secret could not long be hidden. Their problems are unexpectedly solved when superstitious Neves refuses the government post because the document appointing him was dated on the thirteenth of the month.

The illicit love affair continues until Virgilia becomes pregnant. Neither of the lovers doubts that Braz is the father of the child, and he acts very much like a husband who expects to be presented with his first-born. The child, not carried to full term, dies at birth, much to the sorrow of Virgilia and Braz and also of Neves, who thought that the child was his.

One day, Braz receives a letter from Quincas Borba, the begging schoolmate who had stolen his watch. Having improved his finances, the beggar had become a philosopher, a self-styled humanist. Borba's ideas fascinate Braz, who had always fancied himself an intellectual and literary man. He is pleased when Borba sends him a watch as good as the one he had stolen. Braz spends a large amount of time with Borba, for Neves had become suspicious of the relationship between his wife and her lover, and the two are discreet enough to stay away from each other for a time.

Virgilia and her husband leave Rio de Janeiro after Neves receives another political appointment. Lonely, Braz himself turns to public life. Defeated for office, he becomes the publisher of an opposition newspaper, but his venture is not successful. He falls in love and decides to get married. Once more he is disappointed, for his fiancée dies during an epidemic.

The years pass rather uneventfully. Not many

weeks after the death of Quincas Borba, who had become a close companion, Braz falls ill of pneumonia. One visitor during his last illness is Virgilia, whose husband had died, but even her presence is not enough to keep Braz from slipping into delir-

ium. In his dying moments, he casts up the accounts of his life and decides that in the game of life he was the winner by only a small margin, in that he had brought no one else into the world to suffer the misery of life.

Analysis

Machado de Assis has been awarded a unique place in Brazilian literature. Brazilians have called him their sphinx, their enigma, their myth. His writings, including *Epitaph of a Small Winner*, have been contradictorily labeled as brilliant, dry, rich, colorless, ironic, refined, intuitive, pure, limpid, balanced, boring, and elegant. Some Brazilians smell the scent of Brazilianism exuding from his pages, but Pedro Calmon wrote that he did not seem Brazilian, and his works were once described as being psychologically French. In addition to *Epitaph of a Small Winner*, several of his novels and more than a dozen of his other works have been translated into English. Literary critics commonly eulogize him for stylistic purity, perfect linguistic knowledge, and a great inner richness. It was once said that he knew well all the secrets of the art of writing and that his intuitive insight into people's intimate peculiarities was remarkable.

As is evident in *Epitaph of a Small Winner* and the three novels that chronologically followed it, Machado de Assis became steadily more disillusioned with human beings. It is said that these novels, plus his masterpiece, *Dom Casmurro* (1899), supply the most convincing evidence for his ever-continuing disillusionment. Each of Machado de Assis' most celebrated novels paints a wasted human life.

His disenchantment with human beings became universal, and his soul was ever more strained by inner turmoil. He liked to expose human egotism and believed that all nature revealed man's idiocy, that everything in the universe resented what it was and pined to be something else. Sometimes compared to William Somerset Maugham for his inferiority complex, Machado de Assis deliberately withheld information about his personal life and

hinted that it had little to do with his writing. In *Epitaph of a Small Winner*, however, Machado de Assis puts into Braz Cubas' mouth the statement that although many European novelists had made tours of one or more countries, he, Braz Cubas, had made a tour of life. In this tour, added Braz Cubas, he had seen human assininity, human evil, and the sorry vanity of all matter.

Machado de Assis strove for thirty years to master the art of narration. *Epitaph of a Small Winner*, as well as his other early works, gives a hint of the development to come. He usually used short sentences, brief chapters, and deliberately interrupted narrative. He was eventually credited with brilliant manipulation of language and haunting character analysis through skilled use of symbols and metaphors. He cautioned his readers to scrutinize his lines for an interlocking pattern that integrated the various parts. He tinged names of characters with significance and color. He withdrew from the Romanticist movement that was literarily dominant during his youth and became a realist.

Machado de Assis rarely left his native Rio de Janeiro, entwined in its granite mountains and curving bay, and never journeyed far when he did. He remained an autodidact in ideas and cultural values to the end of his life. He died as he lived, loathing the idea of being a bore, a spectacle, or a hypocrite. As he was dying, attended by Brazil's most famous writers of the day, he wanted to call a priest but then reflected that that would be hypocritical. Despite Machado de Assis' celebrated pessimism and bleak insight into human nature, none of his novels alleges that it is impossible to view the world in a more cheerful light than he did; they merely state that it would be difficult.

Critical Context

This novel, written by one of Brazil's leading men of letters, was not made available in English translation until 1951, even though it had long been a favorite with readers in the original Portuguese and in Spanish translations. Machado de Assis was president of the Brazilian Academy of Letters from its foundation in 1897 until his death in 1908. *Epitaph of a Small Winner* is the story of an ordinary man who sums up the profit of living as nothing, except that he had left no children to whom he could pass on the misery of human existence. Because he left no children to endure life, he was, says the author, a small winner in the game of life. Machado de Assis' attitude is one of complete and ironic pessimism. As the English translator points out, the book combines the twin themes of nature's indifference to man and man's own egoism. Readers familiar with eighteenth century fiction will recognize many stylistic peculiarities similar to those in Laurence Sterne's *The Life and Opinions of Tristram Shandy, Gent.* (1759-1767).

THE ESSAYS OF JORGE LUIS BORGES

Author: Jorge Luis Borges (1899-1986)
Type of work: Essays
Principal published works: *Inquisiciones*, 1925; *El tamaño de mi esperanza*, 1926; *El idioma de los Argentinos*, 1928; *Evaristo Carriego*, 1930 (English translation, 1984); *Discusión*, 1932 (revised, with deletions and additions, 1957); *Historia de la eternidad*, 1936 (with additions, 1953); *Nueva refutatión del tiempo*, 1947; *Aspectos de la literatura gauchesca*, 1950; *Otras inquisiciones*, 1952 (*Other Inquisitions*, 1964); *Manual de zoología fantástica*, 1957 (with Margarita Guerrero; *The Imaginary Zoo*, 1969, revised as *El libro de los seres imaginarios*, 1967, *The Book of Imaginary Beings*, 1969); *Introducción a la literatura norteamericana*, 1967 (*An Introduction to American Literature*, 1971); *Seven Nights* (1984)

Arguably the most significant and certainly the most stylistically innovative of Argentine writers, Jorge Luis Borges, a prolific essayist, was also a poet, a short-story writer, and a lecturer. Beginning with *El idioma de los Argentinos* (the language of the Argentines), his third volume of essays, Borges gained critical acclaim. In 1956, his essay collection *Otras inquisiciones* won the National Prize for Literature, and in 1961, he shared the International Publisher's Prize (Prix Fomentor) with Samuel Beckett.

The measure of a writer's work is critical acclaim, which is significantly related to uniqueness of style, to translations made of his or her work, and to the universality of that work's content. In each area, Borges excels. His unique style prompted critics to coin the term "Borgesian" to describe it; such coinage lifts him to a category shared by few writers, among them Franz Kafka and Charles Dickens. Nowhere is his style more obvious than in his mazing of multiple genres; for example, woven in the same sparse, metaphoric form and with the same philosophical themes, his essays are literally indistinguishable from his fiction. His work has been translated into more than a dozen languages, the first of which was French in 1951. The universality of his content rests in its philosophic nature and is measured by its inclusion in new editions of old texts that survey canonical literature.

Both the unique style and the philosophical content are heavily influenced by Borges' childhood; thus knowledge of childhood influences is fundamental for a fully enriched reading of his works. Borges began writing when he was six or seven years old and spent his life with books. He has described his father's library as a chief source of enjoyment and fulfillment, claiming that "I sometimes think I have never strayed outside that library." It was among his father's books that Borges' succinct, clear syntax, central motifs, and major themes began to be shaped. Because many of the books were in English (Borges' paternal grandmother was English), young, myopic, frail Jorge learned to read first in that language. He developed such an affinity with the patterns of English sentences that years later his American translator, Norman Thomas di Giovanni, would say that his work lost virtually nothing in translation because beneath the Spanish language was English syntax.

Borges' favorite early reading was the *Encyclopædia Britannica*, and he never outgrew his enjoyment of those volumes. He bought a set of the eleventh edition—his old favorite—when he won the Second Municipal Prize for *El idioma de los Argentinos*. Borges said that in this collection of essays he tried to tell a "purely Argentine story in an Argentine way," adding that it was a "story" he had retold, with small variations, ever since. He called it a "tale of the motiveless, or disinterested, duel—of courage for its own sake." The leanness of his prose reflects his appreciation for the capsulated form of encyclopedia entries: Most of his essays consist of only two or three pages, and some have but two or three paragraphs; few—if any written for collections—exceed twenty pages.

As Borges' prose works are alike in style, they are also alike in narrative method and in content; indeed, neither method nor content appreciably helps readers to separate his essays from his fiction. All the prose works narrate philosophical concerns long rooted in the writer's mind. Although the content can be heavy, his works are touched with Borges' playful sense of humor. That playfulness, in part, accounts for his deliberate cross-publishing of genres. In fact, Borges published his 1935 short story "The Approach to al-Mu'tasim" in his 1936 volume of essays, *Historia de la eternidad* (history of eternity). He included in the story a footnote, also a fiction, that lent credence to his joke. He enjoyed the story's immediate use by readers as a factual piece. This joke was so good that Borges did not correct the misconception until 1942, when he published the story as fiction in *El jardín de senderos que se bifurcan* (1941, the garden of forking paths). It is this extreme and humorously deliberate sameness of style and content that causes critics to call his stories "essayistic fiction" and his essays "narrative prose."

For all the playfulness, a dark strain—often associated with labyrinths, the essential motif of Borges' works—threads through his texts. He called the labyrinth "a symbol of bewilderment, a symbol of being lost in life." The source of Borges' dark fascination with this symbol is in his childhood. He was captivated by an etching of a labyrinth in a French volume by Robert Garnier in his father's library. Visually handicapped, even as a child, he had thought that, with a magnifying glass, he could find a minotaur in the center of Garnier's labyrinth. Borges was drawn to but frightened by this thought. The fear remained always with him, and it haunts his essays, which typically ponder life as a labyrinth. That is how he saw the universe—as a labyrinth with no center that holds, or if a center, one more frightening than secure.

Borges did, of course, "stray" outside that library, but he took it with him in those notions of maze and minotaur. For example, he describes Androgue, the family's vacation spot where he and his sister played year after year, as "a lost and undisturbed maze of summer homes surrounded by iron fences . . . [and] streets that radiated out of the many plazas." The mirror, a central motif of his essays, also took root here: Investigating a closet, the children saw themselves, unexpectedly, in a mirror. They spent the summer searching the garden maze for the "ghost" they imagined they saw reflected in it. Also in childhood, Borges visited a house that had a large room walled completely around with mirrors. He later called this room a true labyrinth and said that the self, lost in its center, was its own minotaur.

Borges expanded his haunting memories of the minotaur to include a yellow tiger. This extension stemmed from another indelible image of boyhood. On a trip to the zoo, he saw a black-and-gold-striped tiger pacing in a cage. So imprinted was the image that after Borges' eyesight failed completely, he claimed he could see one color: the yellow color of that tiger. Out of these symbols, then, Borges wrote metaphysical essays dealing with dualities of life in themes of time, memory, the self, chaos, cosmos, literature, the universal soul, and God/gods; doing so, he frequently used as symbols the labyrinth, mirrors, and tigers.

Just before World War I began, Borges and his family moved to Geneva, where they remained until after the war. During that period, Borges encountered one more youthful influence. He went to Spain and became involved with a vanguard group of writers who called themselves "Ultraists." This group proclaimed the metaphor as the most significant aspect of any writing. Borges' humorous nature is again revealed when, in maturity, he explained widely that the whole thing was a joke. He said they had been but a group of young men joking around, especially about metaphors. Borges did believe strongly in the use of metaphor, but not in the Ultraist sense of it as the panacea of letters; to him, metaphor was "the momentary contact of two images, not the methodical likening of two things." For Borges, there were only a few "essential metaphors," among them "time and a river; life and dreams; death and sleep; stars and eyes; flowers and women." Their value, he believed, was in their intonation. Such metaphors lend intensity to his works.

Borges returned to Buenos Aires in 1921. In 1925, he published a volume of essays titled *Inquisiciones*. These essays have no relationship to his *Otras inquisiciones* (1952). In 1926, he published a second volume of essays, *El tamaño de mi esperanza* (the measure of my hope), which analyzed the *criollismo* problem as well as Argentine cultural identity. Both these volumes were subsequently suppressed by Borges, who said they were full of purple metaphoric prose. Not completely satisfied, either, with the third set of essays, *El idioma de los Argentinos*, he came to believe it had merit, particularly since, as he relates in "An Autobiographical Essay" (contained in *The Aleph and Other Stories, 1933-1969*, 1970), it won him the three-thousand-peso Second Municipal Prize. (Elsewhere, he says the prize was for his 1929 *Cuaderno San Martín*.) He used his prize money to take a year off to write *Evaristo Carriego*. Carriego, a writer Borges knew from their old neighborhood in Buenos Aires, was fascinated by the gauchos, an antiheroic cowboy class in Argentina. Borges later worked with that subject himself and even published *Aspectos de la literatura gauchesca* (aspects of gauchesa literature). Borges confessed that his book-length essay on Carriego was flat, as he quickly became disenchanted with his subject.

Beginning with *Otras inquisiciones*, Borges' essays fall into three primary groups: philosophical, literary, and miscellaneous. The bulk of them have philosophical themes. Even the literary essays, though frequently critical analyses of the work of writers or a close reading of text, most often focus philosophically on literature as art and deal with such subjects as the hero, genre, writer-as-text, and nature of language. The miscellaneous group includes essays of homage, political essays, Borges' autobiographical essay, and essays on the fantastic.

Otras inquisiciones is the largest single collection of Borges' essays in English translation. Of these, thirteen have philosophical themes, including universal soul, universal mankind, the world as

illusion, the self and its other, God in us, mirrors, and time. Fourteen are essays on literature and/or on writers as text. Ten are miscellaneous essays: six homage pieces, two on war, and two apologetic essays on Argentina.

The essay series *Manual de zoología fantástica* and *El libro de los seres imaginarios* reveals Borges' interest in fantasy, an offshoot of his interest in labyrinths, nightmares, the Minotaur, tigers, and leopards. Included with this series should be *El hacedor* (1960), a tiny volume accumulating pieces from all of Borges' genres. Borges was asked by translators what "hacedor" meant in English. The amused writer told them that "hacedor" was his translation into Spanish of the English word "maker"; thus the title essay in the volume is "The Maker." This five-paragraph prose piece considers the philosophical theme of the universal soul. Ending the piece, Borges writes poignantly of the murmur of the Odysseys and Iliads "it was [Homer's] destiny to sing and leave echoing concavely in the memory of man." He then adds his characteristically dark, dual point: "These things we know, but not those that he felt when he descended into the last shade of all." The content of this work, as Borges writes in his commentary that concludes *The Aleph and Other Stories, 1933-1969* (1970), "may be thought of as autobiographical—Homer as an exaltation of myself, his blindness as my blindness, his acceptance of darkness as my acceptance." Borges called *El hacedor* his most personal and perhaps best collection, as all the writing in it seemed to fall on the page.

Five essays appear in *Antología personal* (1961; *A Personal Anthology*, 1969). Of these, four are philosophical in content, and of those four, three deal with self-identity and one with time. The other, though it addresses dreams and the leopard, is a literary essay, "Inferno I, 32." Borges believed that this collection represented the best of his works and hoped that his canon would be judged by its contents.

His *Introducción a la literatura norteamericana* falls among his literary essays. In it, Borges, who had an immense respect for America and its writers, makes a personal map of American literature as he deals with writers, genres and/or periods, narrative technique, expatriates, poets, the novel (Borges did not, however, like the novel as a form), the theater, the detective story (Borges loved detective fiction and connected it to science fiction), Westerns, and the oral poetry of the American Indians. He used such essays in teaching.

His "An Autobiographical Essay" falls among his miscellaneous essays. In it, he discusses his relationship with his parents, his father's library, his racial heritage, his years away from Buenos Aires, the essay collections he suppressed, external influences on his writing style, his experiences as an underling at the Municipal Library, how he came to write fiction, the Perón and post-Perón years, his career as director of the National Library and professor of English and American literature, his literary fame and travels, and his plans for the future, written when he was seventy-one years old. Reading this essay reveals how consistent Borges was as a person. What he says about himself and his work in the many interviews he gave is consistent with his autobiography.

Seven Nights (1984) contains lecture essays that are uncustomarily long. Of these, two are philosophic discussions and deal with sleep, dreams, and nightmares. Four are on literature and/or writing and deal, variously, with connections between Eastern and Western myths, with supernatural and fantastic literature, and with which came first, speech or writing. The seventh essay is on blindness and concerns itself with the notion of what is gained when something is lost. Borges believed that writing is a metaphysical act, one performed not by a writer alone but by a writer with some-

thing—not necessarily the muse, the Holy Ghost, or the subconscious, perhaps, but something more than self. This self-searching rose out of the inevitable dualities he saw everywhere, nowhere more than within himself. In this regard, for example, he believed that writing consumed the writer, that a writer and his text were self-reflexive. He writes this theme repeatedly, nowhere more clearly than in two short prose pieces. In the first, "Borges and I," he focuses on how Borges (the writer) subsumes borges (the man he might have been). As is his style, he leaves the reader with no certainty of what either [b]/Borges finally concludes, writing (as borges, with Borges as "him") "Thus is my life a flight, and I lose everything, and everything belongs to oblivion, or to him." This may convince the reader that borges is gone, and all that remains visible and material is Borges. The wily writer, however, adds a last one-sentence paragraph: "I don't know which one of the two of us is writing this page." This reopens the philosophical question of self-identity.

In the second piece, the "Epilogue" to *Dreamtigers* (translated from *El hacedor*), he reveals his other side. It is a side that seems to have answered the question that haunted the man and haunts his work. It may be an answer; it also may be a Borgesianism. He writes,

> A man sets himself the task of portraying the world. Through the years he peoples a space with images of provinces, kingdoms, mountains, bays, ships, islands, fishes, rooms, instruments, stars, horses, and people. Shortly before his death, he discovers that that patient labyrinth of lines traces the image of his face.

EVA LUNA

Author: Isabel Allende (1942-   )
Type of work: Novel
Type of plot: Magical Realism
Time of plot: The middle and late twentieth century
Locale: An unnamed South American country
First published: 1987 (English translation, 1988)

Principal Characters

Eva Luna, the narrator. The child of a servant, after her mother's death she is put out to work. Exploited and abused by her various employers and by the godmother who appropriates her earnings, Eva finds her refuge among the lowly and the outcasts. From her mother, Eva Luna learned to invent stories. These not only enable her to escape from the harshness of real life but also eventually to make her way in the world. At first, she simply tells stories to entertain people, but after learning to read and write, Eva becomes a scriptwriter for a successful television series. Eva uses her program to attack her country's oppressive government. In a guerrilla camp, Eva meets Rolf Carlé, who appears to be the man of her dreams. After defeating her old fear of love, she attains her fulfillment as a woman.

Rolf Carlé, an Austrian. The youngest child of a schoolmaster who went to war shortly after his birth, Rolf survives the Russian occupation only to discover that in fact his worst enemy is his father, who has returned to torment his family. After the schoolmaster is murdered by his students, Rolf realizes that he is as guilty as they are and becomes ill. Sent to South America to live with distant relatives in a European settlement called La Colonia, Rolf becomes part of a happy household. Rolf leaves to pursue work as a filmmaker. In the course of making a documentary, Rolf meets Eva Luna and falls in love. Back in La Colonia with her, Rolf discovers that their joy in each other has driven away the ghosts that haunted him for so long.

Consuelo, Eva Luna's mother. A child of unknown parentage reared by missionaries and nuns, she is a quiet, unassuming person who spends most of her brief life as the servant of one eccentric master. It is unclear whether her single sexual encounter is prompted more by her own curiosity or by pity for a man who supposedly is dying. Consuelo's bequest to Eva Luna is the gift of creating imaginary worlds through storytelling.

Elvira, the cook who becomes a second mother to Eva. At heart a revolutionary, Elvira encourages Eva to stand up to her employers. Because her worst fear is of ending up in a pauper's grave, Elvira keeps her coffin handy and frequently sleeps in it.

Melesio (Mimí), a Sicilian forced to emigrate because his family disapproved of his feminine characteristics. When Eva Luna first meets him, he is a teacher by day and a singer dressed in women's clothes by night. Melesio proves his courage by leading the Revolt of the Whores, but he is arrested and thrown into prison, where he very nearly dies. He encourages Eva to write for television.

Huberto Naranjo (Comandante Rogelio), a tough, daring street boy, later a Marxist guerrilla fighter. Although he is briefly Eva's lover and always her friend, Huberto's relationships with women are inevitably superficial, because his *macho* attitude denies women equality while granting them protection. Huberto's victories bring about a change of government.

Riad Halabí, a kindly, intelligent shop owner. Riad seems to be loved by everyone but his wife, Zulema. After admitting to Eva that he loves her,

Riad points out that the vicious gossip attending Zulema's death has made a marriage between them impossible.

Zulema, Riad's wife through an arranged marriage. A self-centered woman, she decides at first glance that she hates both her husband and his town. She refuses to be pleased by anything except the jewels he gives her and the stories Eva tells. After the sudden departure of her husband's cousin, whom she has seduced, Zulema is inconsolable and shoots herself.

The Novel

Eva Luna is the story of a poor girl with a great gift for storytelling who, because of her indomitable spirit, manages to survive a perilous youth and become a successful television scriptwriter. The title character of the novel is also the narrator. Even when Eva herself could not have witnessed what she describes, the implication is that she is faithfully reporting what she has been told by those who were present and thus, in a sense, making those events a part of her own narrative. Since all the people mentioned affect Eva's own history, these stories are an essential part of her life.

The book begins with Eva's birth, the product of the sole sexual encounter of her parents. Her mother, Consuelo, a servant of unknown parentage, had decided to console an Indian gardener who was presumed to be dying from snakebite. When he recovered and went back to the jungle, he left Consuelo pregnant. Even though she died when Eva was only six years old, Consuelo remained an important part of her life, primarily because she told her such fascinating stories.

Allende then moves back in time to introduce Rolf Carlé, the son of Lukas Carlé, an Austrian schoolmaster. Rolf was a baby when his father went to war; during his father's absence, Rolf has made him into a hero. Unfortunately, when Lukas returns, he is so tyrannical that by comparison the Russian occupation troops seem angelic.

Although Allende does not bring Eva and Rolf together until almost the end of her novel, she continues to trace his adventures as well as hers. For example, in one chapter Eva tells about her mother's death, her employment in a household where only the cook, Elvira, treats her with kindness, and her meeting with a street boy, Huberto

Naranjo, who becomes her protector. In the next, she describes Rolf's reaction when his father is murdered by his students: a feeling of guilt by association so consuming that he cannot eat and, as a result, is shipped off to kindly relatives in South America. As Eva points out, when Rolf arrives in the German settlement of La Colonia, he is not far from the place where she is growing up.

Deposited with first one employer and then another by the mad mulatto godmother who rules her life, Eva never feels secure. Nevertheless, she occasionally does exhibit her spirit. On one memorable occasion, because she is disgusted with the cabinet minister who spends every day on an ornate chamberpot that she must empty, she deliberately pours the contents over his head. Fleeing from his wrath, Eva finds her old friend Huberto, who places her in the care of a famous madam, La Señora, and her best friend, Melesio, who calls himself Mimí whenever he performs as a singer, dressed in women's clothes. Eva's life with these two of society's outcasts is supremely happy.

Unfortunately, a political uprising brings the idyll to an end. This time, Eva is rescued by Riad Halabí, called "the Turk" by the people of Agua Santa, the isolated village where he keeps a shop. A man so compassionate that he covers his unsightly harelip with a handkerchief for fear of offending his companions, Riad Halabí has a wife, Zulema, who cannot endure him. During one of Riad's absences, Eva is horrified when Zulema seduces Riad's young cousin Kamel. After Kamel realizes what he has done and runs away, the lovesick Zulema kills herself. Because she was the one to find the body, Eva is arrested, and though she is finally cleared and released, she is forced to leave the village and Riad, even though he is now as much in love with her as she is with him.

In the final section of *Eva Luna*, the lives of Eva, Mimí, Huberto, and Rolf become intertwined. Believing herself to be in love with Huberto, who is now a guerrilla leader called Comandante Rogelio, Eva becomes his mistress. Meanwhile, with Mimí's encouragement, she begins writing and selling scripts for television serials that become so popular that the authorities attempt to influence their content. In the guerrilla camp, Eva meets Rolf, now a documentary filmmaker. When Eva is told that she is in danger from the authorities, Rolf takes her to La Colonia. In that Edenic setting, Eva and Rolf discover that they have at last found the mates they have sought for so long. In time, Eva says, their love eventually wore out, or, if one prefers another ending, it lasted forever.

Analysis

As the niece of Chilean president Salvador Allende, who formed a representative government only to be assassinated in 1973 in a military coup that was immediately followed by a reign of terror, Isabel Allende has every reason to be preoccupied with the abuse of power. In *Eva Luna*, she consistently contrasts the heartlessness of wealthy people such as Eva's abusive *patrona* with the kindness of social outcasts such as La Señora and Mimí. During much of the novel, her characters manage to keep their distance from the sources of power. The tyrannical ruler of the nameless country, the sadistic head of the secret police, and corrupt toadies such as the cabinet minister, however, are always present in the consciousness of her characters, and they become only too real to Mimí when he is thrown into prison for leading the Revolt of the Whores and to Eva herself when she is forced to flee because of her suspected involvement with the guerrillas.

Given her own experience with repression, it is amazing that Allende manages to avoid polemics in her works. She shows that even in the darkest of times, there is always the possibility of fulfillment through love. For Eva Luna, this comes only after she has come to terms with the shock of Zulema's suicide. When, for the first time in years, she feels the pains of menstruation, Eva knows that now her body will once again permit her to function as a woman, thus making possible her total commitment to Rolf. Although this aspect of the plot of *Eva Luna* might be seen as inconsistent with the feminism that pervades Allende's fiction, one must make a distinction between accepting one's gender and admitting inferiority. Implicit in the relationship between Eva and Rolf is the rejection of the patriarchal system. The two are companions and equals.

The fact that, as a creative artist, Eva seems to possess an almost godlike power indicates how closely Allende's attitude toward her art is related to her feminism and to her politics. When Mimí sets Eva down at her typewriter to begin "dusting off memories and weaving destinies" in a world of her own creation, Eva realizes that she has "the power to determine my fate, or invent a life for myself," as well as for other characters. It is this sense of her own power that gives her the strength to disagree with General Rodríguez and finally to refuse him. When the general asserts that there is no such thing as lasting love, Eva replies as one who is in control of her own life and of her own imagination: "I also try to live my life as I would like it . . . like a novel." Thus Allende reminds readers that there is in fact no real barrier between the "real" world and the world of ideas and of idealism.

Critical Context

With *Eva Luna*, Isabel Allende returned to the kind of fiction that had established her reputation. Her first novel, *La casa de los espiritus* (1982; *The House of the Spirits*, 1985), was written in the tradition of Magical Realism, like the novels of Gabriel García Márquez, the noted Latin American author and Nobel laureate to whom Allende acknowledges her indebtedness. Although in *De amor y de sombra* (1984; *Of Love and Shadows*, 1987) Allende continued to explore the theme of repression and political tyranny, in form that novel was realistic or even naturalistic. Although it was an exciting story, it lacked the mysterious, enchanted, and often haunted atmosphere that readers saw again in *Eva Luna*.

Eva and Rolf appear again in *Cuentos de Eva Luna* (1990; *The Stories of Eva Luna*, 1991), a collection of twenty-three stories supposedly invented by Eva at the request of her lover. In the novel that followed, *El Plan Infinito* (1991; *The Infinite Plan*, 1993), for the first time Allende set a work in the United States. Her North American protagonist is a rootless wanderer, not unlike Eva Luna, who searches for love and justice in a world that sometimes seems to contain only brutality and betrayal.

Because of her technical virtuosity and her transcendent humanistic vision, Allende is considered to be one of the most gifted Latin American writers of the late twentieth century. Her importance is perhaps best stated in the frequently quoted words of Alexander Coleman, who wrote in *The New York Times Book Review* (May 12, 1985) that Allende was "the first woman to approach on the same scale as the others [male Latin American novelists] the tormented patriarchal world of traditional Hispanic society."

EXPLOSION IN A CATHEDRAL

Author: Alejo Carpentier (1904-1980)
Type of work: Novel
Type of plot: Historical
Time of plot: The French revolutionary period, 1789-1808
Locale: Cuba, Haiti, France, Guadeloupe, the Caribbean, French Guiana, and Spain
First published: *El siglo de las luces*, 1962 (English translation, 1963)

Principal Characters

Victor Hugues, a robust self-made French entrepreneur and revolutionary living in the Caribbean. Victor helps organize the business of his recently orphaned young Cuban hosts and familiarizes them with the latest liberal ideas. An opportunist, he adapts to the successive stages of the French Revolution, from initial libertarianism through various phases of repression.

Sofía, a wealthy young woman brought up with her brother and male cousin Esteban in a wealthy Havana home situated next door to the retail establishment of her father, who has died just before the action of the novel begins. A spirited woman, she becomes imbued with Enlightenment ideals and stays loyal to them throughout. Sofía's maturation into womanhood is encouraged by Victor's advances, to which she eventually yields before he leaves Cuba. Sofía finally goes to Spain to be near Esteban, who loves her and has been imprisoned there. At Sofía's urging, they join the revolutionary crowd on the day of the Napoleonic massacre in early May, 1808, and are not heard from again.

Esteban, the initially frail, asthmatic younger cousin who from early childhood has lived with Sofía and Carlos. After his cure, Esteban blossoms into an inquisitive, intellectual young man. Under Victor's tutelage, he becomes an enthusiast of the revolution. Later, he becomes disillusioned when the revolution and Victor lose their ideals. Esteban's experiences make up the longest part of the novel.

Carlos, Sofía's brother, a teenage boy when his father dies. Carlos develops into a successful businessman and over the years retains his enthusiasm for the ideals of the French Revolution. It falls to him, traveling in Madrid, to piece together the fate of Sofía and Esteban from accounts of those who knew them there.

Doctor Ogé, a friend of Victor Hugues. Ogé combines traditional beliefs—biblical myths and mystical doctrines—with the progressive liberal credo. He practices folk medicine and cures Esteban of his asthma.

Don Cosme (the **Executor**), initially acts as guardian for the orphaned young people but is effectively displaced in this surrogate father's role by Victor.

Jorge, a slim, handsome Cuban of Irish descent, educated in England, who marries Sofía and works in the family business with Carlos.

Caleb Dexter, a North American sea captain, a friend of Hugues and Ogé. Against the lovesick Esteban's pleas, Dexter respects Sofía's wishes and agrees to take her from Cuba to French Guiana to be with Hugues after her husband dies.

The Novel

Explosion in a Cathedral begins in the sleepy colonial world of Havana, Cuba, where Carlos, his sister Sofía, and their cousin Esteban are reunited following the death of Carlos and Sofía's father.

Sofía nurses her asthmatic cousin in a preference to becoming a nun, and the young adolescents enjoy a chaotic sense of liberation.

Into this backwater comes Victor Hugues, a self-made man, a merchant and revolutionary from Port au Prince, Haiti. He instinctively takes charge, shares in the children's games, and becomes their protector. Through him the others sense the larger world of science and of European and Caribbean revolution. Victor's fellow conspirator, Doctor Ogé, cures Esteban's asthma. During a hurricane that destroys much of Havana, Victor unsuccessfully tries to make love to Sofía. Esteban and Sofía help Victor and Doctor Ogé to escape the local authorities. In Santiago de Cuba, aboard the schooner of Caleb Dexter, Hugues succeeds in making love to Sofía, while Esteban and Doctor Ogé explore Santiago.

The men continue in another boat to Port au Prince, leaving Sofía in Santiago. In Port au Prince, Victor finds his shop burned. A violent revolution of black slaves against all whites makes it imperative that Victor and Esteban leave immediately. They sail to France.

In Paris, the French Revolution is in full course. Esteban joins the Freemasons and observes; Victor succeeds in attaching himself to the Jacobin cause. He finds a position for Esteban as a translator near the Spanish border. The direction of the revolution constantly changes. At a moment of narrow nationalism, Esteban is in danger as a foreigner. He discovers that Victor is about to set sail for Guadeloupe as Augustin Robespierre's agent, with plenipotentiary powers. Hugues agrees to take him along. Esteban finds Victor changed. In the process of jockeying for power, he has emerged as a completely political animal, and he keeps his old friend at a distance.

Victor brings the new order of the revolution with him on his ship: a printing press, a proclamation abolishing slavery, and a guillotine. After courageously defeating the British, who had taken over the island, Victor ruthlessly establishes himself as the supreme power. When he learns of the downfall of Robespierre, he defiantly awaits his own. In the meantime, he has involved France in a

war with the United States. Trusting no one, Victor uses Estaban's mistress to spy on him, finally sending Esteban home, bearing a letter for Sofía.

Esteban arrives in Havana full of criticism for both Victor and the revolution. He finds Sofía married to Jorge, a Cuban of Irish ancestry who has become Carlos' business partner. Esteban is surprised to discover, in spite of his experiences, that Sofía, Carlos, and Jorge are still believers in the revolution, whatever its faults. Esteban discovers that he is deeply in love with Sofía, who rejects him. Her husband is stricken with cholera and dies. Caleb Dexter arrives to inform them that Victor, after having been sent home as a traitor, has been tried and exonerated. Napoleon has named him governor of French Guiana. After her husband's funeral, Sofía escapes in Caleb Dexter's ship, bound for Cayenne, to join Victor. It emerges that in the letter sent with Esteban, Victor had written of his loneliness. Although Esteban tries to stop her, when he is arrested by the local authorities as a dangerous revolutionary and a translator of seditious tracts, he stalls long enough for Sofía to get away. Esteban is sent to a squalid prison in Ceuta.

Sofía enjoys a romantic idyll of complete sexual abandon with Victor in a country house outside Cayenne, but she gradually becomes disillusioned as she discovers how he has changed. As governor, following the orders of Napoleon, he has reestablished slavery and is undertaking a vigorous campaign to capture runaway slaves. Sofía abandons Victor, symbolically reaffirming her sexual freedom by giving herself to a young officer before leaving French Guiana.

In an epilogue, the reader learns of Sofía's moving to Madrid in order to be near Esteban, who is finally released from the Ceuta prison. Carlos visits their apartment on the Calle de Fuencarral. The last that is known of Sofía and Esteban is that they disappeared after joining the people of Madrid fighting Napoleon's army of occupation. Carlos leaves the apartment, where he finds a painting that Esteban had admired as a child: *Explosion in a Cathedral*, which depicts a cathedral in fragments, its roof collapsed, its columns still standing. The cycle of revolution is complete.

Analysis

Carpentier sees human history and revolution as part of a dynamic cyclic process. In this novel, it is the revolution itself, with its inner dialectic. Each revolution is followed by a reaction; mankind advances two steps and then retreats one. There is "progress," although it is not easy to measure; there is also the "eternal return." Hence, Carpentier's novel goes full cycle. The inheritors of the French Revolution (Napoleon Bonaparte and Victor Hugues) become the oppressors, and the people of Madrid, inheritors of the same tradition as that of the stifling and reactionary Havana at the novel's beginning, are revolutionaries fighting for freedom in the streets.

Structure, style, and language are central to Carpentier's presentation. The novel begins with a striking view of the guillotine swaying as it moves over water on the prow of Victor's ship bound for Guadeloupe. This is a flash-forward, an intimation of things to come prior to total immersion among the objects, sounds, and smells of a remote, static, and seemingly immutable Havana at the end of the eighteenth century. The incongruously swaying guillotine symbolizes the uncertainty and violence of life. Above all, it symbolizes the unity and continuity of human history across space and time. It joins France and America and the Caribbean; revolution begets revolution.

The books, instruments, and other objects strewn about the warehouse of Carlos and Sofía's father serve as a compendium to symbolize the eighteenth century, properly absorbed by the young Cubans only when they are joined by Victor. Among these objects, the painting bearing the title *Explosion in a Cathedral* displays the old order in the process of being partially destroyed by the new. Esteban has always been fascinated by the painting, and when he becomes disillusioned by his experience of the revolution, he kicks a hole through it, but the painting is found by Carlos among the objects in the apartment in Madrid.

Critical Context

Carpentier, a musicologist, critic, revolutionary, diplomat, and at one time director of propaganda for the Cuban Revolution of Fidel Castro, is above all remembered for his novels and short stories. In him, European culture and American reality are synthesized in an original way.

His first experimental novel, *¡Ecué-Yamba-O! Historia Afro-Cubana* (1933), revealed the mythic, symbolic perspective characteristic of his works. Nature, primeval rites of sex, and voodoo are contrasted with man's sordid exploitation of man in Cuba. Carpentier did not find his voice as a mature artist, however, until the publication of his novel about Haiti, *El reino de este mundo* (1949; *The Kingdom of This World*, 1957). In the prologue to the latter book is found his aesthetic credo: As opposed to the "magician's tricks" of the surrealists and the "eschatological wallowing" of the existentialists, Carpentier espoused the intense elaboration of American reality, whose marvelous nature lay in the eyes of the beholder capable of appreciating it. This credo is best exemplified in Carpentier's greatest novels, *Los pasos perdidos* (1953; *The Lost Steps*, 1956) and *Explosion in a Cathedral*. Carpentier must be considered one of the principal architects of the so-called New Novel in Latin America, both in a structural, technical sense and in terms of the artistic and philosophical enrichment of the genre.

FACE

Author: Cecile Pineda (1942-   )
Type of work: Novel
Type of plot: Psychological realism
Time of plot: The present
Locale: Brazil
First published: 1985

Principal Characters

Helio Cara, the protagonist and central character of the novel. Helio starts out in the novel as a barber in the huge Brazilian city of Rio de Janeiro. By no means a successful or extraordinarily happy man, Helio nevertheless has the rudiments of life: a job, a girlfriend, and basic acceptance by others. All of this is jeopardized when he falls off a cliff and severely damages his face. Forced to wear a white handkerchief over his face to conceal injuries that other people find repulsive, Helio at first tries to go on with his life as if nothing had happened, but his coworkers and his girlfriend repudiate him, unable to adjust to or to cope with his injury. Helio petitions the city's medical establishment for aid, but he is told that although his face can be physically repaired, his medical insurance will not cover the cost of making him look attractive once again. Helio decides to return to the town where he was born. Motivated to a new brilliance, Helio self-reliantly proceeds to reconstruct his own face using a mixture of medical guides, folklore, and the ingenuity of his own mind. At the end of the novel, Helio has repaired the damage to him, both physical and psychological, and is ready to meet the challenge of living in society once again.

Lula, Helio's mistress, who had been living with him at the time of the accident. Lula leaves Helio even though she still has some tenderness for him; the burden of coping with his injury is too much for her.

Luis and **Mario,** Helio's coworkers at the barbershop. After the accident, they feel empathy for him that is a vestige of their former camaraderie, but they realize that because of the prejudices of their customers, Helio cannot be kept on at the shop.

Cardoso, a barber. Helio's former boss at the shop, Cardoso had taught the younger man to read and had generally acclimated him to the ways of the overwhelming metropolis of Rio de Janeiro.

Senhora Cara, Helio's mother. She dies just before the accident. Helio is bitter toward her for having remarried shortly after his father's death.

Julião, Helio's stepfather. Helio resents Julião for taking the place of his father. Long before Helio's face is injured, he suffers psychically from the trauma of his mother's marriage to Julião.

Godoy, a doctor and hospital administrator. Godoy tells Helio of the insuperable obstacles facing his effort to have his face repaired courtesy of government funding. Later, after Helio has succeeded in convincingly reconstructing his face, Godoy sends Helio a letter at his shack in the hinterlands, presumably offering further help in the treatment.

The Novel

Face is a novel that chronicles one man's effort to rebuild his soul after a devastating calamity changes his life. After a short prologue, the book is divided into two major sections. It is told in the third person through the consciousness of the major character, although there are frequent flashbacks to earlier periods in his life. In addition, the author intersperses the commentaries of doctors and other observers of the novel's action. In the struggle of Helio Cara to repair his badly deformed face, the reader envisages the persistence and resilience of the human spirit.

The book begins with Helio Cara, an ordinary barber with an ordinary life, stumbling as he is running down the rugged rocks of the poverty-ridden, shack-filled Whale Back section of the Brazilian city of Rio de Janeiro. As he makes his way down the multitiered levels of rock, he loses his grip and falls. Although he survives, his face is irretrievably disfigured.

Helio has difficulty remembering the incident after its occurrence. Although his life is forever changed, the exact moment of the injury is clouded by the impact of the trauma. This trauma is so complete that he does not even remember any pain or have clear images of people, such as his coworkers, who were prominent in his life before the tragedy. Wearing a white handkerchief to shield his face from the scorn and mockery of others, Helio reflects on his predicament. The only individuals he perceives clearly are his mother, whom he lost long ago to his stepfather, and his mistress, Lula, whom he suspects he will now lose after this terrible injury.

Helio recalls a time before the accident, when he was living with Lula and enjoying their romantic camaraderie. He is talking idly with his mistress when a telegram comes from Rio Piedras, the remote town in the country that he had left years ago for the large, impersonal city of Rio de Janeiro. The telegram reveals that his mother is dying.

Back in the present, readers witness the attempts of doctors to treat and remedy Helio's condition. The doctors conduct themselves professionally and genuinely try to repair Helio's face. Their scientific discourse does not address the pain Helio feels in his soul.

Helio attempts to return to his job as a barber. Although his superiors and coworkers are not overtly antagonistic toward him, they clearly do not wish to have him around and believe that what has happened to his face has made him, in effect, a different person. Helio remembers his former boss, Cardoso, who had taught Helio to read and had ameliorated his backwoods status, schooling him in the rudiments of urban civilization.

Helio applies to have his face rehabilitated, suffering an embarrassing moment when he goes to the window selling lottery tickets instead; his fate in life is the exact opposite of a lottery winner. Helio becomes increasingly desperate when the doctors, led by an administrator named Godoy, tell him that even though the state-subsidized Brazilian health insurance plan covers the physical and mechanical aspects of his facial rehabilitation, the aesthetic aspects cost extra. In other words, if Helio wishes his face to be beautiful again, or at least as beautiful as it once had been, he will have to pay for it himself. Helio, without a job and with his mother dead, has no money, so this is an impossibility. Closed in and daunted, Helio seems defeated at every turn. Beleaguered and hounded as he is, however, Helio soon has a first glimmer that it will have to be his own initiative, not the assistance of others, that provides his rehabilitation.

Helio relates his abandonment by Lula. Lula still loves him and does not leave him callously, but nevertheless his condition makes it impossible for their romance to continue, and Lula reluctantly severs the relationship. Continuing his odyssey with the Brazilian medical bureaucracy, Helio is admonished that he should have had his workplace issue a letter of disability immediately after the accident; without this, there is no question of full reconstruction being authorized.

Helio decides to take his life fully into his own hands and repair his face himself. Helio leaves the city and returns to the hinterlands, where he was born. Helio finds himself disoriented by the vast difference in scale and lifestyle between city and country. He returns to his mother's shack, and he recalls the pain he experienced after his father's death, when his mother had remarried a man named Julião, an action that Helio had regarded as a betrayal.

Helio once again attempts to find work, but

even the merchants of his hometown disdain him. Bereft of other options, he uses his last remaining money to amass supplies for the reconstruction of his face. Revealing an ingenuity in excess of what could be expected from his largely menial and deprived existence, he slowly remakes his face. It is only when this process is near completion that he is psychologically able to recall the scene of his father's death. Helio receives a letter from Godoy; presumably, the hospital is now ready to subsidize whatever further treatment is needed. Helio imagines encountering Lula and her new boyfriend, and he looks forward to encountering society on his own terms, his identity fully renewed.

Analysis

The themes of *Face* are, from the beginning, symbolic and metaphysical in nature. Although the Brazilian setting, as manifested in Rio de Janeiro and Rio Piedras, is scrupulously drawn, such realistic features are not of the essence in this book. There is little conventional suspense in the action; readers are aware of Helio's plight from the beginning, and there are at least hints of the course the novel will take. What is central to the novel is the examination of psychological issues of identity that Helio's experience provokes. Without a face, Helio is without an identity. Even those who once loved him cannot now recognize him, even though he is still the same person inside. The way in which Helio carries on without a face and succeeds in making himself a new one, however, implies that faces are not indices of truth and authenticity; they are essentially disguises, additions to true identity that people make in order to function socially. Helio's loss of his face calls attention to the conventional, rather than natural, origin of the selves people present to one another.

Helio's self-reconstruction is reminiscent of existential themes of isolation and arbitrary self-projection. Helio is not seen purely as a victim powerless to alter his fate. In reconstructing his face, he displays not only a will to live but also an entrepreneurial assertiveness. Not content to play the role of victim that European philosophies would assign him, Helio reacts to his situation with a committed spirit of Third World resistance. This political and ethical undertone is all the more powerful because of the novel's meticulous avoidance of obvious political themes.

Critical Context

Face was Cecile Pineda's first novel. It was not, however, her first creative effort; for many years previous to the book's 1985 publication, she had been an experimental theater director in San Francisco. This theatrical background permeates the novel in many ways. To act in the theater is to play a part, to disguise one's normal self. Often, as in classical Greek and Japanese drama, this is manifested literally in the use of masks. Pineda's familiarity with drama enables her to understand how even the everyday human face both expresses and masks emotions, how it is both messenger and barrier between the self and the outer world.

Pineda has seldom written about explicitly Hispanic subjects. In both *Face* and *The Queen of the Amazon* (1992), though, she does write about the culture of Brazil. The Brazilian setting of these works enables a dialectic of the strange and the familiar whereby Pineda is able to displace issues that other Latino writers might treat naturalistically onto a more stylized and metaphysical plane. Even in novels that have no thematic relevance to Hispanic experience—such as *Frieze* (1987), a compelling work concerning a medieval Buddhist temple in the East Indies island of Java—Pineda continues to highlight themes, such as the fortitude of the individual against all external obstacles, that occur in the rest of her work.

This emphasis on identity and self-affirmation could be read as obliquely referring to American minority experience. Both *Face* and *Frieze* are taut and parabolic works in which images and themes prevail over conventional narrative. In *The Queen of the Amazon*, though, Pineda displays a looser, more sprawling style that permits a more panoramic view of human experience.

THE FAIR

Author: Juan José Arreola (1918-　　)
Type of work: Novel
Type of plot: Social realism
Time of plot: The mid-twentieth century
Locale: Zapotlán el Grande, in Jalisco, Mexico
First published: *La feria*, 1963 (English translation, 1977)

Principal Characters

Juan Tepano, the oldest of five Indian tribal officials. His designation as Primera Vara (first staff) identifies him as charged with ecclesiastical matters. He provides information about the history and problems of Zapotlán el Grande, the city of thirty thousand inhabitants that is the focus of the action. He works in the fields with his people, who, nominally landowners, are actually tenant farmers subject to eviction. Tepano and his fellow officials are involved in the conflict of legal issues over land possession between the Indians and the Spanish-lineage upper-class residents.

Don Manuel, a shoemaker who lets his business suffer in his unsuccessful attempt at farming. He provides an account of the working of his farm from seedtime to harvest. His inefficacy as a farmer is surpassed only by that of the Indians, who nevertheless agitate for the repossession of their ancestors' land.

Don Salvador, called **Don Salva,** a storekeeper in love with his beautiful employee, Chayo. His determination to propose marriage to her is defeated by his timidity and, finally, by her being seduced and impregnated by Odilón.

Odilón, the handsome playboy and ne'er-do-well son of Don Abigail. His technique of seducing women includes the false promise of marriage. He callously deserts Chayo after she conceives his child.

Gaspar Ruiz de Cabrera (the **Licenciado**), the investor and moneylender who is the sponsor of the fair. Carrying meat that he has purchased for his evening meal, he suffers a fatal heart attack in the street.

Don Abigail, the brother of the *Licenciado*, with whom he was not on speaking terms, and father of Odilón. He is made executor of his brother's estate.

Father Zavala, a parish priest. He carries out the preparations for the fair after the death of the *Licenciado*, calling first upon Don Atilano, the fireworks manufacturer, to produce a huge fireworks display. The *castillo*, as the display is called, is vandalized on the last night of the fair and explodes all at once instead of going off in sections. Father Zavala becomes ill during the fair and is removed to Guadalajara; an assistant priest replaces him.

The Novel

On the literal level, *The Fair* concerns the planning and execution of the yearly fair in Zapotlán el Grande, a small town in Jalisco, Mexico. A complication arises upon the untimely death of Gaspar Ruiz de Cabrera, the *Licenciado*, one of the city's more influential citizens who was to have sponsored the event. The conflicts that develop as the townspeople proceed with the preparations, however, have their real source in the foundations of that society. On another level, then, *The Fair* is an ideological portrait of provincial life in Mexico, in that it examines those foundations.

The novel opens with the voice of Juan Tepano, who locates the origins of his people's plight in the conquest, the spiritual and territorial occupation of the country by a foreign power. An elder of the Indian community, he leads the struggle for restitution of the land to its rightful owners, working side by side with the people in the fields and passing down traditional legends that sustain the community's sense of identity. Through Juan Tepano, the Indians continue their efforts to rectify a five-hundred-year-old injustice, acknowledged but not resolved by the Mexican Revolution.

Similarly, Don Manuel, a former shoemaker, is involved with the land, but he does not belong to it as the Indians do, nor is he capable of profiting from it. To the Indians, he is another boss, the renewed presence of a centuries-old obstacle between them and ownership of the land. On the other hand, Don Manuel marvels at their primitive rituals but dismisses their beliefs as superstitious. He will find, however, that precision, rationality, and modern methods are inappropriate or at least insufficient when dealing with nature. His journal is a testimonial to the enthusiasm and good faith with which he undertakes his new venture, but a lack of experience and much adversity work against him. Don Manuel eventually admits defeat, but not without regret, considerable financial losses, and a sense of disillusionment.

The opposing interests are the subject of the second section of the text, a division signaled by a shift in scene from countryside to town. The *Licenciado*'s funeral serves to introduce his character, along with the rest of his family, representatives of Zapotlán's wealthy, to the reader. Recollections about the usurer evoke sentiments of anger, bitterness, resentment, and fear now that his brother, Don Abigail, is on the verge of taking control, for even the disreputable business practices of the *Licenciado* are only a preface to his brother's treachery. Don Abigail's son, Odilón, promises to be even more unscrupulous, as demonstrated in his hypocrisy, particularly with regard to women. At every opportunity this family succeeds, through illicit means, in subverting the legitimate attempts of the Indians to regain their land.

Another legacy of the conquest is the church, an institution seen to breed flagrant immorality side by side with honest virtue. Among other popular expressions of faith are the hypocrisy of Doña Maria, a brothel madam, as revealed in her comments on the prostitutes; the calumny of the old maids who denounce innocent young girls; and the inhumanity expressed with regard to homosexuals. An earthquake affords an opportunity to appreciate the utility of religion. Church members descend upon the confessionals out of fear for their immortal souls and implore Saint Joseph's protection, promising in return to mend their ways and honor the saint every year in a religious celebration. The church hierarchy itself sets the standard of pragmatism when, for example, Father Zavala is transferred because he threatens to alienate wealthy contributors in his role as advocate of the Indians.

Several stories in *The Fair* concentrate on love and can be said to constitute a fourth unity within the text. Romantic love is considered to be a potential means to an end, but more than that, a temporary condition that will subside sooner or later. The confrontation between idealistic notions and harsh reality can expedite this process. In the microcosm of Zapotlán, love, like all other noble sentiments, is doomed to failure.

As the day of the fair draws near, a series of calamities ensues. Both people and circumstances conspire in order to shatter hopes, plans, and lives. Innocent men are framed and imprisoned; Don Fidencio suffers humiliation upon learning about his daughter's pregnancy; Don Salva decides too late to propose to Chayo; after numerous setbacks and bad omens, Don Manuel is forced to sell his farm and return to his shoe shop; and Father Zavala is transferred to Guadalajara. The fair itself turns out to be a faithful reproduction of life in Zapotlán, where the Indians sustain a machinery that keeps them from advancing, where religion is the veil that shrouds all crimes against humanity, and where even the most sincere, heartfelt efforts will be unrewarded, if not sabotaged. There is a marked discrepancy between the perception of the anticipated event, such as how nice it is to see the town full of strangers, and its actuality: Those strangers have come to seek revenge or will be murdered. From its inauguration (the brutal distribution of the programs) to its closing (the failed display of fireworks), the fair celebrates only the injustice, ignobility, and futility of existence.

Analysis

Through three basic aspects of the society of Zapotlán—land, faith, and love—Arreola conveys a message of hopelessness in the contest between the individual or minority and the superstructure, a struggle that will always end ingloriously with the defeat and disillusionment of the former. A number of dichotomies throughout the text illustrate that, despite the particular nature of such a dispute, be it oppressed/oppressor, will/fate, virtue/vice, altruism/self-interest, or integrity/corruption, power determines victory. The absurdity of the struggle is summed up in the figure of the clown, the only performer of any merit at the bullfight that takes place during the fair.

The novel communicates these ideas through two main structural patterns created with the vignettes of which *The Fair* is composed. One pattern is the evolution of stories about particular people over the course of the book, providing continuity. Sequences also form around topics such as religion and love, which are interpreted by a variety of characters and through different situations and viewpoints. In addition, antithetical or unrelated elements are juxtaposed to contrast or enhance, such as the quiet chess game and the violent confusion of the earthquake, or the literal and figurative suicides of Paulina and Chayo next to Don Manuel's premonitions about his crops. Arreola sometimes reverses time, as when the railroad man murders his wife after the narrative about the incident, or interrupts single units of time and resumes them later, creating an effect of simultaneity. Narrative fragments are manipulated and arranged in such a way as to exhibit or emphasize the underlying meanings of the observable phenomena.

Critical Context

The Fair represents Arreola's first attempt at novel writing. A master of short fiction, his preference for brevity and concision is apparent even in this narrative, which is composed of nearly three hundred fragments of both prose and verse, ranging from partial lines to a few pages in length. This work is also singular within his production because of its subject matter: Mexican life and language as they exist in his hometown of Zapotlán el Grande.

Although the Mexican author began as a realistic writer, by the 1950's he had become a proponent of nonrealistic literature, a new trend that departed from traditional realism as well as the preoccupation with the Mexican Revolution. Although not the leader of a formal movement, both his interest in the fantastic and a remarkable versatility of form and style designated him as a literary model for Mexico's young writers.

Arreola's ambiguous position within Mexican literature can be accounted for in several ways. First, his predilection for timeless, universal themes rather than the country's social, political, and economic problems has given the appearance of indifference toward national concerns. Second, he chose to cultivate short fiction forms at a time when the novel was experiencing unprecedented levels of prestige and popularity in Mexican, and indeed all of Spanish American, literature. Third, his reading public was unaccustomed to, and therefore frequently unwilling to accept, a fantastic rendering of serious subjects. These and other considerations cost Arreola the approval of critics and public alike. Nevertheless, Arreola's contribution to Mexican literature is significant and undeniable.

FIESTA IN NOVEMBER

Author: Eduardo Mallea (1903-1983)
Type of work: Novel
Type of plot: Social criticism
Time of plot: The mid-1930's
Locale: Buenos Aires, Argentina
First published: *Fiesta en noviembre*, 1938 (English translation, 1942)

Principal Characters

Eugenia Rague, a highly respected woman in the society of Buenos Aires. She achieved her position by being very rich rather than by aristocratic birth. She looks down upon all who are beneath her class but also resents authentic aristocrats. She acquires paintings and sculptures as a means of gaining the admiration of members of high society. She is puritan almost to the point of fanaticism, incapable of pardoning human weaknesses, domineering, and ambitious; the role she plays in the family is more that of tyrant than of matriarch. She does not worry about Marta, whom she believes she is able to control, but she feels doubts about Brenda, whom she considers weak and unpredictable.

Marta Rague, Eugenia's twenty-seven-year-old daughter, has traveled extensively, visited the most renowned museums, heard the most famous musicians in concert, and loved intensely, giving herself to those whom she thought were seeking pleasures beyond the mere physical. These activities have left her bored and fatigued.

Lintas, a painter whom Eugenia Rague met at an exhibition. She invites him to her fiesta to get his opinion on the authenticity of three paintings. The painter informs her that the paintings are fakes. During dinner, Marta and Lintas exchange glances that leave both intrigued. Later, after dancing and chatting, they realize that both of them belong to a complex world, full of conflicts, far removed from the fatuous reality that they are living at that instant. After conversing for many hours about life, society, reality, love, and hate, Marta bids farewell to Lintas. She has undergone a transformation: In place of disillusion and boredom, she feels a desire to serve.

Brenda Rague, Eugenia's younger daughter. She leads her own life. As a consequence of her adventures, she has had two abortions, unknown to her mother.

The poet, whose story runs parallel with the overall plot. The nameless character symbolizes those persecuted by association. He has read books prohibited by the regime, has family ties with an executed revolutionary, and has seen innocent people assassinated. He is taken from his home, beaten, and finally riddled with bullets by a patrol.

The Novel

Fiesta in November opens with a passage from the secondary plot, which appears in italics. A young unnamed poet is writing a poem on love late at night. A violent, protracted rapping sounds on the door. As he goes to answer the pounding, he takes with him a piece of bread. Opening the door, he is confronted by the leader of a patrol of armed men in dirty uniforms. The leader states that the patrol has come for him.

The main story begins at eight o'clock on a

warm springlike evening in November. Eugenia Rague has come down the stairs for a final inspection of the setting for her fiesta. English by birth, but Argentine by adoption, she dominates her aristocratic surroundings.

In another room, her husband, George, tries to concentrate on acquiring culture through a phonograph record, but he keeps thinking of how he can persuade Señor Raíces, after dinner, to sign papers regarding a profitable stock purchase. Should delays result, he might lose everything. Intruding into these thoughts come those of his treadmill life, his wife's incessant pressure, and his own desire to relax and perhaps to dream. The arrival of the butler with the afternoon mail interrupts and infuriates him. It is time for him to prepare for the party. Marta, the older daughter, lies naked on her bed, wondering why she had spurned a high-born lover.

At nine, the orchestra tunes up, and the first guests, the elite of Argentine society, arrive. Their conversation is frivolous: the latest scandalous behavior of some politician, the proposal to exterminate the unimportant lower class. The empty conversation and the broken phrases from the more serious exchange of ideas reveal the waste of these people's lives.

Marta makes her entrance, prepared for a boring and perhaps detestable evening among unexciting people she had fully comprehended several years earlier. Her father welcomes her assistance in his social duties. When Raíces appears, Rague gives the signal to proceed to the dining room.

In perplexity, the poet questions the armed men, asking what they could possibly want with him.

At the reception, a painter, Lintas, rushes in, late as usual but in time for the chilled consommé. As he drinks it, he becomes attracted to Marta. Her sudden smile shows her reaction to him. Lintas notices her distraught expression when her mother mentions the fact that Brenda is not there.

After the meal, dancing begins in the garden. Lintas finds himself dancing with Marta as though they are enemies. Later, more friendly, they discuss some of his paintings. Marta remembers that her sister Brenda had sent a message asking for assistance. Marta leaves without a word of explanation.

Meanwhile the leader of the patrol begins to lose patience. His men glare at the young man who is wasting their time. They prepare to march their prisoner away.

Marta's flight takes her to a shabby house and into a stench-filled room where she finds Brenda recovering from an abortion. Brenda needs her sister's help to conceal her situation from her parents and to supply additional money for the operation, which had cost more than the previous one. Marta leaves the house and heads for home.

At the fiesta, no one had noticed Marta's absence. Rague and Raíces discuss the stock deal, and Raíces tries to explain why he does not want to rush into the transaction. Eugenia Rague maneuvers Lintas into visiting her art gallery to pass judgment on some new purchases, which he pronounces to be fakes. Marta returns as Lintas is leaving the fiesta and offers to take him home.

Through the door, the poet sees a fighting cock belonging to a neighbor. He tries to imagine what will happen to him. He is suddenly frightened.

In the car, Marta is impelled to talk. She protests against the sterility of the civilized universe and the difficulty people find in trying to communicate. When they reach Linta's home, he invites her in. The screams of a neighboring woman start him on the story of his life. Poverty had engendered in him a hatred for people like her. He tells her of a gang of ruffians who had beaten up an old bookseller because he was foreign and was selling "subversive books." It was his widow who had screamed. This atrocity had increased his loathing for the governing class, which permitted such crimes to go unpunished. They continue their discussion during a walk at dawn through the woods. As she leaves, they realize that neither has convinced the other.

The prisoner asks for permission to get his hat; what he really wants is time.

Marta dreads returning home. Brenda will be in a troubled sleep; her father will be snoring, and her mother will be sneaking down to the kitchen for a snack. Marta knows that in other parts of the world vigils more painful than hers are going on. She realizes that her trouble is a hatred of herself because of an unsatisfied yearning for something. The thought comes to her that she, who has always been served, ought to serve others. She pauses at a church, but it offers no promise of relief. She stops next at a coffee shop. Although sensing herself to be out of place among the customers, eventually she begins to feel a comprehension of them and a oneness with them all. She goes home.

In her room, she takes stock of herself. She feels a resemblance to her country, with its variety and abundance. Before she falls asleep, she decides that a true change from the horrors of life must come from the tormented people themselves.

Analysis

In a graceful style, rich with vivid, precise images, neither pretentious nor overly decorated, Eduardo Mallea tells the moving story of two people struggling to communicate with each other while lost in the midst of a shallow, violent world. Although the painter Lintas and Marta Rague are the two most sympathetic characters in this short novel, both are held back by their pride from the honesty and openness that would liberate them and enable them to achieve an authentic relationship. They are the only individuals in *Fiesta in November* who care about moral concerns, except for the poet, unnamed and doomed, whose brief story alternates like an almost subliminal theme with the main body of the story, illuminating and commenting upon it.

The two fiestas, one social, the other of blood, are linked thematically by Lintas' account to Marta of the fatal beating of a Jewish book dealer in Buenos Aires by a group of Argentine fascists. An undercurrent of violence also lies behind the conversation and actions of the guests in the house of Marta's mother, Eugenia Rague. The fragments of the condemned poet's story are in italics, suggesting that in spite of its shorter length, this narrative is the more important of the two.

The opening arrest of the poet could be that of Joseph K in Franz Kafka's *The Trial* (1925). There are more than casual similarities between the work

The final pages complete the subplot. The poet's cousin had already been arrested and shot, and his family had been denied permission to bury him. The poet joins the patrol, protesting, but the only reply is rifle butts in his face. The group reaches a deserted house and an open space, and the poet tries to run. The patrol fires after him. He falls to the ground, and blood soaks the piece of bread he drops. One of the men turns over the body to make sure the poet is dead. Members of the patrol, leaving him lying on the ground, walk away with feelings of loathing for one another.

of Kafka and this novel. The contrast between the scene with the poet and the luxurious setting of Eugenia Rague's home is shocking. Eugenia's is a vain, acquisitive character. Her only passions are for her collection of objects from the past and for power. She detests sentiment and everything connected with it, so it is not surprising that she is completely alienated from her two daughters. Her husband, despite his wealth, feels no peace or fulfillment.

The opening picture of the dinner party is a devastating glimpse of empty lives and futile social ritual. The characters struggle with an inner tyranny, a psychic trap more terrible than the cruelty of society, if they only realized it. "All art," thinks Lintas, "is a great and terrible demand for response." This unusual novel demands a response from the reader.

Mr. and Mrs. Rague and their guests would be lost without their ceremonies, but Lintas deliberately walks over their carefully plotted maneuvers. Marta and Lintas recognize each other from the beginning as two of a kind—exiles in a world they detest. Marta, at the age of twenty-seven, still is filled with a passionate curiosity, still is eager to experience life. She hates the pretense of society, the constant betrayal of her own nature.

Mirrors, windows, and polished surfaces constantly reflect faces, oblique views of people, staring eyes. The reflected images seem more real than many of the actual figures and faces. Mallea seems to be asking, What *is* the reality and what is false?

Brenda Rague, Marta's sister, is having an abortion while her mother's fiesta is in progress. This revelation causes Marta to think in a new way about their lives, and her meeting with Lintas continues to stimulate her chain of thoughts. Lintas himself was made suddenly aware by the episode of the brutal beating of the bookseller. Are there social castes, they ask, or only moral castes? Where is the moral answer? The word "serve" appears to Marta as she walks down the empty city streets before dawn. What does it mean? Could it

be the answer for her? She realizes that each individual must, in his or her own way, be heroic and walk alone, bravely and honestly, into his or her fate.

The inner dramas of the novel are not resolved. They move from climax to climax, cumulatively, charged with great lyric tension. Seemingly insignificant individual lives are transformed by Mallea into the very essence of the human condition. *Fiesta in November* is an extraordinary novel by a great author. It is a book that haunts the reader, as Mallea intended, for the questions that it raises are not easily answered.

Critical Context

Keeping several balls in the air at a time is a trick for a juggler. Manipulating several stories simultaneously was the feat of one of Argentina's most brilliant authors, Eduardo Mallea. His early works included the frivolous *Cuentos para una inglesa desesperada* (1926; stories for a desperate Englishwoman) and other volumes more like essays than fiction. Then came a new style, beginning with *Fiesta in November*, classified as "contrapuntal dialogue." It presents a number of characters, each with his or her own problems.

Mallea has been criticized for backing away from narration and substituting psychological analyses or philosophical reflections with the logical steps to a conclusion often omitted. This tendency can be observed throughout *Fiesta in November*, which contains two plots interrupting each other, never being obviously connected.

Mallea's view of life is religious and moral. His works often suggest the European existentialists, though most of his writing anticipated their novels and dramas. He was descended from an old Creole family and attended an English school in Bahía

Blanca, where the majority of his classmates were the sons of immigrants. At the age of thirteen, he moved to Buenos Aires with his family. The city was a revelation for the withdrawn adolescent. His first published stories won immediate attention. In the 1930's and 1940's, he was director of some of the most influential literary publications in Latin America. He was a steadfast opponent of Juan Perón's regime. After the revolution that overthrew the Perón dictatorship, he was named ambassador to the United Nations Educational, Scientific, and Cultural Organization in Paris. Subsequently, he returned to private life to devote himself to writing and lecturing.

Fiesta in November and other novels and stories, such as *All Green Shall Perish* (1941) and *Chaves* (1953), established Mallea as one of Latin America's greatest writers and one of the outstanding prose stylists and moral spokesmen in the world. His works are great art because they are born out of an intense experience of life; they vividly convey this experience to the reader.

THE FIFTH HORSEMAN

Author: José Antonio Villarreal (1924-   )
Type of work: Novel
Type of plot: *Bildungsroman*
Time of plot: 1893-1915
Locale: Mexico
First published: 1974

Principal Characters

Heraclio Inés, the youngest of five brothers born into a family of horsemen, a fact that places him above the peasants in the oppressive social structure of the Hacienda de la Flor but below the owner, Don Aurelio Becerra, his godfather. After mastering his craft and the code of honor that attends it, Heraclio casts off the rigid authority of his family in order to fulfill his individual potential, something that the prevailing sociopolitical tradition in Mexico would deny him. In an assertion of his independence, Heraclio enters into a passionate affair with Don Aurelio's daughter. When threatened with exposure and violence, Heraclio kills a man; thereafter, seeking refuge from the brutality of the rural police, he joins a group of bandits and, eventually, the forces of Pancho Villa. Democratically at one with the people and moved always by his growing sense of justice, Heraclio fights hard for the revolution only to see the cause fail as Mexico falls once again into the grips of easy compromise and corruption. In his last revolutionary act and in order to preserve his integrity, Heraclio executes a traitor. Defeated but not broken, he then leaves Mexico for exile in the United States.

David Contreras, the illegitimate peasant son of Don Aurelio and a healer. David befriends Heraclio while the two herd sheep together, but he begins to turn against Heraclio when Heraclio leaves the flocks in order to learn the craft of the horsemen. Rejected by his natural father and condemned by the social system to a life of peonage, David becomes embittered. After Heraclio sleeps with his half sister, Carmen Becerra, David's bitterness turns to hatred, a hatred that finds its only outlet in lawless violence. Unable to kill Heraclio, the focus of his frustration, David kills Heraclio's wife and child, acts of brutality for which Heraclio, in turn, kills David.

Carmen Becerra, Don Aurelio's daughter, is passionately in love with Heraclio. Like both David and Heraclio, however, she is trapped by the rigid social and political stratification of a system that condemns her to marry the corrupt Domingo Arguiú, a Spanish aristocrat. To Carmen's credit, she attempts to break the barriers that restrain her in order to fulfill her love for Heraclio, but in the end, denied anything beyond a temporary physical relationship, she fails.

Marcelina Ortiz, the innocent girl Heraclio marries, who represents all the best things that life has to offer. Bearing the same name as Heraclio's dead mother, Marcelina represents the continuing embodiment of the pure wife and virtuous Mexican mother. In clear terms, she stands for the sanctity of home and hearth. In a better Mexico, the Mexico for which Heraclio fights, she would not only survive but also prosper. The destructive Mexico into which she is born, however, kills her and her baby.

Xochitl Salamanca, a circus performer who meets Heraclio amid the chaos of the revolution. When Heraclio extracts her from the clutches of Pancho Villa, she becomes his wartime wife and lover. More a symbol than a fully drawn character, Xochitl represents the spirit of the revolution, waxing strong during the period of Villa's victories but dying of smallpox in the sick world that follows in the wake of Villa's defeat.

Teodoro Inés, Heraclio's older brother. Teodoro takes over as head of the family after the death of his father. Proud and brutal within his own family, Teodoro grovels willingly before Don Aurelio, placing the landowner on the level of a god, thereby ensuring the survival of the oppressive social system.

The Novel

Based in part on the experiences of José Antonio Villarreal's father during the Mexican Revolution, *The Fifth Horseman* records the fictionalized education of Heraclio Inés as he moves from relative innocence to war-weary experience. *The Fifth Horseman* falls into two major parts. The first is concerned with peace, while the second is concerned with war. Beginning in the middle of the action, the novel's prologue opens on June 24, 1914, showing Heraclio leading Pancho Villa's attack on Zacatecas. Thereafter, by flashback, the omniscient third-person narrator goes back to 1893, the year of Heraclio's birth, only gradually bringing the protagonist forward through various stages of development to 1911, the year in which Heraclio joins Villa for the attack on Juarez. Subsequently, Heraclio's star rises with Villa in book 2, "The Campaign" and falls in book 3, "Los Desgraciados" (the disgraced ones) after Villa's defeat at Celaya.

Tied by tradition to the feudal social structure of the Hacienda de la Flor, the setting for book 1, Heraclio Inés is born the fifth son to a family of semi-independent horsemen, a factor that places him above the peasantry but below Don Aurelio Becerra, the hacienda's owner. After his father dies while attempting a dangerous feat of horsemanship, Heraclio discovers that he has been born to a code of honor. In 1905, when he ceases herding sheep with David Contreras in order to train as a horseman, he finds his brothers' enforcement of the code to be rigid and brutal. Refusing to let his brothers break his spirit, Heraclio resists; nevertheless, through the various trials that constitute his rites of passage, he makes himself into a master horseman, passing the final test, the ride of death, and surviving. Yet when he sees his oldest brother, Teodoro, grovel before Don Aurelio, Heraclio declares his independence and moves in with Antonio Rivera, a peasant.

Having proved his manhood in terms of the code, Heraclio next realizes the romantic side of his being by falling in love with Carmen Becerra, Don Aurelio's daughter. Disregarding the social gulf that separates them, Heraclio and Carmen plunge into a passionate relationship that is doomed to fail. Believing that love should prevail over class, Carmen reveals her affair to her mother, with the result that her parents rush her marriage to the decadent Spanish aristocrat Domingo Arguiú. Having faced facts, Heraclio knows that marriage to Carmen is impossible; still, the two lovers continue their liaison until one of Don Aurelio's administrators threatens Heraclio with violence and exposure. Heraclio reacts by killing the man, a turn of fortune that forces him to flee to the mountains. He joins a group of bandits led by Ysabel Pulido and his onetime friend David Contreras, who resents Heraclio's liaison with Carmen, his half sister.

Under Ysabel Pulido, Heraclio and the others move north to join Celestino Gámez, a follower of Pancho Villa. When Pulido, who functions as David's spiritual father, dies and Heraclio ascends to leadership of the band, David becomes Heraclio's enemy, never forgiving the horseman for what he believes to have been the theft of his birthright. Thereafter, Antonio Rivera attempts to prevent David from killing Heraclio.

Following Villa's victory at Juarez in 1911 and the apparent end of the revolution, Heraclio returns home and marries the saintly Marcelina Ortiz. When the murder of President Francisco Madero reignites the revolution, however, Villa recalls Heraclio. In the campaigns that follow, Villa and Heraclio fight their way south with the Division of the North. In the course of this march, Heraclio meets and saves Xochitl Salamanca, a young circus acrobat who becomes his wartime wife and who remains with him until she dies of smallpox in the aftermath of Villa's decline. Meanwhile, David Contreras becomes a vicious bandit and, in an act of revenge, finds and kills Marcelina and Heraclio's new daughter. In the fulfillment of his code and in the absence of law, Heraclio then kills David.

After Villa's defeat at Celaya and subsequent retreat, General Gámez goes over to the enemy, an act that Heraclio sees as a betrayal of both the revolution and Mexico. Loyal to Villa and the people, Heraclio finds and executes Gámez; then, with all ties severed, he heads north toward a voluntary exile in the United States.

Analysis

Almost Homeric in scope, *The Fifth Horseman* presents an anatomy of the Mexican Revolution, its causes, its initiation, its fighting, and its results, the whole of the immense event parading before the reader through the effects it brings to bear on a few families and, in particular, the life of a single man, Heraclio Inés. Had Villarreal lived in an earlier time, he might well have attempted to write an epic on his subject; instead, he brings the full weight of his talent to bear in the creation of a unique and telling novel.

In the first half of the novel, with dramatic precision, Villarreal re-creates a picture of what life was like when Mexico still writhed in the grip of the dictator Porfirio Díaz. Under Díaz, the Mexican social structure—a social structure depicted on the Hacienda de la Flor—became stratified and static, the wealthy few ruling the many poor with a heavy authority. At its best, the system preserved a kind of hopeless, immobile order by locking each man and woman into a hereditarily determined place; at its worst, the system produced peonage, slavery, brutality, and intolerable injustice in all phases of life. Heraclio's craft as a horseman places him well above the peons but well below the landowning classes; as a result, he is afforded the opportunity of viewing both stations objectively as he advances toward manhood.

If, in the first half of the novel, Heraclio aspires to and attains a high degree of personal maturity, the novel's second half shows him continuing his moral journey, this time working his way forward toward a state of sociopolitical maturity. Born to be independent of the system, Heraclio might well have turned his back on the revolutionary wind that swept Mexico; instead, when the crisis develops, Heraclio opts for change that will produce good for the whole. When he does, he democratically casts his lot with the people.

With Francisco Madero's elevation to the presidency of Mexico, Heraclio believes that the revolution has succeeded and that the people have won. When Villa is imprisoned and Madero is assassinated, however, Heraclio quickly realizes that a few corrupt men can bring a good thing down. Thereafter, committing himself to Villa, he faces for the first time the chaos of extended war, discovering in the process that the war itself corrupts the men that make it and that the acquisition of power can quickly lead to its abuse.

By means of some fine war writing, Villarreal makes the battles of the revolution spring to life, their violent immensity acting as backdrop for Heraclio's own continuing development. As long as Villa remains strong, hope for the revolution, hope for the people, remains alive. Yet after the battle at Celaya, where the old order unites to defeat Villa, the people's cause is essentially lost. In the period of disillusionment and death that follows, Heraclio learns that the most for which he can hope is the preservation of his own integrity and a period of peace. Rather than compromise with the corrupt new forces that grip Mexico, Heraclio executes the traitor Gámez and marches north into voluntary exile. Heraclio's plan is to return to Mexico when the time is ripe in order to help rebuild his beloved country.

Critical Context

The Fifth Horseman, José Antonio Villarreal's second novel, ends chronologically where *Pocho* (1959), his first novel, begins, with the voluntary exile of its protagonist north of the border. In fact, Juan Rubio, the father of *Pocho*'s protagonist, is often thought to be a portrait of Heraclio Inés in later life; as a result, many readers have enjoyed reading the books together. The novels are not, however, mutually interdependent. *Pocho*, the first major novel in what is sometimes called Chicano literature, has enjoyed continued success since its first publication and remains a unique fictional record of the Mexican American experience. Equally independent as a work of art, *The Fifth Horseman* is an accomplished historical novel about the Mexican Revolution; considered either as Latino or American literature, it is fully capable of holding its own high position independently of *Pocho*.

Experimental in style, *The Fifth Horseman* applies Spanish syntax to English vocabulary, bringing both weight and dignity to the dialogue that normal Anglo-Saxon word order might not have supplied. Some have criticized Villarreal for using this technique, while others have applauded the boldness of his effort, seeing, perhaps, that in elevating the style of his novel, he also broadens the work's scope by giving it a formality of language that recalls heroic poetry.

As a historical novel, *The Fifth Horseman* finds its literary antecedents in works as diverse as *Voina i mir* (1865-1869; *War and Peace*, 1886) and *Gone with the Wind* (1936). At the same time, the special nature of Villarreal's material calls to mind two additional subgenres of North American literature. From the Mexican point of view, *The Fifth Horseman* shows a clear connection with such "novels of the revolution" as Mariano Azuela's *Los de abajo* (1916; *The Underdogs*, 1929) and Martín Luis Guzmán's *El águila y la serpiente* (1928; *The Eagle and the Serpent*, 1930). From a strictly American point of view, *The Fifth Horseman* seems closely related to the Western, to such novels as Owen Wister's *The Virginian* (1902) and Jack Schaefer's *Shane* (1949). Regardless of how one chooses to classify *The Fifth Horseman*, the historical nature of the novel remains dominant.

THE FINAL MIST

Author: María Luisa Bombal
Type of work: Novel
Type of plot: Surrealism
Time of plot: The late 1920's
Locale: A hacienda in the south of Chile and an unnamed city
First published: *La última niebla*, 1934 (English translation, 1982)

Principal Characters

The protagonist, whose name is never revealed, a woman who narrates her feelings of frustration and loneliness. She posits that they are a result of her husband's disinterest in her, in particular, and society's treatment of women, in general. Afraid of old age and incapable of expressing her true feelings to a despotic husband, she withdraws into herself. She consciously opts for a fantasy world in which her repressed sexuality finally finds an outlet. While the logical world limits her, her dream lover liberates her. Her mental activity establishes different mechanisms for self-realization only when Regina, her husband's sister-in-law, shows her how a woman can truly respond to her own innermost desires. The protagonist's flights of fantasy and reliance on reason and practicality, however, only condemn her to the passive existence she had at the start of the novel. She never becomes aware that such constraints can be fought and therefore does not fight what by her own description will be a future full of petty and frivolous worries and undertakings.

Daniel, her extremely sarcastic and bright husband. His wife's passivity makes her an easy mark for his irony and his desire to control her actions. He constantly reminds the protagonist that she will never be more than a weak substitute for his first wife. His arrogance is never undone, even though his everyday concerns are banal and bourgeois.

Regina, Daniel's sister-in-law. She is the barometer of activity, beauty, and self-expression for the protagonist. Regina, a lover of the arts, talkative, and full of life, has taken a lover. She is thus capable of venting her passion much more concretely than is the protagonist. Her fulfillment, like the protagonist's, is postulated as something that cannot come exclusively from her relationships with men. Even Regina's attempted suicide is a source of envy for the protagonist.

The protagonist's lover, who is unnamed. He is not her reason for being, as Regina's lover is to her. More than a concretely described character, he is a representative of the "otherness" in a man for which the protagonist longs. In her mind, he is presumably wealthy and stimulatingly erotic. His mundane end is attributed by his servant to a fall he suffers because of his blindness.

The Novel

The Final Mist begins with symbolism. The protagonist has just married Daniel. They arrive at the hacienda during a storm, the rain and the cold functioning as metaphors for their loveless marriage. From this first night, the protagonist's life is tinged by loneliness and frustration. She wanders through the woods, bitterly anguished by the facts that her life has no purpose and that her body is aging without experiencing real love. The image of a young girl lying dead among artificial flowers in a house surrounded by heavy mist becomes, in the novel, identified with the protagonist's own existence.

One day, Regina, her husband, and her lover come to visit. The protagonist compares her barren life with that of Regina, who becomes a symbol of passion, music, and vitality. From this point on, the protagonist's existential dilemma is symbolized by the dual oppositions of life (sound, light, fire, water, earth) and death (silence, darkness, coldness, deadly mist). One foggy night, she leaves the house and encounters a mysterious young man who takes her to a house and makes love to her. The eroticism of this scene is highly symbolic, as she feels, for the first time, that her life has a true meaning. Because of the surrealistic presentation of this encounter, the reader does not know if the lover really exists or if instead he is a product of the protagonist's mind. Reality and dreams merge in an ambiguous counterpoint between the protagonist's loveless marriage and the mysterious appearances of the lover, who waves at her from a horse-drawn carriage that makes no sound and disappears in the mist.

After many years of lonely passion for a man whose existence itself is deceptive, the protagonist has a final encounter with Regina that throws light on the emptiness of her own life. Regina has attempted suicide because her lover has abandoned her, and now she lies in a hospital bed still calling for her lover. As an adulteress who was brave enough to transgress the laws of her society, Regina had the capacity to choose the course of her life, whereas the protagonist confronts the futility of a love nurtured by dreams. Her only choice is to follow her husband, to live correctly—to cry from habit and smile out of duty, following him to die, one day, correctly. As she and her husband leave the hospital, the fog settles over everything like a shroud. A symbol of darkness, coldness, and sterility, this final mist underscores the tragic fate of female existence irrevocably condemned to death in life by a social system that regulates and represses a woman's essential instincts.

Analysis

The most important theme in *The Final Mist* stems from the surrealist concept of reality. Going against the positivist postulate of reality as a concrete and tangible phenomenon capable of being analyzed through reason and logic, this novel represents reality as a complex and fragmented conglomerate that the human mind is incapable of understanding. Objective reality is only one dimension of a wider microcosmos in which the unconscious, the magic, and the oneiric simultaneously coexist. Thus, the essence of reality is ambiguity. In *The Final Mist*, ambiguity arises from two main phenomena observed in the text: the absence of specific objectivity regarding exterior reality and chronological time, and the elimination of exact and rational limits between oneiric experiences, daydreams, and concrete reality. Because the story is narrated from the protagonist's point of view, the details of concrete reality are important only in terms of her agony and hidden wishes— thus the burning coals in the fireplace become symbols of her lover's eyes.

Time is measured by her subjective perspective and in the context of her feminine experience of approaching old age, which includes a constant and ever-increasing anxiety that the opportunity for love is inexorably receding beyond reach. On the other hand, the encounter with a man who makes love to her in a mysterious house is tinged with ambiguity, arising from the concrete details of the experience mixed with her lover's supernatural qualities: his silence, the halo of light surrounding his body, his uncanny appearance—like an apparition in the wee hours of a misty night. The transition between that love scene and the moment the protagonist finds herself in bed beside her husband leaves the reader in doubt as to whether the lover really existed or was part of a dream. This doubt is never resolved: From that moment on, the reader enters a three-dimensional world with a landscape that is, simultaneously, concrete, oneiric, and supernatural. The leitmotif of mist reinforces ambiguity, darkening reality, producing strange mirages and creating a disquieting uncertainty.

From the aesthetic point of view of representation, *The Final Mist* must be considered a work that questions the traditional conceptions of "real" time, space, and character in order to draw explicit attention to the dynamic quality of a reality simultaneously embedded in the concrete, the oneiric, and the fantastic. By presenting latent meanings or realities behind the reductive "truths" of the positivist cognitive frame, it not only denounces the inadequacies of that frame but also advocates more complex epistemological systems. That the protagonist herself develops doubts about the existence of her lover eliminates the possibility of interpreting the reality presented in the novel as sheer hallucination stemming from a feverish mind, a possibility placed at an even further remove when the protagonist discovers, years later, the house where her lover made love to her. Her anguished question, "How long will it take for these reflections to be erased and be replaced by other reflections?" is, on an explicit level, a defi-nition of a reality the very essence of which seems to be uncertainty and deceptive illusion.

For Bombal, women are primordial human beings intimately united with the cosmic forces of nature, sharing an ancestral bond that has been undermined by the masculine impulse to dominate nature in order to produce civilization. The different spaces depicted in *The Final Mist* become symbols of this basic conflict. The enclosed space of the bourgeois house is often described as a "tomb" or a "coffin," since it represents the order imposed by the patriarchal system; conversely, the open space of nature is unrestrained, free from the moral restrictions that annul the natural essence of the feminine. Within this context, eroticism is conceived as an ancestral instinct to recapture the essence of femininity. Thus, when the protagonist sinks in a pond, she establishes with water—a traditional symbol of fertility—a sensual contact that makes of her nipples dark flowers on its surface. The erotic, then, is presented in the novel as the fulfillment of repressed instincts, as an attempt to reaffirm life in a society that has annulled women's ancestral ties with nature.

Critical Context

Bombal wrote *The Final Mist* while sharing the kitchen table with Pablo Neruda, who at the time was composing the three volumes of *Residence on Earth and Other Poems* (1933, 1935, 1947), books that would revolutionize poetry. As many critics have pointed out, *The Final Mist* was an equally significant landmark for Latin American prose. Published during a period in which the predominant literary trend was *Criollismo*—the nativistic depiction of Latin American prototypes and their peculiar geographic environment rendered through the aesthetic mode of realism—*The Final Mist* presented an avant-garde vision of reality, radically modifying the traditional literary techniques of the period. Subjectivism, poetic elaboration, and the fantastic were elements making the book an outstanding example of the emerging avant-garde in Latin American writing as well as a precursor of the acclaimed Latin American novels soon to follow.

Apart from its importance in the development of Latin American literature, *The Final Mist* is considered to be the most artistic testimony to women's predicament in Latin America. Bombal denounces her society's unfairness to women by presenting the devastating power of patriarchal society. Forced to fulfill the primary roles of wife and mother, women have no choice except to get married and become housewives. Thus, being marginal to politics and economics, they do not have the opportunity to participate actively in society. As Simone de Beauvoir has demonstrated in *The Second Sex* (1949), women's search for love has been conditioned by a system that has equated the condition of being a woman with the imperative of being a mother; even in a love relationship, women stand as the subordinated Other while men represent the Absolute.

Frustration, passivity, and alienation have become, then, the feminine mode of life, and the dilemma of the protagonist in *The Final Mist* must be considered as a true literary representation of a historical circumstance. In the 1930's, women in Latin America did not have the right to vote, nor did they have full access to employment. They were second-rate citizens who depended totally on men, and it is within this context that the protagonist's defeat, at the end of the novel, becomes symbolic of Latin American women's tragic predicament. Although Gertrudis Gómez de Avellaneda in *Sab* (1841) and Terese de la Parra in *Ifigenia* (1924) had denounced marriage as an enslaving bond for women, it was María Luisa Bombal who, by the incomparable excellence of her writing, gave a voice to the oppressed women of the twentieth century.

THE FLIES

Author: Mariano Azuela (1873-1952)
Type of work: Novel
Type of plot: Historical realism
Time of plot: April, 1915
Locale: Mexico
First published: *Las moscas*, 1918 (English translation, 1956)

Principal Characters

General Malacara, the highest ranking individual among the throng of former federal officials fleeing the capital by train. Like the other refugees who share the hospital car, he is a social parasite and a self-serving opportunist whose loyalty evaporates when his political faction loses control. His only concerns are escape, survival, and realignment. Because he is the most promising link to the protection of Francisco Villa, once the train is underway everyone courts his favor. He makes promises of help only in the hope of gaining some advantage, and he rarely delivers. He is a debauched libertine. In spite of the perilous circumstances, he initiates a drunken party and publicly cavorts with Cachucha and Manuela, women young enough to be his granddaughters.

Marta Reyes-Téllez, a strong-willed, essentially silly, middle-aged widow who knows how to take care of her family. Even though she has never worked, she understands better than do her employed children the moral flexibility and hypocrisy required to secure and protect a government job. She believes that she and her family, because of their social and political connections, are morally superior to virtually all others.

Matilde Reyes-Téllez, the older daughter of Marta. She arrogantly but mistakenly assumes that her place in society and her self-professed artistic talent will guarantee both her safety and her future.

Rosita Reyes-Téllez, the younger daughter of Marta. She uses her charms to manipulate men, but she lacks a will of her own.

Rubén Reyes-Téllez, the youngest of Marta's children. He always follows his mother's orders and Matilde's lead. A manly but utterly gullible youth, he is attracted to those in powerful positions and allows their opinions to determine his behavior. His naïveté and simplistic machismo allow his mother and older sister to coerce him to remain in Irapuato, in spite of the extreme danger, to arrange the family's future with the new administration.

Quiñones, a friend of Rubén who understands even less than Rubén of the social rules by which those in power expect their underlings to abide. An arrogant braggart, he demonstrates his careless disregard for Villa's rules and for the well-being of others when he openly criticizes Villa knowing that some of Villa's soldiers can hear him.

Dionacio Ríos, a prosecuting attorney for Villa's government.

Señor Rubalcaba, a corpulent federal schoolmaster. Like the novel's other displaced functionaries, he is utterly bereft of the will to act. More disposed to irony than to anger, he can only sigh with resignation when soldiers make off with his beloved companion, Miss Aurora of the fourth grade.

Don Sinforoso, the blustery former mayor of Turicato. Until he learns that military men are in grave danger, he claims to be a colonel in the federal army.

The Novel

Azuela's story begins in a railway station in Mexico City in 1915 as multitudes of panic-stricken citizens who had thrown their lot with Francisco "Pancho" Villa try to escape the city before Venustiano Carranza's ferocious Indian troops arrive to take over the government. Marta Reyes-Téllez, the widow of a government employee of long standing, is trying to find her children and secure a place for herself in one of the coaches. She frantically seeks help from Dionacio Ríos and General Malacara, whom she believes to be influential. The missing children are finally discovered in a hospital car, where their mother and would-be friends join them.

The doctor in charge regards the pompous family sourly but is unable to keep them out. Throughout the night and following day, the doctor remains the one sensible and calm person among the cowards and opportunists who are revealed to the reader in brief descriptive passages and in their conversations. It is easy to imagine that the doctor of *The Flies* is Azuela himself, sketching a remarkable gallery of characters drawn from his personal experience after the fall of Pancho Villa.

The Reyes-Téllez family forms the central focus of the action in *The Flies*. They are the first people singled out of the crowd in the railway station and the last to act before the story ends. Perhaps, too, they are the most repugnant of a mob of unsavory characters, for they alone have not a trace of intelligence or good humor about them.

Marta, the mother, has sacrificed her virtue for security among the political butchers and bandits, as Rubén, the ne'er-do-well son, intimates when he calls attention to the resemblance between his sister Rosita and the governor. It is no wonder, Rubén comments cynically, that the governor had been good to the family.

In Irapuato, Rubén locates an old acquaintance familiar with members of the new government who may be able to help the family. Rubén betrays his acquaintance to the police without a second thought the moment betrayal appears to be to his advantage.

Matilde, Marta's older daughter, is a silly, shallow girl who reveals her true nature when her pet canary is killed in the confusion of escape. Her reaction is an example of adolescent emotional experimentation. She savors her grief by indulging in screams of profound agony.

Rosita, the younger daughter, follows her mother's example. At a very young age she uses her body to attract men in high places, hoping to be able to use them to her family's advantage.

The crass materialism of the Reyes-Téllez women reaches its peak in the closing pages of the book. They push Rubén off the train as it leaves Irapuato. The boy is deserted with worthless Villa currency and instructions to find a place for the family in the new regime by using Quiñones, the very friend whom Rubén had betrayed.

Analysis   *Grand Hotel - ship of fools*

The action proceeds through fourteen short chapters, each complete within itself and containing the revelation of at least one individual. The characters are associated by accident. Panic flings them together, and fear keeps them together. Azuela has endowed many of them with delightful eccentricities that produce a comic effect. In some cases, this effect is achieved by the device of using ironic names and then playing with the meaning.

General Malacara (translatable as bad face or unpleasant look), for example, is ridiculed by the ironic placing of his name directly after a description of his unfailingly good-natured smile.

A tribute to Azuela's ability to create a pathetic character is the portrait of Don Sinforoso, the arrogant, boastful former federal official. In public he threatens to kill an impudent young soldier, but when fate brings him face to face with the boy alone, he is caught literally with his pants down and reveals himself as a blustery old coward. His days of glory long behind him, he cuts a foolish figure in his efforts to recapture the power and dash of his youth. His name, Sinforoso, is significant; "sin" meaning "without" and "foroso" sounding enough like the Spanish "fuerzo," meaning "strength" or "power," to suggest the Spanish equivalent of "Mr. Powerless."

An outstanding comic character is Moralitos (little morals), a bloated, grotesque little man who runs about the car, flushed and wide-eyed with excitement, spreading rumors of certain destruction. True to the indication of character suggested in his name, Moralitos is a great moralizer. Early in the book his ironic, ranting protestations of sincerity, honesty, and loyalty to the cause on behalf of the refugees provokes an apology from the doctor that explains the theme of the novel. Speaking of the crowd, the flies that buzz frantically about the sources of power and wealth in the capital, he admits that they are no worse than they have to be. They are models of virtue when their bodily needs are satisfied; they are not to be blamed if their morality is inspired by their bellies.

The precarious existence of these people is threatened by every rumor. They have played amateur politics through three regimes and are in the process of throwing in with whomever wins control of the government. Their problem is one of timing. They must turn their allegiance at just the right moment in order to fall in line for the best positions in the new government. They are nervous, insincere people who twitch and fawn before every face on the political horizon, but with the possible exception of the Reyes-Téllez family, they are not evil.

The message of *The Flies* is a bitter one that reflects Azuela's personal disillusionment with the war. The story mirrors a fundamental irony of glorious causes, the great dichotomy between political ideology and social reality. Each person sees the revolution through eyes of self-interest and acts accordingly. The author seems to understand and sympathize with human weakness; he points to faults, but he does not blame.

Azuela's prose style in *The Flies* is journalistic in its direct simplicity. He relates the events in the station, on the train, and in Irapuato as they occur, in plain language suitable to his characters. The choppy, fragmentary dialogue suggests the jerky movement of the train and the nervousness of the fugitives. Although the author's language is not poetic in general, there is a central metaphor running through the work, enriching and unifying it. That image appears as a brief glimpse of a cock with flaming plumage, his head held high, his wings outstretched, perched upon a dunghill. A clear picture of pride and arrogance supported by a "dunghill" of past offenses, this representation is flashed in the train window to indicate the false pride rampant within the hospital car.

The final chapter presents an abrupt change. The town of Irapuato has been evacuated, and the now familiar hospital car of assorted fools has departed. Pancho Villa's official train arrives a moment later, almost exactly twenty-four hours after the story began. He is no longer the man in power. Silence, not madly cheering throngs, now greets him. The sun, says Azuela, died forever with Villa's retreat. The night murmurs that Mexico is saved, but on the horizon the moon looks down, laughing.

The latest swarm of flies is now buzzing about Carranza. So it goes—a new government, a new swarm.

Critical Context

During the Mexican Revolution, Mariano Azuela served in the medical corps of Villa's army. In this peripheral position, he had an opportunity to observe the effects of the war upon every type of person. After Villa's defeat in 1915, Azuela escaped to El Paso, where he recorded recollections of the revolution in poignant but frequently humorous sketches and novels. *Los de abajo*

(1915; *The Underdogs*, 1929) is considered his masterpiece. *The Flies*, a much shorter work written two years after *The Underdogs*, shows less biting criticism, less dismal skepticism, and more good-natured understanding of the author's troubled people.

Azuela joined Villa's forces with the hope of replacing the octogenarian dictator, Porfirio Díaz, with the young idealist, Francisco Madero, whom he believed to be the savior of Mexico. Madero proved to be a disappointment. His mismanagement, poor judgment, and ineffectual personality could not establish a democratic government based upon brotherly love and mutual trust. Those principles, which had attracted Azuela to the revolution, were trampled fifteen months after Madero, backed by Villa and others, entered Mexico City.

THE FOREIGN GIRL

Author: Florencio Sánchez (1875-1910)
Type of work: Drama
Type of plot: Social morality
Time of plot: The early twentieth century
Locale: Near Santa Fé, Argentina
First presented: *La gringa*, 1904 (English translation, 1942)

Principal Characters

Victoria, "La Gringa," the daughter of Italian immigrants. She is in love with Próspero, the son of a creole (native-born) farmer.

Don Nicola, her ambitious immigrant father. He takes over Cantalicio's land when its owner runs into debt.

María, her mother, who distrusts Próspero's attentions to Victoria.

Horacio, Victoria's modern brother, who has studied engineering in the city.

Don Cantalicio, typical of the easygoing land-owners with Spanish blood. He is content to continue to raise cattle unprofitably rather than change over to wheat and make a profit. He is crippled when his horse is frightened by an automobile.

Próspero, his son, who sees the need to improve the land. He takes a job on the farm that was once in the possession of his family. Don Nicola discharges him when he is caught kissing Victoria.

Mr. Daples, an agent for farm machinery and later the employer of Próspero.

The Play

In *The Foreign Girl*, Don Nicola is an Italian immigrant landowner who works hard on his farm in Argentina and expects his laborers to do the same. Privately, his workmen and less ambitious neighbors criticize him because he makes his wife and children get up at two o'clock in the morning to begin their daily chores.

One of his neighbors is Don Cantalicio, an easygoing creole farmer deeply in Don Nicola's debt. Próspero, his son, works for Don Nicola and casts many languishing glances in the direction of Victoria, his employer's pretty daughter. Early one morning, coming to breakfast with the other laborers, Próspero seizes his chance to kiss Victoria when he finds her at her work. She offers little resistance to his embrace. Later, one of the boys reports that he had seen the Italian's white ox in Cantalicio's pasture. Próspero is forced to defend his father against a charge of thievery.

Cantalicio begs his neighbor for a year's extension on a large loan about to come due. Don Nicola says that he intends to foreclose on Cantalicio's property, his reason being that his son Horacio, then studying in Buenos Aires, wants the land for a farm. Cantalicio, although unable to pay the debt, refuses to give up his property. When Próspero comments that his father should have planted wheat instead of trying to pasture cattle, Cantalicio turns on his son and accuses him of becoming a "gringo"—a despised foreigner.

Not long afterward, María, Don Nicola's wife, discovers Próspero hugging her daughter. Told what had happened, Don Nicola discharges the boy. It does no good for Próspero to ask for Victoria's hand; Don Nicola did not intend for any creole son-in-law to squander his hard-earned money.

A few days later, the customers in a nearby tavern are drinking and teasing the waitress when a call comes for the doctor to attend a sick but penniless peon. He refuses to budge, however, until some of the loiterers offer to pay his fee. While Don Nicola was discussing the confiscation of Cantalicio's property with a lawyer, María and Victoria had been in town shopping. They enter the tavern. Próspero also enters, about to leave Santa Fé. He will not listen to Victoria's pleas to stay. He had had another quarrel with his father, who again accused him of taking the side of foreigners against those of good Argentine blood.

Cantalicio, having lost the lawsuit he had brought in an attempt to keep his property, is also preparing to leave the district. He complains bitterly that the immigrants are taking over all the land. When Don Nicola appears at the tavern to pay him the cash difference between the amount of the debt and the value of the farm, Cantalicio refuses to accept a note for a part of the settlement, even though the priest promises to see that the note is made good. The ruined creole trusts no one, and he weeps as he declares that everyone is against him.

Two years later, many changes have been made on the farm taken over by Don Nicola. To make room for a new building, he plans to have the workmen chop down the ancient ombú tree, symbol of the Argentine gaucho.

Cantalicio turns up unexpectedly. Working for others, he is driving oxen to a nearby town and stops to see what his old home looks like. Every change saddens him, but he reacts most strongly to the cutting down of the ombú. Don Nicola had no right to touch the tree, he asserts; it belonged to the land.

Victoria keeps trying to tell him something, but all she can say is that she had been in Rosario for several months. There she had seen Próspero, who missed his father. She also lets slip the fact that she is receiving letters from the boy. Horacio has further word of Próspero. He reports that Mr. Daples, an agent for farm machinery in Rosario, regards Cantalicio's son as his most valued employee. The brother and sister offer to take the old man around the farm. Still resentful, he refuses and hurriedly mounts his horse.

At that moment, the auto of the man who is building the new house chugs over the hill. That symbol of modern progress frightens the creole's horse, which throws Cantalicio in front of the car. Refusing the aid of everyone except Victoria, the hurt man begs her to help him to the ombú. He curses Don Nicola, calling him a gringo.

Several weeks later, everything is going well on the renovated farm. Buyers offer bonuses to get Don Nicola's clean wheat as soon as the thresher arrives to harvest it. Don Nicola tells Horacio that the contractor wants to marry Victoria and has asked for an answer before he leaves that night. The father is anxious to consult her as to her choice, but she is spending most of her time looking after Cantalicio, who had lost his right arm through his accident.

Overhearing a discussion that he might be better off in a hospital, Cantalicio announces that he will leave the farm at once, on foot if they will not lend him a wagon. Victoria refuses to hear of his leaving. Breaking down, she insists that she needs him, for she is carrying Próspero's child.

Próspero, having been sent by Mr. Daples to run the threshing machine, arrives at the farm. María is dismayed when she again catches him embracing her daughter. When she calls for her husband to come and drive Próspero off once and for all, Don Nicola remarks on the young man's industry and calculates that if the boy married into the family they could get their threshing done for nothing. Even Cantalicio becomes reconciled to the gringos—at least to one of them—and lets drop the announcement of his expected grandchild. Everyone is excited, but Don Nicola was never one to waste time, even for such a reason. All right, he declares, Próspero can have Victoria. Meanwhile, there is the threshing to be done. Grandchild or no grandchild, the work must come first.

Analysis

Florencio Sánchez underwent an impoverished and sickly youth. He lived in Bohemian style, dressed poorly, ate scantily, drank lustily, and labored for pittances. He worked for a time in a telegraph office and wrote his first plays on purloined telegraph pads. He suffered heart attacks and nervous seizures, and he died of tuberculosis at the age of thirty-five. Sánchez was thus unable to work systematically or attain intellectual discipline. He read socialist and anarchist tracts but never broadened his political education. The pampa spirit tinges all of his works, both urban and rural; his plots and themes flow from gaucho life with its primitive passions, fatalism, and struggle for survival. His heroes are often gaucho individualists who resist social pressures, or reformers victimized by governmental and bureaucratic tyrannies. His villains are generally oppressors, parasites, rapscallions, bureaucrats, and hypocrites.

The play's theme is the emergence of a hardworking Italo-Creole people who blend the virtues of immigrant and creole-mestizo stock. The rugged and gnarled ombú tree, loved by Argentine poets and once the only tree of the billowing pampa, symbolizes the strength of the pure native. European immigrant attributes are very visible and defended by Sánchez despite traditional Argentine resentment of "gringos." The clashing lifestyles, moreover, are not presented as hopelessly disharmonic. Sánchez's happy ending for *The Foreign Girl* is actually the story of nineteenth century Argentina, where a new people evolved from a combination of Argentines with European immigrants.

Critical Context

In the development of Argentine literature, many early nineteenth-century stories and plays made fun of the foreign-born gringo. Later dramatists, however, realized the foreigner's contribution to the nation's progress and made the immigrant a figure sympathetically presented. *The Foreign Girl* is such a play, written by the short-lived Florencio Sánchez, one of Latin America's greatest playwrights. Born in Uruguay, he spent most of his life on the Argentine side of the River Plate. He wrote rapidly, sometimes completing a play in a single night. His writing time for his eight long and twelve short dramas was only about thirty-five days in all. He gave a new technique to the stage and made it a theater of modern theses. He saw the hope of Argentina in a blending of the creole, or native, spirit and the blood of ambitious, industrious immigrants such as Don Nicola.

Sánchez helped bring European dramatic techniques to the Argentine stage, for he was influenced by Henrik Ibsen and Benito Pérez Galdós. Many Italian dramatic companies visited the River Plate area early in the twentieth century, further molding Sánchez, who was then writing the best current drama of Argentina and Uruguay. Sánchez's works usually contain dramatic intensity and poetic sentiment. They are often constructed laxly and have predictable outcomes, but *The Foreign Girl* is a comparatively hearty and optimistic work. Swollen with emotion, it is beautiful and realistic, with strong dialogue; it evokes familiar features of Argentina's hinterland, such as the *estancia* (ranch), the general store, and the immigrant farm home.

THE FOURTEEN SISTERS OF EMILIO MONTEZ O'BRIEN

Author: Oscar Hijuelos (1951-   )
Type of work: Novel
Type of plot: Family
Time of plot: The twentieth century
Locale: Cuba and the states of Pennsylvania, New York, California, and Alaska
First published: 1993

Principal Characters

Emilio Montez O'Brien, the youngest child and only son of Nelson O'Brien and Mariela Montez O'Brien. Reared and coddled in a household dominated by fifteen women, he serves in Italy during World War II. Following some success on the New York stage, he moves to Hollywood, where he makes forty-two B-films in five years. A vain philanderer, he is seduced by a Montana fan who marries him and soon ends his career in scandal. He flees to Alaska, where he finds true love with Jessica Brooks. Their joyous marriage ends in a fire that kills Jessica and their baby, Mary. Emilio overcomes drinking and depression to take up his father's old profession, becoming "photographer to the stars" in Hollywood.

Margarita Montez O'Brien, the eldest of the fifteen O'Brien children, born in 1902 on the ship taking her parents away from Cuba. Margarita's erotic fantasies are first aroused when a barnstorming aviator is forced to stay at the O'Brien house. Her marriage to the wealthy but abusive Lester Thompson ends in divorce after sixteen years. One of the few siblings to maintain their mother's language, she becomes a Spanish teacher. Still spry at the age of ninety, Margarita does volunteer work for the library, where she meets a gentle pilot named Leslie Howard and marries him, finally fulfilling her adolescent dream of love with a handsome flier.

Nelson O'Brien, patriarch of the clan. Nelson emigrates from Ireland with his sister Kate in 1896. When she dies shortly thereafter, Nelson goes off to Cuba to photograph the Spanish-American War.

When the fighting concludes, he sets up a studio in Santiago. When Mariela Montez sits for a portrait, Nelson begins wooing her. Shortly after their marriage, Nelson and Mariela move to Pennsylvania. Nelson continues to work as a photographer and, with the help of his many children, operates the Jewel Box Movie Theater. Outwardly cheerful, Nelson, a secret tippler, suffers from deep depressions.

Mariela Montez O'Brien, the matriarch of the clan. Soon after their marriage, Nelson takes her back to Cobbleton, a town that mystifies and terrifies the young Cuban woman. Mariela never masters English, becoming even more monolingual with age. After Mariela's death, her daughter Margarita discovers a cache of notebooks in which her mother reveals a complex emotional life unsuspected by the rest of the family.

Katherine Anne (Kate) O'Brien, Nelson's sister. She dies of pneumonia soon after she and her brother settle in Pennsylvania.

Gloria Montez O'Brien, the youngest O'Brien daughter. She suffers from an embarrassing crush on her brother Emilio.

Isabel Montez O'Brien, the second O'Brien daughter. She marries a Cuban pharmacist and settles in Santiago, Cuba.

Lester Thompson, Margarita's wealthy and abusive first husband. He meets her while she is working in her family's theater. They are divorced after sixteen years of marriage.

Betsy MacFarland, Emilio's first wife. Claiming to be an ardent fan of his films, she seduces him. Their brief marriage ends in scandal, causing Emilio's departure from Hollywood.

Jessica Brooks, Emilio's beloved second wife. He meets her in Alaska, where she is running a restaurant. Their joyful marriage is ended by a fire that kills Jessica and their baby.

Leslie Howard, a courtly octogenarian pilot. Margarita meets him in the local library and marries him when she is ninety.

The Novel

The Fourteen Sisters of Emilio Montez O'Brien opens with a chart of those sisters and of Emilio in order of their dates of birth. Their story, though, begins with the migration to the United States of Nelson O'Brien, a young Irish photographer, and his sister Kate. When Kate dies of pneumonia soon after they settle in bucolic Cobbleton, Pennsylvania, a despondent Nelson goes off to Cuba to cover the Spanish-American War. In Santiago, Cuba, he meets and marries Mariela Montez and begins the large and lively family whose experiences are the subject of Oscar Hijuelos' third novel. Concentrating on Margarita, the eldest child, born in 1902, and Emilio, the youngest, born in 1925, the book traces the experiences of the O'Briens throughout most of the twentieth century.

As the opening sentence proclaims, "The house in which the fourteen sisters of Emilio Montez O'Brien lived radiated femininity." That radiation is powerful enough to cause horses to throw their riders, cars to skid into ditches, and a plane to fall from the sky; Hijuelos endows his gynocratic household with Magical Realism. One of the sisters, Patricia, is even explicitly clairvoyant, adept at divining the fates of her many siblings; however, recognizing a rival to his narrative authority, Hijuelos relegates Patricia to a minor role and characterizes her as reluctant to indulge in prophecy.

Patriarch Nelson O'Brien senses himself as being condemned to solitude in his own crowded home, and his proficiency at generating daughters perplexes and perturbs him. He rejoices when his final, fifteenth, child turns out at last to be a son. For Emilio, surrounded and coddled by a mother and fourteen sisters, women set the standards.

Emilio is not born until the middle of the novel. The focus of the first third of the book is on Margarita and her largely erotic longings. Her adolescent fantasies focus on a barnstorming pilot whose plane becomes disabled near the O'Brien house. Margarita's marriage to the wealthy Lester Thompson proves to be a disaster and, after sixteen years, ends in divorce. In later years, Margarita finds fulfillment in teaching and in travel. She becomes the lover of a Cuban she meets in Spain and later, at the age of ninety, marries a pilot named Leslie Howard. In a culmination of her adolescent dreams about the demobilized aviator who came to stay with the O'Briens so very long ago, she learns at last to fly.

As a child, Emilio is especially attached to Margarita, while sister Gloria develops an unseemly crush on him. He eventually breaks free of coddling by the female O'Briens when he enlists in the Army, serving in the infantry during fierce combat in Italy. When World War II concludes, Emilio goes to New York to make his mark as an actor. After some success on the stage, he moves to Hollywood, where, during a career that lasts five years, he makes forty-two B-films. Using the screen name Montgomery O'Brien, he becomes popular playing private investigator Lance Stewart as well as Tarzan, but he is undone by womanizing. Marriage to a manipulative fan ends in ruinous divorce, and Emilio abandons Hollywood stardom for work on an oil rig in Alaska. It is there that he meets and falls in love with Jessica Brooks. Their marriage is joyful, and Emilio is devastated when Jessica and their baby die in a fire. He eventually recovers from severe alcoholic depression to commence a new career in California as "photographer to the stars," thereby resuming the family business that first brought Mariela Montez into the Santiago studio of Nelson O'Brien.

The Fourteen Sisters of Emilio Montez O'Brien is an old-fashioned collation of life studies, a patient record of moments from ten decades. Photography often provides its pretext for narration. At various stages of their lives, Nelson, who continues with his camera work even after opening the Jewel Box Movie Theater, assembles his family for group portraits. Hijuelos proceeds to tell the story behind each picture. After Emilio retires from work in front of a lens and himself becomes a photographer, much of the rest of the story is generated by either the new prints that Emilio produces or the old ones that he ponders.

In the novel's epigraph, Nelson explains to Emilio his preference for the archaic shuttered, folding-bellows camera that, as late as 1937, the older man still prefers to use. He says that it "captures not only the superficial qualities of its subjects but also, because of the time it takes to properly collect light, their feelings, as they settle on the subjects' expressions; sadness and joy and worry, with variations therein, are collected on the plate." It is a manifest parallel to Hijuelos' own device for arresting the fleeting images of existence—the sadness and joy and worry, with variations therein, experienced by each of the O'Briens. For Hijuelos, memory is photographic, if imperfect, and his storytelling is inspired by and analogous to the photographer's dream of retaining traces of light—and life—on paper.

Analysis

The Fourteen Sisters of Emilio Montez O'Brien resumes Hijuelos' project of divulging the sordid secret that all lives are defeated by the treachery of desire. He suffuses his third novel with the melancholy of futile longing. As a B-film actor, Emilio exploits the desires of those who gaze at his bright image in darkened theaters, but his first disastrous marriage occurs when Emilio himself succumbs to the wiles of an opportunistic fan—"once again he had allowed himself to be taken in by his own desire," observes the narrator, explaining both Emilio's seduction by Betsy MacFarland and a general law of the Hijuelos universe, in which characters are forever longing and never achieving satisfaction for long.

The Fourteen Sisters of Emilio Montez O'Brien continues Hijuelos' project of chronicling the experiences of Cuban immigrants in the United States. Cobbleton is not very hospitable to a Hispanic newcomer, and Mariela Montez is obliged to forfeit much of her native culture when she abandons Cuba and follows her new husband to Pennsylvania. The novel dramatizes the process by which her children assimilate into the dominant society, and it suggests a haunting sense of loss felt by both the immigrant generation and its offspring.

Half a dozen years later, Nelson warns his eldest daughter always to use English with him. "'cause in this country it's been my observation that Spanish will be of little use to you, certainly useless to you as far as gainful employment and one day finding yourself a husband." Although Margarita becomes a Spanish teacher and Isabel marries a Cuban pharmacist and moves to Santiago, the youngest of the siblings learn little or none of their mother's mother tongue. In the confluence of Yankee optimism and Latin fatalism, the sanguine blood does not win out. Publicly exuberant, Nelson takes to private tippling, as insulation against his chronic melancholy. Hijuelos' theme, like that of much classic American fiction, is the revenge of the past on the self-assured man.

Critical Context

The first book published by Hijuelos after the huge critical and popular success of *The Mambo* *Kings Play Songs of Love* (1989), *The Fourteen Sisters of Emilio Montez O'Brien* was greeted with the attention and respect appropriate to its author's new prominence. Like Mexican Americans Sandra Cisneros and Richard Rodriguez, Hijuelos owed his public success not only to talent but to timing and a Latino identity as well. His third novel, though, is an ambitious bid to transcend the Cuban American experience. Through the offspring of an Irish father and a Cuban mother, who blend "continents of blood and memory—from Saracen to Celtic, Scythian to Phoenician, Roman to pagan Iberian, African to Dane, a thousand female and male ancestors, their histories of sorrow and joy, of devastated suffering and paradisiacal pleasures linked by the progression of the blood," it attempts to mine particular experience for universal treasure.

THE FRAGMENTED LIFE OF DON JACOBO LERNER

Author: Isaac Goldemberg (1945-   )
Type of work: Novel
Type of plot: Psychological realism
Time of plot: 1923 to 1935
Locale: Peru, primarily Lima and Chepén
First published: *La vida a plazos de Don Jacobo Lerner*, 1976 (English translation, 1976)

Principal Characters

Jacobo Lerner, a Jewish businessman. After leaving Russia as a young man, he settles in Peru, where he attempts to start a business and marry a nice Jewish girl. He has to abandon his first store, however, because in a moment of weakness he gets a Catholic girl pregnant, and he cannot marry her. Eventually, he becomes prosperous as the owner of a brothel. He cannot marry the woman he loves because she is his brother's wife. Her sister, his second choice, breaks their engagement. When he becomes ill, those very people to whom Jacobo has been generous are interested only in the financial impact of his death. At the age of forty-two, he dies.

Bertila Wilson, the mother of Jacobo's son. A shy girl of seventeen when she first meets Jacobo, she is so ignorant that she believes all of his invented adventures and is easily seduced. After Jacobo refuses to take in their son, she turns against the child.

Efraín Wilson, the illegitimate son of Jacobo Lerner and Bertila Wilson. A sensitive, confused boy, he is loved only by his great-aunt Francisca, who has told him that his father is dead. When he becomes aware of his Jewish background, however, he is abandoned by her and by the priest. Eventually, he goes mad and is kept in seclusion.

León Mitrani, a grocer. A friend of Jacobo from the time of their youth in Russia, León precedes him to Peru. A former Bolshevik, in old age León turns back to Judaism. Hated by his blind, Catholic wife and disliked by the neighbors whom he reviles in his prophetic outbursts, he loses his trade. After he is killed by a careless doctor, his casket is lost somewhere on the road.

Moisés Lerner, Jacobo's brother. Smug and hypocritical, he conceals the fact that he cheated Jacobo in a business they owned jointly and that later Jacobo saved him from bankruptcy.

Sara Brener Lerner, the wife of Moisés Lerner. A chatty woman who admits that she cannot make up her mind, she is constantly balancing the opinion of the Jewish community against the possibility of financial gain. Realizing that Jacobo loves her, she is interested only in using him, whether to marry him off to her sister or to make a profit by taking in his son.

Miriam Brener Abramowitz, Sara's widowed sister. In order to regain her social position as a married woman, she is willing to marry Jacobo even though she does not love him. When she learns that he owns a brothel and supports a mistress, however, she breaks the engagement. Unknown to her, she is thereafter supported by Jacobo.

Juana Paredes, Jacobo's Peruvian mistress. A woman whose main concern is her family, she has made sure that Jacobo feels responsible for her widowed sister and her sister's seven children. When he is dying, her primary concern is that she will get enough money for herself and for them.

Francisca Wilson, Efraín's great-aunt and foster mother. A devout Catholic, she loves him deeply until he discovers his Jewish heritage; she then turns against him and consigns him to hell.

Samuel Edelman, a traveling salesman. A friend of Jacobo, he visits Mitrani and checks on Efraín. When he discovers that the boy has gone mad, he resolves not to tell the dying Jacobo.

The Novel

The Fragmented Life of Don Jacobo Lerner, which begins on the night before Don Jacobo's death, recounts the major events of his twelve years as a Russian Jew in Peru through objective narratives and through what might be called the testimony of those with whom his life was involved. The novel traces the steps toward the loss of a sense of self in two major characters, Jacobo Lerner himself and his illegitimate son, Efraín.

When Jacobo arrives in Peru, driven from Russia by a pogrom, he intends to marry a Jewish girl, produce a family, make money, and live to a respected old age in the large Jewish community. By chance, Jacobo hears that his old friend León Mitrani has settled in the village of Chepén. When Jacobo arrives in Chepén, he finds that Mitrani is neither rich nor happy. Married to a local woman, he is alienated both from her narrow Catholic world and from his ancestral faith. Although Jacobo settles in Chepén and becomes prosperous enough to be sought as a son-in-law by the father of Bertila Wilson, he is haunted by Mitrani's misery. When Bertila becomes pregnant and Jacobo must decide whether to marry her and stay in Chepén, he flees.

Although there is an active Jewish community in Lima, Jacobo cannot find the Jewish girl he seeks. Nor do his fortunes improve. Swindled by his brother Moisés Lerner, Jacobo must take to the road as a peddler, moving in fear through the distant villages, where he can disappear without a trace, like the Jews of pogroms and of the Inquisition. When he is offered a share in a brothel business, Jacobo returns to Lima with relief. Still he cannot manage to establish a family. He cannot marry the Jewish woman whom he loves, Sara Lerner, because she is the wife of his brother. He is jilted by her sister, Miriam Abramowitz, after she hears about the brothel and his mistress. He cannot marry Juana Paredes, his devoted mistress, because she is not Jewish, and he cannot reclaim the son he already has lest he be drawn back into the society of Chepén. At last, almost mad, Jacobo

becomes convinced that he is possessed by the dybbuk of Mitrani; exorcised, Jacobo finds himself to be an empty shell, and he dies.

Like Jacobo, Efraín, his son, is an alien in a Catholic society. Hated by his mother and barely tolerated by his grandparents, Efraín clings to his aunt Francisca Wilson and to the local priest. When he grows older, however, he discovers that his father is not dead and damned, as he has been told. When the troubled boy attacks the statue of the Virgin Mary in church for "abandoning" her own son, the priest and Francisca reject Efraín. At the end of the novel Efraín, too, is an empty shell, shut in a solitary room with spiders as companions.

In *The Fragmented Life of Don Jacobo Lerner*, the events of the characters' lives and their own qualities are revealed gradually through four kinds of narration, which alternate as the book progresses. The most objective narrative consists of quotations from the public record—from the birth registration of Efraín, for example, or from *Jewish Soul*, which contains social notes, pleas for taking Peruvian citizenship, and historical comments on past persecutions that reveal the always nervous background of the Jewish community and its attempts to attain some feeling of security in an alien society. In addition, dated "chronicles" reveal public events and private musings in a stylized objectivity. Interspersed with this deliberately emotionless material are third-person accounts, sometimes with limited omniscience. The fourth method, and the most revealing, is the dramatic monologue. Because the monologues are not chronologically ordered but are interspersed among the chronological quotations and "chronicles," there is an alternation between chronological narration and psychological narration that produces suspense somewhat in the mode of a murder mystery. Events are discovered, and therefore characters must be reinterpreted, or characters are revealed by their reactions to events that have already been discovered.

Analysis

Goldemberg has commented that his two persistent themes are the narrowness of village life in Peru and the difficulty for a Jew to find an identity in a society that is perhaps tolerant but is always alien. Both themes involve difficult situations that invite flight. Thus, the Wilson girls, bored with their lives, ignore the official warnings about virtue and run off with whatever men appear. Ephraín's grandmother retreats into dreams; Francisca, into religion; Ephraín, unable to leave, into madness.

For the Jews, the temptation is always to accept provincial life, to assume the mask of a Peruvian Catholic, but thousands of years of tradition are not so easily discarded. León Mitrani cannot forget his heritage, nor can Jacobo, either to become a family man and shopkeeper in Chepén or to become a successful businessman in Lima. Jacobo flees from Chepén. Later, he flees from the small towns where the Jewish peddler is so obviously alien. For a time, with a mistress and a good business, he seems to have found a home in Lima, but still he is pursued by discontent, by the dead León's fear of pogroms, by a terrifying sense of loss, and by the certainty of his death. Throughout his life of flight, Jacobo never finds anything that he can capture. Dying, he cannot remember any happiness; living, he had only fragments without an organizing principle. His very predicament testifies to his idealism: Unlike Sara, preoccupied with her position as First Lady of the Peruvian Jewish community, and unlike Moisés, satisfied with his own success, Jacobo cannot be content with superficials. Nor can he live in illusions. Where once there was the certainty of the prophets of Israel, now there is only the reality of death in a lonely room; beyond it, only a riddle.

Critical Context

This novel can be seen in the context of South American literature. Like Gabriel García Márquez, Goldemberg is interested in the stifling effects of life in a small village where nothing has changed for centuries. The novel should also be seen in the context of Jewish literature, which points out the fear engendered by centuries of persecution and the sense of separateness that persists even after the faith that was its reason has dwindled or disappeared.

Jacobo is a modern version of the legendary Wandering Jew. He also becomes a metaphor for people of the modern world, sentenced to spiritual homelessness for no sin that he can identify. A person wishing to avoid this disease must merge into one community or another, whether the little Catholic community of Chepén or the thriving Jewish community of Lima. Perhaps those who can do so are fortunate. Those who, like Jacobo, recognize the fact that all is not well, who seek a principle by which to organize their lives but who cannot find it, are the contemporary wanderers, regardless of their religious background. In his exploration of universal truths that extend far beyond the limited society of which he writes, Goldemberg has displayed the gifts of a writer worthy of consideration.

FROM CUBA WITH A SONG

Author: Severo Sarduy (1937-   )
Type of work: Novel
Type of plot: Experimental
Time of plot: Undefined
Locale: A simulated Cuba
First published: *De donde son los cantantes*, 1967 (English translation, 1972)

Principal Characters

Mortal Pérez, a common name from Dolores Rondón's epitaph ("come, mortal, and see") turned into a character. He is a blond Spaniard who speaks Castilian Spanish and who always possesses some attribute of power. He starts as an old general, when, in "By the River of Rose Ashes," he falls in love with and relentlessly pursues Lotus Flower. At first a voyeur, he ends as a would-be assassin. In "Dolores Rondón," he is a politician rising from provincial obscurity to national prominence as a senator. His fall comes when it is revealed that the Hawaiian dancer he procured for the president is a mulatto woman from his province. In "The Entry of Christ in Havana," he is a young elusive lover ardently desired by Auxilio and Socorro. Later, he is identified with the wooden statue of Christ found by them in the cathedral of Santiago de Cuba and is brought triumphantly to Havana. He disintegrates on the way and, finally, dies.

Auxilio and **Socorro,** metaphysical twins in perpetual transformation. (Both names mean "call for help" in Spanish, but they appear as *Help* and *Mercy* in some translations.) They start looking for God, only to find all the principal characters in a "self-service" grocery store. In "By the River of Rose Ashes," they are chorus girls, transvestites, and, occasionally, prostitutes. They also help the old general with his passion for Lotus Flower. In "Dolores Rondón," they act as the magic twins, tricksters, of the Afro-Cuban religion. They reveal the senator's fraud. In "The Entry of Christ in Havana," they are two Spanish women in love with Mortal. Having arrived in the Cuba of early colonial days, they learn music in the cathedral of Santiago de Cuba and find there a wooden statue of Christ, with whom they identify their elusive lover. In a triumphant procession, they take the statue to Havana. They are received by gunfire from helicopters.

Lotus Flower, a transvestite who is an actress in the Chinese burlesque opera house in Havana and is desperately pursued by the general Mortal Pérez.

Dolores Rondón, a young mulatto woman from the provinces, mistress and wife of the senator Mortal Pérez. Her new high life is in conflict with the Afro-Cuban religion, and the offended deities cause the fall of the senator. She returns to the province and dies in poverty, summarizing her life in an epitaph she writes for her tomb as a lesson to all mortals.

The Great Bald Madame, Death, a character presented as the final essential ingredient of the cosmic jigsaw puzzle.

Myself, a personal pronoun turned into a character. It represents the authorial voice, which later splits into a dialogue between Narrator One and Narrator Two.

The Novel

From Cuba with a Song is not a novel in the traditional sense; rather, Sarduy's second work of fiction breaks down the novelistic conventions of character, plot, and theme. The innovative thrust of *From Cuba with a Song* lies in its radical alteration of traditional plot. Instead of telling a story in linear fashion, *From Cuba with a Song* reads like a verbal jigsaw puzzle composed of three pieces or narrative sequences attached to a "head"—the introductory "Curriculum cubense."

This first section traces a drawing that helps the reader assemble Sarduy's experiment in the novel form. A Chinese and a black woman surround a blond, white male at the center of the picture. He stands next to Help, half of the pair of twins who reappear throughout the work. Close to them, the "Waxen Woman," the face of Death, absorbs the entire scene. The drawing displayed in "Curriculum cubense," "a giant four-leaf clover, or a four-headed animal facing the four cardinal points, or a Yoruba sign of the four roads," fills in the outline of an empty plot. Each figure in the picture corresponds to one of the three fictions that make up *From Cuba with a Song*. The Chinese and the black woman become protagonists of their own tales—Lotus Flower in "By the River of Rose Ashes," and "Dolores Rondón" in her namesake piece. The white man, Mortal Pérez, fills the center of the drawing since he is in a relation of desire to the two women. He is also the center of his own supreme fiction, "The Entry of Christ in Havana," first as Everyman and then as a baroque Christ figure. The three tales are designed to depict the linguistic and erotic sensibility proper to the racial layers superimposed on the mosaic of Cuban culture: the Chinese, African, and Spanish elements.

Rather than a novel of plot, *From Cuba with a Song* is a novel of language. The linguistic texture of the novel constructs a verbal archetype or reproduction of Cuba. It appears that the pieces of the puzzle fit together in the totality of a culture, a whole Cuba integrated by its racial and ethnic components, as reflected in the drawing. Metaphor and poetic description qualify the Chinese tale; dialogue, colloquial speech, and a mock tragic tone exhibit the African flair for drama in the second tale. The last section testifies to the origins of Cuban lexicon and intonation in Castilian Spanish; it also bears witness to the Hispanic legacy of mysticism.

The presence of language in *From Cuba with a Song* compensates for an absence: Where is Cuba? As the original title in Spanish expresses it, the song may be from Cuba, but "where do the singers come from"? In the Spanish edition, the title is phrased without a question mark, resulting in an affirmative but syntactically ambiguous sentence. "Where do the singers come from?" is a verse from a traditional song by Miguel Matamoros, the "Son de la Loma" (the *son* is a distinctive rhythm that originated in Cuban folk music, reflecting the combination of Spanish and African musical forms). Hence, Sarduy's fiction poses the problem of origin in terms of a question and answer, or an absence and presence. Is there really a "First Cuban Song," an origin of self in culture, a beginning in language? In other words, does a Cuban identity (or that of any nationality) really exist?

At first reading, the four parts of *From Cuba with a Song* lead to an affirmative answer, since the "four different beings" appear as "four who are one." Three races and *etnias* combine in one Cuba, just as the three fictions plus the "Curriculum cubense" result in one novel. The work ends, however, on a final "Note" in which Sarduy explains the mechanism of his novel—three cultures, three fictions, three themes (desire, ambition, religious zeal). This "note" to the song scrambles the puzzle again, leaving the reader with the question asked consistently throughout the work: What is "the definition of being"? Sarduy's fiction underscores the question of cultural identity with a more radical critique. He puts in doubt the transcendental, unified subject invented by Western metaphysics. The novel's four parts turn into five, and the whole of Cuban culture becomes a pretext for revealing the hole inside Being.

Analysis

If *From Cuba with a Song* has a theme, it is best demonstrated in the middle section of the book, dedicated to the tale of Dolores Rondón. An ambitious and attractive mulatto, Dolores leaves her native Camagüey on the trail of Mortal Pérez's political career. After reaching her zenith in the capital (Havana), she suddenly falls from fame and returns, penniless and defeated, to her hometown. The two narrators ask what purpose Dolores Rondón's life serves. The answer solves the riddle of the meaning of Sarduy's fiction: "Nothing. Delicious Nothingness milkshake." The "theme" of the novel, then, is that literature—and all forms of verbal communication—has no meaning, no transcendent message beyond its material substance as language.

In spite of the denial of ultimate categories in Sarduy's fiction, the interweaving stories of *From Cuba with a Song* leave the lingering trace of the author's preoccupation with the transcendent. This is done, however, in the paradoxical "yes and no" style of the novel. For example, the general opens up a store across the street from the Shanghai brothel that is ironically called the Divine Providence. Sarduy's gesture is to disguise the longing for the absolute in terms of erotic desire. The encounter with Divinity is as impossible as the fulfillment of the libido. Both God and the wanted one fade and evade in the look of desire.

Sarduy's characteristic mingling of erotic need and the drive for meaning comes to a climax in "The Entry of Christ in Havana," when Help and Mercy's intense longing for Mortal turns into divine fervor. A wooden statue of Christ appears in the cathedral of Santiago de Cuba, the site where Cuban music originated. Help and Mercy carry the statue in a spiritual journey across the island that ends in a snow-covered Havana. As the journey proceeds, the wooden body of Christ rots away, and the tale "degenerates" into unreality. In the end, Christ enters Havana but steps also into Death, dancing to a mambo beat that brings the novel to a close.

This scene demonstrates that, for Sarduy, the quest for an absolute begins and ends with writing, with the composition of *From Cuba with a Song*. It is writing, the process of inscription that binds the "themes" of the novel together in a "hide-and-seek" game in which the origin, the love object, and the sublime are always pursued but never found.

Critical Context

From Cuba with a Song, Sarduy's second work of fiction after *Gestos* (1963; gestures), marked a turning point in his development as a writer, for soon after the novel Sarduy also proved his talents as an essayist and literary critic. The essays collected in *Escrito sobre un cuerpo* (1969; *Written on a Body*, 1989) expound the theory of literature that makes *From Cuba with a Song* the "novel" novel that it is. Here are Sarduy's views on the equivalences between sex-uality and text-uality, transvestism and literature, and text and body that surface in the fictions of *From Cuba with a Song*.

Sarduy's theory of literature as wordplay and erotic inscription reflects the influence of French structuralist and poststructuralist thought. Critics such as Roland Barthes in *Le Degré zéro de lécriture* (1953; *Writing Degree Zero*, 1967) shaped Sarduy's insistence on the autonomy of language and of the literary artifact. Barthes' *Le Plaisir du texte* (1973; *The Pleasure of the Text*, 1975), like Sarduy's own *Escrito sobre un cuerpo*, conceives of the writing/reading process as an erotic exchange between author and reader. One outcome of these theories is the body/text of *From Cuba with a Song*, a work that unsettles the conventions of the novel genre by its self-referentiality and parodic inversion.

The parodic thrust of the novel is responsible

for its impact in the context of Latin American literature. *From Cuba with a Song* represents one of the most radical rewritings of the Latin American myth of origin. The novelty of *From Cuba with a Song* is that it carries the demystifying tendency in the Latin American novelistic tradition to the point of showing that the only origin of self is the secondary condition of language.

THE FUTILE LIFE OF PITO PEREZ

Author: José Rubén Romero (1890-1952)
Type of work: Novel
Type of plot: Picaresque
Time of plot: The 1920's and 1930's
Locale: Michoacan and Morelia, two provinces in western Mexico
First published: *La vida inútil de Pito Pérez*, 1938 (English translation, 1942)

Principal Characters

Jesús Pérez Gaona, or **Pito Perez,** the protagonist, a thin, long-haired, drunken rogue dressed in rags, a street peddler in Morelia. During his vagabond life, he has assumed various occupations, such as druggist's assistant, sacristan, jailer's secretary, and general store clerk. His adventures inspire his incisive and satirical observations of human nature. He firmly believes that society's injustice and hypocrisy have made him a loser. He feels fully justified to lie, cheat, and steal his way through life. He considers his shamelessness to be a sign of his honesty, and he observes that people can relax only when they have no reputation to maintain.

Jose de Jesus Jimenez, the corpulent and lethargic druggist of Uropa. He is Pito Perez's first master. Pito flees when the druggist discovers Pito's love affair with the druggist's wife.

Father Pureco, the dim-witted priest of La Huacana, who employs Pito as his sacristan. Pito supplies him with Latin phrases to embellish his sermons, as his parishioners appreciate him more when they do not understand what he is saying.

Jose Vasquez, a jailer and champion drinker. Pito becomes his secretary but promptly leaves when Vasquez proves to be dictatorial and selfserving.

Irene, a tall, dark, and slender child of a poor family, Pito's neighbor and first love. Pito serenades her for a year on his flute until he finds out that his brother, Francisco, is already courting her.

Chucha, Pito's olive-skinned cousin. She charms Pito into allowing her to take money from a store's cash box. Pito asks his friend, Santiago, to ask for her hand in marriage for him. Instead, Santiago asks to marry her himself. From this incident, Pito learns that his bad luck in life extends to the pursuit of romance.

Caneca, a female skeleton that Pito calls his wife. Pito claims that she is the perfect mate because she is faithful to him, makes no demands, and has no bodily functions or odors.

The Novel

Romero's purpose in writing *The Futile Life of Pito Perez* was to observe, judge, and criticize Mexican society of the 1920's and 1930's. He realized this goal by casting his story in the form of a picaresque novel, of which a primary characteristic is that the narrative is told in the first-person voice. Appropriately, this novel comprises a series of anecdotes in which Pito tells the unnamed narrator of the various escapades he suffers from childhood until the day of his death. Given this structure, the reader is advised to ignore signs of the traditional plot and rather should imagine himself listening to a good storyteller chatting about the high and low points of his life.

As the town drunk, sardonically, Pito sees himself as life's loser, a pattern established early in his life when his mother adopts a child and ensures that he has more food, comfort, and love than does her own son: "... the day I was born, there was another child who had been left without a mother so mine gave him her full breasts. The stranger grew strong and robust and I was left weak and sickly because there wasn't enough milk for the two of us." By his own account, his life has been "downhill" ever since.

To survive, he assumes any disguise that permits him to close upon his two most enduring friends, food and liquor. With a local, uninstructed, pompous priest, he spouts Latin. With a gross, abject apothecary, he "reformulizes" the prescriptions, keeps the change, and drinks the profits. With the *escribano* (a public writer for the illiterate), his imagination transforms the inarticulate into the most worthy of prose.

As Pito makes his way through these and similar "offices," his character becomes clear. He maintains a gentle and optimistic demeanor that blinds him to the unerring devastation greeting his every turn. Repeatedly, he risks all to better his lovers' lives. His prize unfailingly is to watch them marry someone deemed more socially acceptable.

With each devastation, Pito increases both his hopes for a better future and his expectation of even more cruel results. He finally strikes upon his solution to life's inconstancy: to betroth himself to Caneca, a female skeleton for whom he now works in his last office, that of a street peddler. He says that she is "the most faithful love I have had in all my life," and to her he composes his last verse: "Caneca, my sweet,/ she roams not the street./ And never does she want something to eat!"

The novel ends with Pito's death. His body, significantly, is found on a rubbish heap. In his pocket, Pito has placed his last will and testament, a bitter document that he asks his readers to accept as accurate, since he was mad and therefore able to perceive the truth. In it, he denounces the highly held human sentiments of liberty, equality, fraternity, humanity, friendship, and love. In their lieu, he extols thievery, dishonesty, greed, and ambition.

Analysis

To gain access to the primary theme of *The Futile Life of Pito Perez*, one need only consider the opening and closing scenes. The narrator meets Pito originally in a bell tower: "The dark silhouette of a man was plainly outlined in the luminous arch of the bell tower. It was Pito Perez, intensely absorbed in his contemplation of the surrounding countryside." From this opening image of a man withdrawn temporarily from society and associated with the center of the dissemination of important events, the bell tower, the reader witnesses the downward spiral of a well-intentioned, idealistic man—a bird for whom no thermals exist—to his death. "The early risers ... found the body on a pile of rubbish. Its hair was completely disheveled and caked with mud. Its mouth had contracted into a convulsive grin of bitterness. Its wide-open eyes looked at the heavens with a challenging haughtiness."

Romero's resolutely cynical view of Mexico's infrastructure precludes any characterization based on values of sincerity, loyalty, trust, forgiveness, brotherhood, or love. The inference that madness and death are the principled individual's response to the hypocritical, deceitful world is borne out in Pito's last will and testament, which is a resounding denouncement of all service institutions.

Romero chose the picaresque as the form most suited to his purpose, having detected the baroque premise that underlies the genre—that the greatest sin of man is to be born. With earlier examples of the form, *The Futile Life of Pito Perez* shares the general rhythm and movement of the *engaño/desengaño* (illusion/hope, disillusionment/despair) pattern. Romero's protagonist is cast with a lethal, irreconcilable duality, a born innocent in a deceitful world. As the servant figure, he gains access to all the social strata. Pito's clear view of each group and/or attitude—church, education, justice, business, city, family, traditions, friendship, and patriotism—allows the reader to observe behind the façades, the self-seeking motivations of greed, envy, egotism, and pretense.

The pervasive irony of the work achieves the aim of any social critic, a distance from the text across which the reader becomes objective about the pretenses of the character and his world. Such a serious tone would seem to preclude a wide readership for the novel, yet since its publication Romero's novel has maintained a vast audience as it has been "discovered" by successive generations.

The novel's appeal proceeds directly from its multilayered composition of tones, techniques, and images, each attracting its corresponding readership. It is a "naughty" book filled with outlandish scatological references. It is a "fun" book in which authority is given short shrift, mocked and made ludicrous. It is a "fanciful" book with hyperbole as its major feature. In spite of its general distancing treatment of Pito, the occasional glimpse of affection humanizes him for the sentimental reader. In all, it contains the vitality of the frontier—raucous, strident, and very macho—offset by genuine moments of tenderness.

At a subtler level, the novel's style contains its theme, a goal always desired but rarely reached by authors. Its style is a very mockery of itself, for words, images, scenes, and ideas tend toward inversion, tend to become just the opposite of their normal associations—they become "hypocrites" before the reader's eyes. Of the abounding examples of this uncanny talent of Romero, three stand out. Two already mentioned acquire new power in the context of his style of inversion: the adopted child becomes family whereas the true son becomes orphaned; true love is to the skeletal (life) as false love is to the living (death). The third example is taken from a scene in a jail, which Pito equates with the family. As befits the family, he observes how the prisoners, filled with a "kind of childlike spirit," share with and give support to one another: "When a prisoner doesn't have a blanket, the rest cuss his mother up and down with all kinds of vulgarities, so that he will get boiling mad and thus keep himself warm." In passing, the reader wonders about the appropriateness of the prisoners' reaction if most have received from their mothers the same kind of treatment Pito received from his own.

Critical Context

Critics look at Romero's work in a historical context. At the time the novel was written, the Mexican Revolution, fought to free the individual from the caste system, had recently ended, and it was becoming increasingly apparent to the literati that the early promises of change were illusory; vested interests maintained their power while the disenfranchised were measurably more miserable, since their fresh hope had been destroyed. The general response of Mexican writers to this *engaño/desengaño* process was to write novels of content and theme directly taken from the revolution itself. In contrast, Romero took only the pro-

cess he observed from the deterioration of the revolution's idealism and infused his picaresque narrative with this disillusionment. His novel is regarded, then, as an oblique, ironic exegesis of the revolution, the failure of which accounts for the withering attitude of the author toward Mexico's institutions and values.

Romero's masterpiece was unique in its time and anticipated the exploration of form and content notable in post–World War II Latin American narrative. It remains among the finest novels produced in Mexico.

GABRIELA, CLOVE AND CINNAMON

Author: Jorge Amado (1912-   )
Type of work: Novel
Type of plot: Historical realism
Time of plot: 1925-1926
Locale: Ilhéus, Bahia, Brazil
First published: *Gabriela, Cravo e Canela*, 1958 (English translation, 1962)

Principal Characters

Gabriela, a mulatto girl from the backlands. She comes to Ilhéus, in the Brazilian province of Bahia, to escape the drought. Her physical charms, including cinnamon-colored skin that always smells of cloves, and her ingenuous personality make her irresistible to everyone she meets. She is hired by Nacib Saad, the owner of a local bar. She lacks formal education, but her ability to prepare delicious Bahian dishes and her beauty soon make the bar a popular landmark. Gabriela and Nacib become lovers, a situation that pleases the girl. For her, sex is a natural part of life that should be shared with whomever she chooses. She and Nacib marry, making her a member of an exclusive social circle. The trappings of affluence restrict her physically and emotionally. Their marriage is annulled after Nacib finds Gabriela in bed with another man, but soon the estranged lovers are reunited and resume the same type of relationship they enjoyed before their marriage.

Nacib Saad, the Syrian owner of the Vesuvius Bar. He passionately loves Gabriela and wants to be the only man in her life. He marries her but soon notes that her passion is not as intense as it was before the marriage. When he finds her with Tonico, he wants to kill her, as any betrayed husband should in Brazil. He cannot do so, and in failing, he reflects the modern attitude gradually taking hold in tradition-bound Ilhéus.

Mundinho Falcão, a young businessman from a prominent family in Rio de Janeiro. As the political rival of Ramiro Bastos, Mundinho represents progress in Ilhéus. He hires an engineer to devise a plan to remove a sandbar and obtains accreditation for the local school. Such contributions to the community create changes toward a more modern way of life.

Ramiro Bastos, a wealthy old cacao planter who has controlled local politics for decades. His influence in government has been valuable in the past, but he finds himself challenged by the young, dynamic Mundinho Falcão. Bastos represents the traditional patriarchal system of Ilhéus.

Tonico Bastos, the son of Ramiro Bastos, lacks his father's political talents. A regular at the Mount Vesuvius Bar, he works as a notary public. In this capacity, he prepares the documents for Gabriela's marriage to his best friend, Nacib. Known as a ladies' man, Tonico struggles to keep his affairs secret from his wife.

Malvina, the daughter of cacao planter Melk Tavares. She reads "controversial" books and insists that she does not want the kind of traditional marriage that her parents have. Her love affair causes gossip and precipitates a brutal beating by her father. Unable to tolerate such a repressive atmosphere, Malvina leaves Ilhéus.

Colonel Jesuino Mendonca, a planter whose murder of his wife and her lover becomes the talk of Ilhéus. According to tradition, he acted honorably and should not be punished. As progress spreads throughout the area, however, tradition is replaced by justice, and he receives a prison sentence.

The Novel

As the book opens, one of the "colonels" has just murdered his wife and her lover. If the fact that she had a lover at all reveals some cracks in the old order, the further implication that Colonel Jesuino Mendonca will get off scot-free under the unwritten law indicates that, for the time being at least, it still survives as an effective force.

Meanwhile, Nacib Saad, a fat, gentle Brazilian from Syria and the owner of the Vesuvius Bar, has just lost his cook, whose appetizers and tidbits had largely accounted for his considerable success. Fortunately for him, however, a continuing drought in the backlands has brought a steady stream of homeless migrants to Ilhéus looking for work. Just as Nacib is becoming desperate, he discovers among them Gabriela, whose scent of cloves and cinnamon-colored skin enhance equal talents for cooking food and making love. As a girl of the people, Gabriela represents a way of life that is both older and more essentially Brazilian than any of the ways represented either by the colonels or by Mundinho Falcão, a rich young man from Rio de Janeiro. She embodies the idea of *convivência*—of varied and mingling races and classes mutually dissolving and living together in harmony and absolute democracy—that is at once a Brazilian tradition and a Brazilian ideal. Nacib marries Gabriela.

While Mundinho Falcão, who has rejected the high life of his family, deliberately operates upon the body of society, rechanneling its old systems into new ones, Gabriela unconsciously operates upon its soul. Every man in town adores her, and few of the women, surprisingly enough, are jealous. When election time arrives, the colonels find their influence whittled away. In a last attempt to save their ascendancy, the more reactionary of them attempt to arrange the assassination of a powerful political chief who has defected to Falcão. The killing fails, and Falcão's forces of reform are swept into office, not without his privately acknowledging, however, that even this reform is only temporary and must lead to changes even greater. The nature of the changes still to come, one sees, resides in the musky clove and dusky cinnamon of the beautiful mulatto.

Nacib Saad's attempt to transform Gabriela into a married, respectably shod, and housebroken little bourgeoise ends in the discovery that her love is as naturally democratic as her ancestry: She has slept with any man in Ilhéus lucky enough to be handsome. As her husband, of course, poor Nacib is shocked, but not for long. Gabriela still loves him. He learns, in the course of a short estrangement disastrous for the business of the Vesuvius Bar, that he likewise still loves her. Wild and free, this mulatto girl is as unregimentable as she is desirable, as indomitable as she is beautiful. At the novel's end, she finds herself, though no longer his unhappy wife, once again established as Nacib's happy cook and mistress. All other factions, too,— the colonel's and Falcão's—are reunited in freedom to celebrate new prosperity and progress for Ilhéus. The colonel who had shot his wife is sent, as testimony to a new reign of law, to prison.

Analysis

Gabriela, Clove and Cinnamon is Amado's version of Marxist myth. It is Karl Marx, however, with a considerable difference. Brazil, the writer seems to have recognized, is not a nineteenth century Germany or England; neither is it a twentieth century Russia or Czechoslovakia. If Brazil needs a revolution, says Amado—and even conservatives such as Gilberto Freyre agree that it does—let it be not a puritanical affair, with brigades of workers shouldering picks and marching under banners, but rather a revolution with freedom and harmony as its goals. What Amado wants, in the end, are social changes that will confer upon everyone the freedom of a Gabriela. It is his passionate desire for this freedom that makes *Gabriela, Clove and Cinnamon* so superior to the blind exigencies of any party line. In fable and atmosphere, the novel is a work of robust humanity, sensuous purity, and ultimate universality.

Critical Context

According to Gilberto Freyre, an internationally respected Brazilian historian and social philosopher, Jorge Amado is perhaps the only Brazilian writer of any importance allied with the Communist Party. Winner of a Stalin Prize and a former resident of Communist Czechoslovakia, this great novelist has served as a Communist representative in the Brazilian government. Reputedly disenchanted by the events of 1956, however, Jorge Amado has never been a mere "red intellectual." In *Gabriela, Clove and Cinnamon*, his peculiarly robust, humane, pure kind of "Marxist" thought lies deeply buried in an even more humane, more robust, purer art.

The setting of the novel is perfectly suited to a retelling of that myth by which Karl Marx organized his vision of history. In the middle 1920's, the Brazilian provinces were still suffering under the political, social, and economic dominance of the *coroneis*. These "colonels," who ran unchallenged the local organization of both major political parties, who dictated at whim all manners and morals and who possessed and held, often by violence, the huge estates that supplied the money upon which all provincial life depended, were the direct administrators of what can only be recognized as a feudal society. Like the planters and cattle barons of North America, they ruled vast territories through a complicated system of allegiances built upon favors, kinship, and the naked use of power. In the country around Ilhéus, a seacoast town in the province of Bahia, the grip of the colonels, given sinews by a boom in the international market for cacao, had remained anachronistically strong. What Amado's novel is basically concerned with, then, is the breaking of that grip and the change from a feudal order, as represented by these colonels, to a new bourgeois order, as represented by Mundinho Falcão.

THE GAUCHO MARTÍN FIERRO

Author: José Hernández (1834-1886)
Type of work: Poem
Type of plot: Adventure
Time of plot: The nineteenth century
Locale: Argentina
First published: Part 1, *El gaucho Martín Fierro*, 1872; part 2, *La vuelta de Martín Fierro*, 1879 (English translation, 1935)

Principal Characters

Martín Fierro, an Argentine gaucho who tells in verse the story of his life, to the accompaniment of his guitar. Drafted to fight Indians because he did not vote for the local judge, he returns to find his home destroyed and his family scattered. Finally he is reunited with his sons, whom he sends on their way with advice, after which he lays down his guitar forever.

Cruz, another gaucho, who joins Fierro to fight off the police, who are pursuing him following a cowboy fight. They are comrades during their Indian captivity. Cruz dies while nursing a friendly Indian through a smallpox epidemic.

Fierro's older son, who tells his father his story of government injustice.

Fierro's younger son, who is robbed of his inheritance by his tutor and sent into the army.

Vizcacha, the crooked tutor who robs Fierro's younger son.

Picardia, the son of Cruz, another victim of wicked officials.

A Negro, killed by Fierro in a fair fight.

His brother, who competes with Fierro in a singing match, then tries to kill him to avenge his brother's death.

The Poem

The poem tells of Martín Fierro, a gaucho, born and reared on the rolling plains of Argentina. A gaucho was a mixture of the Spaniard and the Moor, transplanted to South America and mixed again with aboriginal Indians. Gauchos were characterized as God-fearing, brutal, superstitious, ignorant, lazy, and kind. The type passed, but while they roamed the plains, they became legends. Martín Fierro played his guitar and sang his songs, songs that told of his unhappiness and the sorrows of the gaucho all over the land.

Martín once had a home and a wife and children to comfort him. He had owned land and cattle. He rode the plains and lived in peace with his neighbors. Then officers appear to take Martín and his neighbors away from their homes and families to serve the government in wars with the Indians. Martín is among those chosen, because he had not voted when the judge was up for election, and the judge said that those who did not vote helped the opposition. The government promises that the gauchos will serve only six months and then be replaced. Martín takes his horse and clothes and leaves his wife and children.

The men live in filth and poverty. Complaints bring lashes with leather thongs. There are no arms: The colonel keeps the guns and ammunition locked up except when Indians attack. The Indians come and go as they please, killing, plundering, and taking hostages. They pull babies from mothers' arms and kill them for sport. The Indians are not much worse than the officers. The men are not paid, have no decent food, and wear rags. Rats crawl over them while they sleep.

Martín escapes and returns to his home. There he finds his wife and sons gone, the house destroyed, and the cattle and sheep sold by the government. Martín swears revenge and sets out to find his sons. He is soon in more trouble. He kills a Negro in a fight, and when another swaggering gaucho picks a quarrel, Martín kills him as well. These killings bring the police after him. They track him down and are about to kill him when one of their number joins him in fighting the others. Cruz, his new friend, fights so bravely that the two of them drive off or kill their attackers.

Cruz, telling Martín his story, sings it like a true gaucho. He had lost his woman to the commandante of the army and so had left his home. He, too, had killed a man and been hunted by the law before an influential friend got him a pardon and a job with the police. Cruz had no heart for police work. Seeing Martín prepared to fight against great odds, he had decided to join him. The two decide to leave the frontier and go to live among the Indians.

Martín and Cruz travel across the desert to the land of the savages. Before they can make friends and join a tribe, they are captured by a raiding party. For two years they suffer tortures inflicted by the Indians; then they are allowed to pitch a tent and live together, still under guard. They have to ride with the savages on raids against the Christians. When smallpox ravages the tribe, Cruz gives his life by nursing a chief who had been kind to them.

Martín is alone once more. He escapes from the Indians. He rescues a white woman who had been beaten with the bowels of her own baby son. After weeks of weary travel, they return to the plains, where Martín leaves the woman with a rancher.

Martín, returning to his homeland, learns that he is no longer wanted by the government. The judge who had put him into the army is dead, and no one cares any longer about the Negro and the gaucho he had killed in fair fights. In his new freedom, he goes to a racing meet and is reunited with two of his sons. From them, he learns that his wife is dead and that they also had been tortured and cheated by the government.

The older son sings his song first. He had been falsely arrested and convicted for a killing. He spent a long time in the penitentiary. He cautions all who hear his tale to keep away from the law, for the law is not for the gaucho.

The second son sings his song. An aunt died and left him some property. The judge appointed a tutor who robbed the boy of his inheritance, then beat and starved him. Penniless, Martín's son had roamed the land like a tramp until he was sent to the frontier with the army.

A stranger called Picardia appears and sings his song. Like the others, he had been sent to serve in the army and endure the tortures of the wicked officials. Picardia tells Martín that he is the son of Cruz, Martín's old friend. The friends celebrate the meeting with wine and song, and while they sing a Negro joins them. He and Martín hold a singing match, a common thing among the gauchos. The Negro sings that he is the brother of the Negro Martín killed years before and that he will avenge the death. Before they can fight, other gauchos step between them and send Martín, his sons, and Picardia on their way.

They ride only a short distance together, then separate to seek new lives, each man alone. Before they part company, Martín Fierro gives the young men some advice out of his own experience. He tells them to be true to their friends, to give every man his due, to obey the law, and never to cheat. If ever a woman should win their hearts, they must treat her well and be true. The four scatter, each one taking a new name from that day on. Martín, ending his song, advises that gauchos everywhere heed his words, for they come from the wisdom of an old man. Then he lays down his guitar, never to sing again.

Analysis

Martín Fierro is the poetic epic of the gaucho race that settled the rich Argentine pampa. An "ocean of land," pancake flat, the pampa has fertile brown soil and is perhaps the only area on Earth where one could yoke oxen to a plow and slice a furrow for six hundred miles without turning up a stone. Before the Spaniards arrived it was peopled by warlike, nomadic Indians. Its deep grass supported birds and ostriches, and its only tree was the rugged ombú. Cattle and horses introduced by the first Spaniards increased at an amazing rate around the port town of Buenos Aires, on the ocean's edge, and a cowboy type known as the gaucho began to ride the plains near the town. Slowly, the first gauchos pushed inland, rolling back the Indians, thus starting what was to be their historic role of settling Argentina. Gauchos also settled Uruguay and the extensive Brazilian pampa of Rio Grande do Sul, but in Argentina they built a nation.

Usually of Spanish or mestizo blood, the gaucho lived on horseback. He was nervous, restless, and almost always in motion. His games were rough and on horseback; he was tough, ignorant, and despised city folk. His literature was the so-called gaucho poetry, redolent of the pampa, that was sung around campfires at night by illiterate minstrels known as *payadores*. The payador was simply a medieval European minstrel, of Spanish origin, transplanted to the New World, his songs comprising a new, regional literature describing the various types of gaucho, such as the outlaw, the tracker, the tamer of horses, the lover, or the storyteller. This literary genre was to tinge all Argentine literature centuries later, even the drama, and from it came *Martín Fierro*.

José Hernández was born on an Argentine *estancia*, or large ranch. He grew up among gauchos and Indians and loved their free way of life. He knew the gaucho thoroughly—his speech, folklore, psychology, heart, and soul. He also knew the pampa—its beauty, silence, climate, grass, sunrises, and sunsets. As the day of the gaucho began to wane and Hernández realized that the anti-gaucho intellectuals were creating a new Argen-

tina, he decided to tell the dying gaucho's story, to portray his manly virtues and his once-happy way of life.

Martín Fierro tells, thus, of the gaucho's passing. This took place after the 1850's, when the last wild Indian tribes were being pushed up against the setting sun and the Andes foothills. At the same time, the gaucho was being supplanted by progress in the form of barbed wire, railroads, immigrants, wheat, and the herds of purebred cattle, sheep, and thoroughbred horses that have made Argentina famous. The poem includes many epic themes— the fight against injustice, governmental power over individuals, man's struggle against nature, and the yearning for lost freedom and lost loved ones during bitter years of exile in strange country. Present also are such themes as a temporary flight to the land of a hated enemy and the rescue of a maiden in distress. Drenched with the pampa's earthiness, *Martín Fierro* gives pictures of the land and sky, grass, birds, and creatures of the pampa, as well as of the gaucho himself as symbolized by the redoubtable but bigoted Martín. The poem gives the life cycle of a race and is as representative of Argentina as, perhaps, the Mississippi River is of the United States. The poetic style is brisk and clear, even though the language is replete with gaucho vocabulary and flavor of speech. Martín Fierro's character projects itself over the poem. *Martín Fierro* holds one's interest throughout most of its stanzas and is today at the summit of Argentine gaucho literature. It has thus attracted attention in Spanish America, Brazil, and Spain, where the noted Miguel de Unamuno often read it aloud to his classes in the halls of Salamanca University.

Gauchos no longer roam the unfenced pampa's grassy sea. They are often only peons on a mechanized *estancia*, but they still have nostalgic yearnings for the past. At night, around campfires, they often produce old copies of *Martín Fierro*, bound in calfskin. The gauchos speak of Martín himself as if he still lives and might, at any moment, arrive to sing his sorrows.

Critical Context

Although it is not well known in the English-speaking world, the tale of Martín Fierro has had great popularity in the South American countries, particularly Argentina. Fierro gave hope to a people long oppressed by the government and cheated by corrupt officials. He became a legend, and his tale was repeated over and over again. Hernández himself was identified with his hero, and everywhere he went he was idolized as the spokesman for the gaucho. It is said that much of the romantic appeal of the poem is lost in translation; nevertheless, the English version is musical, vigorous, and exciting.

GAZAPO

Author: Gustavo Sainz (1940-   )
Type of work: Novel
Type of plot: Satire
Time of plot: The mid-1960's
Locale: Mexico City
First published: 1965 (English translation, 1968)

Principal Characters

Menelao, a restless, confused, somewhat fearful teenager who resists both parental and religious dicta. Much of the novel focuses upon the sexual awakening of Menelao and Gisela, his girlfriend, and upon the seemingly aimless activities of Menelao and his group of friends. His mother and father were divorced when Menelao was four years old, and he does not see his mother again until he is in high school. None of the adults in the novel sanctions or understands the relationship between Menelao and Gisela, and even Menelao's friends view it one-dimensionally. Brief, interspersed passages, however, suggest that Menelao seeks more than sexual satisfaction from Gisela.

Gisela, Menelao's girlfriend, who awakens sexually over the course of the novel. Seemingly timid and naïve, her bathing in front of an open window and her confident swimming in the presence of a floundering Menelao intimate strong latent feelings.

Vulbo, one of Menelao's friends. Bold in his pursuit of Nacar, Vulbo is one of the few teenagers who openly defies adult authority. When Nacar's mother tells Vulbo that her daughter is already involved with a soldier, Vulbo ignores the mother's wishes. His pursuit of Nacar, told and retold throughout the novel, is one of the major narrative threads.

Mauricio, Menelao's roommate. Mauricio, like Menelao, enjoys using audiotape to record the gang's activities. These stories are altered even as they are told and retold. Mauricio notes the dreamlike quality of life, an outlook that the novel's disjointed, sometimes surreal narration reflects.

Tricardio, a switchboard operator at the Bank of Commerce and Menelao's chief rival. Known for being a voyeur and a seducer of servant girls, he fights Menelao after Menelao learns that Tricardio has surreptitiously seen Gisela bathing. Typically, however, ambiguity marks the interactions of Tricardio, Menelao, and Gisela. Menelao seems to feel some kinship with his rival, and, as Mauricio notes, Gisela appears to find Tricardio interesting.

Matriarca, Menelao's stepmother. Much of Menelao's difficulty at home is caused by the friction between the meddlesome Matriarca and her stepson. Menelao blames Matriarca for turning his father against him.

Nacar, Vulbo's beautiful neighbor. Vulbo pursues Nacar over the course of the novel, thinking for some time that she is an ingenue. He learns, however, that she was married at fourteen and widowed, with a child, at sixteen.

Menelao's mother, a frail woman now hounded by creditors. Menelao is staying in his mother's apartment while she is in Cuernavaca escaping the bill collectors. Throughout the novel, she threatens to return to Mexico City; eventually, she does, disrupting her son's plans with Gisela.

Menelao's father, a husband loath to go against his wife's wishes, even at the risk of losing his son.

Aunt Cripla and **Aunt Icrista,** Gisela's aunts. Aunt Cripla, a Protestant, and Aunt Icrista, a Catholic, loom, specterlike, throughout the novel, passing judgment on many of the actions of Menelao's group.

The Novel

Most of the action of the novel takes place as the characters drive around Mexico City, searching for something meaningful to do. The action centers on the young and misunderstood Menelao, who has been abandoned in a seedy apartment by his divorced mother. Having left his father's home because of his stepmother, Menelao cruises the city with his friends as they all tell stories about their escapades. The narration begins with a collage of actions. Vulbo's telephone conversation with Menelao describes the gang's previous evening's activities; Menelao, in bed, imagines their drive to his father's house in a stolen car to recover his possessions, a fact that he verifies later in a conversation with one of them; Menelao remembers his dream about his girlfriend, Gisela, in which all is well with his family. The vantage point of this series of actions is unclear, although Menelao appears to be piecing the facts together while lying in bed. The first chapter is typical of the narrative as a whole in that events are told from different points of view and are presented in a deliberately ambiguous manner. To these actions are added tape recordings, diaries, and summaries of past events. Menelao retells the history of the fight with his father in an encapsulated version: "a) One day he went on a picnic somewhere and I quarreled with Matriarca. . . . b) Matriarca always manages to get mixed up in my business. . . . c) One evening, after an argument, I piled all my clothes. . . ." He seems to be impatient with his role as storyteller, so he turns to other forms of communication for help.

Two matters preoccupy Menelao and serve as catalysts for the action: his relationship with Gisela, whom he wants to seduce, and the disintegration of his family. He convinces Gisela to go to his apartment, where he makes his advances. The novel becomes humorous when one realizes that Menelao pretends to know more about sex than he does: "I tried to convince her that sharing sexual interests and relations is very natural. 'Every person,' I told her, 'is a coitus brought to a happy climax by his parents. Or an unhappy one, who knows?' 'What is coitus?'" The scenes between

the two young lovers always end badly. Once he writes all over her body with a magic marker that does not wash off; another time they are interrupted by the rent collector, whom Menelao tries to avoid. Although Menelao is thoroughly infatuated with Gisela, he mistrusts her, having caught her showering before an open window with Tricardio viewing from the roof. He also blames her for the break with his father, who dislikes her because she is of a lower social status. The relationship is further complicated by Menelao's lies to his friends about having "scored" with Gisela. When they repeat the story in a taxi, the driver, Gisela's father, overhears and forbids her to see Menelao again. Throughout the entire novel, nevertheless, the two lovers defy the adults by seeing each other when they should be in school.

Menelao's independence is accidental. His mother, divorced from his father, who has married the domineering Matriarca, has gone away, leaving Menelao with no means of support. His father, overcome by his second wife, has let the situation in his home get out of hand and has sacrificed his son to his indecision. Left to his own devices, Menelao divides his time between Gisela and his friends, with no direction or aim. With precision, Menelao traces his routes through the city, giving the reader familiar with Mexico City a very accurate picture of his whereabouts.

The novel has some farcical scenes, especially those between Menelao and his senile grandmother, whom he takes out one afternoon to Chapultepec Park. During this outing, which includes a boat ride, Menelao's grandmother dies, but this is not emphasized in the narration. In *Gazapo*, the things one generally regards as important are trivialized, while banal things are stressed. This is a reminder of the fact that Menelao, his peers, and the society in which they live are disoriented and confused. In the end, nothing happens. Reality, says Sainz, does not have the structure of a conventional novel, with a beginning, a middle, and an end.

Analysis

As a foreword, Sainz defines the word *gazapo* from two different dictionaries. Both give the literal meaning as "a young or newly born rabbit" and its colloquial uses as "a shrewd and astute man" or "a big lie, a whopper." The main themes can be related to any of these interpretations. As the novel describes the world of the young generation and its lack of focus, the naïveté of the young rabbit is evident. Menelao is a displaced person in an urban society that has lost its sense of structure. A victim of circumstances, he fights back with the only tools he has, his imagination and his cleverness; hence the other meanings of the title.

Sainz plays a little with the reader, whom he challenges to find the truth of the action in the novel. In essence, he questions the reliability of anyone who tells a story. If one doubts Vulbo and his boasting about Nacar, why does one believe anyone else in the story, even Menelao? With the diary and tape-recorder accounts, Sainz states the fact that the reader tends to believe taped and written accounts without doubting their validity. The accurate street routes, moreover, compound the illusion, since the person unfamiliar with the city cannot visualize the setting but is convinced of its authenticity. Throughout the novel, Sainz thus contrasts the accuracy of the accounts and the setting with the displacement the characters experience.

Although the treatment of these themes is humorous, Sainz conveys a strong feeling of pathos and destroys many of the myths related to Mexican society. First, the family as a unit no longer exists. Menelao's parents are divorced. His father has remarried, taking a wife who dominates him. Menelao leaves home to go to his mother, who abandons him in a dirty apartment, to be hounded by bill collectors. In Gisela's house, there is no evidence of a mother. She is brought up by two strange aunts and a drunken father. The characters, in relation to their families, appear not to know where they belong. The sense of loyalty within the immediate family seems to be lost. At the same time, the characters seek an independence that they know they will never attain.

The generation gap, the most important theme, isolates one group from another. The young have no use for the adult world except to defy it. The elders make no effort to understand their offspring, and they jump to conclusions easily. No one makes an attempt to respect others. Sainz underscores this lack of communication through the use of external devices (the telephone, the tape recorder), which points to the desperate, useless efforts of human beings to communicate. He also deemphasizes what traditionally would be dramatic and poignant (such as Menelao's grandmother's death) to create a sense of indifference among his characters. The humor reinforces the attempts of a society to cover up its inadequacies with laughter. Although *Gazapo* seems to focus on the trivial, overall it conveys the serious message that urban society has lost its sense of direction.

Critical Context

Gazapo, Sainz's first novel in a prolific career, was one of the pioneer works in a genre that emerged in Mexico in the 1960's as a result of the student movements, the *novela de la onda* or "new wave" novel. Along with other writers of his generation, Sainz sought to take Mexican literature away from historical themes and social protest, instead portraying urban society and the generation gap. Like the other "new wave" works, *Gazapo* experiments with narrative techniques and emphasizes language to convey its message. Because of their humor and their comic-book qualities, these "new wave" novels have not been taken as seriously as those of Sainz's predecessors, including Carlos Fuentes and Juan Rulfo. Nevertheless, *Gazapo* emerged as one of the works that turned the direction of Mexican fiction toward urban settings and universal themes. Most important, as Sainz's other novels have shown, Mexican writers have incorporated in their works a sense of commonality with world literature that has made their works more accessible to those outside their country.

THE GOLDEN SERPENT

Author: Ciro Alegría (1909-1967)
Type of work: Novel
Type of plot: Naturalism
Time of plot: The early twentieth century
Locale: The Marañón River, in northern Peru
First published: *La serpiente de oro*, 1935 (English translation, 1943)

Principal Characters

Lucas Vilca, a young *cholo* (part Indian, part white) from the hamlet of Calemar, located in an Andean valley in northern Peru that is bordered by the mighty Marañón River. As narrator, Lucas voices the *cholos'* deep respect for the land and the river and their identification with nature.

Matías Romero, the head ferryman and owner of the largest house in the Calemar valley. From his long experience, old Matías tells heroic tales of the raftsmen's exploits. He is attentive to nature's signs and has presentiments before the deaths of his son and of Don Osvaldo Martínez. Rogelio's fate depresses Matías, and he becomes less active, passing the title of head ferryman on to his elder son, Arturo.

Arturo Romero, a brawny boatman, son of Matías. Arturo is smitten with Lucinda at the yearly festival in the town of Sartín and with rural Andean directness invites her to return to Calemar with him.

Rogelio Romero, known as **Roge,** Arturo's younger brother. Rogelio's courage is not tempered by good judgment, and he dies on the Marañón, despite Arturo's warning to wait before taking the raft over a rough spot.

Lucinda Romero, Arturo's wife. She has bloomed as a woman in the two years since Arturo last saw her at the Sartín festival, and she captivates him this time with her shining green eyes and graceful figure. In Calemar she has several miscar-

riages, but then she legally marries Arturo at the time of the Feast of the Virgin of Calemar.

Osvaldo Martínez de Calderón, a Lima engineer who has come to study the Marañón area for economic development. Blond, educated, and unfamiliar with the region, he is an outsider, but he is cordially received and adapts well. Osvaldo dreams of organizing a company to extract the mineral wealth of the region and plans to call the firm "The Golden Serpent," in homage to the color and shape of the Marañón. Ironically, Osvaldo is mortally bitten by a golden serpent, a yellow viper, and is buried at Calemar.

Juan Plaza, a cordial and hospitable old rancher. Don Juan is white, and he belongs to the highest social class in the Marañón region. He is a storyteller and a source of regional lore for Osvaldo Martínez.

Mariana Chinguala, a lonely, mature widow who takes in lodgers at her house at the foot of the Calemar valley and cooks for Lucas Vilca.

Ignacio Ramos, an outlaw from Calemar who has to keep moving constantly to avoid prison for slayings he committed twenty years ago. His hard face, calm and steady eyes, and determined jaw mirror his spirit of defiance against an unjust legal system that is harsh on poor men such as him. As he tells it to Lucas Vilca, the several killings he perpetrated were in self-defense.

The Novel

The Golden Serpent is a poetic description of the daily life of a small village on the bank of the mighty Marañón River in northern Peru. Rather than having a single central plot, the nineteen chapters are a series of stories or related episodes told by the narrator, Lucas Vilca, a raftsman and farmer of the Calemar Valley. Lucas Vilca both participates in the incidents recounted and serves as an omniscient narrator who chronicles and generalizes. The stories that Lucas Vilca tells include many adventures on the river, descriptions of festivals and religious celebrations, encounters with state troopers, intense dramas of survival amid natural dangers, and accounts of superstitions, customs, and folklore. Many of the episodes are complete short stories in themselves, but their effect is also cumulative: They are all lyric depictions of the unity of man and nature in the Calemar Valley.

The Marañón River dominates the lives of the villagers who live beside it. The *cholos* (part Indian, part white) of Calemar fish or earn a living by ferrying travelers and cattle across the river. They respect and exult in the power of the huge river as it rushes by them, roaring against the cliffs, churning over the rocks, gliding expansively through open stretches, carrying people and animals to their destinations or to their deaths. Years are measured in terms of rainy seasons, which cause the river to swell and flood, and dry seasons,

when the rapids are treacherous and fish are easy to trap in shallow pools. People live in close harmony with the natural rhythms of the great river, appreciative of the extraordinary beauty of their surroundings and wary of the dangers of this way of life.

Calemar is depicted as a primitive garden of Eden where bananas, avocados, oranges, and coca grow in profusion. It is a fragile paradise, a utopian community dependent on the continuous hard work, positive spirit, and adaptability of the men and women who choose this life. Both natural dangers (snakes, diseases, rapids, landslides) and human threats (state troopers, the inevitability of commercial development on a national scale) menace the autonomous survival of this small, isolated community, yet throughout *The Golden Serpent* the villagers are seen triumphing over one peril after another, not only surviving difficulties but also celebrating their ingenuity, valor, persistence, and good fortune in joyful rituals and tales. As the raftsmen cross back and forth over the raging waters of the Marañón, they sing a song to the river, acknowledging its strength and power but asserting the right to live and thrive in this environment: "River Marañón, let me cross . . ./ River Marañón, I have to cross,/ You have your waters,/ I, my heart." *The Golden Serpent* is a song of celebration of the beauty and nobility of both man and nature.

Analysis

The Marañón River is the force, both symbolic and real, that dominates *The Golden Serpent*. It is the river of life (and of death) and the daily test of fitness for survival. The book is a celebration of lives lived in harmony with the natural world. The lives and deaths of individuals matter much less than the continuing saga of humanity's struggle with the river and the awareness of vitality and freedom that this struggle brings.

The episodes in the book spell out the day-to-day details of the existence of the Calemar villag-

ers; a vast amount of information about currents, rafting, banana growing, goat keeping, fish catching, and household routines is included. All the reader's senses are engaged in myriad details of color, smell, taste, sound, and texture, extensively and lyrically described. General attitudes are illustrated by specific examples: The life story of an outlaw reveals the deep antagonisms between villagers and national law enforcement agencies; the tale of chasing the priest out of town when he tries to cheat people out of their prepaid masses illustrates the villagers' insistence upon justice and their hostility toward outsiders; the folktales about birds and animals show the deep sense of connection with nature felt by those of Calemar. Alegría manages, throughout *The Golden Serpent*, to balance these detailed descriptions of daily life with lyric praise of the beauty of Calemar. This balance works in the novel, without slipping into anthropological accounting on one hand or sentimentality on the other, in part because it is contained within the powerful rhythm of the changing seasons, the

cycle of the year. The primary time period of the novel is that of a full year, although flashbacks and the epilogue extend it into a ten-year span. Events and situations cycle through the novel in repetitive patterns, like the alternating dry and rainy seasons; over and over again, raftsmen go over La Escalera rapids, crops are harvested, couples marry, babies are born, and the festival of the Virgin is celebrated. An overall harmony and tone of well-being are affirmed and sustained despite occasional deaths or disasters.

Critical Context

Ciro Alegría was born in 1909, on a ranch in the Peruvian province of Huamachuco, and he spent his childhood in that region, which is depicted in *The Golden Serpent*. He grew up with people like the Calemar villagers, and from his parents and ranch hands he heard the songs and stories that he retells in this book. He says that these people and these tales "made me understand their sorrows, their joys, their great and overlooked gifts of intelligence and fortitude, their creative ability, their capacity for endurance." Exiled to Chile because of his political activities, Alegría supported himself as a journalist and writer. In 1935, poor, ill, and homesick for Peru, Alegría expanded a short story, "The Raft," into the manuscript of *The Golden Serpent*, which won for him first prize in a contest sponsored by a publisher in Santiago, Chile. His second novel, *Los perros hambrientos* (1938; the hungry dogs), and his third novel, *El mundo es ancho y ajeno* (1941; *Broad and Alien Is the World*, 1941), were also prizewinners. These novels also portray the native people of northern Peru, but they are primarily concerned with the plight of Indians in mountainous areas. Like *The Golden Serpent*, they depict communal village life in harmony with natural forces, but while *The Golden Serpent* reveals the strengths and beauties of traditional val-

ues, often shown in contrast to the motives and actions of outsiders such as state troopers or engineers. Alegría's subsequent two novels portray Indian communities seriously threatened by greedy landowners, exploiters, and twentieth century development. They are much more critical and more political in their focus.

Although *The Golden Serpent* describes the life of *cholos* rather than Indians, it is often considered as part of the Indianist literature of the 1920's and 1930's, fiction associated with regionalism and social protest. Much of this fiction is primarily documentary exposé of the miserable conditions of Indian life, as seen in the stories of the Peruvian Enrique López Albújar and novels by the Mexican Gregorio López y Fuentes and the Ecuadoran Jorge Icaza. Alegría's fiction represents an effort to comprehend the lives of Indians (and, in *The Golden Serpent*, the *cholos*) through an understanding of their values, myths, legends, and daily lives. A few of the other novelists in this tradition are the Peruvian José María Arguedas (*Los ríos profundos*, 1958; *Deep Rivers*, 1978), the Guatemalan Miguel Ángel Asturias (*Mulata de tal*, 1963; *Mulata*, 1967), and the Mexican Rosario Castellanos (*Balún Canán*, 1957; *The Nine Guardians*, 1959).

THE GREEN HOUSE

Author: Mario Vargas Llosa (1936-   )
Type of work: Novel
Type of plot: Social criticism
Time of plot: Between World War I and World War II
Locale: The jungle of eastern Peru and Piura, a small city in Peru
First published: *La casa verde*, 1966 (English translation, 1968)

Principal Characters

Don Anselmo, the founder of the original Green House in Piura. Along with several others, Anselmo provides residents of this barrio with a sense of self-esteem. In the novel, the rise and fall of Anselmo and the Green House are paralleled. Even though he and the Green House are ultimately defeated, Anselmo attains heroic stature as a result of his courage, perseverance, and capacity for sacrifice.

The Sergeant/Lituma, a national policeman from Piura who is stationed near the jungle.

Bonifacia/Wildflower, an Indian girl of mysterious origins who is taken from her home and reared in a convent. Expelled from the convent when she allows other Indian girls to escape, she is ultimately forced into prostitution in order to survive. Largely deprived of her personal and cultural past at the mission, Bonifacia acquires no solid basis on which to fashion an identity or a position in society.

Fushía, a Japanese Brazilian contrabandist who deals in illegal rubber traffic. As the novel's antihero, he embodies both good and evil; he is both victim and victimizer. During Fushía's month-long river voyage from his island to the leper colony of San Pueblo, he seeks answers to vital questions concerning his existence. While many of his illusions are shattered on this trip, Fushía nevertheless clings to the belief that he can control his final destiny.

Aquilino, Fushía's friend. Aquilino engages Fushía in numerous conversations on their river voyage, thereby eliciting the recapitulation of significant events from Fushía's past. Aquilino's primary function in the novel is to act as a moral and spiritual guide to Fushía.

The Novel

The action of *The Green House* takes place principally in the small city of Piura, Peru, and in the Amazon jungle region in the eastern part of the country. Each geographical location has its corresponding characters, who for the most part do not overlap, but when they do, the ties bring jungle and city together through at times tortuous and coincidental ways. In Piura, Don Anselmo has built the Green House, a brothel of great fame that at the time of the narration has become legendary, since the original building has been burned. Its existence is doubted by the town's younger people, for Anselmo, now blind and playing the harp in a new Green House run by his daughter, refuses to discuss his mysterious past. The reader's knowledge of Anselmo's Green House comes from flashbacks that provide information unavailable to any other character.

The jungle and the treacherous rivers of eastern Peru provide the setting for the criminal Fushía's plundering and search for raw rubber, his continual flight along the rivers from the authorities, and his eventual physical downfall (he contracts leprosy and lives out his life literally rotting away in a jungle leper colony). Also inhabiting this inhospitable place is Bonifacia, who is taken from her Indian home and brought up by the Sisters of the Convent of Santa María, only to be expelled for helping other kidnapped Indian girls escape. She meets the Sergeant soon after she is employed locally as a maid, and after the two marry, he takes her back to his native Piura.

The above overview seems sketchy because flashbacks elicited by conversations and interior monologues constitute most of the action. The juxtaposition of different times within a single chapter, paragraph, or speech (through the technique of "telescoping dialogues," in which a question in the present is answered by a character in the time and place with which the question itself deals) forces the reader to piece together the facts of the characters' lives as they become available. The

Sergeant stationed at Santa María de Nieva is identified as Lituma from Piura at about the halfway mark of the novel; only later is it clear not only that Bonifacia and Wildflower are the same person, but also that she is a prostitute in the "new" Green House and awaits Lituma's return from prison. Similarly, other incidents are described in a flowing, stream-of-consciousness narrative with dialogue and description unseparated from each other: the story of Anselmo's arrival in Piura; his constructing the Green House; the indignation of the townswomen that the brothel aroused; his illicit love affair with a blind, deaf, mute, orphaned minor; and her death in childbirth, which when made public incited the women to riot and burn the Green House. In spite of this fragmentation, the episodes of the novel's four chapters reach conclusions in an epilogue that also removes the final vestiges of doubt concerning each character's past and relationships with other characters.

Analysis

One of the principal themes of *The Green House* is civilization versus barbarity: The dominant European-oriented society attempts to control the indigenous people and their land. In one sense, the descendants of the sixteenth century conquerors (the *conquistadores* of Spain's Golden Age) are eminently successful: Anselmo prospers, at least for a time, with his brothel; the Sergeant is able to contribute to the ruling class's domination of the Indian tribes (in one incident the Indian Jum, Bonifacia's father, is tortured for having attempted to organize the Indians into a cooperative so as to garner higher prices for rubber than the exploited tribes are receiving from the white contrabandists); and Fushía plies his trade with abandon. These successes are superficial. Bonifacia never truly adapts to the "Christian" environment, and she is turned into Wildflower, who is manipulated by society. The Sergeant returns to Piura, where he is blamed for the death of a man in a game of Russian roulette and is sent to prison in distant Lima. Fushía is literally "devoured" by the jungle and ends his

life as a rotting mass of flesh repugnant even to his friend, Aquilino.

The constant movement in the novel of characters from city to jungle and along the jungle's rivers—the mythic motif of the river trip redolent of Ulysses' voyage through Hades—accomplishes little. No great recognition of errors or meaning of life is discovered as the characters reminisce about their past or live in a present that offers a bleak future. In one sense, *The Green House* is a chronicle, with the appropriate narrative trappings (Vargas Llosa learned much of his technique from Gustave Flaubert's masterful use of interior monologues), but the traditional time sequence is broken. Events occur simultaneously, as the use of telescopic dialogues bears out. Past and present are fused. The creation of myth through the removal of temporal limitations is the true action of the novel.

Vargas Llosa attempts to write a "totalizing novel," one that presents as many levels of reality as possible. Thus the chronicle tries to document as much social injustice as possible, be it the exploitation of Indians or the deceptive mask of civilized behavior of the citizens of Piura, whose uncivilized violence seethes below the surface until it explodes and swallows up Anselmo's brothel. The memories recounted and the voyages through river and jungle, then, help to constitute a final irony: that of calling one society "civilization" and the other "barbarity."

The title of the novel brings together the disparate geographical locations. Anselmo's Green House and the later Green House, built once the first one has passed into legend, draw the attention of the people of Piura: The men frequent it while the women, as well as the town priest, Father García, crusade against its immorality. Its color symbolizes for Anselmo his supposed origin in the jungle areas while bringing an element of the untamed world into civilization. Another "green house" is the jungle itself, untamed and untamable, a place that dooms to failure all who try to conquer it.

Critical Context

The Green House, Vargas Llosa's second major novel, was awarded both the 1966 Premio de la Critica Española and the 1967 Premio Internacional de Literatura Rómulo Gallegos as the best Spanish-language novel published within the previous five years. His first novel, *La cuidad y los perros* (1962; *The Time of the Hero*, 1966), had earned the 1963 Premio de la Critica Española. Both of these works, as well as his publications since then, have been translated into various major languages.

Vargas Llosa's extraordinary success has made him one of the major contributors to the so-called boom in the Latin American novel, an outpouring of excellent narratives since the early 1960's. Along with Nobel Prize winner Gabriel García Márquez, Vargas Llosa has shown that the Latin American literary culture is capable of producing world-class literature that is not merely derivative of James Joyce, Franz Kafka, and William Faulkner, but that has incorporated the narrative techniques learned from these writers.

Although *The Green House* unquestionably marks a step forward in Latin American letters, it also maintains thematic links to its predecessors: José Eustasio Rivera's *La vorágine* (1924; *The Vortex*, 1935) and Rómulo Gallegos' *Doña Bárbara* (1929). Both novels present the theme of the civilized world against the jungle, but they are at times clearly regional works. Vargas Llosa's infusion of mythic substructures, conflation of time, and creation of new narrative techniques combine to produce a literature that transcends national boundaries. *The Green House* reaches back to Flaubert while providing the impetus for even greater narrative development.

HE WHO SEARCHES

Author: Luisa Valenzuela (1938-   )
Type of work: Novel
Type of plot: Social morality
Time of plot: The 1970's
Locale: Barcelona, Spain; Mexico; and Argentina
First published: *Como en la guerra*, 1977 (English translation, 1979)

Principal Characters

Az, also called **Pepe,** an Argentine semiotics professor and psychoanalyst living in Barcelona. Although married, he is obsessed with a woman referred to only as "she," whom he purports to analyze without her knowledge. Visiting her late at night in a number of disguises, including female costumes, he has sexual relations with her and secretly tapes her conversations. He transcribes the tapes as part of his narration. He pretends to himself that his love interest in her is all in the line of psychoanalytic duty. His own identity begins to merge with hers, especially when he loses track of her and leaves Barcelona to search for her in Latin America.

She, a curly-haired Argentine living in political exile in Barcelona and working as a cabaret waitress and prostitute. She has been at least marginally involved in guerrilla activity in Argentina, has been tortured, and is herself capable of violence. At times, she suspects that Pepe is spying on her for an intelligence agency, and she plans his mur-

der. She collects carved hands and hand symbols from every religion and from all over the world, because she sees in them a relationship to the cosmos. This enigmatic woman is last seen, dramatically and miraculously, in Buenos Aires. She is seen within a fortress, luminous in a glass coffin on a white dais, an image reminiscent of Eva Perón, publicly displayed in the 1970's in a mausoleum.

Beatriz, also called **Bea** and **Bé,** Pepe's jealous but faithful wife. She becomes aware of his infidelity and is eventually reduced to helping him dress for his sexual-analytical exploits and anxiously waiting for him to return home.

Alfredo Navoni, a guerrilla who was the Argentine woman's lover when they both were involved in activism. She remembers her time with him as more real than her time in Barcelona. She tells Pepe two of Navoni's dreams as if they were her own, although she could not have learned them from Navoni himself.

The Novel

He Who Searches opens with a brief scene in which a man is interrogated and is raped with the butt of a gun. This scene ends abruptly, and the novel's first part, entitled "Discovery," begins. A psychoanalyst, Pepe, describes his patient, and the narrative introduces his unusual method of treatment, which includes appearing at her house in various disguises, from postman to transvestite,

and having a sexual relationship with her. Their relationship embraces a variety of fantasies, including one in which he is an insurance man. Valenzuela ironically includes in this section questions such as "Against what can she be trying to protect herself?" The reader knows that there is no insurance for a revolutionary in exile. Eventually, the psychoanalyst's wife discovers the affair that her husband is having with his patient.

In the second part, "The Loss," the psychoanalyst spends time with his wife but longs for his patient, who has disappeared. While reading a story in the newspaper about a banderillero in a barroom brawl, he recognizes his patient in an accompanying photograph. He believes that "a trickle of blood" will lead him to her.

In the third part, "The Journey," the psychoanalyst arrives in Mexico, where he participates in a purification ritual and is guided by Nahuatl-speaking Indian women through the mountains. He meets a woman named Maria Sabina, who gives him sacred mushrooms. This passage recalls the Cave of Montesinos, in which Don Quixote experiences self-revelation through an encounter with the heroes of chivalric novels. The narrator explains that the jungle in Mexico is also the jungle in Argentina.

The psychoanalyst experiences the sensation of living the life that his patient has hidden from him, including hearing the words of her former lover, Alfredo Navoni. Here, the psychoanalyst's character merges with hers. He witnesses an all-night vigil for a dead guerrilla. The guerrillas tell him a story in which there is a bizarre ritual of cannibalism, in which a character named Fatty, who likes things from India, is eaten. In the fourth and final part, the psychoanalyst finds himself in the midst of a political uprising in Argentina. When asked why he is there, he explains that he is searching for a woman and for himself, his feminine counterpart. He proceeds past barriers into the fighting. The fighting takes place in a large park. A revolutionary woman gives him an assignment, to place charges. After he plants dynamite in holes in a box of cement, there is an enormous explosion, and he has a vision of his lover in a coffin that shines like a diamond. At this point, the story ends. It is possible that the very first scene in the novel involves the psychoanalyst sometime after he has planted the dynamite, and that he is being interrogated concerning the whereabouts of his patient.

Analysis

Valenzuela began to treat political themes several years before the publication of *He Who Searches*. As a result of her interest in the secret reality ensconced within people's everyday lives, she began to link her vision of the cosmos, language, and masks to political reality. In *He Who Searches*, masks figure in the hidden identity of "she" and in the multiple identities of the psychoanalyst. Valenzuela has been quoted as saying that the mask that hides in fact reveals. This is a notion shared by poststructuralist critics such as Pierre Macherey, who believes that the text both reveals and conceals, and that the absences are as significant as the presences.

As in *El señor de Tacuru* (1983; *The Lizard's Tail*, 1983), a male character is shown to be blind to his own weaknesses and to treat women as sex objects. Valenzuela uses irony in her choice of a semiotic professor, one who should be able to deconstruct social signifiers, as a main character. For all his psychoanalytic categories, he is unable to detect the true identity of a waitress. Somehow, political commitment eludes psychoanalysis' focus on the individual self. Valenzuela uses feminism to ridicule the excesses of both psychoanalysis and Marxism.

Christian and Indian religious imagery is interwoven with Marxist and feminist references. The eating of Fatty is a grotesque enactment of the ritual of Holy Communion. A link is made between the exemplary life of Jesus and a life of political commitment. The conversion experience of the psychoanalyst, inspired by his love for his elusive patient, results in his decision to engage in a political act and to suffer the consequences of that decision: torture.

There is a discussion of the adoption of invisible fathers. This ambiguous passage suggests that adopted invisible fathers guide revolutionaries yet appear to abandon them to torture. The imagery here evokes both the martyrdom of Christ and the abandonment of Valenzuela's own generation by the Argentine middle class. Pepe confesses that he will never have the courage to adopt an invisible father, but that he is brave to love his patient. Declaring that he exists because of her, he sets off to find her.

Perhaps the most horrifying aspect of *He Who Searches* is that the psychoanalyst takes it upon himself to cure the patient without either her knowledge or her consent. This is analogous to the political situation in Argentina, in which the country was "cured" of the disease of subversives. Many of those considered to be subversives disappeared, some without even knowing why they had been arrested and tortured. Just as the psychoanalyst disguises himself, so the police, during this period, appeared under various pretexts to take away those suspected of being subversives.

Critical Context

Throughout her works, Valenzuela uses feminism and Marxism to interrogate each other. Her familiarity with French poststructuralism is seen in her reference to the work of French psychoanalyst Jacques Lacan. Valenzuela's treatment of characters suggests that she shares with Lacan the notion of the alienated self. Lacan's "mirror phase," in which the child discovers a corporeal unity or form through his or her perception of another human being, accounts for the fascination with the other's image as an anticipation of identification with this image. Considering *He Who Searches*, it can be said that the psychoanalyst searches for himself through his image of his patient. The psychoanalyst is already an adult, but Valenzuela may be somewhat ironic in her treatment of this and other psychoanalytic categories. At a deeper level, she subscribes to the Hegelian and Marxist view that the self cannot be understood except in relation to the other, and she applies this view to the Argentine nation. A family from the country, waiting in line at a political uprising, explains that its members need to be heard and that the people in the city must listen to them. This is a reference to a fundamental division in Argentine society between the urban and the rural populations.

Valenzuela's work cannot be understood apart from the political, social, cultural, and historical context of Argentina, which includes the fact that many Argentines live in exile. The situation of "she," a main character of *He Who Searches*, is a poignant illustration of a character who is forced to deepen her understanding of her own culture in absentia, while living in another country. This situation is not specific to Argentina; it is a metaphor that applies to all political exiles.

In *Cambio de armas* (1982; *Other Weapons*, 1985), Valenzuela also juxtaposes political issues and the male-female relationship. In *He Who Searches*, it is the psychoanalyst who falls in love with the political exile. In "The Word 'Killer,'" a story in *Other Weapons*, the female character falls in love with a torturer. The woman is fascinated and aroused by his violent past and fears that she loves him *because* he is a killer. In both stories, the identities of male and female characters are inextricably bound. These stories lead one to question the nature of the erotic hold on the desire that links individuals to violence. If Valenzuela could tease these links free and examine them, perhaps she could find a cure. In the meantime, it is clear that she believes that the enemy is within our own fascination with violence. The development of a vaccination will probably have to draw from the very traditions that Valenzuela parodies, psychoanalysis and Marxism.

HEARTBREAK TANGO

Author: Manuel Puig (1932-1990)
Type of work: Novel
Type of plot: Psychological realism
Time of plot: Primarily 1937-1939, 1949, and 1968
Locale: Coronel Vallejos, a mythical town in Argentina; and Buenos Aires
First published: *Boquitas pintadas*, 1969 (English translation, 1973)

Principal Characters

Juan Carlos Etchepare, a ladies' man who is suffering from tuberculosis. Although Juan Carlos is the center of the novel, the reader cannot with total confidence know his personality and character. The novel begins after his death, and the reader must reconstruct Juan Carlos through unreliable sources: the letters and memories of persons who loved him too much and understood him too little, his brief comments remembered years after the fact, and a few of his love letters, whose sincerity is at least suspect. Tall, dark, and handsome, Juan Carlos is in a sense a walking cliché. He saw himself as a ladies' man of the Hollywood matinee variety, as did many of the women whom he encountered.

Nélida Enriqueta Fernández, also called **Nené,** a married woman who had been in love with Juan Carlos. Compared to most of her friends stuck back in the dusty hinterlands town of Coronel Vallejos, Nené has done well for herself in life. Nené is a study in frustration. She sees the mediocrity of her emotional and material life. Her constant thoughts of Juan Carlos are an attempt to recover a time of romance that was quite likely more glorious in her imagination than it was in reality. Her letters to Juan Carlos' mother, which comprise a substantial portion of the novel, are not so much an effort to cleanse herself of guilt as they are an attempt to share a hallowed memory.

Celina Etchepare, Juan Carlos' sister. Celina so fiercely defends her brother's reputation from the attacks in Nené's letters that she seems almost to be motivated by jealousy. Strangely enough, considering her defense of her brother's honor, she is no saint herself, having been involved in more affairs, probably, than Juan Carlos himself.

Francisco Catalino Páez, a police officer and friend of Juan Carlos. Francisco gets his way with women largely by intimidation and brute force, and he pays for it with a violent death.

Antonia Josefa Ramírez, also known as **Big Fanny,** a servant girl. Big Fanny is a poor girl with few options in life or in love. Her big "romance" is a hopeless, squalid one with Francisco.

Donato José Massa, Nené's husband. Massa's move to Buenos Aires with his wife is an attempt to move up in the world, but his small dreams and minor successes cannot measure up to his wife's memories of Juan Carlos.

Leonor Saldívar de Etchepare, Juan Carlos' mother.

The Novel

Although *Heartbreak Tango* can be classified as a realistic novel for its representation of an ordinary, familiar reality, it is not at all traditional in the development of its narrative. The portrayal of Juan Carlos Etchepare, dead from tuberculosis as the story begins, is effected primarily through his letters and through the testimony of the other characters of the novel. The interviews, letters, newspaper reports, descriptions of photo albums, objective eyewitness accounts, and stream-of-consciousness passages included in the narrative present Juan Carlos as a childish, lovable, worthless philanderer, as if his personality were the incarnation of the less offensive characteristics of the literary and cultural stereotype of Don Juan.

Ten years after her infatuation with Etchepare, Nené writes letters to his mother, exploring the unfulfilled passion that she feels for him and gradually reconstructing the relationships between the dead man and the people who knew him. The scenario includes Francisco, who tries to emulate the romantic escapades of Juan Carlos but is murdered by Fanny, the young woman whom he impregnates, and Celina Etchepare, who fiercely defends her brother and at the same time tries to live up to his reputation for promiscuous, unbridled sexual freedom. Nené's friend Mabel moves with no hesitation from lover to lover according to her idle whims. All these characters recall the life of Juan Carlos with much nostalgic distortion and exaggeration of his sexual expertise and disarming charm. The woman who was really devoted to him, the widow Elsa DiCarlo, insists on presenting honestly and directly the true portrait of the unfortunate, unhappy consumptive lover whom she nursed through the last stages of his illness.

The letters from Nené to Leonor, Juan Carlos' mother, form the opening section of the novel. They are interspersed with objective narrative passages that portray the reactions of the recipient of the letters. Toward the end of the novel, as the letters of reply from Leonor are presented, it becomes obvious that it is not Leonor but her daughter Celina who has been corresponding with Nené, surreptitiously using her mother's name. As an act of vengeance, Celina sends the letters from Nené to Nené's husband, Donato, in the hope of destroying their marriage. The novel ends with the notice of Nené's death twenty years later, after which Donato honors his wife's request that her private collection of letters (which she received thirty years before from Juan Carlos) be burned without being read by anyone.

Analysis

As in his first novel, *La traición de Rita Hayworth* (1968; *Betrayed by Rita Hayworth*, 1971), Puig explores the phenomenon of popular culture and the force of its fantasies. Jean Harlow loved it when Clark Gable treated her roughly; it was the look in Joan Bennett's eyes that made Edward G. Robinson think of murder. This view of reality is reflected in the written texts produced by the characters of the novel, the letters and diary entries. The police report of the murder of Francisco Catalino Páez, on the other hand, presents a detailed but unemotional account of the crime, and a gypsy's reading of Juan Carlos' future accurately interprets his vapid, opportunistic hedonism.

The novelistic text, then, is a parody of the stereotypes of popular culture, in that the testimonies of many of the characters who are emotionally involved with Juan Carlos create their own stereotype of him. The truth lurking behind that image emerges from the text as a whole. Just as the objective critic of popular culture can understand the conflict of the ideal vision of life and the reality of experience, the objective narrator and reader can perceive the truth beneath the extremes of sentimentality and depersonalized objectivity evident in the various textual fragments of the novel. Puig's extensive use of elements from popular culture, then, is ironic and displaced, for the view of the world that it promotes works its magic directly on the characters but not on the reader. Rather, those cultural elements work on the reader in an inverse way, revealing the disparity of popular fantasies about the fulfillment of needs and the realities of interpersonal relationships.

The novel is divided into two parts, each consisting of eight episodes. This arrangement of the narrative is Puig's preferred method of imposing order on a very disordered narrative, a method that he has used in other novels. In *Heartbreak Tango*, more than in the other novels of similar form, the organization of the material in episodes is essential to the parody of the sentimentalization of life in the manifestations of popular culture. Although the form of the novel reflects that of serialized fiction, the narrative strategies are drastically altered. In place of the chronological telling of events, the calculated suspense tactics, and the carefully structured revelation of facts that are typical of the installment novel, Puig resorts to a synchronic narrative in which the death of the main character is described first; the circumstances of his life are re-created through disparate details scattered throughout the sixteen episodes. The authorial manipulation and deception of the reader characteristic of the serial novel are replaced by other, more complicated authorial manipulations and deceptions. In this way, the parody of the novelistic form reinforces the parody of the influence of popular culture.

Critical Context

From the beginning of his career as a novelist, Puig was an international writer, in that his narrative material and his own experience were not limited to the Hispanic culture of his native Argentina. Puig grew up in a small town, General Villegas, which is transformed into Coronel Vallejos in *Heartbreak Tango*. He was educated in Argentina and in Rome, where he studied cinema and worked as a film director, and he spent much of his life in European cities and in New York City. The titles of his novels indicate both his international experience and the force of North American culture in South American life. One of his narratives, *Maldición eterna a quien lea estas páginas* (1980; *An Eternal Curse on the Reader of These Pages*, 1982), was written first in English, then revised in Spanish for publication, and then rewritten in an English edition that incorporated the Spanish revisions. *Boquitas pintadas* was made into a film in 1974 (known in English as *Painted Lips)* by the Argentine director Leopoldo Torre Nilsson, and *Kiss of the Spider Woman* was filmed in 1985 with an international cast and was directed by Hector Babenco.

Puig's later novels are more clearly political than are *Betrayed by Rita Hayworth* and *Heartbreak Tango*. Although the political themes seem at times to be directed at the oppression of Latin American governments, they are in fact an attack on the cultural oppression that pervades Western societies, an oppression characterized by the rigid definition of sex roles. The prevalence in Puig's novels of references to popular cultural stereotypes is a critique of the influence of the mass media in reinforcing sexual attitudes. The importance of homosexual characters in the later novels is indicative of Puig's interest in the manifestation of those attitudes in the formal and informal institutions of society.

Puig's popularity as a novelist is limited somewhat by the narrative devices that render his novels accessible and attractive only to more sophisticated readers. His view of the mores and prejudices of society and his implied criticism of its attitudes toward sexual roles make his novels somewhat controversial, but at the same time they explain the prominence of his work in the context of the outstanding fiction produced by the important Latin American novelists of the second half of the twentieth century, such as Carlos Fuentes, Julio Cortázar, Ernesto Sábato, Gabriel García Márquez, Guillermo Cabrera Infante, Mario Vargas Llosa, and José Donoso.

HOPSCOTCH

Author: Julio Cortázar (1914-1984)
Type of work: Novel
Type of plot: Experimental
Time of plot: The 1950's
Locale: France and Argentina
First published: *Rayuela*, 1963 (English translation, 1966)

Principal Characters

Horacio Oliveira, an Argentine bohemian living in Paris. An intellectual in his forties who distrusts rationality and the intellect, he is engaged in a never-ending search for self-authenticity. His principal occupation is as philosopher-in-residence to the Serpent Club, a group dedicated to drinking, American jazz, and endless discussions on art and literature.

Morelli, an old avant-garde novelist whose writings have long been debated and admired by the Serpent Club. He is struck down by a car in the streets of Paris and is taken to a hospital. Horacio witnesses the accident, but is unaware of the victim's identity. After Horacio discovers Morelli's identity, Morelli gives the key to his apartment to Horacio and asks him and his friends to arrange the material in his notebooks for publication in any way they see fit. These notes and commentaries form the basis of the second theme of the novel, the writing of the novel itself.

La Maga, Horacio's mistress in Paris. A single parent in her twenties from a typical Uruguayan middle-class background, she suddenly decides to change her life in one bold stroke. She moves to Paris, ostensibly to study singing, and changes her name from Lucía to La Maga. A member of the Serpent Club, she strives to win acceptance but is ridiculed by the others, who laugh at her lack of education and pretensions.

Traveler, Horacio's longtime friend and supposed double. Before Horacio's return to Argentina, Traveler had led a relatively comfortable and placid existence. Content with his unstrenuous job at the circus and secure and happy in his marriage to Talita, whom he loves deeply, Traveler's only quarrel with life seems to be the absurdity of his name, since he has never traveled anywhere. His friend's presence, however, brings to the surface long-submerged feelings of anxiety and incompleteness.

Talita, Traveler's wife. About the same age as La Maga, but better educated, Talita is disturbed by Horacio's confused identification of her with the Uruguayan woman.

Ossip Gregorovius, a member of the Serpent Club. Ossip does not have to work and devotes himself to his chief amusement of role-playing. Both attracted to and jealous of Horacio, he is in love with La Maga, and Horacio believes that he is having an affair with her. He moves into La Maga's apartment after she disappears.

Etienne, a French member of the Serpent Club. A painter, Etienne is probably the only member of the group who could be called Horacio's friend. He accompanies Horacio in his visit to Morelli, and it is to him that Horacio entrusts the treasured key to the writer's apartment.

The Novel

Hopscotch contains two different kinds of action or story. The first plot concerns Horacio Oliveira, an Argentine exile living in Paris. He is one of the founders of the Serpent Club, around which gathers a heterogeneous assortment of foreigners, all of whom revel in the various forms of American jazz and debate the meaning of life and art. The second plot follows the eccentric career and writing of Morelli, who has devoted himself to overturning literary conventions, to inventing what might be called an antinovel. This form of literature exemplifies the view that reality is incomplete and divided, that stories, consecutive accounts of cause and effect, make no sense in a universe that is essentially absurd.

Hopscotch itself is both novel and antinovel. On one hand, chapters 1 through 56 contain a more or less coherent narrative of Horacio Oliveira's disintegration, of his failure to find unity in the universe or to maintain equilibrium in his love life with La Maga. On the other hand, the author provides a "Table of Instructions" that directs the reader to begin at chapter 73 and to jump back and forth (as in the game of hopscotch) among the novel's 155 chapters. In this second way of reading *Hopscotch*, Morelli's writing becomes as important as Oliveira's life—indeed, the experiences of the novel's protagonist and of its novelist become intertwined, so that the boundaries of literature and life overlap, and each is seen as an elaborate fantasy of human contriving.

An extraordinary amusing work for readers who enjoy mind games, *Hopscotch* also demands enormous agility and a simple but determined dedication of the kind children bring to the game for which the novel is named. Although all the principal characters are adults and intellectuals, they are like children in the sense that the "club" becomes a kind of secret hideaway where the members play at being grownups—mature philosophers of the human condition. They are enormously fond of abstractions and esoteric terms. Jazz is played and discussed, and each club member professes an air of authority over his or her favorite music and denigrates the tastes of others.

The center of attraction for these putative thinkers is La Maga. She is no intellectual; indeed, she rarely understands the talk of club members. Although they condescend to her, they also value her directness. Horacio, in particular, sets her up as a kind of spontaneous life force whom he would like to emulate. Unfortunately, he represents the most extreme form of the club's pretensions and cannot seem to let go, to express himself genuinely and directly. He must analyze everything and put himself at a remove from what he experiences.

The moment of crisis for Horacio and the club comes when La Maga's baby dies. She has refused to take the child to a hospital, and Horacio—after discovering that the child has died—allows La Maga to pass several hours in the company of club members without telling her. Although nothing is said before La Maga looks in on her dead child, it is clear that everyone except the mother knows that the child is dead, yet no one has the heart, or the simple human decency, to commiserate with her until she expresses her grief.

Horacio, acutely aware of how he has failed La Maga, drifts away from her and deliberately tries to immerse himself in the life of the streets—first with Bertha Trepat, a broken-down concert pianist, and then with Emmanuelle, the French equivalent of a skid-row bum. Each woman is a kind of experiment that resolves nothing for Horacio, except for his decision to repudiate the club and to return to Argentina.

In Argentina, Horacio is met by Traveler, his double, and Talita, Traveler's wife. He tries to make them over into the couple he made of Ossip Gregorovius and La Maga. In other words, at home or in exile, Oliveira is essentially the same person. Unable to experience himself fully as a human being, he tries to draw life from others. Juxtaposed against his seemingly futile but nevertheless inventive and adventurous playing with other peoples' personalities is the story of Morelli, the novelist who dreads the dissipation of his creative powers and who strives for a prose that would express more directly and honestly the life that has been falsified by too many layers of literary language.

Analysis

More than in most novels, the plots and characters in *Hopscotch* are inseparable. The reader cannot follow Oliveira's absurd behavior, for example, without engaging in the absurd practice of constantly switching back and forth among chapters in various parts of the novel to piece together a complete picture of the protagonist's activity. As this is done, however, the novel also tells the story of a novelist who theorizes about doing exactly what the reader has done—that is, Morelli advocates stripping the novel of its rationality, of the belief that one action or place should reasonably be related to another. Neither life nor literature, he argues, has unity of place or of action. Characters within the novel argue that such a unity exists, and fifty-six chapters of *Hopscotch* tell essentially one story—although Cortázar contends in the "Table of Instructions" that "this book consists of many books." Is life a series of bits and images, or is there such a thing as "reality," a whole to which the parts add up? *Hopscotch* does not answer the question; rather, it is designed to pursue the question by refusing to come to a conclusion. Thus, the "Table of Instructions" not only provides a way of reading the novel but also implies that the story has no end—that it is an antinovel.

Critical Context

A reviewer in the London *Times Literary Supplement* hailed *Hopscotch* as the "first great novel of Spanish America." A recipient of the National Book Award in 1967, *Hopscotch* has been reprinted more than a dozen times and continues to attract new readers and an extensive body of critical commentary. The author of several short-story collections and one previous novel, Cortázar established an international reputation with *Hopscotch*, a reputation consolidated with the steady flow of books he produced until his death in 1984.

Hopscotch is based partly on Cortázar's own experience as an exile in France, where he worked for many years as a translator. Like *Hopscotch*, much of Cortázar's fiction is experimental and playful. Both the political commitment that informed his later works and the love of the fantastic that runs throughout his oeuvre can be linked to this defiance of narrative "rules."

THE HOUR OF THE STAR

Author: Clarice Lispector (1925-1977)
Type of work: Novella
Type of plot: Social realism
Time of plot: The 1970's
Locale: Rio de Janeiro, Brazil
First published: *A Hora da Estrela*, 1977 (English translation, 1986)

Principal characters

Rodrigo S. M., the intensely self-conscious narrator who struggles to write the story of Macabéa. He describes himself as an outsider, essentially classless, as he is considered strange by the upper class, viewed with suspicion by the bourgeoisie, and avoided by the lower class. His financial situation is such that he does not have to worry about where his next meal is coming from. After having caught a glimpse of a girl from the Northeast, he becomes obsessed with creating a life for her. His obsessive self-reflection and marginality suggest to the reader his antecedents in the narrators of Edgar Allen Poe's stories and in Fyodor Dostoevski's Underground Man. He declares that his writing of the narrative is accompanied by a nagging toothache resulting from an exposed nerve and by the music of a street-corner violinist.

Macabéa, a nineteen-year-old orphan from the northeastern Brazilian province of Alagoas. Her parents died when she was an infant, and she was reared by an unloving and abusive aunt. Barely literate, her only education beyond three years of primary schooling was a short typing course. She has migrated to Rio de Janeiro, where she works in an office. Macabéa, born under an unlucky star, covers her blotchy face with a layer of white powder and suffers from a chronic dripping nose and a hacking cough; she emits an unpleasant body odor, for she rarely washes, and she exists on hot dogs, coffee, and soft drinks. Although she affirms her identity by asserting, "I am a typist and a virgin, and I like coca-cola," she is hardly aware of her own existence. What awareness she does have comes strictly through her senses.

Olímpico de Jesus Moreira Chaves, Macabéa's boyfriend, who has also emigrated from the Northeast. In many respects, he is a self-made character, starting with his name, adopted to mask the fact that his true surname, Jesus, marked him as illegitimate. He works in a metal factory transferring metal rods from one area to another, but he insists upon calling himself a metallurgist. By murdering a rival and by becoming adept at petty theft, he has confirmed his manhood to himself. A curious artistic sensibility reveals itself in his carvings of effigies of saints, which he refuses to sell because he finds them so attractive. He has a morbid fascination for funerals, which terrify him but which he attends at least twice a week. Although being a bullfighter is his dream (he is fascinated by blood and knives), his goal is to become a politician.

Glória, Macabéa's much more competent officemate, a voluptuous and self-confident young woman. Although both the narrator and Macabéa describe her as ugly, she is well aware of her charms. The daughter of a butcher, she is well fed and lives on a street named after a general. Her animal magnetism and the attraction of her father's profession prove to be irresistible to Olímpico.

Madame Carlota, a talkative fortune-teller. Madame Carlota is as interested in relating her own history to Macabéa as she is in revealing what the cards can tell about her client's destiny. She credits Jesus with her rise from prostitute to brothel owner to fortune-teller.

The Novel

In *The Hour of the Star*, Clarice Lispector creates a male narrator, Rodrigo S. M., to write the story of a young Brazilian girl who has recently moved to Rio de Janeiro. The narrator has caught sight of this young girl on the street. She is nothing special; the slums of Rio de Janeiro are filled with thousands like her; shopgirls and office workers sharing one-room flats, invisible and superfluous, silent in the clamor of the city.

The first quarter of the book is taken up with Rodrigo's ruminations on why and how he is writing the story of this young girl. He declares that her story must be told by a man, for a woman would feel too much sympathy and end up in tears. The story must be told simply and with humility, for it is about the unremarkable adventures and the shadowy existence of a young girl trying to survive in a hostile city. Rodrigo feels the need to identify with his subject, so he decides to share her condition as closely as possible by wearing threadbare clothes, suffering from lack of sleep, neglecting to shave, giving up sex and football, avoiding human contact, and immersing himself in nothingness. He envisions this identification with his protagonist as a quest for transfiguration and his "ultimate materialization into an object. Perhaps I might even acquire the sweet tones of the flute and become entwined in a creeper vine."

After describing the disastrous physical appearance of the girl, Rodrigo briefly rehearses her early history. She was born, suffering from rickets, in the backwoods of Alagoas, where her parents died of typhoid when she was two years old. Later she was sent to Maceio to live with her maiden aunt. The aunt, determined to keep the girl from becoming a prostitute, enjoyed thrashing her niece at the slightest provocation or with no provocation at all. The child never knew exactly why she was being punished. The only education she experienced beyond three years of primary school was a short typing course, which gave her enough confidence to seek a position as a typist in Rio de Janeiro.

At the moment Rodrigo's story intrudes into her life, the girl is about to be fired. Her work is hopeless—full of typing errors and blotched with dirty spots—but her polite apology for the trouble she has caused inspires her boss to modify his dismissal into a warning. The girl retreats to the lavatory to try to recover her composure. When she looks into the tarnished mirror, her reflection seems to have disappeared; her connection to even her own existence is as fragile and tenuous as is Rodrigo's commitment to identifying her. It is nearly halfway through the text before he even allows her a name.

One day, the girl garners enough courage to take time off from work. She exults in her freedom: the luxury of having the room to herself, of indulging in a cup of instant coffee borrowed from her landlady. She dances around the room and contemplates herself in the mirror. It is a moment of sheer happiness and contentment. On the next day, the seventh of May, a rainy day, she meets her first boyfriend; they immediately recognize each other as Northeasterners, and he asks her to go for a walk. He also asks her name, and for the first time in the text the girl is identified:

—Macabéa.
—Maca—what?
—Béa, she was forced to repeat.
—Gosh, it sounds like the name of a disease . . . a skin disease.

Macabéa explains that her name was a result of a vow her mother had made to the Virgin of Sorrows.

Although the meetings of Macabéa and Olímpico are rain-drenched, their relationship is parched. Conversation is strained, for what little Macabéa has to offer is scorned as foolish or nonsensical by Olímpico. She costs him nothing; the only thing he treats her to is a cup of coffee, to which he allows her to add milk if it doesn't cost extra. The one kindness he has shown her is an offer to get her a job in the metal factory where he works if she is fired. The high point of the relationship occurs one day when Olímpico decides to show off his strength to Macabéa by lifting her above his head with one hand. Macabéa feels that she is flying—until Olímpico's strength gives way, and he drops her into the mud. Not long after, he drops her entirely. Olímpico has become enamored of Macabéa's workmate, Glória.

Maternally sympathetic to Macabéa, Glória recommends a doctor to her when she is feeling unwell and lends her money to consult a fortune-teller who has the power to break bad spells. The doctor diagnoses Macabéa as suffering the preliminary stages of pulmonary tuberculosis, but the words mean nothing to her. He is appalled by her diet of hot dogs and cola and advises her to eat spaghetti whenever possible. Macabéa has never heard of the dish. As for the fortune-teller, Macabéa accepts the loan, asks for time off from her job, and takes a taxi to see Madame Carlota.

The fortune teller cuts the cards to read Macabéa's fortune and immediately exclaims over the terrible life that Macabéa has led; she then sees a further misfortune—the loss of Macabéa's job. Turning another card, though, brings a life change. All of Macabéa's misfortunes will be reversed: Her boyfriend will return and ask her to marry him, and her employer will change his mind about firing her. A handsome foreigner named Hans will fall madly in love with her and shower her with unimagined luxuries. Macabéa is astounded; she embraces Madame Carlota and kisses her on the cheek. She leaves the fortune-teller's house in a daze. When she steps off the curb, she is struck by a hit-and-run driver in a yellow Mercedes.

The narrator observes Macabéa, lying on the pavement bleeding, and wonders about her death. Macabéa gathers herself into a fetal embrace and utters her final words: "As for the future." The narrator lights a cigarette and goes home, remembering that people die.

Analysis

The Hour of the Star begins and ends with passages that prominently feature the word "yes." The "yes" at the beginning of the book is acquiescence to life: "Everything in the world began with a yes. One molecule said yes to another molecule and life was born." The "yes" at the close of the book is an acceptance of death:

> Dear God, only now am I remembering that people die. Does that include me?
> Don't forget, in the meantime, that this is the season for strawberries. Yes.

Even this acceptance of death is interrupted with the insistence that one enjoy life for as long as it offers itself. Lispector died of cancer in the same year that *The Hour of the Star* was published. She characterizes death, "my favorite character in this story," as the ultimate encounter with oneself.

Death, rebirth, and metamorphoses are intimately linked in this twisted fairy tale of a Cinderella whose only transformation into the princess happens at the moment of her death. Lispector hangs Macabéa's story on the frame of the fairy tale, with a wicked stepmother (the aunt), an uncaring father (the boss), a traitorous stepsister (Glória), a false suitor (Olímpico), and a fairy godmother (Madame Carlota). The prince that Madame Carlota promises is only an illusion—at most, he is the driver of the Mercedes that runs Macabéa down. The storyteller cannot conjure a happy ending for this poor girl from the Northeast.

Reality intrudes. On one level, Lispector is exposing the cruelty and difficulties faced by those who have been forced to emigrate from the hinterlands of Brazil into the cities. Northeast Brazil is the poorest region of a country that, though blessed with natural resources, has not been able to devise a system in which wealth can be distributed in any equitable way. Macabéa and Olímpico, products of the impoverished Northeast, present the faces of the victim and the violent—both are devoid of any "civilizing" culture. Olímpico will fight his way into a marginally bourgeois existence, probably by marrying Glória and joining her father in the butchery business. Macabéa hungers for bits of knowledge; she collects advertisements and listens to the culture capsules presented on the radio. This knowledge, though, seems to alienate her even

further from the urban pathways of modern Rio de Janeiro. Her instinctual being does not accord with official reality.

Critical Context

The Hour of the Star was the last book that Clarice Lispector published during her lifetime. She wrote it at the same time that she was writing *Um Sopra de Vida* (1978; a breath of life), a confessional novel bordering on lyrical poetry. *The Hour of the Star* is unique among Lispector's novels in that it deals with contemporary social and political problems in Brazil.

Lispector is best known for moving Brazilian fiction away from regional preoccupations. Like her Argentine contemporary Jorge Luis Borges, she was more concerned as a writer with such major twentieth-century literary preoccupations as existentialism, the New Novel, and linguistic experimentation. Her prose is highly imagistic, and her protagonists develop more through their interaction with everyday objects than through the actions of the plot. In rhythmically developed epiphanies reminiscent of James Joyce and Virginia Woolf, her characters gradually come to an awareness of the isolation and ephemerality of their individual existences. Lispector is one of the early voices of female consciousness in Latin American literature; her protagonists are generally middle-class urban women attempting to find their place in the contemporary world.

The Hour of the Star shares many of these themes and stylistic qualities with such earlier works as *Lacos de Família* (1960; *Family Ties*, 1972) and *A Maçã no Escuro* (1961; *The Apple in the Dark*, 1967), but Lispector's focus on the devastating effects of poverty in contemporary Brazil marked the first time that her very real social concerns (as revealed in her newspaper columns and elsewhere) were addressed in her fiction. Lispector's early death, a day before her fifty-second birthday, silenced one of Latin America's most experimental and original voices.

THE HOUSE OF THE SPIRITS

Author: Isabel Allende (1942-   )
Type of work: Novel
Type of plot: Historical
Time of plot: The turn of the century to the 1970's
Locale: An unnamed South American country
First published: *La casa de los espiritus*, 1982 (English translation, 1985)

Principal Characters

Clara del Valle-Trueba, the most interesting and most discussed character in the novel, who embodies Allende's purpose and meaning. Clara's magical abilities put her on a spatial and temporal plane outside the conventions of society; she is a metaphor for memory, history, time, and inextricability of fiction from truth, and the possibilities of renewal and political harmony. She functions throughout the novel as the hope for the future as well as the necessity of recognizing the past. For example, when Clara knows she is going to die, she is not unhappy, since she understands that memory will live on in her granddaughter, Alba. When Alba needs her, Clara symbolically comes alive to rescue her by reminding her of the importance of memory and respect for the past. Clara affects each character in a positive way, and it is because of her challenge to Alba to record the life of the family that this history is preserved. Clara is a reflection of the author herself, whose goal is to keep the truth alive about Latin American events.

Esteban Trueba, Clara's husband. Esteban's memoirs are scattered throughout the novel by Alba in order to obtain a more accurate and encompassing historical record of her family and her country's past. Esteban is an unsympathetic character until his later years, when it becomes clear that he too has been a victim of rigid authoritarianism and outmoded ideas. Esteban's primary qualities are pride and ambition, and he never learns the tempered reason and compassion that define Clara. He wields power unfairly and cruelly; he represents those who have controlled the fate of others,

primarily the peasant and indigenous populations, since the conquest of Latin America. He cannot change with the times and is destined to live a long life with troubled memories and some remorse. Esteban is a bitter figure, and his written account is a coming to terms, not completely honestly, with the life he has lived.

Alba Trueba, Clara and Esteban's granddaughter. Alba writes the story that preserves the family's history. From the beginning, Alba shares some of her grandmother's positive qualities; she too is life-affirming and openminded. She therefore functions as the legacy of Clara's intimacy with other realities. Alba's nonconformity and her assistance to the resistance movement against the military government reflect the changing times and signal an end to her family's participation in political oppression and wasteful affluence. She is instrumental in forcing her grandfather to contemplate his life and to write it down. She functions as the hope for tomorrow, the unity between political factions, and the fusion of races.

Rosa Trueba, Clara's sister. Rosa intended to marry Esteban until her untimely murder by the hands of political antagonists of her wealthy father. Rosa represents an otherworldly time, a character outside this corrupt time and place. She has green hair and a mermaidlike body that make her figuratively unfit for this earthly un-paradise. Her death shocks Clara into nine years of silence, providing an early lesson into unbelievable realities that Clara will confront throughout her life.

The Count, a fortune hunter who marries

Alba's mother, who has become pregnant by another man. His only function in the text is as a metaphor for the corruption, decadence, and continual encroachment of the Old World on the New. He robs the New World's indigenous inhabitants of their customs, traditions, and soul; his sexual exploitation of the Indian servants reflect his stealing of their histories and their resources. For a minor character, his role in the novel is significant, for it is part of the nonfictional record.

Barrabás, a dog, the closest companion to Clara during her early years. His name is the first word of the novel and one of the last. He shows up at various moments in the text as a unifying symbol that encapsulates time and space and a creature that crosses reality with fantasy. He is a constant reminder of Clara and what she stands for; he also represents circular time, for he never stays in the past but is continually brought forward in the text. In the conclusion, he is brought up from the basement (the past) and will serve as a rug in Alba's room, which was Clara's room. He will thus be a witness to her writing as he was to Clara's. Barrabás functions ultimately as a bridge through time and memory and, along with Alba, as a signifier of the future.

The Novel

The House of the Spirits follows three generations of three families, each of which represents a social class with its particular culture and political outlook. This historical fiction is based on Isabel Allende's own childhood growing up in Chile, her family and relatives, and her experiences as a journalist covering her country's political turmoil.

The House of the Spirits is narrated by Clara's granddaughter Alba, who is piecing together her family's past using the numerous notebooks that her grandmother had written throughout her life and incorporating her grandfather Esteban's memoirs.

The book begins when Clara is a young child. Although she lives in luxury and is pampered by her family, she stands out as the protagonist and as an individual with special qualities. She can communicate with the hereafter, she can foretell events, and most important, she can sense injustice and corruption. She can foresee that Esteban will seek to marry her after the mysterious death of his fianceé, her sister Rosa. Clara knows that she does not love him, but she senses that her duty to others resides with this marriage. This duty begins when they visit Esteban's country estate, Tres Marías, where poverty and neglect of the peasant class are visible to Clara. She knows that Esteban has illegitimate children through one family, the Garcías, and this important relationship enters into the True-bas' lives throughout the novel. From now on, Clara will alternate between living in the reality of the here and now—attending to her family and helping others—and her escape world, where she communes with spiritual forces that allow her to see what is unjust and duplicitous about the real world.

Throughout her marriage to Esteban and the birth of three children, Blanca and the twins Nicólas and Jaime, Clara represents a better tomorrow, a promising and equal society for her country that is not possible now—hence her magical qualities. Esteban becomes a powerful senator and an influential conservative politician who fights against the social reform and political democracy represented by new voices of liberalism and economic equality. He works secretly with other patriarchal figures and foreign governments to overthrow the socialist candidate for president, Isabel Allende's nonfictional uncle by marriage, Salvador Allende, who was president of Chile from 1970 to 1973, when a coup overthrew his government.

The concluding chapters cover the coup and its aftermath. A reign of terror occupies the imaginary country, a parallel to the historical events in Chile. In this novel, Alba is kidnapped and tortured by the right-wing military, but she is able to return home and be united with her grandfather. Her memories and close alliance with her deceased grandmother

Clara enable her to overcome the terror and the suffering; because Alba shares many of the magical properties of her grandmother, she can "hear" Clara's voice and feel her presence in prison. Alba is motivated by Clara to write down her story so it will not be forgotten. Alba represents the future, a time when the country and its people will be at peace with one another and can forgive one another. Alba does not wish for revenge on her enemies, for they are all related and will survive only with the help of each other; she has learned this from Clara. Clara's notebooks, along with her memory, are responsible for Alba's recovery and understanding of the three families that form her past.

Analysis

The House of the Spirits presents the reader with a multiplicity of meanings. First, the Latin American worldview recognizes reality as wearing many faces; it is understood that there are truths above and below the surface. Part of this recognition stems from a political reality in Latin America that has manipulated and distorted the life of the individual. The reader can see this in the discrepancies of wealth and status that define each character. Only a privileged few, such as the del Valles, lead a life of comfort; their opulence is satirically portrayed early in the novel, particularly in regard to their feasts and their leisure. In contrast, even the dwindling middle classes have a difficult time, as shown by the poverty and distress of Esteban Trueba's mother and his sister, Férula. The urban slums are also described in realistic detail; Isabel Allende's purpose is to document this pervasive tragedy, evident not only in Chile but in many other countries as well.

Another meaning of the text is an explication of history. Allende presents the coup and the political events of the 1970's not as isolated, unconnected incidents but as developments with roots far back in the social structure of the country. By encompassing an expansive temporal span and following several families through the generations, Allende gives substance and meaning to what happened; as the past is brought forward and kept alive, the forces of history are made visible. Preserving the memory and the past ensures that the truth will not disappear. The importance of Clara's notebooks and Alba's memoir reflect this: Both women respect history and the role of memory in their lives.

The women's writings then, like the text itself, illustrate the significance of knowing the past and not forgetting it, as Esteban has done. The novel, like history, is not organized and logical; it cannot be confined by dates and times, and it is contingent upon innumerable factors. The historical novel presents the dynamics of social organisms over time in a condensed version that illuminates things that might otherwise be invisible. Allende forcefully reminds her readers of the interconnections between the past and the future as well as of those between fiction and nonfiction.

A third meaning of the text is philosophical. The author anticipates a more peaceful and egalitarian tomorrow not only for the citizens of Chile but also for all Latin America. This is evident throughout the novel. As time unfolds, racial and class barriers disintegrate through marriage and the forming of new relationships. The three main family groups become intermingled in a perceptible development in the author's quest for harmony and change. Clara's son Jaime becomes a doctor and lives among the poor, Blanca marries Pedro and moves to Canada, and Alba's boyfriend Miguel is not from her social class or political background. Clara becomes best friends with Pedro Segundo after an earthquake that foreshadows the fall of the feudal system. Even Esteban must form unusual alliances with people outside his political doctrine to seek assistance for Alba. The novel concludes with Alba's optimism, forgiveness, and expectations for her unborn child in a literary beginning that the author believes will have parallels in reality.

Critical Context

The House of the Spirits is an important contribution to contemporary Latin American fiction. Allende's individual mixture of realism and Magical Realism places the novel firmly in the classical and recent traditions of Spanish-language writers who innovatively respond to the myriad realities of their countries with a complex use of realism on the written page. Latin American novels frequently borrow events, characters, and features from one another in a related, continuing chronicle of the cyclical Latin American reality. Julio Cortázar, Carlos Fuentes, Gabriel García Márquez, and Mario Vargas Llosa periodically refer to one another's fiction. Allende too retropes some of the characteristics of García Márquez's historical fiction, *Cien años de soledad* (1967; *One Hundred Years of Solitude*, 1970). This parodic homage, in the use of repeated time and names, is also a unique aspect of the novel and one that expands its literary horizons.

The House of the Spirits is Allende's first novel, and its readability has made a significant impact on readers previously unfamiliar with Latin American literature or history. In particular, the idiosyncratic character of Clara and the close female connections that she sustains with her daughter and granddaughter have ensured the book's prominence in autobiographical and testimonial literature as well as in gender and feminist studies. Additionally, an interest in metafiction is evident in the work. Allende's use of multiple layers of time, reality, and storytelling combine to form a provocative and interesting literary product that also forms alliances and relationships with other contemporary Latin American texts.

THE HOUSE ON MANGO STREET

Author: Sandra Cisneros (1954-   )
Type of work: Novel
Type of plot: *Bildungsroman*
Time of plot: The mid-1960's
Locale: A Latino neighborhood in Chicago
First published: 1984

Principal Characters

Esperanza Cordero, a preteenage girl and beginning writer who narrates a chronicle of her Latino neighborhood in Chicago. She focuses on the women, describing how some are victimized by men and how others resist traditional roles. As she begins to develop sexually, she idolizes Sally, a pretty girl whose father beats her for seeing boys. Esperanza is raped the night she accompanies Sally to a carnival. Esperanza seeks women in the neighborhood for role models. Alicia, Minerva, and Aunt Guadalupe, for example, encourage her to write. Her family's "sad" house, which embarrasses and pains her, is a catalyst for her imagination. She often describes a dream house and insists on her need for a house of her own. Her insistence and yearning are part of her search for self-identity and artistic expression.

Sally, the beautiful older girl whom Esperanza admires and at first tries to emulate. Sally wears makeup and nylons, dresses in black, and tosses her raven hair. Boys talk about her. Her strict father, who equates beauty with trouble, makes her come straight home after school and often beats her for talking to boys. The night Esperanza is molested at a carnival, Sally has abandoned her to run off with a boy. Sally eventually escapes from her father by marrying a marshmallow salesman, but she finds that she has simply traded one kind of imprisonment for another.

Alicia, a university student struggling to keep up with her responsibilities at home as the eldest daughter in a family whose mother has died. Like Sally, she has a domineering father, but she can escape from the house by taking classes. By convincing Esperanza that Mango Street will always play an important part in her life, Alicia instills in her younger friend a sense of social responsibility and a determination to pursue her dreams.

Elenita, the "witch woman" who reads Esperanza's cards at home. Elenita reads "a home in the heart" in Esperanza's cards. Elenita's divination is the first strong indication in the novel that Esperanza will create a home for herself through her inner life, her writing. Elenita also inspires Esperanza because she knows so much about old folk ways and Mexican magic.

Guadalupe, Esperanza's Aunt Lupe, who is suffering from a debilitating terminal illness. Aunt Lupe becomes the object of ridicule in a game Esperanza plays with her friends. Later, Esperanza feels guilty and sad, so she brings Aunt Lupe books and reads to her. Esperanza shares her own poems with Guadalupe, who is the first person to encourage her to keep writing.

Minerva, a girl only slightly older than Esperanza who has two children and an absent husband. Their friendship blooms when they share each other's poems.

Lucy, Esperanza's friend. Lucy is "the quiet one," truly a little girl, in contrast to Esperanza's other acquaintances in the barrio who have matured as a result of exposure to the adult world and social necessity.

Rachel, Lucy's little sister. Rachel is the talker for the two sisters.

Magdalena (Nenny), Esperanza's little sister. Nenny represents the world of childhood innocence that Esperanza is about to leave behind.

The Novel

Based on Sandra Cisneros' experiences growing up in a Latino neighborhood of Chicago, *The House on Mango Street* is the story of a girl's search for identity as she comes of age. The narrative covers one crucial year in her life. Esperanza Cordero, a young Chicana, is ethnically Mexican and culturally Mexican American. As the first-person narrator of the stories, she describes herself, her neighbors, their dreams, and what goes on around Mango Street. In the process, she gains an understanding of herself and of her true identity.

Cisneros has described the forty-six short vignettes that make up the novel as crosses between poems and short stories. The tiny chapters are intensely lyrical, written in prose that is highly charged with metaphor. Each section has a title, and each could stand alone as an autonomous piece, like a prose poem. Esperanza's voice, however, unifies the narrative. Her quest for identity and purpose shapes the plot, which is otherwise loosely defined.

Esperanza describes her family's house on Mango Street as a "sad" little house with a swollen door and no yard or trees. The red bricks are crumbling, and everyone shares a bedroom. It is not the house she imagined her family would have when they moved. She feels as ashamed of the new house as she felt of the old apartment, the one at which Mother Superior pointed to the boarded upstairs window and said "You live *there*?" Her parents say this house is temporary, but Esperanza knows better. She dreams of having her own house someday.

Esperanza describes her world with a child's innocence, although her innocence is beginning to fade. She is approaching puberty and the longings and confusion it brings. Moreover, she is an astute observer of the world around her, especially of adults and their actions. She intuits human nature and seems to understand well the emotions felt by her friends, family, and neighbors.

In the first few sections of the novel, she introduces her family by describing their hair. She introduces the neighbor girls, Lucy and Rachel, in

a giddy account of the afternoon they met and shared a newly purchased used bicycle. She offers sketches of her neighbors Meme, Louie, Marin, Davey the Baby, and Rosa Vargas, a woman with so many children she does not know what to do. She also describes Alicia, a determined college student who wakes up with the "tortilla star" every morning to pack lunchboxes and who is trying to go to college despite all the duties she has had to shoulder for her siblings since her mother's death. She is portrayed as worn but strong, afraid only of the mice she sees at night and of her dictatorial father.

Midway through the novel, the narrative begins to explore Esperanza's adolescence more closely. Her descriptions and ruminations are emotional, sometimes troubled, sometimes exuberant. She tries on different attitudes and personae. One day Esperanza, her little sister Nenny, Lucy, and Rachel try on old high heels. The grocery man shouts indignantly that high heels are dangerous on little girls, and then a bum tries to bribe the girls for a kiss. They run away frightened. No one complains, Esperanza says, when Lucy's mother throws the old shoes in the trash. In this vignette and others such as "Hips," "Geraldo No Last Name," "Sire," and "Four Skinny Trees," Esperanza tests her nascent sexuality, marvels at her body's changes, and savors the emotions of a first crush. In "The First Job," Esperanza is fooled by an elderly man who takes advantage of her trust and naïveté. He grabs her and kisses her in the lunchroom.

Sally, a beautiful, flirtatious girl, strongly influences Esperanza. Sally, it seems to her, knows how to express her sexuality. Esperanza calls herself the ugly daughter whom nobody comes for, so naturally she is smitten by Sally's self-assurance and by the fact that boys adore her. Emulating Sally, though, does not work for Esperanza. In "The Monkey Garden," she is humiliated when she tries to save Sally from a group of boys only to find that Sally does not desire to be rescued. Sally's betrayal becomes complete when she disappears at a carnival and leaves Esperanza alone and unprotected.

That night, Esperanza is sexually molested by a boy who says only, "I love you Spanish girl." Later episodes focus on Sally's beatings by her father and her attempt to escape by marrying a traveling salesman. This marriage serves only to entrap Sally in a different kind of prison.

As Esperanza matures, her interest in self-identity grows stronger. Latino society limits young women to certain roles. Marriage is acceptable. Esperanza, though, vows not to "grow up tame like the others." She calls marriage a ball and chain. She does not wish to inherit her grandmother's place at the window, where the old woman sat and sighed sadly as she watched the world go by. Esperanza inherited her grandmother's name, but she does not want her circumstances.

Alicia serves as Esperanza's mentor. Kind, older, and supportive, she teaches her protégé that a woman can pursue her dreams despite male domination. Alicia tells Esperanza that she is Mango Street, like it or not; that no matter where she finally finds her own house, she will come back home to Mango Street again. In the end, Esperanza acknowledges this crucial tie, saying that what she remembers most is the sad red house that "I belong but do not belong to." The stories she tells release her from and also tie her to her past and her community. She vows to return, to rescue the women to whom the book is dedicated. She will accomplish this by handing down their stories to others.

Analysis

Esperanza's descriptions focus on the women she knows. Since she is a young adolescent, theirs is a world she will soon be expected to join. Her portraits reveal how women's lives are made difficult by the men who dominate them. Often her perspective, which can be both childish and mature, points to the ways that society at large oppresses Latin Americans. The Latina women Esperanza talks about thus bear a double yoke. Living in a strongly patriarchal society, often in fear of violence, they find their choices for survival and self-expression limited. Meanwhile, many suffer along with their men from all the problems of living in poverty. Their burden is the fate the narrator wants to escape.

Esperanza repeatedly insists, sometimes whimsically, sometimes desperately, that she must have a house of her own somehow. She is also intent on becoming a writer. The two needs are intertwined, and they eventually become inseparable in the narrative. Her two wishes, to be a writer and to own her own house, are her prerequisites for freedom and self-identity. How artistic creation strengthens identity and provides dignity is an important theme.

Esperanza often thinks aloud about her identity, in subconscious or naïve ways. She is Chicana, or Mexican American, and she is Mexican by parentage. This dual identity leads her to perceive two possibilities in everything she encounters. One fundamental example is her name: In English it means "hope"; in Spanish it means "too many letters," sadness, and waiting. She says she would like to create a new name for herself. Esperanza wants to re-create herself from scratch and create the house, too, that will reflect and define her. The house may symbolize the book of her stories that she wants to write.

The house she imagines and describes becomes her symbol for freedom and artistic expression. It also ties her to her community, the anchor of her identity and the source of her stories. In the end, she says that she will leave Mango Street with her books and papers but will come back for those she left behind, meaning that she will not abandon her roots.

Critical Context

The House on Mango Street falls between genres. It could be considered as a series of prose poems, a chain of vignettes, or a set of short stories unified by the narrator's voice and identity. The chapters were written as a series of stories that might be appreciated as single pieces or as parts of the whole. The novel is not linear but moves from one event to another, often revisiting settings and characters in much the same way as a young girl's conversation or inner thoughts might skip from story to story or person to person by association or some other trigger of memory.

Since *The House on Mango Street*, her first book, Cisneros has published *Woman Hollering Creek, and Other Stories* (1991), and *My Wicked, Wicked Ways* (1992), a volume of poetry. These works also explore the themes of feminism, biculturalism, family violence, artistic creativity, and personal identity. All of Cisneros' work offers insights into what it means to be a Latino in the United States.

HOW THE GARCÍA GIRLS LOST THEIR ACCENTS

Author: Julia Alvarez (1950-   )
Type of work: Novel
Type of plot: Family
Time of plot: The 1950's to the 1980's
Locale: The Dominican Republic and the United States
First published: 1991

Principal Characters

Carlos García (Papi), the overprotective Old World patriarch whose part in a failed coup against dictator Rafael Trujillo sends the family into exile. With the help of an intelligence agent and Dr. Fanning, an American colleague, he is able to set up his medical practice in New York City, providing a good life for his wife (Mami) and his four beloved daughters. The youngest of his father's thirty-five children, he is rooted in the old Hispanic heritage and keeps strong control over his family. He establishes the tradition of celebrating his birthday at his house, with the daughters coming without their men. Even as adults, his daughters play the role of the father's little girls.

Laura García (Mami), the energetic mother of the four girls. She is the most comfortable in the exile life because she had studied in America. Her knowledge of English and lack of a heavy accent, along with her temperament, make her the leader of and mediator for the family in the new land. She is ambitious and takes courses that may lead to a successful career. The girls resent her activities, which keep her away from their needs. She calls them each by the generic pet name "Cuquita." Once settled in the United States, she refuses to go back to the island, where she would be considered to be a house slave, oppressed by a society that expects women to have sons. As a good "Mami," she is always giving advice, constantly telling the girls to guard their virginity and avoid drugs. She rears them in an American style but expects them to live by Hispanic cultural values.

Carla, the oldest García sister, remembers Christmas in the native country, with decorations, many activities, and toys brought from New York City by the father. She also thinks of Victor Hubbard, the American consul who prepared the upper class for revolution, and the turmoil of the last day on the island, when the secret police stormed into the house looking for Carlos. She resents the celebration of the first year in exile without understanding her parents' ease in sinking roots. She feels homesick and prays to go back. When the family moves from the city to Long Island, she faces discriminatory treatment by a group of boys and confronts a sexual offender. She grows up to become a psychologist and marries one. Always ready to understand others, she is the family therapist.

Sandra (Sandi), the second sister, is the pretty one. As a child, she exhibits artistic talent and wants to express herself with paintings. In New York City, she hears a woman in her apartment house trying to get the family evicted because of its language, food, and music. At a Spanish restaurant, Sandra sees people paying for the food and music criticized earlier. She wants to be a model as a means of being accepted in the new culture. In order to keep her weight down, she uses drugs that cause addiction and a mental breakdown.

Yolanda (Yoyo), the third of the sisters, learns ghostly tales from Haitian maids as a child, plays with her male cousins, and wanders around restricted places. She remains curious all of her life. Memories of raids by police, violence, and disappearances of uncles stay with her and keep her awake at night. In New York City, she is the only immigrant in her class and is seated apart from the other children as she is tutored in English. Seeking refuge in books and language, she becomes a good student and is chosen in the ninth grade to give a speech. She discovers the power of words and creates poems, eventually becoming a poet and teacher. After suffering from failed relationships and emotional turmoil, she hopes to find her identity in her country of birth, but she is too independent to settle there, in a family compound with guarded walls and a patriarchal society.

Sofia (Fifi), the youngest in the family. She competes with the others to be the wildest. When she is sent to the island to reform her American ways, she falls in love with a cousin who dominates her. She leaves college and runs away with another boyfriend, then finally marries a German chemist. Her father forgives her only when she gives him a grandson.

Chucha, the servant of the family in the Dominican Republic. She came to the grandfather's house to escape from a death decreed for all black Haitians by the dictator Rafael Trujillo. She is disliked by other maids because of her race. Devoted to voodoo, she sleeps in a coffin. When the family leaves, she remains to take care of the house. She worries about the Garcías but is certain that they will know how to invent strategies for survival.

The Novel

In her first book of fiction, *How the García Girls Lost Their Accents*, Julia Alvarez illustrates her own experience growing up in the United States as a Latina immigrant. The novel covers three decades, depicting the survival strategies of an exiled Dominican family and the coming of age of four sisters in the United States.

How the García Girls Lost Their Accents is divided into three parts, of five sections each. Moving backward in time from 1989 to 1956, it begins and ends in the Dominican Republic. The novel uses omniscient third-person narrative as well as first-person narrative.

The novel begins during Yolanda's return to the island after an absence of five years. In her search for roots, she hopes that her "true" home is her native country. As she interacts with her Dominican family, cross-cultural comparisons are made between the island and the United States. Contact with the lush and tropical setting gives her a sense of "home," but the reality of the patriarchal society of the island makes her realize that she has become too independent and Americanized to live there.

The García family had fled the homeland twenty years earlier, escaping a likely death sentence for political subversion. Carlos García, the father, was involved in a coup against dictator Rafael Trujillo. The corrupt regime persecuted the upper class, and the secret police surrounded the family compound. Aided by Americans, Carlos (Papi), Laura (Mami), and their four daughters became exiles in the United States. The girls hold memories of their childhood on their grandfather's property, where adjoining houses were built for uncles, aunts, and cousins while servants lived in shanty shacks. Yolanda liked to play in the forbidden areas of the compound, haunted places with ghostly stories. Their life with chauffeurs, gardeners, maids, and nursemaids is left behind for a life of poverty, uncertainties, discrimination, and prejudice. The woman in the apartment below theirs wants them evicted because of their use of Spanish and the smell of their food. The urban immigrant experience means alienation and loneliness for the girls. While the parents celebrate their first year in the United States, Carla feels homesick and begs to go back.

The move to greener Long Island means that Carla must take the bus to school. A gang of boys chases her, calls her names, and throws stones at her. A man in a car exposes himself to her, and she struggles to explain the situation to the police in English. Bad dreams disrupt her nights. All the family members are haunted by memories of blood in the streets, secret-police cars, and killed or "disappeared" relatives; repeating the names of loved ones and praying makes them feel safer. They fear ridicule because of their accents.

Laura, who was educated in the United States, is the most confident and serves as mediator in the strange land. She tries to invent things to make the family rich, takes courses for a future career, and has no wishes of returning to a society in which she would be only a wife and house slave, ridiculed for not having sons. Carlos, the father, works hard and becomes successful in his medical practice in the Bronx. After four years of waiting to go home, with the possibility of another revolution, he decides to become a "dominican-york" and settle down in his new country.

As the sisters grow up, they want to become Americans and enjoy the new ways of life, so different from those imposed by their parents. They want to understand the puzzling things of the new culture and wish that their mother had more time to attend to their needs. They had been sent to elementary Catholic schools as children, and now they go to boarding schools in Boston as protection from American lifestyles. Adolescence is spent plotting escape from the parents' overprotective, strict control. Unacceptable behavior is punished with obligatory trips to the island during the summers for reforming stays with the Dominican family. The parents hope that the girls will marry homeland boys. What the girls find on the island is a world dominated by macho men who have mistresses and illegitimate children while their wives take care of themselves and their households. Dominican women go to college in the United States, but only for two years, because too much education may harm their chances of marriage. They all criticize the loose American women, but they have no qualms about extramarital affairs in their own country.

The García girls go to college, except for Sofia, and become professional women. They struggle with failed love relationships and marriages, suffering emotional and mental breakdowns in their bittersweet lives. What keeps them together as a family is their devotion to one another. Yolanda and the others will continue to invent strategies for survival after coming of age in America.

Analysis

How the García Girls Lost Their Accents is a family saga illustrating the experience of exile, immigrant life, and coming of age in the United States. Political persecution in the native country forces the García family to leave its home and relatives to start a new life as strangers in a strange land. Fortunately, the parents are familiar with the United States because of previous trips. They have the advantage of financial help from relatives and professional assistance from American friends, who can find a job for Carlos as a medical doctor. The girls grow up in a loving home, although the environment is overprotective. They go to good schools and colleges and spend summers in the Dominican Republic with their upper-class relatives. The circumstances of this family are different from those of other Hispanic immigrants who are not so privileged, both socially and economically, and who do not come to the United States as political exiles. The García family has the option of returning to the homeland after the end of the dictatorship. The family decides to remain in the United States. Other immigrants do not have such a choice.

This deeply human novel is above all an eloquent account, told mostly by female voices, of the experience of growing up in a Hispanic immigrant family. The personal becomes universal when it deals with issues such as alienation, relationships, love, betrayal, prejudice, discrimination, racism, sexism, and search for identity. The issues are not easily reconciled. Love holds the García family together, for example, but the challenges of life in a new country profoundly affect the lives of the protagonists. They survive, but not always with great success. Sandi and Yoyo have emotional and mental breakdowns and will have to struggle to find their identities within the two disparate cultures in which they live.

The narrative builds on the tension between the Old World beliefs of the Hispanic parents and the New World values acquired by the daughters. The interlocked stories reconstruct the conflicts between the two generations and also portray the cross-cultural differences of two countries. The novel explores the feelings of the García girls as they confront the harshness and reality of life at an early age, then mature through their interaction with all kinds of people. The spirit and ideology of the 1960's in the United States are depicted vividly, as they affect the development of the sisters and provoke the most charged moments in the family's life, causing the most harmful trials and tribulations. The themes of female conditioning and feminine roles in the Hispanic and Anglo cultures, and the clash between the two cultures, lead to a meditation about the myths and stereotypes that prevent women from finding fulfillment in patriarchal societies. The novel centers on life in the United States, contemplated also from the vantage point of Dominicans. It provides an often satirical view of life in the Caribbean country, offering testimony and denunciation of all kinds of prejudice in both places.

This bittersweet and honest tale about life in a bicultural and bilingual existence emphasizes the role of writing and the power of words to express ideas and feelings about the world. The use of Spanish words indicates conscious language choices by the author to achieve strategic emotional, ironic, and satirical purposes, as well as offering occasional comic passages to be appreciated by bilingual readers. There is a fluid transition in shifts from one language to another. Alvarez uses the idiomatic resources of both languages, thus expanding her repertoire. Hers is an example of a bilingual text that illustrates sociocultural dualism.

Critical Context

The critically acclaimed *How the García Girls Lost Their Accents* is Alvarez's first novel. It represents the Latino narrative, now being recognized in the United States and abroad for its literary quality. The term "Latino" encompasses a diversity of ethnic, racial, national, and cultural groups, with historic, economic, and social differences. Alvarez offers the voice of the Dominican American, one who came of age in New York as a Hispanic female. Her novel is a valuable contribution to the women's fiction written by Latinas. The American Library Association named it as a Notable Book in 1992, and it won the 1991 PEN Oakland/Josephine Miles Book Award.

The author uses several literary techniques successfully: multiple narrators, flashbacks, monologues and dialogues, and different voices circling around familiar incidents to provide different points of view. These techniques develop a work that holds the reader's attention throughout. The novel moves from one character's story to the next, creating an album of portraits filled with joy and sadness. The story lines of exile, immigration, and coming of age give the narrative universal appeal.

Alvarez left the Dominican Republic as a child, in the 1960's. She received undergraduate and graduate degrees in literature and writing, then began a career teaching writing in schools in Kentucky, California, Vermont, Washington, D.C., and Illinois. In 1984, she published her first book of poetry, *Homecoming*. Some of the stories of the novel have appeared, in slightly different versions, in *The Caribbean Writer*, *The Greensboro Review*, *Third Woman*, and various other periodicals, as well as in anthologies.

Beginning in the 1980's, a new generation of Hispanic writers established a strong literary reputation and received acclaim as members of a boom in Latino fiction. Alvarez is one of these writers. She enriches American mainstream fiction, which is being redefined to reflect changes in the demographics of the country.

HUNGER OF MEMORY: The Education of Richard Rodriguez

Author: Richard Rodriguez (1944-   )
Type of work: Autobiography
Time of work: The 1940's to the 1970's
Locale: California
First published: 1981

Principal Personages

Richard Rodriguez, a writer, lecturer, and former college instructor, the narrator and dominant voice. Richard looks back as an adult on himself as a child, born to Mexican immigrants in Sacramento, California, and known as Ricardo Rodriguez. Ricardo spoke only Spanish until he entered Catholic grade school. The grown-up Richard remembers the fluidity, the naturalness, and the emotional warmth conveyed by the Spanish language of the household, a language that became a refuge against the alien world of the English speakers. The private language of home is not simply a means of communication for Ricardo; the medium of Spanish is also the message itself, that the seven-year-old belongs and is loved as a part of the closely tied organic unit of the family. Richard is truly created when two nuns visit his home and diplomatically suggest that the child is failing to progress because of a lack of practice with his new second language. His parents, willing to sacrifice all for their son's good and unwilling to question the church's authority, immediately agree to give up Spanish at home. The adult Richard derives from this change, acquiring such mastery of his now "public" English that it leads to eventual study in England and published scholarship in British literature.

Richard's father, who never fully acquires the "public language" of English, speaking haltingly and with an accent, embarrassing the teenage Richard. A would-be engineer, his academic progress is frustrated by linguistic and cultural barriers. He remains in a series of manual labor jobs, proud of his son's academic success but skeptical of the trivialization of education.

Richard's mother, more successful than her husband in the U.S. school system, learning typing and office work. She too is limited by education, once losing a desirable job by typing "urban gorillas" for "urban guerrillas." Again somewhat in contrast to her husband, she gains public confidence after the family begins speaking English at home.

Richard's brother and sister, shadowy figures, older siblings whose main function in the book is to precede Richard to school, to come home speaking Spanish, and to fill out the family circle. They are not individualized, and a third, younger sibling, is left undescribed.

The Work

Hunger of Memory comprises a five-page prologue and six chapters of approximately thirty-five pages each. The six chapters that make up the body of the book serve to frame the narrative within a rather loose chronological structure. In the opening chapter, the writer/protagonist/narrator introduces himself to the reader while reminiscing about the time when, as a child of a family of Spanish-speaking Mexicans residing in the United States, -he first experienced English-speaking society. This occurred when he began attending a neighborhood Catholic elementary school in Sacramento, California. The school's population was predominantly white, as was the neighborhood where the Rodriguezes lived. The book closes with a description of the family's annual Christmas gathering some thirty years later, when Rodriguez, now a Ph.D. candidate in English Renaissance literature with brilliant career prospects, acknowledges to the reader—and to himself—the extent to which his development and education have distanced him from his parents, particularly from his father, with whom he is able to share little more than nostalgic longings and inconsequential domestic details. This closing chapter is aptly titled "Mr. Secrets," after the nickname given to the author by his mother in a tone of bittersweet reproach.

The middle section of *Hunger of Memory* provides additional autobiographical detail, but this material is deliberately vague. There is no orderly linear exposition to inform the reader; nor does Rodriguez identify by name the people who influenced him. Substantial portions of his life, such as his adolescence, are hardly mentioned. Instead, each component of the book, while acquainting the reader with an important stage, episode, or insight in the author's development, is more than anything else a discourse on an issue of broad sociological, philosophical, educational, or political relevance.

Although Rodriguez's recollections are interesting enough to capture the reader's attention, his aim is not to entertain. In *Hunger of Memory*, autobiography serves primarily as a backdrop for the discussion of themes of much greater scope. Controversy and tender memories become artfully intertwined to give texture to the work. The book's first chapter, "Aria," for example, examines the relationship between language, family, and intimacy. The third, titled "Credo" discusses Rodriguez's reaction to changes in the Catholic liturgy and explains his deeply felt Catholic faith. Chapter 5, "Profession," recounts the benefits extended to Rodriguez, already an adult, by affirma-

tive action programs. This section is used as a platform for Rodriguez to turn his experience into a case study of how misguided the entire program has been.

During the 1970's, earlier—and at times quite different—versions of some of the book's chapters appeared as individual essays in prestigious journals such as *The Columbian Forum*, *The American Scholar*, and *College English*. Largely because of the controversial nature of Rodriguez's positions on bilingual education and affirmative action, these articles brought their author numerous speaking engagements, much public attention, and a book contract to write an autobiography that eventually became *Hunger of Memory*. Rodriguez tells the reader, in the prologue, that his editor encouraged him to write the book "in stories"— recollecting and reminiscing—not in essays, a suggestion that the writer admittedly ignored. Elsewhere in the prologue he describes the end result of his efforts as "essays impersonating an autobiography," recognizing the fact that *Hunger of Memory* is more a polemic than the story of his life.

A number of controversial themes run through the work. Rodriguez is critical of advocates of bilingual education. He is in favor of cultural assimilation, and he opposes affirmative action programs although he has benefited from them. He argues that race and ethnicity have played too central a role in national debates and in social programs and legislation.

Rodriguez thinks of himself as an individual whose experiences differ radically from those of many other Mexican Americans. He calls the writing of the book an act of contrition. He seeks the forgiveness of those poor, hardworking, and illiterate fellow Mexican Americans who would be the legitimate beneficiaries of affirmative action. He knows that he has left them behind, as he left his parents behind, and in their faces he recognizes little of himself.

Analysis

As an eloquent and accomplished Mexican American with impressive academic credentials,

Rodriguez serves as a model and example of the triumph of the underprivileged individual. His success was achieved through individual and family effort, by overcoming his own past rather than through outside intervention or institutional and governmental supports. Many white readers, especially critics of bilingual education and affirmative action, have embraced him as their spokesperson and point to his rejection of these programs as proof of their worthlessness.

Rodriguez is a vehement critic. He considers bilingual education programs ineffective and even detrimental. He explains his rapid progress in school, to a large degree, by the willingness of his family to abandon domestic intimacy—the use of Spanish, the language of home—and adopt English, the public language. His parents, Rodriguez relates, agreed to speak English at home, even though they had little command of it, when the nuns, their children's schoolteachers, persuaded them that it was in the children's best academic interest. He ceased being Ricardo and became Richard.

As his parents stopped speaking Spanish, Rodriguez perceived a loss of intimacy. At the time, he associated intimacy directly with the language itself and believed that family closeness and warmth were possible only in Spanish. As he matured, he began to believe that the outcome made the sacrifice worthwhile. In the next few years, he experienced academic success and a growing self-assurance in his public persona. He started to read voraciously in English and to rejoice in the sense of mastery, first of words and then of authors and ideas, in the new language. He became disinterested in Spanish and was reticent to speak his native language, even when visitors and relatives who came to his home urged him to do so.

Some years later, upon further reflection, Rodriguez believes that the loss of intimacy experienced in childhood was not caused by the adoption of a new language but was a result of the process of education itself. Education, as he sees it, aims at transforming children as individuals. Bilingual educators, by refusing to acknowledge this fact, contribute to delaying unnecessarily the main function of education. In the case of ethnic groups, bilingual education serves to postpone, if not to interfere with, the process of linguistic assimilation that contributes to an individual's adoption of an identity separate from that of his or her family. It also delays the experience of self-confidence in public society that is essential for success.

Affirmative action is another of Rodriguez's targets, although he openly admits to having been its beneficiary on a number of occasions. As a graduate student in the 1970's, he won several prestigious awards and fellowships, and although he amply met the criteria for such awards, he felt singled out because of his Chicano roots. During his last year of graduate study at the University of California at Berkeley, he was offered coveted teaching appointments at several colleges while equally qualified white fellow students had no such offers. He decided to turn them down. On one hand, he knows that he has devoted his life to becoming a member of English-speaking public society, for which he suffered the losses already discussed. On the other hand, after achieving his goal and distinguishing himself in public society, he is rewarded for being a member of an ethnic minority, the exact thing from which he made it his life's work to escape. He believes that he does not need such rewards; he has already achieved. Affirmative action's largesse should go to the truly underprivileged.

The polemical content of *Hunger of Memory* should not obscure the moving human story it relates. This is the most compelling feature of the work. The reader is easily captivated by Rodriguez's skillful recounting of deeply felt experiences. He is both tender and incisive, public and private. He is able to re-create, in a language that is simple, intimate, and rich, the awkward moments and the sense of excitement distilled from the memories of his youth. In compelling prose, he evokes the mystery of the Roman Catholic Mass. In a tone of contrition, he apologizes for his own success, guilty for having left behind countless Mexican Americans. The pervading tone of the work as a whole is one of nostalgia, of sadness and loss that public success can never erase.

Critical Context

Aside from the intellectual or political merits of the arguments made in *Hunger of Memory*, the autobiography deserves attention on purely literary grounds. When it appeared in 1981, it received favorable notices in major American journals and newspapers. Rodriguez was praised for the grace and clarity of his language and for his ability to communicate his deep understanding of the role and uses of language in the formative stages of an individual.

As a cultural document, Rodriguez's autobiography differs sharply from the works of other American minority writers, such as Claude Brown's *Manchild in the Promised Land* (1965) and Piri Thomas' *Down These Mean Streets* (1967). Those author's stark realism and the graphic language with which they chronicle the violent process of growing up in an urban ghetto contrast sharply with Rodriguez's cool, erudite approach. They recount the frequent terrors experienced in slum neighborhoods; Rodriguez refers to his own domestic situation as "Middle-Class Pastoral." Rather than feeling fortunate for having escaped from the bonds of his youth, Rodriguez is nostalgic for that lost time.

To a large extent, from a literary perspective, Rodriguez's positions appear distinctive because the biographies of many members of minority groups in this country contrast sharply with his own. His views tend to conform to those of social scientists, both black and white, who insist on an emphasis on class as an important social determinant, along with race and ethnicity. Rodriguez's book adds a powerful voice to their argument.

I, THE SUPREME

Author: Augusto Roa Bastos (1917-   )
Type of work: Novel
Type of plot: Historical
Time of plot: 1800-1840
Locale: Asunción, Paraguay
First published: *Yo, el Supremo*, 1974 (English translation, 1986)

Principal Characters

José Gaspar Rodríguez de Francia (Dr. Francia), the supreme dictator of the newly formed Republic of Paraguay. Although he is fundamentally a democratic idealist and believes in the models provided by the United States and France, his experience with the recently ligerated population of Paraguay has frustrated his enlightened intentions. Because of his compatriots' lack of education and the imperialist pressures from other emergent republican states such as Argentina and Brazil, he finds himself forced to assume increasingly greater dictatorial powers. Eventually, he succumbs to the seduction of absolute power, assumes the direct control of all areas of government, and withdraws into the secure isolation of his palace. He spends the majority of his time dictating orders to his subordinates and attempting to justify his betrayal of his own ideals. The last few weeks of his life are filled with a sense of decay and disintegration into absolute impotence and fear for his image in posterity.

Policarpo Patiño, the dictator's constant companion and personal secretary. Essentially a fearful, obsequious, hypocritical mouse of a man, preoccupied more with his creature comforts than with great ideals, Patiño transcribes Francia's dictation and listens to his monologues on a variety of topics. Terrified of the dictator and his tempers, he spends his time contradicting himself in an effort to placate and ingratiate. He is also fond of narrating long tales taken from local superstition and gossip that both interest and enrage his master. He is ignorant and uneducated, and he consistently makes mistakes in the written text of Francia's discourse. At times, his ignorance borders on the comic, as he transposes letters in words to form unconscious plays on words and vulgarities. The dying dictator mockingly sentences him to death and ignominy in one final decree, reducing Patiño to babbling terror.

Juan Parish Robertson, a well-educated English adventurer whose travels bring him and his brother Roberto to Paraguay. The brothers are initially welcomed by the dictator, who befriends them and passes long evenings entertaining them in the palace. They prove to be extremely opportunistic, a characteristic best represented by Juan Robertson's torrid affair with Juana Esquivel, the wealthy octogenarian next-door neighbor of Francia, who showers the young foreigner with gifts and attention. When the dictator requests that they act as intermediaries to sell Paraguayan products to the English Crown, they accept the mission and then betray their benefactor in favor of more lucrative enterprises. Upon their return to civilization, they write two scathing accounts of their adventure, attacking Francia as a monster who maintains his subjects in subhuman conditions and a perpetual reign of terror.

Pilar the Black, Francia's trusted personal valet and general servant. Initially portrayed as obedient, he later becomes rebellious. He steals small items from the government to support an Indian woman he loves and their unborn child. One day, he enters the dictator's office and assumes his clothing and identity, becoming virtually indistinguishable from his master. When Francia returns, Pilar goes wild and attacks him, but the guards cannot tell them apart. The dictator is finally obliged to execute him as a traitor but is haunted by guilt afterward.

General Manuel Belgrano, an Argentine general sent by his government to subdue the Paraguayan provinces. The campaign is not successful; the idealistic Belgrano realizes that the Paraguayan army is prepared to defend the country to the death. He consequently withdraws his forces and later returns as a negotiator to establish a diplomatic alliance. The dictator is touched by the integrity and honor displayed by his former enemy, and they become close friends.

Antonio Manoel Correia da Camara, a treach-

erous and deceitful Brazilian envoy sent to negotiate border disputes. He is the diametric opposite of his Argentine counterpart, Belgrano. Where the latter is honest and forthright, Correia is underhanded and secretive.

Bernardo Velazco, a loyal royalist governor of Paraguay who becomes a lifelong enemy of Francia, primarily as a result of ideological differences. He attacks the dictator's policies and human nature in a series of letters.

Sultan, Francia's idealistic dog and the dictator's alter ego. He enjoys spending his evenings debating the Robertson brothers on diverse political and mythical topics. At the end, he becomes the primary voice of accusation against the dictator's weaknesses.

The Novel

I, the Supeme offers a fictionalized account of the key events and motives behind the nineteenth century dictatorship of Gaspar Rodríguez de Francia (also known as Dr. Francia), who governed in Paraguay from 1814 until his death in 1840. In the novel, Augusto Roa Bastos presents a revision of the accepted interpretations of this period in history, analyzing not only the lingering effects on Paraguay but also the traditional notions of historical writing as the repository of objective truth.

Although *I, the Supreme* is considered to be a novel, it exhibits few of the traditional characteristics of the genre. There is no sense of logical continuity that could constitute a plot and no single voice that could be considered to narrate events. The book is essentially a juxtaposition of different, and frequently contradictory, conversations, monologues, myths, journal entries, circulars, letters, historical documents, footnotes, and anonymous commentaries, all brought together by an unidentified, ostensibly impartial, "compiler." This compiler, who replaces both the traditional narrator and the concept of the author, selects, orders, and presents the diverse fragments that comprise *I, the Supreme.* Although the novel is predominantly fictional, many of the incorporated texts are taken

from authentic historical sources, the value and veracity of which the reader is forced to judge as the novel unfolds.

Besides rejecting the traditional notions of narrator and narrative plot, the novel also eliminates the concept of chronological time. Past, present, and future all merge into a sense of permanent timelessness. The fictional dictator discusses his death and burial as if it were already past, and he argues with historians not yet born and texts not yet written. At other times, two events occurring at vastly different times are telescoped into one moment and presented as simultaneous. This eternal present is emphasized by the insertion of a variety of both European and native Paraguayan myths into historical events as if they were part of the reality being narrated. As a result, the novel offers no progression but rather functions within the timeless dimension of myth.

Insofar as the events of *I, the Supreme* can be said to be located in space and time, the majority of the text is set in the dictator's office and personal quarters in the national palace during the last few months of his life. The novel begins with the appearance on the door of the main cathedral in Asunción of a lampooned dictatorial decree condemning the dictator to death, dismemberment, and oblivion. The outraged Francia, now isolated, ill, and both politically and physically powerless, defends himself and his policies against the judgment of posterity. The rest of the novel consists of this defense before the judge, represented by the reader. Francia's only companion in this enterprise is his naïve personal secretary, Policarpo Patiño, who serves primarily as a scribe taking dictation and as an audience for the dictator's lengthy ramblings and self-justifications. The central action of the text revolves around their extended discussions and arguments on a variety of topics, ranging from real and imagined events to philosophy, writing, and language. A large portion of this dialogue is devoted to the dictation of a "Perpetual Circular," in which Francia recounts his version of events and his ideas on the nation and power. The dialogue and dictation are interrupted with excerpts from the dictator's personal diary, which provide a more intimate self-analysis and critique. Interspersed with this, the reader frequently encounters documents written by the dictator's contemporaries and by future historians; these documents serve as points of departure for further debate between the dictator, his secretary, and his conscience. In this way, all the major events in the novel are narrated, either by the two main characters or by the different historians and historical documents quoted.

Eventually, as the fictional Francia approaches death and the novel becomes increasingly fragmented, the voices of denunciation become stronger and more heavily judgmental. Conversely, the dictator's defense gradually disintegrates until it joins with the detractors and emerges as a self-condemnation. The novel ends abruptly in incoherence, in the middle of a sentence, which corresponds presumably to Francia's physical demise. The "compiler" does provide a curious postmortem to the novel, however, in the form of an appendix of documents that attempt to pinpoint the final resting place of the dictator's bones. The results of the scientific investigation, like those of the novel itself, are inconclusive and only serve to underscore the unsatisfactory nature of any written text. The reader is left with a sense of incompletion and the awareness that the issues presented are left unresolved. In this way, *I, the Supreme* is left deliberately open-ended so that the debate can continue in the reader's mind.

Analysis

I, the Supreme offers a complex interweaving of several themes equally important to the comprehension of the novel. To begin with, the text is a reexamination of the nineteenth century dictatorship of the historical Francia, a figure of primary importance whose ambiguous presence continues to haunt Paraguay more than a century and a half after his death. Alternately revered as the "Karai Guasu" ("great white father") and hated as the instigator of the infamous Paraguayan Reign of Terror, Francia still lives in the imagination of the nation. Roa Bastos challenges these images through the juxtaposition of documentary "fact" and novelistic "fiction," in what he himself calls a "transhistory" or an analysis of the validity of the historical interpretations of that period. This means that he does not attempt to rewrite history, instead demonstrating the shortcomings of historiography (the historian's task of writing the "truth" of history) as a scientific process. The fictional Francia continually argues in self-defense against his historians, revealing their political and emotional biases. This theme is directly embodied in the split of the character into "I" and "HE," an important opposition that permeates the novel. The "I" represents the dictator as human being, while the "HE" symbolizes the image of Francia that has been perpetuated in history books.

Since much of the novel deals with the historical dictatorship of Francia, there emerges a second theme that is also very important: the theme of absolute power. One of the major criticisms that historians have leveled at the founding father of Paraguay is that he became obsessed with the notion of power and set himself up as the supreme and perpetual dictator, the absolute controlling authority, of the newly formed republic. *I, the Supreme* deals directly with this issue; the incorporated documents and characters debate the concepts of democratic versus despotic governments as well as the origins, and dangers, of power itself. In particular, Roa Bastos plays the dictator's ideals of democracy against the reality that was achieved under his rule, revealing his inconsistencies and ultimate self-betrayal.

The historical background of the novel also serves as a point of departure for the author's examination of the boundaries between reality and fiction, another major theme in the text. The constant debate between authentic and fictional documents, as well as between real and imagined events, demonstrates to the reader that reality is difficult to identify and define. In fact, *I, the Supreme* questions the very notion of what consti-

tutes truth and reality, and whether such things as absolute truth or absolute reality exist. The argument between historical reality and the limitations of historical interpretation exposes at the same time the fact that any written text will, of necessity, be fiction, since it is a product of the biases, preconceptions, and even ignorance of the author.

This leads to the central theme of the novel: the inability of language to communicate reality. As the fictional dictator examines his life and argues with his historical interpretations, he realizes that any attempt to convey meaning through words (either written or oral) is doomed to failure, since there is always a gap between the event and the account, as between any object and the word used to express that object. As *I, the Supreme* draws to a close, there is an increasing sense of frustration as Francia's speech becomes disjointed and incoherent and, in the middle of a sentence, finally ceases.

Critical Context

I, the Supreme is Roa Bastos' second novel and his most widely acclaimed work. The author spent much of his life writing short stories and screenplays as well as an earlier novel, *Hijo de hombre* (1960; *Son of Man*, 1965), but this work clearly represents his artistic maturity.

Although it is contemporary to the major works of the Latin American boom era of the 1960's and 1970's, it is not usually analyzed within that context. Instead, it is generally included within the tradition of the "dictator novel" that began in the 1930's with the publication of *Tirano Banderas* (1926; *The Tyrant*, 1929) by the Spanish author Ramón del Valle-Inclán and *El señor presidente* (1946; *The President*, 1963) by the Guatemalan author Miguel Ángel Asturias. This genre focuses on the social, political, and even psychological consequences of dictatorship and its mechanisms for maintaining power, a phenomenon that, unfortunately, has been prevalent in Latin America since the wars of independence at the beginning of the nineteenth century.

Many critics have considered *I, the Supreme* to be the culmination of this genre, along with two other novels in the same category that were published almost simultaneously: *El recurso del método* (1974; *Reasons of State*, 1976) by Alejo Carpentier and *El otoño del patriarca* (1975; *The Autumn of the Patriarch*, 1975) by Gabriel García Márquez. All three novels reject the traditional technique of portraying the dictator as an almost mythical, dehumanized monster constructed by an external point of view and look instead at the internal conflicts of the dictator as a human being. Roa Bastos' creation presents the most radical departure from earlier models. While García Márquez and Carpentier generate a composite or hybrid image of the dictator based on characteristics of actual historical figures from different eras and areas, *I, the Supreme* does exactly the reverse: It begins with one single historical figure (Francia) and presents him through a series of fragmented and contradictory perspectives.

In many ways, this work could be considered a

precursor of the postmodern novel in Latin America. Roa Bastos' experimentations with literary techniques (fragmentation of both space and time; elimination of narrative voice, global structure, and plot; incongruous juxtaposition of a variety of texts and textual styles) work continually to challenge and deconstruct the reader's assumptions and expectations, not only with regard to the book's subject, the historical dictator, but even in terms of the written text itself and the borders between fiction and reality.

In the years after publication of *I, the Supreme*, Roa Bastos established himself as an essayist on a broad range of topics, from his own writing techniques to the sociopolitical and linguistic realities of modern Paraguay. His third novel, *Vigilia del Almirante* (1992; the vigil of the admiral), continues his exploration of the realm of historical revisionism with a timely reconstruction of Christopher Columbus' voyage of discovery in 1492 and affirms Roa Bastos' place in the Latin American literary canon.

INFANTE'S INFERNO

Author: Guillermo Cabrera Infante (1929-   )
Type of work: Novel
Type of plot: Autobiographical
Time of plot: The 1940's
Locale: Havana, Cuba
First published: *La Habana para un infante difunto*, 1979 (English translation, 1984)

Principal Characters

The narrator, a self-proclaimed Don Juan and a lover of the cinema. He selects and reports memories from the past and gives a "continuous showing" of Havana viewed in its physical setting. The plot progresses from descriptions and fantasies to platonic love, rites of passage, and sexual relationships. In them, the narrator passes through many levels of erotic involvement with women in his quest for happiness.

Zoila, the narrator's mother, described as a "beautiful Communist." Besides instilling in her son a love for the cinema, she also instills a fear of sexuality, more specifically, of sexually transmitted diseases.

Margarita del Campo (Violeta del Valle), an actress, a one-breasted, green-eyed beauty who entraps the narrator in a consuming passion. This is the woman with whom the narrator believes he is truly in love for the first time. Margarita's possessiveness finds expression in violent acts; she enjoys wreaking vengeance on men by watching them suffer and die.

Juliet Estévez, a liberated married woman who initiates the narrator into sex. The narrator stresses her euphemistic and pseudoliterary language, language that he finds both annoying and intriguing. While on one hand Juliet employs romantic language to describe her erotic involvements, she also recognizes the banal reality that accompanies her sexual encounters.

Etelvina, a beautiful young prostitute living in the same building as the narrator's family when he was young. The narrator's mother gave him the task of awakening Etelvina every morning. His mother also instilled a fear of coming into contact with the prostitute, or any other woman who might have a venereal disease.

Lolita, a maid and one of the narrator's many sexual conquests in the novel. She imitates the exaggerated, sentimental language of her soap-opera heroes in the hope that she, too, will become the ideal romantic lover. Her true personality comically emerges when she abandons the affected language of the soap opera in exchange for a flood of obscenities while she is in the height of passion.

The Novel

Cabrera Infante's inferno centers on women or, rather, on their ultimate inaccessibility even when attainable. The twelve-year-old narrator dreams about love and cerebrates about sex in a rumpled, one-room tenement apartment. His father, one of the founders of the clandestine Cuban Communist Party, has recently moved the family to Havana and there started to work in the newly created party newspaper, *Hoy*. It is 1941, and the spindly adolescent has the impression that he has died and gone to heaven. He is mesmerized by the trolley cars, dazzled by the lights and by the equally luminous characters who people the tenement building, veritable walking novels who enact the human comedy a mere step from his door. Life can well imitate art because art is so much better than life (at least in the hero's mind) that it need not fear the competition. One art form, especially, has thrilled the narrator ever since a friend of the family took the narrator and his brother to see a double feature one memorable Sunday. Films became his only lasting passion. They are made even better because, in the womblike darkness of seedy and not-so-seedy theaters, the films become amalgamated with erotic experience: "In the pitch-black theaters, platonic caves before the screen, the pursuit of sex interfered with my passion for films, the contact of flesh awakening me from my movie dreams." Watching and feeling his way simultaneously, the hero fulfills the screen dreams that whet his appetite: picking up women in the dark, rubbing elbows, and squeezing thighs.

Time passes, but the heart is a lonely hunter. One passion leads to another, and all that remains of these afternoon loves are memories. The tactile memories become literature (as in *Infante's Inferno* itself); the visual memories are churned out as film criticism when, not surprisingly, the narrator becomes the film critic for a well-known Cuban weekly, *Carteles*. Age can barely keep pace with the hero's ever-mounting lust (even if he seldom gets the many women for whom he pines). His cronies' attempts to initiate him (in a brothel) turn out to be "sour gropes," a complete failure. It is not until he meets a generous, liberated woman— Juliet Estévez—that he shifts his scrimmages from the dark theater to the clear light of the bedroom. The love affair with Juliet is a turning point in the novel. When it is over, the narrator continues his love hunt, but in the instances described thereafter, the liaisons evolve far beyond the casual squeeze in the dark that typifies relationships during the first part of the novel. He marries, but this alliance is portrayed as an event peripheral to the action (which is, after all, about pursuit and not about fulfillment). One such pursuit, the relationship with the actress Margarita del Campo ("Daisy of

the Field"), is, in fact, the culminating adventure in the narrator's eventful life.

The last section of the novel describes in frenzied detail their tempestuous encounters during one hot Havana summer. In the end, they part ways: Margarita, who works for Venezuelan television, invites the narrator to leave everything and return to Caracas with her, but he refuses, steeling himself against the love that they both feel. The impossibility of sustaining love becomes more explicit in this episode than ever before in the novel. It is clear that quests in *Infante's Inferno* are always frustratingly unfinished. One cannot help seeing the novel as a tragicomic meditation on the incompleteness of human experience.

It is impossible not to feel the hero's profound dissatisfaction, to get a sense that he will never obtain what he covets from an ever-disappointing reality. If reality is frustrating, fiction is an exhilarating experience, as the novel makes amply evident. The power of the imagination channeled through art allows the protagonist to transcend the commonplace and transform it into a lasting experience. This transformation is the substance of the long epilogue, an oneiric journey into one last movie house. The narrator enters a theater in hot pursuit of an alluring blonde who seems to give him the eye from the ticket booth. He sits next to her, and their conversation promptly evolves into a fanciful dialogue suggesting, in every way, a return *in utero*. Transported from the theater to a soft cave, the narrator finds a mysterious "book about books," which contains fragments from a ship's log, tales of seamen in hot pursuit of a huge, water-spouting creature that may well be "a projection of the mind, a monster of the id in a forbidden land."

Suddenly the cave begins to heave and toss. The narrator falls, and his body begins to move along the floor, now flooded with a mudlike, red substance. He fears that he is going "to be thrown out, expelled, rejected. . . ." The book concludes with a vivid description of the experience of birth, culminating with the hero's pivotal observation, "Here's where I came in."

Analysis

The three fundamental themes of *Infante's Inferno* are remembrance, the transformational powers of the imagination, and the hardships of love—or, rather, of lust. The novel takes full advantage of the disadvantages of the transient, forgettable nature of things past in order to create the fiction. The entire action takes place in a deceptive present that looks forward to a future while actually taking place in the past. The mature narrator looks over his shoulder to the child he no longer is. (The title in Spanish is literally "Havana for a dead infant," an allusion to the irretrievability of youth as well as to Maurice Ravel's musical composition *Pavane for a Dead Infant*.) Because all action harks back to the past, life in this novel is a primal screen of sorts, filled with sex and films and signifying the—perhaps illusory, undoubtedly elusive—quality of life. To underscore this quality, Cabrera Infante turns to his real-life passion for film, both in his search for form (the novel is a series of vignettes or still compositions) and as a metaphor of the ephemeral: Films, like life, are made up of fleeting images.

For this reason, action in *Infante's Inferno* is often described from the viewpoint of a camera. Life is so much like pictures, in fact, that characters often flow from the make-believe of one medium to the make-believe of another. As one of them notes, "We were so damn close—not to each other but to the screen. So near, in fact, that sometimes we were projected onto the sheet and straight into the picture."

Cabrera Infante makes amply clear that all fiction is made up of half-lies and transformed truths, helping distinguish him from the narrator despite their many similarities. The author may be telling his life story, but because it is remembered, this story is transformed; because it is written down, it is altered, transmuted into art.

Critical Context

Infante's Inferno is undoubtedly the finest work written by Cabrera Infante since his groundbreaking *Tres tristes tigres* (1967; *Three Trapped Tigers*, 1971). Erotic tableaux are central to the development and understanding of this novel as a whole, but they must be seen as vehicles or motives for reflection: on the nature of relationships, on the incompleteness of human experience, and, not least important, on man's (and woman's) artful penchant for fantasy. Like Georges Bataille and William Burroughs, Cabrera Infante portrays sex as a form of expenditure, as the most primal form of expression. This does not mean, in any way, that his erotic fiction should be seen as pornography; he makes evident that the body is in every way the mirror of the soul, the most tangible evidence of being. By depicting the coming together of man and woman and the profound loneliness of both, he has chosen to ponder essential questions, ontological in nature, from a philosophical perspective but with the acerbic wit typical of Menippean satire.

Eroticism as the raw core of human experience is essential to understanding *Infante's Inferno*, but the reader must keep foremost in mind that sex in this novel is always remembered—lived in the past and re-created in the present. For this reason, *Infante's Inferno* is also a witty meditation on that most Proustian of preoccupations: the act of remembrance. The French novelist believed that an accurate, untainted retrieval of the past was possible through the senses. Cabrera Infante makes clear that to remember is to re-create, a notion that he develops with relish as an inquiry into the role of the artist (transformer of facts) and the relationship between life and art. The fact that Cabrera Infante is, as he himself states, "the only British author writing in Spanish" adds yet another nuance to this art of transformations.

THE INVENTION OF MOREL

Author: Adolfo Bioy Casares (1914-   )
Type of work: Novel
Type of plot: Science fiction
Time of plot: The twentieth century
Locale: An unidentified island
First published: *La invención de Morel*, 1940 (English translation, 1964)

Principal Characters

The narrator, an insecure, paranoid fugitive from Caracas, Venezuela. The novel is a quasi-philosophical diary written on an island that he believes to be part of the Ellice, or Lagoon, Islands in the Central Pacific. He believes the island to be deserted until the day he begins the diary, the day when a group of approximately a dozen people appears and inhabits the abandoned buildings. He is afraid that they will discover him or, worse, that they have come in search of him, but he quickly realizes that they have no interest in him. In fact, he seems to be invisible to them. He becomes infatuated with a French woman named Faustine. He discovers that the intruders are the projections of a machine invented by Morel, the leader of the group. The narrator's quest is to discover how to insert himself into the eternally returning period in which his beloved dwells.

Morel, a scientist and technologist, tall, dark-eyed, bearded, and slightly effeminate. He is the inventor of the machines that record and project in space and time and that are capable of capturing feelings and emotions. Morel loves Faustine and is rejected by her, a situation that is the source of hope for the narrator.

Faustine, a dark-haired, tanned French woman given to watching sunsets. She is the object of the narrator's quest and is also pursued by Morel. She remains aloof, in disdain of Morel and completely unaware of the narrator.

The editor, who supplies footnotes to the text of the diary. The notes cast doubt or pass judgment on certain affirmations of the narrator, such as the possibly mistaken assertion that the island is part of the Ellice Islands. The editor also claims to have removed certain extraneous or impertinent material from the diary as published.

The Novel

The text of this short novel is presented as a diary of an unnamed narrator, a fugitive from justice living on an island that he assumes is in the Ellice archipelago. The narrator has found the island with the help of a rug seller in Calcutta who told him about a group of people who came to the island in 1925, built several buildings, and then disappeared. The island is known to be the focal point of a mysterious disease that attacks the body and works inward, its victims losing fingernails, then hair, and finally skin.

After a period of time spent alone on the island, exploring the museum, church, swimming pool, and mill built by the group in 1925, the narrator suddenly sees a group of people dancing and singing. He observes the group unnoticed for several days and becomes fascinated by Faustine, a beautiful woman who sits for long periods of time admiring the sunset. When he finally musters the courage to reveal himself to the woman, he observes that she pretends not to see him. As he becomes more open about his presence on the island, he realizes that he is invisible to the people and that they seem to be repeating at certain intervals their exact actions and words, as if they were acting parts in a play.

As the narrator eavesdrops on a meeting of the group, he hears Morel explain to the group that he has invented a machine that photographs the people through a complex process of recording their senses completely. The machine is then capable of projecting the sights, smells, sounds, tastes, and touch of the objects photographed, so that the images seem to be real. One entire week of their experience has been recorded and will be played forever through a kind of projector powered by the tides, so that the members of the group achieve immortality, forever re-created and forever repeating the actions of that week.

Once the narrator understands the nature of the mysterious images that he has seen on the island, he goes down into the basement of the museum, where the machine invented by Morel is contained. When he tries to leave, he finds that he is imprisoned. As he breaks an escape hole in the wall, it immediately repairs itself to the state of its existence when it was photographed. He must wait until the tides recede and the machine stops projecting the wall.

Desperately in love with Faustine, the narrator decides to try to inject himself into the photographed drama so that he can be with her forever. He observes the images until he has memorized every word and every movement, then sets the sensory receptors of the machine to record the images as he steps into the scenario. He plays to the images as if he were an actor in the scenes that they are playing. In this way, he becomes a part of their drama, so that no observer will suspect that his part has been added later.

Toward the end of the novelistic text, the narrator senses that he is dying and begins to recall his life in Venezuela. He desperately clings to the hope that he will survive and find that Faustine is a living person rather than merely a photographed image, and that they can love each other in a real, eternal existence. Then he awaits his death, at which time his soul will pass over to the image that duplicates and preserves his sensorial experience.

Analysis

Primarily because of the way in which Bioy Casares contains within the text of his novel both the adventure story, with its emphasis on plot, and the plotless, formless, psychological novel, *The Invention of Morel* has been considered to be extraordinarily inventive and original. Bioy Casares develops a psychological study of the narrator's fascination for Faustine first in terms of the narrator's belief that she is a mysterious, elusive woman and then in terms of his knowledge that she exists on another temporal plane. The problem established by the novel, that of two different kinds of reality—one, the sensorial experience of the narrator; the other, the projected record of the sensorial experience of Faustine—is a fantastic one that the narrator proceeds to solve in a rational manner. If it is true, as Morel contends, that the soul passes over to the recorded complex of sensorial experiences when the original photographed object ceases to exist, the narrator can include himself in Faustine's world by photographing himself as he interacts with the images.

The Invention of Morel deals with the very nature of human existence. It also is allegorical, in that the questions posed are equally valid in the ontology of the artistic or literary creation. The images are fictitious inventions, formulated by an exact reproduction of all the senses. When the narrator approaches the problem of the two distinct planes of reality, he is in fact inquiring into the dichotomy between the real, historical experience and the fictional. The narrator, as reader of the "novel" created by Morel, "writes" himself into Morel's creation, hoping that future readers will be deceived into believing that his reality is as fictional—or as real—as is Faustine's.

The mystery of the photographed copy of reality, with its endless variations—what if the machine photographed itself at work, or what if it photographed the tides?—reveals the ambiguous, complex nature of the duplication of experience that is artistic creation. Even the title of the novel suggests this ambiguity, for the "invention" is not only the invented machine but also the replica of Morel created by the machine.

Critical Context

The prologue to *The Invention of Morel* is written by another Argentine, Jorge Luis Borges, the writer with whom Adolfo Bioy Casares has most in common. Borges quotes the Spanish essayist José Ortega y Gasset, who discusses, in *La deshumanización del arte* (1925; *The Dehumanization of Art*, 1956), the impossibility of inventing an adventure story that would appeal to the contemporary British reading public and the predominance of the plotless, formless "psychological" novel. Borges offers *The Invention of Morel* as proof that Ortega y Gasset was wrong. He might have offered his own work, which consists of many stories that fit the description that Borges gives of *The Invention of Morel*, a "perfect" work of "reasoned imagination" that employs allegory, the exaggerations of satire, and, sometimes, simple verbal incoherence.

The Invention of Morel, which is modeled after H. G. Wells's *The Island of Doctor Moreau* (1896), was not well received by the public when it was first published, but it was read and admired by many young writers, including Julio Cortázar, Juan José Arreola, and Alejo Carpentier. Bioy Casares' postulation of the ontology of human existence and of artistic creation places him, along with Borges, in the role of precursor to later Latin American fiction writers who have dealt with the same problem. In particular, Cortázar has portrayed the interdependence of the real and the fictional.

In the second half of the twentieth century, this particular type of fiction has been labeled "metafiction"—the self-conscious fictional work that, within itself, deals with the processes by which fictional literature is created. Bioy Casares has had a significant influence in the development of the Magical Realism of writers such as Gabriel García Márquez, whose *Cien años de soledad* (1967; *One Hundred Years of Solitude*, 1970) initiated international appreciation of Latino writers.

THE ITCHING PARROT

Author: José Joaquín Fernández de Lizardi (1776-1827)
Type of work: Novel
Type of plot: Picaresque
Time of plot: The 1770's to the 1820's
Locale: Mexico
First published: *El periquillo sarniento*, 1816 (English translation, 1942)

Principal Characters

Pedro Sarmiento, nicknamed **Periquillo (The Itching Parrot,** or **Poll),** the young rogue protagonist. As the son of upper-middle-class people of Mexico City, he seeks the easiest way of earning a living. A monk's life is too exhausting. He tries other professions: barber, physician, apothecary, beggar, and secretary to a colonel in Manila. Finally, a schoolmate, now a priest, turns him to a prosperous, honest life, resulting in Poll's marriage and respectability.

Señor Sarmiento, Pedro's father, who wants Pedro to become a tradesman.

Señora Sarmiento, who, wanting her son to be a priest, dies of grief at his many vices.

Januario, a schoolmate who makes a fool of Pedro for his attentions to Januario's cousin, with whom Januario himself is infatuated.

Don Antonio, a good man, unjustly jailed, who helps Pedro. Later, Pedro finds him destitute and aids him.

The daughter of Don Antonio, who becomes the wife of the reformed Pedro.

A scrivener, who arranges Pedro's release from jail so that he can serve as the scrivener's secretary.

The Novel

Pedro Sarmiento, the protagonist of *The Itching Parrot*, was born to upper-middle-class parents in Mexico City between 1771 and 1773; of the actual date, he is not sure. As a child he is willful, and his mother's excessive devotion only makes him worse. He becomes such a scamp that his father sends him off to school. At school, he is nicknamed "Parrot." A little later, when he contracts the itch, his schoolmates nickname him "The Itching Parrot," or "Poll" for short. The name sticks to him through most of his life.

In addition to his nickname, Poll acquires many vicious habits from his schoolmates. Poll's father resolves to put Poll out as an apprentice in a trade, but Poll's mother, not wishing her son to disgrace her family by becoming a vulgar tradesman, insists that the boy be sent to college. Against his better judgment, the father agrees. After learning some

Latin, some Aristotle, some logic, and a little physics, Poll is awarded a baccalaureate degree by the College of San Ildefonso.

Shortly after receiving his degree, Poll goes into the countryside to visit a hacienda owned by the father of a former schoolmate. At the hacienda, he earns the hatred of his former schoolmate, Januario, by making advances to the latter's cousin, with whom Januario is infatuated. Januario takes his revenge by tempting Poll into a bullfight. Poll, who loses both the fight and his trousers, becomes the laughingstock of the hacienda. Still unsatisfied, Januario tricks Poll into trying to sleep with the girl cousin. Through Januario, the girl's mother discovers the attempt, beats Poll with her shoe, and sends him back to Mexico City in disgrace.

Upon his return to the city, Poll is told by his

father that he has to find some means of earning a livelihood. Poll, searching for the easiest way, decides that he will study theology and enter the church. Theology quickly proves uninteresting, and Poll gives up that idea. Trying to escape his father's insistence that he learn a trade, Poll then decides to enter a Franciscan monastery. There he soon finds that he cannot stand the life of a monk. He is pleased when his father's death gives him an excuse to leave the monastery. After a short period of mourning, Poll rapidly exhausts his small inheritance through his fondness for gambling, parties, and women. The sorrow he causes his mother sends her to an early death. After his mother dies, Poll is left alone. None of his relatives, who know him for a rogue, will have anything to do with him.

In his despair, Poll falls in with another schoolmate, who supports himself by gambling and trickery. Poll takes up a similar career in his schoolmate's company. A man he tricks discovers Poll's treachery and beats him severely. After his release from the hospital, Poll goes back to his gambling partner. They decide to become thieves. On their very first attempt, however, they are unsuccessful. Poll is caught and thrown into prison.

Because he has no family or friends to call upon, Poll languishes in jail for several months. He makes one friend in jail, Don Antonio, a man of good reputation who had been unjustly imprisoned. Although Don Antonio tries to keep Poll away from bad company, he is not entirely successful. When Don Antonio is freed, Poll falls in with a mulatto who gets him into all kinds of scrapes. By chance, Poll is taken up by a scrivener in need of an apprentice. The scrivener has Poll released from prison to become his apprentice. Poll's career as a scrivener's apprentice is short, for he makes love to the man's mistress, is discovered, and is driven from the house.

The next step in Poll's adventures is service as a barber's apprentice. He leaves that work to become a clerk in a pharmacy. After getting into trouble by carelessly mixing a prescription, Poll leaves the pharmacy for the employ of a doctor. Having picked up some jargon and a few cures from his doctor-employer, Poll sets out to be a physician. He causes a number of deaths and is forced to leave the profession.

Trying to recoup his fortunes once more, Poll returns to gambling. In a game he wins a lottery ticket that, in its turn, wins for him a small fortune. For a time, Poll lives well. He even marries a girl who believes that he is rich. The life the couple leads soon exhausts the lottery money. After his wife dies in childbirth, Poll sets out once again in search of his fortune. His work as a sacristan ends when he robs a corpse. Poll then joins a group of beggars. Finding that they are fakers, he reports them to the authorities. One of the officials, pleased with Poll, secures him a place in government service.

For a time all goes well, but Poll, left in charge of the district when his superior is absent, abuses his authority so much that he is arrested and sent in chains to Mexico City. There he is tried, found guilty of many crimes, and sent to the army for eight years.

As a result of his good conduct and pleasing appearance, Poll is made clerk to the colonel of the regiment. The colonel trusts Poll. When the regiment goes to Manila, the colonel sees to it that Poll is given an opportunity to do some trading and save up a small fortune. Poll completes his sentence and prepares to return to Mexico as a fairly rich man. His dreams and fortune vanish, however, when his ship sinks and he is cast away on an island. On the island, he makes friends with a Chinese man, in whose company Poll, pretending all the while to be a nobleman, returns to Mexico. When they reach Mexico, the lie is discovered, but the Chinese man continues to be Poll's friend and patron.

Poll stays with the Chinese man for some time, but he finally leaves in disgrace after having introduced prostitutes into the house. Leaving Mexico City, Poll meets the mulatto who had been his companion in jail. Along with the mulatto and some other men, Poll becomes a highwayman. He barely escapes with his life following their first holdup. Frightened, Poll goes into retreat at a church, where he discovers his confessor to be a former schoolmate. The kind confessor finds honest employment for Poll as an agent for a rich man.

Poll becomes an honest, hardworking citizen and becomes known as Don Pedro rather than Poll or The Itching Parrot. Years pass quickly. One day Don Pedro, befriending some destitute people, finds his benefactor of prison days, Don Antonio. Don Pedro marries Don Antonio's daughter, thus completing his respectability. He lives out the rest of his days in honesty, industry, and respect.

Analysis

The Itching Parrot is of special interest to literature students. Besides being the first true novel of Latin American literature and the only important Spanish American representative of the picaresque novel prior to the end of the twentieth century, it is of sociological interest. It compares reasonably well in entertainment value with good modern novels. It paints Mexican society in the last phase of the colonial period and the first years of national independence. *The Itching Parrot* is still widely read and has been published in approximately twenty editions.

The novel's primary aim is to satirize socioeconomic conditions in Mexico. Fernández de Lizardi's criticism of the abuses of his time is sound, and he promotes reform. Realism dominates *The Itching Parrot*, making it primarily a call for social reform, but the book has other virtues as well. It exposes charlatans and fakes at all levels and draws them well. The book is not pessimistic, even though most of its many episodes are depressing. The novel has a cheerful ending, proving that people are capable of reform. Class hatreds are absent, even though the author describes social inequalities and evils. Religious bias is also absent, even though individual Catholic priests are lampooned. The author's patriotism glows throughout the book, in glaring contrast to the selfishly corrupt politicians who mislead Mexico during the initial years of independence and whose stupidity leads directly to the loss of half of Mexico's national territory to the United States.

The book is written in good, basic Spanish. Its three hundred thousand words expose many evils, not only social but also political, for the last Spanish viceroys and the first rulers of independent Mexico were absolute monarchs who failed to use their powers wisely. Fernández de Lizardi flays the town bosses, who wallowed in extortion and corruption. He also exposes court clerks, tax collectors, police, jailers, the swarms of beggars, and merchants who use false weights. Even though a Catholic himself, who defended worthy clerics, he blasts individual priests, such as the one who drinks at a party and squabbles over a woman and another who refuses to interrupt his card game to give the last rites to a dying person.

The author's arrows do not spare the ignorant and lecherous teachers, lawyers, and doctors who infested the unhappy Mexico of his days. Hospitals were often horrible, pharmacists gouged for drugs, and doctors peddled fake nostrums. Nor is the antiquated university system spared—students argued logic all day, as was done in the Middle Ages, and learned little of practical value. Fernández de Lizardi especially resented the fact that the aristocracy and even the middle class scorned manual work, causing their young to waste their time as con men, card sharps, embezzlers, pimps, and the laziest of thugs.

The style of *The Itching Parrot* is direct. Action is never lacking, and a sense of anticipation tinges most of the book, along with episodes of adventure and travel.

Critical Context

This novel, written by the most rabid controversialist among Mexican authors during the unsettled years when Mexico was seeking to become independent of Spain, was suppressed after publication of the eleventh chapter in 1816, and the complete novel was not published until three years after the author's death. Scholars view it as the first Spanish American novel, and it is reputed to have sold more than one hundred million copies. Fernández de Lizardi managed to smuggle into the novel most of the polemical tracts that had earned him nationwide fame as "The Mexican Thinker," pamphlets directed against whomever sat at the head of the Mexican government, whether Spanish viceroy or revolutionist dictator. Fernández de Lizardi, like his fictional hero, spent many months in jail. He considered himself not to be a member of any political party, and many Mexican regimes resorted to prison sentences to silence him. Fernández de Lizardi, always placing Mexico above its rulers, alternately satirized and advised them.

JUBIABÁ

Author: Jorge Amado (1912-   )
Type of work: Novel
Type of plot: Romance
Time of plot: The 1920's and 1930's
Locale: The seaport city of Salvador, in the state of Bahia, Brazil, and neighboring areas
First published: 1935 (English translation, 1984)

Principal Characters

Antônio Balduíno, or **Baldo,** a black street-gang leader who survives successively as a beggar, singer and songwriter, professional boxer, plantation worker, circus artist, and eventually stevedore and strike leader. Antônio sees work as oppression. From an early age he is determined never to earn money by being employed and to become famous through adventurous exploits and thereby get a ballad, an ABC in local parlance, written about himself. When Lindinalva dies, after asking him to look after her son, he is forced to take a job to support the boy.

Jubiabá, an old voodoo priest. He is an important figure for Antônio, both as a friend and as a symbol of wisdom and independence.

Old Luísa, Antônio's aunt, who rears him alone until she goes crazy.

Zé Camarão, a storyteller, singer, and *capoeira* fighter. This mulatto is an important role model for Antônio, who admires him because he is brave and a good ballad singer. He teaches Antônio the guitar and *capoeira* fighting.

Amelia, a Portuguese cook who hates Antônio. She beats him often, declaring that Negroes are subhuman. She precipitates his running away from the house by lying that he has been ogling Lindinalva. Later, however, she takes care of Lindinalva and her son when the family is ruined.

Viriato, a deformed dwarf, part of Antônio's beggar gang and the only one of them who keeps on begging into adulthood. Usually sad because he is alone in the world, he is a successful beggar but eventually drowns himself.

Gordo, Antônio's best friend. Gordo meets Antônio when they are begging and accompanies him on most of his journeys thereafter.

Luigi, an Italian, Antônio's boxing manager and trainer, who later hires him for the circus.

Rosenda Rosedá, a beautiful black dancer whom Antônio meets at the circus. Although he finds her vain and silly, he likes her, and she has a strong character to match his.

Lindinalva Pereira, Antônio's lifelong love, the daughter of the Portuguese couple who take him in when his aunt goes mad. Lindinalva's fiancé, Gustavo, impregnates and abandons her when the family is ruined. She eventually turns to prostitution and dies after asking Antônio to look after her son.

Gustavo Barreira, Lindinalva's fiancé and father of Gustavinho. He is an ambitious lawyer who represents the workers in the strike and unsuccessfully attempts to get them to compromise their demands because the bosses promise to reward him.

Gustavinho, Lindinalva's baby son by Gustavo, later adopted by Antônio.

The Novel

Although *Jubiabá* is named for an old voodoo priest, the novel relates the romantic, adventurous life of Antônio Balduíno, a black hero of the Bahian masses. The loose, episodic story begins with

Antônio's childhood and continues through his mid-twenties. An ABC ballad at the end tells of his death at the hands of a treacherous murderer. Antônio thus realizes his lifelong ambition to become the subject of an ABC ballad.

The novel opens on a brief boxing match, showing Antônio, the Bahian heavyweight champion, beating the central European champion, a blond German, to the delight of the partisan Bahian crowd. Chapter 2 switches back to Antônio's childhood. As an eight-year-old, he lives with his old aunt, Luísa, and roams Capa-Negro Hill with his playmates, whom he leads into mischief. He does not attend school, but he absorbs a rich folklore from the poor people around him, especially Zé Camarão and old Jubiabá. For example, Jubiabá explains that Capa-Negro Hill got its name from a cruel white master who castrated slaves for not reproducing. Jubiabá also tells about Zumbi dos Palmares, a slave who ran away and led a warlike confederation of other runaways. Zumbi dos Palmares becomes Antônio's hero.

When his aunt goes crazy, the twelve-year-old Antônio is adopted by a well-to-do white family, the Pereiras, who live on Zumbi dos Palmares Street. The Pereiras give him some schooling and light servant's duties and make him a companion of Lindinalva, their daughter. Amelia, the white cook, beats him constantly and, when he is fifteen, accuses him of looking at Lindinalva's legs. Antônio is punished severely and runs away. He completes his growing up on the seafront streets of Salvador, where he leads a gang of intimidating young "beggars" and sleeps with girls on the nearby sand dunes. After two years, the police break up his gang by arresting the members and beating them with rubber thongs.

Antônio returns to Capa-Negro Hill, where he learns *capoeira* fighting and guitar playing from Zé Camarão. He earns his livelihood by composing and selling an occasional samba that invariably makes the Bahian hit parade, but he spends most of his time attending parties, festivals, and Jubiabá's wild *macumba* sessions and making love to Joana, Maria dos Reis, and other eager girls. His life takes an exciting turn when, discovered and trained by Luigi, he becomes a professional boxer. Known as Baldo the Negro, he demolishes all competition. He appears to be bound for Rio de Janeiro and North America, but he learns of Lindinalva's engagement on the day of a big bout, gets drunk, and is knocked out by Miguez the Peruvian.

Antônio begins a two-year period of wandering. Ashamed and in disgrace, he sails on the *Homeless Traveler* up the Paraguaçu River to the tobacco country, where he and his pal Gordo work in the tobacco fields. Without women, he becomes so desperate that he lusts after a twelve-year-old girl at her mother's wake, even though the bloated corpse eyes him accusingly. He eventually gets into a knife fight with the boss, Zequinha. Thinking that he has killed Zequinha (who lives but wants revenge), Antônio flees and evades a massive manhunt. He winds up in Feira de Santana, where he again meets Luigi, now part owner of a near-bankrupt circus. Antônio joins the circus, fighting challengers or the bear and falling in love with Rosenda Rosedá, a sexy black ballerina. When the circus fails, he, Rosenda, and the bear return to Salvador.

In Salvador, the bear goes to Gordo, and Antônio and Rosenda eventually split up. Again Antônio hears of Lindinalva, whose fortunes have plummeted. Her father died bankrupt, and her fiancé left her pregnant. After the baby was born, Lindinalva turned to prostitution. Now, physically spent, she is dying, and on her deathbed she evokes a promise from Antônio to help Amelia care for little Gustavinho. Antônio goes to work as a stevedore, just in time to become involved in a bitter strike. Ironically, the workers' negotiator is the lawyer Gustavo Barreira, Gustavinho's father, who sells out to the owners. The workers reject Barreira's watered-down deal, however, as well as Barreira himself; the strike continues, spreads to other workers throughout the city, and becomes violent. With Antônio as one of their leaders, the workers hold out and triumph, winning all of their demands.

Analysis

Antônio's conversion from good-time Charlie to man of commitment embodies the two main themes of *Jubiabá*, which, like Antônio's two phases, seem somewhat inconsistent. On one hand, Amado celebrates the local color of Bahia, particularly its Afro-Brazilian culture. He refers to local history and waxes poetic about the city of Salvador, its environs, and the sea. He incorporates bits of local folklore, songs, and superstitions. The richest of this local culture seems to belong to the poor blacks who inhabit Capa-Negro Hill. They enjoy a sense of community, are fun-loving, and have a priest who wields the powers of African voodoo.

On the other hand, Amado pursues a political theme, championing the downtrodden poor, including residents of Capa-Negro Hill. Beautiful Bahia, it seems, is rife with social injustice, represented most poignantly by the near-bankrupt circus, the performers of which go on display and risk their lives daily but rarely earn enough to make ends meet. Amado suggests that one solution is to fight back—to go on strike, shut down the city, and take power into one's own hands. Why should the circus' hungry lion cry, when it can eat its trainer?

The slumbering power of the poor is symbolized by the drums rolling out over the city, by the fervor of the *macumba* sessions, and, most of all, by the rippling muscles of Baldo the Negro. His fighting spirit is inherited from Africa and handed on to him by Jubiabá. For a long time, Antônio expends his energy in aimless loving and fighting, in boxing matches and circus acts. Even he eventually becomes aware of the lack of purpose in his life. In the end, he learns to love the suffering poor and to direct his fighting spirit at their oppressors.

Critical Context

Any critical estimate of *Jubiabá*, with its rambling plot, its inconsistent characters and themes, its uneven style, and its gross excesses, must take into account that Amado wrote it during his early twenties: It is a fervent young man's novel. For all of its logical disunity and lack of restraint, *Jubiabá* has a powerful unity of feeling, as Amado announces his loyalties to Bahia, to Afro-Brazilian culture, and to leftist politics. This emotional unity makes *Jubiabá* perhaps the best of Amado's early propagandistic works, certainly a representative example.

Amado's early work long remained untranslated into English; therefore, for readers of English familiar only with his mature work—particularly such comic, sexy best sellers as *Gabriela, Cravo e Canela* (1958; *Gabriela, Clove and Cinnamon*, 1962), *Dona Flor e Seus Dois Maridos* (1966; *Dona Flor and Her Two Husbands*, 1969), and *Tiêta do Agreste* (1977; *Tieta, the Goat Girl*, 1979)—his early propagandistic phase may come as a surprise. As a formative novel, *Jubiabá* forecasts much of the later Amado. Although he toned down his politics (after repeated clashes with censors, jail terms, and exiles), no one can deny Amado's continuing interest in local color and sex; nor, if his techniques have become more refined, can he be accused of developing inhibitions or restraint. With his political sympathies, his panorama of local color and characters, and his lack of restraint (whether sentimental or sexual), Amado might be called the twentieth century Brazilian Charles Dickens.

THE KINGDOM OF THIS WORLD

Author: Alejo Carpentier (1904-1980)
Type of work: Novel
Type of plot: Magical Realism
Time of plot: 1750 to after 1830
Locale: Haiti, Cuba, and Italy
First published: *El reino de este mundo*, 1949 (English translation, 1957)

Principal Characters

Ti Noël, a house slave and rebel. He witnessed and at times participated in many of the events in the novel. He is faced with the problem of deciding whether he should use the knowledge he has acquired during the course of many years to answer the needs of his people.

Monsieur Lenormand de Mezy, a plantation owner and Ti Noël's master. He is caricatured as having cheeks caked with powder and a stupid smile. After the slave rebellion led by Bouckman, he is forced to flee to Cuba. He functions as a representative of the oppressive presence of European culture and "civilization."

Mackandal, a fugitive slave, a rebel, and Ti Noël's spiritual mentor. The first of the novel's four sections narrates his exploits. He is finally captured and burned at the stake in 1758.

Pauline Bonaparte, wife of General Leclerc and a symbol of decadent European culture. Her frivolity, sensuality, luxury, and cowardice when the plague strikes, followed by her renewed self-indulgence while escorting her husband's body home to France, climax Carpentier's presentation

of white decadence in contrast to the virility and vitality of the blacks.

Soliman, Pauline's voodoo-practicing black masseur. He rejects his African past, works as Henri Christophe's valet, and travels to Rome with Christophe's wife and daughters.

Henri Christophe, the first black king of Haiti. He governs the country even more oppressively than did the French settlers before him. The third section of the novel deals with Christophe, a hero who becomes a tyrant. His rule is characterized not only by oppression but also by Europeanization and the rejection of local beliefs. The section ends with the collapse of his rule and his loneliness, betrayal, and suicide.

Boyer, a mulatto ruler. The final and fourth part of the novel deals with the government of Boyer (1820-1843), a time of continued oppression but also of reunification after the collapse of Christophe's government. During his rule, many of the old abuses are still perpetuated, and there is a definite need for a renewed struggle against tyranny.

The Novel

Mixing history and fiction, *The Kingdom of This World* recounts the transition of Haiti from slavery to emancipation and from colony to republic. The change occurs through the use of African religion. The novel begins by establishing a difference between black African culture and white

European culture. Although these two systems take on different forms throughout the novel and history, they remain antagonistic toward each other. One is dynamic, the other static. Mackandal, Bouckman, and Ti Noël represent the liberating spirit of African religion and culture, while Monsieur Lenormand de Mezy, Monsieur Blancheland, General Leclerc, Rochambeau, Henri Christophe, and the Mulatto Republicans represent the oppressive force of European culture. The two groups offer conflicting interpretations of history; the novel supports the African perspective.

Mackandal initiates the struggle against slaveowners. After losing an arm in a sugar mill accident, he studies poisonous plants as a means of fighting the whites. Drawing on his knowledge of African lore, he transforms himself into an animal or an insect to elude his pursuers. When Mackandal is captured and burned at the stake, the whites who are present witness his death, but the blacks see him transformed into an insect, and they watch as he escapes. This important passage illustrates clearly the difference between the European and African worldviews.

Bouckman and Ti Noël follow in Mackandal's tradition and continue to fight for the liberation of blacks. Bouckman plays a prominent role during emancipation, and Ti Noël during the struggle against Henri Christophe and the Mulatto Republicans. To Ti Noël, Mackandal is a spiritual father of sorts and a link with the African past.

After the success of the Haitian Revolution, in which the French are ousted from the island, Henri Christophe rules the northern part of Haiti. The ruthless Christophe betrays his own people and continues to oppress them; with his reign, oppression transcends racial designation. Like Mackandal and Bouckman before him, using a knowledge of voodoo, Ti Noël joins the struggle against the enslavement of the Haitian people.

The novel ends by proposing that the cycle of oppression and liberation is ongoing, perhaps endless. Recognizing this cyclic pattern in human history and disillusioned with the prospects for meaningful change, Ti Noël transforms himself and escapes into the animal and insect worlds. He soon discovers, however, that their world, although superficially harmonious, is not any different from the human one. Having gained a greater understanding of his life and destiny through African religion, Ti Noël continues the fight against oppression and for liberation.

Analysis

The Kingdom of This World relates history and fiction. Events in the novel have been documented with precision. In its historical investigation, the novel discloses a cyclical structure: If there are movements of oppression, there will be others of rebellion; if there are movements of rebellion, there will be others of oppression. The cycles documented in the novel continue into contemporary Haitian history. When Carpentier arrived in Haiti in 1943, Élie Lescot was president. Popular reaction against his corrupt government led to the election of Dumarsais Estimé in 1946, but Estimé's benevolent government was soon followed by the dictatorships of François "Papa Doc" Duvalier and his son, Jean-Claude. Using Carpentier's structure, one could foresee the defeat of Jean-Claude Duvalier in favor of a popular government, but also the defeat of that government and the imposition of another ruthless one. The displacement of one by another appears to be inevitable.

The Kingdom of This World offers profound insight into the problems regarding the founding of the first black nation and the first country to receive independence in Latin America and the Caribbean. The racial and cultural tensions depicted in the novel were indeed present from the moment Africans were brought to the New World. These tensions, however, became more intense during the time of the novel, toward the end of the eighteenth century, mainly because of the development of the sugar industry. The Haitian Revolution brought the black struggle to a climax but not to an end. With Christophe and other black and mulatto rulers, the racial confrontation between whites and blacks evolved into a struggle between those who accept and those who reject African religion.

Thus, the black struggle is not only political but also religious. A religious interpretation, which the novel strongly suggests, highlights a broader strategy in which people are but mere participants. During the night of the Solemn Pact, Bouckman, in his final admonition, reveals the following: "The white men's God orders the crime. Our gods demand vengeance from us. They will guide our arms and give us help. Destroy the image of the white man's God who thirsts for our tears; let us listen to the cry of freedom within ourselves." The historical, cultural, and religious themes of the novel complement one another.

Critical Context

In the prologue to the original edition of *The Kingdom of This World*, Carpentier discusses what he calls "Marvelous Realism," anticipating the vogue for the closely related term Magical Realism, which has been widely used to describe the style that brought the Latin American novel to international prominence in the 1960's and 1970's. Only a style that embraces the marvelous, or the magical, he suggests, is capable of doing justice to the reality of the New World. In the novel itself, although not in the prologue, Carpentier emphasizes the African component in the heterogenous culture of the Americas, linking Marvelous Realism to African traditions.

In *The Kingdom of This World*, Carpentier continued the exploration of black history begun in such early works as *Ecue-Yamba-O! Historia Afro-Cubana* (1933) and "El milagro de Anaquillé" (1927), a scenario for a ballet. Of Carpentier's works with a black theme, *The Kingdom of This World* is clearly his best. Within the context of Cuban literature, his concern with blacks and the theme of slavery is not isolated. *The Kingdom of This World* is part of a continuum from the antislavery narratives of the 1830's to the literature of the Cuban Revolution. By writing about the lives of an important but marginal segment of Western society, Carpentier brings the history of blacks to the foreground of literature.

Although many critics regard *El siglo de las luces* (1962; *Explosion in a Cathedral*, 1963) as Carpentier's greatest literary accomplishment, Carpentier himself continued to believe in the historical significance of *The Kingdom of This World*, citing the importance of Mackandal, Bouckman, and the Haitian Revolution for an understanding of Caribbean history and culture. There is no need to choose one novel over the other: They are best read together. *Explosion in a Cathedral* is set during the Haitian transition from colony to republic—that is, from 1789 to 1809—and many of the themes developed in that novel are already present in *The Kingdom of This World*.

KISS OF THE SPIDER WOMAN

Author: Manuel Puig (1932-1990)
Type of work: Novel
Type of plot: Impressionistic realism
Time of plot: The mid-1970's
Locale: Buenos Aires, Argentina
First published: *El beso de la mujer araña* (English translation, 1979)

Principal Characters

Luis Alberto Molina, a window dresser imprisoned for the corruption of a minor. Molina is a homosexual who views himself as a woman. He believes that in any relationship he has with a man, the man should be dominant. He has an exceptional memory for films, and he entertains and distracts Valentin by telling the story lines of romantic films he has seen.

Valentin Arregui Paz, a revolutionary who is being held indefinitely as a political prisoner. Valentin is in many ways the exact opposite of his cellmate, Molina. Valentin is a "man's man," and he believes that emotions are a weakness that, as a revolutionary committed to his cause, he cannot afford. A change occurs in his personality, however, when he finally admits that he is not pining for his equally politically committed girlfriend but, rather, that he intensely misses his former lover, Marta, who had no interest in politics, only in love. Molina's storytelling helps Valentin to become less repressed.

The Novel

Nearly all of *Kiss of the Spider Woman* takes places in an Argentine prison cell. Except for a police report, extensive footnotes to various classic studies of homosexuality, and a few stream-of-consciousness passages, the novel concentrates on several conversations between Molina and Valentin. Valentin never calls his cellmate by his first name, and Molina never calls Valentin by his last. As a radical, Valentin resists the personal advances of Molina and tries to put their relationship on a formal basis, arguing that to show any softness or to enjoy any intimacy is sure to ruin his single-minded dedication to overthrow the government. Molina, on the other hand, favors relationships that are as close as possible, no matter what the political consequences of such romantic attachments.

There is much in Molina's behavior that Valentin finds disgusting. Molina is passive and un-disciplined, and he thinks of himself as a woman who would love to be dominated by a strong man. He is not committed to fighting injustice, and he savors the pleasures of life much too keenly. He exhibits, in other words, all the worst characteristics of people who allow themselves to be subjugated.

Molina, however, is not a selfish person. He derives considerable pleasure from helping others and from sharing whatever he has with them. Although he resents Valentin's rebuffs, he doggedly refuses to remain offended. Molina is naturally outgoing and simply does not believe that Valentin must pursue an ascetic routine of study and self-denial. For all of his seeming weakness, Molina has an extraordinarily strong character that cannot be cowed by Valentin's lectures on manhood and self-determination.

It is not by arguing about Valentin's values, however, that Molina eventually wins him over. Rather, it is through the recounting of motion pictures he has seen. The novel begins with Molina's retelling of one of his favorite films, a film that Valentin obviously enjoys even if he tries to maintain his distance by resorting to jokes, criticisms, and other devices of his rational mind. Like Molina, Valentin is carried away by the film. He begins to care deeply about the characters and eventually admits to comparing his life with theirs.

A struggle then ensues between the two prisoners even as they draw closer to each other. Valentin would have Molina see that he likes precisely those parts of films in which individuals turn into the slaves of others. A man in a film about a panther woman, for example, enjoys his woman precisely because she is helpless and infantile in her fear that she will turn into a panther. Molina, for his part, clearly enjoys involving Valentin in romantic plots in which the lovers (in one case, a French woman and one of the Nazi occupiers of her country) are irresistibly drawn to each other in spite of social and political obstacles.

For both prisoners, the remembered films help to pass the time. Sometimes the films energize them; sometimes the films help them to fall asleep. They exist intact, with their own kind of reality. Valentin is aware of how Molina tends to embroider what he remembers, but all the same the exaggeration is filmlike and absolutely compelling in the intimacy that is established. Soon Valentin cannot live without this kind of romantic intensity, and Molina is called on to retell one film after another.

Analysis

All of Molina's films have to do with romantic entanglements. The characters are caught in webs of passion they cannot escape, as are Molina and Valentin. Molina is like the spider woman of a movie ensnaring her lover, or this, at least, is what is suggested when Molina finally persuades Valentin to kiss him. On the other hand, Valentin has been the woman, for he has been seduced by Molina, who in turn promises to deliver a message to Valentin's political allies shortly after he has been released from prison.

The nexus between politics and art is complex in *Kiss of the Spider Woman*. Cinema is an art form that creates a powerful claim on human emotions, so much so that people try to live their lives as films. At the beginning of the novel, Valentin rejects this kind of devotion to art. He does not want to believe that art is autonomous, for that would mean it creates its own values divorced from the reality that Valentin tries to study and to change. He does not want to believe that women should submit to men, as they do in motion pictures.

Valentin tries to repress his own romantic tendencies. He is abrupt and sometimes pompous with Molina. All of his efforts go toward retaining rigid control over his feelings. He is embarrassed by any signs of physical or mental weakness and is astounded by Molina's nursing of him when he is sick. Like a mother, Molina nurtures Valentin and loves him.

At various strategic points at which Molina's homosexuality is alluded to or is evident by implication in the way he treats Valentin, footnotes summarize conflicting accounts of the causes of homosexuality. Much of the scientific discussion centers on the concept of repression. Various thinkers take issue with Sigmund Freud's notion that repression has been essential in the development of civilization. It seems less important to master each thinker's position than it is to see that the repression of certain forms of sexuality has led to the romantically tense relationship between Molina and Valentin and to the film plots about many different kinds of forbidden love.

Valentin has held back much of himself because that is the way he believes a civilization is built. Molina reacts against this repression by identifying with its traditional targets—women, whom, he believes, represent the caring, giving aspects of humanity on which civilization ought to be built.

Some of the footnotes are pages in length. They indirectly comment on the arguments between Molina and Valentin by showing that there is no agreement on exactly what causes homosexuality.

Some scholars cited speak for a liberation of sexual repression; illustrated, in part, by Molina's efforts to get Valentin to loosen up. At the same time, however, neither prisoner's arguments have been fully endorsed by the scientific studies of sexuality.

Critical Context

Puig studied philosophy at the University of Buenos Aires and in 1957 won a scholarship to study film direction in Rome. His novels reflect a profound exploration of how human beings have tried to transform their lives into art. He has recalled his own immersion in films while living in a small town on the Argentine pampas. For him, politics has to contend with the inclination to escape from reality to a world of the individual's own making.

For Puig, films are the finest example of life escaping into art. *Kiss of the Spider Woman*, his fourth novel, is his most direct use of the film fantasies that have appeared in all of his fiction. Favorably reviewed when it first appeared in the United States, his novel is reflective of the intense interest Latin American novelists have shown in the cinema. The images their characters have of themselves and others have been undeniably shaped by filmgoing, which becomes a reality in itself, a way of seeing that has to be dealt with as seriously as does the philosophy and psychology in the footnotes to *Kiss of the Spider Woman*.

The 1985 film version does not follow Puig's point that Valentin and Molina are using each other. In the film, the story is primarily about Molina's transfiguration through the power of love and happiness. In the novel, that story is there, but it is tempered by the ambiguous motives of the two men. By footnoting their dialogue, for example, the author calls into question the extent to which sexuality per se is understood in Western culture. The characters' speeches are, in part, treated as elaborate rationalizations that the love story of the film would have its viewers accept at face value.

THE LABYRINTH OF SOLITUDE: Life and Thought in Mexico

Author: Octavio Paz (1914-   )
Type of work: Essays
First published: *El laberinto de la soledad: Vida y pensamiento de México*, 1950 (rev. ed. 1959; English translation, 1961)

The Work

Widely acknowledged as the greatest poet of contemporary Mexico, Octavio Paz has led a life that in many ways is typical of the Mexican intelligentsia he describes in *The Labyrinth of Solitude*. He has published ten books of poetry, fought with the Loyalists in Spain, and served his country as a diplomat. Deeply involved in the future of the Mexican land, he has equipped himself to define it to the world by a career that includes the experiences of intense action and even more intense contemplation.

The Labyrinth of Solitude was first published in 1950 by Jesús Silva Herzog's famous and influential magazine, *Cuadernos Americanos*. The version that comes through Lysander Kemp's translation is based upon a second edition, revised and expanded, published by the Fondo de Cultura Económica in 1959. This book is in effect the result of labors that span a decade, labors that show themselves best in Paz's mastery of his own implications: The labyrinth he describes is the modern world.

Paz begins with an analysis of the phenomenon of the *pachucos*, youths of Latin descent who during the 1940's and 1950's alarmed the cities of the American Southwest with their "antisocial" behavior, their peculiar dress, and their hostile acts and attitudes. He sees the *pachuco* as standing between Mexican culture and North American culture, in a limbo, unable to accept the values of

either, equally alienated from both. Moreover, says Paz, the *pachuco* has, without understanding them, reasons: Both cultures have cut themselves off from the flux of life and have failed in their separate ways to reconcile people and the universe. Unable to partake of communion, both the Mexican and the North American have thus become spiritual orphans, imprisoned in the sterility of solitude. If the Mexican seclusion is similar to stagnant water, Paz says, North America is similar to a mirror. Neither contains life.

The forces that confine the North American are summarized in three sets of laws: the seventeenth century religious code of John Calvin, the eighteenth century political code of the American founding fathers, and the nineteenth century moral code of the American Victorians. Caged by these sets of laws, the North American has become a cipher, handling the universe easily by simply denying any part of it that might conflict with these codes. The North American lives, therefore, in a wholly artificial world, creating his psychological mothers and fathers out of a Panglossian delusion. The Mexican, on the other hand—and here Paz has the support not only of innumerable Mexican observers but also of informed outsiders—has no such delusions, but sees himself or herself more or less clearly in orphanhood, without a mother and without a father.

Analysis

For a Mexican, Paz says, life is a combat in which the role as an isolated individual can only

be defensive. To North Americans with some experience of Mexico, the best image for this role is perhaps one that Paz, as a Mexican, is not in an objective position to suggest: the blindfolded child cautiously rushing in, stick raised but head averted, to smash the Christmas *piñata*. Concealing himself or herself behind a mask of reserve, the Mexican is in reality blindfolded, violent, and fearful, like such a child, as well as trapped in the lie of apparent stoicism. Interior turbulence is a torture, while exterior defensiveness destroys even the possibility of the communion that might bring happiness. The Mexican's world is therefore hollow, self-consuming, masochistic, and devoid of love, for what love he or she knows is merely a form of narcissism. Paz says that Mexicans refuse to progress beyond themselves, to free themselves, to expose themselves to the outside world. If North American happiness exists only in neutralizing illusions, Mexican happiness exists only in remotest theory.

Relief comes to a certain extent with the fiesta, a uniquely Mexican plunge into chaos from which the group emerges purified and strengthened, a drunken rapture during which the individual briefly confronts himself or herself. The fiesta, however, cannot wholly offset the lack of communion; it is too impermanent, short-lived, and unstable. The Mexican oscillates between intimacy and withdrawal, shouting and silence, fiesta and wake, without ever surrendering to anything but himself or herself. Despite fiestas, the Mexican never really transcends solitude.

Paz sees this solitude in Mexico as largely the result of the reform movement that, following many years after independence, finally disrupted both the Aztec and colonial traditions. The new Spanish American nations are not new, he claims. Instead, he views them as static or decadent societies, survivals of older, more integrated cultures. Reform was thus an attempt at social reanimation. Its method, however, was based not upon indigenous realities but rather upon abstract and geometrical reasoning imported from Europe. The profoundest effect of the liberal Constitution of 1857 was therefore the creation of a split between the individual Mexican and the native past. The Mexican became inevitably, at the moment of that split,

the orphan that he or she remains.

The revolution that came after reform can be seen as a movement meant to overcome this orphanhood, to reconquer the past, to assimilate it, and to make it live in the present. Paz finds particular significance in the Zapatistas, whose program to reinstitute the ancient systems of land tenure epitomized the revolution on its ideological side. The revolution was above all, however, a "fiesta of bullets," the orgiastic celebration of a total Mexico daring at length to be, and to be in communion with itself.

Mexico's success in maintaining this communion after the shooting ceased has been, for various historical reasons, sharply limited. The essential solitude that Paz describes in his early chapters still stands, as tragic as ever, with its accompanying problems. These problems are not solely Mexican: They are universal. In his view, the crisis of modern times is not the opposition of two great and different cultures but an inward struggle of one civilization that, unrivaled, is shaping the future of the whole world. Each person's fate involves all humanity. Thus Mexicans cannot solve their problems as Mexicans, for they are involved in matters that are universal, not merely national.

The existence of "underdeveloped" countries and of totalitarian "socialist" regimes in the twentieth century Paz regards as equally anomalous, equally scandalous, and equally symptomatic of the social chaos that is the outward and visible sign of the labyrinth of solitude. All too often an underdeveloped country attempting to emerge from its economic prison becomes another victim of totalitarianism. The real cure for chaos and sterility, says Paz, must therefore lie in an outgrowing and a rejection of those false divinities that rule the modern world: endless, infinite work and fixed, finite, chronometric time.

People pretend that they are wide awake when they are thinking, but this is not true; usually thinking leads into the nightmare of reason. After the nightmare is over, one may realize that he or she was dreaming and that dreams of reason are unbearable. With this in mind, one may then close one's eyes to dream once more. The only alternatives to the continuing frustration of labyrinthine solitude are suicide or some new kind of creative involvement and participation, the exercise of loving imagination in communion with the rest of the world.

Critical Context

The Labyrinth of Solitude is a wise book. Years spent in Paris have not seduced Octavio Paz into succumbing to the pathetic charms still held out by a waning existentialism. He avoids the promulgation of a doctrine, achieving instead the kind of essential statement that one should expect from a poet. Not only should the book prove stimulating to anyone who thinks at all about the nature of the world and how its conditions affect humanity; it should also provide perhaps the best gloss yet available on Paz's own work. His great poem *Piedra de sol* (1957), for example, which can be read in English versions, embodies to near perfection the sort of loving and unsolitary imagination for which, in *The Labyrinth of Solitude*, he pleads.

LEAF STORM

Author: Gabriel García Márquez (1928-   )
Type of work: Novel
Type of plot: Magical Realism
Time of plot: The late nineteenth and early twentieth centuries
Locale: Macondo, an imaginary town in Colombia
First published: *La hojarasca*, 1955 (English translation, 1972)

Principal Characters

The doctor, a resident of Macondo for a quarter-century, a grass-eater, an insomniac, and a suicide by hanging. The doctor is variously perceived as lustful and vulgar, animal-like, without pity, hardened, and already dead before death. He is the focus of interior monologues emanating from the colonel, Isabel, and the child. Possibly French, his name is never known. A night of rebellion brings patients to his door, but the doctor refuses to treat wounded men, saying that he has "forgotten" his profession. This denial makes the community long to see his death.

The colonel, a retired military officer. He feels pity and sorrow for the doctor's isolation. As the novella ends, the colonel is about to fulfill his promise to bury the doctor.

Isabel, the daughter of the colonel, an abandoned wife and mother of the child. She is a woman wounded by departures: her mother's death in childbirth, the loss of Meme, Martín's disappearance, and Adelaida's self-effacement. Longing to abide by convention and the town's judgment of the doctor, Isabel fears the result of her father's promise, which she perceives as intolerable.

The child, Isabel's son. Almost eleven, the boy conveys the astonished and colorful perceptions of one who does not fully understand what he sees.

Meme, the colonel's Indian foster child and servant, and the doctor's mistress and servant. Meme creates for Isabel a legendary past in her account of the nineteenth century journey to Macondo. She vanishes about eleven years before the doctor's death; the town suspects that the doctor murdered Meme.

The mayor, the representative of the town, who attempts to delay the burial and fulfill the community's desire for the doctor to remain unburied. He is, however, equally interested in a bribe.

Martín, Isabel's husband. Married to Isabel eleven years before the novel's events, Martín vanished two years later with the colonel's signed notes as financial backing.

Adelaida, the colonel's second wife. The colonel portrays his wife as a once-dominant and vigorous figure who is now sterile, eaten up with religion and superstition.

The pup, a priest. The pup is a mirror image of the doctor, who is disturbed by the idea of a present or absent God. A mysterious resemblance and the coincidence of their arrival in Macondo on the same day connect the two men. The pup's strong grip on the town allows him to protect and save the doctor after he denies treatment to injured men.

The Novel

Leaf Storm is narrated through three alternating interior monologues: those of the colonel, his daughter Isabel, and her son. Through this structure, García Márquez chronicles the founding of the imaginary coastal town of Macondo in the late nineteenth century, its prosperity during the 1910's, and its decadence after 1918. This is the story of the arrival and exit of the "leaf storm," the hordes of outsiders and foreigners who descended on the Colombian coast as the region grew rich on the banana industry during a short period of wealth that ended as quickly as it had begun.

As the novel begins, the doctor has hanged himself and the colonel prepares to oversee the burial of the body. It is learned that ten years earlier, the rest of the townspeople had sworn to oppose this burial, and that the colonel is honoring a personal pledge he had made earlier to the dead man to defy the will of the others. The reason for the town's hostility is only made clear later, as each of the three narrations goes back in time and tells the story of the doctor's twenty-five-year stay in Macondo. At the novel's close, the family prepares to form a funeral cortege with the coffin. The reaction of their neighbors is left unknown.

The three ongoing monologues do not proceed in a linear manner. Many incidents mentioned by one character are taken up later by another. The reader is thus engaged in a constant process of reevaluation and reconsideration of prior clues. The effect is somewhat like that of a mystery novel, in which facts are revealed by one character and corroborated later by another, but in *Leaf Storm* there is no suspense. The plot is circular, for as the twenty-five years between 1903 and 1928 unfold, little changes for the people who describe the events. The colonel and Isabel relate dispassionately the events of those years in a matter-of-fact tone that reveals little emotion. The child provides the perspective of an innocent observer who understands nothing of the facts, while intuitively seeing what exists beneath the controlled exterior of elders.

Leaf Storm, then, serves as an allegory for the broader upheaval in the life of the Colombian coast brought on by foreign investment in the early part of the twentieth century. Through the memories of the colonel and Isabel, the class structure of this society, its patterns of daily life, customs, and religious beliefs are described. The doctor's suicide and his years in Macondo provide the framework for those memories.

Analysis

In *Leaf Storm*, as in many other works of García Márquez, the principal themes are those of the effect of economic forces in the shaping of society in Latin America and of the position of the individual within that society. In Macondo, the class divisions never change, although the town goes through a great upheaval. There is here a somewhat pessimistic view of individual control over destiny, but, at the same time, Macondo is a magical place in its everyday life, and that magic overcomes the harsh realities. The novel begins García Márquez's experimentation with themes of Magical Realism, a kind of writing begun earlier in the twentieth century by Latin American writers. This style incorporates elements of the fantastic (for example, a man who eats grass, a priest who takes his sermons from almanacs instead of the Bible) and combines them with details from daily life. The meaning of this combination is that life in Latin America is often fantastic and somewhat magical, and that this is accepted in a town such as Macondo, which serves as an archetype.

The narrative structure of *Leaf Storm*, the interior monologues that develop the plot and the characters, is inseparable from these themes. The structure reminds the reader at all times of the historical progression in the larger society, juxtaposed with the stagnation of individual lives. García Márquez constructs a narrative to be read both for the pleasure of the story it tells and for its broader message.

Critical Context

Leaf Storm was García Márquez's first novel, following the publication of various short stories. Its themes and characters mark the beginning of the saga of Macondo, a town created in its author's imagination much as William Faulkner created the locales of his novels. Indeed, Faulkner has been recognized by García Márquez as one of his most important literary influences.

This novel is considered by critics of Latin American fiction to be a prefiguration of its author's great work, *Cien años de soledad* (1967; *One Hundred Years of Solitude*, 1970). Along with other shorter tales and novels, *Leaf Storm* introduces characters and situations that will return, in much expanded form, in *One Hundred Years of Solitude*. The story of the doctor's arrival and suicide, for example, is explained in the longer novel. Macondo, at the end of *One Hundred Years of Solitude*, disappears as retribution for its tremendous growth and decadence, providing a final end to the allegory.

In 1982, García Márquez was awarded the Nobel Prize in Literature, following other Latin American writers such as Gabriela Mistral and Pablo Neruda. He is recognized as one of the leading modern novelist/story writers, and he is an active commentator on contemporary Latin American culture, especially in its relationship to society, a theme well begun in *Leaf Storm* and carried out in his later works.

THE LEAN LANDS

Author: Agustín Yáñez (1904-1980)
Type of work: Novel
Type of plot: Philosophical realism
Time of plot: The early 1920's
Locale: A typical, isolated, high-plain, sparsely populated region of Jalisco, Mexico, called Tierra Santa (Holy Land)
First published: *Las tierras flacas*, 1962 (English translation, 1968)

Principal Characters

Epifanio Trujillo, a landowner and patriarch, father of approximately one hundred children by various mistresses. He has spent his life accumulating land, cattle, women, and children. Fat and lethargic in his old age, he comes under the complete domination of his daughter, Plácida. Because he failed to specify how his estate would be divided, he witnesses his heirs struggle among themselves for supremacy.

Miguel Arcángel Trujillo (Jacob Gallo), a son of Epifanio Trujillo and Sara Gallo. He married against his father's wishes, adopted his mother's surname, and sought his fortune elsewhere. Returning to his father's domain a wealthy landowner in his own right, he is determined to use his wealth and knowledge to bring progress to the lean lands. He outwits his half brothers and sister, gains control of his father's estate, and becomes the dominant authority.

Plácida Trujillo, a daughter of Don Epifanio and mistress of his house. As prudish as her father was licentious, she is coldhearted and cruel.

Jesús Trujillo, son of Don Epifanio. He cloaks his evil intentions with fine manners and sweet talk. He instigates the mutilation of Matiana, anticipating that it will result in the fall of Jacob Gallo and allow him to gain complete control over his father's estate. Instead, the peasants rise up to destroy the Trujillos.

Felipe Trujillo, a son of Don Epifanio. In order to prevent Jesús from winning his father's favor and gaining advantage over him in the struggle for the inheritance, Felipe seizes Teófila's sewing machine from Jesús. After Matiana is blinded by Jesús' hired thugs, the enraged peasants hang him and return Teófila's sewing machine to her parents.

Rómulo Garabito, a poor and fatalistic peasant who is the grandson of Teódulo Garabito and the father of Teófila. Don Epifanio gives him the choice of giving up his deceased daughter's sewing machine or losing his farm to pay off his debts. Rómulo is saved from this dilemma by Jacob Gallo, who presents Don Epifanio with a new sewing machine for his birthday.

Teófila Garabito, the saintly daughter of Rómulo. Don Epifanio is obsessed with her and hopes to marry her. When she dies of meningitis at the age of twenty, her parents are certain that God has rescued her from Don Epifanio. The destruction of the Trujillos through her sewing machine is considered to be her most important miracle.

Matiana, an old midwife with a reputation for being a witch. She serves as mediator between the peasants and the supernatural, using her mental powers to execute justice in favor of the weak. Her mutilation at the hands of Jesús' hired thugs precipitates the peasant uprising that destroys the power of the Trujillos.

The Novel

The Lean Lands portrays a transitional moment in the history of the Trujillo family, the sociopolitical center of the region. The action involves an internecine war among the three half-brothers to gain access to the power held by their ill father, Don Epifanio.

Consistent with the *hacendado* system (a parafeudal system of land ownership), throughout his life, Epifanio has conformed majestically to the traditional functions of the *cacique*, the Arawak term for tribal chief. Arrogantly, he has subjugated all in the region to his arbitrary and willful nature in various ways. Chief among them is the long-held prerogative of having multiple "wives" to create an enormous progeny. Sensuality is totally lacking in the "conquests," which are motivated strictly by sociopolitical considerations. Nor is sentiment valued, for Epifanio selects from the children those who show the same uncompromising attitude that he holds toward the weak. These chosen few are brought to the Big House for watchful training to polish their ruthlessness. It is pleasingly ironic that, though the region is impotent to withstand him, his own potency as prolific father and his deficiencies as a guide are the seeds of his demise and of the destruction of the region.

Two of his sons, Don Jesús and Don Felipe, remain in the Big House until they reach majority. They then occupy two extensive ranches and solidify the family's hold over the mountain plain. Quickly, however, they begin to vie for their father's favor and undercut each other's power.

The third son, Miguel Arcángel, has left the valley, changing his name to Jacob Gallo (his mother's surname). He has immersed himself in the political world of the immediate postrevolutionary period. He becomes an officer in the army, establishes himself with the state government, embraces the fruits of progress, such as electricity, and eventually gains immense power. He returns to his birthplace and quickly intensifies the tension between his two half brothers. The peasants, sensitive as victims are to changing forces, give, in varying degree, their allegiance to this prodigal son, whose promise of a better life with technology—electricity, irrigation, and better agronomy—they seem to accept. Thus, the outside world has conquered the valley.

At this level, the novel's general movement is toward progress and suggests an allegorical treatment of good triumphing over evil. Yáñez, a moralist and an intense observer of history, deepens the novel's significance. In fact, Jacob Gallo's purpose is the same as that of his father and brothers—to win dominance over the valley. This view, which the peasants begin to express in murmurs, increasingly sharpens until the final scene in which Gallo's baser character stands revealed. As he prepares to switch on the electrical current initiating progress, the voice of the "old way," belonging to the blind *bruja*, Doña Matiana, prophesies God's punishment for Gallo's hypocrisy and deceit: "I come . . . Miguel Arcángel to remind you that the higher you rise the greater your fall will be. There are no short cuts in the straight and narrow path."

Analysis

The principal themes of this novel are the nature of power, the persistence of feudal patterns, the implications of technology, the dignity of the individual and the family in the face of corruption, and the eternal effort to wrest from the thin soil a life of peace. In the opposing motif to these temporal concerns, Yáñez presents a mystical, spiritual backdrop against which to evaluate and criticize the insanity that is Mexico's inheritance.

Ultimately, this novel's impact rests on the moral view that Yáñez holds. His novel transcends its local limit and presents a universal statement about people, relationships with God, and ultimate personal responsibility. Certainly, Matiana, the blind seer, serves as one indicator of the connection of this local world to the larger, deeper one. The tragic tone is a second link. The innumerable folk sayings, encompassing both collective wisdom and their specific metaphorical relations to nature, represent the penultimate bridge. One critic estimates that more than a third of the novel is composed of these sayings, which are substitutes for rational thinking and are binding in their ritualistic observance by all the characters save Jacob Gallo.

The last relationship of this local story to the universal world is in the retelling of Old and New Testament patterns (that is, Cain and Abel, the return of the prodigal son) and in the naming of the different places in the region (such as Bethlehem, Babel, Jerusalem, Damascus, and Galilea). This powerful parallel is extended through the people's response to the church calendar of holy days. Specifically, the novel is structurally divided by the fiesta celebration of the Easter reenactment, which falls roughly in the middle of the narrative and marks Miguel Arcángel/Jacob Gallo's return to his homeland.

Critical Context

Yáñez is a major figure in the development of both Mexican and Latin American narrative. Particularly significant were his efforts to assimilate international literary techniques to the distinctive materials of Mexican history and culture. He was fascinated by experimenting with simultaneity (as did John Dos Passos), with incorporating the past as a living influence in the present and with blending of subjective and objective reality (as did James Joyce), and with the transference of universal myths and complexes as rationale and foundation for character (as did Sigmund Freud). In addition, his use of unique structural devices to tie together a broad narrative panorama—the music in *Al filo del agua* (1947; *The Edge of the Storm*, 1963) and the religious calendar in *The Lean Lands*—instructs other novelists of similar epic tendencies on how to integrate their works. Finally, in the figures of *The Lean Lands*, he was to achieve a humanistic breakthrough for Mexicans by destroying the stereotypes that distance people from one another.

LEAVING HOME

Author: Lionel G. Garcia (1935-   )
Type of work: Novel
Type of plot: Psychological realism
Time of plot: The early 1940's
Locale: Southern California
First published: 1985

Principal Characters

Adolfo, a poverty-stricken former major-league baseball pitcher who ruins his career with alcohol. Adolfo realizes that he has made no plans for his future, so he decides to see if Isabel, the only woman he has truly loved, will let him move in with her. She refuses him. Adolfo's insecurity is evident in his attempts to appear to be the winner in arguments with his cousin Maria and in his making himself the hero of every baseball story he tells. Adolfo is also insecure about his ability to perform sexually, a problem he never had in younger years. Adding to his insecurity is the cruelty of people telling him that his mouth resembles a rectum whenever he is not wearing his dentures. Although poverty prevents him from improving his appearance, Adolfo is concerned about how he looks. Adolfo has a good sense of humor and wants to be liked by everyone; open dislike crushes him. He loves telling baseball and war stories, but people at the boarding house where he lives start to avoid him so they will not have to hear another story. After his various love affairs fail to lead to true love, Adolfo's search for stability leads him back to Maria's house, where he is happy.

Maria, an emotional yet strong woman who is able to overcome adversity. Maria manages to overcome being jilted by the man she was in love with, the father of one of her children. She carries, delivers, and keeps her illegitimate daughter, also named Maria, despite what others might think. She does, however, experience emotional problems during the pregnancy. Maria loves her family deeply and does not want them to move away from home. She sees no need to seek riches. Maria has

a strong belief in God but also believes in witchcraft. She begins to lose her faith in God when her son, Arnoldo, is killed. By the end of the novel, Maria is unhappy, empty, and bitter. She brightens when she learns that her cousin Adolfo will move back in with her.

Carmen, a strong-willed young woman determined to make something of her life. Carmen is Maria's favorite child but feels no regret when she leaves her mother to move to San Diego to find a job. Carmen works hard, a trait inherited from her mother, and enjoys doing things for others. While she is in a sanitarium being treated for tuberculosis, she helps the orderlies with the other patients and decides to become a nurse. She enters the Navy for training and gets a job at a naval hospital, then later is made an officer. By the end of the novel, Carmen has become engaged to a naval officer and achieved almost all of her goals.

Isabel, Adolfo's former lover. Isabel, like Maria, is left alone by the father of her child, Adolfo. Isabel, however, is not as strong as Maria. Beaten almost to death by her father, Isabel is sent to live with relatives until her baby is born. Isabel is kind and considerate. She takes Carmen in and helps her find a job. When Carmen gets sick, Isabel looks after her. Even though she still has feelings for Adolfo, Isabel tells him that she cannot forgive him for the pain he has caused her.

The Professor (Manuel Garcia), Adolfo's sidekick. The Professor is a small man who feels inferior to Adolfo, even though he finished high school and has taught elementary school. He is willing to take risks and stands up for himself.

The Novel

Lionel G. Garcia's *Leaving Home* offers an intimate view of one Latino family in the early 1940's. The novel examines the pain of breaking family ties, identity crises, and racism.

In *Leaving Home*, Garcia is the narrator, telling the story almost entirely in a third-person omniscient voice. At one point in the novel, the author intrudes into the action using the first-person voice, and at another point, he addresses the audience directly in the second person.

As the novel opens, the aging Adolfo, a former major-league baseball pitcher who ruined his career with alcohol, is preparing to move to San Diego, away from the home of his cousin, Maria, in the Imperial Valley. He is a poor man who has little to live for but his memories. He hopes to move in with his former lover, Isabel, the mother of his son. Carmen, Maria's daughter, goes with Adolfo, hoping to move in with an aunt in order to find a better job. Maria, determined to show her family that no one loves them as much as she does, has burned the letters that Adolfo and Carmen asked her to mail to announce their respective arrivals. Maria hopes that the two will have to move back in with her.

Turned away by her aunt, Carmen is allowed to stay with Isabel. Adolfo, however, is forced to return to Maria's house. Upon his return, Adolfo discovers that he has been swindled out of his beer joint and that he has no prospects for work. Maria promises to help Adolfo find a job, but he is a proud man who considers himself to be a celebrity, and he refuses to work in the fields. Adolfo finally agrees to work as a gardener for a priest, but he soon finds the work demeaning and quits.

Adolfo then travels to Los Angeles, planning to stay with some old friends. On the trip, he meets Antonia, a con artist who easily persuades Adolfo to move in with her so she can get his pension checks. He lives unhappily with Antonia until he gives in to his craving for alcohol, after which she throws him out.

Adolfo then moves in with the Professor, another victim of Antonia's scam. When the health department condemns the men's house, Adolfo and the Professor move into a boarding house, at which they pay their rent in the form of sexual favors to the owner, Anna, a widow.

After the United States enters World War II, the Professor decides that he wants to return to Tijuana to avoid the draft. Even though he is much too old to be drafted, he remembers that during World War I, Hispanics were drafted before Anglo-Americans. The Professor plans to live with his sister, Yolanda. Adolfo accompanies him. In Tijuana, after another failed attempt at love, Adolfo marries a prostitute. He soon leaves her, however, and returns to Maria's house.

While Adolfo travels, Carmen succeeds in improving her life. She contracts tuberculosis while working at a film theater and must go to a state sanitarium to heal, but she discovers through this misfortune that she wants to be a nurse.

Upon her release, Carmen applies for a job at the Navy hospital in San Diego. After some struggle because of her race and her former illness, she is hired to wash pots. She is soon promoted to orderly and shortly thereafter is recommended for nurses' training in the U.S. Navy. She is graduated at the top of her class and becomes an officer. Although Carmen is capable, her promotion is based on the fact that she is Hispanic. The Department of Defense uses her as a symbol.

While visiting her mother, Carmen realizes the differences between the clean, organized military base and her mother's dusty house. Although she loves her mother dearly, Carmen suggests that Maria has not been keeping the house clean. Maria knows that the family tie to Carmen has been broken. When Carmen becomes engaged to an Anglo-American naval officer in the Philippines, Maria believes that she has lost Carmen.

Maria experiences significant changes. She begins to question God's judgment when Carmen gets sick. When Arnoldo, one of Maria's sons, is killed in battle, she loses her faith in God. As her family falls apart, so do her beliefs. She is left alone and lonely. When Adolfo returns to live with her,

Maria feels happy again. The two agree that Adolfo has wasted his life, but they are gratified to have each other. The novel concludes on this positive note.

Analysis

Leaving Home is an examination of poverty, racism, and the family. Garcia presents a group of related individuals in the midst of a changing society. Hispanics had begun to achieve equal rights in the 1940's but were not yet considered to be equal to Anglo-Americans, and hostility against them remained. Not all the characters in the novel want to break away from traditional lives of working all day and drinking all night.

In his novel, Garcia shows a family of diverse personalities. Adolfo was born with talent, a cruel fate according to Maria. Because of his ability to pitch well, Adolfo is able, temporarily, to rise above the expected poverty of his race. His experiences as a famous pitcher cause him to continue to seek better things for himself and his family. After his baseball days, however, Adolfo is never again able to rise above poverty. Maria, on the other hand, is willing to accept her fate. She believes that she should not ask for anything more than she has. She cannot understand Adolfo's pride. When she helps him find a job, it is clear that she does not see a job as a measure of a person's worth.

Garcia presents the plight of farmworkers and those forced to live on pensions. Farmworkers work long hours, yet make barely enough money to live on. Maria lives next to a dump where the children use old tires for toys. Adolfo is not surprised by the shabby furniture at Antonia's house because that is what he is accustomed to. People do not paint their houses, and junked cars litter yards.

The author also shows that Hispanics were treated as second-class citizens, citing the U.S. military's supposed policy of drafting minorities before Anglo-Americans. In the job market, Garcia depicts blatant racism as Carmen is told that not many people of her race become nurses.

Leaving Home is also about breaking family ties and about abandoning the predictable for the unpredictable. Garcia presents various leave-takings throughout the novel. Adolfo and Carmen leave Maria's house to improve their lives. Carmen, unlike Adolfo, almost completely severs the tie to Maria. Another of Maria's daughters, an illegitimate child also named Maria, leaves home several times because she gets angry with her mother, but she always comes back. The death of Maria's son Arnoldo causes a further breakup of the family, almost pushing Maria to insanity. Adam, Maria's other son, also takes permanent leave. Arnoldo dies a hero, but Adam, a victim of syphilis, dies a scoundrel. Arnoldo's death gives Maria much pain, while Adam's gives her relief.

Garcia's novel reveals that in a society of growing equality, people must be willing to take chances, to ignore the fate of their race, to leave home. Doing so may result in success and greater happiness. Such action, however, may also result in anxiety and unhappiness.

Critical Context

Leaving Home is Garcia's first published novel. While the novel was in progress, Garcia won the 1983 P.E.N. Southwest Discovery prize. *Leaving Home* was well received by critics, who forecast a promising future for Garcia. His ability to create believable characters that readers can relate to can be seen in his short stories.

In this novel, Garcia uses several literary techniques. A shifting point of view is evident in the author's use of first-person, second-person, and third-person omniscient points of view. The author also uses indirect interior monologue. Fragmented time sequences add complexity to the novel.

Garcia's theme of moving out of poverty is prevalent in his other two novels, *A Shroud in the Family* (1987) and *Hardscrub* (1990). The author bases his works on human experiences and is inspired by his own familial experiences. *Leaving Home* is part of the body of literary social criticism that examines racism, poverty, and the family.

A practicing veterinarian in Seabrook, Texas, Garcia writes and publishes regularly. Several of his short stories have been published in various magazines. By the early 1990's, he had begun writing and publishing reminiscences revealing the strong ties in his own family.

LIKE WATER FOR CHOCOLATE: A Novel in Monthly Installments with Recipes, Romances, and Home Remedies

Author: Laura Esquivel (1950-   )
Type of work: Novel
Type of plot: Romance
Time of plot: The 1910's to the early 1930's
Locale: Near Piedras Negras, Mexico
First published: *Como agua para chocolate*, 1989 (English translation, 1992)

Principal Characters

Tita de la Garza, the youngest daughter in a ranch-owning family. The rules of her tradition-bound family dictate that the youngest daughter remain single and care for her mother until the latter dies; therefore, Tita grows up in the kitchen, learning about life and cooking from the ranch's Indian cook, Nacha. Her childhood sweetheart marries her older sister Rosaura in order to be near Tita, but Tita's vengeful mother regularly punishes the lovers for their clandestine meetings. Tita rebels against her fate through the marvelous recipes she prepares, which provoke magical reactions. After her mother and sister's deaths, Tita and her lover Pedro are united in a passion so intense that they perish in its blaze. Tita is immortalized in her diary and recipe book, where she had written all of her recipes and the events surrounding their preparation.

Mamá Elena, Tita's tyrannical mother, widowed with three daughters. Her attempts to prevent an adulterous relationship between Tita and Pedro occupy much of Mamá Elena's destructive attention. Fearless in her cruelty, she even intimidates the captain of a marauding band of revolutionary soldiers, thus preserving the ranch's inhabitants and livestock from attack. Later, she becomes paralyzed from a spinal injury she suffers when a group of bandits try unsuccessfully to rape her. She is then forced to rely on Tita to cook for her. Needlessly suspicious that Tita is poisoning her food, Mamá Elena soon dies from an overdose of the emetic she takes to counteract the food's sup-posed noxious effects. She continues to plague Tita and Pedro from beyond the grave. After Mamá Elena's death, Tita discovers her secret past: Her mother had enjoyed an affair with a mulatto man who fathered Tita's sister Gertrudis. When her family discovered Mamá Elena's relationship, they forced her into marriage with a white man and had the mulatto murdered when the affair continued.

Rosaura de la Garza, Tita's older sister, who marries Pedro Muzquiz at Mamá Elena's suggestion. Rosaura lives her life according to her mother's dictates, attempting to maintain the respect and admiration of the cream of society. Jealous of his love for Tita, Rosaura tries unsuccessfully to impress Pedro with her cooking. Rosaura cannot even produce milk to nurse her son and daughter. Her attitude toward cooking and her knowledge of Pedro's undying love for Tita are manifested in Rosaura's obesity and flatulence.

Gertrudis de la Garza, Tita's rebellious older sister, fathered by Mamá Elena's mulatto lover. Loyal and sympathetic to her sister Tita and a great fan of her sister's culinary talents, Gertrudis is so overwhelmed by passion after eating one of Tita's special dishes that she abandons her family and rides off on horseback with a revolutionary soldier. Unable to satisfy her lust with him, she tames her sexual appetite as a prostitute until the soldier returns and marries her. She lives happily, eventually becomes a general in the revolutionary army, and visits the ranch with her soldiers after Mamá Elena's death.

Pedro Muzquiz, Tita's childhood sweetheart, who marries her sister Rosaura to remain near Tita. After her death, Mamá Elena whirls into him in the form of a firecracker, nearly burning him to death, but he recovers under Tita's care. When Rosaura dies, he is finally freely united with Tita, and his ecstasy is so overwhelming that it proves fatal.

John Brown, the de la Garza's family doctor from Texas. A widower with a young son, he visits the de la Garza ranch when Rosaura gives birth. He admires Tita. When she suffers a nervous breakdown, he rescues her and cares for her in his home and later proposes marriage. They become engaged, but when Tita breaks off the relationship, he bows out amicably. He later returns to the ranch happily to celebrate his son Alex's marriage to Rosaura's daughter Esperanza.

Nacha, the de la Garza's Indian cook. One of a long line of expert cooks, she rears Tita from childhood in the kitchen and teaches her secrets to Tita, even whispering recipes to her from beyond the grave. On the day of Rosaura's wedding, after tasting the wedding cake icing in which Tita has shed tears, Nacha dies, overcome with grief and loneliness for the fiancé whom Mamá Elena had forbidden her to marry.

The Novel

Like Water for Chocolate combines the story of a forbidden romance between Tita de la Garza and Pedro Muzquiz with a collection of traditional, mouth-watering Mexican recipes. The title, from a Spanish expression meaning "boiling mad," refers to Tita's anger that an absurd family tradition prevents her from marrying and dictates that, as the youngest daughter, she remain at home to care for her mother, Mamá Elena. Like the title, all the incidents in the novel are related to cooking.

Organized like a recipe calendar, each chapter corresponds to a month of the year and begins with the name and list of ingredients for one of Tita's recipes along with the method of preparation. In its form, the book also imitates the romantic novels presented in monthly installments in women's magazines; each chapter ends with the note "to be continued. . . ." The narrator is Tita's grandniece, who reconstructs Tita's recipes and her love story from the diary in which the protagonist recorded her recipes along with the events that occurred when she prepared each of them.

The novel's plot revolves around the tension between Tita's love for the kitchen, where she creates magic with food, and her rebellion against the tradition that confines her there. The novel opens with the proper method of chopping onions for the January recipe and connects the tears caused by the onions to the flood of tears that accompanied Tita's birth on the kitchen table. The narrator explains that Tita cried her way into the world because she somehow knew her fate, and her tears at birth produced ten pounds of salt for cooking. This beginning typifies the relationship between cooking and the events in Tita's life and introduces into the narrative the recurrent Magical Realism common in modern Latin American fiction.

In the first chapter, Tita's true love, Pedro Muzquiz, requests her hand in marriage. When Mamá Elena explains that Tita cannot marry and suggests Tita's sister Rosaura instead, Pedro accepts in order to remain as near to Tita as possible. The rest of the novel recounts Tita and Pedro's attempts to be together in defiance of authoritarian Mamá Elena and how Tita rebels through her culinary artistry and the unexpected and dramatic reactions her recipes provoke. For example, Tita sheds tears in the batter when forced to prepare Rosaura and Pedro's wedding cake. Her sadness, baked into the cake, afflicts the wedding guests with desperate nostalgia for lost love that causes a mass eruption of vomiting that spoils the wedding reception. One casualty of this nostalgia is the ranch's Indian cook, Nacha, who had nourished and entertained Tita in the kitchen and taught her the secrets of cooking. Later, when Pedro presents Tita with roses to celebrate her first anniversary as the ranch's new cook, the dish Tita prepares with the flowers unleashes such erotic euphoria in Tita's sister Gertrudis that she abandons her family and rides off on horseback, naked, with a revolutionary soldier. Gertrudis ultimately satisfies her lust as a prostitute, then marries the soldier and serves with him in the army.

Tita's sister Rosaura, inept and fearful in the kitchen, cannot even produce milk to nurse her first child, Roberto. Tita rescues him from starvation, but Mamá Elena, suspicious of Pedro and Tita's love, sends Rosaura's family to Texas. Roberto, deprived of Tita's milk, soon dies. Tita suffers a nervous breakdown but recovers in the care of the family's physician, John Brown, who falls in love with and proposes marriage to Tita. Mamá Elena represses Tita until her death from the emetic she uses to counteract poison that she suspects Tita is putting into her food. With Mamá Elena gone, Tita is free to marry John but refuses his offer because of her love for Pedro. Meanwhile, Rosaura attempts to perpetuate the family tradition with her own daughter Esperanza. Tita feeds her from infancy and instills in her an independent spirit. Rosaura eventually suffers a horrid death from intestinal disorders. Esperanza then marries John's son, and at the sumptuous wedding feast prepared by Tita, Tita and Pedro are at last united. Their flames of passion, fanned by the food Tita serves, engulf the lovers in a fire that destroys the entire ranch. Only Tita's diary survives intact. The narrator, Esperanza's daughter, closes the novel with the promise that Tita will live on as long as people continue to prepare her recipes.

Analysis

Like Water for Chocolate playfully imitates the steamy romances included in Hispanic women's magazines and simultaneously pays tribute to the arts of the kitchen. The novel begins and ends in the kitchen, where Tita's grandniece prepares one of Tita's recipes, illustrating that the plot is above all a vehicle for the author to celebrate food and cooking as the center of daily lives and destinies. This message is also evident in the fact that cooking is the root cause for the events of Magical Realism or fantasy that pervade the novel. The importance of freedom for women is the novel's central feminist theme.

Tita learns the most important lessons about life in the kitchen from the Indian cook Nacha. As in the book's title, descriptions of how characters feel in various situations are presented in imagery from food and cooking. In addition, the unique ways in which food is prepared and the ingredients employed are shown as determining or redefining people's fates, as with the wedding cake prepared by Tita that spoils Rosaura's reception and destroys Nacha's life. The novel equates understanding these secrets of the power of food with understanding life. In its language, food-related events, characterization in terms of attitudes toward food and cooking, and cookbook-like form, this novel makes culinary activity itself the captivating stuff of literature.

Central to conveying a message of liberation for Mexican women is the choice of a traditionally female space in Mexican society, the kitchen, as defining characters' lives. To this end, the novel's action is set temporally around the time of the Mexican Revolution, when women's rights in Mexico were also being redefined and reevaluated. Clearly, however, it is not the kitchen but societal codes that have restricted women's independence. Mamá Elena's miserable death from poisoning and Rosaura's grotesque demise testify to the evils of unquestioning allegiance to tradition in the name of keeping up appearances. The novel suggests that Gertrudis' uninhibited happiness, by contrast, is the direct consequence of her rebellious freedom. The plainest evidence of this novelistic message of liberation, even if it applies principally to amorous freedom, appears in the marriage of Rosaura's daughter Esperanza, who, through Tita's guidance, refuses to succumb to the family tradition that has enslaved her aunt.

In the end, the blending of culinary and literary arts, which triumphs most obviously in the survival of Tita's cookbook and diary at the novel's conclusion, offers would-be cooks and writers new recipes for creative expression.

Critical Context

Like Water for Chocolate, Laura Esquivel's first novel, was a runaway best-seller in both the Spanish original and in English translation. In addition to its wide acclaim among nonacademic audiences, the novel was embraced by feminist scholars as a unique and significant contribution to the burgeoning field of Latin American women's writing. In its focus on the kitchen, Esquivel's work finds antecedents in her compatriot Rosario Castellanos' 1971 short story "Cooking Lesson," which denounces how the kitchen imprisons and stereotypes women, and in Puerto Rican writer Rosario Ferré's 1984 essay "The Writer's Kitchen," in which she acknowledges the parallels between recipes for cooking and for creative writing. Esquivel's book introduces novelty both in her narrative technique, which artfully blends recipes into an archetypal love-story plot, and in her lighthearted appropriation of literary genres typically associated with women, the recipe collection and the romance. Other writers who explore the similarities in the creative processes of writing and cooking have not achieved the widespread appeal among diverse audiences that Esquivel enjoys; however, this topic has attracted the attention of female writers both in Latin America and in the United States. Esquivel joins these women in marking a new phase in feminist thought. Instead of rejecting the kitchen as a space that impedes women's freedom, they adapt the kitchen's secrets to literary production.

Esquivel established her reputation as a screenwriter before embarking on her successful foray into fiction writing. In 1985, one of her screenplays received a nomination for the Ariel award from the Mexican Academy of Motion Picture Arts and Sciences. Esquivel also collaborated with her husband on the screenplay for the film based on *Like Water for Chocolate*, which has also enjoyed great praise, capturing eleven awards in Mexico in 1992.

THE LIZARD'S TAIL

Author: Luisa Valenzuela (1938-   )
Type of work: Novel
Type of plot: Social morality
Time of plot: The reign of José López Rega, 1975
Locale: Argentina
First published: *El señor de Tacuru*, 1983 (English translation, 1983)

Principal Characters

The Sorcerer, the protagonist and main narrator, known by several other names. A cabinet minister, he supervises state terrorism. The Sorcerer is a paranoid megalomaniac, living in a continuing delusion of his own divinity and feeling completely self-sufficient. He has a third testicle, which he regards as his twin sister Estrella. The Sorcerer's life story is a representation of the life of José López Rega, who was a minister in Juan Perón's return to the Argentine presidency (1973-1974) and who virtually ran Argentina for a time during the succeeding presidency of Isabel Perón, the general's wife. López Rega was a practitioner of the occult and the leader of a death squad.

Luisa Valenzuela, a novelist with dark curly hair like the author of *The Lizard's Tail*. Valenzuela is also a narrator and a minor participant in the events of the novel. She is writing a fictionalized biography of the Sorcerer.

The Egret, a tall, handsome, young blond eunuch. The Sorcerer uses the Egret for sexual purposes but also reviles him as his dog.

Estrella, the Sorcerer's third testicle, whom he considers his twin sister. Estrella becomes pregnant with the Sorcerer's child and grows to watermelon size. The Sorcerer takes on female bodily characteristics during the pregnancy.

The Dead Woman, a representation of Evita Perón, the charismatic wife of Juan Perón.

The Generalissimo, a representation of Juan Perón.

Madam President, a representation of María Estela Martínez de Perón, who was known as Isabel although like all contemporary historical personages, she is not named in the novel. The Sorcerer calls her the Intruder because she replaced the venerated Dead Woman as the Generalissimo's wife.

Alfredo Navoni, a political dissident and activist who is a friend and former lover of Luisa. Navoni encourages her to continue writing her biography of the Sorcerer when fear deters her.

The Novel

The Lizard's Tail is divided into three parts. The first hundred pages of the novel are narrated by an enigmatic figure known as the Sorcerer, with interruptions by unidentified characters and an omniscient narrator. The Sorcerer claims to be indispensable to the government; it is apparent from the beginning, however, that this is not a realistic political novel but rather a symbolic, mythic, and at times deliberately cryptic allegory of modern Argentina.

The novel opens with a prophecy about a river of blood that will bring twenty years of peace. The first part relates the Sorcerer's childhood in the land of the ants. (He amused himself by sitting on anthills.)

The Intruder, Isabel Perón, organizes a group to

determine with certainty that the corpse thought to be that of Eva Perón is in fact Eva's. A reference is made to the burial of Eva and the disappearance of her body: The Sorcerer says that he and others hid the body after a coup and after the "cult" was forbidden. The Sorcerer says that he is bringing Eva back to life. The Generalissimo, Perón, dies. The Sorcerer decides to make Isabel, Perón's wife, his ally. He makes plans to create a new kingdom that he will rule, the Kingdom of the Black Lagoon. The government begins to persecute him. Rather than fight them, he decides to build a pyramid. In the capital, a plan for national reconstruction is formulated to counter the negative images in the foreign press, which include accusations of torture and "disappearances" condoned by the government. The Sorcerer suggests a masked ball as a preparation for the government's campaign of disinformation. He prepares for the Grand Ball of the Full Moon and plans to invite government officials and journalists.

The second part of the novel, narrated by Luisa, is a declaration of her intention to be a politically committed writer and an examination of the compromised position in which she finds herself while trying to write a biography of the Sorcerer. At the time she receives an invitation to his masked ball, she has been planning a party, at which she wants to introduce certain guests to the ambassador of a foreign country. Her friend Alfredo Navoni, a revolutionary, tells her to continue to write her biography of the Sorcerer. At the Sorcerer's party, guests are to be given terra-cotta masks, which will be broken with clubs distributed among the guests. Meanwhile, a counterceremony is being planned by Navoni's followers. At his own ball, the Sorcerer wears the mask of an ant. At dawn, all masks have been broken and the guests are bloody and beaten. In preparation for their imitation of the

masked ball, the Popular Festival, the people of the town of Capivari build a pyramid and a representation of the Sorcerer.

It is said that the Sorcerer's power has grown while Luisa has written about him, which causes her great concern. The Sorcerer decides to annex Capivari into his kingdom and to cut off its water supply if the townspeople do not agree. Navoni tells Luisa that she should kill the Sorcerer in her book. She believes that it is impossible to do this. The Sorcerer commands that all photographic equipment and mirrors be confiscated. He covers the inside of his pyramid with the mirrors. Luisa's ambivalence about her role finally leads her to decide to stop writing altogether: Fearing that even writing about the Sorcerer will increase his power, she erases herself and, thereby, him.

In the third and final part of the novel, the Sorcerer believes that someone has stopped writing about him. After a ritual with the Egret in which his body is covered with mud and he becomes a woman, he has the pyramid's mirrors covered with white cloth by workers, men blind from birth.

Meanwhile, three mysterious characters move up the river, a teacher who participated in the imitation of the Sorcerer's ball, Luisa, and Navoni. The Sorcerer consummates his marriage to Estrella, his third testicle, by injecting it with sperm and impregnating his sister (himself). In his delirium, he feels his tent closing in on him. Once his protection, he says it is now his torture chamber. The Egret travels to the foot of the pyramid and collapses, exhausted. Something explodes and blood appears. The woman with curly hair (Luisa) says it must be the sign of the twenty years of peace promised by the prophecy. Navoni disagrees and says that once one president falls, another is ready to take over, and that the little thread of blood is not the one mentioned in the prophecy.

Analysis

The symbols of the novel are rather difficult to understand without some historical background. Valenzuela found it strange that Argentina, a country with most of its population of European descent, could have fallen under the power of a sorcerer. It appeared to her that Argentina was more "Latin American" than the Argentines had supposed. She chose the structure of a myth for her book in order to show the absurd extremes that could be reached when people allow themselves to be ruled by an insane leader. Valenzuela wrote *The Lizard's Tail* to cure Argentina of its conspiracy of silence, its inability to speak out against the torture of dissidents and the *desaparecidos*, the "disappeared ones."

Having decided to focus on López Rega in *The Lizard's Tail*, she formulated a response to his discourse and to that of the generals, some of whose language appears in the book. Valenzuela does not pretend to be a physician or healer who is unscathed by the disease. She, too, has been tortured by the memories of the disappeared, whose silhouettes have been stamped on the walls of Buenos Aires.

In *The Lizard's Tail*, the reader participates in the creation of and is cured by the poetic text. Valenzuela chooses to exorcise the demons that have destroyed the country from within. Rather than rid the country of subversives, she would rid the consciousness of her reader of identification with the repressive regimes that have countenanced the torture and the disappearances of the 1970's. In her novel, the sick body of Argentina is transformed into a symbolic landscape upon which Valenzuela performs the exorcism. She creates an allegory in which the Argentine psyche can view the pain that the body can no longer tolerate.

Critical Context

The critical context for Luisa Valenzuela's work must be defined to include the political situation in Argentina in addition to works of other writers. In France, Valenzuela came into contact with the group of poststructuralist critics associated with the avant-garde literary journal *Tel quel*. Poststructuralists in France were critical of orthodox Marxism and its failures. The rise of French feminism coincided with the breaking away from orthodoxy on the Left. In Argentina, women made gains in terms of working conditions and democratic rights during the Perón period. Ideological contradictions in the movement allowed a broad spectrum of women, from traditional to radical, to call themselves Peronists. At the time Valenzuela wrote *The Lizard's Tail*, Argentine women were actively engaged in political struggle. The military government did not make allowances for gender in its torture of women.

In an interview in 1983, Valenzuela mentioned that Jacques Derrida, Michel Foucault, and Roland Barthes had been her colleagues at the New York Institute for the Humanities. It is within this context of postmodernist debates about language and the political situation in Argentina that Valenzuela chooses to situate herself as a writer.

Valenzuela's work is grounded in the contemporary writing of Argentina, including the work of such writers as Jorge Luis Borges and Julio Cortázar. These writers also incorporate the themes of dream, death, magic, and desire. In fact, it was not until *Aquí pasan cosas raras* (1975; *Strange Things Happen Here*, 1979) and *Como en la guerra* (1977; *He Who Searches*, 1979) that Valenzuela began to address political issues in her work. Existentialism and psychoanalysis have become woven into the fabric of contemporary letters in Argentina. Valenzuela's attitude toward these traditions is irreverent on occasion, and at least equally informed by feminism and a belief that only truth and justice can exorcise the phantasms in her country. Several critics have noted that it is very important that one not read Latin American literature as merely symbolic or magical; Latin American writers are faced with the problem of conveying a political reality that is frequently "unbelievable," especially to readers from another culture. Nevertheless, Valenzuela wishes her work to be read for its metaphors, as literature, not only as political commentary.

THE LOST STEPS

Author: Alejo Carpentier (1904-1980)
Type of work: Novel
Type of plot: Psychological realism
Time of plot: The late 1940's
Locale: An unnamed metropolis (probably New York City), a South American city, and the South American jungle
First published: *Los pasos perdidos*, 1953 (English translation, 1956)

Principal Characters

The narrator, a composer and music theoretician now writing for films and advertisements. Despising his job, bored with a marriage that is only a convenience, and unable to create anything worthwhile, he is terrified at the prospect of a vacation, which will force him to confront the sterility of his existence. An old friend, the curator of a museum, offers him a reprieve by asking him to travel to South America to acquire some primitive instruments. As he travels into an increasingly primitive environment, his own modern alienation gradually slips away. He begins to compose again and finds a woman whom he admires and loves. Compelled by outside forces and the pressure of his music, he leaves but insists that he will immediately return. When he finally does return, he finds the doors to his happy life closed.

Mouche, an astrologist, the narrator's French mistress. Mouche's intellectual pretensions and superficiality are stripped away by the authenticity of the jungle. Unable to tolerate her any longer, the narrator takes advantage of her illness to send her away.

Rosario, the narrator's ideal of the true woman. The narrator continually compares the earthy mestizo woman to the more civilized Mouche. Rosario cannot comprehend his compulsion to write music.

Ruth, an actress, the narrator's wife. Ruth and her husband see each other only on Sunday mornings. When he does not return from his trip, she claims he is lost in the jungle and stages his rescue as a gigantic publicity stunt. Enraged by his request for a divorce, she frustrates his efforts to get back to Rosario.

Fray Pedro de Henestrosa, a Capuchin friar and martyr admired for his courage and willingness to help others. Knowing it means certain death, he undertakes a mission to the lands of savage Indians. They kill him and horribly mutilate his body as a warning to others.

The Adelantado, a man who has founded his own city.

The Curator, the narrator's friend and former employer. An admirer of the narrator's theories on the origin of primitive music, he gives him the task of finding some primitive instruments for his museum.

Marcos, the Adelantado's son. Against his father's wishes, he had once left the settlement and gone to seek his fortune in the city. Humiliated and mistreated, he returned home filled with resentment and scorn for everything he had seen in the outside world.

Simon, a shoemaker turned itinerant river merchant who tries to help the narrator find his way back to the village.

The Novel

The Lost Steps narrates a journey, through space and back through time, to the most remote origins of Latin American history. The novel, written in the first person, can be read as a diary kept by the unnamed narrator-protagonist as he flees mechanized civilization in search of a more primordial existence. The dated entries that provide the basic structure for the novel are augmented by the narrator's fragmented recollections of the past and his meditations on art, culture, and history.

As the novel begins, the narrator is surveying the set of a long-running play about the antebellum South; in this play, his wife, Ruth, has a leading role. The play is a resounding commercial success despite its banality. As he surveys the soiled costumes and the dwarf magnolias, the narrator is overcome by boredom and loneliness. Once a promising young composer and musicologist, he now prostitutes his talents in an advertising agency. Neither the automatic nature of his weekly sexual relations with Ruth nor the frenetic, pseudo-intellectual gaiety of Mouche and her friends can satisfy him. Every aspect of his life seems mechanical and uninspired. Faced with the beginning of a three-week vacation, he feels empty and disoriented.

A chance encounter with his old friend and employer, the Curator, whom he has not seen for several years, presents the narrator with a unique opportunity. The Curator reminds him of his earlier work on primitive instruments and of his theories on the origins of music and asks him to travel to South America during his vacation to acquire a number of indigenous clay instruments for the museum. The narrator initially rejects the offer. Mouche convinces him to go, announcing that she will accompany him.

The second chapter opens with their arrival in an unspecified South American city. The central role that geography will play in the novel becomes more explicit. The narrator hears once again the language of his childhood and is haunted by memories of his early years. In these new surroundings, he begins to feel more alive, to recover his spiritual equilibrium. At the same time, Mouche's urban pretensions strike him as increasingly false and ridiculous. When he meets the mestizo woman Rosario during the bus ride to the interior, he is captivated by her strength, simplicity, and obvious connection with nature. He and Rosario become lovers and Mouche, bedraggled and weak with malaria, is dispatched home.

The small group—which now consists of the narrator; Rosario; a Capuchin friar; Yannes, a Greek prospector and miner; and their guide, the Adelantado—presses its way by boat into the jungle. When the Adelantado appears with magnificent specimens of the primitive instruments for which he has been searching, the narrator is suddenly overcome by the realization of "the first outstanding, noteworthy act of my life to that moment." He decides to continue on the expedition. In a small village that seems to exist before time and before history, the narrator hears a funeral lament that convinces him that he has witnessed the birth of music. He resolves to remain in the jungle, never to return "back there." With Rosario, he sets up housekeeping in Santa Monica de los Venados, the town founded by the Adelantado, and begins to compose a new work, *Threnody*, based on the text of Homer's *Odyssey*.

The narrator is increasingly troubled, however, by a number of misgivings: the Adelantado's establishment of a civilized order in what has been an idyllic, natural place; his own failure to deliver the prized instruments to the Curator; Rosario's refusal to marry him; and, most important, the growing scarcity of the paper he desperately needs in order to complete his composition. The unexpected arrival of a small plane, part of an expedition sent by Ruth to find her lost husband, offers him the irresistible chance to return briefly to the city in order to settle his affairs and stock up on those items he considers indispensable for his new life in Santa Monica de los Venados.

The return occasions a series of personal and professional difficulties: a messy divorce from an embittered Ruth, loss of both job and credibility, and financial troubles brought on by his mounting legal expenses. The "tentacular city" alienates him more than ever. He stumbles through an almost apocalyptic landscape that underscores the bankrupt quality of the city's inhabitants and their art, religion, work, and relationships.

When the narrator is finally able to return to the jungle, it is too late. The incision that marked the path to Santa Monica de los Venados has disap-peared beneath the rising waters of the river. Yannes tells him that Rosario is now pregnant by another man. The narrator immediately recognizes his error: "One day I had made the unforgivable mistake of turning back, thinking a miracle could be repeated, and on my return I found the setting changed, the landmarks wiped out, and the faces of the guides new."

Analysis

Recapturing lost origins—of humanity itself, as well as of art, language, and history—is a central theme in *The Lost Steps*. As both the title and the conclusion of the novel suggest, such a recuperation is impossible. The narrator is driven by the need to discover in the past some essential truth about himself and his culture but is prevented from doing so by his commitment to the present. Thus, in the final pages of the novel, he comes to the realization that "the only human race to which it is forbidden to sever the bonds of time is the race of those who create art." The novel examines the relationship between the artist and his creation, as the narrator-protagonist struggles to find a balance between his desire for an audience for the *Threnody* and his painful awareness of the pitfalls of perverting his creation to suit an uncomprehending public.

The Lost Steps presents a Spenglerian view of modern civilization as decadent and moribund, especially when contrasted with the exuberant fertility of the New World jungle. Given the truncated nature of the narrator's idyll in Santa Monica de los Venados, the novel cannot be read as a Utopian romance. The narrative is divided among three readily distinguishable locales—a modern city, a civilized zone in Latin America, and the marvelous and mysterious jungle—in the manner of many works that trace a symbolic journey. The epigraphs that introduce each chapter mirror the narrator's thoughts and emotions.

Carpentier is a highly symbolic writer, and his novel is structured around three mythic figures who bear some resemblance to the protagonist: Sisyphus, condemned to spend his life pursuing an endless and fruitless task; Prometheus, the rebel condemned to eternal suffering because of his godlike aspirations; and Ulysses, whose long journey home takes him to far-off lands and unimagined adventures. Carpentier examines the relationship among people, nature, and history. The protagonist realizes that nature, like history, is a text to be read, a text Rosario can read but he cannot. Thus his concluding meditation on his own odyssey: "I had lived to make straight a destiny that was crooked because of my own weakness, and a song had welled up in me—now cut short—which had led me back to the old road, in sackcloth and ashes, no longer able to be what I had been."

Critical Context

The Lost Steps is Carpentier's most important work, and it represents a turning point in his development as a writer. Latin America in the 1940's beckoned to avant-garde writers as a place of ar-tistic and spiritual rebirth. Carpentier took the surrealist concept of Magical Realism and attempted to redefine it as a purely Latin American phenomenon. His theories were published in the form of a prologue to *El reino de este mundo* (1949; *The Kingdom of This World*, 1957). In *The Lost Steps*, Carpentier confronts this issue directly within his narrative: The protagonist struggles to come to terms with questions regarding the origins of language and tradition. *El siglo de las luces* (1962; *Explosion in a Cathedral*, 1963) represents a further attempt to write Latin American fiction based on the history of the New World. In *El recurso del método* (1974; *Reasons of State*, 1976), Carpentier paints a hilarious yet biting portrait of a Latin American despot caught between his European pretensions and the reality surrounding him.

The Lost Steps is often mentioned as one of the forerunners of the "boom" in Latin American literature, the explosion of literary activity in the 1960's and 1970's that brought authors such as Gabriel García Márquez and Jorge Luis Borges to the attention of readers outside Latin America. The language of *The Lost Steps*, rich in metaphor and cultural allusions, is as dense and prolific as the jungle it describes, making the novel a primary example of the Latin American neo-Baroque.

LOVE IN THE TIME OF CHOLERA

Author: Gabriel García Márquez (1928-   )
Type of work: Novel
Type of plot: Romance
Time of plot: The late 1870's to the early 1930's
Locale: A fictional Caribbean coastal city in northern Colombia
First published: *El amor en los tiempos del cólera*, 1985 (English translation, 1988)

Principal Characters

Florentino Ariza, a romantic poet and president of the River Company of the Caribbean, who at the age of eighteen courts and is rejected by Fermina Daza. He continues a clandestine lifelong devotion to her that culminates in their reunion in old age. The illegitimate son of a philandering father and a resourceful single mother, Florentino becomes a mysterious "hunter" of innumerable women in an effort to substitute sexual desire for his more spiritual fidelity to Fermina. His determination to regain Fermina and consummate their love is fraught with constant pitfalls, including his own physical decrepitude (he grows bald, breaks his leg, and is left lame) and the violent deaths of two of his former mistresses. Ultimately, however, he is rewarded for his persistent love.

Fermina Daza, the daughter of a disreputable mule dealer, who as a teenager jilts Florentino. She then marries Dr. Juvenal Urbino, who is well above her class, for socially pretentious reasons but not for love. She almost entirely forgets Florentino and his desperate suit for her, and she throws herself into the social responsibilities and familial obligations of the Urbinos. She lives a strangely unformed life, a mixture of accommodation and revolt, until she is finally liberated in widowhood to pursue her own inclinations, which include a rekindling of love, now more mature and tempered by the realities of old age, for Florentino.

Dr. Juvenal Urbino, a European-educated physician and member of one of the city's shabby-genteel families. Urbino conspires with Fermina's father to marry her shortly after she rejects Florentino. Respected for his civic activities and his commitment to ending the cholera epidemic that had ravaged the community in the previous century, he holds his wife as a social adornment for most of their nearly fifty-year marriage, though in his death throes he does profess his divine love for her. His elitist values and misplaced faith in the powers of reason are undermined throughout the novel, however, and even he himself is conscious of his status as the "last of a line." His diagnostic methods toward both professional and personal life cannot withstand the spontaneity and love that Florentino and Fermina's reunion celebrates.

Jeremiah de Saint-Amour, a Caribbean refugee who gains Urbino's camaraderie as an accomplished chess player. He takes his own life in chapter 1 because of his "gerontophobia": He loved life and his secret Haitian mistress with such passion that he thought he could not survive the prospect of old age and decay.

Tránsito Ariza, Florentino's mother, who operates a lucrative pawn shop in her home and who shelters and nurses her son following the devastation he feels from his jilting by Fermina. She encourages her brother-in-law to help establish Florentino in a career with the River Company of the Caribbean. Her progressive senility disturbs Florentino less than her eventual death, since she had been one of his few confessors concerning his lost love.

Lorenzo Daza, a shady entrepreneur and the father of Fermina. Lorenzo finds out about his daughter's relationship with Florentino and, having higher hopes for her, threatens her young lover, who refuses to be dissuaded. Lorenzo recruits the wealthy and respectable Urbino for his daughter's hand. His criminal business dealings revealed, Lorenzo is finally expelled from the country.

América Vicuña, a schoolgirl placed in the charge of the elderly Florentino by distant relatives. América commits suicide at the end of the novel, unable to bear the rejection of her former lover, Florentino, and in essence dying from the bitter cliché of a broken heart. Her death parallels the suicide of Jeremiah de Saint-Amour at the beginning of the book; both episodes suggest the price that must be paid for the triumph of love that Florentino and Fermina have achieved.

The Novel

The first novel to be published by Gabriel García Márquez since he was awarded the Nobel Prize in Literature in 1982, *Love in the Time of Cholera* chronicles the nearly sixty-year relationship between Florentino Ariza and Fermina Daza, who finally consummate their love in old age during a boat trip down the Magdalena River in Colombia.

Love in the Time of Cholera is divided into six lengthy, discursive chapters, ranging in form from the chronologically linear to frequent flashbacks and reprises. The novel has a single narrative voice that relates certain events in duplicate order to capture the overlapping experiences of its protagonists: Florentino, Fermina, and her husband of some fifty years, Dr. Juvenal Urbino.

The book begins with the bizarre suicide (by gold cyanide) one Pentecost Sunday of Jeremiah de Saint-Amour, the elderly Urbino's longtime friend and chess companion. The event coincides with the silver wedding anniversary of Urbino's most eminent medical student. Urbino's own accidental death later the same day (he falls while trying to retrieve his wife's pet parrot from a mango tree) sets in motion a second level to the narrative. Because the deceased physician had been one of the provincial capital's most prestigious residents, mourners from town swarm the Urbino household to console his widow, seventy-two-year-old Fermina Daza. One of those visitors is seventy-six-year-old Florentino Ariza, the president of the River Company of the Caribbean, who repeats to Fermina the vow of eternal love that he first expressed to her more than half a century earlier.

This chain of events is the springboard for the rest of the novel, which flashes back to tell the story of Florentino's passionate three-year courtship of Fermina Daza when they were still teenagers. Their romance is conducted entirely through clandestine letters and the complicity of Fermina's spinster aunt and her coquettish cousin, but Florentino's swooning preoccupation and progressive physical distress over Fermina arouse the concern of his mother, Tránsito, and his Uncle Léo XII. Florentino's romantic love remains unrequited, however, since the beautiful but fickle Fermina abruptly jilts him and later marries Urbino, a member of a fading aristocratic family.

Subsequent chapters of *Love in the Time of Cholera* account for the contrasting backgrounds of Florentino, Fermina, and Urbino, who together represent a stereotypical three-cornered love relationship. A broad temporal and spatial perspective registers the main social developments that shape the postcolonial community, and the book also surveys the political history of Colombia since its independence in the early nineteenth century. Even after Fermina has wed Urbino, at the coaxing of her father, and settled down into a life of social ostentation and domestic boredom, Florentino remains in the city of their star-crossed romance, a setting that is a social and racial microcosm of a formerly prosperous Spanish city situated at the mouth of the Magdalena River. The action of the novel centers on this provincial capital, a rough composite of Cartegena de Indias, Barranquilla, and other locations on the Caribbean coast.

Despite the fact that Fermina has married another man, the doctor famous for ending the ravages of cholera in the region, and has learned to cherish if not altogether love him, Florentino never abandons his devotion to the love of his youth and dedicates his life to preparing for Fermina's return. This is not to say, however, that he has forsaken heterosexual love during his half-century wait for her: In fact, while many of the townspeople suspect him of homosexuality because of his secretive ways, Florentino has earned a reputation as the lover of widows, shop clerks, madwomen, and even schoolgirls in his effort to find a substitute for Fermina. If he has resolved to keep himself spiritually pure for the day when he will possess Fermina, he nevertheless amasses and records in his diary hundreds of liaisons and sexual adventures with other women. Both he and Fermina hence cross the line into old age leading parallel lives in the same locale. Florentino has risen over the years from lowly messenger to president of the prosperous River Company (and continues his sexual exploits, despite the failings of his body and the tragic murder, by a cuckolded husband, of one of his mistresses), while Fermina endures her husband's infidelity, obsessiveness, and patriarchal domination to achieve at least the guise of conjugal contentment.

The final chapter of the work circles back to the beginning, to the elderly Florentino's repeated vow to Fermina on the first night of her widowhood and her initial rage at and outright rejection of him. Yet because of a lifetime of experience and a more mature perspective tainted by intimations of his own mortality, Florentino persists in his veneration of her, and the meditational letters he now writes to Fermina are tempered, sympathetic, and comforting in the first years following the death of her husband. Eventually, against social conventions and disabused of their earlier illusions, Florentino and Fermina fulfill their desires on the *New Fidelity*, an aptly named boat that sails up and down the Magdelena River. Their dogged achievement over old age, fate, and the prejudices of their society stands as a final affirmation of life, hope, and persistent love.

Analysis

The novel is a balanced portrayal of romantic love, irrespective of age and in a variety of forms, and devotion against all odds, even the threat of impending death. It highlights the themes of marriage and old age, human dignity and compassion, and sensual pleasure in defiance of prejudicial societal constraints, as Florentino and Fermina must overcome countless obstacles before their eventual reunion. Such consummation of love in old age rejects the idealism of youth and is based instead upon a fatalistic brand of humanism that rests on a mature recognition of social and personal realities, including the certainty of mortality.

The novel is also underlaid with feminist and "Americanist" themes and motifs. Fermina's marriage, while ultimately fulfilling, reveals the strictures placed on women's freedom and sense of individuality in a patriarchal society. In essence, Fermina is a slave to her husband's and family's demands, and she finds self-empowerment and liberation only in widowhood. Furthermore, the novel's postcolonial setting implies the theme of America: García Márquez's considerations of history, politics, race, class, and culture are conveyed in both literal and symbolic terms. The era of Spanish rule has left the city an open cesspool "forgotten" by the rest of the world, and the postcolonial milieu is evoked in the once-aristocratic Urbino family's economic and social decline. The vital potential of the town's impoverished mulattos contrasts with the *criollo* class's decadence, thus celebrating the possible revival of Latin American peoples (despite the death of América Vicuña, who may allegorically represent the natural and political life of the continent).

Critical Context

Love in the Time of Cholera, unlike García Márquez's phenomenally successful *Cien años de soledad* (1967; *One Hundred Years of Solitude*, 1970), diverges from the Magical Realism that marked the author's early development and that of other "boom" generation Latin American writers of the 1960's and 1970's. Although the novel experiments with fictional techniques, such as temporal flashbacks and simultaneity, it remains more in the tradition of the *follétin*, the lachrymose, sentimental nineteenth century love story. In this respect, García Márquez's work is similar to Colombian Jorge Isaacs' *María* (1867), which enjoyed wide popularity with readers in Europe and the Americas. García Márquez's novel is more a pastiche of the *follétin* genre, since the book's verbal clichés, character types, and narrative situations finally transcend the melodramatic through an acute sense of irony and tragicomic style. The novel's thematic emphases upon love, solitude, old age, and death, however, place it well within the context of García Márquez's other fictions, including *El coronel no tiene quien le escriba* (1961; *No One Writes to the Colonel*, 1968), *El otoño del patriarca* (1975; *The Autumn of the Patriarch*, 1976), *Crónica de una muerte anunciada* (1981; *Chronicle of a Death Foretold*, 1982), and *El general en su laberinto* (1989; *The General in His Labyrinth*, 1990). Perhaps the most recognized Latin American writer, García Márquez has achieved a range and empathetic flexibility in his work that make him one of the most important novelists of the twentieth century.

MACHO!

Author: Victor Villaseñor (1940-   )
Type of work: Novel
Type of plot: *Bildungsroman*
Time of plot: The late 1960's
Locale: Mexico and California
First published: 1973

Principal Characters

Roberto Garcia, the eldest child in a large family of poor farmers, natives of a rural village in Michoacan, Mexico. Because of his father's drinking, Roberto, not yet eighteen when the story begins, must provide for his mother and the other children by doing most of the farm labor. His maturity, strength, and intelligence are immediately evident. Roberto embodies the best of the Spanish male/macho tradition: He silently accepts his father's condition and does his work for him; he competently oversees the older men with whom he works, offering no excuses for anything; and he tactfully deals with those who challenge him—but fights when necessary. Roberto's struggle between tradition and change quickly becomes the novel's central conflict. Roberto meets every test with honor, and, in the process, shows that a real man, while honor-bound, may choose not only how he honors his traditions but also how he may change them.

Juan Aguilar, the most experienced and most dominant of the village *nortenos*, who travel north across the Mexican border illegally each year to work seasonally on United States farms. Like most *nortenos*, Juan returns to the village each year to squander his earnings. Prematurely old, Juan is feeling the effects of his hard and dissolute life; thus, mostly out of predatory self-interest, he asks Roberto to accompany him north. Although the extent to which Juan will exploit Roberto remains uncertain, Juan sees in Roberto an image of the son he never had and gradually develops a genuine sense of responsibility for him. Ironically, it is often Roberto who protects Juan on their travels.

Pedro, Juan's *norteno* companion of the past ten years and Roberto's sworn enemy, as he humiliated Roberto's father. Roberto exacts a measure of revenge, and Pedro literally loses face midway through the novel, but their differences remain unresolved.

Esperanza, the eldest, at sixteen, of Roberto's younger siblings. Her desire for improvement, coupled with her natural intelligence and resourcefulness, has allowed her to transcend the educational constraints normally imposed upon females of her village. She supports and encourages Roberto's efforts to challenge tradition whenever it impedes progress. Despite his belief that Esperanza is too idealistic and too hopeful, Roberto is closer to her than to anyone else in his family.

Don Carlos Villanueva, Roberto's *patrón*, the aged owner of the land Roberto and the others work. The don was the first in the local community to see that the volcanic dust of a newly formed volcano had improved the soil. With his erect bearing and intelligence, his love of horse racing, and his success without compromise, Don Carlos represents the finest of old Spanish Mexico.

Gloria Sanchez, the potential romantic interest who is most similar to Esperanza. Although Roberto and Gloria are greatly attracted to each other, Gloria's Americanized and outspoken personality naturally clashes with Roberto's traditional values of hard work and stoicism. Their cultural conflict makes it difficult for a relationship to develop.

Lydia Sanchez, Gloria's much less studious younger sister. Lydia has not seriously evaluated

Roberto's or Gloria's values. Although both sisters are physically attracted to Roberto, Lydia, unencumbered by ideology, has the advantage when it comes to developing a romantic relationship.

Antonio, the aging ex-foreman who chooses Roberto as his successor. Antonio represents the Mexican male traditions of hard work and deceptively clever resourcefulness. He is a respected older worker, though a minor stock character.

Pablo Reyes, the eldest of the thirteen Reyes brothers. Together, Pablo and his brothers personify the age-old Mexican tradition of violence and revenge. When the Reyes brothers retaliate in ambush for a humiliation, the resulting deaths initiate a *nortenos*-Reyes feud.

The Novel

This fictional account of approximately a year in the life of a young man dramatizes the real plight of the migrant Mexican farmworker attempting to enter and work in the United States. *Macho!* is divided into three major parts, each labeled as a book and further subdivided into chapters. Books 1 and 3 are short, with the action set in the rural Mexican village of the principal characters; book 2 chronicles the odyssey of the protagonist, Roberto Garcia, into the violent underworld of the illegal migrant farmworker. Although the omniscient third-person narrator occasionally reveals thoughts of other characters, the narrative perspective is almost entirely Roberto's.

In addition to the main fictional narrative, each chapter begins with a brief quasihistorical preface, designed to inform and to persuade the reader. The first and longest of these prefaces describes the dramatic 1943 appearance of the volcano Paricutin one hundred miles from Roberto's village and the volcano's far-reaching effects. Through these prefaces, Villaseñor suggests that the natural threat of Paricutin, a blessing in disguise for Roberto's community, has been replaced by the less visible, more insidious threat of airborne industrial pollution. The threat of pollution lingers before being dismissed summarily, like dirt in the wind, at the story's end. Most of the novel's remaining prefaces indict American agribusiness interests for exploiting cheap Mexican migrant farm labor and chronicle César Chávez's challenge to the status quo during the tumultuous 1960's.

The novel itself begins well into Roberto's seventeenth year, during the planting season of his native Mexican village. Roberto's father has over the past year begun drinking heavily, leaving Roberto, as the eldest child, to support his mother and seven younger siblings. Although Roberto is humiliated by his father's weakness, he can do nothing to change it; he must simply work hard and well, for his culture does not allow him to complain—or even to think about complaining. It would not be respectful or manly. It would not be *macho*.

Roberto's strength of character is revealed immediately, not only through his uncomplaining silence in response to his father's behavior but also by his interaction with the nine older men he works with and oversees. For example, on the morning the story begins, Roberto, on his way to the fields, falls into an irrigation channel with his horse and nearly drowns. Arriving for work a few minutes late, dripping wet, he denies, when taunted by one of the other men, that anything untoward had happened. A man's personal condition should be of no concern to another. Yet his responses to the older man must tread carefully between nonservile amicability and nonprovocative bravado. Too much servility would cost him his job (not to mention his self-respect); too much arrogance would cost him his life.

The need for balance between servility and arrogance, dependence and independence, is emphasized throughout the novel—along with the impossibility of maintaining perfect balance in a world of violent passion and conflict. Moving Roberto and the other *nortenos* into an American setting adds further conflict, in the form of different cultural expectations, while simultaneously placing them in the middle of the ongoing farm-labor conflict.

In addition to the obvious intercultural conflicts of the novel are the conflicts between the traditional local farmers and the village *nortenos*, who at great risk become temporarily wealthy (by local standards) by leaving the community and journeying north to work on U.S. farms. Although the *nortenos*' dissolute and violent lifestyle does not appeal to Roberto, a persuasive offer from the *norteno* leader, Juan Aguilar, to travel north in the coming work season and thus provide for Roberto's family draws Roberto reluctantly away from

his home and traditional way of life.

As book 2 begins, the novel explodes into violence with an episode that forces Roberto and the *nortenos* to leave abruptly for the United States. Among the *nortenos* is Pedro, Juan's companion of the past ten years. Pedro, who had already earned Roberto's enmity for publicly humiliating his father, continually goads Roberto. Although Juan keeps peace between the two for some time, Pedro and Roberto eventually clash openly and decisively. Final resolution of their conflict, however, must wait until the setting returns, in book 3, to the village in Michoacan.

Analysis

Paralleling the narrative plot is the novel's larger political conflict, one that directly affected—and still affects—all United States farmworkers, legal or otherwise. The battle had presumably been resolved in 1963, when legal importation of braceros (migrant farmworkers) from Mexico into the United States was stopped, largely because of the efforts of farm-labor organizers such as César Chávez. The end of the bracero program had what should have been predictable results: an increase in the demand for cheaper Mexican workers by American agribusinesses and an increase in the incentive for Mexicans to enter the United States illegally. Men south of the border grew so desperate for work in the United States that they fell easy prey to those who promised to get them across any way possible—in many cases, to be deported soon anyway.

As political lines were being drawn, the issues for the starving Mexican workers remained so basic that political ideologies were irrelevant. One must work to eat. Who among the poor Mexicans ever heard of refusing to work in order to improve their working conditions? If offered a fair wage, why not take it and perform uncomplainingly? To the Mexican worker, American wages, no matter how low, were always better than Mexican wages. Is it Roberto's fault that he was born a poor Mexi-

can farmer? Can it be expected that he should see an American problem through American eyes? He is by circumstances concerned, above all else, with providing food for his family. Abstract ideological concerns are for him a luxury beyond comprehension. The reader accepts Roberto's limited understanding but also sees the larger context as a moral dilemma of which Roberto is unaware: that better pay and working conditions for American workers, however much needed, may penalize humans born elsewhere (in this case, Mexico).

Villaseñor's resolution of Roberto's plight may not completely satisfy those who want an American success story or those who like perfect resolutions to difficult problems. The ending does provide the reader with a sense that both the protagonist and the reader have learned and matured, that the power and the immediacy of life itself, though it may at times depend on political expediency, ultimately transcends political boundaries.

For Roberto, whose physical journey ends with a cyclical return to his origins, the passage to manhood is complete. He has survived the initiation rites of his male society, rites shared by the male warrior/worker (here one and the same) of many, perhaps all, cultures: the Japanese samurai code of *bushido*, the Finnish tacit and unyielding *sisu*, the Roman warrior's stoicism, and the American marine's code of death before dishonor. Arguably, none of those masculine traditions can be fully appreciated or fully defined except by those who have lived them, but Victor Villaseñor offers the reader a glimpse of understanding through the eyes of Roberto Garcia.

Critical Context

Macho!, published under the name Edmund Victor Villaseñor, was the author's first novel. Part of a larger outpouring in the 1960's and 1970's of Latin American literature, it was critically acclaimed when it appeared in 1973.

Each chapter of *Macho!* begins with a prefatory sociopolitical comment on the times immediately preceding (and including) the turbulent American milieu of the late 1960's. Villaseñor's intent is to heighten the reader's awareness of the historical context within which the novel's fictional characters come to life. The novel's main character, serious and intelligent but naïve, endures the type of coming-of-age conflicts that young men in many societies have traditionally encountered. The resulting story dramatizes the struggles of the migrant Mexican farmworker in much the same way that John Steinbeck dramatized the plight of the displaced Okies in *The Grapes of Wrath* (1939).

Villaseñor's later works also rely heavily on dramatization of history. In 1977, Villaseñor's account of the trial of the convicted California serial murderer Juan Corona stirred even more controversy. At issue was the concern that Villaseñor's interpretation of historical events was more creative than present authorial conventions allowed.

Having captured the public's attention, Villaseñor's dramatic talents were given full rein in his 1981 television screenplay *The Ballad of Gregorio Cortez*, which won first place in the National Endowment for the Humanities television drama category that year. The film was subsequently released to theaters and on videocassette. Villaseñor's 1991 *Rain of Gold*, the story of his family's immigration from Mexico to California, is also historical, yet charged with the author's fictionalized personal drama.

Although Villaseñor has established himself as an important and principled chronicler of the Mexican American experience, he has received relatively little critical notice to date. Part of the reason may be that he writes in English about people whose first language is Spanish. That argument may be put to rest by his readers, who immediately recognize the universal appeal of his *Macho!* hero, who challenges the limited stereotypical image of the Latino male. That appeal lifts Villaseñor's work beyond narrow regional or linguistic boundaries, to a genuinely international level of human understanding.

MACHO CAMACHO'S BEAT

Author: Luis Rafael Sánchez (1936-   )
Type of work: Novel
Type of plot: Social satire
Time of plot: The early 1970's
Locale: San Juan, Puerto Rico
First published: *La guaracha del Macho Camacho,* 1976 (English translation, 1980)

Principal Characters

The Heathen Chinky (The Mother), a woman who has been used sexually since she was five years old. Her brother was killed in the Korean War, and her mother died of grief shortly thereafter. When her husband deserted her for a Chicano woman, he left her alone with her encephalitic, retarded son. She prostitutes herself to pay for the boy's food and medical expenses and calculates the price of her material wants in terms of the number of tricks she will have to turn. At the suggestion of the Old Man, she has taken to leaving her child in a nearby park for a beneficial "sun bath" while she meets him. Ironically, she is waiting for the senator's arrival when her child is hit and killed by the car driven by his son, Benny.

Senator Vincente Reinosa (The Old Man), a Puerto Rican politician. Reinosa prides himself on supporting the U.S. involvement in Vietnam, and on his coining of the phrase "Yankee this is home" in response to the "Yankee go home" sentiments of the nationalist movement for independence. He has an inflated sense of his sexual prowess, classing himself within a great tradition beginning with Don Juan and coming down to him through Ricardo Montalban and other Latin lovers. The senator's wife allows him in her bed only on rare occasions, and she is quick to make the sign of the cross immediately thereafter. His relations with his son are limited to providing material goods and immunity from the law. While he waits in traffic, creating inane campaign slogans ("Vince is a prince and easy to convince"), his son, Benny, kills the child of his mistress.

Graciela Alcántara y López de Montefrío, Reinosa's wife. Having been sheltered from the world of men by her widowed mother and sent off to finishing school in Switzerland, she remains ignorant of sexual matters until the day of her wedding. She has since become resigned to this fact of life with the attitude of a Christian martyr. Her relations with her son are limited to admonishing him to keep his friends' motorcycles out of her garden and to prodding him to observe the social graces. She does not care for native Puerto Rican artists who depict the sordid reality around her; she claims that she was not born to look at ugly things. Yet she will not be able to avoid the reality of her life for long. As her son is out on the street mourning the fact that the Kid's brains have stained the door of his Ferrari, Graciela discovers to her dismay that even her posh psychiatrist has become enchanted by Macho Camacho's vulgar *guaracha*.

Benny, the son of the senator and Graciela. Benny is a lazy and reluctant university student and a budding terrorist. He is responsible for plotting and carrying out with his friends the firebombing of the office of a local nationalist group, causing at least one death. His father has presented him with a brand-new Ferrari, which becomes the object of Benny's sexual fantasies; he masturbates in his bed each night with visions of the car dancing in his head. When Benny kills the Kid, his only regret is that the door of his Ferrari is dirtied with the child's blood and brains.

Doña Chon, the Heathen Chinky's friend and neighbor. Doña Chon is enormously overweight and is constantly conjuring up some traditional Creole concoction in her kitchen. She pours forth platitudes and prayers as she pontificates on the problems of the world. She is genuinely kind; she shows concern for the welfare of the Kid; and she mourns deeply the unjustifiably long imprisonment of her daughter Tutú on a minor drug charge. It is because Doña Chon is delayed at the office of her daughter's inept attorney that she is unable to reach the child in time to take him safely home.

The Kid, the encephalitic and mentally retarded son of the Heathen Chinky. He consumes three lizards and innumerable flies per day and lives in a constant puddle of vomit and drool. He is tortured mercilessly by the neighborhood children when he is left in the park, and he is killed as he runs away from his own reflection in a broken mirror.

The Novel

Macho Camacho's Beat is a fictional portrait of life in San Juan, Puerto Rico, at a time when the country is inundated with the sound of Macho Camacho's *guaracha*, or dance tune, "Life Is a Phenomenal Thing." Framed by a notice that reveals the subject of the novel and an appendix that provides the reader with the entire text of the *guaracha*, *Macho Camacho's Beat* is a montage of fragmented narrative sections interrupted by a series of radio announcements that track the meteoric rise in popularity of the rhythmical and irrepressible Afro-Antillean tune.

The entire plot of *Macho Camacho's Beat* occurs within the few minutes before, at, and just after five o'clock on a steamy Wednesday afternoon. As an immense traffic jam paralyzes San Juan, the novel's characters are depicted in the act of waiting. Through the fragments of sounds, images, thoughts, and experience, the reader is able to piece together a composite picture of Puerto Rican culture.

The Heathen Chinky (whose name is never mentioned) is introduced through the device of an omniscient third-person narrator whose relation with each of the characters in the novel is so intimate as to allow the narration to pass fluidly between the third and first-person voices. As she awaits the arrival of her lover, the Old Man (Senator Vincente Reinosa), the Heathen Chinky indulges in sexual fantasies of her virile triplet cousins, Hughie, Louie, and Dewey, and anesthetizes her body with a sea of cubalibres and her mind with the incessant, insistent, and sensual salsa beat of Macho Camacho's *guaracha*.

Senator Vincente Reinosa swelters in his Mercedes-Benz, stuck in the enormous traffic tie-up, impatient to meet his sultry and accommodating dark-skinned mistress (the Heathen Chinky), who waits for him every Monday, Wednesday, and Friday afternoon in a studio apartment rented specifically for convenient fornication. The news of a bombing at the university in San Juan interrupts the senator's lustful fantasies and political self-aggrandizements only long enough for him to worry whether he will lose votes in the next election. As the occupants of the hundreds of immobilized automobiles that surround him dance in the street with a frenzied abandon brought on by the *guaracha*'s irresistible beat, the senator's thoughts quickly return to the schoolgirl he has been ogling, and he wonders if he has time to make her his next conquest.

The senator's aristocratic wife, Graciela Alcántara y López de Montefrío, waits for her appointment with her trendy psychiatrist, Dr. Severo Severino. In her elegant compact mirror, Graciela scrutinizes her face to detect signs of aging and dwells on the absolute abhorrence she has of sexual relations with her husband. Graciela flips through the pages of *Time* magazine, deliberately ignoring the ugly reality of the war in Vietnam and concentrating instead on photographs of Elizabeth Taylor, Richard Burton, and Jacqueline Kennedy Onassis. Finally driven to distraction by the vulgar receptionist who constantly plays the *guaracha* on her radio, Graciela, in an uncontrollable fit of temper, rails against the devastating reality that she can never be truly like her ideal, Jackie O.

The Mother, by a number of similarities—the desire to be Iris Chacón, the affair with the Old Man—is identified as being one and the same person as the Heathen Chinky. In this guise, she is shown in her own home, apparently moments before leaving to keep her appointment with the Old Man. Because the Mother cannot bring her encephalitic three-year-old son, the Kid, with her, she leaves him alone to "sunbathe" on the steps of a basilica in a nearby park—a treatment that the Old Man himself has prescribed. The Mother's neighbor, Doña Chon, agrees to pick the Kid up after the Mother offers to share the money she receives from the Old Man. Before Doña Chon arrives at the park, however, the Kid, cruelly abused by the neighborhood children, runs away from them into the street. Doña Chon arrives just in time to see the Kid hit and killed by a speeding car.

Benny, the spoiled son of the Reinosas, is also stuck in the five o'clock traffic. He sits in his beloved Ferrari, frustrated and furious at being compelled to keep his foot on the brake and restrain the power of his high-speed sports car, the object of his sexual fantasies. Benny's thoughts return obsessively to ways in which he can convince his father that what Puerto Rico's youth really needs are cars and fast tracks on which to race them. When Benny finally breaks free of the traffic, he roars down a narrow side street. The threads of the plot are tied together as Benny, privileged son of the wealthy and aristocratic Reinosas, hits and kills the retarded son of his father's poverty-stricken, lower-class mulatto mistress.

Analysis

Macho Camacho's Beat is a razor-sharp, deep-cutting indictment of Puerto Rican culture. Sánchez's prose is rich with the colorful and often obscene language of the streets, loaded with the language of consumerism, and abundant in references to the lifestyles of the rich and famous, fictional and otherwise. The fragmented, baroque surface of Sánchez's highly allusive prose is a brilliant reflection of the kaleidoscopic confusion caused by the indiscriminate acceptance of the material values espoused by a profit-oriented consumerist society. Language defines thought, and in this novel, language is the product of a largely American-controlled mass media. The resulting inability to communicate on an intimate, personal level creates in the reader a sense of the moral and spiritual poverty of Sánchez's characters.

Macho Camacho's Beat clearly calls for a radical reformation of Puerto Rican society and of the ways in which individuals perceive themselves. The political push to Americanize Puerto Rico and the corruption of government officials are exemplified in the character of Reinosa. The moral decay of the population is sardonically expressed in the Mother's prostitution and Benny's love affair with his Ferrari, which supersedes his affection for any human being. Even the personal physical reality of the people is being transformed and Americanized. This is clearly expressed in Graciela's obsession with makeup, hair, and fashion, in her social life, and in her absurd proposed design for typical Puerto Rican dress: a tailored suit in spotted calfskin.

The key metaphor of the monstrous traffic jam symbolizes the stagnation of a Puerto Rican society that constantly denies its own seedy reality as it becomes obsessed with the fleeting distractions offered by a sensationalist media and subscribes to the seductive but clearly false philosophy of the seductive *guaracha*. No element of Puerto Rican society is immune from Sánchez's irreverent and biting sense of humor. The sins of elitism, racial discrimination, and denial of self are laid bare before the grotesque feet and obtuse minds of the sinners. Just as the Kid is forced to confront his ugly and deformed reality reflected in the surface of a fragmented mirror, Sánchez compels his fellow Puerto Ricans to confront themselves in the fragmented and glittering surface of *Macho Camacho's Beat*.

Critical Context

Luis Rafael Sánchez's first full-length novel, *Macho Camacho's Beat* was written after Sánchez had already been acclaimed as an important Puerto Rican playwright. A critic of literature and the arts, Sánchez has published many articles in newspapers and magazines and has also published a collection of short stories under the title *En cuerpo de camisa* (1966; in casual dress).

Macho Camacho's Beat was an immediate bestseller. Sánchez's use of language and symbol, his irreverent sense of humor, his incisive social criticism, and his ability to explore a culture that is uniquely Puerto Rican has led some critics to consider *Macho Camacho's Beat* the single most important Puerto Rican novel of the twentieth century. In his second novel, *La importancia de llamarse Daniel Santos* (1989; the importance of being named Daniel Santos), Sánchez continued to explore mass culture and society. This second novel goes beyond Puerto Rico to include Latino communities in the United States, Central America, and South America as well as the Antilles, a much broader scope than that of the distinctly Puerto Rican *Macho Camacho's Beat*.

MACUNAÍMA

Author: Mário de Andrade (1893-1945)
Type of work: Novel
Type of plot: Fantasy
Time of plot: The early twentieth century
Locale: Brazil, principally the Amazon jungle and São Paulo
First published: *Macunaíma, o Herói Sem Nenhum Caracter*, 1928 (English translation, 1984)

Principal Characters

Macunaíma, the mock hero. He is lazy, selfish, and abusive, a liar whose main interests are women and money. Even as a child, he already shows an incredible capacity to metamorphose himself into different appearances in order to fulfill his needs and desires. After killing his mother unintentionally, Macunaíma, along with his two brothers and Iriqui, leaves his homeland. They encounter Ci, the Mother of the Forest, who is raped by Macunaíma with the help of his two brothers. As a consequence, he becomes the Emperor of the Dense Jungle. Later on, in a fight against a lake monster, he loses the magical amulet that Ci has given to him. The stone accidentally comes into Venceslau's possession, precipitating the hero's journey to São Paulo in order to recover it.

Maanape, Macunaíma's elderly brother. He is a sorcerer and uses his knowledge and power to cure Macunaíma of the many diseases acquired by the latter in São Paulo. He brings his brother back to life following the first fight with Venceslau.

Jiguê, Macunaíma's witless brother. He is the permanent victim of his brother's tricks. Jiguê's loyalty to Macunaíma motivates him to follow his brother to São Paulo. When they return to the forest, Jiguê, fed up with his brother's mockeries, decides to take vengeance on him but fails.

Ci, the Mother of the Forest. Ci, raped by Macunaíma, gives birth to a child.

Venceslau Pietro Pietra, a man-eating giant. Macunaíma decides to recover his amulet from Venceslau's hands, and, after several attempts, he is able to destroy the giant by throwing him into a boiling pot of macaroni.

Vei, the sun, represented as a female entity. At the beginning, she protects the hero, but, in return for her kindness, she receives his ingratitude. Macunaíma, instead of accepting one of Vei's daughters as his wife, seduces a Portuguese fisherwoman. Vei takes vengeance on him by injuring his private parts with heat rays and leading him to the treacherous arms of a siren.

The Novel

This unusual work is an antirealist fantasy drawn from Amazonian Indian mythology, Afro-Luso-Brazilian folklore, and the author's imagination. Thus, much of what occurs is fablelike, magical, or illogical, with no spatial or temporal bounds. The action centers on the hero's struggle to recover a magical amulet given to him by Ci.

Macunaíma is born an ugly black baby to a Tapanhuma Indian mother. Although he is destined to be a popular hero, his mother notes that all names beginning with "Ma" bring bad luck. The sadistic and mischievous child soon discovers magical powers, transforming himself into a comely prince to seduce his brother Jiguê's first wife. When Jiguê distributes meat after a successful hunt, the hero receives tripe and vows revenge.

During a famine, the hero's acts show him to be vindictive and greedy. As punishment, his mother expels him from the jungle, and he must return home by his wits. Back home, he goes through several metamorphoses to seduce Iriqui, Jiguê's new wife. Tricked by the gods, Macunaíma kills his mother. The three brothers and Iriqui then set off for "our world." They soon encounter Ci, whom the hero rapes, thus becoming the new emperor of the virgin forest. The two engender a son. A venomous serpent causes the death of Ci and son; before ascending to become a bright star, she gives the hero a special amulet. The precious stone is lost as Macunaíma defeats the Water Mother in battle. When the hero learns that the man-eating giant Venceslau has obtained the coveted charm, he sets off for São Paulo to recover it, accompanied by his brothers and a flock of royal parrots.

In the metropolis, the trio trade beans for currency and discover that money rules all. The hero picks up some white women only to discover that they are prostitutes. They explain to Macunaíma that the goblins, spirits, and animals that he thinks he sees are actually buildings and machines. Macunaíma surmises that white people are the Children of Manioc and ruminates on the monumental struggle between urban people and machines; he decides that the contest is a draw and that the two are equivalent. The hero confronts the villain for the first time but is killed, diced, and stewed. Maanape employs his powers to revive him. Posing as a French prostitute, the hero again attempts to lure the amulet from the giant, whose vicious dog pursues Macunaíma through all regions of Brazil. During this chase they encounter several figures from the nation's colonial past. By now the hero is overcome by rancor and attends a voodoo rite in Rio de Janeiro, in which he beseeches devil spirits to punish Venceslau. At the halfway point of the book, the emperor writes a pedantic letter to his subjects recounting his adventures and explaining his impressions of civilization and the Portuguese language.

As Venceslau recuperates, the hero is captured by the giant's wife, whose lustful daughter allows him to escape. The ensuing chase traverses Brazil's varied geography and cultural landscape. After unsuccessful attempts to get a scholarship to finance a trip to Europe, the hero searches for buried treasure, purchases a bogus goose that lays golden eggs, and is tricked into a fatal smashing of his own testicles. Resuscitated again, Macunaíma imagines a European ocean liner in a fountain; his plea for passage is rejected. The giant returns, however, and the hero tricks him into falling into his own stew. Amulet in hand, the emperor heads back home with his brothers.

During the torturous return trip, the hero finds Iriqui again but rejects her in favor of a princess he created from a tree. He cannot find his old conscience, stowed before he left, so he assumes that of a Spanish American. Illness and hunger plague the hero in his new hut. His brothers discover magic food-producing agents, but Macunaíma loses them. A poison hook that he devises turns his brothers into ghostly shadows, who begin persecuting him. This antagonism results in the creation of folk dances and rites. In his solitude, Macunaíma feels remorse and recalls his former glory. Vei the Sun lures him into mortal combat with the Lady of the Lake. He loses the amulet and a leg. Macunaíma decides to give up life and ascends to heaven as the Great Bear constellation. Many years later, a man wanders into the jungle to be told these great tales by a parrot. That man is the omniscient narrator of this work.

Analysis

Mário de Andrade is as well known for his work in music as for his literary endeavors. He called *Macunaíma* not a novel but a "rhapsody." This classification suggests both sung epic poetry (such as the *Iliad* and the *Odyssey*) and an instrumental fantasy based on popular or traditional melodies. In literature, the term also connotes an ecstatic, highly emotional, or irrational work. All these meanings of "rhapsody" have a direct relation to *Macunaíma*. Although Andrade's fundamental approach is comic, it is clear that the saga of Macunaíma is a reflection on questions of Brazilian nationality. The work playfully brings into question the character and psyche of Brazil as a young American nation and of its people as a diverse population. Thus, the contradictory qualities of the turbulent hero himself are central to any evaluation of the novel. Orality is emphasized throughout the work; that which the narrator relates has been learned from a parrot, and characters constantly relate deeds, accomplishments, or myths of origin. Popular, traditional, or indigenous elements inform the entirety of the novel, and linear logic is subordinated to unbridled fantasy throughout.

One of the work's central themes is language itself, the primary vehicle of culture. The author blends, often arbitrarily, the vocabulary and structure of standard Portuguese, colorful street language, and many regional varieties into a unique linguistic style. In the original, many passages are unintelligible even to native Brazilians. The author's aim was to raise readers' consciousness about the diversity of their New World language, in which thousands of indigenous and African words were added to the European mother tongue. Enumeration is frequent and meaningful in *Macunaíma*. When biting insects or parrots are mentioned, for example, dozens of kinds are listed. This technique calls attention to a copious rural vocabulary and emphasizes geographical differences between the New World tropics and the dominant culture of Europeans who came to conquer.

Another of the principal aims of *Macunaíma* is to poke fun at the classical rhetoric dominant in Luso-Brazilian letters until the 1920's. The letter that the hero writes to his Amazon subjects midway through the novel is the high point of stylistic satire. This effort is particularly effective because the letter writer is an ingenuous native looking at urban culture as an outsider in his own country. Macunaíma writes in the pedantic, verbose academic style of Brazil's traditional intellectual leaders, employing Latinate structures, eloquent vocabulary, and erudite allusions. On the surface, the letter appears to be constructed impeccably, but there are many grammatical errors, misuses of words, and stylistic abuses. The letter also satirizes mores, customs, and São Paulo society. The innocent hero describes things as he sees them, and many aspects of urban life are seen in a comic light. Corruption, prostitution, bad public health, and faulty services, among other elements, emerge from the hero's explanations of civilization.

Cultural satire and contrast play an important role outside the letter. The figure of the villain, a cannibalistic giant and wealthy merchant, incorporates a satire of the many Italian immigrants who became rich in São Paulo and suggests the rapacious nature of business in Brazil as well as the dominant role of foreign nations in its commerce.

Critical Context

Andrade wrote *Macunaíma* during a six-day frenzy and underwrote its publication. The literary establishment was perplexed by the work and gave it a bad reception. The leading critics of the time called it barbarous, outrageous, disconnected, fragmented, and excessive. Most failed to see the unity of the interwoven motifs, and some reacted negatively to its flamboyance and obscenity. *Macunaíma* was one of the most forceful affronts to literary decorum of the 1920's. This was the decade of modernism in Brazil, an iconoclastic and nationalistic movement of literary renovation that sought to break sharply with the past, to challenge the influence of Portuguese letters, and to make national reality the focus of literary endeavor. With his rhapsodic novel, Andrade made a major contribution to a radical literary faction known as "Anthropophagy," which used the practice of cannibalism as a metaphor for their project of modern Brazilian writing.

It was not until 1955 that *Macunaíma* began to be fully appreciated by critics and the reading public. In that year, a detailed explanation of Andrade's sources, cultural references, and allusions was published, showing the thematic unity of the work and its complicated background. This critical defense acknowledged that *Macunaíma* was frightening and astounding, but for its erudition and craft and not for its supposed incoherence or immorality. *Macunaíma* is now regarded as one of the most representative and influential works of Brazilian modernism and a foremost example of literary rebellion and nationalism in Latin American literature in general. In 1969, *Macunaíma* was made into a film, one of the most successful productions of Brazil's New Cinema.

THE MAMBO KINGS PLAY SONGS OF LOVE

Author: Oscar Hijuelos (1951-   )
Type of work: Novel
Type of plot: Historical realism
Time of plot: The 1950's to the 1980's
Locale: New York City
First published: 1989

Principal Characters

Cesar Castillo, the novel's protagonist, born and reared in a poor family in Oriente, the eastern section of Cuba. During his childhood, Cesar suffers the violence of his abusive father. In Oriente, Cesar marries Luisa, with whom he has a daughter, Mariela. Their marriage is rather unstable, and after several separations, Cesar finally leaves Luisa permanently and goes to Havana. In 1949, Cesar decides to emigrate to New York City with his brother Nestor in the hope of succeeding as a musician. Upon arriving in the United States, Cesar and Nestor form the Mambo Kings, an orchestra that enjoys moderate success in dance halls and theaters. Cesar's greatest accomplishment in show business is his appearance on an episode of *I Love Lucy* in 1955. Soon after, however, Nestor is killed in a car accident. This event changes Cesar's personality; he is transformed from an apparently happy fellow into a sad, alcoholic man who tries to become more like his late brother. As Cesar becomes older and less attractive, his already low self-esteem (only temporarily bolstered by his extreme good looks) begins to worsen, and his life sinks into a series of escapes that finally ends in a melancholic remembrance of his past experiences.

Nestor Castillo, the younger of the two Castillo brothers. He spends most of his life mourning for a lost love named María back in Cuba. Although he is mainly a follower of his brother Cesar, it is Nestor who composes "Beautiful María of My Soul," the most popular song of the Mambo Kings' repertoire. In spite of his melancholia, Nestor manages to marry a girl named Delores in New York, and they have two children, Eugenio and Leticia.

Nestor tries to overcome his sadness and be a good husband and father, but he is unable to overcome his basically unhappy disposition.

Eugenio Castillo, Nestor and Delores' son. Eugenio appears in the novel as a sort of alter ego of the author; his role in the story itself is secondary. Eugenio becomes important to the plot only after his father's death, when he becomes closer to his uncle Cesar. Nevertheless, Eugenio is an important element in the book, because he narrates the prologue and epilogue. In the epilogue, moreover, Eugenio becomes the main character of a brief narrative sequence set in Los Angeles, where he goes to meet Desi Arnaz after Cesar's death.

Delores Castillo, Nestor's wife. Delores is an interesting woman who, unlike Nestor and Cesar, is eager to study and attend school. She firmly believes that her role as a mother and wife is not in conflict with her impulse to learn from books. This interest in studying is one of the main causes of her marital problems, but she manages most of the time to do what she wants without provoking a major break with Nestor. After Nestor's death, she remarries, to a quiet man who is tolerant of her aspirations.

Desi Arnaz, a real-life musician from Oriente who became the most well-known Cuban entertainer in the United States. In *The Mambo Kings Play Songs of Love*, the fictional Desi invites Cesar and Nestor to appear on his television show. Years later, both Desi and Eugenio recall the past and express sorrow for a life that does not give any meaning to the act of dying.

The Novel

The Mambo Kings Play Songs of Love is the fictionalized story of two Cuban brothers, Cesar and Nestor Castillo, who emigrate to New York City from Havana in 1949 hoping to succeed as musicians. The novel is divided into five sections, three of which are extensive and tell the main story in detail; the other two are very short and appear as a prologue and epilogue to the narration. An omniscient third-person narrator tells the story in the three large sections, while Eugenio narrates the prologue and epilogue in the first person.

The book begins in 1980. Eugenio recalls how in 1954, when he was not yet five years old, his father Nestor (now deceased) and his uncle Cesar (now old and disenchanted with his life) had appeared on the *I Love Lucy* television program as Ricky Ricardo's singing cousins fresh from Cuba. For Eugenio, this moment is more than just the high point in Nestor and Cesar's musical career; it is "a beautiful night of glory, beyond death, beyond pain, beyond all stillness." This great moment of success does not reveal the many sorrows that the two brothers experience after their arrival in New York in 1949, also the year when the two Castillo brothers form the Mambo Kings, an orchestra that is relatively successful for a time in nightclubs, dance halls, and theaters along the East Coast. Nestor is never happy after leaving Cuba; he is obsessed with the memory of a former girlfriend named María who broke his heart. It is precisely this sad memory that inspires Nestor to compose the Mambo Kings' most successful song, "Beautiful María of My Soul."

Nestor dies in a car accident in 1957. Although Cesar and one of his girlfriends are also in the car when the accident occurs, they are not injured.

Cesar, who has always seemed happy, concerned only with music, women, and drinking, starts to become as unhappy as his late brother was. Cesar feels responsible for Nestor's death, and these feelings of guilt cause him to become an alcoholic. After Nestor's death, Cesar becomes very close to Nestor's wife, Delores, and their children, Eugenio and Leticia. Cesar attempts all kinds of solutions and escapes in order to overcome his great sadness: He goes back to visit his family in Cuba; he joins the merchant marine for eighteen months; he tries to revive his musical career; he continues his obsessive womanizing; and above all, he drinks more and more heavily.

The richness of *The Mambo Kings Play Songs of Love* stems not only from the story of the two immigrant brothers but also from the book's detailed descriptions of life in New York City. The discussion of historical events and the use of real names of important Latin musicians and other public figures of the time help to re-create the ambience of both New York City and Cuba. The events of the Cuban Revolution of 1959 and the resulting waves of exiles from Cuba to the United States are an important part of the novel's second section.

Near the end of the novel, readers learn about Cesar's death. In the epilogue, Eugenio tells how he went to Los Angeles one year after Cesar's death to meet Desi Arnaz, who had sent Eugenio a letter of condolence. Desi ended this letter with an invitation to his home, where he receives Eugenio affectionately. As the two men recall days gone by, their reminiscing gives way to Eugenio's intense daydreaming of a fantastic, wonderful world where he, his father, and his uncle are blissfully happy.

Analysis

From a psychological point of view, the main meaning of Cesar and Nestor's story has to do with the disastrous results of being reared in an abusive environment. Cesar and Nestor are unable to overcome the low self-esteem produced by the abuse their father inflicted upon them. Nevertheless, the novel has another main theme that transcends the psychological or individual perspective: the search for the American Dream. In the novel, however, the American Dream appears void of any meaningful fulfillment. The two Castillo brothers search in vain for happiness; American society does not provide more than a materialistic solution for most of their aspirations. Consumerism—manifested in cars, carnal pleasures, and a sense of financial prosperity—is all that the American Dream has to offer the Castillo brothers.

The story of the two musician brothers and their Mambo Kings orchestra coincides with a historical, worldwide increase in interest in Latin music and culture. This fact gives special importance to the events narrated in *The Mambo Kings Play Songs of Love*, because the Latin music of the Castillo brothers introduces the reader to an important historical period in the relationship between American and Latin cultures. During the three decades covered by the story, moreover, both U.S. and Cuban society underwent radical changes; the novel thus helps to vivify such epochal developments as the Cuban Revolution and the U.S. Civil Rights movement.

Critical Context

The Mambo Kings Play Songs of Love, Oscar Hijuelos' second novel, was his first commercial success; his first novel, *Our House in the Last World* (1983), although welcomed by critics, did not sell well. Nevertheless, Hijuelos won the Rome Fellowship in Literature of Arts and Letters in 1985, mainly on the strength of *Our House in the Last World*. One of Hijuelos' main concerns as a writer is a deep desire for an understanding of his parents' lives prior to his birth; in his first book, Hijuelos tried to penetrate the Cuban cultural world in which his parents lived.

The Mambo Kings Play Songs of Love is a sort of continuation of Hijuelos' search for his parents' lives and culture. This time, however, Hijuelos concentrates his artistic imagination on fictionalizing a generation of Cubans in New York City in the 1950's. The character Eugenio is a kind of alter ego of Hijuelos himself. Eugenio appears as the author of the novel's prologue and epilogue, and there are some suggestions in the rest of the work that Eugenio might have written the entire story of the Castillo brothers.

The Mambo Kings Play Songs of Love enjoyed enormous critical and commercial success. The novel won Hijuelos the 1990 Pulitzer Prize for fiction, the first such prize won by a Cuban American writer, and was adapted to film in both English and Spanish.

A MANUAL FOR MANUEL

Author: Julio Cortázar (1914-1984)
Type of work: Novel
Type of plot: Social morality
Time of plot: 1969 to 1972
Locale: Paris, France, and Buenos Aires, Argentina
First published: *Libro de Manuel*, 1973 (English translation, 1978)

Principal Characters

Andres Fava, the main narrator, an Argentine intellectual living in Paris. He is connected to the members, though not much to the activities, of a principally Latin American activist group, the Screwery.

The one I told you, an Argentine writer who is quietly chronicling the activities of the Screwery. His narrative, together with the clippings and other documentary materials collected by Susana for her son Manuel, seems to correspond to the book Cortázar has written, so "the one I told you" can be seen as a surrogate author.

Marcos, the Argentine head of the Screwery, a dedicated revolutionary who is also something of an intellectual. Under Marcos' direction, the members of the Screwery create small provocations in Parisian public places, aimed at raising consciousness among ordinary citizens. They also undertake the kidnapping of a police official.

Ludmilla, an actress of Polish descent who has been Andres' lover and who begins a relationship with Marcos shortly before the kidnapping.

Susana, an Argentine member of the Screwery, married to Patricio. They are the parents of the infant Manuel. Susana is putting together a scrapbook of political clippings that is to serve as a kind of primer for Manuel.

Patricio, Manuel's father and Susana's husband, an active member of the Screwery.

Manuel, the son of Susana and Patricio, an energetic infant who keeps his parents and the members of the Screwery busy attending to his needs and steering him away from household hazards.

Lonstein, an Argentine who works at the morgue but cultivates intellectual interests and occasionally writes a poem. At the end of the novel, Lonstein is at the morgue cleaning the corpse of an unspecified friend—whether Marcos, the one I told you, or Andres is unclear.

Francine, Andres' French lover, university-trained, a well-organized woman who owns a bookshop and lives in a well-appointed apartment.

Gomez, a Panamanian member of the Screwery who is considered to be a conventional, unimaginative Marxist militant by intellectuals in the group. He is the lover of Monique, a French member of the group.

Lucien Verneuil, a French member of the Screwery. He participates in both the group's antic disruptions of Parisian street life and the kidnapping.

The Vip, the Screwery's name for the portly Latin American police official in charge of international antiterrorist operations. He is kidnapped by the Screwery and held in exchange for a number of political prisoners to be freed from Latin American jails.

Higinio, a Latin American secret police official entrusted with protecting the Vip. Higinio is called the Gi-ant by the Screwery, whose code name for the secret police is the ants. He is prepared to have the Vip shot so as to ensure that the kidnappers will be charged with the maximum offense.

The Novel

As the novel begins, Susana translates and discusses articles from the newspaper with other members of a revolutionary group called the Screwery. A telegram from London and a reference to something called the "Vincennes business" constitute the readers' introduction to the group's plan to smuggle counterfeit money in order to finance a political kidnapping. The target is a top Latin American police official, referred to as the Vip, whose headquarters are in Paris. He is to be held for ransom until Latin American political prisoners are released.

As the kidnapping preparations are under way, Andres takes Francine to a sleazy bar. He then tells her about a dream in which he sees himself in a film theater that has two screens at right angles. He is there to see a Fritz Lang thriller. A messenger arrives and tells him that a Cuban wants to speak with him. Andres follows the messenger until he enters a room where he sees a figure on a sofa. It is the Cuban. At this point, the most important point in the dream, the dream's narrative is interrupted. The next thing that Andres sees is himself, now spectator of and participant in a thriller, leaving the room. Andres interprets the dream to mean that since he has spoken to the Cuban, he now has a mission to fulfill. He has no idea, however, what the mission might be. Andres' quest is directed toward one goal: to find the message cut from his dream, a message that will show him the road he should elect between the beloved solitude of his life as an intellectual in Paris and total political commitment.

The kidnapping does not occur until three-quarters of the way into the book, and the account of the actual moment, provided by the unnamed character identified only as "the one I told you," is no more than "a general impression of total confusion." The details that would have "made a good narrative" are missing. Andres, who is not present at the kidnapping, is awakened from sleep when the Cuban from his dream says to him, "Wake up." He arrives at the scene of a police shoot-out where the Screwery is holding the Vip. The Vip is released, saved by the police. Gomez and Heredia are next seen in prison. They discuss the fact that "Marcos would have thought" that the operation went well. Proceedings of a press conference on human rights follow this scene. Accounts from Argentines who had been tortured appear in one column, juxtaposed to testimony from North American soldiers who witnessed or participated in torture in Vietnam. The novel ends with two glimpses of the return to everyday life: Monique cares for the baby and waits for news from Gomez; Andres tells Susana that he must pick up a Joni Mitchell record and put the notes of "the one I told you" in order, and that the water pitcher story must be added. It is implied that "the one I told you" has died. Lonstein returns to his job washing bodies in the morgue.

The novel ends with a fantastic twist. The body that Lonstein washes, after picking up a water pitcher, is not identified, but Lonstein recognizes him and says, "It had to be us, that's for certain, you there and me with this sponge, you were so right, they're going to think we made it all up." The reader must link "the blackish stain," which Lonstein removes with the sponge, to the character who went out to pick up a Joni Mitchell record, Andres.

Analysis

A Manual for Manuel is a novel about the continuing war between Latin American guerrillas and Latin American government. It is literally a collage of fragments. Using newspaper clippings, testimony from human rights commission hearings, advertisements, recipes, and musings on literary criticism, Cortázar interrogates his own identity through the character of Andres; he questions his life as an intellectual and the role of the intellectual in relationship to political commitment. As an Argentina who lived in Paris after 1951 and as a translator for the United Nations Educational, Scientific, and Cultural Organization, Cortázar was acutely aware of the ideological as well as the directly confrontational warfare in Argentina and elsewhere. Selecting and translating from newspapers was part of his job. His transformation of these newspaper texts into a novel can be understood as his attempt to recapture the subject he had to translate for others. He was aware of the difficulty of writing about the themes of *A Manual for Manuel*, which include political torture; in one passage, he points out that Latin American readers are already aware of the issues, rendering the novel useless as a didactic device, while North American readers do not usually have the background to understand the political references. In *Hopscotch* (1963), he discusses the dilemma of the man of action and the intellectual. He condemns both for the unforgivable sin of conformity. One conforms to the party while the other capitulates to the dictates of everyday life. The dilemma is presented again in *A Manual for Manuel*, but this time, the work centers on a group devoted to political action. Andres, the narrator, is not present at the moment of political action, the kidnapping of the Vip. He is always on the outside. This is the problem of the modernist writer. Cortázar seeks to overcome it to some extent by actively involving what he calls the "reader accomplice."

Critical Context

A Manual for Manuel was awarded the Prix Médicis. One critic has called it a necessary second volume for *Hopscotch*. The narrative structure of *A Manual for Manuel*, although less complex than that of *Hopscotch*, is experimental and similar to the structure used by twentieth century musicians, both classical and jazz. It proceeds in a more or less linear manner, but there are certain questions left unanswered, certain unfilled gaps, because of the way in which the story is told. There is no omnipresent narrator. Rather, the story is told primarily through the eyes of a narrator, "the one I told you," and Andres. The fact that the modernist cannot get inside the historical event, rendering modernist literature helpless as a political educational tool, is of concern to Cortázar. His novel is about this problem, making the work postmodernist in that it examines the structure of the modernist novel.

Philosophically, Cortázar's refusal of the role of omniscient narrator implies that there is no essence to be distinguished from appearance. Two possible conclusions arise: He is a Kantian, who believes that the object is unknowable, or he is a postmodernist, who refuses to distinguish between art and its object. The implication of this method is that reality becomes intelligible through the combined activity of the writer and reader, who write or read the text. In *A Manual for Manuel*, "the one I told you" sees the kidnapping as a "multilenticular and quadrichromatic picture of the ants and the Vip himself. . . ." This "multilenticular" view joins the imaginings of "the one I told you" with the "sparser" information possessed by Marcos and Ludmilla. The active reader of the book must then take all of this and attempt to reconstruct the event.

In terms of genre, Cortázar's work has been linked to the literature of fantasy and Magical Realism, both by critics and in his own writing. He sees his activity as a writer and the active participation that he demands on the part of the reader as a form of political practice that transcends the boundaries of traditional genres to become a testimony of Latin American reality. Certain critics have interpreted the freedom embodied in his characters as a model for overcoming alienation and shaking epistemological assumptions. Cortázar sees the "Other," the dimension of the fantastic, as the only salvation from conforming to the role of obedient robots that technocrats would like people to accept and that they continue to refuse. In his own life, the political form of Cortázar's refusal can be seen in his support for the Cuban revolution, Salvador Allende's regime, the Russell Tribunal, and the Nicaraguan revolution.

A Manual for Manuel marked a turning point in Cortázar's career, toward political literature. Not all critics greeted this change favorably, and many still believe that *Hopscotch* is a more successful literary work.

MEMORY OF FIRE

Author: Eduardo Galeano (1940-   )
Type of work: History
Time of work: *Genesis*, the pre-Columbian period to 1700; *Faces and Masks*, 1700-1900; *Century of the Wind*, 1900-1984
Locale: Principally Latin America, but also North America and Europe
First published: *Memoria del fuego I: Los nacimientos*, 1982 (*Memory of Fire I: Genesis*, 1985); *Memoria del fuego II: Las caras y las máscaras*, 1984 (*Memory of Fire II: Faces and Masks*, 1987); *Memoria del fuego III: El siglo del viento*, 1986 (*Memory of Fire III: Century of the Wind*, 1988)

The Work

Although the trilogy *Memory of Fire* has been classified as a work of history, it is a supremely personal and subjective history. The author, Eduardo Galeano, makes no claim to being a historian; in fact, he specifically states the contrary. In school, he found history courses to be like visits to a "waxworks" or "the Region of the Dead," with the past "lifeless, hollow, dumb." His literary efforts have been a reaction to such a view of history and the desire to make history vital again. The title *Memory of Fire* reflects the author's purpose: "to contribute to the rescue of the kidnapped memory of all America, but above all of Latin America, that despised and beloved land." To preserve this important memory, Galeano wrote a unique series of three books containing short episodes that form a mosaic of the many elements contributing to America's past.

The format of the trilogy underlines the subjective nature of the work. Although many voices are taken into account, the work reveals one vision, that of the author. It is not an anthology, Galeano maintains, but to classify it as a novel, essay, epic poem, testament, or chronicle is equally difficult— probably because it contains elements of each of these. Every fragment is based on documented information, with a series of sources listed in the back of each volume and referred to by number at the end of the episode involved. The information upon which each fragment is based comes from many types of sources, but the choices of what to include and how to tell what happened reveal Galeano's own bias. The author recognizes that he is not "neutral" in his reporting; he "takes sides." The side he takes is clearly that of the oppressed groups, whether Indian, black, poor, or female. Finding traditional textbook history filled with lies and made to serve the function of teaching people to "resign [themselves] with drained consciences to the present," Galeano presents his history as a vital part of stimulating change, using the repetition of ideas, episodes, and motifs so that the three volumes form one vision of the rich Latin American tradition as well as the history of exploitation of people and natural resources.

Genesis, the first volume of the trilogy, is divided into two parts, "First Voices" and "Old New World." The "First Voices" are Indian myths of pre-Columbian America, starting appropriately with a creation myth and ending with a prophecy of the "rule of greed." In between, the harmonious relationship of the Indian with nature is given a full range of expression through stories of many different tribes. As the section closes, a tale called "Authority" introduces a recurring theme, that the power of one group over another (in this case, men over women) is often based on a lie that is passed from one generation to the next. In this way, he suggests, the rule of master over servant is maintained, once violence and murder have established it. Galeano then introduces three sections, titled "Dangers," "The Spider Web," and "The Prophet," in which the arrival of the Europeans is foretold: "Men wearing clothes shall come, dominate, and kill." In contrast to the domination to come, the pre-Columbian Indians' life resembles paradise.

The remainder of *Genesis* relates a series of historical moments, starting in 1492 on board Christopher Columbus' ship and ending in 1700 at the deathbed of Charles II. Each episode, whether focusing on a specific incident or an individual, has a heading with the year and location in addition to a title. Galeano consults various sources for his information and occasionally interpolates literal transcriptions, which appear in italics.

Faces and Masks continues the same format as the second part of *Genesis*. This volume begins with an entry titled "Promise of America"—the search for paradise that the land of America stimulated in Indians as well as in the conquistadores—and ends with a second prophecy, speaking of the end of greed through struggle and the establishment of freedom. This book covers the years 1701 through 1900 and contains an almost overwhelming amount of violence and betrayal that the positive tone of the final section cannot counterbalance.

Century of the Wind picks up at the beginning of the twentieth century. "The World Goes On," as the title notes, in spite of the belief of many that the world would end at midnight on the last day of 1899. Galeano traces modern developments in Latin America and its relations with the United States. Freedom is crushed repeatedly, but each time there is new rebellion. Galeano traces the cycle through many turns and ends on the positive note of the irresistible life force, symbolized here by the "Maypole fiesta" and the "tree of life." As with the second volume, Galeano reaffirms the positive despite the horrors presented in the historical chronicle of this period.

This trilogy is a mixed composition drawn from mythology, literature, historical accounts, newspapers, and other varied sources. The sheer number of sources—227 for *Genesis*, 361 for *Faces and Masks*, and 475 for *Century of the Wind*—shows the volume of material that went into creating this mosaic, intended to represent the whole of Latin American history and experience.

Analysis

That *Memory of Fire* is a personal statement on the part of the author quickly becomes clear. Galeano is not aloof from politics and the struggles of the poor and powerless. Although the tone is controlled and the prose often stripped down to an essential statement of facts, the choice of episodes and persons as well as the vocabulary quickly reveals his sympathy with socialist aims. Some critics have reacted to the political overtones, while others have focused on the enormity of the task of writing a complete Latin American epic of this type. The majority seem to believe that, viewed as a subjective, personal collection of moments in history, *Memory of Fire* is extremely successful in making history live, in capturing its electricity.

Because of the length of time involved, from pre-Columbian times through 1984, a format of connected fragments was used. These are joined together in a type of symphonic structure, with themes or motifs that appear and reappear. The language of the individual entries, which often read like stories told as part of the oral tradition, is often poetic and musical, though never florid. It has been suggested that a series of fragments is the most appropriate form for a history of Latin America: The land itself is splintered into individual countries, themselves splintered into factions and classes, with the result that there is no one Latin American identity, only a multitude of voices and faces. Galeano visualizes this history as one of conflict, a record of resistance to injustice and oppression.

Because *Memory of Fire* is clearly a personal chronicle, it is inevitable that the choice of documentary sources reflects a personal bias. Because the work is also a presentation of history, that choice is significant. The several hundred sources involved in the three volumes are a heterogeneous collection involving everything from myths and stories to newspaper reports and data gleaned from standard texts on conquest and colonization. Galeano borrows from each as it fits his total vision. The result underlines the fact that this is not a historian's history, not an objective analysis or an attempt to weigh the validity of documents. In his sources are tales of magic along with reports and opinions based on insufficient evidence or even possible misinterpretation. The questions of what really happened and how to interpret it are important, particularly as Galeano attempts to unmask how the lies of history become the official version, as in "The Government Decides That Peronism Doesn't Exist" and "The Government Decides That Truth Doesn't Exist." Another humorous illustration is the episode in which the president of Guatemala proclaims the Santa María volcano to be dormant despite the lava destroying Quetzaltenango. The ironic title reads, "The Government Decides That Reality Doesn't Exist."

The cyclical format of *Memory of Fire* is introduced in *Genesis*; in Spanish, *los nacimientos* ("beginnings" or "births"). Appropriately, the first fragments deal with the "birth" of creation in a dream by God. The myth introduces the idea of cyclical time because woman and man will be born and die again and again: Much of the first section of *Genesis* focuses on indigenous myths of nature. Only toward the end of the section is the prophecy of the "rule of greed" introduced: "Men will turn into slaves," and "the world will be depopulated, it will become small and humiliated."

Genesis then presents historical moments to illustrate the fulfillment of this prophecy. From the beginning, the Indians lose in the clash of cultures that Columbus' discovery causes. In a report ironically titled "Day of Glory," the few surviving Indians brought to Europe as trophies are paraded before a hostile audience that would have preferred gold or spices.

Religion and greed as causes of tremendous suffering in the Americas becomes the theme of *Genesis*. In separate fragments, six Indians are burned alive for the sacrilege of burying images of Christ and the Virgin (to fertilize their crops), and Aztec human sacrifices are juxtaposed to the burning of heretics by the Spanish Inquisition. In reaction to mistreatment of the Indians, protests begin to arise—first from Antonio de Montesinos and then from Bartolomé de las Casas.

European diseases and overwork wipe out whole populations of Indians, and the slave trade brings blacks from Africa to do manual labor. The desire for freedom arises repeatedly, and the oppressed revolt. Revolt is followed by repression, which in turn will be followed by another revolt.

The irony of the Spanish exploitation of America's resources is a theme introduced early and followed through the wars of independence in *Faces and Masks*. Although the conquest was accomplished by Spaniards and many Indians and blacks paid with their lives for the gold sent to Europe, "the metals arriving from Mexico and Peru do not even leave a smell in Spain." European merchants and bankers outside Spain profited instead.

Galeano does not paint pre-Columbian America as a garden of Eden, but he presents an image of a lost paradise, with hope for the future, in *Faces and Masks* and *Century of the Wind*. Already in *Genesis*, there is an episode in which Mancio Serra de Leguízamo, one of the conquistadores of the Incas, is dying. He confesses the inherent goodness he sees in the Indian way of life, with its community property and lack of greed. *Faces and Masks* starts with the idea that people have sought paradise in America and continues with a series of episodes illustrating that this hope for paradise remains unfulfilled. Galeano argues the case of the oppressed, demonstrating the crushing weight of history against the powerless while admiring the spirit of those who resist. The motif of runaway slaves recurs, as does the question of the oppression of women.

As the wars of independence rage, the oppressed groups show their courage in the resistance against Spain, but the wealthy Creoles fear a real revolution of the underclasses. "Agrarian reform" alternately inspires hope in the poor and is suppressed by the wealthy, who fear the loss of their economic advantages. This reform is connected clearly with the Indians' idea of common property: "All belongs to all."

A main figure of *Faces and Masks* is José Martí, whose ideas are important to Galeano. Martí sees Latin America fighting to revive its "hidden and betrayed identity" rather than accepting the one imposed by Europe or the United States. Here the theme of the mask from the title is most clearly emphasized. Galeano quotes Martí as writing: "We were a mask, with trousers from England, Parisian vest, jacket from North America, and cap from Spain." Latin America does not recognize the value of its own customs and language. Starting in *Genesis*, Galeano interpolates episodes showing the devaluing of anything Indian or mestizo. The attitude continues even after independence to apply to art, clothing, dance, customs, and literally anything that is an American product. The image left at the end of *Faces and Masks* is of an American plundering its raw materials to send overseas, working Indians, blacks, and the poor to do it. Nevertheless, freedom and the end of the rule of greed strike the last chords of the volume.

Century of the Wind reintroduces many of these themes as they apply to the twentieth century. Here the United States becomes the outside power with the strength to crush rebellions. At the same time, the question of the appeal of Marxism is introduced. The Peruvian poet José Carlos Mariátegui sees the depths of his country in the Indian communities, which are "unconquered in their socialist traditions of work and life." The events of Cuba and Nicaragua continue that thread.

Many grotesque dictators are introduced in short vignettes, and the suffering of the individual who resists is shown in the person of Miguel Mármol, who escapes death many times during the years of his long life. Events of modern Latin American history show a fragmented continent with individual countries waging war against their neighbors and thus squandering their resources, with the result that debts to foreign powers control their economies. Violent repression occurs when-

ever the questions of agrarian reform, divorce laws, higher wages, or nationalization are raised, since each of these challenges one or more powerful groups. A president who "dares to commit" reform, for example Salvador Allende (Chile) or João Goulart (Brazil), is eliminated.

The many atrocities are recounted in tones of sadness and irony. The humor inherent in the human condition, specifically in the Latin American condition, is used to relieve the stark portrait the author paints. Even here, however, irony is Galeano's strongest weapon. "The Soccer War," for example, between El Salvador and Honduras seems impossibly absurd at one level yet horribly ironic at the same time, as two fragments of what was once a single republic define each other as the enemy and leave thousands dead in battle. In another example, the words "bad luck, human error, bad weather" from official reports become an ironic litany in the account of the deaths of President Roldós of Ecuador, Omar Torrijos of Panama, and General Rafael Hoyos Rubio of Peru, all of whom had opposed powerful economic groups and died in suspicious plane crashes for it. To round out the irony, Galeano uses ironic juxtaposition of words ("benevolent multinational corporations"), a stylistic device that is almost a trademark of this trilogy.

Against the chronicle of torture, repression, and wars, Galeano repeatedly infuses an element of hope: Things could change. He writes of the Indians who are "guided by the ancient certainty that someday greed and arrogance will be punished," and he includes many episodes of brave individuals and groups who stand up for their beliefs in spite of almost certain death. At the end of *Century of the Wind*, Galeano closes with nine fragments, starting with "Against Forgetting," that express his purpose in compiling this personal epic. Believing with Carlos Quijano (publisher of the *Marcha* magazine) that forgetting is "the only death that really kills," Galeano makes *Memory of Fire* his pledge that this massive history and tradition will not be forgotten.

Critical Context

Modern Latin American history has often seemed to the outside world like an unending series of dictatorships, atrocities, and economic problems. Galeano's work attempts to balance that view with a vision of the dormant potential inherent in the people. For the Latin American, he gives expression to the turbulent history of the region. At the same time, he allows the outsider an insight into the many fragments of the Latin American experience. He reminds the reader of a rich culture outside that of Europe. Although greatly influenced by European civilization, it has its own unique characteristics.

Galeano's work stresses political and social questions that result from economic problems and the brutality of dictatorships. Politically engaged, he admires the heroic individuals who fight against oppression and uses his work to plead for solidarity against those who abuse power. His sympathies lie with the poor, and he sees in socialism a continuation of the Indian custom of common property, which he finds so admirable compared to the greed of big business and wealthy landowners. For expressing such opinions, he spent many years in exile. He finally returned to his homeland of Uruguay in 1984.

As a journalist, he contributed to *El Sol*, a socialist weekly, and was editor of *Marcha* and *Época*. His first international recognition came from his book *Las venas abiertas de América Latina* (1971; *Open Veins of Latin America: Five Centuries of the Pillage of the Continent*, 1973), which discusses the problem of underdevelopment in Latin America. From his collection of stories to his important novels, *La canción de nosotros* (1975; our song) and *Días y noches de amor y de guerra* (1978; *Days and Nights of Love and War*, 1983), Galeano writes in the tradition of contemporary Uruguayan fiction, which attempts to deal with the harsh realities of dictatorship and economic crisis along with the political movements demanding change. With *Memory of Fire*, he writes an epic history of Latin America, showing the destructive forces in the clash of traditions that produced it and in the division between rich and poor that still dominates it. Bringing together history, literature, mythology—in fact, fragments of everything he finds significant—he produces a kaleidoscope of impressions, joined together through repeated themes and by the author's own desire to keep alive the memory of the past, whose influence continues to be felt as Latin America forges its future.

MEN OF MAIZE

Author: Miguel Ángel Asturias (1899-1974)
Type of work: Novel
Type of plot: Social morality
Time of plot: The twentieth century
Locale: Guatemala
First published: *Hombres de maíz*, 1949 (English translation, 1975)

Principal Characters

Gaspar Ilóm, an Indian guerrilla leader poisoned by the Machojóns. He fights against the maizegrowers, who are destroying the forests. The Indians believe that he rose from the dead to continue to curse those who burn down the forest to cultivate maize as a cash crop instead of a sacred food.

Piojosa Grande, the "Great Fleabag," the wife of Gaspar Ilóm. She tries unsuccessfully to escape the massacre of her husband's men with their son. According to Indian lore, she is the rain and her son is the maize.

Tomás Machojón, an elderly landowner and maizegrower. He believes himself and his son to be under a curse for having poisoned Gaspar Ilóm.

Machojón, the son of Tomás Machojón. He dies in a fire on his journey to claim the hand of Candelario Reinosa.

Colonel Gonzalo "Chalo" Godoy, the foulmouthed, blue-eyed commander of the Mounted Patrol. The Indians believe that he is cursed for having led the massacre of Gaspar Ilóm's men. He

dies seven years after the massacre in a forest fire that the Indians believe is caused by the Deer of the Seventh Fire.

Goyo Yic, an elderly blind Indian beggar abandoned by his wife, María Tecún.

María Tecún, the freckled, red-haired wife of Goyo Yic, saved by him when the rest of her family was slaughtered. Not wanting any more children, she abandons her husband. She is reunited with him many years later, when she comes to visit their son in prison.

Dionisio "Nicho" Aquino, the postman of San Miguel Acatán. He neglects his postal duties to search for his missing wife.

The Deer of the Seventh Fire, also identified as the curer and the firefly wizard. When a deer is killed by Gaudencio Tecún, the curer also dies because the deer was the curer's *nagual*, or animal protector. Indian legend holds that it avenges the death of Gaspar Ilóm and his destruction of the land by killing Godoy and destroying the Machojóns.

The Novel

The action of *Men of Maize* is divided into two periods. In the first part of the novel, Gaspar Ilóm wages war against the professional maizegrowers who set fire to the brush and ruthlessly exploit the land. According to the Indians of Guatemala, the first people who were created, their ancestors, were made of corn. Therefore, this grain is sacred; it may

be consumed but never exploited, eaten but never sold. The maizegrowers, however, prefer profits to traditions. This is why Gaspar and his Indian guerrillas revolt against them, gaining the upper hand until the maizegrowers call in the Mounted Patrol. The commander of the Mounted Patrol lures Gaspar and his men to a feast. During the celebration, Gaspar is tricked into drinking poison, but he dives into the river and manages to "extinguish the thirst of the poison in his intestines." He returns after dawn, only to discover that the soldiers have taken his men by surprise and massacred them. Gaspar dives into the river once again, and the maizegrowers return to the mountains of Ilóm, unaware that a curse has been cast. The yellow-eared rabbit sorcerers who accompany Gaspar condemn all the perpetrators of the massacre to die before the seventh year is ended. One by one, in the chapters that follow, they are all punished.

The second part of the novel describes the adventures of three men whose lives become intertwined. The first, Goyo Yic, is a blind beggar whose wife, María, runs away, taking with her their many children. Goyo cannot live without her and seeks the help of a curer, who removes the veil of blindness from his eyes. He has, however, never seen María. For this reason, he becomes a peddler and travels from fair to fair. He coaxes women to buy his wares in order to hear their voices. He hopes to recognize his missing wife. Goyo invokes O Possum, patron saint of peddlers, to guide him on his search, but to no avail. One night, he gazes at his shadow by the light of the moon, and "it was like seeing the shadow of a she-opossum." The moonlight turns him from a man into an animal. He wanders into the forest so long as a fugitive that his skin turns black. One day, he is lured by the lights and the laughter of the big fair in the town of Santa Cruz de las Cruces. He returns to the world of men and teams up with Domingo Revolorio to start a business selling liquor by the glass. They buy a demijohn and take turns carrying it on their backs to a distant fair. It is a hot day and they soon get tired. They start selling glasses of liquor to each other until, finally drunk, they lose their permit and are sent to jail for selling liquor without a license.

Time passes. People preserve and repeat the legend of the blind man and his runaway wife, María Tecún, immortalizing it by referring to all runaways as "tecunas." One day the wife of Nicho Aquino, the postman in the little town of San Miguel de Acatán, suddenly disappears. Nicho is overcome with grief. On his next trip to the capital, mail pouch on his back, he meets a wizened old man with black hands who offers to tell him the whereabouts of his wife. Nicho follows him into some caves, where the old man brings to life the tale of creation according to Maya tradition. He reveals to Nicho why maize is sacred and explains the import of Gaspar Ilóm's death and of the cycle of retribution that it has for a sequel. Nicho is enlightened. Upon discovering his origins, he regains a sense of self. For a moment he becomes a coyote, his *nagual*, or animal protector.

Meanwhile, in San Miguel, the townspeople are worried that the postman—and especially their letters—may never reach their destination. They send the muleteer, Hilario Sacayón, to look for Nicho and steer him onto the right path. Hilario looks everywhere and on his way ponders the nature of tales and the difference between reality and fiction, but he never finds Nicho. The former postman ends up burning the mail and running away to the coast, where he becomes a factotum for a hotel proprietress. One of his duties is to ferry people to the Harbor Castle, fitted out as a prison, where Goyo Yic is serving a sentence for selling liquor without a license. Once again, years have passed. Goyo's own son is serving time in the same prison, and one day his mother, María Tecún, comes to pay him a visit. Nicho ferries her across and is astounded to discover that the women he knows as a legend really exists. The members of the Yic family are reunited, and when the men are set free, they all go back to harvest corn in Pisigüilito, where the action started.

Analysis

There are three major themes in *Men of Maize*: struggle, paternity, and the genetic process of myth.

The first of these is the most readily apparent and one that is a factual reflection of social conditions in twentieth century Guatemala. When Asturias conceived this novel, his country's society was divided into two factions: the haves and the have-nots, who were Indians for the most part. In the vision of the novel, the differences between these two factions are not simply economic but, more profoundly, ethical. Essentially, what distinguishes them is an attitude toward life. The Indians live in harmony with nature; the outsiders (represented by the commercial maizegrowers) exploit nature to make a living. The exploiters of the land have the upper hand, while the Indians are portrayed as a strayed race, wandering and blind but by no means lost. Asturias points the path to salvation by underscoring the need to return to the land, the natural harbor and seedbed of the race. The first step in restoring the lost order of the Mayan forefathers is to eradicate evil; the second is to heed the voice of tradition, of the past. Salvaged people will establish a nexus with the roots of their culture, as do Goyo and Nicho, who both transform themselves into their protective animals as a sign of their conversion.

The second major theme in the novel is paternity. Man and maize are one. The enemies of the Indian engage in commerce with maize; they sell "the flesh of our children" and are punished with sterility for this sin. Meanwhile, the prototypical

Indian family, that of Goyo Yic, flourishes. At the end of the novel, when they all return to Pisigüilito to harvest corn, they are a full-bodied clan "because their married children had many children and they all went there to live with them." As Asturias indicates, it is a "wealth of men, wealth of women, to have many children." He clearly portrays the moral poverty of the maizegrowers and exploiters of the Indian by depicting their sterility.

The most original thematic feature of *Men of Maize* is that the reader is allowed to participate in the genetic process of myth. Characters encountered in the first sections of the novel (Gaspar Ilóm, Machojón, María Tecún) are referred to, later in the action, as figures from a legendary past (even while some of them, such as María, are still alive). Tales in *Men of Maize* have a way of being repeated until they are believed and filter into the collective unconscious of all characters. The message becomes a medium, a link in the chain of shared traditions that binds people together and that is known as culture. By showing fellow Guatemalans that culture (and, more important, the ability to forge it) is a collective enterprise, Asturias wished to encourage them to take an active hand in transforming the society that was being recast during the years he spent writing his novel (1945-1949).

Critical Context

Men of Maize is, without a doubt, Asturias' most controversial novel as well as his best. It has been disparaged and misunderstood by critics since its publication. Given its unique narrative structure and the fact that Asturias underplays character and chronological development, many readers have believed it to lack unity. In fact, the conception of *Men of Maize* is so revolutionary (in form as well as in content) that unity must be found in features other than those dictated by convention.

As James Joyce did in *Ulysses* (1922), Asturias turned to an earlier, classical work for the infrastructure for his groundbreaking novel. He borrowed from the past but actualized it in the present

and, most important, developed his novel through an association of key themes. For example, all Indian characters in *Men of Maize* are associated with water, and all their enemies with fire. Three sets of three animals each also play primary roles in the novel, and each set is associated with one of the three elements that anchor Asturias' pyramid to Meso-American people: fire, water, and corn. Finally, four numbers—four, seven, nine, and thirteen—enter the alchemy of *Men of Maize*. Each is associated with an animal and a color, in keeping with Mayan mythology. At the end of the harvest, Goyo and his family become ants, one of the animals responsible for the discovery of corn, according to the Meso-American mythic tradition. Goyo's animal protector is also the opossum (god of dawn in Meso-America), known in Maya as Zach Och, the white animal (white betokens the beginning of something, specifically, of civilization). The novel starts with a cycle of struggle and retribution and then picks up the thread of a wandering blind man, a beggar, who ends up fully healed, as a farmer and a begetter of many children. Thematically speaking, Asturias shifts the action from chaos to order and concludes with a return that is in every respect a beginning, a hope-filled eulogy to the common people of Meso-America.

THE MIXQUIAHUALA LETTERS

Author: Ana Castillo (1953-   )
Type of work: Novel
Type of plot: Epistolary
Time of plot: 1970's-1980's
Locale: The United States and Mexico
First published: 1986

Principal Characters

Teresa, a Mexican American woman married to Libra. She is bored with her marriage. She meets Alicia during a summer trip to Mexico while in search of her roots and her purpose in life. She wants to be a writer and keeps notebooks of her daily impressions. Having met Alicia, she becomes a virtual nomad, going through a series of painful separations from men she once trusted. Unlike Alicia, who has a light complexion despite her gypsy background, Teresa is dark and has attractive Indian features, indicative of her ancestry. The rivalries as well as the close friendship between Alicia and Teresa result from differences in skin color, appeal to men, and temperament. What unite the friends are their many shared experiences and their dedication to their own art.

Alicia, a New York artist whose ancestry goes back to Spain through a grandmother who is from Andalucía and is part gypsy. Alicia's parents come to the United States and adopt the prejudices of that country toward people of color, forgetting that, through Alicia's father, they are related to gypsies. In her rebellion toward her parents, Alicia goes through a sexual quest, always involving herself with men with dark complexions. She helps Teresa get over her first husband and initiates her into a similar erotic quest, one that ends with Teresa's second and very happy marriage in the conformist reading of the novel. Alicia's nomadism and sensuous lifestyle result in a life devoted to art and personal isolation from society.

Libra, Teresa's first husband. A high school dropout, Libra makes numerous attempts to start a business but is always duped by his associates. He is a weak person who is easily intimidated by men with strong personalities. It is clear that Libra will never achieve anything in life. He is inconsiderate to women, even his wife. Teresa's bohemian life and search for herself is a direct response to Libra's opinions and way of life.

Rodney, Alicia's black boyfriend. He represents defiance against her racist father. Alicia gets pregnant by Rodney and gets an abortion that results in unintended sterilization. She takes a trip to Mexico to get over the shock of her sterilization and entrusts Rodney with the care of her New York apartment, only to find on her return that Rodney has been taking his black girlfriend there for romantic trysts. This begins a series of sentimental and erotic mishaps that serve as indications that the only spiritual fulfillment Alicia will find will be through her career as an artist.

Alexis Valladolid, a flamenco singer and distant gypsy relative of Alicia who comes to New York in search of stardom. He moves in temporarily with Alicia and shortly thereafter begins a stormy relationship with Teresa when she arrives for a short visit. When Teresa moves back to Chicago, Alexis follows her. They move in together, and Teresa becomes pregnant and eventually goes through an abortion. That leads to their separation and mutual manipulation, until Alexis leaves her when assured of a contract in a local nightclub. They come in contact again five years later in the same nightclub, while both are involved with different people. Alexis represents the artist who loves only his music, allowing nothing and no one to interfere with his art. Teresa is envious of Alexis, admiring his dedication and his passion, but feels inadequate in her many failed attempts to excel in her craft as a writer while simultaneously searching for a man's love. The hurt caused by Alexis and his abandonment brings Teresa back to reality. She abandons a bohemian life when she meets someone who finally, in the conformist reading, gives her the stability she always sought, through marriage, a son, and a home.

El Gallo, a close gypsy friend of Alexis Valladolid who accompanies him on his trip to the United States. Estranged from his wife, El Gallo becomes Alicia's lover and live-in companion, thus helping Alicia endure the pain caused by the news that Rodney is having a child with a black girlfriend. El Gallo eventually leaves Alicia when he decides to return to Spain and his wife.

Vicente das Mortes, Teresa's Brazilian boyfriend who abandons her after he develops an interest in Alicia. He appears only in letter 38.

Abdel, an anguished Vietnam veteran from New York who is a mediocre artist. He meets Alicia in art school while Alicia is trying to forget and transcend her past love affairs through the attainment of a degree. Abdel befriends Alicia and confesses his many problems with the wife he is divorcing. He soon moves in with Alicia. Their love affair becomes a struggle because of Abdel's insecurities and expressed envy of Alicia's artistic talent. Letter 40, read only in the conformist reading, reveals the end of this relationship. Abdel becomes a nuisance, particularly when he destroys Alicia's paintings and sculptures. Alicia decides to throw him out of her life. As a form of revenge, he commits suicide in Alicia's apartment while she is attending school one evening; ironically, Alicia had just changed her mind about Abdel and decided to make their relationship work.

The Novel

Ana Castillo is a true pioneer in the area of Chicana feminism, charting in *The Mixquiahuala Letters* the hopes, temporary disillusionments, and partial fulfillment of Hispanic and Chicana women living in the United States in the 1970's and 1980's. In her first novel, Castillo experiments both with point of view and with narrative structure, as if to suggest the ways in which the tortuous and open-ended existences of her two heroines unfold.

Dedicated to the memory of Julio Cortázar, *The Mixquiahuala Letters* follows a narrative plan which is similar to that of *Hopscotch* (1963), the novel by the Argentine writer. Instead of reading the novel's forty letters only in the order presented, Castillo proposes three different readings, for the conformist, cynic, or quixotic reader. The proposed options represent an ironic sequence, beginning with apathy for the conformist reading and concluding with madness or complete ineffectiveness in the "real" world for the quixotic reading. The result is a novel with three different conclusions, as if to underscore the importance of personal experience over ideology and of choice and contingency in the lives of Castillo's two heroines.

The experiential core of the novel recounts the lives of two women who, in selected features, represent opposites. Alicia has family roots in Sapin; Teresa, in Mexico. The former is slender and passes for Anglo-American; the latter is voluptuous and has experienced racism because of her dark skin. Alicia attracts men during the day, but men prefer Teresa after sunset. These differences divide and unite these characters in a whirl of experiences that take place in the U.S. cities of New York, Chicago, and Los Angeles as well as throughout Mexico, from Yucatán to the pre-Columbian town of Mixquiahuala. This town, almost ignored by history despite its Toltec ruins, is the place where they become friends shortly after their first meeting in a summer program in Mexico City. Teresa's forty letters to Alicia carry the title of this ancient village, itself representative of the cultural achievements of Toltec civilization. In search of themselves, the women do not realize that Mixquiahuala, the location of their initial friendship, is a symbolic homeland and founding place of their true identity as artists in the making, Alicia as a painter and sculptress and Teresa as a writer.

Their travels throughout Mexican cities and villages reveal the inability of Mexican people to accept these two women in search of emancipation. As they continue on their journey, they deliberately commit transgressions against patriarchal or traditional values by dressing in jeans, hitchhiking, and engaging in ephemeral love affairs. While Teresa learns to feel liberated from her first husband, Alicia progressively grows more morose and taciturn, unable to forget Rodney, her first lover. Although the novel contains three different conclusions and therefore three different futures for each character, readers can be sure that Alicia and Teresa will find it difficult, or almost impossible in the case of Alicia, to find lasting communion with a man.

The novel covers approximately ten years in the lives of both heroines and describes two consummated trips to Mexico. A third journey is planned in letter 1, read only by the quixotic reader. The conformist reading ends with Teresa happily married, living in Cuernavaca, Mexico, with a career as a teacher. She is somewhat distanced from Alicia, who, although successful as an artist, continues on her search for her own home, as symbolized by her art exhibit entitled "La casita," or "the little house." The cynic reading ends with Teresa and Alicia in conflict over the same man, Vicente das Mortes, thus showing a cynical world devoid of virtue and self-control. The quixotic reading ends with both Alicia and Teresa planning a third trip to Mexico in order to start another journey of self-discovery. In this reading, the friendship continues.

Analysis

The novel is an extended reflection on the counterculture of the 1960's in the United States, offering a critical view of its alleged ideals of social justice and racial equality that, ironically, exclude women. The trips to Mexico are a search to adventure and an erotic quest that becomes easily identifiable as an explicit reference to one of the central notions of the cultural era: the "trip" and its possibilities of expansion of the mind. Alicia and Teresa yearn for an antimaterialistic life that turns on the values of making life an artform in its own right.

Castillo's novel confronts truths that give stridency to the political discourse expressed by U.S. minorities. The relationships that Teresa and Alicia have are all with men of color; thus, the obstacles that these women find in their self-fulfillment are not necessarily posed by the Establishment or those who represent it. The journeys of self-discovery are much in the masculine mode, particularly in the Freudian sense: If one's erotic life, as encoded in the subconscious mind, truly represents a dark continent that must be discovered before self-mastery is achieved, then the journeys of Teresa and Alicia are driven by an erotic quest the real purpose of which is their attainment of full consciousness. Seen from this angle, the lives of both characters are far from being existential failures.

Critical Context

The Mixquiahuala Letters, Ana Castillo's first novel, brought immediate attention to this Chicana writer who until then was known only as a poet. Published when Castillo was thirty-three years old and a mother of a three-year-old son, this novel placed Castillo at the forefront of Chicana feminist literature and earned her the Before Columbus Foundation American Book Award. In this novel, Castillo draws on her readings of Latin American writers, primarily Octavio Paz, Carlos Fuentes,

Gabriel García Márquez, and Julio Cortázar. She develops a highly experimental novel that produces three different conclusions, depending on the reading chosen. The narrative is in epistolary form, and the intimacy of the one-way correspondence (the letters written by Alicia are absent) lends itself to introspection and confession.

The figure of the artist attains prominence in this novel, almost as a herald of Castillo's second novel, *Sapogonia* (1990), in which the main character, Máximo Madrigal, is a composite of Alexis Valladolid (as a flamenco singer) and Alicia (as a sculptor). In this novel, however, Castillo chose to focus on the theme of masculine misogyny more so than on the portrait of the artist as a young man. In 1993, Ana Castillo published her third novel, *So Far from God*, through W. W. Norton, becoming one of the first Chicana writers to achieve such recognition by a major mainstream publisher.

MULATA

Author: Miguel Ángel Asturias (1899-1974)
Type of work: Novel
Type of plot: Allegory
Time of plot: The 1960's
Locale: Quiavicús and Tierrapaulita, Guatemala
First published: *Mulata de tal*, 1963 (English translation, 1967)

Principal Characters

Celestino Yumí, a poor woodcutter whose desires for riches and social position lead him to sell his wife, Catalina, to the corn devil, Tazol. Overwhelmed by passion, he marries the Mulata but cannot endure her. Disenchanted with his life as a rich man, he recovers Catalina and returns to his life as a poor woodcutter. Catalina turns him into a dwarf and then into a giant. In the guise of a pockmarked Indian, he accepts the challenge of a priest to do battle. The priest almsot defeats Yumí, but the Mulata saves him.

Catalina Zabala, Yumí's happy, uncomplaining wife. Through Yumí's pact, she is abducted by Tazol. Yumí recovers her, but she is a dwarf. Her desire to become a sorcerer takes her and Yumí to Tierrapaulita. She becomes a powerful witch, changing Yumí into a dwarf out of revenge and then into a giant to prevent Huasanga from enjoying his love.

The Mulata, a sensual, wild, and violent hermaphrodite. Yumí impulsively marries her. She is so destructive and demanding that Yumí tries to kill her. They eventually engage each other in a battle of wits, and she saves Yumí.

Huasanga, the dwarf wife of Yumí.

Tazol, the corn devil, who covets Yumí's wife. Tazol impregnates Catalina through her navel, resulting in the birth of Tazolín.

Cashtoc, the earth devil of the Indians. He destroys Tierrapaulita and abandons it to the Christian devil.

Candanga, the Christian devil. He promotes the repopulation of Tierrapaulita after its destruction by Cashtoc in an earthquake, so that his hell would not lack inhabitants.

Mateo Chimalpín, a priest. Chimalpín challenges Candanga for urging the inhabitants of Tierrapaulita to procreate. He is transformed into a spider with eleven thousand arms to battle Candanga with his eleven thousand horns. Yumí becomes a hedgehog and pocks the priest's face.

Timoteo Teo Timoteo, a friend of Yumí whose riches and good fortune make Yumí envious. Yumí forms a pact with Tazol so that he can be richer than his friend.

The Novel

Miguel Ángel Asturias bases *Mulata* on a popular Guatemalan legend—that of a man who sells his wife to the devil in exchange for unlimited wealth. The novel begins with Celestino Yumí parading through the religious fairs of the countryside around Quiavicús with the zipper of his pants open, in compliance with a bargain he has struck with Tazol, the corn-husk devil. In this way, Yumí will cause women to commit sins by looking at his private parts and then compound those sins by their accepting Communion without going again to confession. Successful in luring the women, Yumí is next informed by Tazol that, to complete the bargain whereby Yumí will become wealthy beyond his dreams, he has to hand over his wife, Catalina Zabala, to Tazol. Yumí is hesitant at first, but the promise of riches, importance, and power proves too much, and he finally consents. Tazol takes possession of Catalina and grants Yumí his fondest wishes—lands, crops, and money in abundance.

Once rich, Yumí discovers that what Tazol had told him is true: Everyone asks for and respects his opinion on anything and everything. Yumí finds that riches and power cannot compensate for the loss of his wife; he yearns for her love and takes to drinking and carousing. While at a religious festival with his friend Timoteo Teo Timoteo, he encounters the Mulata. Drunk and instantly overcome with lust for this ripe and haunting woman, Yumí marries her in a civil ceremony and carries her home. There, in their marriage bed, Yumí discovers that the Mulata, much to his chagrin and embarrassment, is bisexual and dangerous. As much animal as human, she dominates and torments him in such a way that Yumí finds it terrifying to lie with her. He tries to undo the bargain with Tazol, and he succeeds in reacquiring Catalina, who has been turned into a dwarf by Tazol. Catalina comes to live with Yumí and his new wife. The Mulata at first accepts her as a living doll with which to play but quickly tires of the idea and prefers to mistreat her. Yumí and Catalina hope to rid the household of the Mulata. Catalina, in a clever ruse, lures the Mulata to the cave of the Grumpy Bird and seals her in, but the Mulata eats the bird and escapes, provoking in the process a cataclysmic volcanic eruption that destroys Quiavicús and all of Yumí's wealth.

Now even more destitute than before the bargain with Tazol, Yumí has no idea of what to do. Catalina, who in her dealings with Tazol and the Mulata has acquired a taste for witchcraft, convinces Yumí to journey with her to Tierrapaulita, the city where all those who wish to learn the black arts must go. They make their way to Tierrapaulita with an image of Tazol protecting them.

Yumí and Catalina find Tierrapaulita such a fantastic and terrifying place that, despite their lust for the power that witchcraft will bring them, they decide to leave. Cashtoc, the Immense, the red earth demon of Indian myth, prevents them from leaving, employing other demons from Xibalba, the Mayan hell. Catalina gives birth to Tazolín (having been impregnated through the navel by Tazol) and is pronounced the great Giroma, the powerful mother witch. Taking vengeance on Yumí for his bargain with Tazol and his marriage to the Mulata, Catalina turns him into a dwarf, only to change her mind later, when, jealous of the attentions paid him by the dwarf Huasanga, she transforms him into a giant.

This act and Huasanga's cries precipitate an earthquake during which Cashtoc calls his legions together and removes all the sorcerers from Tierrapaulita, destroying the city in the process. Cashtoc empties the town because he realizes that the Christian demon Candanga has arrived and with him "the ones who will demand generations of men without any reason for being, without any magic words, unfortunate in the nothingness and the emptiness of their ego."

Yumí and Catalina, along with other witches, wizards, and sorcerers, return to Tierrapaulita, only to find that their powers are nonexistent now that Candanga, the Christian demon, is dominant. In a nightmarish ceremony, Yumí, in the guise of a pockmarked Indian, representing the Christian demon Candanga, does battle with the Mulata, in the form of the new sexton, representing Cashtoc. Recognizing each other despite their disguises, Yumí and the Mulata engage in a battle of wits, during which the Mulata, in order to save Yumí (who has become a hedgehog and is fighting with the priest, who has become a spider with eleven thousand legs and arms), resumes her form and with a magic mist immobilizes the combatants. In a subsequent Requiem Mass, the Mulata is married to Yumí (still in hedgehog form) for an eternity of death.

As punishment for her betrayal, Cashtoc deprives the Mulata of one leg, one eye, one ear, one hand, one arm, one lip, one teat, and her sex, then sends her crawling away like a snake. Cashtoc and his legions once again take leave of Tierrapaulita, leaving it and its citizens to the Christian demon Candanga, who incites the populace to breed because his hell is in need of souls. The novel ends with a horrific cataclysm in which Tierrapaulita and all of its inhabitants are destroyed by earthquakes and volcanic eruptions.

Analysis

In *Mulata*, as in the majority of his works, Asturias concerns himself with the effects of the continuous clash of two cultures, the Spanish Christian culture and the culture of the Mayans and their descendants. In Asturias' view, this clash has left the Indian and mestizo suspended between the past and the present, between myth and reality, a suspension where myth can be reality and reality myth, where the past is the present and the present the past. Their daily reality is dominated by tradition saturated with legends, myths, and superstitions. In such a world, anything is possible: Dead animals may arise and speak, woman may change into dwarfs, and boar-men may counsel humans. It is this magic reality that, in Asturias' work, the people use as a defense against the four and a half centuries of persecution to which they have been subjected since the conquest. Unfortunately, this response to the Spanish Christian culture precludes an amalgam of the two cultures.

It is no accident that the clashes in Tierrapaulita between the ancient Indian myths and the Spanish Christian beliefs are conducted by demons, Indian and Christian, and not by the deities of either. The deities are no longer available to do battle since the beliefs that have survived are dominated by demons on both sides, each side bent on the destruction, physical and spiritual, of the people. Asturias sees clearly that the clash between cultures has resulted in deep conflicts and confusion in the psyche of the Indians, who have served as the battleground for these opposing forces. Although the two competing cultures form one, at the same time each cancels out the other, with neither making a whole by itself. The resulting hybrid mentality of the Indians is symbolized by the Mulata's persona. She has no proper name, she is simply a Mulata; a hybrid of neuter gender, she has both and so has none. Dominated by the phases of the moon, she is in constant turmoil, doing battle with antagonistic forces within herself.

Later on, when mutilated by Cashtoc and left only half of what she was, the Mulata joins with a skeleton woman in order to make a whole. In this way, the two opposing cultures have mixed, an imperfect half clinging to a substanceless frame. In this same way, the Indians ensure that the protection they seek from the Christian saints is effective, endowing them with features and characteristics of their own Nahuatl animals derived from the ancient beliefs. In Asturias' view, these acts are attempts by the people to impose a wholeness to their existence, a universal harmony that they once knew and is now but a psychic memory.

Any subversion or disobedience to the laws of universality eventually will result in chaos or destruction. When Yumí abandons his wife for wealth and power, he sets into motion the chain of events that leads to his tragic end. The same result lies in wait for Catalina when she attempts to set herself apart from all others with the knowledge and use of sorcery. It is this deflection from universal love that Asturias deplores and that, if not corrected, will result in the destruction of humanity.

Critical Context

Asturias' work has long been recognized by critics throughout most of the literary world as being in the forefront of the Latin American literary movement. It was not, however, until the English publication of *Mulata* in 1967, the same year that saw Asturias awarded the Nobel Prize in Literature, that English-speaking readers became aware of his prodigious talent. *Mulata*'s success and the Nobel Prize led to the publication in English of Asturias' other works. In these are found the style and themes that are incorporated in *Mulata*, most notably in the novels *Hombres de maíz* (1949; *Men of Maize*, 1975), *Viento Fuerte* (1950; *The Cyclone*, 1967, better known as *Strong Wind*, 1968), and *El papa verde* (1954; *The Green Pope*, 1971).

Long concerned with what he considered the continuous isolation of man from nature and the resultant conflicts that arise from this isolation, Asturias incorporated nature into his novels, not as background setting but as a constant presence that must be taken into account. Using ancient Mayan myths and legends, many of which still carry much weight within the consciousness of the Guatemalan people, Asturias personified the different elements of nature (as did the ancient civilizations) in order to show how his characters and these elements are inextricably bound.

Although these elements have appeared in his other novels, in *Mulata* Asturias achieves a more profound synthesis of myth and reality than in his other works. Through his skillful use of language, the suspension between myth and reality in which his characters conduct their lives is brought vividly to the forefront. In this way, he shows not only how wide the split between modern people and natural elements has become but also the resultant conflicts. The inescapable truth of *Mulata* is modern people's urgent need for a balance between spirit and matter, instinct and reason, a wholeness that can be achieved by a reexamination of barely remembered or long-forgotten truths inherent in the myths and legends of the ancients.

NO ONE WRITES TO THE COLONEL

Author: Gabriel García Márquez (1928-   )
Type of work: Novel
Type of plot: Ironic
Time of plot: October to December, 1956
Locale: An unnamed village in Colombia
First published: *El coronel no tiene quien le escriba*, 1961 (English translation, 1968)

Principal Characters

The colonel, an extremely poor retiree who has waited fifteen years for his military pension. He is extremely careful, respectful, and formal, and his hair is metallic, like his joints. His not having a name in the novel fits perfectly with his wish to remain anonymous, which to him is a way of keeping his dignity. His meager possessions are displaced by a prizefighting cock whose value is mainly symbolic. Liked by most of the townspeople, who know his true state, he lives in a dream world and on hope. To the very end, he feels unbeatable, believing that even though he is starving his rooster will win and feed him.

His wife, the colonel's conscience, guide, and subtle protector. She is a practical woman whose asthma attacks do not prevent her from imagining every conceivable means to support her family. The memory of their son, Agustín, is the only thing that gets her out of her constant nagging.

Don Sabas, Agustín's godfather. A corrupt businessman who takes money from any source or person without blinking an eye, he is short and unappealing. Everyone knows that he has gotten rich through illegal means. They also know that corruption is so widespread that to take on Don Sabas may actually create more political repression.

The physician, a part of the subversive movement. A kindly, practical man, he does not harbor illusions about the political situation that represses him and the others. He does not charge the colonel or his wife, and his good sense of humor is mainly produced at the expense of Don Sabas.

The Novel

The plot of this short novel is simple. The elderly and impoverished colonel has been waiting for fifteen years to receive a pension check for his service in the army. The cultural context of the story is what is known as *la violencia*, a civil war between liberals and conservatives in Colombia that lasted from the late 1940's into the 1960's. Nine months prior to the opening of the story, the colonel's son, Agustín, had been killed at a cockfight for distributing secret political literature. The colonel is torn between his desire to keep his son's prizefighting cock in order to enter it into cock-

fights in January and his need to sell it to provide food for himself and his wife. The story focuses primarily on the colonel's pride in trying to conceal his indigent state and his often ironic and bitterly humorous response to his situation.

The central metaphors in the story are the pension, which never arrives, but for which the colonel never ceases to hope, and the fighting cock, which also represents hope as well as his son's and the whole village's political rebellion. In desperation, he decides to sell the cock to the exploiter Sabas, who gives him considerably less money than he originally promised. When the villagers snatch the bird and enter it in the trial fights and the colonel sees that it lives up to its reputation as a prize-fighter, he decides to give the money back and keep the bird. Even though his wife nags him to change his mind, he holds out, realizing that the animal belongs to the whole community. When his wife asks him what they will eat until the time of the cockfights, he replies with an expletive that ends the story.

Although the story is lacking in plot—mainly concerned as it is with the colonel's stoic pride, his wife's nagging, the venality of Sabas, and the tense political situation of a people under martial law—the character of the colonel sustains the reader's interest. The atmosphere of the story is also arresting, for it seems summed up by the colonel's intestinal complaints—"the colonel experienced the feeling that fungus and poisonous lilies were taking root in his gut"—and his wife's remark—"We're rotting alive."

Moreover, no summary of the events of the story can adequately account for the sense of a fully contained fictional world created here, a world as completely realized as that of William Faulkner, one of García Márquez's admitted influences. It is not the plot that makes this story powerful, but rather the combination of understated realism with a sense of a folklore reality that creates a unique combination that has been called Magical Realism by some critics. Although there is little background for the simple events that make up the story, García Márquez's recognized masterpiece, *Cien años de soledad* (1967; *One Hundred Years of Solitude*, 1970), provides a complete picture of the mysterious world of superstition, fantasy, and stark reality that the colonel inhabits. Finally, what characterizes the story is the understated style of the third-person limited point of view, which filters the fictional world through the minds of the characters, along with the laconic speech of the colonel, who, innocent though he may be, is wise in his stoic acceptance of an immediate reality that he cannot change and an ultimate reality that he can only encounter with wit and wry humor.

Analysis

Although the background for the story is *la violencia*, the protracted civil war in Colombia, and although the colonel's problems stem from being a member of the losing party in that civil war, this is not a political novel except in an indirect way. Although García Márquez is a committed leftist, he is by no means a propagandist. His interest in this novel is in the heroic dignity of his protagonist and in his work's carefully controlled style—the style of the colonel himself. The atmosphere of the story is more pervasive than the social world of political repression and futile underground resistance would seem to suggest. It is a world of decadence and decay as concretely felt as the world of William Faulkner, yet it is a world of individual pride and understatement as pure as the style of Ernest Hemingway.

Although the past in the story is as distant as sixty years, when the colonel was a young man in the army, it is as close as the motheaten old umbrella the colonel's wife won in a raffle many years earlier. The only thing that it is good for now, says the colonel, is "counting the stars," but he has only two stars to count, and to count on—the hoped-for pension check and the prizewinning rooster. The bird becomes the most immediate symbol of hope for the colonel. Although he knows that it is his only source of capital, he also knows that it has more important value than staving off hunger. Because it belonged to his dead son and because it represents the emotional hope of the village, he holds on to it and waits for the coming cockfights.

Although this short novel is more realistic than *One Hundred Years of Solitude*, it is nevertheless distinguished by the hybrid of fable and fact, of dream and gritty reality, that characterizes that epoch-making work and that led to the Nobel Prize for García Márquez in 1982.

Critical Context

García Márquez has said in interviews that his characteristic storytelling style is the style of his grandmother and that some of his best characters are patterned after his grandfather, whom he calls the most important figure in his life. Discussing literary influences, he has acknowledged his debt to Franz Kafka, William Faulkner, and Ernest Hemingway—all of whom lie behind the style of *No One Writes to the Colonel*.

Although García Márquez is a novelist, working within that genre's basic pattern, his style is that of the modern romancer. It is lyric rather than realistic, highly polished and self-conscious rather than concerned with mere external reality. His characters exist not in an "as-if" real world, but rather in a purely fictional world of his own making—a combination of the folklore conventions of his South American heritage and the realism of the great modernist writers. The result is that reality is seen as more problematic and inexplicable than everyday experience would suggest.

That his fictions take place in a political culture that seems unstable and adrift is not so thematically important as the fact that this unorganized social world makes possible his exploration of reality as governed by inexplicable forces. Thus, his characters, deprived of the props of established social order, have only their most elemental and primal virtues to sustain them. He is a metaphysical and poetic writer, not a propagandist or a social realist.

García Márquez, primarily because of the popular and critical reception of *One Hundred Years of Solitude*, is perhaps the best-known writer in the Latin American explosion of talent that began in the 1960's. Others in this tradition are Julio Cortázar, Carlos Fuentes, and José Donoso, all of whom have created their own version of a Kafkaesque modernist world that has fascinated general readers and critics alike. *No One Writes to the Colonel* is a minor masterpiece in this tradition, a precursor to the complexity and control of *One Hundred Years of Solitude*.

THE OBSCENE BIRD OF NIGHT

Author: José Donoso (1924-   )
Type of work: Novel
Type of plot: Psychological symbolism
Time of plot: One year in the 1960's, with major flashbacks to the eighteenth century and the periods during and after World War I
Locale: Chile
First published: *El obsceno pájaro de la noche*, 1970 (English translation, 1973)

Principal Characters

Humberto Peñaloza, also known as **Mudito** (or "Little Deaf Mute"), who has served as Don Jerónimo Azcoitía's secretary, the Azcoitía family historian, and the overseer of Don Jerónimo's estate, La Rinconada. He has worked for the family most of his life. As a youth, in an effort to "be someone," Humberto imagines a fusion between his personality and that of Don Jerónimo. Humberto serves as the story's schizophrenic narrator-protagonist, taking on multiple identities (including that of a female, a large papier-mâché head, and a phallus) before becoming, ambiguously, a sexless and timeless bundle, the contents of which, at the conclusion, are emptied and tossed on a fire.

Don Jerónimo Azcoitía, a powerful and influential politician for whom Humberto works and with whom Humberto has fused his own personality. The relationship between the two is strangely symbiotic, as virtually all of Humberto's power (limited as it is) derives from his relationship with Don Jerónimo, while Don Jerónimo's sexual potency is mysteriously tied to his relationship with Humberto.

Doña Inés de Azcoitía, Don Jerónimo's wife. A pious woman early in the novel, she works diligently to have the family's home for retired servants beatified because of an eighteenth century

miracle said to have occurred there. After receiving the transplanted organs of her servant, Peta Ponce, she becomes an inmate of the home herself. Rather than dedicate the rest of her life to prayer, as she had intended, she sets about winning the belongings of her fellow inmates in a strange dog-racing game. After being sexually attacked by Humberto, she is taken away to an insane asylum.

Peta Ponce, a crafty servant woman and apparent possessor of demonic powers. Among her many bizarre activities is the mysterious encounter she arranges with herself, Humberto, Doña Inés and Don Jerónimo so that Doña Inés might be impregnated, presumably by Humberto (since Don Jerónimo is thought incapable of the act himself). Later, Peta's organs are said to be transplanted into Doña Inés.

Boy, the deformed son of Doña Inés and either Don Jerónimo or Humberto, conceived during a mysterious and intentionally unclear encounter. Boy lives on the family's estate, La Rinconada, where he is surrounded by other deformed people so that he will be sheltered from the outside world. When Don Jerónimo announces his intention to close the estate and take Boy back to the city with him, Boy and the others conspire against him, leading to Don Jerónimo's symbolic death.

The Novel

This work relates the tangled story of Humberto Peñaloza, the schizophrenic narrator-protagonist,

and his strange relationship with the Azcoitía family, for whom he has worked during most of his adult life and in whose shelter for the aged he is living at the beginning of the novel. Because of the extremely unstable psychological state of the narrator, the events of the story are related out of sequence, from various perspectives (reflecting the narrator's various personalities), and with no regard to what is real as opposed to what is merely the narrator's illusion. The novel, therefore, resists any ordered, detailed plot summation. A brief sketch of some of the major events of the story can be offered.

Urged by his socially conscious father to "be someone," Humberto fuses his identity with that of Don Jerónimo Azcoitía, an influential politician for whom Humberto becomes a secretary as well as family historian. Sometime later, after Don Jerónimo has not been able to provide his wife, Doña Inés, with a child, the mysterious family servant, Peta Ponce, whose very appearance unsettles the already psychologically unbalanced protagonist, arranges a nocturnal encounter attended by herself, Humberto, Doña Inés, and Don Jerónimo. In a scene shrouded in ambiguity, Doña Inés is impregnated by either her husband or Humberto, the real answer to this question being known only to the crafty servant woman. Boy, the child conceived during this bizarre meeting, is born deformed. Don Jerónimo sends the child to an estate called La Rinconada, where he surrounds the boy with other human monsters to shield him from the world of normal human forms. Humberto is placed in charge of La Rinconada, where he spends much of his time working on the Azcoitía family history. After several years on the estate, Humberto is forced to give up his position, when, in part because of the psychological pressures of living in a world of the deformed, he develops a bleeding ulcer. He has surgery but is convinced that the one-eyed physician who performed the operation has removed eighty percent of his organs to use as transplants.

More disturbed than ever, Humberto, now in the identity of the emasculated Mudito, is sent to live in the Casa, a former convent-prison owned by the Azcoitía family and used as a home for the retired female servants of rich families. While Doña Inés works to have the building beatified (legend has it that the Casa was the site of a miracle in the eighteenth century), Mudito witnesses and participates in the strange activities of the inhabitants of the home. Humberto's narration of these activities—as Mudito—occupies a significant portion of the novel and represents what may be considered the "base" narrative in the work.

Later, the rapidly aging Doña Inés becomes an inmate of the Casa herself, having just returned from Europe, where she received the transplanted organs of Peta Ponce, whom, much to the displeasure of Mudito, she begins to resemble more and more every day. Although she had planned to dedicate the remainder of her life to prayer, she goes about winning the belongings of the other inmates in a bizarre dog-racing game. One of her victims is Iris Mateluna, a prostitute whom the old women ironically suspect of being the expectant virgin mother of a holy child. Mudito eventually assumes the identity of Iris' baby. When Doña Inés wins possession of him in one of the games, he attempts to attack her sexually, an act that precipitates her entry into an insane asylum. This last turn of events pleases Mudito, who is glad to be rid of the shadow of Peta Ponce once and for all.

Mudito, now viewed by the old women as the holy child who will guarantee them a place in heaven, is wrapped in a cocoon. When the Casa is scheduled for demolition, the women are taken away in buses, but Mudito, now a sexless, impotent, and timeless bundle, is left behind. He occasionally manages to open a small hole in the layers of material that surround him, but each time he does this the opening is immediately sewn up by a mysterious, gnarled hand. He remains in this state of limbo "for centuries" until an unidentified old woman takes the bundle down to the riverbank and empties its contents onto a dying fire. Moments later, all that remains of Mudito is "the black smudge the fire left on the stones."

Analysis

There is more than one possible theme to be found in Donoso's novel. The most superficial is that concerning the relationship between the employer and the employee in Latin America's surviving feudal system. The work shows well, though in unconventional terms, the exploitation and victimization of those in the employ of the upper class.

In attempting to discern a more profound theme, however, it is important to consider the complex and unusual nature of the novel's story. Because of the narrator's mental state, the narration is governed not by conventional logic based on objective reality but by an irrational mind functioning in a world of illusion, a world in which reason and logic are nonexistent, as the reader is presented with the narrative meanderings and psychotic hallucinations of Humberto. The narrator's perception of reality, his subconscious concept of time (characterized in large measure by free association), and his multiple personalities and identities (which may lead the reader to believe that there are multiple narrators) destroy any semblance of a traditional narrative.

It is possible that Donoso's intent is simply to convey a close-range, realistic account of the psychological state of his unbalanced narrator, in an attempt to demonstrate the fragmented nature of the human psyche, particularly that of the schizophrenic. If such is the case, it is clear that he achieves his goal. On a larger scale, however, it is more probable that both the disjointed presentation of Humberto's story and the story itself represent the disintegration of convention, personal security, and the individual identity in modern life. In this way, the story and the manner of its telling are symbolic of the anarchical modern world in which conventional order, logic, and objective reality are being replaced by a collective chaos in which the individual is pushed perilously close to infinite nothingness.

For all of its apparent chaos, the novel is a skillfully assembled narrative, possessing a defined structure (in three parts) not readily apparent to the first-time reader and a masterfully developed code of symbols (which not only reveals the conscious planning put into the narrative by the author but also allows the work to be classified as psychological symbolism). As impressive as the novel's subtle structure and its symbolic content is Donoso's use of intentional ambiguity, which both reflects the uncertain nature of Humberto's inner world and discourages any attempt at a definitive interpretation of the meaning of the work and its plot, as events remain forever shrouded in mystery.

Critical Context

The Obscene Bird of Night is a prime example of the Latin American version of the New Novel. In the tradition of this particular narrative form, it presents a highly complex narrative characterized by an unconventional use of narrative voice, a nonchronological rendering of time, and indirect and incomplete character development. Also in keeping with the characteristics of the New Novel, it is a work in which the reader must actively participate in order to discern even the most basic elements of the story, a work that demands multiple readings, and a work that, rightly or wrongly, frequently inspires more discussion concerning the presentation of its story than of the story itself.

Within the context of Donoso's literary canon, this novel is his masterpiece. This is not to say that his other works, such as *Coronación* (1957; *Coronation*, 1965) and *El lugar sin límites* (1966; *Hell Has No Limits*, 1972), are not fine pieces in their own right. It is *The Obscene Bird of Night*, however, that represents the high point of Donoso's career as a writer, a work that would have earned for the author lasting fame had he written no others.

THE OLD GRINGO

Author: Carlos Fuentes (1928-   )
Type of work: Novel
Type of plot: Historical realism
Time of plot: 1913-1914
Locale: Chihuahua, Mexico
First published: *El gringo viejo*, 1985 (English translation, 1985)

Principal Characters

Harriet Winslow, the character who "sits and remembers" the story of her adventure in Mexico. Harriet, a spinster, agrees to go to Mexico in the service of the Miranda family to teach English to their three children; she hopes thus to escape a stultifying existence in Washington, D.C. Arriving in Mexico, she is used by revolutionary leaders, and she finds the country in turmoil and the Miranda hacienda in ruins. She becomes involved with a revolutionary general, whom she ultimately betrays.

Ambrose Bierce, the "old gringo," a famous, real-life writer whose true identity is only gradually disclosed to the reader. Notorious for his bitterness and cynicism, Bierce has worked for the newspaper mogul William Randolph Hearst for more than twenty years and now regrets having misused his talents. During the fall of 1913, Bierce retires to Mexico, a seventy-one-year-old alcoholic and asthmatic seeking Pancho Villa and the

adventure of revolution. *The Old Gringo* makes Bierce a heroic figure but sidetracks his mission through his encounter with Tomás Arroyo, whom he serves briefly and who then murders him.

General Tomás Arroyo, a simple peasant who symbolizes Hispanic virility and machismo. Arroyo is driven by revolutionary idealism and a personal quest for revenge against Miranda, whose bastard son he is. After his army takes over the Miranda estate, however, Arroyo begins to think of the Miranda lands as his own birthright and becomes obsessed with documenting his claim. As he seems to lose his revolutionary focus, the old gringo takes action to shake his complacency, and the enraged Arroyo kills him.

Pancho Villa, the bandit turned revolutionary leader and wily politician. Villa is troubled by the political crisis caused by Arroyo's murder of Bierce. Villa is forced to execute Arroyo in order to avoid an embarrassing international incident.

The Work

The Old Gringo is a novel fashioned as a tribute by one writer to the memory and courage of another, the cynical American journalist and storyteller Ambrose Bierce; the book offers a fictive speculation about Bierce's mysterious disappearance in Mexico in 1913 during the civil war. Carlos Fuentes imagines that Bierce, at first referred to only as the "old gringo," went to Mexico seeking Pancho Villa. His motives for going are ambiguous. He is seeking a new frontier and the adventure

of fighting for the revolution, but what he seems to be seeking most is a heroic death. As Fuentes repeatedly states, the "old gringo came to Mexico to die," preferably with dignity.

The story is grounded in a factual framework. Bierce crossed the border at El Paso, Texas, in November of 1913. On December 26, he wrote that he intended to ride a troop train to Ojinaga seeking Pancho Villa. He was never heard from again. According to one legend, Bierce found Villa, became a senior staff adviser, and was later shot as a deserter, alienated by the bandit's cruelties. Fuentes works a variation on this legend.

Although named for the old gringo, the novel is mainly the story of Harriet Winslow, a spinster who leaves her mother in Washington, D.C., and goes to Mexico to work as a governess for the wealthy, landowning Miranda family, teaching English to the three Miranda children. She is seeking liberation, adventure, and independence, but she is manipulated by the Miranda family. They put her in the middle of the revolution by summoning her to their hacienda as they are making plans to depart themselves; the family uses her to create a diversion. She is also manipulated by General Tomás Arroyo, who uses her to gain entry to the Miranda estate. The Mexicans who exploit her consider her a fool. The story is framed by Harriet's memory.

The old gringo has concluded, to his shame, that he had also been manipulated and exploited during his career as a muckraking journalist by his employer, William Randolph Hearst. Bierce has contempt for his own accomplishments done in the service of a millionaire who has profited by his talent. He describes himself as a "contemptible, muckraking reporter at the service of a baron of the press as corrupt as any I denounced in his name." He also considers himself a personal failure and blames himself for the deaths of his sons. He has turned his back on his country and on his former life. He is a would-be idealist, as Fuentes imagines him, who carries in his saddlebags a copy of the story of *Don Quixote*. Significantly, though, he has not yet read the book as he leaves El Paso to go tilting after windmills in revolutionary Mexico.

The gringo goes looking for Pancho Villa but instead finds General Tomás Arroyo, whom he antagonizes with his brutal honesty. His courage is unquestionable, and he is useful to Arroyo during the siege of the Miranda hacienda. Arroyo, himself a bastard son of the Mirandas, is conflicted. His quest to kill his father, Miranda, is frustrated by the family's escape, but after he has conquered the estate, he is derelict in his duty to return his army to Villa. He discovers Spanish documents that he believes to be sacred, for he thinks that whoever possesses the documents owns the land. The gringo has a more sophisticated understanding of political power than Arroyo, and he attempts to teach Arroyo that the documents are in fact worthless. When Arroyo refuses to believe him, the gringo burns the papers, and Arroyo, in a rage, shoots him in the back, killing his spiritual father, whom the gringo has become.

Harriet Winslow is also searching for a father. Her own father deserted the family to serve in the Spanish-American War and never returned. Harriet confesses to the gringo that her father had not died in combat, as her mother prefers to believe, but remained in Cuba to live with a black woman. She and her mother had reported him dead in order to collect his pension: "We killed him, my mother and I," she confesses, "in order to live."

Harriet too, becomes conflicted in Mexico; she is torn between the young Arroyo and the seventy-one-year-old gringo, who treats her with both respect and affection. She surrenders herself to Arroyo, claiming that she did so to save the gringo's life, a rationale that the gringo refuses to accept or believe. His disposition is always to force those around him to face the truth. Arroyo, therefore, has exploited Harriet sexually, and she comes to hate him for that. She gets her vengeance, however, by reporting the gringo's death to the United States consulate, claiming that the gringo was her father, and demanding that his body be returned to Arlington National Cemetery for a military burial.

This lie creates a political problem for Pancho Villa, who is liable to be held responsible for the death of a captain of the United States Army. Politically, Villa and his allies will need the support of the United States government if their revolution is to succeed, and Villa must take measures to rectify the situation. The body of the gringo is exhumed, propped up against a wall, and shot by a firing squad at Villa's command. Arroyo is ordered to administer the coup de grâce; he is then executed by the same firing squad. Harriet claims the body of the gringo and takes it home, where she continues to live with her memories. "She sits and remembers," Fuentes explains repeatedly.

Analysis

The novel is a cross-cultural meditation that demonstrates the differences between the Mexican and North American national temperaments. The freedom fighter Arroyo is an innocent undone by the inexperienced Harriet and the experienced gringo, both of whom make demands that he is unable to satisfy. In the novel's preoccupation with Mexico and Mexican history, apart from the way it explores the relationship of Mexico and the United States, *The Old Gringo* resembles Fuentes' earlier novel *La muerte de Artemio Cruz* (1962; *The Death of Artemio Cruz*, 1964).

The two novels also share a tendency to experiment with nonlinear storytelling, shifting points of view, consciousness, and structure. The point of view of *The Old Gringo* is predominantly third-person omniscient, but Fuentes rapidly shifts the focus from character to character without regard to linear chronology. Sequences and conversations started early in the novel are continued later, after the reader has developed a better and more complete sense of context. The narrative technique is sophisticated and challenging.

In the novel, the elegant Miranda hacienda becomes a symbol of the old order, which must be destroyed but which casts a hypnotic spell over Arroyo, who has links to the family, and threatens to seduce him from his revolutionary purpose. This could partly explain his sexual attraction for Harriet as well, since she is linked to the world of the Mirandas. The hacienda is a repository of historic memory and fantasy, its many mirrors serving as windows to the past. The peasants gaze into these mirrors and are enjoined by Arroyo to "see themselves," but the mirrors can also distort what they reflect. Harriet Winslow, a city woman from another culture, looks into the mirrors but can only see herself. For her, the mirrors cannot have the same cultural significance, since they will not reflect her history. What she sees is a thirty-one-year-old Gibson Girl in a Mexican setting.

The novel has been praised for its vivid treatment of the peasants' revolt against their masters but it has also been criticized for its mannered, dreamlike surrealism and its portentous symbolism and rhetoric. The legend of Ambrose Bierce is a dominant symbol. Bierce represents uncompromising honesty, which drives him out of the United States but is also not tolerated in Mexico, where his honesty is the destroyer of dreams. Harriet Winslow seems to represent both American innocence and American duplicity. The lesson she learns is that she cannot adjust to the "other," to a simple life in a different culture.

The novel is shot through with irony: Harriet and her mother have been living a lie in the United States, and Harriet goes to Mexico to find a new life; there, she finds only death and disappointment, and she returns to the United States to live another lie. Arroyo is obsessed with the idea of murdering his actual father, but he pays with his life for murdering his spiritual father. The old gringo wants to be put up against a wall and shot by Pancho Villa; he gets his wish, but only after he is already dead, shot ignominiously in the back by Arroyo. Harriet's journey to Mexico is framed as a spiritual quest, but the novelist turns it into a sexual one. She is not honest with the gringo or with herself about her sexual surrender to Arroyo.

The theme of children searching for fathers and a father searching for his children is carefully crafted but ultimately overworked. The theme of memory and its consequences and the notion that one's home can only be found through one's memories is developed in an interesting manner.

Critical Context

The Old Gringo was first conceived as a film project. Although the story was effectively simplified and clarified by the film version directed by Luis Puenzo and produced by Jane Fonda in 1989, the film was a box-office failure, perhaps because the novel's value resides not so much in its story and relatively wooden archetypes as in its psychological complexity, which cannot conveniently be brought to the surface and visualized. The film makes the story more easily comprehensible—the identification of the gringo with Ambrose Bierce is made clear to the viewer from the very beginning, for example—but it cannot be as well understood, except on the most superficial level.

The Old Gringo is more than merely a colorful and passionate revolutionary epic that resembles a classic Western featuring archetypal characters. It is both a psychological novel and an intercultural meditation disguised as popular fiction that seems to exploit sensuality, romance, and adventure, and its varied strengths made it the first novel by a Mexican writer to become a U.S. best-seller.

ON HEROES AND TOMBS

Author: Ernesto Sábato (1911-   )
Type of work: Novel
Type of plot: Psychological realism
Time of plot: 1841 and 1946-1955
Locale: Buenos Aires and Patagonia, Argentina
First published: *Sobre héroes y tumbas*, 1961 (English translation, 1981)

Principal Characters

Martín del Castillo, the sensitive young man whose relationship with the mysterious Alejandra Vidal Olmos provides the focus of the book. Until he meets Alejandra, he regards women as either pure and heroic or as gossiping deceivers. He has some weeks of happiness with Alejandra, but his enigmatic lover finally brutally casts him aside. His attempt, with Bruno's help, to heal himself and to understand what has happened to him and to Alejandra provides the intellectual problem of the novel.

Alejandra Vid..l Olmos, the daughter of a decayed branch of an old family of the Argentine oligarchy. Alejandra is eighteen years old when she meets Martín and is an exotic beauty. She is a mysterious figure, exerting an almost occult influence on Martín. Her family is lost in a time warp. They possess the manners and memories of the old Argentina; their aristocratic gentility only brings ruin in the materialistic modern world. Alejandra realizes that her family lives in a world that no longer exists, yet she detests the new Argentine elite. Martín finally understands that she is locked into an incestuous relationship with her father. She kills her father with a gun and then commits suicide by setting fire to the family home.

Fernando Vidal Olmos, Alejandra's father. Alejandra is his daughter by Georgina, his first cousin. Fernando's obsessions dominate his life. He narrates the third part of the book, "Report on the Blind," which takes the reader into the mind of the paranoid madman. He has been obsessed by blindness from the days of his youth, when he blinded birds with a needle. He believes that the world is controlled by a secret sect of the blind: The blind spy, persecute, and determine everyone's destiny.

Bruno Bassán, an unpublished writer from a prosperous family. Bruno, pensive, with a gentle, ironic air, grew up with Fernando and Georgina, whom he loved. He provides the philosophic comments of the book, helps Martín understand the nature of the trauma of his relationship with Alejandra, and also helps him reconcile himself to the inevitable tragedies of the doomed Vidal and Olmos families.

The Novel

In an introductory note to his linguistically and ideologically complex novel, Ernesto Sábato admits that the narrative represents his attempt to "free himself of an obsession that is not clear even to himself." This admission is borne out by the novel's extraordinary display of unusual imagery, puzzling events and characters, and conflicting political and ethical points of view.

The text of *On Heroes and Tombs* is presented in four parts. In "The Dragon and the Princess" and "Invisible Faces," Martín del Castillo meets Alejandra Vidal Olmos, a young woman for whom he develops an immediate fascination. After a long period of pursuit, he finally convinces her to begin a love affair with him. In an attempt to understand the strange behavior of Alejandra, Martín follows her and sees her with another man, whom she later admits is Fernando, her father. Although she seems to be an innocent, introverted woman, Alejandra (who turns out to be the daughter of a decadent aristocratic family) is a prostitute who caters to the wealthy members of Juan Perón's administration. At the same time, she maintains an incestuous relationship with Fernando, who is her father but was never married to her mother, Georgina.

Fernando Vidal Olmos has written a mysterious document that narrates his frequent hallucinatory experiences, a document incorporated into the text in the third part, "Report on the Blind." After finishing the report, Fernando goes to his daughter's home, even though he knows that he is going to his death. Alejandra shoots him and then commits suicide by setting fire to the house.

In the fourth part of the novel, "An Unknown God," Martín seeks the help of Bruno Bassán as he attempts to understand his relationship with Alejandra. Martín falls into an alcohol-induced stupor, in which he envisions himself in a world likened to a dung heap or sewer. He is saved and nursed back to health by Hortensia Paz, who instills in him the hope for a better life. Martín meets a truck driver, Bucich, who takes him on a trip to Patagonia. Interpolated in the narrative of the trip are passages that depict the struggle of the revolutionary forces of General Juan Lavalle against the regime of Juan Manuel de Rosas, the dictator of Argentina from 1829 to 1852. Two ancestors of Fernando and Alejandra Vidal Olmos carry the body of Lavalle toward the Argentine-Bolivian border in 1841 as Martín flees to Patagonia in 1955 and finds that the crystal-clear sky and the fresh air make him feel free and reborn.

The story of Alejandra, Martín, and Fernando is told through a variety of narrative points of view. The foreword of the novel is an objective police report of the death of Alejandra and Fernando. "The Dragon and the Princess" and "Invisible Faces," narrated by an unnamed omniscient narrator, include many long passages that portray the thoughts of the characters and scenes from the early life of Alejandra and Martín. The "Report on the Blind" is a text written by Fernando as a memoir or confession, a narrative of his own experience. In the last section, "An Unknown God," it becomes clear that the narrator of the first two sections is someone who knew the characters and has obtained most of the information from Bruno and from Martín years after the death of Alejandra and Fernando. The narrator acts as an organizing consciousness of the material—the episodes of the contemporary history of the characters, the recollections of the earlier years, the interpolated passages of the history of Alejandra's ancestors, and the text of Fernando's psychotic, paranoic report on the activities of the blind.

Analysis

The treatment of the central characters as representatives of abstract notions of masculine and feminine traits is a manifestation of a principal theme of the novel, the search for the meaning of human existence. Sábato creates from a common, almost trivial concern—that of the inability of one sex to understand the other—an exploration of an ontological problem. As Martín, Bruno, and Fernando attempt, each in his own way, to understand the mysterious Alejandra (who is likened to Argentina itself), they seek through the elusive feminine psyche a justification for their own experience. Fernando's hallucinatory document about the blind is presented in terms of a harrowing journey through the vaginal canal of a woman, and Martín is rescued from his despair by a warm, maternal savior, Hortensia Paz. Bruno works out his answers to the mystery vicariously, by piecing together the story of Martín, Fernando, and Alejandra. Fernando finds his solution in his own madness, justifying the irrationality of existence as a plot perpetrated by blind people. Martín resolves his anguish by escaping to the free, open spaces of Patagonia, out of the reach of women, and by experiencing the exhilarating sense of masculine communion as he and the truck driver urinate together under the stars.

In the conflict of man and woman, then, is contained the insoluble mystery of existence. The elaboration of the conflict in *On Heroes and Tombs* is complicated by the fact that this is a novel about incestuous relationships, both sexual and nonsexual. Fernando and Alejandra, father and daughter, are lovers. Bruno has been sexually involved with Alejandra and with her mother, Georgina. Fernando fathered the child, Alejandra, by the daughter of his mother's brother, and the child looks like Fernando's mother, whose husband—Fernando's father—Fernando hated and tried to poison when he was a child. Martín becomes involved in a love affair with Alejandra, the former lover of his friend Bruno.

The fact that Alejandra works as a prostitute serving the Peronists, the longtime enemies of her aristocratic family, indicates that the incestuous relationships and the exploration of the meaning of existence itself have a political symbolism in the novel. The counterpoint provided in the narrative that shifts between the twentieth century condition of these characters living under the dictatorship of Perón and the struggles of the nineteenth century rebels fleeing the tyranny of Manuel de Rosas further develops the political implications of the story of Martín, Fernando, Bruno, and Alejandra. As Fernando dies, murdered by his daughter, at the same moment that Perón is deposed, Martín finds his freedom, aided by the maternal figure that nurses him and gives him the spiritual strength to escape his depression.

Critical Context

Ernesto Sábato first received international acclaim with the publication of his short novel *El túnel* in 1948 (*The Outsider*, 1950). In the author's note at the beginning of *On Heroes and Tombs*, Sábato says that in the thirteen years between the first novel and the second, he continued exploring the mysterious labyrinth that leads to the secret of human existence. *The Outsider* is a pessimistic, oppressive story of a man who murders his married mistress when he finds out that she has deceived him. Many of the details and themes of the second novel are contained in the first—the mistress' husband is blind, the protagonist's love for the woman is obsessive and violent, and his behavior is at times distorted by paranoia.

As Sábato suggests, *On Heroes and Tombs* seems to be a development of the obsessive concerns of the first novel. The pessimism of *The Outsider*, however, is tempered somewhat by the optimism of the ending of the second novel. The more promising vision of human existence offered by Hortensia Paz and the portrayal of potentially rewarding relationships in the conversation and communion of Martín and Bucich in Patagonia are indications that Sábato sees some salvation for his characters despite the apparent meaninglessness of life.

Sábato's novel is a stylistic tour de force that inevitably evokes a comparison with the work of many of his Latin American contemporary novelists. There are many passages that are precursors of the narrative complexities of the work of Carlos Fuentes, Julio Cortázar, and Guillermo Cabrera Infante, and the ontological problems suggested by the novel reflect similar preoccupations of the most influential Argentine writer of the twentieth century, Jorge Luis Borges. In spite of the development of a concept of life in *On Heroes and Tombs* that is more optimistic than the ontology of *The Outsider*, the later novel continues to suggest the impossibility of resolving the conflict of human rationality and human existence. The stylistic and ideological complexities of Sábato's work, which confirm his confession of the obsessive nature of his narrative impulse, render his novelesque work very difficult and not at all clear in its communication of the central mystery of life.

ONE DAY OF LIFE

Author: Manlio Argueta (1936-   )
Type of work: Novel
Type of plot: Social criticism
Time of plot: 1979
Locale: El Salvador
First published: *Un día en la vida*, 1980 (English translation, 1983)

Principal Characters

Guadalupe (Lupe) Fuentes de Guardado, a forty-two-year-old, superstitious, earthy, traditional matriarch of a peasant family in Chalatenango, El Salvador. She displays a sense of humor, humaneness, and generosity in the account of a day in her life, in which she tells of her son Justino's murder by special military forces, the search for her granddaughter by the same forces, and the capture, beating, mutilation, and apparent murder of her husband.

José "Chepe" Guardado, an enthusiastic activist and leader in the Christian farmworkers' federation, an excellent storyteller and folksinger capable of good humor and self-effacement. Chepe, like most men in this area, must spend nights in the hills for fear of being apprehended in his own home by the military authorities.

Adolfina Hernández Guardado, the fifteen-year-old granddaughter of Lupe and Chepe, well educated (to the fifth grade), independent, and extremely active in the federation.

María Pía Guardado Fuentes de Hernández, the oldest of Lupe's surviving children. Her husband, Helio, has disappeared after participating in a bank demonstration. She fears for her daughter and sends her to spend time with her grandmother in Chalatenango. María Pía is beaten up by the authorities in a night raid in which they also destroy her house.

María Romelia Ramírez, a protester wounded in the hand at the bank demonstration. She gives the most chilling account of Justino's decapitation and praises the stoic patience of Lupe and Chepe.

Rubenia Fuentes, Lupe's mother, who tells of the 1932 massacre that occurred in Santa Tecla.

The Novel

The narrative thread recounts one day in the life of a middle-aged peasant woman, from 5:00 A.M., when she arises at dawn, until 5:00 P.M., when she lights candles as darkness closes in. The chapters divide the day's segments as she goes about her routine activities of cooking, child care, house and garden work, and musing about the people and events that have shaped and informed her life. This interior monologue reveals her past—the unremitting, wretched poverty as well as her simple, humble acceptance of the inhuman conditions under which she and the other peasants in the village live.

She muses about her childhood, her betrothal to José (Chepe) Guardado, their marriage, their children, their work, and their efforts to better their lot. By exercising extreme frugality, they have bought a small piece of land. The carefully tended crops have enabled Lupe and Chepe to provide a few comforts for their meager existence; for example, they are able to buy a few toys and candies for the children at Christmas. Lupe recalls the early hardships, as when their child died of malnutrition, dysentery, and worms as many of the peasant children do, and how the "old priests" advocated resignation and hope of eternal happiness in heaven.

Then the "new priests" came and offered instruction and help in forming cooperatives, recommended pharmaceuticals to treat worms and dysentery, and suggested cheese as food for malnourished babies. They encouraged the farm laborers to seek higher pay and the peasants to sell their goods in town, where they could get higher prices than the local merchant offered. Then she remembers how the authorities came and began abusing the peasants and finally attacked the priests. The priests were sent away, but the changes they had wrought could not be stopped. The authorities became increasingly abusive as the peasants became increasingly assertive.

As the hours pass, Lupe reminisces about the increasing involvement of her family members in protest activities. Chepe has become a leader in the farmworkers' movement. Helio Hernandez, Lupe's son-in-law, has been seized by the guards for his activist involvement, and the family can get no information as to his whereabouts or fate. Lupe's granddaughter, Adolfina Fuentes, who is a child of fifteen years, is the most outspokenly militant. She took part in a week-long demonstration in which a cathedral was seized and occupied by the peasants. As she was returning home, the bus in which she and other demonstrators were riding was attacked by guards and most of the passengers were killed. She and another girl escaped, and on the day of the narrative, she arrives to visit her grandmother for a few days until the situation cools down.

Later, the authorities come to question Adolfina about a man whom they have apprehended and beaten; the man murmured her name as he slipped into unconsciousness. They must wait for an hour or so with Lupe until the girl and Lupe's smaller children return from the store.

In her interior monologue, Lupe recapitulates the fears, compliance, hopes, anger, human kindness, and resignation that follow one another as she waits helplessly for Adolfina's return. Later, however, when the guards want to take Adolfina away to identify the man they are holding, she defies them and insists that they not take Adolfina away alone. Finally, they bring the man to the hut for the girl to see, but only Lupe recognizes Chepe. He is dying from the brutal and disfiguring beating he has received. To protect her family, she denies knowing who he is, and they take him away. Lupe resolves to carry on and to encourage her granddaughter also to continue such resistance as they can offer to the authorities.

The novel is detailed and often moving in its description of the miseries and brutalities of life in El Salvador. The ignorance and hopelessness of the peasantry are palpable in the lifestyles portrayed. Lupe's random associations are simplistic yet believable, and there is an occasional contrast to the misery: the surprise of joy at the beauty of dawn, the pleasure of watching and hearing the tropical birds, the affection for a dog. These poignant flashes of delight remind the reader that Manlio Argueta established his reputation first as a poet.

In addition to Lupe's own chapters, in which her point of view and experiences are dominant, other chapters are interspersed in which the interior monologues and events of other characters' lives are revealed. The voices of three other women are heard in these chapters, and their experiences parallel Lupe's own and confirm her justification for hating the authorities. The guards are afforded two chapters in which their point of view is presented. These men are drawn from the peasant class themselves and are in truth turning against their own families, friends, and neighbors in order to uphold the brutally oppressive regime of a handful of wealthy families in El Salvador. Ironically, the voices of the guards, reflecting their confusion about loyalties and their wistful desire for a bit more power, a few more possessions, and a modicum of respect, are more believable than those of Adolfina, Lupe, and Chepe.

Analysis

The novel is written to recount and extol the birth of a sense of self-worth among the Salvadoran peasantry. This central theme illuminates the narrative and asserts that human dignity can and does transcend misery, brutality, and oppression. Beyond the misery of *One Day of Life*, beyond the carnage and despair, the novel holds forth hope for social justice in the future. Neither the peasants nor the guards seem able to comprehend or discuss the complex problems they face, or even their own attitudes toward these questions. No solutions are proposed; no real focus of effort to accomplish any concrete goals ever appears to emerge. For each small action—a demonstration, a rally, an act of defiance—harshly brutal reprisals follow immediately. The book suggests that such measures serve only to strengthen the resolve of the peasants to continue to seek ways to make their lives better, but the position of the peasants appears precariously weak, beset by enemies both at home and abroad.

This novel asserts that the dignity of the human spirit will not be destroyed by misery and oppression, that it will resist and ultimately triumph. It is a splendid hope, providing a luminescent thematic unity to this tale of how the human spirit flourishes in one of the most economically depressed and politically unsettled areas of the Americas.

Critical Context

One Day of Life was Manlio Argueta's third book but his first one to address in such direct fashion the social conditions in El Salvador. He is known principally as a poet, and critics have commented favorably on this book with respect to his lyricism, his poetic and moving imagery, and the authentic flavor of the vernacular language. They have also found the characterizations flat and the story line thin, as is often the case with novels of social and political protest. The book was first published in 1980 in El Salvador and quickly excited so much interest there that Argueta was forced into exile and the book was banned. Since then, it has been translated and published in Italy, Germany, the Netherlands, and the United States. Argueta was not known widely outside his own country prior to the publication of this book, which established him as a new and dynamic voice in Central American literature.

ONE HUNDRED YEARS OF SOLITUDE

Author: Gabriel García Márquez (1928-   )
Type of work: Novel
Type of plot: Magical Realism
Time of plot: The 1820's to the 1920's
Locale: Macondo, a mythical town in an unnamed Latin American country
First published: *Cien años de soledad*, 1967 (English translation, 1970)

Principal Characters

Melquíades, a wise and honest gypsy. He makes annual visits to Macondo, a remote, mythical village in Latin America. He introduces the people of Macondo to new inventions such as magnets, telescopes, magnifying glasses, and false teeth. He leaves a precious parchment manuscript, the history of both the past and the future of Macondo.

José Arcadio Buendía, the family patriarch, the founder and colonizer of Macondo. He becomes enthralled with the knowledge and inventions of Melquíades, but his spirit of initiative disappears.

Úrsula Iguarán, the wife of José Arcadio Buendía and the matriarch of the Buendías.

José Arcadio, their gigantic older son, who marries Rebeca, the adopted daughter of his parents. Born on the journey to found Macondo, he does not share his father's interest in inventions. Initiated into the mysteries of sex by the family's servant, Pilar Ternera, he quickly leaves town when she becomes pregnant. One day he is shot. It is not clear if it is an accident, suicide, someone's clever revenge, or a murder by Rebeca.

Rebeca, their adoptive daughter. She arrives on the Buendías' doorstep, with her parents' bones in a sack, when she is eleven. Rebeca is courted by and becomes engaged to Pietro Crespi; then the manly presence of José Arcadio overwhelms her. Her subsequent marriage and banishment and the death of José Arcadio leave her a recluse.

Colonel Aureliano Buendía, the younger son of José and Úrsula. He, too, is introduced to the

wonders of sex by Pilar Ternera. He leads the Liberals in revolt and launches thirty-two unsuccessful rebellions against the central government. He becomes supreme commander—the heart and soul—of the revolutionary movement throughout the country and a legend in his own time.

Amaranta, José and Úrsula's daughter. In love with her sister Rebeca's fiancé, Pietro Crespi, she does everything in her power to prevent the wedding. When Rebeca suddenly marries José Arcadio instead, Pietro Crespi is free to court Amaranta, which she encourages. Amaranta's enveloping tenderness leads Pietro Crespi to propose, but she scornfully rejects his offer, and he commits suicide. In remorse, she plunges her hand into a stove of hot coals. She wears a bandage of black gauze on her burned hand until her death as a sign of her virginity.

Pietro Crespi, an Italian music master. He is first engaged to Rebeca, then becomes Amaranta's suitor, but he commits suicide when she rejects his proposal of marriage.

Pilar Ternera, a part-time servant of the Buendías. A generous woman of easy virtue, her lovemaking skills and ability to read the fortunes of others in the cards are sought out by the inhabitants of Macondo.

Arcadio, her illegitimate son by José Arcadio, reared by the Buendías. He is placed in charge of Macondo by Colonel Aureliano Buendía.

Aureliano, a member of the sixth generation of Buendías in Macondo. Locked up and ignored as a child, he pores over and deciphers the manuscripts and books in Melquíades' room.

Aureliano, the seventh generation of Buendías. Born with a pig's tail—reminiscent of an ancestor who was also the product of a union of close relatives—he dies when eaten by ants and fulfills the prophecy of Melquíades' manuscript.

The Novel

One Hundred Years of Solitude chronicles the rise and decline of Macondo, a mythical Latin American town, and of its leading family, the Buendías. Located in a country resembling the author's native Colombia, Macondo, by symbolic extension, suggests not only Colombia but also Latin America generally, much as William Faulkner's Yoknapatawpha County is a microcosm of the Deep South. The novel covers roughly the first century of South American independence and appears to be a judgment on this historic period, an era marred by violence, exploitation, stagnation, and disillusion. Just as six generations of Buendías eventually bring forth a child with a pig's tail, so García Márquez seems to see a pig's tail as the end product of Latin America's first one hundred years of independence.

The problems of independence have their roots, to some extent, in "the era of the first pig's tail," the colonial period. For the Buendías, the roots reach to the sixteenth century, when "the pirate" Sir Francis Drake raids Riohacha, causing Úrsula Iguarán's great-great-grandmother, frightened by the English with "their ferocious attack dogs" and "red-hot irons," to sit on a hot stove. To escape the English pirates, the Iguaráns migrate from the seacoast to a peaceful Indian village in the foothills, where they intermarry with the Buendías for three centuries. Such inbreeding produces the first pig-tailed boy, near the end of the colonial period, from the union of Úrsula Iguarán's aunt and José Arcadio Buendía's uncle.

Married first cousins, Úrsula Iguarán and José Arcadio Buendía are afraid of breeding another pig-tailed child or, even worse, iguanas. Another migration comes about because Úrsula Iguarán wears a chastity belt for the first eighteen months of marriage and, taunted by an angry cockfighting opponent for his rumored impotency, José Arcadio Buendía kills the man. To escape the man's ghost and make a fresh start, José Arcadio Buendía leads a hardy band of young pioneers across the mountains. After wandering aimlessly for more than two years, the band settles in the middle of a rather allegorical swamp when José Arcadio Buendía has an equally allegorical dream of a city built of mirrors.

On such auspicious foundations rises Macondo. At first only an isolated village, Macondo is happy and prosperous, especially proud that it has no need for a graveyard. From the first, however, Macondo is plagued by gypsies who come bearing gifts, some the products of the new science and others the remnants of old superstitions and frivolities. This hodgepodge forms the village's learning, yet, except for old Melquíades, the gypsies are not so much teachers as hucksters intent on gulling the ignorant villagers. The gypsies are precursors of the latter-day Anglo pirates, the American banana entrepreneurs who appear later in the century, transform Macondo's society, and then leave it stagnant.

Even without rapacious outsiders, Macondo eventually creates plenty of trouble for itself. The second generation of Macondo Buendías includes a colonel who starts thirty-two revolutions and loses them all; the third generation produces a petty town dictator who rules Macondo by decree and firing squad; and in the fourth generation, a Buendía labor leader succeeds only in getting his followers murdered. After this massacre in a town that once bragged about not needing a graveyard, the banana company leaves, and Macondo slips into a sleepy decadence. The businesses close, houses fall, and young people depart.

At the Buendía mansion, the weeds and termites are encroaching while the fifth Buendía generation, returned from abroad, entertains itself with homosexuality and incest. The sixth generation, a reclusive scholar deciphering Melquíades' writings, is also involved in the latter entertainment, thereby producing the lucky seventh generation, a pig-tailed boy appropriately named after his father. When the mother dies, the father goes off to soak himself in a whorehouse, and the unattended baby is eaten by an army of red ants. It is time for Macondo to call it quits. A whirlwind rises and wipes the town off the face of the earth, just as the sobered scholar deciphers Melquíades' prediction of the end.

Analysis

The main theme of *One Hundred Years of Solitude* is the awful disappointment of Latin America's first century of independence: One can bear to think about the disappointment only by treating it as a joke. The causes of the disappointment are no joke: ignorance, violence, exploitation, and rigid conventionality. García Márquez seems to see these causes arising, in turn, from the ingrown nature of Latin American society, as suggested by his novel's title and by other indications. Latin America is represented as Macondo, a small town whose inhabitants possess a small-town mentality. The Buendía family names are repeated through different generations to the point of mass confusion. Throughout the novel, there is an obsession with inbreeding and incest. José Arcadio marries Rebeca, his adopted sister, and Arcadio lusts after Pilar Ternera, his mother (though unknown to him), and Amaranta, his aunt. Even Pilar Ternera is a sort of mother surrogate for the boys she beds. A soldier sums up the obsession when he jokingly says that the Liberal revolutions are for the right to marry one's mother. The pig's tail is the unnatural result of such an incestuous society, the apocalyptic ending an appropriate punishment.

Some readers of *One Hundred Years of Solitude* have been included to see the novel as the reactionary retreat from the leftist sympathies that García Márquez has expressed elsewhere, particularly in his nonfiction. García Márquez's condemnation of Latin American history in *One Hundred Years of Solitude* not only is consistent with his leftist views but also undergirds them. What could be more revolutionary than the novel's ending, which seems to call not for the Liberal variety of revolution but for one that destroys the old order?

The revolutionary potential of art is implied by the novel's secondary theme, which explores the relationship of art and life. On one hand, art imitates life—to the point in *One Hundred Years of Solitude* in which García Márquez includes playful references to himself, his wife, and the work of fellow novelists. On the other hand, life imitates art: Melquíades' writings are both record and prophecy. Telling the story being lived in the novel, Melquíades is a stand-in for the author, who records, prophesies, entertains, and presumably influences events just as the old gypsy does. More ironic aspects of the author are suggested by the bookish Aureliano, who interprets history only as he suffers it: by Aureliano's best friend, Gabriel, who is last seen leaving Macondo—for good reason—to become a starving writer in Paris; and by Aureliano's mentor, an old Catalonian bookseller who writes three boxes full of purple prose.

Critical Context

Internationally read and admired, Gabriel García Márquez was awarded the 1982 Nobel Prize in Literature. Even the Nobel Prize does not adequately denote his achievement, which ranks with that of James Joyce and William Faulkner. Like these two writers, García Márquez has staked out his literary territory. He himself acknowledges the strong influence of Faulkner, especially apparent in *One Hundred Years of Solitude*.

In *One Hundred Years of Solitude*, widely regarded as his masterpiece, García Márquez solved the main problems of the modernist writer better than Joyce and Faulkner did—how to cover complex material and pessimistic themes and still be accessible and entertaining. Unlike Joyce and Faulkner, García Márquez also gives his work political direction, which provides an antidote to modernist nihilistic tendencies.

García Márquez solved his problems in *One Hundred Years of Solitude* by dropping some of the duller, more obscure modernist techniques and returning to earlier modes of narration, modes possibly suggested by his native background. Adopting the role of omniscient author, García Márquez, like Faulkner in *The Hamlet* (1940), sounds like a spinner of tall tales drawing on local folklore. His Magical Realism was antedated by François Rabelais and Voltaire, as was his fast-paced action. García Márquez integrated these older techniques into his modernist outlook, making *One Hundred Years of Solitude* a work that no reader should miss.

OUR HOUSE IN THE LAST WORLD

Author: Oscar Hijuelos (1951-   )
Type of work: Novel
Type of plot: Family
Time of plot: 1929-1975
Locale: Cuba and New York City
First published: 1983

Principal Characters

Hector Santinio, the youngest son of Mercedes Sorrea and Alejo Santinio. Born in New York City in 1951, Hector spends part of his childhood in Cuba with his parents. A near-fatal infection contracted in Cuba turns him into a sickly, lonely, and overprotected boy. Hector grows up in a dingy apartment in New York City resenting his overprotective, superstitious mother and his violent, alcoholic father. Although his parents are Cuban, he rebels against their Cuban ways and refuses to learn Spanish. In his mind, Cuba is associated with illness and with his unhappy home life. At the same time, however, he considers himself inferior to his father, whom he fears. Even after his father dies, Hector remains haunted by Alejo, who appears to him in dreams and visions. Only after Hector moves out of the apartment is he able to achieve a measure of autonomy and spiritual peace.

Alejo Santinio, the head of the Santinio family. A mail carrier in Cuba, he meets and marries Mercedes Sorrea; shortly after the wedding, they emigrate to the United States in search of a better life. Although Alejo is at first full of hopes and ambitions, material success eludes him, and he resigns himself to being a cook in a large hotel, where he works from the mid-1940's until his death twenty-five years later. Seeing other members of his family arrive in the United States and prosper, Alejo becomes embittered and turns to drink and to other women for temporary solace. A big, friendly man with a winning manner and a tendency to live beyond his means, Alejo has many friends. At home, however, he is sullen and authoritarian. Often coming home drunk in the evenings, he brutalizes his wife and his two children. When he dies suddenly of a stroke, his children are relieved as much as aggrieved.

Mercedes Sorrea, Alejo's wife and Hector and Horacio's mother. Although initially in love with her husband, Mercedes soon comes to resent him for being a failure. A poet in her youth, Mercedes is frustrated at not being able to cultivate her literary inclinations. In New York, she leads a life of drudgery and poverty. Considering herself something of a medium, she finds consolation in a fantasy world of spirits. Even though her life with Alejo is full of discord, after he dies she loses touch with reality and retreats further into her fantasies.

Horacio Santinio, Alejo and Mercedes' eldest son. Unlike his brother Hector, Horacio is tough and independent. He is not intimidated by Alejo and learns very early to take care of himself. When he is old enough, Horacio joins the Air Force, thereby escaping the unhappy Santinio household. Horacio cannot understand why his brother does not distance himself from Mercedes and Alejo. The contrast between the infirm Hector and the strong Horacio is a principal theme in the novel.

Buita, Alejo's sister, who also emigrates from Cuba and spends some time living with the Santinios. Buita, who never approved of Alejo's marriage to the eccentric Mercedes, is a stern and unforgiving woman who does not miss any opportunity to humiliate her sister-in-law. After Alejo's death, Buita tries to convince Hector to leave his mother and live with her in Miami.

Luisa, Mercedes' sister, who also spends some time living with the Santinios after arriving from Cuba. Unlike the Santinios, Luisa and her husband do very well in the United States and soon are able to afford a nice house in the suburbs. Of his relatives, Luisa is the one Hector likes best, for he has fond memories of her kindness to him when he was a small child in Cuba.

The Novel

Based in part on the author's own experiences growing up in New York City during the 1950's, *Our House in the Last World* is a fictional memoir that follows the fortunes of the Santinio family over several decades, first in Cuba and then in the United States. Divided into fourteen unnumbered chapters that cover events between 1929 and 1975, the novel begins with the meeting of Hector's parents, Alejo and Mercedes, in Holguín, a small town in Cuba's easternmost province. Mercedes, whose family's fortunes declined sharply after her father's death a few years earlier, lives with her mother and works as a ticket girl in a theater. Alejo is a tall, robust man and something of a dandy; he lives in a neighboring town and makes a living as a mail carrier. The romance begins in the theater on a Sunday afternoon and culminates in marriage several years later. Although Alejo and Mercedes do not seem particularly suited for each other, they enter into their new life full of dreams and hopes.

Shortly after their marriage in 1943, Alejo decides to try his luck in the United States. At first, he and Mercedes live with his sister Margarita and her husband Eduardo, but soon they get a small apartment of their own. After trying several odd jobs, Alejo lands a position as a cook in a large New York hotel, where he works for the rest of his life. The Santinios' first son, Horacio, is born in 1945; the second son, Hector, in 1951. Several years after Hector's birth, the Santinios go back to Cuba to see their families; during the stay, Hector contracts a mysterious infection that nearly kills him. Back in the United States, Hector spends a year in a hospital for terminally ill children. Because the hospital is in Connecticut, his mother visits him infrequently. During his long stay in the hospital, Hector is forced to learn English by one of the nurses, who locks him in a closet and refuses to release him unless he asks to be let out in English. Eventually, he gets well and rejoins his parents in their New York apartment.

The Santinios' life in New York is not a happy one. Alejo likes his job as a cook, but he is frustrated that he is not doing as well as some of his relatives. He makes plans to buy a store and go into business for himself, but his plans never come to fruition. The high point of Alejo's career as a cook occurs one day when Soviet Premier Nikita Khrushchev has dinner at the hotel and Alejo brings the food out. The next day, a picture of Alejo standing alongside Khrushchev appears in the newspaper, and Alejo becomes a celebrity in the neighborhood for a few days.

Mercedes is no happier than her husband. Constantly pressed for money, she hunts for bargains and rummages through the neighbors' castoffs in search of usable clothes for her children. Alejo and Mercedes fight endlessly. Alejo criticizes her for not being a good wife and mother; she criticizes him for being a drunk and for not providing adequately for the family.

Horacio and Hector grow up in the midst of constant battles between their parents. Often, when Alejo comes home drunk, Horacio and Hector have to undress him and help him into bed. After they go to bed, they hear their parents screaming in the next room. Horacio reacts to this unhappy situation by becoming a tough, street-smart kid. Spending as little time as possible in the apartment, he is defiant of his parents and neglectful of his brother. When he gets his girlfriend pregnant, he quits school and enlists in the Air Force.

Hector, who lacks his brother's toughness, is an obese and sickly boy who is tortured by his home situation but cannot do anything about it. Because his mother fears for his health, she does not let him out of her sight. Seeing him as his mother's ally, his father ignores him until Hector reaches adolescence. Alejo then seeks him out and tries to get to know him, but Hector wants nothing to do with his father. In the mid-1960's, Hector spends several months with his Aunt Buita, who lives in Miami. In Miami, though, Hector feels equally out of place; he cannot speak Spanish like the other Cubans, who mistake him for an American. Much as he tries, Hector cannot act and sound Cuban. In Miami, he falls in love with a Cuban American girl named Cindy, but she does not pay any attention to him. When Alejo collapses unexpectedly at work, Hector returns to New York for the funeral.

The novel concludes with an excruciating description of Alejo's funeral and the family's reaction. After Alejo's death, Mercedes retreats into a fantasy world of Cuban ghosts. Although she hated Alejo in life, once he is dead, she cannot seem to live without him; she pretends that he visits her in the middle of the night. Hector lives for a while with his mother, but eventually he moves out and enrolls in a university.

Analysis

This novel tells the story of the disintegration of a family. Somber and unsparing, the narration details the miserable existence of the Santinios as they try to adapt to life in a new country. Almost every chapter chronicles a new misfortune—a child's illness, an episode of drunkenness or adultery, a violent squabble between husband and wife or father and son, or a new setback for the family's finances. The reader emerges with a painful portrait of a troubled family on the way toward dissolution. There is little love or tenderness here, either between spouses or among parents and children.

At the center of it all is Hector. The great theme of Hector's childhood and adolescence is becoming a Cuban man like his father. Over and over, Hector harps on the fact that he is not as Cuban as Alejo or Horacio. He does not speak Spanish, he is blond, he is frail, and he is a mama's boy. Unlike Horacio, who follows in his father's footsteps by becoming a hard-drinking, brawling, macho womanizer, Hector develops into a shy and overweight "American" teenager. Making things worse is Hector's striking physical resemblance to his father. As he grows up, Hector develops the conviction that he is a defective replica of his father, a reproduction exact in outward details but lacking Alejo's Cuban spirit. Too Cuban to be completely American but hardly Cuban enough to resemble his father, Hector sees himself as freakish and deformed.

An important facet of Hector's struggles with his father is language. For Hector, Spanish is his father's tongue, a language that he both desires and abhors. When Hector speaks Spanish, he becomes Alejo; when he becomes Alejo, he turns into the monstrous man who comes home drunk in the middle of the night. Since the Spanish language focuses his ambivalent feelings toward his father, it is a wound, a handicap. When he tries to utter a Spanish sentence, he feels as if the words wrap themselves around him like hospital tape. Spanish immobilizes him, ties him up in knots; try as he might, he cannot speak it fluently.

The circumstances in which Hector learns Spanish certainly shape his pathological view of the language. The most wrenching scenes in a book full of wrenching scenes are those that describe Hector's prolonged stay in the sanatorium (Hijuelos suffered a similar illness when he was four years old). During his convalescence, he sees his mother intermittently and his father not at all. Separated from his parents, he comes under the care of nurses who make him speak English. Hector enters the sanatorium as a Cuban boy; by the time he is released a year later, Spanish has become identified with the illness he caught in Cuba. In the five-year-old boy's mind, Spanish is disease, and English is health. This feeling was to stay with him for many years. Like other immigrant memoirs, *Our House in the Last World* is a conversion narrative, for it narrates a character's passage from one culture to another. What is unusual is that the conversion takes place in a hospital and is portrayed as a cure.

Our House in the Last World is best seen as a valedictory to Cuban culture. The voice that speaks in this novel, and which may be close to that of Hijuelos himself, is that of someone who retains ties to Cuban culture but who is no longer Cuban.

The novel pays tribute to Cuban culture even as it bids it farewell. As the title makes clear, Cuba is the "last world," a world that the characters have left behind. This work is Hector's complex and conflicted valedictory to the Spanish language, to his Cuban parents, and to the island's customs and culture.

Critical Context

Our House in the Last World, Hijuelos' first book, has been overshadowed by the success of his two subsequent works, *The Mambo Kings Play Songs of Love* (1989), which won for the author the 1990 Pulitzer Prize for fiction, and *The Fourteen Sisters of Emilio Montez O'Brien* (1993). For this reason, although the book was well reviewed

upon publication, it has received scant critical attention. *Our House in the Last World*, however, is certainly a significant accomplishment in its own right. As a sensitive and moving portrait of an immigrant family's difficult adaptation to life in the United States, it ranks with the best immigrant memoirs written by U.S. Hispanics.

THE OUTSIDER

Author: Ernesto Sábato (1911-   )
Type of work: Novel
Type of plot: Psychological
Time of plot: 1946
Locale: Buenos Aires, Argentina, and a ranch in the countryside
First published: *El túnel*, 1948 (English translation, 1950)

Principal Characters

Juan Pablo Castel, the narrator, a well-known and critically admired painter. He sees María Iribarne in a gallery, seemingly transfixed by one of his paintings. He becomes obsessed with her and becomes her lover. Finally convinced that María is having an affair with Luis Hunter, he breaks into her room and stabs her to death.

María Iribarne, a beautiful, young, wealthy woman. The reader knows her only as an enigmatic figure described entirely by Castel.

Allende Hunter, María's blind husband. When Castel kills María, he rushes to Allende to tell him that María has betrayed him with Luis Hunter and others. Allende attacks him, calling him an imbecile and fool, but does not contradict Castel's charges. Allende neither explains his relationship with María and Luis Hunter nor reveals his perception of any of these events. He commits suicide.

Luis Hunter, an architect and Allende's cousin. He lives on the family *estancia*, where María often stays. Castel believes that Luis has an affair with María, but perhaps that is only a paranoid fantasy.

The Novel

The Outsider is an intense psychological novel concerning a passionate crime, narrated in the first-person-singular form, using techniques found in detective fiction. The opening line of the novel unveils the outcome of Juan Pablo Castel's desperate attempt to reach out of his inner confinement through a total physical and spiritual communication with María: "I am Juan Pablo Castel, the painter who killed María Iribarne." The plot of the novel unfolds in a very simple way. A tormented artist enters into a passionate affair with the wife of a wealthy blind man. Frustrated by his inability to experience María's absolute love or to possess her, Castel murders her. The protagonist confides the recollection of his story to readers in a direct, personal style, forcing them to enter his tunnel of absolute isolation.

The painter first sees María at one of his art exhibits, viewing a painting entitled *Maternity*.

Although the artwork centers on the figures of a mother and child, there is a small window in a corner of the painting. Through that window, one can see an anxious woman on a desolate beach. She seems to be waiting for someone's response. Castel observes María's attraction to the remote scene and is certain that finally someone equal to him understands his cry for communication. While he is lost in a web of meditations, however, she leaves the gallery. The reader is then thrown into Castel's frantic search for María through the streets of Buenos Aires. By this time, one realizes that the anecdote is being told from the point of view of what could be considered a madman, the protagonist. The series of hypotheses, questions, and digressions that go on in Castel's mind, however, intrigue and hold the reader's interest.

The next encounter with María, as well as subsequent ones, confirms the tumultuous nature of

Castel's personality. The intense and cruel interrogation that María is forced to undergo at every meeting reveals the futile struggle of Castel to possess her. She seems reluctant to surrender to Castel's passion, fearing to cause him more harm. The only common thread between them seems to stem from the mutual understanding of Castel's art.

María's sudden departure for the country leaves Castel in greater depression. The painter goes to her fashionable apartment. While waiting in the library, Castel is confronted by the inexpressive stare of the eyes of María's husband, Allende. He acts courteously toward Castel and hands him a letter from María. The extreme discomfort of the situation for Castel comes from the discovery that María's husband is blind. At this point, the author brings out one of his reiterated themes, his obsession for the "subworld" of the blind. As Sábato has admitted, blindness produces in him both profound intrigue and repulsion.

An unexpected discovery is the fact that María has gone to the country to visit her cousin, Luis Hunter. Hunter is a man publicly known to be a mediocre writer and a womanizer. María's frequent trips to Hunter's ranch become a new source of anguish for Castel. The rest of the novel fluctuates between Castel and María's exasperating meetings at his studio and the absences of María because of her visits to Hunter. Castel's repeated accusations and intense questioning seem to frighten her and even drive her away. In desperation, the protagonist tries to possess her through physical love. Every sexual encounter is now marked by hatred and violence, followed by moments of remorse and humility on Castel's part.

The protagonist decides to see María at Hunter's estate. He is convinced that Hunter feels

jealous. One night, he seems to distinguish the sound of a woman's footsteps entering Hunter's room. Without any doubt about the love relationship between María and Hunter, he leaves the ranch at dawn. Once in Buenos Aires, he spends nights and days in a phantasmagoric world of bars, prostitutes, and fights. His mental incoherence becomes evident and is shown in the difficulties he finds writing an insulting letter to María, accusing her of being Hunter's lover.

The author next details the deterioration of Castel's mind. Castel goes to the studio and destroys his paintings with a knife. He tears the canvas of *Maternity*, with its little window, into small pieces, anticipating perhaps the final separation from María. He then drives wildly to the ranch in a borrowed car, waiting until dark to approach María. In this agonizing interval, Castel summarizes his relationship with her, concluding with the fact that María never shared with him the feeling of isolation. She merely looked through one of the windows of his tunnel out of curiosity and saw him suffering, helplessly waiting to end his tormented existence. He misunderstood her compassion for love.

Castel waits outside Hunter's ranch during a violent storm. When the light of María's bedroom goes on, Castel enters and stabs her to death. Before turning himself in to the authorities, the protagonist confronts an astonished Allende, to whom he reveals that María has been his lover, Luis Hunter's lover, and the lover of who knows how many other men. Castel also tells Allende that he has killed her. In the concluding paragraph, Castel learns of Allende's suicide. He ends his story in abject isolation.

Analysis

The principal theme of the novel is the isolation of a man in a world ruled by reason and logic. Throughout the novel, the contradiction between the tormented, complex world of the protagonist and the hostile, external reality is present and obvious. It is important to point out that "objective"

reality is only one element in Sábato's narrative, whereas "subjective" reality permeates the work. Most of the action takes place in the tumultuous mind of Castel. The novel's original title, *El túnel* (the tunnel), reveals the inner confinement and entrapment of the protagonist, who has become totally estranged from his exterior world. His desperate attempt to liberate himself from such a condition leads him to believe that María has spent her existence in a similar tunnel, parallel to his own. Physical possession and subsequent jealousy gradually become frantic obsessions for Castel and seem to be the only means of bridging their inner lives. The theory that love, and finally sex, leads only to more extreme anguish and solitude has been analyzed by Sábato in a lucid 1953 essay entitled "Solitude and Communication."

It becomes apparent to the reader that Castel painted the little window in *Maternity* to represent his own limited exposure to the world—one of his tunnel's windows. Looking through it, he found María, who seemed in turn to be searching for a way out of her own secluded world. The painter perceived conflicting images of María in each one of their encounters, however, and the reader must ponder her real identity. She is presented as tender and passionate as well as detached and cynical. It is precisely this confusing perception of his lover that leads Castel to his gradual mental deterioration.

The painter eliminates María, and with her his only hope of escaping solitude. At the end of the novel, the reader sees him looking through a small cell window while listening to the sounds of outside, everyday life. The exterior world seems to him more remote and indifferent than ever. Castel comes to the realization that he has always been alone in his inner labyrinth and, what is more frightening, that he is doomed to remain alone in his own tunnel forever. Such is the fate of a man whose anguish and loneliness are oblivious to the rhythm of an orderly world where reason prevails.

Critical Context

When Sábato's *The Outsider* was published in 1948, his name instantly gained international recognition. The novel was translated into French, English, Polish, Portuguese, Swedish, Romanian, Japanese, Danish, and German. Sábato's first public exposure was through his incisive essays published since 1940. These diverse essays have been collected in several volumes. They are encyclopedic in nature and cover art, literature, politics, philosophy, history, education, religion, science, mathematics, and literary style.

To understand the vastness of his writings, it is necessary to remember Sábato's academic background. He earned a doctorate in physics in 1938 and worked at the Curie Laboratory in Paris as well as at the Massachusetts Institute of Technology. Many of his essays reveal his disillusionment with the sciences early in his professional career. After all, according to the writer, pure science has not been able to alleviate man's anguish at the prospect of death. In his essays and novels, Sábato shows the futility of expressing the subjective world of the individual—feelings and emotions—through orderly and logical reasoning.

Other essays deal with the writer's convictions on the role of literature. His disenchantment with communism also becomes apparent in several political essays. The most controversial, however, are the ones related to Argentina's unstable situation before and after Juan Perón's regime.

All the themes of Sábato's essays are masterfully interwoven in his three novels. Thirteen years after *The Outsider*, Sábato finished his second fictional work, *Sobre héroes y tumbas* (1961; *On Heroes and Tombs*, 1981), unanimously acclaimed by critics. This novel presents the same conflict found in *The Outsider*: the study of people in an irrational universe. Instead of projecting the vision of the world through the mind of a tormented individual, however, the reader is exposed to a panoramic view of Argentine society—explored from historical, demographic, and geographical points of view—by four main characters. *On Heroes and Tombs* ends with bleak hope for the future of humankind. A similar mood informs Sábato's less successful novel, *Abbadón, el exterminador* (1974). *The Outsider* remains his most widely read creation and an outstanding example of the Latin American psychological novel with existentialist overtones.

THE PALACE OF THE WHITE SKUNKS

Author: Reinaldo Arenas (1943-1990)
Type of work: Novel
Type of plot: Family
Time of plot: The late 1950's
Locale: Holguín, a small provincial town in the rural Oriente province of Cuba
First published: *Le palais des très blanches mouffettes,* 1975 (English translation, 1990)

Principal Characters

Fortunato, a sensitive and restless adolescent desperate to escape from a closed social and familial circle in which he feels trapped. He is the most complex character in the novel, fragmenting himself in order to give voice to the suffering of the other family members. As a writer, he creates and imagines other levels of reality in order to escape the poverty, hunger, war, intolerance, and prejudice around him. His failed attempt to join the rebel forces leads to his death at the hands of the government police.

Polo, Fortunato's grandfather, an impotent patriarchal figure. A Spaniard who emigrated to Cuba from the Canary Islands looking for a better life, he is a frustrated and embittered old man disillusioned by the poverty and misery of the Cuban countryside. Moreover, wishing to have had boys to help him with his struggles, he considers himself cursed for having engendered only daughters. As an act of defiance, he resorts to silence, refusing to talk to anyone except Tomasico, the owner of the only factory in town. Through Polo's chats with Tomasico and his interior monologues about the ups and downs of his fruit and vegetable stand, the reader becomes aware of the collective misery of the local economy.

Jacinta, Polo's wife, a Cuban peasant woman who must cope with the stresses and misfortunes of a harsh rural lifestyle without the help of her uncaring and selfish husband. Uneducated and superstitious, she places her hope on some miracu-lous intervention that will change her life and that of her family. There is no escape from the misery that surrounds her, from the problems facing her daughters and fatherless grandchildren. Throughout the novel, she alternates between prayers begging for God's help and blasphemies insulting God for his indifference.

Adolfina, "the spinster daughter," Fortunato's feminine double. She and Fortunato share sensibilities, experiencing feelings of extreme loneliness, dissatisfaction, and helplessness. Adolfina identifies with Fortunato's liberating spirit and his ability to express himself freely. Fortunato expresses himself openly; Adolfina, by contrast, must bury her emotions. As the oldest daughter in a traditional Hispanic family, she takes on the role of the responsible caretaker who must abandon her dreams and hopes and sacrifice herself for her family. Adolfina makes one last attempt to find a man, but she returns home defeated, still a virgin, and sets herself afire.

Celia, "the half-mad daughter," driven to madness after her only daughter, Esther, commits suicide.

Digna, "the abandoned daughter," abandoned by her husband Moisés and left to rear her two children, Tico and Anisia.

Onerica, "the banished daughter," Fortunato's mother, who abandons him and goes to the United States in search of her own "fortune."

The Novel

The Palace of the White Skunks is a stylistically rich experimental novel that tells of the desolation, despair, and vicissitudes of a Cuban family prior to the 1959 Cuban Revolution. The novel, which deliberately and systematically undermines the conventions of the realistic novel tradition, is centered on Fortunato, a sensitive and restless young man living through a turbulent political period in Cuban history: the insurrectional struggle against the dictatorial government of Fulgencio Batista. Desperate to escape the disappointments and cruelties of his family (the members of which he refers to as "creatures" and "wild beasts"), as well as to escape from Holguín, a small, conservative town, Fortunato attempts to join Fidel Castro's revolutionary forces. This flight for freedom, however, ends tragically when the young man is arrested, tortured, and executed by the government police.

The novel is divided into three parts. In the fourteen pages that make up part 1, "Prologue and Epilogue," the reader is introduced to the squabbling and self-pitying voices of the characters, all members of the same family. At this point, the crisscrossing of voices is entangled, difficult to decipher during a first reading. These fragments of voices, however, will be contextualized and expanded during the second and third parts of the novel. With the (con)fusion of what is traditionally the first word (prologue) and the last word (epilogue) of the traditional novel, the suggestion is made that there is no first or final word on any given matter; rather, discourse is open-ended, without finalization.

Part 2, "The Creatures Utter Their Complaints," constitutes the major portion of the novel. This section is divided into five "agonies" in which family members take turns articulating their own intimate sufferings. These accounts are presented as a rambling of voices that often conceals the identity of the speaking subject. Temporal-spatial realities are filtered through the turbulent voices of the family members, who do not concern themselves with providing objective reference points. It appears as if the same state of instability and crisis that is assaulting the country exists internally in each family member.

Part 2 also introduces fragments from newspaper accounts, bulletins of guerrilla activity, advertisements, film announcements, and beauty magazines; these fragments are juxtaposed alongside and serve to parallel the babel of voices of the family members. In "Fifth Agony," there appear twelve versions of the two most significant episodes within the novel: Fortunato's decision to escape from home to join the Castro-led rebels and Adolfina's unsuccessful attempt to lose her virginity during a night on the town. The contradictions in the different versions of these two fruitless quests reveal the difficulty of attempting to record any reality faithfully. This lack of precision is irrelevant to the emotional intensity, dreams, and desires of both characters. In the end, any reader searching for objectivity in *The Palace of the White Skunks* will be at a loss and will consequently miss the artistic and creative intensity of the novel. To appreciate this text, one must surrender to its hallucinatory situations, implausible incidents, and disjointed digressions.

In part 3, "The Play," the reader discovers the insertion of a play within the novel. This change of genre (from novel to drama) is accompanied by a significant change from interior monologue to dramatic dialogue. In this phantasmagoric theatrical representation, the family members become performers who reenact their own lives and obsessions. Immediately following the play, there appears "Sixth Agony," which recounts yet another version, of Fortunato's escape. The omniscient narrator of this last agony describes the young man's torture and death at the hands of government soldiers. Earlier, however, this same omniscient narrator, traditionally a reliable voice, had expressed doubt over whether Fortunato had ever joined the rebel forces. Regardless of what indeed happened, it is significant that no version denies Fortunato's reasons for wanting to escape from home: hunger, poverty, repression, lack of opportunities, and the suffocating demands of his family.

Analysis

The Palace of the White Skunks is embedded in a concrete historical event, the fight of the Sierra Maestra rebel forces against the Batista regime that culminated in Fidel Castro's revolutionary victory in 1959. The presentation of the characters' other levels of experience is never sacrificed for any type of accuracy or transparency, or for any hope of reproducing historical reality faithfully at a referential level of language. Arenas' concern is not to rewrite history but to subordinate history to fiction, thus allowing free inquiry into the nature of human existence. The novel does not support the concept of an "official" history of a collective consciousness that simplifies human experience by reducing it to facts or figures; rather, the book examines the enigma of individual human existence.

The ironic and ludicrous title, *The Palace of the White Skunks*, alerts the reader to the unconventionality of the story. In this novel, the notion of a well-structured plot is subverted by the presentation of a narrative time-space of multiple possibilities that invites the reader to sort out the various narrative threads and, thus, to work out a larger meaning. The text requires a flexible approach to reading, a letting go of traditional expectations. The reader is asked to make the text intelligible in spite of its violations and transgressions, to accommodate the shifting codes of a multifarious reality. Hence, the initial image of death riding on a bicycle around the family home is presented as being equally as "real" as the protagonist's frustrated attempt to join the revolutionary struggle. Fortu-

nato's walking on the roof while stabbing himself, Esther and Fortunato's chats beyond the grave, demons and spirits dancing in the living room, the extreme poverty of the rural town, the insurrectional struggle against Batista, the grandmother's blasphemies and insults, Adolfina's sexual frustrations—all are presented side by side and contribute equally to the novel's textual validity.

Utilizing a narrative strategy that fragments the story into bits and pieces, *The Palace of the White Skunks* invites the reader to re-create a bewildering collage that, although it at first disorients, ultimately reforges the life-art connection on the level of the imaginative. In this, his third novel, Arenas provides the reader with a disturbing portrait of the poverty and misery that were present in rural Cuba shortly before the triumph of the revolution. While many Cuban novelists during the 1970's were writing testimonial realistic works that idealistically presented the revolution as the decisive moment that radically transformed Cuban society for the better, Arenas, undermining this rather utopian vision of history, portrayed the revolution as the catalyst responsible for the death of his protagonist and the emotional destruction of a family.

In *The Palace of the White Skunks*, Arenas clearly had no intention of writing a closed, linear text that presented a coherent, objective representation of empirical reality. The novel is a daring compositional experiment that subverts and challenges authoritarian and reductionist attitudes toward literature as well as life.

Critical Context

While living in Cuba, Arenas published only one novel, *Celestino antes del alba* (1967; *Singing from the Well*, 1987), and a few short stories. The author's refusal to articulate revolutionary propaganda in his writings forced the cultural policymakers of the Cuban Revolution—individuals who defined the function of literature as political and of immediate practical utility—to censor his

texts and designate them as counterrevolutionary. After Arenas' fall from favor with the Cuban government, his work was no longer published on the island; moreover, his manuscripts were repeatedly confiscated and destroyed by the Cuban secret police. As a result, Arenas secretly began to send his manuscripts abroad. *The Palace of the White Skunks* thus first appeared in 1975 in French translation before appearing in its original Spanish version, *El palacio de las blanquísimas mofetas*, in 1980.

The Palace of the White Skunks is the second novel of a five-book sequence—*Singing from the Well*, *The Palace of the White Skunks*, *Otra vez el mar* (1982; *Farewell to the Sea*, 1986), *El color del verano* (1991; the color of summer), and *El asalto* (1991; the assault)—that constitutes a unique intradependent unit within the author's total novelistic production.

This quintet, which the author insisted on calling a *pentagonía* ("pentagony")—a playful but revealing neologism that underscores the despair and *agonía* (agony) suffered by the characters in each novel—reflects different historical periods of Cuban society as well as providing an imagined futuristic vision of the Cuban island and its people. In each novel of the series, the main character is destroyed—only to be resurrected under a new name in the subsequent text, where he suffers a whole new set of ordeals. With *The Palace of the White Skunks*, Arenas continued the family saga that he had begun with *Singing from the Well*. *The Palace of the White Skunks* explores the protean main character's adolescent world, a chaotic world of torment and spiritual hardship played out against a backdrop of revolutionary upheaval.

PARADISO

Author: José Lezama Lima (1910-1976)
Type of work: Novel
Type of plot: *Bildungsroman*
Time of plot: The early twentieth century
Locale: Cuba, Florida, Jamaica, and Mexico
First published: 1966 (English translation, 1974)

Principal Characters

José (Joseíto) Cemí, the protagonist, at the novel's opening a five-year-old, skinny asthmatic. After his father's death, he is drawn to his Uncle Albert, whose language skills enchant Cemí. He studies law at Havana University, though his vocation is poetry. His friendship with Fronesis and Foción at the university help him to define his emotional needs as a poet. Oppiano's instruction is a climactic fulfillment for him and the novel.

Colonel José Eugenio Cemí, his father. A respected engineer and much-admired Cuban army officer, he dies while on military assignment at the age of thirty-three.

Rialta Olaya de Cemí, his mother. Ten years after his father's death, she tells Cemí what she hopes for him: not to avoid danger, but always to try what is most difficult.

Leticia, Rialta's petulant sister. She introduces Cemí to Fronesis while Cemí is visiting her home.

Doña Augusta, Rialta's mother. Her story about her father's body being exhumed strongly affects Cemí. She dies of cancer while Cemí is at the university.

Ricardo Fronesis, the provincial friend of Cemí and Foción. He impresses Cemí with his stoical dignity and ineffable charm. At the university, he impresses all with his articulate discussions of philosophical issues.

Eugenio Foción, a homosexual student, older than Fronesis and Cemí. He vehemently defends homosexuality in discussions with Fronesis and Cemí at the university. Although he has erotic feelings for Fronesis, he never succeeds in a sexual relationship with him. He loses his sanity after Fronesis' father warns him to stay away from Fronesis; after a brief hospitalization, he is cured when lightning destroys a tree that he has identified with Fronesis.

Oppiano Licario, a tall, Sorbonne-educated poet and notary. Cemí meets him ten years after the death of Cemí's father, an occurrence witnessed by Oppiano. He writes his last poem for Cemí.

Ynaca Eco Licario, the wise Cuban sister of Oppiano. She gives Oppiano's last poem to Cemí when he visits her house of mourning.

The Novel

Paradiso is both the story of a Cuban upper-middle-class family during the first quarter of the twentieth century and a *Bildungsroman* that traces a young man's path to artistic creation. Although the novel focuses on the protagonist, Cemí, and begins with a description of an asthma attack that he suffers in early childhood, from chapter 2 to chapter 6 it tells the story of his parents' families, their meeting, and the death of his father, the colonel, at the age of thirty-three.

The death of the colonel is the event that endows his widow, Rialta, and his son Cemí with a spiritual mission in life. She becomes convinced that the loss of her husband cannot have been meaningless and that her son, in some way, will fulfill his father's truncated destiny. Cemí seems to accept that destiny without question, but he does not know how he will fulfill it. Through a series of mystical experiences precipitated by Cemí's intense observation of objects and by his meditation about particular images and ideas, he comes to realize that he will make his contribution through the cultivation of poetry and the search for poetic images that will lead to truth. Poetry fills the vacuum left by the death of Cemí's father, and it endows that seemingly purposeless death with meaning.

The rest of *Paradiso* follows Cemí's education in art and in the ways of the world. Leaving behind the safety of family life, Cemí enters the outside world, first at school and then at the university, where he is introduced to the allure of sex and the life of the intellect. In this stage of his education, his guides are his friends, Fronesis and Foción.

With them, he explores all the vital issues that the embalmed lectures of the university professors never broach.

Having survived the dangers of this phase of his education—the pursuit of wanton eroticism and the abuse of intelligence as an instrument of power—Cemí is ready to undertake his poetic apprenticeship under the guidance of Oppiano Licario. This enigmatic character appears at several crucial moments in *Paradiso*. Licario, the only one present when Cemí's father died, accepts the colonel's dying request: "I have a son. Get to know him, and try to teach him something of what you have learned through your travels, suffering, and reading." Licario becomes Cemí's poetic mentor. By the time he dies, he has led the young man to the very threshold of artistic creation. As Cemí sits alone, late at night, in a café, he remembers his mentor's assurance that he is now prepared for poetic creation. *Paradiso* ends with Licario's words: "We may now begin."

Analysis

The principal theme of *Paradiso* is the power of poetic language to transform life. For Cemí, the quest for poetic images is also the road to spiritual salvation. For him, as for Lezama, the poetic image is a vehicle to reach truth, in particular, divine truth. Although extremely unorthodox in his views, Lezama always maintained his adherence to Catholicism. *Paradiso* (and all of Lezama's work) must be understood in the context of the author's mystical concept of artistic creation. The artist must always attempt the impossible, for it is only by working at the limits of capacity that he or she can hope to catch a glimmer of truth. The writing of poetry is therefore dependent on mystic revelations that often occur unannounced and that make use of the prosaic material of everyday life. *Paradiso* is a stylized autobiography in which Lezama utilizes the structures of the family novel and the *Bildungsroman* in order to expound his system of poetic mysticism.

Lezama's concept of illumination through difficult poetic images owes much to the practice of Zen Buddhism, in which, under the guidance of a *roshi* (Zen master), the disciple meditates on paradoxes (*kōan*) that lead to flashes of insight. Similarly, the stages that Cemí must pass through before he reaches the state of mind where artistic creation is possible recall the purification that a Buddhist must undergo through successive lifetimes before reaching nirvana.

Taoism also plays a major part in the characterization of Cemí; particularly important are the central concepts of yin and yang, the opposing but complementary principles that make up the universe. Cemí is in essence a personification of the yin and yang. Unlike his friends Fronesis and Foción, who are dynamic and represent either of these principles, Cemí is static because he contains them both. He is the balance of reason and passion, light and dark, heterosexuality and homosexuality.

Cemí never engages in sex in *Paradiso* because he represents the principle of androgyny, which for Lezama means sexual self-sufficiency.

Sexuality in *Paradiso* functions as a parable of artistic creation and of salvation. Homosexuality represents a destructive turning upon oneself, symbolized in the novel by the image of the circle (for Lezama a symbol of false immortality). Heterosexuality is viewed in a positive light, but the concomitant procreation is considered an acceptance of mortality. Only asexuality is seen as compatible with artistic creation and true immortality.

From the point of view of twentieth century philosophy and literature, the most striking aspect of Lezama's worldview is his faith in language and in poetic expression. Many others have seen language as a prison and poetry as mere wordplay; Lezama believes in their ability to reveal truth.

Critical Context

The publication of *Paradiso* launched Lezama into international fame. Prior to the novel's publication, Lezama was virtually unknown outside Cuba, where he was known as a major poet, an essayist, and the founder of *Orígenes*, the most important literary journal in the years before the revolution. *Paradiso*, which was read and praised by leading Latin American writers such as Julio Cortázar, Octavio Paz, and Mario Vargas Llosa, earned a place for Lezama among the writers of the "boom" of Latin American literature.

Although *Paradiso* has been hailed by novelists and critics as a seminal work that offers previously unsuspected rich avenues for the development of the novel, it has never enjoyed a wide readership. The novel's great originality and richness have also been its bane. Lezama's highly metaphorical language, his idiosyncratic handling of characterization and plot, and his mysticism have presented insurmountable obstacles for many readers. *Paradiso* has also elicited heated polemics because of its treatment of sex and of homosexuality in particular, and it has been attacked on political grounds. Upon its first publication in Cuba, it was received by some as a counterrevolutionary work. Nevertheless, Lezama's first novel is firmly entrenched as one of the classics of Latin American literature. *Oppiano Licario* (1977), an incomplete continuation of *Paradiso*, was published posthumously.

THE PASSION ACCORDING TO G. H.

Author: Clarice Lispector (1925-1977)
Type of work: Novel
Type of plot: Epiphany
Time of plot: The 1960's
Locale: An apartment in Rio de Janeiro, Brazil
First published: *A Paixão Segundo G. H.*, 1964 (English translation, 1988)

Principal Characters

G. H., a Brazilian woman identified only by her initials. G. H. narrates the story, which is largely concerned with recording her psychological reactions during a moment of self-reevaluation and turmoil. She is a middle-aged, middle-class amateur artist living in Rio de Janeiro who has enough income from investments to live well and amuse herself by sculpting. She has many friends and loves to go to parties, restaurants, and dance clubs, yet she has never formed any but shallow relationships. Although she has had a number of lovers, it seems that none of them has touched her deeply or established a long-term alliance with her. When she accidentally became pregnant, she hurried to have an abortion so that she would not be tied down. Nothing is told about her parents or early years, but it is hinted that she has had one lover in particular for whom she developed a profound affection; unfortunately, she was blind to her own feelings at the time. The novel focuses on G. H.'s thoughts one morning when she begins reconsidering the philosophical basis of her life. In the end, G. H. resolves to live in accordance with her newly enriched vision of the world, but it is left teasingly unclear whether, and how, she will keep her promise to herself.

Janair, G. H.'s maid, whose abrupt and unexplained departure leads G. H. to clean the servant's room and find that Janair has altered it in unusual ways, stripping it of all decorations except for primitive figures she has drawn in charcoal on the wall. Janair's name perhaps recalls the name of the city, Rio de Janeiro, where the action takes place.

The cockroach, an old insect that scares G. H. by coming out of Janair's wardrobe and is squashed to death; the incident sparks G. H.'s philosophical reflections.

The doctor, who performed G. H.'s abortion. The doctor temporarily becomes an addressee of her written record, but he is not further described.

The crying man, a former lover who also temporarily becomes G. H.'s addressee. In recalling a moment of silent communion between the two of them, she realizes that he was the one man she really loved. He is only described as he appeared in this incident, with none of his past or future relations with the narrator mentioned.

The Novel

Although the book is heavy with Christian allusions, especially to the Old Testament, what *The Passion According to G. H.* presents is a completely secular description of a spiritual rebirth. The trivial act of squashing a cockroach as she cleans her maid's room strangely rattles the story's narrator and leads her into a cascade of profound reflections on the scheme of things.

The book centers on a few hours in the life of the narrator, who is identified only as G. H., as she sits in her servant's room and thinks. The bulk of the text is taken up with a precise delineation of her thought processes as she reevaluates her life. This reevaluation, however, is not of the sort found in psychological novels, in which a character might reconsider past actions and resolve to make up for past lapses. What concerns G. H. is not any specific incident but rather the tenor of her life. Thus, for example, thoughts on the animality of the cockroach lead her to ponder her own humanness, which, she learns, can be truly appreciated only by understanding its linkage to nature. This facet of her existence she has previously overlooked.

Abstruse as such a concentration on abstract issues may seem, the heroine's spiritual journey is correlated with the specifics of her present lifestyle, her relation to her maid, and her past history. Concurrent with the unraveling of her previous, faulty spiritual constructions occurs a gradual revelation of her material circumstances.

G. H.'s life is ripe for enlightenment because it is one of extreme artificiality. She is a rentier, that is, one who lives off the dividends of her investments. She sculpts, not as serious artistic activity but to pass the time. Her friends are fellow idle bohemians, isolated from the daily life of the average Brazilian, and G. H.'s relationships extend no further than friendships. She has no relatives or long-term interpersonal commitments. She is without real work, hobbies, or intimacies with others.

Such facts are scattered throughout the story, but G. H.'s connection to her maid, Janair, is given in a lump at the beginning. Although the servant had been employed for some time G. H. knows nothing about her and has not been in her quarters since she was hired. Going into the room to clean up after the maid has abruptly left, G. H. is startled to find that the occupant had stripped the place of its clutter and sketched rude, primitive pictures on the wall, depictions that reveal Janair's hatred for her mistress. Finding her superficial understanding of her employee to be so wrong sufficiently disorients G. H. so that she can begin a reconsideration of her relations with the world.

Forced to see one relationship in a new light, the narrator is enabled to more purposefully allow herself to look at major events from her past in a new light. Her casual killing of a cockroach in the maid's wardrobe leads her to remember an abortion she had undergone just as casually. Her quiet moments in the servant's quarters lead her to think back to quiet times with an ex-lover and to acknowledge for the first time the depth of the love they had, which was expressed best in silence. In keeping with the novel's philosophical bent, however, G. H. thinks of her abortion not to blame herself for the choice she made in eliminating her unborn child but rather in order to condemn herself for the offhanded, thoughtless manner in which she made the decision. This condemnation links to the central spiritual perception with which she leaves the room at the end: She must henceforth try to live without preconceptions so that she can approach every moment with heightened authenticity.

To crown and close this chapter in her life, these few hours in which she has thought and functioned more intensely than ever before, G. H. bends down and eats the cockroach. In this bizarre act of "communion," G. H. both thanks the bug for being the guide to her spiritual reinvigoration and, more important, physically acts out her new rejection of traditional social stereotypes, such as the belief that insects are inherently disgusting. After this ritual, G. H. is ready to leave the room and confront life with an altered and enriched perspective.

Analysis

Before writing this novel, Lispector had lived extensively outside her homeland of Brazil, in the United States and in European countries, and she had a cosmopolitan, nonsectarian outlook. In depicting G. H.'s epiphany, Lispector draws on Christian imagery and citations available to her from her upbringing but presents the situation nondenominationally. She translates religious terminology into a secular vocabulary. In G. H.'s moment of truth, the name of God frequently comes up, but "God," G. H. explicitly states, is a word she is using to name the constantly emergent life force of the world, not a higher being attached to some religious creed. To someone like G. H., who has lived out of touch with nature and her own animal side, an awareness of this life force strikes with as much power as a religious revelation.

Part of the reason for Lispector's desacralization of this experience is to remove it from its doctrinal trappings. Above all, she wants to bring spiritual exaltation down to earth and make it seem realizable for anyone. Through such techniques as the use of homely details and realistic characterization, Lispector strives to indicate that every person who has ever thirsted for a richer life has the potential to undergo a genuine rebirth. Stated obversely, the book argues that no one has the right to shrug off such intangible events as are captured in the volume, since every person is liable to vital renewal.

Metaphysical experiences are often described in unconvincing and unsatisfying ways by those who went through them. Lispector confronts the issue of the possibility of representing nearly imperceptible happenings head on by having G. H. keep a written record. Everything in the novel describes the events of the narrator's extraordinary morning, but without revealing what has occurred since then, G. H. tells the reader that it is the day after her revelations; she is trying to write down what took place so that she will never forget the particulars. She runs into manifold problems in trying to find the words to embody what are resolutely nonverbal experiences. This is where redefinition comes in. She finds that many words that she formerly used, such as "God" and "love," no longer seem meaningful according to her new understanding of reality. Her wrestling with expression also provokes her to draw constantly on biblical imagery, as when she describes the maid's room as a desert where a saint is tested. She does this not because the experience is especially Christian but because this imagery accurately conveys the subtleties of mental nuance felt by those undergoing spiritual ordeals.

Thus, though Lispector is intent on showing readers how close anyone is to mystical discovery, this does not persuade her to downplay the complexity or ambiguity of such discovery. The writer is unflinching in accepting the challenges of attempting to put the ineffable into words.

Critical Context

The Passion According to G. H. can be connected to two intellectual currents of the period. The first was the rising prominence of "liberation theology" in Latin America. This theology was a Christianity, largely Catholicism, that had become more concerned with social justice and trying to ensure the poor an adequate life than with getting them to take the sacraments and register doctrinal purity. This religious trend partook of some of the spirit of the Cuban Revolution and of the urban guerrillas who fought corrupt dictators in many South and Central American countries, though it differed fundamentally from these movements in choice of means. Where the guerrillas depended on firepower, the liberation church eschewed violence in favor of preaching and having its leaders set examples of simple, dignified living in the communities of the impoverished. Although Lispector does not directly promote such ideas in her book, she shows that she is influenced by them in her double act of translation. She places a woman's moment of life-shattering vision in a mundane setting, and she drops religious phraseology in favor of everyday language. She translates a moment from specialized religious experience to place it in the common stream of life. By this tactic, she follows the wave of liberation theology in an insistence on the relevance and worldliness of spiritual concerns.

Second, Lispector is inspired by Continental

existentialism, to which she had been exposed in the fiction of the twentieth century French philosopher and novelist Jean-Paul Sartre. Sartre's novel *La Nausée* (1938, *Nausea*, 1949) is highlighted by a scene that recalls the one in which G. H. is transfixed by a cockroach. Sartre's protagonist is horrified by the roiling, inexhaustible life revealed to him by a tangle of tree roots. Although his feeling is one of revulsion, Sartre suggests that such moments are constructive, since one can live in authenticity and freedom only if one breaks the brittle surface of conventions—conventions that would ignore, for example, the life force in the tree and see it as merely another object. Lispector shares Sartre's belief that the passageway to authenticity leads through a realization of the estranging foreignness of the natural world, though her vision is not so unrelievedly dark as his.

This novel added to Lispector's reputation as a writer's writer. She did not garner as much popular support as did many of her contemporaries in Latin American fiction. Although some of them, such as Julio Cortázar and, to a lesser extent, Mario Vargas Llosa, were as tenaciously experimental as she was, their works had more conventional plots (though they were not always unfolded in a traditional way) and seamier themes, being concerned with such matters as sex or political corruption. Lispector's reputation has continued to grow, as discriminating readers increasingly appreciate the exquisiteness of her writing and the depth and precision she brings to her treatment of philosophical and aesthetic issues.

PEDRO PÁRAMO

Author: Juan Rulfo (1918-1986)
Type of work: Novel
Type of plot: Magical Realism
Time of plot: The late nineteenth and early twentieth centuries
Locale: Comala, Jalisco, Mexico
First published: 1955 (English translation, 1959)

Principal Characters

Juan Preciado, the protagonist and point-of-view character of the novel. A young, curious man, Juan decides to research and discover his past after the death of his mother. Juan returns to the dusty provincial town of Comala in search of the man he knows to be his father, Pedro Páramo. Although he finds the town virtually deserted and Páramo dead, he continues to investigate the events that have brought the town to its current state. He talks with the local inhabitants who remain. Literally suffocated by the paralysis and despair of Comala, Juan dies in the middle of the novel. Even after his death, his consciousness remains alive and gives reports on the life and fate of his cruel father.

Pedro Páramo, the local chieftain of the village of Comala, dead by the time the novel begins. Pedro Páramo is a loveless man, without soul or pity, who lives to control and dominate others. Although he lacks a distinguished family background, Pedro rises to the top of the village hierarchy by a ruthless process of exploitation. Pedro bullies more timid men and through force and deceit neutralizes other potential power centers in the village such as Father Rentería and Bartolomé San Juan. Pedro gathers all power to himself and uses it neither to benefit others nor to improve the quality of life in the desperately poor village. Pedro's rampaging, promiscuous sexuality leads him to affairs with many women and the fathering of several children. Unscrupulous, insensitive, and dedicated to graft and tyranny, Pedro has one emotional soft spot: his love for Susana San Juan. When she dies, Pedro, through his semimagical

powers, leaves the town dead in revenge. Pedro is finally killed in resentment by one of his many sons, Abundio. Pedro's death marks the end of any sign of life in Comala.

Miguel Páramo, Pedro's impetuous son. Miguel has all of his father's machismo and boorishness without his calculating cruelty. He is symbolic of human appetite incarnate, complementing his father's embodiment of cruelty. The only one of Pedro's many sons to be fully acknowledged by him, Miguel is employed as a tool in his father's schemes. Filled with lust and rage, he rapes the young Damiana Cisneros and kills the brother of Father Rentería. An avid horseman, he is killed while riding. Although he is hated by Comala, his death further saps the waning life force of the town.

Susana San Juan, Pedro's idealized lost love. She is the daughter of Bartolomé San Juan, a dead miner. Susana represents the lost innocence of childhood and youth to Pedro. He cherishes her memory even though he stands for the corruption of all the qualities she represents. Susana is the only figure in the novel exempt from Comala's snares of despair and death.

Abundio Martínez, one of Pedro's illegitimate sons. He kills his father out of resentment and frustration.

Father Rentería, the local priest whose potential to present opposition to Pedro's domination of Comala is short-circuited by his own unwillingness to challenge authority. He is the uncle of Damiana Cisneros, who is raped by Miguel, who also murders the brother of the priest, Damiana's father. Through his charitable act of convincing Pedro to accept responsibility for his illegitimate son Miguel, Father Rentería ironically seals the doom of Comala. Father Rentería is a symbol of the subordination of church to state in anticlerical, twentieth century Mexico.

Damiana Cisneros, Father Rentería's niece. She is raped by Miguel Páramo as a young girl. She becomes a domestic servant of Pedro and takes care of Juan Preciado as a boy, surviving to encounter him years later and provide him with am-

biguous information regarding his father.

Dolores Preciado, the mother of Juan. Dolores is seduced and abused by Pedro, as one of his many female conquests. She lives in devastated sorrow the remainder of her life. Her death initiates her son's quest to find his father.

Dorotea, "La Curraca," a local woman who offers a kind of passive resistance to Pedro Páramo and after his death is the vehicle that the novel uses to portray the collective meditation of the town's inhabitants.

The Novel

The story opens when Juan Preciado, a peasant, Pedro Páramo's son, arrives in Comala looking for his father. During his journey, another walker joins him. The traveler turns out to be another of Páramo's sons. He tells Preciado that their father was a "kindled rancor" and that he is dead. Preciado finds only one other person in Comala, Eduviges Dyada, an old friend of his mother. She gives him shelter. The reader soon begins to realize that this woman is a dead being, as was the companion of Preciado during his journey.

Suddenly, the action changes. Pedro Páramo appears as when he was a boy, dreaming of his childhood sweetheart, Susana San Juan, and doing some domestic chores. Susana, who will appear later in the story, is the only true, deep love of Páramo, in contrast to the many other women whom he seduced or raped.

The action then returns to Eduviges Dyada and Juan Preciado. From this point on, the back-and-forth changes of time, situation, and characters constitute the structure of the novel. The reader must be alert in order to follow the subplots contained in the main general theme.

Eduviges tells Preciado that she should have been his mother, for on her nuptial night his true mother, advised by a superstitious soothsayer, asked Eduviges to take her place beside Pedro Páramo. Little by little, the main character's moral profile is drawn by Eduviges, who keeps telling

Preciado what kind of man his father was. Through her, readers learn of Miguel Páramo, the only son whom Pedro acknowledged. He is a violent depredator and sexual young man who dies in an accident. Father Rentería, the local priest, now enters the plot. He is perhaps the most tormented of all the characters. His brother has been murdered and his niece raped by Miguel Páramo, but he must celebrate a funeral mass and perform the last Catholic rites for the soul of Miguel. He believes that he has betrayed his priestly state because he has not presented a firm stand against the abuses committed by wealthy people, chiefly those of Pedro Páramo, and he has not given true hope and consolation to the poor. Once, when he went to confess to the parish priest of Contla, he was reprimanded for this and denied the absolution because he had allowed his parishioners to live lives of superstition and fear.

Later in the story, Pedro Páramo appears again, no more as a child but as an adult. He has grown, as Father Rentería says, as weeds do and has obtained all that he ever wanted—women, children, lands—by such unscrupulous means as unfulfilled promises, threats, violence, and murder. His only redeeming trait is his love for Susana San Juan, who after becoming a widow agrees to become Páramo's wife. She goes insane, and a change begins to transform Pedro's soul. He now feels old, sad, and impotent. His situation becomes worse after Susana dies in his hacienda. On her deathbed, she believes herself to be with her dead husband. Páramo's life begins to disintegrate; he suspects that death will come soon. Soon thereafter, another son of Pedro Páramo appears. Abundio Martínez, griefstricken because of his wife's death, gets drunk and goes to his father to ask for money for the burial. Blinded by wine, Abundio stabs his father to death. Páramo falls as if he were a pile of stones.

Analysis

Pedro Páramo is written in modes of modern narrative techniques and style: stream of consciousness and consequent monologues, directness and realism of expression, multiple and intermingled recording of facts, and flashbacks of action. Juan Rulfo's work also shows the quality of having delved into the complex, atavistic, desolate, fatalistic life of the Indians of Mexico.

Pedro Páramo is a strange novel. Somber in its harsh realism, poetic in its deep feeling of compassion for the anxieties of the human soul, it is a book of voices—voices of people, voices of nature, voices of circumstance and morality and passion. All of its characters are dead, only voices or murmurs that live in a town, Comala, that is a village of echoes. All these dead people, souls in pain, are presented as if they were living in another world, in a strange limbo of memory. Everybody in the village remembers his or her own life and those of the others. At the same time, intemporality pervades all the story. The town itself, Comala, where they paradoxically live, although dead, is a place where the only noise is that of the spider and the echoes of silence.

From these figures and his rural setting, Rulfo creates his work. He declared the original title for the book was "The Murmurs." He changed that title because it seemed to him that Pedro Páramo is in fact the pivot of the story. The author stated that all these dead people were roaming about Comala because the parish priest, also existing in sin, was not able to absolve their sinful souls. With these assumptions, the book can be understood.

In spite of being a novel of monotony and evocation, *Pedro Páramo* interests and moves the reader because of its vigor and intensity. Violence, sex, love, fatalism, and solitude combine to give a portrait—or at least a portion of a portrait—of the Indian soul. Rulfo, a native of Jalisco, spent part of his youth among peasants and Indians on his father's haciendas and had the occasion of learning at first hand their true, authentic spirit. It is not a picturesque folkloristic account of Indian life that runs through the pages of his book. Its qualities of insightful realism and introspection had already appeared in his previous work, *El Llano en Llamas, y Otros Cuatos* (1953, *The Burning Plain and Other Stories*, 1967), a book that introduced to Mexican literature a new treatment and style of rural and Indian fictional characters.

This unfolding of the Indian spirit is not only ethnographic but also artistic. The characters possess a double profile, both real and spectral. Sharing a concrete, physical life and a strange, immaterial, dreamlike vitality, they embody and combine both realism and idealism, the two poles of Rulfo's art. The popular expressions of the characters are also elevated to aesthetic rank. Although sometimes Rulfo takes liberties with language in his style, the intentional and affective charge of the words produces an effect of primary and calm beauty.

There are flaws in the novel, such as its lack of a nucleus and a true unfolding of plot, its confused intersection of temporal and local planes, and its emphasis on the pejorative aspects of experience. Rulfo's work, however, marks a milestone in Mexican fiction for the novelty of his treatment and the depth of his appreciation of the Mexican Indian, who after centuries of cultural and political history is still not sufficiently known or understood.

Throughout its odd mixture of fantasy and reality, *Pedro Páramo* contains thematic threads that together illuminate Rulfo's pessimistic vision of life. The vision is essentially a nihilistic one. Each inhabitant of Comala relives a single moment of pain or guilt over and over again, but the experience never brings increased self-awareness, insight into the causes of behavior, or any suggestion of possible remedies for dilemmas. The characters have no individuality; they are instead symbolic figures, standing for people as powerless victims of both external and internal forces. Rulfo's men and women are helpless in the face both of outside circumstances and of their own psychic problems. The world of Comala thus is a microcosm for a universe that is in a state of irremedial chaos, of inescapable disintegration. The despair of this situation is conveyed powerfully through the author's style, which is based on the basic rhythms of common speech; characters' lives and emotions come alive through the reality of their language. As poet Octavio Paz put it, Rulfo is "truly a very gifted writer," one who has created a "strange and fascinating language."

Critical Context

Few recognized Latino writers have been so limited in production as Juan Rulfo or, at the same time, received higher praise for artistic performance. Two books compose his total literary production: *El Llano en Llamas*, a collection of short stories, and *Pedro Páramo*, a novel.

Since the second half of the nineteenth century, novels have appeared portraying the character, environment, and vicissitudes of Mexican peasants, both *mestizos* and Indians. Most of the novels that take the Mexican Revolution as their principal theme have rural settings and *peones* as main or secondary characters, or present the situations in which they live and their violent, cruel reactions to a world of despotic oppression. Mariano Azuela, José Rubín Romero, and Gregorio López y Fuen-tes, to mention a few, emphasize country life and rustic or provincial characters. The last of the above-mentioned writers introduced the Indian, through his novel *El Indio* (1935), as an important though frustrated participant in revolutionary deeds. Later, Augustín Yáñez dealt with rural settings and lives in his novels, including *Al Filo del Agua* (1947, *The Edge of the Storm*, 1963). Later, anthropology and ethnology pervaded Mexican fiction. Based on their personal experiences, some writers have told, closer to reality than to fiction, of the Indian world. No previous writer, however, had used vanguardistic formal techniques and developed so intimate an approach to rural Indian life as Rulfo. This is the merit and the place of this novelist on the Mexican literary scene.

PHILOSOPHER OR DOG?

Author: Joaquim Maria Machado de Assis (1839-1908)
Type of work: Novel
Type of plot: Social criticism
Time of plot: The late nineteenth century
Locale: Rio de Janeiro, Brazil
First published: *Quincas Borba*, 1891 (English translation, 1954)

Principal Characters

Pedro Rubião de Alvarenga, a simple school-teacher known simply as Rubião. He befriends the eccentric and dying Quincas Borba, from whom he unexpectedly inherits a substantial fortune and the obligation to care for the deceased's dog, also named Quincas Borba. While traveling to Rio de Janeiro, he meets Christiano and Sophia Palha, who bring him into Rio's high society. He suffers from his unrequited love for Sophia. A generous man, he lends money freely, gives lavish gifts, and frequently entertains his many new friends, gradually dissipating his fortune. His rise in social status thus leads to his downfall. His descent into madness parallels his descent into poverty. He comes to believe that he is Napoleon, emperor of France.

Christiano Palha, a friend of Rubião. Christiano lives beyond his means, borrowing money from Rubião many times. He goes into partnership with Rubião and tries to restrain Rubião's impractical generosity. Christiano is particularly proud of his wife Sophia, whose beauty he displays—and uses—at every opportunity. The capital provided by Rubião gives him social mobility. As he rises up the social ladder, he leaves many old friends behind, but he does honor, to some extent, his promise to his wife to see to the care of Rubião.

Sophia Palha, the beautiful and gracious wife of Christiano Palha. Very attentive to Rubião, she manages to avoid any indiscretion. She smooths over her husband's less graceful behavior and knows how to cultivate those of use to her while ignoring old friends no longer of import. She toys with the idea of adultery, perhaps with Carlos Maria or Rubião, but she is a chaste and faithful wife.

Carlos Maria, a pretentious young man beginning to enjoy the fruits of his mother's fortune. Narcissistic and egotistical, he finds the perfect mate in Maria Benedicta, who adores and literally worships him.

Doña Tonica, the unmarried daughter of Major Siqueira, a friend of the Palhas until they rise in social status. She is finally engaged to be married, at the age of forty, but her fiancé dies just three days before the wedding.

Doctor João de Souza Camacho, a lawyer and politician who draws Rubião into politics, using the latter's money to fund the newspaper in which he publishes his own opinions. Camacho promises Rubião a position in the ministry, thus feeding his delusions of grandeur.

Maria Benedicta, Sophia's cousin from the country. Sophia gently acclimates her to city life. Maria falls in love with Carlos Maria and eventually marries him.

Quincas Borba, a man who considers himself to be a philosopher of the school of thought he calls Humanitism, which states that above all people must eat. Rubião takes care of him in Barbacena, but Quincas leaves for the capital, where he dies soon after writing a letter to Rubião in which he claims to be St. Augustine. His dog, also named Quincas Borba, is his constant companion. As Rubião descends into madness, he suspects that Quincas Borba, the dog, is host for the spirit of Quincas Borba the man.

The Novel

The novel begins with a flashback of the almost completely happy forty-year-old former teacher, Rubião, in his luxurious Rio apartment. The death without heirs of his benefactor Quincas (Joaquim) Borba, while Borba was visiting his old friend Braz Cubas, left Borba's money to Rubião, his nurse and disciple. A condition of the inheritance was that Rubião care for a mongrel dog that he had given to Borba. The dog is also named Quincas Borba, in the hope that it would perpetuate the millionaire's name among those who could not understand the book in which he had developed his system of thinking.

Machado de Assis presents as a sample of Borba's philosophy the fable of two hungry tribes and a small field of potatoes. If they all try to share, both tribes will perish. For one to survive, it must drive off the other. Thus peace is destructive and war is a preservative. With Borba's message of "to the victor belong the potatoes," and with a determination to be hard and implacable, Rubião goes off to Rio de Janeiro.

The rest of the novel deals with his life there. Of special interest are the well-phrased thumbnail sketches of the characters, for example that of young Carlos Maria, who each morning thinks over the events of the previous day to find some word or thing to his credit. His discoveries are like inns where he stops, a weary traveler, for a drink of cool, refreshing water. Chief of those who seek to use the millionaire's wealth are Christiano Palha and his wife Sophia, who meet Rubião on the train en route to the capital and help settle him in a luxurious home. Palha wants him as a partner, and the naïve Rubião, infatuated with Sophia, agrees to everything. A cycle of misunderstandings and confusion joins Carlos, falsely suspected of being Sophia's lover, and her cousin, Maria Benedicta, who vainly adores the wealthy bachelor because he is the only person kind to the bashful country girl.

The grain of insanity that made Borba think himself St. Augustine shows up in his disciple, giving him the delusion that he is Napoleon III. He buys a statue of Napoleon and sacrifices his beard to resemble the emperor. Unfortunately, by now his acquaintances have separated him from most of his money. Palha disassociates himself from his partner. Sophia, who has been encouraging him, though privately calling him a tiresome man, outgrows him as she has outgrown all of her other friends. At last Rubião loses everything: money, friends, and mind. Even the little boy he snatched from under the hoofs of a horse in the early part of the story joins with the rest of the youngsters to scream that he is crazy when he appears.

Returning to his old home, with only the dog to keep him company, the man who thinks he is Napoleon dies. The look on his face at the moment of death is serious, like the expression of an emperor abdicating. As for Quincas Borba, he whimpers and looks frenziedly for his master. One morning he is found dead in the street. The author says that those who have tears may weep for these two, while those who have only laughter may laugh.

Analysis

Philosopher or Dog? develops through the accumulation of unrelated details in more than two hundred brief chapters. There is one in which the author talks to the readers about Sophia's laughter at the sight of a fallen mailman. He makes a digression on why long explanatory chapter titles would be useful. The story is sometimes told from the viewpoint of the dog and by a woman's conversation with two roses. No threads of plot, however, are left dangling at the end.

Knowing of the novelist's own idyllic life with his wife Carolina, one wonders at the many unfaithful and unpleasant wives that stray into his pages. The chapter in which Sophia confesses to her husband that Rubião made love to her in the garden is cynical and ironic. Torn between jealousy and covetousness, Christiano finally tells her that he owes her lover a great deal of money.

None of the characters is admirable as a person, unless one can feel admiration for the generous hero, too blind to see the motives of the sycophants who hang around his table and bring him their financial worries. The politician Camacho solicits funds to publish a newspaper and builds Rubião's hopes of entering politics as a representative of his native Minas and of receiving a title from the emperor.

Some suspense is created by the struggle between Camacho and Palha for control of his wealth and friendship, but other episodes and characters intervene. Doña Tonica, thirty-nine years old and unmarried, sets her cap for the rich man. Sensing his attachment to Sophia, she does everything possible to kill it, but she ends as the fiancée of an undistinguished government employee who dies three days before the wedding.

Critical Context

Machado de Assis, now considered Brazil's greatest novelist, was the mulatto son of a black house painter and a Brazilian laundress. Born in the slums of Rio de Janeiro, dark of skin and with a stuttering tongue, he became a writer whose pen made him president of the Brazilian Academy of Letters and the admired acquaintance of the aristocracy. Any Brazilian family with pretensions to culture took care to have his complete works on its shelves.

Three of his four important novels have appeared in English. *Dom Casmurro* (1899) is probably the easiest for North Americans to comprehend. Then came *Memórias Póstumas de Braz Cubas* (1881), which appeared in English as *The Posthumous Memoirs of Brás Cubas* in 1951 and as *Epitaph of a Small Winner* in 1952. Its sequel, *Philosopher or Dog?*, requires thoughtful perusal before all of its facets can be properly understood.

In his posthumous memoirs, the ghost of Braz Cubas, made wealthy by cornplasters, decides that his good deeds outweigh his bad. Braz is happy in the fact that, though he had successfully pursued the wife of his best friend, he left no children behind him to inherit the miseries of the world. This book helps interpret its sequel, *Philosopher or Dog?*. The heroes of both are naïve and reveal Machado de Assis' preoccupation with insanity. Both novels seem to preach that only megalomaniacs are capable of grasping happiness. Both scorn the pattern of life of the novelist's contemporaries. Critics see in their realism and flashes of ironic humor the influence of Voltaire, Montaigne, and especially Laurence Sterne's *The Life and Opinions of Tristram Shandy, Gent.* (1759-1767) in matters of technique. In an illuminating preface, the translator of the present volume shows its similarity to Desiderius Erasmus' *The Praise of Folly* (1511).

THE PLAYS OF DOLORES PRIDA

Author: Dolores Prida (1943-   )
Type of work: Plays
Principal published works: *Beautiful Señoritas*, pr. 1977, pb. 1991; *The Beggars Soap Opera*, pr. 1979; *La era latina*, pr. 1980 (with Víctor Fragoso); *Coser y cantar*, pr. 1981, pb. 1991; *Crisp!*, pr. 1981; *Juan Bobo*, pr. 1981; *Savings*, pr. 1985, pb. 1991; *Pantallas*, pr. 1986, pb. 1991 (*Screens*, pr. 1992); *Botánica*, pr. 1990, pb. 1991; *Beautiful Señoritas and Other Plays*, pb. 1991

Born in Caibarién, Cuba, in 1943, Dolores Prida established herself in the United States principally as a playwright, although her early writings embraced the genres of poetry, the short story, and journalism. She went to New York City with her family in 1961 and continued to live there, studying at Hunter College and subsequently working in the publishing business as a writer and editor. Following the production of her first play, *Beautiful Señoritas*, at the Duo Theatre in New York City in 1977, Prida remained active in theatrical circles. Her plays have been performed in New York City as well as in other cities of the United States, Puerto Rico, Venezuela, and the Dominican Republic.

Prida's identity as a displaced Hispanic woman plays a major role in defining the themes of her work. Discrimination against women, the difficulties of overcoming stereotypical images of women's roles in society, the conflicts inherent in living in two cultures simultaneously, and the struggle not to destroy one's cultural roots while assimilating into a new society that speaks a different language and has a different cultural tradition are all themes that run through her dramatic output. Her characters usually represent people who are exploited for some reason, primarily social class, gender, or ethnic origin. The problems that they confront as a result of this exploitation form the basis for the action of her plays.

Although Prida deals with complex social issues, she incorporates humor, music, and satire into her plays. References to everyday life in Cuba and the United States abound. For example, there are allusions to popular music, colloquial expressions, food items, and dating practices. Frequently such references highlight the cultural differences between the two countries. Prida's fascination with the musical comedy of the United States, coupled with her love of Cuban musical theater, provided the impetus for using music as an integral part of her dramas. The use of witty dialogue and musical interludes creates a tension with the serious aspect of her message of sympathetic understanding of the plight of the alienated and disadvantaged members of society.

Despite the depth of the problems that she addresses, Prida exhibits a hopeful and optimistic outlook, choosing to examine alternatives to the present situation in a future, ever-changing society. Both in her plays and in personal statements, she anticipates that Hispanic culture, language, and theater will have an increasingly beneficial influence in the United States and that the country will acquire a broader, more diversified social structure because of that influence.

Prida's first play, *Beautiful Señoritas*, is a musical set in the context of a beauty pageant with competitors from the Caribbean and South America. Through the use of humor and satire, the playwright gives examples of male chauvinism and female repression in Hispanic societies, beginning with the disappointment and bitter anguish of a father upon learning that his first-born child is a girl. Throughout the play, as she matures, the allegorical Girl observes scenes that depict the role allotted to women in the Latin world. Four Beautiful Señoritas, representing Carmen Miranda, Iris Chacón, Charo, and María la O, sing "The Beautiful Señoritas' Song," the ringing refrain of which is "Always ready for amor." The pageant contestants are dressed in typical costumes of their countries, their fixed smiles showing that they have learned well the lesson of how to present themselves in the best light. Their interviews with the Master of Ceremonies reveal how they have reconciled their hopes to the reality that their future depends on their physical attractiveness and their ability to snare a rich husband.

As the story progresses, four older women lament their plight, four "Catch" Women give advice on how to catch a man, the Nun chides the Girl for having sinful thoughts, the Priest hears confessions from the Beautiful Women, and three female Martyrs get traditional advice from the Mother and hear the Woman Agitator (*Guerrillera*) urge them to rebel against the repression that they suffer. Finally, all these women understand that they must establish their own identities. The musical ends on a note of hope, with the Girl singing "Don't deny us the music."

Prida emphasizes stereotypes by having the actors play multiple roles. She enhances the impersonal nature of the characters by calling them by generic, rather than specific, names, thereby making them allegorical. This technique adds tremendously to the impact of the drama.

The Beggars Soap Opera, which opened in 1979, is one of several adaptations that Prida has made of plays by other writers. In this case, the piece is a musical comedy based on Bertolt Brecht's *The Threepenny Opera* (1928). Here Prida adopts the form of the soap opera, or *telenovela*, a popular form of entertainment in Latin America. She uses this familiar aspect of Hispanic life as a vehicle to showcase the problems of underprivileged minorities.

In 1980, Prida and Víctor Fragoso coauthored *La era latina*. The thesis of this drama is that Hispanics ought not to sacrifice their values and identity in order to be successful on Broadway. The plot concerns two New York dramatists, Chago and Manny, who try to write a play inspired by their own Hispanic culture that will be acceptable to a Broadway producer. The work that they create is written while the play progresses, as they imagine the scenes that are represented by a group of actors and musicians. The result of their efforts is a play that criticizes the expectations of Broadway pro-

ducers who are motivated only by monetary success and who entertain unflattering stereotypes of Hispanics. At the same time, it recognizes the failure of New York's Hispanic artists to express themselves fully in their art forms. The play ends on a positive note of hope that Latinos will be able to portray their culture authentically rather than sacrificing their values for success on Broadway, since "Broadway es sólo una calle" (Broadway is only a street).

Coser y cantar, presented in New York City in 1981, is called "A One-Act Bilingual Fantasy for Two Women." It is, in fact, a dialogue between the two sides of the protagonist's character, her traditional Hispanic being and her newly acquired Anglo identity. Although two actresses play these roles, the audience soon becomes aware that together they represent only one person, a transplanted Cuban woman who is struggling with the conflict of her two cultures. To reinforce the idea of her biculturalism and fragmentation, Prida calls the Hispanic entity "Ella," which is the Spanish equivalent of "she"; the Anglo personage is referred to only as "She." Ella speaks in Spanish; She in English. Their conversation appears to be a dialogue, in that their comments follow each other's logically, but the actors neither face nor confront each other until the end of the play. In fact, they appear to be completely unaware of each other until that moment.

During the course of the play, the two characters cover a broad range of topics, including food, music, sex, magazines, their fantasies, their memories, their disorientation, and their boyfriend, whose presence is limited to the other end of a telephone line. From the first lines of the play, the viewer realizes the different perspectives offered by the two cultures. While She expounds on U.S. obsessions such as eating properly and exercising regularly, Ella consumes a huge breakfast, rejects She's idea of seeing the new Rainer Fassbinder film, and remembers her fears at the airport as she left Cuba. The intrusions of concerns such as world problems and finding one's way around New York City preoccupy both characters. Each continues to speak in terms appropriate to her orientation, both linguistic and cultural, using colloquial, idiomatic speech. Each responds angrily and dejectedly to the man on the other end of the telephone line when he rejects her. At the end of the play, She and Ella face each other in anger, each blaming the other (and symbolically the culture that she typifies) for her inability to resolve the conflict between her Hispanic roots and the new Anglo culture. When the confrontation is interrupted by sirens, shots, and screams, they unite in an effort to escape from their apartment and begin to look frantically for the map that will show them the way. This ambiguous ending clearly denotes the strain that the protagonist is under as she attempts to find her way in a new, alien society. The map serves as a symbol of the hope that in the future the central figure will be able to devise a plan to integrate the two aspects of her personality into a whole and escape from her cultural dilemma.

Of lesser interest from 1981 are *Crisp!* and *Juan Bobo*. The former is an adaptation of *Los intereses creados* by Jacinto Benavente, with added musical numbers that help the development of the characters and emphasize the satire of the original version. *Juan Bobo* is a bilingual children's musical that focuses on a Puerto Rican folk figure, Juan Bobo, who is transported to New York City and learns an appreciation for the world he discovers there.

Prida's next play, *Savings*, a musical, was first performed in 1985 in New York City. Although the plight of the Hispanic in the city forms the background, in this case the cultural conflicts are secondary to the economic exploitation of the Puerto Rican community. The neighborhood is being bought up for gentrification by developers aided by an ambitious young Hispanic. The residents of the barrio are being forced to move away because they cannot afford the high rents that are being demanded by the new owners of the properties. In trying to solve their dilemma, they display an awareness of community and their own interdependence, as well as a sense of humor. As frequently occurs in Prida's drama, an element of hope is injected into the gloomy situation, in this case by the appearance of Ms. Wong, a young attorney who grew up in the area. She announces that she is the new executive director of the Neighborhood Tenants' Association and that the tenants have decided to fight to save the neighborhood. The play ends on a positive note as they all sing "We won't be moved."

Prida's next two plays are written in Spanish and mark a significant change in her technique and the audience that she addresses. *Pantallas* was produced in 1986 and appeared in an English translation entitled *Screens* in 1992. *Botánica* dates from 1990. In *Pantallas*, Prida returns to the *telenovela*, or soap opera, as the setting for the action. The play is set in an indefinite future time that the author hopes will never arrive. The action apparently follows a catastrophic event. The three characters continually change roles as they endeavor to create a new soap opera to be presented after the world returns to normal. As they move from portraying one story to another, they occasionally return to their true identities and make ironic comments about their situation. These transitions are so well integrated into the dialogue that at times the audience has difficulty in discerning the difference between the characters' reality and the fictitious dramas that they create. As the play ends, the stage becomes dark, while the actors continue their search for new, creative ideas. The spectators are left with a sense of the futility of an ever-repeating scene that holds little hope of ending happily.

This work shows a more mature Prida, who has created a dark drama using the *telenovela* as the vehicle for conveying her preoccupation with the possibility of world destruction. Her pessimism is somewhat attenuated by occasional humor; for example, the audience sees the dismay of one of the characters when he discovers that their one remaining audio tape is by Julio Iglesias, hardly a favorite among young Hispanic males.

The theme of *Botánica* is the generational conflict between young Puerto Ricans born and reared in the United States and their older, more traditional parents and grandparents. Milagros, who after finishing her education at a college in New Hampshire prefers to be called Millie, returns to the *botánica* that her grandmother runs. She has chosen to reject her cultural heritage as a Hispanic, has accepted a position at a bank in the city, and plans to move out of the barrio and into an apartment downtown. She attempts to modernize her grandmother's business and even goes so far as to open discussion with a real estate entrepreneur who wants to buy the property for what seems to be a huge sum of money but is really only a fraction of what it is worth. During the course of the play, Pepe el Indio, a neighborhood denizen who appears to be crazy, keeps complaining about how "they" have killed all the buffalo, clearly symbolizing the destruction of the traditional Hispanic culture by the dominant Anglo one. Finally, brought to an awareness of the importance of her heritage when her grandmother becomes ill, Millie realizes that she cannot entirely desert her family's hopes and dreams for her. She decides to live in the empty apartment in the building owned by her mother and grandmother and to help them keep their business while working at her bank job in New York City. Millie thus achieves a balance between the two cultures, so that she does not have to reject the old completely in order to embrace the new. Her grandmother sees this change of heart as a miracle, a *milagro*, bearing out the significance of Millie's Spanish name.

As Prida's drama has evolved, her focus has broadened and she has tackled more universal human problems, such as world peace and exploitation of the poor. In so doing, however, she has not abandoned her cultural heritage and has continued to incorporate Hispanic themes, points of view, and characters into her works. Underlying all of her work is a strong concern for social injustice, underscored by her own awareness of herself as a female member of an ethnic minority.

THE PLAYS OF LUIS RAFAEL SÁNCHEZ

Author: Luis Rafael Sánchez (1936-   )
Type of work: Plays
Principal published works: *Farsa del amor compradito*, pr., pb. 1960; *Los ángeles se han fatigado*, pr., pb. 1960; *La hiel nuestra de cada día*, pr. 1962, pb. 1976; *O casi el alma*, pr. 1965, pb. 1966; *La pasión según Antígona Pérez*, pr., pb. 1968; *Teatro de Luis Rafael Sanchez*, pb. 1976; *Quintuples*, pr., pb. 1985

Puerto Rican playwright Luis Rafael Sánchez is also known as an accomplished novelist, essayist, and short-story writer. He is perhaps best known for his novel *La guaracha del Macho Camacho* (1976; *Macho Comacho's Beat*, 1980), which epitomizes Sánchez's primary concern in all of his writings: the experience and depiction of Puerto Rican language and culture.

Sánchez's first work to be performed, *La espera: juego del amor y del tiempo* (the wait: a game of love and time), was produced in 1958 at the University of Puerto Rico. An experimental work, *La espera*, on one level, explores the consequences to an individual who is unwilling or unable to come to terms with a rapidly changing society. La Hermana wants to keep herself within the safe cocoon of her home, secure in her old way of life. All of society outside of her home is, in her eyes, *muy mala* (very bad). The audience comes to understand that what it has witnessed is actually La Hermana's dreaming of the events of the past fifteen years. Sánchez's gift for language and love for his native cultural forms of song and verse are apparent even in this early work. On a more universal plane, Sánchez meditates on the nature of time and love, life and death. Death herself, in the character of La Sombra, tells that life is a lie of which all people are a part, that time exists only in the present moment, and that the only way to achieve freedom is to destroy the veil of illusion.

Cuento de Cucarachita Viudita: tragedilla popular de los tiempos de Maria Castaña (story of the little widowed cockroach: a popular little tragedy from the times of Maria Castaña), produced under similar circumstances in 1959, was awarded the prize for the best new work for children's theater by the Academia del Arte Escenico Santo

Domingo. The play is a dramatization of a folktale in which a young cockroach, the lovely, primped, and powdered Cucarachita Martina, must marry because the family's cheese supplies are becoming depleted. It is important that she marry soon because, as her aunt reminds her, Cucarachita Martina is a glutton. She accepts an offer to marry the lizard, Largatijón. The fact that she has already agreed to marry the Rat, Ratoncito Pérez, it seems, has completely slipped her mind. The two suitors fight a duel in which Largatijón dies. Cucarachita Martina marries Ratoncito. Their honeymoon is scarcely over, however, when disaster strikes and Ratoncito Pérez falls into the pot in which he is making soup, then dies.

Although it is essentially a children's fable, *Cuento de Cucarachita Viudita*, like *La espera*, can be read as an allegory of Puerto Rican society at a time when the country was undergoing major social and economic upheaval. Like La Hermana, Cucarachita Martina is caught up in forces beyond her control; her efforts to alleviate her own and her family's economic difficulties by marrying come to naught. Many of the theatrical techniques of *La espera* are put to a more whimsical use here.

Farsa del amor compradito (farce of an ill-begotten love) was the first of Sánchez's plays to be published. Using characters drawn from the Italian and French *commedia dell'arte* traditions, along with a Puerto Rican version of the *zanno* (clown), Goyito Verde, Sánchez creates puppetlike, grotesque personages akin to those created by the great Spanish playwright Ramón del Valle-Inclán in his *esperpentos* (loosely translated, "grotesque plays"). Like Valle-Inclán, Sánchez holds up a "funhouse mirror" to the people of his country. Puerto Rican society, it seems, has little compassion for its brethren and little respect for the prevailing authority, as demonstrated by Columbina's refusal to continue playing in this particular drama. At one Pirandellian moment, Columbina walks off the stage and sits in the audience, next to a fat lady. At the play's finale, she insists on a happy ending; Pirulí Pulcinello, the director of the work, loses control over the action. Sánchez's use of the *commedia dell'arte* tradition of "people's theater," in which audience and actors interact directly and spontaneously, is aimed at the creation of a truly national *teatro puertorriqueño*.

Still working in an experimental mode, Sánchez begins to deal in depth with specifically Puerto Rican topics in the 1960 *Los ángeles se han fatigado* (the angels are weary). The play dramatizes the inner life of its heroine, Ángela Santoni Vicent, in the form of an extended monologue. As Ángela speaks to her landlady Petra, who is neither seen nor heard, the audience learns that Ángela comes from the *latifundista*, or class of major landowners, in Yacuo, but was forced by economic necessity to move to San Juan, where she makes her living as a prostitute. That Ángela has lost contact with reality is clear from the fact that she cradles an imaginary child and speaks to her imaginary bird, "Hitler," as well as from the fact that she says repeatedly that "Mi nombre es Ángela, pero me dicen Ilusión" (my name is Ángela, but they call me Illusion).

Ángela has sunk progressively lower over the years, in every sense of the word: emotionally, physically, socially, and economically. The wealthy North Americans that used to come to her, her "angels," no longer seek her out, and she has been reduced to selling herself to the locals for a pitiful three dollars. Moreover, she has murdered her pimp, Santiago, out of jealousy. By the end of the second act, it is clear that Ángela is insane. As she frees her imaginary bird from its cage and takes up her imaginary baby in her arms, she exits, according to stage directions, "like a queen," to be taken away to an asylum. Her last words, "spoken like a hallelujah," are "¡Libre! ¡Libre!" (Free! Free!).

In 1962, *Los ángeles se han fatigado* was published along with *La hiel nuestro de cada día* (our

daily bitterness) under the title *Sol 13, interior*, which is the address the protagonists of both plays have in common. Like *Los ángeles se han fatigado*, *La hiel nuestro de cada día* is biting social criticism. The protagonists, Píramo and Tisbe (Pyramus and Thisbe), are a childless couple in their seventies and are poverty stricken. The only way out of their situation is to win the lottery. They believe that the spirits of the dead would predict the winning number for them if only they had money to purchase a ticket. Píramo refuses to beg, so the couple attempts to sell a sofa for the money they need. In the end, Píramo commits suicide in the hope that he can help Tisbe from the afterlife, leaving Tisbe completely alone in the world.

Both pieces in the suite *Sol 13, interior* depict characters who are victims of the economic and spiritual poverty of Puerto Rican society. Ángela has lost touch with reality and has succumbed to madness. Píramo and Tisbe live for a dream they will never achieve, the little home in which they will live, happily ever after, once they hit the number. They are all characters who have become deformed puppets, grotesque versions of human beings, made grotesque by their efforts to adapt to a world in which they no longer have a secure place. In both works, Sánchez continues his experiments with language, using word games, rhythms, and repetitions that are reminiscent of works from the Theater of the Absurd, such as Eugène Ionesco's *The Bald Soprano* (pr. 1950, pb. 1954) or Samuel Beckett's *Waiting for Godot* (pb. 1952, pr. 1953). Sánchez's linguistic virtuosity, relying heavily on Puerto Rican dialect, slang, and popular culture, has since become one of the hallmarks of his work.

In *O casi el alma* (or almost the soul), Sánchez grapples with religion and the deformation of the relation between people and God. The heroine, a prostitute named Maggie (a name suggestive of Magdalene) has lived most of her life alone. El Hombre (the man) visits her and tries to convince her that he is the Son of God. He does convince her to tell the story of this "visitation" and of her subsequent redemption to the local church authorities, who become convinced that the story is true.

When Maggie, unable to go on living the lie, confesses to the local priest, she is urged to keep the truth to herself, since this "miracle" has brought many people back to the church and made many souls happy.

Drawing on the tradition of the medieval Spanish *auto de fe* (one-act religious play), *O casi el alma* is a religious allegory. Sánchez's language, very often a hybridization of street language and the rhythms of Christian ritual, has been widely admired. El Hombre, the "Son of God," uses the language of commercialism to sell his concept. Maggie, he tells her, is about to embark on a wonderful new career as a "Misionara . . . salvadora de almas . . . socio fundador de Dios, S.A." (Missionary . . . savior of souls . . . associate founder of God, Inc.). Dramatizing the relation between people and God as a distortion of what was once held sacred, *O casi el alma* is considered by some to be among Sánchez's finest literary works.

La pasión según Antígona Pérez (the passion according to Antígona Pérez) is probably Sánchez's best-known play. The drama, like the *Antigone* of Sophocles (441 B.C.) and that of Jean Anouilh (pr. 1944, pb. 1946), wrestles with the issues of the individual versus the state and of religious law versus civil law. Sánchez's drama, more particularly, depicts a state in the grips of a modern military dictatorship.

Unlike the heroines of Sophocles and Anouilh, Sánchez's Antígona is imprisoned from the beginning of the play for the crime of having buried the bodies of the Tavarez brothers, revolutionaries fighting against Creon's dictatorship. She is visited in turn by her mother, Aurora; her best friend, Irene; Creon himself; Creon's wife, Pilar; and the Monsignor Bernardo Escudero, all of whom try to convince her to reveal the burial site of the Tavarez brothers. None of them succeeds, and Antígona is executed.

With *Antígona Pérez*, Sánchez uses certain techniques developed by Bertolt Brecht for his Epic Theater, or Theater of Alienation, that have become a somewhat traditional form used by writers of modern agitprop dramas. This is particularly true of many Latin American dramatists. As Augusto Boal observes in his *The Theatre of the Oppressed* (1985), the traditional Aristotelian dramatic structure of Western drama tends to reaffirm the social values of the ruling class. Because the Brechtian model aspires to create a dialect in which issues are shown from a variety of viewpoints across various social strata, it is designed to make its audience watch the play with a critical eye, always aware of the fact that it is watching theater rather than becoming completely drawn into an illusion.

That Sánchez wishes to keep his audience aware of its personal investment in the drama is demonstrated by his opening stage directions, which indicate his wish that topical events from the recent political life of Latin America be used as the posters and newspaper headlines that decorate the set. Antígona keeps the audience engaged at this level as she addresses it directly and very often reveals what is to occur in each scene before it is played. From the beginning of the play, Antígona knows that she will die tomorrow, and she informs the audience of that fact.

As the title suggests, the work may also be taken as a Passion play. That Antígona suffers and dies for the rights of individuals (as Christ did for the sins of humanity) is evident from her final speech:

> Antigone is another name for the living, haunting, eternal idea of freedom. Ideas don't succumb to a hail of bullets, nor do they retreat disoriented before a trained gun. Nor suppress their existence because a vain dictator has decreed their extinction. (Ardently.) To kill me is to give me new life, to make me new blood for the veins of this bitter America. (Urgently.) Quickly, Creon, quickly. Give it to me. Give me death.
> (These last words have been a rejoicing alleluia.)

The final irony is not only that the press give Antígona's death an importance equal to that of Pierre Cardin's latest fashions but also that the press falsely reports that Antígona, finally, did confess to Creon the place where the Tavarez brothers are buried.

The *Parabola del Andarín* (the parable of the

walker) is, as its title suggests, a parable about life in Puerto Rico. The protagonist, El Andarín, is another character out of Puerto Rican folklore. The play is set in the 1940's during ten consecutive days in which El Andarín visits the towns of the island accompanied by El Hombre Orquestra (the one-man band), La Futura Estrella del Cine Mexicano (the future star of Mexican films), El Empresario (the impresario), and La Autoridad (the authority), there to observe. El Andarín is on a personal quest for meaning. La Futura Estrella has only her dreams of becoming a film star. El Empresario, however, dictates their every move, and to gain freedom from him, El Andarín and La Futura Estrella finally murder him. After only five days of freedom, the two are captured and imprisoned. El Andarín dies in jail. La Futura Estrella, once she is free, vows to bury herself, day after day, in the darkness of a film theater.

Much of the play is written in poetic verse. Sánchez makes use of advertising jingles and popular music to dramatize the ways in which the mass media can distort the expression of life. La Futura Estrella, for example, finds the definition of true love in the pop tune "Besame mucho" (kiss me a lot). Because the mass media tends to inhibit individual thinking, the characters in *Parabola del Andarín* are deformed in personality and alienated from their own reality, responding to ethics and ideas imposed on them from without. They are ultimately unable to communicate effectively.

Quintuples (quintuplets) is a piece written for one actor and one actress who, between them, play the roles of the Morrison quintuplets and their father. Although unaware of the fact at the top of the show, the audience is implicitly part of the work, a convention gathered to discuss family matters. At times, audience members become participants in the action of the play itself.

The play is structured as a series of six monologues. The first introduces Dafne Morrison, the oldest of the quintuplets. Tonight, she explains to the conference members, the Morrison family's performance will be totally improvised. As Dafne "improvises," the audience learns that, like Elizabeth Taylor, she has been married six or seven times. She has recently become involved with the dwarf Besos de Fuego (kisses of fire) and will join his Antillean Circus, not as the glamorous Chinese Queen, as she had hoped, but as a fire eater in the side show.

Baby Morrison is the youngest of the quintuplets. He is pathetically shy, and his appearance is gaudy and disheveled. He wears spectacles so large that they make him look like an extraterrestrial. Baby Morrison's closest friend and confidante is his cat, Gallo Pelon, who writes books about children for cats to read. Desperate to escape from his family, Baby Morrison will join the Antillean Circus as a lion tamer. More precisely, he will tend to the needs of some feline creature that Besos de Fuego has chemically altered.

Bianca Morrison, self-abusing and suffering from nicotine withdrawal, lets her secret slip in public—she is a lesbian. She loses control of herself and ends her turn with a spectacular chain-smoking finale, after having begged a light from an audience member. Mandrake al Mago Morrison is the older of the two male quintuplets. Sardonically abusive to his siblings, he has made a deal with the devil: For six pounds of bread, he has been given his irresistible good looks and three toy tops. Carlota Morrison is in her ninth month of pregnancy and will deliver her child at any moment. She selects various audience members to assist her should she go into labor and deliver the child onstage. Papa Morrison, El gran divo (superstar) or Semental (stud), enters on a motorized wheelchair equipped with a portable oxygen tank and wet bar. Keeping up his macho image to the end, he tells the audience that he has done what he could for his children; the audience understands that he has exploited them for everything they are worth.

Sánchez explores the very nature of theater and theatricalism in *Quintuples*. Although all of the characters declare that they are improvising, they are in fact actors playing out a script that has been carefully written and rehearsed. Both performers play three different characters apiece, deliberately obscuring the boundaries between actor and character. At the end of the work, the two actors appear on stage as "themselves" and begin to remove their makeup in full view of the audience. The irony is that this moment of apparent reality is also an illusion, as the actors are still delivering scripted lines and following scripted stage directions.

Rich with literary allusions and with images, sounds, and ideas of popular culture and pop psychology, *Quintuples* also explores the nature of family relations, social prejudices, distortions of self-image, and the nature of reality itself. With this work, Sánchez returned to writing drama after several years away, during which he wrote his two highly acclaimed novels, *La guaracha del Macho Camacho* and *La importancia de llamarse Daniel Santos*. *Quintuples* reaffirms his place as one of the great Puerto Rican dramatists of the twentieth century.

THE PLAYS OF LUIS MIGUEL VALDEZ

Author: Luis Miguel Valdez (1940-   )
Type of work: Plays
Principal works: *The Theft*, pr. 1961; *The Shrunken Head of Pancho Villa*, pr. 1965, pb. 1967; *Las dos caras del patroncito*, pr. 1965, pb. 1971; *La quinta temporada*, pr. 1966, pb. 1971; *Los vendidos*, pr. 1967, pb. 1971; *Dark Root of a Scream*, pr. 1967, pb. 1973; *La conquista de México*, pr. 1968, pb. 1971 (puppet play); *No saco nada de la escuela*, pr. 1969, pb. 1971; *The Militants*, pr. 1969, pb. 1971; *Vietnam campesino*, pr. 1970, pb. 1971; *Huelguistas*, pr. 1970, pb. 1971; *Bernabé*, pr. 1970, pb. 1976; *Soldado razo*, pr., pb. 1971; *Actos*, pb. 1971 (includes *Las dos caras del patroncito*, *La quinta temporada*, *Los vendidos*, *La conquista de México*, *No saco nada de la escuela*, *The Militants*, *Vietnam campesino*, *Huelgistas*, and *Soldado razo*); *Las pastorelas*, pr. 1971 (adaptation of a sixteenth century Mexican shepherd's play); *La Virgen del Tepeyac*, pr. 1971 (adaptation of *Las cuatro apariciones de la Virgen de Guadalupe*); *Los endrogados*, pr. 1972; *Los olivos pits*, pr. 1972; *La gran carpa de los rasquachis*, pr. 1973; *Mundo*, pr. 1973; *El baille de los gigantes*, pr. 1973; *El fin del mundo*, pr. 1975; *Zoot Suit*, pr. 1978, pb. 1992; *Bandido!*, pr. 1981, pb. 1992; *Corridos*, pr. 1983; *"I Don't Have to Show You No Stinking Badges!,"* pr., pb. 1986; *Luis Valdez—Early Works: Actos, Bernabé, and Pensamiento Serpentino*, pb. 1990; *Zoot Suit and Other Plays*, pb. 1992

Actor, director, and dramatist Luis Miguel Valdez has devoted his life to Chicano theater, from the grade-school puppet shows of his youth to the improvised street theater of his union days as an organizer for the United Farm Workers; from his founding of, directing, and writing plays for El Teatro Campesino (The Workers' Theater) to his Broadway and Hollywood productions; and from his lectures on Chicano history and theater arts at the University of California (both Berkeley and Santa Cruz) to his essays on Chicano theater and its place in national theater. Many consider him to be the single most important figure in Chicano theater. He has sped its development from a limited tool of unions to a forceful satiric weapon in the national arena and has, as he hoped, "put the tools of the artist in the hands of the humblest, the working people." He began his writing career with a one-act play, *The Theft* (pr. 1961), which received the Obie Award for "demonstrating the politics of survival," and went on to write by 1993 three screenplays, two musicals, more than a dozen plays, and numerous *actos* or short dramas. His works mark him both as a spokesman for "La Raza" (Chicanos) and as a distinguished and uniquely American playwright. The praise gar-

nered by the 1993 productions of *Corridos* is typical. Eleven awards from the Bay Area Theater Critics Circle led to a version produced by the Public Broadcasting Service (PBS) titled *Corridos: Tales of Passion and Revolution*, starring Linda Ronstadt and featuring Valdez as narrator. This charming, well-received television tribute to Chicano heritage won the coveted Peabody Award.

Valdez's early works are guerrilla theater reflecting conflicts and alienation within the Chicano community, in forms that Valdez claims have more in common with Kabuki (Japanese drama) than with Broadway. His later works combine a sophisticated sense of dramatic technique and strategy with an empathy for the common person, an awareness of human limitations, and an ability to laugh at himself that make his political message encompass universal concerns. Jorge Huerta compares Valdez's early drama to that of Clifford Odets, while David Savran finds his dramatic "sleight of hand" and interest in illusions that hide reality to share much with Luigi Pirandello. Valdez himself acknowledges the influence of Bertolt Brecht in form, approach, and theme; most particularly he enjoys "communicating a concept, an abstraction." His method is to start with abstract ideas and, after a period of free associations, move toward character development and structure. The result is an intriguing mix of the realistic and the surreal, using allegory and symbol to make forceful political statements and to lend greater depth and universality to works with a clear-cut ethnic base. His merging of realism and metaphor (shrunken heads, swarming cockroaches), his catchy verses and exaggerated stereotypes, his plays within plays, and his multiple possible endings shock, amuse, intrigue, and challenge.

Overall, Valdez has taken as his personal goal to involve Chicanos in mainstream American theater, for he believes that Chicano contributions to American culture "are vital and necessary to a true perception of our national reality." Thus, despite the facts that his characters speak a mix of Spanish and English; that his women are often either the traditional mother or prostitute of Latin American literature and spend their time making tortillas, having babies, worrying about their men, and carrying on the conservative essence of the culture; and that there is usually a self-destructive character, a "picaro" or rascal in whom Valdez projects a part of himself, his works have a broad mainstream appeal. Valdez sees art as a social right; the expression of art should explore the human condition, penetrate beneath superficial differences to expose universal significance, and ultimately improve the lot of humanity.

The first stage of Valdez's theater career was one of *actos*, short comic and satiric skits based on *commedia dell'arte*, Mexican folk culture, Plautus (whose wily Roman servants provided models for strikers), and Valdez's experience as a member of the San Francisco Mime Troupe. The *actos* were improvised street plays conducted in the fields and along the highways, wherever migrant workers might assemble. These were agitprop (agitation/propaganda) theater. Their goals were to raise political awareness, to persuade workers to join the Farm Workers Union, to foster strikes, and to inspire action. Loosely conceived as single-page dramatic guides to direct action, they grew out of real-life encounters between field workers, bosses, and landowners, and they depended heavily on stock types to provide a ready-made character base. With time, the communal themes acted out in these group productions and Valdez's own experience living in a barrio nicknamed "¡Sal si puedes!" ("Leave if you can!") provided a realistic and topical base for Valdez's own personal dramatizations, dramatizations still aimed at educating and motivating. For example, *Los Vendidos*, which grows out of this tradition, attacks tokenism through a Chicana secretary for California Governor Ronald Reagan who is assigned to buy a "Mexican-type" as a front for the main office. After checking out several "types" at "Honest Sancho's Used Mexican Lot," she rejects the Farm Worker, the Revolutionary, and the Pachuco (street punk), and chooses instead an assimilated Mexican American businessman who drinks dry martinis and sings "God Bless America." Once installed, however, he malfunctions, shouts union slogans ("Viva la huelga!"—"Long live the strike!"), chases her away, and divides up the office funds with his cohorts, the other "stereotypes."

The next stage in Valdez's artistic career was a more formalized extension of the labor theater, El Teatro Campesino, which was eventually housed in San Juan Bautista. During this period, Valdez began to experiment with *mitos*, parables that drew on the pre-Columbian heritage for Indian myth and ritual in order to reveal myth as "the supporting structure of our everyday reality." His works continued to focus on political activism but added to it a sense of religious ritual and ethnic heritage, a search for meaning that partook of the allegorical. Peter Brooks finds many of the religious plays performed at the San Juan Mission during this period to be in a medieval tradition, as the Chicano production of *Las pastorelas* confirms. *Bernabé*, a combination *mito* and *acto* about the prostituted land being reclaimed by the field worker who loves it, is typical of this period, as it merges realistic dialogue and relationships with symbolic characters and acts. Set in California's San Joaquin Valley, it begins with a bet between the owner of a cantina and the cousin of a prostitute, Consuelo, about whether they can get a retarded campesino named Bernabé into bed with Consuelo. Once there, Bernabé beats up the cousin, who tries to eject him. In the ritualistic ending, La Luna (brother Moon, a 1945 pachuco in a zoot suit), La Tierra (sister Earth), and El Sol (father Sun, dressed like the Aztec sun god, Tonatiuh) together make Bernabé mentally whole when he is united in marriage with the revirginized Earth and blessed by Sun and Moon. Bernabé vows to protect the land he loves from rapacious landowners and bankers, and even to face death for her sake. At the end, the newlywed La Tierra stands revealed as Coatlicue, the Aztec goddess of life, death, and rebirth.

The late 1960's and the 1970's marked Valdez's experimentation with a third form, a mix of action, song, and dance with a unifying narrative based on the Mexican *corrido* or folk ballad. Valdez says that his goal with this form was "to claim a cultural heritage." His most popular *corrido* was *Zoot Suit*, which had a long successful run in Los Angeles and was the first Hispanic play to reach Broadway. *Zoot Suit* received awards from the Los Angeles Drama Critics Circle, and its film version was nominated for the Golden Globe for best musical film of 1981. Centered around the Los Angeles zoot suit riots and the related Sleepy Lagoon murder trial of 1942, it contrasts the racist public treatment of events with what Valdez depicts as the harmless reality.

According to the newspapers, hordes of armed zoot-suiters battled over turf, knifing and killing, until stopped by the U.S. Navy and Marines and deservingly imprisoned. What Valdez shows on stage is lively singing and dancing, interrupted by police violence and mass arrests; an interrogation in which the police sergeant says, "You can't treat these animals like people"; the yellow journalistic shouts of an allegorical figure called "The Press"; and the hero, Henry Reyna. Henry is scheduled to ship out to the Pacific the next day but instead finds himself as a scapegoat, bearing the crimes of others. The action is narrated by Pachuco, a zoot-suiter "master of ceremonies" who is proud of his attire. He swaggers, interprets illusion and reality, and stops the action to insert telling commentary whenever he pleases. He calls himself an "existential . . . Actor in the streets" and claims that it will take more than the U.S. Navy to beat him down. Valdez calls him a "Jungian self-image," "the superego," and "dean of the school of hard knocks" and dresses him in the colors of Testatipoka, the Aztec god of education.

At Pachuco's direction, the audience is carried in flashbacks to Henry's joyous celebration with his girlfriend Della and a minor scuffle with a rival gang. Newsboys cry out lurid headlines, and the trial proves a farce. The testimony (presented by flashbacks that explain the misunderstandings) becomes twisted by the manipulations of the prosecution. The "gang" is convicted and becomes a "cause" for white liberals who use the situation for personal ends. The pachuco narrator himself, overpowered and stripped by servicemen, reverts to his Aztec ancestry—clad in loincloth and heralded by the blowing of a conch—to provide Henry with *nahual* strength to endure prison. The winning of the war and the release of the gang simply begins a repeat of police persecution. Valdez leaves viewers with the choice of multiple possible endings, based on the Mayan philosophy of multiple levels of existence: Henry retaining his calm while facing new charges with the support of his united family; Henry as social victim, reincarcerated and killed in a prison fight; Henry the born leader killed in Korea and winning a congressional Medal of Honor; Henry married with kids; and Henry as El Pachuco, a living myth.

La gran carpa de los rasquachis (the tentshow of the underdogs) depicts, with music, the hard life of and the indignities suffered by a farmworker from his border crossing to his death. *El fin del mundo* (the end of the world), rewritten yearly over a ten-year period, captures the Chicano urban scene. Valdez argued in moving political theater that Chicanos should stay out of Vietnam in *Vietnam campesino*, *Soldado Razo*, and *Dark Root of a Scream*. *Soldado razo*, narrated by La Muerte (Death), explores reasons why young Chicanos fought willingly in Vietnam, while *Dark Root of a Scream* uses the wake of a Chicano who died in Vietnam to suggest that Chicano soldiers should have fought the more important battles in the barrios.

Valdez has always been interested in the political and existential implications of acting and role-playing in theater and society. His plays in the 1980's and 1990's have reflected this interest. In *Bandido!*, a play within a play, the realistic interior of a brick jailhouse is contained within a fake melodrama stage on which the "reality" of the bandit Tiburcio is reinterpreted. In order to call into question "history" and "legend," the action alternates between the real Tiburcio, viewed sympathetically through Valdez's eyes, and the stereotypical Tiburcio of stage and legend, with the legend reinforced by narrative songs extolling his notorious deeds and distorting his exploits. Like *Zoot Suit*, *Bandido!* contrasts public images with private reality: the slick, womanizing, murderous bandido of legend, who even seduces the wives of his own supporters, with the kindhearted social bandit of "fact" who was forced into crime by Anglo-American invaders, whose associates are responsible for the murders in question, and whose affection is focused on the one love of his life. Melodrama and reality merge at the end, when Tiburcio becomes the last man to be publicly hanged in California. According to the melodrama, the hanging is for vicious murders; according to the "reality play," it is for being Mexican in the wrong place at the wrong time. The Tiburcio of the inner play ("reality") is no saint and admits to being both good and bad, comic and tragic.

I Don't Have to Show You No Stinking Badges! was produced in both Los Angeles and San Diego. It takes place in a television studio set up to film an episode of *Badges!*, a show set in a 1985 Southern California suburban home where Buddy and Connie Villa, assimilated middle-class Chicanos, live. They have made themselves a comfortable life playing maids, gardeners, and bandits, being "the silent bit king and queen of Hollywood." Buddy's most memorable role was the leader of a group of Mexican bandits in *The Treasure of the Sierra Madre*. In order to ensure for their son (Sonny) upward mobility and a better life than their own, they have sent him, at great personal expense, to Harvard to study law. Their daughter studied medicine. The play begins with Sonny's arrival

home with an older, newly acquired Asian American girlfriend. Sonny fantasizes about Hollywood success only to suffer an identity crisis and degenerate into a gun-slinging *cholo* (street punk). Beset by the police, he starts to commit suicide but is stopped by a director who calls "Cut!", steps into the scene, and demands an entertaining ending, claiming that laughs are more important than reality. Sonny and his girlfriend return to Harvard in a flying sombrero from Buddy's dreams, tragedy is averted, and the question of whether or not Chicanos can attain the American Dream is left unanswered. The pat sitcom solution cannot dispel the nightmarish images of the young man chased by bulky Anglo-American policemen, his guilt unquestioned, his home violated, his ruin inevitable, his assimilated parents unable to help or understand. *La Bamba*, in a way, is a realistic treatment of this same question, with intimate and credible scenes despite Valdez's claims of pre-Columbian symbolism, with Ritchie Valens corresponding to Quetzalcoatl, the Aztec feathered serpent. A successful 1987 film, it traces the rise of Ricardo Valenzuela (Ritchie Valens) from a migrant field worker family playing in local music halls to a singer of national fame, describing the social and familial conflicts created by this rise in class and status and his sudden tragic end.

The Shrunken Head of Pancho Villa is perhaps Valdez's most inspired play. It explores the conflict between ethnic heritage and assimilation into Anglo-American society, with the heritage of Pancho Villa—romanticized bandit and revolutionary—conflicting with the adoption of a new culture. The shrunken head becomes an absurdist metaphor for the shattering loss of identity involved in acculturation. The Mexican heritage, the head, is protected and nourished by the women in the family, the traditional center of conservative values. Supporting that "head," however, consumes the family income and time as it demands more and more tortillas, and it engenders more "heads" that are equally demanding. One son, Joaquin Murrieta, begins as a social bandit, imagining himself as a Villista, as his father wished he were, but jail turns him literally into a headless body. The other son, Mingo, who seeks assimilation, serves in the military, rejects Spanish, and gets a job with the welfare service. He begins to cheat his family and friends and to pursue a private fortune by exploiting the poor. Ultimately, as a result, he rejects his family, turns his brother over to the police, and metaphorically becomes another headless (and heartless) body. In other words, when the Anglo- American side dominates, something is lost, but when the Mexican side dominates, something is also lost. In either case the family is torn apart. The popular Mexican Revolution song *La Cucaracha* (the cockroach) plays off and on throughout the play. Cockroaches swarm over the shrunken head, but the final dream is that one day Pancho Villa will return, social justice will be restored, and the headless bodies and bodiless heads will be united into whole persons.

Valdez dramatizes Chicano families in crisis to reflect the community crisis. He deals with serious questions in a comic-satiric way, as if to say that where there can be laughter there can be hope. His plays are good theater—lively and engaging, with song and dance and compelling stage business. Their natural mix of attitudes, languages, and cultures makes them all-American. Despite their ethnic concerns, they speak to all Americans about the distortions of history, the racism latent in a "melting pot" that is in fact a gumbo of different flavors that do not always blend easily, and the limitations inherent in the American Dream.

THE PLUM PLUM PICKERS

Author: Raymond Barrio (1921-   )
Type of work: Novel
Type of plot: Social criticism
Time of plot: The 1960's
Locale: The Santa Clara Valley, California
First published: 1969

Principal Characters

Manuel Gutierrez, a Chicano farmworker from Texas. Seeking to assert his Mexican heritage and its celebration of the land's potential, Manuel struggles to define himself through the value of his work. He is not ashamed of physical labor, viewing himself as the crucial link between the ripening plums that will either provide sustaining nutrition or, left unattended, will fall to the ground and rot. Unconvinced by the rhetoric of the growers that the conditions of his life are steadily improving and that he will someday reap the benefits of his labor, Manuel clings to his integrity of self-identity, even when he is reduced to the status of a caged animal.

Lupe Gutierrez, Manuel's wife and the mother of his three children. She cleans their tiny shack on the compound, obsessed with providing the best possible conditions for the children's health. Although she realizes the ever-present threat of agricultural accidents and the narrowness of her children's lives, she keeps hoping to escape the probable destiny of her children of following their father into farm labor.

Ramiro Sanchez, a mestizo who urges the crews to claim their independence from the abuse of the growers. Cynical toward any particular ideological salvation, Ramiro pieces together various bits of revolutionary ideas while vociferously protesting any denigration of his crew or himself. He sees himself as heir to Mexico's revolutionary heritage. His strength and courage rest in his image of himself as Tenochtitlan, a god reborn to lead his people into salvation.

Frederick Y. Turner, the owner of the Western Grande migrant compound. Turner believes he is the triumph of American business and the embodiment of the self-made man. He has lied so much that he has come to believe his own lies. Eccentric in his hobbies and brash in his political manipulations, Turner has lost any recognition of the humanity of the migrants who make him rich.

Morton J. Quill, the Anglo manager of the Western Grande compound. Caught between his self-loathing and his fantastic projections of power, Quill opens the novel in fear of being attacked and closes it with his lynched corpse dangling from a tree. He never seems to grasp the fake realities that Turner constructs all around him, including that of his own importance.

Jim Schroeder, a local Anglo nursery owner. Defiant of Turner's ruthless attitude and disgusted by his exploitation, Schroeder supports the workers in their quest for labor reforms. He works beside his farmworkers, whom he pays a fair wage. Not fearful of physical work, he embodies the pastoral ideal struggling to survive corporate indifference.

The Novel

Detailing the daily lives of Chicano migrant farmworkers trapped in low-paying, dead-end, back-breaking roles within the corporate agricultural system, *The Plum Plum Pickers* protests their exploitation and degradation. While exploring the hierarchy of oppression, the novel attacks the greed, racism, and injustice leveled against workers and reveals the unfulfilled hopes of the workers, who suffer from self-deception, disillusionment, and self-destruction.

Written with a loosely framed narrative but carefully designed coherent structure, the novel consists of thirty-four chapters that are like fragments in a collage of episodes, broken by graffiti, picking instructions, newspaper articles, radio broadcasts, popular songs in both Spanish and English, and government announcements to the pickers. The reader not only receives a complete description of daily routines in the migrant compound and of the pickers' futile labor in the fields of plums and tomatoes but also feels immersed in the emotional tension between hope and despair and engulfed by the juxtaposition of a lush landscape with the brutality of harsh, racist exploitation.

As the novel opens, Morton J. Quill, the Anglo manager of the Western Grande migrant compound, receives an anonymous death threat. Quill, behaving more like a merciless plantation overseer than a competent manager, fears the ruthless power of his boss, Frederick Y. Turner, the compound's greedy owner. Blind to the squalor in which the migrant children live, Quill measures his success by the number of boxes of fruits and vegetables; the less overt resistance from the pickers, the greater Quill believes his status to be. To insulate himself from confrontations with the pickers, he relies on Roberto Morales, his Mexican assistant.

Much of the novel proceeds not so much by plot as by unabashed—even didactic—social protest that documents migrant pickers' routes from state to state, their desperate and self-deceptive dreams, their self-destructive conflicts among themselves, their increasing entrapment by the growers and their political allies, and their increasing rage. Manuel and Lupe Gutierrez recall their brutal treatment at the hands of the Texas Rangers and try to believe that their life in California's Santa Clara Valley is really better. Manuel works himself to exhaustion and fears never being able to provide

his wife and three children with a stable life of human dignity and worth; Lupe, however, dreams of a bigger house, regular schools, and greater opportunity for her children. Although she can sustain her fantasies of freedom and security during her own daily grind amid the harsh conditions, she must often be awakened from nightmares of seeing her children plowed alive under the earth by the noisy tractors.

When the pickers seek a Saturday night escape at the Golden Cork, their frustration, fueled by alcohol, erupts into a near brawl. Zeke Johnson, an Anglo mechanic and sometime picker from the South, provokes Ramiro Sanchez, a vocal critic of the system from Texas, with racist taunts. He passes out before fists fly, and Sanchez's crew unceremoniously carries him outside and dumps him in the garbage.

Throughout the narrative, Manuel and the other pickers move closer to embracing the collective bargaining power of the farmworkers' union and the threat of strikes. Turner and his cohorts, such as the bigoted, right-wing radio announcer Rat Barfy and the governor Howlin Mad Nolan, continue to assert their paternalistic delusions that they are preserving the freedom of the pickers and their right to work without government interference. Any reform, in their minds, would mean the arrival of communism.

Meanwhile, Turner's wife, Jean Angelica Turner, becomes trapped in her own isolating fantasies of a career on the stage. To hold back the stark reality of suffering that surrounds her lonely mansion, she "acts" as an organizer of the rich growers' wives to provide hollow deeds of charity.

When Quill, his ego inflated by a meager raise, decides to confiscate some of the pickers' few possessions to pay off their food and rent debts, his own nightmare of death becomes reality. Seized by unidentified vigilantes during the night, he is lynched behind his own apartment. When Turner arrives at the compound, he is greeted by Lupe's scream announcing discovery of the body twisting in the sun. Despite the workers' rage, little has changed, save that their nightmare existence has emerged into daylight.

Analysis

The Plum Plum Pickers closely parallels the historical exploitation of California farmworkers, whether Mexican, Chicano, or Anglo. Both the fiction and the history testify to the paradox of abundance that buries the humanity of those who have the least and are exploited the most. Barrio strips the mask from the face of the ruthless capitalism that curses the pickers and proclaims its own benevolence, convincing those businesspeople and politicians who are prone to believe in their own racial superiority that the agricultural corporate combines are the guardians of lesser human beings than themselves. The owners of plum and apricot orchards or of vast acres of tomatoes see only the green of profits, denying the reality of rotting human lives in deference to the appearance of a lush green paradise. They convince many of the pickers either that their lives are meant to end in futility or that their salvation rests in copying the corrupt success and fraudulent goodness of the rich.

What the greedy owners do not see is their psychological and spiritual self-destruction. Quill lives in suspended terror, never sure whether he is alive and dreaming of death or instead living death and dreaming of having a life that he can call his own. Despite his power and influence, Turner isolates himself in fantasies of his days as a Hollywood extra in cowboy roles, obsessively constructing his own false reality by turning the Western Grande compound into an absurdly "authentic" old Western town, complete with false fronts on the migrant shacks.

In the process of revealing that slavery inevitably leads to revolt, Barrio shows that the pickers, once forced to act against their enslavement, achieve a higher human dignity and self-worth than any imagined by the owners. In their struggle to overcome physical misery, the Chicano pickers find humanity precisely in the struggle for a self-determined identity and a fragile existence. They see themselves in the cycles of life and death that surround and threaten them. Their unshakable faith is symbolized by Lupe's careful watering of the avocado plant she nurtures in her shack. Their faith in themselves is defiantly symbolized by Lupe's refusal to accept Jean Turner's old dresses and her implicit condescension.

The novel does not indulge in blind optimism, for although hope may survive, it does so in the ambiguity of Barrio's principal symbol of the omnipresent summer sun. The symbolic sun is both destruction and resurrection, reality and appearance, futility and hope. Rising with the sun, Manuel feels the hope of a new day, but he knows the reality of the searing sun that waits in the fields. That ambiguous reality is too dark to accept fully, but too bright to deny completely.

Critical Context

Having its origin in Barrio's friendship with a migrant family that he met in Cupertino, California, *The Plum Plum Pickers* failed at first to reach publication. Although Barrio wrote at the time that César Chávez's movement to unionize farmworkers was making national news, every major publishing house to which he submitted the novel rejected it as too didactic, too narrow in its topic, or too regional in its significance. He was forced to publish it himself. Only after the novel had sold more than ten thousand copies through five printings in less than two years did Harper and Row inquire about purchasing publishing rights. The novel emerged as an underground classic, its impact spreading largely by word of mouth.

The Plum Plum Pickers serves as a foundation in the development of the Chicano novel over the next twenty-five years. The first Chicano novel to explore social issues through literary innovation and experimental techniques, its forerunners are the North American proletarian novels of the 1930's, the literary extravagance of the Beat poets in the 1950's and 1960's, and the early 1960's Magical Realism of South American writers. Now widely acclaimed and more anthologized through brief excerpts than almost any other Chicano fiction, the novel is one of the first issued in the Chicano Classics series published by the Bilingual Press. Despite its favorable reception in brief reviews, the novel has received scant in-depth analysis and focused critical attention.

Barrio has continued publishing, though none of his subsequent works have gained the reputation of *The Plum Plum Pickers*. His interest in the visual arts resulted in a collection of essays on art, *Mexico's Art and Chicano Artists* (1975). In *The Devil's Apple Corps: A Trauma in Four Acts* (1976), he cast Gore Vidal as the public defender in a mock trial of Howard Hughes, perhaps the industrial parallel to the fictional Turner. Barrio makes it clear that he remains a harsh critic of those who exploit the rank and file of American workers. His editorials in *A Political Portfolio* (1985) consistently attack exploitive figures from all professions; among the pieces in this collection are three selections from the novel *Carib Blue* (1990). That novel further develops, in broader contexts, the potential for aesthetic experimentation to reveal the exploitation behind the masks of the practical approaches to resolving social issues.

POCHO

Author: José Antonio Villarreal (1924-   )
Type of work: Novel
Type of plot: *Bildungsroman*
Time of plot: 1923-1942
Locale: Santa Clara, California
First published: 1959

Principal Characters

Richard Rubio, a young man of Mexican heritage who aspires to be a writer while growing up in the farmlands of California. The only son of a disillusioned soldier of the Mexican Revolution who is in exile as a nomadic day laborer, he is indulged by his doting mother, eight sisters, and proud father. He is ridiculed by playmates as a "dirty Mexican" and forced by his father to accept a challenge to fight in defense of his male dignity and national pride. Richard is not a typical boy; his is a sensitive, observant, contemplative, and questioning mind that finds escape from shame, and shelter from violence and crudity, in books. When his father abandons his family for a young Mexican woman, Richard becomes the head of the household. He chooses, in self-defense, to throw off this responsibility. Only by enlisting in the Navy and heading into the unknown of World War II can he escape his mother's clutches and the captivity of her insular world. *Pocho* stands as eloquent testimony to Richard's successful escape, on the wings of language, from the poverty, lack of education, cultural oppression, and social injustices that pervade the world into which he was born.

Juan Manuel Rubio, a fiercely passionate patriot in the Mexican Revolution who settles into family life as a migrant worker in the United States during the Depression. In his role as soldier at the beginning of the novel, Juan is a cold, ruthless killer whose only real sentiment is dedicated to his worship of Pancho Villa and the cause of the Mexican Revolution. After the assassination of Villa, Juan escapes criminal prosecution by flight across the Rio Grande. Settled with his family in Santa Clara, California, he seems a different man, hardworking, loyal, and generous. The one aspect of his personality that remains unaltered is his fierce attachment to his native land and his intention to return. So powerful is this intention that he cannot bear seeing his family assimilate American culture, and he abandons them.

Consuelo Rubio, Juan's submissive wife and Richard's doting mother. Consuelo experiences twelve pregnancies by the age of thirty-four; she is very much a product of male-dominated Mexican tradition. In her years in America, however, she absorbs new attitudes. She finds that she does not have to acquiesce to physical abuse, and she learns that she can enjoy sexuality, not just suffer it. Although Consuelo is far from "liberated" by her discoveries, she does become more possessive of her husband and more assertive of her own needs. Refusing to get a divorce from her husband when he abandons her is consistent with her religious tenets, but it is also an act of defiance and independence.

João Pedro Manõel Alves, a forty-year-old Portuguese aristocrat. Known familiarly as Joe Pete Manõel, this older man is teacher and fellow-poet to the child Richard. Through him, Richard learns much of other places, other social classes, and other lifestyles. To the town's horror, however, it seems that Joe Pete Manõel has abused a twelve-year-old female, Genevieve Frietas. Her pregnancy and Joe Pete Manõel's commitment to an asylum leave Richard shocked and disillusioned.

Richard Malatesta (Ricky), a schoolmate of Richard who appears fearless and destined for great social success. Richard claims him as his best friend. Ricky is revealed as shallow, materialistic, and generally conventional as he matures, and he and Richard grow apart.

Zelda, the tough female leader of the neighborhood gang of boys. At puberty, the aggressive battling tomboy becomes the sexual property of the males she has terrorized. Richard claims her as his steady girlfriend and commits her to sharing her sexual favors exclusively with him.

Mary Madison, a Protestant schoolgirl. Three years younger than Richard, she befriends him and shares his enthusiasm for writing. Although her family is moving away, she declares that she intends to marry him.

Marla Jamison, the daughter of the owner of a pear farm. Admired for her courage in the face of defiant laborers, the older Marla becomes a mentor for Richard, encouraging his interest in reading by sharing her interests and her library with him.

The Novel

Pocho recounts the lives of Mexican migrant farm laborer Juan Rubio, his wife, and their nine children as they attempt to hold their family together, survive the Depression, and adjust to American culture. As family bonds disintegrate, the only son, Richard, defines himself against both Mexican and American cultures and affirms his determination to become a writer. The first of eleven chapters introduces Juan Rubio, a colonel in Pancho Villa's army, and depicts his grief over the Mexican Revolution's failure, his flight from Mexico, and his resettlement in California. The chapter ends with the birth of Juan's only son, Richard. Richard's background and development from childhood to young adulthood in chapters 2 through 9 strongly resemble experiences of José Antonio Villarreal's own life. The division of each chapter into two or three sections emphasizes the tensions, conflicts, and multiple perspectives associated with the construction of Richard's personal identity. These involve family, church, school, language, sex, friendship, career, money, prejudice, injustice, and, most important, dual cultural allegiances. Dramatic events of chapters 10 and 11—including Juan's leaving home, Richard's high school graduation, and his enlistment in the U.S. Navy—move Richard to the brink of adult responsibility and an uncertain future as a man and as a Mexican American.

As early as age nine, Richard is aware of his attraction to books and his interest in writing. In contrast to his soldier father, he shrinks from fights and sex and finds shelter in reflection and escape in reading and imagination. He is in love with words, words such as "sundries," which is painted on the window of his home, an abandoned store, and he shifts easily between English and Spanish as his context requires.

As Richard matures, he consciously rejects large parts of his Mexican heritage, including some of the "macho" privileges offered him by his father, his mother's faith in God, and obedience to religious dogma. At the same time, he rejects pressures in Anglo culture to devalue his own intelligence, neglect his own education, and settle for menial and meaningless labor. Such negations are in fact affirmations of his own self-worth and his own aspirations to be a writer. Free of many of the ideological constraints of both cultures, he may at last be able to write his novel and his life.

Richard's liberation of consciousness as man, Mexican American, and artist is in the foreground of the novel. The backdrops to his personal growth include the dissolution of the traditional Mexican family, the chaos of a nationwide depression, a vast panorama of social unrest and prejudice, and, finally, world war.

Analysis

Three questions dominate *Pocho*: What is a "man"? What does it mean to be Mexican in American society? How does a writer come to be? For Richard Rubio, answers to each are found in negations. Richard finds his manhood not in the esteemed tradition of fighting but in feeling and weeping, and he finds his male dignity not in acts of valor but in reading and thinking. To define himself in an alien culture, he negates the macho tradition of his father's world, refuses the comforts of insularity in a Mexican barrio, rejects the reassurances of religious faith, and opts for joining "the melting pot." As a writer, he immerses himself in the books and the language of Anglo culture and relinquishes dependence on the language of his forefathers. Yet he rejects as well Anglo social pressure to make do, to leash his dreams and settle for the life of a welder or a policeman. Without support or encouragement, he affirms for himself the less conventional aspiration to write, to labor with head and heart rather than hands. Ironically, Richard seems less a Mexican American than a man without a country. What is, after all, the origin of a man's nationality? Is it the accident of his place of birth or the geography of his residence? Is a man's nationality determined by his past, by his present, or by his future? What physical or mental borders separate a Mexican from an American identity? Shedding gender, familial, religious, linguistic, and social skins, Richard slowly builds a liberty of mind and perception that frees him to be an artist.

The title *Pocho* suggests one of the major themes of the novel: the complexity of the immigrant's dual existence in language, culture, and values. The term *pocho* has many resonances. Among loved ones, it can be a term of affection acknowledging the practical and emotional difficulties of surviving as an alien in an alien world. Used by a stranger, the term is an ethnic slur or a shaming label suggesting a Mexican who is a would-be gringo. As a descriptive term, it can mean the hybrid language used by the immigrant or it can mean a person, a kind of hybrid who lives with simultaneous powerful attachments to two cultures. This one word and Richard, the *pocho* of the novel, represent the many tensions in personal identity that exist in a man undergoing the metamorphosis of acculturation.

Although Richard is a *pocho*, a man who thinks in two languages and lives in two cultures, the language of the novel itself is very much English, a relatively formal and academic English at that. Richard the writer was never Ricardo, and the language of his novel is never *pocho*, never hybrid. Its language bespeaks complete assimilation.

The dominant tone of the novel is elegiac. An adult evokes his lost youth, innocence, parents, and culture. This is a tale of exile characterized by a profound sense of loss. Losses—of homeland, culture, and language, even of family, faith, and friends—pervade every chapter. It is small wonder that lamentations, profuse weeping by men and women alike, occur repeatedly. Richard's personal sacrifices and negations of his heritage are only a solitary, individual portion of one family's disintegration, of Mexico's impoverishment, of America's panoply of social ills and racial fears, and of worldwide poverty, prejudice, and cataclysmic violence.

Critical Context

Pocho is widely recognized as a literary landmark; it was the first novel written in English by a Mexican author about the Mexican experience in the United States to be printed by a major publisher. At its publication in 1959, however, the novel received little attention and went quickly out of print. After the social activism of the 1960's, the novel was reprinted, and discussion focused on the book's social and political import.

Pocho was Villarreal's first novel. His second,

The Fifth Horseman (1974), takes place in Mexico and deals with interpretation of the Mexican Revolution. Although in that work Villarreal decried the excesses of the Mexican Revolution and affirmed its spirit, in *Clemente Chacón* (1984) he showed how high the cost of success in the United States can be for the Mexican immigrant.

THE POETRY OF JIMMY SANTIAGO BACA

Author: Jimmy Santiago Baca (1952-   )
Type of work: Poetry
Principal published works: *Immigrants in Our Own Land*, 1979; *Swords of Darkness*, 1981; *What's Happening*, 1982; *Poems Taken from My Yard*, 1986; *Martín; &, Meditations on the South Valley*, 1986; *Black Mesa Poems*, 1989

Many critics consider Jimmy Santiago Baca to be one of the most important contemporary Chicano writers. Although he has written essays, plays, and screenplays, he has received most of his praise and renown for his poetry. He was awarded a National Endowment for the Arts grant for poetry in 1987 and the Before Columbus Book Award for his poetry collection *Martín; &, Meditations on the South Valley*. He has served as poet-in-residence at prestigious universities such as Yale and the University of California, Berkeley.

In order to understand Baca's poetry, which is extremely autobiographical, it is essential to know at least the outlines of his life. Baca was born in 1952 in Santa Fe, New Mexico, to a Chicana mother and an Apache father. His parents were divorced soon after his birth, and Baca stayed with his grandmother and other relatives from the ages of two to six. He was placed in various detention centers and orphanages from the ages of six to twenty. He ended up living on the streets of Albuquerque's barrios. At the age of twenty, he was sentenced to prison for possession of drugs, and he remained in prison until 1979. It was only in prison that Baca became completely literate, received his high-school diploma (the General Equivalency Diploma, or GED), and began his interest in poetry. Baca's difficult background is like that of few other poets writing in the United States.

Through poetry, Baca has been able to forge a new life for himself, to transform himself, and to redirect his energy away from drug addiction and despair toward communion with others and dedication to his art. "In language," he says, "I have burned my old selves and improvised myself into a new being." His poetry, however, is not in any way simply therapeutic. His writing also bears witness to the suffering of his people and to the negating power of oppression and materialism. A modern Walt Whitman, he has "no use for the pampered poets of the academy, or the darlings of fashion. Real poetry comes from and expresses the common energy of the people." Baca's poems, written in free verse with passion and straightforward language, are dedicated to the people on the streets rather than the elites in universities.

Baca's first full-length collection of poetry, *Immigrants in Our Own Land*, written while Baca was still in prison and published in 1979, is filled with tremendous energy and passion. If these early poems do not show Baca's full powers as a poet, they make up for the occasional slack line or flat image with their incredible urgency and their convincing modulation between rage and compassion, despair and hope. Early in the collection, the poet admits that he is "Scared of what might become/ Of me, the real me,/ Behind these prison walls," but the book as a whole shows a progression as the poet reflects on the power of poetry to change his life. In his collection of personal essays *Working in the Dark* (1991), he comments on this situation: "They sent me to prison for drug possession. And there, out of suffering, I found a reprieve from chaos, found language. . . . I discovered a reason for living, for breathing, and I could love myself again, trust myself again, trust what my heart dreamed and find the strength to pursue those dreams."

The title of *Immigrants in Our Own Land* refers, at least in part, to the movement of convicts away from their old world, the barrios and ghettos and reservations, and their "immigration" into the world of the prison. This newfound land, in which the warden ignores "the blood of these cellblocks, bucketfuls weekly . . . cutoff fingers/ caught in doors of cages, often, dead men thrown to the hoofed mud/ like chewed corn husks," provides a locale in which, remarkably, Baca establishes his identity and finds the power of compassion. He centers himself in this new world by writing poems about the land in which he grew up, his grand- mother who reared him, and his father—the "child with a warrior's heart"—who offered Baca and his siblings

> to the wind,
> to the mountains, to the skies of autumn and
>   spring.
> He said, "Here are my children! Care for them!"
> And he left again . . .

Baca remains committed in the poems to forming these links with his past as well as to forming strong bonds with the people in his present. He writes poems for fellow convicts, for Joe, his cell- mate, who had been sent "to Vietnam to serve a country/ Whose heels only he had seen." He speaks of the power of drugs in "It Goes by Many Names," sympathizing with the people locked behind bars "for taking heroin/ But they are not criminals." To the addicts, he speaks as a brother and says, "I will . . . weep for you, be silent for you, assist you." It is in these poems that Baca offers his assistance. When he discovers that poetry can be a vehicle for anger and solidarity, he is able to offer himself as the voice of the people. In an interview, Baca said that he wrote the poems in *Immigrants in Our Own Land* as a "weapon against sterility, mental and spiritual and emotional sterility"; the poems can also be used by readers to fight a similar kind of emptiness and despair they might find in their own lives.

Baca continued his explorations into his prison experiences in the first five poems of *What's Hap- pening*, a small book of only nineteen pages and ten poems published in 1982. The book's title comes from the first poem in the collection, in which "What's Happening" is not a question but a statement of current conditions in prison. What's happening is grotesque: Murders and beatings take place, and the dignity of the incarcerated men is

stolen from them, all in the name of rehabilitation. The poem chronicles these abuses, but it too is a poem in praise of solidarity. The men are on strike, protesting conditions, and all through the prison "fires burn and burn before each cell,/ voices scream and scream, We Want Justice!" As usual, Baca is able to make something good come out of all this suffering. In "Who Understands Me But Me," he remarks that in "the midst of this wreckage of life . . . I have found parts of myself never dreamed of by me."

The last five poems of this collection leave the prison world, but Baca maintains his loyalty to the underclass, the oppressed. His career is focused on the marginalized, the poor, the ethnic minorities. In "There's Me," he attacks the upper-class world in which people make large amounts of money by using their brains and other people's bodies. Baca wonders, "What if there weren't no bodies/ to work for them? Huh?" He also decides that he and his friends are better off than the wealthy because, although he wakes up in the morning to curse cockroaches, he decides "it's a good/ life, better, because we know we're human beings. Know/ what I mean?" To some readers, Baca may seem to romanticize poverty and demonize the wealthy, but his voice is convincing even if the language of the poems is not particularly arresting. His heart is good.

Martín; &, Meditations on the South Valley (1986), Baca's most critically acclaimed book, joins two self-contained works that complement each other. *Martín*, the first section, is a fifty-page autobiography in verse in which Baca recasts his own life by employing fictive names and eliminat- ing whole sections of his life story; in *Martín*, for example, no mention is made of the seven-year imprisonment.

The poem moves in time from the speaker's childhood to his adulthood, and in mood from despair and abandonment to hope and commit- ment. Martín, like Baca, recounts his years of hopelessness as he is abandoned in Pino Wells, New Mexico, by his sexually abused mother and his alcoholic father. He wanders between orphan- ages and relatives' homes, learning finally of his mother's murder by her new husband and his father's death in a gutter from alcoholism. The death of his father, who had submerged his "feelings/ for forty years/ like embryos in whiskey bottles," hurts Martín terribly because he believes that "there is no reprieve/ from the pain/ from not having embraced each other,/ just once." After his parents' deaths, he takes to the open road, traveling by motorcycle across the United States. He eventually returns to Albuquerque, ready to begin again. He prays at Quaraí, a site of Indian ruins, and promises himself to "learn the dark red Apache words/ and wind burnished chants,/ the blazed red Spanish names of things/ that absorb centuries of my blood." He attempts to rebuild his life by attaching himself to his cultural past, and, most important, by finding love and establishing a family.

Thus, *Martín* ends on a triumphant note. Martín finds love with Gabriela, feels an attachment to "Mother Earth," builds a new home, and witnesses his wife giving birth to their son, Pablo. Martín promises his son that he, unlike his own parents, will never abandon the boy. He extends this promise to all living things, bringing to a very moving conclusion the almost mythic journey from a kind of chaotic hell to the constructed pleasures of domestic tranquillity.

In the second section of this linked collection, *Meditations on the South Valley*, the narrator, again Martín, begins in despair because the new house just completed in *Martín* burns to the ground, destroying hundreds of Martín's poems in the process. The book ends, though, with another birth, this time of a newly repaired house with Martín serving as a kind of mother. As he says matter of factly, "I gave birth to a house." The collection also ends with Martín's reintegration into his community.

Baca frames this collection with the story of the burned house and the new house rising, like a phoenix, out of the flames, but the majority of the poems are reflections about the South Valley in New Mexico. Because of the fire, Martín and his family are forced to move from their home temporarily to the section of town called the Heights. Martín cannot leave the barrio behind him. The

Heights, a wealthy community, does not attract Martín; he hates the newness, the impersonality, and the empty perfection of the place, preferring the warmth and personality of the South Valley, where his friends live. Each poem in this section is an attempt to recall the character of the Valley and the characters who inhabit it with such gusto.

Because Baca is trying to capture the authentic voice of the people in the Valley, this section contains many examples of Chicano Spanish in it, giving the poems an authenticity they would otherwise lack. Martín recalls the "vatos," or guys he hung out with: one who died swimming drunk in the Rio Grande, and another, a janitor, who fights against land developers for the people's right to clean water. He remembers the "ancianos," or old people, who "slowly wean themselves/ from this life,/ and prepare for the next." He recalls Pancho, "the barrio idiot," who would always fill Martín's heart with delight. He imagines the dreams of the immigrants from Mexico or thinks of the "viejos," the old men, who have endured poverty and "made a rich dream land/ out of a small garden plot."

In *Black Mesa Poems* (1989), a collection that includes poems from the previously published chapbook *Poems Taken from My Yard* (1986), Baca drops the mask of Martín and speaks of his own wife and children, not the characters Gabriela and Pablo. The book begins, like *Meditations on the South Valley*, with the reconstruction of a house, this one outside the valley at Black Mesa, in New Mexico. The poems also follow a chronological progression, as they did in *Martín*, but in this volume the seasons, not the central character's growth and wanderings, loosely control the progress of the book. In this collection, Baca begins with the purchase and refurbishing of the house in fall and winter, and then he chronicles his life for a year, finishing the book with fall and winter again. Memories are interspersed throughout the book, so that the chronological movement in the collection is balanced nicely with a movement across time, back into the past.

In these sixty-five poems, Baca's prison experience is, once again, not mentioned. It is as if he sweated out the poison of his previous life by writing the earlier collections of poems. In *Black Mesa Poems*, Baca focuses on the most basic aspects of life, and he revels in them: the seasons of the earth and the crops he grows; the animals that graze and give birth on the mesa; his wife and his second son, Gabriel, whose birth he celebrates; and his friends and neighbors, including Mr. Abaskin, "a gray-haired prophet in overalls" who is conspicuous in the collection because he is welcomed into Baca's circle even though he is a Russian immigrant rather than a Chicano or a Native American.

Although Baca has always had an attraction to the elemental aspects of life, in this collection more than in any other he pays special tribute to the earth, seeing it and the creatures on it as metaphorical emblems to be studied:

> I await the burning books
> of lilac buds
> to flame. This year I promise myself
> to read them
> as they are opening
> before they burn away.

Because of Baca's devotion to the forces of nature, anyone who allies himself with the "enemies of the earth" earns Baca's wrath. He distances himself from a former friend who "sells out" and becomes a weapons engineer at Los Alamos Laboratory. He gives the finger to a driver of a car with a bumper sticker that reads, "Jet Noise, The Sound of Freedom."

The poems here, as in *Martín; &, Meditations on the South Valley*, pay special tribute to the courage, dignity, and humor of people who live lives that are rich in passion and commitment. Perhaps a third of the collection focuses on individuals who live lives not of quiet desperation but of difficult happiness. These characters, people from the barrio or the mesa, are praised in Baca's poems because of their tenaciousness, their ability to survive with dignity. Baca is no longer the poet of futile rage as he was in his earliest poems; he is able to mix his anger against the injustices of a system with fierce compassion for those who have suffered and have endured. He is the true poet of his people, one who sees their shortcomings (and his own) and still manages to sing a hymn of praise for them and for life. The reader has a sense that Jimmy Santiago Baca, despite the hardships he has endured, will never abandon his family, his people, his art, or the earth.

THE POETRY OF ERNESTO CARDENAL

Author: Ernesto Cardenal (1925-   )

Type of work: Poetry

Principal published works: *Hora cero*, 1959 (in periodicals; in book form, 1960; *Zero Hour and Other Documentary Poems*, 1980); *Gethsemani, Ky.*, 1960; *Epigramas*, 1961; *Oración por Marilyn Monroe y otras poemas*, 1965 (*Marilyn Monroe and Other Poems*, 1975; contains samples of previous poems not appearing in separate translation); *El estrecho dudoso*, 1966; *Salmos*, 1967 (*Psalms*, 1971); *Homenaje a los indios americanos*, 1969 (*Homage to the American Indians*, 1973); *Canto nacional*, 1973; *Oráculo sobre Managua*, 1973; *Cristianismo y revolución*, 1974; *El evangelio en Solentiname*, 1975 (*The Gospel in Solentiname*, 4 vols., 1976-1982); *Apocalypse and Other Poems*, 1977 (contains samples of previous poetry published only in Spanish); *Poesía y revolución*, 1979; *Tocar el cielo*, 1980; *Vuelos de victoria*, 1984 (*Flights of Victory / Vuelos de victoria*, 1985); *Los ovnis de oro*, 1988 (*Golden UFOs: The Indian Poems*, 1992); *Cántico cósmico*, 1989 (*Cosmic Canticle*, 1993); *The Music of the Spheres*, 1990; *Obras completas*, 1991

Ernesto Cardenal, a poet, priest, and revolutionary figure, was born on January 20, 1925, in Granada, Nicaragua, to a prominent family. Writing was a part of his inheritance: On his mother's side, he is a cousin of established author José Coronel Urtecho; a paternal cousin is the well-known poet Pablo Antonio Cuadra. Links are always established between Cardenal and his predecessor, famed poet Rubén Darío (1867-1916), the father of Latin American *Modernismo* writing and one of the major literary figures of Spanish American letters in the twentieth century.

Cardenal himself is considered an innovator and an outstanding literary figure of his generation of poets, in the same sense as César Vallejo (Peru), Pablo Neruda (Chile), and Nicanor Parra (Chile). Critics frequently compare the stylistic and thematic contributions of Cardenal to these world-class writers. He has achieved much fame for his unique style of verse, a style he has labeled "exteriorist." His language is free of obscure symbols, metaphors, and references. The poet's life goal has always been to make his writing understandable to even the most simple peasant of his country; lines read as easily as prose and are most easily understood when recited aloud. Exteriorist poetry is objective; it talks about real, concrete things in daily life. One finds in the text names of people and of places, abbreviations, initials, and numbers; in some ways, this poetry is conversational.

Cardenal studied literature at Columbia University from 1947 to 1949. During this period, his style was strongly influenced by Ezra Pound and T. S. Eliot. Most of Cardenal's theoretical grounding, the basis of his aesthetic, is credited to Pound. This basis makes his poetry distinctly different in style and technique from that of any other author writing in the Spanish language.

Cardenal wrote a variety of loose poems in his youth, in the period before his studies in New York. These are rarely anthologized and are difficult to locate. These poems were heavily emotional and technically weak. *Epigramas* (1961; epigrams) was Cardenal's first real collection of poems, written between 1952 and 1956. The long single poem *Hora cero* (zero hour) was conceived almost simultaneously. Neither work was published until many years later.

In *Epigramas*, one finds a characteristic present in all Cardenal's subsequent poetry, the adaptation of a pre-existent literary genre and language for his own purposes. Here it is the epigrammatic form of Catullus and Martial (Roman poets before the Christian era)—brief pithy poems of four or five lines, with a poignant message about love or hatred for the dictator, as in "Epigram XXXV."

Our poems cannot be published yet.
They pass from hand to hand, in manuscript
or cyclostyled. A day will come, however,
when the name of the dictator they attack
will be forgotten,
and they will still be read.

In *Zero Hour*, the poet's political involvement becomes evident. Conceived in the years 1954-1956, the lengthy poem, divided into four sections, artistically recounts a social-political reality, denounces social injustice, and puts forth a message of hope for the future. By this time in his career, Cardenal was in control of his technique, a unique artistic fusion of the languages of advertising, politics, and war that becomes a verbal and imagistic collage yet never becomes propagandistic. The text retells, using vivid descriptions, the events of a popular rebellion and conspiracy in April, 1954, to depose dictator Anastasio Somoza. The poet himself was involved in the events and went into hiding after the coup failed and the military began reprisals.

A salient characteristic that sets Cardenal's writing apart from that of his contemporaries is his deep Christian rooting and commitment, directed to transmitting a message that will help change humanity. *Gethsemani, Ky.* is a short collection of poems that first make public the poet's religious "conversion" (as Cardenal himself describes it) and depict a variety of his experiences while he lived from 1957 to 1959 as a novice monk in a Trappist monastery in Kentucky. Cardenal's original intention was to live a secluded monastic life. He describes those years as the happiest of times, a period when he had close contact with another monk, the noted spiritual novelist and poet Thomas Merton. Life in this community of men was "communistic," devoted to prayer, physical farm labor, and very little writing; in fact, Cardenal had to promise that he would not officially write during this period of training and initiation. The ideas shared by Merton and Cardenal at this time, their thoughts about a better society, took shape years later in the founding of a religious commune on the remote island of Mancarrón, Archipelago of Solentiname (the community was named Our Lady of Solentiname), in Lake Nicaragua. In 1966, Cardenal was ordained to the Catholic secular priesthood, with the understanding of his bishop that the poet/priest was to found this social/religious commune. The community operated successfully until October, 1977, when it was destroyed by Somoza's national guard.

It is impossible to separate the life of the author, his all-encompassing religious worldview, and the events in his native Nicaragua from his poetic texts. A clear example of intermingling is the collection *Salmos* (*Psalms*), a book that has been translated into many languages. These poems were composed between 1961 and 1965 in La Ceja, Colombia, while the poet studied theology in preparation for ordination to the priesthood. They began as an exercise in exegesis and meditation and are Cardenal's attempt to make these ancient prayers relevant to the twentieth century. The poet reflects on twenty-five of the Old Testament Psalms, rewriting the text in a form parallel to the biblical one but updating the language and references to reflect the joys and terrors of contemporary societies. Cardenal's technique parallels the rhetorical and rhythmical characteristics of the Hebrew text. A hymn of praise, Psalm 150, "The Cosmos Is His Sanctuary," ends the collection, a group of texts that extends beyond the troubled conditions in Nicaragua and Latin America to encompass World War II, Hiroshima, and all suffering persons:

Praise the Lord in the cosmos
                                    His Sanctuary
. . . .
Praise Him with blues and jazz
                    and with symphonic orchestras
with Negro spirituals
                    and with Beethoven's Fifth
    with guitars and marimbas

This collection of poems can be grouped according to their nature and message. Those with the nature of wisdom allow the reader to gain insight and solace for a particular existential situation. Other poems are texts of protest and lament, and still others are songs of praise.

El estrecho dudoso (the doubtful strait) is an integral part of the poet's production yet very different in content and nature from his other works. The twenty-five segments, or "cantos," as fellow Nicaraguan poet José Coronel Urtecho calls them, are essentially taken directly from historical chronicles, letters, and other documents of the early Spanish explorers who discovered this region of Nicaragua. There are texts from explorers Hernán Cortés, Pedrarias Dávila, and Pedro de Alvarado, as well as from Spanish queen Juana la Loca, all in their original sixteenth century Spanish. The reference to the "doubtful strait" is to the watercourse between Lake Nicaragua and the Atlantic Ocean. Early explorers of the Spanish crown dreamed that this course, the San Juan River, could be the route that would permit easy access to the trade routes in the East, functioning as the Panama Canal later would.

The outstanding achievement of this epic account of the exploration of Central America is the utilization of a pre-existent documentary text, not a fictional one, for the creation of a new poetic text. Cardenal achieves in poetry what other contemporary Latin American authors have done so successfully in the novel: the fictionalization of history. Cardenal does not simply copy or paraphrase. He cautiously selects segments of documents, phrases that reflect his own worldview and values and that help convey his message. He fuses several historical epochs and even looks to the future. The archaic sixteenth century Spanish blends with the poet's contemporary lines to reveal a new interpretation of history. The epic poem's underlying theme is the violence and injustice of the Spanish conquest, contrasted to the docility and ingenuousness of the indigenous population. In this poem, Cardenal becomes the new chronicler who states in capital letters, in archaic Spanish, that "the chronicler must not cease to exercise his office." That is, as protest poet, Cardenal indicates that his new role, in accord with his committed Christian perspective, is to denounce the injustices imposed on his country's native people throughout their history.

Homenaje a los indios americanos (*Homage to the American Indians*) has enjoyed considerable international success as it praises and portrays, although idealistically, the customs and value systems of the original peoples of the Americas. This collection was completed while the poet lived in his commune in Solentiname, drawing upon previous years' anthropological study, travel, and work among various Indian groups. *El estrecho dudoso* offers an external view of events and persons during the conquest years; the speaker of each poem in *Homenaje a los indios americanos* appears to be a member of a given Indian community, before the arrival of the Europeans. Literary critic Audrey Aaron called Cardenal the new and contemporary Mayan prophet (or *chilam*) in view of the poems rooted in the Mayan tradition. Peoples represented in the poems are the Aztec, Mayan, and Inca, as well as several North American tribes. In one poem, after including a quote from the prophetic book of the Mayan, the poet composes his own modern prophecy:

> And I therefore say that Mayapan will fall
>   Mayapan the walled city always falls in this
>   katun
>
>   Mayan rubber for Goodyear
>   Mayan chicle for Adams Chiclets
>   The military are to blame

This unique blend of political statement is the salient characteristic of Cardenal's writing. It has earned him the title of "poet and prophet of liberation," and it is what sets him apart from other Latin American poets of the twentieth century. In interviews and in his prose writings, such as *En Cuba* (1972; *In Cuba*, 1974), *Vida en el amor* (1970; *To Live Is to Love*, 1972), and *La santidad de la revolución* (1976; the holiness of revolution), the poet explains that the Christian gospel is what led him to embrace Marxism: He sees no contradiction between the two. Likewise, in preaching revolution for the poor and oppressed of Latin America, calling for the overthrow of oppressive capitalist regimes, he advocates that revolution must start with the interior renewal of each individual, the shaping of a new person in the best Christian sense. From that, a new society built on love, fraternity, and equality can emerge, one akin to those he selectively depicts in the Indian civilizations before the European conquest. The Cuba of 1970, as viewed by Cardenal during his visit and later described in the book *En Cuba*, is an ideal social model. The poet chose to overlook and omit any negative aspects he found; he does mention an obvious lack of a religious basis and practice.

Two lengthy poems, *Canto nacional* and *Oráculo sobre Managua*, have not been translated in their entirety, perhaps because of their complexity and length. Both offer prophetic messages to Nicaraguans on how to take pride in their identity, their heritage, and even their present condition, and how to direct their society along Christian lines to reshape it, rebuild it, and ultimately make it new. *Oráculo sobre Managua*, written as a response to the enormous destruction suffered by the capital, Managua, during the earthquake of 1972, is a modern prophecy and call to action, as evidenced by the title of "oracle," which roots the poem in both biblical and Greek traditions. The closing lines depict an indigent, homeless woman giving birth. Cardenal's message is one of hope, trusting in God's promise: "Behold I make all things new." Therein lies the possibility for the reconstruction of Managua.

When the Nicaraguan revolution began in 1979 and the Sandinista Front took control of the government, Cardenal was called back from exile to serve as one of nine cabinet ministers to the president. In most of his poems until this time, the poet had exalted and privileged young poets and revolutionaries who were killed for the political cause; these young heroes, particularly Augusto Cesár Sandino himself, assume messianic roles in the poems. In his role as the government's minister of culture, Cardenal had the opportunity to be a visible and public revolutionary, rather than one in hiding or exile. He saw new freedom for Nicaragua become a reality. As minister of culture, Cardenal implemented poetry writing workshops throughout the country, in an attempt to rescue and restore national pride and culture as well as to give voice to a natural inclination and talent found in all Nicaraguans. During these years (1979-1990),

Cardenal was able to secure enough private time to write two collections, *Vuelos de victoria* and *Cántico cósmico*. The latter in particular demonstrates a new direction in the poet's themes.

Labeling these forty-three lengthy poems as canticles places them in a religious context. Ever present are his Christian view of the world, the cosmos, and all the cycles experienced by created matter. Many of the poet's religious and scientific interpretations of the universe stem from the French philosopher and scientist Pierre Teilhard de Chardin. The poems contain many references difficult for the uninitiated to comprehend, including those to quantum theory and principles of physics, astronomy, and other sciences. The poet's technique is familiar, including juxtaposed images, learned references and abbreviations explained a few lines later in lay language, flashbacks, and collages of seemingly unrelated images that become a new way of seeing reality for the reader. Selected lines from the poem "The Music of the Spheres" convince the reader of the underlying unity in God's creation:

A single rhythm in planets, the sea, atoms,
   apples
which ripen and fall, and Newton's head.
     Melody, arpeggio, chord.
       The harp of the universe
. . . .
Nothing is or is not,
        everything in the process of being.
And what is real?
            Is jealousy real?
Love is real.

In *Cántico cósmico*, all the familiar themes and beliefs of Cardenal appear again against this backdrop: the ideal life of God-centered Indian populations, the hatred of capitalism and exploitation, the view of community or "communism" as a better condition, and above all, cycles of evolution that lead to the unification of all humanity and ultimately to union with the Godhead.

Cardenal's writing has evolved, with later works showing a fusion of elements from earlier work. This colorful poet/priest, who has distinguished himself by his singular costume of blue jeans, cotton peasant shirt, sandals, and wool beret worn over shoulder-length hair, has traveled exten-sively, reciting and proclaiming, through poetry, his unique message of liberation, nonviolent revo-lution, and personal and societal renewal.

THE POETRY OF ROSARIO CASTELLANOS

Author: Rosario Castellanos (1925-1974)
Type of work: Poetry
Principal published works: *Apuntes para una declaración de fe*, 1948; *Trayectoria del polvo*, 1948; *De la vigilia estéril*, 1950; *Dos poemas*, 1950; *El rescate del mundo*, 1952; *Poemas (1953-1955)*, 1957; *Al pie de la letra*, 1959; *Salomé y Judith: Poemas dramáticos*, 1959; *Lívida luz*, 1960; *Materia memorable*, 1969; *Poesía no eres tú: obra poética 1948-1971*, 1972; *Looking at the Mona Lisa*, 1981; *Meditación en el umbral*, 1985 (*Meditation on the Threshold*, 1988); *The Selected Poems of Rosario Castellanos*, 1988; *A Rosario Castellanos Reader: An Anthology of Her Poetry, Short Fiction, Essays, and Drama*, 1988

Rosario Castellanos is among the best known of all female Mexican writers of the twentieth century. As a poet, novelist, short-story writer, essayist, and literary critic, Castellanos became the voice of her generation, focusing attention on the social, political, and racial conflicts of her native land. Her fame derives mainly from her narratives, *Balún-Canán* (1957; *The Nine Guardians*, 1959), and *Oficio de tinieblas* (1962, service of darkness), which rank among the most notable *indigenista* (indigenous) novels of Latin America. José Donoso, in his treatise on the "boom" period of Latin American literature of the 1960's, mentions Castellanos as one of a host of writers that the public has associated with this literary current. Her narrative fiction merited three prestigious national awards during her lifetime.

Poesía no eres tú (you are not poetry), which encompasses twenty years of her writing, is the only complete collection of her poetry in existence. Published in 1972, this volume examines the concerns of a generation of Mexicans bred on the need for social justice according to the principles of the Mexican Revolution of 1910. At issue is Mexico's social construct, which becomes the quintessential polemic of her thematic focus. Infused with revolutionary spirit, Castellanos' poetry is her personal testimony of a fragmented society that has yet to achieve any meaningful sense of equality in terms of race or gender.

Her first poetic works, *Apuntes para una declaración de fe* (notes for a declaration of faith) and *Trayectoria del polvo* (trajectory of dust), appeared in publication in 1948. In the former, Castellanos

underscores the cultural alienation of upper-class Mexicans from their own indigenous heritage. She criticizes the current generation of "Coca-Cola drinkers" whose dedication to European fashion is in high contrast to the values of Indian culture. The revolutionary fervor of an earlier generation that threw off the political yoke of European imperialism years earlier seems to have dissipated in contemporary Mexico: "They work, they become rich and they rot/ without ever asking what is this all about/ . . . and without repenting of their stupid contentment." Her message is both dramatic and potent as she chastises her peers for their adherence to meaningless values.

Trayectoria del polvo explores a more personal theme and reflects her studies in philosophy. Stylistically much like *Apuntes para una declaración de fe*, this is a free-flowing poem also written in the first person. Heavily laden with contemplative overtones, the work recounts the narrator's personal journey from birth to death.

> It is here that death is late like forgetfulness.
> It invades us slowly, pore by pore.
> It is useless to run, to anticipate it,
> to flee even to invent new roads
> and it is also useless to be quiet
> without blinking even so that it does not hear us.

These reflections show a depth of thought that characterizes her poetry, which is both abstract and intimate. Elena Poniatowska, a contemporary Mexican writer, asserted that Rosario Castellanos talked more about death than any other Mexican writer. The death of her younger brother Benjamín when she was a child, in addition to her parents' sudden demise in 1948, most likely contributed to this preoccupation with death.

As Castellanos developed her poetic style, social and political themes became integrated, with an emphasis on the sometimes antagonistic relationships between men and women. It is during this period that she finished her master's degree thesis in philosophy, titled *Sobre cultura femenina* (1950, about feminine culture). After this, she received a scholarship to study a postgraduate course in aesthetics at the University of Madrid. The poems of *De la vigilia estéril* (of the sterile vigil), published in 1950, evince themes of abandonment, rejection, and solitude. "Dos poemas" (two poems) illustrates the substance of the collection with its scrutiny of both the positive and negative aspects of relationships between men and women in a patriarchal society. Although love is possible, her ultimate destiny is to be alone. Thus, she writes: "Solitude, my enemy. She rises/ like a sword to strike me, like a rope/ around my throat." Such imagery serves to further show the development of a feminist perspective that will be much in evidence in later works.

In 1952, Castellanos returned to Chiapas and began work as director of cultural affairs at the Institute of Arts and Sciences in Tuxtla, Gutiérrez. Her poetry during this period was published under the title *El rescate del mundo* (1952, rescue of the world), and it typifies her continuing examination of the social class structure within Mexico. This work actually contains three separate collections of poetry: *Cosas* (things), *Invocaciones* (invocations), and *Diálogo con los oficios aldeanos* (dialogue with rustic professions). In general, these brief poems provide impressionistic accounts of village life as Castellanos acquaints the reader with the spirit and values of mainstream Mexico. For example, poems such as "Lavanderas del Grijalva" (washerwomen of Grijalva) and "Tejedoras de Zinacanta" (weavers of Zinacanta), both of *Diálogo con los oficios aldeanos*, highlight the women whose everyday labors give a poignant look at life among the poorer working classes.

"Oración del indio" (prayer of the Indian), the most pointed piece from the collection *El rescate del mundo* also emphasizes social class issues, since the lower classes of Mexico are typically of Indian descent. This is the legacy of the Spanish conquest, that a once proud and strong people must now live as subservient members of a society that prizes its European roots more than its own Indian ancestry.

> The Indian climbs the temple staggering,
> inebriated by his sobbing as in some strong
>   alcohol.
> He stops in front of God in order to express his
>   misery
> and he yells with a cry of an animal in pursuit
> and he hits his head with his fists.
>
> The gushing of blood that flows from his mouth
> leaves his body quiet.

The forceful imagery of this poem illustrates her concern for social, political, and racial injustice still inherent in a society founded on the principles of the Mexican Revolution.

With a scholarship in 1953 from the Rockefeller Foundation through the Mexican Writers' Center, Castellanos wrote both poetry and essays during her next period, which culminated in the publication of *Poemas (1953-1955)*. Her themes include women's issues such as abandonment, submission, betrayal, and loneliness, described through imagery loosely associated with the Malinche myth. Malinche is a derogatory name given to doña Marina, the Indian slave who aided Hernán Cortés in his bid to conquer the Aztecs. At present an icon within the Mexican national conscience, she has been cast as both the traitor to her own people and the victim of both figurative and literal rape by the conquering Spaniards. It is this story that the poet depicts as her own experience in "Eclipse total" (total eclipse):

> Because I loaned my flesh
> so that the treason could take form
> and so that revenge would acquire volume
> I am here, worse than the captive
> carried in the presence of her owner
> and that, upon showing her bare feet, cries.

Like doña Marina, who became Cortés' mistress, the narrator gives herself to her captor: "And I open my hands. And I consent." She is at once a slave and free. In this way, Castellanos attempts to redefine this image in feminist terms that empower women within male-dominated society.

In her next book of poetry, *Al pie de la letra* (1959, word for word), her imagery takes form once again from these historical roots, although this time her focus is more clearly on the conquest itself. Castellanos' work as an editor at the National Indigenous Institute of Mexico City, beginning in 1959, coincides with the publication of this work, which may explain the evident sense of nationalism. "Crónica final" (final chronicle), from this collection, casts the poet in the role of modern chronicler, recording the history of Mexico in the twentieth century. With language that reflects indigenous roots, she laments the state of a once great civilization: Words such as fraud, solitude, disgrace, captivity, and inequality further develop her social themes within their cultural and historical context.

"Salomé" and "Judith," labeled "dramatic poems," also appeared in print in 1959. They are two portraits of women within the confines of Mexican society who become politicized through their own domestic oppression. Situated in San Cristóbal during the era of the dictator Porfirio Díaz, "Salomé" is a protest of feminist merit. A young woman of the upper class, Salomé is in conflict with her mother over the love of an Indian rebel. Embodying the role of the traditional, submissive Mexican woman, her mother opposes the match because of the Indian's lower social status and revolutionary bent. When the Indian strikes the woman, Salomé realizes that he is as domineering a man as was her father. For this, she betrays him to the government, and he is summarily executed for crimes against the state. Salomé interprets her individual act against the Indian as a form of collective female rebellion against the *machista* or patriarchal society.

> Mother, all women that before me and with me supported the yoke of humiliation, you drank

> an unjust drink, you are revenged by me!
> I have ransomed your slavery
> at the price of my tears.

In this manner, Salomé's betrayal becomes her rallying cry to others of her station and experience. Unlike her passive mother, she acts and, in this one moment, achieves the liberation she seeks for herself and all women. Castellanos' other dramatic piece, "Judith" is similar in both style and theme.

It is important to note that these poems are a stylistic departure for the poet. In 1956, Castellanos was beginning a post as director of the Guiñol Theatre in San Cristóbal. It was here that she spent free time reading the *Popol-Vuh* and translating the Mexican Constitution into the Tzotzil language of her Indian friends so that they might understand the principles of equality and justice promised by the revolution of 1910. Two years later, she was to receive the Chiapas award for *Balún-Canán*, her first *indigenista* novel.

Beginning in 1960, the poet worked as the director of information services at the National Autonomous University of Mexico. At about this time, she received the Xavier Villarrutia prize for *Cuidad real* (1960; *City of Kings*, 1992), a collection of short stories. In her poetry of the same period, which includes *Lívida luz* (1960, livid light), she continues to explore women's roles. "Monólogo en la celda" (monologue in the cell), for example, equates the lack of liberty for women with a lack of personal identity.

> They forgot about me, they left me aside.
> And I don't know who I am
> because no one has said my name; because no
>   one
> has given me form, looking at me.

Her cell becomes the world in which she must live. Thus women, like the Indians, are marginalized members of Mexican society. They live their lives isolated from power, wealth, and decision making. The resulting sense of alienation becomes a potent and oft-repeated image in her poetry.

Materia memorable (memorable material) was published in 1969, when Castellanos began teaching the contemporary Latin American novel at the National Autonomous University of Mexico and at the Iberoamerican University. At this time, her poetry begins to reflect more nationalistic themes. "Ultima crónica" (last chronicle), for example, labels the conquest as a fraud in which the conquerors are "mutilators/ the hucksters" who enslaved a great Indian nation. Such imagery serves to affirm both the sense of lost grandeur of the Mexican civilization and its annihilation at the hands of the European invaders.

The poem "Malinche" typifies the spirit of social protest through a reinterpretation of the popular national cult of doña Marina. Castellanos presents this historical figure in feminist terms that exemplify not only the enslavement of the Indian by the conquerors but also that of women by men: "I was sold/ to the merchants, on my way as a slave,/ a nobody, into exile." As she is presented to her new owner, Cortés, her humiliation echoes the death knell of all Mexicans: "I advance toward destiny in chains/ leaving behind all that I can still hear,/ the funereal murmurs with which I am buried." Castellanos presents, in this manner, a dual perspective, defined by the oppression Malinche experiences as a woman and as an Indian.

Highly delineated motifs of rebellion against the social and political structure of Mexico characterize the later phase of her work. "Memorial de Tlatelolco" ("Memorandum on Tlatelolco"), for example, poetically recounts the events of October 2, 1968, when government forces massacred hundreds of students at the National Autonomous University in Mexico City. Her account of the attack becomes a cry for retributive action: "I remember, we must remember/ until justice be done among us." She sought, like many Mexican writers of her era, to make sense out of a national tragedy that seemed devoid of meaning.

In "Meditación en el umbral" ("Meditation on the Threshold"), the poet rejects passive female figures whose response to feelings of entrapment and stagnation within patriarchal societies is self-destructive. Thus, she criticizes Anna Karenina for "throwing herself underneath the train," Madame Bovary for committing suicide, and Mexico's Sor Juana, who accepted her "cell of solitary confinement." Castellanos seeks role models that empower women instead of conditioning them to accept their fate: She demands "Another way to be human and free./ Another way to be." Her feminist criticism of the male system has become by this time strongly defined and more universal in scope.

In summary, the poetry of Rosario Castellanos presents the dissonant voices of Mexican society, evoking motifs of social and political protest. Castellanos, as the national conscience of her generation, wrote with deep personal conviction of the ongoing social struggle of her nation and of her people. As she wrote in "Ultima crónica," her poetry witnesses the need for social and political change: "And I continue here, abject, the work/ of repeating *greatness, liberty, justice, peace, love, knowledge/* and . . . and . . . I do not understand yet/ that demented and slow stuttering." On August 7, 1974, while serving as Mexican ambassador to Israel, Rosario Castellanos died in a tragic accident. Her revolutionary spirit, evident in all of her writings, lives on in her poetry and contributes to her ever-growing popularity as well as to her importance within contemporary Latin American literature.

THE POETRY OF LORNA DEE CERVANTES

Author: Lorna Dee Cervantes (1954-   )
Type of work: Poetry
Principal published works: *Emplumada*, 1981; *From the Cables of Genocide: Poems on Love and Hunger*, 1991

As an editor of *Mango*, Lorna Dee Cervantes has contributed to the visibility of her generation of Mexican American poets, but it is her own poetry that has won her acclaim. The 1970's saw a renewal of the poetry associated with the Chicano movement in the United States, a renewal arising both from feminist concerns of the Chicana movement and from increased interest in poetic craft. Cervantes' poetry addresses concerns of the Chicana, or feminist Chicano, movement, and her use of language and imagery reflect a commitment to poetic craft. She received the American Book Award from the Before Columbus Foundation for her first book, *Emplumada* (1981), and the Paterson Poetry Prize for her second, *From the Cables of Genocide: Poems on Love and Hunger* (1991).

In *Emplumada*, Cervantes anchors politics and poetics within the concrete imagery of lived experience. She writes from her own experiences but does not limit herself to autobiography or confession. Her poems and their images link the disparate and contradictory elements of Chicana experience, but the poet performs these linkages with an eye to the outside influences on that experience. *Emplumada* conveys the complexity of specific moments, revealing the nature of oppression and its resistance.

The opening poem, "Uncle's First Rabbit," serves as an example of Cervantes' encompassing narrative: In it, she provides a vivid narrative that culminates in her uncle's abusive relationship with his dying wife. It begins, "He was a good boy," then describes him at the age of ten, "hunting my grandpa's supper." When shot, the rabbit screams. The uncle "dreamed of running," of selling the rifle and leaving town on the next train. The poem jumps ahead fifty years, when the uncle "still hears/ that rabbit 'just like a baby.'" The poem

mixes the gory image of a "blood soaked jacket" with a sensitive child's tears. This leads to a revelation: The ten-year-old has connected the "terrible singing" associated with hunting with "his dead baby sister's,/ remembering his father's drunken/ kicking that had pushed her/ into birth."

Cervantes makes clever use of repetition to build the narrative. She frequently uses ambiguity and enjambment (continuing a sentence across line breaks) to complicate her meaning. For example, "He dreamed/ of running, running/ the bastard out of his life." The uncle dreams of pure escape, of "running," and of the power to drive out the abuser: "running the bastard out of his life." The uncle's impotent ambivalence comes through from the repetition, subtly because Cervantes has broken the sentence across lines.

Cervantes often uses imagery to convey a deeper understanding or to reveal the hidden, as in the imagery of the shark described below. Eventually, the uncle escapes, enlisting in "the war," yet at war's end "he could/ still hear her, her soft/ body stiffening under water/ like a shark's." He cannot leave behind the trauma of his sister's death, and though she is innocent, the death itself (the stiffening body) lingers like a shark, a threat. Finally he awakens "to find himself slugging the bloodied/ face of his wife," the threat realized. The uncle comes full circle, becoming the abusive husband his father once was. Again the poet reminds readers that the present is fifty years after the rabbit hunt, and now she shows the dying aunt, the uncle cursing her. In the last lines, he still dreams of leaving on the next train, this time selling the new pickup truck on the way. Repetition connects the past and the present.

The poet has brought together in this single poem, as in many, a complete narrative history for a present moment—in this case, that of the uncle cursing his dying wife. Without defending or justifying the abuse, she reveals its nature and the perversity of its transmission. With subtle images, she connects it to blood sport (the hunt), to the military (the uncle's military service), and to economic need (the uncle's selling a gun or a pickup truck to fund his escape). Although he has turned his rage and pain unjustly against his wife, the rage and pain has its causes and roots within the uncle's powerlessness. Cervantes conveys this sympathetically but without making excuses. In this way, she presents a complex yet clear statement with poetic craft, rather than by resorting to slogans. The poetic statement carries with it the necessary and messy complexity of reality.

All the poems in *Emplumada*, taken together, reveal complexity from the specific perspective of Cervantes' Chicana experience. She intends readers to consider *Emplumada* as a whole, having said in an interview that she thought it should be read in one sitting. The whole reveals a process of development, a way by which the poet records her barrio beginnings as well as her family's pain and suffering. In the process of recording, she transforms and transcends those things through the act of writing; with language, image, and metaphor. Most of the transformation comes from the act of making poetry itself, from building her own world and writing herself into it.

Although Cervantes intended the book to be read as a whole, it is still worthwhile to consider each of the three untitled sections separately in discussing the book. The first section gives a context, weaving three main threads: the beginnings of her own personal history growing up in the San Jose barrio, events in her life growing up, and celebrations or recollections of significant people from her past. The first section is largely reflective, set in the past.

The poem that best brings these three threads together is "Beneath the Shadow of the Freeway." Cervantes presents clear images of her home: "Across the street—the freeway,/ blind worm, wrapping the valley up/ from Los Altos to Sal Si Puedes." The names she chooses to mark the ge-

ography of the freeway highlight America's divided culture: Los Altos means "The Heights," and Sal Si Puedes is translated as "get out if you can" and is a barrio (neighborhood) in East San Jose, California. Further emphasizing the divide, Cervantes ironically describes her "woman family" in royal terms, her grandmother as "our innocent Queen" and her mother as "the Swift Knight, Fearless Warrior." Her mother is dissatisfied with her lot: "Mama wanted to be Princess instead." Her grandmother is down to earth; she "trusts only what she builds/ with her own hands." Her mother is down to earth in a more blunt way, warning "You're too soft . . . always were./ You'll get nothing but shit./ Baby, don't count on nobody." Such descriptions echo through the whole first section, which gives the context of the poet's beginnings. They also foreshadow important themes of *From the Cables of Genocide*.

Cervantes also reveals images of herself in "Beneath the Shadow of the Freeway": "I turned to books, those staunch, upright men./ I became Scribe: Translator of Foreign Mail." These lines anticipate the second section of *Emplumada*, which describes Cervantes becoming "scribe" and "translator," her obsession and fascination with language, its abilities and inabilities, strengths and weaknesses. Language, however, divides Cervantes from her world. Cervantes as Chicana poet lives between an Anglo-American world (Los Altos) and the Hispanic world (Sal Si Puedes). The last two poems of the section in particular convey this: "Oaxaca, 1974" and "Visions of Mexico While at a Writing Symposium in Port Townsend, Washington." Mexico rejects her in the first poem: "México gags,/ ¡Esputa!/ on this bland pochaseed." *Es puta* translates to "is a whore," with a play on *espuca* (to spit). Pochaseed, or pocha, is slang for an assimilated Mexican American. Mexico does not provide, by this account, the comforting homecoming she thought it would for her. In the second poem, she laments: "I don't belong this far north." She longs to dispel society's stereotypes of Hispanics and their culture, yet to do so she needs the language she distrusts. In the end, she goes north in order to write her poems. She comes to the

Anglo-American world and its written poetry, but as shown above, her poems contain a mixture of languages and cultures. She is, in the end, Chicana, not pocha.

Poetry, for Cervantes, describes, inscribes, creates, and transforms. It contains the magic of ritual and healing. Within it, she gives magical images: birds and feathers take on significance, and mystical connections are frequent. Although much of this is imagery and metaphor, the rich and varied use of these images within the poetry conveys a sense of the power, magical or otherwise, within poems themselves. It is the power of language to transform, along with a more spiritual power, as often as not connected with the image of Cervantes' grandmother. That is the power of connection and understanding.

Cervantes' grandmother remembers some of the old stories, she wears her hair in a loose braid, and she remains true to herself. Her mother, on the other hand, comes from another generation and rejects who she is; she wants to be a princess rather than the swift knight. Her mother has suffered at the hands of men and warns her daughter that that will be her lot as well. Cervantes, in the end, rejects this warning. Although her mother and her experience warn her about male violence and the untrustworthiness of men, in "Beneath the Shadow of the Freeway" the poet persona comes back to her old home "with a gentle man." She recognizes in herself—and connects with—images of her grandmother, and "trust[s] only what I have built/ with my own hands." Her poems are what she builds, and in the final section of *Emplumada*, those poems are love poems, perhaps for the "gentle man"—possibly John, to whom the book is dedicated.

Ten years after *Emplumada*, *From the Cables of Genocide: Poems on Love and Hunger* appeared in print. This book focuses much more tightly on individual experience and emotion than does the more epic *Emplumada*. *Emplumada* contains many narrative poems with rich context; *From the Cables of Genocide* relies more on the confessional lyric. The imagery remains strong, and if anything is denser. The language and craft ap-

proach but do not quite reach overelaborated self-consciousness. The overall effect is that the reader comes to feel the depth of suffering and the darkness of moods; one follows the poetry up for air, if only a gulp. While *Emplumada* transforms the desolation of the barrio and an abusive family into images of hope and love, the much more introspective *From the Cables of Genocide* follows the poet into and part way out of despair, through four sections. The book centers on two explicit traumas in the poet's life: the breakup of her marriage and the abortion of a child. These two events are closely linked: The father of the child is her husband, John, the man who deserts her.

It is through reconnection with her cultural heritage that Cervantes finds some redemption. She again uses images of her grandmother, but this time more closely linked with poetic craft through her homage to Latino poets Pablo Neruda and Federico García Lorca. The rich mix of her cultural awareness is reflected in the wide range of her acknowledged influences. She quotes, for example, African American blues singer Billie Holiday and dedicates the book to author Sylvia Plath (among others). In the end, it is her ability to connect to the poetic language that brings her out of total despair, though not totally out of despair.

If the instrument of redemption in *Emplumada* is the quill, in *From the Cables of Genocide* it is again her pen. Poetry allows her to make her experience into transforming metaphors and images, and again (new) love brings the possibility of salvation. This time, however, her very life seems to depend on this salvation, as suicide becomes a recurring image in the early poems. This time, Cervantes tempers the salvation—and thus love itself—considerably with uncertainty and self-doubt. Love is not the only answer. It may not even be an answer.

Often Cervantes leaves ambiguity as to whether the new lover addressed in a poem is an actual lover, poetry, or—in the four poems with the epigram "after Neruda"—Neruda himself. When she appears to discuss her actual new love, she brings out contradictions within their relationship, her own doubts, and her own sense of emptiness within. This relationship is scrutinized more carefully than, and not accepted as completely as, the first had been. In *Emplumada*, Cervantes came to realize the messy complexity of the world around her; in *From the Cables of Genocide*, she realizes the complexities of herself and her relationship with men.

In her new relationship she holds back, and although she does not feel the same emotional satiation as with her earlier lover, she seems to see this new man more clearly than the last. The poems about the new lover are dedicated "for Jay," which invites the question of whether the new lover is a new way of seeing John, as Jay is a plausible nickname for John. The depth of emotion conveyed in the poems seems authentic, though, and it seems unlikely that the events in the book are anything but autobiographical, yet the question remains because of the apparent coincidence.

Cervantes begins again to trust only what she has built herself, and her self is all that she has built. Cervantes wants to distinguish hunger (and its satiation) from love. She wants to survive both. She has taken the reader through despair to the brink of suicide and back from that edge by making experience into a metaphor, thus making it malleable and understandable, something with which she can cope. In the process, the poet has presented her reality with such clarity that she subjects the despair to a certain scrutiny. *From the Cables of Genocide*, taken as a whole, interrogates the nature of romantic attachment.

Cervantes writes provocative and well-crafted poetry that reveals her own specific experiences in ways that allow readers access to the truth and familiarity of her images. Her poems remain accessible on many levels, but it is her intelligent and careful attention to poetic craft that has earned attention for her work. Her ability to understand the complexities of experience and relate those complexities in language marks her work, as does her ability to write inclusively, using history, time, and all the elements of her universe within each book.

THE POETRY OF SOR JUANA INÉS DE LA CRUZ

Author: Sor Juana Inés de la Cruz (1648-1695)
Type of work: Poetry
Principal published works: *Inundación Castálida de la única poetisa, musa décima, sor Juana Inés de la Cruz*, 1689; *Fama y obras póstumas del Fénix de México y Dézima Musa*, 1700

[handwritten: La respuesta / Los empeños de una casa]

Sister Juana Inés de la Cruz, a celebrated Mexican nun, was arguably the greatest literary figure in the colonial New World, not only because of her lyrical ability but also because of her delightful personality. In the early seventeenth century, there were few women in Hispanic America who could even sign their names, but as the culture developed more and more girls received a sort of education in schools called "Amigas." It was only a primary education. The University of Mexico, founded in 1551, was only for boys. Girls were not believed to have any need or desire for extensive learning.

This was not true, however, of Juana Inés de Asbaje y Ramírez de Santillana, born in San Miguel Nepantla, Mexico, in 1648. To keep her out of mischief, her mother sent her with an older sister to one of the Amigas. There the three-year-old unblushingly told the teacher that her mother wanted her to be taught how to read. The teacher, at first as a joke, then amazed at Juana's quickness, taught her to read before her mother learned of the deception.

A craving for knowledge followed Juana throughout life. A few years later, having heard that cheese, of which she was very fond, stupefied the brain, the girl stopped eating it. When she thought she was not learning grammar as rapidly as she should, she cut her hair, vowing not to let it grow long till she conquered the subject, "since a head so naked of knowledge ought not to be adorned with pretty hair." Hearing about the university for men in the capital, she importuned her mother to let her disguise herself in men's clothes and attend classes. At the age of eight, when she finally went to Mexico City to live with her grandparents, she learned Latin so that she could read all the books in their library.

Turning suddenly to the religious life, she entered the convent of Santa Teresa la Antigua at the age of sixteen, but the rigorous discipline of the order proved too strict for her frail health, and she was released. In 1669, she entered the convent of San Jerónimo. She remained a member until her death.

[handwritten: Rococca]

She discovered her versifying ability early and practiced it for formal and informal occasions. The late seventeenth century was the Baroque period, with poetry and even prose full of distorted syntax, Latinisms, mythological and classical allusions, and an abundance of metaphors and ridiculous conceits. This was the result of imitation of the Spanish poet Luis de Góngora y Argote.

Because of her wide reading, Sor Juana was bound to imitate the prevailing literary fashion when she began to write. Before long, however, she found other models. Critics find in her work the influence of the great lyric poet Garcilaso de la Vega, who wrote in the Italian style with love as his chief theme. Although limited in number, his verses achieved perfection. His thirty-eight harmonious sonnets, in which emotion mingles with beauty, established that form in Spanish verse. At times Sor Juana also followed Lupercio and Bartolomé Argensola, brothers who were among the most classic of poets.

Sor Juana experimented with every type of verse: sonnets, lyrics, ballads, *redondillas* of four-line stanzas and a specific rhyme scheme, *villancicos* or rustic Christmas carols, and drama, both short *autos sacramentales* and full-length plays. She synthesized many of the poetic currents: learned and popular, Renaissance and baroque, even traces of mysticism. Her subject matter ran from the deeply spiritual to such humor as the *ovillejo* concerning the beauty of Lisarda.

[handwritten: abba]

Mostly she wrote love poems. Love versus reason was a favorite theme. Of her sixty-five sonnets, twenty-two deal with love. Critics argue about how much of her work is autobiographical and how much is the result of either her observation or conformity to literary trends. There is speculation that she had an unfortunate early love affair with the Count of Mancera. The Mexican playwrights José Rosas Moreno and Octavio Meza have dramatized the story for the stage.

Was her well-known example of *Redondillas* founded on fact? It begins:

> Stupid men, quick to condemn
>   Women wrongly for their flaws,
>   Never seeing you're the cause
> Of all that you blame on them!

Was she talking of her own experiences when she went on?

> She who's modest cannot hold
>   Man's esteem. We're all thought naughty.
>   If we don't accept, we're haughty;
> If we welcome you, we're bold.

Is it her personal pronoun in the final stanza?

> Women need be strong, I find,
>   To stay safe and keep unharmed
>   Since the arrogant male comes armed
> With Devil, flesh, and world combined.

Ermilo Abreu Gómez, editor of a volume of her poetry, declared that her poetic reputation rests essentially on her lyric verse, which is for the most part amorous. During her lifetime, her personality so charmed everyone that she was called Mexico's Tenth Muse, and everything she wrote was accepted uncritically. Before she became a nun, she was lady in waiting to the Marquesa de Mancera, wife of the viceroy. Later, after she had taken her vows, her cell in the convent became a meeting place for the leaders of Mexico's intellectual life.

Two books of her poems were published during her lifetime. The first appeared in Spain in 1689 under the title *Inundación Castálida de la única poetisa, musa décima, sor Juana Inés de la Cruz* (the Castalian flood of the unique poetess, the tenth muse, Sister Juana Inés de la Cruz). Three years later, a second volume was published in Seville. In 1700, five years after her death, a Madrid publisher printed *Fama y obras póstumas del Fénix de México y Dézima Musa* (posthumous fame and works of the Phoenix of Mexico and the Tenth Muse.)

What is known of her early life can be read in one of the greatest autobiographical letters in Spanish literature, *A Reply to Sor Philotea de la Cruz*, written in 1691. An acquaintance, Bishop Manuel Fernández de Santa Cruz, of Puebla, wrote her some admonitions under the signature of Sor Philotea, suggesting that to be holy she spend less time on worldly things and more on religious matters. The letter brought a reply from her telling of her lifelong craving for knowledge and of childhood episodes. She stated that she had never written anything of her own volition, always writing in response to outside urging, except in the case of "Primero Sueño" (first dream), the subtitle of which declares it to be an imitation of the *Soledades* or *Visions* of Gongora. Although much of the poem is an arabesque of interwoven images and thoughts made difficult by artificial grammar, many of the thousand lines are pure poetry and show her intellectual knowledge of her art. In the Silva meter of irregular lines, Sister Juana tells how in a dream her soul caught a glimpse of the whole of creation and in dismay returned in humility to undertake a further search for knowledge, simple and complicated, with attendant doubts and uncertainties. Apparently no one has ever put its baroque verses into an English translation.

A number of her sonnets appear in English form. From one of them, a reader can get an idea of her style, with its Gongoristic ornaments:

> This trickery of paint which you perceive
> With all the finest hues of art enwrought,
> Which is false argument of colors taught
> By subtle means the senses to deceive—
> This by which foolish woman would believe
> She could undo the evils years have brought
> And conquering in the war against time fought
> Could triumph over age, and youth retrieve—
> Is all a futile ruse that she has tried,
> A fragile flower tossed against the wind,
> A useless bribe the power of fate to appease,
> A silly effort of mistaken pride,
> A base desire, and viewed in rightful mind,
> Is dust, a corpse, a shade,—is less than these.

3 years later

The admonitions of the bishop brought results. Sor Juana sold her private library of four thousand books, surely the largest collection in the New World, concentrated on religious work, and died four years later nursing sisters in the convent during a plague.

No. He commissioned the critique.
Archbishop Francisco Aguilar y wrote the letter

THE POETRY OF VICTOR HERNÁNDEZ CRUZ

Author: Victor Hernández Cruz (1949-   )
Type of work: Poetry
Principal published works: *Snaps*, 1969; *Mainland*, 1973; *Tropicalization*, 1976; *By Lingual Wholes*, 1982; *Rhythm, Content & Flavor*, 1988; *Red Beans*, 1991

Victor Hernández Cruz emigrated with his family to New York City from the rural Puerto Rican town of Agua Buenas at the age of five. After publishing his first volume of poetry, *Snaps* (1969), Cruz became a central figure among the New Yorican (or Nuyorican) poets, Puerto Rican poets who, like Cruz, grew up and began writing in New York City. It is this collision of cultures, between Puerto Rican and New Yorker, and of languages, between Spanish and English, that gives Cruz's poetry tension, flavor, and ultimately a voice of convincing personality and insight.

In his essay "Mountains in the North: Hispanic Writing in the U.S.A.," contained in his book of poems *Red Beans* (1991), Cruz claims that he wishes to "change the English and give it spice, Hispanic mobility. . . ." He writes, "we are the sons and daughters of campesinos, fishermen, farmers who cultivated café and tobacco, cutters of cane whose eyes contain the memory of ardent green vistas out of wooden windows within the hottest tropicality." Although he writes primarily in English and frequently focuses his attention on his surroundings in New York and the United States, Cruz recognizes that his roots are in the Spanish language he learned as his native tongue and in Puerto Rico, the source of his earliest memories and family history. From these roots, Cruz envisions his poetry becoming a potent force, an agent of creation and change.

His first book, *Snaps*, is a collage of language capturing the energy and danger of life in the New York City of Cruz's youth, a life of drugs, dance clubs, and knife fights over loaded dice. At the same time, the book brims with Cruz's attention to details, details in the world and in language, told in a bold rhythmic structure that resembles popular Latin music. Poems in this book such as "Mega-

lopolis," "The Eye Uptown & Downtown (three days)," and "going uptown to visit miriam" blend images, sounds, thoughts, and insights characteristic of the streets of New York, with a style forged in the rhythm of steel drums and salsa music. In the poem "latin & soul," Cruz re-creates the chaos of urban night life. Although the language of the poem captures the feeling of the chaotic, the structure builds upon a definite rhythmic alternation between chorus line and verse. The rhythm drives steadily toward the realization at the end of the poem that it is the music itself that is the force behind his writing:

> a sudden misunderstanding
> > a cloud
> > full of grayness
> a body thru a store window
> > a hand reaching
> > into the back
> > pocket
> a scream
> > a piano is
> > > talking to you
> > thru all this
> > why don't you
> > > answer it.

Although the young Cruz hears the music in *Snaps* and uses the music to provide order to his poetry, he only begins to recognize clearly that the music echoes from his Puerto Rican origins.

In *Mainland* (1973), Cruz's second book, he acknowledges two distinct elements of his personality, one Puerto Rican and one New Yorker. The book opens with a quote from Luis Palés Matos that reads, in part, "Sometimes, from its hidden hoarse-voiced high sea, from those unexplored distances, come echoes . . . cries for help, voices, moans like those from a huge ship that is being wrecked in the distance." In these poems, Cruz begins to answer the distant echoes of memory's wreckage, wreckage strewn with details and bits of language from his Puerto Rican childhood and ancestry. The two landscapes, as well as the two elements of the poet's identity, remain separate, and he realizes that they need to come together. These poems lament Cruz's fragmentation and express his desire to unify his voice and his person. In "From the Secrets I," he hears his ethnic identity inside himself, but it remains isolated from his environment: "Thoughts in Spanish run through/ the mind/ The buildings speak broken English." Aware that the two landscapes and languages must interact, even blend, if he is to become a unified person, Cruz remains unable to hear a version of Puerto Rico in New York; most of the scatterings of Spanish used in the book do not integrate into the poems but stow away in titles, quotes, and proper names.

Still, *Mainland* does chart the wellspring of Cruz's poetic imagination as Puerto Rican in poems such as "Aguadilla," one of his first with a completely tropical setting and theme.

> We carry the drums on our backs
> We go to the edge of the ocean
> just where the water reaches
> We turn around to look for the house
> But it is not there
> All we see is green rhythm coming
> to eat us

Although the specific images do not yet come into focus (the house is beyond sight), what he has brought with him (or, more accurately, what has followed him) is the rhythm, the creative force of Puerto Rico, an energy that he anticipates overtaking and engulfing him.

If the poems in *Mainland* are written by a Cruz looking over his shoulder at an approaching poetic sensibility built on the rhythms of the Caribbean and Spanish, those in *Tropicalization* (1976) depict a poet at the moment just before he is overtaken by that sensibility. In this book, Cruz's New York and Puerto Rican sensibilities have not yet begun to blend, but face off as equal forces competing for

his voice. Here is a poet in exile, surrounded by a cold city where, as he writes in "Side 2," "ice hugs the glass" and the announcer "Murray the K he says over radio/ 2 below outside." In these poems, New York, although still described in authentic, personal, believable detail, becomes a cold, sexless sort of wasteland in which creativity must somehow take root, a place in which he finds himself "telling stories of the hot sun" and longing for that other place of "walking around half naked/ Suave moon lifting skirts." Puerto Rico—warm, sexual, fertile Puerto Rico—is no longer a distant, vaguely remembered homeland but a presence that comforts him through his exile by providing imagination and rhythm. The first line of "Side 2" reads "Out the window the window looking out," a variation on that most traditional of English lines, the iambic pentameter; upon closer inspection, however, it becomes clear that the line also has a salsa rhythm.

As the title of Cruz's fourth book, *By Lingual Wholes* (1982), implies, Spanish and English blend in a single poetic voice. Cruz reapproaches not only New York but also the United States (as he experiences it), from the imaginative and cultural perspective of Puerto Rico. In the poem "Art This," Cruz offers a free-flowing discourse (with some urgency, as if he is relearning his native language on that very page) on Spanish names and how, when they change from masculine to feminine, their meanings as words change. In the middle of this thought he stops himself:

> This
> is all in Spanish and something is being
> lost in the translation just like you lose
> your natural color when you leave a tropical
> country and come to a city where the sun
> feels like it's constipated

Not only does Cruz express his plight as an outlander, and thereby achieve some strengthened sense of self, a self comprising elements that blend as languages blend, but he also exposes the reader/poet relationship, exploding the illusion that the reader has entered the poem, exactly as the illusion is exploded that he, as a Puerto Rican, has assimilated and entered fully the culture of the United States. This is an exciting moment in Cruz's development as a poet, both because he achieves some resolution of the fragmented self through a unified language and voice and also because this resolution frees his poetry to explore aesthetic and philosophical issues, such as the poem's own relationship to experience in "Art This."

Cruz is also free to turn his poetic attention to matters of culture beyond his own immediate experience. For the first time, he becomes that potent political voice he aspired to as a younger poet, concerned with oppression and disharmony beyond mere realities reflecting his own developing psyche. The poem "Prescriptions from the Plantnet" reads as a sourcebook of remedies and affective substances in which seemingly every possible condition in the human experience has a corollary or cure in some herb or root. Clearly, the physical world is prepared to deal with all of humankind's spiritual, physical, and psychological needs; all that is needed is knowledge in the form of a tradition for encountering the natural world.

Many poems in this book are social and historical accounts: of the kidnapping to the Hawaiian canefields of a shipload of Puerto Rican immigrants in "Borinkins in Hawaii"; of failed Portuguese colonization in "Bacalao and Society"; and of the collision between the rational, scientific thinking of Columbia University professors and a Hispanic family for whom the miraculous is almost commonplace in "The Physics of Ochun." These are fairly direct narratives, reflecting a less fragmented poet able to absorb and respond to the world lucidly and with passion. Clearly, at this point in his development, as he writes in "The Process of Bolero," "Pushing a big heart through a small/ pen is not difficult."

The poems in *Islandis*—a section of new poems in Cruz's selected poems *Rhythm, Content & Flavor* (1988)—and the book *Red Beans* (1991) that closely followed continue to speak with the voice of a poet no longer tormented by contrary elements of self. The poet has become whole, able to draw on and blend his diverse ethnic and linguistic experiences. In the poem "To El Grupo Folklórico y Experimental Nuevayorquino" (to the folklore group of experimental New Yorkers) from *Red Beans*, he writes, "This is a poem that combines/ the memories of several cultures into one unique juice." The description is an apt one for the poet as well as for this creation. Puerto Rico has become a large enough presence in his understanding of himself that its three primary ethnic groups, Taíno (Native), Spanish, and African, begin to take on roles of their own, as in the poem "Root of Three" in *Islandis*:

> I walk New York with a fan
> in my pocket
> Made with the feathers
> of three continents
> It blows African feet
> It blows Spanish heart
> It blows Taíno head space.

A Puerto Rican sensibility, comprising the combined power of three cultures' rhythm (feet), passion (heart), and imagination (head space), has become as accessible as his hip pocket. Spanish has become so integrated into his voice that *Islandis* contains two entirely Spanish poems, "Estudios Mentales" (mental studies) and "La simplicidad de la imagen" (the simplicity of the image).

So much of Cruz's energy has been spent building his single, unified language that the language has become for him a reality in itself. The poems from *Islandis* and *Red Beans* are frequently so loose, so natural and unplanned, that they convey the feeling that their insights and meanings occur in the very act of the writing. In "Puerta Rica," "A Skirt in the Distance," and "Caribbean Glances I," Cruz explores social, emotional, and experiential reality via an exhaustive and free-flowing exploration of language. It seems natural to wonder if, in these poems, he sees a difference between experience and language, between "Puerto Rico as thing/ Puerto Rico as word." In "The Troubadour's Heritage," one word from the troubadour, the right word, "descansa" (rest), is able to lure a passing beautiful young woman over to where he sits in the plaza. Language has the power to alter reality, to make reality, and for this Cruz loves it passionately.

The power of the word to create reality has applications far beyond the ability to capture the attention of women. For Cruz, the associations of language often lead to political and religious truths. In his essay "The Bolero of the Red Translation" (a sort of introduction to *Red Beans*), Cruz writes, "A poem about a pair of eyes can become the history of a civilization. . . . Air stops being ether and becomes angels." The commonplace becomes religious throughout Cruz's poetry precisely because of the language he assigns it. Because he understands the everyday as religious and assigns to it religious words, he sees that "We have been breathing angels, our lungs are temples." Compare this to a section from "Is It Certain Or Is It Not Certain Caso Maravilla" in *Islandis*, a poem about the brutal killing of two young revolutionaries in Puerto Rico:

> Be careful
> Cause look what is loose
> And possessive of power
>
> . . . .
> Christians
> Of the kind that sold themselves to Rome
> Who maintain the language of the killers
> Of Christ
> As the ceremonial language of the very
> Church of Christ

The holy in the everyday, or the wretched and oppressive in the wrappings of the supposedly holy—language makes all the difference. The language of the church that allows oppression creates a reality in which "Mercy means the opposite." The language of the everyday things, the people's tongue, is the tongue of religious truth and grace, the tongue that calls for political liberation.

In the poem "An Essay on William Carlos Williams" (in *Red Beans*), Cruz praises Williams for his quality of language, praise that could just as easily be about his own work: "The tongue itself carries/ the mind/ Pure and sure." From some fragments of a remembered Puerto Rico, street life in New York, and two languages, Cruz has achieved a voice "sudden and direct" that gives him access to experience. Like music, his language is an experience itself, "like the appearance/ of a green mountain/ Overlooking a town." That "green rhythm" that Cruz saw coming to engulf him back in *Mainland* has caught up with him and has become language. By writing words as a composer writes notes, to be played upon the ear, Cruz brings to poetry in the United States an urgent voice reminding readers that poetry should have power to liberate nations, power to reconcile clashing cultures, power to make people move.

THE POETRY OF RUBÉN DARÍO

Author: Rubén Darío (Félix Rubén García y Sarmiento, 1867-1916)
Type of work: Poetry
Principal published works: *Azul*, 1888; *Prosas profanas*, 1896 (*Prosas Profanas and Other Poems*, 1922); *Cantos de vida y esperanza, los cisnes, y otros poemas*, 1905; *Canto a la Argentina, oda a mitre, y otros poemas*, 1914; *Selected Poems of Rubén Darío*, 1965 (Lysander Kemp, translator)

Nicaraguan poet Rubén Darío is perhaps the most important Hispanic writer of the nineteenth century. He headed a movement, *Modernismo*, that in the 1880's and 1890's became Latin America's declaration of independence in literature. Today, his achievements are compared to those of the great Spanish poet Garcilaso de la Vega, who in the early sixteenth century helped bring the Renaissance from Italy to Spain. Darío brought a new Renaissance, in the form of *Modernismo*, to the Hispanic world. Three major publications mark Darío's development as a writer: *Azul* (1888; blue), a collection of short stories and poems; *Prosas profanas* (1896; profane hymns), generally considered to be his most decadent work; and *Cantos de vida y esperanza, los cisnes, y otros poemas* (1905; songs of life and hope, the swans, and other poems), which focuses more on real-life problems while continuing to develop the fundamental themes presented in the first two works.

In 1888, when many Latin American authors were still writing about the world of nature around them—the pampa, the mountains, the jungle—Darío published *Azul*, a work written for the most part while he was living in Chile. The title may have been inspired by a line from the nineteenth century French romantic poet Victor Hugo, "L'art c'est l'azur" (art is blue). The color symbolizes many things in Darío's poetry: an ideal, a dream, a mystery, infinity. Along with the swan and Venus (both the statue and the planet), blue was one of his favorite symbols.

Azul gained instant notoriety for Darío when the Spanish novelist and literary critic Juan Valera reviewed it in 1888 for the newspaper *El Imparcial* in Madrid. Valera criticized Darío for his excessive dependence on French writers and culture for in-spiration and for his failure to include more from his own Hispanic heritage. At the same time, however, he brought Darío's work to the attention of the Spanish literary establishment.

France was not the only source of Darío's inspiration. His poetry also draws extensively on the world of Greek and Roman culture and mythology. Although Valera's criticism was directed only at Darío and *Azul*, later critics transformed the criticism into accusations of escapism. Darío and the modernist writers who followed him were falsely accused of ignoring the social realities of their world while closing themselves away in the ivory towers of art. Only one poem from *Azul*, "Caupolicán," has any direct connection with Latin America. It is a sonnet written in honor of the native hero of Alonso de Ercilla y Zúñiga's sixteenth century epic poem "La Araucana," about the wars between the Spaniards and Indians in Chile. Darío tries to give Caupolicán even greater stature by comparing him with Hercules and Samson.

Darío first demonstrated his potential for innovation in the short stories contained in *Azul*. Many have an atmosphere that is both highly rarefied and distinctly foreign to Darío's Nicaragua. Today, literary critics see stories such as "La Ninfa" (the nymph) and "El rubí" (the ruby) as forerunners of the literature of the fantastic that flourished in the works of the Argentine modernist Leopoldo Lugones and his more famous countrymen Jorge Luis Borges and Julio Cortázar. Beneath the surface, though, the reader will find ample evidence of Darío's social conscience in his stinging commentaries on society's obsession with material wealth and its indifference toward the problems of the artist and the working class.

The role of the artist in an increasingly utilitarian and materialistic society is the theme of the story "El Rey Burgués" (the bourgeois king). In this story, people and things exist only in terms of their potential value in dollars and cents. The fictional poet of this story, like the world of ideals he represents, is cast out of the king's warm castle to die in the bitter cold because his poetry is of little monetary value and he, therefore, of little use. The sarcastic story "La canción del oro" (money's song) echoes this same theme: Money buys everything, and without it one is nothing.

"El velo de la reina Mab" (Queen Mab's veil) once more examines the fate of artists—in this case a painter, a poet, a sculptor, and a musical composer—in a society preoccupied with material goods. The four artists have the same complaint: They have to create not for the sake of art itself but for the sake of survival. At the end of the story, Queen Mab wraps them in a blue veil of hope, an illusory hope for a better future.

The most social of the short stories in *Azul* is "El fardo" (the crate). Darío strikes up a conversation with an old man, Lucas, on the docks of Valparaíso, and introduces his readers to the life of a poor but honorable working-class family. Lucas tells how, at the age of fifteen, economic necessity forced his son to abandon his education and join Lucas in working to support the family. The father and son first became fishermen, but their boat was destroyed during a storm at sea. Later, they worked as stevedores, unloading oceangoing ships in the port until Lucas fell victim to rheumatism, leaving his son as the sole supporter of the family. One Saturday, while unloading a ship, a large crate came loose from the crane that was lowering it and crushed Lucas' son. Darío describes the accident in almost slow-motion detail. On that day, everything stopped: food, medicine, income, and, consequently, any future for Lucas and his family. In the closing paragraph, as Darío leaves the old stevedore Lucas and heads for home, a bitterly cold wind lashes at his face. Symbolically, this wind is the chilling response of a society grown indifferent to anything incapable of producing material wealth, something neither Lucas' poor working-class family nor the poet of "El Rey Burgués," a

man of ideals, would ever be able to do.

The final prose section of *Azul*, "En Chile, en busca de cuadros" (in Chile, in search of paintings), is the most innovative from a technical point of view. Here, painting with words instead of a brush, Darío tries to bridge the gap between literature and visual art in a series of short narratives with titles meant to draw associations with painting: "Acuarela" (watercolor), "Paisaje" (landscape), "Aguafuerte" (etching), "Naturaleza muerta" (still life), and "Al carbón" (charcoal).

The poetry of *Azul* is more traditional in its form, though its content reveals basic themes that run through Darío's later works. The first poem, "El año lírico" (the lyrical year), presents four seasons of love that range from the tender and reflexive loves of "Spring" and "Autumn" to the tempestuous loves of "Summer" and, paradoxically, "Winter," a season that commonly is symbolically associated with death.

"Summer" takes place in a poetic jungle far from Darío's Nicaragua. Three figures appear: a tigress in heat, a tiger on the prowl, and a hunter, the Prince of Wales, who in Darío's time was a symbol of beautiful youth. The tigress and tiger meet and mate, and the heat of their passion fills the air. The hunter, unmoved by the scene before him, coldly takes aim, measures the distance, shoots, and kills the tigress. The two animals and the hunter represent a profound contradiction in Darío's mind and a repeated theme in his works: the constant sexual attraction that women held for Darío (the tigress) and his efforts—always fruitless—to control those desires (the calculating hunter).

Although there are other poems in *Azul* (additions to the 1890 edition) dedicated to French authors such as Leconte de Lisle and Catulle Mendès, North American Walt Whitman, and Latin Americans J. J. Palma and Salvador Díaz Mirón, only the sonnet "Venus" merits additional commentary. Just as the planet Venus is simultaneously the morning (Lucifer) and the evening (Vesper) star, announcing both light and darkness, woman in Darío's poetry is presented as being the giver of both pleasure (light and life) and pain (darkness and death). Although the Venus of this sonnet is an object of desire that forever remained just beyond the poet's reach, he never ceased pursuing her, a pursuit that in *Prosas profanas* Darío frequently described in terms of a religious experience.

Prosas profanas combines the exotic with the erotic. Darío composed most of its fifty-four poems between 1893 and 1898, while he was in Buenos Aires, Argentina, working for the newspaper *La Nación*. In *Prosas profanas*, Darío created a new and distinct poetic language that came to characterize not only his work but *Modernismo* in general as well. It glowed with diamonds, precious metals, and objects of art. It borrowed from French and Latin and from the Spanish baroque in an effort to revive the language of poetry. Darío was at his innovative best in the use of metric combinations. He eventually used almost all the metric forms available in Spanish: some thirty-seven meters in 136 kinds of stanzas.

In the use of "proses," Darío refers to hymns that used to be sung in the Catholic liturgy that have to do with cycles of suffering, death, resurrection, and victory over death. Darío's poetic hymns sing the triumph over death, which he personifies as a virgin, desired and desiring, who seeks in each man the one who is capable of wresting the secret of immortality from her.

Throughout *Prosas profanas*, there are references to the Catholic liturgy, which Darío converts into a rite of sensual pleasure. The title of "'Ite, Missa Est'" ("go, the Mass is ended") contains the last words of the priest at the end of the service. The poem is a celebration of pleasure in which the woman (presented as the enigmatic Sphinx) is the "host" of his sacrifice, and in which the poet's lovemaking causes her to reveal her secret.

Woman is a constant presence in *Prosas profanas*. She is flirting, distant, seductive, passionate, and mystic. She is the object of analysis in one of the major "hymns," "Coloquio de los centauros" (colloquium of the centaurs). The centaur is but another symbol of Darío himself: the head of a man (reason) on the body of an animal (desire). The subject of the centaur's poetic colloquium is the

enigma of life itself, which is quickly linked to woman. Different centaurs relate their encounters with women and how sexual attraction led them to their deaths. Man, like the centaurs, is eternally motivated by his physical desires. The centaur Medon claims to have seen death: She is not the grim reaper but is more like the mythological Diana, chaste and virgin. She wears a wreath of starry roses and holds the palms of triumph in one hand and a cup of the water of forgetfulness in the other. At her feet, love lies like a sleeping dog. She is death, desired (her beauty) and desiring (Diana, the huntress with her dogs). Man is thus trapped between opposites: life (Venus, sexuality) or death (Diana, chastity).

Many of the other poems of *Prosas profanas* merit attention. "The Swan," for example, is a poem that uses one of the most frequently abused symbols of modernist poetry. "Sinfonía en gris mayor" (symphony in gray major) uses synesthesia, a crossing of the senses that is frequently found in modernist poetry. "El reino interior" (the inner kingdom) is another poem that analyzes the contradictions in the poet's mind.

"Yo persigo una forma . . ." (I pursue a form . . .) is a sonnet that closes *Prosas profanas*, ending the volume, as *Azul* ended, on a note of frustration. Despite all he has achieved, Darío has only found the beginning of things, the "bud that seeks to become the rose," and not the fulfillment or triumph for which he had hoped.

Darío left Argentina during the last days of 1898 and went to Spain where, as a reporter for *La Nación*, he wrote about life there at the end of the Spanish-American War. He already had an international literary reputation, and his trip to Spain is a milestone in the development of Latin American literature. Darío carried *Modernismo* with him, and Latin America for the first time began to influence literary and cultural developments in Spain. During his years in Spain, Darío wrote many of the poems collected in the last of his greatest works, *Cantos de vida y esperanza, los cisnes, y otros poemas*.

The volume opens with the autobiographical poem "Yo soy aquel . . ." (I am the one . . .), in which Darío reviews his life and work. It refers to *Azul* and to *Prosas profanas* as well as to the development of a strong, erotic vein in a man who had been a very timid and introverted youth. Darío speaks of the frequent temptation to escape from the ugly reality around him to the ivory tower of art and, above all, to his "sacred jungle." He had just cause to want to escape. Spain was a country in decay and Darío, despite being at the peak of his career, was frequently penniless. He was also plagued by continuing marital problems resulting from his forced marriage in 1893 to Rosario Murillo and his ongoing affair in Spain with Francisca Sánchez. Despite this, Darío closes the poem on an optimistic note, rededicating himself to art because only it, like Jesus, can say: "I am the light, the life and the way."

The poems of *Cantos de vida y esperanza* turn more and more toward Darío's own culture and his own times. Although the poems to Miguel de Cervantes and Francisco de Goya and the "Salutación del optimista" (salute of the optimist) contain Hispanic themes, it is the long poem "A Roosevelt" (to Roosevelt) that constitutes Darío's most memorable political statement. "A Roosevelt" addresses a subject on the minds of many of Darío's fellow Latin Americans: the power and ambitions of the United States. Darío admires the material wealth, energy, and progress of the United States, but he is wary of its recent success in the war with Spain and of its intervention in Panama. Darío warns President Theodore Roosevelt against invading Latin America. He reminds him that Latin America has its ancient heroes and poets, its religion and racial heritage, and that the cubs of the Spanish lion are ready to defend themselves. He also claims that God, a Catholic God, is on their side against the Protestants from the north.

Other poems show Darío becoming increasingly preoccupied with death. In "Melancolía" (melancholy), he wanders blind in search of light. In "Spes" he asks Christ to forgive him after death, and in "Song of Hope" he calls on Christ to save

the world. The flight of time is the theme of "Canción de otoño en primavera" (song of autumn in spring); its famous verse "youth, divine treasure,/ you are going away to never return" is a repeated lament. Woman continues to attract Darío, as the reader finds in "Carne, celeste carne de la mujer" (flesh, heavenly flesh of woman), where she is the "host" of yet another sacrificial offering. In "En el país de las alegorías" (in the country of allegories), woman beckons the poet with the sensual attraction and spiritual enigma of her "sexual rose."

Cantos de vida y esperanza closes with one of Darío's most significant and troubling poems, "Lo fatal" (fatalities). The poet calls the tree and the stone "happy" because they have no feelings. He tells the reader that there is no greater pain than being alive and no greater grief than being conscious. He fears being and not knowing his path in life, or perhaps having already been, or other terrors yet to come. He worries about the certainty of death, the temptations of the flesh, and the open grave that awaits his body. His greatest concerns, however, are more existential: knowing neither where the human race has come from nor where it is going.

The major themes of *Cantos de vida y esperanza* carry over into later collections of Darío's work. *El canto errante* (1907; the wandering song), for example, contains the now-infamous "Salutación al águila" (salute to the eagle), written in 1906 in a moment of optimism and inebriation. Darío invites the United States into Latin America to teach its youth character, persistence, and efficacy. This was a mistake, the mistake of a poet, not a diplomat, and it was not the last political mistake of twentieth century Latin American authors. "Poema del otoño" (autumn song), from a 1910 collection, fairly well depicts the remaining years of Darío's life, in which he was still troubled by the temptations of the flesh and the proximity of death. The poem closes with classic lines in which Darío decides that if he must enter the kingdom of death, he will do so by the road of love.

THE POETRY OF CARLOS DRUMMOND DE ANDRADE

Author: Carlos Drummond de Andrade (1902-1987)
Type of work: Poetry
Principal published works: *Alguma Poesia*, 1930; *Brejo das Almas*, 1934; *Sentimento do Mundo*, 1940; *Poesias*, 1942; *A Rosa do Povo*, 1945; *Poesias até Agora*, 1948; *Claro Enigma*, 1951; *Viola de Bôlso*, 1952; *Fazendeiro do Ar & Poesia Até Agora*, 1955; *50 Poemas Escolhidos pelo Autor*, 1956; *Ciclo*, 1957; *Poemas*, 1959; *Lição de Coisas*, 1962; *Antologia Poética*, 1962; *Obra Completa*, 1964; *In the Middle of the Road: Selected Poems*, 1965; *Versiprosa*, 1967; *José & Outros*, 1967; *Boitempo & A Falta Que Ama*, 1968; *Reunião: 10 Livros de Poesia*, 1969; *Seleta em Prosa e Verso*, 1971; *Poesia Completa e Prosa*, 1973; *Souvenir of the Ancient World*, 1976; *The Minus Sign: Selected Poems*, 1980 (United States; published in England as *The Minus Sign: A Selection from the Poetic Anthology*, 1981); *Traveling in the Family: Selected Poems*, 1987

Poet, essayist, short-story writer, and critic Carlos Drummond de Andrade ranks as one of Brazil's most influential modernist intellectuals. His work, however, is not widely translated into English. Drummond was born in the small town of Itabira, in the iron mining state of Minas Gerais. His work has a mineral clarity through which he examines the self, the world, and the past. Throughout his poems, there is an ironic detachment that often corresponds to a skeptical vision of everyday life.

Drummond's lyric poetry can be divided into four phases. With his diffidently titled first collection *Alguma Poesia* (some poems), he demonstrates an extreme detachment of the self. With the appearance of this collection in 1930, Drummond ushered in the second phase of Brazilian modernism, which eschewed the excesses of the earlier avant-garde. The poems in this collection suggest a reticence in establishing any connection between the self and one's society and thus describe an unresolved tension with the world outside the self.

In 1934, after he had worked as a teacher and journalist, his second collection of poems, *Brejo das Almas* (swamp of souls), was published. At about the same time, he became an adviser to the minister of education. With *Brejo das Almas*, there is a shift from the extremism of the enclosed self—often humorously cavalier—to that of the precarious and diminishing possibilities of the self.

With the advent of World War II, Drummond's poetry became much more socially engaged. In 1945, he left the Ministry of Education and joined the Office of the National Historical and Artistic Heritage, where he remained until his retirement in 1962. With his third and fourth collections, *Sentimento do Mundo* (1940, grief of the world) and *Poesias* (1942, poems), Drummond moved from what is typically described as his individualistic irony to an acute awareness of the world. The fourth and final phase of his poetry begins in the postwar years. In these poems, acceptance of and resignation to one's condition coincide with the awareness of the enigma of things themselves.

The poem "No Meio do Caminho" ("In the Middle of the Road"), from *Alguma Poesia*, demonstrates his initial opposition to a poetic language that deviated from unadorned, direct language. The poem remains startlingly new and provocative in its compression and in its repetition; it clearly announced the challenge offered in Drummond's first book of poems:

In the middle of the road there was a stone
there was a stone in the middle of the road
there was a stone
in the middle of the road there was a stone.

Never should I forget this event
in the life of my fatigued retinas.
Never should I forget that in the middle of the road
there was a stone
there was a stone in the middle of the road
in the middle of the road there was a stone.

As one of his best-known poems, it reveals the sensibility and singular voice found throughout his poetry. The repetition creates a claustrophobic quality: The poem implodes upon itself, becoming as stony as the stone in the middle of the road. The stone is less an ordinary stone than a representation of something within the poet that obsesses him. Such an obsession creates an enclosed self, discontinuous with the world around him. The obsession, like a stone, is enduring and tautological; there is no escape from this condition. Language does not offer any transcendence: It is as concrete, arbitrary, and limited as the stone it attempts to describe.

The possibility of communication is regarded with fatigued skepticism, a hallmark of Drummond's irony. Only the idealist or perfectionist—which describes Drummond—can invoke this ironic need to communicate but to also express the insufficiency of communication. This poem also reveals his distinct view of the word: Like the stone, the word is a concrete entity; it is irreplaceable and has its own enigmatic possibilities. As he writes in a later poem, "Procura da Poesia" ("Search for Poetry") from his 1945 collection *A Rosa do Povo* (the rose of the people), each word "has a thousand secret faces under a neutral face/ and asks you, without interest in the answer,/ poor or terrible, which you will give it:/ Have you brought the key?" The work, like the stone, is indifferent but demanding, an impasse but also an enigma.

An offhanded ease and humor mask the extremism of the belief in self-sufficiency found in many of the poems of *Alguma Poesia*. "Poema de Sete Faces" ("Seven-Sided Poem") opens with the disarmingly comic lines, "When I was born, one of the crooked/ angels who live in shadow, said:/ Carlos, go on! Be *gauche* in life." The angel—who is doubly hobbled by the qualifier "crooked" and its residence, "in shadow"—dismisses the world, goading the narrator to be "*gauche* in life." Like a cubist painting, the succeeding six stanzas present different aspects of a personality, each discontinuous from the others. Drummond refuses any resolution. Instead, he closes the poem with mock intimacy: "I oughtn't to tell you,/ but this moon,/

and this brandy/ play the devil with one's emotions." Through the subversive junction of the high romantic symbol of the moon and the colloquial phrasing of the last line, the poet refuses to construct a coherent, unified self; instead, Drummond presents readers with a multiplicity of selves or states of mind. The modern self, as suggested in this poem, is not so much alienated as fractured and discontinuous in its insularity.

Before turning away from this remarkable first collection of poems, it is important to point out the thematic focus on family and memory that Drummond would develop throughout his poetry. In the poem "Infância" ("Infancy"), the poet creates dramatic irony by showing an absorbed child unaware of the history of colonialism that surrounds him and that he reads in "the story of Robinson Crusoe,/ the long story that never comes to an end." The aura of nostalgia for one's birthplace—the poem invokes fields, horses, mango trees, and family—masks the countermemory of slavery. The servant's voice that "called us for coffee" had "learned/ lullabies long ago in the slave-quarters—and never forgot." Within the insularity of nostalgia, this intrusion of historical or social memory is momentary: "*Shh*—don't wake the boy./ She stopped the cradle when a mosquito had lit/ and gave a sigh . . . how deep!" The final couplet—"And I didn't know that my story/ was prettier than that of Robinson Crusoe"—is profoundly paradoxical. Is the narrator completely smug, or is he self-deprecatingly ironic, as conveyed through the comparative "prettier"? Perhaps this is ironic in a more literary sense, in that the narrator invokes that archetype of colonial self-sufficiency, Robinson Crusoe, who ironically made his fortune, in Daniel Defoe's novel, through his Brazilian plantations?

In 1934, after self-publishing his first collection of poems, Drummond published *Brejo das Almas*. With this collection begins the breakdown of the defiant, but defensive, stance of self-sufficiency. Realizing the failure of such a stance, the speakers in the poems of *Brejo das Almas* yearn for connections with the world. Connections with the world, however, are doomed, as expressed in the hyperbolic lines opening "Sonêto da Perdida Esperança"

("Sonnet of Lost Hope"): "I missed the streetcar and my hope./ Pale, I return home./ The street is useless and no car/ would run over my body." The poem equates everyday frustrations with larger, inner emotional failures, which leads to a perception of the insignificance of oneself. The poem expresses a condition of not knowing one's true condition; thus it invokes the terrifying element of the absurd: "I don't know if I am suffering/ or if somebody is just having fun." These lines suggest omnipotent forces manipulating the speaker. The lines are tinged with the sense of persecution and paranoia. The poem closes with the reflection that affirmation once was possible, but that impulse is now lost: "And yet, long ago long ago/ we cried: yes! to the eternal." The loss of hope suggests the withdrawal of the ideal, the idea of truth, or the eternal.

The loss of the eternal also implies a theological retreat. This theme arises in "Romaria" ("Pilgrimage"), found in Drummond's first collection, where "Already tired of so many petitions, Jesus/ sleeps dreaming of another humanity." Although this earlier poem suggests the insularity of the divine and a rejection of creation, in *Brejo das Almas*, this rejection becomes apocalyptic and destructive. In "Aurora" ("Dawn"), the narrator reports that "Everything was beyond repair./ Nobody knew that the world was going to end"; or from "Segrêdo" ("Secret"), "Suppose that an angel of fire/ swept the face of the earth/ and the sacrificed men/ asked for mercy." This apocalyptic sensibility is most often translated into the act of suicide, the extreme response to a world that seems useless and to the uselessness of suffering in such a world. Such a response is seen as mundane, as exemplified in "Poema Patético" ("Pathetic Poem"). The narrator responds once to the question "What kind of noise is that on the stairs?" that "it is the man who closed the door/ and hanged himself in the curtains." His subsequent responses to this repeated question, however, become more enigmatic and suggest the secret, incomprehensible world outside the self. The noise "is the still moon upon the plates/ and the cutlery shining in the pantry" or it is "the virgin with a trombone."

The ambivalence of the poems in *Brejo das Almas* can be summarily described in these lines from "Não Se Mate" ("Don't Kill Yourself"): "It's useless to resist/ or to commit suicide." Any action is seen as futile; the possibility of any relationship, the idea of love, is equally frustrated: "today a kiss, tomorrow no kiss,/ day after tomorrow's Sunday/ and nobody knows what will happen/ Monday." The ordinary, colloquial language of these lines furthers the skeptical sensibility that informs so much of Drummond's poetry. This skepticism, however, prepares Drummond for the poems that follow these first two books. The destructive stasis of "Não Se Mate" forces the later poems to turn outward.

In the third phase of Drummond's work, he writes in "Mãos Dadas" ("Hand in Hand"), from *Sentimendo do Mundo*, that "I will not be the poet of a ruptured world," nor will he be either sentimental or a utopian; instead "Time is my matter, time now, men now,/ life now." This marks his turn toward social commentary as the dominant element of his poetry. This turn away from the inward, self-sufficient, and nihilistic is enunciated in what becomes his *ars poetica*, the poem "Procura da Poesia" ("Search for Poetry"). In this poem, Drummond advises future poets: "Do not tell me your feelings,/ which capitalize on ambiguity and attempt the long journey./ What you think and feel, that is not yet poetry." Poetry is not merely the rendering of powerful feelings; rather, it is centered on language and the accuracy of the words themselves.

Among Brazilians, "José" from *Poesias* is perhaps one of Drummond's most popular poems. It exemplifies his sociopolitical poetry, in which he becomes increasingly colloquial and realistic as well as depending on repetitive structures that serve as refrains. The poem creates in the figure of José a human symbol of Brazil, with constant struggles with its economy, poverty, the despoliation of its environment, and its corruption:

> What now, José?
> The party's over,
> the lights are off,

> the gang has gone,
> the night has grown cold,
> what now, José?

After these opening lines, the poem catalogs the social failures of Brazil. This poem not only reveals Drummond's political beliefs but also typifies the antibourgeois sentiments of his generation's intellectuals.

If "José" offers a vision of social failure, the long poem "Canto ao Homem do Povo Charlie Chaplin" ("Song to the Man of the People: Charlie Chaplin"), from *A Rosa do Povo*, provides a vision of compassion. Drawing on the visionary capacities of the American poet Walt Whitman, especially his *Leaves of Grass* (1855), Drummond assumes an all-embracing stance:

> Through me speak those who were dirty with
>   sadness and a fierce disgust for everything,
> who entered the movie house with the anguish
>   of rats running away from life,
> there are two hours of anesthesia, let's listen to
>   some music
> let's visit the images in the dark—and they
>   discovered you and were saved.

The poet, like Chaplin through film, assumes the socially ethical role of being the voice through which those who are voiceless can be heard. The long lines and the inclusive lists of those the poet speaks for—"those abandoned by justice, the simple of heart,/ the pariahs, the failures, the mutilated, the deficient, the downtrodden"—recall Whitman's lines. As Chaplin portrayed so many men, he became a cinematic version of this Whitmanian voice, this "friend/ we would like to hold on to/ in the rain, in the mirror, in the memory,/ and yet whom we have lost." By reinvoking Chaplin and Whitman, the poet hopes to instill again a sense of compassion, to invoke again the possibility of a socially redemptive love.

After World War II, Drummond's poetry developed yet another voice that had been otherwise far less dominant, one more reflective and philosophical. As a response to the previous period of his poetry, the poem "Amar" ("To Love"), from his 1951 collection *Claro Enigma* (clear enigma), asks rhetorically, "What else can a creature do/ among creatures but love?" The difficulties of love in the earlier phases of Drummond's poetry are overcome here, in that the poet sees in the Whitmanian embrace, in the unconditional love for the other, the only resolution to social injustice. The poems become conciliatory, though always on the rigorous terms of the language. The poet does not acquiesce but remains always honest about himself. In so doing, he enables himself to love or to offer love.

The remarkable long poem "A Mesa" ("The Table"), also from *Claro Enigma*, exemplifies the conciliatory potentials of memory and love. In this poem, as in many of his poems of this later phase, the speaker is surrounded by his family as he silently addresses his dead father. Here the process of experience, complete with its discord and frustrations, provides the speaker with the capacity for love. The image of the shared meal conveys the idea of communion and the necessity of sharing in life and hope. The emphasis on the family indicates Drummond's turn from the social to the intimate, for it is here that he finds life. His language in "A Mesa" is almost the language of belief. It is not, however, a theological belief or a return to his early Jesuit education, but a belief—even after death—of life and the capacity, however tenuous, to love:

> Now you are above us,
> and above this dinner
> to which we summoned you
> so far—at last—to love you
> and loving, delude ourselves
> at a table that is
>
>   empty.

Drummond's skepticism remains, but overshadowing it is a consummation, an embrace of self and other.

THE POETRY OF NICOLÁS GUILLÉN

Author: Nicolás Guillén (1902-1989)
Type of work: Poetry
Principal published works: *Motivos de son*, 1930, 1980; *Sóngoro cosongo: Poemas mulatos*, 1931, 1981; *West Indies, Ltd.: Poemas*, 1934; *Cantos para soldados y sones para turistas*, 1937, 1952, 1957; *España: Poema en cuatro angustias y una esperanza*, 1937; *El son entero: suma poética, 1929-1946*, 1947; *Cuba Libre: Poems by Nicolás Guillén*, 1948; *Elegía a Jesús Menéndez*, 1951, 1962, 1982; *Elegía cubana*, 1952; *La paloma de vuelo popular. Elegias*, 1948, 1959, 1965; *Buenos días, Fidel*, 1959; *Sus mejores poemas*, 1959; *Poesías*, 1962; *Poemas de amor*, 1964; *Tengo*, 1964 (*English translation*, 1974); *Che comandante*, 1967; *Cuatro canciones para el Che*, 1969; *El gran zoo*, 1967, 1971; *El diario que a diario*, 1972, 1979 (*The Daily Daily*, 1989); *La rueda dentada*, 1972; *Man-Making Words: Selected Poems of Nicolas Guillen*, 1972; *Patria o muerte! The Great Zoo and Other Poems by Nicolás Guillén*, 1972; *Obra poética, 1920-1972*, 1974 (2 vols.); *El corazón con que vivo*, 1975; *Poemas manuables*, 1975; *Por el mar de las Antillas anda un barco de papel*, 1977; *Sol de domingo*, 1982

Although Nicolás Guillén's poems are rooted in Cuba's specific cultural and political circumstances, this local focus has by no means limited their international appeal. Guillén's work has been widely anthologized in Latin America, and his poems have been translated into more than thirty languages.

Even before he was named Cuba's poet laureate and president of the National Union of Cuban Writers and Artists in 1961, Guillén had been closely identified with the anti-imperialist movements that, in 1959, culminated with the Cuban Revolution. If much of his later, postrevolutionary poetry was dedicated to exalting the achievements of Fidel Castro's regime, his earlier poems' repeated calls for a classless and raceless society earned him a reputation as prophet of the revolution. Even though Guillén's commitment to Cuban Marxism lends a certain thematic coherence to most of his poetry, to cast that poetry purely in this particular political mold does not do it justice. Critics who read Guillén's poems primarily as sociopolitical documents tend to neglect the fact that Guillén was an important literary innovator and a meticulous cultural historian.

Perhaps the best description of Guillén's poetic writings is that they are attempts at unraveling what he calls, in his preface to *Sóngoro cosongo* (1931), Cuba's (and the Caribbean's) intricate cultural "hieroglyphics." His poetry as a whole is engaged in distilling a distinctive literature from the many disparate and conflicting ingredients that make up what his compatriot and teacher Fernando Ortiz termed the cultural stew of the Hispanic Caribbean. A mulatto from one of Cuba's black middle-class families, Guillén was keenly aware that modern Cuba was not, as has often been claimed, the "whitest" island in the Caribbean and that his country's national literature had to take into account both African and Hispanic cultural contributions.

Unlike the Francophone Caribbean Negritude poets who were his contemporaries, Guillén was interested neither in proclaiming black superiority nor in nostalgically recovering Africa as a lost diasporic origin. Nor did he create in his poetry a symbolic system comparable to that of the Black Arts movement that emerged in the United States during the 1960's. Guillén, as he proclaims in "La voz esperanzada" (the hopeful voice) at the end of *España* (1937), is a "son of America,/ son of [Spain] and of Africa." He was a poet preoccupied with cross-cultural phenomena and with the challenge of translating the complexities of Cuban race relations into equally complex literary forms.

A prime example of such formal complexity is the *poema-son* (or *son*-poem), perhaps Guillén's most significant literary accomplishment, which he used for the first time in *Motivos de son* (1930). This collection of eight short poems written in Afro-Cuban vernacular, which were eventually set to music, provoked a controversy unparalleled in Cuban literary history. Although their initial reception was largely enthusiastic, some critics were disturbed not only by Guillén's dramatization of topics such as racial stereotyping, prostitution, and urban poverty but also by the aesthetic and social implications of Guillén's literary use of the *son*, a popular musical form with a strong black component. Guillén's *poemas-son* were indeed a daring literary experiment, one that amounted to a bold symbolic statement about the racially mixed origins of Cuban culture and literature.

Popularized in the 1920's and 1930's by, among others, the famous Trio Matamoros, the *son* foregrounds the question of what constitutes Cuba's national identity. This question is central to all of Guillén's poetry. A vital expression of Cuba's fundamental *mestizaje* (miscegenation or transculturation), the *poema-son* is also part of a larger framework: It exemplifies the interaction among European, African, and Amerindian cultures in the New World and thus encourages readers to acknowledge such sustained cross-cultural exchanges as the origin of American literatures. Guillén's insistence on African contributions to a culture that regarded (and still regards) itself as white was at least as upsetting to some of his contemporaries as the overtly racial themes of the *Motivos* and the resemblance of their poetic voices to those of certain black and mulatto characters who were popularized in nineteenth century Cuba's antislavery novels.

Motivos de son, along with *Sóngoro cosongo* and *West Indies, Ltd.* (1934), is considered as part of the Afro-Antillean movement that evolved in Cuba during the mid- to late 1920's, partly as a consequence of postwar Europe's anthropological interest in and artistic "rediscovery" of African and African American cultures. In Cuba, the anthropologist Fernando Ortiz was instrumental in preparing the path for the Afro-Antillean movement, the members of which included the novelist-to-be Alejo Carpentier, the Puerto Rican poet Luis Palés

Matos, and the Cuban poets Emilio Ballagas, Ramón Guirao, and José Zacarías Tallet.

With *Motivos* and *Sóngoro cosongo*, Guillén turned away from the more conventionally modernist, often trite, sonnets and ballads he had written during the early 1920's, poems that were collected as *Cerebro y corazón* (brain and heart) in 1922 but not published until 1962. He began to develop a form of vernacular poetry distinctly his own. What distinguished these poems from those of the Latin American modernists who had influenced Guillén's earlier verse, notably Rubén Darío and José Asunción Silva, was their consistent use of African and particularly Afro-Cuban words and phrases such as the untranslatable *sóngoro cosongo* and "Mayombe, bombe, mayombé" from "Sensemayá: Canto para matar una culebra" (sensemayá: chant for killing a snake). The latter quotation is an example of a poetic line that, for rhythmic purposes, ends on a stressed syllable. To the ears of a Spanish reader, this would have a cacophonous rather than a pleasing effect. A break with Spanish poetic convention, this peculiar Africanized accentuation became one of the hallmarks of Guillén's Afro-Cuban poems. The so-called *jitanjáfora* that Guillén used amounted to more than (presumably) nonsensical words employed simply for their rhythmic properties. It was both a literary and a political strategy in the battle against racial discrimination and neocolonialism in a prerevolutionary Cuba largely controlled by the economic and political interests of the United States.

More so than *Motivos* and *Sóngoro cosongo*, the 1934 collection *West Indies, Ltd.*, which includes "Sensemayá," is a veritable microcosm of all the major forms and themes that Guillén would chisel and hone during the long course of his poetic career. Focusing not only on Cuba but on the economic plight of all Caribbean countries as well, the long title poem, "West Indies, Ltd.," emphasizes the value of shared cultural practices as a possible antidote to U.S. imperialism. A collage of many different poetic forms, "West Indies, Ltd." is also the first example of Guillén's peculiar use of the long poem, a form he develops further in the *elegías* (elegies) during the 1940's and 1950's and perfects in *El diario que a diario* (1972; *The Daily Daily*, 1989).

West Indies, Ltd., like the two volumes that preceded it, is a systematic effort to call attention to "the fleeting tender dark shadow of the [African] grandfather,/ who put an indelible curl into your yellow hair," as Guillén put it so well in "El abuelo" (the grandfather). By contrast, his next two books, *Cantos para soldados y sones para turistas* (songs for soldiers and *sones* for tourists) and *España: Poema en cuatro angustias y una esperanza* (Spain: poem in four anguishes and one hope), strike a much more overtly militant note. These poems' more aggressive political tone may well have resulted from the changing intellectual climate in Cuba after the downfall of dictator Gerardo Machado in 1933. What moves to the forefront of Guillén's poetry in those years is a strong advocacy of solidarity across racial, class, and national boundaries, a theme that echoes his own political activities. In 1937, the year during which these two volumes were published, Guillén officially joined the Cuban Communist Party. In *Cantos*, dedicated to Guillén's father, who had been the victim of a political assassination in 1917, Guillén portrays the soldier as potential revolutionary and ally of the *sonero*, the singer who confronts American tourists in poems such as "José Ramón Cantaliso." The most popular of his soldier poems, "No sé por qué piensas tú" (I don't know why you should think), once again returns to the *son* form.

Although poems such as "Soldados en Abisinia" (soldiers in Abyssinia) explicitly contextualize Guillén's revolutionary concerns within an internationalist framework by linking Latin America's neocolonial situation with Africa's, *España* shifts the focus to the Spanish Civil War. At once a political declaration of solidarity and a literary homage, especially to the Andalusian poet Federico García Lorca, who had visited Cuba in 1930, *España* closes on an optimistic note, in "La voz esperanzada" (the hopeful voice), and with a reaffirmation of Guillén's identity as not merely a Cuban but an American poet.

In the 1940's and 1950's, Guillén traveled extensively and almost incessantly, both within and outside Latin America. He attended writers' and peace conferences all over the world. In 1954, he was awarded the Lenin Peace Prize. His anti-Batista activities in Cuba during the early 1950's forced him into a six-year exile in Chile, Paris, and Buenos Aires, respectively. *La paloma de vuelo popular* (the dove of popular flight), which was published in 1958 together with a collection of six *elegías*, indirectly comments on those travels by combining an acute sense of exile, in "Exilio" (exile) and "Canción puertorriqueña" (Puerto Rican song), with the desire to embrace Latin America, Europe, the Soviet Union, and China in an abiding gesture of peace enscribed in the title's image of the flying dove. On the other hand, topics already familiar from the early Afro-Cuban volumes, particularly United States imperialism and racism, recur both in *La paloma* and in the *elegías*. Guillén's tone is more urgent, and his language, especially in "Pequeña letanía grotesca en la muerte del senador McCarthy" (short grotesque litany on the death of Senator McCarthy), "Little Rock," and "Elegía a Emmett Till" (elegy for Emmett Till), is often that of bitter satire.

Upon his return to Cuba only weeks after the triumph of Castro's rebel army, Guillén undertook a variety of projects on behalf of the revolution. He worked as a journalist, gave numerous public poetry readings, and helped found the National Union of Cuban Writers and Artists. In 1964, he published *Tengo* (I have) not only to praise revolutionary achievements but also to articulate the need for a solid cultural foundation that would nourish the revolutionary spirit. Rather than categorically rejecting a past marked by neocolonial dependence on the United States, *Tengo* revisits Cuban history to highlight those of its aspects that had often been ignored, notably the undeniable and sustained influence of Afro-Cuban popular culture on Cuba's national culture. Guillén's sweeping, yet very detailed, historical and literary revisionism continues in *La rueda dentada* (the gear) and especially in *El diario que a diario* (*The Daily Daily*), both of which appeared in 1972.

Extravagant experiments in form characterize *El diario* much more so than they do *La rueda*, which remains closer to the more familiar lyricism of *Tengo*. *El diario*'s most immediate precursor is the 1967 volume *El gran zoo* (the great zoo), a long poem as raucously humorous as it is viciously satirical. Both poems stand in a direct line of descent from *Motivos*. To combine the two different literary traditions and genres with ease and elegance has been typical of Guillén's poetry from the very start; *El gran zoo* is no exception in this regard. This poem is a bestiary in the long tradition of Aesop, Jean de La Fontaine, Guillaume Apollinaire, Jorge Luis Borges, and Pablo Neruda. Guillén's bestiary specifically harks back to the chronicles of the Indies, the initial accounts of the New World that told of the existence of all kinds of fabulous creatures that, for Guillén, become the stuff of a "marvelous American reality" (in Alejo Carpentier's well-known phrase). *El gran zoo* announces what *El diario que a diario* will confirm, that the chronicles are important foundational texts for Latin American novelists and poets alike.

After the *Motivos de son* and its poetic use of popular musical forms, *El diario que a diario* is Guillén's most radical poetic experiment. A sixty-four-page collage that joins Guillén the poet with Guillén the journalist, this poem poses as both a newspaper and a historical chronicle. It assembles myriad fragments from all walks and periods of Cuban life: editorials, newspaper clippings, advertisements, public announcements, and sonnets. *El diario* is an extensive and intricate play on language, poetic convention, and traditional boundaries between the literary and the nonliterary. Although the poem's five-part structure, in which each part corresponds to a different stage in Cuba's historical development, and its epic range from the island's discovery and conquest by Spain to the months just prior to the revolution, suggest chronology as an organizing principle, Guillén's real interest lies with ordering history differently, imaginatively. This new order seems frequently to border on chaos, and its result is a satirical anti-epic that indulges in the kind of baroque "stylelessness" that Carpentier regarded as the most salient feature of Latin American cultural realities. What confer some sense of order in this unwieldy poem are references to Afro-Cuban carnival, specifically to the "Día de Reyes" (Day of Kings), on which, during the nineteenth century, African slaves were symbolically freed for one day. Guillén had used this colonial carnival as a model for resistance to cultural and political oppressions as early as the poem "Sensemayá," where it undermines the official image of Cuba as culturally "white." In *El diario*, this same image and strategy of resistance, in this case to Spanish colonialism and to U.S. imperialism, asserts Cuban cultural and political independence. It becomes the basis for a distinctive poetics of "Cubanness."

A close reading of *El diario* shows that Guillén is no less preoccupied in his late work with exploring the salient contributions of Afro-Cuban culture to his country's national identity than he had been at the beginning of his poetic career. *Sol de domingo* (Sunday's sun), a collection of previously unpublished prose and poetry from as early as the 1920's, printed in celebration of Guillén's eightieth birthday, seconds the poet's ultimate refusal to place his writing in the service of any one political doctrine or regime. According to Guillén, the task of the poet, and especially of a national poet laureate, is both that of the careful chronicler and of the relentless critic of society. As he put it succinctly in the "not strictly necessary little prologue" that opens *El diario*:

> In the beginning I was the notary,
> dust-covered and in no hurry,
> inventor of the inventory.
> Today I play a different part:
> I am the Daily that daily
> forewarns you and puts you on guard.

THE POETRY OF JOSÉ-MARÍA DE HEREDIA

Author: José-María de Heredia (1842-1905)
Type of work: Poetry
Principal published work: *Les trophées*, 1893 (*Sonnets of José-María de Heredia*, 1897)

José-María de Heredia produced translations, discourses, and critical works, but it is for his poetry that he is most noted. Winner of the prize of the Concours Archon-Despérouses in 1893 and elected to the Académie Française in 1894, Heredia became one of the most respected poets both in France and in his native Cuba. Although his sonnets were mainly written in French, Heredia published three sonnets in Spanish that were dedicated to his famous cousin, a romantic poet, for whom he was named. The memorial sonnets composed for this cousin's centenary in 1903 brought attention throughout the Spanish American literary world. These Spanish sonnets later formed part of Heredia's only collection, *Les trophées*. *Les trophées* became an immediate success and was translated into Spanish in South America and Mexico as well as into other languages, including Norse, Russian, Romanian, Serbian, Czech, Polish, Greek, Japanese, and English.

Heredia's goal was to create a perfect model of beauty in poetry. He used the strict rules of the sonnet to perfect artistic form. Heredia explained why he used the sonnet form in a letter to Edmund Gosse in 1896.

> If I have kept to the sonnet it is because I find that in its mystical and mathematical form . . . it demands through its brevity and difficulty an awareness in its execution and a concentration of thought which cannot but rouse and spur on to perfection an artist worthy of that fine name.

Through his concise sonnet form, Heredia adhered to the Parnassian tendency of precision of method while acknowledging the significance of Symbolist poetry. As a Parnassian, Heredia found the ideal of beauty in classical Greece, but he thought that all effective poets were Symbolists. Heredia evoked the past in an impersonal, objective manner and, on an aesthetic level, treated themes such as love, death, and the transience of life.

Heredia divided *Les trophées* into five sections: "La Grèce et la Sicile" ("Poems of Greece and Sicily"), "Rome et les barbares" ("Rome and the Barbarians"), "Le Moyen Age et la Renaissance" ("The Middle Ages and the Renaissance"), "L'Orient et les Tropiques" ("The Orient and the Tropics"), and "La nature et le rêve" ("Nature and Dream"). Heredia unified these five divisions through historical development. *Les trophées* depicts the heroic moments of previous epochs that show the fragile condition of humanity.

In "L'Oubli" ("Oblivion"), the introductory poem of the first section, Heredia introduces the message indicated by the title of the work through the image of a ruined Greek temple. This temple refers to a ruined monument that reflects the poet's nostalgia for past eras. The first quatrain equates humanity's perishable condition with the ruined temple: "The ruined temple crowns the promontory./ By death commingled in this wild domain/ Bronze God and marble Goddess long have lain;/ their only shroud the grass that hides their glory." Heredia suggests the perishable condition of humanity by juxtaposing the ruined temple with the decaying God and Goddess, relics formed from durable materials. In the second quatrain, he contrasts them with the permanence of nature's elements such as the sky, the sea, and the earth: "Alone, at times, some shepherd flutes their story,/ Leading his flock to drink, the old refrain/ Filling the tranquil skies that arch the main,/ His figure limned against them, dark and hoary." Heredia insists on human fragility by indicating that even the grass has more durability. Heredia does, however refer to the shepherd's "old refrain," thereby affirming the survival of humanity. This first quatrain is linked to the first tercet by synecdoche in order to show the role of nature in protecting the temple with its traditions. Heredia replaces the term "temple" in the first quatrain with "capital," the top part of the temple's column: "Yet to the Gods maternal earth is kind;/ With fresh acanthus, vain solitude,/ Each shattered capital she strives to bind." It is the acanthus that holds together the ancient temple. This plant also suggests a covering that hides the temple, because in the last tercet the poet indicates that people are oblivious to the destruction of the temple, which represents the ancient traditions: "But man, now careless of the ancient mood,/ Serenely hears, with no ancestral fright,/ The wild sea mourn the Sirens in the night." Here, Heredia underlines the main idea of the sonnet: The memories of the past disappear without any regrets. The final line concisely summarizes the sonnet and provides nasal sounds that emphasize the sorrow of this oblivion.

Heredia also uses the Greek sonnets to introduce two recurring themes: the purity of the freshly created world and the savage condition of primitive life. "La Naissance d'Aphrodite" ("The Birth of Aphrodite") embodies these two themes. In this sonnet, Heredia portrays the purity of the freshly created world through the beauty of spring and summer. "And never Spring brought stormy skies nor bright/ Suns bursting from the clouds with sudden light,/ Nor Summer came, her bounty to disburse." Heredia associates Aphrodite's birth with the creation of art: "The Ocean opened! From its clasping flood/ Rose Kypris, radiantly nude, the true,/ The foam-born blossom of celestial blood." Heredia also shows the uncivilized condition of primitive life through the gods of Olympus: "The High Gods, knowing neither mirth nor sport,/ Upon Olympus' snows held their wild court./ But heaven let fall the germinating dew." "The Birth of Aphrodite" thus reveals Heredia's positive attitude toward life in an objective manner, with nature triumphing over the brutal behavior of these gods.

Heredia develops the theme of the brutal condition of primitive life in several other Greek sonnets, a theme discussed in the following examples. "La Chasse" ("The Chase") portrays Artemis, goddess of the hunt, who terrorizes the people of the woods: "The hounds of Artemis the pathway take,/ Baying deep-mouthed for slaughter and for blood;/ While on their track, shafts hurtling from her bow,/ Hair streaming, breathless, furious, all aglow,/ The Goddess bounds and terror fills the wood." "Nemée" ("Nemea") presents a struggle between a lion and Hercules:

> He shrieks. Nemea's terror he descries
> > With jaws agape against the bloody skies,
> > Ferocious fangs and ruffled mane erect;
> For, towering through the shade crepuscular,
> His figure in the frightful skin bedecked,
> > More beast than man seems Hercules afar.

"Jason and Medée" ("Jason and Medea") depicts the jealous wrath of Medea: "Love smiles upon them, but the fatal Bride,/ Bearing her philtres and her jealous pride,/ Her father and her Gods will not forsake." Finally, "Thermodon" ("The Thermodon") reveals the defeat of the Amazons in a bloody battle: "Toward flaming Themiscyra, which all day/ Has trembled with the shock of cavalry,/ Thermodon's sombre flood bears mournfully/ The slain whose arms and chariots drift away."

Heredia further illustrates the themes of primitive violence in the Greek sonnets through the presentation of passion and animal instinct. In fact, many figures are both animal and human or divine. These creatures include the centaurs, Pan, and the Sphinx; they underline the struggle between animal instincts and the higher goals of humans. Although "La Centauresse" ("The Centauress") reflects animal instincts and "Nessus" reflects human desire, both poems depict the nostalgia of the lost innocence of an unattainable paradise. In the following two poems, Heredia uses the technique of ascribing the violent qualities in humans to a Greek supernatural figure. "Pan" presents the carnal desire of an insensitive god to abduct a naked nymph, carrying her into the forest: "But from the copse the God, with one great bound,/ Bursts, grasps her, vanishes, and as the sound/ Of mocking laughter dies the wood is still." "The Sphinx" illustrates the destructive effects of desire. Heredia changes the mythological Greek Sphinx who killed the Thebans for not solving her riddles into an appealing monster who kills the victims she embraces:

> —Approach me not! Ah, my lips thirst for
> thine!—
> —Then come! My arms that clasp can
> strangle too;
> My talons rend thy flesh. . . . —But if thy kiss
> I conquer, let the penalty be mine!—
> —In vain thy triumph!   Kiss and
> die!—O bliss!

The sonnet associates desire with pleasure and suffering.

In the second division of poems, "Rome and the Barbarians," Heredia modifies the themes previously introduced. The brutality of the primitive Greek world is changed into more organized violence, and the newness of creation is replaced by the nostalgic dream of a simpler life in which people can communicate with the gods. In fact, the gods are scarcely represented in the Roman poems.

Heredia's knowledge of the history of the Roman Empire becomes especially apparent in his treatment of organized violence in "La Trebbia" ("The Trebbia") and "Après Cannes" ("After Cannæ"). Based upon Livy's historical account of the Punic wars, the two sonnets describe Hannibal's victories over Rome. "La Trebbia" establishes nature's ominous warnings concerning the outcome of the organized violence. The Roman Consul Sempronius, desiring glory, plans to attack Hannibal who, in contrast, is confidently waiting for the appearance of the Roman legion:

> Scornful of Scipio and of augured ill,
>   Of Trebbia's rage, of wind and rain, once more
>   Sempronius bids his lictors march before
> His host as new-won glory fires his will.
>
> . . . .
>   From afar is heard
> An elephant. Beneath the bridge's arch,
> Hannibal harks, by victory unstirred,
>   The hollow thunder of his legions' march.

In "After Cannæ," Heredia portrays the paralyzing fear and helplessness of the people of Rome through the stylistic techniques of enjambment and truncated rhythm: "One Consul slain, one to Liter-

num fled/ Or to Venusia." The enjambment of the third line into the fourth adds auditory and visual effects: "Heaven frowns, a bolt, lays low/ The Capitol. Toward the end of the sonnet, Heredia's characteristic flexibility of the caesura, or pause, of the twelve-syllable alexandrine line and the enjambment re-creates the sounds of the Roman people rushing to their deaths: "Each evening to the aqueducts the spawn/ Of the Subura, all the rabble, rush,/ From prison and cloaca vomited." In these two sonnets, the poet associates death with both eternal life and heroic actions. The death of the soldier thus appears to acquire meaning because of his heroic actions, which become monuments to his earthly endeavors.

In the third division, "The Middle Ages and the Renaissance," Heredia indicates that artistic achievement is also worthy of being termed a monument. Although "Le Vieil Orfèvre" ("The Old Goldsmith") and "Sur le livre des amours de Pierre de Ronsard" ("For Ronsard's 'Book of Loves'") specifically reflect Heredia's concept of artistic survival, the second sonnet clarifies it:

> All die; Cassandre, thou, Marie, Hélène!
>   Dust, too, would be your bodies once so fair,
>   (No morrow, rose nor lily, may be thine)
> Did not Ronsard, by yellow Loire or Seine,
> Around your foreheads, with immortal care,
>   Love's myrtle and the bays of glory twine.

The above sonnet thus links artistic achievement with immortality.

In "The Middle Ages and the Renaissance," Heredia considers his Spanish heritage to be another monument. The poet was directly related to the conquistador Don Pedro de Heredia from Aragon, who sailed with Christopher Columbus to the New World. Heredia's Spanish heritage supplied him with a vivid imagination. The quatrains of "Les Conquérants" ("The Conquistadores") portray the conquistadores in their preparation for the voyage to the New World, and the tercets reveal the beauty of the New World that makes people dream. The first line of the poem, "As from their native eyries hawks take wing," creates the tone of the sonnet. The image of the flying birds of prey suggests the conquistadores, who want to find lasting glory through their discoveries. These discoverers dream of the grandeur of unknown lands: "Sail drunk with dreams that brutal conquests bring./ They seek the treasure fabulous to wring/ From the far mines Cipango's mountains bear,/ The trade winds fill their sails and waft them where/ Mysterious western shores lie beckoning." The final line of the poem, "Strange stars ascend from Ocean's depths unseen," signals Heredia's innovative style. Instead of summarizing the thematic development of the poem, as in a traditional sonnet, the final line focuses on the conquerors' amazing discovery.

The fourth division, "The Orient and the Tropics," contains two themes: the mysterious beauty of life and eternity. The sonnets concerning the Orient or Egypt illustrate both themes by the animation of the ancient sphinx, whereas the poems pertaining to the tropics not only portray the mysterious beauties of life but also reflect the tropical setting of the author's childhood in Cuba. The theme of the mysterious beauty of life is especially exemplified in "Le Récif de corail" ("The Coral Reef"), which induces the reader to envision marine life at the bottom of the ocean. Although Heredia does not present any concrete idea in the sonnet, he begins with a logical description of the immobile coral reef by means of the precise selection of vowels and consonants, thereby adding visual and auditory emphasis to the mysterious atmosphere: "The sun beneath the sea, mysterious dawn,/ Illumes the dusk the coral forests keep,/ Where mingled thrive in Ocean valleys deep/ The quickened flora and the growing spawn." The immobility of the above scene suggested by the alexandrine line is broken in the second tercet to show the fish's mobility: "Then swift his fin strikes flaming from below/ And makes across the unrippled surface run/ Tremors of pearl, of emerald and gold." The final line returns to the regular alexandrine form, indicating the diminished energy of the fish. The beautiful ocean will again resume its calm display of colorful imagery.

Heredia continues his presentation of the mysteries of nature in his final division, "La nature et le rêve" ("Nature and Dream"). The first part of this section deals with the role of the sea in the lives of the people of Brittany, and the later sonnets emphasize the main themes of *Les trophées*: death, heroism, superior achievement, and immortality. "La Mort de l'aigle" ("Death of the Eagle") illustrates these themes with a soaring eagle that, because of lightning, dies while trying to ascend to greater heights. The tercets clarify this concept:

> A wild scream, and the vortex whirls him down;
>   Sublime, he drinks the flames that round
>   him hiss
>   And plunges, shriveled, into the abyss.
> What joy, for Liberty and Glory's crown,
> In pride of might and ecstasy's uplift,
>   To die a death so dazzling and so swift!

The eagle portrayed in the above quotation represents the higher aspirations of humans and dies a heroic death because of its lofty ideal. In "La Vie des morts" ("Life of the Dead"), Heredia also relates the idea of death to immortality and achievement on Earth.

The final sonnet of *Les trophées*, "Sur un marbre brisé" ("On a Broken Statue"), returns to the theme of the initial Greek sonnets: human fragility. It presents the deteriorated marble figure of an ancient god that is covered with vegetation. This god miraculously comes to life for a short time, but, like people who have hopes of attaining high goals, he cannot endure nature. Heredia describes this condition in the following manner:

> The pious moss has closed its mournful eyes;
>   In this drear wood, its task to once define,
>   They seek in vain the Nymph that poured
>   the wine
> On the idyllic spot where now it lies.
> Erewhile, viburnum and the ivy rise,
>   Careless, around the wreckage once divine,
>   If Pan, or Faun, or Hermes they entwine,
> Or what green horns its broken brow surprise.
> Behold! A slanting beam, caressing yet
>   Its flattened face, inserts two orbs of gold,
>   The vine a red lip laughing from the sod;
> And wind and leaf in moving magic met,
> And sun and shadow as they shift and hold,
>   Of this old marble make a living God.

"On a Broken Statue" concludes the thematic presentation in Heredia's work. Since history has not changed the fragile condition of humanity, people must act heroically if their achievements are to be worthy of eternal recognition.

THE POETRY OF JOSÉ MARTÍ

Author: José Martí (José Julian Martí y Pérez, 1853-1895)
Type of work: Poetry
Principal published works: *Abdala*, 1869; *Ismaelillo*, 1882; *Versos sencillos*, 1891; *Versos libres*, 1919; *Obras completas de Martí*, 1936-1953 (74 volumes); *The America of José Martí, Selected Writings*, 1954; *José Martí: Major Poems*, 1982

José Martí was a journalist, essayist, poet, teacher, activist, revolutionary leader, and soldier who is considered the "apostle" of Cuba and the driving force behind the Cuban struggle for independence from Spain. Remembered more for his political prose than for his poetry, Martí nevertheless produced a sizable and striking body of verse that was an integral expression of his political and personal sensibility and that helped to define the uniqueness of Hispanic American poetry.

José Julian Martí y Pérez was born in Havana, the capital city of Cuba, on January 28, 1853. His father, Mariano, was a gruff colonial artillery sergeant from Valencia, Spain. It was from his mother, Leonor, that the young José derived his passionate and perceptive nature. His first exposure to poetry came at the Escuela Superior Municipal de Varones (the Municipal Superior School for Boys), where he became a favorite student of the maestro (director), Rafael María de Mendive, a controversial and well-known poet and supporter of Cuban independence. Under Mendive, Martí gained an appreciation of poetry as well as an awareness of Cuban society's political and social inequities.

When the First Cuban War of Independence broke out in 1868, Martí was too young to join the revolutionary forces, but he regularly attended revolutionary gatherings, often at Mendive's home, where political discussions were interspersed with readings of revolutionary poetry. It is believed that Martí wrote his first poem during this period, a piece entitled "A mi madre" (to my mother). A longer dramatic poem, *Abdala*, was published in 1869 in a revolutionary journal, *La Patria Libre*, under Martí's editorship. *Abdala* dealt with a young man (Martí was still a teenager at the time) torn between his love for his mother and his patriotic duty; ultimately, the protagonist chooses the latter and dies fighting for independence. It was a romantic, melodramatic exploration of the idea of glory, composed in an artificially rebellious tone.

Such sentiments were early on embedded in the young poet's mind and soul. As revolutionary activities increased, the Spanish colonial authorities became stricter and more oppressive. Mendive was one of many people arrested and taken away on suspicion of revolutionary activities. Losing his mentor further steeled Martí's support for the movement and his determination to devote his life and work to Cuban liberation. In 1871, the discovery of a letter chastising a schoolmate for pro-Spanish activities resulted in Martí's imprisonment in Havana's prison, the Presidio, and then later in his permanent exile from his native isle. Martí was sent to Spain, where he continued to pursue his studies and develop his craft.

The tradition of Spanish-language poetry into which Martí emerged was one of classical rigidity and ornate embellishment. Martí, as a young poet, adopted the practices of the time. His early poems, most of which went unpublished during his lifetime, consisted of family sketches and explorations of his imprisonment and exile. They are characterized by adherence to classical meter, extended metaphors, and an artificial pomposity. Forty-eight of his poems of this period are grouped under the title *Flores del destierro* (flowers of exile). In his preface (translated here) to the collection, Martí strikes a note of shame, an awareness of the tendency toward unnecessary excess: "I feel contempt for everything that is mine, but these anguished, rebellious, sullen and querulous poems I indulge and love." In this collection, there is already the seed of what he calls "Contra el verso retórico y ornado/ el verso natural," ("The opposite of rhetorical and ornate poetry/ Natural poetry"). These poems establish themes that would remain with Martí throughout his career: the pain of exile, the desire for return, the value of poetry, and the sadness of injustice and oppression. They are full of elemental imagery as well as powerful oxymorons and juxtaposed contradictions: poetry, like life, is "estrella y gozque" ("star and mongrel"), and the poet respects "mi modo brutal, un modo manso" ("my brutal way, a gentle way").

Martí's true career as a poet began in 1882, with the publication of *Ismaelillo*. Martí spent the 1870's in various nations, having gone from Spain to Mexico and then to Guatemala, with a brief return to Cuba in 1878 under the general amnesty for political criminals. He married Carmen Zayas Bazan in 1877; their son José Francisco was born the following year. In 1881, because of her own homesickness and growing philosophical discomfort with Martí's revolutionary sentiments and activities, Carmen returned permanently to Cuba, taking with her the baby, affectionately called Pepe. Martí missed his wife and son sorely. These emotions, commingled with his revolutionary fervor, led to *Ismaelillo*.

Written during a sojourn in Venezuela, *Ismaelillo* consists of fifteen poems dedicated from father to son. Ismaelillo, or "little Ismael," is portrayed as a dwarfish, sometimes mischievous prince whose image rests on his father's shoulder like an angel or hovers in the distance like a guiding lighthouse. Martí connects his son's blond hair with the innocence of both childhood and political purity. Pepe becomes a symbol of the homeland to which the poet longs to return; the child's gradual journey to adulthood is equated with Cuba's journey toward freedom. The poems, written with lightness, love, and humor, are also imbued with Martí's unflagging moral beliefs. In "Mi reyecillo" (my little king), he writes, "Mas si amar piensas/ El amarillo/ Rey de los hombres,/ ¡Muere conmigo!/ ¿Vivir impuro?/ ¡No vivas, hijo!" ("But if you consider loving/ The yellow/ King of men,/ Die with me!/ Live impurely?/ Don't live, my son!"). Implicit is the belief that Martí will not be truly reunited with his son until he is freely re-

united with his homeland, and that he may very well die in the effort.

Although thematically consistent with the earlier poems, *Ismaelillo* contrasts stylistically in its simple language, short lines, and sincerity of emotion. As Martí wrote in his preface to the volume, "If someone should tell you that these pages resemble others, tell them that I love you too much to thus dishonor you. . . ./ These rivulets have coursed through my heart." While focusing on his relationship with Pepe, Martí avoids excess and sentimentality. Just before his death, Martí characterized this period of his career by saying, "None of my verses should be published before *Ismaelillo*. None of them are worth bothering with. Those which come afterwards to the end are worth something. They are sincere." Sincerity became a true test of the value of poetry for Martí.

Nicaraguan poet Rubén Darío described *Ismaelillo* as a book of poems on the art of being a father. Many critics have hailed the appearance of *Ismaelillo* in 1882 as the beginning of the *Modernismo* movement in Hispanic American poetry, a movement that came into full force with the publication of Darío's *Azul* (blue) six years later. In *Ismaelillo* are evident the abandonment of classical form and rigidity and the wider exploration of the power of word, image, simplicity, and honesty that characterize the movement.

Versos libres (free verses) consists of forty-six poems written, it is believed, in the late 1870's and early 1880's but not published until 1919. In the preface to *Versos sencillos* (simple verses), Martí mused, "Why do they publish this simplicity, written as if in play, and not my boisterous *Free Verses*, my hirsute hendecasyllables born of great fears or great hopes or the indomitable love of freedom or a painful love of beauty . . . ?" *Versos libres* continues Martí's development in the direction of greater formal and thematic freedom. Martí uses the eleven-syllable line throughout most of the poems but abandons rhyme and refines his use of striking imagery.

More important, his poetry itself becomes a central subject, a metaphor for the political freedom he envisions for Cuba and a weapon to be used in the struggle for liberation. In his dedication to the collection, Martí wrote:

> As long as I could not lock up my visions whole, in a form worthy of them, I allowed them to fly. . . . A poem should be like a shining sword that leaves the spectators with memories of a warrior bound for the heavens; when he sheathes his sword in the sun, it breaks into wings. . . . These poems—my warriors—are cut out of my very entrails.

The poems of *Versos libres* evidence a classical tradition set free. Martí's themes are grandiose. Like classical odes, the poems reflect the various episodes of epic struggles. The love of country, the squalor of prison, the power of poetry, and such concepts as death, honor, and oppression are portrayed with deep emotion and great nobility. The poems contain a wealth of exclamation points, poetic catalogs, and apostrophes.

At the same time, the imagery is drawn from the tempestuous and powerful realm of nature, and many of the images have a sharpness and uniqueness that mark a clear departure from the systematic, ordered imagery of classical poetry. Indeed, the movement of ideas and images is often obscure, disordered, and seemingly random. In "Pollice verso" (prison recollections), Martí writes, "¡Zarzal es la memoria; mas la mía/ es un cesto de llamas!" ("memory is a bramble patch, but mine/ is a basket of flames!"). There are Whitmanesque catalogs in a populist vein, such as in "Medianoche" (midnight):

> Oh thirst for love! Oh heart captivated
> By all of life that inhabits the Universe:
> The little green worm into which a leaf
> On a tree twists itself; the rippled jasper
> Into which the waves of the ocean thicken;
> The imprisoned trees that from my eyes
> Always draw tears; the handsome elegant
> Rogue who with bare feet in the mud
> And snow, hawks newspapers or flowers.

Behind all the poems is, again, sincerity, now enforced by a more mature and fiery passion. The yearning for freedom, love, peace, and clarity is more angry, urgent, profound, and reckless. It is as if Martí truly let his poetic imagination run free, maintaining all the while a vigorous emotional connection. In "Crin hirsuta" (bristling mane), Martí compares his poetry to "espantado/ Caballo que en los secos troncos mira/ Garras y dientes de tremendo lobo" ("a frightened/ Horse that among the dry trunks sees/ The claws and fangs of a dreaded wolf"), concluding that, nevertheless, "Solo el amor engendra melodías" ("Only love engenders melodies").

In 1889, Martí, living in New York City, began publication of a children's magazine called *La Edad de Oro* (the golden age), combining poetry, essays, and stories on a wide variety of themes and topics. Although only four issues ultimately appeared, *La Edad de Oro* included several poems notable for their deceptive simplicity. Accessible to children, such poems as "Dos milagros" (two miracles) are nevertheless sophisticated in their imagery and structure. *La Edad de Oro* carried one of Martí's most striking poems, "Dos principes" (two princes), in which the death of a prince is juxtaposed with that of a peasant boy. In the mournful castle and the solemn mountain cottage, the simultaneous deaths obliterate superficial distinctions of class and wealth.

The crowning achievement of Martí's poetic oeuvre came in 1891 with the publication of *Versos sencillos*. The forty-six untitled poems were written during the previous summer, when Martí was in the Catskill Mountains of New York State for rest and relaxation, on his doctor's advice. (Throughout his life, Martí was plagued by ailments that traced back to his early imprisonment and hard labor.) In the preface to *Versos sencillos*, he wrote, "I love simplicity, and I believe in the need to put feelings into plain and sincere forms."

Versos sencillos contains some of Martí's most unadorned and yet most moving poetry. It begins with the bare stanza, "Yo soy un hombre sincero/ De donde crece la palma/ Y antes de morirme quiero/ Echar mis versos del alma." ("I am a sincere man/ From where the palm tree grows,/ And before I die I want/ To pour out the poems of my soul"). The numbered poems of the collection vary in form, subject, and length; many rhyme, though the rhyme schemes vary and Martí never lets the rhyme become more important than the idea of the poetry. In the vein of *Modernismo*, the verse is simpler and the thought more complex than ever.

Martí fills these poems with intimate memories of his parents and his childhood, and with his retrospective feelings about them. Scenes of oppression or pain, such as reminiscences of the harsh treatment of Negro slaves being taken off a ship, are not met with the "boisterous" and "hirsute" passion of *Versos libres* but rather with stillness and vulnerability, along with a heightened sense of pathos. The populist impulse receives full play: "Yo vengo de todas partes,/ Y hacia todas partes voy" ("I come from everywhere,/ To everywhere I'm going"). Martí's disdain for artifice is explicit: "Callo, y entiendo, y me quito/ La pompa del rimador" ("I am silent, I understand, and I cast off/ The pomp of the rhymer"). The poet takes on organized religion, challenging the Spanish bishop to leave his columns and altar and join the poet in the church of nature to be found among the mountain poplars. Friendship, always valued by Martí, is honored in stark terms: "Tomo a un amigo sincero/ Y pongo a un lado el amor" ("I take an honest friend/ And put love to the side").

Among the most telling poems is poem IX, one that has become a classic love poem. It concerns the death of "La niña de Guatemala" (the Guatemalan girl). During his stay in Guatemala in 1877, just before his marriage, Martí had become intimate with Maria García Granados, daughter of a former governor. Already engaged, Martí could not pursue the mutual attraction. After he left Guatemala, the shy and sensitive young woman grew ill and eventually died. In poem IX, Martí mixes memories of their tender friendship with the emotions he experienced at her funeral, marked with the refrain, "Ella se murió de amor" ("She died of love"). Writing mostly in the third person, he moves into the first person to proclaim that hers was "¡la frente/ Que más he amado en la vida" ("the face/ I loved the best in all my life!").

This poem is followed in the sequence by "La bailarina española" (the Spanish dancer), whose fiery eyes captivate the tremulous soldier who seems to be taking some risk to see the dance. The story of the poem is sketched hazily, but the details of the dance and its emotional effects are clear. Another of the *Versos sencillos*, numbered XXXIX, has become a well-known rhyme among Latin American children. It begins "Cultivo una rosa blanca" ("I cultivate a white rose") and carries a simple message of compassion and tolerance in the face of cruelty.

In many of these poems, as in Martí's earlier poetry, colors play an important role in establishing the power of images. White is the innocence of the rose of friendship or the pale locks of the child. Yellow is disease or corruption, like the yellow of the king that Martí warns his son not to love in *Ismaelillo*. Red is the heat of passion or the blood of life, the red of the desert sun shining on a hanged slave; gold is sublime, often divine, beauty, a golden bird miraculously flying forth from a sycamore tree in "Dos milagros." Blue, the sky, is freedom; black is death. Perhaps the most significant color is the rose (pink) embodied in the natural beauty of the mountain chapel, in the poignant generosity of the little girl's slippers, and, of course, in the flowers that blossom in the beloved child's kisses. Martí found great poetic power in a palette of simple colors. He writes, in *Versos sencillos*, "Mi verso es de un verde claro/ Y de un carmín encendido" ("My poetry is of a clear green/ And a flaming scarlet").

Martí's love of poetry, born in the revolutionary fervor of the First Cuban War of Independence, provided both a weapon and a refuge for him during the great battles of his life. He died in a real battle, at Dos Rios on May 19, 1895, in the opening days of Cuba's successful Second War of Independence. Had he lived, it is likely that he would have given the world volumes more of his simple and profound verse. Poetry was part of the lifeblood that drove his passion for freedom. In his essay on Walt Whitman, Martí wrote:

Who is the ignoramus who maintains that people can dispense with poetry? . . . Whether it unites or divides the soul, strengthens it or causes it anguish, props it up or casts it down, whether or not it inspires a man with faith and hope, poetry is more necessary to a people than industry itself, for while industry gives men the means of subsistence, poetry gives them the desire and courage for living.

THE POETRY OF GABRIELA MISTRAL

Author: Gabriela Mistral (Lucila Godoy Alcayaga, 1889-1957)
Type of work: Poetry
Principal published works: *Desolación*, 1922; *Ternura*, 1924, 1945 (enlarged); *Nubes blancas*, 1930; *Tala*, 1938; *Antología*, 1941; *Lagar*, 1954; *Selected Poems of Gabriela Mistral*, 1957; *Poesías completas*, 1958; *Poema de Chile*, 1967

Gabriela Mistral was born Lucila Godoy Alcayaga, on April 7, 1889, of Spanish and Basque lineage. Her father, who deserted the family when Lucila was but a child of three years, was a teacher and poet. Her early years were spent among the peasants, and the poet, who spoke of herself as one of the *campesinos*, put the peasant's love of the land and the countryside into her poetry.

To understand the poetry of Gabriela Mistral, one must know something of her life. She always thought of herself as a teacher first and a poet second, even after she had been awarded the Nobel Prize in Literature in 1945. She began her teaching career at the age of fifteen, with unusual success. In 1912, she became a teacher in secondary schools, moving up from primary schools, with the help of Pedro Aguirre Cerda, who later became president of Chile, the poet's native land. During the years 1918-1922, the poet served as director of schools at Punta Arenas, Temuco, and Santiago. By 1922, she had become so well known in educational circles that she was sent to Mexico to help in the educational reforms in that country. Her fame spread, and in later life she held a host of educational and official positions. She taught in the United States at Columbia University, Vassar, and Middlebury College. She was the Chilean representative on the Committee of Intellectual Cooperation of the League of Nations. She was Chilean consul in Naples, Madrid, Lisbon, Nice, and Santa Barbara, California. She died in New York City in 1957.

Gabriela Mistral's first fame as a poet came when three sonnets on death were read for her (though she was in the audience) at Chile's Juegos Florales in 1914. These poems, which brought her national acclaim, were ironically the indirect result of a suicide. Gabriela had fallen in love with a young man about five years earlier. The young man, Romelio Ureta, killed himself with a gunshot when he was unable to repay money he had "borrowed to help a friend in need of funds," from the railroad that employed him. Also ironically, her first published volume of poems appeared, not in her native Chile, but in the United States, in 1922, after interest in her poetry had been generated by Federico de Onís in a lecture on her poetry at the Columbia University Instituto de las Españas. This volume was *Desolación*.

Part of the poetry in *Desolación*, in the section entitled "Dolor," was also the direct result of the death of the young man she loved. There are also poems that show the poet's interest and feeling for religion, her deep maternal feeling for children, and her inspiration in teaching. There are also some poems for children as well as those written for the adult public. The poems about love show that love, for her, at least as a poet, was not sensual gratification, nor was it joy. The poet tells the reader that it is a bitter experience that ends with death, unless it is the kind of love that becomes almost a religion, so that it can transcend mortality. Her own love, as she writes about it, was an overpowering, jealous love, so strong that it made her, a plain woman, into one of beauty. She describes in "El Ruego" (the prayer) how she wants her dead lover, a sinner because he took his own life, admitted to the presence and grace of God, despite his sinful end. She pleads humbly, but at times forcefully, for him. Another side of love that Gabriela Mistral celebrated, even though she was childless, is maternity, as the fruit of love. The poet says that sterility that brings forth no child is a source of shame, and the woman who suffers it is a tragic figure. Women, she says, are instinctively maternal.

Maternity and teaching fused for Gabriela Mistral. In her "Teacher's Prayer," she begs God to make her more maternal than an ordinary mother, so that she may love her young charges as a mother, though they are not of her flesh and blood. In "La Maestra Rural," she compares the rural schoolteacher with Christ, saying that the teacher's kingdom, like Christ's, is not of men. She exclaims that the teacher must be pure and glad of heart, that she must be willing to accept misunderstanding and hurt, if necessary, to be a successful teacher of children. This same love of children is also reflected in her poems for children. Along with her love for children, she reveals in her poetry and in her public statements about her career as a teacher and educational administrator a love for the poor and the unfortunates of the world that is akin to maternal love.

As a poet, Mistral began with the theme of death, following the loss of her beloved. Death recurs in her work throughout her career. Death often appears in the poetry as impurity, or as a process of disintegration. In writing of death, as in writing on other topics, she uses concrete details. Her figures of speech and her descriptions of death are graphically specific. She seems often to emphasize a lurid aspect of death.

Life, death, and religion are for the Chilean poet inextricably intertwined, as they are for most poets in the Christian tradition. Religion seems for her to be an emotion rather than a ritual of faith. She seems to believe that Christianity is the hope of the peoples of the world, not of the individual alone, but it is a Christianity that is neither doctrinal nor conventional. She is reputed to have regarded herself as strongly anticlerical, though very religious. Some of her poems are actually prayers or hymns.

In the early poetry of Mistral one finds little lightness or gaiety: She is sad, or at least serious, when her tone is not tragic. Her poetic vocabulary is filled with words of suffering and pain; notably, she uses verbs of violence and pain. Her language is suggestive, too, of underlying violence and turbulence. Even when she writes of nature, it is viewed as the peasant knows it—not a smiling nature, but one from which a living must be wrung.

Mistral's later poetry, as one finds it in *Tala* (1938), is more complex, showing greater maturity of view and craft. The reader notes immediately a greater objectivity and a wider scope of subject matter in the later poems. One whole section of *Tala* is called "América" and is devoted to the country that Gabriela Mistral knew and loved. One also finds a wider interest in the other sections of the volume. Her America is a larger land than is her native Chile; it is the whole of Latin America, a land of many mountains, a land of varied climates, and a land of many people with long histories. She writes of the Indians of her America, their tragedy, their poverty, and their hopes. In her poems, writing about the Incas, the Mayas, the Quiches, the Quechuans, and the Aymará, she displays her love of people and her concern for the poor and the unfortunate. In her later poetry, she could write of her own experience as well. The death of her mother, which affected the poet deeply, is the subject of a poem in this volume.

By 1938, the poet had become conscious of her craft. This fact is borne out by the notes she included with *Tala*. She comments on her poetic vocabulary, justifies her use of certain words, and notes her use of specific rhyme schemes. Her choice of words with a distinctly rural flavor receives comment. She notes that she is influenced by the popular dialect of her own region and country, as distinct from the language from the Spanish classics.

Among historians of Hispanic American literature, Gabriela Mistral has been regarded as a female poet who simply ignored the traditional place of women in her culture and, by so doing, became a great writer and public figure. She has been regarded as a romantic (in the literary sense) rebel against the formality of the literary trends of the 1880's and 1890's, one who began as a poet of disillusion but became a voice of love for the suffering people of her time—the children, the mothers, the peasants, the Indians, and the Negroes. Critics have seen in her work such varied influences as the Bible, the poetry of Rabindranath Tagore, the poetry of Amado Nervo of Mexico, and the poetry of Rubén Darío of Nicaragua. Her best-known poems are reputed to be her *Canciones de Cuña* (lullabies) and *Rondas de Niños* (songs of children), known and sung throughout South America. Even before she was awarded the Nobel Prize, she was heralded and acclaimed as a moral force throughout the South American continent, both as a poet and as a teacher.

THE POETRY OF PABLO NERUDA

Author: Pablo Neruda (Neftalí Ricardo Reyes, 1904-1973)
Type of work: Poetry
Principal published works: *Crepusculario*, 1923; *Veinte poemas de amor y una canción desesperada*, 1924 (*Twenty Love Poems and a Song of Despair*, 1969); *Tentativa del hombre infinito*, 1926; *El hondero entusiasta*, 1933; *Residencia en la tierra*, 1933, 1935, 1947 (3 volumes; *Residence on Earth and Other Poems*, 1946, 1973); *España en el corazón*, 1937 (*Spain in the Heart*, 1946); *Un canto para Bolívar*, 1941; *Alturas de Macchu Picchu*, 1946 (*The Heights of Macchu Picchu*, 1966); *Canto general*, 1950; *Los versos del capitán*, 1952 (*The Captain's Verses*, 1972); *Odas elementales*, 1954 (*The Elementary Odes*, 1961); *Las uvas y el viento*, 1954; *Nuevas odas elementales*, 1956; *Tercer libro de odas*, 1957; *Estravagario*, 1958 (*Extravagaria*, 1974); *Cien sonetos de amor*, 1959; *Navegaciones y regresos*, 1959; *Canción de gesta*, 1960 (*Song of Protest*, 1976); *Canto ceremoniales*, 1961; *Las piedras de Chile*, 1961; *Plenos poderes*, 1962 (*Fully Empowered*, 1975); *Memorial de Isla Negra*, 1964 (5 volumes; Isla Negra, 1981); *Arte de pájaros*, 1966; *Una casa en la arena*, 1966; *La barcarola*, 1967; *Las manos del día*, 1968; *La espada encendida*, 1970; *Selected Poems*, 1970; *Geografía infructuosa*, 1972; *New Poems (1968-1970)*, 1972; *El mar y las compañas*, 1973; *La rosa separada*, 1973; *El corazón amarillo*, 1974; *Defectos escogidos*, 1974; *Elegía*, 1974; *Five Decades: Poems, 1925-1970*, 1974; *Jardín de invierno*, 1974; *Libro de las preguntas*, 1974; *El mal y el malo*, 1974

Pablo Neruda was an essayist, translator, playwright, and novelist as well as a poet, but it is for his poetry that he is most remembered. Winner of the Nobel Prize in Literature in 1971, Neruda became one of the most widely read poets not only in Latin America but also internationally. One of his most popular collections, *Twenty Love Poems and a Song of Despair*, appeared in more than one million printed copies and was translated from Spanish into more than twenty languages.

Neruda's goal was to liberate Spanish poetry from the literary strictures of the nineteenth century and bring it into the twentieth century by returning verse to its popular sources. He states in the prologue to one of four editions of *Caballo verde* (a literary review that he founded in 1935 with Manuel Altalaguirre) that he was seeking a poetry that would contain the "confused impurities" that people leave on their tools as they wear them down with the sweat of their hands. He would make poems like buildings, permeated with smoke and garlic and flooded inside and out with the air of men and women who seem always present. Neruda advocated an impure poetry whose subject might be hatred, love, ugliness, or beauty. He sought to bring verse back from the exclusive conclave of select minorities to the turmoil from which words draw their vitality.

Neruda's work is divided into three discernible periods, the turning points being the Spanish Civil War (1936-1939) and his return to Chile in 1952 after three years of forced exile. During the first phase of his work, from 1923 to 1936, Neruda published six rather experimental collections of verse in which he achieved the poetic strength that carried him through four more decades and more than twenty books. He published *Crepusculario* (twilight) himself in 1923 while a student at the University of Santiago. *Crepusculario* is a cautious collection of poems reflecting his reading of French poetry. Like the Latin American *Modernistas* who preceded him, he consciously adhered to classical forms and sought the ephemeral effects of musicality and color. The poem that perhaps best captures the message indicated by the title of the book is very brief: "My soul is an empty carousel in the evening light." All the poems in *Crepusculario* express Neruda's ennui and reveal his experimentation with the secondary qualities of language, its potential to create the effects of music, painting, and sculpture.

One year after *Crepusculario*, *Twenty Love Po-*

ems and a Song of Despair appeared. This collection has become one of the most widely read collections of poems in the Spanish-speaking world. In it, Neruda charts the course of a love affair from passionate attraction to despair and indifference. In these poems, Neruda sees the whole world in terms of the beloved:

> The vastness of pine groves, the sound of beating
>   wings, the slow interplay of lights, a solitary bell,
> the evening falling into your eyes, my darling,
>   and in you the earth sings.
> Love shadows and timbres your voice in the
>   dying echoing afternoon
> just as in those deep hours I have seen
>   the field's wheat bend in the mouth of the wind.

Throughout these twenty poems, Neruda's intensity and directness of statement universalize his private experiences, establishing another constant in his work: the effort to create a community of feeling through the expression of common, universal experience.

In 1926, Neruda published *Tentativa del hombre infinito* (venture of the infinite man), his most interesting work from a technical point of view. In this book-length poem, Neruda employed the "automatic writing" espoused by the Surrealists. The poem celebrates Neruda's discovery of the city at night and tests the capacity of his poetic idiom to sound the depths of his subconscious. Ignoring the conventions of sentence structure, syntax, and logic, Neruda fuses form and content.

The poem opens in the third person with a description of the poet asleep in the city of Santiago. It uses the same image of the sleeping man and the hearth fires of the city three times, changing person from third to second to first, creating a circular or helical structure. The imagery defies conventional associations: "the moon blue spider creeps floods/ an emissary you were moving happily in the afternoon that was falling/ the dusk rolled in extinguishing flowers."

In the opening passages, Neruda explores the realm between wakefulness and sleep, addressing the night as his lover: "take my heart, cross it with your vast pulleys of silence/ when you surround sleep's animals, it's at your feet/ waiting to depart because you place it face to face with/ you, night of black helixes." In this realm between motive and act, Neruda's language refuses to acknowledge distinctions of tense: "a twenty-year-old hold to the frenetic reins, it is that he wanted to follow the night." Also, the limits that words draw between concepts disappear, and thoughts blend like watercolors: "star delayed between the heavy night the days with tall sails."

The poem is a voyage of exploration that leads to a number of discoveries. The poet discovers his own desperation: "the night like wine enters the tunnel/ savage wind, miner of the heavens, let's wail together." He discovers the vastness of the other: "in front of the inaccessible there passes by for you a limitless presence." He discovers his freedom: "prow, mast, leaf in the storm, an abandonment without hope of return impels you/ you show the way like crosses the dead." Most important, He discovers wonder: "the wind leaving its egg strikes my back/ great ships of glowing coals twist their green sails/ planets spin like bobbins." The abstract becomes concrete and hence tractable: "the heart of the world folds and stretches/ with the will of a column and the cold fury of feathers." He discovers his joy: "Hurricane night, my happiness bites your ink/ and exasperated, I hold back my heart which dances/ a dancer astonished in the heavy tides which make the dawn rise."

When the poet finds his beloved, he begins to acquire a more logical grasp of objective reality, but when he realizes that he is still dreaming, his joy becomes despair. He gradually awakens; his senses are assaulted by the smell of the timber of his house and the sound of rain falling, and he gazes through the windows at the sky. Interestingly, his dream visions do not abandon him at once but continue to determine his perceptions:

> birds appear like letters in the depth of the sky
> the dawn appears like the peelings of fruit
> the day is made of fire
> the sea is full of green rags which articulate I am
>   the sea
> I am alone in a windowless room
> snails cover the walk
> and time is squared and immobile.

In this experimental work, Neruda mastered the art of tapping his subconscious for associative imagery. Although he never returned to the pure Surrealism of *Tentativa del hombre infinito*, it is the union of strikingly original and often surreal imagery with earthly realism that gives Neruda's mature poetry its distinctive character.

In *Residence on Earth and Other Poems*, Neruda first achieved that mature voice, free of any derivative qualities. One of the greatest poems in this collection, "Galope muerto" ("Dead Gallop"), was written in the same year as *Tentativa del hombre infinito*, 1925, although it was not published in book form until 1933. "Dead Gallop" sets the tone for the collection, in which Neruda repeatedly expresses a passionate desire to assimilate new experiences: "Everything is so fast, so living/ yet immobile, like a mad pulley spinning on itself." Many of the poems in *Residence on Earth* begin in the same manner, recording those peripheral and secondary sensations that reside on the fringe of consciousness. They work toward the same end, resolving the new into understandable terms. As the poems come into focus, the reader participates in the poet's assimilation of his new world. For example, the significance of his vague memories of saying good-bye to a girl whom he had left in Chile gradually becomes clear in one poem:

> Dusty glances fallen to earth
> or silent leaves which bury themselves.
> Lightless metal in the void
> and the suddenly dead day's departure.
> On high hands the butterfly shines
> its flight's light has no end.
> You kept the light's wake of broken things
> which the abandoned sun in the afternoon throws
>   at the church steps.

Here, one can see Neruda's gift for surreal imagery without the programmatic irrationality and dislocation of the Surrealists.

In *Residence on Earth*, too, there are magnificent catalogs in the manner of Walt Whitman: "the angel of sleep—the wind moving the wheat, the whistle of a train, a warm place in a bed, the opaque sound of a shadow which falls like a ray of light into infinity, a repetition of distances, a wine of uncertain vintage, the dusty passage of lowing cows."

Like Whitman, Neruda in *Residence on Earth* opens Spanish poetry to the song of himself: "my symmetrical statue of twinned legs, rises to the stars each morning/ my exile's mouth bites meat and grapes/ my male arms and tattooed chest/ in which the hair penetrates like wire, my white face made for the sun's depth." He presents uncompromising statements of human sensuality; he descends into himself, discovers his authenticity, and begins to build a poetic vision that, although impure, is genuinely human. He manages in these sometimes brutal poems to reconcile the forces of destruction and creation he had witnessed in India in the material world of buildings, work, people, food, weather, himself, and time.

Although Neruda never achieved a systematic and internally consistent poetic vision, the balance between resignation and celebration that informs *Residence on Earth* suggests a philosophical acceptance of the world. "Tres cantos materiales" ("Three Material Songs"), "Entrada a la madera" ("Entrance to Wood"), "Apoges del apio" ("Apogee of Celery"), and "Estatuto del vino" ("Ordinance of Wine") were a breakthrough in this respect. In "Entrance to Wood," the poet gives voice to wood, which, though living, is material rather than spiritual. Neruda's discovery of matter is a revelation. He introduces himself into this living, material world as one commencing a funereal journey, carrying his sorrows with him in order to give this world the voice it lacks. His identification with matter alters his language so that the substantives become verbs: "Let us make fire, silence, and noise,/ let us burn, hush and bells."

Neruda was writing the last poems of *Residence on Earth* in Madrid when the Spanish Civil War erupted. The catastrophe delayed the publication of the last book of the trilogy by twelve years. More important, the war confirmed Neruda's stance as a defender of oppressed peoples, of the poor. Suddenly, Neruda stopped singing the song of himself and began to direct his verse against the Nationalists besieging Madrid. The war inspired the collection of poems *Spain in the Heart*, a work as popular in Eastern Europe as is *Twenty Love Poems and a Song of Despair* in the West. These poems, such as Neruda's 1942 "Oda a Stalingrad" ("Ode to Stalingrad"), were finally published as part of *Residence on Earth*. They were written from the defensive point of view of countries fighting against the threat of Fascism. In them, the lyric element almost disappears before the onslaught of Neruda's political passion. Indeed, from 1937 to 1947, Neruda's poetry served the greater purpose of political activism and polemics:

> You probably want to know: And where are the
>   lilies?
> the metaphysics covered with poppies?
> And the rain which often struck
> his words filling them
> with holes and birds?
> I'm going to tell you what has happened.
> I lived in a neighborhood in Madrid
> My house was called
> the House of Flowers. . .
> And one evening everything was on fire
> . . . Bandits with planes and with Moors
> bandits with rings and duchesses
> bandits with black friars giving blessings
> came through the sky to kill children.

More than ten years had to pass before Neruda could reaffirm his art above political propaganda.

During the 1940's, Neruda worked by plan on his epic history of Latin America, *Canto general*. Beginning with a description of the geography, the flora, and the fauna of the continent, the book progresses from sketches of the heroes of the Inca and Aztec empires through descriptions of conquistadores, the heroes of the Wars of Independence, to the dictators and foreign adventurers in twentieth century Latin America. Neruda interprets the history of the continent as a struggle toward autonomy conducted by many different peoples who have suffered from one kind of oppression or another since the beginnings of their recorded history.

Neruda, however, did not disappear entirely from his work during these years. He published

anonymously *The Captain's Verses* to celebrate falling in love with the woman with whom he would spend the rest of his life, Matilde Urrutia. Unlike previous women in his life, Matilde shared Neruda's origins among the poor of southern Chile as well as his aspirations. These poems are tender, passionate, and direct, free of the despair, melancholy, and disillusionment of *Twenty Love Poems and a Song of Despair* and of *Residence on Earth*.

While working in exile for the European Peace Party, Neruda recorded in his book *Las uvas y el viento* (grapes and the wind) impressions of new friends and places, of conferences and renewed commitments made during his travels through Hungary, Poland, and Czechoslovakia. Neruda warmly remembers Prague, Berlin, Moscow, Capri, Madame Sun Yat-sen, Ilya Ehrenburg, Paul Éluard, Pablo Picasso, and the Turkish poet Nazim Hikmet. The most interesting works in the collection re-create Neruda's return to cities from which he had been absent for more than thirty years.

Neruda's travels through the East ensured his fame. His fiftieth year signaled his return to Chile in order to fulfill the demand for his work that issued from three continents. In 1954, he built his house on Isla Negra with Matilde Urrutia and published the first of three remarkable collections, *The Elementary Odes*, followed by *Nuevas odas elementales* (new elementary odes) and *Tercer libro de odas* (third book of odes). In these books, Neruda returned to the discoveries made in the "Material Songs" of *Residence on Earth*. In the odes, Neruda's poetry regained ascendancy over politics, although Neruda never ignored his political responsibilities.

In the elementary odes, Neruda learns to accept and celebrate the common gift of happiness, "as necessary as the earth, as sustaining as hearth fires, as pure as bread, as musical as water." He urges his audiences to recognize the gifts they already possess. He sings of such humble things as eel stew, in which the flavors of the Chilean land and sea mix to make a paradise for the palate. Against those who envy his work and its unpretentious message of common humanity, Neruda responds that a simple poetry open to common people will live after him because it is unafraid and healthy as a milk-maid in whose laughter there are enough teeth to ruin the hopes of the envious.

The language of the elementary odes is very simple and direct, but, because Neruda writes these poems in brief, internally rhyming lines, he draws attention to the natural beauty of his Spanish, the measured rhythm of clauses, the symmetry of sentence structure, and the solid virtues of an everyday vocabulary. In the tradition of classical Spanish realism, the elementary odes require neither the magic of verbal pyrotechnics nor incursions into the subconscious to achieve a fullness of poetic vision.

After the collection *Extravagaria*—in which Neruda redirected his attention inward again, resolving questions of his own mortality and the prospect of never again seeing places and people dear to him—the poet's production doubled to the rate of two lengthy books of poems every year. In response partly to the demand for his work, and partly to his increased passion for writing, Neruda's books during the last decade of his life were often carefully planned and systematic.

Navegaciones y regresos alternates a recounting of his travels with odes inspired by remarkable people, places, and events. *Cien sonetos de amor* collects one hundred rough-hewn sonnets of love to Matilde Urrutia. *Isla Negra* is an autobiography in verse. *Arte de pájaros* is a poetic ornithological guide to Chile. *Las piedras de Chile*, *Cantos ceremoniales*, *Fully Empowered*, and *Una casa en la arena* are all-inclusive, totally unsystematic collections unified by Neruda's bold style, a style that wanders aimlessly and confidently like a powerful river cutting designs in stone. *Las manos del día* and *La espada encendida*, written between 1968 and 1970, attest Neruda's responsiveness to new threats against freedom. *Geografía infructuosa* signals Neruda's return again to contemplate the rugged coast of Chile. As Neruda remarks in his memoirs concerning his last decade of work, he gradually developed into a poet with the primitive style characteristic of the monolithic sculptures of Oceania: "I began with the refinements of Praxiteles and end with the massive ruggedness of the statues of Easter Island."

THE POETRY OF JUDITH ORTIZ COFER

Author: Judith Ortiz Cofer (1952-   )

Type of work: Poetry

Principal published works: *Latin Women Pray*, 1980; *The Native Dancer*, 1981; *Among the Ancestors*, 1981; *Peregrina*, 1986; *Reaching for the Mainland*, 1987; *Terms of Survival*, 1987; *Silent Dancing: A Partial Remembrance of a Puerto Rican Childhood*, 1990; *The Latin Deli: Prose and Poetry*, 1993

Judith Ortiz Cofer undertook a new direction in continental Puerto Rican literature by removing herself from the Puerto Rican literary circles of the so-called "Nuyorican" group of New York City. Nuyorican poet Julio Marzán succinctly described her innovative style as "different." She broke away from many Latino writers' tendency to produce sociohistorical documentaries of life in the barrio. Instead, her poetry engages in a more personal and intimate exploration of her ethnicity.

Among the awards that Ortiz Cofer has received are a fellowship in poetry from the Florida Fine Arts Council (1981), a Bread Loaf Writers' Conference Fellowship in poetry (1987), and a grant from the Witter Bynner Foundation for Poetry (1988-1989). Further national recognition came in 1989 with a National Endowment for the Arts Fellowship in poetry. Her novel *The Line of the Sun* (1989) was nominated for a Pulitzer Prize and was selected as one of the "Twenty-Five Most Memorable Books" by the New York City Library System. Ortiz Cofer has combined a busy reading tour throughout the United States with teaching English and creative writing.

A self-described Navy brat, she was born in Hormigueros, Puerto Rico. She arrived in Paterson, New Jersey, at the age of two, when her father joined the Navy. She, her mother, and a younger brother returned to Puerto Rico every time her father sailed with a cargo fleet. During those long visits, she lived with her maternal grandmother, who entertained her with local folktales and with her own stories. The transition to contact with another culture was always abrupt and traumatic, but the arrangement allowed the young girl to keep in touch with Puerto Rican culture and with the Spanish language. The transitions, she says, caused her to become an observer of life.

High points of Ortiz Cofer's childhood experiences in New Jersey included repeated attempts to master English and her introduction to American life in ethnic barrios. Although the "Puerto Rican period" of her life was short (she was fourteen when the family moved to Georgia), its influence has been felt throughout her life.

Shortly after the Paterson riots and her father's retirement in 1968, Ortiz Cofer's family moved to Augusta, Georgia. In 1977, she received a master's degree in English literature from Florida Atlantic University. At that time, she started to write poetry for local journals and became a member of several poetry groups. The young writer soon realized that active Nuyorican writers were publishing almost exclusively for Latino or Puerto Rican markets. Her distance from the Nuyorican circles led her to start publishing in mainstream literary journals, which began to request more submissions. She has proudly pointed out that she was the first Puerto Rican author to be published by distinguished mainstream publications in the United States.

Key events of her childhood are the thematic center and main inspiration of Ortiz Cofer's poetry. Her poetry gives voice to her own experiences and to those of the people who shared those memories, in poems that are about "people, places, and things, not necessarily about philosophical abstractions; I write about people." Ortiz Cofer moves beyond the traditional social documentation of the Puerto Rican experience in the United States and dwells on the relationship between ethnicity and the literary process.

Linguistically, Ortiz Cofer's poetry stands out for its use of standard American English. She rejects the Spanish-English hybrid form commonly referred to as "Spanglish," a popular street code-switch talk used by most Nuyorican poets. Her choice of language has accelerated her recognition as an important voice of the Puerto Rican in urban America, but it has also set her apart from the Nuyorican group. This apparent split has caused discussions about whether her work belongs to Puerto Rican literature or to American literature.

Her acculturation process, fully verbalized in English, proves that expressions of Puerto Rican ethnicity can take shape in a language other than Spanish. This is the case for *Latin Women Pray*, her first poetry collection, published as a chapbook by The Florida Arts Gazette Press, house of *The Florida Arts Gazette*, a literary journal for which she served as poetry editor. Ortiz Cofer describes the poems in *Latin Women Pray* as the best ones of her early production. The eleven poems stand out for their clarity of expression, in contrast to the experimental linguistic constructions of the poetry of other Latino writers. Another key difference is that she prefers to give testimonial voice to typical, ordinary characters, many of them Latinas, who are often ignored as a source of poetic inspiration in Latino literature. In keeping with her *ars poetica*, her characters are not necessarily political activists, nor are they metaphysical abstractions. Their lives and their particular outlooks on existence and on society (including issues of racism and of chauvinism) provide the poetic tension. "Latin Women Pray" and "Grace Stands in Line for Saturday Confession" are of particular thematic importance because they show a feminist line of thought that would become an essential part of her future work.

Social problems faced by the Hispanic community constitute a major theme of *The Native Dancer*, also a chapbook. The struggle for survival in a foreign land is ever-present, but the twenty-four poems carry on the existential exploration of the Latino experience. In a technique that has become a trademark, the poetic process depends on her childhood memories. The process of recollection has a dual purpose. First, memory brings forward poetry's internal mechanisms, as the adult poet identifies and meditates on those moments

that helped to shape her poetic craft. Second, those instants of revelation are also her poetic inspiration. The recognition in mainstream criticism that these childhood vignettes by a Hispanic poet are authentic material for literature—and not merely sociological material—may be a major contribution of Ortiz Cofer's poetry.

The Native Dancer concentrates on people who contributed to her personal development as a poet and as a woman with a feminist conscience. Her mother, her father, and her grandmother in Puerto Rico are remarkable for their formative roles and are figures to whom the poet will return in her future poems. This volume also starts a more defined metaphysical phase. Hispanic characters such as those in the poem "The Native Dancer," aided by their ethnic boundaries (many imposed by mainstream society), transcend their physical reality to achieve higher spiritual dimensions.

Although strongly attached to her Puerto Rican heritage, Ortiz Cofer's production also includes poetry inspired by her experiences in the South, an area that she knows well. This phase is visible in *Among the Ancestors*, a chapbook of fourteen poems in honor of her husband's family. As do her Puerto Rican poems, *Among the Ancestors* shows characters (Southerners, in this case) in personal touch with their traditions. In "Among the Ancestors," she observes strong attachment to family land, a devotion that had contributed to the development of a rich regional culture.

With the publication of *Peregrina*, Ortiz Cofer moved away from the local poetry markets of Florida and Georgia. *Peregrina* was the winning manuscript in the 1985 Riverstone International Poetry Chapbook Competition, organized by the Poets of the Foothills Arts Center in Colorado and judged anonymously by poet Linda Pastan. It was a significant literary prize for Ortiz Cofer, since it gave her the kind of exposure that could open up nationally known publishing markets.

Peregrina's fourteen poems take the reader into a journey through developmental phases of the feminine psyche as it is reflected in the title word, which is Spanish for "pilgrim." The opening poem, "Quinceañera," begins the journey with a teenage girl who resents having turned fifteen, an age at which Hispanic tradition considers a girl to have become a woman. The responsibility of womanhood is heavy and unnerving. Feminine voices of different time periods and ages ponder their own experiences within social and religious structures. The cycle closes with "Holly," addressed to and dedicated to Ortiz Cofer's eleven-year-old daughter, who stands as the woman of the future, empowered by multiple options, choices that were fought for by women like her mother and by the anonymous women of the previous poems.

National attention came to Ortiz Cofer's work with *Reaching for the Mainland*, the first book-length collection of her poems. The poems collected in that volume date from 1980 and were published elsewhere in journals and in *The Native Dancer*. The volume appeared in *Triple Crown* (1987), a poetic trilogy with Roberto Durán, a Mexican American, and Gustavo Pérez Firmat, a Cuban American. In the preface, Gary Keller, a critic of Latino literatures, describes the works as "serious poetry by three important young poets," representatives of the largest, most influential Latino populations in the United States. For Ortiz Cofer, this praise meant her independence from the Nuyorican poetry school and her acceptance by critics as part of the Puerto Rican diaspora.

Reaching for the Mainland is a metaphorical allusion to Ortiz Cofer's physical and psychological journey to the United States, reflected in the internal divisions of the book. The first section, "The Birthplace," is a celebration of her place of birth, using childhood memories in Hormigueros, family anecdotes, and folk stories—all key elements in Ortiz Cofer's poetry, which becomes her "emotional and intellectual connection to [her] heritage." For example, the opening poem, "They Say," inspired by stories of her difficult birth and near death, initiates the journey into the Puerto Rican culture that has determined her unconscious existence. Also from her early experiences on the island, the poet created several characters who were uprooted and, therefore, considered to be social outcasts. These inarticulate people became *dramatis personae* in Ortiz Cofer's poems. For

example, the protagonists of "The Woman Who Was Left at the Altar" and of "The Man Who Lost His Handwriting," the town's notorious crazy people, have already started their own journeys into the visionary world of their inner selves.

The second part, "The Crossing," continues the metaphysical quest for one's true essence. The opening poem's epigraph, by Mexican poet and Nobel Prize winner Octavio Paz, stresses that the personal search for the "other" is the burden of all humankind and constitutes a lonely process. Such an existentialist position must have appealed to Ortiz Cofer because of its approximation to her own experience as a child. The poems in "The Crossing" address her own crossing into a new metaphysical dimension, represented by American urban culture. She was not alone. Along with her early tendency to present *dramatis personae*, she created other people close to her childhood as participants in this coming-to-terms process. Two of them, her mother and father, became characters of key importance in her poetry. They underwent various degrees of acculturation to American society. Another influential person was her grandmother, who became a connector to the life Ortiz Cofer had left behind and the source of many of the stories retold in poetic form.

"The Habit of Movement," the last section, begins a political trend. Ortiz Cofer attempts to illustrate the social problems faced by the Latino population, and especially by Latinas, by revealing the psychological dimension of the exiled persona. The poem "The Other," echoing Octavio Paz's theory of the "other," presents the split personality of a woman who, as she dresses herself up in a mirror, sees her Latina side putting on clothing more to her ethnic liking. A new theme appears in two poems, "In Yucatán" and "Returning from the Mayan Ruins," written after a trip to the Mexican peninsula of Yucatán. These two poems show the poet's interest in Latin American aboriginal cultures and histories.

Terms of Survival uses Spanish words to represent features of Hispanic culture that find no literal translation into English. The trend had already shown up in *Peregrina* and in *The Native Dancer*, books that provided some of the poems published here. Organized around the idea of a cultural dictionary, this collection is divided into two parts. "Palabras" (words), the first section, assembles thirty-five poems inspired by Puerto Rican notions of social life and family relationships. In "El Mal," for example, the voice of a teenage girl remembers a gloomy phrase, "le hizo el mal" (evil befell her), used by her mother to explain why her daughter could no longer be with her favorite friend. In recollection, the young woman transforms the source of "el mal," her friend's pregnancy, into "an old sorcerer's trick that begins/ by mixing man, woman and moon."

The second part, "Common Ground," returns the poetic persona to the United States in an existential quest for the meaning of "being." The change of language for the titles corroborates her acceptance that Puerto Rican identity can take shape in English. Although her ethnicity might have added a special dimension to her life experiences, these experiences are not in any way more significant solely because of her Puerto Rican background. The poem "Common Ground" illustrates this point with its emphasis on the fact that "blood tells the story of your life." Family ties and relationships, in clear echoes of Virginia Woolf, a literary model for Ortiz Cofer, determine one's adult perspective. Her adult perspective also shapes Ortiz Cofer's poetic craft.

Silent Dancing shows a new facet of Ortiz Cofer's career, although some of the poems were published originally in *Terms of Survival* and in *Reaching for the Mainland*. Thirteen personal narrative essays accompany the eighteen poems, which are related in subject matter. The idea came from New York-based novelist Hilma Wolitzer. After hearing Ortiz Cofer's poetry reading at the Bread Loaf Writers' Conference in 1987, she suggested that Ortiz Cofer write as stories the anecdotes about her mother and her grandmother that she was using as background information for her poems.

Clearly influenced by her grandmother's folktales, Ortiz Cofer's poems and essays explore the process by which reality is perceived and remembered at various moments of one's life. They also reflect on the process by which Puerto Rican culture apprehends the American reality that is so different from the Caribbean world, converting it into diverse symbols that merge into new ethnic concepts. Specifically, the poetry in *Silent Dancing* aims to rediscover dear memories in a process described in the subtitle as *A Partial Remembrance of a Puerto Rican Childhood*. In the preface, Ortiz Cofer explains her concept of recollection by insisting that her work is more than family history, that it is "creative explorations of known territory." In this "tapestry that is my memory of childhood," as inspired by Virginia Woolf, memory is triggered by numerous factors. For example, "Claims" recalls the moment that her grandmother decided to stop having sexual relations, in order to avoid pregnancy and to protect her health. The poem's inspiration was the grandmother's caution to her daughters: "Children are made in the night and/ steal your days/ for the rest of your life, amen."

The struggle of individuation, whether it is ethnic or personal, is a unifying theme of all the poems in *Silent Dancing*. The testimonial reconstruction of images from the past provides the poet with a fuller mosaic of her own poetic persona. Within this frame, previously published poems find in *Silent Dancing* their natural place within the context that inspired them. For example, "The Habit of Movement," a poem that addresses her many trips to the island, now stresses that Puerto Ricanness is a state of mind manifested through multiple cultural signifiers.

The Latin Deli reflects Ortiz Cofer's commitment to literary experimentation by setting together thirty-seven poems, stories, and essays in an effort to complete the complex mosaic of the Latino experience in the United States. The book is divided into two sections, "From the Book of Dreams in Spanish" and "The Medium's Burden." "The Latin Deli," the opening poem, stresses immigrants' nostalgia for their motherland. A maternal proprietress of a Latin deli provides consolation and, by catering to people's spiritual needs through food, becomes a goddess-like figure. The poet may perform the same service. The ability to identify people's internal struggles has a price, however. "The Medium's Burden," the last poem, closes this metaphysical cycle as the poetic voice, clearly that of a woman, expresses resentment of her own role in unveiling her friends' problems. The poet's responsibility to provide a social voice is draining and overwhelming.

THE POETRY OF HEBERTO PADILLA

Author: Heberto Padilla (1932-   )

Type of work: Poetry

Principal published works: *El justo tiempo humano*, 1962; *Fuera de juego*, 1969; *Provocaciones*, 1973; *El hombre junto al mar*, 1981; *Legacies: Selected Poems*, 1982; *A Fountain, a House of Stone: Poems*, 1991

Widely regarded as Cuba's foremost living poet, Heberto Padilla has also written novels and a memoir depicting his complicated and ultimately antagonistic relationship with the regime of Fidel Castro. Although he had previously published a signal collection of poems, *El justo tiempo humano* (1962, just human time), and a novel, *Buscavidas* (1965, seeking lives), he gained worldwide attention with the publication of *Fuera de juego* (1969, outside the game), which was awarded Cuba's National Prize for Literature by the Unión de Escritores y Artistas de Cuba. Although the prize brought him widespread fame throughout the Latin American literary world, his criticism of the Cuban government's increasing preference for innocuous, Party-minded literary figures over less doctrinaire artists and intellectuals resulted in a decade of ostracism, prison, house arrest, and, since 1980, exile in the United States.

Padilla has merited sustained attention not for his eponymous leading political role but for his artistic role in transforming the poetic vocabulary of contemporary Cuban poetry, as well as his role in, roughly speaking, broadening the thematic range available to poets. From the onset of his literary maturity in the 1950's, Padilla sought to provide a corrective to the baroque proclivities of prerevolutionary Cuban poetry. His own energetic, direct-speaking, often aphoristic poems derive not from modernist forebears but from European surrealist and even, in their compression, hermeticist models. Padilla's poetry, far from evincing the counterrevolutionary traits for which it earned the state's opprobrium, looks authentically revolutionary in its emphatic turn away from the highly wrought toward the egalitarian, from complicity in theoretically sanctioned change toward a freshly imagined, and perhaps newly revived, humanistic empathy.

Born in Pinar del Río in 1932, Padilla published his first collection of poems at the age of sixteen, before taking up study of the law, which he quickly abandoned for journalism. By the 1950's, he was working in the United States as New York correspondent for Prensa Latina, the Cuban press agency. With the overthrow of Fulgencio Batista, he returned to Cuba to work on a new paper, *Revolución*, and to help found the Unión de Escritores y Artistas de Cuba as well as a literary magazine, *Lunes de Revolución*. Subsequently working for both press organizations, he was sent to Moscow, where he resided until 1968. He was then recalled following the controversy surrounding the national literary prize awarded his soon-to-be-published collection, *Fuera de juego*. In poems highly critical of the revolution, Padilla found himself the target of government attacks, a situation not ameliorated in 1971, when attacks against him occasioned a new book defiantly entitled *Provocaciones* (1973). During the decade of his imprisonment and house arrest (1971-1980), Padilla worked on translations of the English Romantic poets, principally Percy Bysshe Shelley, William Blake, Samuel Taylor Coleridge, and Robert Burns. After taking up residence in the United States, Padilla published two collections of poems and a memoir. His poems appear frequently in translation in English-language literary journals. The two collections in English, *Legacies: Selected Poems* (1982) and *A Fountain, a House of Stone* (1991), make available to English readers poems from across Padilla's career, but especially from the fertile period of the 1960's and the period of exile.

Beginning with the appearance of *El justo tiempo humano*, Padilla's poems strike a strongly contrastive note with modernism, which by the 1950's was firmly entrenched as the reigning aesthetic in nearly all Western literatures. Whereas modernist doctrine encouraged impersonalism and polished, ironic surfaces, Padilla's best poetry gets its effects from the immediacy of directly stated emotions. One feels not only that the poet stands directly behind his words but also that he deploys those words with the very intention of providing transparent access to an emotional state, as though he wishes readers to feel what he feels, not just the effects of feelings transcribed and left in evidence. It is not difficult to imagine just how this desire (what, in another poet, would be described as "technique") for immediacy could affront the corporate sensibilities of the state, for not only must immediacy itself be held in disrepute, since the emotional pressure behind it implies a weight of "bourgeois" individualism, but in addition the feeling of immediacy—the feeling of the moment— opens the door to doubt. For example, in "A ratos esos malos pensamientos" ("Occasional Wicked Thoughts") Padilla asserts that "there's a bunch of guys/ who work against your liberty, who grab/ your most sincere poem and indict you." Similarly, in "Canción del juglar" ("Song of the Juggler"), the speaker addresses a general in this way: "I don't know how long this war will last/ but every night one of your orders dies/ without being followed,/ and, undefeated, one of my songs survives." Although the feeling of spontaneity derives some of its power from a strong sense of individualism, Padilla is careful not to hang his hat solely on this premise. To do so would be to leave his poems open to the suspicion that they were merely the quirky by-products of an aberrant vision. Instead, he clearly wishes to invoke a tradition of literary ancestors whose collective poetics of strong selfhood can be opposed to seductive modern abstractions, such as "history," against which individual endeavor stands in danger of being interpreted as only an instance of puny narcissism. Padilla does not try to leap outside history; rather, he makes of it a human matter open to human interpretation, not

an impersonal force. As a result, he is often tempted to view the events of history, particularly revolutionary history, from a slightly more stable and sometimes bemused perspective. He is not, however, free of engagements of his own. In "El relevo" ("Relief"), he glosses the irony of his "wicked thoughts":

> Every time a generation
> comes in or goes out, slamming doors,
> the old poet tightens his belt
> and tunes up his cornet like a little rooster.

The rooster, aside from his other whimsical traits, is self-delegated to give humanity a wake-up call. The poet—as ancient, as musician—revels in the mischief of time, and his I-told-you-so, while it has the rooster's fierce determination to be heard, also leavens the message: The passage of generations need not be the subject of a grim poetry. After all, people live in history, and while it perhaps makes available the range of responses at any given historical period, people also make history, by virtue of living in it.

For Padilla, it is the tendency to get things backwards that sets his poetry on edge. It is precisely to the degree that it is on edge that his poetry takes on a polemical cast: Machine guns go off in the name of abstractions, after all, and to the poet it does not matter whether these abstractions are called "History," "The Motherland," or "Progress." The point is that an important relationship has suffered a reversal. Concepts, which were the inventions of people, suddenly in the twentieth century precede them. Subject and object have exchanged places, and few seem to have noticed that the ironies proceeding from this mistake are monstrously omnipresent. As the speaker in "Cantan los nuevos césares" ("The New Caesars Proclaim") says with the conviction of blind, corporate bravado, "We are still building, building/ with all the legality of the law."

Padilla's extended sojourn in the Soviet Union appears to have sharpened his sympathies for the suffering population and their great poetic voices, rather than for the Soviet system, whose existence provided the occasion for his being there. His poems of that period, such as "Canción de la torre Spáskaya" ("Song of the Spasskaya Tower"), "Los enamorados del bosque Izmailovo" ("The Lovers of the Izmailovo Forest"), and "El abedul de hierro" ("The Birch Tree of Iron"), show an increasing awareness of the brutalizing effects of statism gone haywire in its zeal to promote revolution in the face of the suffering of numberless individuals. With his awareness has come the poet's increasing insistence on the dignity of suffering, since suffering is always a matter of individual pain. Individuals, for so long howlingly pressed into the abstraction "the masses," come back in a brilliant natural figure of the birch tree, a symbol of Russia itself. The birch tree is "bulletproof, time-proof," it "dreams and groans," and "All the dead in Russia/ rise up through its sap." The recognition of these dreams and groans is both life-giving and value-bearing.

It would be a mistake to think that the poet's solidarity with the suffering masses—even when individuated—springs from a merely intuitive revulsion against authority and its ever-refined (or not) methods of coercion. Padilla knows that, even with Marxian refinements in "human engineering," it is death that makes the inevitable point when the larger phenomenon of diabolical worship of philosophical abstractions (the subject/object switch) is allowed to go uncorrected. In a striking poem, "Una pregunta a la escuela de Frankfurt" ("A Question for the Frankfurt School"), Padilla indicts the well-meaning, social-minded philosophers of that famous school, who refuse to consider the real effects of abstract justifications. Describing a man about to be executed, "who trembles between a rifle and a wall," who will be erased from life "by a blow/ that the mother who bore him/ could never have dreamed of," the poet puts the question squarely: "what does he think?" In setting up an appropriate response, Padilla, like Aristotle, distinguishes between immediate and remote causes. The immediate cause of the man's death is the blow, and he could therefore be standing in anticipation of his death. Behind this likely response stands the remote cause, the philosophical justification; hence, the answer is sharpened into

an accusation of murder: "Answer preferably/ in the following order:/ Horkheimer/ Marcuse/ Adorno."

What then does one do in a world obsessed with its own history, that promotes its problematic past to the status of Hegelian godhood ("History")? Padilla's response is a skeptical one, for although he reveres his literary ancestors and the history of the stories they have created, he also suggests in "Lo mejor es cantar desde ahora" ("Best to Begin This Minute to Celebrate") that, just as modernity saw fit to invent the machine gun to settle contentions decisively, so can he promote the seemingly unpoetic feat of rejecting the past in the name of the here-and-now, where he can "forget the world of my ancestors./ For them ashes, for me life." Although this assertion may strike readers' ears as shockingly disrespectful toward the dead, Padilla's unsentimental abruptness has an underlying ironic point: In a violent time, it is not the living who have all the advantages. In "Herencias" ("Legacies"), the dead are better dead because "they will never have memory, nostalgia,/ never have remorse, as we have." Padilla singles out remorse because it is a sense of bearing the weight of the past without a means to convert it into meaning: it is only a weight, or in the metaphor of "El que regresa a las ergiones claras" ("Returning to Bright Places"), an illness. In this poem, the speaker finds himself incapable of intimacy or authenticity until he has banished his own haunted image "which now the sun has cured,/ the last symptom of that sickness,/ thank heaven, transitory."

As one would expect from a poet reared in the tropics, the sun figures importantly in Padilla's poetry, as it does in that of his Mexican friend, Octavio Paz. As Padilla has come to concentrate on the possibilities of the present, in contrast with meditations on the black-and-white past, readers will note the increasing appearance of colors. The sun becomes a figure for the present, for it is only in the present that the sun can shine and reveal color. The poet, in turn, juxtaposes a third term: poetry. It is in focusing on the present that one can discover the pleasures of the sun, pleasures linked both to warmth and to revelatory possibilities of light, and it is poetry that is the vehicle giving the present-in-the-sun its significance. Conversely, the forces of progress (the future) and the past (history) find in the sun an enemy. By linking these terms, Padilla can also suggest that these same forces are unnatural in their opposition to any of the terms. The sun's revelatory powers also improve vision; in fact, they are responsible for it, as in "A veces me zambullo" ("Sometimes I Plunge"), in which "the country appears/ that for so long we thought/ we were carrying on our shoulders: white, like a warship,/ shining against the sun and against poets." The initial suggestion is that the country's whiteness connoted a pristine mission, but in the clear light of day it appears rather to have been a blankness, the same blankness revealed in the image of Moby Dick, and with the same futile result.

A poet so turned to investing the present with significance will naturally be inclined to talk in terms of "essences" and to find things that are "essential." This same poet will reject suggestions that so-called essences are made up and cleverly inserted into objects in order to fit other conceptions. The verse of this poet will be one of discovery of what is already there, not one of spiritual or philosophical superimposition from without. Padilla's essentialism is, like his opposition to the tyranny of abstraction, not merely an intuitive matter (though one gathers he would prefer it so), but also one subscribed to after much travail. In "Los últimos recuerdos de Sir Walter Raleigh en la Torre de Londres" ("The Last Thoughts of Sir Walter Raleigh in the Tower of London"), the Renaissance discoverer's last words are "Things shine in themselves alone./ It is men who need their jesters and their mirrors." Similarly, in "Andando" ("Walking"), the speaker is suffused with the ardor of essences: "You love this field, these rocks and brambles,/ flowers, beasts, birds of this country." Commonplaces are sustaining, and since these commonplaces are present ones in the light of the sun, they are all the more worth the effort of discovery. A twisted palm tree—Padilla's Cuban equivalent to the Russian birch—withstands even the most feverish effects of tropical weather "until night smothers its flames,/ but the green fronds,

high in the wind, rise above the fire,/ and the trunk, though blackened, nourishes them and sustains them." In this poem, "night" begins to sound like "history," but the trunk, itself nourished by many years of sunlight, has stored up enough sustenance to nourish, in turn, the weak fronds for future growth. The present with its sunlight must have, after all, a way of bridging any temporary darkness—even, as in this case, when the darkness is precisely as recurrent as daylight.

It is hard to tell sometimes whether Padilla is a domestic poet who has been forced to deal with history or a historically determined poet who has found his own contingent nature embarrassing. Whichever the case (and there is some indication that he falls into the latter category), a poet of the present is in a good position to be a poet of domesticity. Padilla's collection *A Fountain, a House of Stone* begins to exchange the world-ranging poems of *Legacies: Selected Poems* for the local, specifically those of Princeton, New Jersey, Padilla's home. In spite of this circumstance, which itself surely points to the steady accompaniment of historical events, Padilla has secured a voice that is richly resonant of his past quest for spontaneous authenticity. The curious fact is that spontaneity, by its very nature, seems to abjure the notion of resonance, of sounding back through time in search of echoes of a larger speech. Spontaneous speech (and "spontaneous" poems) generate their energy by leaving the impression that there is no other speech sponsoring them, historical or literary. Part of Padilla's special importance as a poet is the fact that he manages to communicate this very impression, even as he leaves awareness that his oeuvre, as with any major poet, becomes self-referential; that is, it will increasingly echo its own utterances. The accumulation of these effects becomes, over time, that poet's characteristic voice. In settling down, so to speak, to a less tumultuous life stateside, Padilla still addresses his reader in direct accents, devoid of the reductive niceties of domesticated speech of the sort decried by American poet Theodore Roethke as the signal danger attending any settled-down verse. That the emotional urgency of Padilla's voice has not faded, in spite of his new surroundings and acceptance, in turn directs attention to what is likely to be of enduring value in his poetry, namely his ability to arrest the moment by matching its essential quality with his equivalent summoning of words drawn from the vocabulary of natural human response, a quick-witted yet emotional and unhesitating language. In the poem "Entre el gato y la casa" ("Between the Cat and My House"), the poet confronts his past: "Between the cat and my house/ there is a ramp full of people/ got up as harlequins." Although there is "no longer any sun" to distinguish these figures particularly, they are not invisible, just "blurred and tangled." They have become part of the poet's mental furniture and, like furniture, can be stored. These figures threaten to enter on the "ramp" and become part of his present. Although he notes with documentary plainness that he is "writing in Princeton,/ in a house on Markham Road," this acknowledgement provides no guarantee that domesticity equals privacy. On the contrary, "between one lost country and another still to appear/ I stay still, ready to pounce." Vigilance is the price that the feeling person pays to the persistence of memory. At the same time, Padilla suggests that, though his responsive voice is at the ready, life is not done with changing him in other ways.

One of these ways pertains to one of the few universal facts about all human life: humans die. The current nervous sequestering of the poet serves only to reinforce this theme. It is the biggest theme of all and equally relevant to all, whether actual death occurs with heroic honor or with the mere cessation of breath in small-town America. In "El cemeterio de Princeton" ("Princeton Cemetery"), Padilla remarks, "A town can be a fortunate assembly of many souls,/ but it is also a steady contemplation of death." Even in the midst of lights going on in a house and the rustle of curtains, "we have another casualty." The fact that the "tiled tombstones/ coexist with our workdays" implies that the greatest mystery accompanies each present moment, regardless of its particular circumstances, whether it be a man executed or simply "an empty algebra" of mortality. In other words, it occurs to the poet that the lightly ironic circumstance of his current genteel surroundings spells a huge irony, in that there is always the universal groundswell of death reaching all with such finesse, and yet such ordinariness, that "the routine of our lives/ skips over this thin grass," separating us from oblivion. Suddenly brought into horrible proximity to this fact, where neither sun nor poetry can rescue him, he erupts into a *cri du coeur*: "O God, tell us where, tell us why." One suspects that the "why," should one emerge, belongs, like the harlequins in the cat poem, to "one of my fictions." Because one also suspects that the poet, in spite of the sudden emotional heightening, has something of the same suspicion, he turns a self-promise, in "Para que te liberes de un viejo pensamiento" ("To Free Yourself from Obsessions"), into a directive: "Do not forge any more darkness." Any suspicion about death, any metaphysical "why" directed at its supposed "purpose," is automatically a deathly suspicion.

Although communism may have lost the lead in stripping humanity of its old sense of the fullness of the self, there are plenty of other candidates gathering on the horizon to move in and renew the assault. Padilla's importance as a poet rests not only with the sense apparent to all readers that here is a self—doubting, suffering, fully aware, real person, addressing one as if one also were such a self. It rests as well with the felicitous wedding of this selfhood to themes that seem, as they accumulate, combine, and divide off into numerous permutations, as urgent as the man who seems to be tugging at one's sleeves. It was perhaps fated that so gifted a poet would run afoul of the Cuban authorities sooner or later. Regardless of the embarrassing, Galileo-like "confessions" of ideological "errors" coerced from the man, it is precisely the man for whom the poet comes to the rescue, sustaining the belief that the possibility of rescue from oneself is still one of the nobler tasks that humanistic art cannot help trying to realize.

THE POETRY OF NICANOR PARRA

Author: Nicanor Parra (1914-   )

Type of work: Poetry

Principal published works: *Cancionero sin nombre*, 1937; *Poemas y antipoemas*, 1954 (*Poems and Antipoems*, 1967); *La cuenca larga*, 1958; *Versos de salón*, 1962; *Discursos*, 1962 (coauthored with Pablo Neruda); *Canciones rusas*, 1967; *La camisa de fuerza*, 1968; *Obra gruesa*, 1969; *Artefactos*, 1972; *Poemas de emergencia*, 1972; *Sermones y prédicas del Cristo de Elqui*, 1977 (*Sermons and Homilies of the Christ of Elqui*, 1984); *Nuevos sermones y prédicas del Cristo de Elqui*, 1979; *Ecopoemas*, 1982; *Ultimos sermones*, 1983; *Poesía política*, 1983; *Antipoems: New and Selected*, 1985; *Poemas*, 1988; *Chistes parra desorientar a la policía*, 1989; *Sinfonia de cuna*, 1992

Nicanor Parra is one of the most famous living Spanish American poets. His fame largely rests with his creation of what he called the "antipoem," that is, the poem that rejects the artificial and high-flown language normally associated with poetry and attempts to speak with a voice that is recognized by everybody, not only the elite. It is helpful to know a little about Parra's life in order to understand the main themes of his poetry.

Parra was born in Chillán, a small town two hundred miles south of Santiago, Chile, in 1914. His education gave little indication that he would become a poet. In 1938, he finished his studies of mathematics and physics at the University of Chile in Santiago. For two years (1943-1945), he studied advanced mechanics at Brown University in the United States, and in 1948 he was appointed director of the school of engineering at the University of Chile. He subsequently went abroad for further study, working under one of England's foremost cosmologists, E. A. Milne, at the University of Oxford in England from 1950 to 1952. In 1952, Parra returned to his alma mater in Chile and was awarded the chair of theoretical physics there, a position he held until retirement. Parra's subsequent invitations to lecture and teach abroad were based on the merits of his poetry, which was attracting increasing attention. He was invited in 1963 to the Soviet Union, where he spent six months supervising the translation into Spanish of an anthology by Soviet poets. In 1966, Parra was a visiting professor at Louisiana State University, and in 1971 he was a visiting professor at New York, Columbia, and Yale Universities. Parra's work has been awarded a number of prestigious literary prizes. His *Poemas y antipoemas* (poems and antipoems) was awarded the Premio del Sindicato de Escritores (Writers' Union Prize), and his *Obra gruesa* (solid work) the Premio Nacional de Literatura (National Literary Prize).

The best way to discuss Parra's poetry is to use a chronological evaluation. Parra's poetry is not like that of César Vallejo (1892-1938) and Pablo Neruda (1904-1973), for which there is a clear watershed (in their cases the year of political commitment, 1927 for Vallejo and 1936 for Neruda). His work is more even in the sense that the world-vision expressed and the techniques used to express that vision are more or less constant throughout his poetic career. His work has been bracketed under the term "antipoetry," and much of his later work is a natural outgrowth of the primary objective. One of the incidental advantages for Parra's work of its consistent focus of vision is its ability to be translated into English relatively easily. Despite its relative uniformity, however, there are four discernible stages in Parra's work: juvenilia (1937-1950), antipoetry (1954-1967), social criticism (1968-1976), and poems in a prophetic voice (1977 on).

In the juvenilia stage, Parra is still attempting to find his poetic voice and is still largely derivative. In *Cancionero sin nombre* (ballads without name), for example, Parra imitates the style, verse form, and imagery of *Romancero gitano* (1928; *The Gypsy Ballads*, 1951, 1953) by Spanish poet Federico García Lorca. His ballads of this period do not yet show the "strong poet" (to use Harold Bloom's term) of later years; in these early years Parra is still a derivative poet.

In the antipoetry stage (1954-1967), there is evidence of the maturity and originality of Parra's poetic voice. In the poetry of this period, Parra rejects the conventions of poetry, in many ways coinciding, in spirit if not in practice, with the call for "impure poetry" enunciated in 1935 by his compatriot, Pablo Neruda, in the journal he founded called *Caballo verde para la poesía* (a green horse for poetry). That poetry would be "worn out as if by acid by everyday labor, suffused with sweat and smoke, smelling like urine and white lily," a poetry from which no element, however unpoetic, had been screened. Parra gives an individual twist to this idea, perhaps the result of the scientific, anti-abstract nature of his mind; after all, his professional and educational training was in the sciences and not the arts. Parra saw poems as mathematical theorems; "Maximum content, minimum of words," he once said; "Economy of language, no metaphors, no literary tropes." Parra's work, true to this definition, does not refer to the poetic tradition. He writes as a nonqualified poet who nevertheless hits the nail on the head every time. He is thus the absolute opposite of a poet such as T. S. Eliot, for whom literary resonance—allusion to other works of poetry—is of utmost importance. Parra, on the contrary, tries to wipe the poetic slate clean.

"Advertencia al lector" ("Warning to the Reader"), the opening poem from *Poemas y antipoemas*, is a type of *ars poetica* in the sense that it enunciates the aims of Parra's poetry. The opening line of this poem ("The author is not responsible for any inconvenience caused by his work") gives a good indication of the iconoclastic tone of this collection. The second stanza sets down precisely what Parra's poetry is about:

> The doctors of the law say this book shouldn't
>   see the light of day:
> The word *rainbow* can't be found anywhere in it,
> Much less the words *sorrow*
> Or *torquate*.

> Sure there's loads of chairs and tables.
> Coffins! Desk Supplies!
> All of which makes me burst with pride
> Because, as I see it, the sky is falling in on us,
>   bit by bit.

Parra rejects words such as "rainbow," "sorrow," and "torquate" because they are typical of a romantic and sentimental type of poetry that purports to be above the toils of everyday life. His poetry has ordinary things such as chairs and tables, coffins and desk supplies. Notice how Parra will mention "coffins" but not "sorrow"; the intermediary image here is death, and to express that image Parra prefers to use the concrete term "coffin" rather than the abstract term "death." This choice reflects the concrete and anti-abstract nature of his mind.

The iconoclastic theme returns later in the same poem, when Parra invites his readers to "burn" their "boats" (using the historical reference to Hernán Cortés' conquest of the Aztec empire as a means of suggesting the imaginative leap into the unknown). That he is trying to write poetry without relying on antecedents is clear when he describes his project as similar to that of the Phoenicians. As he says: "Like the Phoenicians I'm trying to develop my own alphabet." Other poems from the same collection emphasize a similar thematics. In "Los vicios del mundo moderno" ("The Vices of the Modern World"), for example, Parra uses the technique of chaotic enumeration, popularized by Walt Whitman, to describe the vices of the modern world, which include "racial discrimination," "the manipulations of high finance," "the clandestine white-slave trade carried on by international sodomites," "the deification of the phallus," and "the gory humor of the theory of relativity." Parra's enumeration, which forms the middle part of the poem, is able to express the frantic and disjointed all-inclusiveness of the modern world.

Perhaps Parra's most famous poem is "La montaña rusa" ("The Roller Coaster"), from *Versos de salón* (salon verses). The poem is worth quoting in its entirety, since it is able to capture like none other the iconoclasm of his poetic stance:

For half a century
Poetry was the paradise
Of the solemn fool.
Until I came along
And built my roller coaster.

Go up and have a ride, if you feel like it.
But don't blame me if you come down
Bleeding from your nose and mouth.

The idea of this poem is that Mount Olympus, where traditionally the poets went to drink inspiration in the spring of Castalia, has been exchanged for the roller coaster. Parra's poetry has more in common with the modern world: It is neither gentle nor uplifting; it may even lead to a nosebleed. "La poesía terminó conmigo" ("Poetry Ends with Me"), from the same collection, echoes the same theme in that it emphasizes how Parra's new poetics has nothing to do with the traditional concept of poetry. "Conversación galante" ("Lovers Talk"), likewise from the same collection, uses irony to deflate the notion of romantic love. Although the title might engender expectations of a conversation between two lovers declaring eternal love for each other, there is nothing more than a hurried, angular conversation that concludes with the words: "Stop talking and put your clothes on/ Before your husband comes home."

"Ultimo brindis" ("The Final Toast"), from *Canciones rusas* (Russian songs), reveals a facet of Parra's verse that is often overlooked: its conceptual complexity despite the impression it gives of lexical clarity. It addresses the eternal conundrum of time, specifically its division into the three realms of past, present, and future, none of which, as the poem points out, can truly be grasped.

There are only two cards
In the deck:
The present and the future.

And not even two
Because everyone knows
That the present only exists
To the degree that it becomes the past
And then it's gone . . . ,
                                    like youth.

Although this is a conceptually difficult poem, Parra manages to express its scientific complexity in clear language. "Aromos" ("Acacias"), from the same collection, is another example of the lexical simplicity of Parra's poetry. It re-creates the poet's sensation of sadness on hearing that an old flame has married someone else, but does so without recourse to metaphor. "Nadie" ("Nobody"), from the same collection, focuses on existential sadness, particularly the loneliness that is part of modern urban life. It describes the poet's feelings on hearing a woman in an adjacent apartment sobbing for lost love. It makes its point without using metaphors; it simply describes the curtains in the poet's room as they move and the rows of poplars that are rocking in the wind. It ends with a description of how the poet is "dead tired from so much sobbing."

In the social critique stage (1967-1976), Parra expands his poetic repertoire to include the merciless exposure of the ills of society in a way reminiscent of the caustic poetry of one of the most famous poets of the colonial period, the Peruvian Juan de Valle y Caviedes. "Inflación" ("Inflation"), for example, addresses the social theme directly. It takes a hard look at inflation not from the point of view of economists but from the man in the street who suffers its consequences directly.

The cost of bread goes up so the cost of bread
   goes up again
Rents go up
So in a flash all rents double in price
The cost of clothes goes up
So the cost of clothes goes up again.
There's no way out
We're caught in a vicious circle.

This poem rejects the explanation of the phenomenon given by politicans and economists and simply states the facts of economic life as they are. "Tiempos modernos" ("Modern Times"), from *Poemas de emergencia* (emergency poems), likewise addresses a political theme. Written in 1972, at the height of the Cold War, the poem suggests how the world is trapped by the opposing forces of the superpowers.

We're living through horrible times
it's impossible to say anything without contradicting
    yourself
it's impossible to hold your tongue without being
    a pawn of the Pentagon.
Everyone knows there's no other choice
all roads lead to Cuba
but the air is filthy
and breathing is a waste of time.

The poem simply states things as they are for the average citizen of Latin America. It ends on a note of pessimism. Even the new hope of social justice embodied by Cuba leads nowhere, since "everything is contaminated from the start." Parra rejects capitalism as well as communism for being straitjackets. Two short poems that appear in *Artifactos* (artifacts) in a sense speak for themselves. The first is titled "USA" and reads simply: "Where liberty/ is a statue." The second, which immediately follows it, runs as follows: "If Fidel Castro played it fair/ he would believe in me/ in the same way I believe in him: history will absolve me." Parra turns on its head one of Castro's famous statements ("History will absolve me"), which the Cuban used to justify his revolutionary activity. In both these poems, Parra uses ironic humor to criticize a political system. He is a friend of neither communism nor capitalism.

In the prophet's voice stage (1977 on), Parra adopts the tone and imagery of the Old Testament prophets and also of Christ of the Sermon on the Mount in order to expose the ills of contemporary society, particularly in terms of its spiritual dimension or lack of it. Parra follows a long line of Latin American poets who use biblical imagery as a social commentary; examples abound but the best known are Vallejo in *Poemas humanos* (1939; *Human Poems*, 1968) and Neruda in *Canto general* (1950; the general song). In *Sermones y prédicas del Cristo de Elqui* (*Sermons and Homilies of the Christ of Elqui*), Parra adopts the persona of an itinerant preacher he had seen preaching in his childhood in Chile during the 1920's. Domingo Zárate Vega, who left his job as a construction foreman in order to preach to the masses on streetcorners, was known popularly as El Cristo de Elqui

because he made no secret of his belief that he was the reincarnation of Christ. He was something of a Groucho Marx character in real life, and this is the impression that Parra's poetry gives of him. The Christ of Elqui in Parra's poetry, for example, starts off by giving his flock some advice of a "practical nature," which includes "early to rise," "don't wear tight shoes," "don't make the mistake of eating shellfish," "don't kill birds unless absolutely necessary," and "don't retain gas in your stomach." In section 23, he dares his audience to take communion without first making confession, use the Bible for toilet paper, and spit on the Chilean flag.

Parra's *Nuevos sermones y prédicas del Cristo de Elqui* (new sermons and homilies of the Christ of Elqui), which was published two years later, carried on in the same iconoclastic vein. Section 28 begins with the Cristo de Elqui exhorting his flock to obey traffic lights. In section 29, he asks them not to clip the wings of their chickens, and in section 35, he asks them to stop confusing him with Santa Claus. Section 53 is particularly sardonic. The Christ of Elqui predicts that "very soon the Left will be victorious" but the Right will attempt to curb their influence in "any way they can/ assassination - dollars - ITT," and finally that "he will commit suicide/ once he finds himself betrayed and alone." The irony of this is that Parra is referring to the rise and fall of the first Marxist president elected to power in Latin America, Salvador Allende, who was president of Chile from 1970 until 1973. All the details the Christ of Elqui gives are correct; however, when this poem was published, the events described had already happened. *Nuevos sermones y prédicas del Cristo de Elqui* can therefore be seen as a veiled critique of Augusto Pinochet, who at that time was in power.

Parra combines the spiritual with the political in his poetry of this period. In *Chistes parra desorientar a la policía* (jokes to mislead the police), Parra again turns his irony on society and accuses the traditionalist, bourgeois society ushered in by the independence movements of the early nineteenth century of being a straitjacket for the twentieth century: "Terrific! Now who'll/ save us from our liberators?/ Our backs are against the wall."

In *Ultimos sermones* (last sermons), Parra once more attacks capitalists, taking up the persona of the Christ of Elqui. In "Cristo de Elqui se lanza contra los patrones desvergonzados" ("The Christ of Elqui Takes on the Shameless Bosses"), savage irony is directed at the bosses who take their employees for a ride. Parra's anger is suggested by the words he puts into the boss's mouth: "iron this shirt for me asshole/ bring me a tree from the forest/ get down on your knees you little shit/ go check those fuses." The answer to "But what if I get electrocuted?" is "Oh! that's no big deal." In later works, Parra remains as iconoclastic as ever. He rejects rhetoric, lies, and the rich, standing for antipoetry, truth, and the underdog.

THE POETRY OF OCTAVIO PAZ

Author: Octavio Paz (1914-   )

Type of work: Poetry

Principal published works: *Luna silvestre*, 1933; *Bajo tu clara sombra y otros poemas sobre España*, 1937; *Raíz del hombre*, 1937; *Entre la piedra y la flor*, 1941; *Libertad bajo palabra*, 1949, 1960; *¿Aguila o sol?*, 1951 (*Eagle or Sun?*, 1970); *Semillas para un himno*, 1954; *Piedra de sol*, 1957 (*Sun Stone*, 1963); *La estación violenta*, 1958; *Agua y viento*, 1959; *Salamandra*, 1962; *Selected Poems*, 1963; *Blanco*, 1967 (English translation, 1971); *Discos visuales*, 1968; *Topoemas*, 1968; *La centena*, 1969; *Ladera este*, 1969; *Configurations*, 1971; *Renga*, 1972 (in collaboration with three other poets; *Renga: A Chain of Poems*, 1972); *Early Poems*, 1973; *Pasado en claro*, 1975 (*A Draft of Shadows and Other Poems*, 1979); *Vuelta*, 1976; *Selected Poems*, 1979; *Airborn/Hijos del Aire*, 1981 (with Charles Tomlinson); *Selected Poems*, 1984; *Arbol adentro*, 1987 (*A Tree Within*, 1987); *The Collected Poems of Octavio Paz, 1957-1987*, 1987

Octavio Paz is a poet and essayist of international stature. His literary career has spanned more than sixty years, producing more than twenty books of poetry in addition to more than twenty prose books on a wide range of subjects. Perhaps the greatest living poet of the Spanish-speaking world, Paz in 1990 became the first Mexican to be honored with the Nobel Prize in Literature.

Although recognized as an intellectual leader of Latin America, Paz takes greatest pride in his identity as a poet. He assigns a special, vital function to poetry in human life. In Paz's view, writing and reading poetry contribute to the creation of a better world. Poetry remedies the isolation and spiritual desolation of humanity by facilitating the experience of unity beyond the grip of time, history, and alienation.

Many different cultures and literatures have influenced Paz's poetry: Mexico's pre-Columbian culture and heritage, Mexico's Spanish colonial legacy and modern revolution, Spanish art and literature, the French Surrealism of André Breton, the writings of Stéphane Mallarmé, and Eastern myth and philosophy. Paz is particularly indebted to French Surrealism and Eastern philosophy for helping him to articulate the role of poetry in combating the alienation created by modern society.

From the beginning of his literary career, Paz maintained that the values of poetry need to be lived. He met many poets during his first visit to Spain in 1937. He directly experienced, among the anti-Fascist forces loyal to the Spanish Republic, how poetry restores the human spirit, awakens consciousness, and destroys alienation. He supported the anti-Fascist cause in Spain's Civil War through his poetry and other literary activities. When the Fascist forces of General Francisco Franco triumphed against the Spanish Republic in 1939, Paz realized that political action could not stop the spread of evil in the world. In spite of his disillusionment, Paz affirmed that the poet's function is to remind readers of the inner values of love, communion, and solidarity so necessary in a world dominated by war, hatred, and death.

While serving in the Mexican diplomatic service in Paris immediately after World War II, Paz became friends with the founder of Surrealism, André Breton. Disenchanted with politics and the course of history in the aftermath of the war, Paz was attracted to Surrealism because it maintained that the exercise of poetry could reestablish the primordial innocence of humanity. Although Paz did not adopt the techniques of Surrealism, such as automatic writing, he shared Surrealism's view that poetry could subvert the established order and bring positive social change. Poetry invites the reader and poet to experience ecstatic union with "the other" (woman, nature, or language), thereby bringing liberation from the tyranny of alienation and the world's corruption.

Masterpieces of Latino Literature

Surrealistic themes are evident in Paz's earliest poetry. In "Más allá del amor" ("Beyond Love"), the poet invites a woman to escape with him to a realm of existence beyond time and duality. He reminds her that she belongs to the night, which knows no boundaries, and that she can enable him to experience oneness and transcend alienation. In another early poem, "Himno entre ruinas" ("Hymn Among the Ruins"), the poet credits poetry with the power to renew a world destroyed by war. The poet seeks to conquer decay, death, and injustice by taking his awareness beyond irreconcilable opposites. This experience allows him to recover a pristine level of language, one with the power to make fully present what it signifies.

In *¿Aguila o sol?* (1951; *Eagle or Sun?*, 1970), composed shortly after World War II, Paz struggles against words that have been corrupted by serving the interests of the agents of death and destruction. He evokes figures from Mexico's pre-Columbian past and memories of his own childhood in his attempt to regain a state of primordial innocence. The poet transcends corrupt language and the evils of history to find a state of inner silence from which he is empowered to create a new pure language capable of changing consciousness and creating an ideal society.

Piedra de sol (1957; *Sun Stone*, 1963) marks the end of the first period of Paz's poetic work, before he began to be influenced by Oriental philosophy as Mexico's ambassador to India (1962-1968). This poem expresses Paz's principal themes: alienation and its banishment through union with "the other," and the quest for transcendental experience. The poet seeks to experience the poetic moment beyond the duality of self and other through making love.

Piedra de sol imitates the form of the Aztec sun stone, a circular calendar of 584 days. The poem, composed of 584 lines, opens and closes with the same six lines. These opening and closing lines, while suggesting that time is cyclical as the Aztecs believed, evoke a reality outside the passage of time, an edenic realm where duality has no place. In the rest of the poem, however, the poet is ejected from this paradise and confronted with the evils of

history. The poet momentarily escapes alienation through lovemaking only to encounter again the dehumanizing forces of modern life. The poet praises the role of women in his life. Through the ecstasy of lovemaking, they redeem him from his alienation and free him from the evils of human history.

Piedra de sol is generally considered to be Paz's most important poem. While evoking an eternal present before time and history, the poem presents a complete time cycle dominated by alienation and the horrors of history. Through the intervention of women, the poet periodically escapes the cycle in poetic moments of ecstatic love.

Salamandra (1962) represents a change in Paz's poetic expression. He began to recognize the importance of the space that surrounds the words of the poem, thereby acknowledging the role of silence in poetry. The space surrounding the words of poetry suggests the silent awareness beyond words that both the poet and the reader can enjoy. The white space refers to the multiple meanings that the words can evoke. Paz's poems were no longer primarily verbal, becoming visual as well.

Paz identifies the literal, scientific mentality that can only fathom one meaning for language, as the enemy of poetry. In the title poem, "Salamandra," the poet works to subvert scientific discourse and free language from its contamination by history. Paz reveals multiple meanings for the word "salamander" and thus enlivens language's latent possibilities. Through such liberated and purified language, the poet and the reader both savor a realm of all possibilities available in the eternal present of an alert but serene awareness.

Paz began integrating Oriental thought, especially Buddhist philosophy, into his poetry during his tenure as Mexican ambassador to India. The poetry of Mallarmé also influenced his writing in this period. Both Buddhist philosophy and Mallarmé advocate the negation of the ego, viewing it as the root of personal alienation and suffering. By applying this notion to the process of writing poetry, Paz understood writing poetry to be an ascetic process in which the poet denies the ego and disappears into the poem, so that its words can take on their own life. Surrounded by the silence of white space, the words are freed to take on an infinite play of meanings.

Ladera este (1969) investigates Indian philosophy, religion, and art through love and travel poetry. In the long poem *Blanco* (1967), also greatly indebted to his stay in India, Paz experiments more boldly with the interplay of poetic text and space. It was first published on one continuous sheet of paper, printed in black and red ink with various typefaces. A central column of text alternates with two parallel columns on either side. The three columns are either spaced separately or combined, and are distinguished from each other only by their distinctive typefaces. The typographical layout of the poem, with its different typefaces, ink colors, and columns, allows for many alternative readings. Although it is one long poem, *Blanco* has fourteen texts that can be read separately or in various combinations.

The poem opens in the central column with an evocation of language's origins in a level of consciousness undefiled by time and the corruption of history. A lamp represents the poet's alert but silent state of consciousness that patiently waits for language to emerge from the transcendental silence. When the words of the poem finally flow forth, the poet dissolves with his beloved in the ecstasy of pure language. The side columns are love poems that separate and join like two lovers. When the poet penetrates the woman, he fertilizes the words that create the poetry in the central column.

Blanco reflects Paz's study of the Buddhist Tantric tradition, which understands lovemaking to be a means for spiritual liberation. The words of the poem are erotic objects free to repel or unite with each other in the white space that surrounds the poetic text. The poet compares writing poetry to making love to a woman. Like Mallarmé, Paz maintains that living language is made of flesh, as is the human person. In *Blanco*, erotic love and the creation of poetry are aspects of the same experience of transcending time and language.

In 1968, Paz resigned from his ambassadorship to India in protest against the massacre of student protesters in Mexico City by government troops.

Paz records his reaction to Mexico upon his return in *Vuelta* (1976). "Vuelta" means "return." After a long absence, Paz reencounters his past and is confronted by the degradation of life in Mexico City. He finds himself in the grip of alienation, overwhelmed by feelings of separation and emptiness. Nostalgic for the experience of oneness, the poet laments the absurdity of modern life. He decries the absurdity of Mexico City's unchecked growth. In asking himself how he should relate to the world's afflictions, the poet responds by affirming the need for ethical action informed by a keen sense of social responsibility.

Vuelta reveals Paz's ongoing preoccupation with the relationship between the poetic text and space. Although the title poem does not demonstrate an obvious experimentation with space, as do other poems, notably *Blanco*, space makes a vital contribution to the poem's message. The poem is organized spatially to create a counterpoint to the poet's memories, impressions, and reflections, suggesting the instability of existence. The space breaks the linear development of the poetic text.

> Wind
> on the dusty corners
>   turns the papers
> Yesterday's news
>   more remote
> than a cuneiform tablet smashed to bits
> Cracked scriptures
>   languages in pieces
> the signs were broken
>   atl tlachinolli
>   was split
>   burnt water

By scattering the words in space, the poet displaces the syntax of the text and breaks the flow of meaning. As in earlier poems, space functions to offer the reader a free zone where multiple meanings can spring from the text.

In another poem from *Vuelta*, "Nocturno de San Ildefonso" ("San Ildefonso Nocturne"), the poet evokes his days as a student in the preparatory school housed in the eighteenth century building of San Ildefonso. The poet denounces religious and political intolerance and asserts that everyone is implicated when those who refuse to submit to political or religious orthodoxy are persecuted. Paz identifies politics and ideological absolutism to be the antithesis of the ethics of poetry that he espouses: love and union with "the Other," who should be valued as much as oneself. After portraying Mexican reality and the poet's own past in such bleak terms, he takes refuge in his wife as "the Other" who anchors him and helps him to overcome his despair.

In *Pasado en claro* (1975; *A Draft of Shadows*, 1979), a long autobiographical poem, Paz assumes a markedly confessional tone. The poet reviews his past and the influences that shaped him. He evokes very specific memories about his parents, his grandfather, and the places he knew as a child. He examines not only his childhood memories but also his relationship with poetry and with himself.

The poet reflects on his own life and on language. He was never motivated by the usual material or spiritual goals of money, power, or holiness. Erotic love brought him wholeness, an enfleshed spiritual experience. God did not speak to him from the clouds. His body spoke to him from the leaves of the fig tree.

Death has an important relationship with language and poetry in *Pasado en claro*. He reverses the opening image from the Gospel of John. For him, the word did not take on flesh, but flesh became word and discovered that it could not escape its own mortality. In death, the poet discovered language, yet death is not the only possible escape from history: In the purification of language, pronouns dissolve as the self unites with "the Other."

Although the poet reveals poignant memories and impressions from his childhood, ultimately all that remains of his memories, his poetry, and his identity are shadows. The words that capture his memories are rippling shadows. His poems are traveling houses made of reflections. They are made of air that sculpts itself. The shadows that constitute his poetry create him; he is the shadow that his words hurl. The things that are most important to him are made of shadows: his personal identity, his memories, and his poetry.

Paz demonstrates that his poetic inspiration continues unabated in *Arbol adentro*, 1987 (*A Tree Within*, 1987). The nature of language and poetry remain central themes for him. In the title poem, the poet describes a speaking tree growing within him. Its tangled foliage is its thoughts.

The wind is the central protagonist in "Un viento llamado Bob Rauschenberg" ("A Wind Called Bob Rauschenberg"). The wind makes mute paralytic objects sing, laugh, and dance. The wind makes the landscape open its eyes, stand up, and begin to walk, creating dark murmurs as it goes. The wind understands what the universe says. The poet speaks of the interminable conversation of the universe and identifies the sounds of nature as its language.

In "Entre lo que veo y digo . . ." ("Between What I See and What I Say . . ."), the poet finds poetry in the gaps between words and concepts, where meaning can only be intuited: between speech and silence, existence and nonexistence.

The poet's own death is the subject of "Pequeña variación" ("Little Variation"). He reconciles himself with his eventual death by telling himself that it will be like the timeless experiences that occur in lovemaking. In death, the poet will be consumed by pure time, by eternity.

Over the span of Paz's career as a poet, certain themes have remained constant. Poetry celebrates the ecstasy that takes the poet into an infinite dimension in which time and history are transcended. Poetry is a vehicle of liberation for the poet and the reader, making the experience of a primal unified reality accessible. Poetry re-creates for the reader the experience of oneness the poet enjoyed. Poetry is a solution to the isolation and alienation of humanity in the modern world. Writing poetry that fosters the experience of transcendence contributes to creating a better world.

THE POETRY OF ALBERTO RÍOS

Author: Alberto Ríos (1952-   )
Type of work: Poetry
Principal published works: *Whispering to Fool the Wind* (1982); *Five Indiscretions* (1985); *The Lime Orchard Woman* (1988); *Teodoro Luna's Two Kisses* (1990)

Albert Ríos was born in Nogales, on Arizona's border with Mexico, to a Mexican father and an English mother. He grew up learning Spanish but had lost command of the language by early adolescence. The distance between those two languages he metaphorizes in one poem as "a third animal." In his poems, Ríos investigates both worlds, or perhaps more accurately the space that exists between them. Critics have mentioned Magical Realists such as Gabriel García Márquez when speaking of the surreal element in Ríos' poems, and in a review David Barber describes Ríos as "a writer who smudges the lines between the actual and the marvelous as a matter of course."

Ríos began producing a book roughly every two years after the appearance of *Whispering to Fool the Wind*, which won the Academy of American Poets' Walt Whitman Award for 1981. *The Iguana Killer* (1984), a book of short stories, appeared between his first two poetry collections. Gary Soto and Lorna Dee Cervantes have been mentioned among the Chicano poets whose work bears similar bicultural traits. Ríos blends the miraculous with the everyday through a fusion of his talents as storyteller and master of the deep image or metaphor. The result is most often either an eccentric character or a startling story or drama in miniature that is immediately accessible, but only up to a point, so that despite the apparent familiarity of language and image, the poems are rarely easy reading.

Ríos' first collection, *Whispering to Fool the Wind*, offers an eccentric cast of characters including the woman "who wore her purse close like an arm/ in a third black sleeve"; the man who grew a new tooth each year, until he looked "like the old cartoon wolf/ in a zoot suit flipping a coin and whistling"; and the impatient man "who had grown once/ so angry/ his look had terrified/ even the harvest."

Among these people are the persona of the poet, the first-person speaker whose mother takes him at the age of ten to the frighteningly buxom fortune teller in one of Ríos' most frequently anthologized poems, "Madre Sofía." Ríos' fascination with physical detail is obvious throughout the poem and lends to it an almost visceral reality at the same time that it taps into the resources of the bizarre:

> Central in that head grew unfamiliar poppies
> from a face mahogany, eyes half yellow
> half gray at the same time, goat and fog,
> slit eyes of the devil, his tweed suit, red
> lips, and she smelled of smoke, cigarettes,
> but a diamond smoke . . .

Reading such a passage, one feels that one can "see," yet somehow not quite "visualize," the scene. Mingled with the exotic images in the poem are humorous references to Oral Roberts and baseball. Ríos' subtle sense of humor also figures in poems such as "The Purpose of Altar Boys" and "The Arroyo, Sergio, and Me," in which the description appears to be autobiographical.

Ríos' relatives also inhabit his books. His grandmother, in by far his most frequently anthologized poem, "Nani," becomes something of a metaphor or symbol for a recurrent theme in his poems: the difficulty of communication, even with those to whom one feels closest. Now able to understand only about a third of the Spanish that "dribbles down her mouth as she serves/ me albondigas [meatballs]," the speaker perceives that, standing at the stove, "she does something with words/ and looks at me only with her/ back." He discovers that he can understand her by watching her, as if he can read her gestures, her face:

Near her mouth, I see a wrinkle speak
of a man whose body serves
the ants like she serves me, then more words
from more wrinkles about children, words
about this and that, flowing more
easily from these other mouths.

The "man whose body serves/ the ants" is his grandfather, now deceased (from "Mi Abuelo"). The speaker also discovers that much of himself "will die with her," and that hers were the words for what he was and what he could have been.

The passages quoted above exemplify one facet of Ríos' free-verse line: It is largely end-stopped or grammatical, with line breaks occurring somewhat predictably within the sentence, for example, prior to a prepositional phrase. "Nani" is of particular interest formally, as it is a sestina that is not set up in sestets and not composed in the conventional iambic pentameter. Several poems in his next book of poetry, *Five Indiscretions* (1985), in which he extends his play with form, are composed with the entire left margin capitalized, a practice that Ríos continued in subsequent collections and that some readers would associate with increasing attention to "line integrity." Ríos, however, is by no means predictable. In his first book, he offers an unconventional, nonstanzaic, eighteen-line villanelle, "La Sequía" (the drought). The traditional villanelle, one of the most taxing of all fixed forms, requires nineteen lines set up as five tercets and a quatrain. In *Five Indiscretions*, "The Language of Great-Aunts" is cast in the challenging sestina form, this time using sestets.

In poems such as "A Man Walks as if Trapped," Ríos employs the open or run-on (enjambed) free-verse style, which emphasizes unpredictable line breaks: "No hunter can catch him/ lithe and properly built/ hatless like a steep hill." Occasionally, as in "The Mouths of Two People" and "The Carlos Who Died, and Left Only This," he composes an entire poem in a single sentence. The reader is almost always aware in such poems of the tension between sentence and line; moreover, Ríos often fractures his stanzas by allowing lines to flow across the space that separates them rather than ending a stanza with terminal punctuation. Ríos

also includes two prose poems in the collection.

It is not so much the technique and craft of Ríos' poems that strike the reader, however, as his creation of a world that is strange to non-Hispanics but from which he does not allow the reader to feel estranged. In "Snow Cones from the Old Carnival," he alternates lines of Spanish, so that about a third of the poem is in his "other" language. "Old Man on the Hospital Porch" appears in both English and Spanish (as "Anciano en el porche del hospital"). Readers enter his world through people's names: Panfilo, Carlos (the recurring alter self), Mariquita, the boxer Reies Madero, Flora Carrillo, Father Torres, El Santo the wrestler, and Doña Carolina. Readers then come to know his world by the peculiar music of its place names: Chiapas, Guaymas, Oaxaca, the Tacaná volcano, the Santa Cruz River, the movie houses (Kino Viejo, El Dorado, Buena Vista), and the bar known as El Molino Rojo (The Red Mill, or the Moulin Rouge, to use its familiar French name).

"Five Indiscretions," the 155-line title poem of his second poetry collection, is Ríos at his best, taking risks with both content and language. Flora Carrillo, whose fifth indiscretion leads to the birth of her only child, a daughter, avenges herself on her lover with a knife "Long as the member of this man" by taking from him "his rolled tongue/ Hanging there between his thin legs/ . . .This small and second body of his/ Which had found its way to her second mouth." The "power" she derives, and what makes her "happy," is "Never once making love to a man," as the last line says. Metonymically concealed in this lyric narrative of castration and fellatio—often beautiful and frequently humorous (but never painful, even for a male reader)—is her discovery of the power of words, of tongue and mouth.

For no apparent reason, Ríos' third collection of poems, *The Lime Orchard Woman* (1988), has attracted less critical attention than his other books. The dozen poems that make up the first section are sensual and passionate. They are not so much poems of love and romance as they are of carnal desire and lust. In nine of them, the central character is a woman. The initial poem, "The Industry of

Hard Kissing," can be said to set the pattern, beginning as it does with a comical observation, "Knocking cows over when they sleep/ They get mad." It moves quickly to a more serious proposition, that "Ordinary life falls the quickest/ Is the easiest to make/ Breathe hard." This perception arises from "The quiet of a sad desire/ For someone/ You cannot have/ Again, this small cancer/ Of the happy soul."

Other poems in the opening section range from the playful "Dressing for Dinner," in which the first-person speaker tries to imagine being a woman but can "only pretend," to the woman who gives "tourniquet kisses." As in many of his poems, oral imagery is reiterated, with references to lips, tongues, and mouths that are often quite sensual. A Freudian symbolist would detect various female or vaginal symbols in, for example, piñatas and Mason jars. Without pursuing that angle of approach to Ríos' poems, it is worth noting that the mouth as a symbol can be seen as simultaneously and sometimes ambiguously both creative (in the act of speech, for example, or as it relates to kissing and procreation, particularly as Ríos refers in "Five Indiscretions" to the woman's "second mouth") and destructive (the devouring mouth of hell, for example, and the so-called *vagina dentata* or "vagina with teeth" that reoccurs in Indian lore).

In the title poem, María, "the lime orchard woman," responds angrily at the age of twelve to her developing breasts, and she dreams of wearing "High heels backward on her feet" in order to keep her balance. At the age of twenty-eight, her concern has moved to her broad thighs, the result of her "Years of crying/ When she was all mouth and chewing/ To feel better, all without boys." When her husband Miguel deserts her and invests his passion in the orchard, she dreams again of high heels and of the time "When her breasts were those small animals,/ Just big enough/ To touch him with their mouths/ Not angry."

Most of the poems in the second section of *The Lime Orchard Woman* involve male personas, especially relatives (cousins, grandfathers, and uncles). Two are clearly in the Magical Realist vein: "Incident at Imuris," in which watermelons are

found to be cocoons from which thousands of green moths emerge, and "The Sword Eusebio Montero Swallowed, and Kept There," in which an opera singer uses his mouth (rather than his voice, it would appear) to sing down a tornado.

The third section of the book mostly entails the first-person speaker and includes some of Ríos' most lyrical poems, such as "I Drive While Kissing You" and "Piece for Flute and Clarinet." Several of the poems in that section directly involve music or dance, including "Practicing the Cornet," "Edith Piaf Is Dead," and "Like This It Is We Think to Dance." The last part of the collection sustains the presence of the first-person speaker, who is even more consistently and obviously autobiographical than elsewhere. The signal is given in the first poem, "Nogales, 1958," in which Ríos flirts with nostalgia. In the final poem of *The Lime Orchard Woman*, "Listening for Tonight," Ríos listens to the "noises of the house" and then imagines the "Noise that will be," until he can conjure a "pointillist dream" in which he can hear the future.

Teodoro Luna's Two Kisses (1990), the first of Ríos' books to be published by a large commercial press (Norton), drew more critical attention, nearly all of it positive, than any of his earlier work, with the possible exception of his collection of short stories, *The Iguana Killer* (1984), for which he won the first Western States Book Award for fiction. Throughout Ríos' poems, but insistently in *Teodoro Luna's Two Kisses*, he employs metaphors of fragmentation and dismemberment, pieces of things, and for people in particular, of body parts. This representation of the whole by way of various parts is called synecdoche and was once described by Robert Frost as his favorite figure of speech. It functions poetically in a metonymic fashion rather than metaphorically. Cordelia Chavez Candelaria has commented on Ríos' "imagery of fragmentation and dismemberment" in his first two books, suggesting that the "detached body parts may even be seen as a kind of cubistic language, one especially suited to the outrages and even to some of the more benign outcomes of the twentieth century." David Barber indicates an undercurrent in the poems, a "maddening pattern of carnal wear and tear, the manhandling and possession of women eerily depicted as literal disfigurement."

Most of the poems in *Teodoro Luna's Two Kisses* do involve detached body parts, including the short title poem, in which the lusty Teodoro makes love to his wife "Not so much with his lips as with his brows." In the next poem, "Teodoro Luna's Old Joke," he is described as having lost an ear in the war and the use of an arm from years of milking cows. Now his wife can see in his eyes "the second white parts/ Of what he was becoming./ First his hair, and his eyes, and his flatfish tongue." She waits for him to the end, wearing her red dress and ready "That he would be young enough again for both of them,/ That he might lift her,/ The way he had lifted her the first time with his many eyes."

For Teodoro Luna's brother Anselmo, the man who becomes a priest after he burns the eggs for lack of a spatula, that object becomes over the years "The Hand of God." Most often in the poems, the body parts are associated with eros, as in "Mr. Luna in the Afternoon":

> She put her body in his mouth.
> Some things persist, without
> Written instruction. He knew
> What to do.
> This was not the hard bosom
> Of a small wife, but he knew
> What to do, his mouth
> As if it held a saltine.

This sort of gentle sensuality can become overtly comical, as when, in the next poem, "Mr. Luna and History," readers are told that in 1932 Teodoro Luna "Invented the making of love," so "There was talk after his death of a statue," where pigeons would not land on his head or arms, "But rather on his fame,/ Two dozen of them."

"Some mouths have the custom of food," Ríos observes, "Some of words. Most go with food./ Mr. Luna's mouth had the habit of women." The cause of his death is not known, nor what became of his body, but in the process he is transformed:

> It is said he gave some of himself each time,
> From the inside and then out,
> Awake but also in dream.
> It is said he became a thousand women.

In many of his best poems, Ríos demonstrates this remarkable power of metamorphosis, the transformation of simple things by the creative powers of the poet. One is reminded of the ninth of Rainer Maria Rilke's *Duino Elegies* (1923), in which readers are encouraged to show the angel "some simple thing shaped for generation after generation/ until it lives in our hands and in our eyes, and it's ours." In Ríos' poems, especially those in *Teodoro Luna's Two Kisses*, the things transformed are intensely intimate, those owned most personally (sometimes painfully, very often comically): the parts of one's own body.

THE POETRY OF LUIS OMAR SALINAS

Author: Luis Omar Salinas (1937-   )

Type of work: Poetry

Principal published works: *Crazy Gypsy: Poems*, 1970; *From the Barrio: A Chicano Anthology*, 1973 (editor, with Lillian Faderman); *4 Entrance: Chicano Poets*, 1975 (with others); *I Go Dreaming Serenades*, 1979; *Afternoon of the Unreal*, 1980; *Prelude to Darkness*, 1981; *Darkness Under the Trees: Walking Behind the Spanish*, 1982; *The Sadness of Days: Selected and New Poems*, 1987

Luis Omar Salinas was born in Robstown, Texas, in 1937. He spent some time with his parents in Mexico, but from early elementary school days he was a resident of the area around Fresno, California, where he became the ward of his uncle and aunt.

Salinas held many different jobs before enrolling in Fresno State University in 1967. He edited the school's literary magazine, *Backwash*, in 1969 and 1970. He began writing poetry in the late 1960's, becoming part of the Fresno literary community and part of the Chicano literature movement of that place and time. His first collection, *Crazy Gypsy*, was published in 1970. He was awarded the California Teachers Prize for his poetry in 1973 and the Stanley Kunitz Poetry Prize in 1980 for *Afternoon of the Unreal*. This book also won the Earl Lyon Award in the same year. Salinas won an award from the General Electric Foundation in 1983.

During the 1970's, many of Salinas' poems found their way into anthologies, particularly anthologies of ethnic American writers. Both his production and his publications decreased beginning in the late 1980's. *The Sadness of Days* (1987), his first book since 1982, included many of his early poems and a few new ones.

Salinas is unique among Chicano poets in his favoring, at least in his earlier and better-known poems, a surrealistic vision rather than social and political concerns. He writes about "the strange fullness of the unreal," as he calls it. Salinas links things from the social and political worlds with very different things from the world of ideas and visions. These unusual metaphors are his answer to the marginal position of the Chicano in American society, to the suffering and poverty that are his birthright. These images are often striking and difficult to follow, but in the best poems they work together to make both a social and poetic statement.

Salinas' style owes much to metaphysical poets of the seventeenth century such as John Donne, George Herbert, and Richard Crashaw, who linked things from the physical world with things from the spiritual world. His poetry contains such images as "the flesh of night is torn into small, little children," "Midnight and I'm between/ a pastrami and a dream," "There are drunk cemeteries/ in my heart," and "It is Sunday and I look for you/ a meteor wandering, lazy/ simple as dust."

One of Salinas' major influences is the Spanish poet Miguel Hernández, who admitted to basing his work on early metaphysical poets of his country, most notably Luis de Góngora y Argote. Another influence is the great Latin American poet Pablo Neruda. Although it is a stretch to call Neruda a metaphysical poet, he does bring together disparate images and asks his readers to make imaginative connections among them. Hernández, Neruda, and Salinas experimented with these surreal images in their early poetry, but they were able to allude to the suffering of their people and to social and political issues. Analysis of their work tends to emphasize these social and political ideas at the expense of the technique and form with which they are achieved. This is unfortunate, since form and technique make Salinas stand out among the Chicano poets of the 1960's and 1970's who were crying out against injustice. The reader has to work to get the point of a Salinas poem. The meaning is in the subconscious, but very often, the effort to find it is worth the work.

Crazy Gypsy was Salinas' first book. Although

it was published in 1970, some of the poems go back to the early 1960's. It has many of the marks of the time it was published. Some of its better-known poems reflect the political concerns of a young poet struggling with his own and his people's identity during a time when the pursuit of civil rights and the importance of protest were vital. The rebel leader Che Guevara is invoked in "Guevara . . . Guevara": "Guevara . . . Guevara wake up/ it is raining in Bolivia." The "Secretive Gods with sharpened axes/ look for your body." The Secretive Gods who want to find and destroy Che's body and thus bring an end to revolution are, however, defeated by the common folk, the revolutionaries:

> Guevara . . . Guevara
> we have found you
> your blood fills our throats
> our lungs
> our belly
> with a smell as fresh
> as yesterday's fallen snow.

In "Death in Vietnam," a Mexican American soldier dies and comes home to a country where "mothers sleep in/ cardboard houses." Injustice becomes evident, a realization made more horrible by the idea that it will continue:

> tomorrow it will rain
> and the hills of Viet Nam
> resume
> the sacrifice is not over.

The volume's most famous poem is "Aztec Angel," in which Salinas' surrealism is more readily observed. Salinas here adopts a persona, as he often does in his poetry. Sometimes it is an angel, sometimes a crazy gypsy, sometimes just Salinas. The Aztec angel is the "dangling man" that the Chicano becomes in American society: He is an outsider, "criminal/ of a scholarly society": "forlorn passenger on a train/ of chicken farmers/ and happy children." He

> socializes with spiks
> niggers and wops
> and collapses on his way
> to funerals.

The poem as published in *The Sadness of Days: Selected and New Poems* ends with a remarkable tragic cry: "I am an Aztec angel/ offspring of a woman/ who was beautiful." It is interesting to note that in the original 1970 poem, the Aztec angel was "offspring of a tubercular woman." The change is for the better, because it underlines the suffering of the Chicano, caught between two worlds, with less bitterness and greater impact.

The title poem is a variation of "Aztec Angel," with Omar assuming the role of a "crazy gypsy—another outsider who writes poems on walls, ends up in jail and composes dances using his nightmares for inspiration, then sells them for a bottle of tequila." The poem makes fewer references to being a Mexican American and stresses surrealistic images, the most striking the last: "I speak of hate/ as something nibbling my ear."

Salinas later wrote many more fine poems, but few have the freshness and the power of the material in *Crazy Gypsy*. Almost all of his anthologized poems are from this volume, published in a limited edition by the tiny Origenes Publications.

During the 1970's, Salinas continued to publish in periodicals and placed several *Crazy Gypsy* poems in anthologies of Chicano and ethnic writers. In 1975, a group of his poems appeared in *4 Entrance: Chicano Poets*. Gary Soto, whose work entered the mainstream of American poetry much more readily than did Salinas', was also included in the book.

Salinas published four books of poetry between 1979 and 1982. Three were small collections: *I Go Dreaming Serenades*, *Afternoon of the Unreal*, and *Prelude to Darkness*. These poems were followed by *Darkness Under the Trees: Walking Behind the Spanish*, a more substantial collection published by the University of California.

It is difficult to look at these poems without seeing differences from the *Crazy Gypsy* group. Most obvious is the appearance of the poems on the page. The lines are fairly regular, not spread all over the page. There still are some striking discordant images, but not nearly as many. The poems are not necessarily easier to read, and the surrealistic element is still present, but not to the extent nor to the effect of the best of *Crazy Gypsy*.

If Neruda was Salinas' guide in the early going, it is not difficult to find another muse hovering in these poems, a poet Ezra Pound said every American poet had to make his peace with—Walt Whitman. In "Ode to the Mexican Experience," Salinas "celebrates himself and sings himself," much as the "good, grey poet" did:

I know you in bars
In merchant shops, . . .
in the smile of her eyes,
in the tattered clothes of school children

At the end of the poem, the singer is still cataloging, in Whitman's style:

I was an altar boy,
a shoeshine boy
an interventionist in family affairs . . .
To all the living things I sing
the most terrible and magnificent
ode to my ancestry.

In another poem from *Afternoon of the Unreal*, "Salinas Sends Messengers to the Stars," the poet talks about weaving blankets and telling them (the stars) that he loves them "so dearly." In "Salinas Is on His Way," along with many other poems in these four books, the poet uses the image of the road, quite probably the "open road":

After dreams get through with me
I shall devour books, sing arias,
walk on snow
have arguments with darkness
and crawl into the corner of the sea

A poem dedicated to the American poet Delmore Schwartz ends with the poet saying "I am the best/ of my age." Another poem is titled "I am America." All are Whitmanesque.

Salinas' work of the early 1980's shows a philosophical change. The poet no longer is the marginal figure of the early poems. He seems better poised, more a part of the group. In many poems, it seems that he has looked into the abyss and pulled himself back. One could argue that Neruda's later poetry also showed this change.

Does it help? The better poems still seem to have that anger, that news from the barrio. An "Aztec ghost" hovers over "For Armenia," and uneven lines dominate in "I Go Voyaging Afternoons" and "I Sigh in the Afternoon." Striking images still dominate "It Was Sunday" and the love poem "An Evening Lies Dying." "By the Elms" talks of a "heart walking on all fours," and "Romance in the Twilight" tells readers that they must learn to trust "this devil/ whose heart knocks/ birds to their death." The anger and the disparate images predominate in a series of poems, particularly in *Darkness Under the Trees*, that speak of madness. "My Quixotic Bang Up," with its coming to relative peace with the world and insanity, is very effective. Less effective are optimistic pieces written to favorite writers: Lorna Dee Cervantes, Federico García Lorca, César Vallejo, and Miguel Hernández. The positive tones in these poems seem forced and inauthentic.

In 1987, Arte Público Press at the University of Houston published *The Sadness of Days: Selected and New Poems*. It includes selections from all of Salinas' books except *I Go Dreaming Serenades*. Except for an underemphasis on the *Crazy Gypsy* poems, it serves as a comprehensive summary of Salinas' poetry to that date. The new poems in that volume, except for two or three, lack focus and are repetitive in their message. Salinas seems to be saying "Life is chaos, but I've looked into the abyss and pulled myself out. Life is still sad, but I'm alive at least." A notable exception is "Come Pick Up My Body," which offers some of the excitement of the old surrealist poems and images such as "Come with the quickness of deer,/ Jumping over a tooth"; "This afternoon is inside a box, in tears"; and "as if madness were a drunk neighbor or a dog on fire." The images come together as a plea to be loved, to be cared for. "In Life," despite several failed Shakespearean allusions, is a beautiful tribute to the poet's father. "Letter to Soto" is a plea to his old friend and fellow Chicano poet Gary Soto to flee the city and find somewhere out of time and space, where "the heart is silent."

"Letter to Soto" ends with the poet found "on bad elbows by the meadow/ With a copy of Omar Khayyam, whiskey,/ And my poems that can't find an ear." This last line has proven true. Salinas remains a relatively obscure poet, rarely mentioned even among Chicano poets in the many volumes published about them in recent years. Twenty years after his first book, there still had been no major critical appraisal of his work. Soto has moved into the mainstream but kept his Spanish heritage and the language deeply engaged in his poetry. Soto's poetry looks forward, however, not back. There is no resignation. Whether his old friend and mentor Salinas will be able to recover his imaginative gift and get the attention he deserves, certainly at least for the early poems, remains to be seen.

THE POETRY OF GARY SOTO

Author: Gary Soto (1952-   )
Type of work: Poetry
Principal published works: *The Elements of San Joaquin*, 1977; *The Tale of Sunlight*, 1978; *Father Is a Pillow Tied to a Broom*, 1980; *Where Sparrows Work Hard*, 1981; *Black Hair*, 1985; *A Fire in My Hands*, 1990; *Who Will Know Us?*, 1990; *Home Course in Religion*, 1991; *Neighborhood Odes*, 1992

Gary Soto is perhaps the best Chicano poet of his generation and one of the best young poets in the United States. One of the first Chicanos to be nominated for a Pulitzer Prize and a National Book Award (1978), he has received numerous awards and recognitions, including the Academy of American Poets Prize (1975), the Bess Hokin Prize from *Poetry* magazine (1978), and a Guggenheim Fellowship (1980). He became an associate professor of Chicano Studies and English at the University of California, Berkeley, in 1977.

Born on April 12, 1952, in the heart of California's agriculturally rich San Joaquin Valley, Soto finds his richest imagery and material in the memories of his Fresno childhood, in the "elements" of San Joaquin, as he calls them in the title of his first volume of poetry. A third-generation Chicano growing up in the largely Hispanic and poor west side of the city, he attended the Fresno public schools and went on to California State University, Fresno, to study poetry under Phillip Levine. He was graduated in 1974 with a degree in English. Levine was a major influence on Soto's early poetry. Like Levine—who grew up in the poor, mean streets of Detroit—Soto exhibits a tough realism in his poetry, as well as a terse precision of language, a strong awareness of social injustice, and a vivid sense of place.

Soto's poems are populated with the poor, the lonely, and the marginal, with relatives who worked long hours picking fruit and cotton in the fields around Fresno or spent their lives in the packing houses. His poems tell of Leonard Cruz, who scrubbed toilets for a living and slept at night in cars, and Tony Lopez, a barber and drug pusher shot to death in 1958. He writes of the soil that "sprouts nothing," the staggering Fresno heat, and the fog that hides the young thief prying open a window screen. Soto's vision is of a relentless wasteland of aggressors and victims caught in a desperate struggle, and of hard-working people doomed to an invisible existence. He left Fresno to study at the University of California, Irvine, where he received a master of fine arts degree in creative writing in 1976, and to teach at San Diego State University and later at Berkeley, but it is Fresno and the San Joaquin Valley that haunt his best poetry.

The Elements of San Joaquin (1977), Soto's much-admired first volume, typifies the structure and style of his poetry. The thirty-one poems of the volume are broken into three sections, each informing the other two. The first poem, "San Fernando Road," and the final poem of the book, "Braly Street," suggest movement, exit, and entrance, making the volume circular in structure and suggesting the circular and repetitious lives of his characters. Abandoning rhyme and conventional meter, the poet speaks in the casual and intimate voice of a friend and in the simple language of the personas he often assumes. Soto's San Joaquin is presented in a vision that is objective, fragmented, and chillingly cold.

The opening poem, "San Fernando Road," points to a journey: The poet seeks his Chicano heritage and Fresno childhood, his characters seek escape from the lonely roads they trudge as migrant farmworkers and laborers, and all seek the sources of the social evils that entrap them. Four of the six poems in the first section, for example, involve rape. Women are victimized in underground parking lots, in cars, and on the hard earth of vacant lots. They become wards of the county, live in nightly fear within their own homes, and are left beaten and naked in vineyards. Misogny is the natural offshoot of a machismo Latino culture, a dark undercurrent in the Chicano culture that the poet must come to grips with.

The six poems of the first section of the volume alternate between victim and aggressor, concluding with the murder of Tony Lopez, who as drug pusher is aggressor and as dead barber is victim. In the opening poem, Leonard Cruz, a persona of the poet who reappears throughout the volume, is surrounded by unflushed toilets, rubber dust, and the grime of the factory he sweeps and cleans. He is one of the invisible poor who have no home, no life, and no future. In the second poem, "The Underground Parking," a whimpering woman—perhaps "your wife," the poet suggests to male readers—is raped by a tattooed stranger who holds an ice pick to her throat. The man is much like Leonard.

In each of these first six poems, Soto uses precise language to link poem to poem and theme to theme. Circular imagery reinforces the circular structure of the entire volume and the circular lives of the characters, who are going nowhere. Images of sleeping also appear in all six poems. The poems move from dawn in "San Fernando Road," through morning in "The Underground Parking" and late afternoon in "County Ward," to night in the final three poems.

In the second section's thirteen poems, character gives way to more impersonal elements. Soto uses the word "elements" in several senses. The poems are named simply, with titles such as "Wind," "Sun," "Rain," "Harvest," and "Summer." Essentially, the section describes the natural forces and persistent destructive elements that created the wasteland world of the first section; the wind, fog, and heat that are as much a part of the location as are the people and place names. They are the irreducible constituents of the San Joaquin Valley.

If the first section of the volume is an urban vision, the second is predominantly rural, dotted with bursts of natural beauty, but no less negative. The dirt sprayed by the wind covers everything in a fine silt. The sun blazes in the sky, driving even

the lizards into hiding, while the autumn rain, flattening the sycamore leaves and flushing ants from their holes, brings no solace, for it means no harvesting and no work for the farm laborers. The fog and mist drift in, hiding everything, including the young thief prying loose a window screen and even the very lives of individuals who time, like the fog, will obliterate.

The last poems of the second section give glimpses of the farmworkers' lives after the hoeing and harvesting. The poems are filled with ominous and menacing images: a Filipino standing under a streetcorner neon light, turning a coin in his pocket; a dog snapping at the ankle of a woman carrying bricks; a woman with a cane tapping her way along the railroad tracks. Each suggests a world as menacing and full of threat as the earlier world of aggression and rape.

The final twelve poems, in the third section, bring the poet closer to Braly Street where he was born and to memories of his childhood: spotted dogs, a doll's head with a chipped nose, his brother and sister, a photo of his dead father. Once again readers encounter Leonard, collecting copper in dirt alleys, but this time there is hope, for the copper provides a soft glow that shows "the way back." The way back for Soto, Leonard, and the other characters is clearly through the prism of memory and the mirror of poetry.

Hope is provided in the poems about the poet's grandmother—"History," "Remedies," and "Spirit." A proud survivor who was pulled from Mexico to the San Joaquin Valley, she is both the poet's muse and the central feminine figure that brings together the suffering victims of earlier poems. She is, above all, that which gives *The Elements of San Joaquin*, in its final poem, "Braly Street," its final resounding word—"alive."

The concluding optimism of *The Elements of San Joaquin* is continued in Soto's second volume of poetry, *The Tale of Sunlight* (1978), a book as drenched in sunlight as the first one was wrapped in darkness. The first poem, "El Niño," sets the tone of the volume, which is again divided into three parts. Appearing as if by magic when a spark is struck from a rock, Molina, the poet-persona of the first eleven poems, opens up the poet's childhood recollections like a magician parting a curtain. Magic, mystery, and fantasy lead the poet into cellars, through doors, and into distant regions on a journey from remembered childhood to the realities of present adulthood. The poet is explorer and adventurer, and Molina is his guide, taking him via map and story to Panama, Bogota, Lima, the Orinoco River, and, in the final poem of the first section, back to "The Street." In that poem, the poet confronts the equally mysterious and hidden lives of Julio, the retired butcher; Theresa Fuentes, palm reader and washerwoman; Emilio Zaragoza, who stuffs chorizo into pig gut; and Mother Luisa, who threads a needle's eye with sunlight.

In the ten poems of the second section, the brutal heat and chilling fog of the San Joaquin Valley are replaced by autumn sunlight, clear water, and dazzling snow. Although there are still "elements" to contend with, the Latinos of Soto's imaginary landscape survive the harshness of their lives with dignity. Their world is filled with the kind of Magical Realism found in the fiction of Gabriel García Márquez, one of Soto's favorite authors, to whom Soto dedicates the final poem of the section.

The final eleven poems of *The Tale of Sunlight* are entitled "The Manuel Zaragoza Poems." The poet-persona in them is a cantina owner in Taxco, Mexico. Forty years old, having survived a young wife who died in childbirth, Manuel lives out his life in a fly-ridden cantina of six tables, drinking himself to sleep and fantasizing himself as a circus impresario or a famous guitarist. The final poem, "The Space," finds Manuel sleeping in a hammock, content with smells, rustling grass, cooing birds, and the space between the trees, the same inner space in which poets find imaginary worlds and where anyone can find escape from the boredom and sadness of outer lives.

Soto's next two volumes, *Como Arbustos de Niebla* (1980), a chapbook of eight poems translated into Spanish by Ernesto Trejo, and *Father Is a Pillow Tied to a Broom* (1980), contain poems that either appeared in his first two volumes or would appear in his next volume published in the

United States, *Where Sparrows Work Hard* (1981). In that work, there is again a three-part division of poems that balance and inform one another. The first poem, "The Trumpet," finds the poet-persona reading the newspaper want ads and imagining himself as a trumpet player in an East Los Angeles band. Childhood, the reality of the Fresno streets, and the fantasy world of escape: These are the conflicting themes of the volume. In this collection, the poet comes closer to speaking in his own voice than in the earlier volumes.

Fire is one of the principal metaphors of the book, as if Soto's glimpses of childhood, burned in the memory, must be purged and destroyed in order to grow. A child draws a crayon portrait of God in a frying pan, an image that will be eradicated through flame. In "Burning Many Things," the poet-persona sets a Christmas tree on fire and dances among the flames. In "The Street," he is a child who flicks matches into a jar of flies. Fire, like memory, both purifies and destroys.

The final two sections of the book are populated with memorable characters and objects, each captured in Soto's sharply etched imagery. Joey the Midget rummages through trash cans for other people's discards so that nothing will be wasted "In a world where sparrows work hard/ To prove there is enough." Chuy is armed with "an equator" of fat, while his dog is "a suitcase of fur." A man's face is "a yard of loose skin," and a condor drops from the sky "like a coat." Soto's wonderful eye for detail and precise language makes his characters—the Widow Perez, Beto, Frankie Torres, Juan Rodriguez—come brilliantly alive.

Soto's next volume of poetry, *Black Hair* (1985), represents a growing maturity in the poet's vision. This maturity is particularly apparent in the second section of twenty-five poems, centering on his wife, Sadako, and his daughter, Mariko. The responsibilities of marriage and parenthood give all forty-nine poems of this volume a new richness and personal involvement, even at times a confessional tone. The poet-persona moves in age from eight years in the opening poem, "Black Hair," through adolescence and thoughts of love in "Morning on This Street," the final poem of the first section, in which the poet watches an old man pull his wife and cart through neighborhood streets. Marriage, the poet concludes, is "a man and a woman, in one kind of weather."

The remainder of the volume elaborates the weather of marriage through an adult persona. The poems move from sunlit October mornings, through rainy Saturdays and serious storms, to late-night walks beneath blossoming trees. Although *Black Hair* contains an undercurrent of sadness and despair, its final word is "smiles" and its central focus is love.

Much of Soto's writing since the early 1980's has been prose reminiscences and fiction for young adults that expresses the same guarded optimism found in *Black Hair*, though he continued to publish serious poetry in such prestigious journals as *The Nation* and *The New Republic*. Soto is no longer a promising young poet but instead a mature artist who has learned his craft, who has a deep, rich vision of the world and human relationships, and who cuts across narrow ethnic boundaries with a clear and powerful voice that speaks of a common humanity.

THE POETRY OF CÉSAR VALLEJO

Author: César Vallejo (1892-1938)
Type of work: Poetry
Principal published works: *Los heraldos negros*, 1918 (*The Black Heralds*, 1990); *Trilce*, 1922 (English translation, 1973, 1992); *Poemas humanos*, 1939 (*Human Poems*, 1968); *España, aparta de mí este cáliz*, 1939 (*Spain, Take This Cup from Me*, 1972); *César Vallejo: The Complete Posthumous Poetry*, 1978; *Selected Poetry*, 1981

Peruvian poet César Vallejo wrote essays, short stories, novels, and plays. Although these deserve examination in their own right, Vallejo's poetry is probably his most important and is certainly his best-known work. He is considered to be one of the foremost poets of the twentieth century in Latin America. The very complexity and difficulty of his poetic language have contributed to making Vallejo a celebrated poet in Latin America but a relatively little-known writer outside the Spanish-speaking world; problems of translation limited the accessibility of his work until translations began appearing in the late 1960's. It took decades for his major works to be translated.

Vallejo's poetic work evolves through a span of influences, ranging from Spanish Romanticism and Latin American *Modernistas* such as Rubén Darío to the Symbolist, avant-garde, and Surrealist work coming from Europe. Vallejo's continual questioning of any source of poetic authority and his preoccupation with language resulted in poetry that is not merely a matter of influences but strives to be something not seen before. His poetry must be counted among the first internationally "modern" works in the sense that it responds to specific concerns unfolding in Europe as well as in North and South America around the beginning of the twentieth century. Vallejo saw in the beginning of the twentieth century the crystallization of a nineteenth century loss of faith in both Christian and traditional ideas of salvation, harmony, and transcendence. His own loss of faith was impelled in large part by his exposure to scientific and philosophical ideas such as positivism and evolution theory; his education in these matters contrasted violently with his upbringing, which had been strictly Catholic—both of his grandfathers were Jesuit priests from Spain. Friedrich Nietzsche's death of God, almost seventy years earlier, echoes in Vallejo's seemingly softer but more ironic claim in his "Sentencing": "The day I was born/ God was ill,/ Seriously."

Another, more personal, sense of loss for Vallejo was the death of his mother in 1918. The absence pervades his *Trilce* collection. This profound loss of faith in spiritual sources of power and authority, including his mother as a source of spiritual strength, implies a loss of faith in traditional ideas of the function and structure of poetry itself. Vallejo found that the protection of the mother, the sanctuary of the church, and the consolation of poetry were radically undermined by questions about humanity's place in the scheme of things. Although thinkers of the early twentieth century might hail scientific knowledge as that which would replace spiritual knowledge, for Vallejo neither could be a source from which to derive a poetics. In his work, then, Vallejo asked himself the poetic question of where to derive the (poetic) authority to begin to write again. In a sense, Vallejo's first two books of poetry address both the necessity and the impossibility of an individual poetics in the face of a modernity that has undercut all traditional sources of authority and left none in their place. It was not until he was older, and living in Paris, that his poetry turned outward to a celebration of the value of ordinary, mass humanity.

Vallejo saw only two of his books of poetry published during his lifetime. He published the first edition of *Los heraldos negros* (*The Black Heralds*) himself in 1918 in Trujillo, Peru, to a surprisingly good critical reception. The reception accorded *Trilce*'s appearance in Lima in 1922, however, was hostile. Even the most avant-garde of the Peruvian poets there could not understand a poetry filled with neologisms, archaic words, and medical, scientific, and legal terminology, and that often abandoned even poetic syntax for more opaque, difficult patterns. As Vallejo wrote to a friend, "The book has fallen into a total void."

After a 1920 incident in which he was jailed on trumped-up charges of instigating a riot in Trujillo, and following the hostility accorded *Trilce*, Vallejo decided to leave Peru for Paris in 1923. In Paris, he participated in the ferment of artistic and intellectual life that made Paris a mecca for the arts in the early part of the century, even sitting to be sketched by Pablo Picasso. It was in Paris that his political conscience was born, and he became committed to socialist ideals. All of this is reflected in the poetry he wrote in Paris but never managed to get published. After his death, his Paris poems were published as one collection, called *Poemas humanos*, except fifteen poems under the title *España, aparta de mí este cáliz*. The latter collection contains his most overtly political poems, fiercely dedicated to the ordinary soldiers who fought against the Fascists during Spain's civil war.

Vallejo's first collection, *Los heraldos negros* (*The Black Heralds*) shows his Romantic and Modernist influences. God, if not dead, is at least very sick and very sad. In a gesture of romantic alienation, the poet then must take on Christlike overtones, standing in for an endangered transcendent authority and appropriating the Christian image of bread and its connotations of spiritual nourishment in poems such as "The Black Heralds," "Agape," and, as below, in "Our Daily Bread":

> You want to knock on all the doors,
> and ask of who knows who; and then
> to see the poor, and, crying quietly,
> give little pieces of fresh bread to all.
> And to strip the rich of their vineyards
> with the two blessed hands
> that with a blow of light
> flew off unnailed from the Cross!

Much of *The Black Heralds* is devoted, in two sections titled "Agile Ceilings" and "Of the Earth," to women and to the poetic persona's love affairs.

The sexual act is almost exclusively shown in deliberately profane ways, reversing the Christian religious tendency to make of sexual love a metaphor for spiritual relations. For example, "The Poet to His Beloved" likens the speaker's lips to the Cross and the pain of love to the pain of crucifixion: "Beloved, tonight you have sacrificed yourself/ on the two curved timbers of my kiss;/ and your grief has told me that Jesus has wept."

The section titled "Imperial Nostalgias" is a group of poems dedicated to Latin America's indigenous Indians. This poetry shows the beginnings of a sensibility toward oppression, a sensibility marked by Vallejo's own Peruvian Indian heritage (both his grandmothers were Indian) and that would later find its expression in his commitment to Marxism.

The family poems of this collection, grouped under the title "Songs of Home," are some of the best of the book, as they show a sensibility not so concerned with a deliberately romantic, alienated poetic "stance." Many show a preoccupation with the age and impending death of his parents. In "Feverlace," Vallejo's parents are the anchor of that spiritual faith which is being eroded by scientific knowledge:

> My father sits in an old armchair.
> Like a Sorrowing Mary, my mother comes and
>   goes.
> And, seeing them, I feel a something that won't
>   go away.
>
> Because before the wafer, host made of
>   Knowledge,
> is the Host, wafer made of Providence.
> And the visit begins, it helps me to live right . . .

In this collection, Vallejo alters conventional forms such as the sonnet by using far-fetched metaphors and difficult, tortured syntax. He inherited from Symbolists and Modernists a preoccupation with language itself—its look, its sound, its musical and dissonant qualities. What Vallejo finds, however, is that the poetic language he inherited cannot support a loss of faith, and the Christlike wound that crops up in poems such as "The Black Heralds" and "Absolute" will become, in *Trilce*, a deep and unhealable wound in poetic language itself.

Trilce crystallizes what was begun in *The Black Heralds*. As *Trilce*'s language becomes ever more opaque and its poetic forms more experimental, *The Black Herald*'s Christian/romantic themes are largely abandoned in favor of a poetic examination of the domain of the "given," the specifically corporeal body in its various moods: sexual, hungering, mourning, abandoned, absurd, evolutionary. The continuing hunger of this poetic body invests the formerly religious theme of bread with a sense of mourning. *Trilce* mourns the poetic inability to "eat," or incorporate the security of an earlier poetic harmony, and the passing of the primary source of nourishment, the mother herself.

Thinking back to his first sight of Vallejo, the Peruvian novelist Ciro Alegría remarked that he thought "there was something deeply ripped apart in this man." In *Trilce*, the theme of the wound—which also manifests itself as rips or tears in clothing, in time, and in the world—again makes its appearance. As in poem XLII, it is obliquely related to Christ's own wound in His left side: "Is the death star reeling?/ Or are strange sewing machines/ inside the left side." This theme of wounds and rips marks the poetic comprehension of a fundamental "tear" both in life and in poetry—a tear, or rip, between the spiritual and the mundane.

For Vallejo, language itself suffers under this fundamental breach. In using scientific language, archaic words, and neologisms, Vallejo's poetry acknowledges that such an "unpoetic" language is more fitting in describing the contemporary, abandoned body. The ambiguity, and sometimes outright opacity, of many of *Trilce*'s poems serves to point up the problem of a modern language that, in its quest to describe scientific or objective "truth," dissects and renders humanity itself absurd and without meaning, as in *Trilce*'s poem X:

How destiny,
mitred monodactyl, laughs.

How at the rear conjunctions of contraries
destroy all hope. How under every avatar's lineage
the number always shows up.

How whales cut doves to fit.
How these in turn leave their beak
cubed as a third wing.
How we saddleframe, facing monotonous croups.

This poem, which speaks of the inevitable but seemingly senseless evolutionary nature of things, uses a language that resonates more with Vallejo's studies in mathematics, botany, and anatomy than with received notions of a poetic or lyrical vocabulary.

One of the best-known poems of this collection, poem XXXVI, takes the ruined body of the Venus de Milo for its subject, making ironic commentary on the figure of Venus as goddess of love and beauty and on the time's passion for all things classically Greek. Vallejo's Venus is maimed and incomplete; she is, finally, the dissected, "ruined," evolutionary human body of the new modern age. As *Trilce*'s "ars poetica," this poem glosses nearly all the concerns that make up *Trilce*'s poetic catalog: the problem of the feminine laboring under the absurdity of evolution's mandate to blindly reproduce the species, the crippled imperfection of material existence, the overt refusal of a poetic or philosophic harmony or symmetry, and celebration of the idea of abandonment, or "orphanhood":

Are you that way, Venus de Milo?
You hardly act crippled, pullulating
enwombed in the plenary arms
of existence,
of this existence which neverthelessez
perpetual imperfection.

. . . .
Refuse, all of you, to set foot
on the double security of Harmony.

. . . .
Make way for the new odd number
                              potent with orphanhood!

Vallejo wrote the poems making up *Poemas humanos* over the last fifteen years of his life, when he lived mostly in Paris, with some visits to Spain and the Soviet Union. As one reads through the trajectory of these poems, a growing theme in the collection becomes a marked sense of an acceptance of, and even affection for, the suffering implicit in being alive. In many poems, the speaker examines his own body with an ironic or rueful acceptance of its impure fleshiness, as in "Epistle to the Pedestrians": "this is my arm/ that on its own refused to be wing;/ these are my scriptures,/ these my alarmed balls." For this Vallejo, there is "never so much painful tenderness" as in the nine months of human, corporeal gestation, what he will ironically call in the title of another poem the "nine monsters" of birth. Much of this poetry painfully celebrates the "delightful weight" of the material body.

As Vallejo became more committed to Marxism, his poetry turned away from the despairing individual and toward an examination of how the poet and his poem stand in relation to other human beings, as in "A Man Walks By": "A bricklayer falls from the roof, dies, and no longer eats lunch./ After that innovate the trope, the metaphor?" Speaking of humanity in general, the persona of "Considering Coldly" understands "that he knows I love him,/ that I hate him with affection."

Although the sentiments that drive much of this poetry were politically motivated, the poetry itself is never crudely political, continuing instead to voice its concerns through its preoccupation with language and syntax. In "Intensity and Height," the two concerns of language and of humanity's material evolution and existence are linked:

I want to write, but I feel myself, puma!
I want the laurel, but I'm wreathed in garlic.
There's no cough spoken that doesn't end in
  mist,
no god or son of god, without evolution.

This sonnet encloses within its formality the stuttering inability of the speaker to transcend to the laurel wreath of poetry; language, the "spoken cough," fails once again. He is left not with God but with the evolutionary animal body and the faintly ridiculous garlic.

Finally, Vallejo was able to bring together and at least partly reconcile the poetic rift between language and the given, life and death, in his paean to the Republican fighters of the Spanish Civil War, *España, aparta de mí este cáliz* (*Spain, Take This Cup from Me*). In this short collection, the stutterings and hesitations of the poet are put aside, the writing takes on a new rootedness, and it is the text that will survive death and carry on the fight, as can be seen in "A Small Response to a Hero of the Republic":

Poetry of purple cheek, between speaking
And silencing,
Poetry in the moral letter which should accompany
his heart.
The book and nothing else remained, for there
  are no
Insects in the tomb.
And the air remained at the edge of his sleeve,
  soaking
Turning itself into vapour, infinitely.

The message of heroism, written in a "moral letter" in the heart and on the sleeve, will remain after the death of the individual hero. "We" will speak his actions: "and bodily, fatefully his mouth entered into our breath/ . . . a book above, sprouted from the body." The tone of these poems is no longer ironic, nor in the end despairing, though pain is present and the language is still complex and sophisticated. In these last poems, Vallejo began to find that poetic place of "authority" for which his work had always searched.

THE POETRY OF BERNICE ZAMORA

Author: Bernice Zamora (1938-   )
Type of work: Poetry
Principal published work: *Restless Serpents*, 1976

Bernice Zamora's book of poems, *Restless Serpents*, is really two books: Zamora's own book of seventy-four pages and that of José Burciaga, sixty-four pages inverted next to Zamora's. Burciaga's closing piece, entitled "The Last Bastion," is a prose critique of the art scene, both in his own town of East Menlo Park and in the United States as a whole. "Art," he says, "is the last bastion of racism and prejudice in this country." Burciaga may be guilty of overstatement; certainly there were other bastions remaining in 1976 when *Restless Serpents* was issued. His statement can be applied to Zamora's career as a poet and critic determined to weaken the racism and sexism rooted, although secretively and in bad faith, in the art establishment and in its offshoot, academia. She has not contented herself with remaining outside the establishment: Having obtained a doctorate and having taught for many years in universities on the West Coast, she has worked from the inside as well. This can be a difficult fence to straddle, but she has done it well, maintaining her own integrity as a Chicana who has a body of ethnic tradition to draw upon in the writing of her poetry as well as certain political and social obligations to her Chicano/a audience. Although conscious of her roots and obligations, she is conversant with English and American literary traditions.

Bernice Zamora was born and reared in the farmlands of southern Colorado, where her ancestors had lived and farmed for a number of generations. After earning a master's degree at Colorado State University, she moved to northern California to continue her studies at Stanford University. She remained in the region, writing, teaching, and on occasion editing journals of Chicano literature. Although she has not published widely, her influence is evident, especially as a Chicana, a female poet of Mexican American heritage. She has been

the subject of a lengthy chapter in an academic study and has received extensive notice in other arenas. This is perhaps because her poems have a literary quality clearly influenced by the canon of American literature in a way that is rare in Chicano literature, which has more often defined itself in its own terms, ignoring those of the dominant culture except insofar as to critique and turn away from them. This is not to say that Zamora places herself as a poet within the dominant tradition; rather, through her familiarity with the tradition, she can turn it back upon itself as a method of critique and analysis. Thus, her best poems are at once social and literary critiques, and because she is a Chicana, a women in a dominant Chicano culture, her social critiques often turn upon the politics of sexuality as well.

This overview of her work does not do justice to her entire oeuvre; Zamora is not to be pinned down so easily. Although she usually works within a fairly defined group of themes, she sometimes employs one of these themes alone, sometimes mixes them together in varying degrees, and sometimes stretches outside these themes altogether. Her treatments vary as well. She often uses narratives or realistic monologues, but she is no stranger to abstractions or surrealism. As a characterization of her work, one might take her own brief poem "So Not to Be Mottled." She is not, she says, schizophrenic: "*My* divisions are/ infinite." Where there are infinite divisions, there are no divisions; there is pure flux from one aspect of reality to another, with each part being part of each other. Thus, Zamora is not to be mottled; her work is not cleanly divided between different areas of color. Nor is her language to be easily pinned down, with each word pointing cleanly to one meaning. Her recurrent use of puns is one indication of this. The word "mottled" can also be read as "modeled," with its suggestions of sculpting into one form to the exclusion of others.

Some of the poems in *Restless Serpents* are one-of-a-kind performances, using techniques or themes that go unrepeated in the rest of the book. An obvious example is "Sin Titulo," a one-line poem that merely poses the question "What if we survive?" "Girded Us," with its Dadaistic language—"aged escapists reflux/ arthritic currents"—is another example. With "The Sovereign," Zamora turns aside from her typically critical and analytical stance to commemorate and praise the work of César Chávez, a stance she takes nowhere else in the book.

On one hand, it would be difficult to point to any two poems as being typical Zamora poems; it could be said that each poem stands alone. On the other hand, recurrent themes, treatments, and stances do emerge. For example, Zamora often uses small poems of about ten lines or less to tell what might be described as poignant jokes. "Martha," whose character's favorite phrase is "doesn't know shit from Shinola," and "El Burrito Cafe," a description of a greasy spoon in which the cook is grandiosely called a chef, are examples of these. "Denizens" adds to the joke a quick social comment. Sometimes humor is attained through the juxtaposition of two poems on facing pages. The titles of the two poems "41 Trinkets" and "At Hand" can be read as one title, and the poems have river themes in common. Add to this the likelihood that the forty-one trinkets are the preceding poems, of which there are exactly forty-one, and the effect is of a strange, suggestive, and ultimately surprising joke.

Although Zamora is often darkly humorous in her longer efforts, she does not merely strive for comedic effects. Sometimes she concentrates on pruning the literary establishment down to size. "Supping On . . ." and the poem on the facing page, "Morning After," are examples. In the first, she attacks poets and artists, including herself among them, who are self-satisfied with their role as artists while at the same time seeking "to be admired by/ the pawning apes/ of state." This last clause offers a multilayered pun. The pawning apes, who pawn the artists' work, are also fawning apes, who fawn, as do the artists, upon the higher powers, those of the state. The apes of state are the ship of state, suggesting that the artists pawn their art to the powers that be. "Morning After" attacks an unnamed poet who finds in his work a "bargain, prostitute" for which he pays "one mind for one sleep," sleep here acquiring both the sense of a loss of consciousness and of "sleeping with." "Pico Blanco" takes on the twentieth century California poet Robinson Jeffers, by whom Zamora is heavily influenced, and simultaneously criticizes his language and thematics while asking, in a guarded way, for his blessing in her own work, which she characterizes as "chipping the/ crust of the Pico Blanco." Each of these poems, while directing energies primarily at the literary establishment, also carries implicit judgments concerning the larger culture in which that establishment is located.

These cultural critiques constitute a large part of Zamora's work. Poems such as "On Living in Aztlan," "Chaff," and "Stone Serpents" are readable primarily as social critiques. The first poem, had it been titled "On Living," would make a statement universal to all human beings. Zamora shuns easy universalisms and instead focuses on the realities of living in Aztlán, that is, in a culture rooted in Mexico before the Spanish came. The law "which is not ours" becomes the law of the usurpers, whether Spanish or Anglo-American. The speaker of "Chaff" accepts the challenge to "recreate man" but finds him "unyielding," a play on "chaff," which likewise yields nothing. Man is found to wear nothing "save for his past"; that is, he wears what he used to when, presumably, he had a fruitful, yielding kernel. "Stone Serpents" takes a look at the "weary wealthy" locked within a castle lined with "stone serpent balustrades" and "filled with the/ temple's rusting treasures." The men inside see, but lifelessly, and the women do not dare raise their eyes. Not even the idea of a child can be born inside. The overall effect is one of impotence and enclosure within the balustrades. Implicit here is also a critique of this dominant culture's sexuality, a critique expanded upon and modified throughout Zamora's work.

By definition, these sexual critiques embody social critiques as well. In "When We Are Able," Zamora locates an impotence in the oppressed paralleling that of the oppressors which she dissects in "Stone Serpents." Where the oppressors are weary and blind, the oppressed are fearful and unable to protect their rights. Furthermore, they are also enmeshed in the confusion of property relations found in the dominant society. In "our bed," the speaker says to her lover, is found "what is yours," that which the stranger ravishes each night. Whether this stranger is an emblem of the dominant culture or of the lover himself, perhaps exercising the influence of that culture, is left purposely vague.

What should be remembered is that Zamora, as a Chicana, is subjected to the demands of two dominant cultures, the European/Anglo-American and the Chicano. This latter dominance is set forth clearly in the short poem "Pueblo, 1950," in which a girl is shamed by everyone, including herself, for being kissed by a boy who goes unshamed. In the following poem, "Bearded Lady," Zamora renders a portrait of the obsessional mystifications that come alive in this environment of shame. In "Gata Poem," written entirely in Spanish except for one line and the English word in the title, these mystifications are placed in the mouth of a man who paints visions of the romantic bliss possible if the speaker would come away with him. The speaker herself is caught up in mystification, picturing the man glistening "in the sun like a bronze god." These romanticizations stand out in contrast to the flatness underlying the relationship. The man says "come, woman," and the speaker at the end states simply "and I went." Whether she leaves with the man or without him is left unclear; either way, the flowery language of the courtship is reduced to bald reality.

Zamora often successfully brings together in one poem her three dominant subject areas—the social, the sexual, and the literary. "California" builds off the last lines of the Jeffers poem "Roan Stallion" and renegotiates the relations put forth there. In "Roan Stallion," Johnny wants to treat his wife, California, as he has seen his stallion treat the mare. California runs from him to the corral, where she shoots his dog; the stallion tramples Johnny, and she shoots the stallion. Zamora's poem picks up at this moment with California's monologue, describing the violence from her perspective. The two dead gods are the stallion—the one shot—and Johnny, the "one killed by the other." Both were beasts, the stallion a beast "of the wind and rein," and Johnny "of the night and wine." Both these beasts are emblematic of the divisions Zamora refuses in "So Not to Be Mottled," insofar as they have been guilty of "splitting hairs, splitting atoms." California's action has not freed her, though; it has "plunged/ [her] wailing will to the center of the bloody corral." She has assumed responsibility, without perhaps meaning to, for determining the course of her relationships within "the bloody corral," the dominant culture. She has become, in short, a feminist.

Feminism for a Chicana is a more difficult trek than for an Anglo-American because the Chicana must fight her way out of two "bloody corrals." Zamora forcefully states this fact in "Notes from a Chicana 'Co-ed'," a poem not found in *Restless Serpents*, having first been published in the small magazine *Caracol* in 1977. The speaker criticizes her Chicano boyfriend for glibly claiming "the gringo is oppressing you, Babe" while earning a good living off the system. Meanwhile, she works two jobs, seven days a week, worrying if she will be able to feed her children. Worse, the boyfriend claims that her "Women's Lib trip" only divides them, making it harder for them to work together for the movement. His concern is betrayed, though, by the fragrance of another woman's perfume on his collar. Nevertheless, she colludes with him. She is dependent on his love to give meaning to her life, and to some extent she remedies the flaws he finds in her writings, which he finds too full of flowers instead of "social reality." Still, her consciousness struggles to assert itself as she continues to write of flowers, though now they are redolent "of oppressing perfume." "Tere," included in the anthology *New Chicana/Chicano Writing* (1992), takes Zamora's literary and social critiques into an otherworldly universe. A letter written by one scribe to another, "Tere" seems on one level to evoke the voice of Zamora's muse, who has been reborn among the tribe of Aztlán. She is doomed to think in a language she did not create and to confront problems in which she has no ultimate interest. Female scribes, after all, have their "tortured souls full." Still, she is tempted to break her silence, to stop merely copying bibles, because she is "the one with most experience."

Certainly it is true that, among Chicana poets, Zamora has the greatest understanding of the dominant culture's literary traditions. Her ability to turn the oppressor's language back against the oppression, whether it stems from Chicano or Anglo-American, has earned for Zamora a well-deserved recognition among her Anglo-American and Chicana sisters and the more enlightened of her Chicano and Anglo-American brethren.

RAIN OF GOLD

Author: Victor Villaseñor (1940-   )
Type of work: Family
Time of work: The early twentieth century
Locale: Mexico and the United States
First published: 1991

Principal Personages

Lupe, the author's mother. Conceived during the night of a miraculous comet, Lupe is a beautiful and blessed child. Her great beauty sets her aside from her sisters and makes her much hated by other schoolgirls, and later by other field-workers. Lupe shares her mother's tremendous faith in life and God. Her resolve is tested by Juan Salvador during their courtship. She has to overcome her suspicions of him in order for them to marry.

Juan Salvador, the author's father. Juan appears headed for a bad end, but he shows his strength of character at the age of eleven, when he misses the train on which his family is emigrating out of Mexico. He runs for an entire day and night and catches the train. In the United States, he goes to prison in another man's place so that his family will have enough money to live. Later, he becomes a successful gambler and bootlegger. Once he meets and falls in love with Lupe, he has to hide his profession so that she and her family will not be frightened away. He has to put aside his overwhelming anger and dreams of revenge in order to win his bride.

Doña Guadalupe, Lupe's mother. A Yaqui Indian whose family was killed by soldiers because they were Indian, she was adopted by a soldier who felt pity for her. She marries twice and has a total of eight children. Lupe's father must work away from the family, so Doña Guadalupe becomes the family's leader. Once her husband returns, however, she turns over the leadership to him, although she retains her role as the spiritual teacher. She instills in Lupe a strong love of God and a quiet courage.

Doña Margarita, Juan Salvador's mother. An indomitable and crafty woman, she holds her family together at the cost of her own dignity. The low point in her life comes in Ciudad Juarez. Rather than see her children starve, she goes into town and begs the townspeople for money. Her religious faith is as strong as Doña Guadalupe's, but more irreverent, and she is not above threatening God and the Virgin Mary should her prayers not be answered.

Carlota, Lupe's sister. Mischievous, gossiping Carlota is forever interested in parties and dances and never misses an opportunity to torment Lupe.

Sophia, Lupe's oldest sister. Sophia goes to the United States after the death of her first husband and is presumed dead when the ship she was thought to be aboard is lost at sea. Doña Guadalupe never loses faith that Sophia still lives. Eventually Sophia is reunited with he family in the United States.

Maria, another of Lupe's sisters. Maria elopes with her first husband Esabel during the aftermath of the revolution. After he disappears, she marries again, only to see Esabel return. She mortifies her sister Lupe by wanting to keep both husbands.

Victoriano, Lupe's brother. When still a child, Victoriano is forced to be the man of the family when his father leaves the home to find work in the lowlands. While picking through discarded mine tailings looking for gold, he is falsely arrested and nearly hung. Doña Guadalupe smuggles a gun to him so that he can escape.

Luisa, one of Juan Salvador's older sisters. Luisa is sarcastic and hot-tempered, though good-hearted. During the journey to the United States, she is deserted by her husband Epitacio. When he returns, she beats him soundly but makes it clear that she still loves him. She opposes Juan Salvador's marriage because she thinks that Lupe is conceited.

Domingo, one of Juan Salvador's brothers. Domingo is separated from his family for many years. While he is away, he loses his common sense and his pride. His recklessness nearly exposes the family bootlegging business.

Archie Freeman, a deputy sheriff. Freeman is sympathetic to both sides of the law, since he is also Juan Salvador's partner in a gambling business. He provides Juan Salvador with protection from other lawmen.

The Work

Rain of Gold is a history of the author's parents, told in story form. The sections of the book alternate between Lupe (the author's mother) and Juan Salvador (his father) until they meet and begin their courtship. The first and third sections are concerned with Lupe's childhood in northwestern Mexico. Juan Salvador is the subject of the three chapters that compose the second section. In these first three sections, Lupe and Juan are living in different areas of Mexico. In the fourth section, both of their families have been forced by events following the 1910 Mexican Revolution to emigrate to the United States, where Lupe and Juan Salvador meet. The fifth and final section focuses on the obstacles that Lupe and Juan Salvador overcome in order to marry. The story ends with their wedding.

Villaseñor has included material in the book to make things easier for the reader and increase the story's sense of authenticity. He provides family trees for both Lupe's and Juan Salvador's families. The genealogy charts are helpful, because many of Villaseñor's family members had the same or very similar names. Two useful maps show the areas of Mexico where his grandparents lived. The book's foreword explains Villaseñor's writing process and the tradition of oral history that inspired him to write his family's story. Photographs show Lupe, Juan Salvador, and several of the important people in the story, adding to the sense that the events in the book really happened. At the end are author's notes that explain Villaseñor's relationship to Lupe and Juan Salvador and tell what eventually happened to many of the people in the book.

The story starts with the discovery of gold in a box canyon in northwestern Mexico. The gold leads to the construction of a mine, La Lluvia de Oro (The Rain of Gold). Lupe is born in the settlement that springs up around it. Despite her family's poverty, which forced Lupe's father to live away from his family because there was no work in the village, Lupe lives happily there. She is taught by her mother to believe that every day is full of miracles that are gifts straight from God. Waking, eating, and even working are all miracles. Later, this attitude steels her and her family for the depredations of marauding soldiers and the privations of the journey to the United States.

Villaseñor vividly depicts the poverty of the Mexican peasant class at the turn of the century, using the village of La Lluvia de Oro as an illustration. The villagers are exploited as laborers by the American company that owns the mine, and things get even worse with the coming of the revolution of 1910. The soldiers conduct terrifying raids, destroying villages, raping, and killing. Lupe's sisters and brother repeatedly have to hide in a large pile of manure kept near the house for this purpose. The result of the violence and chaos caused by the revolution was a huge wave of immigration into the United States. Villaseñor shows how his mother's and father's families came to be part of that influx.

Once in the United States, their struggle changes. Work, and thus food, is available, though it involves long, brutal hours in the fields and a nomadic lifestyle following the harvest seasons from state to state. As Mexicans, they are discriminated against and assumed to be stupid, dirty, and lazy. Because they are seldom long in one place, many of the children lose their chance for an education. Lupe nearly quits school altogether after being shamed and sexually harassed by one of her teachers. In one instance, Juan Salvador's life is threatened because he defies racist stereotypes and dares to be the best worker at a mine.

Lupe and Juan Salvador have different reactions to the opportunities and difficulties of life in America. Lupe hopes to escape the fields through education, one day becoming an office worker or an accountant. Lupe's family is shockingly poor, but they live within the law. In contrast, Juan Salvador supports his family through pool hustling and bootlegging. He is determined to make a lot of money, so that he can buy a flashy car and show his nephews that a Mexican can be an important, respected man. Ironically, he extols education and a nonviolent life to his nephews, who are attracted to what they see as the more glamorous gangster elements of his life. Born in the United States, his nephews demonstrate one of the problems of assimilation. They have absorbed all too well the message that Mexicans are worthless, and they want nothing to do with reminders of Mexico.

Juan himself is torn between the exciting life created by his easily, but illegally, obtained money and the stability he would have with a wife and family. Seeing his indecision, his mother compels him to promise to marry during her lifetime. Once he falls in love with the beautiful Lupe, he has to hide his illegal actions from her. He cannot easily change his ways. His desire for revenge against two men who nearly killed him is almost as strong as his desire to fulfill his vow to marry. He misses key meetings in his courtship of Lupe in order to pursue the men; only his promise to his mother drives him to mature and forget how he was wronged.

The language of the book is simple and straightforward. Villaseñor writes in the tradition of oral history: Storytelling is far more important than any stylistic concerns. Although some Spanish words are used, they are easily understood. Some words, such as *sombrero*, are immediately recognizable to non-Spanish speakers. Others are defined for the reader and then repeated throughout, or they are understandable in their context. The book does not require an understanding of Mexican history or of Mexican American culture. Villaseñor assumes that for many readers his book will be a first exposure to the subject; for example, he explains that beans and tortillas are staples of the Mexican diet.

Analysis

Although *Rain of Gold* presents many of the social issues common in Chicano literature, such as discrimination and the mistreatment of fieldworkers, it does not dwell on the episodes of injustice. Villaseñor tells an intensely personal story, and the book is more an oral history than an obvious political statement. Much of the anger that characterizes his earlier work has been toned down, and instead there is a sense of wonder and a deep thankfulness for the opportunities that life affords in even the most terrible circumstances.

Villaseñor has stated in interviews that one of his aims for the book was to create heroes for Mexican American children, just as his family members were heroes to him. The heroism in *Rain of Gold* comes in many different varieties. Juan Salvador is a traditional masculine hero almost in the style of the Western cowboy: courageous, disciplined, courteous, and respectful of women. His counterpart, Lupe, is an old-fashioned feminine heroine of a type often found in European fairy tales: beautiful, kind, and capable of patiently withstanding suffering. Doña Guadalupe and Doña Margarita are both powerful mother archetypes: No sacrifice is too great if it will keep their children alive and their families together.

Accordingly, one of the strongest themes in the book is the importance of family and family honor.

One's allegiance is to one's relatives, rather than to the law or to a country. There are some unexpected consequences of the allegiance. Juan Salvador is unable to get other workers to stand up for their rights at a quarry pit because they will endure any indignity before they will risk losing the jobs that support their families. When he desperately needs to borrow money, he cannot get it from his closest friends because of the custom of not lending money outside the family. One of the turning points in the book comes when he sees his mother, who was from a fine, educated family, begging in the streets of Ciudad Juarez so that he and his siblings can eat. He swears to God that even if he must kill or steal, his mother will never have to beg again, and the family honor will be restored. The supreme importance of the family is also seen in Doña Guadalupe's words of advice to her daughter Lupe: "No man, no matter how wonderful, is to be put before woman's first loyalty, which is her family."

In one of the many ironies of the work, fellow Mexicans treat their compadres as badly as do the non-Mexicans in the United States. The character of the *vendido*, someone who sells out his own people, recurs throughout the book. At one point, Don Tiburcio, one of Lupe's brothers-in-law, comments that although his countrymen have a rich culture and strong traditions, they have little compunction against killing one another as easily as they would a dog.

Villaseñor raises the question of what makes a man truly a man. Juan Salvador thinks that a real man has to be both "soft and tender, hard and tough, all at the same time." His employee Julio demonstrates the dangers of being only soft. He is unable to control the hysteria of his wife, Geneva, and as a result nearly destroys Juan Salvador's bootlegging business.

Villaseñor has insisted on the veracity of the events in *Rain of Gold*, but he uses certain novelistic devices more commonly seen in fiction. For example, there are strong parallels in the ways that Lupe and Juan Salvador are depicted. Lupe has a pet deer that is sacrificed so that starving people can eat, and Juan's beloved burro meets the same end. They each have a sister who is sarcastic and prone to fits of violent temper, and at least as presented in the story, their mothers, Doña Guadalupe and Doña Margarita, are very similar as characters in their religious faith, inspirational qualities, and willingness to do anything for their children.

Another example of a novelistic device is the use of foreshadowing, which is especially prominent in the beginning of the book. For example, the stressing of the story of La Lluvia de Oro mine prefigures events to come. Educated American engineers are brought in and are given permanent housing in a compound of their own. The people of Lupe's village who provide the manual labor that makes the mine possible live in stone houses and mud-and-stick lean-tos at the bottom of the canyon. Later, as field-workers in the United States, they are once again badly housed and fed while their labor makes others wealthy.

Critical Context

Rain of Gold has had a troubled publishing history. A major mainstream publisher originally planned to publish it, but as the book entered the editing process, the publisher wanted to make changes that Villaseñor found unacceptable, such as shortening it and changing the title. Worse still, the book was to be presented to the public as a work of fiction, not as a true story. Villaseñor withdrew the book, and it was published first in hardcover by the Chicano press Arte Público. Arte Público is a small but important publisher that is considered by some in the literary community to have the responsibility of defining the Chicano literary canon: that is, if a book is published by Arte Público, it must have literary merit. Later, the book was reprinted by a different major publisher and thus received much wider circulation and greater exposure to a non-Hispanic audience.

After the publication of *Rain of Gold*, Villaseñor became heavily involved in public speaking and political activism. Although critical reaction to the book was mixed, he has commented that he was greatly moved by the general public's reception of it. Inspired by a vision, in 1992 he founded a global Thanksgiving movement that aimed to make the American holiday of Thanksgiving a worldwide holiday for peace and brotherhood. Like his grandmothers and parents before him, he seemed determined to make the impossible a reality.

REBELLION IN THE BACKLANDS

Author: Euclides da Cunha (1866-1909)
Type of work: Historical
Time of work: The 1870's through the 1890's
Locale: The backlands of northeastern Brazil
First published: *Os Sertões*, 1902 (English translation, 1944)

Principal Personages

Antonio Vicente Mendes Maciel, also called **Antonio Conselheiro,** the fanatic religious leader of the backlands rebellion. Quiet and withdrawn, this former store clerk vanishes into the backlands in the aftermath of a disastrous marriage, only to reappear years later. Roaming from town to town, Maciel, now known as Conselheiro (the Counselor), preaches an apocalyptic religious message and is asked to settle disputes. In the process, he attracts an increasingly large following of the dispossessed poor, including numerous outlaws, who eventually settle with him in Canudos in 1893. Threatened by what they perceive as Conselheiro's antirepublican message, the state and federal governments organize four different expeditions to destroy the rebel town. Conselheiro dies two weeks before the final surrender of Canudos.

Lieutenant Manuel da Silva Pires Ferreira, the leader of the government's first expedition. He sets out from Bahia with roughly one hundred troops. Before they are able to reach Canudos, they are ambushed by the rebels in Uauá. Although casualties are relatively few, Pires Ferreira's troops must face a demoralizing retreat.

Major Febronio de Brito, the leader of the government's second expedition. Ambushed by the backlanders, de Brito's troops are completely disabled and forced into a humiliating retreat.

Colonel Antonio Moreira Cesar, the leader of the government's third expedition. His overconfidence and impetuosity prove to be his downfall. Displaying downright contempt for the backlanders, Moreira Cesar sees his victory as certain, but, despite some initial success, his exhausted and hungry troops are eventually driven back by the crafty and resilient backlanders. Moreira Cesar is wounded in combat and dies.

General Arthur Oscar de Andrade Guimarães, the leader of the first column of the government's fourth expedition. A highly respected officer, he sees his expedition as a crusade to save the young republic from the supposedly antirepublican rebels of Canudos. Although known for his restless, bold character and for his incomparable tactical skills, he uncharacteristically fails to act soon enough. As his troops are encircled and immobilized by the rebels, he decides simply to hold out and wait for reinforcements.

General Claudio do Amaral Savaget, the leader of the second column of the fourth expedition. More flexible than the other commanders, Savaget, although attacked on his way to Canudos, is able to reach the entrenched forces of the first column to free them from their precarious position, and to force the rebels to retreat into Canudos. After he is wounded at Cocorobó in June, 1896, he leaves the front.

Marshal Carlos Machado de Bittencourt, the war minister and eventual commander of the fourth expedition. Cold, quiet, calculating, and practical, he lacks the disastrous overconfidence of his predecessors. He plans the final attack on Canudos in an organized and methodical way. He is in command when Canudos finally surrenders on October 5, 1897.

Form and Content

Rebellion in the Backlands is a factual account of a historical event. The event—a rebellion led by a charismatic religious fanatic against the federal government of Brazil—might have sunk into obscurity but for Cunha's account, which does not merely report the event but also defines and interprets its significance. As a result, *Rebellion in the Backlands* has been called Brazil's national epic, and its influence on Brazilian fiction—indeed, South American fiction—has been substantial. The work itself, with its plot buildup, might be said to anticipate the so-called "nonfiction novel" of later decades.

Cunha does not, however, begin with plot but with extensive essays on the land and the people of the backlands region. Taking up approximately one-third of the book and covering geography, geology, rainfall, flora and fauna, race, ethnology, psychology, and other subjects, these two long essays are burdened by outdated nineteenth century theories of environmental influence and race. Cunha draws a daunting picture of the hot, rugged, semidesert *sertão*, periodically stricken by killing droughts, and speculates that the *sertanejo*'s personality has been formed by this harsh environment and by mixed racial heritage (white, black, and Indian). Whereas the admixture of "superior" and "inferior" racial stocks (as Cunha expresses it) has resulted in universal "degeneration" along the Brazilian seaboard, the *sertanejo*, through isolation in the primitive backlands environment, has become "a retrograde, not a degenerate, type," physically robust but morally backward. The *sertanejo*'s atavistic tendencies are superbly represented by the undying devotion to the religious fanatic Antonio Conselheiro, himself a spiritualized version of the backlands mentality. In the *sertanejo*'s simple view, "Anthony the Counselor" is a backlands saint.

These long introductory essays serve to romanticize the subject matter and to set the stage for the narrative of the rebellion. The introductions make clear that the underlying causes of the conflict are cultural differences between the isolated backlands and the developed seaboard. These cultural differences first cause religious friction between the established Catholic church and Antonio Conselheiro. Later, the Counselor begins preaching against the recently established Brazilian Republic (proclaimed in 1889), with new taxes and new laws regarding civil marriage and the like that offend him. The Counselor's idea of proper government is a vague theocracy, ruled by the law of God rather than civil law. He and his followers label the republic an Antichrist, call its laws "the law of the hound," and rip down its tax notices.

In 1893, a contingent of thirty Bahian police officers comes after the Counselor for preaching insurrection. They catch up with him in Massete, where his band routs them in a shoot-out. Another contingent of eighty soldiers turns back when the Counselor fades into the forbidding backlands. He and his followers withdraw to distant, inaccessible Canudos, where they establish their theocracy and military stronghold. It is a fairly inadequate theocracy, since the motley backlands population rallying to Canudos includes not only thousands of the religiously devout but also hordes of bandits, who raid the surrounding countryside. Despite such depredations and the Counselor's growing power, the government leaves Canudos alone until October, 1896, when a trivial incident—a dispute between the Counselor and the Joazeiro magistrate over a load of lumber—precipitates the military phase of the rebellion.

With the Counselor's forces threatening to attack Joazeiro, the town's magistrate wires for help from the Bahian governor, who dispatches one hundred troops under Lieutenant Manuel da Silva Pires Ferreira to put down the nuisance. This ridiculous expedition arrives in Joazeiro, sets out for Canudos, and, after marching for days through the backlands heat, encounters perhaps thousands of the Counselor's *jagunços* at Uauá. The encounter is fierce and swift, and the surviving troops escape only because the *jagunços* do not pursue.

The government immediately begins organizing a second expedition, involving more federal troops and artillery. After some organizational delays, the second expedition of 560 men, led by Major Febronio de Brito, sets out for Canudos from Monte Santo. Again, there are days of marching through the torrid heat, this time with the *jagunços*, from the cover of the roadside *caatinga* (tangled scrub forest), sniping and making running attacks on the advancing column. The expedition's provisions give out just as, somewhat demoralized and depleted, it arrives in the vicinity of Canudos. Outside Canudos, it runs into an ambush and, the following morning, a full-scale enemy attack. Forced to retreat, the expedition has to fight its way back along the same roads on which it fought its way in. Of troops arriving back in Monte Santo, not a single one is able-bodied.

Sterner government measures to quell the rebels are called for, as well as a forceful leader. The man of the moment is Colonel Antonio Moreira Cesar, a ruthless hero of the republican wars whose fame is guaranteed to strike fear into the hearts of the *jagunços*. He is called to head the third expedition, consisting of thirteen hundred men with artillery.

Colonel Moreira Cesar's aggressive tactics live up to his reputation. From Monte Santo to Canudos, he leads a series of long forced marches through the backlands heat; as a result, his troops arrive quickly and relatively intact, but exhausted. The colonel decides to storm Canudos immediately, sending columns of his troops charging across the dried riverbed into town and expecting to rout the quivering *jagunços*. The results, however, are not as encouraging as expected: The troops who survive the enemy fire spread out and disappear down the narrow alleyways and into the wood-and-mud huts. As the attacking troops continue to be absorbed, Colonel Moreira Cesar decides to lead an inspiring cavalry charge. He is shot down, however, and the command falls to timid Colonel Tamarindo. Amid the mounting confusion and faltering attack, Colonel Tamarindo and his fellow officers decide on a retreat that becomes a panic as the *jagunços* turn and pursue the fleeing troops, who abandon their equipment and wounded along the road. The *jagunços* line the roadsides with soldiers' heads and hang the decapi-

tated corpse of Colonel Tamarindo from a bush.

Stunned by the defeat, the whole nation panics, with rumors flying of a monarchist conspiracy behind the backlands revolt. The republic calls for full mobilization of its military resources, which prove to be embarrassingly limited, but within three months a fourth expedition is organized. The expedition divides into two columns. The first column, consisting of 1,933 men under General Arthur Oscar de Andrade Guimarães, leaves from Monte Santo, while a second column, of 2,350 men under General Claudio do Amaral Savaget, departs from Geremoabo. The second column must fight its way to Canudos, but it arrives in time to rescue the first column, pinned down on the town's outskirts. After the columns link up, a state of siege begins, though sometimes it is difficult to tell who is besieging whom. Since the army has a foothold only on one side of Canudos, the town has easy access to supplies, while the army has trouble getting its supplies through. Meanwhile, the army's casualties are horrendous.

Seeing the supply problem, Marshal Carlos Machado de Bittencourt, the war minister, steps in and takes charge of the situation. He buys one thousand mules, sets up regular supply trains, and sends in troop reinforcements. Saved by the mules, the army begins asserting itself. Through various forays and attacks, it extends its line further into and around Canudos, eventually surrounding the city. After that, Canudos is doomed, though the *jagunços* continue to resist strongly and to inflict heavy casualties. The army's artillery bombards the city, starting extensive fires, but somehow the huts absorb the cannonballs and shrapnel. When the army tightens its circle, it has to stop the bombardments to avoid endangering its own troops and resort to close fighting, including hand-to-hand combat. The army tries dynamite bombs briefly, but their effects fall so heavily on the civilian population that, even in this vicious war, they are discontinued. Only one truce is called, to allow some two hundred women, children, and old men to surrender. The remaining defenders of Canudos die to the last man, conveniently falling back into a mass grave that had been dug earlier.

Analysis

Rebellion in the Backlands should be required reading for all military students, since it clearly points out the dangers to a cumbersome army, with outmoded tactics and long supply lines, of fighting a guerrilla war on the guerrillas' home turf. The *sertanejos* utilize classic guerrilla procedures, including local intelligence networks, hit-and-run maneuvers, enticement into ambushes, recycling of captured equipment, and psychological demoralization. Most of all, the *sertanejos* are expert at using their terrain against the army, striking after the troops are exhausted or have marched into cul-de-sacs. Finally, the *sertanejos* illustrate the determination of guerrillas fighting for a fanatical cause or for their homes.

Notwithstanding Cunha's interest in military lessons, *Rebellion in the Backlands* is ultimately an antimilitaristic work. Besides showing the military to disadvantage, Cunha condemned his country for using military power against its own citizens, poor people living in a neglected region that might be termed the Appalachia of Brazil. His condemnation may seem unfair under the circumstances, but Cunha believed that integrating the *sertanejos* into the national culture was a matter of time and education, not military force. Furthermore, Cunha's admiration of the *sertanejos* suggests that such integration does not simply mean conformity of the "backward" *sertanejos* to the "civilized" national culture. How civilized, asks Cunha, is a culture that must prevail through superior brutality? This paradox continues to plague not only Brazil but also the superpowers and "civilization" generally.

Critical Context

Rebellion in the Backlands is Brazil's own *Iliad*, with soldiers and *sertanejos* replacing Greeks and Trojans. A monumental work of the early Brazilian Republic, *Rebellion in the Backlands* contributed to the rediscovery of Brazil's colorful regions, particularly the Northeast, and to the creation of the *sertanejo* myth. Cunha thereby helped lay the groundwork for the modern flowering of the Brazilian novel. Cunha's influence can be seen, for example, in such novels as Jorge Amado's *Terras do Sem Fim* (1942; *The Violent Land*, 1945) and *Gabriela, Cravo e Canela* (1958; *Gabriela, Clove and Cinnamon*, 1962), with Gabriela as a modern embodiment of the *sertanejo* myth.

The influence of *Rebellion in the Backlands* does not stop at Brazil's borders. It inspired, for example, a fictional retelling of the Canudos story, *La guerra del fin del mondo* (1981; *The War of the End of the World*, 1984), by Peruvian novelist Mario Vargas Llosa. More generally, Cunha and other nonfiction writers, particularly sociologists, have helped to define the subject matter of Latin American fiction and have influenced its tendency to incorporate sociology, local color, and other factual material. The bizarre nature of some Latin American fact (especially political fact), as depicted by Cunha and others, has also influenced fictional interest, by novelists such as Argentina's Julio Cortázar and Colombia's Gabriel García Márquez, in the interplay of illusion and reality, fact and fantasy.

EL SEÑOR PRESIDENTE

Author: Miguel Ángel Asturias (1899-1974)
Type of work: Novel
Type of plot: Social criticism
Time of plot: The early twentieth century
Locale: Central America
First published: 1946 (English translation, 1963)

Principal Characters

El Señor Presidente, a dictator partially modeled on Manuel Estrada Cabrera, a ruler of Guatemala during Asturias' lifetime. His government runs on webs of political intrigue and corruption involving rumors, rigged elections, spies, secret police, hired assassins, false imprisonment, and torture. Since childhood, he has enjoyed tormenting weaker beings. Now he takes brutal revenge on all those who oppose or hinder him, including his former associates. He initiates a plot to frame his rival, General Canales, for murder. He at first appears to accept the relationship between Miguel and Camila, but he steadily works against them in secret.

Miguel Cara de Ángel, the handsome protagonist, called "as beautiful and as wicked as Satan," who serves as aide and favorite adviser to the dictator. His character changes when he falls in love with and later marries Camila Canales, whom he had earlier kidnapped while engaged in the dictator's plot against her father. His efforts to protect her lead him deeper into conflict with the regime and into a web of deception that the dictator suspects and eventually unravels, causing disaster for the young couple. Arrested while supposedly leaving on a foreign mission for the government, Miguel is tricked, betrayed, tortured, and finally thrown into prison, where he eventually dies in anonymity and despair after hearing lies about his wife's involvement with the dictator.

Camila Canales, the innocent young daughter of an influential general. During a plot against her father, she is kidnapped by Cara de Ángel, who wants her for himself. He is charmed by her and comes to pity her situation. They soon fall in love and marry, despite obstacles. She is separated from her husband and relatives through the dictator's deceits. She and her son finally leave the city to live in seclusion in the countryside, believing that Miguel abandoned them after he supposedly goes abroad on a secret mission for the dictator.

General Eusebio Canales, an opponent of the dictator who is falsely accused of murder. He flees, learns of more abuses by the government, organizes a failed revolution, and finally dies of shock upon hearing lies about his daughter's connections with his enemies.

Lucio Vásquez, a low-level employee of the secret police. His killing of Pelele, under orders, causes a series of events culminating in the downfall of Cara de Ángel. He is eventually imprisoned by his own regime.

Genaro Rodas, a misguided friend of Vásquez who wants to join the secret police. He witnesses the killing of Pelele without understanding all of its implications. Beaten and imprisoned by the authorities, he agrees to spy against Cara de Ángel. He is involved in Miguel's eventual arrest.

Fedina de Rodas, the wife of Genaro and a friend of Camila. Thought to know too much about the plot against General Canales, she is tortured by the authorities. After her baby dies of neglect, she is sold into prostitution and driven to madness.

Pelele (Zany or **Idiot),** one of several unfortunate beggars found around the cathedral early in the novel. His demented killing of one of the dictator's officers sets the plot into motion, as the dictator tries to blame the crime on General Canales. Pelele is aided by the unwitting Miguel but is eventually killed by Vásquez under the pretext that he is a public danger infected with rabies.

El Auditor General de Guerra, the Judge Advocate General, a military counselor, one of several powerful, brutal, corrupt, anonymous officials. He is successful in undermining Cara de Ángel, thus fulfilling his own political ambitions

and gaining favor with the dictator.

Doña Chon, a brothel madam who knew the dictator in the old days. She bargains with the Judge Advocate General to buy Fedina de Rodas for her establishment.

Abel Carvajal, a lawyer summarily executed for supposedly aiding General Canales. His wife tries desperately to save him but cannot.

Major Farfán, a minor officer who is aided by Miguel but who eventually betrays and arrests him.

The Novel

The novel provides no clue as to its time or locale, beyond the mention, when Cara de Ángel is searching the pages of *El Nacional* for an announcement of his wedding, that he sees mention of the Battle of Verdun, at a time when Manuel Estrada Cabrera was the Guatemalan president. Apparently Asturias had no special target in mind.

The novel is concerned with the unnamed president of an unnamed Latin American nation. He is a dictator who maintains himself in power by cruelty and ruthlessness, although his portrait, pasted everywhere—with punishment for its removal—makes him appear to be a youthful charmer. In the portrait, he wears huge epaulets and is about to be crowned with a laurel wreath by a smiling cherub. The Judge Advocate General sums up the President's theory of control: Never let anyone have grounds for hope; make them realize, by brutal beatings and kickings if necessary, that there is none. The President, lamenting the murder of his hatchet man, Colonel Parrales Sonriente, killed by a crazy beggar named Zany whom he had taunted on the cathedral steps, also reveals his philosophy by declaring that he had intended to make Parrales a general because of his ability to trample on the populace and humiliate them.

The killing of the officer provides the President with an excuse for getting rid of a political rival, General Canales, along with a fellow plotter, Lawyer Abel Carvajal. The Judge Advocate General gathers up all the beggars from the cathedral where the killing had taken place and beats them until

they are willing to swear they had seen Canales commit the murder. The only one refusing to sign the accusation, Mosquito, a legless blind beggar, is beaten to death. To prevent discovery of the true facts, Lucio Vásquez of the secret police finds Zany, the real murderer, and silences him with two bullets.

Further evidence of the merciless nature of the President is revealed as he orders the beating of his personal physician, Dr. Barreño, for uncovering political graft that has caused the death of soldiers at the hospital. Even worse, he has his secretary whipped to death for spilling ink on a document. It is easy to understand how such a man could mark the innocent General Canales for death.

In order to carry out his scheme against General Canales, the President involves his crony, Miguel Cara de Ángel, in an elaborate plot, first ordering the police to shoot the general if he attempts to flee, then sending Cara de Ángel to warn him of his danger and urge him to escape. The crony, in love with the general's daughter, betrays his master by getting his victim safely across the frontier. The general dies, however, before he can recruit an army for invasion.

Complications, including acceptance of bribes by the Judge Advocate to put Camila Canales into the Sweet Enchantment brothel and her rescue by Cara de Ángel, result in the arrangement of the marriage of Camila and Miguel by the President to ensure the loyalty of his crony. Through treachery, Cara de Ángel is illegally imprisoned and soon dies. Other rebels against the President also die. As opposition continues, so does the atmosphere of terror that allows the dictator's favorites to thrive

in a generally corrupt society. With the secret police in power, El Señor Presidente continues to have his way.

Analysis

A dictatorship in Latin America can have several aspects. It is frequently viewed by the outside world as a comic opera sort of thing. O. Henry and others have written of its amusing moments and its romantic and adventurous episodes such as gun running, but frequently it is much more tragic and cruel. The stakes are high and the financial returns enormous. History records many long-term Latin American dictatorships. Asturias' novel shows how fear and terror can make such longevity possible.

As if to lighten the unpleasant pictures of oppression and the exploitation of the poor, the author includes bits of folklore; references to Tohil, Giver of Fire; folk poetry; and descriptions that might have come from Asturias' earlier French impressionist poetry period. Local color and regional words are so numerous in the novel that Asturias felt the need to include a vocabulary and glossary covering eight pages.

Critical Context

Miguel Ángel Asturias, born in Guatemala, spent much of his life elsewhere. After finishing his studies as a lawyer at the University of Guatemala, he traveled to France in 1923 and remained there for ten years, writing poetry in the French style and completing a novel about a Spanish American dictator that he had started before leaving home. He also served as Guatemala's diplomatic representative in France, Argentina, El Salvador, and Mexico. Following the increasing success of his writings, he retired to Buenos Aires

with his wife and two sons.

It is chiefly for this bitter picture of a morally sick Latin American nation under dictatorship, a disease suffered by many Latin American nations, that he is recognized as an important author. The pictures of human misery in this novel make a powerful impression even on those critics who find it aesthetically weak. *El Señor Presidente* is an example of *esperpéntica*, a mixture of satire and the grotesque.

THE SEVEN MADMEN

Author: Roberto Arlt (1900-1942)
Type of work: Novel
Type of plot: Magical Realism
Time of plot: The 1920's
Locale: Buenos Aires, Argentina, and its suburbs
First published: *Los siete locos*, 1929 (English translation, 1984)

Principal Characters

Augusto Remo Erdosain, the protagonist, a hapless dreamer who, at the beginning of the novel, loses both his wife (to a virile military captain) and his low-paying job as a bill collector for a sugar company (because he has embezzled funds). Frustrated, humiliated, and emotionally overwrought, Remo surrenders himself to fantasies of amorous and financial success, and to the crackpot schemes of a subversive group that he joins.

The Astrologer, a charismatic charlatan who leads a pseudorevolutionary group of down-and-outers and plans to take over Argentina in a coup d'état. His plan for revolution is elitist in intention: The happy few will benefit from the labor of the masses, who will be regimented for maximum productivity.

Arturo Haffner, called the **Melancholy Ruffian,** a pimp and member of The Astrologer's activist cell. Haffner despises women, seeing only potential earnings in them. He befriends Erdosain and gives him the money he needs to pay back the funds he has embezzled.

Elsa, Erdosain's wife, a woman brought up in some luxury who has sacrificed herself to live with him but reaches the end of her patience with the poverty and hopelessness of his life. She goes off with Captain Belaúnde after a tense scene with Erdosain at his apartment. She leaves the captain almost immediately, after he makes an offensive

pass at her, and ends up in a nervous crisis at a hospital, unbeknown to Erdosain.

Eduardo Ergueta, a corpulent pharmacist who is a compulsive gambler, religious fanatic, and member of The Astrologer's group. A deluded small-time prophet, Ergueta has married a prostitute, Hipólita, in order to save her. Ergueta's ravings eventually land him in a mental hospital.

Hipólita, a prostitute married to Ergueta and befriended by Erdosain. Hipólita is not physically impaired, but she is called a Lame Woman or Lame Whore by Ergueta because she has, as he says, gone astray. This sobriquet sticks to her. She has a prostitute's cynical view of men but seems to adopt an almost motherly attitude toward Erdosain.

Gregorio Barsut, Elsa's cousin, who is locked into an ongoing contest of wills with Erdosain. He punches Erdosain upon learning of Elsa's departure and then confesses that it was he who denounced Erdosain to the sugar company. Then and there Erdosain resolves to have Barsut killed. The revolutionaries kidnap Barsut on Erdosain's suggestion. Barsut is saved from death by The Astrologer, who arranges with him to simulate the execution in front of Erdosain.

The Major, an army officer affiliated with The Astrologer's group who plans to use the revolutionary movement as a provocation for a military coup.

The Novel

The Seven Madmen chronicles the disaffiliation of Remo Erdosain from normal, middle-class life and his increasing involvement with the mysterious conspiracy of The Astrologer. During a period of only a few months, Erdosain moves from being a clerk with a pretty, respectable wife to being the colleague of various denizens of the underworld, occultists, and political fanatics. The novel closes with Erdosain among these dangerous companions, under the charismatic sway of The Astrologer, working on an invention that, if successful, would be fatally toxic to the population of Buenos Aires. A footnote promises that the outcome of these circumstances will appear in a sequel, *Los lanzallamas* (the flamethrowers), which in fact was published in 1931.

While Erdosain becomes more deeply enmeshed in The Astrologer's schemes, the reader of *The Seven Madmen* finds it increasingly difficult to distinguish the realistic from the magical and fantastic elements in the novel. It is unclear whether The Astrologer is a Socialist revolutionary, a Fascist, or the leader of a religious revival.

His followers, with the exception of the earnest protagonist, often seem not to believe in the worth of The Astrologer's project. They hint that no serious revolution is being planned and that the conspirators are merely distracting themselves from boredom with the shared fiction of a grand undertaking. It is this mix of realistic descriptions and plot elements with bizarrely imaginative ones that has won for *The Seven Madmen* its fame as an important early example of Magical Realism.

The Astrologer announces a goal of providing modern humankind, alienated from traditional sources of spiritual orientation, with a renewed sense of purpose. To achieve this end, he is willing to resort to demagogy, deceit, and "mind games." The Astrologer often hints that he is indifferent to the viability or outcome of his conspiracy, so long as those involved can escape the pervasive meaninglessness of modern existence.

Analysis

The Seven Madmen is an existential novel, a novel full of myth and magic; at the same time, it includes realistic descriptions of social circumstances. The fact that no reader can say definitively what the novel is "about" gives it its lasting appeal. New meanings and themes continue to surface as new readers come to the work.

One of the work's most unmistakable statements is that modern people, without the guidance provided by religion and tradition, are unstable creatures, easily swept up in totalitarian movements, mass manias, and occultism. The character who upholds traditional values, Elsa, Erdosain's wife, is not very appealing. The only figures mentioned as leading spiritually meaningful lives belong to earlier eras. The novel's comment on twentieth century life is a sour one, for its characters experience a fullness of meaning only when they are engaged in dangerous and self-deluded enterprises or lost in vivid fantasies.

Another strong theme is the power of imagina-

tion. The novel contains numerous tributes to earlier times in which human beings were transformed by a transcendent vision—for example, the days of chivalry. Even in the impoverished modern era, individual characters have brief moments when they rise above the banality of their circumstances through inspired eloquence.

Even though *The Seven Madmen* often leaves the reader unsure as to the reality of the events of the plot, it is a realistic work in two important ways. First, it accurately describes Buenos Aires of the late 1920's, with special attention to the precarious situation of the lower-middle class in the poorly balanced economy of the times. Second, it shows, through fiction, some of the forces behind the 1930 military takeover. The resemblance to real-life events is so strong that Arlt needed to add a note to post-1930 editions pointing out that he wrote the novel before the military coup and had been unaware of the gathering conspiracy.

Critical Context

Both as an early example of Magical Realism and as a literary achievement in its own right, *The Seven Madmen* is held in high esteem. It is the most widely discussed work by Roberto Arlt, generally deemed a great original figure in Latin American writing. Although Arlt produced three other novels, two volumes of short stories, many journalistic pieces, and several plays, none is quite as successful at fusing realism, existential preoccupations, and wild imagination as *The Seven Madmen*.

Arlt was a newspaper writer whose style was often rough, though he also was capable of lyric prose. The varieties of language and style in *The Seven Madmen* have irritated some readers and fascinated others. Even Arlt's greatest admirers concede that his writing is of very uneven quality; some passages of *The Seven Madmen* are simply too histrionic, "purple," or sentimental.

Any reader of the Latin American New Novel, especially novels of the magical vein worked by such authors as Gabriel García Márquez and Julio Cortázar, should turn to Arlt's novel to understand the beginning stages in the development of this highly original form. Indicative of Arlt's role in the development of Latin American literature is the changing degree of recognition accorded his work. During the 1920's and 1930's, Arlt won considerable attention as an unusual and flamboyant figure on the Buenos Aires literary scene, but his work was not always considered to be of lasting significance. For example, although *The Seven Madmen* won for Arlt the Municipal Prize in the category of novels published in its year in Buenos Aires, it also had many detractors who deemed the novel to be too rough in language and irregular in its construction.

After Arlt's death, many of his titles went out of print for considerable lengths of time. An interest in Arlt and his work was considered to be a sign of literary bohemianism and of a taste for the per-

versely experimental. Arlt's declining reputation can be attributed in great measure to the rise of realistic fiction during the 1940's and 1950's. The prominence of existential themes in Argentine fiction of the 1950's contributed to some revival of interest in Arlt, but his wildly imaginative fiction has a very limited resemblance to the sober exposition favored by 1950's-style existential novelists.

It was in the late 1960's that Arlt's reputation began to rise dramatically. The upsurge of interest in Arlt, and especially in *The Seven Madmen*, is directly attributable to the widespread success of the Latin American New Novel of the 1960's and 1970's. This movement was characterized by a mingling of realistic and fantastic or magical constituents, by an inclusion of rougher language (and indeed by a thoroughgoing willingness on the part of writers to transgress the constraints of decorum), and by puzzling narrative arrangements. The traits of the New Novel were, in effect, those of Arlt's novel; it is not surprising that many writers of the new form, such as Cortázar, expressed a debt to this neglected forebear. Readers had been schooled in the abilities needed to appreciate Arlt's work. The New Novel taught its readership to piece together plots from fragmented bits of information, to accept unexplained elements in the narrative, and to grant the novel license to use diverse registers of language and a variety of styles. These readers were prepared to understand Arlt's irregular novelistic practices, and the cult figure now assumed the status of a much-read and much-cited staple of Argentine (and Latin American) literature. *The Seven Madmen* has been filmed, translated into various languages, lampooned, discussed, and generally given a prominent place in Argentine literary culture. Ahead of its era and slow to be accepted, this is a work whose time has come.

THE SHIPYARD

Author: Juan Carlos Onetti (1909-   )
Type of work: Novel
Type of plot: Allegory
Time of plot: The late 1950's
Locale: The fictional city of Santa Maria and its hinterland, modeled after the River Plate basin towns of Argentina and Uruguay
First published: *El astillero*, 1961 (English translation, 1968)

Principal Characters

E. Larsen, the antihero, a stout, balding, late-middle-aged former pimp. He wishes to reintegrate himself legitimately into the area of Santa Maria, the river city from which he was exiled five years before for establishing a brothel there. Larsen is appointed general manager of an idle, bankrupt shipyard nearby at Puerto Astillero and, feeding self-delusion to justify his existence, tries to make something out of its rusting plant, which has not received an order or paid its managers in years. He courts the boss's mentally defective daughter in the hope of possessing the seignorial house where she and her father live. Apparently dying, he rides upriver on a ferryboat.

Jeremías Petrus, the elderly owner of the defunct shipyard. Petrus, too, is self-deluded. He keeps up the role of willful pioneer of industry. When he is jailed for forgery, Petrus ages further overnight, calls the cell his office, and continues to make empty plans for the business with his visitor, Larsen.

Angélica Inés Petrus, the idiot daughter of the shipyard owner. Tall, blonde, and childlike, she emits involuntary bursts of laughter from her perpetually open mouth and is generally incapable of making coherent conversation. Larsen courts her with comic formality, but Angélica Inés barely comprehends what is happening.

A. Gálvez, the bald young administrative manager of the shipyard. Receiving no salary in his purely nominal job, with nothing to do but occasionally sell spare parts from the plant, he lives in poverty with a wife and dogs in a shack on the shipyard grounds. He becomes increasingly humorless, denounces Petrus to the police for forgery, and then commits suicide, as if he were no longer able to live the lie of the shipyard.

Gálvez's wife, a tall, attractive, but unkempt woman who wears a man's overcoat and shoes. At the time of the action, she is pregnant. Larsen is attracted to her, considering her a real woman, perhaps by comparison with the childish Angélica Inés.

Kunz, the older, corpulent, hairy technical manager of the shipyard, a German immigrant. Like Gálvez, Kunz is cynical and sarcastic about the phantom enterprise and spends his supposed work time looking over his stamp album.

Dr. Díaz Grey, a middle-aged bachelor physician from Santa Maria, formerly acquainted with Larsen. Díaz Grey's impressions of Larsen and recollections of the string of predecessors Larsen has had at Petrus Limited provide another perspective. Informed of Larsen's absurd engagement to Angélica Inés Petrus, Díaz Grey soberly recommends that they avoid having children.

Josefina, Angélica Inés' servant, whom Larsen bribes and romances in order to get access to Petrus' daughter.

The Novel

The narrative focus of *The Shipyard* provides a closely detailed, agonizing, but simultaneously ironic inside view of Larsen's doomed attempt to make a comeback and acquire respectability in the Santa Maria area, from which he was exiled five years earlier for his connection with a brothel there. Having returned to Santa Maria for a day at the beginning of the novel, Larsen goes upriver to Puerto Astillero and obtains the meaningless post of general manager of an idle shipyard. Its decayed plant is presided over remotely by its owner, Jeremías Petrus. The only employees on hand are the administrators Gálvez and Kunz, who do not receive their salaries and perform no work except occasional clandestine sales (for their own survival) of the rusted parts that remain from the days when Jeremías Petrus, Ltd., was a bustling enterprise.

Larsen throws himself into a senseless routine at the several degraded locales that provide the grotesque setting and the recurring chapter titles of the novel: Santa Maria, the shipyard, the summerhouse, the house, and the shack. At the shipyard, he pores over yellowing contracts and faded blueprints from times past and continually tells himself that a good managerial hand is all that is needed to set the phantom enterprise in motion again. Each afternoon, he visits the summerhouse of the Petrus estate in a comically decorous ritual of courtship with Petrus' feebleminded daughter, Angélica Inés. From the grounds, Larsen gazes at the Petrus house, which he hopes to inherit and occupy, as part of devoting "the rest of his life to revenge without consequences, to sensuality without vigor, to a heedless, narcissistic power"—aspirations that reflect the severe limits of Juan Carlos Onetti's fictional world.

With no salary, Larsen soon finds it necessary to take his meals in the shack occupied by the sardonic Gálvez and his wife, a Faulknerian stoic female, whom Larsen also courts. Larsen slips back into Santa Maria in an attempt to save Petrus from imprisonment for an old forgery, and despite the vague danger of apprehension and new expulsion, he cannot resist looking up former acquaintances such as Dr. Díaz Grey, whose conversation fills Larsen with memories of his Santa Maria past. The river—reminiscent of the tributaries of the actual River Plate—also functions as an important symbolic setting, most notably when a defeated (or, in the alternate ending provided, a still somewhat game) Larsen takes his last, presumably fatal trip north on the ferryboat, away from the Santa Maria country.

Analysis

Larsen and all the characters, in reflection of and in relation to him, face an existential void: Their lives lack purpose, and they are reduced to doing what Larsen in meditation refers to as "one thing and another and another, all alien, without worrying about whether they turned out well or badly." The need to maintain narrative impetus does generate some tension between the characters' faith in the future and the sense that there is no future, but the essential tone is a lucid pessimism, the atmosphere one of disintegration and death-in-life. The shipyard acts as the central metaphor of these themes right up to Larsen's final departure from Puerto Astillero, when, "deaf to the din of the boat, his eager ear could still make out the whisper of moss growing among the piles of bricks and that of rust devouring metal." Throughout, the human body is visualized in decay; interaction among the characters is pure theater, devoid of the vitality of real life. Gálvez's suicide in this context seems like an attainment of authenticity.

Positive values in the Onettian world exist mainly as absence or nostalgia. This world lacks true community, sense of purpose, and any conventional religious sense of a power that would confer a higher meaning of life. Some remote nostalgia for religion can be felt in the abundant (though degraded and ironic) Christian allegory of the novel, which appears not only in the names of characters but also in their functions. Larsen, the debased Christ figure, nurtures the ambition of acceding to Petrus' house, "the empty form of a paradise he had coveted and had been promised; the gates of a city he longed to enter." Petrus is not a divinity, but he holds the keys to the coveted kingdom. Angélica Inés is linked to the Petrus faith not only by her name but also by her characteristic backward-leaning gait, compared with that of someone carrying a figure in a religious procession. Gálvez's wife seems to be named Maria, and Larsen realizes the significance of her name when the calendar tells him it is the feast of the Immaculate Conception. This significance is noted as such but not explained in the narration; Onetti's allegory differs from the medieval variety in that it does not serve to confirm but ironically serves to mark the absence of an effective communal faith.

Another allegorical level of the novel can be found in the Freudian depths of its presentation of women from Larsen's male point of view. The visualizations of the Gálvez woman and even of Angélica Inés stress their maternal aspects. Larsen's alienation may ultimately be generic, traceable to expulsion from the womb. Passing by the shack as he is about to leave on his last journey, he spies Gálvez's wife in labor. One can predict that her child is about to be initiated into the trauma of life outside the mother.

The Shipyard is dedicated to Onetti's friend and political patron Luis Batlle Berres, who was the last leader of the long-reigning liberal Colorado Party before its historic defeat in the 1958 elections, a defeat attributed to the financial ruin experienced by Uruguay in the 1950's. Some critics have chosen to read the dedication as a satiric statement, seeing the story of Petrus' bankrupt shipyard an allegory of the decline of the Uruguayan welfare state built by the Colorados in the approximately fifty years preceding the publication of *The Shipyard*. Certainly the novel's tone of disillusionment fits the public mood of Uruguay since the mid-1950's, a mood in which alienation has not needed to be metaphysical in nature.

Critical Context

In 1963, Onetti deservedly won the William Faulkner Certificate of Merit for *El astillero*. The novel is an innovative transmutation of the themes and techniques of Faulkner, the Uruguayan author's most influential literary model. Onetti's Santa Maria country is a fictional locale suggested by but not simply copied from Faulkner's Yoknapatawpha County. The religious allegory of *The Shipyard* is Hispano-Catholic in content, but it has technical precedents in Faulkner novels such as *Light in August* (1932). The multiple points of view of *The Shipyard* also can be traced to Faulkner. Criticism has not always pointed out the differences between Onetti and Faulkner, but *The Shipyard* displays some, such as the greater measure of pessimism present in Onetti's work and the Uruguayan writer's more pointed reflexive dimension. The distinctive Onettian narrative voice repeatedly comments on the progress of its narration, which itself seems tainted by the arbitrariness and insubstantiality of the lives being told:

> Now, in the incomplete reconstruction of that night, as part of the whim of giving it historical importance or meaning, as part of the inoffensive game of cutting short a winter evening, manipulating, combining and playing tricks with all those things which interest no one and which are not indispensable, there comes the testimony of the bartender of the Plaza.

Onetti is the best of the River Plate writers who, quite independently of the French, developed an existential fiction in the 1940's and 1950's. He is one of the earliest and most redoubtable craftsmen of the Latin American New Narrative. For all of its reminiscence of Faulkner, the Santa Maria saga was itself highly influential long before the 1980's, when Onetti's life work was awarded Spain's Cervantes Prize and Uruguay's National Literature Prize. Onetti stimulated the equally ambitious projects of younger writers such as Gabriel García Márquez and Mario Vargas Llosa. No novel of the saga is as intense as *The Shipyard*, or more successful in maintaining Onetti's ambiguous play between disintegration and imaginative attempts to prevail against it, between the somber theme of mortality and the comic treatment of it.

THE SHROUDED WOMAN

Author: María Luisa Bombal (1910-1980)
Type of work: Novel
Type of plot: Surrealism
Time of plot: The first half of the twentieth century
Locale: The southern part of Chile and the fantastic realm of Death
First published: *La amortajada*, 1938 (English translation, 1948)

Principal Characters

Ana María, a dead woman who alternately views her mourners, the memories they arouse, and the dramatic landscape of death. Ana María finds that in death her perceptions are amplified; her emotions are fully realized. Her early beauty returns, and she sees herself as pale, slender, and unwrinkled by time. Following heart attacks and a stroke, Ana María dies and witnesses her wake, a journey to the family vault, and her fall to surreal subterranean landscapes. Flowing back to the surface, she roots herself to the world and longs for immersion in death.

Ricardo, Ana María's adolescent lover and neighbor. Ricardo deserts Ana María when he goes to study agricultural farming in Europe. On his return he fails to approach her, then says that he is not to blame for her pregnancy. From this time on, each avoids the other.

Antonio, Ana María's rich, handsome, and charming husband. After marriage, his young bride feels lost in his sumptuous, labyrinthine house; she resists both his home and the pleasure that Antonio arouses in her. Antonio allows her to visit her father's home, but when she returns, he is indifferent to her presence. Fated now to love a man who seems only to tolerate her, Ana María suffers from

Antonio's constant pursuit of other women.

Fernando, an older man who woos Ana María and becomes her confidant in her later years. Fernando—ill, luckless, unhappy, swarthy, and lean—repulses Ana María, although she needs to confide in him.

Alberto, the son of Ana María and Antonio. Handsome and taciturn, he loves only life on his southern hacienda until he meets María Griselda. Her overwhelming beauty and appearance of self-containment drive him to agony and drink. Jealous, he walls her up in the family hacienda.

María Griselda, Alberto's wife. Her beauty causes her to suffer from early childhood as she draws the adoration of men and women, children, and nature. Left lonely by her husband's searching love, she remains solitary. Only Ana María can forgive her great beauty.

Fred, the son of Ana María and Antonio. Ana María dearly loves this child, who fears mirrors and speaks an unknown language in dreams.

Silvia, Fred's wife. Silvia makes the tragic decision to spend her honeymoon at the forest hacienda. The new bride shoots herself in the temple when Fred confesses that he has been transformed by the presence of María Griselda.

The Novel

In *The Shrouded Woman*, María Luisa Bombal skillfully juxtaposes the unknown and supernatural realm of Death with concrete reality. At the beginning of the novel, Ana María lies dead and is surrounded by those who once had relationships with her. Although she is dead, Ana María can still hear and see those who are mourning her. Simultaneously, while she lies in her casket, the protagonist is led into the past as she recalls events significant to her life. She enters the supernatural space of Death, inhabited by mysterious voices, uncanny landscapes, and strange insects and flowers. The juxtaposition of Life and Death is created in the novel through the cinematic technique of a montage, capturing the coexistence of elements of reality traditionally conceived as separate entities: the past binds to the present, both merging into a single instant; consciousness survives beyond death; and concrete objective reality fuses with the mysterious zone of Death.

In addition to the omniscient narrator, there are several other narrators who give their own testimony on Ana María, in this way adding conflicting views and interpretations to the story of her life. Thus, Ana María becomes a multifaceted charac-

ter: a passionate lover, a selfish woman, a naïve girl, a strict mother, and an intuitive human being with mystical doubts about God. In the same manner that the shrouded woman acquires a new understanding of her life through the fragmented memories of the past, the reader adds these different perspectives about Ana María to realize finally that human beings are what they think of themselves as well as the different images they project on others. The protagonist's journey into Death is the ultimate act of Life, not only because she now comprehends the real meaning of her existence but also because Death has allowed her to annul the worries of everyday life, penetrating thereby into the mysteries of people and nature. Ironically, then, the burial of Ana María at the end of the novel becomes a symbol of what true Life should be: the profound and wise experiences of the self as part of a wider cosmic order.

Analysis

As a true exponent of the avant-garde movement, *The Shrouded Woman* expresses a preoccupation with those mysterious aspects of reality that lie beyond the limits of scientific and rational parameters. Shortly after the publication of the novel, María Luisa Bombal said: "I think people have willingly ignored that we live on the surface of the unknown. We have organized a logical system on a well of mystery. We have chosen to ignore what is primordial to Life: Death." Therefore, the literary representation of Death is not only a supernatural locale of the novel but also an important theme that enlightens the conception of Life. Death is seen as a process of immersion in the primordial cosmos. The archetypal motif of the journey into death is presented in counterpoint to other experiences in the realm of the living. Only in death does Ana María comprehend the tragic and profound significance of her life and those of others. Thus, Death is a spiritual experience that leads not only to the hidden meaning of life but also to an integration with the cosmic forces that are the origins of Life.

A mysterious voice invites Ana María to abandon her coffin and explore a magical zone that belongs to the unknown. Light and darkness, Life and Death emerge in the supernatural gardens underground, as in the primordial stage of biblical Genesis. The dead protagonist descends into the origins of the universe, going down into the earth where she encounters flowers of bone and marvelously intact human skeletons with their knees drawn up as if once again inside the womb. After she is buried, she feels an infinity of roots spreading from her body into the earth like an expanding cobweb through which the constant throbbing of the universe rises. Immersed in the ancient flow of Life and Death, she now feels new islands emerge; far-off mountains of sand tumble down to give rise to other forms of life in a cyclic movement of death and regeneration. Her dead body disintegrating in the earth becomes a new source of life in the cosmic cycle, in which matter never dies but only assumes new forms.

The Shrouded Woman is also a denunciation of Latin American women's predicament in the twentieth century. The theme of love as the sole gratification for women is conceived in the novel as a spiritual search, which is achieved in society only through a subordinate relation regulated by men. Moreover, María Luisa Bombal, in a view very similar to that of the French feminist Simone de Beauvoir, states that women's total dependence on love deprives them of the right to mold their lives in a truly independent way. Ana María is a prisoner of love, and, very symbolically, she realizes at a later stage in her life that her concept of love has been a deception created by a culture in which women are supposed to be sentimental and pas-

sive. Therefore, the message of the novel implicitly makes a distinction between love as a spiritual and innate drive in human beings and love as a social activity that reinforces the primary roles of men and women in a patriarchal society. At the end of the novel, after Ana María has returned to the ancestral realm of the earth, she recapitulates her life in a highly symbolic statement—she believes that while she was alive she lived the life of a dead person, restricted by her society, which only allowed her to attain the goal of marriage without ever allowing her the opportunity to overcome subordination.

Critical Context

When María Luisa Bombal published *La última niebla* in 1934 (*The Final Mist*, 1982), she was immediately acclaimed by critics as one of the outstanding writers of Latin America. Radically departing from the realist mode in vogue, she constructed this first short novel on the ambiguous juxtaposition of dreams and reality experienced by a female protagonist who escapes her tragic social predicament through alienation. The publication of *La amortajada* in 1938 reaffirmed her position as an innovative writer. In 1942, her second book was awarded the National Prize as the best novel in Chile. In 1948, the English version, *The Shrouded Woman*, was published in the United States, and it was subsequently printed in Sweden, Germany, Great Britain, and Japan. The Spanish version of *The Shrouded Woman* has gone through more than ten different editions and remained a best-seller in Latin America for decades after its initial publication.

Although literary criticism of Latin American literature has undergone changes and revisions, *The Shrouded Woman* continues to be acclaimed as one of the most significant Latin American novels ever published. Its impeccable technical elaboration and the presentation of a reality in which the concrete and the marvelous coexist have made this novel a landmark of surrealistic accomplishment in Latin America.

It is also a remarkable expression of women as second-class citizens with no right, or possibility, to change society. Its protagonist has been excluded from active participation in history. It is precisely this marginal status that has caused a basic alienation, rendered through daydreaming, erotic fantasies, and an immersion in the primordial realm of the cosmic. As feminist studies have demonstrated, Bombal's images of women not only denounce feminine subordination but also represent the innate essence of women as deeply rooted in nature. According to her worldview, men regulate natural forces to produce civilization and women, as individuals of an intuitive nature, grasp the mysterious irradiations of the universe in search of ancestral harmony. Power, violence, and civilization are, for the author, the basic expressions of the masculine, which, as opposed to the erotic and ancestral feminine, become irreconcilable forces doomed to noncommunication and sterility. Ana María in *The Shrouded Woman*, as well as the other women presented in María Luisa Bombal's works, are subjected to the dominant male order, and the defeat of the female is the real source of their tragic destiny. While in *The Shrouded Woman* the only exit is death, in *The Final Mist* it is death in life, conceived as a shrouded and oppressive mist that symbolizes social regulations imposed on women. If on the surface this appears to be a highly pessimistic view of women, subsequent works written by Latin American women have consistently coincided with María Luisa Bombal's lucid testimony, which is presented through an artistic elaboration that is considered exceptional.

62: A MODEL KIT

Author: Julio Cortázar (1914-1984)
Type of work: Novel
Type of plot: Experimental
Time of plot: Uncertain; possibly the 1950's or the 1960's
Locale: Paris and Arcueil, France; London, England; Vienna, Austria; and an imaginary city
First published: *62: Modelo para armar*, 1968 (English translation, 1972)

Principal Characters

Juan, an Argentine interpreter who works for an international agency. He has an almost surrealist vision of the world, which he shares with most of the characters, all of whom are among a group of friends who meet habitually in the café Cluny. Juan is interested in metaphysical matters, especially in the ways in which reality is perceived. During his stay in Vienna, as he works at an international conference and shares his life with Tell, he is obsessed with the story of an old woman, Frau Marta, who vampirizes an English girl who is touring Vienna. Always mixing fantasies with real life, he tries to save the English girl from an imaginary danger, and everything becomes a metaphor of his relationship with Hélène, the woman he loves.

Hélène, a young French anesthetist, aloof and distant but a sensible and tender person. She invites Celia to her small apartment and, having no control of her feelings and senses, forces Celia to make love with her. After this disturbing experience, she has a sexual encounter with Juan, but she cannot forgive herself for the disgraceful incident of the night spent with Celia.

Marrast, a French sculptor. In order to forget that his lover, Nicole, has revealed to him her love for Juan, he invents absurd situations in a museum, situations in which almost all the members of the group, now in London, are engaged. All the members of the group are together at the inauguration of his Vercingetorix statue. He continues loving Nicole and tries to get her back.

Nicole, a French illustrator of children's books. She has a good relationship with Marrast, but their happiness is destroyed when she confesses that she is in love with Juan. They live together for a while, but she decides to go to bed with Austin in order to destroy Marrast's love.

Tell, Juan's lover, a young, beautiful, and independent Danish woman. She shares Juan's friends and travels with him, trying to enjoy their relationship even though she knows that Juan is in love with Hélène. She participates joyfully in the surrealistic games in which Juan is engaged, such as following Frau Marta and the English girl in their wanderings across Vienna and trying to protect the girl from impending danger.

Calac and **Polanco,** two Argentines, the first a writer and critic, the second a worker in unusual jobs. Both have a ludicrous sense of life and are always engaged in absurd dialogues in which they have nothing to say. Sometimes they use a language of their own. They are, in some respects, as Juan is in others, the alter ego of the author.

Celia, the youngest member of the group. She is rich and spoiled and decides to leave her parents' home. She runs into Hélène in the Cluny. She accepts Hélène's invitation to her place with curiosity, because Hélène is a mystery to most members of the group. She suffers a tremendous shock when she accepts Hélène's sexual assault, and she decides to go to London to join the others. She meets Austin and falls in love with him.

Austin, a young English lute player who receives French lessons from Marrast and joins the group. He is handsome and self-confident, having a casual affair with Nicole and initiating Celia into the delights of heterosexual love. He meets the group in London and they travel to Paris, attending the inauguration of Marrast's statue in Arcueil.

The paredros, an abstract entity that sometimes functions as an alter ego of a main character.

The Novel

The novel begins on the twenty-fourth of December in Paris. As Juan spends Christmas Eve alone in a gloomy restaurant, he examines the relationship between thought, word, and action, and he questions the value of reasoning itself. The deceiving nature of memory is then explored in passages that change swiftly and without warning from a first- to a second- and third-person narrator. Glimpses of specific details of what is going to happen, or has already happened, are introduced mostly through Juan's thoughts. In the midst of a labyrinthine beginning, which sets the tone of the text, some explanation is provided as to what constitutes the city and the paredros, key elements in the book.

For much of the novel, the friends are scattered in different European cities. In London, Marrast, Nicole, Calac, and Polanco amuse themselves at the expense of the British and their sense of decorum. A museum and the streets of London offer the possibilities of freedom and games, but inside their room of the Gresham Hotel Marrast and Nicole live their last days together. Nicole is in love with Juan, and Marrast becomes the frustrated witness of her melancholy. Their state of mind is portrayed carefully through the use of dialogue, inner reflections, and letters.

At the same time, Juan is translating for an international conference in Vienna, accompanied by Tell. Tell, the crazy Dane, as Juan calls her, makes him forget the treachery of language, and her sense of humor relieves him from the pain of his unrequited love for Hélène. In their pursuit of play, they decide to follow the steps of Frau Marta—a gray, repulsive old lady—whom they have watched develop a bizarre friendship with a young English female tourist. Tell and Juan couple their wish for adventure with the historical background of a legend and become detectives in a modern story of vampirism.

In Paris, the attention is focused on Hélène, an anesthetist, and the teenage Celia. The same day that Celia runs away from home, Hélène has lost a young man—who reminds her of Juan—at the operating table. The anesthetist invites Celia to her apartment; the prose switches back and forth between Celia's surprisingly mature and thoughtful analysis of Hélène and Hélène's memories and her actual displacement to the streets of the imaginary city. In the city she searches for a certain hotel and for a certain room where she is to deliver a package. Dialogue and interior monologue cut into each other constantly, and any attempt to establish a rational continuity is doubly frustrated by the tale of Juan and Tell in Vienna, which alternates with the episode in Paris. That night, Hélène seduces Celia in a scene presented in both a lyric and violent fashion. A broken doll in the morning and Celia's horrified scream at its sight stress the dark and mysterious aspect of the plot.

Shortly before the final gathering of the group, the various tensions produced by desire and adventure and play come to their conclusion. Nicole attempts suicide; Celia falls in love with Austin, the young English lutenist adopted in fun by Calac and Polanco in London; and Hélène and Juan finally confront each other and see themselves reliving the myth of Diana and Acteon. Near the end of the novel, all the friends, including Feuille Morte (an indefinite entity with a female voice) and Osvaldo, a pet snail, converge in France. The occasion is the unveiling of the statue of Vercingetorix, sculpted by Marrast and commissioned by the city of Arcueil. The sculpture turns out to be quite scandalous, for it appears that the hero of Gaulle has its backside pointing heavenward. On their return to Paris, Hélène and Juan keep repeating the same words, their language and themselves unable to advance anywhere except toward the city, the imaginary city that has haunted them from the start. It is in the room of a hotel where Hélène had a date, where she was to make a delivery, that Juan finds her, Austin's dagger in her chest, her body crushing the package, which contains a doll. As their train approaches Paris, Calac, Tell, and Polanco wait anxiously at the gate for Feuille Morte, who appears to have been forgotten. Feuille Morte is delighted to be rescued. Echoes of the initial fragments of the book come to mind. To find out if all the parts of the model kit are really there, at this point in the novel, the reader is tempted to return with Juan to a gloomy Parisian restaurant on Christmas Eve.

Analysis

Cortázar's writings are marked by an effect of discontinuity and fragmentation attained through various literary means. In *Rayuela* (1963; *Hopscotch*, 1966), the sequential modality of chapters is broken by altering the continuity of their numbers. In *Libro de Manuel* (1973; *A Manual for Manuel*, 1978), the typical page is distorted by the including of journalistic passages and by other devices. *62: A Model Kit* is no exception to the experiment that seeks to break away from the established institution of the novel. Cortázar, through *Hopscotch*, supposedly composed by the fictional Morelli, proposed that some of the main elements of this genre need to be revised or discarded in order to provide space for the "final mutation" of human beings. These new people, as writers and readers, yearn to dislodge themselves from old, worn forms such as realism, psychology, reason, feeling, and pragmatism. Cortázar willfully deviates from the "true-to-life" feature that is expected to produce an identificatory reality in fiction. In this case, the transgression is done at the level of the genre itself. The characters, however, constitute a group whose rebellious stand reaches beyond the limits of the book to criticize some aspects of Western culture and society.

The group, for example, takes precedence over the concept of the individual. Play and eroticism, two important concepts in the novel, require more than one person in order to take place. The voice of the paredros, an impersonal entity, decenters the discourse of any given subject, and since the paredros could be a number of characters, it affirms the group at the expense of the individual figure. The doll, like the anthropological *mana*, is a gift (transgressive in this case) that binds Juan, Tell, Celia, and Hélène; by extension, it binds all the friends except Feuille Morte. The imaginary city, known to all of them, but where meetings never occur, is enveloped by an aura of darkness and death. There one is alone. It is in the city, also, where the characters cease to laugh and play. Cortázar, throughout the novel, attacks the idea of the serious in a dionysian, joyous vein, and he stresses the importance of the game.

Critical Context

Cortázar's *62: A Model Kit* is his third novel, following *Los premios* (1960; *The Winners*, 1965) and *Hopscotch*. It also follows two books of poetry and five books of stories. Cortázar appears to have left unfinished business in *Hopscotch*. As he states in the introduction to *62: A Model Kit*, the novel is based on chapter 62 of *Hopscotch*. Critics widely agree that it is not nearly as successful as the earlier work, but the two share characteristics.

Juan, the Argentine interpreter, could be acting out the role of the author himself, who worked as a translator in France. Horacio Oliveira plays a similar role in *Hopscotch*. The two novels also share a treatment of time. Events do not take place linearly—in *Hopscotch*, the author invites the reader to rearrange chapters—and events are not firmly connected. The times at which events take place often are vague. Finally, both books can be seen as antinovels, violating the norms of novelistic form. The paredros, for example, acts as a noncharacter.

Cortázar's message changes with *A Manual for Manuel*, with his concern switching to politics. He retains many of his experimental methods but makes his plot more nearly linear. Characters are abstractions of real people, though retaining some of the fantastic features of those in his earlier books. Instead of asking readers to sort out abstract puzzles of existence, he focuses more narrowly on interpreting the real labyrinth of Argentine politics.

SO FAR FROM GOD

Author: Ana Castillo (1953-　　)
Type of work: Novel
Type of plot: Impressionistic realism
Time of plot: The 1970's to the 1990's
Locale: Tome, a small town in New Mexico
First published: 1993

Principal Characters

Sofia, a strong, resilient family matriarch whose marriage to Domingo was doomed from its inception. Long pitied as *la Abandonada* (the abandoned), Sofia struggles to hold on to her family home while she rears and later buries her four daughters. A quick-witted, dance-loving woman, Sofia is the vitalizing force whose drive, commitment, and faith help inspire and nurture a new spirit in her community—a spirit that recognizes that resistance is the secret of joy.

Esperanza, the mainstreamed yuppie newscaster who tries to bring her two worlds, the Chicano and the "white," together. Her choices to dump Ruben and accept a dangerous job in Saudi Arabia are ultimately framed by the realizations that she cannot bridge the gap between her two worlds and that her accomplishments will not guarantee success in love. The only one of Sofia's daughters to complete college, Esperanza is posthumously honored as an American hero.

Caridad, the family beauty, a hospital orderly who dulls the pain of her failed marriage with nightly binges of alcohol and promiscuous sex. Caridad is transformed by a violent attack into an intuitive mystic and healer whose extraordinary powers are honed by her exile in the desert. Afraid of love because everyone and everything she had given her heart to has gone away, Caridad discovers that her love for Esmeralda will defy death and exalt them both in Acoma mythology.

Fe, a prim and proper bank employee who is in constant quest of the good life. The supposedly "normal" daughter, Fe goes into a year-long screaming trance after receiving a letter breaking her engagement. Her lifelong quest for the good life and its amenities eventually leads Fe to accept a job with a chemical company; that job and her exposure to toxic chemicals kill her. When confronting death, Fe finally comes to appreciate the wonders of the lives her family had led, and she loses her embarrassment regarding her family.

La Loca, the family's youngest daughter, gifted with supernatural foresight following her death and resurrection. Shunning people in favor of her animals and the visits of mysterious astral personages, La Loca intercedes on her family's behalf and routinely performs miracles through her prayers.

Domingo, the mustached dandy who swept Sofia off her feet. Simultaneously the great love of Sofia's life and her greatest disappointment, Domingo, although a caring and compassionate man, is also a compulsive gambler. After he returns, he eventually gambles away the family's remaining land and house and is finally divorced by Sofia.

Doña Felicia, Caridad's ancient, eccentric landlady and mentor. She is instrumental in helping Caridad learn to recognize, accept, and use her healing gifts.

Francisco el Penitente, doña Felicia's godson. His obsession with Caridad leads to her death; he later takes his own life.

Ruben, Esperanza's activist boyfriend. Afraid to commit to a relationship with her, only after her death does he finally admit that he loves her.

Esmeralda, a mysterious woman who becomes romantically involved with Caridad. Their relationship leads to Esmeralda's abduction and rape by the obsessed Francisco.

The Novel

Medieval Christian mythology transformed the story of Sofia, the Greek goddess of wisdom, into the inspirational story of a heroic mother and her martyred daughters. *So Far from God* is Ana Castillo's modern reinterpretation of the lives and struggles of Sofia and her four daughters, Esperanza, Caridad, Fe, and La Loca. Set in contemporary New Mexico, the novel chronicles how this family, its neighbors, and their community confront and essentially prevail over the obstacles of racism, poverty, exploitation, environmental pollution, and war. The novel, covering two decades in the family's lives, unfolds through a series of flashbacks woven into the central narrative. Blending ironic humor with scathing social commentary, the novel is told from the perspective of a highly opinionated, omniscient third-person narrator.

Beginning with a flashback to the mysterious death and equally mysterious resurrection—*El Milagro*—of La Loca at the age of three, the narrative quickly shatters any boundaries between the real and the unreal, the natural and the supernatural. La Loca's miraculous resurrection and ascension to a church rooftop elevates the child to the status of folk saint. Left with an aversion to people, La Loca withdraws from the world and devotes her life to prayer and to the spiritual care of her family.

From this flashback, the novel moves into the more recent past as the narrator details the stories of Sofia and her daughters. Like their mother, Sofia's three older daughters have painful, failed relationships. While at college, Esperanza, a college activist, lived with her activist boyfriend, Ruben, who upon graduation elected to trade his Chicano cosmic consciousness for a *gabacha* (a white woman) with a Corvette. The most sensible of Sofia's children, Esperanza turns her failed relationship into the catalyst for an advanced degree and a successful journalistic career. Esperanza's younger sister Caridad also experiences problems in her marriage to her unfaithful high-school sweetheart, Memo. Rather than use that failure to improve herself, the self-destructive Caridad resorts to alcohol and nightly anonymous sex.

Unlike her two older sisters, who seem doomed to failed relationships, Fe, the third daughter, appears fine until she receives a letter breaking off her engagement. Unable to cope with this loss, Fe suffers a nervous breakdown, and only a miracle eventually restores her. Before that miracle, Sofia, Esperanza, and La Loca have to deal with yet another crisis—the vicious attack, horrible mutilation, and near death of Caridad. The simultaneous miraculous restoration of Caridad and cure of Fe trigger a series of changes in the family. Following the incident, Domingo, the girls' wayward father, reappears and tentatively resumes his life with Sofia; Esperanza accepts a dangerous assignment to cover the Persian Gulf War; Caridad—now gifted with foresight and prophecy—moves out and apprentices herself to doña Felicia, an eccentric *curandera*, or witch woman; Fe also moves out and resumes her job at the bank. La Loca remains at home and prays.

While covering the war, Esperanza and her news crew disappear and are presumed captured in Saudi Arabia. Her unknown fate becomes the focal point for both her family and the media community until La Loca informs her mother that Esperanza has been killed. Without the attendant news coverage, Caridad also undergoes a profound, life-changing encounter: Accompanying doña Felicia on her yearly pilgrimage to Chimayo, Caridad unexpectedly falls in love with Esmeralda, a mysterious woman. Unsure how to deal with the effect of Esmeralda and with her renewed emotions, Caridad also disappears. The fate of Sofia's missing daughters is partially resolved when Caridad is discovered exiled in the desert. For a time following her return, Caridad is regarded as a local folk saint. Although severely tested by the fates that have befallen her daughters, Sofia, who continues to believe in the power of faith and in the principles of social change advocated by her war-hero daughter, decides to run for mayor of Tome. Protected from the world in the cocoon of her mother's *rancheria*, La Loca continues to pray.

Fe appears close to achieving her quest for the

American Dream in her marriage to her cousin Casimiro. The epitome of middle-class consumer utopia—complete with a three-bedroom, two-car-garage tract home and new sedan—deteriorates into a horrid nightmare. In order to afford the amenities of the good life, Fe quits her dead-end job at the bank and takes a job with a mysterious chemical company; the result is her slow, excruciating death from toxic poisoning. While her sisters have been victims of misguided social policies, Caridad becomes the victim of the misguided obsession of one man, Francisco el Penitente. Viewing Caridad as his God-chosen mate, Francisco begins to stalk her. Completely unbalanced after he uncovers Caridad's friendship with Esmeralda, Francisco abducts and rapes Esmeralda. When he continues to stalk them, the women commit suicide by leaping from a cliff.

The final tragedy that Sofia must face is the death of her youngest daughter, La Loca, from acquired immune deficiency syndrome (AIDS). Facing death as she had lived, with courage and acceptance, La Loca, once again elevated to the status of saint, becomes the patron of her community. Rather than end tragically, the novel returns to the themes of survival, endurance, and heroic triumph in Sofia's founding of MOMAS, an eccentric organization for the mothers of martyrs and saints.

Analysis

So Far from God, a complex, multidimensional novel, blends elements of New Mexican mythology, pueblo stories, and European Catholicism with home remedies, recipes, and Castillo's bitingly sardonic humor to tell the story of a remarkable family. The subtext of the novel examines the brutal poverty and discrimination faced by Hispanic and indigenous peoples in the Southwest.

The novel is a probing critique of the racism, sexism, and materialism of American society in general and of social institutions such as the government, the church, and large corporations in particular. Woven into the narrative is a pointed examination of such contemporary issues as political oppression, economic exploitation, and environmental pollution. One of the novel's main thematic focuses is environmental racism and the lack of protection afforded to minorities and the poor by the policies and agencies intended to safeguard them. The powerfully poetic chapter 15 juxtaposes brutal sociopolitical realities with the deep feelings of people making a Way of the Cross procession, presenting a catalog of social and environmental ills: minority families living below the poverty level, growing unemployment, deaths from toxic poisoning, radioactive dumping on reservations, birth defects and cancers linked to uranium contamination. The critique is not limited to sociopolitical issues, for the narrative also examines the problems of socially defined sex roles, sexuality, and women's struggle for self-respect. Throughout the novel, women strive to define themselves outside restrictive, socially acceptable roles: Esperanza struggles to succeed in a male-dominated profession, Caridad struggles to reconcile her feelings for Esmeralda with her internalized expectations, and Sofia struggles to keep her family together and her faith intact in the face of repeated challenges and tragedies.

The novel is also about interpersonal and family relationships; about loyalty, honesty, compassion, and love as the basis for successful relationships. A compulsive gambler who cannot control his addiction, Domingo nevertheless loves Sofia and his daughters; a victim of *susto* (shock) who cannot commit to a relationship, Tom clearly loves Fe; a nearly textbook-perfect *machista* (male chauvinist) who refuses to admit his feeling and vulnerabilities, Ruben finally realizes that he truly loves Esperanza. Although the men love the women, their relationships fail because they lack mutual respect, loyalty, and compassion. These very qualities form the basis of the women's relationships with one another. Even Fe, who is originally estranged from her family, grows to appreciate the importance of compassion and acceptance.

Castillo's novel is also a powerful study of personal heroism, of honor, courage, and determination. *So Far from God* is a remarkable celebration of survival with dignity and joy. The power of the novel lies in the women's ability not only to survive adversity but also to triumph over it. In the midst of death and tragedy, Castillo affirms life and the human will that sustains it. Refusing to give in to despair, the women discover that within themselves they have the power and the vision—both spiritual and political—of the saints they love.

Critical Context

So Far from God is Ana Castillo's third novel. The book's favorable reception by critics and the public alike secured her place among the writers at the forefront of the wave of Chicana fiction that came to mainstream consciousness in the late 1980's and 1990's. The novel's publication marked the author's move from small presses to larger publishing houses.

In the novel, Castillo successfully continues the experimentation with literary techniques that characterized her previous novels, *The Mixquiahuala Letters* (1986), which received the American Book Award in 1987, and *Sapogonia* (1990). In *So Far from God*, Castillo uses a distinctive participating narrator, flashbacks, introspective asides, and digressions from the central narrative to create a rich, complex, mythic tale.

Internationally recognized as a poet, novelist, essayist, and translator, Castillo started as a "protest poet," and she continues to explore the issues—racism, sexism, oppression, inequality—to which she first gave voice in her poems. In *So Far from God*, she also continues to explore the feminist themes that have been recognized as central not only to her other two novels but also to her poetry and nonfiction.

SON OF MAN

Author: Augusto Roa Bastos (1917-   )
Type of work: Novel
Type of plot: Social criticism
Time of plot: From 1910 to the mid-1930's
Locale: Itapé, Sapukai, and the site of the battle of Boquerón, all in Paraguay
First published: *Hijo de hombre*, 1960 (English translation, 1965)

Principal Characters

Miguel Vera, the narrator of the odd-numbered chapters, a member of the educated upper middle class in Paraguay. He can never seem to make a commitment to any cause. He joins the military at an early age and becomes an official but later sneaks away to help a group of rebel peons whom he subsequently betrays. Later, when fighting in the Chaco War, he and his men become stranded and are dying of thirst. When, after a treacherous journey, Cristóbal Jara arrives with a water truck, Vera, delirious with thirst, shoots him down. In the end, Vera is killed by a bullet from his own gun in an apparent suicide.

Cristóbal Jara, a rebel leader of the Paraguayan campesinos. A brave, silent young man, he works selflessly to better the lives of the peons, of which he is one. He organizes a peon rebellion to fight for rights in the Chaco War. After Vera's betrayal, he ingeniously escapes the persecution of the military. He later embarks on a final selfless mission of carrying water across the enemy lines to a group of isolated soldiers, one of whom is Vera.

Casiano Jara, an indentured plantation worker. Weakened from abuse, he and his wife Natí escape with their infant son, Cristóbal, from their forced labor. They flee to their hometown of Sapukai, where they make their home in an old train car. Demented by their harrowing experiences, they continue their flight by pushing the car up and down old and forgotten rails.

Gaspar Mora, a leper who has isolated himself in the woods so as not to contaminate townspeople. To assuage his loneliness, he busies himself by carving a life-size wooden image of himself. After his death, this statue is cherished by the townspeople as a Christlike symbol of Mora's sacrifice for his fellow people.

Alexis Dubrovsky, an exiled Russian doctor. He comes to live in the town of Sapukai and establishes a ranch for the lepers of the town. He begins caring for the sick, from whom he rarely accepts payment until the day he discovers a coin in the neck of an ancient image he receives from a patient. He begins demanding these images from his patients and ultimately breaks them all open, then goes on a drinking spree financed with the coins from within the images. He disappears from the village, never to be seen again.

Crisanto Villalba, a soldier who fought in the Chaco War. After the war, he returns to his hometown of Itapé as a broken man. Although he is reunited with his son and is now able to return to his ranch, he is depressed and dejected. He no longer wants to be a farmer. He had found his identity and his purpose in life as a soldier. He returns to his ranch with his son and blows it up with hand grenades.

The Novel

Son of Man is a novel of "man crucified by his fellow man." The plot includes nine stories, or chapters, not in chronological order, each appearing at first to be independent of the others. The novel jumps from one time to another to introduce an important event or to present a character, acquiring its unity from the repetition of certain symbols and events and from the voice of Miguel Vera, who acts as the protagonist-narrator in five of the stories (the odd-numbered chapters) and the omniscient spectator-narrator in the other four (the even-numbered chapters).

Miguel Vera begins by remembering his childhood in Itapé. He recalls the figure of Macario Francia, a blind old man, and the stories that he would tell the youngsters, particularly Gaspar Mora's story, in which Mora, Macario's nephew, leaves the village for the nearby hills after contracting leprosy. When Mora dies, an image that Mora carved is found in his house. The peasants take the image to the town, where it presides over their lives.

In the following chapter, a little town near Itapé, called Sapukai, has suffered an enormous explosion during an insurrection. In the blast, thousands of people have died. One day, Alexis Dubrovsky, a Russian doctor, suddenly appears in the Sapukai railway station. He dedicates his life to curing the peasants and takes care of a colony of lepers. Leprosy was common in Paraguay at that time.

Miguel Vera next narrates his train journey to Asunción, where, as a young boy, he is going to enter military school. During his trip, Vera listens to the passengers' conversations, which reveal a variety of characters. Alexis Dubrovsky is among them. Vera witnesses the moment when Alexis is thrown off the train in Sapukai, the moment at which the previous chapter begins.

In chapter 4 comes a description of the terrible conditions on the Paraguayan *yerbales* (plantations on which cocaine, marijuana, and other drug-producing plants are grown). Cristóbal Jara is introduced. Casiano Jara, his wife, Natí, and their newborn baby boy, Cristóbal, flee the brutality and the inhuman life that they have been forced to endure on the *yerbales*. At the end of Vera's narration of their odyssey, they obtain their freedom.

In the fifth chapter, Miguel Vera has been confined in Sapukai because of disciplinary problems, and there he meets Cristóbal Jara, who is also called "Kiritó" (the Guaraní word for Christ). Kiritó asks Vera to be a military instructor for a rebel group, but, at the beginning of chapter 6, the rebel conspiracy has failed. All the rebels have been shot or taken to prison except Kiritó, who hides in the cemetery and escapes, disguised as a leper.

Vera, in diary form, next narrates his imprisonment and the Chaco War in which he voluntarily enlists. In the Chaco War, Kiritó has been given the mission of bringing water to Vera's company, which is besieged at the front. After all kinds of adversities, Kiritó manages to arrive, but Vera mistakes him for a mirage and kills him.

Finally, the war has ended, and Vera has become the mayor of Itapé. Life has not changed much. The spirit of rebellion is growing again. Vera feels his solitude and puts an end to his life.

Analysis

Son of Man is not simply a historical or a mythical novel, yet it presents Paraguayan history from the regime of José Gaspar Rodríguez de Francia to the Chaco War against Bolivia. The story and its structure reveal a concern for individual human beings, and at the same time, they show a clear vision of the history of the Paraguayan people.

The main theme in the novel is the desire for the social redemption of a country. Characters are moved not by their reason but by their hearts. Their hearts lead some of them to take heroic actions that are symbolic for others.

Like many writers, Roa Bastos sees the Christ figure as a powerful symbol of redemption. The figure of the "son of man"—Cristóbal Jara, or Gaspar Mora—appears throughout the book as an outstanding individual who reveals himself in death. His death may not reduce the people's oppression, but it supports them by reinforcing their belief in brotherhood. The carved Christ of Itapé is one of the most important symbols of redemption, symbolizing man crucified by men, a man who must be avenged. At the same time, it is a symbol of the individual who sacrifices himself for others.

Roa Bastos does not give answers in his book. He presents facts; unfortunately, these facts are repeated throughout time. The world spins like a whipping top: The more it spins, the more static it looks. Nothing changes in spite of the passing of time. "Everything is the same, it seems the time does not move over the enormous slow whipping top."

Critical Context

Son of Man won first prize in Editorial Losada's International Novel Contest in Buenos Aires in 1959 and was published in 1960. It was a great success, in spite of the dissatisfaction the author himself felt with the book. In 1960, Roa Bastos wrote the screenplay for *Son of Man*. The film received the first prize of the Argentine Institutode Cinematografía, and it was considered the best film in the Spanish language for that year.

In his novel, Roa Bastos presents his country, his people, and his own experiences. He was sent to military school in the capital at the age of eight, like Miguel Vera, the narrator of the story. Roa Bastos fought in the Chaco War against Bolivia. In the early 1940's, he traveled among the *yerbales*, where he learned about the exploitation and the degradation of the *yerbales* workers. All these facts make *Son of Man* a realistic novel with a historical base transformed by the magical imagination of the author.

Roa Bastos, like other South American writers, wants to present in his novel the essence of his country, yet the novel is more than history. The author presents, at the same time, his vision of the world and his vision of people: "Man has two births. One when he is born, the other when he dies. . . . He dies, but he remains alive in others, if he has dealt kindly with his neighbours. If he has helped others during his lifetime, when he dies, the earth may devour his body, but his memory will live on. . . ."

SPIDERTOWN: A Novel

Author: Abraham Rodriguez, Jr. (1961-   )
Type of work: Novel
Type of plot: *Bildungsroman*
Time of plot: The 1990's
Locale: South Bronx, New York City
First published: 1993

Principal Characters

Miguel, a sixteen-year-old crack cocaine delivery boy. At one time in his life, he wanted to become a writer, but he abandoned this dream when he realized that there were no famous Puerto Rican writers. In the seventh grade, his English teacher asked him to compose an essay about his father, but he could only think of negative things to say; he then dropped out of school. On the streets, he turned to Spider for support, regarding the crack czar as a surrogate father. Miguel is well read, intelligent, and uncommonly sensitive, but he is also self-deluded. He misconstrues money and power as success and considers himself to be an adult. His relationship with Cristalena forces him to see the perversion and ugliness of his life. Gradually, through a process of self-analysis, he redeems and defines himself. By the end of the novel, he has attained considerable self-awareness and crossed the threshold of maturity.

Amelia, a twenty-one-year-old crack user and psychology major at City College (though she has taken a brief respite from her studies). She is Firebug's girlfriend and Miguel's best friend. Miguel describes her as "funny and twisted and sometimes sad." She has sex with Spider in exchange for crack. Although she suffers from low self-esteem, she is intelligent, sensitive, and independent. She reads books by Charles Dickens and Jean-Paul Sartre, whose existential philosophy appeals to her. She describes herself as a "Latino girl with brains." Unlike her two older sisters, obsequious husband-hunters, Amelia set her sights on a career as a therapist and a marriage of equality, but

the men in her life discouraged her, treated her contemptuously, and drove her to society's fringe, where she lives with junkies, prostitutes, and outcasts. As she counsels Miguel to self-awareness, she undergoes a parallel transformation, finds herself again, and returns to college.

Cristalena, Miguel's sixteen-year-old girlfriend, a preacher's daughter. She is rebellious, sexually repressed (though not a virgin), and intelligent. Her parents are oppressive religious fanatics. To dress fashionably and date boys, she must resort to subterfuge, changing clothes at school and pretending to spend her evenings at her aunt's apartment. She pursues Miguel aggressively, initiating their first sexual encounter. Miguel is fond of saying that she has a name like a poem, and Amelia describes her jealously as a "Latino Barbie Doll." Her father's fiery sermons on sin continue to haunt her, causing her occasional pangs of guilt. Although naïve and pristine, Cristalena is extremely sensible, a planner by nature. She rejects Miguel's suggestion that they move in together because she knows that they will not be able to support themselves. She is realistic about her age and education and recognizes the necessity of staying in school. Her ambition is to become a dress designer and work in Paris.

Spider, an ambitious crack czar who is both a "Streetwise Patton" and a latter-day Fagin. To dissociate himself from his boring father, who worked for years as a postal employee and then retired to a life of dominoes, Spider entered the exciting, lucrative world of drugs and staked his claim aggressively. Now he considers himself to be an important crime boss. He loves corporate paraphernalia such as business cards, which in his organization are appropriately vague. He boasts that he can "grab a ten-year-old kid and turn him into a successful businessman faster than IBM or ITT." He talks like a successful entrepreneur drunk on the American Dream, yet he dresses poorly and smells bad. Through flattery, bribery, and lies, Spider lures children into his web and devours them.

Firebug, Miguel's roommate, a teenage arsonist. Abused by his father, who used to burn him as punishment, he grew extremely fond of fire. In school, he would throw fiery "scrunchballs" at the teacher, and once he set a girl on fire. He makes a living by burning down tenement buildings for businessmen. He requires his friends to attend his "wienie roasts" to witness his art; he depends on their accounts of the fires to inflate his ego. Because he wants to be ready to move at a moment's notice, he shuns possessions, keeping his few belongings in a gym bag. He seldom displays emotion and may be incapable of genuine emotion.

The Novel

Spidertown is a *Bildungsroman* that recounts the intellectual and spiritual growth of a teenage boy. Sixteen-year-old Miguel falls in love with Cristalena, a preacher's daughter who despises crack cocaine and the criminals who are terrorizing her neighborhood. Because he works for Spider, the local crack czar, Miguel fears that Cristalena will reject him. Consequently, he lies about his work, and his guilt and shame propel him on a journey of self-discovery and redemption.

As the novel opens, Miguel and his roommate, Firebug, are drinking and talking in their nearly unfurnished apartment. Firebug, a professional arsonist, invites Miguel to a "wienie roast," which is a euphemism for the torching of a building. Although he agrees to escort Firebug's girlfriend, Amelia, Miguel would prefer to stay home. He no longer enjoys the commotion of the crowd, the fire engines, and the flames. His relationship with Cristalena has shown him the perversion and ugliness of his world.

At the fire, Miguel and Amelia sit in his car and discuss his growing disenchantment with the drug culture. Amelia says that he has too much heart to be a criminal, confesses that she has fallen in love with him, and tries to explain her relationship with Firebug, who is incapable of love.

The next day, as he makes his usual deliveries for Spider, Miguel stops several times to call Cristalena, but she is unavailable to speak with him. Angry and dejected, he starts drinking heavily and gets behind in his deliveries. His tardiness almost costs the lives of several drug dealers, who have to dodge bullets to get to his car.

In the morning, Miguel visits Cristalena at the boutique where she works and learns the reason for her evasion. She has not yet told her parents about him, and they are very strict and watch her closely. Miguel proposes to Cristalena, and they make plans to celebrate her birthday in bed at his apartment.

At Spider's request, Miguel delivers ten thousand dollars to a police car parked across the street from his apartment building. One of the officers sticks a pistol in his face and threatens him. After this humiliating experience, Miguel walks to his car and discovers that the tires have been slashed by Spider's spies to prevent him from running off with the money. Enraged by Spider's lack of trust in him, Miguel resolves to quit his job at the right moment.

Starting another day of deliveries, he meets with Spider to pick up the crack. When Spider asks him to deliver more money to the police, he refuses. He does not take Spider's threats seriously because he intends to quit soon anyway. At his last stop, a group of street thugs, led by a boy named Richie, drag him from his car and beat him severely. It is Spider's way of teaching him a lesson. When he returns to his apartment, only Amelia shows sympathy for his bruises. That night, she drugs Firebug and sleeps chastely with Miguel in his bed.

In the morning, Miguel telephones Spider and informs him that he is quitting, but Spider refuses to believe him. When Miguel picks Cristalena up that night, he starts to tell her the truth about himself, but he is interrupted by Spider, who emerges from the darkness and pounds on the windshield. Miguel gets out of his car, and they argue. After Spider leaves, Miguel tries to tell Cristalena the truth about himself, but she says he is too late and runs back into her building.

Upset by Cristalena's reaction, Miguel visits Amelia; she takes him to her private apartment, where they finally have sex. Miguel still loves Cristalena, however, and resolves to win her back. Knowing that he must first straighten out his life, he goes to see his mother, Catarina, who is living with a well-to-do importer named Nelo. She agrees to let Miguel move in with them if he will submit unconditionally to their authority. He reluctantly accepts her terms. After begging for and receiving Cristalena's forgiveness, Miguel takes Cristalena to his apartment, and they have sex.

The next day, he encounters Richie, who tries to persuade him to betray Spider. Miguel refuses emphatically. When he gets back to his apartment, he discovers that Firebug is moving out. Firebug gives Miguel a gun for protection, tells him to meet Spider at a bar, and leaves. Wanting to break with Spider amicably, Miguel foolishly goes to meet him, and he is shot twice in the back during an attack on the bar.

At the hospital, Miguel is questioned by a police officer named Sanchez and visited by Amelia and Cristalena. After his release from the hospital, he moves in with his mother and Nelo. He decides to burn his car as a symbol of his independence from Spider. Amelia, Cristalena, and Miguel create a funeral pyre for the car and set it ablaze. As the three friends walk away from the fire, Sanchez drives up, and Miguel hands him a tape of Spider's life story, narrated by the drug lord himself.

Analysis

The theme of deception is central to the novel's meaning. With their lies and subterfuges, the characters weave hopelessly tangled webs and often snare themselves. Cristalena deceives her parents about her clothes, boyfriends, and parties. To sustain the deception, she must expend vast amounts of energy and creativity, even enlisting the aid of her cousin and aunt, who provide alibis and a refuge for the "little child of Christ." Fearful of losing Cristalena, Miguel lies about his profession, telling her that he works for a lumber company. He goes to great lengths to conceal the truth about himself; in the end, he almost loses Cristalena because of his deceit. By pretending to be estranged from Spider, Firebug deceives Miguel, but only for a short while. Eventually, Miguel figures out the truth on his own.

Deception is Spider's modus operandi. He lures children into his operation by promising them exaggerated wealth and power. He lies repeatedly to Miguel, first about the car tires, then about the beating. When he is caught in his lies, he reacts with insouciance and moves on to another deception, supremely confident in his abilities as a machinator. He summons Miguel for a meeting and has his thugs shower the bar with bullets. The betrayal, once realized, prompts Miguel to cooperate with Sanchez, and the cost to Spider's organization is potentially great, because Miguel can provide damaging and detailed information about the drug kingpin's operation.

At one point in the novel, Amelia talks bitterly of self-deception, accusing the people in Spider's world of deluding themselves with guns, stereos, and gold chains. They act like millionaires and generals and pretend to be important, yet they live in squalor. Like rodents and insects, they scurry from one abandoned building to another, dodging sunlight. Amelia blames white people for creating the illusion of success for African Americans and

Latinos and for encouraging them to deceive and kill themselves. Miguel used to revel in the "fringe benefits" of his job such as money, women, and drugs. When he realizes that it is all a "sick pretend game," however, he stops playing.

Deception perverts friendships, undermines trust, and fosters paranoia. It will inevitably cause Spider's destruction. More repugnant still, self-deception imprisons the soul and impedes individual growth and development. The only antidote for deception, of course, is truth. Miguel cures his self-deception by holding up a mirror to himself and seeing the truth.

Rodriguez uses Charles Dickens' *Oliver Twist* (1837-1839), which is also concerned with decep-tion, as a model for *Spidertown*. Amelia reveals that she gave Spider a copy of the novel and that he devoured it. At their first meeting, Spider questioned Miguel about the book, and Miguel demonstrated his familiarity with it by comparing Spider to the crafty Fagin, who uses children to commit crimes, and himself to the Artful Dodger. In *Spidertown*, Miguel is actually more like the young Oliver than the Artful Dodger. Both Oliver and Miguel wander the streets of a big city until they are befriended by exploitive criminals. Because he arranges the first meeting between Miguel and Spider, Firebug is like the Artful Dodger, who introduces Oliver to Fagin.

Critical Context

Spidertown is Rodriguez's first novel but not his first book. In 1992, he published *The Boy Without a Flag*, a critically acclaimed collection of short stories about Puerto Rican Americans in the South Bronx. Several of the characters in *Spidertown* have prototypes in the stories. For example, Spider is a minor character in "Birthday Boy," and Careta makes an appearance in "The Lotto." Miguel is similar in many ways to Angel in "Birthday Boy" and to the narrator of "The Boy Without a Flag." Likewise, Cristalena resembles Dalia in "The Lotto." It is obvious that Rodriguez borrowed situations and characters from his first book to create continuity between the works.

As a *Bildungsroman*, or apprenticeship novel, *Spidertown* is a descendant of such established novels as Johann Wolfgang von Goethe's *Wilhelm Meisters Lehrjahre* (1795-1796; *Wilhelm Meister's Apprenticeship*, 1824), Dickens' *David Copperfield* (1849-1850), W. Somerset Maugham's *Of Human Bondage* (1915), James Joyce's *A Portrait of the Artist as a Young Man* (1916), and Thomas Wolfe's *Look Homeward, Angel* (1929). These novels all trace the youthful development of a male protagonist, often an artist or a writer.

By having his characters discuss *Oliver Twist*, Richard Wright's *Native Son* (1940), and Ken Kesey's *One Flew Over the Cuckoo's Nest* (1962), Rodriguez creates another context for his novel. These works depict the underbelly of society and constitute sophisticated protest literature, of which *Spidertown* is an example. It is interesting to note that the literary tradition represented by these works is distinctly male, though not exclusively white or American.

Finally, *Spidertown* belongs to a body of recent literature by Latino authors. As a New York Puerto Rican writer, Rodriguez has an affinity with Nicholasa Mohr and Piri Thomas, who also write about Puerto Rican Americans in the South Bronx. *Spidertown* has been compared to Thomas' *Down These Mean Streets* (1967), an autobiography of one man's struggle with drugs and crime in New York. Rodriguez's novel can also be grouped with the works of other Latino authors, such as Mexican American author Sandra Cisneros' *The House on Mango Street* (1989) and Cuban American author Oscar Hijuelos' *The Mambo Kings Play Songs of Love* (1989), which won the 1990 Pulitzer Prize for Fiction.

THE STORIES OF JORGE LUIS BORGES

Author: Jorge Luis Borges (1899-1986)

Type of work: Short stories

Principal published works: *Historia universal de la infamia*, 1935 (*A Universal History of Infamy*, 1972); *El jardín de senderos que se bifurcan*, 1941 (the garden of forking paths); *Ficciones, 1935-1944*, 1944 (English translation, 1962); *El Aleph*, 1949 (translated in *The Aleph and Other Stories, 1933-1969*, 1970); *El informe de Brodie*, 1970 (*Doctor Brodie's Report*, 1972); *El libro de arena*, 1975 (*The Book of Sand*, 1977); *Veinticinco agosto 1983 y otros cuentos*, 1983 (August 25, 1983, and other stories)

It is virtually impossible to overstate the importance of Jorge Luis Borges within the context of Spanish American fiction, for he is, quite simply, the single most important writer of short fiction in the history of Spanish American literature. This is true not only because of his stories themselves, chiefly those published in *Ficciones, 1935-1944* and *El Aleph*, but also because of the important contributions his stories made to the evolution of Spanish American fiction, both short and long, in the latter half of the twentieth century.

Borges was the father of Spanish America's "new narrative," the type of narrative, practiced by the likes of Julio Cortázar, Gabriel García Márquez, Carlos Fuentes, and Mario Vargas Llosa, that put Spanish American fiction on the world literary map in the 1960's. Prior to Borges, and particularly between 1920 and 1940, Spanish American fiction was chiefly concerned with painting realistic and detailed pictures of external Spanish American reality. Description frequently ruled over action, environment over character, and types over individuals. Social message was often more important to the writer than was narrative artistry. Spanish American fiction after Borges (that is, after his landmark collections of stories of the 1940's) was decidedly different in that it was no longer documentary in nature, turned its focus toward the inner workings of its fully individualized human characters, presented various interpretations of reality, expressed universal as well as regional and national themes, invited reader participation, and emphasized the importance of artistic—and frequently unconventional—presentation of the story, particularly with respect to narrative voice, language, structure (and the closely related element of time), and characterization. This "new narrative," as it came to be called, would have been impossible without Borges' tradition-breaking fiction.

This is not to say that Borges' stories fully embody each of the characteristics of Spanish America's "new narratives" listed above. They do not. For example, Borges' characters are often far more archetypal than individual, his presentation tends to be quite traditional, and reader participation (at least as compared to that required in the works of other "new narrativists") is frequently not a factor. The major contributions that Borges made to Spanish American narrative through his stories lie in his use of imagination, in his focus on universal themes common to all human beings, and in the intellectual aspect of his works. In the 1940's, Borges, unlike most fiction writers in Spanish America at the time, treated fiction as fiction. Rather than use fiction to document everyday reality, Borges used it to invent new realities and to toy with philosophical concepts, in the process creating truly fictional worlds governed by their own rules. He also chose to write chiefly about universal human beings rather than exclusively about Spanish Americans. His characters are often European and Chinese, frequently of no discernible nationality, and only occasionally Spanish American. In most cases, even when a character's nationality is revealed, it is of no real importance, particularly with respect to theme. Almost all of Borges' characters are important not because of the country from which they come but because they are human beings, faced not with situations and conflicts peculiar to their nationality but situations and conflicts common to all human beings. Finally, unlike his predecessors and many of his contemporaries, Borges did not aim his fiction at the masses. He wrote instead, it seems, more for himself, and by extension for the intellectual reader. These three aspects of his fiction—treating fiction as fiction, placing universal characters in universal conflicts, and writing for a more intellectual audience—stand as the Argentine writer's three most important contributions to Spanish American fiction in the latter half of the twentieth century. To various degrees, virtually every one of Spanish America's "new narrativists," from Cortázar to García Márquez, followed Borges' lead in these areas.

Borges' stories are more aptly called "fictions" than "stories," for although all fit emphatically into the first category, since they contain fictitious elements, many do not fit nearly so well into a traditional definition of the second, since they read more like essays than stories. They are sophisticated, compact, even mathematically precise narratives that range in type from what might be called the "traditional" short story (a rarity), to fictionalized essay (neither pure story nor pure essay but instead a mix of the two, sometimes containing both fictitious characters and footnotes, both fictitious and factual), to detective story or spy thriller (though always with an unmistakably Borgesian touch), to fictional illustration of a philosophical concept (this last type being, perhaps, most common). Regardless of the specific category into which each story might fall, almost all touch on either what Borges viewed as the labyrinthian nature of the universe, irony (particularly with respect to human destiny), the concept of time, the hubris of those who believe they know all there is to know, or some combination of these elements.

Most of Borges' fame as a writer of fiction and virtually all of his considerable influence on the Spanish American "new narrative" are derived from his two masterpiece collections, *Ficciones, 1935-1944* (1944) and *El Aleph* (1949). Of these two, the first stands out as the more important and is the single most important collection of short fiction in the history of Spanish American literature.

Ficciones, 1935-1944 contains fourteen stories (seventeen in editions published after 1956). Seven of the fourteen were written between 1939 and 1941 and, along with an eighth story, were originally collected in *El jardín de senderos que se bifurcan* (1941; the garden of forking paths). The other six stories were added in 1944. Virtually every story in this collection has become a Spanish American classic, and together they reveal the variety of Borges' themes and story types.

"La muerte y la brújula" ("Death and the Compass") is one of the most popular of the stories found in *Ficciones, 1935-1944*. In it, detective Erik Lönnrot is faced with the task of solving three apparent murders that have taken place at exact one-month intervals at locations that form a geographical equilateral triangle. The overly rational Lönnrot, through elaborate reasoning, divines when and where the next murder is to take place. He goes there to prevent the murder and to capture the murderer. Instead he finds himself captured, having been lured to the scene by his archenemy, Red Scharlach, so he, Lönnrot, can be killed.

This story is a perfect example of Borges' ability to take a standard subgenre, in this case the detective story, and give it his own personal signature. The story is replete with Borgesian trademarks. The most prominent of these concerns irony and hubris. Following the first murder and published reports of Lönnrot's line of investigation, Sharlach, who has sworn to kill Lönnrot, constructs the remainder of the murder scenario. He knows that Lönnrot will not rest until he deciphers the apparent patterns and then, believing he knows all there is to know, will blindly show up at the right spot at the right time for Scharlach to capture and kill him. Ironically, Lönnrot's intelligence and his reliance (or overreliance) on reasoning, accompanied in no small measure by his self-assurance and intellectual vanity, which blind him to any potential danger, bring him to his death. Other trademark Borgesian elements in the story include the completely non-Spanish American content (from characters to setting), numerous references to Jews and things Jewish (a Talmudic congress, rabbis, and Cabalistic studies, to name a few), and an intellectual content and ambience throughout not typical of the traditional detective story.

"The Garden of Forking Paths" is another story from *Ficciones, 1935-1944* that in the most general sense (but only in the most general sense) fits comfortably into a traditional category, that of spy thriller. Like "Death and the Compass," in Borges' hands it is anything but a story typical of its particular subgenre. In this story, Doctor Yu Tsun, a Chinese professor of English working in England as a spy for the Germans during World War I, has been captured and now dictates his story. Once again, neither the setting nor the characters are Spanish America. Yu tells of how he had needed to transmit vital information to the Germans concerning the name of the town in which the British were amassing artillery in preparation for an attack. Yu's superior, however, had been captured, thus severing Yu's normal lines of communication. Identified as a spy and pursued by the British, Yu tells how he had selected, from the telephone directory, the only man he thought could help him communicate his message, one Stephen Albert. The reader at this point is not aware of exactly how Albert could be of help to Yu. Yu tells of how he traveled to Albert's home, hotly pursued by a British agent. Yu had never met Albert, but Albert mistook him for someone else and invited Yu in. The two talked for an hour about Chinese astrologer and writer Ts'ui Pên (who happened to be one of Yu's ancestors) and Ts'ui's labyrinthian book *The Garden of Forking Paths* (which, given its content, provides a story-within-a-story element). Yu stalled for time to allow the British agent to catch up with him. Yu says that as the agent approached the house, Yu killed Albert and then allowed himself to be captured by the agent. The final paragraph of the story reveals that Yu had chosen to kill Albert and then be arrested so that news of the incident would appear in the newspaper. He knew that his German colleagues would read the small news item and would divine Yu's intended message, that the British had been amassing artillery near the French town of Albert.

"Las ruinas circulares" ("The Circular Ruins") is one of a number of examples in *Ficciones, 1935-1944* of Borges' frequent practice of using a story to illustrate (or at least toy with) philosophical concepts, in this case most notably the Gnostic concept of one creator behind another creator. In this story, a mysterious man travels to an equally mysterious place with the intention of creating another person by dreaming him. The man experiences difficulty in this at first, but eventually he is successful. The man instructs his creation and then sends him off. Before he does, however, the man erases his creation's knowledge of how he came to be, for the man does not wish the creation to know that he exists only as the dream of another. Soon after the man's creation has left, fire breaks out and surrounds the man. He prepares for death, but as the flames begin to engulf him he cannot feel them. He realizes then that he too is but an illusion, not real at all but simply the dream of another.

"Pierre Menard, autor del Quijote" ("Pierre Menard, Author of Don Quixote"), also from *Ficciones, 1935-1944*, is one of Borges' most famous stories that can be classified as a fictionalized essay. It contains fictive elements, but by any traditional definition of the term, it is not a story. In it, a pompous first-person narrator, a literary critic, presents an essay of literary criticism that tells of the writer Pierre Menard, fictional in the real world but completely real in Borges' fictive universe. After considerable discussion of Menard's bibliography (complete with titles and publication dates, all fictional but with titles of real literary journals) as well as other facts about the author, the critic discusses Menard's attempt to compose a contemporary version of Cervantes' *Don Quixote de la Mancha*. Menard accomplishes this not by writing a new *Don Quixote* but simply by copying Cervantes' original text word for word. The critic even examines identical passages from the two versions and declares that Menard's, though identical to Cervantes, is actually richer. The critic pursues the reasons for and ramifications of this fact. The result is, among other things, a tongue-in-cheek send-up of scholars and literary critics and the snobbish and often ridiculous criticism they publish.

Finally, "El Sur" ("The South"), from *Ficciones, 1935-1944* as well, is a classic Borges story that demonstrates the author's ability to mix reality (at best a relative term in Borges' world and in Spanish American "new narratives" as a whole) with fantasy and, more important, to show that the line between the two is very subtle and of no real importance, for fantasy is just as much a part of the universe as is so-called reality. This story, which Borges once said he considered his best, concerns Juan Dahlmann, a librarian in Buenos Aires. Dahlmann, the reader is told, has several heroic military ancestors, and though he is a city-dwelling intellectual, Dahlmann prefers to identify himself with his more romantic ancestors. In that spirit, Dahlmann even maintains a family ranch in the "South" (capitalized here and roughly the Argentine equivalent, in history and image, to North America's "Old West"). He is, however, an absentee landowner, spending all of his time in Buenos Aires, keeping the ranch only to maintain a connection, though a chiefly symbolic one, with his family's more exciting past. Entering his apartment one night, Dahlmann accidentally runs into a doorway, an accident similar to one Borges' himself suffered in 1938. The resulting head injury develops into septicemia as was the case with Borges, and he is sent to a sanitarium. He recovers well enough to travel, at his doctor's suggestion, to his ranch in the South to convalesce. His train trip to the South is vague to him at best, as he slips in and out of sleep. Unfamiliar with the region, he disembarks one stop too early and waits in a general store for transportation. While there, he is harassed by a group of ruffians. He accepts the challenge of one among them, and as the story ends he is about to step outside for a knife fight he knows he cannot win.

If the above were all there were to "The South," the story would be interesting, perhaps, but certainly nothing spectacular, and it would probably fit fairly comfortably into the type of Spanish American narrative popular before Borges. There is more, however, that places the story firmly within the parameters of Spanish American "new narrative." The story is the literary equivalent of an optical illusion. For those who can perceive only one angle, the story is essentially that described above. For those who can make out the other angle, however, the story is completely different. There are numerous subtle though undeniably present hints throughout the second half of the story, after Dahlmann supposedly leaves the sanitarium, that suggest that the protagonist does nor step out to fight at the end of the story. In fact, he never leaves the sanitarium at all, but instead dies there. His trip to the South, his encounter with the ruffians, and his acceptance of their challenge are nothing but a dream. Dahlmann, the librarian who likes to identify himself with his heroic and romantic ancestors, would have preferred death in a knife fight to dying in the sanitarium. This added dimension as well as the subtle manner in which it is suggested separates both the story and its author from the type of fiction and fiction writer that characterized Spanish American fiction before Borges. It is this type of added dimension that makes Borges' fiction "new" and him a truly fascinating writer to read.

Borges continued to write short fiction after *Ficciones, 1935-1944* and *El Aleph*, but the stories produced during this period never approached the popularity among readers nor the acclaim among critics associated with the two earlier collections. This resulted in part from the fact that most of the stories the Argentine writer published in the 1960's, as well as in the 1970's and 1980's, lacked much of his characteristic style. Most are decidedly more realistic. They are more often Argentine in focus and in general are less complex. Some of this, particularly the change in complexity, has been explained through his loss of sight in 1955, after years of declining vision. Borges turned to dictation, which made editing and polishing more difficult. Regardless of the reason, most of Borges' fiction after his two landmark collections of the 1940's is largely ignored. When one thinks of Borges' fiction, with rare exceptions one immediately thinks of those stories included in *Ficciones, 1935-1944* and *El Aleph*. These two collections, particularly the former, are enough to make Borges the single most important writer of short fiction in the history of Spanish American literature.

THE STORIES OF ROSARIO CASTELLANOS

Author: Rosario Castellanos (1925-1974)
Type of work: Short stories
Principal published works: *Ciudad Real*, 1960; *Los convidados de agosto*, 1964; *A Rosario Castellanos Reader: An Anthology of Her Poetry, Short Fiction, Essays, and Drama*, 1988

Rosario Castellanos characterized herself foremost as a poet, even in her prose works. Although she chose to focus on her style and mode of expression, her readers know her best for the sharp social critique inherent in the content of her works. Castellanos utilized every literary genre, as well as journalistic means, to promote awareness of and appreciation for the plight of the disenfranchised and marginalized in Mexico. Her works won numerous literary prizes and awards in Latin America but were little known outside Latin America, or even outside Mexico, until about 1980. Castellanos' works are now staple components of the Hispanic and feminist literary canons throughout the Western world. Translations of individual works in anthologies continue to multiply in most romance languages and particularly in English.

Although Castellanos was a product of an economically privileged, European immigrant heritage, her personal experience with prejudice and discrimination made her an avowed egalitarian with a literary social conscience to match. She frequently linked the lot of the Mexican indigenous population to that of women at all socioeconomic levels. Seeing the treatment of the exploited indigenous workers as a child growing up on a rural farm in the state of Chiapas, along with her awareness of her parents' marked preference for her brother, the male heir, caused Castellanos to forge such a link early in life. Her later experiences reiterated her concerns on both fronts. Although the emphasis varies, these components of her biography thread through her works in all genres.

Early critics and those not so familiar with the whole of her work have sometimes unjustly limited and classified Castellanos as an "indianist" writer. Her early works do in fact justify her reputation as a social critic more in terms of racial inequality than of gender inequality. Her first short story

collection, *Ciudad Real*, contains ten stories and emphasizes the indigenous aspects of her society. "La muerte del tigre" traces the virtual genocide of a representative indigenous tribe (whose totem animal is the tiger), either by death or forced social and physical integration or absorption into the more powerful immigrant culture.

Male protagonists and central characters abound in these stories, whereas in Castellanos' later work, they become uncommon or merely symbolic of the oppression of the greater patriarchal society. So-called "luck" often results in a cycle of disadvantage to, if not outright mistreatment of, the indigenous characters. "La suerte de Teodoro Méndez Acubal" plays off two male characters, one of European descent and one indigenous, in a cycle of stereotyping that dooms the latter. The story literally and figuratively revolves around economics. Teodoro considers himself to be lucky when he finds a valuable coin. He tries to spend the coin in Don Agustín's store. The action then comes to a halt, as does Teodoro's luck. The authorities assume that the coin is stolen because Teodoro, in their eyes, could not possibly have obtained it legally. They arrest him and put him in jail. Because he is such an unimportant and common "criminal," they forget about him, and Teodoro remains forever after in jail.

"El advenimiento del águila" is similar, though the protagonist is of European descent. In this plot, Héctor, a no-good loafer, finds luck: He secures a minor official's position in the titular *Ciudad Real*. Via deceit, he manages to fleece an entire group of indigenous inhabitants.

"La rueda del hambriento" and "El don rechazado" repeat the pessimistic tone of the collection, though well-intentioned social-reformer characters attempt to make changes. They, too, are thwarted in the end, and the heart-rending cycle continues. This overwhelming sense of hopelessness colors all the other stories in the collection, which includes "La tregua," "Aceite guapo," "Modesta Gómez," "Cuarta vigilia," and "Arthur Smith salva su alma."

Castellanos' novels and early short stories contain significant indigenous content. On the other hand, her master's thesis, *Sobre cultura femenina* (about feminine culture), and her essays, dramas, and poems are overtly feminist. Her later works of short fiction reiterate this focus on intra- and inter-gender relations as the source of the social alienation of women. The first hints of this realignment of emphasis appear in her short fiction published in periodicals between the publication of her first and second books of stories, in 1960 and 1964. In each decidedly pessimistic story line, a more-or-less triangular "rivalry" characterization focuses on female descendants of European immigrants who are literally or figuratively thwarted or "ruined" by male characters or patriarchal society itself as a result of the conflict between their images of what constitutes "proper" female behavior. Such a plot and its variations have long been traditional in Hispanic literature on both sides of the Atlantic. Castellanos, however, treats it with a sense of firsthand emotion guaranteed to engage the reader's empathy.

"Three Knots in a Net" (1961), published in the *Revista de la Universidad de Mexico*, anticipates Castellanos' second prose collection, *Los convidados de agosto*, which contains three stories and a novella. The stories have practically no indigenous content apart from background details and implications. In "Three Knots in a Net," Juliana tries her best to do what society demands, deferring to her husband and properly socializing her daughter. Despite her efforts, her husband treats her with disdain, and her daughter all but ignores her. Although she does not attempt to break out of her ascribed social role, Juliana finds "reward" in an ignominious death in the terminal cancer ward of a charity hospital. As a nurturing martyr to the end, she saves her family the financial and emotional expense of watching her die by pretending to be off on a visit to relatives.

The first story in Castellanos' second collection, "Las amistades efímeras," features many of Castellanos' characteristic elements, including a nameless female narrator and a female character somehow "ruined" by a man or by male-inspired prejudice and limitations. The story is unique in her works for its portrayal of a female friendship and in its slightly more hopeful implications for the future, at least for the narrator's future. The friendship of the nameless narrator and Gertrudis completely surrounds the seemingly interpolated story of Gertrudis' escape from a boring existence by running away with a minor criminal, being forced into a shotgun wedding, standing by her new husband through his jail term, being divorced by him for his childhood sweetheart, and seeing his eventual death in the commission of another act of public vandalism. This is a classic Castellanos representation of female experience. The physical circumscription of the friendship around Gertrudis' experience leads the reader to focus on the relationship between the friends rather than on Gertrudis' own trials and tribulations. Castellanos uses this technique and the unusual (for her) appearance of female friends to urge readers to pay close attention. The uncharacteristically positive note is that, through the two friends' correspondence by letter, the narrator discovers her vocation in an independent identity as a professional writer. Furthermore, Gertrudis' fate is left unresolved, rather than sealed as a result of her "sins" against social convention, as typical in Castellanos' work.

In the second story of the second collection, "Vals 'Capricho,'" two sisters attempt to socialize their niece, Reinerie, the intensely unconventional and resistant daughter of their brother. The brother's mysterious wife was almost undoubtedly Mexican; that "bad blood," implicitly, is at the root of the niece's problem. Despite the sisters' best efforts, their local society cruelly refuses to incorporate Reinerie, who simply disappears into the countryside (which can be read as the margins of society) because she does not "fit."

The third story, "Los convidados de agosto," presents two spinster sisters, one of whom, the discontented one, has determined to enliven her life and picks up a stranger at a bar. At the last moment, her brother, unbidden and unwelcome, "saves" her, to her everlasting regret. She remains on the margins of life experience, condemned to perpetual virginity.

One of the few later Castellanos stories with a male protagonist is "El viudo Román," a novella that is the last story in the collection. Román rejects his young bride falsely as lacking virginity in vengeance for the imagined sins of her brother with Román's deceased first wife. Reminiscent of the Spanish *Comedia*, seventeenth century honor-based tragedies, this plot is the clearest modernization of the traditional triangular rivalries for which Hispanic literature is famous. This story recalls those of *Ciudad Real* in its inescapable cycle of random "luck" that always results in disadvantage to, if not outright mistreatment of, the less powerful characters, in this case female rather than indigenous.

Castellanos' third collection, *Album de familia*, also contains three stories and a novella. All four works are noteworthy for their few references to Mexican culture and people. The first three stories function together as a sort of triangular discussion of the chronological course of a marriage of middle-class people of European descent. In each story, the wife battles her husband or society for control of her identity and spirit, if not her physical being.

"Lección de cocina" is narrated in stream-of-consciousness style by a nameless adult female who recounts her first days as a traditional wife directly to "you," the reader. This story clearly supports Castellanos' characterization of her own prose work as "poetic," as it contains extended metaphors of cooking and traditional household tasks. The protagonist's resentment strongly colors her portrayal of her rivalry with her husband and society concerning her spiraling loss of identity.

Edith, the jaded wife in "Domingo," symbolizes the interim stage of the prototypical marriage. Bogged down in routine, she takes up painting and fantasizes about Rafael, a former lover. During the course of the characters' interaction during one of the married couple's Sunday afternoon "open houses," the reader learns how Edith's life has come to this point, as a result of the unavoidable conflicts in "normal" heterosexual relationships. Castellanos manages to broach such normally taboo subjects in Mexican culture as homosexual relationships, drinking to excess, adulterous flirting on the part of women, and abortion, in addition to reiterating social attitudes toward women as either whore or mother. Edith has brief moments of respite from convention, but it does not appear likely that she will escape the traditional cycle of life and its lack of options for women.

Finally, a wife as a widow in "Cabecita blanca" ties up the marriage sequence. Again laced with food metaphors, the story traces Justina's bad marriage to a cheating husband, the father of her two dysfunctional daughters and her too-devoted son, characterized as having a hint of homosexuality. In this story, Castellanos branches out and verbalizes some usually covert deprecating attitudes of women toward men, even showing widows being secretly delighted to be wives of dead husbands, as that status provides the best of both social acceptance and some degree of self-determination. Furthermore, Castellanos addresses the role of the Church in reinforcing traditional discriminatory attitudes.

"Album de familia," the novella of the collection, features female protagonists working through socialized competitive attitudes to realize a sense of the family of women, the greater sisterhood to which all women belong as a result of their common experience as marginalized members of the human family. The atypically upbeat ending has much to do with women relying on themselves and on each other, with a notable lack of male influence.

The progression of Castellanos' short prose works bears more than a little resemblance to the course of her life: a lonely, rural childhood with much influence from the indigenous culture, an alternately thwarted and successful career, a late and problematic marriage and motherhood, the inevitable conflict between the two roles, and finally her tragic, accidental (and somewhat mysterious) electrocution while working as a Mexican ambassador to Israel.

THE STORIES OF DENISE CHÁVEZ

Author: Denise Chávez (1948-   )
Type of work: Short stories
Principal published work: *The Last of the Menu Girls*

Denise Chávez is a public artist, devoted to creating works of fiction, drama, and poetry that both engage with and represent the Chicano/Chicana culture from which her writing stems. Chávez is best known for her short-story cycle *The Last of the Menu Girls* (1986), the title story of which won the Puerto del Sol fiction award for 1985, but she has always defined herself as a community artist, performing her plays and reading her poems in prisons and senior centers as well as directing writing workshops for children and adults. As Chávez commented, "It's not enough to write something. . . . The important thing is being able to communicate, making the connection between the writer and the audience." The rich, evocative style of Chávez's writing connects her to her community and to her role as a communal and public artist.

The Last of the Menu Girls connects writer and audience through the overlapping of different kinds of writing, through a style at once both engagingly simple and multifaceted, and through careful evocations of the New Mexico and Texas landscapes her characters inhabit. The collection is loosely bound by the narrator, Rocío Esquibel. The stories in *The Last of the Menu Girls* depict Rocío's movement toward maturity and wisdom, her search for a female role model, and her memories of her family, hometown, and community. Although Chávez's collection does not ignore the poverty, pain, and alienation of the world she describes, the overall tone of *The Last of the Menu Girls* is affirmative, for Chávez's characters find hope in the events of everyday life. In "Space Is a Solid," for example, Rocío prevents her nervous breakdown through the simple action of making tacos. The final story in the collection, "Compadre," tells a bleak history of families growing apart yet ends with a ritual, that of buying and eating tamales, that reestablishes kinship.

Moving back and forth in time and in and out of the lives and minds of various characters, *The Last of the Menu Girls* is a stylistically complex work reflecting Chávez's long training in drama and poetry. Much like a series of dramatic monologues, the collection arranges its vignettes thematically but not chronologically. Thus the collection begins when Rocío is seventeen, but the second story tells of Rocío's childhood, and the third tells of her adolescence. Rocío's maturation is presented imagistically and dramatically, rather than as a series of linear events. Stylistically, the collection also provides a collage of techniques, interspersing traditional narratives with, for example, a menu from a hospital and a young girl's journal entries, and moving back and forth between a lyrical, highly metaphorical and poetic style and more direct, straightforward language meant to capture the day-to-day musings of the people Chávez describes.

The title story, "The Last of the Menu Girls," begins in an unusual way, listing the first four lines of Rocío's employment application for her job at Altavista Memorial Hospital. It quickly moves to Rocío's thoughts on her only other experience with the sick and dying, the death of her great-aunt Eutilia. Chávez's stories often do not have traditional plots. In this first narrative, Rocío's application for employment is interspersed with the "events" of Rocío's summer employment as a menu girl (someone who writes down patients' food preferences). Rocío is seventeen, preparing to go to college, and she has difficulty seeing what this desolate world of pain and suffering has to do with her own youthful sense of joy and potentiality. Through her contact with those who are ill, Rocío learns much about herself and her world.

Rocío discovers, for example, that the pain she sees in the hospital is everywhere in the outside world, and even everywhere in her own life. She also learns that life and death are interconnected, influencing and shading into each other. Rocío imagines, for example, dancing a dance of life that connects her youthful and sexual body with the decaying and decrepit body of her great-aunt. Chávez's rich and powerful style graphically captures both the beauty and the pain of such moments of growth and connection: "I danced around Eutilia's bed. I hugged the screen door, my breasts indented in the meshed wire. In the darkness Eutilia moaned, my body wet, her body dry. Steamy we were, and full of prayers. Could I have absolved your dying by my life? Could I have lessened your agony with my spirit-filled dance in the deep darkness?" Through her dance, Rocío comes to understand that her life and her great-aunt's are interconnected, and later she realizes that although dead physically, Eutilia lives on as a part of her consciousness.

Throughout the summer, Rocío has such moments of epiphany, moments that help her to understand pain, suffering, and death. Rocío also has moments of growth and self-realization, moments in which she begins to see some of the outlines of the self she wishes to become. Rocío makes a leap into herself and discovers that she does not want to spend the rest of her life serving people and being the Florence Nightingale of Altavista Memorial Hospital. Rocío rebels against traditional roles for women yet can formulate no alternatives. Perhaps this is why Rocío describes herself as continually angry.

The second story in the collection, "Willow Game," delves into an early stage of Rocío's childhood, perhaps to understand the roots of her teenage dissatisfaction. The story describes in loving detail three trees that hold a tremendous meaning for Rocío and the other neighborhood children. One tree, a willow, is destroyed by a disturbed youth who must later be institutionalized. The willow's destruction teaches the children important lessons about pain and loss, lessons that help the children mature. Looking back on these memories, Rocío realizes that through them she came to understand the way time and memory can both

wound and heal. Through vivid imagery, Chávez evokes the texture of memory, the searing pain of loss, and the healing balm of time. "Time, like trees, withstands the winters, bursts forth new leaves from the dried old sorrows—who knows when and why—and shelters us with the shade of later compassions, loves. . . ."

Chávez's themes of time, memory, and feminine growth are articulated most clearly in "Shooting Stars," which describes Rocío's search for a role model through her friendships with a series of women. Rocío dreams of a beautiful and powerful female face, a face full of clear words and acts, and awakens to find that this face is her own. Finally she models herself on herself, rejecting the versions of femininity offered to her by other women. Rocío admires the women she sees and knows, women whose youth and beauty are destroyed by difficult marriages, multiple pregnancies, and poverty. Although Rocío chooses not to become like these women, she still loves them, cherishes them, and memorializes them in her writing.

The next two stories in *The Last of the Menu Girls*, "Evening in Paris" and "The Closet," continue to examine Rocío's maturation and her search for a feminine role model, but they focus more specifically on Rocío's relationship with her mother. In the first of these stories, a young Rocío buys her mother, Nieves, a Christmas gift of cologne and bath water. Rocío's mother and father are separated, and Rocío hopes the perfume will somehow compensate for her father's absence. Rocío's mother does not attach the same importance to the perfume; in fact, she never uses it. Rocío's dreams for her mother and for herself do not materialize, and she is left believing that she lacks the right words and the right gifts to compensate her mother for the emptiness that surrounds them, the emptiness that no bottle of cologne can ever fill.

In "The Closet," Chávez again examines the ways women attempt to fill the emptiness of their lives. In this story, the closets in Rocío's house become emblems and metaphors for the lives of the Esquibel women. At times, the closets represent the way women's dreams can be crushed by a brutal world. Nieves' closet, for example, holds the shoes of a woman with furious bitter hopes, the shoes of a woman who has waited all her life for better things to come. The closets also take on more positive symbolism, becoming the realm of dreams, fantasy, religious ecstasy, and imagination. Rocío imagines that she travels through the hall closet to a world that is spacious, blue, and light. She exercises her imagination to create and define this alternative world, a space that is her own and does not confine her. Imagistically, she rejects the confined and limited closets of her mother and her older sister Ronelia (married and pregnant at the age of eighteen), seeking instead to define her own closet, her own psyche, her own model of self. Rocío tells her younger sister Mercy that everyone has their own rooms, their own house; in effect, Rocío is teaching Mercy that she need not be defined and limited by the rooms, the closets, the houses—the identities—given to her by the external world.

In "The Closet," space itself is embodied, taking on physical and metaphorical meanings. The closets of the house become characters, identities, personas that the women inhabit or choose not to inhabit. Rocío describes a house of women, a house in which women are defined and sometimes delimited by the spaces they inhabit. Space thus becomes a metaphor for self-definition, maturation, and the actual or symbolic possibilities of an individual's life. In the next story, space is again a metaphor for individual potentiality. "Space Is a Solid" is one of Chávez's most interesting and powerful stories. It uses "crossover" narration, telling the story from multiple points of view, but mainly switching between the perspectives of Kari Lee, a young schoolgirl, and Rocío Esquibel, now a struggling graduate student teaching drama appreciation classes. The story chronicles the growth of Rocío and Kari Lee's friendship, as well as Rocío's own attempt to find a space (again, an identity) that is her own.

Kari Lee and Rocío, although at different stages of their lives, are on parallel voyages of self-discovery. Kari Lee comes from a dysfunctional family, and it is only in Rocío's classes that she begins to explore who she is and what she wants. Rocío, too, is seeking a safe space in which to explore her psyche. When the story begins, she literally lacks any space of her own and is living in her boyfriend Loudon's spaceship-shaped room. Rocío moves in and out of a series of apartments, and as she does so her psyche splinters and fragments, leaving her on the verge of a nervous breakdown. Rocío does finally take control of her life, find a space of her own, and recover her equilibrium.

Throughout the story, various spaces are marked with different and often distinctly feminine images of physical and mental trauma. Kari Lee's home, for example, is dominated by her bitter and paranoid mother, Nita. Nita sees her radical mastectomy as a direct punishment from God, a direct punishment that she feels in her "female flesh." Rocío's pregnant and schizophrenic cat dominates and destroys Rocío's first apartment. Even Rocío's classroom is marked by disease. Kari Lee is often distressed by the presence of Arlin Threadgill, a boy who has no arms because his mother took thalidomide during her pregnancy. In the end, however, Kari Lee is able to stop seeing Arlin as a "cripple" and begin treating him as an individual, and Rocío is able to heal herself and her psyche. The images of disease and death recede as both Kari Lee and Rocío find spaces in which they can be whole and healed.

In "Compadre," the final story in *The Last of the Menu Girls*, Rocío moves closer to self-definition and integration, deciding to become a writer and chronicle the lives of her family and friends. This story also examines the relationship between Rocío's mother, Nieves, and her compadre, Regino Suárez. *Compadrazgo* is not a familial relationship but a relationship structured around affiliation. Regino, the neighborhood handyman, and Nieves have a protective and supportive relationship that spans their lives and even outlasts the ties between husband and wife, parents and children. More diffuse than Chavez's other stories, "Compadre" has themes that are more broad and universal, offering a fitting conclusion to the collection as a whole. Again, Rocío's maturation is an important focus, yet Chávez places this theme in the larger context of difficult and often fragmented familial relationships. Regino Suárez's family abandons him, and Rocío's mother lives in the Southwest while her two daughters live in the North. The story is marked by alienation and loneliness but also by the enduring bonds of *compadrazgo*.

Stylistically and imagistically, the story is one of Chávez's most complex. Images of the Southwest landscape abound, but in this piece the landscape is presented as dry and desiccated, ancient like the people who inhabit it. The cultural world of this landscape is evoked through a blending of Spanish and English prose and by an effortless movement between these two languages. As in "Space Is a Solid," Chávez also moves in and out of different characters' minds, telling the story from the points of view of Rocío, Nieves, Regino, and other characters. The story presents a rich mixture of imagery and language, functioning as a strong encapsulation of Chávez's main themes of maturation, the search for feminine role models, the meaning of time and memory, and the vividness of Rocío's spatial and cultural worlds.

Chávez's later stories continued to explore the vivid worlds and themes of her earlier fiction. "The McCoy Hotel" (1990) returns to themes articulated in *The Last of the Menu Girls*: time, memory, and growth—especially female maturation. Other works by Chávez, however, explore new areas of perception and characterization. "Chata" (1992), for example, is a powerful and moving story that gives voice and dignity to those who perform "menial" labor, like the title character, a cleaning woman. "The King and Queen of Comezón" (1988) is a descriptive excerpt that takes as its focus a male character, Arnuflo Olivárez. "Grand Slam" (1987), a powerful dramatic monologue, describes a middle-aged woman's attempts to come to terms with a faded romance from her past and with her own sense of loss and mortality. Stories such as these show that Chávez can extend her strongly evocative style and her optimistic and humorous tone in new directions. The beauty and strength of *The Last of the Menu Girls* will be retained as Chávez moves into new fictional spaces, making these spaces her own.

THE STORIES OF JULIO CORTÁZAR

Author: Julio Cortázar (1914-1984)
Type of work: Short stories
Principal published works: *Bestiario*, 1951; *Final de juego*, 1956; *Las armas secretas*, 1959; *Historias de cronopios y de famas*, 1962; (*Cronopios and Famas*, 1969); *End of the Game and Other Stories*, 1963 (also known as *Blow-Up and Other Stories*, 1967); *Todos los fuegos el fuego*, 1966 (*All Fires the Fire and Other Stories*, 1973); *Octaedro*, 1974 (included in *A Change of Light and Other Stories*, 1980; *Alguien que anda por ahí y otros relatos*, 1977 (included in *A Change of Light and Other Stories*, 1980); *Un tal Lucas*, 1979 (*A Certain Lucas*, 1984); *Queremos tanto a Glenda y otros relatos*, 1980 (*We Love Glenda so Much and Other Tales*, 1983); *Deshoras*, 1982

Julio Cortázar was a novelist, essayist, translator, and short-story writer. He wrote one of the most important Latin American novels of the twentieth century, *Rayuela* (1963, *Hopscotch*, 1966), but he is most highly regarded as a writer of short stories. Together with his compatriot Jorge Luis Borges, Cortázar brought inventiveness and imagination to the short-story form, deliberately challenging the rationalism and realism that have dominated Western literary and intellectual traditions. Despite his experimentation in style, language, and form, Cortázar differs from other avantgarde artists in his accessibility. Always intriguing and entertaining, Cortázar's work manages to be both serious and playful at the same time. His fiction, especially his more than eighty short stories, has universal appeal and has been widely translated. Cortázar was himself something of an international figure. Born in Brussels, Belgium, reared and educated in Argentina, well traveled, and long a resident of Paris, Cortázar perhaps more than any other writer of his day easily crossed boundaries, cultures, and ideologies. His influence on world literature has been enormous.

Cortázar's influence is a result in part of the wide range in content and style found in his stories. He wrote masterpieces in virtually every short-story genre—fantasy, horror, political and psychological realism, mystery, and the quintessential Latin American genre of Magical Realism. Because of his innovation in exploiting the conventions of these genres, it is perhaps best to label Cortázar, if a label is necessary, as an experimental writer. The experimentation one encounters in Cortázar's stories is almost never trite or fatuous; that is, Cortázar did not experiment for the sake of experimentation. In story after story, he found new technical, stylistic, and formal approaches to his material; more important, Cortázar used those approaches to heighten psychological insights and truths. His genius is the rare combination of technical virtuosity and philosophical incisiveness. Cortázar deepens one's understanding of art and human nature in even the slightest of stories.

An example from Cortázar's early work is the story "Axolotl," which was first published in 1954. As in many of Cortázar's stories, the technical brilliance of "Axolotl" comes from a clever and careful manipulation of a schizophrenic point of view. The story is narrated by a man who has become, or thinks he has become, an axolotl, a kind of Mexican salamander that he is fond of observing in the Paris zoo. Every day he visits the zoo and stares for hours at the salamanders through the glass of the aquarium. One day, he recognizes that he is feeling the pain and suffering of the axolotls, "that stiff torment at the bottom of the tank." His extreme empathy for them results in a transmigration of souls: He trades places, so to speak, with axolotl. As usual in Cortázar's stories, this extraordinary and inexplicable phenomenon is accepted as quite ordinary and inevitable by the character: "So there was nothing strange in what happened."

Technically, Cortázar controls this transmigration, and the reader's acceptance of it, by a careful blending of points of view. First the man is narrating, then the point of view shifts rapidly back and forth between man and salamander ("Recognizing him, being him himself, I was an axolotl and in my world"), and finally the narration remains entirely reptilian. The transformation is smooth, natural, and believable. Moreover, the transformation makes sense psychologically as well as technically: "every axolotl thinks like a man inside his stony semblance," the narrator concludes, and the statement itself, grammatically ambiguous, does not clarify whether the "stony semblance" is man's or axolotl's. Inside, people all experience a reptilian isolation, "incapable of expression, limited to the golden splendor of our eyes."

Several of Cortázar's stories continue this experiment with the schizophrenic point of view. In some of his most renowned fiction, the persona of one reality yields consciousness to the persona of an altogether different reality. Such is the case in "The Night Face Up" (1956), a widely anthologized story about a young man who is badly injured in a motorcycle accident. The accident, and his subsequent loss of consciousness, triggers a strange slippage of realities for the protagonist. He is vaguely aware of the ambulance ride to the hospital and the preparation for surgery on his severely damaged arm, but this "reality" is distant and confusing. Once anesthetized, the protagonist finds himself in a dream. Curiously, the dream, full of sensuous details, is much more distinct and real than is the hospital. In the dream, he is a Moltec Indian, trying to escape from Aztec headhunters. Occasionally the hospital reality penetrates this deep dream—a voice or a smell draws him back to his familiar and painful circumstances—but that reality seems increasingly strange, while the dream seems increasingly real. In the climactic moment, the two worlds draw parallel: In the hospital, the protagonist is lying on his back in traction, and in the dream, he is lying on his back, tied to an Aztec altar for sacrifice. All the correspondences now become apparent: the bed and the altar, the Aztec priest with his knife and the doctor with his scalpel, and so on. Then another slippage occurs, as dream and reality are transposed: The Moltec Indian, in the moment of his sacrifice, recalls in fear a con-

fusing and terrifying dream "in which he was going through the strange avenues of an astonishing city, with green and red lights that burned without fire or smoke, on an enormous metal insect that whirred away between his legs." This is a quintessential Cortázar passage in its technical virtuosity and in the suggestiveness that emerges from its ambiguity. Cortázar does more than raise the possibility of metempsychosis. Through the device of temporal parallels, "The Night Face Up" brings to light the underlying barbarism of modern life. Through the protagonist's estrangement, the reader's sense of reality is disturbed and destabilized.

This confusion of temporal and spatial realities is a recurring device in Cortázar's work and is often, as in "The Night Face Up," the source of the schizophrenic point of view. "Secret Weapons" (1959), one of Cortázar's masterpieces, follows a similar pattern. In this story, "reality" is post-World War II France, and the protagonist is a young Frenchman named Pierre. Pierre's sense of reality is invaded by strange visions that have something to do with his new girlfriend, Michèle. On his way to spend a weekend with Michèle, Pierre's consciousness is taken over by that of a young German soldier who had raped Michèle during the war and was later caught and executed by her friends. The story reaches a chilling yet ambiguous climax, and the reader is left in doubt as to which reality, Pierre's or the soldier's, will emerge victorious.

"Secret Weapons" explores one of Cortázar's favorite themes, the *Doppelgänger*, or double. As in classic double stories, such as Edgar Allan Poe's "William Wilson" (which Cortázar, Poe's translator, greatly admired), the protagonist is haunted, pursued by, and sometimes tormented by a previously unknown corporal or psychical twin, an alter ego. In "The Distances" (1951), Cortázar's protagonist searches out her double, a beggar woman, only to discover that in embracing they have switched places and she is now the crippled beggar. Cortázar called this switch "a psychic exchange." The narrator of "A Yellow Flower" (1963) finds in his double, a young boy, evidence of reincarnation. In a twist, the narrator has allowed his double to die, and in so doing has unwittingly destroyed the only possibility of his own reincarnation. His immortality is thus canceled, and he is condemned to live out in despair "his poor stupid life, his imbecile, abortive life."

The archetypal Cortázar story challenges notions of reality, most particularly faith in the logical and consistent operation of physical laws. Most of metaphysics concentrates on what is knowable and explicable, but Cortázar had an unwavering interest in the inexplicable and harbored a suspicion—perhaps even a hope—that the "true world" or "reality" manifests itself in the exceptions to what is understood to be the orderly universe. In other words, Cortázar's work suggests that what is commonly called reality may not be real at all, and that the only insights to the true world come on those rare occasions when something inexplicable takes place, such as the random appearance of a tiger in a country house ("Bestiary") or the usurpation of a house by some unidentifiable force ("House Taken Over"). Cortázar called the belief that all things can be described and explained by reference to a harmonious system of laws or principles "a false realism." Opposed to this false realism was the fantastic, and in his stories Cortázar made the fantastic his own territory.

Almost all of Cortázar's best stories explore some aspect of the fantastic. In "Bestiary" (1951), one of his earliest stories, the reader is introduced to what appears to be a mundane world in which characters are preoccupied with rice puddings and long-division problems. Even the first mention of the fantastic intrusion upon this world, a tiger that roams through the house, does not hint at anything unusual. In most cases, Cortázar's characters accept the fantastic as a normal part of their world. Gradually, however, the reader realizes that all is not normal—the tiger is a killer and must be avoided by the occupants of the house. "Bestiary" also illustrates how Cortázar uses the fantastic not as a gimmick but as a means of heightening a story's psychological insight. The central conflict in the story is not between the tiger and the family but between a little girl, Isabel, and Nene the Kid, an adult relative who is cruel and abusive, especially toward Aunt Rema. To save Rema, Isabel

deliberately deceives Nene the Kid, and he is subsequently devoured by the tiger. The story explores the realm of the fantastic, but its principal themes—incest, family violence, and machismo—are rooted firmly in the human experience.

One aspect of human experience that particularly attracted Cortázar was play. Thus, games and children's play figure as prominent motifs in his fiction. For example, in "End of the Game" (1956), Cortázar's narrator is a young girl who plays a game with her two sisters. Every day the three girls draw lots to see who will "play the statue." The girl who is the statue must hold a certain pose during the passage of the afternoon train. Eventually, their game attracts the attention of a young man aboard the train, who declares himself to be a great admirer of the sister named Letitia. Letitia is crippled, but because the game does not involve movement, the young man is unaware of her disability. On the day that he has promised to descend from the train to visit with the girls, Letitia refuses to meet him and instead sends a letter. The next day, Letitia performs a pose that is stunning but that reveals her deformity. The young man is never seen again, and the game is ended forever.

Another aspect of human experience that Cortázar explores in his fiction is the nature of art. He was particularly drawn to the complexities inherent in the relationship of the artist to his or her art. This is the theme of one of Cortázar's best and longest stories, "The Pursuer" (1959). The story of an American jazz saxophonist named Johnny Carter (based on the life of jazz great Charlie Parker), "The Pursuer" focuses on the relationship of the artist to his art, or in this case, the musician to his music. Johnny Carter is a tormented soul whose torments prove to be the greatest inspiration for his music. He is destroying himself in pursuing or seeking his art. Ironically, at least for the narrator, Johnny is unable to articulate his quest, nor does he understand—at least in critical terms—what he discovers in his pursuit of pure musical expression. Bruno can express it, though somewhat reductively, and thus feels superior to Johnny. Bruno has garnered fame and wealth from his ability to analytically describe what for Johnny is intuitive expression. Thus, Johnny's torments and his eventual death give Bruno the opportunity to reap rich rewards.

"The Pursuer" has much in common with other stories about tormented artists (such as Thomas Mann's 1912 "Death in Venice") who pursue their art even though it means self-destruction. Cortázar undoubtedly identified with his main character—the similarity of the names J. Cortázar and J. Carter suggests such a bond. When Bruno says that Johnny tried "to explore himself, to bite into the reality that escapes every day," he describes Cortázar as well. Carter and Cortázar are also similar in their struggles with form: "I see here the ultimate paradox of his style, his aggressive vigor. Incapable of satisfying itself, useful as a continued spur, an infinite construction, the pleasure of which is not in its highest pinnacle but in the exploratory repetitions, in the use of faculties which leave the suddenly human behind without losing humanity."

Here Bruno is speaking of Johnny Carter's saxophone style, but he may just as well have been speaking of Julio Cortázar's fiction, and in particular Cortázar's story "Blow-Up" (1959). This complex story, Cortázar's most famous after Michelan-
gelo Antonioni made it into a film (*Blowup*, 1966), illustrates what the narrator of "The Pursuer" calls "the paradox in style." "Blow-Up" is a quintessential metafiction, a story that conspicuously and paradoxically calls attention to its own construction and narration. Roberto Michel, a photographer, tells the story, but he is the very definition of an unreliable narrator, for he is not sure himself whether what he tells is truth or whether he "is guilty of literature, or unreal fabrications." Ultimately, the story compares reality to art and questions whether the interpretation of anything—art or reality—is possible given the essential ambiguity of experience and people's inevitable unreliability as narrators of that experience.

These problems are at the core of Cortázar's best work. His short fiction turns on an irreducible ambiguity in both "real" experience and in the artistic re-creation of experience, an ambiguity that implies the ultimate failure of attempts to impose a rational framework on what people choose to call reality. His ability to express this ambiguity through stunning technical innovations made him one of the representative voices of twentieth century literature.

THE STORIES OF ALBERTO RÍOS

Author: Alberto Ríos (1952-   )
Type of work: Short stories
Principal published work: *The Iguana Killer: Twelve Stories of the Heart*, 1984

Alberto Ríos is a poet and storyteller, born and reared in the border town of Nogales, Arizona. Although his first language was Spanish, he was forced to speak English upon entering first grade, and only during his years in high school did he relearn his first language. Probably because of these early experiences, he chooses to write in English and does not align himself with the outsiders of the Chicano movement in literature. This is not to say that he is uncritical of his second culture and language. Many of his stories show the Anglo culture impinging on the natural world of children. Still, Ríos has established himself as working from within the system. He has received prestigious awards and fellowships and has earned much recognition for his work, especially his poetry, though his stories reward the careful reader.

The title story of his collection *The Iguana Killer: Twelve Stories of the Heart* (1984) is also the first story of the collection. It concerns an eight-year-old Mexican boy who receives, as a Christmas gift from his grandmother in Arizona, a baseball bat. At first he is puzzled, because he does not know about baseball. He does know about killing iguanas, the meat of which is locally prized, and he instantly divines the proper use of the bat; proper, that is, in his culture. A description of his iguana-killing exploits follows. His lethal expertise with the bat wins status for him among the other children. Not only does this status confer wealth on him—he is able to rent the bat out for a *centavo* a day—but it also pushes him a step closer to maturity, as illustrated when he presents a cradle he has made from a tortoise shell to a mother in confinement, someone he feels obligated to help. By the end of the story, he has acquired a sense of responsibility. He is not a dependent child, but a person on whom others can depend. This development comes through the agency of the bat, an artifact from another culture recast to fit its new milieu.

This theme of cultural adaptation is given a brutal turn in the next story, "The Child." Two elderly widows board a bus in Mexico headed for the border town of Nogales, Arizona. The talkative one makes it her business to find out all she can about the nervous man across the aisle who has carried on a sleeping boy, but the man is guarded in his replies. At a rest stop, everyone leaves the bus except for the child, who is still apparently asleep. The talkative widow decides to bring him some water. She discovers that he is dead. Later it is found that his insides have been cleaned out and replaced with bags of opium. In these first two stories, Ríos takes two major concerns of the United States, baseball and drugs, and shows how they can insert themselves into Mexican culture, suggesting at the same time that those most affected are children.

The next five stories deal with typical themes of childhood such as revenge for insults, first thoughts on sex, and friendship, mixing them in various combinations. In "Pato," a chubby boy takes his revenge on a friend named Wienie who makes insinuations about his mother and older brother sleeping in the same room. They do sleep in the same room, but it is because Pato's body gives off a strange smell of which he is proud but that his brother cannot bear. Pato is too naïve to understand Wienie's insinuation, which he takes as a suggestion that his brother is scared of the dark. Still, he is bothered enough by an undercurrent he does not comprehend that he tells his mother what Wienie said, hoping that some clarification might slip out. Naturally, none does. Pato defines the situation for himself by throwing a rock at Wienie, demonstrating that he is no longer scared of his tormentor.

First dealings with and thoughts about sex are expanded on in the next story, "His Own Key," which is about a self-confident young boy whose view of the world is turned upside down when he learns from his friends a few of the facts of life. His self-assuredness comes in part from being trusted by his parents with his own key to the house. As he learns from his friends, there are other, more important, keys that only adults seem to have. His first impulse is to deny what his friends tell him. He cannot believe, for example, that such an act would feel good. When he is alone, his denial turns to bewilderment. He is frightened by what he does not know, especially in regard to what his new responsibilities might be. Suddenly he is no longer the big boy he though he was with his own little key, but a little boy with a key too big for him to handle.

The next two stories focus on friendship, specifically on unlikely friendships. In "A Friend, Brother Maybe," Frankie, a boy prone to fighting, is made the subject of an experiment in which a padded machine is placed in his room. The machine emits a laughing sound when first touched and continues to do so even as Frankie, infuriated, kicks and punches it. Finally, it begins to sob. The sobs infuriate Frankie more, at least for the first few days. Eventually, Frankie learns compassion and decides to beat up the machine no more. His attacks on the machine awaken him to the fact that his fighting is a response to the abuse he has suffered. The machine becomes a friend of sorts; together they can stand against the abuse of the world.

The narrator of "Johnny Ray" befriends the title character, an Anglo who is an outcast among the students of the predominantly Latino school he attends. It is not merely that he is Anglo that makes him an outsider. More incriminating are his pastimes: He makes bread, reads for fun, raises bees, and even sews. Nevertheless, the narrator befriends him, ostensibly because he himself is self-confident and sees that same trait in Johnny Ray, respecting him for it. One day, Johnny Ray proves his strength of character by refusing to dress up for *Dia del Vaquero*, the Day of the Cowboy. When

some seniors arrive to mete out punishment for nonparticipants, Johnny Ray fights them off. The narrator learns from Johnny Ray to stand up for his own ideals and understandings against the demands of the world.

"The Way Spaghetti Feels" combines all these themes in the story of a young girl, Mari, who conducts a secret correspondence with an unknown boy who, through his writing, proves himself witty and charming and thereby wins her heart. The vehicle for their letter writing is, curiously, a cow, one in a herd Mari passes on her way to school. One day, Mari notices a piece of paper attached to the cow and finds that it is a note that reads, "Hi. Is anyone out there? Put the answer back on the cow." Thus begins an exchange of notes in which, eventually, both reveal intimate details of their lives. Mari describes her first period, and the boy his first wet dream. When the two finally decide to meet, Mari is shocked to learn that the boy is one in her class who, with his friend, had insulted her. Ruben, the boy, swears that his friend had made him do it, but the memory is enough to dispel any further development of the romance, though they try half-heartedly to advance it. Poised at the very beginnings of adulthood, they each learn how vital it is that appearance and reality at least somewhat match up.

In "Then They'd Watch Comedies," a boy acquires this same knowledge through seeing the disparity between what his father teaches and what he actually practices. Coming home one day after a scuffle, he explains that he was defending his name, Leocadio, from mockers who would shorten it to Leo. His father, also named Leocadio, had always told him not to allow anyone to call him Leo. That night, the boy discovers a pay stub on which his father is identified as Leo. The father, whom Ríos portrays walking around in his underwear to symbolize the boy's new insight, weakly defends himself, suggesting that there are certain compromises that adults must make that Leocadio cannot understand.

This introduction to the complexities of the adult world as seen through the eyes of children provides Ríos with the theme of the next three stories. In "La Boda" (the wedding), Ríos switches between the adults making preparations for a wedding, with all the confusions that result, and the adventures of two little boys related to the couple being married. One of the boys, Jorge, has trouble staying clean and yet is nominated to be the ring-bearer. The other, Tonio, has a tremendous problem with flatulence; he is banished to sit in the balcony. Predictably, he passes wind at a crucial quiet moment in the ceremony and Jorge arrives dirty. More important, though, they have wrapped as a present a rusty loaded gun they had found by a river. The adults pretend that the gun is fake, but the effect is to show the disasters, natural and unnatural, that await children in their interactions with the adult world.

This adult world is fraught not only with danger but also with destruction. In "The Secret Lion," a group of boys learns how adults govern and control the environment. For example, they enjoy swimming in the arroyo, except on those days when the sewage plant releases sewage into the river, sometimes catching them unaware. Then, they have to invent excuses for coming home smelling so bad. One day, they decide to forgo the arroyo and explore the mountains instead. After a long trek, they arrive at what they decide must be heaven, a seemingly endless expanse of cut grass and beautiful trees. They lie down, pretending to be the owners, and the narrator finds a small hole in which to place his soda. Two men show up with metal sticks in bags and shout at the boys to leave. Their heaven is instantly destroyed, becoming a golf course. Adults thus not only lay claim to and destroy the best that life offers but also create in children's minds fantasies that, like the story's lost heaven, do not exist.

In the following story, "Eyes Like They Say the Devil Has," the narrator discovers that adults save their best effects precisely to recruit children, as well as other adults, into these realms of fantasy. This humorous story relates the experience of a boy who is taken to a gypsy fortune-teller, an imposing and theatrical woman. Scared simply by the thought of going to see her, he is horrified to find himself, once in her home, crushed in his seat

as she bends over him. He nearly faints, surviving the ordeal having heard only that the future would make him tall. As he notes, children only wish, whereas adults decide. What he as a child could only wish for was supposedly decided for him through the impressive display of the gypsy woman. He doubts the decisiveness of the woman's prophecy; by implication, the ability of all adults to make decisions that affect the course of events comes under question.

The hoax of adult decisiveness is further exposed in the final story, "The Birthday of Mrs. Pineda," the only story in which no children appear. The story is a touching exploration of the consciousness of Alfredo Pineda, a middle-aged man, as he reads and chats with his wife. Through flashbacks, Ríos sketches the important moments of Pineda's life. Readers learn that he aggrandized himself in order to win his wife's hand in marriage. Meanwhile, Mrs. Pineda tries to tell him of a friend's visit. She realizes that she must likewise aggrandize the importance of this visit in order to keep her husband's attention. Ríos seems to suggest that adults do not impress their wills directly upon the world. Rather, they create versions of themselves and of reality that they hope prove true, ones that match, and therefore seem to determine, the desired outcomes.

Besides the stories in *The Iguana Killer*, Ríos has published stories in literary magazines such as *The Ohio Review* and *Ploughshares*. There was, however, a lapse of six years between the appearance of *The Iguana Killer* and the publication of these later stories, which show an advance in maturity over the earlier work. In "All-weddings," published in *The Ohio Review* in 1990, Jose, a carpenter, is making a coffin in a funeral home when the coffin's intended occupant, lying nearby, sits up. Jose runs away frightened and swears never to return, though he is later assured by the mortician that what he saw was simply a manifestation of gases building up in the body. Because he can find no other work, his marriage falls apart, and he leaves town. He returns decades later as an old man, about to die because, as he explains, he knew his wife was "capable of sitting up herself when she passed away," seeking him out and dragging him back to her. Although this story is on one level a human comedy, on another it is a parable of the artist such as one finds in many of the stories of Henry James. The dead man is named Luna, or the moon, emblematic of the imagination. Jose's wife is Rosa, or rose, emblematic of the artist's work. These names combine with certain narrative details to suggest a story of a storyteller who finds that he cannot leave his work behind.

"Waltz of the Fat Man," published in the Summer, 1991, issue of *The Kenyon Review*, marks another departure for Ríos' fiction. Its surrealistic narrative is reminiscent of the Magical Realists. A simple story of a man who "did not think himself fat, but felt himself heavy" and who, alienated from his fellow townspeople, leaves to join a cir-

cus, "Waltz of the Fat Man" takes on the quality of a tone poem with its imaginative use of language. Both these stories are evidence of the advances that Ríos has made over his earlier work.

Ríos stands at midcareer as a storyteller coming into his full power. At the same time, he straddles two cultures and successfully joins them, melding the language of one with the heart of the other. In his stories and poems, he makes sure the reader knows that, to paraphrase the words of James Joyce, "the language in which we are speaking is yours before it is mine." The English he was forced to speak as a child was his teacher's language, not his, yet he has emerged more powerful in the language than its original purveyors, able to aim that medium back at its source through the content of his own feelings, his heart.

THE STORIES OF TOMÁS RIVERA

Author: Tomás Rivera (1935-1984)
Type of work: Short stories
Principal published works: *. . . y no se lo tragó la tierra*, 1971 (*. . . and the Earth Did Not Part*, 1971); *The Harvest: Short Stories by Tomás Rivera*, 1989; *Tomás Rivera: The Complete Works*, 1991

Born on December 22, 1935, in Crystal City, Texas, Tomás Rivera has been considered to be the father of Chicano literature. The Chicano movement in the 1960's sparked an awakening of self-realization and human potential of which Rivera was a large part. Rivera was both a scholar of languages and a teacher. His teaching experience included working at the elementary level; teaching Spanish and English at the junior high school level; and teaching Spanish, English, and French at the college level. He drew attention to his dedication to improve Mexican American life by presenting himself as an example of human potential.

His life was a struggle as he tried to obtain higher education in a society that provided segregated colleges for African Americans and women though denying the opportunity for education to Latinos. Financial difficulties often made it a struggle to pursue higher education even for those Chicanos that had the opportunity. Born into a migrant family atmosphere, Rivera learned to adapt to his situation, never giving up his ambition. He struggled with educational and language barriers.

Rivera surpassed those obstacles and attended Southwest Texas Junior College, then went on to Southwest Texas State University and obtained a bachelor of science degree. He obtained master's degrees in education and literature and then a doctorate in literature. He worked in administrative positions as a counselor in the department of modern languages and the department of education at the University of Oklahoma, then as associate professor of Spanish at Sam Houston State University from 1968 to 1971. In 1971, he became a professor of romance languages at the University of Texas at San Antonio.

His honors include membership on the board of directors of the Pan American Student Forum in 1965, presidency of the Sigma Delta Pi chapter at the University of Oklahoma in 1968, the Premio Quinto Sol, and the National Chicano Literary Award for 1969-1970. In 1979, he became the first Mexican American to be appointed as a chancellor of the University of California, Riverside.

Rivera fought for reform in academic curricula and encouraged the Chicano community to rise and seek opportunity. He hoped to be a role model, not of how a successful a Chicano could become, but for understanding the need to succeed with an education. He was a man of character who, through his works, illustrated understanding of fellow Mexican Americans and aspirations for a better life. He believed that the search for identity is everlasting but that with the help of literature, identity can be understood.

His most notable work is *. . . y no se lo tragó la tierra* (1971; *. . . and the Earth Did Not Part*, 1971). It was awarded the first U.S. national award for Chicano literature and has since become a standard text in U.S. Hispanic literature courses. In it, Rivera examines the typical history of the first Mexican Americans in early American society. His work presents many of the social and cultural aspects found in literature written by Mexicans and their descendants who live or lived in what is now the United States, work that has come to be known as Chicano literature. Rivera presents in his work the concepts of spiritual strength and justice so prevalent in Chicano literature. He portrays vividly the experiences and struggles of the economically, politically, and socially deprived Mexican migrants who kept moving, never staying in one place to suffer or to be subdued, always searching for work. Having lived in that milieu, Rivera documents through fiction the lives of the Mexican and Mexican American migrant workers of the 1940's.

The characters in the work are presented as having to exist in a hostile social environment from which they are trying to liberate themselves. The only way that they can find freedom, according to Rivera, is by confronting the reality of their situation and, in the end, knowing who they really are.

The work was highly praised by Mexican American novelists. It has been characterized as a summary of the past, a living present, and a base for the future of Chicano literature. It has also been called a landmark in the present and a point of departure into the future of the Chicano literary tradition. Rivera's work has been considered to be an important piece of prose fiction and genuine "literature of liberation." Several authors have claimed that Rivera renders an authentic account of the Chicano experience. It has been said that Rivera's narrator/hero embraces the totality of his experience as a Chicano.

The book comprises fourteen short stories about migrant lives, each introduced by an anecdote. The stories range from prayers for sons in Vietnam to a narrative about a young child stricken with thirst out in the fields. The first story, "The Children Were Victims," sets the stage for the presentation of the struggles endured by migrants. The story deals with the struggle against nature in order to survive. Children as young as five years old were considered to be adults and worked as adults in the hot sun. As the story develops, a child goes to get a drink at the end of the rows of crops, and the foreman sees him. To scare him from drinking, he shoots at the child. Instead of being scared, the child drops to the ground dead, with a bullet in his frail body. Apparently, the foreman did not want his workers to catch a disease from drinking the filthy water, but his prevention proved far more deadly. The effect of this simple description points out clearly the tragedy of the people Rivera writes about: "He didn't even jump like the deer; he just fell into the water like a dirty rag and the water became saturated with blood." The story has been described as expressive of the painful, humble condition of a people reduced to an inferior position in American society and of the exploitation at the hands of their bosses.

In the story, the child questions his beliefs in God and the potential for his people to survive:

> Why is it that we are here on earth as though buried alive? Either the germs eat us from the inside or the sun from the outside. Always some illness. And work, work, day in and day out. And for what? Poor father, he works just as hard as the rest of us, perhaps harder. . . . Barely five years old and he was already out there planting corn with his father. After feeding the earth and the sun for such a long time, . . . unexpectedly he is felled by the sun. And powerless to do anything. And to top it off, praying to God. God doesn't even remember us. . . . There must not be a God. . . .

Although these people believe that God does not forsake his people, when the feeling of being forsaken comes, it takes a miracle to overcome the feeling. The child does not understand that people can be good and yet still suffer. Later, his father becomes better. Looking down at the ground, the child "kicked it and said to it, 'Not yet, you can't eat me yet. Someday.'"

In "It Is Painful," Rivera examines the struggle for education:

> It's always the same in these northern schools. Everyone just stares at you up and down. They laugh at you, and the teacher with that popsicle or eskimo pie stick trying to find lice on your head. One feels shame. And when they turn up their noses, one feels anger.

A child gets in a fight with an Anglo boy who says that he hates Mexicans because they steal. The Chicano boy hits him and is expelled. Here children are presented as being different from adults because they want change. Migrant children experience feelings that they do not know how to deal with. In this story, the child feels alienation, a common theme in Chicano literature. The story gives the reader an understanding of how success is categorized and of the limited potential for Hispanic children at the time. No dreams of becoming lawyers, doctors, or powerful businesspeople are possible.

In the last story of the book, "Under the House,"

a Chicano boy examines the year that has just passed. In his remembrance, he comes to understand more about his family, his culture, and himself. Looking back at the previous year, he examines his growth:

> One has to be alone in order to bring everyone together. . . . I needed to isolate myself in order to understand many things. From here on all I have to do is come back here in the dark and think about them. And I have so much to think about, and so many years to catch up on. I think that today I wanted to remember this past year. But that's just one year. I'll have to come here to remember all the others.

The story contains two main "characters," the young boy and the Chicano entity that surrounds him. This community is the base upon which Rivera molds his work. It has been stated that Rivera tells the story of his people on a level that is more than simply writing about "the oppressed." He leaves the day-to-day battle against the odds of language, religious mysticism, and Anglo bigotry to the reader.

Although the central protagonist is the community ("el pueblo"), the strongest voice is that of the child narrator, who is part of the first generation whose members can no longer accept mystical and religious explanations of life and the quiet resignation of their parents. In this work, as well as in most Chicano literature, the Chicano is characterized as an outsider, one who feels and expresses alienation from not only society but also from his or her family and culture.

Rivera's work has been praised for capturing the simplicity and feeling of his people in the fight for existence against two main enemies: the sun that draws at their life and the earth that, watered by their sweat, does its utmost to swallow them. In his stories, the "pueblo" continues to live while attacked by disease, exploitation, oppression, and persecution, all of which have been the daily experiences of Mexican Americans.

Rivera also published literary essays and poetry. In 1973, a short collection of poems appeared under the title *Always and Other Poems*. His best-known poem is titled "The Searchers," and was published in 1977. It has been called an epic poem. Rivera said that through this poem he wanted to portray migrants as searchers, as his grandfather and father had been. He hoped to be a searcher in the same sense, seeking for spiritual justice for his people. A parallel with the child protagonist of . . . *y no se lo tragó la tierra* can be seen throughout the poem. The migrants are on a quest for being and in search of an understanding of their existence and selves. Again Rivera presents the act of remembering; he declared that it is from the past that one is able to perceive, create, and give life to rituals.

Rivera's works have been categorized as a mixture of remembering the past and accounts of discrimination, alienation and cultural conflict, and the concepts of otherness and unity. The past, to Rivera, is the tool for discovery within oneself. Rivera used remembrance, and his works are full of realism, since memory, for him, is the filter of reality.

When Rivera died in 1984, he left a collection of unpublished poems and an unfinished novel titled *La casa grande*. His legacy is that of a master of reflection and the father of Chicano literature. His work has been considered the foundation of modern Chicano literature.

THE STORIES OF HELENA MARÍA VIRAMONTES

Author: Helena María Viramontes (1954-   )
Type of work: Short stories
Principal published work: *The Moths and Other Stories*, 1985

Helena María Viramontes is best known for her short stories, but she is also an essayist who has discussed topics ranging from writing to the role of women in Chicano culture. She has been winning prizes for her short stories almost since she began writing them. Her "Requiem for the Poor" won first prize in a contest sponsored by California State University, Los Angeles, in 1977. She won first prize with "The Broken Web" the following year. In 1979, she won the Chicano Literary Contest at the University of California, Irvine. Even though she has only one collection in print, Viramontes has gained critical recognition and has been credited as being in the forefront of the growing feminist Chicana movement, which is changing both the way Chicanas write and how others view them.

Viramontes writes about the people she has known since her childhood, when she would "wake up at midnight and hear the voices and listen to the soft music, see the light under the door." There, in the house already filled with her parents, five sisters, and three brothers, late-night meetings and card games would take place among the adults, the visiting friends and relatives. In the morning, she would rise early and watch her mother go about stretching the limited food to fill all the hungry mouths.

Viramontes notes that her stories are colored by her father as well as by her mother: "[I]f my mother showed all that is good in being female, my father showed all that is bad in being male." This dichotomy is something that she has consciously considered, recognizing her own preconceived notions concerning gender and gendered roles. The struggles of Chicana women in Chicano households, in Chicano culture, and in society at large remain at the center of her creativity. The stories in *The Moths and Other Stories* (1985) constitute detailed examinations of the ways Chicana women suffer and how they endure.

In "Growing," Viramontes presents Naomi, an adolescent poised between childhood and maturity, between stickball and clandestine kisses. Naomi has unwittingly committed an offense, one without mitigating circumstances, in the eyes of her father and his culture. When she asks her father what this crime is, he "thunders" his response, "*TÚ ERES MUJER*" (you are a woman). Unable to understand why this is a crime and saddled with the task of chaperoning a younger sister who will one day face the same dilemma, Naomi for a moment longs to return to the days when her only decision was "what to play next." She wishes to forget "her age, her menstruations, her breasts." The condemnation of gender reaches beyond Naomi's father to their entire culture, which is patriarchal, and by extension to other patriarchal cultures. Naomi represents any woman confronted with male rules and condemnations, which cross borders and time to keep women in "their place." Despite Naomi's wistful thinking and her perceived notions about American life, not even in the United States do "parents trust their daughters," if those daughters happen to be Chicanas.

The title story, "The Moths," depicts a maturing girl's need for the society and support of other women. The girl in this story lacks the "female" skills of her sisters, their ability to crochet and to please their father through obedience and religion. Instead, she finds herself burdened with "bull hands" and an apparent inability to show her love to either her grandmother or her mother. Recalling each, she says, "I never kissed her."

In her father's house, this girl cannot join forces with her sisters or her mother because the divisive force of the father's expectations and judgments is too strong. Failing to live up to his expectations, she is overshadowed by her older sisters, who seem to embody all accepted and acceptable feminine virtues. It is only when she escapes to the home of her *abuelita* (grandmother) that she can find solace. Her grandmother helps her to reshape her hands and gives her tasks that those hands can accomplish—caring for a garden and for an invalid. She learns that there are womanly tasks that even her hands can accomplish and experiences an unstated warmth of familial acceptance. When her *abuelita* dies, the girl uses those hands to stroke the dead face and to take the body into the bath with her. She uses those hands to wash both of their bodies in a joint rite of passage: the grandmother's journey away from life, and the daughter's return to her mother, for whom she can now cry and feel longing. Finally, in grief, mother and daughter have something to share, something uncorrupted and incorruptible by patriarchal rules.

Two other young protagonists are presented in *The Moths and Other Stories*. Both face the question of abortion, although for very different reasons. Alice, in "Birthday," is in no position to care for or to rear a child on her own. Almost as soon as she tells her boyfriend, Mike, of her pregnancy, he makes it clear that abortion is the only option he is willing to consider. Her friend, Terry, older at twenty-one, gives her advice, personal testimony, and a clinic's telephone number. Even though the story allows Alice easy access to safe and legal abortion, the shock of having to make this decision is not lessened.

Abandoned by Mike, who does not give her support or financial assistance, and by the God she thinks is punishing her for "loving," Alice struggles to retain her composure at the clinic. Even as she prepares herself for the procedure, her inner monologue shows her turmoil as she discovers that she cannot love God or herself. She is losing her child, her religion, and her self-respect.

In "The Long Reconciliation," Viramontes introduces Amanda, who must make a decision similar to Alice's but who has even less support. Unlike Alice, Amanda is a married woman, although even her husband considers her as more of a child. The important thing to him is that she is "one that can

bear children." Sons are of vital importance to him as proof of his virility, and even his neighbors take an interest. When Amanda has not yet announced a pregnancy three months into the marriage, the neighbors are ready to declare her "useless."

Amanda actually is pregnant and is beginning to grow up. She recognizes that her husband has been cheated and that his land will not support a child since it barely supports the two of them. She turns to a priest for help and asks him why God is not helping his poor as he promised to do. The priest can only offer vague platitudes about woman's lot. In desperation, she chooses an abortion that ultimately ends not one life but four. The child's loss causes Amanda to lose her husband's love and forces her to turn to the man who cheated him, Don Joaquín, with whom she "begins to die." Her husband, Chato, abandons her and later realizes that he "never saw life again" after that day. Don Joaquín himself is killed by Chato. Amanda's action, meant to keep the child from suffering and to keep Chato and herself from suffering, merely changes the form that suffering takes. Chato cannot accept a woman "who acted like God" when he acts "like a man should."

In "The Broken Web," Viramontes tells the story of four women, each changed by the life and death of one man, Tomás. The four women are his wife, his daughter, his mistress, and his sister-in-law. Tomás is unfaithful to his wife, who recognizes too late that when men are unfaithful, God, who is a man, understands, but that no one understands when a woman is unfaithful. When she shoots her husband in self-defense, during a brutal beating, the bullet goes straight through him and hits a statue of Jesus. Viramontes thus shows the shattering of both the immediate physical and the more distant metaphysical male authorities by a woman who has been pushed too far.

The death, and especially the broken Jesus, haunt the woman's older daughter, Martha. Her aunt tries to explain the early courtship and marriage of Tomás and his wife so that Martha can escape her nightmares. The story is not a pleasant one, showing the mother to have had a closer relationship with Olivia, the mistress, than she would perhaps have wished to admit or have known. By seeking to explain the seemingly unexplainable, that which is beyond the help of the powerless priest whom Martha tries to ask for guidance in confession, the old aunt hopes to give her niece back the peace that the simultaneous deaths of her father and "Jesus" shattered.

Two of Viramontes' stories in *The Moths and Other Stories* address the subject of older women. The first, "Snapshots," tells the story of a woman who spent her life becoming the best possible wife and mother she could be, only to find herself as a divorced woman with a grown child. She has perfected a role that is of no use to anyone and now sees her role-playing as wasted effort.

The second story about an older woman is "Neighbors," in which a woman finds herself at the mercy of young men. Aura has lived her life peaceably with her neighbors and only desires that they should live peaceably with her. Driven to distraction by the pain in her aged body, she calls the police to come and take away the young men who laughingly refuse to give her the quiet she needs. Even as the police arrive, she realizes her mistake. When the gang members, the Bixby Boys, return to take their promised revenge. Aura's first solace is the thought, "I'm so glad I'm going to die soon." Her further attempts to defend herself only lead to more tragedy.

The most poignant story in the collection is "Cariboo Cafe." In this story, a Salvadorana (woman from El Salvador) who has lost her small son to death squads in her native country finds a lost boy and believes, with all the anguish of her desolate motherhood, that this boy is her Geraldo. The child is not hers: He is the child of other illegal immigrants. When his six-year-old sister, a latchkey child caring for her younger brother while their parents work, loses the key to their apartment, the two children are suddenly forced into the open, fleeing from the police they have been taught to fear as agents of *la Migra* (the immigration authorities). Even when the Salvadorana grabs at "her" son, his sister never lets go of his hand.

The two female characters are united by their claims on the boy, although neither seems to understand what the other represents. The Salvadorana makes plans to return to her home, to the way life was before her son was lost. She is so happy that the idea that her old world is not safe for either of them never seems to cross her mind. Tragically, her new world is not safe either. The owner of a café who has turned other immigrants over to the authorities remembers seeing the two children's pictures on television. Although his thoughts return again and again to his own dead son, Jojo, he does not seem to have any sympathy for the parents of these two missing children, and by extension the Salvadorana, nor does he make an effort to get involved until he must.

This time, however, the authorities are faced not with frightened factory girls but with an angry mother on the defensive. She has lost her son once and will not do so again. Nothing the men can do will persuade her to let him go now that she has found him again, and they are not willing to negotiate. It never occurs to her that she is mistaken, that this is another child. If the police wish to take this boy, as they took "him" before, they must go through her. Even though they are supposed to be rescuing the children, one policeman ignores the proximity of the children—the Salvadorana is clutching one of the boy's hands, and his sister has a tight hold on the other hand—and shoots the woman point blank in the face.

The United States and El Salvador thus become equivalent countries in which the police and other authorities are dangerous to the common people. The two countries are places where children can disappear and suffer from violence. In El Salvador, children are made to work among corpses; in the United States, they are forced to watch a woman who has fed, bathed, and housed them have her head blown off, and they are made to suffer her blood and brains being spilled over them. The two countries are places where women have little chance to speak and less chance to be heard, where they cannot defend their children from criminals, from danger, or from the police. This inability to protect their children is the worst suffering that Chicana women must endure. They do not have the power, the training, or the temperament to fight.

The Moths and Other Stories encompasses a range of the Chicanas' trials. Faced with authority in the form of family, church, *la Migra* and tradition, they must endure because they know no other way, because they are not offered choices, and because they have duties. Using multiple voices, stream-of-consciousness narrative, and elements of magic, Viramontes brings her characters' strengths and weaknesses before her readers, showing the Chicanas she presents to be human and fallible, and therefore, also valiant, genuine, and worthy of love and of respect. Viramontes' Chicanas live and grow.

THE STORYTELLER

Author: Mario Vargas Llosa (1936-   )
Type of work: Novel
Type of plot: Philosophical realism
Time of plot: The 1950's to the 1980's
Locale: Lima, Peru; the Peruvian Amazon; and Florence, Italy
First published: *El hablador*, 1987 (English translation, 1989)

Principal Characters

The narrator, a middle-aged Peruvian writer who is similar to and virtually a stand-in for the author. He is a novelist, essayist, and television writer and producer. A consummate intellectual, he is defined by his ideas and his intellectual pursuits; little else of his life is portrayed. The narrator is a man driven by curiosity and his need to clarify mysteries that have hung over his life for decades. His fascination with and affection for his old friend Saúl resulted in a void when Saúl retreated from the narrator's life. The narrator's sense of loss and rejection translate into a nearly obsessive desire for answers, about both Saúl and the Machiguengan people. As a writer, he believes that satisfaction will come through his writing, and he sets for himself the challenge of coming to a logical understanding of what has transpired over the years.

Saúl Zuratas, a striking, tall man with bright red hair and a consistently disheveled appearance. As a Peruvian Jew, he is somewhat marginalized from the social mainstream. Furthermore, he has an enormous purplish birthmark covering half his face. He has great interest in and sympathy for others who are threatened or marginalized, including endangered peoples and cultures such as the Machiguengas of the Peruvian Amazon. Saúl's nickname, "Mascarita," or "Mask-face," appropriately conveys his detached, distant quality. He is committed to his studies and increasingly to the history of and issues surrounding the indigenous peoples of the Amazon. A fierce debater, Saúl strongly expresses his views to his friend, the novel's narrator, and does not hesitate to let their intellectual differences come between them. Ultimately, Saúl disappears from the narrator's life and becomes something between a memory and a phantom.

The Storyteller, the narrative voice of the novel's interspersed chapters relating the beliefs and customs of the Machiguengas. The storyteller is a wise and humble man who speaks in a simple, unassertive language that conveys important information without self-consciousness or sophistication. The storyteller has learned all he knows by listening to the Machiguengas. He ultimately takes no responsibility for the stories he tells, following anecdotes and bits of lore with the disclaimer, "That, anyway, is what I have learned." The storyteller relates his fears, emotions, and doubts with candor and a touch of humor. As a storyteller, his life is one of wandering among the jungle from community to community, accompanied by his mascot, a disfigured parrot that sits on his shoulder, regaling his listeners with stories that last for hours on end. He tells of his facial marking and his acceptance into the tribe. It is strongly suggested, but never specifically confirmed, that the storyteller is actually Saúl Zuratas; within the world of the novel, however, they are presented and function as two distinct characters.

Tasurinchi, the benevolent Machiguenga creator. The Machiguengas believe that their god is evident in each male, so in referring to one another, and in recounting their stories, they call each man Tasurinchi, differentiating among them with identifiers such as "Tasurinchi, the herb doctor" or

"Tasurinchi, the one who used to live by the Mitaya and now lives in the forest up the Yavero." Tasurinchi is many different characters; the use of the name unifies them into a coherent persona. Tasurinchi is a generally good man who takes lessons from the world around him, lords over his wife, and avoids contact with white people. He has a deathly fear of sneezes, knowing from experience that the white man's common cold means tragedy for the Machiguengas.

The Schneils, a husband-and-wife team of American linguists working with the Machiguengas.

Don Salomón, Saúl Zuratas' aging father.

The Novel

The Storyteller is an intriguing, often disturbing exploration of the Machiguengas, a real, indigenous nomadic tribe in the Peruvian Amazon, and of the encroachment of modern life and values into their environment and culture. Mario Vargas Llosa frames this exploration as a quest for information about both the tribe and a Jewish student from Lima who may have been absorbed into it.

The narrator resembles Vargas Llosa himself. Like the author, he is a Peruvian novelist who vacations in Florence, Italy, and who once hosted a Peruvian television magazine. Although the narrator is never explicitly identified as Vargas Llosa, such identification is neither denied nor contradicted. Within the fictional world, many factual particulars of the novel suggest that it is written in the author's own voice.

At the beginning of the novel, the narrator, on vacation in Florence and immersed in a reading of the works of Dante, wanders into a photographic exhibit on the Machiguengas, an indigenous people of eastern Peru. The tribe has long fascinated him and once played a central role in an ongoing debate he had with a friend at the university, Saúl Zuratas. In one of the photos, the narrator sees a native storyteller who strongly resembles Saúl. This prompts an account by the narrator of the two students' friendship.

Saúl was an intense young Jewish man with an enormous purplish birthmark that covered half his face and earned him the nickname La Mascarita, or Mask-face. He was deeply concerned about the survival of indigenous peoples in Peru and had strong criticism for those who sought to evangelize, assimilate, or "culturally advance" such peoples under the guise of scientific, anthropological, and linguistic research. Saúl turned down a lucrative scholarship to study in France, choosing instead to remain with his aging father and continue his studies in Peru.

The narrator and Saúl shared discussions on many issues, including the Machiguengan people. The narrator found Saúl's views too strident. The narrator went to study in Europe; although he tried to maintain contact, he never heard from Saúl again. Upon returning to Peru, the narrator learned that Saúl and his ailing father supposedly had moved to Israel.

The account of the students' relationship is rendered in a speculative, impressionistic fashion. Few scenes or conversations are presented in detail; all is filtered through memory and, to a degree, emotion. Plot and action are outpaced by a wealth of information and meditation on the Machiguengas, Peruvian politics, and modern life.

Interwoven into the account of Saúl Zuratas are chapters written in the voice of the Machiguengan *hablador*, or traditional storyteller. In these chapters, Vargas Llosa employs a language that is at once naïve and wise, suiting Machiguengan lore, beliefs, and rituals. The storyteller describes Kientibakori, the spirit of evil; Kashiri, the sometimes benevolent; the seripigari, or wise men; the Viracochas, or dangerous outsiders; and Tasurinchi, the Machiguengan creator whose name is also used to refer to any Machiguengan man.

The storyteller chapters relate story after story of Tasurinchi after Tasurinchi: their family relationships, their lifestyles, and the lessons they have learned from the environment and animals that surround them. Some of the stories are amusingly scatological, while others clearly establish the Machiguengan cosmogony. The Machiguengan people come into focus as a loose society of wanderers, "the men that walk," believing that their walking keeps the sun in the sky. In addition, the storyteller relates his own experiences as the link among the scattered Tasurinchis.

As the novel alternates between the narrator's account and the storyteller's tales, the two sequences, already linked by the photograph in Florence, begin to merge. The narrator describes his interest in Machiguengan storytellers and the unavailability of pertinent information. In the early 1980's, as host of a television program called *The Tower of Babel*, he ventured back into the jungle to report on the Machiguengas. There he encountered the Schneils, a husband-and-wife team of American linguists working with the Summer Institute for Linguistics. He had met them once before: It was Edwin Schneil who had first mentioned Machiguengan storytellers to the narrator. During this later visit, to the narrator's amazement, Schneil described an "albino" storyteller with a large birthmark on his face. In speaking with a Jewish coworker, the narrator also discovered that Saúl did not go to Israel as rumored. After his father's death, he disappeared.

In the following chapter, the storyteller relates how he found that vocation. He refers somewhat cryptically to his birthmark, his previous life elsewhere, his acceptance among the Tasurinchis, and his transformation from a studious listener to an itinerant teller of stories. It is strongly suggested, though not explicitly articulated, that the storyteller is Saúl Zuratas.

By the end of the novel, the narrator returns to the present moment in Florence, where he repeatedly visits the photography exhibit to view the singular image. He contemplates his friend's destiny, puts together the pieces of the puzzle he has been investigating, and decides for himself that the storyteller in the photograph is none other than his lost friend Saúl Zuratas, La Mascarita.

Analysis

The Storyteller questions the basic values of modern, Western culture by placing it in direct juxtaposition with the Machiguengas. Organizations such as the Summer Institute of Linguistics (a real entity) are charged with the disruption of natural prerogatives. In researching indigenous peoples of the Amazon, they appropriate native languages and ways while imposing Christianity, technology, and the Spanish language. Also implicit is criticism of the destruction perpetrated on precarious natural habitats such as the Amazon jungle. Vargas Llosa offers an evenhanded examination of these issues and effectively avoids sentimentalizing the plight of indigenous peoples. The questions, nevertheless, loom large over the novel.

Balance is a key element in *The Storyteller*. The alternating narrative voices balance one another, as do their respective cultures. Saúl and the narrator are balanced in their friendship and discussions. Saúl, the arrogant, impenetrable Jewish university student, contrasts sharply with the wise, humble, and candid Machiguengan storyteller that he allegedly has become. Machiguengan history is compared to Jewish history, with the storyteller recounting Biblical cosmology in Machiguengan terms. The narrator's journey into the heart of Machiguengan culture is placed in relief against the often-unwilling journey of Tasurinchi into knowledge about the world outside the Amazon jungle. For Vargas Llosa, transformation requires balance; the worlds of modern Peru and the traditional Machiguengas can only meet through slow and mutual accommodation and respect.

The novel is concerned with what is right. In the same way as Saúl and the narrator search intellectually for ethical ways of interpreting their world, the various Tasurinchis and the Machiguengan people as a whole strive to make the world right. Their entire cosmology makes sense of a natural world often riddled with contradictions, and they are aware of how human words and acts put natural elements and heavenly bodies out of order.

In such a world, the storyteller is essential as a preserver of order. Among a people whose mandate is to wander incessantly, the storyteller is a link to the past, to the environment, and to the whole community. He is also the retainer and definer of the indigenous language (even if he, as suggested, is not a native speaker himself). Storytelling becomes a much larger cultural institution: It is the foundation of society.

The power of storytelling grows further when considered in the context of the novel as a whole. Vargas Llosa, through his narrator, sets out to learn about the Machiguengas, to create a stylistically viable language for them, and to tell their story as part of his own. In doing so, he highlights his own role as a storyteller in Latin American culture. His invocation of Franz Kafka and his reading of Dante in Florence place his present writing in the tradi-

tion of Western literature. At the same time, he is asserting not only the need for inclusion (rather than appropriation) of native history and culture, but also the speculative quality that such inclusion must take. Vargas Llosa cannot solve the mystery for certain: If the storyteller is indeed Saúl, he is inaccessible to his old friend. Machiguengan stories are inherently incompatible with Peruvian novels, so the storyteller chapters are by necessity inventions, and the coincidences—the birthmark and the recounting of Jewish history among them—are, by the rules of the game, not clues encountered in the narrator's investigation but rather manufactured results of an intellectual process. Thus, Vargas Llosa's efforts to inform and stimulate certainly succeed, but whether the two worlds do or can meet—and whether or not the elusive Machiguengan storyteller is indeed a transformed Saúl Zuratas—is a question that the reader, like the narrator, must in the end decide.

Critical Context

Vargas Llosa has always drawn from personal experience to document the injustices and uncertainties of life in modern Peru. His earliest novels, *La ciudad y los perros* (1962; *The Time of the Hero*, 1966) and *La casa verde* (1966; *The Green House*, 1968), explore themes of repression and corruption in the military academy of his adolescence and a small jungle town of his youth. *Conversación en la catedral* (1969; *Conversation in the Cathedral*, 1975) is a panoramic portrait of Peru in the 1940's and 1950's under the dictator Manuel Odria. In these early novels, Vargas Llosa began to experiment with an interweaving, nonlinear narrative style.

His next two novels, *Pantaleón y las visitadoras* (1973; *Captain Pantoja and the Special Service*, 1978) and *La tía Julia y el escribidor* (1977; *Aunt Julia and the Scriptwriter*, 1982), incorporate hu-

mor and farce and draw on the author's knowledge of military life and the television industry. Both use the technique of incorporating fictional documentary material into the body of the novel.

With *La guerra del fin del mundo* (1981; *The War of the End of the World*, 1984) and *Historia de Mayta* (1984; *The Real Life of Alejandro Mayta*, 1986), Vargas Llosa returned to his serious, political writing, focusing on turn-of-the-century religious zealotry in Brazil and contemporary radicalism in Peru. For Vargas Llosa, writing is a political act; in 1990, the author ran unsuccessfully for the presidency of Peru. *The Storyteller*, not surprisingly, gives evidence of the political leader that Vargas Llosa has become, concerned with the larger issues confronting Peruvian government, society, and culture.

STRONG WIND

Author: Miguel Ángel Asturias (1899-1974)
Type of work: Novel
Type of plot: Social criticism
Time of plot: The early twentieth century
Locale: An unnamed Latin American country; Chicago, Illinois; and New York City
First published: *Viento fuerte*, 1950 (English translation, 1968)

Principal Characters

Lester Mead (Cosi, Lester Stoner), the millionaire organizer of a banana growers' cooperative in an unnamed Latin American country. He left his life as a millionaire for adventure in the tropics. Under the name of Cosi, he is an itinerant salesman of sewing supplies. After his marriage to Leland Foster, he became known as Lester Mead. He buys land and becomes an independent banana grower. When the Tropical Banana Company (Tropbanana) refuses to buy the independent growers' bananas, he organizes them into a cooperative. He goes to Tropbanana headquarters to try to convince the company executives to stop exploiting the banana growers. When members of his cooperative are jailed for heading an uprising against Tropbanana, he bribes an official to release them. Under his true identity as Lester Stoner, millionaire and major stockholder in Tropbanana, he travels to New York City to urge stockholders to pressure the company to treat the growers justly and honestly and thereby ensure for themselves a profitable and stable investment. When he returns to his banana farm, he is killed by the strong wind conjured up to destroy Tropbanana.

Adelaido Lucero, an overseer on a banana plantation. He saves his money to buy land for his sons. They become Mead's partners in the independent banana growers' cooperative. His son Juan is imprisoned for leading an uprising against Tropbanana.

Leland Foster, the wife of Lester mead. She dies with him in the strong wind. She does not realize that her husband is a millionaire until their trip to New York.

Sarajobalda, an old witch. Her beating and rape at the hands of representatives of Tropbanana trigger the uprising led by Juan Lucero and Bastiancito Cojubul.

Rito Perraj, the shaman who conjures up the strong wind to satisfy Hermenegilo Puac's desire for vengeance on Tropbanana for refusing to buy his crop.

Bastiancito Cojubul, a highlander who migrated with his wife to the coast to become a banana grower. He is arrested with Juan Lucero for the rebellion against Tropbanana.

The Green Pope, the president of Tropical Banana Company. He orders the company's representatives to stop buying bananas from the growers. He maintains that the stockholders are only interested in dividends and would not be upset if they knew that the company's profits came from exploitation of the growers.

The Novel

The antagonist in *Strong Wind* is Tropbanana, a North American fruit company. The novel begins as Tropbanana is establishing banana plantations on the Pacific coast of an unnamed Latin American country. Adelaido Lucero is one of many natives of the highlands drawn to work in the great enterprise of taming the tropical lowlands and carving plantations from them. He remains in the company town, marries, and rears his family there. He will work for the company all his life, but he buys land for his sons so that they will be able to be independent.

Lester Mead, an American, also buys land, and he, along with Lucero's now grown sons, finds himself in conflict with Tropbanana. These independent growers prospered while the company bought their bananas at a good price. When the company decides to cut the price by more than half, however, Mead refuses to sell at a loss. He goes to Chicago to talk to the head of the company, but he fails to win any concessions for the independent growers.

When Mead returns to the plantations, he suggests that the independent growers form a coopera-tive. The efforts of the members of the cooperative to preserve their independence from the company form the core of the novel.

The company retaliates by taking over all the cooperative's markets and then has two of the cooperative members arrested during a demonstra-tion of workers who are protesting against the company's policies. Mead finds that the only way to secure their release is through bribery: There is no legal recourse, and the company controls the press and the government.

By the end of *Strong Wind*, neither the company nor the growers have won a clear victory. The growers still own their land, and the company still controls its plantations. The strong wind of the title has devastated the land, however, and has claimed the lives of Lester Mead and his wife.

Analysis

The central theme of *Strong Wind* is anti-imperialism. The plot revolves around the struggle of local growers to maintain their dignity and independence in the face of the power of Tropba-nana. By not naming a real place or company, Asturias has extended his attack to all monopolistic exploitation in all of Latin America.

In this novel of the independent growers' strug-gle against the company, which initiates his banana trilogy—the other novels in the trilogy are *El papa verde* (1954; *The Green Pope*, 1971) and *Los ojos de los enterrados* (1960; *The Eyes of the Interred*, 1973)—Asturias anticipates the rebellion of the workers that will occur in *The Eyes of the Interred*. Mead says that the members of the cooperative may not see the fruits of their struggle but that those who will follow them will benefit. Thus, the theme of the endurance of the people, the hope that even-tually justice will triumph in spite of the odds, underlies the action of the novel.

Mead proposes changes in the company man-agement to other stockholders in terms of educated self-interest. To protect their investment and guar-antee a stable source of profits, they must curtail the abuses by the company. He is not a pure idealist seeking only the welfare of the exploited; rather, he seeks solutions that will benefit all involved, investors as well as workers and independent growers. The strong wind that takes the lives of Mead and his wife implies the inadequacy of these solutions. A greater force for change must blow through the plantations.

Although he portrays many Americans who work for the company negatively, Asturias has not written an anti-American novel. The main charac-ter, Lester Mead, is an American who transcends stereotypes and struggles for justice and dignity for all people. Mead is portrayed as very human. He loves his wife and is drawn to a woman whom he meets in the capital. He rails against injustice, struggles with his frustrations, and cares for his friends.

In addition to the social themes that are domi-nant in the work, nature, myth, and magic are present as powerful forces throughout the novel. Nature is a force to be confronted, not merely a setting or background. The tropical coastlands must be put to the service of humanity, and nature must be respected. Myth and magic, so much a part of the lives of the native people, are also to be respected and put to service. Sarajobalda, the witch, and Rito Perraj, the shaman, are sought out by the people for solutions to all manner of problems. Asturias affirms the importance of magic by having the strong wind, the force of nature, summoned by the magic of Rito Perraj. People are not merely social creatures in contact with one another; they must maintain relationships with nature and with the magical reality that surrounds them.

Critical Context

The work of Miguel Ángel Asturias was more widely known in Europe and Latin America than in the United States prior to 1967, the year in which Asturias was awarded the Nobel Prize in Literature. Increased interest in his work then prompted the translation of *Strong Wind* into English in 1968. The other works of the banana trilogy, which *Strong Wind* initiates, were translated soon afterward. *Strong Wind*, along with the rest of the trilogy, represents the height of Asturias' social concern. Although it is related to his other works in its shared characters and the common theme of anti-imperialism, *Strong Wind* can be read profitably without recourse to the other two books of the trilogy.

Strong Wind has not received the critical attention accorded to Asturias' widely acclaimed first novel, *El señor presidente* (1946; *The President*, 1963), or *Hombres de maíz* (1949; *Men of Maize*, 1975). Less innovative and less concerned with myth than are his earlier works, *Strong Wind* represents Asturias' turn toward realism as a vehicle for social commentary. Much of the criticism of *Strong Wind* reflects the posture of the critic with regard to "committed" literature, literature written with a social purpose. Critics who value such committed literature fault *Strong Wind* for excessive allusions to myth and popular beliefs, which, they claim, dilute the direct impact of the novel's social message. Others attack the work as journalistic because its social theme overshadows the artistic elements.

Strong Wind is not limited to social realism. Because the social reality he presents is in intimate contact with nature and its forces, and because the people about whom he writes attribute tremendous power to myth and magic, Asturias has produced a novel of social realism, Magical Realism, and nature.

A SUMMER LIFE

Author: Gary Soto (1952-   )
Type of work: Memoir
First published: 1990

Principal Personages

Gary Soto, a typical boy, full of mischief, curiosity, and adventure. Two issues in particular concern and disappoint him. First, he discovers that except in wrestling, he is unskilled in athletics. Second, he is not particularly attractive, which leads to awkwardness around girls. The fact that he marries and becomes a successful writer and professor, however, proves his adolescent worries to be ephemeral.

Rick Soto, Gary's brother, two years older. He plays cruel tricks on Gary, punches him, and snatches his glasses. Throughout their teens, there is no evidence of closeness between the two brothers, yet Soto dedicates *A Summer Life* to Rick, suggesting that they may have grown more compatible as adults.

Debra Soto, the only girl in the family. From the age of four or five, Debra is a "little lady," first painting her tiny nails and gradually progressing to makeup. She also appears to be Gary's closest sibling. The two of them are able to work together on a school project or sit on the porch, eating fruit, without fighting. In addition, Debra is helpful and motherly. She entertains the fourth child, the baby brother, when no one else will, and teaches Gary an innovative way to tie his shoes.

Mrs. Soto, a working-class mother, juggling her various factory jobs with the responsibilities of homemaking. It is quite likely that corporal punishment is the only discipline she knows. On the whole, Mrs. Soto is a protective mother who establishes safety rules and invents stories, such as that of the dogs on Sarah Street, to protect her children. She appears to enjoy her family. Her pleasure in her children is seen when she sings popular songs along with them and treats them to a drive-in movie when they have been especially good.

Shorty, Gary's uncle, a war veteran who probably retains heinous memories of his time in Korea. Having returned safely, he wishes to put the war behind him. For a while, he resides with the Sotos. He enjoys entertaining the children. He takes pride in displaying his panther tattoo, which evokes awe in the children, but shows no desire to relate war tales. He moves from familiar Fresno to Los Angeles, where he finds work in a foundry.

Grandfather, a lover of money as well as avocados. Green is his favorite color, as it is the color of dollar bills. Apparently not trusting American banks, Grandfather, a native of Mexico, keeps the cash he earns at a raisin factory safely tucked behind calendars, inside sofas, and in his clothing. He misses Mexico and blames the slow development of his avocado tree on the fact that the wind is blocked by tall buildings; in Mexico, he says, buildings "grew" only so tall, allowing the sun and wind to reach the growing plants.

The Work

A book for children, *A Summer Life* consists of three parts, each containing thirteen memoirs concerning Soto's childhood and adolescence in the industrial section of Fresno, California. Part 1 takes place when Soto is four and five years old, prior to his admission to kindergarten, the event that would take him from the protection and circumscription of early childhood to the greater freedom of his school years. Part 2 takes Soto from the age of six (following his initiation into school) to about twelve, and part 3 covers his years from junior high school to the age of seventeen.

Although at first glance the autobiographical narratives seem like a series of unconnected scenarios, a closer reading reveals a theme of emotional as well as chronological maturity running through the work as a whole, with an overall tone of optimism. There is a loosely woven pattern within each part. Part 1, for example, begins and ends on a note of security and peace. The first story, "The Buddha," concerns a ceramic statue of Buddha that Soto's Uncle Shorty brought home from the Korean War. Thinking that the Buddha, with its huge, gilded belly, is one of the most beautiful objects he has ever seen, Soto carries the statue everywhere, wiping the dust from its face and regarding it as a mentor, using it to help reinforce his parents' rules. When approaching busy Van Ness Avenue, Soto tells Buddha, "We can't go over there," as if the silent agreement of the icon will strengthen his own reserve.

The second story in part 1 describes Soto's grandfather, a model of patience and optimism. Loving avocados, Grandfather plants his own tree, tends it faithfully, and waits twenty years for it to bear fruit, never doubting that one day it will.

Part 1 ends in the narrative entitled "The Shirt." Uncle Shorty, a Korean War veteran, owns a polo shirt that young Soto especially admires because it does not require fussing with buttons. One of his happiest moments, and the scene with which part 1 ends, occurs when Uncle Shorty rinses his dusty polo shirt with the garden hose, allows it to dry in the sun, and then lets his nephew wear it around the house and even outside on the block. Seemingly trivial things, such as the Buddha and the shirt (both connected with Uncle Shorty), lend joy, structure, and stability to the life of the young child.

Between the second and last stories in part 1, however, are episodes signifying adventure to a curious five-year-old. Although at this stage Soto's physical world is circumscribed by parental mandates—he is not allowed to cross the street and is permitted to play only on his own block—it is not without danger and daring. For example, there is a

railroad track near the Sotos' home. By placing a large rock on the track, five-year-old Gary thinks he can make the train derail and burst into flames, igniting the nearby houses and a pickle factory. He is mildly surprised and disappointed when nothing happens. In another episode, Gary and his brother and sister deliberately set fire to a stack of newspapers in the living room. Fortunately, the fire extinguishes itself, but the children attribute a near escape from death or serious injury to the brother's self-proclaimed mastery of magic

Part 1 relates the days of Soto's early childhood, with its restraints and emblems of security; part 2 is transitional. Soto is growing up, enjoying greater physical freedom and a wider range of activities, such as a pool party and many afternoons of swimming and playing board games at the neighborhood park. The majority of the stories in this section concern rites of passage that most children undergo as they progress from middle childhood into their teens. The pool party, related in the first episode, "The Inner Tube," is Soto's first "grown up" party, consisting of more than birthday cake and ice cream. Other indications of sophistication and maturity include his first theft (a pie from a neighborhood grocery); his first confession; and the fascination of his sister, Debra, who is close in age, with rock stars, jewelry, cosmetics, and her own developing body. The final story in part 2 concerns Debra getting her first boyfriend, which epitomizes her being grown up.

In part 2, Soto begins to develop a moral conscience and sensitivity toward creatures. He is sorry, for example, for not sharing his stolen pie with a neighbor and is scrupulous about remembering all of his sins in the confessional. Whereas he used to delight in squashing red ants, he now feels contrite for neglecting a pet hen, which is seized by a cat, and shrinks from the sight of a gasping, newly caught fish.

Despite his new experiences and personal growth, however, Soto is still a child. This is particularly evident in "The Haircut." An older boy trims Soto's hair in a supposedly fashionable style, but the effort is not successful. Consequently, Mrs. Soto recuts his hair, so short that the blue tint of his skull shows through. The significance of short and long hair may carry over from Soto's poem "*Black Hair*," in which he associates long, flowing hair with freedom and the beginning of manhood. In *A Summer Life*, the cropping of his hair can be interpreted as a check on his growth: He must not grow up too soon or acquire too much freedom, but must remain a boy for a few more years. The blueness of his skull suggests the skin of a newborn, while its "bumpiness," which Soto laments, is reminiscent of newly budding antlers on the head of a young buck.

During the years of part 2, Soto's father, fairly prominent in part 1, dies in an industrial accident, an incident that Soto does not describe. He simply states that his father died. After more than two years, his mother remarries, but the narrator portrays his stepfather only as an indolent man who consumes beer after beer while sitting in front of the television, glaring critically at the Beatles, who, he thinks, resemble girls.

Part 3 begins and ends with references to war,

a concern of many young men, especially during the time of conscription. In the first memoir, "The Hero," Tony, Soto's baseball coach, whom he regards as a role model, declares his wish to die for the president. By the end of part 3, Soto himself, now seventeen years old, is contemplating his own role in Vietnam.

The undercurrent of impending conscription or enlistment runs through all the youthful concerns of Soto and his best friend, Scott: worries about their appearance, the desire to attract girls, learning to drive, and debates over which rock group is best. Again Soto mentions having his hair cropped, this time at the insistence of his stepfather, who thinks long-haired boys look like hippies. Both Soto and Scott seem optimistic about their probable future in Vietnam. Each assures the other that he will not die in battle. Perhaps the optimism of Soto's grandfather regarding the slow growth of his avocado tree has made an impact on his grandson's attitude toward life.

Analysis

Soto wrote *A Summer Life* primarily for Mexican American children, in an attempt to make them realize that their lives and experiences (some of which are quite similar to those of all American children) are worth writing about. In the long run, he hoped to inspire some of these young Chicanos to become writers themselves, sharing their culture with the rest of the nation. In an interview with Nancy Needham, a staff writer for *National Education Association Today*, Soto claimed that his children's stories were the first written specifically for Mexican American youngsters and that Mexican Americans as a group were not writers.

To portray the physical world of Mexican Americans in industrial Fresno, Soto uses a number of oft-repeated visual and tactile images that emphasize the hot climate of the city: the constantly beating sun, asphalt that turns soft and sticky from the heat, swarms of mosquitoes and red ants, hair saturated with perspiration and dust,

sweat and dirt in the creases of necks and elbows, and his mother's glasses steaming up as she prepares a hot Mexican meal of beans and tortillas, despite the weather. In addition to portraying the climate of Fresno, Soto injects a realistic sense of danger and enmity in this area of factories, diesel trucks, and workers struggling to subsist.

In his adult poetry, Soto frequently presents city streets—especially in the poorer parts of town—as being odious and dangerous. This literary characteristic carries over into his autobiographical narrative for children. Braly Street, on which the Sotos live, consists of factories, run-down houses, and a junkyard. Its sidewalks, gutters, and road are littered with paper trash, bottle caps, and broken glass. On one end of the block is busy Van Ness Avenue (on which the pet dog of one of Soto's uncles lost its life), and on the other end is Sarah Street, the setting for "The Bike," in part 1. Wishing to keep her five-year-old son in sight, Mrs. Soto tells Gary not to ride his two-wheeler onto Sarah Street, warning that there are hungry dogs there that devour little boys on bikes. Letting his curiosity get the better of him, Gary rides around the corner onto Sarah Street anyway, encountering not a dog but a boy about his own age riding a tricycle. Considering this boy to be a "baby," Gary challenges him to ride over his (Soto's) leg. This dare results in a badly skinned and bruised ankle. Although the "accident" is the consequence of Soto's own doing, the incident nevertheless casts Sarah Street as a sinister place in which one might get hurt. Even as Soto grows older and acquires more freedom, the streets are still sites of danger. He relates several episodes in which he narrowly escapes being hit by cars as he rides his bike through the heavy traffic.

Soto writes in the first person, matter of factly and without moral judgment. In his adult recollection of the fire-setting incident, for example, he does not comment that the attempt to use "magic" might have destroyed a home and three young lives. Nor does he reflect on the fact that tampering with railroad property is a federal offense.

Although all Soto's children's stories contain a subtle angst, or tone of fear and anxiety, that adult readers can easily perceive, children rarely pick up on it. Despite their lives filled with poverty and danger, Soto's characters in *A Summer Life* almost always seem to be happy and carefree. This is probably because the author deletes traumatic and disappointing occurrences. For example, he does not directly recount the death of his father, but simply states in part 2 that two years after his father died, his mother remarried. Similarly, when twelve-year-old Debra gets a boyfriend, Soto does not narrate his sister's probable disappointment when the relationship breaks up, an almost inevitable consequence of very young love. Finally, he avoids discussion of the horrendous realities of war. Uncle Shorty comes back from the Korean War tired but not inclined to retell his ordeal. All he brings home with him, that the children can see, is the statue of Buddha, a relic of beauty from the East. Furthermore, although Soto and Scott realize that they could die in Vietnam, their innocence makes death appear as a remote possibility; thus, they look forward to a full life ahead.

Critical Context

Although Soto is primarily a poet for adults, he began writing children's books in 1985. Many Chicanos who belong to the class of unskilled labor see themselves as living on the fringe of society, rather than in the mainstream; therefore, they assume that their lives have little value or interest to Americans at large. Young people, in particular, frequently feel doomed to a future in a factory job. In his children's books *Living Up the Street* (1985), *Baseball in April* (1990), and *A Summer Life*, Soto strives to change this negative attitude by bringing out the beauty of Chicano life, such as the closeness of the extended family often lacking among other groups, as well as its commonalities with American culture as a whole. Since his characters are similar to his readers, his stories cover familiar topics and may encourage reading on the part of children who are unaccustomed to regarding books as sources of entertainment. For children whose primary language is Spanish, Soto has adapted to stories from *A Summer Life*—"The Inner Tube" and "The Bike"—into films. The scripts are in Spanish, and all the actors are Mexican American. Both the books and the films help young Chicanos to believe that they are important and have something to share with the rest of America.

Soto's works have also filled a gap in children's literature. During the past several decades, authors have begun including African and Asian American characters in their works, dispelling the stereotypes associated with these ethnic groups. Mexican Americans remained underrepresented. Perhaps *A Summer Life*, along with Soto's other children's books, will help to make young readers more aware of this particular group of American citizens.

TATTOO THE WICKED CROSS

Author: Floyd Salas (1931-   )
Type of work: Novel
Type of plot: Social realism
Time of plot: After World War II
Locale: Golden Gate Institute of Industry and Reform, a prison farm in California
First published: 1967

Principal Characters

Aaron D'Aragon, a Latino adolescent, a pachuco, and a gang leader sent to prison for fighting. He is the protagonist of the novel. Although Aaron is small for his age, he is quite a fighter, like a bantam rooster. Upon entering prison, he is not sure of himself and is intimidated by the director of the prison. He looks forward to seeing an ally while he is in prison, his good friend Barneyway. He hears disturbing rumors that Barneyway is a "queen." Aaron's main tormentor is Buzzer, a cruel and ruthless prison leader. Aaron is raped by Buzzer and his gang, and Aaron vows to Barneyway that they will no longer be victims of Buzzer and his gang. Aaron must reconcile his religious beliefs, which say to "turn the other cheek." He decides to take revenge on Buzzer and his gang by poisoning them, but he inadvertently kills Barneyway as well. Because of these acts of murder, he gains the respect and attention of the other inmates, and he begins to serve his time with dignity.

Buzzer, the antagonist of the story. Buzzer represents evil, and Aaron represents good. Buzzer is ruthless and mean, and anyone who crosses his path is dealt with severely. Aaron wants nothing to do with him, but eventually Aaron is brutally sodomized and beaten by Buzzer and his gang. After being hospitalized because of the beating, Aaron feels humiliated, not so much because of the beating but because he has been "gang banged." Buzzer has always had his way and does not think he has anything to fear from Aaron, but he does not reckon with Aaron's fierceness.

Barneyway, Aaron's friend. Barneyway was quite a fighter and tough guy on the streets, but in prison he fell victim to Buzzer's ruthlessness and became a "queen." He learns how to survive in the cruel prison system. Even though he has become a victim of Buzzer and the prison system, Aaron continues to be his friend. Because of Buzzer, their friendship is not the same as it was on the streets.

Rattler, a member of Buzzer's gang. Although he too can be ruthless and cruel, he is only a shadow to Buzzer.

Big Stoop, the brutal giant who runs the institution with a conviction that he is right and the prisoners are wrong. He believes that harsh treatment will strengthen the prisoners' character. He is unaware that the prison system has made him a cruel overseer.

Judith, Aaron's girlfriend. She represents the stabilizing element in Aaron's life while in prison. Aaron thinks that she has failed him because she appears for a visit with a tattoo on her cheek. She is no longer a symbol of purity and virtue. There is a close connection between the way Aaron feels toward Judith and the way he feels about his mother's death. He thinks that his mother was taken away by God unfairly and that he has been betrayed by Judith. Aaron believes that he has nothing to hold on to anymore.

The prison chaplain, a Protestant minister who is weak and effete. Ostensibly he is there to save the souls of the young men, but he is no spiritual leader. In fact, the chaplain is in the service of the state because he acts as an informant. Aaron hates him both because he finds out that he is an informant and because the chaplain has not fulfilled his function as a man of God. His role as an informant makes him a cruel man, exhibiting the opposite of the Christian goodness that he is supposed to represent.

The Novel

Floyd Salas' *Tattoo the Wicked Cross* takes place in a boys' prison farm. The novel is divided into ten parts. As Aaron D'Aragon enters the prison, he sees its sign: GOLDEN GATE INSTITUTE OF INDUSTRY AND REFORM. The prison looks almost like a cemetery, and the entrance resembles the "pearly gates" of heaven. Aaron has been sent to prison for gang fighting. The story encompasses approximately six months and shows the changes that Aaron goes through during that time. He changes from an idealistic, religious youth who believes in God and honor to one who learns that to survive he must change and learn a different code of honor. He learns that in prison there is a code that must be followed: One does not snitch, and one takes care of himself.

Aaron is apprehensive when he arrives at the prison. His good friend Barneyway is in prison, and Aaron is looking forward to seeing him. Part 1 is titled "Dead Time," referring to the stage of a prison sentence during which an inmate is not yet acclimated to prison life. Aaron is placed in a cell with a limited view of the prison and other inmates. He hears people but cannot see them, and his food is brought to him. While in this cell, he discovers that someone has carved a heart with the message RICHIE DE LA CRUZ + EVA, Richard of the Cross and Eve. Along with the heart is a pachuco cross with three lines, suggesting rays of light, emanating from it. From his initial contacts with other inmates, he learns about the prison and also learns he must be cautious, especially when inquiring about his friend Barneyway.

In part 2 "Buddies and Bad Actor," he learns that Buzzer rules the prison ruthlessly and brutally and that he sodomizes whomever he wishes. When Aaron learns that Barneyway is one of Buzzer's victims and has become a "queen," he becomes determined not to be a victim.

In the third through eighth parts, Aaron learns of the brutalities occurring in the prison and must make decisions about how to respond. Aaron's family visits him and encourages him to do what they believe is right. They tell him to avoid trouble and do his time quietly. Aaron's girlfriend, Judith, gives him hope in a seemingly hopeless brutal place.

Aaron finds himself in a dilemma: How can he live up to his ideals and beliefs if he is beaten and sodomized by Buzzer? Aaron does not want to be a hapless victim like Barneyway. He wants vengeance but cannot seek it while remaining true to his Catholic faith.

Judith appears for one of her visits with a tattoo on her cheek. Because she has a tattoo, Aaron now views her as lost, no longer the ideal pure person who gave him hope. His faith was already slipping because he was angry with God for taking his mother; now his girlfriend has been taken away from him.

Part 9 prepares the background for the final chapter. Aaron is in the prison hospital recovering from a savage beating and rape by Buzzer and his gang. He is aware that he has been beaten badly but knows that he fought bravely. At this point he does not know that he has been "gang banged." When he is told, he does not feel anger; he only feels shame. He is asked for the names of the people who jumped him. He says he does not know. Barneyway visits Aaron, and Aaron says he must make sure that Buzzer does not bother them again. It is then that he decides he must have revenge.

Buzzer and his gang attack Aaron again. Hot with anger, he remembers that there is poison in the supply room to feed Buzzer and his gang. He pours the white powder into the soup. Buzzer dies a horrible death at the chapel altar; unfortunately

Barneyway also dies of poisoning.

Tattoo the Wicked Cross ends with part 10, titled "Good Time." Aaron's revenge does three things for him: He has gotten back at Buzzer, has earned the respect of his fellow inmates, and will finally be left alone. He is a mass murderer, but because he is a minor, he is not sentenced to the gas chamber or a state prison. He will remain in the institute doing "good time," remaining on his best behavior.

Analysis

Tattoo the Wicked Cross is a complex novel with many themes and meanings. Ostensibly it is about what happens to a fifteen-year-old delinquent, Aaron D'Aragon, while in a boys' prison farm. The prison is supposed to teach him to be a "good citizen," to reform. Aaron and the other boys in prison have a different code of ethics, the ethics of the streets. Salas shows the reader that prison is a dehumanizing place, one that offers corruption instead of the promised rehabilitation. When Aaron enters prison, he is an "innocent" boy who still has beliefs and a sense of right and wrong. He soon realizes that he cannot hold on to his ideals. His good friend Barneyway is also in prison, and Aaron is eager to see him. He remembers Barneyway as a tough gang member but soon learns that he was not tough enough to withstand the brutality of Buzzer. Barneyway falls victim to Buzzer and thus to the system that created this cruel person.

Another theme is the loss of faith. Aaron tries to pray as he has been taught and tries to remain true to his Catholic faith. When he is beaten and violated by Buzzer and his gang, a dilemma develops. How can he remain true to his faith, which does not allow retaliation? How does one remain nonviolent in a violent world? Aaron finds it impossible to abide by his old moral code and makes a decision to take vengeance on his tormentors. Aaron poisons his tormentors, forsaking his faith and becoming a mass murderer.

The outside world and the visitors who once gave him hope have changed. Judith, his girlfriend, was once a symbol of purity and virtue, of love and goodness. Aaron sees her differently when she tattoos her cheek. She is now a symbol of fallen feminine perfection, no longer the biblical symbol that bears her name, "the praised one." She is also not the symbolic heroine of the apocryphal Book of Judith. Aaron becomes angry with God for taking away his mother and for allowing Judith to fall from purity. Even the death of Buzzer has religious overtones. Buzzer dies in the prison chapel, at the altar. It is ironic that Buzzer, the one who torments and "crucifies" Aaron, is now the crucified.

In the kind of prison system in which Aaron is placed, the murders elevate him. As a killer, he will be respected by his peers. Salas asks whether this is the kind of system in which youths should be placed.

Another main point made in the novel is that society destroys its "innocent" children under the guise of helping them. If these children are to be rehabilitated, this will not be accomplished by placing them in dehumanizing prisons with dehumanized authorities and dehumanized inmates. The result will be tragedy. Salas makes his point by chronicling the changes that the main character goes through during his first six months in prison.

Critical Context

Tattoo the Wicked Cross is an important novel because it deals with universal themes of honor, faith, good and evil, survival, and identity. Much of the fiction by Latinos and Chicanos during the 1960's deals with their experiences with authority figures such as the police, the church, schools, and parents. Fiction of that period also addresses issues of poverty, insufficient social and health services, lack of education, and discrimination. Although Salas' novel touches on some of these concerns, he has concentrated on the environmental factors that send young people to prison and what happens to those youths while they are incarcerated. Salas' novel speaks eloquently and graphically about the injustices of the penal system, especially as it concerns youthful offenders. Placing them in prisons does not rehabilitate them; it corrupts them. It turns youths into incorrigibles unfit for society.

Salas' book gives the reader a glimpse of the penal system that destroys youth. He speaks from some of his own experiences in a youth camp. Since publication of his book, there has been a movement to treat youthful offenders with an eye toward rehabilitation rather than punishment. Perhaps Salas' book has influenced some members of the penal and judicial system.

Tattoo the Wicked Cross, Salas' first published novel, set him apart from other Latino and Chicano writers of the time. The novel set the tone of his writing, which rebelled against the literary world. Two other works that show his rebellious bent are the novels *What Now My Love* (1969) and *Lay My Body on the Line* (1978). He writes about issues that concern him, even though the resulting works may not readily find publishers. He remains true to himself and to his art.

Tattoo the Wicked Cross was honored with the Henry Joseph Jackson Award and the Eugene F. Saxton Fiction Fellowship. The novel was reissued in 1981, and it was translated into French in 1969 and into Spanish in 1971. Salas' recognition as a writer goes beyond the sphere of Latino and Chicano writing, but his works are becoming part of the canon of Latino and Chicano literature.

In addition to writing Latino fiction, Salas has also published poetry and numerous essays on the craft of writing. In 1986, he edited *Stories and Poems from Close to Home*, a collection of writings by San Francisco Bay writers, and in 1992 he published *Buffalo Nickel: A Memoir*, an autobiography that reads like a novel. Although his roots are Latino, of Spanish stock, he has not limited his writings. He has contributed much to Latino literature, but his writings are truly contributions to the wider American literature.

THE TEACHINGS OF DON JUAN: A Yaqui Way of Knowledge

Author: Carlos Castaneda (1925-   )
Type of work: Anthropology
Time of work: 1961-1965
Locale: The southwestern United States and northern Mexico
First published: 1968

Principal Personages

Carlos Castaneda, a graduate student in anthropology at the University of California, Los Angeles, who is collecting information on medicinal plants used by the Indians of the Southwest. On one of his research trips, he is waiting in a border town for a Greyhound bus with a friend, who points out a white-haired Indian man to him and tells him that he is very knowledgeable about plants. This person is don Juan Matus, a Yaqui sorcerer and a practitioner of an ancient system of knowledge.

This meeting between Carlos Castaneda and don Juan moves from a case study between an anthropological observer and a practitioner into a relationship between teacher and apprentice. Don Juan tells Castaneda that he possesses knowledge taught by his teacher or "benefactor." Moreover, he informs Castaneda that he has chosen him as an apprentice to learn this knowledge.

This passage from observer to participant and practitioner of this way of knowledge forms the narrative of this work and succeeding ones. The experiences related in this book occurred between 1961 and 1965.

Castaneda's field notes are the core of the narrative. Through his diary entries, he relates his encounters with three psychotropic "power" plants—peyote, Jimson weed, and a mushroom—that he ingests under don Juan's guidance. The state of heightened awareness that Castaneda attains during these sessions opens up perceptual possibilities that Castaneda describes with extraordinary clarity and detail. On one occasion, he becomes a crow and gives a detailed description of the sensation of growing wings and of developing peripheral vision from eyes that look out to the side.

Castaneda affirms that the psychotropic experiences were only an initial stimulus, a device don Juan utilized in an attempt to break Castaneda's stubborn insistence on commonsense explanations and his tenacious bonds with a concrete cause-and-effect linear thought process. What he actually experienced in these states of awareness and in don Juan's world is recapitulated from the depths of memory and slowly unfolds during the course of the rest of his writing.

Don Juan Matus, a Yaqui Indian and a practitioner and teacher of an ancient way of knowledge unique to the American continent. He relates to Castaneda that he was born in the Southwest in 1891 and had lived most of his life in Mexico. In 1900, his family had been exiled to central Mexico by the Mexican government. He lived in central and southern Mexico until 1940.

Don Juan's knowledge is conveyed through a series of challenging tasks that he sets before Castaneda. The first of these is motivated by Castaneda's repeated request to learn more about peyote and don Juan's insistence that he has to learn to respect the power of Mescalito (his name for peyote). He then instructs Castaneda to find a comfortable place on the floor, pointing out to him that his restlessness and agitation reveal his discomfort. Castaneda then spends about eight hours rolling on the floor until he finds his spot. The incident illustrates don Juan's pragmatism and his ability to begin training his apprentice by forcing him to observe his surroundings not merely by observing visually but also by learning to use his entire body to understand reality.

This pragmatism, which is based on a respect for nature and the universe, is the basis of don Juan's knowledge. Once the commitment to the pathway of knowledge is affirmed, it must be steadfastly upheld. There is no turning back.

Don Juan's teachings are exemplified through his words and, more important, through his sense of self-discipline, courage, and humor. He is the counterbalance to Castaneda in that he embodies a unique and non-Western way of being and action that contrasts with Castaneda's Western theories of reality. The basis of the work lies in this ongoing conflict.

The Work

The Teachings of Don Juan: A Yaqui Way of Knowledge reads like a novel, but it was Carlos Castaneda's master's thesis. While gathering information about medicinal plants used by southwestern Indians, Castaneda was introduced to the enigmatic and supremely confident don Juan Matus. This Yaqui *brujo* (a medicine man, sorcerer, or witch) was to become his mentor in the arduous process of becoming what the Indian called "a man of knowledge."

Mescalito, the spirit of the peyote plant, has indicated to the *brujo* that Castaneda is the person to whom he should act as "benefactor" and pass on his age-old knowledge. As a youth, don Juan was selected similarly. There is no indication where his knowledge originates or how old it may be. As teacher, guide, and interpreter, don Juan introduces his student to an extraordinary world by teaching him the principles necessary for entering and utilizing "nonordinary" reality. Castaneda's unusual experiences during his apprenticeship both terrify him and make him violently ill, but they disclose marvelous possibilities.

Near the end of the fourth year of his apprenticeship, Castaneda experiences a particularly traumatic lesson. Late one evening, suddenly fearing for his life, he becomes convinced that the don Juan he seemingly observes is in fact a diabolical imposter bent on destroying him. With this experience, Castaneda's implicit sense of everyday reality is severely undermined. He begins to have what might be described as a nervous breakdown and abruptly breaks off his relationship with the *brujo*. *The Teachings of Don Juan* recounts events that took place during the first four years of the author's apprenticeship.

The book is divided into three parts: "Introduction," "The Teachings," and "A Structural Analysis." "The Teachings" (the largest section, comprising 131 pages of the book's 196) consists of dated field notes that describe the "ordinary" and "nonordinary" experiences Castaneda has with don Juan. In addition to descriptions of the procedures or rituals used to induce nonordinary experiences, these notes include question-and-answer sessions between teacher and student both before and after perception-altering experiences. In these conversations, Castaneda tries to clarify his encounters with nonordinary reality as well as reveal the content of don Juan's beliefs. Because "The Teachings" includes the subjective version of what he experiences, this section is emotionally charged and reveals the author's confusion, amazement, and, at times, abject fear.

"A Structural Analysis" was written after Castaneda's experiences as an apprentice. An abrupt change of style is evident, as this section reflects the objective and detached language of an anthropologist. In it, the author attempts to establish criteria for analyzing the lessons, perceptual attitudes, and psychological states reported in "The Teachings" and to "disclose the internal cohesion and cogency of don Juan's teachings." A discussion of suggestibility is a prominent part of this section. Appendices briefly discuss the process of validating nonordinary reality and include a detailed outline of "A Structural Analysis."

Analysis

Like Aldous Huxley's psychedelic literature, Carlos Castaneda's *The Teachings of Don Juan* attempts to examine rationally what escapes the limits of logic. Unlike other works of the genre, however, which generally describe and discuss drug-altered experiences, this book identifies a structure to which hallucinatory experiences conform and teaches a coherent way of experiencing the world that is utterly foreign to Western consciousness. For this reason, the work intrigued an entire generation interested in both hallucinogens and altered states of consciousness and is considered a classic addition to the literature chronicling the psychology of drug-altered perception.

Used separately and on different occasions, the hallucinogenic substances *mescalito*, *yerba del diablo*, and *humito*—peyote, Jimson weed, and mushrooms—play a significant role in Castaneda's introduction to the system don Juan attempts to elucidate. The bulk of his teachings, in fact, involve the preparation and use of these hallucinogenic plants. Each plant possesses different perceptual properties. In explaining the use of the "allies," as don Juan calls the entities present in these plants, the *brujo* warns Castaneda that they are powerful but dangerous teachers that can accept or reject the recipient. The capacity of these plants to produce a peculiar state of perception is an essential element in the learning process, guiding the initiate to a level of conceptualization allowing comprehension of nonordinary phenomena. Castaneda learns further that the realm of nonordinary reality is not illusory but real, with its own inherent properties. Moreover, it can be utilized to draw points of reference that have value in ordinary reality. That this nonordinary reality has a form, structure, and logic of its own and that one can actually move around in it is undoubtedly one of the author's most startling and controversial revelations.

The interrelation of mind and matter, the processes of perception and knowing—these are some of the themes of don Juan's lessons. Again and again he forces his student to question the validity of his assumptions: Nothing can be taken for granted. Don Juan's epistemology is as exacting and subtle as that of any contemporary theory, requiring the precise performance of sophisticated and complex techniques. Because these procedures collapse the façade of illusions on which most people depend, learning them demands the courage and discipline of a warrior. "A man goes to knowledge," don Juan tells his student, "as he goes to war, wide-awake, with fear, with respect, and with absolute assurance. Going to knowledge or going to war in any other manner is a mistake, and whoever makes it will live to regret his steps."

"Going to knowledge" also brings with it an ongoing reevaluation of the everyday world and one's role in it. What constitute worthwhile goals and what constitutes the highest knowledge must be reformulated to synthesize with the insights acquired in the learning process. Castaneda discovers, for example, that for the man of knowledge there are no regrets in the struggle for understanding, even though he is acutely aware that if he does achieve his goal, it will be only for a fleeting moment, and death will claim the final victory. Thus, for the man of knowledge—as for all enlightened individuals—the journey itself must provide the meaning and the rewards.

The epistemology and ethics of the system don Juan teaches are founded on metaphysical presuppositions that differ radically from Western conceptions of reality. In fact, the prevailing notion of reality in the West is merely a facet of the more fundamental and holistic world to which don Juan is privy. The Cartesian duality of mind and matter, a supposition of Western metaphysics, is ignored. In the Indian's ontological paradigm, physical and cognitive being are considerably more diverse than traditionally conceived by Westerners.

The companion world Castaneda is shown is not transcendental in the sense that it lies beyond the sensorium; rather, it is apprehended by utilizing and understanding sensorial data in a different way, guided by the insights provided with psychedelics. Mastering the *brujo*'s more sophisticated level of perception allows the apprentice to see the world's complexity more completely. Even something as innocuous as the light of day has deeper significance. The evening twilight, for example, is seen as an avenue to a separate reality, "the crack between the worlds."

Someone who has mastered the principles of the *brujo*'s system can see the future, leave his or her physical body, be in two places simultaneously, and transform himself or herself into a bird, dog, coyote, or any other creature. Castaneda is skeptical that such possibilities exist. His own experiences, however, seem to corroborate the claims of his benefactor. After having smoked the hallucinogenic mixture *humito*, for example, he recounts his apparent transformation into a crow and his subsequent sensation of soaring above the mountains with other birds. Returning to ordinary reality, he finds himself naked in the open desert.

After such strange experiences, Castaneda is at times ecstatic, but more often exhausted and confused. The uncertainty about what he has actually experienced is apparent at every step of his apprenticeship, particularly when he begins to shift in and out of ordinary and nonordinary states without hallucinogenic mixtures. He describes these phenomena as they occurred—subjectively. Only afterward, during dialogues with his teacher (which are interpretive debriefings as well), does Castaneda attempt to understand what he has experienced. Rather than applying the methodology of modern scientific investigation, however, he and his teacher conduct these discussions using terms of the Indian's world. Although Castaneda's questions to his teacher are at times fumbling and redundant, they are a concerted effort to comprehend don Juan's order of conceptualization.

Castaneda's unique approach to his subject, as well as his considerable talent as a writer, results in a vivid and compelling exploration of an experiential paradigm. By describing the events of his apprenticeship with the same terror, ecstasy, wonder, and bewilderment he experienced as they occurred, he has made don Juan's amazing world tangible. The book is a story of discovery and revelation delineating a mysterious and fully elaborated worldview that differs radically from Western cosmology but provides as much, if not more, cosmological satisfaction. As a story of discovery, it incorporates a familiar archetypical theme, Hesse-like in its presentation, of a young man's initiation into another way through the kind but emphatic tutelage of a wise old man.

Critical Context

The Teachings of Don Juan provided the foundation for Castaneda's further conversations and experiences with don Juan, related in the widely popular works that followed: *A Separate Reality: Further Conversations with Don Juan* (1971), *Journey to Ixtlan* (1972), *Tales of Power* (1974), *The Second Ring of Power* (1978), *The Eagle's Gift* (1981), *The Fire from Within* (1984), *The Power of Silence* (1987), and *The Art of Dreaming* (1993). The most frequent criticism leveled against these works, particularly the first, questions their basis in fact: How much of the study is true?

The Teachings of Don Juan has the momentum and suspense of fiction and a narrative power unmatched by other anthropological studies. Castaneda himself calls his book an anthropological field study, but the testimony of leading scholars is mixed. Detractors claim that the book is a fraud, the work of a novelist rather than a scientist, although one with a unique knowledge of the desert and Indian lore. For example, how could an observer, under the conditions experienced by Castaneda, write down everything don Juan says verbatim?

Other criticisms revolve around three themes. First, there is no proof that don Juan really did what he said he did—or that he even exists; there is no bibliography, no corroboration at all, beyond the book itself. Because there is virtually no information about don Juan's past (nothing is learned about his family), it is impossible to decide whether his "way of knowledge" has genuine ethnic roots or he is a harmless crank who fabricated his stories as mood and occasion suggested. That Castaneda never considers don Juan's motivation is seen as another weakness of the study.

Weston LaBarre, a distinguished researcher of peyoteism, is particularly critical of Castaneda's report, noting that it does nothing to advance the knowledge of ritualized hallucinogenic experiences. Finally there is the controversy concerning the source and originality of don Juan's teachings. Scholars have called attention to the striking similarity between the ideas of the *brujo* and those of Taoism, American Indian folklore, and European existential philosophy. It is no wonder, then, that experts can recognize in Castaneda's book much that is of anthropological validity.

Those who find the book enlightening are not only convinced of its cultural and historical accuracy but also believe it represents superior ethnographic scholarship. Because Castaneda attempts to go within rather than merely observe don Juan's world, the book's place among contemporary anthropological studies is unique, and the author has been seen as a major figure in the evolution of the

discipline. Defenders of the work point out that don Juan's ancestry is unimportant because he is, after all, a loner, an outcast sorcerer who neither speaks for nor represents Yaqui culture or religion.

The work's supporters find that the similarities between don Juan's ideas and those of others in no way undermine the credibility of the study; in fact, such similarities point to the universality and profound truth of don Juan's way of knowledge. Castaneda himself has responded to the charges by pointing out that Westerners are generally unwilling to look at another culture on its own terms, particularly when it conflicts with the vision of reality they have been reared to perceive and accept.

The question of its authenticity remains unanswered, but whether castigated or celebrated, *The Teachings of Don Juan* was widely read by a generation of young people in the 1970's and continues to fascinate readers. By providing a glimpse into another way of experiencing the world, it suggests that reality is not absolute but is instead a culturally determined package of illusions. With this glimpse comes flexibility, curiosity, and an open mind.

TENT OF MIRACLES

Author: Jorge Amado (1912-   )
Type of work: Novel
Type of plot: Magical Realism
Time of plot: From 1968 to 1969, with flashbacks to the years from 1868 to 1943
Locale: Salvador, in the state of Bahia, Brazil
First published: *Tenda dos Milagres*, 1969 (English translation, 1971)

Principal Characters

Pedro Archanjo, a writer and self-taught anthropologist. A brilliant mulatto who loves good conversation, riotous celebration, women, and social justice, he earns his living as a runner at the Bahia School of Medicine yet writes four insightful anthropological works about the beloved mulatto culture of his native Bahia. One highly controversial work traces the impurities in the aristocratic bloodlines and infuriates white supremacists. The 1868-1943 frame of the novel follows the fight against white supremacy. The 1968-1969 frame relates the perverse whitewashing of his image when it becomes profitable to make the neglected writer a national hero.

Fausto Pena, a poet. The first-person narrator of the 1968-1969 frame, Fausta, with his beard, long hair, and blue jeans, prides himself on the nickname "Wicked Cobra," given to him by the lady poets. When Ana Mercedes betrays him, he experiences doubts about his masculinity, literary significance, and political integrity. Faust accepts a commission from Levenson to research Archanjo's life, but he later realizes that the commission was merely a ruse to clear Levenson's access to Ana Mercedes.

Nilo d'Ávila Argolo de Araújo, a professor of forensic medicine at the Bahia School of Medicine. Argolo uses his considerable force of character to advance racial hatred. He persecutes Archanjo, inciting Archanjo's arrest and the destruction of the Tent of Miracles. His arrogant world falls to pieces when Archanjo's research reveals that Argolo is related to Archanjo.

Lídio Corró, a painter and printer. Lídio is Archanjo's best friend and owner of the art and print shop called the Tent of Miracles, where Archanjo and his circle gather to celebrate and converse.

Ana Mercedes, a poetess, reporter, and Pena's girlfriend. Mercedes exudes sexiness and voluptuous insouciance. Mercedes seduces Pena into writing poems over her name, then betrays him for a prestigious affair with Levenson.

James D. Levenson, a scholar. The North American Nobel Prize winner disrupts Bahia in 1968 by declaring that he has arrived to study the neglected writer Archanjo. Everyone suddenly clamors to become Archanjo's champion.

Pedrito Gordo, the chief of the secret police. The cane-wielding bully wages brutal war against the mulatto element of Bahia.

Zèzinho Pinto, a newspaper publisher. A worldly man who thinks of nothing but selling newspapers, he spearheads and profits from the new acclamation of Archanjo and instigates the whitewashing of Archanjo's image.

The Novel

Most of the story takes place during different time periods in the neighborhood of Pelourinho, where a type of free university of Afro-Brazilian culture holds sway, owing to the practices of popular mestizo poets, artists, storytellers, musicians, craft workers, singers, *capoeiristas* (dancers of a self-defense sport), black magicians, cult priests, and folk healers. This natural campus, situated near the state's official school of medicine, has as its main building a shop called the Tent of Miracles, where Lídio Corró runs his printing press and paints miracle pictures for those who wish to acknowledge their gratitude for having had their prayers answered.

The chancellor of this unofficial university is the protagonist, Pedro Archanjo, a mestizo whose knowledge, books (published by Corró), camaraderie, honor, generosity, and sexual feats command the respect of this community. Pedro Archanjo's story is told in 1968, one hundred years after his birth, by Fausto Pena, an unappreciated poet hired by James D. Levenson, a handsome blond American scholar, winner of the Nobel Prize, and professor at Columbia University. Pena is to do research on Pedro Archanjo for an introduction to the professor's English translation of the mulatto's works. Unknown to the rest of Brazil literati until Levenson's discovery, Pedro Archanjo's works earn praise through the famous American's recognition of their overall ethnological merit. Now considered to be indispensable reading for understanding the racial problem in Brazil, these acclaimed works spark a local and national campaign for institutionalizing Pedro Archanjo as a Brazilian hero. In counterpoint to the fanfare and ultimate fictionalization of Archanjo as a national hero in 1968, a factual historical account, narrated by an omniscient voice, traces the hero's humble beginnings from 1868, when his father was killed in Brazil's

devastating war with Paraguay, up to his position as messenger in the school of medicine in 1900, and during the time of his main publications (1904-1928), which cause a reactionary debate by the racist professor Nilo d'Ávila Argolo de Araújo, who espouses theories of Aryan superiority.

Argolo epitomizes the prejudice and hatred engendered by a black/white dichotomy that incites racial, economic, social, and political divisiveness. Archanjo's defense of miscegenation leads to his imprisonment and the destruction of the Tent of Miracles by the vigilante police chief, Pedrito Gordo. Fausto Pena's narrative closes with the protagonist in prison. The omniscient narrator resumes the story, paralleling the indigent mulatto's death in 1943 with allusions of Nazism and the impact on the world of its belief of Aryan supremacy. Before dying, Archanjo, always the crusader, reminisces over his lifelong battle against the forces of bigotry and exhorts those who are to come after him to close the "gates" of division between the races by making the mixture of blood complete.

As the narrative draws to a close with the hypocritical pomp surrounding the centennial celebration of Archanjo's birth, promoted by Bahia's politicians, businesspeople, and pseudointellectuals, the novel ends with the carnival of 1969, at which Archanjo's glory is celebrated. More festive and authentic, this popular tribute in the form of a samba school's musical theme, symbolizes Archanjo's humane, real-life mulatto existence in the colorful streets of Bahia.

Analysis

The novel's central theme is the struggle for racial equality within a society manifesting insidious prejudice and practicing covert and overt discrimination that at times becomes unexpectedly violent. Plagued by the turn-of-the-century spurious theories of Joseph-Arthur, comte de Gobineau on the inferiority of the black race, Brazil is portrayed here as a country striving to eradicate an image that might label it as a backward nation.

Ironically, it is an American, bestowing a foreigner's approval of Archanjo's worth, who ignites Brazilian interest in the country's own racial history and resources. Brazil's society and government, concerned about projecting the right national image, are mocked and satirized by Amado as dependent on foreign influence.

The issues of image, racial bigotry, and socioeconomic inequities surface via Amado's deft treatment of shifting points of view, rich symbolism stressing the spontaneous mixture implicit in carnival and miscegenation, and contrastive narrative techniques. For example, the true account of Archanjo's humble beginnings, life, and death are told by an omniscient narrator, in direct contrast to the first-person version developed, almost uncontrollably, by the naïve, well-intentioned, but unreliable narrator Fausto Pena, a middle-class poet used in 1968 by local politicians, businesspeople, and the state to create a profitable and "safe" myth out of Archanjo's bawdy but noble life.

The preoccupation with a correct and proper image leads to questions about the interpretation of social history and the relativity of points of view. The reader questions this process as Amado illustrates how the pernicious powers of the media and the state reinterpret history for their own aims. This problem has more subtle implications, brought out by the hidden realities of the violent 1868 and 1968 periods in Brazilian history and their "official" images as promoted by the government. Added to this sense of history and "image-making" are allusions to the rampant presence of Nazism and its racial campaign within Brazil and abroad in the 1930's and 1940's, during Archanjo's time. The historical parallels are more than coincidental. By underscoring a local incident, Amado, with the use of contrastive techniques and a historical framework, undermines the inhumanity of racism and violence, thereby raising important questions that accord his novel true universal meaning.

Critical Context

Tent of Miracles, Jorge Amado's sixteenth novel and twenty-sixth book, has been printed in more than twenty editions and translated into every major language, including English and Russian. This novel, considered to be one of Amado's most technically sophisticated creations, is representative of his second literary phase, which is commonly recognized as beginning with the critically acclaimed *Gabriela, Cravo e Canela* (1958; *Gabriela, Clove and Cinnamon*, 1962), a novel that announces Amado's closer attention to character development, narrative techniques, and lyric prose while deemphasizing the overt thesis formula of his earlier social realist works. This phase is also marked by Amado's allegiance to Brazil's rich literary oral tradition, the *literatura de cordel*, poetry composed and sung by popular balladeers of the Northeast, stressing the time-honored values of the common folk. *Tent of Miracles* illustrates many of these themes and techniques in Amado's development as a novelist, including a panoramic depiction of numerous Afro-Brazilian rituals and practices in which spiritual events magically play upon the destinies of his characters.

Known primarily as a popular, best-selling novelist, Amado proves himself to be a skillful craftsman in *Tent of Miracles*, frequently referred to as one of his masterpieces. In 1977, a feature-length Brazilian film based on this novel was made by the well-known Brazilian director Nelson Pereira dos Santos.

Always a first-rate storyteller, Amado infuses his social criticism with humor, irony, and sex. Praised as well as criticized for his portraits of "sensual mulattas" and for alluding to Brazil as a racial democracy, Amado in *Tent of Miracles* provides through symbols and characterization an implicit explanation of his stand on these issues. *Tent of Miracles* also constitutes one of the first examples of Amado's allegorical documentation of violence, bigotry, and repression in Brazil. This novel accentuates Amado's overriding theme of individual freedom while proving the author to be one of Brazil's master novelists of the twentieth century.

TERRA NOSTRA

Author: Carlos Fuentes (1928-   )
Type of work: Novel
Type of plot: Allegory
Time of plot: From the first century A.D. to New Year's Eve, 1999
Locale: Rome, Italy; Paris, France; Mexico; and Spain
First published: 1975 (English translation, 1976)

Principal Characters

Pollo Phoibee, a young man in Paris in 1999 who works as a sidewalk hawker carrying a sandwich board. He is proclaimed in the novel as the seeker of ultimate truth and is perhaps the possessor of some mysterious knowledge. He is transformed into one of the three bastard sons of Felipe the Fair and becomes the lover of Joanna Regina, the widow of that king. At times, he seems to be one of the narrators of the novel. At the end of the novel, he performs an ecstatic act of love with Celestina, through which the two become one hermaphroditic being who gives birth to a new creature, the New World of the twenty-first century.

Celestina, a female pimp, a twentieth century transformation of the female procuress of the same name from the Spanish Renaissance play *Comedia de Calisto y Melibea* (1949; the play of Calisto and Melibea), by Fernando de Rojas. She accompanies Pollo Phoibee on his search through history for eternal truth. At times she seems to be a narrator of the novel as she tells her story, which forms a large part of the narrative. She is also transformed into a bride, raped by Felipe the Fair on her wedding night, who gives birth to one of his three bastard sons.

Felipe, also called **El Señor,** the king of Spain from 1556 to 1598, portrayed in the novel as the son of Felipe the Fair and the Mad Lady Joanna Regina. Educated from birth to be a strong monarch, Felipe is a tyrant intent on creating a perfect building, the royal palace and monastery, the Escorial. He desires to contain in one place all time and space and to preserve an ascetic way of life, shutting out all lasciviousness and evil. When one of the bastard sons of Felipe the Fair returns from an encounter with the Aztecs in the New World, Felipe refuses to admit the possibility of an unknown world beyond the oceans.

Isabel, also called **La Señora,** Felipe's wife. Frustrated and confused by her husband's attempt to preserve an ascetic way of life within the walls of the royal palace, the Escorial, Isabel remains closeted away in a hidden room of the palace, in which she has created a Moorish pleasure salon furnished with white sand, blue water, and a bed of total sexual abandon. As she cultivates her hedonism, seeking in vain to ward off the devastating effects of the passage of time, she is haunted by a recurring nightmare.

Felipe the Fair, King Philip I of Spain, married to Joanna Regina. He is the father of three bastard sons and of Felipe II.

Joanna Regina, the widow of Felipe the Fair. Always dressed in mourning, heavily veiled, she travels in a caravan across Spain bearing the embalmed body of her dead husband and finally takes as her lover one of his bastard sons.

Tiberius Caesar, the emperor of Rome. Tiberius' death is accompanied by a curse, which dictates that Agrippa would be revived in the form of three Caesars, represented in the novel as the three bastard sons of Felipe the Fair, each with a red birthmark in the shape of a cross on his back and six toes on each foot.

The Novel

Although the narrative of this complex novel begins on July 14, 1999, in Paris, and ends on New Year's Eve of the same year in the same city, the historical time frame of the events spans many centuries. In Paris, Pollo Phoibee meets Celestina, a naïve young woman with tattooed lips, who asks him to explain to her the mysteries of chaotic modern civilization. As Pollo slips and falls into the river Seine, the time of the narrative shifts to the first century A.D. and the assassination of Tiberius Caesar, and to the sixteenth century of Felipe, King Philip II (also called El Señor), who is engaged in building the Escorial, the massive palace and mausoleum near Madrid. Pollo, transformed into one of the three mysterious, illegitimate sons of El Señor's father, Felipe the Fair (Philip I), becomes the lover of Isabel, Felipe's wife (Queen Elizabeth I). Another of the sons washes up on a beach in the New World and is welcomed by the Aztecs as the promised redeemer. When he returns to the court of Philip II with news of the discovery of America, the king refuses to accept the possibility of a world beyond the confines of the known Old World, all of which he has sought to reproduce and preserve in the Escorial.

Meanwhile, Joanna Regina has had the body of Felipe the Fair embalmed and preserved against the ravages of time. She then takes as her lover the third illegitimate son of her dead husband. Felipe continues to build the Escorial, in an attempt to enclose within the enormous structure all times and all spaces and thereby defeat the forces of change and preserve his ultimate power. His wife, Isabel, remains secluded in her room, in which she has re-created a Moorish pleasure palace furnished with white sand, blue water, and a bed of total sexual abandon. As she cultivates physical pleasure, she seeks in vain to escape her nightmare of lying prone in the courtyard at the mercy of a mouse that incessantly gnaws at her genitals and "knows the truth."

Toward the end of the novel, Felipe climbs the endless stairs of his mausoleum. On every step, he encounters the opportunity to make new choices and change the course of his past life. Instead, he reinforces his refusal to accept the possibility of a New World that would disrupt the totality of his hermetic space. The last chapter of the novel portrays a return to Paris at the end of the twentieth century. In the ruins of the city, devastated by riots and famine and the collapse of Western civilization, Pollo and Celestina unite in an ecstatic act of love and become one hermaphroditic creature who gives birth to a new creature, the New World of the twenty-first century.

Analysis

Through the fictional manipulation of history and the Hispanic literary tradition, Carlos Fuentes creates an allegorical interpretation of the Iberian experience from the time of the Roman Empire to the end of the twentieth century. The episode that dominates the novel is a narrative of the building of the Escorial. As the novel moves in a complex temporal mosaic through the periods of the Roman Empire, the destruction of the Aztec civilization in pre-Columbian Mexico, the sixteenth century Spanish Empire, and the apocalyptic Paris of 1999, the Escorial becomes a symbol of the denial of both worldly pleasure and the passage of time. Felipe attempts to contain all historical experience in his monument to the ascetic ideal, duplicating within its walls everything that exists and gathering together all knowledge, thus creating a space that contains all spaces and a time that embodies all time. Meanwhile, Felipe's wife cultivates her hedonism, seeking in vain to ward off the devastating effects of the passage of time.

The Escorial represents Felipe's attempts to solidify and protect his power in the face of threats from all sides. Within the central narrative are many other narratives, all concerning the eternal struggle for power. The Roman emperor Tiberius Caesar dies at the hands of the reincarnated Agrippa, the ruler that he himself had assassinated. In pre-Columbian Mexico, the struggle for power is played out in human sacrifices and assassinations. In the time of Felipe, the mythical sons of Agrippa are reincarnated in the three mysterious bastard sons, each with the mark of the cross on his back and six toes on each foot, whose individual identity can be established only by the manuscript contained in each of three green bottles floating in the ocean.

Terra Nostra is an interpretation of Iberian civilization as a quest for supreme power, exemplified in Felipe, who is portrayed as the quintessential despot. Knowledge is power, and the king's desire to create a repository of all things and all times is a desire to gain ultimate knowledge, which implies ultimate control. His denial of the possibility of a New World is an attempt to negate the existence of anything beyond the limits of his own ordering of the universe. The truth contained in the manuscripts and the truth held by the mouse in Isabel's nightmare are threats to the king's ordered world.

Critical Context

Fuentes is one of Latin America's leading writers. His most successful novel, *La muerte de Artemio Cruz* (1962; *The Death of Artemio Cruz*, 1964), is a stylistically complex revelation of the life of a twentieth century Mexican who helped shaped the image of his country. In *Terra Nostra*, Fuentes turns to sixteenth century Spain as the historical moment in which the whole of Hispanic cultural and political history can be revealed. Just as *The Death of Artemio Cruz* is directly related to the ideas developed by the Mexican essayist Octavio Paz in *El laberinto de la soledad: Vida y pensamiento de México* (1950; *The Labyrinth of Solitude: Life and Thought in Mexico*, 1961), *Terra Nostra* is a fictive narrative of the ideas developed by Fuentes in his essay *Cervantes: O, La crítica de la lectura* (1976; *Cervantes: Or, The Critique of*

Reading, 1976). As Fuentes says, his novel reveals an attempt to reconcile the dual history of liberal Spain and reactionary Spain, a concept also explored by Paz in *The Labyrinth of Solitude*.

Terra Nostra attempts to be a "total novel" not only in its interpretation of the whole of Hispanic history but also in its stylistic complexity. In *Terra Nostra*, Fuentes treats "memory as total knowledge of a total past," not only what actually happened but also "what could have been and was not." To convey this complex vision, he employs a dazzling array of narrative devices, so that, in the words of Milan Kundera, the novel becomes "an immense dream in which history is performed by endlessly reincarnated characters who say to us: it is always us, we are the same who go on playing the game of history."

THIS SUNDAY

Author: José Donoso (1924-   )
Type of work: Novel
Type of plot: Social realism
Time of plot: The late 1950's
Locale: Santiago, Chile
First published: *Este domingo*, 1966 (English translation, 1967)

Principal Characters

Josefina Rosas de Vives, called **Chepa,** the well-to-do daughter of Alejandro Rosas and the wife of the lawyer Alvaro, who likens her to a bitch constantly nursing a vast litter. In her preoccupation with giving aid and sustenance to slum dwellers, she envisions herself as a many-breasted nurturer who, in giving suck to a multitude, is bitten and consumed. Her ostensible charity is actually an obsession with making others completely dependent upon her. In her passion to control others, she develops a strange attachment to a convicted murderer, Maya, whose release from prison she secures and whom she sets up in a leather business.

Alvaro Vives, a fifty-five-year-old lawyer and husband of Chepa, who is the same age. His cancer, evidenced by an enlarging mole above his left nipple, will take his life within five months. His youthful sexual affair with Violeta had been followed by dates with many girls and by his marriage to Chepa. His extramarital affairs attest his loveless marriage. Both he and Chepa, each self-centered, are incapable of love.

Maya, a convicted murderer. Maya exploits Chepa's fascination with him by prevailing upon her to secure his release from prison. Once released and set up in a leather business, which Chepa provides for him, he resents his subjection to her. He loses all of his money and subsistence by betting on racehorses. Ultimately, he can assert his individualism only by committing another murder as a means of being returned to prison.

Violeta, a maid in the household of don Alvaro and his wife Elena, the parents of Alvaro. She had continued to serve without pay after a household staff retrenchment and was rewarded upon Elena's death with the legacy of a house. She is four years older than Alvaro (the son), although on the Sunday that she initiates him in sexual union, she is said to be twenty-two (instead of twenty) to his sixteen. She remains the young Alvaro's sexual partner for six years, until he marries Chepa. She is murdered by Maya in his determination to be returned to prison.

The grandson of Alvaro and Chepa. He narrates the three shorter sections of the novel.

The Novel

The plot of *This Sunday* is divided into five parts, presented through two different narrative voices. The first narrator, one of the grandchildren of Chepa, remembers, many years later, the weekends spent as a child at the house of his grandparents. His narrative includes the parts entitled "In the Fishbowl," "Legitimate Games," and "Sunday Night." The second voice is that of a third-person narrator who presents certain aspects of the life of Alvaro and Chepa unknown to the grandchild, and who relates the chapters entitled "Part One" and "Part Two."

The third-person narration begins when Alvaro Vives is a high-school student. While his family is vacationing at a nearby resort, he must stay at home to prepare for exams. In the solitude of the house, sexual relations develop between Alvaro and Violeta, the maid in charge of taking care of him. Years later, Alvaro marries Chepa, but the marriage fails very soon because of temperamental incompatibilities. Both Alvaro and Chepa immerse themselves in selfish existences, isolated from each other, each of them solely concerned with his or her own interests. Alvaro takes refuge in himself, and Chepa hides her sexual frustrations behind charitable concerns for others. As the years pass, their marriage is reduced to a routine governed by the rules imposed by Chepa.

In a visit to the penitentiary, Chepa meets Maya, a brutal murderer. She experiences a dark and irresistible attraction toward the convict and decides to obtain his freedom. Once she has achieved her goal, Chepa projects onto Maya all of her secret frustrations, hoping to exert absolute dominion over him, as she does with all those who surround

her. Maya cannot cope with this type of life, and after a turbulent relationship of deceit and falsehood, he disappears.

The novel begins on a Sunday morning (its title alludes to this particular day), when Maya reappears several years later, seeking help from Chepa. Alvaro, however, impedes their meeting and, in doing so, sets in motion a fatal sequence of events. Maya kills Violeta as a means of reasserting his independence, ironically through a return to prison. On the same day, Chepa, who has gone in search of Maya, is traumatically abused by others of her slum constituents.

The bulk of the novel concentrates on the relationship between Chepa and Maya. Expanding from this point, the novel illuminates the distorted world of human relations that envelops all the characters, along with its unavoidable breakdown.

Analysis

This Sunday offers a powerful treatment of the theme that has obsessed Donoso throughout his career: the conflict between the dominant and visible order of society and the marginal or repressed. The way of life of Alvaro and Chepa, as well as that of those who surround them, reflects the former. For them, everything has been established once and forever. Chepa, for example, submerged in her own reality, is incapable of understanding that society does not conform to her personal will. The same occurs not only with the rest of her

relatives but also with Violeta, who considers herself to be a member of the family.

Isolation, lack of communication, and ambiguity are some of the literary motifs introduced by Donoso to bring to light the existential condition of the Vives family. As is usual in his novels, Donoso concentrates on the moment when a disruptive element suddenly appears to violate the dominant order, revealing the presence of another reality.

Critical Context

José Donoso belongs to the tradition of critical realism characteristic of many Chilean authors, for whom revealing the fragility of the dominant social order has been a constant, significant achievement. The fictitious world presented in most of Donoso's novels is predicated on conflict between upper and lower levels of society.

Donoso's ultimate concerns are not with class

struggle or any other kind of social conflict but rather with a metaphysical conflict between two different modes of consciousness: that of human beings who do not wish to face reality and who seek to impose their own order on it, and that of those who meet reality without such artificial constructs. Donoso shows that, sooner or later, the former will always pay painfully for their hubris.

THE THREE MARIAS

Author: Rachel de Queiroz (1910-   )
Type of work: Novel
Type of plot: Social realism
Time of plot: The 1930's
Locale: Fortaleza and Rio de Janeiro, Brazil
First published: *As Três Marias*, 1939 (English translation, 1963)

Principal Characters

Maria Augusta (Guta), the narrator, a student in a girls' boarding school and later a typist in the city of Fortaleza, Brazil. Awkward and fearful, she is relieved to find friends during her first days at the nuns' school. She, Maria Jose, and Maria da Gloria share one another's hopes, enthusiasms, fantasies, and discouragements. After graduation, Guta tires of the monotony of home life, gets a job in Fortaleza, and soon moves in with Maria Jose. After a miscarriage and illness, she returns home to Crato, in the Cariri region, where her father, her dull and virtuous stepmother, and her younger half brothers and half sisters live.

Maria Jose, Guta's closest friend and the first girl to befriend her at the nuns' school. After they have left school and are working, Maria Jose, who teaches school and is devoutly religious, shares her room in her mother's house with Guta.

Maria da Gloria, Guta's other close friend at the convent school and afterward. An orphan at the age of twelve, she venerates the memory of the poet-father who reared her, and her friends admire her passionate mourning and her talent as a violinist. Soon after they are graduated, she becomes engaged to Afonso, a young college graduate, and she centers her emotional energy upon him.

Jandira, a friend of the three Marias at the school. The illegitimate daughter of a married man and a prostitute, she has been cared for and sent to school by her father's sisters. She marries a seaman during their last year at school, but the marriage is an unhappy one. She is left a house and money by her aunt, takes a lover, and is much happier.

Aluisio, an emotional young student, a friend of Guta and Maria Jose who commits suicide and leaves a letter in which he alludes to an unhappy love affair. Everyone assumes that his passion was for Guta.

The Novel

The novel consists of a retrospective view of the lives of the narrator, Maria Augusta (Guta); her two close friends, Maria Jose and Maria da Gloria; and other boarding school companions. After recounting with great sensitivity their first encounter at boarding school, Guta goes on to tell about their school adventures and about the choices they make about their lives. In the crucial years before and after graduation from high school, each of the schoolgirls searches for a direction for her life.

Each of the girls makes a very different choice. The three Marias epitomize this difference of choice. Maria da Gloria becomes "a happy wife and mother," Maria Jose becomes a schoolteacher, and the narrator remains "a frustrated seeker of satisfying values."

As the novel begins, Maria Augusta makes a fearful entry into the convent school. Frightened and insecure, she wants to hold on to the sister who escorted her in, especially when she discovers that all the commotion and excitement that she observes on arrival is not caused as much by the arrival of a "new" girl as by her silly-sounding name, Guta.

As the girls torment and tease her mercilessly, Guta bashfully responds to their barrage of questions, timidly explaining the facts of her life, such as her age, her hometown, her parents, and the origin of her nickname. "Guta" is simply a degeneration of "Augusta," a name that Guta was unable to pronounce as a small child; the baby-talk substitute, "Guta," stuck with her for life.

Gradually the girls lose interest and stop questioning her. Only one, Maria Jose, remains at her side, obviously interested in Guta's well-being. Advising Guta not to pay attention to such mistreatment, she persuades the reluctant newcomer that she is not like the other girls and that she can be trusted. As Guta aptly observes, her newly found friend has taken charge. As they walk through the schoolyard, Maria Jose points out her main enemies while singling out her "only" friend, Maria da Gloria, whom she introduces to Guta. Thus, the three girls begin their life together.

To the homogeneous milieu of the school, each Maria brought with her the baggage of her past life, which in turn conditioned how each girl responded to circumstances in school and after school. Following graduation, each girl searches for and finds a different life. Each choice is influenced by the girl's own life and by the lives of the other girls. Thus the novel focuses on the growth and development of each of the three Marias through the critical years of her life.

Analysis

Through Guta, Queiroz poses the fundamental question of what a woman is to do with her life in the traditional Brazilian society of the Northeast, where the only honorable options are marriage or joining a religious order. It is particularly relevant that Queiroz asked this question in the 1930's, when a career was not available as a choice to women in that society. The novel attempts to create awareness of the fact that not all women can be satisfied with marriage or nunhood, and that other honest options should become available to women. A choice of life as a single schoolteacher should be as legitimate and fulfilling as any other, and other choices must be made available for those women who are not cut out for the career of schoolteacher, the choice made by Maria Jose.

The novel is one of the first works to pioneer the cause of women in Brazil. By focusing on Guta, a woman who cannot be either a satisfied wife and mother or a successful teacher, Queiroz calls attention to the fact that there are women who do not fit the traditional pattern, that they should not be ridiculed for that, and that simply because they desire to be different, their lives should not be wasted, as Maria Augusta's is bound to be. Rachel de Queiroz joins her contemporary, writer Graciliano Ramos, in deploring the options available for women in the Brazil of the 1930's.

Critical Context

Until 1975, *The Three Marias* was Rachel de Queiroz's best work, but it never received the appropriate critical acclaim. The lack of a decisive ending left critics confused with regard to its main purpose, leading them not to include it among the great works of its period. It was not until the 1950's and 1960's that the novels of Jorge Amado, Clarice Lispector, and Lygia Fagundes Telles depicted with equal depth the problematic condition of growing up female in traditional Brazilian society. Fred Ellison's excellent translation of Queiroz's novel and the 1985 paperback edition by the University of Texas Press constitute appropriate if somewhat tardy recognition of the author's achievement. In 1975, Queiroz's *Dôra, Doralina* was published. It expanded on the theme of life in Brazil's Northeast while encompassing a broader scope.

Critics praised its return to the psychological realism of *The Three Marias* and considered it to be a better work.

THREE TRAPPED TIGERS

Author: Guillermo Cabrera Infante (1929-   )
Type of work: Novel
Type of plot: Satire
Time of plot: The summer of 1958
Locale: Havana, Cuba
First published: *Tres tristes tigres*, 1967 (English translation, 1971)

Principal Characters

Bustrófedon, a character who embodies language and its creative potential. His name, of Greek origin, means "to write alternately from right to left and left to right." During his lifetime, he has been fascinated with anything that was reversible, including words, numbers, or concepts. He represents an appreciation of the sheer joy of spontaneous and uninhibited creation. He is a character in the process of discovering and creating himself through language.

Silvestre, a would-be writer. Estranged from the present, he is obsessed with the past, preferring his memories over experiencing life. He is particularly concerned with ordering the chaos of existence by means of the written word.

Arsenio Cué, a professional actor, Silvestre's closest friend. His personal and professional lives merge to such an extent that they seem one and the same. He is so often playing a role that it is difficult to know who he is. His humor, his continual role-playing, and his dark sunglasses protect him from the outside world.

Códac, a photojournalist. He is first a superficial recorder of the social scene, then later becomes involved in the more realistic and distasteful journalistic duties of photographing political reality during the last months of the dictatorship of Fulgencio Batista. Although sensitive to visual reality, he is also able to appreciate the beauty beneath appearances, underscoring one of the novel's major themes: the importance of re-creation instead of duplication, creation rather than sterility, change rather than permanence.

La Estrella, a huge mulatta singer of boleros. Although she is obese and generally unattractive, she is an outstanding singer. La Estrella is a combination of the ugly and the beautiful, a symbol of life itself.

The Novel

The plot of *Three Trapped Tigers* is conceived as a nightclub show, introduced by the frenetic multilingual wordplay of the emcee of the famous Tropicana cabaret in Havana. His first word is "Showtime!"; his last ones are "Curtains up!" At this point a number of characters, some of them present in the club and introduced by the emcee, narrate sections of the text, with no further introduction or explanation. Episodes include a one-sided telephone conversation, a letter, a story appearing as a series of fragments placed at various points in the text, and another story in two translations (only in the Spanish original) and complete with "corrections" by the author's wife, who turns out to be a fictional creation of her husband. There are even fragments of a woman's sessions with a psychiatrist. The author has said that the text consists of a series of "voices," and that voices have no biography, which means that the only possible coherence results from the reader's ability to assemble the fragments into a more or less meaningful whole.

There is a certain symmetry to the fragments, in that several characters, stories, and themes introduced in the first half are mirrored in the second, in some cases approximately the same distance from the end as their initial appearance is from the beginning. Thus, a story about Silvestre, in which he and his brother witness a murder on the way to the cinema, is related by him to his friend Arsenio Cué near the conclusion, with some significant details reversed. Silvestre then vows that he will one day write the incident as a story. Presumably, the result is the version that appears earlier in the text. A character named Beba Longoria, whose rise in the society world has led to a serious "confusion of tongues" in her manner of speaking, is called "Babel" near the book's conclusion. Arsenio Cué completes a story near the book's end that he narrated in unfinished form near the beginning.

The incidents related generally have to do with false appearances and resultant disillusionment. Relations between the sexes are not functioning in a normal manner, and significant persons in the lives of the principal characters are dying. There is a definite theme of what Mikhail Bakhtin calls "carnivalization," which brings about a reversal of values. One of the most important models for the novel is the work of Lewis Carroll; mirrors, both literal and figurative, play an important role in effecting reversals. The transition between the two halves of the book is a segment entitled "Headcracker," in which Bustrófedon is viewed as a sort of Antichrist figure, or mirror image of Christ. Whereas the latter is presented as "the Word become flesh," Bustrófedon is the man who "tried to be language." He dies, and the text, which begins with an outburst of linguistic activity, ends in a manifold repetition of the word "silently." The text too has reversed itself.

Analysis

Although politics might be expected to take on considerable importance in a novel concerning the months immediately prior to Castro's takeover of Cuba, such is not the case with *Three Trapped Tigers*, which the author himself has described as "the least political book ever written in Latin America." This is probably a reflection of the fact that Cabrera Infante had worked fairly closely with the Castro government for a time but then became disillusioned, not only with it but also with political ideologies in general.

Instead, one of his major concerns in this work is the way in which the essence of a society can be re-created through that society's popular language. He insists that the novel is not written in Spanish but in "Cuban," as spoken in 1958 by the "voices" that make up the text. Thus, the work's language is preoccupied mainly with itself as a creative phenomenon. The text consists largely of puns and other types of wordplay, which has caused some readers to conclude—very wrongly—that the novel is frivolous and not to be taken seriously.

Although it is consistently humorous, it is no more frivolous than Miguel de Cervantes Saavedra's *Don Quixote de la Mancha* (1605, 1615). In both *Don Quixote de la Mancha* and *Three Trapped Tigers*, humor becomes a tool for the attainment of some very serious ends. The joke, according to both Aristotle and Immanuel Kant, operates by presenting the hearer with something unexpected. It appears that the creative possibilities inherent in that situation are not lost on the characters of this novel, who are in search of some viable new reality as the old reality seems about to disappear.

Reality is presented as a fundamentally linguistic phenomenon, so that, as both language and the other phenomena of daily life are perceived as breaking down, the characters appear to be searching for creative new combinations among the fragments, just as one might go on turning a kaleidoscope, fascinated by the endless procession of new symmetrical patterns formed by the shards inside.

Related to the linguistic quest is a rejection of the artificiality that characterized Havana nightlife in 1958. The combination of cosmetic techniques and creative lighting were able to produce illusions very disturbing to those in search of the essential. At times the principal male characters are troubled by the fact that, while relationships between the sexes appear to be increasingly sterile, homosexu-ality seems to be on the increase among both men and women. For Cabrera Infante's characters, a return to creative language represents their only hope of escape from a world they perceive as having been turned upside down.

Critical Context

In his book *La nueva novela hispanoamericana* (1969; the new Spanish-American novel), Carlos Fuentes first mentions *Three Trapped Tigers* in connection with its use of humor, which he considers "one of the notable features of the creation of the true Latin American language." He goes on to say that Cabrera Infante's novel "allows us to carry out the verbal transition from the past to the future," in that "Cabrera's savage intent to demolish goes to the roots of a Latin American problem: our language has been the product of uninterrupted conquest and colonization—a conquest and colonization whose language betrayed an oppressive hierarchical order." Such a statement is perhaps typical of the thinking of authors and critics in evaluating this author's contribution to Latin American prose fiction. During the years following its publication, this novel has come to occupy an important place among the trend-setting novels of Latin America, especially where language and humor are concerned.

One of the major forces at work within the novel is the Cuban *choteo* tradition, which has been described as the tendency to mock everything that represents any form of authority. In this case, if Fuentes is correct, much of the text is concerned with an unrelenting attack on the Spanish language because that language is expressive of certain structures that Latin America must leave behind in its quest for a modern identity. Still, the author has repeatedly stated that the novel should not be taken too seriously, since it is nothing more than a joke that got out of hand. This is also in the *choteo* tradition, to attack even one's own work if one fears that it may be considered in an overly serious manner.

THE TIME OF THE HERO

Author: Mario Vargas Llosa (1936-   )
Type of work: Novel
Type of plot: *Bildungsroman*
Time of plot: The 1950's
Locale: Leoncio Prado Military Academy in Lima, Peru
First published: *La ciudad y los perros*, 1963 (English translation, 1966)

Principal Characters

Porfirio Cava, a cadet in the Leoncio Prado Military Academy in Lima, Peru. A highlander with a peasant background, he has chosen to attend the academy because he plans a career in the military. He is one of four members of "the Circle," a group of cadets formed for mutual protection and support. After a losing roll of the dice, he is obligated to steal a chemistry examination for the Circle. During the late-night theft, he accidentally breaks a window. This evidence, coupled with information supplied by the informant Arana, leads to his court-martial and expulsion, ending his chance for a career in the military and for the resulting economic and social mobility.

Alberto Fernández Temple (the Poet), the bourgeois intellectual of the Circle, a cadet whose wit and skill at writing love letters and pornographic stories are admired by the other cadets. His father is a womanizer, his mother a complainer. Like his father, Alberto is preoccupied with women. First he was infatuated with Helena; after she broke off their relationship, his grades suffered and his father sent him to the academy to teach him discipline. Alberto has his first sexual experience with Golden Toes, a prostitute who has serviced half of his class. At the request of Ricardo, who cannot get a pass, he agrees to meet with Teresa. He takes her to see films, is smitten, and continues to date her. Sustaining a friendship with Ricardo and a relationship with Teresa troubles his conscience. When Ricardo is murdered, Alberto is so overwhelmed with guilt that he denounces the murderer before Lieutenant Gamboa. Academy officials ignore the facts, and nothing is done. As the novel ends, Alberto has finished the academy

with high marks, has received a gift from his father as a reward, and will probably go to the United States to study engineering. Influenced by his circle of bourgeois friends outside the academy, he drops Teresa and begins dating Marcela. He will probably repeat his father's philandering ways.

The Jaguar, the leader of the Circle, a violent, fearless cadet who shows his class how to stand up to and beat the system. Before entering the academy, he fell in love with Teresa, but after an argument, they went their separate ways. Poor, his father dead, and his mother old, Jaguar was living with the criminal Skinny Higueras and was leading a life of crime until most of his cohorts were caught during a robbery attempt. After going without food and sleeping in the open, Jaguar finally turned to his godfather, who put him to work in exchange for room and board. With the help of his godfather's wife (whom he had to satisfy sexually), Jaguar has entered the academy, where he has become a natural leader and fighter. He organizes the class and his followers to resist the upperclassmen. He teaches them that there are no moral limits to protecting the group. When Cava is betrayed, Jaguar murders the betrayer, Arana. Jaguar's subsequent ostracism from the group, however, makes him aware of how lonely Arana must have been. Remorseful, Jaguar confesses his crime, but the academy is not interested. In the end he marries Teresa.

Ricardo Arana (the Slave), a timid and shy cadet whom the other cadets ostracize. He has been reared by his mother and his Aunt Adelina in the regional town of Chiclayo; his father was absent during his early upbringing. Suddenly uprooted from this environment and brought to Lima, where his mother moved to live with his father again, Ricardo learned to avoid his father and most social interaction. His father concluded that Ricardo was a mama's boy, ill-adapted to face the world, and saw the military academy as a remedy for these shortcomings in his son. Ricardo has willingly agreed to enroll, but he is not accepted by the other cadets. They make fun of him, abuse him, and exploit his unwillingness to fight back. He finds some solace in his friendship with Alberto and is infatuated with Teresa, but having been confined to the academy, he becomes so desperate for a pass to see his mother that he informs the authorities that Cava stole the examination. In revenge, Ricardo is murdered in an "accident" during a field exercise. The authorities cover up the incident and blame the death on the cadet himself.

The Boa, a cadet who sexually molests chickens and his dog Skimpy. He is a member of the Circle and a loyal follower of its leader, Jaguar.

Lieutenant Gamboa, a tough, no-nonsense, model officer, who believes in a fair and consistent application of the rules and discipline. He reports the murder but finds his career threatened by superiors, who cover up the scandal.

Teresa, a young woman whose interest in Ricardo and Alberto probably results from their higher economic and social background. She finally marries Jaguar.

The Novel

Based in part on Vargas Llosa's experience as a cadet in the Leoncio Prado Military Academy in Lima, Peru, from 1950 to 1952, *The Time of the Hero* is a fictionalized portrayal of a group of adolescent boys at the school during a three-year period that coincides, roughly, with the author's own stay there. *The Time of the Hero* is divided into two parts, of eight chapters each, and an epilogue. It has four narrators: an omniscient third-person narrator; two first-person narrators, the Jaguar and the Boa, whose identity is discovered only in the last part of the book; and a fourth voice, that of Alberto, who communicates with the reader through several internal monologues.

The book begins during the boys' third and last year at the school. They are there for various reasons. Alberto's father, a middle-class dandy, somewhat dismayed at his son's interest in books, decides that what the young man needs is an education that will prepare him for adult life in the real world; the Leoncio Prado, the father believes, will do precisely that. Ricardo Arana is there because his absentee father considers him effeminate; the boy has been reared by a devoted mother and an aunt, and the father insists that he is in need of the discipline and toughening that a military education can provide. The Jaguar, who comes from a family of thieves and is a budding juvenile delinquent, ends up in the academy as an alternative to reform school after he is caught stealing. As the novel begins, an omniscient third-person narrator relates how several boys are about to carry out a carefully planned maneuver designed by the Jaguar, the undisputed leader of the school's student gang known as "the Circle." Their aim is to steal an important chemistry exam. They succeed in getting the exam but break a window in the process, thus exposing the theft. Pending the discovery of or confession by the guilty parties, school authorities suspend all leaves.

The severing of the lifeline with the outside world becomes the catalyst for the novel, testing the partnerships, relationships, and loyalties that had been established and upon which the Circle was built and impelling the characters to act in ways that express their true nature. Ricardo Arana, "the Slave," so called because of his lack of aggressiveness and courage as defined by the other boys, cannot bear giving up his plan to get away from the school and the boys whom he detests and visit his beloved Teresa. He informs the authorities about the theft and thus breaks the honor code of the Circle. He is subsequently wounded by a bullet during the school's military exercises. He dies shortly thereafter. Following a superficial investigation of the incident, school authorities conclude, wrongly, that the Slave's death was caused by the accidental firing of the victim's own gun.

Alberto, "the Poet," Ricardo's only friend among the cadets, is certain that Ricardo's death was not an accident but rather the Jaguar's revenge against the Slave for informing. The Poet, in turn, informs Lieutenant Gamboa of his suspicions about the Jaguar and takes advantage of the opportunity to expose all the petty infractions and violations of the regulations carried out by the group: the gambling, drinking, illegal furloughs, and contraband. Although Gamboa believes Alberto, he is unable to persuade his superiors to reopen the case. They are concerned about the good name of the school and the bad publicity that a full investigation might attract. They urge Alberto to withdraw his accusations, threatening to expose him as a pornographer, a reference to Alberto's sideline as a writer of erotic tales. Alberto succumbs and withdraws his charges. The lieutenant, in turn, is transferred to a distant post, a plan that causes him and his beloved family great hardship. He accepts the transfer with true dignity, which serves to highlight the contrast between the corruption of the upper echelons of the military hierarchy and the naïve honesty of its humbler ranks. Alberto himself also becomes an informer when he tells Gamboa the truth about the Jaguar. As for the leader of the Circle, his own comrades turn on him, give him a severe beating, and accuse him, falsely, of having revealed the details of their illegal rackets.

The epilogue of the work serves to tie loose ends. Alberto, feeling no guilt over his retreat from responsibility, plans to pursue technical studies in the United States and will eventually marry a suitable young middle-class woman. The Jaguar confesses about the shooting to Gamboa before the lieutenant leaves the school; the latter decides not to expose him. The Jaguar also becomes "respectable." He works at a bank and marries his childhood sweetheart Teresa, the same Teresa who had moved Ricardo to inform, setting off the chain of events described above, and who, at the same time, had been romantically ensnarled in a relationship with Alberto behind the Slave's back.

Analysis

The novel is a scathing critique of the hypocrisy and corruption of Peruvian society in general, of which the Leoncio Prado is a microcosm, and of its military establishment in particular. The events of the book transpire during the real dictatorship of General Manuel Odría, who ruled Peru for eight years beginning in 1948, after a military coup. Although the novel appeared several years after the Odría regime, its publication touched a raw nerve. The novel was attacked as antipatriotic and, presumably, several copies of it were burned in the courtyard of the Leoncio Prado.

The novel is also about growing up; about honor, loyalty, bravery, and love. The group of adolescent boys whose stay at the school the book chronicles is a cross section of Peruvian—and Latin American—society, from a sociological and political perspective. The boys will grow up, which in the novel means that they will fulfill the roles that society has designed for them. There will be no surprises, and not one of the boys will ever go beyond his assigned task. This sense of fatalism pervades the novel, in which growing up means coming to terms with this reality, conforming to one's fate. The first-year recruits, the "dogs" of the novel's original Spanish title (literally "the city and the dogs"), receive from the Jaguar the impetus to challenge their script. He offers to protect them from the system that seeks to humiliate those at the bottom of an inevitably cruel hierarchical structure. The boys accept his leadership and its benefits only when he is strong; the moment he needs their help and support, they turn on him and break their dependence—in preparation for life outside the school—on what is, after all, a lower-class boy.

Critical Context

The Time of the Hero, Vargas Llosa's first full-length novel, was also his first commercial success. The book was published when the author was not yet thirty, yet its favorable reception by critics and public alike placed Vargas Llosa—along with Julio Cortázar and Carlos Fuentes—in the mainstream of the exciting wave of Latin American fiction of the 1960's and 1970's known as the "boom." In this novel the author experiments, rather successfully, with a number of literary techniques. He uses multiple narrators, flashbacks, fragmented time sequences, introspective monologues, and breaks in the structure of the narration, all of which contribute to making this book a complex work of literature whose story line is that of a rather simple *Bildungsroman*. Although the figure of the writer appears in this novel, repre-

sented by the Poet, Vargas Llosa has not yet begun to explore the role of the writer in the creation of reality and the relationship between reality and fiction, themes that will become central to some of his future celebrated novels, such as *La tía Julia y el escribidor* (1977; *Aunt Julia and the Scriptwriter*, 1982) and *La guerra del fin del mundo* (1981; *The War of the End of the World*, 1984).

Vargas Llosa has also been a prolific writer outside the area of fiction. He has established a reputation as an erudite and respected literary critic and has been a frequent contributor to important news and cultural publications throughout the world. He has become one of the most important novelists, in any language, of the last quarter of the twentieth century.

THE UNDERDOGS

Author: Mariano Azuela (1873-1952)
Type of work: Novel
Type of plot: Historical
Time of plot: 1914-1915
Locale: Zacatecas, in northern Mexico
First published: *Los de abajo*, serial, 1915; book, 1916 (English translation, 1929)

Principal Characters

Demetrio Macías, a peaceful Mexican Indian driven by the cruelty of Federalist soldiers to take up arms. He eventually becomes a general. Home after two years, he is killed by the Federal soldiers.

Camila, his pretty nurse, who at first prefers Luis Cervantes to Demetrio.

Luis Cervantes, a pseudointellectual journalist who encourages Demetrio to fight.

Venancio, a barber-surgeon who cures Demetrio's wounds.

President Madera, the first political leader Demetrio follows.

President Huerta, the leader of the Federalists.

General Orozco, the Federalist commander at Jalisco.

Pancho Villa, a rebel leader who is defeated at Celaya.

General Natera, a rebel leader.

Solís, an idealist who is killed in battle.

Whitey Margarito, a sadistic soldier.

La Pintada, a camp follower who stabs Camila.

Don Mónico, Demetrio's landowning enemy, raided by the rebels.

The Novel

Demetrio Macías is a peaceful Indian who knows nothing about revolutions as *The Underdogs* opens. When, as a follower of Madera, he is hounded by the political leader of Jalisco, he flees with his wife and child to the mountains. There some Federal soldiers come upon the fugitives. Wild and lawless, they would have raped his wife if he had not returned with a gun. Being no killer, the Indian lets them go free, only to have them come back with reinforcements and burn his fields. Demetrio then joins a band of sixty sharpshooting rebel outlaws and helps them to drive off twice as many soldiers. During the fighting, two of the rebels are killed and Demetrio is shot in the leg.

For two weeks, the outlaws remain hidden in a native village, looked after by Indians who hate the government. Venancio, a barber-surgeon tends Demetrio's wound. An attractive young girl named Camila is his nurse.

One day, the pseudointellectual Luis Cervantes blunders into the village and explains that he has deserted the government forces because his commanding officer had assigned him to menial duty. Distrusting Cervantes' glib tongue and big words, the rebels pretend to condemn him to death. One outlaw dresses in a priest's robes and pretends to hear the deserter's last confession in order to determine whether he is a spy. Accepted eventually as a revolutionist, Cervantes then urges the rebels to join the great revolutionary leaders of Mexico. Camila falls in love with him. Although she makes her feelings evident, Cervantes never encourages her, not even on the night of the outlaws' departure. The girl has never responded to Demetrio's attention: He was only an Indian.

Hearing from messengers that Huerta's Federalists had fortified the city of Zacatecas, Cervantes urges the band to hurry to join the besiegers and be in at the capture. He also flatters Demetrio by telling the Indian that he is more than a common rebel; he is a tool of destiny to win back the rights of the people.

Demetrio plans a surprise attack on one of the towns along their march, but an Indian guide betrays the scheme, so the Federalists are prepared to resist. A friendly citizen shows the rebels a back way into the town, however, and the garrison is overwhelmed.

By the time rebel leader General Natera arrives in the district, Demetrio's reputation has grown so great that he is made a colonel in the revolutionary army. Failing to take Zacatecas, the rebels are forced to retreat, discarding their booty along the road. Demetrio thinks of going back to Camila until news of Pancho Villa's coming excites the rebels and gives them a fresh incentive.

During the next battle, Cervantes and Solís, an idealist, take refuge in a place where they think they are safe. While they discuss the significance of the revolution, a stray bullet kills Solís. Demetrio's gallant charge turns the tide of battle and he is promoted to the rank of general.

While drinking and boasting in a tavern after the battle, Demetrio meets Whitey Margarito and La Pintada, a prostitute with whom he goes looking for a hotel room. Her insistence that as a general he should occupy a house of his own makes him decide to commandeer a fine residence. During the ransacking, Cervantes finds a valuable diamond ring. Whitey, joining Demetrio's forces, runs off with Cervantes' girl while Demetrio argues the matter of taking her instead of La Pintada, of whom he has tired.

Soon afterward, the rebels raid the house of Don Mónico, Demetrio's landowning enemy, and burn the estate. Cervantes suggests that he and Demetrio hide their loot in case they are forced to leave the country. Demetrio wishes to share it with the others. Still an idealist, he believes that the rebel cause will triumph. Cervantes promises to get Camila for his leader.

Cervantes goes to the village and persuades the girl to return with him. Believing that Cervantes is in love with her, she is surprised to find herself in Demetrio's bed. The next morning, La Pintada discovers Camila and offers to help her escape. Camila refuses. She has found that she likes Demetrio and has decided to stay with him and the army.

During the march against General Orozco at Jalisco, Whitey shows his cruelty by tightening a rope around a prisoner's neck until his eyes bulge. Later, when kindhearted Camila persuades Demetrio to return ten bushels of confiscated corn to a starving villager, Whitey gives the man ten lashes instead. Camila's protests at the incident win her the enmity of La Pintada, who had taken up with Whitey after Demetrio and Cervantes had discarded her. When Demetrio, siding with Camila, orders the camp follower away, La Pintada becomes enraged and stabs Camila.

By the time Demetrio and his men reach Aguascalientes, they find Villa and Carranza, once allies, fighting each other. The Federal forces, taking advantage of the disunity, defeat Villa at Celaya. The defeat is a terrible shock to Demetrio's followers, who cannot bring themselves to believe that their idol has been beaten. The rebels are forced to retreat.

Cervantes escapes safely across the border. From El Paso, he writes to Venancio, the barber-surgeon. He says that Whitey had shot himself, and he invites Venancio to join him in Texas, where, with the barber's money, they could open a restaurant.

After Villa's defeat, Demetrio finds the villagers no longer willing to help the rebels. Somewhat discouraged, he decides to return home. He has been away two years and has seen much, but he cannot answer his wife's question when she asks him why he kept on fighting. He lacks Cervantes' glib tongue to put his true feelings into words.

Trying to pacify the landowners of the region, the government sends troops into the uplands after the outlaw band. Once more, the rebels and the Federal troops clash. Outnumbered, the outlaws die on the spot where two years before they had won their first victory. After the fighting ends the soldiers find the body of Demetrio Macías. His eyes, forever fixed, still sight along the barrel of his gun.

Analysis

This fictionalized chronicle of the Mexican Revolution merits its international fame. Vivid and deep, it has literary and sociological worth. Azuela's honesty glitters in it, since he does not overly caricature his enemies even while lampooning them and bares the hypocrisies of his own side. His characterization is true to life, and his action scenes are fast and clear. Violence, pathos, beauty, and tragedy are etched against Jalisco's night-blackened hills, so that the reader receives an indelible image of revolutionary pageantry with its women *soldaderas*, bandoliered rebels, uniformed *federales*, and greedy nouveau riche who muddy the pond of revolutionary ideals. Thus, while painting only local vignettes of a nationwide holocaust, *The Underdogs* presents the seedy as well as the inspiring aspects of the entire contortion well enough to be a historical document.

The genuine worth of this novel was not recognized until almost a decade after its publication. By the mid-1920's, it had been translated into various languages and was considered to be a Latin American classic. It was written when Azuela was in black despair because he saw that the revolution was drowning some injustices in blood only to spawn others as bad and as self-perpetuating. The virtue of the novel thus lies in its eyewitness impressions of intense, futile events.

An elliptical style selects and spotlights a few specific characteristics of a person, a scene, or a situation so as to describe it deftly. Disjointed scenes are thus used, rather than systematic chapters, so as to strengthen the overtone of violent eruption. Selfishness wins, idealism is crucified, and the novel's true protagonists—Mexico's poor—do *not* march out of misery into a sunny horizon.

Although fragmented into many swift scenes, the novel is divided into three basic sections. The first section has twenty-one chapters and reflects hope; the last two sections have a total of twenty-one chapters and reflect failure. It is in the last two portions that the filth, nastiness, lewdness, and garbage of war arc bcst painted; when personalities such as Cervantes realize that the revolutionary issues will not be decided by logic or delicacy but by brute power as symbolized by self-made, upstart generals who care little for ideals.

Azuela uses colors and details well. The natural dialogue is regionalistic but not difficult and, even though each personality uses special shades of language that subtly characterize him or her, there is a high percentage of standard Spanish.

Azuela's masterpiece became the standard novel of the Mexican Revolution. Most revolutionary movements of the preceding years had not sought to aid the submerged masses—the mestizo, the Indian, the laborer, "the underdog" in general. Following Azuela's example, many Mexican and other Latin American novelists took up the fight for reform, denouncing tyranny and championing the cause of the "forgotten man."

Critical Context

Noted for its "Mexicanness," and still ranked internationally as the best novel of the Mexican Revolution, *The Underdogs* helped transform the Latin American novel (which before 1910 had inspired few translations or fame beyond the local region that had produced each novel) into the most important literary genre of Latin America. *The Underdogs* is also possibly the first Latin American novel in which literary style was engendered by the subject matter. For example, time is telescoped to reflect the rapidity of events, while linguistic nuances tinge different aspects of the novel, including characters, scenes, and episodes. Individual members of Demetrio's command symbolize certain features of Mexican society. One soldier is a former waiter and another a former barber; others include peons, prostitutes, and virtuous country women.

Azuela knew at first hand the materials of this novel, for he had served as a military doctor with Pancho Villa's Golden Boys. His vivid account of revolutionary Mexico was first published serially in a small El Paso newspaper. Almost forgotten, it was revived in 1924 and won immediate fame for its author. Pessimism marks this story of those coming up from below—*Los de abajo*—at the beginning of the Mexican Revolution. This is no overall picture of the struggle, but a blending of excitement, cruelty, and beauty as seen through the eyes of a man practically pushed into the struggle, a soldier who fought because the enemy was in front of him. *The Underdogs* is the best known of Azuela's sixteen novels.

THE VALLEY

Author: Rolando Hinojosa (1929-   )
Type of work: Novel
Type of plot: Social realism
Time of plot: The 1920's to the 1970's
Locale: The Texas-Mexico border
First published: *The Valley* (1983; revised from *Estampas del valle y otras obras/Sketches of the Valley and Other Works*, 1973)

Principal Characters

Rafa Buenrostro, the autobiographical narrator in many of the sketches in *The Valley*. Rafa is a self-assured young man who has served in the military and soon will go to the University of Texas at Austin. He was born and reared in Belken County, but having been exposed to some of the world outside it, he realizes the need to make a break from its confines. He understands the people of the area, observing them carefully and presenting them with considerable objectivity. He usually reserves his judgments about others.

Jehú Malacra, an orphan who comes of age in *The Valley*. Jehú's parents die before he reaches puberty, so he is reared with his Briones cousins. Through Vicky Briones, he is introduced to the life of the circus and becomes don Víctor's helper in transporting circus props from place to place.

Don Víctor, a former revolutionary. As a lieutenant colonel in the Mexican armed forces, he married a Mexican Jew, Lía Samaniego, by whom he had a son, Saúl. After an epidemic of Spanish influenza claims the pregnant Lía and their son, don Víctor retires from the military, eventually makes his way to Belken County, and there is connected with the circus, where Jehú comes to work with him.

Don Manuel Guzmán, a former revolutionary who knew Pancho Villa and Álvaro Obregon. Don Manuel can trace his U.S. citizenship through his family to 1845, when a new boundary was drawn between the United States and Mexico. Despite his citizenship, don Manuel is thoroughly Mexican. Later in life, he owns three dry-cleaning estab-

lishments and part of a bakery. He is a free spirit who was once a bronco buster. He dies suddenly in his mid-forties, from a stroke that hits him when he is in the middle of telling a joke.

Gilberto (Beto) Casteñeda, the friend and brother-in-law of Baldemar (Balde) Cordero. Beto is present when Balde fatally stabs Ernesto Tamez. Called upon to give a deposition that details his recollection of the barroom stabbing, Beto tells the truth, although he never forsakes his friend. Orphaned early when his parents are killed with twenty others riding in a farm truck that is struck by a train, Beto knows the fields well and works hard in them. He dies at the age of thirty, leaving Marta Cordero a widow.

Baldemar Cordero, Gilberto's brother-in-law and friend. Baldemar kills Ernesto Tamez in a brawl over one of the hostesses of a local bar. He is tried, found guilty, and sentenced to fifteen years in prison. Drunk when he committed this rash act, he cannot remember what he did but has to pay the price for having done it.

Chedes Briones, Jehú Malacra's aunt, who helps to rear Jehú. Distressed when her daughter Vicki joins the circus, she is soon soothed by getting free tickets to its performances.

Juan Briones, Chedes' husband, a stoic who, when he learns his children have left home, drinks another beer and orders another dozen oysters.

Panchita, Rafa Buenrostro's aunt, who practices folk medicine and incantations to treat those who are ill, including Rafa.

The Novel

This collection of sketches about Rolando Hinojosa's fictional Belken County, situated just north of the Mexican border in Texas, was Hinojosa's first major publication. Originally, it was rendered in Spanish with English translations by Gustávo Valadéz and José Reyna under the title *Estampas del valle y otras obras/Sketches of the Valley and Other Works*. Hinojosa himself translated it under the present title in 1983, adding some material and a set of photographs from his family album.

The collection constitutes a novel by some definitions of the term, but it also is the first major segment of Hinojosa's evolving multivolume "Klail City Death Trip" series. Hinojosa focuses on the area around his birthplace of Mercedes, Texas (Klail City in his series). In these sketches, he attempts to capture the ambience of the area and its people.

The Valley lacks the real plot, the dramatic climax, the carefully planned denouement, and the clearly identifiable protagonist found in conventional novels. Nevertheless, it contains pervasive characters, including the frequent narrator, Rafa Buenrostro, the biographical details of whose life closely approximate Hinojosa's. It also presents Jehú Malacra, seen through many eyes at various stages of his development. The last pages of the book, "A Life of Rafa Buenrostro," focus on Rafa.

Three early sketches—a total of twenty-three printed lines—focus on Rafa's elementary school experience and evoke the sense of separation Mexican American children feel from their Anglo-American classmates and teachers. The three paragraphs that constitute these sketches are not directly related to one another. Rather, each provides a snapshot of something connected with that early school experience: the teacher, Miss Moy, is described in five lines; a Hispanic girl lies about what she had for breakfast to make herself seem more like her Anglo-American classmates (eight lines); Rafa punches Hilario Berrago in the mouth during recess (ten lines).

From these school sketches, Hinojosa moves directly to a short vignette about a man from the water company coming to shut off the Ponce family's water supply because they have not paid their bill. The next sketch moves to a neighboring town, Flora, and has no direct connection with what has preceded it.

A six-line sketch follows, telling about how in Edgerton the narrator's father had once fired three shots at a man who was trying to knife him. As these sketches unfold, readers, probably at first bewildered at encountering unfamiliar characters in unfamiliar towns, begin to develop a sense of the region about which Hinojosa is writing. The individual sketches may lack plot, yet from them emerge details useful elsewhere throughout this book and the others of the "Klail City Death Trip" series.

One sustained narrative among the sketches focuses on Baldemar (Balde) Cordero's fatal stabbing of Ernesto Tamez in a barroom brawl. Balde's friend, Gilberto (Beto) Castañeda, is married to Balde's sister, Marta. They all live together in Klail City. Beto, witness to the stabbing, gives a deposition recounting what happened. Through it, readers learn the backgrounds of Balde and Beto and of other characters they have previously encountered in the book. A sketch of Beto Castañeda follows.

Some characters in this collection emerge more fully developed in subsequent volumes of the series. Jehú Malacra is a typical example. In this book, readers first meet Jehú's grandfather, an unnamed narrator, and his long-dead great-grandfather, Braulio Tapia. Jehú's father, Roque Malacra, visits the narrator, a widower, requesting his daughter Tere Noriega's hand in marriage.

In fewer than twenty lines, the narrator consents to this request and reflects upon his having visited Braulio Tapia many years before seeking permission to marry Braulio's daughter Matilde, Tere's mother. He also recalls that Braulio's wife, doña Sóstenes, was dead when he approached his prospective father-in-law, as the narrator's wife is dead when Roque approaches him.

In these parallel circumstances, one senses the

recurrence of human events that is part of continuance in a county such as Belken. Hinojosa's family lived in the south Texas area from the 1740's and became "accidental" American citizens in 1845, when the boundary between Mexico and the United States was redrawn a few miles south of where they had previously lived as Mexicans. *The Valley* and subsequent volumes follow Jehú Malacra from his birth through his childhood, his war experiences, and his rise as an officer in the local bank and second husband of Becky Escobar, to whom Hinojosa later devotes a full volume, *Becky and Her Friends* (1990).

Analysis

Hinojosa's main thrust in this first volume of the "Klail City Death Trip" series has to do with establishing the sense of recurrence and continuity that characterizes his fictional (and actual) county in south Texas. The boundary changed in 1845, but the drawing of a line on a map cannot change the hearts, souls, or heritage of a citizenry.

Hinojosa's sketches, if viewed in the light of the full series, also have to do with how people mature into what they eventually become. If his characters are inconsistent, Hinojosa makes no apology, saying that people are not consistent as they go through life. Some things about them remain the same, some change. In Hinojosa's eyes, consistency of character is not a valid human trait.

In this volume, as in the others in the series, there is really no dominant character; even in *Becky and Her Friends*, Becky Escobar cannot be called a dominant character in the usual sense. Rather than writing about one or more protagonists, Hinojosa writes about a community of people. Readers meet most of them without being given much background: They simply appear on the page engaged in living some small part of their lives.

Some critics disdain this approach, yet it replicates the way people come to know and understand society in real life. People happen upon scenes and draw from them what they can with the information available to them.

Those who judge Hinojosa negatively should remember that when Gertrude Stein replicated actual speech patterns with great accuracy in *Three Lives* (1909), readers accustomed to having authors run interference for them between actual speech and the dialogue of most novels were appalled. Yet in that experimental novel, Stein broke new stylistic ground that led many subsequent authors to reconsider how they would present dialogue in their fiction.

Hinojosa has reassessed the ways human beings derive information from actual occurrences in their lives. In the volumes in his series, he has no misgivings about plunging directly into ongoing action. If one suddenly is plunged into a scene that depicts an event in Flora, Hinojosa does not pause to tell his readers where Flora is or what kind of town it is. He does that elsewhere in the book, but he does not interrupt the ongoing action of his story to provide details without which his readers can still perceive the action.

One cannot deny that an initial reading of a book such as *The Valley* bewilders and confuses readers. Hinojosa, who holds a doctorate in Spanish literature from the University of Illinois and is well schooled in literature, is bent on achieving a depiction that mirrors reality. Upon completing this book, readers have a sense of community that few more conventional novels impart.

Critical Context

The 1960's were crucial to Rolando Hinojosa's development as a writer. He completed a five-year stint as a high-school teacher and factory laborer in Brownsville, Texas, and in 1962 began graduate studies at New Mexico Highlands University, receiving a master's degree in 1963. He then moved to the University of Illinois at Urbana for doctoral work.

Hinojosa and his wife arrived in Illinois just before the strident racial uprisings of the 1960's, a period that focused attention on the problems of African Americans. Out of this period grew a hospitable atmosphere for black protest literature and, subsequently, for black literature that had been produced earlier. In this climate, all minority literatures began to be encouraged and reevaluated.

Just before completing his doctorate, Hinojosa accepted a teaching job at San Antonio's Trinity University, where, fortunately, he came under the influence of Tomás Rivera. Rivera encouraged Hinojosa's writing, urging him to submit a manuscript to the Quinto Sol competition, which Rivera had won in 1970. Hinojosa submitted the original version of *The Valley*, which took the prize in 1972 and resulted in the book's publication the following year.

THE VILLAGERS

Author: Jorge Icaza (1906-1978)
Type of work: Novel
Type of plot: Social criticism
Time of plot: The twentieth century
Locale: Ecuador
First published: *Huasipungo*, 1934 (English translation, 1964)

Principal Characters

Alfonso Pereira, a debt-ridden Ecuadoran landowner who cheats the Indians and sells timber rights on his estate.

Blanca, his wife, who uses Cunshi as wet nurse for their baby.

Andrés Chiliquinga, an Indian who dies defending his *huasipungo* (a small plot of ground given workers on an estate) against the greedy whites.

Cunshi, his wife, wronged by Pereira.

Lolita, their seventeen-year-old daughter, in love with a mestizo.

Don Julio, Pereira's uncle, who demands repayment of a loan.

Policarpio, Pereira's overseer, who is somewhat sympathetic toward the Indian tenants.

Padre Lomas, the avaricious, lustful village priest who overcharges for masses and burials. He tricks the Indians into building a road to open their territory.

Mr. Chapy, a North American promoter interested in timber and oil.

Jacinto Quintana, the proprietor of the village store and saloon.

Juana La Chola, his wife, who is forced to accept the attentions of Pereira and the priest.

Juancho Cabascango, a prosperous Indian, cursed by the priest and killed by the Indians.

The Novel

Alfonso Pereira is an Ecuadoran landowner in *The Villagers*, one who is plagued by domestic and financial troubles. His wife Blanca nags him, and he is worried about his seventeen-year-old daughter Lolita, who wants to marry a man who is part Indian. Don Julio, his uncle, adds to his difficulties by demanding repayment of a loan of ten thousand sucres, a debt already three months overdue.

When Pereira confesses that he is unable to repay the loan, Don Julio suggests that his nephew try to interest Mr. Chapy, a North American promoter, in a timber concession on Pereira's mountain estate. Privately, the old man suspects that Mr. Chapy and his associates are on the lookout for oil and are using their lumber-cutting activities in the

region as a blind. In order to interest the North Americans, however, it would be necessary to build fifteen miles of road and get possession of two forest tracts. In addition, the Indians would have to be driven off their *huasipungos*, the lands supplied to them in return for working on the master's estate.

Pereira assures his uncle that such a course would be difficult. The Indians, having a deep affection for their lands, would never willingly give them up. Don Julio ridicules Pereira's sentimentality and tells him to return to the estate at Tomachi and build the road. Back home, Pereira discusses his problem with Padre Lomas, the village priest. The padre agrees to persuade the Indians to work on the road; he will tell them that the labor is the will of God.

Andrés Chiliquinga, an Indian workman, is unhappy because Pereira has returned, for he has gone against his master's and the priest's wishes by taking Cunshi as his wife. He is one of thirty Indians sent to start cutting wood and clearing the roadbed.

To find a wet nurse for her baby, Blanca Pereira examines some of the Indian mothers. Their undernourished babies are diseased, some with malaria or dysentery; others are idiotic or epileptic. Policarpio, the overseer, finally chooses Cunshi, mother of the healthiest child in the village, and takes her to the Pereira house. Pereira, seeing the young Indian woman, forces her to sleep with him.

One night, Andrés makes the long trip home to see his wife. Finding no one in their hillside shack, he becomes suspicious and angry. The next day, he deliberately lets his ax fall on his foot. The Indians treat the cut with spiderwebs and mud, but when the bandage is removed three days later, the foot is so badly infected that Andrés is sent home. A medicine man poultices the sore and saves Andrés' life, but the wound leaves him lame.

One day, while Pereira and the priest are at the store discussing the building of the road, they send Jacinto Quintana, the proprietor, on an errand. After his departure, both men force Juana, his wife, to accept their attentions.

Storms make life miserable for the Indians working on the road, unprotected as they are in their camps. Some die when they try to drain a swamp; others perish in quicksand. Pereira, choosing to risk the Indians rather than follow a longer, safer route, keeps the workmen drunk and entertains them with cockfights. The ignorant laborers continue to toil.

The priest goes to Juancho Cabascango, an Indian with a prosperous *huasipungo* beside the river, and asks for one hundred sucres to pay for a mass. When the Indian refuses, Padre Lomas curses him. A short time later, a flash flood drowns some of the Indians and their cattle. Blaming the disaster on Juancho, his superstitious neighbors beat him to death. The priest declares the affair the will of God and easily collects several hundred sucres for his mass.

At last the road is completed, but the Indians receive none of the benefits Padre Lomas had promised. He buys a bus and two trucks, taking transport business from those who used to drive mule teams into Quito with the products of the region. Young Indians ride the bus to the city and there end up as criminals and prostitutes.

Because of easy transportation and the possibility of a profitable sale in Quito, Pereira decides not to give the Indians their customary grain from his plentiful harvest. Policarpio's protests do no good. When the hungry Indians go to Pereira's patio and beg their master to relieve the hunger of their families, he tells them that their daily pay of fifty centavos is generous enough. Besides, the proceeds from the ton and a half of corn needed to feed the Indians will help considerably in reducing his debts. He does, however, heed his overseer's warning and asks that guards for his estate be sent from Quito.

Hunger stalks the region. When one of Pereira's cows dies, the famished Indians beg for the carcass. He refuses, because they might be tempted to kill other cows, and he orders Policarpio to bury the dead animal. Desperate, Andrés digs it up. After he and his family eat some of the meat, the tainted flesh kills Cunshi. Padre Lomas demands twenty-five sucres, more than the Indian could ever earn, in payment for burying the dead woman. That same night, Andrés steals one of his master's cows and sells it to a nearby butcher. Tracked down by dogs, the Indian is captured and flogged in Pereira's patio.

A score of foreigners arrives in Tomachi. The Indians welcome them timorously, thinking that these new white men could certainly be no more cruel than their Spanish masters. One of their first acts is to order the Indians driven from their *huasipungos* to make room for company houses and a sawmill.

When Andrés' son brings news of the order, the Indians rebel. They had stolidly accepted the white man's cruelty, even his lechery toward their women, but they believe that the land is theirs.

Jacinto tries to stop them when they march on the village. The enraged Indians kill six of the white men. The others, including Mr. Chapy, flee in their autos.

The white men return, over the road the Indians had built, with three hundred soldiers, under a leader who had killed two thousand Indians in a similar rebellion near Cuenca. Troops hunt down and machine-gun Indians of all ages, both men and women. The few survivors, taking refuge in Andrés' hillside shack, roll rocks down on the soldiers and shoot at them with bird guns. Finally, the soldiers set fire to the shack's thatched roof. When the Indians run from the burning house, the troops shoot them without mercy.

Analysis

This brutal novel flows swiftly. Technically, it is one of the better Spanish American novels. Its virtues are legion, among them interesting dialogue, bitter irony, sardonic humor, interesting plot, effective use of detail, exposure of social injustice, and crispness of style, with short sentences that get to the point. *The Villagers* presents the Ecuadoran Andes clearly. Even the sounds of the sierra are heard, and the odors, temperature changes, and direction of the night wind are experienced. The book's crowning virtue is its defense of Ecuador's oppressed Indians. For this reason, it is considered to be Jorge Icaza's most significant novel. It helped launch the cycle of so-called *Indianista* novels, devoted to telling the story of the long-abandoned Indians. The novel's protagonist is the Indian, who is characterized collectively but clearly, even to the peculiar flavor of his Spanish.

Decay is a prominent and depressing note. Images of garbage, filth, mold, slime, and rotten meat are frequent. Trash, dirt, and profanity are always present; everything is sloppy and unkempt, reflecting life's hopelessness. Depression is thus a constant note, accentuated by dismal mountain fogs, clammy cold, foul speech, and superstition. *Soroche* (altitude sickness) occasionally strikes, as do other afflictions. Alcoholism is the Indian's bane, for the *huasipunguero* abandons everything—chickens, corn, potatoes, children—for alcohol.

The characters generally fail to change or develop. Icaza implies that the mestizo or mulatto suffers from a psychological inferiority complex in Ecuador, as is exemplified by Juana la Chola's (Juana the Half-breed) inert submission to rape by a landowner and a cleric. Those villains, unfortunately, are crudely drawn. Don Alfonso Pereira is a second-rate Simon Legree, a consistent rascal, self-server, hypocrite, and uncomplicated brute from start to finish of the novel. He snarls, curses, and brutalizes Indians, but he cringes from those above him. The priest is worse: He is so utterly depraved as to be comical. He extorts money from hungry Indians, sells passages out of purgatory or burial plots "close to Heaven" at alarming prices, and builds a lucrative trucking business on illicitly obtained money. The priest is a symbol of Icaza's disenchantment with religion. It is puzzling that this "larger-than-life" caricature has not aroused disdain or even criticism from college students and professors.

Other ogres in the book are wealthy people, businessmen, whites, property owners, and gringo capitalists. The gringos career about in Cadillacs, oblivious to Indians; they relish money and lack human feelings. The novel was intended as a tirade against the social injustice that then blighted Ecuador. Icaza possibly had the illusion that his novel would bring a better life to the Indians, but initially his work was better received and lauded abroad than in his own country. In any event, Icaza exposed the plight of Ecuador's peons as well as the decay of the rural aristocrats, who had left the work of their fathers to live luxuriously in the city. The novel also promotes the conflict of red race against white. Some critics think that Icaza's work had political motivations; others compare him to John Steinbeck and consider him to be a social reformer.

No one in *The Villagers* apparently wishes to

live in the country, since life in Quito is much richer. The countryside is backward, isolated, and uncomfortable; the city is cultured and far superior. Nature is unattractive; its beauties are never mentioned and unextolled. Nature's dangers are stressed, however, as in a scene in which a man dies horribly by drowning in mud. Tints of sunrises, sunsets, mountains, skies, fields, or towns are generally lacking, and even the grayness of the constant mountain mist is assumed rather than described. The author's treatment of color is a deliberate stylistic device to increase the feeling of dismal hopelessness.

Critical Context

Stark, brutal realism overlies the artistry of this novel of protest against the enslavement of the Indian in rural Ecuador. Icaza is only one of many Latin American novelists who, influenced by Fyodor Dostoevski, Maxim Gorky, and other European realists, used the indigenous theme and showed the white man's cruelty toward the Indian. *The Villagers* is the best of these polemic works. Greater as a social document, perhaps, than as a work of fiction, it is made up of a series of episodes with power lying in graphic accounts of the lives and trials of the Indian. Icaza writes carelessly, with a scorn of syntax, but with a keen ear that reproduces the difficult dialect of the Quichua-speaking inhabitants of the Andean region near Quito. Types symbolizing classes, rather than clearly realized individuals, fill his pages. In spite of its defects, *The Villagers* is a powerful novel, with many pirated editions in Spanish, an English translation printed in the Soviet Union, and even a version in Chinese.

Although of Spanish blood and comfortable background, Icaza decided as a youth to champion Ecuador's poor of all races. Having attracted international attention, his novel *The Villagers* eventually won acceptance in Ecuador and undoubtedly helped the Indians. Some of the political attention has been lip service, but the life of Ecuador's highland Indians is today improved over that described in this book. Icaza's novel has, in spite of its propagandistic qualities and superficial characterization, attracted much attention through its readability.

THE VIOLENT LAND

Author: Jorge Amado (1912-   )
Type of work: Novel
Type of plot: Romance
Time of plot: The late nineteenth century
Locale: The state of Bahia, Brazil
First published: *Terras do Sem Fim*, 1942 (English translation, 1945)

Principal Characters

Colonel Horacio da Silveira, a barbarous cacao planter of Bahia, Brazil. He schemes to get more land. His wife sleeps with his lawyer, who is murdered when found out.

Colonel Sinhô Badaró, another wealthy plantation owner. He has more power until a change of government takes place.

Doña Ester, Horacio's unfaithful wife, who dies of a fever.

Doña Ana, Badaró's wealthy daughter, who fights to defend the plantation.

Captain João Magalhães, a professional gambler who marries Ana.

Doctor Virgilio Cabral, Horacio's cultured lawyer and Ester's lover, who is shot by order of Horacio.

Margot, Cabral's mistress before she turns to Juca.

Juca Badaró, the colonel's younger brother, who admires Magalhães. He spreads anti-Silveira scandal until shot by a hired gunman.

The Novel

This novel, skillfully plotted and impressive in its evocation of the spirit of a region, reflects the violence of the struggle to produce and market the raw materials for chocolate. The action covers the early years of cacao production in the state of Bahia, Brazil, a corner of the world that was a late frontier. Like most frontiers, it was a lawless area that attracted people anxious to get rich quickly, people who did not care whether others, or they themselves, lived or died. Bahia was, at the same time, a land where courageous men carved fortunes out of the wilderness and the labor of other men, a place where the strong lived and the weak succumbed. Its history is the Brazilian counterpart of an era in the development of the western United States. Wherever it is found, the frontier is always a violent land.

In the minds of most Brazilians, the São Jorge dos Ilhéus was a semibarbarous country ruled by a handful of rich planters who styled themselves colonels. These men had risen, almost without exception, from humble origins by means of courage, bravado, and murder. The two most important planters in *The Violent Land* are Colonel Horacio da Silveira and Colonel Sinhô Badaró. Between their lands lies a large forest, upon which both men have long cast covetous eyes. The forest, actually a jungle, could be cleared to uncover productive cacao-growing soil.

Among the strangers who pour into the region in search of wealth at the time are several people who are to range themselves on one side or the other in the coming struggle. Dr. Virgilio Cabral, a cultured and talented lawyer, allies himself with da Silveira. With the lawyer comes Margot, a beautiful prostitute who had fallen in love with him and become his mistress while he was a student. Another arrival is Captain João Magalhães, a professional gambler and a courageous opportunist who calls himself a military engineer. Among his admirers are Juca Badaró, Colonel Badaró's younger brother, and Doña Ana Badaró, the colonel's daughter, also the heiress to the Badaró fortune.

Soon after his arrival, Cabral falls in love with Ester, da Silveira's beautiful wife. The woman, who hates her husband, quickly returns the affection of the more cultured man. When she becomes his mistress, both know that they will be killed if the husband finds out. As his ardor for Ester da Silveira increases, the lawyer's affection for his former mistress wanes. Soon Margot finds herself unwanted by her lover. In retaliation, and because she needs someone to support her, Margot becomes the mistress of Juca Badaró. Out of spite, she also furnishes him with scandal about the opposition, gossip he uses in the newspaper, which favors the Badarós.

Professionally, as well as amorously, Cabral is a success, for he finds an old survey of the contested lands and registers the title in da Silveira's name after bribing the registry officials. The Badaró family quickly retaliates by burning the registry office and all the records on file. In addition, the Badarós hire Magalhães to run a survey for them. He makes the survey, even though he lacks the proper knowledge to do so. His presence at the Badaró plantation earns him the respect of the Badaró brothers and the love of Doña Ana Badaró. The self-styled captain, always an opportunist, permits himself to fall in love with the girl and pay court to her.

Because the Badaró family is the more powerful of the two factions, da Silveira goes to several small planters and promises to let them divide half of the forest land if they, as a group, help him hold it against the Badarós. There is bloody fighting on both sides of the forest and within it, for both factions hire assassins and bodyguards to back up their interests with bullets.

Juca Badaró is assassinated by a hired gunman after insulting Cabral. Juca had found the lawyer dancing with Margot, at the girl's request, and had insulted the lawyer for daring to do so. Both Cabral and da Silveira are deterred in their plans when the colonel falls ill with a fever. The planter recovers but his wife, the lawyer's mistress, becomes ill as

a result of nursing her husband. Her death removes one incentive in the efforts of both her husband and her lover, but they stubbornly continue the fight.

As the struggle in the courts and in the fields continues, the Badarós spend more and more money. They sell their current crop of cacao pods as well as next year's crop in order to raise funds immediately. Before his assassination, Juca Badaró had seen to it that his niece, Doña Ana, was married to the gambler, for he saw in Magalhães an ambitious man willing to fight for money and power. So tempting was the proposal the Badarós made that the captain agreed to take his wife's name, her father insisting that he do so in order to carry on the Badaró line.

At first, by tacit consent, the contending parties do no damage to one another's cacao trees, but as the Badaró's become desperate, they instruct their desperados to burn the cacao groves. Their opponents see that the matter has to be settled at once, lest both parties be irretrievably ruined and become victims of someone stronger. Colonel da Silveira and his forces attack the Badaró plantation in force and drive off the family, after killing all the men except a handful led by Magalhães.

Da Silveira and his men believe that the women of the Badaró household have been sent away, but the attackers are greeted by gunfire from Doña Ana herself as they enter the house. When she runs out of ammunition, she gives up, expecting to be killed. The attackers let her go, however, because she is a woman.

The rout is completed by an announcement from the Brazilian capital that the political party favoring da Silveira has come into power and is sending troops and government agents to the district to quiet the violence. The jungle lands are ceded to the da Silveira faction by the government's action. Da Silveira is forced to stand trial for the murder of Juca Badaró, but the trial is staged more to clear the colonel than to find him guilty.

The district quickly settles down after the great feud ends and the new government starts its operations. There is to be one more assassination. While going through his dead wife's effects, da Silveira discovers letters Cabral had written to her. He is horrified and embarrassed to learn of her infidelity, which he had not suspected, and his lawyer's duplicity. After thinking about the matter for some time, he sends a gunman to clear his honor by killing the man who had made him a cuckold.

Analysis

Jorge Amado's novel is the standard-bearer of the cacao cycle in Brazilian literature, a series of novels exposing exploitation of cacao workers. *The Violent Land* is the story of Bahia's panhandle, where a balmy climate, fertile soil, and lack of high winds make it one of the few areas on Earth well suited for chocolate trees, whose weak stems and heavy pods need heat but cannot stand strong winds. Amado's characterization of the raw frontier of the panhandle of Bahia, a narrow strip stretching southward toward the mountains of Espirito Santo, is particularly apt. The reader sees not only an area where "the colonels" and their heavily armed cohorts oppress the weak but also the Bahian *sertão* (backlands) in general, brimming with blood, old feuds, religious messianism, and fanaticism. Even today, the colonels, cowboys, professionals, and workers that sprinkle the novel's pages can be seen around the old town of Ilhéus and elsewhere in the panhandle. Amado's characters are thus flesh-and-blood realities from rural Bahia. His principal characterization flaw is an error of omission, for the warmly human types so common everywhere in Brazil, including Bahia, are lacking in the violent pages of *The Violent Land*.

This novel refreshingly explodes the oft-heard myth that Brazil, unlike Spanish America, is a bland and frivolous land not given to violence. Amado's novel bristles with the violence and mystery endemic to the *sertão*. It is for this reason that the book's English translation is titled *The Violent Land*; a true translation of the Portuguese title is "the endless lands." Amado paints a land fertile with blood, as his preface indicates. Set in the late twentieth century, when cacao was power, wealth, and life, the novel's action portrays the enslavement of everything and everyone to the cacao pod. The shadow of cacao darkens every heart. It smothers finer instincts and levels all characters, from aristocratic Colonel Horacio da Silveira to the more common Badarós.

The Violent Land reflects progress, however, for the colonels are drawn as a crude but civilizing force in Brazil's historic "march to the west" that, a century later, was opening up the once trackless *sertão*. Amado himself was born on a cacao plantation in 1912 and admired the ranchers, such as his own father, who settled the raw panhandle, built roads, and founded towns. The novel's first scene, symbolically enough, is aboard a ship drawing away from the baroque city of São Salvador de Bahia. The passengers aboard are immigrants to the rich but violent lands of the panhandle, and they discuss land, money, cacao, and death. They sing a sad song that presages disaster, but that night, in their staterooms and steerage quarters, they dream of laden cacao trees.

Landscape is an important factor in *The Violent Land*. Amado paints the golden mornings dawning over green palms, the red soil under the cacao trees, the blue-green waves of the sea, and indigo skies. One also sees stormy nights, wild Brahma cattle, birds, and snakes. Trees are almost idolized, especially the cacao. Above all, Amado lyrically paints the forest in the uninterrupted sleep that it enjoyed before the colonels came. The waiting forest is like an unexplored sea, locked in its own mystery, virginal, lovely, and radiant. Amado also presents the varied Bahian racial types, from Scandinavian-like blondes to Latin brunettes and Hamitic blacks. One also sees the colonels in khaki trousers, white hats, and gun belts, as well as the leather-clad gunmen, legendarily ferocious *onças* (wild cats), and ranch tools.

Fear is an additional element in the story. The forest's mysteries incite fear—Ester hysterically fears snakes and is haunted by the phobia that they will one night invade her house en masse. The backlanders tell many snake stories, while dogs howl at night, rain clouds are dark, and nights are jet black.

Critical Context

Lamentably, the storied and colorful old city of São Salvador de Bahia does not loom in *The Violent Land* as Atlanta does in *Gone with the Wind* (1936). Little São Jorge dos Ilhéus, "a city of palms in the wind," is depicted well. Its streets are lined by palms, but it is dominated by the cacao tree, for the scent of chocolate is in every conversation and each colonel's fortune can be measured by the size of his estate. Inland from the pastel town, on every red-dirt road leading into the cacao lands, are crosses without names.

Brazilian novelists complained for decades that the harsh, nasal Portuguese language in which they wrote was "the graveyard of literature," a literary cul-de-sac. *The Violent Land* has been translated into more than twenty languages and translations of other novels into foreign languages have opened Brazilian literature to the world. Amado's masterwork also helps reveal that the key to Brazilian literature is not chronology, style, or study of influences, but geography. Brazil is a literary archipelago with six literary "islands," and *The Violent Land* is to be read and regarded as a work of the "island" of Bahia.

VISIÓN DE ANÁHUAC

Author: Alfonso Reyes (1889-1959)
Type of work: Essay
First published: 1917

The Work

Anáhuac was the Nahuatl name for the Valley of Mexico, site of the great city of Tenochtitlán and the center of the Aztec civilization that fell to the conquistadores under Hernán Cortés in 1521. In a style that is subtle, evocative, and varied, Alfonso Reyes re-creates the wonder of that place and time when two races and two societies confronted each other and the feudal barbarism of the Old World performed its act of violence upon the Indian barbarism of the New. Years later, Bernal Díaz del Castillo, chronicler of the conquest, voiced his lament for a despoiled culture that was passionate and cruel but also beautiful and splendid: "Now all is lost, razed, so that there is nothing."

In the epigraph to his essay, Reyes welcomes the traveler to the most crystalline region of the air. In this luminous prose and vivid imagery, every object stands out, distinct and immaculate in color and form, bathed in the blue and gold intensity of sky and sun. For the sake of analogy, Reyes invokes the name of Giovanni Battista Ramusio, who began to publish his collection *Delle Navigazioni e Viaggi* in Venice in 1550. Among the illustrations in this old work are scenes of the New World as the explorers saw it and wrote about it. These pictures, ingenuous in conception and meticulous in design, present an exotic world of nature in the vegetation of New Spain: the ear of corn, the clustered banana, the strange tropical fruits distilling their own fragrance and honey, and in stiff array the varieties of cacti, emblematic plants of a semi-arid land where the cactus, the eagle, and the serpent are the appropriate heraldic devices for a coat of arms.

To the priests and warriors of the tribe that entered the valley early in the fourteenth century— the last of such migrations into Anáhuac—the legendary vision of the eagle and the serpent was the fulfillment of a prophecy. Behind that roving band lay a history of many wanderings and wars in which memory and fact faded into a primitive myth of warriors who came out of the Seven Caves to which the seven tribes traced their dim beginnings. There they built a city, a flower of stone on water. The city became an empire, cyclopean like those of Egypt and Babylon, over which Moctezuma the magnificent but weak ruled in the ill-omened days that heralded the coming of the white man. The stage had been set for the last act in an ancient drama of conquest and settlement when Cortés and his followers crossed the snow-capped mountains and descended through fields of maize and maguey to the valley floor.

Ahead of them, connected with the mainland by three stone causeways two lances in width, Tenochtitlán rose like a mirage from waters that caught and held the color of the sky. In that clear atmosphere, every detail of the city and its environs could be viewed as if through crystal, an intricate pattern of temples, palaces, public squares, streets, canals, and gardens bright with flowers. Over the city loomed the bulk of the great temple, with wide streets radiating from its four corners. Smoke rose from the sanctuaries atop the holy pyramid, and through the still air came the echoing rumble of drums and the thin music of flutes.

To the Spaniards, the sight was like some vision of enchantment, for the conquistadores carried in their blood the same strain of wonder that had produced the romantic story of Amadís of Gaul. "As soon as we saw so many cities and towns in the water," Díaz del Castillo wrote, "we were struck with amazement and said that it seemed like things from the book of Amadís because of the great towers and temples and houses which they had built in the water, and all of them of stone and mortar, and even some of our soldiers spoke of what they saw as if they were in a land of dreams."

As Reyes points out, the life of the city revolved around three central points: the temple, the marketplace, and Moctezuma's palace. In all sections of the city, the pattern was repeated in the smaller shrines, the market squares, and the palaces of the nobles. The proud, somber Indian of Anáhuac was a worshiper of fierce gods, a shrewd trader, and a lover of ceremony and display.

Within the serpent-carved wall of the sacred enclosure stood the great temple, a terraced, monolithic pyramid built of basalt and porphyry slabs quarried from the surrounding hills. Inside this precinct, the apartments of the priests, the study halls, and rooms for the storage of sacrificial utensils and books of ritual covered an area that could have enclosed a village of five hundred persons. One hundred fourteen steps led to the highest platform, on which were images of the gods, housed in sanctuaries decorated with carvings of men and monsters in wood and stone. The giant idols, made of cereals and blood, were decorated with precious metals and jewels. Sacred fires burned on the altars. Close at hand were trumpets, censers, flutes, conch shells, and the flint knives used for human sacrifice. There also was the ceremonial serpent-skin drum, which could be heard two leagues away. Blood spattered the altars and floors. The priests wore black robes, and their hair was matted with gore. They were the guardians of savage rituals, the ministers of a faith reaching downward toward that concept of earth and blood that is the dark mystery at the heart of humanity's remote origins.

From the horrors of the temple, the Spaniards turned to the bustle of the marketplace. It was, said Cortés, twice as large as that of Salamanca. Every day some sixty thousand people engaged in buying and selling under the supervision of inspectors and twelve presiding magistrates. All the produce of the land was offered for sale, each in its separate quarter under deep porticoes: jewelry of precious stones and metals, including collars, bracelets, earrings, and lip plugs of jade, crystal, emerald, turquoise, gold, silver, and copper; beautiful feather-

work, shimmering as a hummingbird poised in sunlight; flowers from Xochimilco; textiles that reminded Cortés of the silk market in Granada; game of all kinds, including partridge, quail, wild ducks, rabbits, deer, and small dogs bred for eating; vegetables of every description, including onions, leeks, cresses, sorrel, artichokes, beans, and golden thistles; corn of red, black, yellow, and blue, sold green on the ear or dried or ground or baked into loaves and tortillas; fish, fruits, cacao, syrups of corn and maguey; building materials of stone, bricks, and timber; firewood and charcoal for cooking and heating; pottery for every use, painted and glazed; eggs, cakes, sweets, hides, and tobacco. There was a quarter for apothecaries—Indian herbalists acquainted the Spaniards with more than twelve hundred medicinal plants and roots—and another for barbers. There were houses where food was cooked and served. In another quarter was the slave market. The Indian market, according to Díaz del Castillo, surprised even those who had been to Constantinople and Rome.

Those familiar with the Spanish court were equally astonished by the pomp and splendor that surrounded Moctezuma. To their awed gaze, he seemed another Midas, whose touch turned everything to gold. It was necessary for him to uncover himself to show Cortés that he was of human flesh. Moctezuma, in his palaces, had reproduced in precious stones, gold, silver, or feathers every natural object in his kingdom. Six hundred lords attended him daily. When he dined, three hundred noble youths were needed to serve him, for he had put before him every variety of meat, fish, vegetable, and fruit in the land. Four times a day he changed his dress, and his garments, like the dishes from which he was served, were never used again. Those who approached his person wore poor clothing and abased themselves in humility. When he relaxed, dancers, buffoons, and acrobats entertained him.

In his great palace the walls were of porphyry, jasper, and marble, roofed with carved beams and richly carpeted with cotton rugs, skins, and featherwork. Fountains played in the courtyards. He had other palaces for his recreation. One contained pools of water, salt and sweet, for every kind of aquatic bird. Another section contained birds valued for the beauty of their plumage. Still another housed birds of prey, for the king was skilled in falconry. There was a palace in which wild animals and reptiles were kept. Another was given over to the raising of flowers (no vegetables or fruit trees ever grew in the Indian garden), fragrant shrubs, and scented herbs.

In a land where nature was so inseparably joined to the daily lives of the people, the flower, not the snakeskin drum or the sacrificial knife, was the symbol of culture, a symbol of the love of art and beauty that redeemed in part the cruelty of the religion. The Aztec noble carried flowers in his hand when he walked abroad; garlands decked him on ceremonial occasions. Flowers filled the markets, the palaces, and the adobe houses of the poor. Floral designs decorated the pottery of Cholula. Floating gardens covered the lakes. In the calendrical codices a shower of flowers is shown descending upon the earth at the end of the fourth sun-cycle. The flower also had its consecration in art. Stylized in picture writing and in sculpture, it appears in place names and as the designation of the exquisite qualities of things. As surviving fragments and translations show, the flower provided themes and imagery in both secular and religious poetry of the period before the conquest.

Analysis

Reyes laments the loss of the indigenous poetry of the Indians. Although scholars may unearth portions of their hymns, rituals, or festive songs, and although others still exist in the versions of the Spanish friars, nothing can ever compensate for the loss of the body of literature that reflected the religious and social experience of the people of Anáhuac. Findings and reconstructions contain only suggestions of what that poetry must have been, for even altered and indirect in the surviving versions, it exhibits a degree of sensibility not characteristic of the translating Spanish missionaries who possessed more pity than imagination. One poem, "Ninoyolonotza," is quoted as an example of man's search through the world of the senses for a concept of the ideal. Another, paraphrased in part from the Quetzalcoatl cycle, contains echoes of an ancient fertility myth similar to those of Tammuz and Adonis. The likeness becomes cause for reflection. The promise of rebirth in the Quetzalcoatl legend, if fulfilled, might have destroyed the blood-drinking gods of the Aztecs and so altered the somber history of Anáhuac.

Discussion can do no more than suggest the magnificence of the writing in *Visión de Anáhuac*. All of preconquest Mexico is seen here, evoked out of a vast and prodigal storehouse of history and legend, every detail viewed through the eyes of a poet conferring impressions of sense and details of fact like a radiant gift. The style is in keeping with the theme, language rising from the page to the slow swing of its rhythms and the sudden thrust of its images, a mingling of grace and violence, of the concrete and the hauntingly allusive. It has been said that *Visión de Anáhuac* set a standard for a new kind of poetry. Certainly its auditory and visual effects have been echoed by a number of modern poets. Among others, Valéry Larbaud and Juan José Domenchina have called attention to the similarities of tone and style between this prose poem by Reyes and the *Anabasis* (1924) of St.-John Perse. It should be pointed out also that *Visión de Anáhuac* is the antecedent work.

Critical Context

For more than fifty years, in book after book, Reyes demonstrated the excellence and universality of Hispano-American letters. Poet, short-story writer, essayist, critic, theoretician, metaphysicist, and scholar in the best humanist tradition, he has ranged for his themes and materials from Athens in the classic age to the Indian pueblos and the history of his native Mexico. Under these circumstances it may seem somewhat arbitrary to let a single essay, even one commonly found in separate publication, represent a writer of such variety and scope. *Visión de Anáhuac*, written in Madrid in 1915 and published in San José de Costa Rica two years later, is one of those seminal works for which significance or influence bears no relationship to bulk. It is a prose poem, a landscape painting, a patriotic invocation, a study in history, an archaeological reconstruction, a literary critique, and an exercise in style. The late Chilean poet Gabriela Mistral called it the best single piece of Latin American prose.

THE WAR OF THE END OF THE WORLD

Author: Mario Vargas Llosa (1936-   )
Type of work: Novel
Type of plot: Historical realism
Time of plot: The late 1890's
Locale: Brazil, primarily the backlands
First published: *La guerra del fin del mundo*, 1981 (English translation, 1984)

Principal Characters

Antonio Conselheiro (the Counselor), a tall, thin, bearded man of mysterious identity and origins who proclaims that he has been sent by God to become the lord of Canudos. This backlands mystic begins to develop a following in the interior of the state of Bahia, Brazil. Predicting the end of the present world and the beginning of a new one, he gradually becomes a symbol and leader for those who remain committed to the monarchy. He and several thousand of his followers establish a community at an abandoned cattle ranch called Canudos, where they plan to wait out the apocalyptic developments that he has predicted. Rejecting the advances of the encroaching Republican civilization, they refuse to pay taxes and also shelter numerous backland outlaws. The insecure new federal government eventually crushes this "revolt" in 1897.

Galileo Gall, the alias of a Scottish-born utopian anarchist and phrenologist. This libertarian intellectual views Canudos idealistically as a model of human fraternity, only superficially cluttered by religion. In his view, the Canudos movement is the beginning of a revolution that will ultimately end the tyranny of the state.

Baron de Canabrava, an unscrupulous politi-

cian and head of Bahia's Autonomist Party. He represents the local elite. He attempts to turn matters to his own favor by accusing the republicans of inciting the entire episode.

Rufino, a tracker and guide. A young, suspicious man, he has been hired by Galileo Gall to take the latter to Canudos.

The nearsighted journalist, an inept and unnamed individual whose mission is to report on the campaign against Canudos. He breaks his glasses and cannot see anything during the destruction of the religious community, symbolically taking a myopic view of historical events. His character, one of the most memorable and believable in a novel devoted to the clash of monolithic social forces, performs a consistently subversive function in the narrative by indulging in self-parodying remarks. He also serves as one of Vargas Llosa's surrogate authors.

Jurema, Rufino's young wife, Gall's victim, and the journalist's lover. Considered as nothing more than a domestic animal by Gall, she is raped by him in an intense scene of physical violence. Her rape underscores the relationship between sexual and political repression in the novel.

The Novel

Using the epoch-making historical work of Euclides da Cunha, *Os Sertões* (1902; *Rebellion in the Backlands*, 1944), Vargas Llosa re-creates the turbulent events of late nineteenth century Brazil in a novel of revolution that has a clear relationship to the continuing history of revolt in Latin America.

As he elaborates the facts and biases of Cunha's "Bible of Brazilian Nationality," he follows the career of the millenarian preacher Antonio Conselheiro, his sectarian community at Canudos in the backlands of northern Brazil, the military campaigns to destroy the anti-Republican stronghold of the Counselor's followers, and the political intrigues of the monarchists and Republicans in a newly independent Brazil. When he departs from Cunha's social history, he carefully maintains a fidelity to the historical details and backgrounds against which his characters act.

Like much late twentieth century fiction, the novel is, in part, a work about writing. The efforts of the unnamed nearsighted journalist (likely modeled on Cunha himself, to whom the novel is dedicated) to explore, record, and explain the facts and hypotheses of a revolt doomed to failure are central to the plot. The journalist is himself caught up in the campaign against Canudos and becomes a questionable eyewitness to the events, as he loses his eyeglasses there. As the journalist encounters each of the figures whose exploits and intentions he will later seek to note, classify, and explain, so Vargas Llosa develops his own story by notation, classification, and explanation. At one point in the process of conducting his research into the revolt, its antecedents, and its consequences, the journalist exclaims that Canudos is filled with stories. The telling of those stories becomes his obsession, and the telling of the journalist's story is a major portion of the novelist's objective.

This work combines these many stories into a version of history that merges imagination with fact and provides a complete fiction that clearly embroiders the facts yet also rests upon the facts of the siege of Canudos. The story of the Counselor, for example, is a fully articulated exercise in hagiography that includes such standard elements as a mysterious birth, a period of childhood isolation, a time of itinerancy that includes wanderings in deserted places, the gathering of a band of unlikely followers, the performance of good works for the poor and oppressed, the function of preaching, the foundation of a community of believers, and martyrdom at the hands of the established political force. This overarching fictionalization of the Counselor's life contains overtly biblical dimensions as well as elements common to many aspects of the Acta Sanctorum, with the difference that Vargas Llosa's clear-eyed reconstruction of history eschews a pietistical viewpoint usually associated with hagiography. The novel also works on a political level, pitting the ostensibly hapless band of Canudos against the inexorable military machine of the Brazilian Republic. In this phase of the narration, Vargas Llosa creates an unrelieved and intensely stark chronicle of the dehumanizing aspects of military campaigns and warfare. From the first pitched battle, in which the republic suffers ignominious defeat, to the virtual extermination of the sect, the novel explores the effects of the politics of confrontation upon all who engage in it and does so by using the vehicle of fiction to comment on the meanings of historical events.

The stories of the many characters intersect in the apocalyptic battle of the siege of Canudos, which pits the fanatic band that follows the Counselor's anti-Republican teachings against the military strength of the Brazilian Republic. This climactic "war of the end of the world" represents, for followers of the Counselor, the triumph of the Antichrist as embodied by the republic and its trappings: the census, the metric system, civil marriage, and the separation of church and state.

Analysis

The principal theme of the novel is one implicit in most serious historical fiction, the attempt to make sense of a series of historical events and, in so doing, to assess their meanings for the present. In this sense, the novel works as a metafiction, as the author writes of an author who writes of the actions and written reports of actions of the revolt in the backlands. Two other equally forceful themes borrowed from the epic tradition are concerned with the metaphors of life as journey and life as warfare. Vargas Llosa also manipulates the traditional themes of fiction—love, honor, revenge, adventure, idealism, the education of naïve characters, lost innocence, trial by experience, and the effects of a rapidly changing social context on individuals caught up in those changes. In the treatment of all these themes, Vargas Llosa relentlessly seeks the meaning of events and actions, the individual meaning for each of his characters, the larger meaning for the Brazilian Republic in the aftermath of Canudos, and the meanings that lessons of history hold for the present.

Frequently, Vargas Llosa introduces themes and, through the magical interaction of characters, allows them to play themselves out without authorial comment. Thus, for example, the love theme not only is particularized in the romantic love of the journalist for Jurema but also extends to such varied aspects of love as that between Rufino and Jurema (a relationship of power and control), between Gall and Jurema (again, a power relationship), the love of the Counselor for his followers, the love of God, and the love of country. All these loves are motivating factors for the characters and work together to illustrate the potentially destructive force of love as a ruling passion. So, too, the theme of messianism that is at the very core of the work plays itself out in the actions of the Counselor and his followers on one side and in the lives of Brazilian politicians and generals on the other. Messianism, itself an exaggeration, possibly a necessary one, draws to itself both adherents and disbelievers who must engage one another militantly until only one party can emerge. It is worth recalling that although Vargas Llosa chronicles the events of some generations ago, the chronicle itself can be viewed as a parable for contemporary Latin America, where the lines of a new messianism are clearly drawn between those intent on carrying out a sort of ideological revolution in a practical, political, and military forum and those who would cling to and support an equally powerful ideological base. In the novel's terms, this is a clash between the oppressed Christian commune and the forces of an implacable democratic republic; in contemporary terms it is a clash between Marxist thought and capitalist thought. One key to viewing the novel as an allegory of current events is the character Galileo Gall, who is intent on spreading the international revolution of Marxism in the backlands of Brazil but who is mistaken in thinking that Canudos is part of that revolution. So, too, the modern reader may wonder whether any of the ideologies at war with one another take into account the individuals who must suffer and die for them.

Critical Context

In *The War of the End of the World*, Vargas Llosa continues a probe of Latin American history, life, and culture that has occupied his works for more than a quarter of a century. Long recognized as some of the more important works coming from Latin America, his works include volumes of plays, literary criticism, and nonfiction. He has steadily gained in reputation as a remarkable novelist of international stature for such earlier achievements as *Conversación en la catedral* (1969; *Conversation in the Cathedral*, 1975), *La ciudad y los perros* (1963; *The Time of the Hero*, 1966), *La casa verde* (1966; *The Green House*, 1968), and *La tía Julia y el escribidor* (1977; *Aunt Julia and the Scriptwriter*, 1982). *The War of the End of the World*, like Vargas Llosa's earlier novels, presents a vision of Latin American life and culture that has, in the last half of the twentieth century, provoked considerable attention in the English-speaking world.

THE WEDDING

Author: Mary Helen Ponce (1938-   )
Type of work: Novel
Type of plot: Social realism
Time of plot: The 1950's
Locale: Taconos, a fictional town in Southern California
First published: 1989

Principal Characters

Blanca Muñoz, a young Mexican American woman who plans her wedding. She is originally determined to stay away from *pachucos*, tough young Latino men, but when she becomes interested in men, she chooses from the available selection. Enjoying the fights and excitement of Saturday night dances, she admires Cricket's physical prowess and status among the Los Tacones gang. On several fronts, Blanca manages her life well. After several rejections in the job market, she gets a highly regarded job at a poultry farm. She is not afraid to talk back to an Anglo-American woman who disparages Mexican Americans. With her mother as a model, she respects her relatives and compliments her aunt on hand-embroidering special kneeling cushions, which Blanca secretly considers "low-class Mexican." Planning the wedding, Blanca manages her money and even crosses Cricket in making advance arrangements for the orchestra to play the fast dance music she loves. When things go wrong, Blanca adopts a passive optimism: If she pretends everything is all right, maybe no one will notice. She takes this attitude toward her pregnancy, never mentioned specifically in the novel.

Samuel (Sammy-the-Cricket) Lopez, the barely literate leader of Los Tacones who marries Blanca. Engaging in vandalism in grammar school, Cricket aspires to be meaner than any of his tough, mean brothers. His favorite pastime is kicking and stoning dogs. Sullen and given to tantrums, Cricket cannot handle mainstream society. After failing at several jobs involving manual labor, he keeps a job as a garbage worker by smoking marijuana to get the energy that impresses his boss. After buying a bad used car, Cricket retaliates by throwing a brick through the dealership window. Completely selfish, he uses others to enhance his status. With fights and insults, he keeps the gangs on the edge of conflict. Ignoring Blanca, he refuses any financial responsibility for the wedding. Although Los Tacones respect "the chicks" and pay for the bridesmaids' bouquets, Cricket scorns their values. Collecting money from Los Tacones to pay the dance band, he spends it on tailor-made shirts for himself. After the wedding, he cleans his "boppers" (dark glasses) on Blanca's wedding dress and will not let her lean against him lest she wrinkle his "drapes." At the dance, he resents Blanca's dancing ability. He ends the evening securely in his field of expertise, brutally kicking the leader of the rival Planchados gang and passing out, convinced he is winning.

Father Francis Ignatius Ranger, Taconos' parish priest, whose hypocrisy reveals the irony of his name (Francis, presumably for St. Francis of Assisi, and Ignatius, for the founder of the Jesuit order). Father Ranger feels betrayed at being assigned to Taconos amid needy Mexican Americans. He seeks the cultured life of Los Angeles. His fairly innocent pleasures—attending jazz concerts and enjoying the meetings of the parish's teenage girls—betray his spiritual charge. He hates and is hated by the *pachucos*. After calling the police when a fight occurs, he must live down the label of "stool pigeon." Father Ranger is bright enough to characterize the *pachucos* and to see the connection between the women's minimal lives and the life of marriage and children the church advocates for them. Offering no practical help to Blanca and Cricket, he decides that all he can do is pray and prepare the paperwork for the wedding. Disapproving of their marriage, he enjoys his center-stage role in the church's mighty event of the wedding mass.

Lucy Matacochis, Blanca's maid of honor and bossy best friend. She wins the reader's respect because of her energetic ability to survive. Having led a rough life since the age of fourteen, she works in her Aunt Tottie's bar and looks for a man with a steady job and a fine car. Lucy tries to take over the wedding arrangements while shrugging off responsibilities that divert attention from herself. Ignoring the maid of honor's responsibility to provide the kneeling cushions for the wedding mass, Lucy eagerly helps Blanca dress on the wedding morning because that is a status task. Lucy enjoys her position among the bridesmaids as the authority on makeup, men, and birth control. She anticipates the wedding dance as a place to meet men. Beautified by "falsies" that give her skinny figure a spectacular bustline, she enthusiastically fights at the dance. When Blanca miscarries, Lucy, who sees Cricket's viciousness, tells her to leave him. Realistic and tough, Lucy voices the reader's hope that Blanca will free herself from her stereotyped future.

The Novel

The Wedding fictionally re-creates a small-town barrio (neighborhood) near Los Angeles in the 1950's and traces events surrounding the wedding of Blanca Muñoz and Sammy-the-Cricket Lopez. Ironically contrasting a young woman's romantic dreams with her world's reality, the novel portrays working-class Mexican Americans' ability to live spirited lives on the fringes of society.

The Wedding's two parts, told by an omniscient narrator, focus mainly on Blanca. The first part ranges from the characters' childhoods to just before the wedding. The second part narrates the traditional events of the barrio wedding day.

The novel begins when the eighteen-year-old Blanca and the twenty-two-year-old Cricket start dating. Both are junior-high-school dropouts with menial jobs: Blanca plucks turkeys, and Cricket collects garbage. Blanca, living at home, helps her mother with expenses. She and her friends fantasize about romance and excitement—specifically, an ideal man with a steady job and a "cool" car. Unglamorous and inexperienced, Blanca lacks criteria for judging men. She finds Sammy-the-Cricket impressive because in fights he knocks his opponents senseless. Cricket is a *pachuco*, one of the 1950's Mexican American youth who wore tailored, baggy "zoot suits" and often were involved in street gangs. Cricket, the leader of Los Tacones, the neighborhood gang, had earned his nickname by stomping a member of a rival Planchados gang after beating him up.

On their first date, Blanca and Cricket see *Gone with the Wind*, a film Blanca has seen ten times, at the drive-in with their friends Tudi and Sally. Tudi, driving his own car, refuses Cricket's urging to ram a car full of Planchados who are peacefully leaving the drive-in. During the courtship, Cricket gets Blanca pregnant. Her condition apparently prompts Cricket's offhand suggestion that they marry; however, since the narrative does not mention the couple's intimacies, Blanca's pregnancy becomes obvious only at the wedding dance.

As Blanca plans the wedding, her life's realty intrudes upon her romantic hopes. Blanca wants to be the first in her family to marry ceremonially and thus make her family respectable. Blanca also confronts Cricket's silent, obsessive will to dominate. Cricket sees a wedding as a means of increasing his own social status. Realizing that he will not contribute toward expenses, even an overnight honeymoon, Blanca works overtime at turkey plucking to earn extra money. Traveling by bus to

Los Angeles, she buys her wedding dress at a bridal store that sells refurbished factory seconds to Mexican American brides. She selects a *Gone with the Wind*-style gown that allows her to see herself as a real bride and trendsetter, the first bride in Taconos to wear a "colonial" wedding dress. The marked-down veil, adorned with *azares* (wax orange blossoms traditionally worn by Mexican American brides), symbolizes Blanca's yearnings for the wedding and her future.

The wedding day occurs against Blanca's ambivalence: excitement at the day's events; irritation with her expanding body; regret at surrendering her independence and her future paychecks to Cricket; anticipation of her wifely status. During the morning wedding mass, said by Father Ranger, misfortunes undercut romance. Cricket, hung over from partying with his friends, wears his dark glasses, and Blanca must hold him upright. The junior bridesmaid vomits on the hand-embroidered kneeling cushions. Neither bride nor groom receives the sacrament of communion because Cricket, in a screaming fit, had refused to prepare by going to confession.

After the mass, the high-spirited events proceed ceremonially. The wedding party cruises the barrio streets in the Tacones' cars, festooned with paper flowers. After the wedding breakfast at maid-of-honor Lucy's, the cars parade into Los Angeles to have wedding pictures taken. The afternoon reception features a meal provided with dignity by Blanca's mother and the neighborhood women. Los Tacones speculate about the possibility that the Planchados might crash the evening's dance. The prevailing opinion among the young people is that only dances with fights are any good.

The wedding dance presents a panorama of guests and wedding participants who are hoping that something will happen. Blanca, recognizing Cricket's ugly egotism, feels unwell but eager for the splendid occasion. She revels in dancing, especially fast numbers. Cricket, threatened by Blanca's skill, sulks because his inept dancing endangers his reputation. As the celebration heightens, Blanca starts to miscarry. When the Planchados arrive, a melee of fighting and dancing ensues. Two ambulances are required: one for the groom and the Planchado leader, and one for the miscarrying bride, who insists that Cricket will change and is worth keeping. Blanca enters the hospital emergency room talking about her beautiful wedding.

Analysis

With humor and sympathy, *The Wedding* treats themes important to Latinos, women, and a multicultural society. The novel is a coming-of-age story that tells of a teenage girl's maturation as a woman. Developing this universal theme, the novel strikingly dramatizes adolescent girls' preoccupations with their physical appearance, their future as women, and men. Since Blanca succeeds within her frame of reference, the novel also dramatizes the reality that many women face quite limited possibilities.

Ponce establishes the themes of *The Wedding* mainly through the Mexican American cultural context. One way she establishes background is through names, the meanings of which may be ironic—"Blanca" and "Taconos," for example.

Ponce also ironically develops the novel's cultural themes. She celebrates Blanca's great event while depicting the flaws of Blanca's and the community's frame of reference. In the larger arena, the straightforward narrative reveals the real poverty of the Taconos community. The characters have no myths, superstitions, or dreams to guide them. On the outskirts of "Los," as the young people call Los Angeles, they are cut off from the imaginative past of their Latino heritage. The young men have only posturing *machismo*; the women, scraps of stories and current misinformation about contraception and abortion.

The narrative implies a related social and historical theme: that mainstream institutions have stunted Mexican American minorities by colonizing (isolating and dominating) them to keep them out of the way. The setting of the 1950's, a period of relative complacence and prosperity for American society, creates a backdrop for this concept. Ponce exemplifies the young people's wish to join the mainstream in the fact that they speak their own barrio English rather than Spanish. The schools should provide linguistic and cultural transitions to the larger society; however, they include Blanca and the other Mexican Americans only halfheartedly, with the result that all the young people drop out by the eighth grade. The church, which could provide continuity with a spiritual past and strength to reestablish cultural identity, continues its rituals without seriously engaging the lives of the people in its charge. Blamed for not having skills, the characters have access only to dangerous or physically unpleasant jobs. The novel suggests that though the young people are fascinated by Los Angeles, they have learned to be wary of contact with the larger world and prefer to stay in their neighborhood.

Ponce proposes that, lacking expectations, deprived communities find ways to keep themselves alive. Taconos creates a high-spirited life in events themselves, in spectacle, not in the meaning behind events. At weddings or fights, whatever happens is important. The gangs, which trade insults and punches rather than bullets or knifings, tangle more from boredom and the wish to create action than from hostility. Each event of the wedding day—the mass, the breakfast, the parading cars, the reception, the dance—is important to the participants as ritual, though none is endowed with overarching meaning. Dramatizing the reasons for the physical and inner poverty of the barrio and its women, Ponce respectfully acknowledges their vitality. Capturing the details of the characters' lives, Ponce's humor touches serious issues.

Critical Context

Focusing on Mexican American women, *The Wedding* enlarges the themes of Ponce's volume of short stories *Taking Control* (1987). Ironic narratives of sometimes unrecognized failure, these stories depict women attempting to live out their own standards in relation to their Latina culture. Ponce participates in the vigor of Latino fiction writing in the late 1980's, years when Latino writers reflected on their identity in relation to the United States literary mainstream, to mainstream feminism, and to their own heritage.

Ponce's straightforward narrative, focusing on the characters' actions and conscious lives, distinguishes her method from the dream-sequence and stream-of-consciousness techniques of Latina authors writing in English such as Lucha Corpi in *Delia's Song* (1989) and Cristina Garcia in *Dreaming in Cuban* (1992). Like a number of Latina writers, Ponce takes risks with the English language. Using Spanish phonetic spellings for words in conversations, Ponce veils meaning momentarily and thus reveals the characters' cultural difference. Although she narrates with sometimes broad comicality in *The Wedding*, Ponce's use of humor links her with an aspect of Latina writing that is beginning to receive critical attention.

The Wedding treats the special bicultural reality of Latina women at the same time that it connects with the feminist mainstream. An obvious but important focus of the novel is female subjectivity (woman as the subject of events and of her own life). The novel also expresses the feminist interest in perceptions of the female body. Constantly evoking the body, its dampness, its smells, and its visceral reactions, Ponce "writes the body." The young women's inscribing of their faces and nails with vivid 1950's cosmetics proclaims their sexuality, the color they wish their lives to have, and their outsider status. In her 1990 essay "The Color Red," Ponce observed that in the 1950's, lower-class Mexican Americans wore bright colors that Mexican Americans wanting an "American" look regarded as too vivid.

Through constant references to Blanca's uncomfortable flesh, the novel emphasizes the basic, physical level of reality that women in the community occupy. In its silences, the novel also encompasses the concept of women's secret knowledge—about Blanca's intimacy with Cricket, her pregnancy, and her most private emotions.

WHERE THE AIR IS CLEAR

Author: Carlos Fuentes (1928-   )
Type of work: Novel
Type of plot: Allegory
Time of plot: 1910-1954
Locale: Mexico City, Mexico
First published: *La región más transparente*, 1958 (English translation, 1960)

Principal Characters

Federico Robles, a wealthy and powerful business tycoon. Robles is born to peons working on the Ovando hacienda but has the opportunity to go to Morelia with a priest to serve as his sacristan. They go to the Zamacona hacienda, where Robles meets fifteen-year-old Mercedes Zamacona, with whom he begins sexual relations. After the lovers are found out, Robles flees and never again sees Mercedes, whom he made pregnant. Robles fights in the Mexican Revolution and later becomes a wealthy lawyer working for North American companies. Robles finally meets his son, Manuel Zamacona, who is later killed by an unknown assailant. Robles marries the beautiful Norma Larragoiti in order to complete his success. Robles begins a sexual and emotional relationship with Hortensia Chacón, whose Indian mother was a servant in the Ovando household. Although Hortensia is a typist in Robles' office, they do not meet until he begins to visit her in the hospital, where she is recovering after being beaten by her estranged husband. Robles takes care of Hortensia, who is now blind. She later stands by him when he goes bankrupt as the result of rumors and the dirty dealings of other businessmen. Norma, crazed by the thought of losing her wealth and social position, threatens to leave him. After Norma dies in a fire, Robles marries Hortensia, who is pregnant. The two withdraw to the countryside to grow cotton. Robles represents the corrupt businessman who sheds his false self to return to an authentic existence.

Ixca Cienfuegos, a mysterious Indian who appears everywhere and knows all the characters. As he moves in the various social classes, he listens to the characters' life stories. He performs humanitarian acts but almost lets Norma drown in the ocean. He may have been responsible for her death, a sacrifice demanded by Teódula Moctezuma, his mother. After the fire, Teódula informs Ixca that he can go back to his true life, having performed the sacrifice. His wife is to be Rosa, Norma's maid and the recent widow of a taxi driver. Ixca disappears for three years, but reappears at the end of the novel. He waits for Rodrigo in the latter's car and explains that Teódula believed that Norma's sacrifice was necessary. He forces Rodrigo's foot onto the accelerator but finally allows him to stop the automobile.

Norma Larragoiti de Robles, Robles' wife, Ixca's lover, and Rodrigo's former girlfriend. Norma pretends to be the daughter of an aristocratic family that lost everything during the revolution, but her mother is a maid and her father had been a small businessman before his suicide. She becomes Ixca's lover while married to Robles. Although she knows that he wants to destroy her, she loves him. After an argument with Robles about his bankruptcy, she locks herself in her room, throws herself on the bed, and laughs hysterically. When the house catches on fire, she is unable to find the key and dies.

Rodrigo Pola, a failed poet. When his father returned to the revolutionary troops, he left his bride of two weeks pregnant. Rodrigo is reared by his mother, who works hard to educate him. He falls in love with Norma, who later tires of him. He feels unfulfilled and often complains of his bad luck. Toward the end of the book, he begins to write screenplays of little value, but they make him rich. He is now respected and marries the aristocratic Pimpinela de Ovando.

Pimpinela de Ovando, a member of the fallen landed aristocracy. She is innocent, dignified, and well-mannered. She lives reasonably well but tries to get back the family's lands. She falls in love with a young lawyer, Roberto Regules, but does not marry him because her mother objects. She later regrets this decision when he becomes rich. She marries Rodrigo after he becomes wealthy.

Teódula Moctezuma, an Indian woman who represents the great mother figure of Aztec mythology. She keeps the coffins of her dead husband and sons in her house and performs Aztec rites over their cadavers. Believing Norma to be the victim of the sacrifice she demands from Ixca, she goes to Norma's burning house and throws her ritualistic jewelry into the fire as she gives thanks for the sacrifice.

Gabriel, a border crosser who returns to Mexico with gifts for his family. He is stabbed in the stomach during a party.

The Novel

Where the Air Is Clear is divided into three parts of different lengths. The first presents the most important characters: Ixca Cienfuegos, Federico Robles, his wife Norma Larragoiti de Robles, Rodrigo Pola, and the Ovando family. In the second section, the largest of the book, these men and women meet, intermingle, interfere, and collide. In the third section, the shortest, new secondary characters appear. The book closes with an intent to synthesize Mexican history.

Ixca Cienfuegos opens the book. He is the spokesman of the city or perhaps is the city itself, as is suggested almost at the end of the book. From his words readers learn that the ancient Indian spirit remains always and everywhere present in all phases of Mexican life. The ancestral forces operate mainly in Mexico City, cradle of the strongest old Indian culture. The old gods have not died: They look upon the people of every condition and sooner or later devour them all.

After this initial monologue by Ixca, the parade of characters begins to file in, sometimes in a consecutive linkage, sometimes with abrupt jumps. Beginning early in the day, Gladys García, a poor but not depraved prostitute, seeks food. While roaming downtown, she starts to remember her life, her parents, and her lovers. On the night of the same day, she sees a group of fashionable, snobbish people who engage in a wild party. Federico Robles, a lawyer and banker, then appears

in the book. He is a nouveau riche, a despotic man with no social concerns who has climbed to high social esteem by his cunning and by his wealth, obtained through dishonest means during the days of the Mexican Revolution. He was pushed to enter this movement without consciousness of its purpose, but at the end of it he found himself with money, prestige, pride, and reasons to justify his holdings. Later, he marries Norma Larragoiti, an unscrupulous, status-seeking woman who thinks she is doing a favor for Federico by remaining married to him. Robles has a lover, Hortensia Chacón, a long-suffering woman blinded by her first husband. She loves Robles with compassion and without self-interest. Another jump in the plot sends the reader to meet Rodrigo Pola, son of a revolutionist shot to death without knowing his child. Just as abruptly, other characters are introduced: the Ovandos, an aristocratic family of the days of Porfirio Díaz that struggles to no avail to keep its haughtiness and money; Manuel Zamacona, an idealist, original thinker, and poet; and many other people of lesser importance. All of them are met by the omnipresent Ixca Cienfuegos, who appears in the crucial moments of frustration or confession of the characters.

The second part of the book constitutes the section of frustration. All the main people of the novel, Ixca excepted, fall into disaster. Robles becomes bankrupt and is repudiated by his wife;

Norma perishes in a blaze in her home; Pola climbs the social staircase but is unhappy; the Ovandos are forced to work in the humblest jobs and live in secluded and poor rooms; and Manuel Zamacona is killed in a bar. In this way, Fuentes proves that the ancient Mexican deities—always in control— and the hatred that is part of human lives have taken their revenge. Every life has been little more than a hideous play, as in the past days of human sacrifices.

The last pages of the book are perhaps the most successful. They are a tight, energetic synthesis of the tragic, painful history of the Mexican people. Many people of decisive importance to the Mexican country and its society appear as do representatives of the common people. There also stand Gladys García and Ixca Cienfuegos, symbol of the city and of Mexican history. He says fatalistically that these things have happened, that they could not be avoided or halted.

Analysis

The original title of the novel corresponds to a phrase taken from *Visión de Anáhuac* (1917) a study written by the Mexican essayist Alfonso Reyes, who described the high Mexican plateau as the clearest region of the air. Fuentes gives a different, almost sarcastic interpretation to the phrase. The moral and physical atmosphere of Mexico, as seen by Fuentes, is quite contrary to that contemplated by Reyes. It is hard to think of a darker environment than this one, involving all the characters in a cloud of fumes, rain, dust, corruption, and frustration.

This novel constitutes a vast, chaotic synthesis of the society of the Mexican capital. It is written with demolishing impetus, dialectic assumptions, and modern formal techniques; through its pages the reader attends, in a crisscross itinerary and with accelerated movement, to the drama of the urban inhabitants. All of them are marked with a deterministic sign—they cannot act in a different way or escape their environment and past. They were born in Mexico City, in a given spot, and must submit to their destiny. Immersed in this geographic fatalism, Fuentes creates a great fresco depicting men and women, real or semifantastic, belonging to different ethnic groups, social and economic strata, professions, and environments. Around them and at the same time partially constituted by them, solemnly and cruelly stands the city, with its unquenchable thirst for human lives, its old mythology, and its irrationality.

The characters of the novel are prostitutes, snobs, pseudo-intellectuals, aristocrats, international opportunists, cab drivers, braceros, underdogs, nouveaux riches, politicians, and social climbers. In one way or another, their lives are linked by a character of penumbral profile, Ixca Cienfuegos. He is the only figure who escapes undamaged by physical or moral disaster, and he does so because he is more a symbol than a real entity. He ubiquitously appears everywhere, is known by most of the characters, talks with them, listens to their autobiographical confessions, and expresses the voice of the old, instinctive Indian ancestry. He, perhaps, represents the anonymous Mexican.

In spite of the concreteness of many pages, the novel cannot be classified as belonging to the realistic tradition. Fuentes belongs, as do other Mexican writers of his generation, to the school of symbolic realism. He tries to perceive, behind the feel of things and situations, a reality closer to truth than is the evident daily reality. This makes his novel a surrealistic and naturalistic story, with characters close to fantasy as well as to life, well-known places and others without local fixation, dialogues made up of uncommon words and others built up with platitudinous and cheap sentences, temporal situations of the present and of the past. The reader is cast into a sad, rotten, turbulent, intemporal carnival, in which every character is merely a player acting in a set role.

The novel employs stream of consciousness, dislocation of time, social protest, interference of characters, and crudity of expressions. There is not a plot, a development, or a climax. It could be said that Fuentes wrote a novel of loosely linked frag- ments, with the intention of creating a kaleidoscopic panorama of people, environments, and situations.

Critical Context

Nature is a popular theme among Latino novelists of the twentieth century. The great masters of fiction, such as Mariano Azuela, Tomás Rivera, Rómulo Gallegos, Ricardo Güiraldes, and Ciro Alegría, undertook to depict more the landscape than the people. As Alegría suggests in his title *Broad and Alien Is the World* (1941), the world is too wide and alien for people, who have no room on this planet in spite of its size.

A new trend emerged in the fiction of Latin America. Nature and its inhabitants became a secondary subject, their places in fiction replaced by the city and its dwellers. The work of God gave way to the works of men; the rural setting was forgotten, and the urban environment grasped the preoccupations of the writers of fiction. Instead of objective presentations of farmers, settlers, and Indians who struggle in vain against a jungle of greenness and obstreperous rivers, narrators inserted characters into a jungle of iron and cement. Juan Carlos Onetti, Eduardo Mallea, Julio Cortázar, and Mario Vargas Llosa exemplify the new trend.

Carlos Fuentes inaugurated the new urban novel in Mexico. Born in Mexico City and a resident in many major cities of the American continents—Rio de Janeiro, Montevideo, Washington, D.C., Santiago, Lima, Buenos Aires—he chose the city as his main concern in his writings. His Mexico City is an urban conglomerate often visited and departed from, tasted and remembered, lived in and yearned for because of his frequent trips abroad accompanying his father, a Mexican diplomat. Very often, after beginning his literary career, he wanted to concretize and condense the multiform, variegated, tumultuous, vital stream of the city, but he could not organize a fit scheme. Finally, in *Where the Air Is Clear*, his first novel, Fuentes was able to seize upon and bring into being his desire.

Fuentes has written a singular novel, told in an overflowing, contrasted, negative, black protesting tone. It cannot be denied that *Where the Air Is Clear* is also a book born out of passion and love for his city and country. To echo the words of one of his characters, when a person writes about Mexico, the work must be done with joy, anger, compassion, hatred, and the fire of passion. This novel is a work of genuine, if undisciplined, achievement.

THE WINNERS

Author: Julio Cortázar (1914-1984)
Type of work: Novel
Type of plot: Satire
Time of plot: The 1950's
Locale: Buenos Aires and a cruise ship along the coast of Argentina
First published: *Los premios*, 1960 (English translation, 1965)

Principal Characters

Gabriel Medrano, a dentist and a womanizer. He allies himself with a group that does not accept the official explanation of why the passengers have not been given complete access to the ship. When Claudia Lewbaum's son Jorge becomes ill, he storms the radio room and forces the operator to send a message to Buenos Aires about Jorge's condition. The radio operator then kills Gabriel. The passengers are asked to sign a statement that Gabriel died of typhus instead of gunshot wounds.

Carlos López, a leftist high school Spanish teacher who refuses to believe that the passengers are being denied access to the entire ship because of an outbreak of typhus. He threatens one of the ship's officers that he will storm the other side of the ship if the restrictions on passenger movement are not lifted; he agrees with Gabriel Medrano about the need to send a radio message because of Jorge's illness.

Persio, a short, bald eccentric proofreader and aspiring writer. He is a dreamer who lives in a world of philosophical speculation. He is so engrossed in his own thoughts that he does not involve himself in the controversy among the passengers about their treatment on the ship.

Raúl Costa, a homosexual architect who tries to seduce Felipe Trejo. During his secret explora-

tion of the other side of the ship, he steals three guns and ammunition from the sailors' quarters. He gives Medrano and López guns and helps them storm the other side of the ship.

Paula Lavalle, an attractive redhead who writes poems and stories. Costa's close friend and traveling companion, she is courted by López.

Claudia Lewbaum, the divorced mother of Jorge. Her son's high fever precipitates the assault on the other side of the ship.

Felipe Trejo, a high-school student learning to deal with his sexual feelings. His fantasies of sexual conquest remain unfulfilled because there are no young ladies his age on board. Although contemptuous of homosexuality, it intrigues him. He rejects Costa's advances, only to be raped by a sailor, an incident he represses by fabricating a tale in which he seduces an insatiable Paula.

Dr. Restelli, a conservative colleague of Carlos López who teaches Argentine history. He speaks up for the passengers who accept the restrictions imposed by the ship's authorities.

Don Galo Porrino, a successful Galician businessman confined to a wheelchair. He speaks in defense of the authorities and considers those who are unwilling to submit to their demands to be guilty of insubordination and anarchy.

The Novel

The novel is divided into four chapters, entitled "Prologue," "Day One," "Day Two," and "Epilogue." In the opening section, eighteen people, representing a broad spectrum of Buenos Aires society, are gathered in the Café London. They are the winners, with their invited guests, of a mysterious lottery whose prize is an ocean cruise with a secret itinerary. They are greeted courteously but evasively by an inspector from the "Ministry of Cultural Affairs" who tells them about certain "technical problems" that have complicated the arrangements. They are taken to the *Malcolm*, a freighter of uncertain nationality, where they discover that the whole aft portion of the ship is barred to them. The prohibition, at first unexplained, is later implausibly blamed on an outbreak of "Typhus 224." The only contact with the other part of the ship is provided by the waiters, a bartender, a single officer who represents the invisible captain, a doctor, and a few uncommunicative seamen who speak an unrecognizable language.

On the first day at sea, the motley group of passengers becomes acquainted, developing attractions, and enmities, social and sexual, but the mysterious prohibition becomes the focus of a major division into two groups, sometimes referred to as "the group of the damned" and "the peace party." The latter are the partisans of the establishment, who accept without question any explanations offered by the representatives of Magenta Lines. The former band, composed of the more unconventional, socially critical thinkers, rejects the explanations, suspecting something much more sinister, and makes plans to confront the forces of evil directly.

On the following day, the determination of the rebellious party to act in the face of what it sees as at least official high-handedness leads to two attempts to cross the barrier, both of which result in violence. Felipe, anxious to prove his manhood, tries to exploit the interest shown in him by one of the sailors named Orf and is raped by him, and a direct armed assault designed to reach the telegraph leads to the death of Medrano at the hands of the crew.

In the epilogue, which narrates events that take place on the morning of the third day, the inspector arrives by seaplane to offer the passengers air transportation back to Buenos Aires on condition that they sign a document ratifying an official version of the incident, absolving the shipping line and the ministry of responsibility. All must agree to sign or they will all be endlessly delayed. The defenders of authority declare themselves immediately ready to sign and beg to be allowed to continue their cruise. The rebels refuse to sign, but the reader is left with the clear impression that their defiance will not lead to action.

The novel is narrated in short scenes relying heavily on dialogue provided by a third-person narrator clearly more interested in the rebels. The constant silly pretentiousness of the conversations of the conservative party contrasts with the sympathetic, although frequently ironic, presentation of the deliberations of the rebels. Felipe's battle with his emerging sexuality, for example, is treated with sensitivity and in detail. The reader's sympathy is enlisted on the side of the nonconformists in the most obvious way; for example, the official version of Medrano's disappearance flatly contradicts the narrated events.

Interspersed throughout the narrative scenes are passages in italics that convey the meditations of Persio on the nature of perception and the relationship between experience and imagination. These sections employ an avant-garde, associative, modernist style that contrasts with the conventional language of the remainder of the novel, which relies for much of its effect on slightly parodic imitation of a range of Argentine voices.

The novel is basically comic. There is a great deal of humor in the satiric treatment of the snobbish and intellectually arteriosclerotic and much wry humor in the portrayal of the thinkers. Even the culminating violent events are treated completely without sentiment, without any sense of tragedy.

Analysis

The novel must be read, in part, as an allegory of the political situation in the Argentina that Cortázar had left in 1951. This shipload of fools at the mercy of an authority that is perceived as sinister and arbitrary, with its bureaucratic nonsensicalities, is a microcosm of Argentina. As is usual in Cortázar's work, however, it is not so much the political situation itself that concerns him as it is the uncritical, even unheeding, acquiescence of the average person, who, confronted with such a situation, does nothing. It is the impact of the oppressive regime on people whose lives are ruled by received opinion and cultural conventions that fascinates Cortázar. Complacency in the face of abuses of power and the dilemma of the contemplative mind confronted with the violence of the world are common enough problems to make the book more than a political allegory of a particular situation or moment.

Through the meditations of Persio, the reader is led to contemplate another of Cortázar's major themes, the relationship between art and reality, between artistic contemplation and political involvement. Although *The Winners* is not as clearly an "antinovel" as *Rayuela* (1963; *Hopscotch*, 1966), it foreshadows it in its ironic treatment of the themes of the European literary tradition (Orf as Orpheus at the gates of the underworld, for example) and particularly in the experiments in nonlinear narrative that comprise the passages in italics.

As in much of Cortázar's fiction, the central characters are involved in a quest for personal fulfillment. The need to enter the forbidden zone of the ship assumes symbolic significance. The leaders of the party of the damned suffer in varying degrees from a sense of incompleteness, which they seek, unsuccessfully, to remedy by their action. As everywhere in Cortázar's world, this sense of alienation is felt both in its intensely personal aspect and in relation to the social context. The need to discover personal integrity involves an encounter with the other and otherness. The group's quest for the truth about the mysteries of the aft end of the ship parallels Felipe's more personal adventure in self-discovery; both lead to a loss of innocence too painful to be openly admitted. As Felipe returns to Buenos Aires, concocting stories of wild shipboard romances with which to regale his friends, the others bluster unconvincingly about their intention to make their discoveries of official abuses public.

Critical Context

Although *The Winners* is not as great a novel as *Hopscotch*, it is a witty and intriguing treatment of the themes of Cortázar's later novels and is particularly relevant to the study of his development as a novelist. It treats for the first time the major themes of Cortázar's long fiction and shows him struggling with the question of form as well. The sections in which the narrator expresses Persio's meditations in a radically experimental style are perhaps not convincingly integrated into the body of the narrative. On the other hand, Cortázar's gift for imitating voices and for recording in a way that always rings true the variety, richness, and frequent silliness of human consciousness is already well developed in this work.

The Winners can be seen as an early contribution to the body of Latin American literature that began to invade the North American and European literary consciousness in the 1960's. Written, like many other books of the period, by an exile from a country in political turmoil, it reacts boldly but ironically, with humor and without ideology, creatively and wittily in such a way that readers anywhere in the world can identify with its central dilemmas.

WOMAN HOLLERING CREEK AND OTHER STORIES

Author: Sandra Cisneros (1954-   )
Type of work: Short stories
Type of plot: Primarily self-discovery
Time of plot: Primarily the second half of the twentieth century
Locale: Primarily southern Texas and Mexico
First published: 1991

Principal Characters

Rachel, the narrator in "Eleven" who tells what it is like to be a girl of that age.

Michele, a young American girl of Mexican heritage in "Mericans," who feels strange in a family of boys and in a culture whose language she cannot speak.

Cleófilas Enriqueta DeLeón Hernández, a Mexican woman in "Woman Hollering Creek" who follows her husband to the United States and there uncovers her own oppression.

Clemencia, a Mexican American artist who tells of her relationships with a white man and with his teenage son in "Never Marry a Mexican."

Inés Alfaro, the women who ran away with Mexican general Emiliano Zapata as a young girl; a character in "Eyes of Zapata."

Rosario De Leon, a young woman who offers her own version of the power of the Virgin of Guadalupe in "Little Miracles, Kept Promises."

Lupe Arredondo, a Mexican American artist who moves from San Francisco to San Antonio and comes to terms with her heritage and her talent in "*Bien* Pretty."

The Stories

Woman Hollering Creek and Other Stories includes twenty-two selections, divided into three sections. The narrators, almost all female, offer inside looks at the lives and thoughts of Mexicans and Mexican Americans who live on both sides of the border. The narrators in the first section are mostly young girls. In "Eleven," Rachel is in school musing about what age really means—with wisdom beyond her years—when her teacher insists that she wear an ugly, abandoned sweater. Rachel says that it is not hers but finally puts it on, deeply humiliated. Phyllis Lopez eventually remembers that the sweater is hers, but by then, Rachel is wishing she were anything but eleven years old, wishing she were much older and already far away.

This sense of separation runs through most of Cisneros' stories. Michele, the young narrator in "Mericans," and her brothers are visiting in Mexico, playing outside a church while waiting for their Mexican grandmother. When the boys taunt her as "sissy" and "girl," Michele goes inside. She comes back out to find one brother speaking Spanish with tourists. He addresses Michele in English, shocking one tourist, who thought the boys were Mexican children. Junior explains to her that they are "Mericans." Michele is left wondering where she really does belong.

In the second section, which comprises only two stories, the narrators begin to wade into the river of sexuality and love. In "One Holy Night," the unnamed narrator—a Latina eighth grader living in the southwestern United States—gets to know a man who buys from her pushcart every Saturday. After a few weeks, she visits Chaq Uxmal Paloquín (also known as Baby Boy) in his rented room, where he tells the girl that he is descended from Mayan kings and initiates her into the mysteries of sex. She knows she is supposed to be ashamed, but instead she runs home jubilant with her secret knowledge. Eventually, the truth comes out. The family goes to confront Baby Boy but finds him packed and gone. In the meantime, the girl learns she is pregnant, and the family learns the truth about Baby Boy: He is thirty-seven years old, really named Chato (which means fat face), and not of Mayan blood. Her family sends the girl to live with relatives in a small Mexican town, where she counts the months until her child's birth, staring at a picture of the man she thinks she loves.

Most of the narrators in the third section are older, are sometimes harder, and are always resilient. In "Woman Hollering Creek," Cleófilas moves with her husband across the border to live near San Antonio, Texas. There she gives birth to a son and also becomes fascinated by the name of an arroyo called Woman Hollering. She wonders if the woman is hollering for joy or in pain, but there is no one who can tell her. As time goes by, Cleófilas learns what it is like for love between a man and woman to go sour. When a woman at the medical clinic sees Cleófilas' bruises and knows her husband is beating her, she makes arrangements to help Cleófilas escape back to Mexico. On the way to the bus station, Felice drives Cleófilas and her son across Woman Hollering Creek and unexpectedly lets out a yell like Tarzan. This act amazes Cleófilas, as does Felice herself, who drives a pickup truck and does not have a husband. At that moment, Cleófilas feels a long ribbon of laughter coming out of her own throat.

In "Never Marry a Mexican," Clemencia, a Mexican American artist, does not paint a pretty picture of her parents' marriage or marriage in general. Clemencia has remained single, but she has not spent her life alone. She tells of Drew, a white man like the man her mother married when her Mexican father died. Their affair is long over, but Clemencia still spends time painting his image, making him into whatever she wants him to be. Clemencia also keeps the connection lively by befriending—and then bedding—Drew's teenage

son. She wants to make the boy love her the way she still loves Drew, and she succeeds in getting him under her power. Rage spills out of Clemencia sometimes at night, when she has an urge to communicate but no language with which to form words. At these times, she telephones Drew, waking him and presumably his wife. Both loving and hating Drew, Clemencia is frightened away by his voice. In the mornings sometimes, she says, all of humanity strikes her as lovely, and she wants to tell someone that everything is really all right.

Inés Alfaro, tells of her life with Emiliano Zapata in "Eyes of Zapata," perhaps the strongest story of the collection. He is asleep beside her in bed, on one of his infrequent visits, and she thinks about their past. Zapata loved her but never said he would marry her; he never did. She made a life for herself and their two children, while Zapata spent months away at a time. He married and fathered two children with another woman, and he had many other "pastimes." Through the years, he continued to return to Inés. The villagers think that Inés is a witch, and she does have inner vision. She describes how, heartsick, she once left her sleeping body and flew far away to watch Zapata asleep beside another woman. Inés is from a family of women, she says, who never forget a wrong but who love as strongly as they hate. As she reviews the past, even as she flies into the future and sees its trials, Inés knows that she belongs to Emiliano, that she has belonged to him from their first kiss, and that she knows real love.

"Little Miracles, Kept Promises" is a series of petitions and notes of thanks left on the altar in a Mexican church. These range from requests for help in finding a man who at least knows how to pronounce the petitioner's name correctly in Spanish to requests for clothes and furniture after a house fire. The last note in the story is from Rosario De Leon, a young female artist. It is attached to a braid of her hair, which she offers along with other relics left on the altar. The reader is privy to Rosario's silent musing about her previous feelings of alienation from the church and from herself, then her deepening understanding of the many facets of the feminine divine in different countries and cultures, and finally the relief and freedom symbolized by her short hair, now that she is no longer ashamed to be her ancestors' child.

The last story in the collection, "*Bien* Pretty," tells the story of Lupe Arredondo, a well-educated Mexican American artist who leaves a professorship in San Francisco to spend a year in San Antonio trying to get over a broken heart. Lupe throws herself into her job at the community center and neglects her own artwork until she meets Flavio Munguía, a pest exterminator who writes Spanish poetry and looks like an Aztec god. He agrees to pose for a portrait, and they become first friends, then lovers. Eventually, Flavio tells Lupe that he has to leave to take care of family obligations, his many children by two wives back in Mexico. Lupe is devastated and stops painting, spending her evenings instead watching television soap operas. When she starts to dream of slapping those silly women to bring them to their senses, Lupe's inner strength grows. She again starts to paint, living each day as it is, no more and no less, learning that it is she who charts her own direction in life.

Analysis

The selections in *Woman Hollering Creek and Other Stories* deal with how women are seen, and how women see themselves, in the Latino culture. Most of the stories deal with relationships between men and women. They paint powerful pictures of the details of ordinary life, as women try to come to terms with, then eventually learn that they have the right to redefine, their own lives. The essence of what happens in these stories occurs inside the hearts and minds of the narrators. Although the stories are not tied together with a single narrator, as are the intertwined vignettes that comprise Cisneros' *The House on Mango Street* (1983), the different female narrators are played off each other skillfully to suggest a sense of development of Latinas as a group. The stories are sequenced such that the main characters move from the innocence of childhood into the confusion and even cynicism of adolescence and young womanhood. Girls who, like Michele in "Mericans," feel confused about their place in the world they see around them may grow into disturbed women like Clemencia in "Never Marry a Mexican." They may also grow into women like Lupe Arredondo and Rosario De Leon, digging deeply into themselves and their heritage to create a blend of Mexican and American that works for them.

The power that Cisneros uncovers in Latinas in this collection can best be seen in Lupe and Rosario from the final two stories. Rosario learns to be the liberated woman of her generation that she wants to be and at the same time to link arms with her mother's patience and her grandmother's endurance. Lupe also experiences healing through greater understanding of individuality as well as cultural roots. She finally finds a man who can love her in Spanish, only to be abandoned by him, and she falls into wrenching despair. Lupe ultimately realizes, as does Cleófilas in "Woman Hollering Creek," that love cannot be synonymous with torment. She understands that women can be people who make things happen, not only to whom things happen.

Cisneros' stories present a female perspective of Mexican heritage as it is seen from both sides of the border. They investigate the interactions between the Mexican and the Mexican American cultures as well as the alienation that occurs when women must maintain their Mexican heritage in order to keep their self-identity but are influenced daily by the values of America. Cisneros does not use the words "alienation" and "identity." Rather, she uses the conversational, often playful language of her people as her literary voice. Cisneros is determined to bring into mainstream American literature the real voice of her people, which she says is the Latino voice, rather than the Hispanic. "Hispanic," Cisneros has said, is English for a person of Latino origin who wants to be accepted by the white status quo. Cisneros writes powerful messages of feminism and cultural oppression, but they do not overshadow her rich powers of observation and the vibrant, poetic images that abound, such as the set of wooden dolls—nested one within the other—that appears in several stories. The meaning of Cisneros' work will best be appreciated by those who can catch the subtle innuendos of her language, primarily Latinas themselves. At the depths of these stories, however, Cisneros is speaking of a universal experience: the inevitable search inside oneself to find what the outer environment, including other people, can never provide.

Critical Context

Woman Hollering Creek and Other Stories followed the publication of Cisneros' semiautobiographical novel *The House on Mango Street* and her book of poetry *My Wicked, Wicked Ways* (1987). When the short-story collection appeared, *The House on Mango Street* had just been reissued by a press devoted to writers of Latin American origin working in English. Cisneros was being hailed as the *enfant terrible* of Chicano letters. The rarity of Mexican American women writers helped propel Cisneros to the forefront of the Hispanic literary world. Although she has been criticized by some for her stereotypic portrayals of Mexican men, Cisneros has been celebrated for breaking the stereotype of the Latino culture's passive, fatalistic woman. Her prose has been welcomed as refreshing, sometimes even hypnotizing. Critics note that Cisneros has made no compromises in language as she moves between poetry and prose, and her work has been described as a mosaic of Mexican American voices that leaves a series of almost visual images resonating in the reader's mind.

In *Woman Hollering Creek and Other Stories*, Cisneros successfully combines interior monologues, fragments of dialogue, letters, flashbacks, dream images, and Mexican folklore to create sophisticated structures in which the narrative curves back on itself, enticing the sensitive reader to find deeper levels of meaning. Cisneros' language is rich, but her style is bare. She provides the threads but leaves the reader to weave them together. This fosters a sense of intimacy, as does her liberal intermixing of Spanish words with English, creating a tapestry that is stronger for the contrasts. Her use of Spanish acknowledges the primary audience, but she uses it in such a way that there is sufficient context for the non-Spanish speaker to make sense of the meaning, even to gain something from the sounds of the language.

Cisneros has been classed with other strong ethnic women writers such as Denise Chavez, Gloria Anzaldua, Christine Garcia, and Julia Alvarez. She has also been compared with Alice Munro and Joyce Carol Oates, in that all three are at their best when writing in a young girl's voice. Cisneros' books are used in classes from the junior high school to the graduate level and were included in the multiethnic "new curriculum" at Stanford University. Cisneros believes that Chicano writers have a lot to say, and she predicts that the Spanish language is going to contribute something very rich to American literature.

WORKING IN THE DARK

Author: Jimmy Santiago Baca (1952-   )
Type of work: Autobiographical essays
First published: 1991

Principal Personage

Jimmy Santiago Baca, the author. The name Baca is well known in New Mexico, which has seen the Spanish explorer Cabeza de Vaca and nineteenth cavalry lawman Elfego Baca. To see the name in print as Chicano is surprising because many New Mexicans pride themselves on being Hispanic, some claiming "pure" Spanish bloodlines. Even more astonishing is to hear a Baca proudly state "soy chicano hasta los huesotes" (I'm Chicano clear down to the bone marrow).

Baca suffered throughout his childhood and young adulthood, first as an orphan and later as a prison inmate. Clearly, this Chicano author has a remarkable story to express. Few prison writers succeed, but Baca does in his starkly clear illustration of harsh, degrading prison life.

As do other Chicano writers, Baca spins a narration of barrio life, poverty situations, and racially discriminatory school life. Despite negative experiences, including exploitation and degradation in prison, he emerges as a unique, creative poet. His stories and poetry reflect not only his own defeats and sorrows in his involvements with women, alcohol, and drugs, but also his determination and his courage in fighting a justice system grossly unfair to Chicanos. Baca's penetrating indictment of the brutality toward and human debasement of inmates contrasts with the loving and tenderness he describes as part of Chicano character. It is this strong faith in "La Raza" that highlights Baca's testimony throughout his "meditations" and soul searching in prison.

Baca petitions for a different connection with other humans, a different relationship based on trust and love, not on drugs and greed. The extended family and his sons provide Baca's innermost strength and support. He portrays Chicano family life as positive despite the cruel oppressive dark hovering over it. Baca identifies strongly with poverty, with its condition of lacking and with its pain as well as with the power of pride that can emerge out of this state.

Form and Content

Working in the Dark is an honest, evocative, barrio-rooted work consisting of chapters that range in content from personal thoughts to criticism of the prison system. It is an autobiography that could have been written by a large number of Chicano youths. It is bold and terribly self-analytical, as far as Chicanos are concerned, and is likely to evoke sentiments close to home in Chicano readers. Fifteen realistic essays and a diarylike narrative at the end create a unique view of Chicano life and prison experience. Most of the essays are based on very personal experiences of failures and successes as a man and as a poet. Some describe Baca's memories and the women and men who made an impact in his life.

Baca employs first-person narrative throughout. His prose is clear and distinct, marked by some symbolism and imagery. It contains some words from the "Caló" dialect. Baca stresses that his life and his views on the prison system are critical to his work. He might be considered to be an "ideal" prison writer. His attempts to free himself from the paranoia, hates, and horrible memories of incarceration—what he calls a radical disorientation—led to a realization that America is two countries; one society has opportunity, and one is deprived.

The book concerns four main topics: The author's infancy and youth, his prison experience, his female acquaintances, and his success. His infancy, tragic as it was, still had highly positive meaning because of his relationship with his grandmother. Baca's experience illustrates that Chicanos, through their extended families, are enriched and supported despite the poverty and oppression that prevail in American society. Early in his adolescence, women enter Baca's life in a negative manner. His reaction is to punish himself through antisocial behavior. He describes these experiences as fulfillments of an emptiness in his adolescence and as touching God. He saw himself as a forgotten person, isolated from the basic supports that a father and mother offer. The world of the barrio, according to Baca, contained work and laughter. His grandmother's love and influence, her gentleness, and her caring nature left an enduring strength in his character.

There is also a dark side to the poet's life. In Baca's New Mexico, "Hispanic" thought has been that of assimilation. Baca affirms his status as a Chicano poet, manifesting his pride in being Chicano and having Mexican background. When he writes about the dark, he refers to his loneliness, his drinking, and his use of drugs. He admits to becoming the coauthor, with his oppressor, of his own destruction. Baca's night involves his own ignorance as a youth and his efforts to become Anglo. He encounters rejection from both white and Raza societies. Baca writes from the perspective of a Chicano freed from his Anglo oppressor and his oppressor's ties.

This freedom was acquired at great cost to the individual's soul and with a great loss of a young man's time. Baca tried to make something of his time in prison, insisting on instruction toward his high school equivalency diploma. He was put into solitary confinement for his efforts. His defiance led directly to a series of brutal treatments, resulting in his acquisition of the powerful tool of language. This dynamic transformation is described vividly by the author.

Poetry becomes a powerful, defiant weapon. Entering the degrading prison system before he is eighteen years old, Baca becomes an innocent victim of a "suspicion of murder" charge. In prison, he hears men reading Octavio Paz, Pablo Neruda, Howard Nemerov, and Ernest Hemingway. At the age of twenty, again in prison, he discovers William Wordsworth and Samuel Taylor Coleridge, the latter an opium addict. In solitary confinement, fighting mental destruction and insanity, he disappears into an imaginary world of language that empowers him and thus helps him to escape the destructive and enslaving forces.

This new power, the written word, enables him to form a defense against his prison enemies. It also educates him to the Chicano resistance. Baca argues strongly for any further Anglo encroachment on Chicano culture in the chapter on "Chicanismo," wherein he affirms values that have aided "La Raza." He labels Chicano prison inmates as "spiritual warriors" yet also refers to himself as a "vato loco" (literally, wild guy). He repeatedly illustrates rank discrimination and oppression and describes the resistance he has displayed against them. In the chapter "Past present," he questions the value of prison rehabilitation and the myth that prison alters criminal behavior in a positive manner. He asserts that life in prison distorts reality and that every skill a man needs to live productively is destroyed by the conditions and brutality inflicted in prison.

Inside or outside prison, Baca eventually would have become a poet and writer. In the tragic reality of incarceration, however, he realized a rebirth that transformed him into a powerful, skilled craftsman of language, a strong voice for "La Raza's" least socially accepted. In the process, he personally found a new, proud Chicano identity with a strong message of hope.

This message resounds with the strength of a culture that has resisted assimilation while participating in America's wars and achievements. Baca issues a call to recognize the value and heritage of a people that has struggled for liberation since pre-colonial times, a proclamation against racism and injustice. Baca has described his poetry as a meditation on the beauty of his culture and a protest against the forces of assimilation. He states further that his responsibility as a Chicano is to carry his vision so that all people can share in it. That vision entails writing about his barrio.

Baca states that he has scars and wounds from the birth of poems, and that he has had to struggle against his culture, which sees sex as bestial and degrading. He hides nothing as he readily admits how shamed, lonely, and shy he was with women as a young man. It was in prison, writing to a female poet, that he experienced a release of his negative feelings about sex. This release altered his perspective toward sex and matured him. His new attitude toward the opposite sex even changed his male role, increasing his sensitivity toward himself, allowing admittance of weakness, pain, and hurt.

Male poets often are perplexed and inspired by the feminine mystique, and Baca is no exception. He admits that his fears and negative attitudes toward women were influenced by Chicano culture. He now realizes that he had been taught to look at women as sex objects. He addresses his change to a more positive and "sacred" view as part of the creative force. He acknowledges poetry's feminine power, describing himself as half man and half woman when he writes. The women in his life—his wife, his grandmother, his sister, his deceitful sixteen-year-old girlfriend, a woman poet, and the nuns from his childhood—have left him with different impressions. In a poignant and loving memory, his grandmother is described as warm

and nurturing, kind and caring, leaving him a heritage of truth, kindness, giving, and compassion. His love for poetry is characterized in a challenging narrative. He led a dog's life in trying to love Lolita; he is also poetry's dog. He continuously expresses, through beautiful prose demonstrating his creativity, a union of his masculine and feminine attributes. The sensuous, soft, womanly virtues dominate the birth of poems, his children. This birth fulfills his manhood, which previously was incomplete and now is shared with a woman in a sacred experience.

American careers are valued in dollars. Few poets measure their success by that standard. Baca claims that the worst thing that can happen to a poet is to achieve fame and become rich early in his or her career. His assertion is that the poet must undergo challenges that test courage, as he must be truthful to himself, his close ones, and his humanity, drenching his lips and tongue in the blood of life. Baca is successful not only as a writer and poet, achieving fame and financial security, but also as a husband and father. Close friends still picture him as the same sensitive and courageous Chicano, still close to the barrio. One cannot fail to see a certain parallel between the dog Baby Face, described by Baca as a meek animal that commits "felonies" and is rescued at the last minute by a "conned" owner, and the humble Chicano poet felon who lies at poetry's feet. Baca states that the dog has earned his bone.

Analysis

Autobiography, very often, is extremely biased. Baca's work is based on a true picture of a Chicano life, with all of its weaknesses and strengths. It is a distinctive and valid story of barrio and prison incidents that reflect the author's preoccupation with the issues of assimilation and self-identity. It is based on opposition to assimilation and on the establishment of a future "Aztlán," a country free of racism and oppression.

Another view is expressed in Richard Rodriguez's *Hunger of Memory: The Education of*

Richard Rodriguez (1981). Rodriguez suggests a need to assimilate and, by doing so, to become American. He contends that if he functions as an isolated, private individual, disconnected from his ethnic group, social class, and family, yet with a public identity, doors will open to the greater network of American rewards. Rodriguez has emerged as the right-wing establishment's Hispanic voice, opposing bilingual education and affirmative action programs.

Baca's book breaks new ground through its

strong affirmation of the Chicano culture's stature in an ever-changing world. Baca repeatedly points out the strong values of the Chicano, in and out of prison, while also noting his errors and sins. He recognizes that Chicanos constitute a low socio-economic group in the United States, suffering from oppressive immigration policy and practice, deficient and underfinanced education, and voiceless leadership. Baca, with this literary work, provides a tiny beacon of light, working in the dark, struggling to turn night to day for Chicanos. He narrates tales of true Chicano heroes, blood-and-meat models of whom his people can be proud.

Baca presents a symbolic "marca" of "La Raza," a mark full of spiritual connotations for Chicanos akin to the Native American nonmaterialistic essence of harmony with the universe that focuses on health and sanity. He shows a way of life very different from that assigned to Chicanos by television and other media of Anglo culture. His message is valuable because it is an honest, frank portrayal of the raw life of the poor and dispossessed. It gives the barrio warriors a true, brave reflection of their valid struggle. It creates a heritage nurtured by the blood of prison inmates, dignified by the poor campesino, and formalized by the barrio grandmothers. Baca enriches this heritage.

Critical Context

The Chicano minority in the United States is the largest segment of the Latin population in the country, the one with the highest birth rate and with an economic potential that will eventually become a powerful political force. Baca's work is important because it lays a philosophical base, through its interpretation of the beliefs of Chicanos, that will demand further interpretation and discussion. It will introduce fundamental experimentation in the barrios, prisons, and rural areas in the realms of education, social work, and justice systems. A true translation into Spanish is a must.

Baca's literary work, along with a venture into the film industry, constitutes a major step for the Chicano perspective. Certainly it is a critical attempt to introduce a more humane, less male chauvinist, model for Chicano youth. Future writers can lean on Baca's beautiful description of creative feminist though as it pertains to the "vato." It is a distinct guidebook of leadership and courage, a model for many suffering Chicanos involved in alcohol and drugs, living in constant anxiety and fear. It is a beacon of hope for many Chicanos caught up in the current, assimilating into the traditional American "rat race" full of misery and false joy.

Baca presents true images of the Chicano barrio man, in opposition to the colonized barrio image that many other authors have portrayed. At the very least, his work serves as an initial exposition of a man's transformation as a result of his faith in his fellow barrio "vato." It is based on the immense volume of neglected, rejected, and omitted narratives of countless voiceless Chicanos. It is still too early to measure the impact of *Working in the Dark*. Chicano barrio workers and organizers, however, will surely use it as a tool in dealing with drug addiction, alcoholism, and antisocial behavior.

EL ZARCO, THE BANDIT

Author: Manuel Altamirano (1834-1893)
Type of work: Novel
Type of plot: Romance
Time of plot: 1861-1863
Locale: The province of Morelos, Mexico
First published: *El Zarco*, 1901 (English translation, 1957)

Principal Characters

Nicolas, a Mexican blacksmith of Indian descent. Infatuated by Manuela, Nicolas realizes, while he is imprisoned for accusing an officer of shirking his duties, that Pilar is his true love. Released from jail, he joins Martín Sánchez and assists in El Zarco's capture.

El Zarco, a bandit. Taking advantage of the troubled times during the War of Reform, El Zarco leads his cutthroats through the countryside, murdering and plundering. Flattered by her devotion, he takes Manuela as his bride.

Manuela, Doña Antonia's impetuous daughter. In love with the bandit El Zarco, she refuses to believe the stories of his cruelty. After she runs away with him she sees his sordid side, but she remains true to him. When he is executed, she falls to the ground dead.

Martín Sánchez, a rancher. Enraged by the death of his father and his son at the hands of El Zarco, Martín swears to track down the bandits. At La Calavera, he captures El Zarco, but the outlaw is rescued. Undaunted, Martín again captures the bandits and executes them.

Pilar, Doña Antonia's godchild, in love with Nicolas.

El Tigre, El Zarco's bestial lieutenant.

Doña Antonia, Manuela's mother.

The Novel

During the War of Reform, and after, bands of robber outlaws took advantage of the troubled times to overrun those districts of Mexico where the local authorities, in a land still disturbed by civil war, were powerless to make effective reprisals against them. Roaming the countryside in armed bands, the *plateados*, as they were called, waylaid and murdered travelers, kidnapped wealthy estate owners for ransom, and levied tribute on the villages and haciendas. For their amusement they often wantonly burned the canefields and inflicted brutal tortures on their prisoners.

A town terrorized in this fashion was Yautepec, a pleasant village in the province of Morelos, in which *El Zarco, the Bandit* is set. By day the people maintain lookouts in the church towers to give warning of approaching marauders; at night they barricade themselves in their houses, so that after sunset the little town in the middle of its circling orange groves resembles a place of the dead. The bandits, some five hundred strong, have their headquarters at Xochimancas, a nearby ruined hacienda from which they make forays. Their leader is El Zarco, a man of savage temper and cruel disposition whose bloody exploits cause all respectable and decent people to fear him. The bandits sometimes enter the town and ride boldly through the streets.

On an evening in August, 1861, Doña Antonia sits in the inner courtyard of her house with her daughter Manuela and her godchild Pilar. The two girls are plaiting flower garlands for their hair.

After a time, Manuela begins to tease Pilar, because her friend is making a wreath of orange blossoms, the flower of weddings. When Manuela complains of her dull life, her mother rebukes her sharply, saying that the girl ought to forget fiestas and dances and take a husband who will protect her. Doña Antonia's choice is Nicolas, the sober and industrious blacksmith of the estate at Atlihuayan. At this suggestion, Manuela begins to speak scornfully of the Indian, as she calls him, and declares that she would rather have El Zarco as a suitor. She adds that Nicolas might be good enough for Pilar, but she herself would never have him. Pilar blushes but says nothing.

Before Doña Antonia can reprove her daughter further, Nicolas, a nightly caller, arrives with the news that the night before bandits had robbed and killed an English family traveling to Acapulco and that a cavalry detachment is being sent from Cuernavaca to pursue them. Alarmed at this latest outrage, Doña Antonia decides that she and Manuela will go to Mexico City until times are better. They will travel with the troops as their escort for part of the dangerous journey.

Later, while Nicolas is on his way back to Atlihuayan, another rider is traveling toward Yautepec. The horseman is El Zarco. In the village, he turns down a dark lane that leads to a stone wall surrounding Doña Antonia's orange grove. Drawing rein beneath a giant sapota tree, he whistles twice. An answering whistle comes from the darkness under the tree, where Manuela is waiting for her lover.

El Zarco had met Manuela in Cuernavaca during a brief period when he and his men were aiding the government forces, and the two had been strongly drawn to each other. After he had established himself at Xochimancas, the bandit learned that the girl and her mother had returned to Yautepec. Through his spies in the village, he had arranged to see her regularly. El Zarco finds her devotion flattering to his vanity. Manuela, refusing to believe the stories of his violence and cruelty, sees him only as a handsome, brave caballero. Now, unwilling to leave Yautepec, she tells him of Doña Antonia's plans and asks him to take her

away. Before they part that night, they arrange for him to carry her off to Xochimancas. In parting, El Zarco gives her several small boxes for safekeeping. After his departure, she notices that one is bloodstained. The boxes contain a diamond ring, two bracelets, and earrings. Putting them on, she goes to a pool in the garden and looks at her reflection by the light of a lantern. She buries the jewels with other gems and money that El Zarco had already entrusted to her.

The next night, Manuela flees with El Zarco to his hideout, leaving behind a note in which she tells her mother goodbye. Heartbroken, Doña Antonia asks Nicolas to go with her to beg that the cavalry troop from Cuernavaca hunt down the bandits and rescue Manuela. When the commander refuses, Nicolas charges the officer with shirking his duties. The blacksmith is placed under arrest and ordered held for trial.

Pilar, upset by the news of Nicolas' arrest, tries to visit him in prison but is turned back by his guards. Nicolas, hearing her pleas, realizes that it is Pilar and not Manuela whom he truly loves. When the commander sets out to take his prisoner to the capital, a large party accompanies the troops to see that the blacksmith receives full justice. Through the intercession of the owner of Atlihuayan, Nicolas is finally released. He returns to Yautepec in time to see Doña Antonia on her deathbed. The woman is dying of grief over her daughter's disgrace. After her death, Nicolas continues to ride into the village each evening, but now to visit Pilar.

Meanwhile, at Xochimancas, Manuela lives a different and sordid life of lawlessness and violence. Forced to associate with disreputable women, ogled and showered with lewd compliments from the men, she is at first terrified by her new surroundings. She realizes that she had been attracted to El Zarco by infatuation and greed, not love. In particular, she is horrified by the condition of a French prisoner, tortured daily to extort from him a greater ransom. At a fiesta to celebrate one of El Zarco's raids, Manuela is forced to dance with El Tigre, a repulsive creature who tells her that El Zarco will tire of her eventually and turn her over to one of his lieutenants. El Tigre intends to be that man.

A short time earlier, El Zarco had killed the father and son of a rancher named Martín Sánchez. Swearing revenge, Sánchez sells his property and buys arms and equipment for twenty men he recruited to track down the bandits. After he makes several successful raids on the outlaws, other men are roused from their apathy and fears to join him. In an encounter at La Calavera, in which Nicolas takes part, El Zarco is wounded and taken prisoner. With him is Manuela.

In spite of Martín Sánchez's protests, El Zarco cleverly arranges to have his trial held in Cuernavaca. While the prisoners are being taken there, bandits fall on the escorting troops and set El Zarco and Manuela free. Sánchez, determined to end lawlessness in the region, obtains from President Benito Juarez authority to hang without trial any bandit who falls into his hands.

The wedding day of Pilar and Nicolas arrives at last. After the mass, they start by coach for Atlihuayan with friends invited to the feast to be held there. On the way, they meet a troop of horsemen led by Martín Sánchez, who asks the party to drive on without stopping. At that moment, Manuela appears from behind the horsemen and begs helps of Nicolas and his bride. El Zarco and El Tigre, she says, have been captured and are to be executed. Sánchez tells how he had saved the wedding party from an ambush. Pilar, filled with pity for Manuela, wants to take the unfortunate creature into the coach, but the distraught girl cries out that she would rather die with El Zarco than see Pilar in her wreath of orange blossoms. Saddened, the wedding party rides on.

Shot down by a firing squad, El Zarco's body is hung from the branch of a tree. Manuela, seeing her lover dangling there, gives a loud cry and falls to the ground, dead.

Analysis

El Zarco, the Bandit has beauty, action, and clarity. It paints the subtropical mountains of Morelos between 1861 and 1863, when political conditions were chaotic, a potentially rich economy stagnated, and social justice was unknown. Readers see the traditional reasons for Mexico's sluggish progress, which stemmed from bad government but which has been blamed on the rich, on bloated landlords, and on narrow-minded priests. The novel clearly depicts the dichotomy between a virtuous social element—as represented by Nicolas, Antonia, and others—and the various corrupt types that were crippling Mexico through laziness, greed, and dishonesty. The negative minority is in sociopolitical control, while the healthier majority is excluded from the levers of control. The same theme appears often in Mexican literature, implying that Mexican revolutions have often been meaninglessly destructive, and that even some of the glorified patriotic victories have blocked as well as unleashed progress. This, for example, is a theme of Mariano Azuela's *The Un-*

derdogs (1915), which, in describing the civil strife that took place half a century after the events of *El Zarco, the Bandit*, condemns the nouveau riche of a popular revolution as much as it does their opponents.

El Zarco, the Bandit suffers from the inevitable limitations of the nineteenth century in which it was written. Some of its characterizations are simplistic. Nicolas, for example, seems faultless and is not presented convincingly, while Antonia, Pilar, and El Tigre are one-dimensional. El Zarco is presented in greater depth, since his motivations for vengeance and power—stemming from his sorry past as a stable boy and menial drudge on large estates—are convincing. Altamirano even makes it clear that El Zarco's menial tasks were given to him because he was too lazy to learn higher skills. Manuela is initially callous, greedy, spoiled, and even deliberately evil. Sorrow, frustration, and total defeat finally goad her into psychological transformation. Disillusioned and hapless, knowing that she has sinned, she receives the attendant punishment without self-pity as she dies at the foot of El Zarco's corpse.

The real person that Altamirano was in his daily life stalks though these pages. The novel reflects his youth—for which he yearns, oddly enough—and its memories of slights, offenses, and the indifferences of calculating women who were frivolously incapable of seeing in him anything more than an impoverished boy. Altamirano's novels, even while reliving the memories that make these novels authentic, are not basically autobiographical. El Zarco's reaction to his humble past is the opposite of Altamirano's, while Nicolas' reaction to life is Altamirano's—he does not live as an abject and servile Indian but as a cultured man dignified by work and conscious of his own personal worth.

Altamirano is the first Mexican who can truly be called a novelist, working with an awareness of and within limitations imposed by a clearly defined literary form. A patriot and a veteran of three Mexican wars, he found the materials of his fiction in the life of his turbulent period. *El Zarco, the Bandit* illustrates his intention to present Mexican life and to interpret faithfully the spirit of the people. It is a somber work, historical in background, deeply probing in psychological depth, and suffused with the beauty of the Mexican landscape. Two characters stand out from the background against which they move: Manuela, an impulsive, headstrong girl brought to folly and ruin by infatuation and greed, and Nicolas, an Indian representative of the class in which Altamirano saw a bright promise for the future of his nation. Completed shortly before the writer's death, the novel appeared posthumously eight years later.

Altamirano used his novels in favor of his political views, which were liberal in a nineteenth century sense. He thus followed the tradition of Argentina's Domingo Sarmiento and Bartolomé Mitre, who were literary presidents of the Argentine Republic. Like them, Altamirano was politically active as a theoretician and campaigner.

ZERO

Author: Ignácio de Loyola Brandão (1936-   )
Type of work: Novel
Type of plot: Surrealism
Time of plot: The late 1960's
Locale: A large city in Latin America
First published: 1974 (English translation, 1983)

Principal Characters

José Gonçalves, also called **Zé,** a vagabond worker and later an assassin and subversive. Although seemingly apathetic, he is violent, feeling trapped, conscious of systematic oppression and his own mundane, captive life. José is relatively content as long as he retains his solitude, but when he marries, he is thrust into a confusing world that both beckons him and rejects him, threatening his individuality. In an atmosphere of rising political turmoil and violence, he is picked up and questioned regarding various small crimes. He begins robbing, then killing, and he gets the material goods he desires, but it seems not to be worth it. He joins the Communs, an antigovernment terrorist group, but comes to realize that the group threatens his identity as much as does the oppressive government.

Rosa Maria, José's wife. Short and plump, she is seen as unattractive by José's friends. Reared as a good Catholic, she answers José's personal advertisement and they marry, though her people do not approve. Immediately she begins to pressure him for material comforts for them and their unborn child. Rosa Maria is abducted by members of a cult and, in a grotesque ritual, is sacrificed as a means of ridding the earth of evil.

Gê, the leader of the Communs, a terrorist group. Self-sacrificing and charismatic, he is a well-known fighter with an obscure background, apparently a medical school graduate turned rebel. Gê takes José under his wing and lectures him on the necessity of living for the group cause and not for individual action, a necessity that José never accepts.

Atila, José's friend and fellow subversive. His nickname derives from his tendency toward violence when drinking. When José goes to join the Communs, Atila goes along for the fun. He joins in robbing and killing and is eventually caught and brutally tortured, but he will not divulge information on the group and is finally released.

Malevil, José's friend and fellow subversive. Atila tells José that Malevil is the first case of reanimation after having been frozen. He betrays José.

Carlos Lopez, a textile worker. A patriot with a sick son, he keeps running up against a bureaucratic government as he tries to find treatment. When his son finally dies without care, he turns against the system.

The Novel

Zero was written in Brazil in the late 1960's, during the first years of the repressive military regime that took power in 1964. The setting of *Zero* as a "Latindian American country, tomorrow," stated on the introductory page, is a thin disguise for Loyola Brandão's contemporary Brazil. Certain dates, historical names, geographical references, and institutional acronyms link the novel to that country, although many of the events and the atmosphere could fit several other Latin American countries ruled by authoritarian military regimes. Finished in 1969, *Zero* was too controversial for

Brazilian publishers in the early 1970's, despite the author's previous respected and successful publications, and was first published in Rome in Italian in 1974. The following year, during the beginning of the regime's political opening, it was published in Brazil to the acclaim of critics and a public thirsty for a literary treatment of the country's dark period, during which censorship was in effect.

The salient characteristic of *Zero*, as a novel, is unconventionality. It is an extensive prose narrative containing a degree of character and plot development and thus may be deemed a novel. Its unconstrained language, its bizarre characters and episodes, and especially its chaotic structure, however, clearly set it apart from the norm. This unconventionality is the critical element for the author's creation of a critical, surrealist portrait of the times in his homeland.

Zero is a series of titled, disjointed narrative units, lists, drawings, and graphs, the majority of which sketchily relate major events in the characters' lives, but many of which serve to convey social, political, and philosophical commentary linked to the plot only as a backdrop to reinforce tone and atmosphere. The plot revolves around José Gonçalves' evolution from vagabond to subversive. At the outset of the work, the reader sees José doing the first of his odd—both diverse and strange—jobs, killing rats in a rundown film theater. Later, he writes slogans for Coca-Cola bottle caps and books acts for a national freak show that makes up an entire neighborhood. Finally, he car-

ries out robberies and assassinations for Gê, the leader of the subversive "Communs." Other significant events in his life are his residence in an abandoned book warehouse, where he reads and gains political consciousness; his courtship of and marriage to Rosa, whose dubious background causes him anguish; his murder of individuals whom he believes are doing him wrong; and his arrest, torture, and subsequent escape.

Plot development is secondary to tone and atmosphere, and the reader is required to piece it together from frequent but disjointed and transitionless glimpses that are intercalated among unrelated but equally chaotic observations and commentaries made by the narrator. These latter elements include statistics on Latin American countries, subplots on exploited individuals, a labeled drawing of a malnourished man, ludicrous Orwellian government pronouncements, plentiful ironic footnotes and "Free Associations," and even strings of nonsense syllables. Attention is focused naturalistically on torture, pain, sexual acts, deformities, and the like through detailed listings.

The chaotic nature of the novel's structure is underscored by the deliberate breaking of convention in punctuation and spelling, seen, for example, in the placement of commas between verbs and their objects and the phonetic rather than normative spelling of many words. The novel's emphasis on the base and the ugly is heightened by frequently coarse and brutal language almost devoid of lyric quality.

Analysis

Zero's chaotic structure, brutal language, pathetic characterization, and bizarre plot all point up the major theme of the novel—that the society it depicts is chaotic, brutal, pathetic, and bizarre. The novel portrays the regime's baleful effects on that society in its devastation of the individual, whether through malnourishment, torture, constant fear, or violent death. The tragedy inherent in this sociopolitical order is underscored by the constant depiction of abnormal behavior and physical de-

formities, to the point, in fact, that they become commonplace and expected. An instance of biting irony comes when José recognizes that a healthy, well-adjusted, normal man who applies for a position in the freak show is indeed the greatest freak of all because of his very wholesomeness.

The specific targets of the author's criticism are the military rulers' moral hypocrisy, indiscriminate brutality, and paranoia, which subsequently affect the fabric of society, shaping it to the regime's mold. There is no philosophical commentary on the absurdity of the human condition in general or the alienation and dehumanization of people in modern society. The macabre, the absurd, and the grotesque in *Zero* are a clamor of protest against brutal conditions in a specific place and time— conditions in which a few people are responsible for the suffering of many.

Critical Context

Zero is the best known of Loyola Brandão's works. It continues the themes and attitude of his previous novel, *Bebel que a Cidade Comeu* (1968), but evinces an evolution into a more audacious, experimental creation. Some subsequent works— the novel *Dentes ao Sol: Ou, A Destruiçao da Catedral* (1976) and the stories of *Cadeiras Proibidas* (1979), for example—also have certain parallels in theme and perspective but are much more conventional in structure, language, and development of characters and plot.

Zero represents a significant landmark in modern Brazilian prose fiction, with its bold structure, contumacious tone, and unrelenting indictment of the military regime. Numerous other Brazilian novels have rendered a critical portrayal of life under this repressive regime with similar themes, techniques, and tone, notably Ivan Angelo's *A Festa* (1976; *The Celebration*, 1982), Carlos Heitor Cony's *Pessach: A Travessia* (1967), and Roberto Drummond's *Sangue de Coca-Cola* (1983), but *Zero* stands out as the most innovative and powerful of the literary protests of those dark times.

Indexes